D1327523

CORRUPTION AND MISUSE OF PUBLIC OFFICE

CORRUPTION AND MISUSE OF PUBLIC OFFICE

Colin Nicholls QC
Tim Daniel
Martin Polaine
John Hatchard

OXFORD
UNIVERSITY PRESS

Great Clarendon Street, Oxford OX2 6DP

Oxford University Press is a department of the University of Oxford.
It furthers the University's objective of excellence in research, scholarship,
and education by publishing worldwide in

Oxford New York

Auckland Cape Town Dar es Salaam Hong Kong Karachi
Kuala Lumpur Madrid Melbourne Mexico City Nairobi
New Delhi Shanghai Taipei Toronto

With offices in

Argentina Austria Brazil Chile Czech Republic France Greece
Guatemala Hungary Italy Japan Poland Portugal Singapore
South Korea Switzerland Thailand Turkey Ukraine Vietnam

Published in the United States
by Oxford University Press Inc., New York

First published 2006

British Library Cataloguing in Publication Data
Data available

Library of Congress Cataloging in Publication Data
Data available

Typeset by Newgen Imaging Systems (P) Ltd., Chennai, India
Printed in Great Britain
on acid-free paper by
CPI Antony Rowe, Chippenham, Wiltshire

978–0–19–927458–1

3 5 7 9 10 8 6 4

To our families

ACKNOWLEDGEMENTS

The following material is reproduced from the Council of Europe website, and every effort has been made to contact the copyright holders:

(1) Council of Europe Civil Law Convention on Corruption
(2) Council of Europe Criminal Law Convention on Corruption
(3) Council of Europe Resolution (97) 24 on the Twenty Guiding Principles for the Fight Against Corruption
(4) Council of Europe Recommendation No R (2000) 10 of the Committee of Ministers to Member States on Codes of Conducts for Public Officials
(5) Council of Europe Committee of Ministers Recommendation Rec (2003) 4 of the Committee of Ministers to Member States on Common Rules against Corruption in the Funding of Political Parties and Electoral Campaigns
(6) Statute of the GRECO

The following material is reproduced with the kind permission of the Commonwealth Secretariat:

(1) Framework for Commonwealth Principles on Promoting Good Governance and Combating Corruption
(2) Commonwealth Report of Expert Group on Good Governance
(3) Commonwealth Working Group on Asset Repatriation

The Joint Action of 22 December 1998 Adopted by the Council on the Basis of Article K.3 of the Treaty on European Union, on Corruption in the Private Sector (98/742/JHA) is reproduced with the kind permission of Europa and the European Communities from their website. Disclaimer: only European Community Legislation printed in the paper edition of the Official Journal of the European Union is deemed authentic.

The International Monetary Fund Revised Code of Good Practices on Fiscal Transparency is reproduced from the International Monetary Fund, and every effort has been made to contact the copyright holder.

Text of the Anti-Corruption Action Plan for Asia and the Pacific from ADB OECD Anti-Corruption Division, 2004, updated 18 October 2005, http://www1.oecd.org/daf/ASIAcom/index.htm is reproduced with the kind permission of the OECD and the ADB.

The Bangalore Principles of Judicial Conduct are reproduced from the-Transparency International website, and every effort has been made to contact the copyright holders.

The ICC Rules of Conduct to Combat Extortion and Bribery (Part II of Extortion and Bribery in International Business Transactions—1999 Revised Version) are reproduced with the kind permission of the International Chamber of Commerce.

The World Customs Organization 'Declaration of the Customs Co-operation Council', done at Arusha, Tanzania on the 7th day of July 1993 (81st/82nd Council Sessions) is reproduced with the kind permission of the WCO.

The following material is reproduced with the kind permission of the United Nations Office on Drugs and Crime:

(1) African Union Convention on Preventing and Combating Corruption
(2) Council of the European Union: Convention on the Fight Against Corruption Involving Officials of the European Communities or Officials of Member States of the European Union
(3) Council of the European Union: Convention on the Protection of the European Communities' Financial Interests
(4) Second Protocol to the Convention on the Protection of the European Communities' Financial Interests
(5) Council of the European Union Framework Decision on Combating Corruption in the Private Sector
(6) Council of the European Union: Protocol to the Convention on the Protection of the European Communities' Financial Interests
(7) Inter-American Convention Against Corruption
(8) Revised Recommendation of the Council on Combating Bribery in International Business Transactions
(9) Convention on Combating Bribery of Foreign Public Officials in International Business Transactions
(10) Southern African Development Community Protocol Against Corruption
(11) United Nations Convention Against Corruption
(12) United Nations International Code of Conduct for Public Officials Resolution Adopted by the General Assembly [on the report of the Third Committee (A/51/610)]
(13) Economic Community of West African States Protocol on the Fight Against Corruption

The Wolfsberg Anti-Money Laundering Principles on Private Banking are reproduced with the kind permission of The Wolfsberg Group.

FOREWORD

The World Bank estimates that 6% of the world's economy was paid in bribes in 2004. Is it any wonder that a global consensus appears to be emerging as to the need to condemn corruption and to take effective steps to combat it not merely in individual countries but across borders? A host of international and regional initiatives are currently being pursued aimed at stamping out corruption. Appointment to public office and behaviour in public office are now regulated by codes of conduct which reflect core principles and which are open to public scrutiny. A recent example is the Guidelines to Judicial Conduct produced by and for the judiciary of England and Wales.

Attitudes have changed since a future Prime Minister, a future Lord Chief Justice and the Government Chief Whip thought it appropriate to use their inside knowledge that the Government had just concluded a lucrative contract with Marconi to buy shares in that company, and to do so with impunity and little newspaper comment. In a fascinating and informative chapter, the authors of this book describe, with examples, the shift in morality and trace proposals for reform that have culminated in the draft Corruption Bill, which is awaiting its turn in the legislative queue.

Meanwhile the lawyers and judges have the task of applying our patchwork of civil and criminal measures in order to combat the pernicious effect of corrupt business practices and address head on any lingering perception of corruption as a victimless crime. In making our way through this thicket we shall now have the assistance of this comprehensive but practical guide, written by authors with a vast and varied professional experience in this field. The substantive criminal, civil and public law relating to corruption is explored in depth, as are the procedures for investigating and prosecuting criminal misconduct and for obtaining civil remedies.

The authors look at international initiatives for fighting corruption and devote a chapter to the corruption laws of the United States, selected Commonwealth countries and other jurisdictions and regions.

This book fills a large gap and will, I predict, prove to be a valuable tool for those bent on attacking an evil that, if unchecked, can infect the life of a nation.

Nicholas Phillips
Royal Courts of Justice
London, WC2A 2LL

PREFACE

Writing a book on corruption may be compared with taking on the many-headed Hydra of Greek legend. Cut off one head of this gigantic monster and two appear in its place, with the central head immortal. Hercules needed an assistant (Iolaus) to tackle this most taxing of his twelve Labours: we at least are four, but burning out the roots of corruption, and severing the immortal head from the body are, unfortunately, not likely to be options in the lifetime of these authors.

Institute a daily press search on the internet using 'corruption' as the Find word and there will likely be over 100 'hits' each day of the year. Some of those who read this book will themselves have had personal experience of corruption of the 'petty' variety, especially when travelling. Even if they have not had first-hand experience of 'grand' corruption, they will almost certainly have read about it: it tends to make headlines when it is uncovered. One has only to think of the Volcker investigation into the UN's handling of the Iraqi oil-for-food programme, or the failure by the European Union in November 2005 to obtain a 'clean certificate' from its auditors for an eleventh consecutive year to appreciate that corruption is not a problem confined to far-away developing countries.

In today's world, the role of Hercules must be assumed by political leaders. The display of a strong political will to combat corruption by those who govern is central to the fight. Like Hercules, however, the political leaders cannot stand alone in this battle: they must have Iolaus at their side. In the context of corruption the role of Iolaus surely falls to the lawyers. This book deals primarily with the law and practice relating to corruption and misuse of public office in the United Kingdom, but, with corruption being a global issue, the book also encompasses the international initiatives which have been taken in the past ten years or so and the corruption laws of some other jurisdictions. These have assumed increased importance with the coming into force in December 2005 of the United Nations Convention against Corruption. It is still too early to say how effective this will be but international recognition of the problem is a major step forward; it will still be down to individual states to make good all that is in the Convention. One has to look no further than the United Kingdom itself to see just how fraught with difficulty even the drafting of a modern law on corruption can be. It is the authors' hope that this book will stimulate discussion and debate, as well as giving practical assistance to legal practitioners and others involved in the fight against corruption.

The authors are honoured that the Lord Chief Justice, Lord Phillips of Worth Matravers, took time away from his onerous duties as President of the Courts of England and Wales to write the Foreword.

The authors are indebted to many colleagues and others who have assisted them in a whole variety of ways, whether conducting additional research, reading and commenting on early drafts, or making suggestions and giving encouragement. The views expressed in the book are the authors' own, unless otherwise stated, and responsibility for errors and omissions rests solely with them.

Particular acknowledgment is due to the following for their advice and assistance with criminal and international practice and initiatives covered in the book: Alan Bacarese of the CPS, who leads policy in the field of anti-corruption law and practice and is a UK delegate on the OECD Bribery Working Group, and who has unstintingly shared his great knowledge and expertise in relation to these bodies, as well as practice before the European Court of Human Rights; Mark Carroll of the CPS, and Greg McGill, Prosecutor with Revenue and Customs; Paul Stephenson of the Home Office Criminal Policy Unit; Arvinder Sambei, Head of the Criminal Law Section, Commonwealth Secretariat; Jeremy Pope, Director of Policy, TIRI; Francis Fitzgibbon of Doughty Street Chambers; Ailsa Williamson of 3 Raymond Buildings; Dr Karen Brewer of the Commonwealth Magistrates and Judges Association; Charles Caruso of the Asian Law Initiative of the American Bar Association; Ian McWalters SC of Hong Kong; David Perry, a Senior Treasury Counsel at the Central Criminal Court; Professor Mark Pieth, Professor of Law at Basle University and Chair of the OECD Working Group on Bribery; Mary Waldron, and especially Karen Smith for their typing, patience, and research.

For input and comment on reform, the civil law, and remedies in England and the United Kingdom, thanks are due to Graham Rodmell of Transparency International; Colin Joseph; James Maton; and particularly Victoria Murray for uncomplainingly fielding an endless series of requests for information and sources.

Thanks are also due to the team at Oxford University Press, particularly Jane Kavanagh and Louise Kavanagh and Annabel Moss for keeping the authors to the deadlines they set themselves and for their assistance and advice in the production of this book.

Two of the authors are in full-time practice, the third is employed in the public sector and the fourth is a full-time academic. No book of this kind can be written without the understanding and support of colleagues: heartfelt thanks are due to all those who practise and work at 3 Raymond Buildings, partners, fee earners and staff at Kendall Freeman, and colleagues at the Centre for Law at the Open University.

The law is stated as at 31 October 2005, but, where possible within the context of the final editing process, reference has been made to later events.

Colin Nicholls QC
3 Raymond Buildings
Gray's Inn
London, WC1R 5BH
colin.nicholls@3raymondbuildings.com

Tim Daniel
Kendall Freeman Solicitors
43 Fetter Lane
London
EC4A 1JU
timdaniel@kendallfreeman.com

Martin Polaine
Barrister, Senior Crown Prosecutor,
currently seconded to the
Commonwealth Secretariat
m.polaine@commonwealth.int

John Hatchard
The Open University
Walton Hall
Milton Keynes MK7 6AA
J.Hatchard@open.ac.uk

22 November 2005

CONTENTS—SUMMARY

CONTENTS

TABLE OF CASES

TABLE OF LEGISLATION, TREATIES, AND CONVENTIONS

Secondary Legislation – United Kingdom Statutory Instruments

LIST OF ABBREVIATIONS

ACPO	Association of Chief Police Officers
ADB	Asian Development Bank
ADR	alternative dispute resolution
ARA	Assets Recovery Agency
ASB	Accounting Standards Board
ATCSA 2001	Anti-Terrorism, Crime and Security Act 2001
CBI	Confederation of British Industry
CDPC	European Committee on Crime Problems
CDCJ	European Committee on Legal Co-operation
CFA	Commission for Africa
CFPOA	Corruption of Foreign Public Officials Act (Canada)
CHIS	Covert human intelligence sources
CIB	Companies Investigation Branch (of the DTI)
C(IC)A 2003	Crime (International Co-operation) Act 2003
CJ(IC)A 1990	Criminal Justice (International Co-operation) Act 1990
CJA 1948, 1988	Criminal Justice Act 1948 and 1988
CJPOA 1994	Criminal Justice and Order Act 1994
CLA 1977	Criminal Law Act 1977
CLP	City of London Police
COE	Council of Europe
CPS	Crown Prosecution Service
CRA 2005	Constitutional Reform Act 2005
CSOs	civil society organizations
CSPL	Committee on Standards in Public Life
CTL	Commission on Transnational Corporations (UN)
DPP	Director of Public Prosecutions
DTI	Department of Trade and Industry
EAW	European Arrest Warrant
ECGD	Export Credits Guarantee Department
ECHR	European Convention on Human Rights
ECOSOC	Economic and Social Council (UN)
ECOWAS	Economic Community of West African States
ECtHR	European Court of Human Rights
EEIGs	european economic interest groupings
ERA 1996	Employment Rights Act 1996
FCPA	Foreign Corrupt Practices Act 1977 (US)
GA	General Assembly (of the United Nations)

GMC	Multidisciplinary Group on Corruption (COE)
GPAC	Global Programme against Corruption
GRECO	Group of States against Corruption
HRA 1998	Human Rights Act 1998
HSB	Honours Scrutiny Board
ICAC	Independent Commission Against Corruption (HK)
ICC	International Chamber of Commerce
ICSID	International Centre for the Settlement of Investment Disputes
ICTA 1988	Income and Corporation Taxes Act 1988
IOCA 1985	Interception of Communications Act 1985
IPCC	Independent Police Complaints Commission
LLPs	limited liability partnerships
LSPBs	local spending public bodies
MDGs	Millennium Development Goals
MDP	Ministry of Defence Police
MPS	Metropolitan Police Service
NCIS	National Criminal Intelligence Service
NCS	National Crime Squad
NDPBs	non-departmental public bodies
NGOs	non-governmental organizations
OAS	Organization of American States
OECD	Organization for Economic Co-operation and Development
PACE 1984	Police and Criminal Evidence Act 1984
PHSC	Political Honours Scrutiny Committee
PIDA 1998	Public Interest Disclosure Act 1998
POA 1985	Prosecution of Offences Act 1985
POCA 2002	Proceeds of Crime Act 2002
POGAR	Programme on Governance in the Arab Region
PPERA 2000	Political Parties, Elections and Referendums Act 2000
PRA 2002	Police Reform Act 2002
Quangos	quasi-autonomous non-governmental organizations
RICO	Racketeer Influenced and Corrupt Organizations Act (US)
RIPA 2000	Regulation of Investigatory Powers Act 2000
RPA 1983	Representation of the People Act 1983
RPPA 1998	Registration of Political Parties Act 1998
SADC	South African Development Community
SEC	Securities and Exchange Commission (US)
SFO	Serious Fraud Office
SOCPA 2005	Serious Organised Crime and Police Act 2005
SPAI	Stability Pact Anti-Corruption Initiative for South-Eastern Europe
UNCAC	United Nations Convention against Corruption
UNODC	United Nations Office on Drugs and Crime
UNDP	United Nations Development Programme
WGB	Working Group on Bribery (OECD)

BIOGRAPHIES

Colin Nicholls is a Bencher of Gray's Inn, and Queen's Counsel, whose specialist experience includes high profile complex corporate and commercial crime cases, extradition, criminal mutual assistance and human rights, with much of his work having an international element.

He has advised and acted for companies, prosecuting authorities, and defendants in corruption cases involving the United Kingdom, the Channel Islands, France, Italy, the United States, the Middle East, Hong Kong, and South America, and in the Bofors litigation in India and mani puliti trials in Italy.

He has given expert evidence in Ireland and the United States and written and lectured extensively on corruption, ethical governance, terrorism and human rights.

He was a Recorder of Crown Courts from 1983–2000, and is the immediate Past President of the Commonwealth Lawyers Association.

Tim Daniel is a litigation partner in the City law firm of Kendall Freeman (formerly D J Freeman). For the past thirty years he has represented the Government of the Federal Republic of Nigeria and ten years ago founded the Public International Law group at his firm, which has represented two states in cases before the International Court of Justice in the Hague.

His practice has also covered acting in many leading UK insolvency cases involving substantial international fraud and asset tracing exercises. With the return of civilian rule in Nigeria much of his focus has been on the fight against corruption and the recovery of looted state assets. He has assisted developing states in drafting proceeds of crime and anti-money laundering legislation and represents and advises a number of states in relation to asset recovery. He speaks and writes regularly on anti-corruption and recovery issues.

He is currently Joint Secretary of the British Branch of the International Law Association and Hon. Treasurer of the Commonwealth Lawyers Association.

Martin Polaine is a Crown Prosecutor with the Crown Prosecution Service of England & Wales, currently seconded to the Commonwealth Secretariat. A barrister, he has previously practised at the criminal bar and as a lawyer at the IPCC.

He is a member of the OECD Working Group on Bribery (WGB) and has been a 'lead examiner' for the WGB's peer review process. In the field of anti-corruption, he has also undertaken country evaluations and training on behalf of the EC/EU, UN and other international and regional bodies, and has advised on law, procedure and drafting in Central and Eastern Europe, Asia and the Pacific.

He has written and spoken widely on anti-corruption law and practice, and on related topics, including anti-money laundering, economic and financial crime, international co-operation and proactive/covert evidence gathering.

John Hatchard is Professor of Law at The Open University and Secretary General of the Commonwealth Legal Education Association. He has held senior academic positions at universities in the United Kingdom, United States, Zambia and Zimbabwe. He has also served as Chief Mutual Legal Assistance Officer at the Commonwealth Secretariat and was a Senior Fellow at the British Institute for International and Comparative Law.

He has published extensively in the area of criminal law, constitutional law and human rights, with particular reference to the Commonwealth. He has undertaken consultancy work for a wide range of international organisations, particularly in the field of corruption, good governance and human rights.

He is the Editor of the *Corruption Case Law Reporter* and *Commonwealth Legal Education*, Joint Editor of the *Journal of African Law* and a member of the Editorial Board of the *Commonwealth Law Bulletin and Journal of Commonwealth Law and Legal Education.*

1

THE MEANING AND SCOPE OF CORRUPTION

A. The Meaning of Corruption

1. Definition of Corruption

The word 'corruption' is derived from the Latin word 'corruptus' meaning to break. Its derivation emphasizes the destructive effect of corruption on the fabric of society and the fact that its popular meaning encompasses all those situations where agents and public officers break the confidence entrusted to them.[1] **1.01**

[1] G Moody-Stuart, 'The costs of grand corruption', in G Moody-Stuart (ed) *Grand Corruption in Third World Development*, prepared for the UNDP Human Development 1994 Report (Berlin: Transparency International, 1994).

1.02 The *Oxford English Dictionary* defines corruption as the 'perversion or destruction of integrity in the discharge of public duties by bribery or favour; the use or existence of corrupt practices, *esp.* in a state, public corporation etc'. It defines the adjective 'corrupt' as 'perverted from uprightness and fidelity in the discharge of duty; influenced by bribery or the like; venal'. It defines the verb 'corrupt' in a similar way, except that it extends it to any duties, 'public' or not, and offers a further definition: 'to induce to act dishonestly or unfaithfully, to make venal; to bribe'. It defines the verb 'bribe' as 'to influence corruptly, by a reward or consideration, the action of (a person), to pervert the judgment or corrupt the conduct by a gift'.[2]

1.03 These definitions correctly emphasize the essence of corruption in its legal sense, which is the inducement to show favour, rather than showing of the favour itself. They also demonstrate the use of the word to cover acts other than what is popularly termed bribery. The restriction of the definition of 'corruption' to 'public' duties no longer reflects the state of English law,[3] or of most modern states. The absence of the restriction in the definition of the verb 'corrupt', reflects the extension of corruption to include all persons who are induced to act corruptly, whether in the discharge of public duties or otherwise. The fact that the restriction appears in one definition and is omitted from the other indicates a tendency, even in modern times, to restrict the use of the word to the acts of public officials, having regard to the public nature of the crime and the gravity of its consequences.

1.04 The United Nations Convention Against Corruption (UNCAC) does not define corruption. It requires each State Party to adopt legal measures to establish certain criminal offences, including bribery, embezzlement, misappropriation or other diversion of property by public officials, trading in influence, abuse of functions, illicit enrichment, bribery in the private sector, embezzlement in the private sector, money laundering, concealment of property obtained as a result of any of those offences, and obstructing justice.[4] The Council of Europe Criminal Law Convention on Corruption contains similar provisions.[5] The provisions reflect the tendency of international bodies to regard offences of corruption as including offences beyond the confines of bribery as popularly understood.

1.05 Similarly, legislators in South Africa have unbundled the offence and attempted to criminalize specific acts of corruption where no bribery occurs, for example, abuse of power, conflict of interest, patronage, nepotism, theft of state assets, the diversion of state resources, insider trading, illicit enrichment, and money laundering the proceeds of corruption.[6]

---

[2] 1989 edn. [3] Prevention of Corruption Act 1906. [4] Arts 13–31, See 9.10ff.
[5] ETS No 173. [6] See 11.54ff.

Transparency International has defined corruption as 'the misuse of entrusted power for private gain'. The definition reflects the current approach to the topic, but its usefulness is debatable. It has the advantage of simplicity as it embraces offences of corruption strictly so-called and related offences such as misconduct in public office, extortion, embezzlement, fraud, and theft, which are distinct offences, albeit usually committed in the course of corruption and for that reason are included in this book. The question for the authors is where the topic ends. One of the reasons for the current approach is the prevalence of grand corruption in addition to petty corruption. **1.06**

2. Grand and Petty Corruption

The term grand corruption is used 'to describe cases where massive personal wealth is acquired from States by senior public officials using corrupt means'.[7] It arises mostly where high officials have power over the granting of large public contracts and a local agent receives a commission if the transaction is won. It has three main criteria: size, immediacy of its rewards, and mystification; the more technical and complicated a transaction the less likely it is that questions will be asked.[8] Some of its key mechanisms have been very fully described in George Moody Stuart's book, *Grand Corruption in Third World Development*.[9] **1.07**

The Society of Advanced Legal Studies Anti-Corruption Working Group, concluded that grand corruption involves two main activities: bribe payments and the embezzlement and misappropriation of state assets. The bribe can either be a direct payment in return for showing favour or payment of part of the proceeds of a contract granted as a result of the bribe, called a kickback. For example, Benazir Bhutto's husband, Asif Zardari, was convicted in Pakistan of taking secret kickbacks from airline, power station, and pipeline projects, rice deals, customs inspections, defence contracts, land sell-offs, and even government welfare.[10] Many kickbacks paid by European firms never leave the United Kingdom and are simply moved from one account to another. An example of embezzlement and misappropriation of state assets concerns the late President Abacha, who, in addition to taking hefty cuts before approving contracts, siphoned off fortunes from sales of Nigerian crude oil as well as diverting huge sums from four state-owned oil refineries, leaving them in near-total collapse.[11] **1.08**

[7] Report of the Anti-Corruption Working Group of the Society for Advanced Legal Studies, 'Banking on Corruption, the legal responsibilities of those who handle the proceeds of corruption', February 2002.

[8] ibid paras 2.1 and 4.1.

[9] Berlin: Transparency International, 1994.

[10] The court in Pakistan convicted Mr and Mrs Zardari of corruption, sentenced them to 5 years' imprisonment, ordered fines of US$8.6m, and disqualified both from holding public office, *Eastern Economic Review*, 29 April 1999.

[11] Davi Orr, *The Scotsman*, 4 December 1998.

1.09 The term 'petty corruption' is sometimes used to distinguish between grand corruption practised by senior officials and the petty corruption to which, for example, magistrates and judges, are subject due to inadequate remuneration and facilities. The term is more usually used, however, to describe 'facilitation' or 'grease payments' sought by officials for services the public are entitled to free of charge, for example, payments to customs officers to pass goods through a road border, to immigration officers to have travel documents accepted, to medical staff to receive prescription drugs or other benefits, payments for fictitious services, or to avoid prosecution for traffic offences, real or imaginary.[12] The key distinction from grand corruption is that an official may be being paid for doing what he is lawfully required to do. The sums involved are usually small and paid to cut through bureaucratic red tape. In most cases it is assumed that the service required would not be obtained without the additional payment, so there is an element of extortion.

3. Systemic Corruption

1.10 Systemic corruption, or institutional or entrenched corruption, as it is sometimes called, is corruption brought about, encouraged, or promoted by the system itself. It occurs where bribery on a large scale is routine. The causes are usually brought about by inefficiency, inadequacy, or undue laxity in the system.

1.11 It arises where corruption permeates a country's political and economic institutions and is no longer restricted to a few dishonest individuals. It thrives where institutions are weak or non-existent and it is closely related to poor governance; where there are inadequate legislative controls, no independent judiciary, or oversight; and where independent media and civil society agencies are absent. For example, the position in Russia has been described as follows: 'What you really have is a kleptocracy, a Government that has institutionalised theft at its heart'.[13]

B. The Scope of Corruption

1.12 Although this book was originally intended for use by UK practitioners, it became increasingly obvious to the authors that the book had a wider significance having regard to the increasingly transnational nature of corruption and ongoing international and regional efforts to combat corruption and its

[12] Evidence to the Select Committee on International Development (Transparency International) 4 April 2001.

[13] Congressman Jim Leach, Chairman of the House of Representatives Banking Committee, TL O'Brien, 'Russian says officials funneled cash to bank in laundering case', *New York Times*, 28 August 1999.

insidious effects. It was also apparent that, whereas in the United Kingdom at least, corruption had been regarded as relating solely to what is commonly called bribery, it was regarded internationally as including other offences such as misuse of public office, embezzlement, and misappropriation of state assets. The meaning of corruption was therefore much wider than was originally contemplated.

The publication of this book was originally to coincide with the arrival of a new Corruption Act for the United Kingdom. Whilst the Act has yet to materialize, several factors make such a book necessary at this time. **1.13**

First, a wider examination of the existing law on corruption is needed. This is especially so in that common law bribery overlaps with the ancient offence of misconduct in a public office, which has become one of the offences of choice for prosecutors with conduct of police and public official corruption cases in common law jurisdictions. In any event, given the fact that the new Corruption Act will not have retrospective effect and that corruption investigations are often lengthy, the existing offences will remain relevant for some time to come. **1.14**

Secondly, combating corruption demands a multifaceted approach that goes beyond a consideration of the criminal law alone. Thus, for example, the use of civil remedies in tackling corruption now provides a potentially highly effective mechanism for the restraint and recovery of proceeds of corruption. Further, whilst ten years ago it would have appeared strange that a book on corruption and misuse of public office should include a chapter on the regulation of conduct in public life, this is no longer the case, especially given the impact of the Committee on Standards in Public Life and the extent to which its recommendations have been embodied in legislation and codes of conduct. **1.15**

Thirdly, global efforts to combat corruption continue apace and increasingly have an impact in domestic law and practice. For example, the Organization for Economic Co-operation and Development (OECD) Convention on Combating Bribery of Foreign Public Officials in International Business Transactions, to which the United Kingdom is a party, is a concerted international attempt to address bribery offences committed wholly or partly abroad. This has already led to the passing of the Anti-Terrorism Crime and Security Act 2001 (ATCSA 2001) and the taking by the UK of nationality jurisdiction. Such a trend is also reflected in the work of the Council of Europe and the European Union. Moreover, the coming into force of the United Nations Convention on Corruption in 2005 and its ratification by the United Kingdom will have considerable implications for the public and private sector alike. This is illustrated by Article 1, which sets out the purposes of the Convention: (a) to promote and strengthen measures to prevent and combat corruption; (b) to promote, facilitate, and support international cooperation in the prevention of **1.16** and fight against corruption, including asset recovery; and (c) to promote integrity, accountability, and proper management of public affairs and public property. Thus the impact of international developments on domestic law and practice is already profound.

C. Arrangement of the Book

1.17 The arrangement of chapters in the book falls into five main categories, as follows:

- Chapters 2–5: UK criminal law relating to the prosecution of corruption offences;
- Chapters 6 and 7: UK civil law relating to bribery, corruption, and recoveries;
- Chapter 8: Regulation of conduct in public life in the United Kingdom; and
- Chapters 9–12: International anti-corruption conventions, foreign jurisdictions, and the role of civil society organizations in fighting corruption in the United Kingdom and abroad.

A summary of the content of each chapter is given below.

1. UK Criminal Law Relating to the Prosecution of Corruption Offences

i. Chapter 2: Offences of bribery and corruption

1.18 The criminal law relating to bribery and corruption in the United Kingdom comprises a common law bribery offence and a series of statutory offences, the most important of which are set out in the Prevention of Corruption Acts 1889–1916 as amended by ATCSA 2001.

1.19 The common law offence of bribery and the 1889 Act deal with public sector corruption; the 1906 Act covers corruption by agents and covers both the public and private sector. The 1916 Act simply extends the classes of public bodies covered by the 1889 Act and introduces a presumption of corruption in cases involving the employees of public bodies involved with public contracts.

1.20 The chapter examines the definition and scope of common law bribery offences and considers various aspects of the offence, including the treatment of facilitation payments, the mental element, entrapment, defences and immunities, and the distinction between bribery and other common law offences.

1.21 The chapter considers the elements of the offences under the Prevention of Corruption Acts, and other statutory offences, including the sale of public offices, offences relating to honours, and election offences. It also considers jurisdiction, the liability of corporate and unincorporated bodies, and sentencing.

Finally, it examines anti-money laundering and confiscation provisions under the Proceeds of Crime Act 2002 (POCA 2002) as amended by the Serious Organised Crime and Police Act 2005 (SOCPA 2005), and the powers of the Assets Recovery Agency, and mechanisms for gathering evidence in criminal matters through international cooperation. **1.22**

ii. Chapter 3: Misconduct in public office

The common law offences of bribery and misconduct in a public office apply only to public office holders. After falling into disuse during the middle of the twentieth century, prosecutions for misconduct in a public office have undergone a revival in common law jurisdictions. The offence is flexible and can be used in a variety of situations. It has the advantage of enabling the prosecutor to bring a single charge in order to cover an entire course of conduct. **1.23**

The chapter considers the case law governing the nature and elements of the offence, including 'public office' and 'breach of duty'. It examines culpability and the mental element in the context of what amounts to an abuse of public trust in the office holder. **1.24**

The chapter also includes the tort of misfeasance in public office, a topic which had been neglected until the liquidators of BCCI commenced their proceedings against office holders at the Bank of England. **1.25**

iii. Chapter 4: Investigation and prosecution of corruption offences

This chapter examines criminal investigation of corruption by the police, the Serious Fraud Office (SFO), the Department of Trade and Industry (DTI), and the Independent Police Complaints Commission (IPCC). The roles of the Crown Prosecution Service (CPS) and the prosecuting authorities in Scotland are also dealt with. **1.26**

The chapter focuses on the reporting obligations of public servants in relation to corruption, the Civil Service Code, the obligations of persons serving in the diplomatic service abroad, and the opportunities for reporting by the Inland Revenue as a result of new legislation introduced under ATCSA 2001. It also deals in detail with whistleblower protection under the Public Interest Disclosure Act 1998 (PIDA 1998). **1.27**

It examines the comparative merits of reactive and proactive investigations, along with the role of informants, covert methodologies, the impact of the European Convention on Human Rights, the necessity for covert methods in a democratic society, and the use of the Regulation of Investigatory Powers Act 2000 (RIPA 2000) and covert human intelligence sources (CHIS). It considers surveillance in depth, together with the pitfalls of entrapment and the comparatively recent use of integrity tests as an investigative tool in anti-corruption investigations. **1.28**

1.29 The chapter ends with an extensive review of extradition and its use in investigating and prosecuting corruption offences, including the criteria that have to be met for successful extradition applications.

iv. Chapter 5: The movement for reform

1.30 This chapter sets out the history of steps taken by the UK Government, mainly in the last half-century, to tackle corruption. It covers the setting up of a series of government committees and commissions appointed to look into the issues, and their identification of the need to draw up codes of conduct.

1.31 Ultimately the Law Commission was charged with the task of examining reform of the law. It conducted the most extensive review of the law of corruption ever undertaken and produced a draft Bill. In its Consultation Paper and later Report the Law Commission analysed for the first time the precise nature of corruption as a separate and identifiable offence, distinguishing it from theft, fraud, and dishonesty. Its recommendations, leading to the draft legislation, centred on the principal-agent relationship, widening considerably the meaning hitherto given to that relationship by introducing the concept of 'public' agents where the functions performed are of a public nature. The Commission identified a need to define corruption and carried out a rigorous examination of situations which may give rise to corrupt activity taking place, for example the use of corporate hospitality.

1.32 The Law Commission's recommendations were in large part accepted by the Government, but when the draft Bill was submitted to the Joint Committee of both Houses of Parliament a number of far-reaching objections to the proposed legislation were advanced. The Government has rejected the majority of these objections but the passage of the Bill is unlikely to be a smooth one.

2. UK Civil Law Relating to Bribery, Corruption, and Recoveries

i. Chapter 6: Civil remedies

1.33 This chapter deals with the development of the civil case law relating to corruption. The objective in bringing civil proceedings is to recover the proceeds of corruption. The possibility of recoveries from both agents and bribers is examined, as is the nature of the recovery with its implications for claiming more than the amount of the bribe itself.

1.34 Those who assist in corruption and those who receive the proceeds of corruption are also dealt with. Finally, the chapter has a review of some of the main arbitration cases which have had corruption at their centre.

ii. Chapter 7: Civil recoveries

1.35 Chapter 7 deals with the practicalities of effecting recoveries, interim relief, jurisdiction, and conflict of laws. It deals with the recovery and repatriation of looted state assets and the effectiveness of mutual legal assistance. POCA 2002 has introduced civil recoveries as a method to be used by the newly created Assets Recovery Agency (ARA) for recovery of the proceeds of crime: the proceedings are *in rem* and the standard of proof is the civil one. This is particularly useful in corruption cases, where evidence is often hard to obtain. The chapter also deals with the UK tax treatment of bribe payments.

3. The Regulation of Conduct in Public Life

i. Chapter 8: The regulation of conduct in public life

This chapter considers the importance of self-regulation in preventing corruption—in particular, the work of the Committee on Standards in Public Life (CSPL) and the extent to which the Committee's recommendations have been adopted by the Government and embodied in legislation. The chapter deals extensively with the rules regulating both Houses of Parliament, the Executive, the Prime Minister's Office, ministers, civil servants, lobbyists, special advisers, local government, quangos, and local spending public bodies. Finally, the chapter deals with the recent reforms relating to the independence of the judiciary set out in the United Kingdom in the Constitutional Reform Act 2005 and, internationally, in the Bangalore Principles of Judicial Conduct (2003). **1.36**

4. The International Fight Against Corruption

i. Chapter 9: International and regional initiatives

This chapter looks at the efforts of international bodies to achieve uniformity of approach and maximum cooperation between states in combating corruption worldwide. It considers in detail the United Nations Convention Against Corruption, which came into force on 14 December 2005, the work of the Council of Europe, the European Union, and the Group of States against Corruption (GRECO). It examines the African Union Convention on Preventing and Combating Corruption, the South African Development Community (SADC) Protocol Against Corruption, and the Economic Community of West African States (ECOWAS) Protocol. The Inter-American convention against corruption is examined, as are initiatives such as the Asian Development Bank/OECD Anti-Corruption Action Plan for Asia and the Pacific, the work of the International Chamber of Commerce, the World Bank and the International Monetary Fund. The chapter ends with an overview of initiatives taken and the progress which has been made, particularly in the last ten years. **1.37**

ii. Chapter 10: The bribery of foreign public officials

This chapter deals with the OECD Convention on Combating Bribery of Public Officials in International Business Transactions, including the requirement for **1.38** peer review of state legislation resulting in a proactive and coordinated approach to the criminalization of corruption.

1.39 The chapter contains an extensive review of the findings of the Bribery Working Group (BWG), which conducts the reviews and summarizes the differences in approach taken by OECD countries over such issues as defences, jurisdiction, mutual assistance, enforcement, limitation periods, money laundering, accounting, extradition, and tax deductibility. The future work of the BWG is considered, as are the possibilities for extension of the coverage given by the OECD to countries outside the immediate group.

1.40 Finally, the last section in the chapter deals with lessons learned from the Lesotho Highlands Water Project, which has seen some of the most high profile and proactive anti-corruption litigation undertaken in recent years. The tiny Southern African State of Lesotho pitted itself against a range of multinational companies which had bribed extensively to secure the Highlands Water Project.

iii. Chapter 11: The corruption laws of other jurisdictions

1.41 This chapter examines key provisions in the anti-corruption laws of a number of leading jurisdictions including: the United States, Australia, Canada, New Zealand, South Africa, Ireland, and Hong Kong. Other countries and regions are referred to in outline, including the GRECO member states, Russia, Eastern Europe and Eurasia, South-Eastern Europe, the Baltic countries, Asia Pacific and the Arab states. Lastly, anti-corruption commissions and related institutions in the various countries are examined and their operations compared.

iv. Chapter 12: The role of civil society organizations in combating corruption

1.42 This chapter focuses on the increasingly pronounced involvement of civil society organizations (CSOs) in the fight against corruption. It identifies the main players in the field in order to assist the reader in identifying bodies concerned with tackling different areas of corruption around the world. The chapter also refers to publications, research materials, and education and training opportunities.

D. The Prevalence of Corruption in the World Today

1.43 At the meeting of the G8 countries in Gleneagles, in July 2005, it was stated that the Millennium Development Goals cannot be achieved, particularly the eradication of poverty and disease, unless the developing countries rid themselves of corrupt regimes and establish effective strategies to combat corruption.

1.44 The Lord Chancellor, Lord Falconer, wrote in his Foreword to the UK draft Corruption Bill in 2003: 'Corruption worldwide weakens democracies, harms economies, impedes sustainable development and can undermine respect for human rights by supporting corrupt governments with widespread consequences'. Having in mind, no doubt, the conduct of some British companies and recent reforms in the UK he added: 'We are bound to promote high standards of fairness and propriety and to ensure that UK citizens do not contribute to corruption at home or abroad.'

He was referring to obligations that the United Kingdom and most other countries have undertaken under the OECD and other conventions to promote and strengthen measures to prevent and combat corruption worldwide; facilitate international cooperation and asset recovery; and promote integrity in public life and international commerce. **1.45**

Lest anyone should be in doubt about the scale of the corruption problem worldwide, it was estimated by the World Bank, in 2004,[14] that in 2002 the equivalent of over one trillion US dollars was paid in bribes.[15] This extraordinary figure, calculated using 2001–02 economic data, compares with an estimated size of the world economy in those years of US$30 trillion and *only* includes estimated bribe payments, ie it does not include embezzlement of public funds or theft of public assets. Much of the money paid out corruptly belongs to governments, many in the developing world: the World Bank quotes estimated embezzlement figures published by Transparency International of between US$15 and 35 billion for Suharto of Indonesia, and up to US$5 billion each for Marcos of the Philippines, Mobutu of Zaire, and Abacha in Nigeria.[16] In June 2005, Nigeria's own anti-corruption commission put forward a figure of £210 billion as its estimate of the amount stolen or misused by corrupt leaders and politicians since Nigeria gained independence in 1960.[17] This figure is said to equal the entire amount of aid donated by Western countries to Africa between 1960 and 1997, or six times the amount of American aid given to post-war Europe under the Marshall Plan.[18] **1.46**

The World Bank acknowledges that the cost of corruption constitutes a major obstacle to reducing poverty, inequality, and infant mortality in emerging economies. Its research shows that countries which tackle corruption and **1.47**

---

[14] World Bank Group, The Costs of Corruption, 8 April 2004: External News on http://web.worldbank.org.

[15] A trillion is 1,000,000,000,000. It can be expressed as 10^{12}, ie one thousand billion or a million millions. The writer, mathematician, and astronomer, Carl Sagan has calculated that it would take 32,000 years (longer than there has been human life on earth) to count to one trillion from one at a rate of one count per second, night and day: counting to one billion takes a mere 32 years: C Sagan, *Billions and Billions: Thoughts on Life and Death at the Brink of the Millennium* (New York: Ballantine, 1997.)

[16] See further 7.50 below.

[17] Projection released by Mallam Nuhu Ribadu, Chairman of Nigeria's Economic and Financial Crimes Commission, which was set up in 2002.

[18] David Blair, *The Daily Telegraph*, 25 June 2005.

improve their rule of law can increase their national incomes by as much as four times in the long term, and that child mortality can fall as much as 75 per cent. 'We have found what we label as the 400 percent governance dividend' said Daniel Kaufmann, Director for Governance at the World Bank Institute.[19] The United Nations, in a Note issued by the UNDP in June 2005,[20] states that 4.8 million children in sub-Saharan Africa die before the age of five every year, ie nine deaths every minute. The Note goes on to state that, if current trends continue, there will be 5.1 million child deaths in 2015, with Africa's share of the world total rising from a current 45 per cent to 57 per cent. It is no coincidence that the two countries that account for the largest number of child deaths per annum, Nigeria (nearly one million) and the Democratic Republic of Congo (more than half a million), are also the ones which have been most heavily looted by their leaders.

1.48 The UNDP Note was issued in the context of achievements in the five years since the Millennium Development Goals (MDGs) were set in 2000 with the objective of halving world poverty by 2015. In April 2005, the British Government published the Report of the Commission For Africa (CFA), 'Our Common Interest', ahead of Prime Minister Tony Blair's Chairmanship of the G8 countries. The Report deals with corruption, stating that:

> Corruption is a by-product of weak governance . . . much of it takes place at a grassroots level and affects people's daily lives, for example through bribes paid to bureaucrats, or non-delivery of services to poor people. The corrosive effect of corruption undermines all efforts to improve governance and foster development . . . African governments, together with their development partners, should broaden their investigation of means to address corruption at all levels . . . The initial focus should be on tackling corruption in those sectors where it is most pervasive, such as in the lucrative natural resource sector . . . and in the area of procurement.
>
> Procurement—the way that governments buy in goods and services—suffers particularly severely from corruption. Abuse of this system takes many forms. Though public sector contracts are widely put out to sealed tender, bribes—known by euphemisms such as 'signature bonuses'— can be requested or offered which result in the accepted bid not being the best available. Quotations can be doctored to build in false costs. It is not only the politicians and public officials who create the problem: it is also the bankers, the lawyers and the accountants, and the engineers working on public contracts.
>
> Experts estimate that systemic corruption can add as much as 25 per cent to the costs of government procurement, frequently resulting in inferior quality

[19] The Costs of Corruption (n 15 above).

[20] UNDP Human Development Report Office: *Sub-Saharan Africa—the human costs of the 2015 'business as usual' scenario*, Draft Background document, issued 9 June 2005 in advance of the full global trend projection in the 2005 *Human Development Report*. UNDP, the United Nations Development Programme, is the UN's global development network; for more information, visit http://www.undp.org.

> construction and unnecessary purchases. Transparency International's most recent Corruption Perception Index suggests that, of the US$4 trillion spent world-wide on government public contracts every year, some US$400 billion is lost to bribery.[21] Since this money comes out of the public purse this means a major loss of resources that could otherwise be spent on education, healthcare and the reduction of poverty.[22]

The CFA Report cites a European Commission Report which estimates that stolen African assets equivalent to more than half of the continent's external debt are held in foreign bank accounts.[23] The CFA recommends that: **1.49**

> Countries and territories with significant financial centres should take, as a matter of urgency, all necessary legal and administrative measures to repatriate illicitly acquired state funds and assets. We call on G8 countries to make specific commitments in 2005 and to report back on progress, including sums repatriated, in 2006.[24]

The recovery of these monies could indeed help to 'Make Poverty History'.[25] **1.50**
The world's civil courts have a huge role to play in effecting such recoveries. Very often the only redress that an overseas party will have is to take civil action. In the case of foreign governments there is the option of requesting mutual legal assistance but experience has shown that in the United Kingdom the process can be slow, cumbersome, and uncertain in outcome. In general the problem may have been that governments are not that keen on spending taxpayers' money pursuing claims on behalf of foreign governments which have little chance of winning votes at home. This is now showing signs of change in the UK,[26] with the growing realization that corruption is genuinely a global problem, and the coming into force of the United Nations Convention Against Corruption, which has the potential to produce a significant shift in the attitude of governments to providing international assistance will, the authors hope, produce further widespread, change.

---

[21] *Corruption Perception Index 2004* (Berlin: Transparency International) http://transparency.org/publications/index.html. [22] 'Our Common Interest', para 4.5.1.

[23] Commission of the European Communities, *EU Africa Dialogue, 2003*, 7.

[24] 'Our Common Interest', para 4.5.3.

[25] 'Make Poverty History', http://www.makepovertyhistory.org/.

[26] See 7.69 below.

2

OFFENCES OF BRIBERY AND CORRUPTION

A. Introduction

2.01 This chapter describes the criminal offences which may be committed by persons who engage in corrupt practices in England and Wales or, if they are United Kingdom nationals or corporations incorporated under the law of any part of the United Kingdom, engage in corruption outside the United Kingdom.[1] The Law Commission has recommended that the existing offences be replaced by new legislation which is currently reflected in the Draft Corruption Bill 2003 which, at time of writing, is still the subject of consultation. Detailed consideration of the nature and extent of the proposed reforms is included in chapter 5 below.

2.02 Apart from bribery, which is a common law offence,[2] the English law relating to what are called 'offences of corruption' is set out in two main statutes, the Public Bodies Corrupt Practices Act 1889 and the Prevention of Corruption Act 1906, as amended by the Prevention of Corruption Act 1916 and Part 12 of the Anti-Terrorism, Crime and Security Act 2001 (ATCSA). The three corruption statutes are known as the Prevention of Corruption Acts 1889 to 1916.[3] Corruption offences are, however, to be found in at least 11 statutes.[4]

[1] See ATCSA 2001, which is dealt with further at 2.78 below.

[2] The common law and statutory offences were misdemeanours. The distinction between felonies and misdemeanours was abolished by the Criminal Law Act 1967, ss 1 and 12(5) and 6.

[3] See App 28 below

[4] Sale of Offices Act 1551; Sale of Offices Act 1809; Public Bodies Corrupt Practices Act 1889; Prevention of Corruption Act 1906; Prevention of Corruption Act 1916; Honours (Prevention of Abuses) Act 1925; Licensing Act 1964, s 178; Criminal Law Act 1967, s 5; Local Government Act 1972, s 117(2); Customs and Excise Management Act 1979, s 15; Representation of the People Act 1983, ss 107, 109 and 111–115.

The common law offence of bribery is limited to public sector corruption. The Public Bodies Corrupt Practices Act 1889 is also limited to public sector corruption, particularly the officers and employees of public bodies. The Prevention of Corruption Act 1906 is concerned with corruption by agents and covers both public and private sector corruption. The Prevention of Corruption Act 1916 did not create any new offences. It extended the meaning of public bodies and introduced a presumption of corruption where money has been received by employees of public bodies in connection with public contracts.[5] Part 12 of ATCSA 2001 extended the jurisdiction of English courts over bribery and corruption offences to include corruption involving foreign public officials abroad. **2.03**

In practice, most corruption cases coming before the courts are for offences under the 1906 Act, rather than under the 1889 Act or for the common law offence. Following an extensive review of the English corruption laws, the Law Commission recommended the abolition of the common law offence of bribery, the repeal of the offences under the Prevention of Corruption Acts, and their substitution by an entirely new set of offences under a new Corruption Act. A Draft Bill was introduced to Parliament in October 2003 and considered by a Joint Committees of both Houses (the 'Joint Committee'). Evidence received by the Committee severely criticized the bill, its drafting, clarity and comprehensiveness. The Committee invited the Home Office to bring forward a revised Bill taking account of the points it had made, and the Government gave a robust response.[6] No new draft Bill has been introduced. For the time being, therefore, the offences of corruption remain as described in this chapter.[7] **2.04**

In the Prevention of Corruption Acts the offering or giving, and the soliciting or receipt, of a bribe are treated as distinct offences. Offering or giving a bribe is sometimes described as active corruption and soliciting or receiving a bribe is sometimes described as passive corruption.[8] Where an offence of corruption is complete, it is likely to have been committed by the person who pays the bribe as well as the person who receives it. In such a case they may both be prosecuted for the full offence or for conspiracy to commit one of the statutory offences, together with any other persons who have knowingly participated in the offence. They may also be prosecuted for conspiracy to defraud, on the basis that they conspired dishonestly to cause loss, for example, to the principal of the person bribed.[9] **2.05**

[5] The 1916 Act increased the maximum penalty for corruption relating to government contracts from two to seven years, but this was repealed by CJA 1988 s 170(2), Sch 16, when the maximum penalty for all offences against the 1889 and 1906 Acts was increased to seven years for any corruption offence; see 2.34, 2.45, 2.59 below.

[6] House of Lords, House of Commons Joint Committee on the Draft Corruption Bill, Report and Evidence, Session 2002–03, HL Paper 157, HC 705.

[7] The proposals for reform are set out in Ch 5 below.

[8] See the OECD Convention, Commentary 1.

[9] *R v Whittaker* [1914] 3 KB 1283; 10 Cr App R 245 CCA and see 2.12 n 23 and 3.30 below.

2.06 Because the commission of corruption offences usually involves the commission of other criminal offences, this chapter attempts to distinguish between corruption offences in the strict sense and other offences, such as theft, obtaining by deception, false accounting, money laundering, and conspiracy to defraud, which are usually also committed by persons performing corrupt acts. In some cases persons are not able to be prosecuted for bribery or corruption, but they are nevertheless guilty of fraud, false accounting or some similar offence.

B. Common Law Offences

1. Bribery

i. Definition and scope of the offence

2.07 Bribery is a common law offence which has developed over the centuries. The result is that opinions differ as to whether it is a general offence applying to a range of different offices or functions, or whether it is comprised of a number of specific offences distinguished by the office or function to which the particular offence applies.[10]

2.08 David Lanham, in *Essays in Honour of J C Smith*, adopting with minor amendment the definition in *Russell on Crime*, defines bribery as 'the receiving or offering [of] any undue reward by or to any person whatsoever, in a public office, in order to influence his behaviour in office, and incline him to act contrary to the known rules of honesty and integrity'.[11] It is an offence of bribery not only to give or receive a bribe, but also to offer or solicit a bribe. Offering and receiving are unilateral acts and do not depend on any state of mind on the part of the person offering the bribe or the person solicited.

ii. Any undue reward

2.09 The bribe is defined as 'any undue reward'. A reward, which is so small as not to be considered a reward at all, cannot be regarded as 'undue'.[12] In the *Bodmin Case*[13] Willes J mentioned that he had been required to swear that he would not take any gift from a man who had a plea pending, unless it was 'meat and drink and that of small value'. In *S v Deal Enterprises (Pty) Ltd*,[14] a South African case,

[10] D Lanham, 'Bribery and Corruption' in P Smith (ed) *Criminal Law: Essays in Honour of J C Smith* (London: Butterworths, 1987) 92–93; Law Com Report, para 2.2.

[11] Sir William Oldwell Russell, *Russell on Crime* Turner (ed) (12th edn, 1964) 381; Law Commission Report, para 2.5. Lanham (n 10 above) 93, prefers Russell's definition in Sir William Oldwell Russell, *A Treatise on Crimes and Misdemeanours*, (4th edn, 1865) vol 1, p 382, see *Hawkins* 1 PC, ch 67, s 1; Coke 3 Inst 145, on the basis that it is wider and more satisfactory.

[12] See 10.42 below, in relation to the OECD Convention.

[13] (1869) 1 O'M & H 121. See also the approach to treating in elections at 2.102 below.

[14] (1978) 3.42 SA 302, 311.

Nicholas J distinguished entertainment from bribery on the same basis. It seems that entertainment and treats, which are things of small value are not prohibited because they cannot be regarded as having been conferred in order to influence a person, or incline him to act contrary to the known rules of honesty and integrity.[15] In every case, however the distinction must depend on the particular circumstances. According to Lanham, treats, if regarded as an exception to the rule against bribes, are narrowly construed and are not to be considered as a defence.[16]

iii. Facilitation payments

The common law definition of a bribe clearly covers facilitation payments, ie payments made to petty officials to induce them to perform their public duties where otherwise they may be disinclined to do so. UK law has never recognised facilitation payments (nor indeed corporate hospitality gifts)[17] as a distinct category of payment or reward.[18] However, the Government has publicly stated that it is difficult to envisage circumstances in which the making of a small facilitation payment, extorted by a foreign official in countries where this is normal practice, would of itself give rise to a prosecution in the UK.[19] The Corner House, a UK NGO which participated in the Draft Corruption Bill consultation process, has recommended that the Government should operate a zero tolerance policy except in exceptional circumstances in which the life of an employee may be at risk if a payment is not made.[20] **2.10**

Although bribes usually take a tangible form such as money, they can also take the form of services including sexual services.[21] **2.11**

iv. Acting in an official capacity or performing a public function

The offence of bribery is limited to persons acting in an official capacity or performing public functions. It does not extend to public officers performing private functions.[22] The obvious example of a person who performs a public function is a public officer. A public officer is an officer who discharges any duty in the discharge of which the public are interested, irrespective of whether his office is judicial, ministerial or otherwise.[23] **2.12**

---

15 *Woodward v Maltby* [1959] VR 794. See also treating in elections at 2.102 below.

16 Lanham (n 10 above).

17 For an analysis of the nature of corporate hospitality gifts see 5.128 below.

18 *cf* FCPA at 11.15 below

19 See http://www.ukti.gov.uk.

20 International Development Committee, Fourth Report, 'Corruption', vol 1, para 186, p lix; Joint Committee on the Draft Corruption Bill, Written Evidence, Memorandum from The Corner House (DCB1).

21 *Scott v State* 141 NE 19 (1923) (Supreme Court of Ohio); see also *US v Girard* 601 F 2d 69, (1979); *Zalla v State* 61 So 2d 649 (1952) (promise of illegal lottery tickets).

22 *HM Advocate v Dick* (1901) 3 F (Ct Sess) 59.

23 *R. v. Whitaker* [1914] 3 KB 1283, 1296; 10 Cr App R 245, CCA. See further 2.04 above and 3.06, 3.30 below.

2.13 Bribery appears to have been concerned originally with persons holding judicial office.[24] It was subsequently extended to persons exercising ministerial functions[25] which now include any functions which are not judicial. The result is that it includes any person who is in the position of trustee of public functions, for example, an army officer as in *R v Whitaker*.[26] It is not necessary that the person bribed should be paid for his or her services and it includes persons who discharge ad hoc public duties. Thus it has been held to include justices of the peace,[27] jurors,[28] and electors at local and parliamentary elections.[29]

2.14 Bribery of judges, magistrates, or other judicial officers may also be punished as contempt: *R v Harrison*.[30] Bribery of jurors also constitutes the offence of embracery, which is now almost obsolete. Bribery of a customs officer is a summary offence, contrary to section 15 of the Customs and Excise Management Act 1979.[31]

v. The object of the bribe

2.15 The object of a bribe is to secure a benefit, for example to obtain a contract, or service, or to secure a prize or appointment.[32] The purchase and sale of a public office can constitute bribery.[33] It can also constitute the separate offence of sale of a public office.[34]

2.16 Trading in influence, ie offering a person a bribe to induce him to exercise his influence to obtain an appointment for a person offering a bribe, is not unlawful unless an agency relationship exists between the person who is offered the bribe and the person making the appointment, in which case an offence may be committed under the Corruption Act 1906.[35]

2.17 Although definitions and understanding as to what amounts to trading in influence have tended to differ from jurisdiction to jurisdiction, there is now the

[24] eg a coroner in *R v Harrison* (1800) 1 East P.C. 382. Two Lord Chancellors and one Lord Chief Justice have been prosecuted for taking bribes; *R v Bacon* (1620) 2 State Tr 1087; *R v Earl of Macclesfield* (1725) 16 State Tr 767; *Thorne's Case* Coke 3 Inst 145. See also *Judicial independence - Its History in England and Wales*, an essay by Brooke LJ, Court of Appeal England at http://www.jc.nsw.gov.au/jb/fbbrook.htm.

[25] eg a First Lord of the Treasury and Privy Councillor; *R v Vaughan* (1769) 4 Burr. 2494, 98 ER 308.

[26] [1914] 3 KB 1283, 1296.

[27] *R v Gurney* (1867) 10 Cox 550.

[28] *R v Young* (1801) 2 East 14, 16.

[29] *Pitt and Mead* (1726) 3 Burr 1335; 97 ER 861.

[30] (1800) 1 East PC 382.

[31] See 2.93 below.

[32] The Law Commission gives extensive consideration to the object and purpose of bribes; see 5.40 below.

[33] *R v Pollman* (1809) 2 Camp 229n.

[34] See 2.92 below.

[35] The Corner House believed that it should have been included as an offence in the Draft Bill, as the Government had noted in its consultation that it was broadly welcomed as an offence; Report of the Joint Committee on the Draft Bill—Written Evidence, Memorandum from the Corner House (DCB1) para 6. See also UNCAC, Art 18 which provides that states shall consider criminalization of trading in influence.

benefit of the definition contained within Article 18 of UNCAC[36] to the effect that trading in influence comprises:[37]

(a) The promise, offering or giving to a public official or any other person, directly or indirectly, of an undue advantage in order that the public official or the person abuse his or her real or supposed influence with a view to obtaining from an administration or public authority of the State Party an undue advantage for the original instigator of the act or for any other person; or,
(b) The solicitation or acceptance by a public official or any other person, directly or indirectly, of an undue advantage for himself or herself or for another person in order that the public official or the person abuse his or her real or supposed influence with a view to obtaining from an administration or public authority of the State Party an undue advantage.

On the basis of that definition, there will be occasions where a case proceeds under the 1906 Act, but amounts to trading in influence on the UN definition.

vi. The mental element

2.18 Russell describes the mental element of bribery in terms of a briber intending 'to influence the behaviour of a public officer' and 'to incline him to act contrary to the known rules of honesty and integrity'.[38] It includes giving a bribe to induce the recipient to act in breach of his duty, ie to do something he would not otherwise do, or to exercise his discretion in a way he would not otherwise exercise it, and giving a bribe to induce the recipient to perform a duty which he is required to perform by the terms of his office, but which he is disinclined to perform without payment of the bribe. The latter is called a 'facilitation' or 'grease payment'.[39]

2.19 In *R v Gurney*,[40] a case involving a justice of the peace, the mental element was held to include an intention to produce *any effect at all* on his decision. In *HM Advocate v Dick*[41] it was held that the decision must relate to the duty of the person receiving the bribe. Thus it was not unlawful for a councillor to receive a bribe to use his influence to procure the grant of a licensing certificate by a magistrate, as the use of the influence was no part of the councillor's official functions. However, if a person uses his position to get a commission corruptly, it does not matter whether the work in respect of which he gets commission is work to which his duties relate or not.[42] If he keeps the money, he can be convicted of theft. In *R v David*,[43] a case under section 87 of the Queensland Code, it was held not to apply to a police officer, who was paid a bribe to

[36] See also 9.28 below. [37] Set out in full at App 29 below.
[38] See 2.08 above. [39] See 2.10 below.
[40] (1867) 10 Cox CC 550; *contra* see *Williams v R* (1979) 23 ALR 369 (a case under the Australian Crimes Act 1914, s. 73). [41] 1901 3F (Ct of Sess) 59.
[42] *R v Dickinson and De Rable*, (1949) 33 Cr App R 5, CCA, a case under the Corruption Act 1906. [43] 1931 2 QWN 2.

destroy evidence as it was no part of his duty to destroy evidence. In *Attorney-General for Hong Kong v Ip Chiu*[44] it was held not to apply to a suspect who paid a policeman a bribe to avoid having evidence planted on him as planting evidence could be done equally well by a person not in the police force.[45]

vii. Entrapment

2.20 Difficult issues can arise in entrapment cases,[46] as the prosecution only have to prove the defendant offered a gift in order to get the offeree to agree to enter a corrupt transaction. In *R v Smith*,[47] a case under the Public Bodies Corrupt Practices Act 1889, the Court of Criminal Appeal upheld the decision of a trial judge to withdraw from a jury the defence that offering a bribe in order to expose corruption was not corrupt, as 'corruptly' required merely an intention to corrupt and motive was irrelevant.[48] Similarly, in *R v Carr*,[49] a case under the Prevention of Corruption Act 1906, it was held that the prosecution have to prove only that the offeree received a gift as an inducement to show favour, not that he actually showed favour. Thus a person who accepts a gift knowing it is intended as a bribe enters into a corrupt bargain even if he makes a mental reservation not to carry out his side of the bargain. He cannot avoid liability on the basis that he did not intend it to influence him. Double-crossing is not a defence.[50] However, if the offeree merely pretends to respond to the approach, he has no intention to corrupt and if he receives money to entrap the giver or to provide evidence for the police and does not intend to keep the money, it is not corrupt.[51]

2.21 Before the Joint Committee, the Newspaper Society was concerned that 'newsgathering practices could effectively be criminalized, thereby potentially inhibiting investigative journalism'.[52] It suggested such conduct should be excluded from the definition of corruption or that there should be a public interest defence. The Crown Prosecution Service (CPS) did not favour the suggestion, as it considered it would open the door to all sorts of spurious defences. It pointed out, however, that public interest was one of the factors taken into account when deciding whether to prosecute.[53]

2.22 The solution for persons involved in entrapment situations is for them to invite the involvement of the police, where possible.[54]

---

[44] [1980] AC 663, PC. [45] See also *R v Patel* 1944 AD 51.
[46] See, generally, 4.195 below. [47] [1960] 2 QB 423
[48] See also *S v Van Der Westhuizen* 1974 (4) SA 61; *R v Dillon* (1982) VR 434; *S v Ernst* 1963 3 SA 666. [49] (1956) 40 Cr App R 188, Ct MAC.
[50] Sir Francis Bacon, Lord Chancellor in 1618, pleaded guilty to bribery, but claimed, in mitigation only, that he had not done any of the things for which he had been paid the bribes.
[51] *R v Mills* (1979) 68 Cr App R 154 (CA); *R v Carr* (1956) 40 Cr App R 188, Ct MAC.
[52] Joint Committee (n 6 above), Evidence 138 DCB 8.
[53] Joint Committee Report, paras 59–60. [54] See 4.195–4.210 below.

viii. Defences and immunities

The common law defence of duress, which requires proof of threats of physical violence[55] unless the conduct is carried out, is a defence to bribery and also to offences under the Prevention of Corruption Acts. **2.23**

There is a degree of uncertainty as to the extent to which Members of Parliament are immune from the criminal or civil law in respect of what is said or done in Parliamentary proceedings, due to the protection granted by Article 9 of the Bill of Rights.[56] The Committee on Standards in Public Life has recommended that Parliament should legislate so as to make it clear that MPs have no immunities where allegations of corruption are concerned.[57] The common law of corruption applies to MPs in Canada[58] and Australia.[59] **2.24**

The Diplomatic Privileges Act 1964, which incorporates the Vienna Convention on Diplomatic Relations 1961 grants diplomatic agents of foreign missions in the United Kingdom immunity from the jurisdiction of UK courts while they are in office in respect of their official acts. Sections 20(1) and 27 of the State and Immunity Act 1978 grant immunity from criminal jurisdiction to foreign sovereigns and heads of state and their families and servants. The extent of sovereign immunity and immunity in respect of acts of state was considered in *R v Bow Street Metropolitan Stipendiary Magistrates, ex p Pinochet Ugarte (No 3)*.[60] The immunity of foreign ministers was considered in *Democratic Republic of the Congo v Belgium*.[61] **2.25**

ix. Penalty and mode of trial

Common law bribery is triable only on indictment and is punishable by fine and/or unlimited imprisonment,[62] irrespective of whether the bribe is accepted or not, and in the case of office holders by loss of office.[63] The convicting court can make a confiscation order under the Proceeds of Crime Act 2002 (POCA 2002).[64] **2.26**

2. Bribery Distinguished From Other Common Law Offences

i. Misconduct in public office

Receipt of a bribe by a public officer can also be charged as the common law offence of misconduct in a public office.[65] Misconduct in public office was **2.27**

---

55 *R v Howe* [1987] AC 417, HL. 56 See 5.161 and 8.15 below.
57 Nicholls Report, paras 1.35–1.42; Nolan report (Cm 28.50–1, 1995) paras 103–104.
58 *R v Bunting* (1885) 7 OR 524.
59 *R v Boston* (1923) 33 CLR 386; see also *A-G for Ceylon v de Livera* [1963] AC 103; *R v Boston* (1992) unreported but noted at [1998] PL 356. 60 [2000] 1 AC 147 HL.
61 [2002] ICJ 1 (14 February 2002). 62 See n 119 below.
63 3 Co Inst 147. The imprisonment is unlimited by virtue of it being a common law offence.
64 See n 5 above.
65 *R v Llewellyn-Jones* [1968] 1 QB 429. For the definition of misconduct in a public office, see 3.07 and 3.49 below.

described in the Salmon Report as a 'breach of official trust', an offence which 'embraces a wide variety of misconduct including acts done with a dishonest, oppressive or corrupt motive'.[66]

ii. Extortion

2.28 The common law offence of extortion was abolished by section 32(1)(a) of the Theft Act 1968 and replaced by blackmail, an offence contrary to section 21 of the same Act. The importance of blackmail in the context of bribery and corruption has increased having regard to the Government's approach to prosecuting in cases involving facilitation payments.[67]

iii. Embracery

2.29 Bribery of a juror, or any attempt to bribe or influence a juror out of court, constitutes the almost obsolete common law offence of embracery. Such conduct is normally charged as perverting the course of justice or contempt of court.[68]

iv. Contempt of court

2.30 Bribery or intimidation of a witness and an attempt to bribe or intimidate a witness is a contempt of court and may be dealt with by summary procedure.[69] It also constitutes the indictable offence of perverting the course of justice.[70]

C. Statutory Offences

1. Introduction

2.31 Statutory offences of corruption in the United Kingdom were created in response to specific events and not as part of any general legislative scheme. They are set out in three statutes, known collectively as the Prevention of Corruption Acts 1889 to 1916.[71] The jurisdiction of the English courts for offences under those Acts is the same as in the case of common law bribery.[72]

2.32 The first of the Prevention of Corruption Acts 1889 to 1916, the Public Bodies Corrupt Practices Act 1889, was enacted following revelations by a Royal Commission on malpractice in the Metropolitan Board of Works, the body which exercised the powers of local government in London at that time.[73] As

[66] Salmon Report, para 194, citing *Borron* (1830) 3 B & Ald 432.
[67] See 2.10 above. [68] *R v Owen* [1976] 1 WLR 840.
[69] *Moore v Clerk of Assize, Bristol* [1971] 1 WLR 1669 (CA, Civil Division); *R v Owen* 63 Cr App R 199, CA. [70] *R v Stevenson* (1802) 2 East 362; *R v Bassi* [1985] Crim LR 671, CA.
[71] Prevention of Corruption Act 1916, s. 4(1). [72] See 2.77 below.
[73] P Fennell and PA Thomas, 'The Law Relating to Corruption in England and Wales, An Historical Analysis' (1983) 11 *International Journal of Social Law* 167, 172 and see, generally,

a result it was limited to corruption in local bodies. The second statute, the Prevention of Corruption Act 1906, followed a report published by the Secret Commissions Committee of the London Chamber of Commerce, calling for the criminal law of corruption to be extended to the private sector. Although it purported to deal with corruption in the private sector, it also covered corruption in the public sector. The third statute, the Prevention of Corruption Act 1916, was passed following a series of First World War scandals involving contracts with the War Ministry.[74]

The manner in which the Corruption Acts were enacted has led to a number of anomalies between them, particularly where agents of public bodies are involved. For example, councillors in local government are not agents and cannot be prosecuted under the 1906 Act and the Crown is not a public body for the purposes of that Act, however, because there is an agency relationship between the Crown and Crown servants, they must be dealt with under the 1906 Act. Conversely, public servants cannot be dealt with under the 1906 Act and must be dealt with under the 1889 Act.[75] **2.33**

The 1916 Act extended the 1889 Act to include corruption in central government, increased the maximum sentence in cases of public corruption to seven years[76] and introduced a presumption of corruption in cases involving government contracts. The descriptions in this chapter of the offences in the 1889 and 1906 Acts incorporate the amendments made by the 1916 Act, ATCSA 2001 and other statutes. **2.34**

2. The 1889 and 1906 Acts and the meaning of 'corruptly'

The word 'corruptly' appears in all three Corruption Acts, but is not defined in any of them. In *Cooper v Slade*,[77] a case of bribery at an election by paying voters travelling expenses under the Corrupt Practices Prevention Act 1854, Willes J, in the course of his advice to the House of Lords, interpreted 'corruptly' as not meaning dishonestly, but meaning purposely doing an act which the law forbids as tending to corrupt. In *Bradford Election Case (No 2)*[78] Martin B, commenting on this interpretation, said the word was not otiose and had been given some meaning which was akin to an evil mind. In *R v Lindley*[79] and *R v Calland*,[80] two cases under the 1906 Act, it was held to mean dishonestly weakening the **2.35**

A Crew, *The law Relating to Secret Commissions and Bribes: The Prevention of Corruption Act 1906* (London: Pitman & Sons, 1913).

74 P Fennell and PA Thomas (n 73 above) See Salmon Report, para 46 and para 5.01 ff below.

75 *R v Natji* [2002] 1 WLR 2337; [2002] 2 Cr App R 20.

76 This provision was repealed by CJA 1988, s 170(2), Sch 16, when the maximum sentence for offences under the 1889 and 1906 Acts, was raised from two to seven years.

77 (1858) 6 HL Cas 746, 773.

78 (1869) 19 LT 723, 728.

79 [1957] Crim LR 321.

80 [1967] Crim LR 236.

loyalty of an agent to his principal and, in the latter case, it was said that if the defendant's action amounted to sharp practice and not dishonesty, he was not guilty of corruption. In *R v Smith (John)*,[81] a case under the 1889 Act where the defendant claimed to have offered a bribe with a view to exposing corruption, the Court of Appeal approved the dictum of Willes J in *Cooper v Slade* and upheld the trial judge's direction that 'corruptly' meant with intention to corrupt and that motive was irrelevant. Lord Parker CJ, recognised that this construction arguably rendered the word 'corruptly' redundant, but suggested that even if this were so in cases involving inducements, the word might have an independent function in the case of rewards. In *R v Wellburn*[82] and *R v Harvey*,[83] both cases under the 1906 Act, the Court of Appeal expressly disapproved *R v Lindley* and *R v Calland* and followed the interpretation of Willes J in *Cooper v Slade*, the court stating in *Wellburn* that 'corruptly' was an ordinary word, the meaning of which would cause a jury little difficulty.[84] In *R v Harvey* the court held that dishonesty was not an element of the offence and that the word 'corruption' for the purposes of the section is to be construed as deliberately offering money or other favours with the intention that it should operate on the mind of the offeree so as to encourage him to enter into a corrupt bargain. In *R v Godden-Wood*,[85] a case under the 1906 Act, it was held that the test was the same whether it was in the public or the private domain

2.36 The interpretation of 'corruptly' in *Cooper v Slade* followed by the Court of Appeal in *Wellburn* has been subjected to criticism, not least by Professor Smith, who said it would leave the word 'devoid of any functional significance' and Lanham, reviewing the authorities in England and Australia, described the authorities in both countries as in 'impressive disarray'.[86]

2.37 The Law Commission, took the view that the court's view in *Wellburn* that the meaning of 'corruptly' would cause a jury little difficulty was unduly optimistic. It said the meaning was unclear and decided to include a definition of 'corruption' in its draft Bill which differed according to whether the offence was involved with an inducement or a reward.[87]

---

[81] [1960] 2 QB 423. It has been submitted in Sir Gerald H Gordon, *Criminal Law* MGA Christie (ed) (3rd edn, Edinburgh: W Green & Son, 2001–1) para 44.08, that *R v Smith (John)*, was wrongly decided and that the court was wrong to rely on *Cooper v Slade*, as the situation in *R v Smith* was altogether different from the situation in *Cooper v Slade*.

[82] (1979) 69 Cr App R 254, CA.

[83] [1999] Crim LR 70, CA.

[84] *Ibid* at 265 *per* Lawton LJ.

[85] [2001] Crim LR 810, CA.

[86] Lanham, *Bribery and Corruption in Criminal Law: Essays in Honour of J C Smith* P Smith (ed) (London: Butterworths, 1987) 92–93, 104; Law Com Report, para 2.2.

[87] Law Com Report, para. 2.29; Law Commission Consultation Paper No 145, paras 4.15–4.17.

3. The 1916 Act and the presumption of corruption in government contracts

Section 2 of the 1916 Act introduced a presumption of corruption in cases under the 1889 and 1906 Acts where a bribe has been received by an employee of a government department or public body from a person holding or seeking to obtain a government contract.[88] **2.38**

Section 2 provides: **2.39**

> Where in any proceedings against a person for an offence under the Prevention of Corruption Act 1906, or the Public Bodies Corrupt Practices Act 1889, it is proved that any money, gift, or other consideration has been paid or given to or received by a person in the employment of [Her] Majesty or any Government Department or a public body by or from a person, or agent of a person, holding or seeking to obtain a contract from [Her] Majesty or any Government Department or public body, the money, gift, or consideration shall be deemed to have been paid or given and received corruptly as such inducement or reward as is mentioned in such Act unless the contrary is proved.

The presumption does not apply to conduct which amounts to an offence only by reason of sections 108 or 109 of ACTSA 2001, ie offences committed by UK nationals and UK registered companies abroad.[89] The effect of the presumption is to place the burden of proving that a payment was not a corrupt payment upon a defendant, who can only discharge the burden if he satisfies the jury of the probability that the gift was made innocently.[90] The burden was originally the full legal burden.[91] **2.40**

It has been suggested that the presumption violates the presumption of innocence contained in Article 6(2) of the European Convention on Human Rights incorporated into domestic law by the Human Rights Act 1998 (HRA 1998), and the Law Commission therefore recommended that it (ie the presumption) should be abolished.[92] However, in *R v Lambert*[93] and *R v Matthews*,[94] cases not relating to corruption, where there were similar presumptions, it was said obiter that they would not do so, as the provisions only imposed an evidential or persuasive burden.[95] The problem may be avoided by charging conspiracy to commit an offence under the 1889 or 1906 Acts, contrary to section 1 of the Criminal Law Act 1977, which is an offence separate and distinct from the ulterior offence and to which the presumption does not apply.[96] **2.41**

---

88 See App 28.
89 ATCSA 2001, s 110. See 2.80 below.
90 *R v Carr-Briant* [1943] KB 607, 29 Cr App R 76, CCA.
91 *R v Braithwaite* [1983] 1 WLR 385; *Evans v Jones* [1923] 17 Cr App R 121. For further cases on this area see paras 5.90 ff and 11.78 below.
92 *Legislating the Criminal Code: Corruption*, Para 4.78.
93 [2002] 2 AC 545, HL.
94 [2003] 3 WLR 693.
95 See also *R v DPP, ex p Kebilene* [2000] 2 AC 326; *Sheldrake v DPP; A-G's Reference (No 5 of 2002)* [2004] UKHL 40.
96 *R v A-G, ex p Rockall* [2000] 1 WLR 882.

2.42 The Law Commission recommended that the presumption should be abolished. Transparency International argued before the Joint Committee that the public expects its servants to be incorruptible and nothing should be done to ease the pressure to maintain integrity standards. It stressed the fact that corruption is necessarily a covert offence, the seriousness of which may merit special measures. A redrafted 'presumption' or 'inference' should not offend the Convention and could prove useful to prosecutors whilst not being unfair to defendants. The Joint Committee considered that there may be an argument for extending the inference to the private sector on the basis that private sector corruption raises similar concerns and share many of the same characteristics as its public sector counterpart.[97]

2.43 The Home Office favoured careful consideration of an extension of the presumption to include foreign officials: 'It may be reasonable to expect a person in these circumstances [namely a government official] to justify any questionable payments made to them. The Government therefore considers it right to consider carefully any extension to the presumption of corruption. If it is extended to government officials, there can be no reason for not applying it to foreign officials as well'.[98]

4. Corruption in Public Office

i. The offences

2.44 Section 1 of the Public Bodies Corrupt Practices Act 1889, as amended by the Prevention of Corruption Act 1916 and ATCSA 2001, provides that:

> (1) Every person who shall by himself or by or in conjunction with any other person, corruptly solicit or receive, or agree to receive, for himself, or for any other person, any gift, loan, fee, reward, or advantage whatever as an inducement to, or reward for, or otherwise on account of any member, officer, or servant of a public body as in this Act defined, doing or forbearing to do anything in respect of any matter or transaction whatsoever, actual or proposed, in which the said public body is concerned, shall be guilty of [an offence].[99]
>
> (2) Every person who shall by himself or by or in conjunction with any other person corruptly give, promise, or offer any gift, loan, fee, reward, or advantage whatsoever to any person, whether for the benefit of that person or of another person, as an inducement to or reward for or otherwise on account of any member, officer, or servant of any public body as in this Act defined, doing or forbearing to do anything in respect of any matter or transaction whatsoever, actual or proposed, in which such public body as aforesaid is concerned, shall be guilty of [an offence].[100]

---

[97] Joint Committee, Evidence 3, para 3.8. See n 6 above.

[98] The Home Office Report, *The Prevention of Corruption*, at para 3.11.

[99] The 1889 Act provided that the offence was a misdemeanour. The distinction between felonies and misdemeanours was abolished by the Criminal Law Act 1967 ss 1 and 12(5) and (6).

[100] ibid.

ii. The penalties

Section 2 of the Act[101] provides that: **2.45**

Any person on conviction for offending as aforesaid shall, at the discretion of the court before which he is convicted,

(a) be liable—
  (i) on summary conviction, to imprisonment for a term not exceeding 6 months[102] or to a fine not exceeding the statutory maximum, or to both; and
  (ii) on conviction on indictment, to imprisonment for a term not exceeding 7 years or to a fine, or to both;[103] and

(b) in addition be liable to be ordered to pay to such body, and in such manner as the court directs, the amount or value of any gift, loan, fee, or reward received by him or any part thereof; and

(c) be liable to be adjudged incapable of being elected or appointed to any public office for five years from the date of his conviction, and to forfeit any such office held by him at the time of his conviction;[104] and

(d) in the event of a second conviction for a like offence he shall, in addition to the foregoing penalties, be liable to be adjudged to be for ever incapable of holding any public office, and to be incapable for five years of being registered as an elector, or voting at an election either of members to serve in Parliament or of members of any public body, and the enactments for preventing the voting and registration of persons declared by reason of corrupt practices to be incapable of voting shall apply to a person adjudged in pursuance of this section to be incapable of voting;[105] and

(e) if such person is an officer or servant in the employ of any public body upon such conviction he shall, at the discretion of the court, be liable to forfeit his right and claim to any compensation or pension to which he would otherwise have been entitled.

Section 3(2) provides that 'a person shall not be exempt from punishment under this Act by reason of the invalidity of the appointment or election of a person to a public office'. **2.46**

iii. Consent to prosecution and mode of trial

Section 4(1) provides that 'a prosecution for an offence under this Act shall not be instituted except by or with the consent of the Attorney General'. The expression 'Attorney General' means the Attorney General or Solicitor General, and as respects Scotland means the Lord Advocate.[106] **2.47**

---

[101] As amended by the 1906 Act and ATCSA 2001.

[102] As from a day to be appointed, the maximum period is to be extended to 12 months, but only in respect of offences committed after that date; CJA 2003, s 28(2)–(4).

[103] Para (a) was inserted by CJA 1988 s 47(1) and (3) in respect of offences committed after 29 September 1988.

[104] Inserted by the Representation of the People Act 1948, s 52(7).

[105] Inserted by the Representation of the People Act 1948, s 52(7).

[106] Section 4(2) was repealed in part by the Statute Law (Repeals) Act (Northern Ireland) 1954; the Criminal Jurisdiction Act 1975, Sch. 6; and the Law Officers Act 1997, s 3(2) and

2.48 Where two persons are charged respectively with offering and accepting bribes and are tried separately, the conviction of one and the acquittal of the other, does not by itself render the conviction unsafe on the ground of inconsistency.[107]

2.49 Offences contrary to section 1 of the 1889 Act are arrestable offences under section 24 of the Police and Criminal Evidence Act 1984 (PACE 1984), and are triable summarily or on indictment. When tried on indictment they are Class 4 offences.[108]

iv. Definitions and interpretation

2.50 **Gift, loan, fee, reward or advantage** Section 1 of the 1889 Act, defines a bribe as a 'gift, loan, fee, reward or advantage'. The words 'gift', 'loan' and 'reward' are not defined in the Act.

2.51 A 'reward' includes a gift for a past favour irrespective of whether there was any previous agreement to provide it.[109] The offence lies in accepting the reward, not in the showing of the favour.[110] The reward must be given in respect of favours shown by the recipient in respect of a matter in which the public body in which he is concerned is interested.[111]

2.52 An 'advantage' is defined in section 7 as including 'any office or dignity, and any forbearance to demand any money or money's worth or valuable thing, and includes any aid, vote, consent, or influence, or pretended aid, vote, consent, or influencc, and also includes any promise or procurement of or agreement or endeavour to procure, or the holding out of any expectation of any gift, loan, fee, reward, or advantage, as before defined'.

2.53 **The object of the bribe** The bribe must be given or received 'as an inducement to or reward for or otherwise on account of any officer doing or forbearing to do' something in respect of which the public office is concerned.[112] It has been held under the 1906 Act to include a 'sweetener' designed to secure *generally* more favourable treatment.[113]

2.54 **Public body** Section 7 of the 1889 Act, defines a 'public body' as 'any council of a county of county [sic] of a city or town, any council of a municipal

Sch.1. On 20 May 1999 the Lord Advocate ceased to be a Minister of the Crown and certain of his functions passed to the to the Secretary of State for Scotland or the Advocate General for Scotland; Scotland Act 1998, s 44(1)(c); Transfer of Functions (Lord Advocate and Secretary of State) Order 1999, SI 1999/678 and Transfer of Functions (Lord Advocate and Advocate General for Scotland) Order 1999, SI 1999/679.

107 *R v Andrews-Weatherfoil Ltd* (1972) 56 Cr App R 31, CA, a case under the 1889 Act.
108 For current sentencing practice see 2.70 below. 109 See n 107 above.
110 *R v Parker* (KR) (1986) 82 Cr App R 69, CA, a case under the 1889 Act.
111 ibid. 112 See 2.44 above. 113 Law Comm 248, para 2.11.

borough, also any board, commissioners, select vestry, or other body which has power to act under and for the purposes of any Act relating to local government, or the public health, or to poor law or otherwise to administer money raised by rates in pursuance of any public general Act'.

The meaning of 'public body' in the 1889 Act was extended by section 4(2) of the 1916 Act to include 'in addition to the bodies mentioned in the [1889 Act], local and public authorities of all descriptions'. It was held in *DPP v Holly and Manners*[114] to include any body which has public or statutory duties to perform and which performs those duties and carries out its transactions for the benefit of the public and not for private profit. It does not include either the Crown or a government department, as section 2 of the 1916 Act, distinguishes between 'the Crown and any government department' and a 'public body'; *R v Natji.*[115] **2.55**

The expression 'public body' also includes companies, which, in accordance with Part V of the Local Government and Housing Act 1989, are under the control of one or more local authorities.[116] The meaning of 'public body' has been further extended by section 19(1) of the Civil Aviation Act 1982 to include the Civil Aviation Authority, and by section 108(4) of ATCSA to include in respect of offences committed after 14 February 2002, 'any body, which exists in a country or territory outside the United Kingdom and is equivalent to any body described above'. **2.56**

Section 4(3) of the 1916 Act provides that a person serving under any public body, as defined in the 1889 and 1916 Acts, is an 'agent' within the meaning of the Prevention of Corruption Act 1906, and the expressions 'agent' and 'consideration' in the 1916 Act have the same meaning as in the Prevention of Corruption Act 1906, as amended by the 1916 Act. **2.57**

The expression 'public general Act' in section 7 of the 1889 Act includes the Metropolitan Police Acts.[117] Section 7 of the 1889 Act also provides that the expression 'public office' means any office or employment of a person as a member, officer, or servant of such public body, and the expression 'person' includes a body of persons, corporate or unincorporated. This latter provision accords with the general provision to that effect in the Interpretation Act 1889.[118] **2.58**

---

[114] [1978] AC 43 HL. [115] [2002] 2 Cr App R 20, CA.

[116] These words were inserted as from a day to be appointed by the Local Government and Housing Act 1989, s 194(1) and Sch 11, para 3.

[117] *R v Silbertson* (1899) 129 Cent Crim Ct Cas 372.

[118] Interpretation Act 1978, ss 5 and 11, and Schs 1 and 2, Pt 1, para 4(5).

5. Corruption with Agents

i. The offences and penalties

2.59 Section 1(1) of the Prevention of Corruption Act 1906 creates two offences of corruption with agents and a further offence relating to false documentation. It applies to all 'agents' whether employed in the public or private sector. The first two limbs of section 1(1) provide:

> If any agent corruptly accepts or obtains, or agrees to accept or attempts to obtain, from any person, for himself or for any other person, any gift or consideration as an inducement or reward for doing or forbearing to do, or for having after the passing of this Act done or forborne to do, any act in relation to his principal's affairs or business, or for showing or forbearing to show favour or disfavour to any person in relation to his principal's affairs or business; or
>
> If any person corruptly gives or agrees to give or offers any gift or consideration to any agent as an inducement or reward for doing or forbearing to do, or for having after the passing of this Act done or forborne to do, any act in relation to his principal's affairs or business, or for showing or forbearing to show favour or disfavour to any person in relation to his principal's affairs or business.
>
> he shall be guilty of [an offence] and shall be liable:
>
> (a) on summary conviction, to imprisonment for a term not exceeding 6 months or to a fine not exceeding the statutory maximum, or to both; and
> (b) on conviction on indictment, to imprisonment for a term not exceeding 7 years or to a fine, or to both.[119]

2.60 Although the 1906 Act provides for no disqualifications as in the 1889 Act, the provisions relating to the disqualification of company directors and the confiscation provisions under POCA 2002 apply where appropriate.[120]

2.61 Section 1(4), inserted by s.108(2) of ATCSA 2001 and section 68(2) of the Criminal Justice (Scotland) Act 2003 provides that for the purposes of those Acts, it is immaterial if (a) the principal's affairs or business have no connection with the United Kingdom and are conducted in a country or territory outside the United Kingdom; (b) the agent's functions have no connection with the United Kingdom and are carried out in a country or territory outside the United Kingdom.

---

[119] Section 1(1)(a) and (b) was substituted in relation to offences committed after 29 September 1988, by the CJA 1988, s 47(2) and (3). The 'statutory maximum' fine is the prescribed sum within the meaning of the Magistrates'Courts Act 1980. As from a day to be appointed, the maximum period of imprisonment on summary conviction is to be extended to 12 months, but only in respect of offences committed after that date; CJA 2003, s 28(2)–(4).

[120] The Company Directors Disqualification Act 1986, s 2; see as to confiscation 2.121 below.

ii. Consent to prosecution and mode of trial

Section 2 of the 1906 Act as amended[121] provides, in subsections (1), (3), and (6) respectively: **2.62**

- 'A prosecution for an offence under this Act shall not be instituted without the consent, in England, of the Attorney General or the Solicitor General.'
- 'Every information for any offence under this Act shall be upon oath.'
- 'Any person aggrieved by a summary conviction under this Act may appeal to the Crown Court.'

Offences contrary to section 1 of the 1906 Act are Class 4 offences and triable either way. The Act applies to Northern Ireland. Section 2 does not extend to Scotland.[122]

iii. Definitions and interpretation

Gift or consideration: section 1(2) 'Gift' is not defined. Section 1(2) provides that 'for the purposes of this Act the expression "consideration" includes "valuable consideration of any kind" '. It connotes the legal meaning of the term in the sense of a bargain or contract.[123] In *Currie v Misa* it was said that 'a valuable consideration, in the sense of the law, may consist either in some right, interest, profit or benefit accruing to the one party, or some forbearance, detriment, loss or responsibility, given, suffered or undertaken by the other'.[124] **2.63**

Agent: section 1(2) and (3) section 1(2) defines 'the expression "agent" ' to include 'any person employed by or acting for another'.and under section 1(3): 'a person serving under the crown or under any corporation or any borough, county, or district council, or any board of guardians, is an "agent" within the meaning of this act.' in determining whether a person is 'serving under the crown' the question is not whether he is employed by the crown but whether the duties he performs are performed by him on behalf of the crown, it being necessary for the crown to exercise its functions through human agency.[125] a police officer serves under the crown.[126] **2.64**

Section 4(3) of the 1916 Act extends the definition of 'agent' in the 1906 Act to include a person serving under any public body as defined in both the 1889 and 1916 Acts. Section 4(2) of the 1916 Act extends the definition of 'public body' **2.65**

[121] The Courts Act 1971, s 56(1) and Sch 8, para. 2; the Criminal Jurisdiction Act 1975, Sch 6, Pt II; and the Law Officers Act 1997, s 3(2) and Sch. Section 2(2), (4), and (5) of the 1906 Act were repealed by the Administration of Justice (Miscellaneous Provisions) Act 1933, the Costs in Criminal Cases Act 1908, and CLA 1967, respectively.

[122] *Halsbury's Statutes* (4th edn, reissue, London: Lexis Nexis (Butterworths, 2002) vol 12, paras 165–166. See Law Officers Act 1997, s 3(2), for Scotland.

[123] *R v Braithwaite* (1983) 77 Cr App R 34, CA.

[124] (1875) LR 10 Exch 153, 162.

[125] *R v Barrett* (1976) 63 Cr App R 174, CA.

[126] *Fisher v Oldham Corporation* [1930] 2 KB 364.

in the 1889 and 1906 Acts to include in addition to the bodies mentioned in the 1889 Act, local and public authorities of all descriptions and companies which in accordance with Part V of the Local Government and Housing Act 1989 are under the control of one or more local authorities.[127]

2.66 **'Principal' and 'in relation to his principal's affairs'** Under section 1(2) the expression 'principal' includes an employer.[128] The words 'In relation to his principal's affairs' are to be widely constructed.[129]

6. The offence of using a false document to deceive a principal

2.67 The third limb of section 1(1) of the Corruption Act 1906 provides that 'If any person knowingly gives to any agent, or if any agent knowingly uses with intent to deceive his principal, any receipt, account, or other document in respect of which the principal is interested, and which contains any statement which is false or erroneous or defective in any material particular, and which to his knowledge is intended to mislead the principal' he shall be guilty of an offence and subject to the same penalties as a person guilty under the first and second limbs of section 1 (1) of the Act.

2.68 The offence of using a false instrument to deceive a principle applies only to documents which are intended to pass between a principal and a third party. It does not apply to an internal document which was never intended to go to a third party and had not come from one.[130] Where a third party gives a false document to an agent with a view to deceiving his principal, it is irrelevant whether the agent knows of the falsity. The offence is not limited by the title to the Act which contains the word 'corruption', nor by the context of the section.[131] The offence does not require a person to act corruptly and it is not affected by the provisions of ATCSA 2001.

D. Theft, false accounting, fraud, and conspiracy to defraud

2.69 Persons who commit offences of bribery or offences contrary the Corruption Acts usually commit offences involving dishonesty in the course of their corrupt conduct, such as theft, obtaining property or services by deception, and false accounting. When two or more persons are involved, they may be guilty of a conspiracy to defraud, or to commit a statutory offence of corruption or some other statutory offence. Because of the breadth of the offence of conspiracy to

[127] Part V has yet to come into force.

[128] This section is printed as amended by CJA 1988, s 47; and as repealed in part by the Local Authorities, etc (Miscellaneous Provisions) (No 2) Order 1974, SI 1974/595.

[129] *Morgan v DPP* [1970] 3 All ER 1053, 1058 DC. See also *R v Dickinson and De Rable* (1948) 33 Cr App R.

[130] *R v Tweedie* [1984] QB 729; 79 Cr App R 168, CA.

[131] *Sage v Eicholz* [1919] 2 KB 171, DC.

defraud, ie agreeing dishonestly to cause loss to another, prosecutors sometimes charge that offence in preference to charging bribery or one of the Corruption Act offences. A disadvantage of prosecuting for these other offences is that on the offender's conviction, disqualification from public office and similar sanctions,[132] which can be imposed for bribery and for corruption in public office under the 1889 Act, are not available to the court.

E. Sentencing in Bribery and Prevention of Corruption Acts Cases

As already indicated, the sentence for common law bribery is unlimited but as a matter of good practice a sentencing court will be guided by that available for the comparable statutory offence. For offences under the Prevention of Corruption Acts the maximum sentences on indictment are seven years' imprisonment.[133] Bribery is punishable by loss of office and an offence contrary to the 1889 Act is punishable by disqualification from office, disqualification from registration as an elector, and forfeiture of any right to compensation and a pension.[134] Persons convicted of bribery or of an offence contrary to the 1889 or 1906 Acts are subject to the confiscation procedures, interim measures and civil recovery procedures referred to in 2.121 below. **2.70**

There are no guideline sentencing cases.[135] Corruption invariably attracts prison sentences because of its seriousness, but the sentences vary widely according to the circumstances of the case and the offender.[136] Important factors in determining their length include whether the defendant pleaded guilty or not guilty, and if guilty, at what stage; and the personal circumstances of the defendant. There appears to be no distinction between sentencing for corruption in the public sector and sentencing for corruption in the private sector. **2.71**

The variation in sentences is illustrated by cases involving police, prison, and immigration officers. In *R v Donald*[137] a total sentence of eleven years (the court having imposed consecutive sentences) was upheld in the case of a detective **2.72**

---

[132] See 2.26 and 2.45 above.

[133] 1916 Act, s 1 increased the penalty for corruption relating to government contracts to 7 years, but this was repealed by CJA 1988, s 170(2), Sch 16, when the maximum penalty for offences under the 1889 and 1906 Acts was raised from 2 to 7 years (CJA 1988, s 47(1), (3)).

[134] See 2.26 and 2.45 above.

[135] See D. Thomas, *Current Sentencing Practice* (4th edn), London: Sweet & Maxwell, 1982) B9–1.3; R Banks, *Banks on Sentencing*, (London: Butterworths Lexis Nexis, 2003) paras 37.1–37.4.

[136] See 9.93 below. OECD Convention on Combating Bribery of Foreign Public Officials, Art 3 requires parties to ensure that sentences for bribery of foreign officials are 'effective, proportionate and dissuasive'; see discussion at 10.90 below. The Council of Europe Criminal Law Convention on Corruption (ETS No 173) Art 19.1 contains similar provisions, but is not limited to the bribery of foreign public officials.

[137] [1997] 2 Cr App R (S) 272.

constable who pleaded guilty late to four counts of corruption for agreeing to accept £50,000 (he only received £18,000) from a defendant for disclosing confidential information and destroying surveillance logs. In *R v McGovern*[138] a defendant charged with burglary who offered a £200 bribe to a police officer had his sentence reduced by the Court of Appeal to nine months. In *R v. Oxdemir*[139] an offender who offered a free meal or £50 to a police officer for not reporting a driving offence had his sentence reduced to three months' imprisonment. In *R v Garner*[140] the Court of Appeal upheld sentences of eighteen months and twelve months respectively imposed on prison officers who pleaded guilty to providing luxury items to a prisoner. A sentence of two years' imprisonment was imposed in a similar case.[141] In *R v Patel*[142] an immigration administrator was sentenced to two years' imprisonment for accepting a £500 bribe to stamp a passport granting leave to remain, and ordered to forfeit the bribe.

2.73 A similar variation exists in public procurement cases. In 1974, when the maximum sentence for an offence under the 1889 and 1906 Acts was two years, the architect, John Poulson, was sentenced to a total of seven years imprisonment for paying bribes to members of Parliament, police officers and health authorities to obtain building contracts. T Dan Smith, the Labour leader of Newcastle-upon-Tyne, was sentenced to a total of six years imprisonment and William Pottinger, a senior civil servant in the Scottish Office was sentenced to a total of five years' imprisonment.[143] In *Foxley*[144] a 71-year-old Ministry of Defence employee, convicted of four counts of corruption under the 1906 Act, was sentenced to four years' imprisonment for receiving over £2 million in the placing of defence contracts. A confiscation order was made for £1,503.901.08. In *Dearnley and Threapleton*[145] a council employee and supplier of security services who was convicted of misrepresenting a loan to pay off a personal debt, had his sentence reduced to twelve months because of strong mitigation. In *R v Allday*,[146] a case under the 1889 Act, council employees accepted bribes from waste contractors to tip waste. They were sentenced to eight and six months imprisonment each and the contractors were sentenced to three months each.

---

[138] [1980] 2 Cr App R (S) 389.

[139] [1985] 7 Cr App R (S) 382.

[140] [1988] 10 Cr App R (S) 445.

[141] *R v Sanderson* [1980] 2 Cr App R (S) 147.

[142] (1992) 13 Cr App R (S) 550.

[143] The Poulson Case lasted for 52 days and was the longest running corruption case in England at that time. It led to the resignation of the Home Secretary, Reginald Maudling, who was the subject of a parliamentary inquiry, which concluded that he had indulged in conduct inconsistent with the standards the House is entitled to expect from its members. Poulson's conviction was influential in the forcing the House of Commons to initiate a register of its members (HC 57 (1969–70), and HC 102 (1974–5); see 8.20 below. See M Gillard, *Nothing to Declare, The Political Corruption of John Poulson* (London: John Calder, 1980); J Poulson, *The Price* (London: Michael Joseph, 1980).

[144] (1995) 16 Cr App R (S) 879.

[145] [2001] 2 Cr App R (S) 201.

[146] (1986) 8 Cr. App. R (S) 288. See also *R v Jones* (1981) 3 Cr App R (S) 238.

In *R v Hopwood*[147] a sentence of three and a half years' imprisonment was upheld on an employee for accepting bribes of £200,000 not to disclose frauds on his employer involving £1.75 million. In *R v Wilcox*[148] an agent for suppliers for competitive bids, who received bribes of £32,000 in respect of contract renewals, had his sentence reduced from twelve to six months. His co-accused were sentenced to two years and six months respectively. In *R v Wilson*[149] a sentence of three years was reduced to eighteen months in the case of a chief buyer for a manufacturing agent who accepted £2,500 for showing favour to one of his employer's suppliers, where there were strong personal mitigation circumstances including the break-up of the defendant's home and loss of his business. **2.74**

F. Jurisdiction

1. The General Rule

The common law rule is that, subject to the rules of international comity, English courts have jurisdiction over an offence if any part of it, either the prohibited conduct or its consequences, takes place in England or Wales.[150] This means, so far as the common law offence of bribery and the statutory offences of corruption are concerned, that the jurisdiction of English courts is limited to acts committed in England and Wales except in so far as English jurisdiction has been extended by statute. Thus English courts have jurisdiction wherever an offer, acceptance, or agreement to offer, or accept a bribe takes place in England or Wales. For these purposes, sending an email or making a telephone call into England and Wales, and an act committed by a person abroad through the agency of a person in England and Wales, will suffice to confer jurisdiction, irrespective of the nationality of the offender and whether the agent has committed an offence.[151] It is immaterial that any intent, which is an element of the offence, is to do something outside the jurisdiction.[152] Corresponding rules apply to the jurisdiction of Scottish and Northern Ireland courts.[153] The Prevention of Corruption Acts apply to Scotland and **2.75**

147 (1985) 7 Cr App R (S) 402.

148 (1994) 16 Cr App (S) 197.

149 (1982) 4 Cr App R (S) 337.

150 *Treacy v DPP* [1971] AC 537; *Liangsiriprasert v. Government of the USA* [1991] 1 AC 225. *R v Sansom* [1991] 2 QB 130, 92 Cr App R 115, 119, CA; *R v Smith (Wallace Duncan) (No 4)* [2004] 3 WLR 22, CA.

151 *R v Baxter* [1972] QB 1.

152 *R v Hornett* [1975] RTR 256 CA: *R v El Hakkaoui* (1974) 60 Cr App R 281, CA. See also *R v Arud* [1989] Crim LR 809 where the issue was raised whether the English Courts have jurisdiction if all the ingredients of the offence occur in a foreign embassy, but no decision was required on the facts found by the court.

153 For the Scottish rules, see Sir Gerald H Gordon, *Criminal Law* (3rd edn.) vol 1, paras 3.41–3.50 (n 81).

Northern Ireland, in which case the Scottish or Northern Ireland courts have jurisdiction.[154]

2.76 Sections 1 to 6 of the Criminal Justice Act 1993 provide in relation to certain offences of dishonesty in the Theft Act 1968—such as theft, obtaining by deception, the use of false instruments, false accounting, and offences of blackmail, referred to as Group A offences—that English courts have jurisdiction where any one of the elements of the offence occurs in England or Wales, irrespective of the nationality of the defendant, and in the case of Group B offences—such as conspiracy to defraud, conspiracy and incitement and attempts to commit Group A offences—that they have jurisdiction where any one of the elements of the intended offences or the fraud is to take place in England and Wales.

2. Extraterritorial Jurisdiction

2.77 Section 1A of the Criminal Law Act 1977 (CLA 1977)[155] extends the jurisdiction of English courts to include conspiracies to commit statutory offences abroad, provided the intended conduct would amount to an offence in the country where it is to be committed and a party to the agreement has done something in England relating to the agreement before its formation, or became a party to the agreement in England and Wales by joining it in person or through an agent, or has done or omitted to do something in England and Wales in pursuance of the agreement. This Act would apply to cases of conspiracy to bribe a foreign public official.

2.78 Part 12 of ATCSA 2001, which came into force on 14 February 2002,[156] extends the jurisdiction of English courts in respect of offences committed after that date to include the corruption of foreign officials abroad and corruption abroad by UK nationals and UK incorporated companies. For the purposes of any common law offence of bribery it is immaterial if the functions of the person who receives or is offered a reward have no connection with the United Kingdom, and are carried out in a country outside the United Kingdom.[157] ATCSA 2001 extends the definition of 'public body' in the Public Bodies Corrupt Practices Act 1889 to include any body which exists in a country outside the United Kingdom and is equivalent to a body defined in the 1889 Act,[158] and extends public bodies included in the Prevention of Corruption Act 1916 to include authorities existing in a country or territory outside the United Kingdom.[159]

[154] 1889 Act, ss 8 and 4(2); 1906 Act, s 3; see para 1(4). *Halsbury's Statutes* (4th edn. Vol 12 (1)) *Criminal Law* 159, 164, 188.

[155] As inserted by the Criminal Justice (Terrorism and Conspiracy) Act 1998, s 5(1).

[156] Anti-terrorism Crime and Security Act (Commencement No 3 Order) 2002, (SI 2002/228) See 2.02 above.

[157] ATCSA 2001, s 108(1).

[158] ibid s 108(3).

[159] ibid s 108(4).

2.79 ATCSA 2001 also extends the jurisdiction of UK courts to include anything done outside the United Kingdom by a UK national or a body incorporated under UK law where the act would, if done in the United Kingdom constitute an offence of common law bribery or an offence under section 1 of the 1889 Act or the first two offences under section 1 of the 1906 Act.[160] For the purposes of the section, the act constitutes the offence. A UK national is an individual who is a British citizen, a British Dependent Territories citizen, a British National (Overseas) or a British Overseas citizen; a person who under the British Nationality Act 1981 is a British subject; or a British protected person within the meaning of that Act.[161] Part 12 of ATCSA 2001 does not apply to Scotland.[162] It does apply to Northern Ireland.[163] The 2001 Act put beyond doubt that the Corruption Acts 1889–1916 apply to the bribery of foreign public officials in respect of offences committed after 14 February 2002. However, there are differing views as to whether complaints of corruption alleged to have occurred before that date require either a relevant act of bribery to have occurred within the UK to trigger an investigation, or would need to be prosecuted as other offences such as false accounting, deception or money laundering. The Home Office has argued consistently that they could have been prosecuted if they satisfied common law principles of jurisdiction prior to ATCSA 2001 under the then existing legislation. The Serious Fraud Officer, however, has been reported as believing that there remains a fundamental uncertainty as to whether the Prevention of Corruption Acts apply to foreign public officials prior to 2001, thereby making it doubly hard and high risk to prosecute such allegations.[164]

2.80 The presumption of corruption under section 2 of the Corruption Act 1916, does not apply in relation to anything which would not be an offence apart from Part 12 of ATCSA 2001.[165]

3. Offences by Crown Servants

2.81 Section 31(1) of the Criminal Justice Act 1948[166] provides that 'any British subject employed under Her Majesty's Government in the United Kingdom in the service of the Crown who commits, in a foreign country, when acting or purporting to act in the course of his employment, any offence, which, if committed in England, would be punishable on indictment, shall be guilty of an offence . . . and subject to the same punishment, as if the offence had been committed in England.' The reference to 'indictable offence' relates not to

[160] ibid s 109(1) and (2).

[161] ibid s 109(4).

[162] ibid s 128(1)(b): for Scotland the Criminal Justice (Scotland) Act 2003, ss 68 and 69 extends the jurisdiction of the courts in relation to such offences to Scottish partnerships as well as UK nationals and companies.

[163] ATCSA 2001, s 128(2).

[164] S Hawley, The Corner House, *Enforcing the law on overseas corruption offences: towards a model for excellence*, a discussion paper, 24 June 2004.

[165] ATCSA 2001, s 110.

[166] As amended by CJA 1948, Sch 3, Pt III.

whether the offender was tried on indictment, but whether he could have been tried on indictment.[167] British officials can be tried in England for oppression, crimes, and lesser offences committed outside Great Britain under the Criminal Jurisdiction Act 1802 and section 14 the Sale of Offices Act 1809.[168]

G. Liability of Corporate and Unincorporated Bodies

1. Corporations

2.82 English law recognises a variety of legal persons, all of whom are distinct from their members and may become involved in corrupt transactions either as offenders or as victims. Foremost amongst them are public and private companies; limited liability partnerships (LLPs), whose partners enjoy limited liability; and European Economic Interest Groupings (EEIGs).[169]

2.83 Subject to obvious exceptions, such as murder, the criminal liability of corporations is the same as that of natural persons. Corporations can be convicted of common law[170] and statutory offences including offences requiring *mens rea*.[171] Some statutes, such as the Companies Acts 1985, expressly impose criminal liability on corporations. In other statutes, whenever passed, subject to a contrary intention, the word 'person' is construed as including corporations, and in the case of statutes passed after 1889, bodies incorporate.[172]

2.84 A corporation is vicariously liable for offences committed by its servants or agents in the same way as a natural person, subject to its possessing the necessary *mens rea*. It is also liable where an offence is committed in the course of its business by a person in control of its affairs, so that it may fairly be said to think and act through him and his actions and intent are the actions and intent of the

[167] *Hastings & Folkestone Glassworks v Kalson* [1949] 1 KB 214, 221–222.

[168] *R v Hodgkinson The Times*, June 26 1900. They include members of the Royal Air Force; Air Force (Application of Enactments) (No 2) Order 1918, SR & O 1918/548.

[169] EEIGs are a form of association between companies or other legal bodies of individuals from different EU countries needing to cooperate together across national frontiers. EEIGs have unlimited liability status and are governed by Council Regulation (EEC) No 2137/85 and SI 1989/638.

[170] *R v JG Hammond & Co Ltd* [1914] 2 KB 866 (contempt of court); *R v ICR Haulage Ltd* [1944] KB 551 (conspiracy to defraud).

[171] Article 2 of the OECD Convention requires parties to take such measures as may be necessary to introduce the 'responsibility' of legal persons. Art 3 para 2 indicates however, that non-criminal sanctions against a corporation are acceptable, provided they include monetary sanctions and that they are overall 'effective, proportionate and dissuasive'. See para 10.69 below. This may be important from the point of view of mutual legal assistance. See para 2.147ff. Note that Art 18 of the Council of Europe Criminal Law Convention and Art 26 of UNCAC seeks to hold legal persons liable for corruption and related offences.

[172] Interpretation Act 1978, ss 5, 11, and Schs 1, 2, and Pt 1, para 4(5).

corporation. In such a case the natural person whose action and intent are the action and intent of the corporation is also liable.[173]

2.85 Not every 'responsible agent' or 'high executive' or 'agent acting on behalf of a company' can by his actions make a company criminally responsible. The criminal liability of a corporation for bribery or corruption will depend on whether the natural person who performed directed or authorised the prohibited act with the requisite state of mind was part of its 'controlling mind or will', and it is necessary for a judge to invite the jury to consider whether or not there were established those facts which he decides as a matter of law are necessary to identify the person concerned with the company.[174] No intention to benefit the legal person or any of its leading persons is necessary and in theory a legal person can be convicted of an offence even though no proceedings have been brought against a natural person. In fact, it is rare in England for legal persons to be prosecuted for offences such as corruption and their officials are usually prosecuted for their individual criminal acts.[175]

2.86 The penalty for corporations found guilty of corruption is an unlimited fine. Apart from their liability for bribery and offences under the Prevention of Corruption Acts, corporations, for example banks and financial institutions may incur liability under the money laundering provisions in POCA 2002.[176]

2. Liability of UK Companies for Offences Committed by Intermediaries

2.87 A survey conducted in 1997 found that 56 per cent of European companies and 70 per cent of US companies said they 'occasionally' used middlemen such as agents, joint venture partners or subsidiaries to make corrupt payments,[177] while 44 per cent of European firms and 22 per cent of US firms admitted doing so regularly.[178] The OECD Convention does not address the issue specifically, but the OECD Working Group on Bribery in International Business issued a questionnaire on the role of foreign subsidiaries in September 2001 and set up a taskforce on Foreign Subsidiaries. The taskforce reported back to the Working Group and, on the strength of the report back, the Working Group concluded that in its current format the OECD convention adequately addresses the

[173] *Mousell Bros Ltd v London and North Western Railway Co* [1917] 2 KB 836 DC; *Tesco Supermarkets Ltd v Nattras* [1972] AC 153, 176; *Lennards Carrying Co v Asiatic Petroleum Co* [1915] AC 705; *Meridian Global Funds Asia Ltd v Securities Commission* [1995] 2 AC 500, PC.

[174] *R v Andrews Weatherfoil Ltd* (1972) 56 Cr App R 31, CA.

[175] GRECO Evaluation Report on the UK 2nd Evaluation Round, Strasbourg, 30 September 2004, para 89.

[176] See 2.112 below.

[177] The Business Risk Group, Control Risks Group (see GRECO Report above).

[178] John Bray, *Beyond Compliance: Corruption as a Business Risk*, paper presented to the conference on Fighting Corruption in Developing Countries and Emerging Countries: the role of the private sector, Washington, February 1999.

issue.[179] In reviewing ATCSA 2001, the Working Group specifically stated that UK legislation should make it an offence to commit an offence for the benefit of a third party, as is required in Article 1 of the OECD Convention on Combating Bribery.[180] Although the lead examiners in the Phase 2 Review, noted that the common law offence was not expressly applied where the third party receives the benefit, they appear not to have disputed the United Kingdom's view that such a transaction is indeed criminalized and that, in relation specifically to the 1906 Act, the legislation (when read in accordance with general principles) criminalized a corrupt payment made to a third-party beneficiary. The lead examiners stopped short of recommending a specific change to the law in that regard, but recommended that the Working Group follow up on the issues of the complexity and uncertainty which they felt characterized the present state of the law.

2.88 English law does not automatically impute to UK companies absolute control over or knowledge of the actions of their intermediaries or subsidiaries. In order for a company to incur liability, evidence would be required that the company in some way directed or otherwise influenced the subsidiary to commit the offence.[181] Transparency International recommended that Clause 13 of the Draft Bill, relating to corruption outside the United Kingdom, should be extended to include subsidiary companies of UK companies if the subsidiaries were under actual control of their parent companies, and that in the case of other subsidiaries, associated companies and joint ventures. United Kingdom incorporated companies should be held responsible if they fail to take adequate measures to satisfy themselves that the foreign registered companies or joint ventures are implementing suitable anti-corruption policies in the conduct of their business.[182] This approach is similar to that of the Exports Credit Guarantee Department (ECGD), which requires applicants for support to warrant that neither they nor anyone acting on their behalf have engaged or will engage in any corrupt activity in connection with the supply contract.[183] The Confederation of British Industry (CBI) argued that the Bill should not apply to overseas subsidiaries because they were subject to the law of the other country.[184]

2.89 UK jurisprudence in cases such as *Connelly v RTZ*[185] case reference shows that the courts are reluctant to assume jurisdiction simply on the grounds that a

[179] See further 10.75 below.

[180] OECD Working Group on Bribery in International Business, Country Report, 'United Kingdom Review of the Convention and 1997 Recommendation, Phase 1 bis Report', March 2003, 18 and phase 2 Report, at 60. (http://www.oecd.org/pdf/M0003000/M00039418.pdf). For further discussion on 'red flags' and corporate responsibility in relation to intermediaries, see para 10.149 below.

[181] Price Waterhouse Coopers to Joint Committee, Evidence 50, DB 16 para 4.1.

[182] Joint Committee (n 6 above) Evidence 4 DCB 18, DCB 31.

[183] Ibid, Evidence 141, DCB 10, para 9.

[184] ibid DCB 17.

[185] [1998] AC 854 (HL).

multinational parent company is based in this jurisdiction. The government has specifically stated on several occasions that the new corruption offences are not intended to cover subsidiaries of UK companies. The Corner House has argued for specific provision for intermediaries in the draft Bill on the basis that although attempting, conspiring or inciting to commit a criminal offence, and aiding and abetting, counselling or procuring go some way towards ensuring the situations are covered, companies are bound to defend themselves on the basis that the use of intermediaries is common business practice and that they had no knowledge the intermediary would pass on a bribe. It recommended that the words 'whether directly or through intermediaries' should be included at appropriate parts in Clause 5 of the draft Bill.[186]

3. Avoidance of Liability Through Company Restructuring

Although leave of the court is required before proceedings can be commenced against a company which is the subject of an administration order or a winding up order,[187] English company and insolvency law provides a wide range of sanctions and investigative powers to ensure that companies and their officers cannot evade penalties through restructuring and reformation.[188] These include specific investigation powers for mandatory production of documents;[189] mandatory investigation of a company's affairs where it is being wound up by a court;[190] restriction on the re-use of company names;[191] provisions whereby assets transferred from an insolvent company can be recovered by a liquidator; and the disqualification of company directors under the Company Directors Disqualification Act 1986. Section 557A (1)(b) of the Income and Corporation Taxes Act 1988, denies tax relief for any payment the making of which constitutes a criminal offence. Section 68 of the Finance Act 2002, extended section 557A to include payments taking place wholly outside the United Kingdom 'where the making of a corresponding payment in any part of the country would constitute a criminal offence there' in relation to expenditure incurred as from April 2002. The Inland Revenue has wide powers[192] since the introduction of the ATCSA to disclose information to other law enforcement bodies of any crime, including corruption. The Inland Revenue has its own powers to investigate, confiscate and prosecute tax and money laundering offences and provides assistance to the Assets Recovery Agency.[193] **2.90**

[186] Joint Committee Memorandum from the Corner House DCB1.

[187] Insolvency Act 1986, ss 10 and 130.

[188] GRECO 2nd Evaluation Round, 27–30 September 2004.

[189] Companies Act 1985, P XIV. [190] Insolvency Act 1986, s 132

[191] ibid ss 216–217. [192] See paras 4.72 and 7.80 below.

[193] The Evaluation Report on the UK, 2nd Evaluation Round, Group of States against Corruption, September 27–30 2004, para. 111, vii, urged the UK authorities to make statistics available on the use of corporate sanctions.

4. Unincorporated Bodies

2.91 Unincorporated Bodies are not legal persons so far as common law offences are concerned and cannot incur criminal liability for bribery. Their members, however, may be personally liable. Unincorporated bodies are criminally liable for offences of corruption contrary to the 1889 Act[194] and for offences under the 1906 and 1916 Acts.[195]

H. Other Statutory Offences Involving Corruption

1. Sale of Public Offices

2.92 It is an indictable offence at common law to buy and sell offices of a public nature.[196] It is also an offence under the Sale of Offices Act 1551 and the Sale of Offices Act 1809,[197] to buy or sell or to pay any money or reward for any office in the gift of the Crown, and any military or naval commission or place under the control of any public department, whether it be in the United Kingdom or in a British possession abroad.[198] The punishment is a fine and/or imprisonment, forfeiture of the office and absolute disqualification from holding office again.[199] Purchases of the offices of sheriff and bailiff are punishable under Sections 27 and 29 Sheriff's Act 1887.[200]

2. Corruption of Customs Officers

2.93 It is a summary offence contrary to section 15 of the Customs and Management Act 1979, to bribe or attempt to bribe a Customs officer.[201]

3. Offences Relating to Honours

2.94 The Queen is the sole fountain of honour and she alone can create peerages and confer honours. In fact she is advised by the Prime Minister and sometimes

---

194 Interpretation Act 1889, 7.

195 ibid s 19; Interpretation Act 1978, Sch 2, para 4(5). In *A-G v Able* [1984] QB 795, 810 Woolf J, dealing with an offence under the Suicide Act 1961, said there could be no question of an unincorporated body committing an offence under that Act. However, an unincorporated body has been held liable for a fixed parking offence (*Clerk to Croydon Justices, ex p Chief Constable of Kent* [1989] Crim. LR 910 DC), and the Banking Act 1987, s 98(1) simply assumes that offences under the Act may be committed by unincorporated associations; Smith, Hogan, D Ormerod, *Criminal Law* (11th edn) Lexis Nexis UK 208–209.

196 *R v Vaughan* (1769) 4 Burr 2494, 2500; *Russell on Crime* (n 11 above) 374.

197 ss 1, 3. The Act applies to Scotland; s 1.

198 The latter Act is extended to the Air Force by SR & O 1918/548, as amended by SI1964/488. See 2.11 above.

199 *Earl of Macclesfield's Case* (1725) 16 St Tr 767.

200 There appear to have been no reported cases under the 1551 and 1809 Acts for 130 years and it is generally agreed that the Acts should be repealed. Law Com No 145 para 2.33.

201 Customs internal officers can only investigate if corruption relates to an assigned matter under the Customs and Excise Management Act 1979, otherwise there will have to be a police investigation. An 'assigned matter' is 'any matter in relation to which the Commissioners are for the time being required in pursuance of any enactment to perform duties'; ibid s 1.

by other ministers, such as the Foreign Secretary and the Defence Secretary.[202] In 1917 public concern that political honours were being conferred in exchange for financial contributions to political parties led to a resolution in the House of Lords that the government should ensure that whenever an honour was conferred on a British subject, other than Royalty and members of the Forces or permanent civil service, a public statement of the reasons for its recommendation should accompany it, and the Prime Minister should satisfy himself no payment or expectation of payment to any political party or party fund was associated with it. Political honours continued to be bought and sold during the Premiership of Lloyd George, and public outrage following the Birthday Honours List in the summer of 1922[203] led to the appointment of a Royal Commission under the Chairmanship of Lord Dunedin to advise on the procedure to be adopted in future to assist the Prime Minister in making recommendations to the Sovereign. The Commission found no fault in the system in general, but expressed concern about honours for political services, particularly the activities of touts who offered to procure honours for 'political services' in return for a contribution to party funds.[204] The result was that, in 1923, a Political Honours Scrutiny Committee (PHSC) was appointed by Order in Council, consisting of three Privy Councillors, to enquire into the backgrounds of persons put forward for political honours and to decide whether they were. 'fit and proper persons'. It was followed by the Honours (Prevention of Abuses) Act 1925.

The 1925 Act makes it a criminal offence to deal in honours, either as broker or **2.95** purchaser.[205] Section 1 of the Act provides that:

(1) If any person accepts or obtains or agrees to accept or attempt to obtain from any person, for himself or for any other person, or for any purpose, any gift, money or valuable consideration as an inducement or reward for procuring or assisting or endeavouring to procure the grant of a dignity or title of honour to any person, or otherwise in connection with such a grant, he shall be guilty of an offence.

(2) If any person gives, or agrees or proposes to give, or offers to any person any gift, money or valuable consideration as an inducement or reward for

[202] AW Bradley and KD Ewing, *Constitutional and Administrative Law* (13th edn, London: Longmans, 2003, 250).

[203] Committee of Standards; Fifth Report, paras 14.1–14.3. A South African millionaire, Sir Joseph Robinson, who had been convicted of fraud paid £50,000 for a peerage, but the Prime Minister, Lloyd George, was forced to forced to withdraw his nomination following objections by King George V. When Sir Joseph heard the news, he is alleged to have responded by producing his chequebook and asking 'how much more'? Beaverbrook, *The Decline and Fall of Lloyd George* (London: Collins, 1963) 127; *The Times*, 15 November 2005

[204] See also ATH Smith, *Property Offences* (Thompson Professional Publishers, Canada, 1994) paras 2503, 2507.

[205] In spite of the 1925 Act, the trade continued into the 1930s and one notorious tout, Mr Maundy Gregory, continued to operate until his conviction in 1933. Committee of Standards, in Public Life Fifth Report, para 14.11; T Cullen, *Maundy Gregory: Purveyor of Honours*. (Bodley Head, London, 1974).

procuring or assisting or endeavouring to procure the grant of a dignity or title of honour to any person, or otherwise in connection with such a grant, he shall be guilty of an offence.

(3) Any person guilty of an offence under this Act shall be liable on conviction on indictment to imprisonment for a term not exceeding two years and/or to a fine of any amount, or to both such imprisonment and such fine, or on summary conviction to imprisonment for a term not exceeding three months and to a fine not exceeding the prescribed sum, or to both such imprisonment and such fine, and where the person convicted (whether on indictment or summarily) received any such gift, money, or consideration as aforesaid which is capable of forfeiture, he shall in addition to any other punishment be liable to forfeit the same to [Her] Majesty.[206]

2.96 Although the Honours (Prevention of Abuses) Act 1925 imports some of the language of the 1889 and 1906 Acts, it differs in that it is directed at any person who bribes or is bribed by another with a view to the grant of an honour and is not focused on agents or public bodies. Also, it does not use the word 'corruptly', although trafficking in honours is, of its nature, corrupt. The Law Commission made no proposals about honours in general. Its view was that the offences in the 1925 Act are specific offences for a highly specific mischief which do not fall naturally within the scheme of the offence of bribery.[207]

2.97 In the 1980s and 1990s it was widely believed that substantial political donations buy goodwill and substantially enhance the likelihood of being considered for an honour, and of receiving one, particularly a life peerage.[208] The Committee on Standards in Public Life (CSPL) was concerned by public disquiet about abuse of the honours system. It recommended in its Fifth Report, that life peerages should be referred to the PHSC, which had not happened previously, and that the PHSC should in future scrutinize all honours from CBE and above where there has been a political donation by the nominee of £5,000 or more. The CSPL also recommended that the PHSC's remit should be extended to enable it to monitor and review the whole of the honours system and that the PHSC should in future be called the Honours Scrutiny Board (HSB) to reflect the change. The HSB was intended to scrutinize nominations for peerages on grounds of propriety, but the committee was abolished early in 2005. The House of Lords Appointments Commission, a non-statutory, non-departmental public body, attached to the Cabinet office, is responsible for recommending non-party political nominees to become life peers and for vetting non-party political nominations.[209] The Commission is chaired by a peer

206 This section is printed as amended by CLA 1977, s 32(1); and the Magistrates' Courts Act 1980, s 32(2). The Act applies to Scotland.

207 See Law Com No 145 para 2.36.

208 R Blackburn, *The Electoral System in Britain* (Macmillan Oxford 1995) 323.

209 PG Richards, *Patronage in British Government* (Toronto: University of Toronto Press, 1963) ch 10; J Walker, *The Queen has been Pleased* (Secker & Warburg, London, 1986). In spite of recent reforms, public disquiet about the grant of peerages in return for political donations

and its members include nominees of the three main parties and three independent members.[210]

4. Corrupt Practices at Elections

Bribery, treating, undue influence, and personation at elections are common law offences and punishable as corrupt practices. If proved, they are punishable on indictment by fine and imprisonment and the election is avoided.[211] An attempt to bribe is an offence.[212] Corrupt practices are distinguished from 'illegal practices' in that, except in the case of offences of incurring prohibited expenses, it is necessary to prove a corrupt intention. A person guilty of a corrupt practice is disqualified from being elected to the House of Commons for five years. A person guilty of an illegal practice is disqualified for three years.[213] The common law offences have been superseded by express statutory provisions. **2.98**

Electoral procedures in England are prescribed mainly in legislation, in particular the Representation of the People Act 1983, which consolidates legislation dating back to the nineteenth century. RPA 1983 creates a number of offences relating to corrupt and illegal practices at elections and contains extensive provisions relating to candidates' election expenses. All the offences also apply to European Parliamentary elections.[214] Although the statutory offences have now largely superseded the common law offences, the common law offences still exist and are referred to briefly in this section. Following the extension of the remit of the CSPL in 1997 to consider the funding of political parties, and the CSPL's Fifth Report, the Political Parties, Elections and Referendums Act 2000[215] introduced extensive new provisions relating to party funding, and an independent Electoral Commission was appointed with widespread executive and investigative powers. **2.99**

continues. An investigation by *The Times* in November 2005 revealed that at least 15 of the 292 peers created by Tony Blair since 1996 have made political donations ranging from £6,000 to £13m and that two of the most generous donors are now ministers. According to *The Times*' report the pattern is set to be repeated in a list to be published in December 2005.

[210] www.house of lords appointmentscommission.gov.uk.

[211] *Guildford* (1869) 1 O'M. & H 15 (bribery); *Bradford Case (No 2)* (1869) 1 O'M & H 35 (treating); See also R Mates and A. Scallan, *Schofield's Election Law* (Shaw and Sons, 1996) vol 1, pt 3.

[212] *R v Vaughan* (1769) Burr 2494. Asking for a bribe has been held not to be an offence; *Mallow Borough Case* (1870) 2 O'M. & H 18; Mates and Scallan (n 211 above) para 14.02.

[213] RPA 1983, ss 160, 163.

[214] European Parliamentary Elections Regulations 1986, reg 5(1) and Sch 1.

[215] See 2.110 below.

5. Bribery at Elections

2.100 Section 113 of RPA 1983 provides:

> (1) A person shall be guilty of bribery if he, directly or indirectly, by himself or by another person on his behalf—
> (a) gives any money or procures[216] any office to or for any voter or to or for any other person on behalf of any voter or to or for any other person in order to induce any voter to vote or refrain from voting; or
> (b) corruptly does any such act as mentioned in head (a) above or on account of any voter having voted or refrained from voting; or
> (c) makes any such gift or procurement to or for any person in order to induce that person to procure, or endeavour to procure, the return of any person at an election or to vote for any voter; or
> if upon or in consequence of any such gift or procurement he procures or engages, promises or endeavours to procure, the return of any person at an election or the vote of any voter.
> (2) A person is guilty of bribery if he advances or pays or causes to be paid any money to or for the use of any other person with the intent that that money or any part of it shall be expended in bribery at an election or knowingly pays or causes to be paid any money to any person in discharge or repayment of any money wholly or in part expended in bribery at any election.
> (3) A voter is guilty of bribery if before or during an election, he directly or indirectly by himself or by any other person on his behalf receives, agrees or contracts for any money, gift, loan or other valuable consideration, office, place or employment for himself or any other person for voting or agreeing to vote or refraining or agreeing to refrain from voting.
> (4) A person is guilty of bribery if after an election, he directly or indirectly by himself or by any other person on his behalf receives any money or valuable consideration on account of any person having voted or refrained from voting or having induced any other person to vote or refrain from voting.

2.101 The term 'voter' includes a proxy voter and it is irrelevant whether he has the right to vote.[217] If the prohibited act is done to induce the voter, the offence is committed irrespective of whether it was successful.[218]

6. Treating at Elections

2.102 Treating, in addition to being a common law offence, is an offence under section 114 of RPA 1983. Section 144 states that:

> . . . a person is guilty of treating if he corruptly by himself or by another person, either before, during or after an election, directly or indirectly gives or provides, or pays wholly or in part the expense of giving or providing, any meat, drink, entertainment or provision to or for any person—
> (a) for the purpose of corruptly influencing that person or any other person to vote or refrain from voting; or

[216] *R v Johnson* [1964] 2 QB 404.
[217] RPA ss 202(1) and 113(7).
[218] ibid s 202(1); Mates and Scallan (n 211 above).

(b) on account of that person or any other person having voted or refrained from voting, or being about to vote or refrain from voting...

The offence of treating also extends to the person who corruptly receives any such meat or provision. There must be an intention to corrupt and to influence the voting.

7. Using Undue Influence

Undue influence, in addition to being a common law offence, is a statutory offence contrary to section 115(1) of RPA 1983, and is the using or threatening to make use of any force, violence or restraint, or the infliction or threat to inflict damage, harm, or loss on a person, or resorting to any fraudulent contrivance in order to induce or compel him to vote or refrain from voting. **2.103**

8. Personation at Elections

A person is guilty of personation at an election, contrary to section 60 of RPA 1983, if he: **2.104**

(a) votes in person or by post as some other person, whether as elector or as proxy, and whether that person is living or dead or is a fictitious person; or
(b) votes in person or by post or by proxy—
    (i) for a person who he knows or has reasonable grounds for supposing to be dead or to be a fictitious person, or
    (ii) when he knows or has reasonable grounds for supposing that his appointment as proxy is no longer in force.

9. Election Expenses

It is a corrupt practice knowingly to make a false declaration as to election expenses. It is also a corrupt practice for a person other than a candidate, his election agent, or persons authorized in writing by the election, to incur certain election expenses.[219] In *Bowman v UK*,[220] the applicant, an anti-abortion campaigner, was prosecuted under Section 75 of RPA 1983 for incurring unauthorised expenditure during an election campaign by printing and distributing the candidates' voting record on abortion. The court accepted the legislation pursued the legitimate aim of controlling the expenditure of individual candidates so as to ensure that they were on an equal footing in the financing of their own campaigns. The European Court of Human Rights held that the provision violated Article 10, relating to freedom of information, as it was disproportionate to the aim which the legislation sought to achieve. **2.105**

[219] RPA 1983, s 82(6). For a recent examination of the provision see *Sharma v Director of Public Prosecutions* [2005] EWHC 902 (Admin)

[220] 26 EHRR 1.

10. Mental Element

2.106 *Mens rea* is an essential element of all the offences referred to above and requires that to be guilty of an offence, a person must have acted 'corruptly', ie done 'that which the legislature forbids',[221] and that he must have an intention to influence the voting.

11. Penalties

2.107 A person guilty of a corrupt practice is liable on conviction on indictment to imprisonment for a term not exceeding one year or to a fine or to both, or on summary conviction to imprisonment for a term not exceeding six months or to a fine not exceeding the statutory maximum, or to both. A person convicted of a corrupt practice or an illegal practice is disqualified from being registered as an elector or voting at any parliamentary election in the United Kingdom, or at any local government election in Great Britain. Such a person is also incapable of being elected to the House of Commons and of holding any elective office for five years in the case of a corrupt practice and three years in the case of an illegal practice.[222] A person already elected to Parliament who is found guilty of a corrupt practice must vacate his seat.[223]

12. The Funding of Political Parties

2.108 The funding of political parties has been a source of public concern and not infrequently been accompanied by allegations of corruption, particularly relating to honours.[224] On 12 November 1997, the Prime Minister, the Rt Hon Tony Blair MP, extended the terms of reference of the CSPL and asked it to consider how the funding of political parties should be regulated and reformed. The CPSL's Fifth Report *The Funding of Political Parties in the United Kingdom*, was published on 13 October 1998.[225] It reaffirmed the need for controls to ensure political parties are properly accountable and that elections do not become a matter of who can spend the most. It proposed a new framework, overseen by an independent Electoral Commission with widespread executive and investigative powers. It recommended clear rules on full public disclosure of

---

[221] For cases on the meaning of 'corruptly' in corrupt practices' offences, see Mates and Scallan (n 211 above) 2nd loose leaf edn, para 14.03.

[222] RPA 1983, s 173.

[223] ibid s 137, as inserted by the Political Parties, Elections and Referendums Act 2000, s 136. See *A-G v Jones* [2000] QB 66.

[224] See 2.94 above. Also AW Bradley and KD Ewing, *Constitutional and Administrative Law*, p37 (13th Edn, London: Longmans 2003); KD Ewing, *The Funding of Political Parties in Britain* and M Pinto-Duschinsky, *British Political Finance 1830–1980*, American Enterprise Institute, Washington DC, 1981. London HMSO session 1991–92 no 726 20 July.

[225] Cm 4057. The Committee drew on the experience of a number of other countries, undertaking study tours of Germany, Sweden, Canada, the US and Ireland (CSPL, First Seven Reports, para 35).

donations; donations to political parties to be allowed only from a 'permissible source' defined so as to ban foreign donations; a ban on anonymous donations to political parties in excess of £50; a limit of £20 million on national campaign expenditure in a general election by a political party; and wider scrutiny by an Honours Scrutiny Committee of all proposals where there might be perceived to be a connection between the honour and a political donation.[226]

In July 1999, the Government published a White Paper and a draft Bill[227] in response to the Report. The Bill was introduced into Parliament in January 2000. It received the Royal Assent in November the same year. **2.109**

The Political Parties, Elections and Referendums Act 2000 (PPERA 2000), provides for applications to be made for registration as a political party to the Electoral Commission and sets out regulations relating to its financial affairs.[228] Only candidates representing a registered political party may be nominated for elections—other candidates must be nominated as independents without description.[229] The Act imposes reporting requirements on party funding and prohibits foreign donations. All donations to a political party in excess of £5,000 nationally and £1,000 locally, must be reported to the Electoral Commission on a quarterly basis with the names of the donors and the amount of the donation published by the Commission.[230] Donations may only be received from permissible donors, ie individuals who are on the electoral register in the United Kingdom or organisations that are based here and conduct business activity in the United Kingdom.[231] Companies must secure shareholder approval at least every four years for political donations and expenditures.[232] PPERA 2000 contains a number of offences relating to the making of false statements relating to registration[233] and failure to submit proper statements of accounts.[234] It contains provisions for forfeiture of donations made by impermissible donors,[235] offences concerned with evasion of restrictions on donations,[236] and corrupt and illegal practices in election campaigns and proceedings,[237] and consequences for persons convicted of such practices.[238] It also provides for the punishment of persons convicted of such offences,[239] summary proceeding, and offences committed by bodies corporate and unincorporated associations, and the duty of the court to report convictions to the Commission. **2.110**

226 ibid para 37. 227 Cm 4413.

228 Registration was introduced by the Registration of Political Parties Act 1998, (RPPA 1998) which has been superseded by the PPERA 2000. It is not compulsory, but it is necessary to enjoy a number of prescribed benefits; Bradley and Ewing (n 224 above).

229 PPERA 2000, ss 22, 28. 230 ibid ss 69, 149. 231 ibid s 54.

232 ibid s 139, Sch 19. 233 ibid Pt II, Registration of Political Parties, s 39.

234 ibid Pt III, Accounting requirements for political parties, s 47.

235 ibid Pt IV, control of donations to political parties, s 58. 236 ibid Pt IV, s 61.

237 ibid Pt VIII, ss 136–137. 238 ibid ss 150–154. 239 ibid Pt X Supplemental.

I. Recovering the Proceeds of Corruption

1. Introduction

2.111 The procedures for recovering the proceeds of corruption, referred to in this section, are distinct from the civil remedies referred to in Chapter 7 below, not least because their object is to deprive offenders of the proceeds of their crimes, as opposed to restoring property to the victims and compensating them for their loss. The result is that the procedures described in this section can only be instituted by a prosecutor or a judge following a criminal conviction or on the initiative of the Assets Recovery Agency (ARA). In the case of the former, the property or moneys which are recovered belong, not to the victim, but to the State.[240] Proceedings brought by the ARA are civil proceedings and recoveries can be paid to the victim.[241]

2. Money Laundering

2.112 The Proceeds of Crime Act 2002 (POCA) consolidated and enhanced the provisions of the previous money laundering legislation[242] by abolishing the distinction between drugs related and non-drugs related offences and replacing the previous provisions by three new money laundering offences;

(1) concealing, disguising, converting, transferring and removing criminal property from the jurisdiction (section 327);
(2) entering into or becoming concerned in an arrangement which a person knows or suspects facilitates the acquisition, retention, use or control of criminal property by another person (section 328); and
(3) acquiring, using or possessing criminal property, without making an authorized disclosure under the Act (section 329).

2.113 'Criminal property' is defined as property constituting a person's benefit from criminal conduct or directly or indirectly representing such benefit where the alleged offender knows or suspects it is such.[243] 'Criminal conduct' is defined as conduct which is either an offence in the UK or would be if it occurred there.[244] Bribery and corruption, like all other criminal offences, amount to criminal conduct for the purposes of money laundering, including when they have been committed abroad (save that there will be a defence when the conduct aboard is legal under local law).[245] For the purposes of the POCA 2002 it is immaterial who carried out the conduct, who benefited from it and whether the conduct pre-dates the Act.[246]

240 See 6.01 below. 241 See 7.71 below.
242 CJA 1988, ss 93A–93C; the Drug Trafficking Act 1994, ss 49–51; and the Criminal Justice (International Cooperation) Act 1990, s 14. 243 POCA 2002, s 340(3).
244 ibid s 340(2). 245 SOCPA 2005, s 102 (eg bull fighting).
246 For the detailed provisions of the Act see N Padfield, S Biggs, and S Farrel *The Proceeds of Crime Act 2002*, (London: Butterworths LexisNexis, 2002).

2.114 Sections 330 to 332 of POCA create a new failure to disclose offences and introduce a new negligence-based criminal offence which applies to professionals, including legal practitioners and accountants who deal with other people's money and fail to make a disclosure when there are reasonable grounds for knowing of, or suspecting money laundering. Section 102 of SOCPA 2005 amends these offences so that it will not usually be necessary to *report* offences that take place overseas provided that the conduct is not unlawful in the country in which it occurred. The Government has not yet worked out which 'serious' offences will need to be reported, even if they are legal overseas.

2.115 The National Criminal Intelligence Service (NCIS) receives and processes suspicious transaction reports of money laundering. It works closely with the Police in ordinary cases and with the Serious Fraud Office (SFO), a separate governmental agency, when investigating and prosecuting high value cases. The GRECO Evaluation Team was informed during its Second Evaluation Round in 2003, that 15 per cent of the 100,000 suspicious transaction reports it receives a year lead to investigations by law enforcement authorities.[247]

2.116 Persons wishing to avoid prosecution for non-disclosure offences must make disclosure as soon as is practicable; and if disclosure is made before the activity in question takes place, they must seek consent to proceed from the relevant authorities wherever possible. Failure to report is a criminal offence, punishable by up to five years's imprisonment.[248]

2.117 The Money Laundering Advisory Committee, a public/private sector forum[249] for key stakeholders, including the Law Society and Consultative Committee of Accountancy Bodies, coordinates the anti-money laundering regime and reviews its efficiency and effectiveness. It examines industry–produced guidance notes[250] and makes recommendations prior to submission for government approval.

3. The Proceeds of Crime Act 2002

2.118 The procedures whereby the State recovers the proceeds of crime in the United Kingdom are now governed mainly by POCA 2002, as amended by SOCPA 2005. In addition to introducing new and stricter money laundering offences, POCA 2002 enhanced the courts' post–conviction confiscation powers, transferred to the Crown Court powers formerly exercised by the High Court, established an ARA and introduced civil proceedings in the High Court allowing for forfeiture of assets where on the balance of probabilities, there are

[247] The role of NCIS as the UK's FIU and 'intelligence gatekeeper' is discussed at para 4.07 below.
[248] POCA, s 330 to 332.
[249] http://www.imf.org.
[250] eg the Interim Guidance for Accountants, March 2004.

'reasonable grounds' for 'suspecting' they are the proceeds of, or to be used in, criminal activities.[251]

2.119 The United Kingdom has five different schemes for the recovery of the proceeds of crime by the State. They are confiscation, deprivation, civil recovery, taxation and the seizure and forfeiture of cash. Interim measures are available for the preservation of property liable to confiscation and civil recovery.

2.120 The POCA 2002 confiscation provisions came into force on 24 March 2003.[252] They apply only in respect of offences committed on or after that date. Offences committed before that date are governed by the Drug Trafficking Offences Act 1994 and the Criminal Justice Act 1988. Confiscation procedures depend on the conviction of an offender. Civil recovery measures are *in rem* proceedings. They do not depend on the conviction of an offender. Their essential character is that they are the product of criminal conduct.

4. Confiscation

2.121 The confiscation provisions in POCA 2002 are contained in Part 2, sections 6 to 91. Application to commence the confiscation process is usually made by the prosecutor or the Director of the ARA. The trial judge can commence the process if he considers it is appropriate. The procedure is mandatory once the confiscation process has commenced.[253]

2.122 The court must first consider whether the defendant has a 'criminal lifestyle'.[254] A defendant has a criminal lifestyle if either he is convicted of an offence listed in Schedule 2 of the Act; or the offence constitutes conduct forming part of 'a course of criminal activity'; or was committed over a period of at least 6 months and the defendant has benefited from the conduct constituting the offence.[255] In the latter two cases the benefit must be at least £5,000. An offence constitutes conduct forming part of a course of criminal activity (a) if the defendant has benefited from it and in the proceedings in which he was convicted he was convicted of three or more other offences and each of the three or more of them constituted conduct from which he had benefited, and (b) if the defendant has benefited from the conduct and in the period of six years ending with the day when the proceedings in which he was convicted were started, he was convicted on at least two separate occasions of an offence constituting conduct from which he has benefited.[256]

---

[251] See further 7.69ff below.

[252] POCA 2002 (Commencement No 5, Transitional Provision, Savings and Amendment) Order 2003 (SI 2003/333) and see n 246 above.

[253] POCA 2002, Pt 2, s 6(4).

[254] ibid, s 6(4).

[255] ibid s 75(2).

[256] ibid s 75.

Schedule 2 lists a considerable number of offences including blackmail[257] and money laundering offences under sections 327 and 328 of POCA 2002, but does not include bribery or offences under the Corruption Acts or offences under those Acts as extended by sections 108 to 110 of ATCSA 2001. The result is that a court considering whether to make a confiscation order on the basis of a defendant's 'criminal lifestyle' cannot consider an offence of bribery or corruption unless the offence constitutes conduct forming part of a course of criminal activity, or the offence has been committed over a period of at least six months and the defendant has benefited from the offence. The situation is different when the court is considering whether to order confiscation for the offence of which the defendant has been convicted. At the House of Lords Committee Stage of the Bill, Lord Goldsmith, Attorney-General, said that the inclusion of blackmail was aimed at extortion rather than simple cases of blackmail.[258] **2.123**

If the court decides the defendant has a 'criminal lifestyle', it must decide whether he has benefited from his general criminal conduct whether occurring before or after the passing of the 2002 Act or whether he obtained it before or after the passing of the Act. For the purpose of deciding whether he has benefited from his criminal conduct, the court is required to make a series of assumptions unless the assumption is shown to be incorrect or there would be a serious risk of injustice if the assumption were made.[259] If the court decides he has benefited from his criminal conduct, it must then decide the recoverable amount by taking the benefit from the general criminal conduct and making any reduction where the amount available is less than the benefit. **2.124**

If the court decides the defendant has not benefited from his general criminal conduct, it must decide whether he has benefited from his particular criminal conduct. If it decides that he has benefited from his particular criminal conduct,[260] it must determine the benefit and make an order for the recoverable amount, which is the amount of the benefit or such lesser sum as is available.[261] **2.125**

There are thus two forms of confiscation; the traditional 'criminal conduct confiscation', which requires the court to be satisfied beyond reasonable doubt of a 'causal link' between the specific crime and the specific benefit; and the 'criminal lifestyle confiscation', which allows the court to assume that all of the defendant's properties held over the previous six years are the proceeds of his criminal conduct. In this case no causal link is required. In the case of criminal conduct confiscation, there is no *de minimis* threshold below which sums cannot be confiscated. **2.126**

257 Theft Act 1968, s 21.
258 HL Committee Stage, 22 April 2002, col 20.
259 POCA 2002, s 10.
260 ibid s 6(4)(c).
261 ibid s 7(2).

2.127 As a confiscation order is treated as part of the criminal sentence, the convicted defendant has a right of appeal in the same way as against the judgment, governed by the legislation relating to the appealing of convictions and sentences. The appeal does not necessarily suspend the enforcement of the order, but in practice the courts have awaited the outcome of appeals before commencing their action. The confiscation order may also be appealed separately by the prosecution or by the Director of the ARA. Either the court or the Director of the ARA acts as the enforcement authority to ensure that the confiscation order is carried out, ie that money is paid.

2.128 Over the last three years (2000–01 to 2002–03), under pre-existing legislation, 4,068 confiscation orders have been made with a total value of £235 million. There are no specific figures for corruption offences.

5. Deprivation Orders

2.129 The courts also have power to make an order under section 143 of the Powers of Criminal Courts (Sentencing) Act 2000 against an offender following his conviction to deprive him of anything that was used in the commission of the offence.

6. Civil Recovery

2.130 Part 5 of POCA 2002 introduced a civil recovery scheme and established the ARA which empowers the Director of the Agency to sue by way of a civil proceeding to recover the proceeds of unlawful conduct.[262] 'Unlawful conduct' is 'conduct occurring in any part of the United Kingdom, which is unlawful according to the law of that part and conduct occurring outside the United Kingdom which is unlawful by the law of that country and which if it occurred in a part of the United Kingdom would be unlawful by the law of that part'.[263] Thus corruption offences would fall within the ambit of Part 5.[264]

2.131 Cases can be referred to the Director of the ARA by the law enforcement authorities. The Director may apply to the High Court for an interim receiving order, freezing of assets, or, at a full hearing, for full recovery.[265] The Director must establish that the property derives from unlawful conduct. As the scheme is civil law–based, the standard of proof is the civil standard of the balance of probabilities. Proceedings must be brought within twelve years from the moment when the property was obtained.

---

[262] Civil recovery under POCA is dealt with in more detail at 7.69ff below,
[263] POCA, s 241. [264] See, also, 7.73, 7.74 below. [265] POCA 2002, s 243.

Civil recovery is not pursued below a threshold of £10,000. According to the Government, the scheme will only be instituted when criminal proceedings are not felt to be available or appropriate,[266] including where there is insufficient evidence for a prosecution.[267] **2.132**

7. Taxation

Part 6 of POCA gives the Director of the ARA power to tax the proceeds of crime when there are reasonable grounds to suspect that a person has received income or profit from unlawful conduct, as previously defined. In such cases, the Director exercises the functions of the Inland Revenue and assesses a person's income and tax. **2.133**

8. Seizure of Cash

Police and Customs officers, can seize, detain and seek the forfeiture of cash of not less than £5,000 which they suspect of being the proceeds of crime or intended for such use.[268] Although this power can be exercised in respect of the proceeds of corruption, it is primarily aimed at conduct, such as drug dealing in the street, where large sums of illegally obtained cash are carried by the perpetrator. It is, however, starting to be used increasingly by the police when they find large cash sums which are suspected of being the proceeds of corruption.[269] **2.134**

9. Interim Measures

POCA 2002 also provides for interim measures, such as restraint orders and the summary seizure of cash, and introduces significant investigation powers enabling the seizure, or compelling the production of material and information. These include the ability to compel a bank to produce documents, produce information as to whether a person holds an account and details thereof, and to produce information on transactions through an account over a period of time. **2.135**

10. Seizure

Section 19 of the Police and Criminal Evidence Act 1984 (PACE 1984) authorizes police constables in the course of a search to seize anything they believe it is necessary to seize in order to prevent it from being concealed, lost or destroyed, provided they have reasonable grounds for believing that it has been **2.136**

[266] HC 2R, 30 October 2001, col 846.

[267] The Republic of Ireland introduced civil forfeiture and established a Criminal Assets Bureau in its Proceeds of Crime Act 1995. For comments on the legislation and its conformity with the ECHR see N Padfield, S Biggs, and S Farrell (n 246 above).

[268] POCA Part 5, Ch 3, sections 289–303.

[269] £1 m was seized by the police in a raid on the London apartment of the Governor of Bayelsa State in Nigeria, *The Times* September 2005.

obtained in consequence of the commission of an offence or if it is evidence in relation to an offence that they are investigating. This would clearly include seizure of the proceeds of bribery.

11. Management of Seized Assets

2.137 Section 40 to 47 of the POCA 2002 authorize a prosecutor or the Director of the ARA to apply to a Crown Court for a restraint order[270] in respect of all realisable property held by a specified person, where an investigation or prosecution has commenced. Section 48 authorises the court or the Director to appoint a management receiver over the property, if an asset requires overseeing and active involvement to prevent its value being diminished.

12. The GRECO Evaluation Report

2.138 The GRECO Evaluation Team (GET), in its Report on the United Kingdom in September 2004, [271] was impressed by the amount of money recovered as a result of suspicious transaction reports. However, it criticised the confiscation and recovery schemes so far as cases of corruption are concerned as they are not mandatory; the 'criminal lifestyle confiscation' is not in practice used for values below £5,000; and the threshold for civil recovery is set even higher, at £10,000. It concluded that the schemes do not apply to corruption when the bribe is less than these amounts and considered that, subject to exceptions, confiscation or similar measures, for preventive reasons, should be used wherever possible in all corruption cases, and not only when it is 'economically defensible' in an individual case.

2.139 The GET approved the use of restraint orders at the early stages of a criminal investigation to protect assets, but criticized them on the basis that they are merely to restrain property, except where it is possible to seize cash. It disapproved of restrained property remaining in the hands of a suspected offender who has full use of it until a subsequent confiscation takes place and the fact that a confiscation order would never be enforced before a final decision had been reached. The Team considered the lack of the possibility to deprive a suspected offender of a particular object, such as a bribe which is not paid in cash, is a wrong signal to the offender.

---

[270] The order is to *restrain* property, rather than to *freeze*, in that the property in question remains in the hands of its owner.

[271] Group of States against Corruption (GRECO); Second Evaluation Round, Evaluation Report on the UK, adopted by GRECO at its 20th Plenary Meeting (Strasbourg, 27–30 September 2004) see further para 9.118 below. GRECO is responsible for monitoring the Guiding Principles for the Fight against Corruption and implementation of the Council of Europe Criminal Law Convention on Corruption and the Civil Law Convention on Corruption and Recommendation R (2000) 10 on Codes of Conduct for Public Officials.

2.140 The GET recommended that the United Kingdom should:

(1) take measures to encourage the wider use of confiscation and civil recovery schemes by reducing the financial thresholds for the schemes;
(2) make wider use of measures which would ensure that the value of property representing the proceeds of crime is conserved at an early stage in order to satisfy a subsequent confiscation order;
(3) and consider enhancing the National Criminal Intelligence Service (NCIS) communication with, and feed back to, the providers of suspicious transaction reports.

2.141 While there is no automatic procedure for the use of confiscation and interim measures, the GET was told that the Government is committed to these means being used much more widely than is currently the case. The Government has committed itself to doubling the amount of proceeds recovered, from £29.5 million in 1999–2000 to £60 million by 2004–2005, with further increases in later years. The GET was also told that parts of the recovered money will be added to the criminal justice budget.

2.142 It is, however, worthy of note that the lead examiners conducting the OECD Phase II review of the United Kingdom, in their report which was presented to the Working Group in December 2004, although recognizing that it was too early to judge practical effectiveness, welcomed the adoption of the new and consolidated powers of seizure and confiscation as contained in POCA 2002.[272]

13. International Cooperation for Interim Measures and Confiscation

2.143 A prosecutor or the Director of the ARA may send a request for assistance to the Secretary of State with a view to its being forwarded to the government of the receiving country to secure that any person is prohibited from dealing in realizable property.[273] The United Kingdom Central Authority (UKCA), which is part of the Home Office, acts as the 'gatekeeper' for channelling all provisional and confiscation measures in relation to corruption offences, whether the United Kingdom is the requesting or the requested party. The UKCA may allow a restraint order or confiscation order to be made by a court in the United Kingdom and registered and enforced in an overseas State.

2.144 Information and evidence for confiscation proceedings can be obtained on a government-to-government basis by virtue of the United Kingdom's bilateral confiscation agreements. Beyond this lies the framework of the Crime (International Co-operation) Act 2003 (C(IC)A 2003) and the Criminal Justice

[272] Phase II review, 74–76.

[273] POCA 2002, ss 74, 141, 222.

(International Co-operation) Act 1990 (CJ(IC)A 1990) allowing the United Kingdom to co-operate in overseas criminal proceedings and investigations.[274]

2.145 Both the CJ(IC)A 1990 and section 376 of POCA 2002 allow for requests to be made for evidence from overseas in confiscation investigations. A confiscation order may be registered and enforced in an overseas jurisdiction. There is no need for a requesting country to have entered into a convention, treaty or agreement with the United Kingdom to apply for the restraint of assets, or confiscation, but it must have been designated under section 9 of CJ(IC)A 2003, proceedings must already have started, and the authority must be in a position to give a comprehensive account of the proceedings. Thus, the state must provide in its request a *Commission Rogatoire* or 'letter of request', the appropriate legislation, details of the property, current holder of the property, the link between the subject and the property, brief details of the property, a certificate from the UKCA confirming that proceedings have been started, and if the confiscation order has not yet been made, what its value will be, and a confirmation that such an order is expected to be made in the proceedings.

2.146 Where an order has been made, a similar procedure with supporting documentation can be used by an overseas jurisdiction to enforce a confiscation order. Part 11 of POCA 2002 provides that secondary legislation will be made setting down arrangements for the UK to assist overseas jurisdictions in the investigation, freezing and recovery of criminal proceeds at the stage of investigation, rather than that at the stage of having charged the suspect. Moreover, the GET was informed that the need for countries to be designated under section 9 of CJ(IC)A 1990 ceased on 1 January 2006.

14. International Cooperation Generally: Mutual Assistance and Mutual Legal Assistance

2.147 Evidence may be obtained from abroad by informal (mutual assistance) or formal (mutual legal assistance) means. A formal letter of request is not necessary for all requests for evidence from abroad, but will usually be required if another state is being requested to exercise a coercive power (for example search and seizure) or to obtain an order of the court.

2.148 Prosecutors and investigators sometimes have recourse to mutual legal assistance without exploring whether mutual assistance would, in fact, meet their needs. It is often forgotten that the country receiving the request might welcome an informal approach that can be dealt with efficiently and expeditiously.

[274] C(IC)A 2003, ss 7–9 and CJ(IC)A 1990, ss 13–15 respectively relating to evidence requested by the UK and evidence requested of the UK were brought into force on 26 April 2004. The provision in relation to freezing orders, ss 10–12, are not yet in force.

Prosecutors must thus ask themselves whether they really need a formal letter of request to obtain a particular piece of evidence.

The extent to which countries are willing to assist with an informal request does, of course, vary greatly. In many cases, it will depend on a particular country's own domestic laws, on the state of the relationship between that country and the requesting state and, it has to be said, the attitude and helpfulness of those on the ground to whom the request is made. **2.149**

i. Informal requests (mutual assistance)

Although no definitive list can be made of the type of enquiries that may be dealt with informally, some general observations might be useful. Variations from state to state, must, however, always be borne in mind: **2.150**

- If the enquiry is a routine one and does not require the country of which the request is made to seek coercive powers, then it may well be possible for the request to be made and complied with without a formal letter of request.
- The obtaining of public records, such as land registry documents and papers relating to registration of companies, may often be obtained informally.
- Potential witnesses may be contacted to see if they are willing to assist the authorities of the requesting country voluntarily.
- A witness statement may be taken from a voluntary witness, particularly in circumstances where that witness's evidence is likely to be non-contentious.
- The obtaining of lists of previous convictions and of basic subscriber details from communications and service providers that do not require a court order may also be dealt with in the same informal way.

ii. Formal requests (mutual legal assistance)

Conversely, the sorts of request where a formal letter will, ordinarily, be required will include: **2.151**

- obtaining testimony from a non-voluntary witness;
- seeking to interview a suspect under caution;
- obtaining account information and documentary evidence from banks and financial institutions;
- requests for search and seizure;
- internet records and the contents of e-mails; and
- the transfer of consenting persons into custody in order for testimony to be given.

In criminal matters, there is no universal instrument or treaty which governs the gathering of evidence abroad. However, the framework for formal requests is the conventions, schemes, and treaties that states have signed and ratified. Thus, for an anti-corruption investigation, the UNCAC and the OECD Convention **2.152** each make specific provision for mutual legal assistance and the encouragment of international cooperation.

2.153 Similarly the person making a request must take care to ensure that his or her own domestic law allows the request that is actually being made. For instance, a piece of domestic legislation might, in fact, disallow some requests or types of request that many conventions, treaties, or other international instruments would appear to allow. For some countries, the domestic legislation will have primacy. To make a request otherwise than in accordance with domestic law in such circumstances would be to be invite arguments for exclusion of evidence. Above all, it should not be forgotten that a formal letter of request is a means of requesting evidence, not intelligence or other law enforcement assistance.

2.154 The requesting judicial authority should compile a letter that is a stand-alone document. It should provide the requested state with all the information needed to decide whether assistance should be given and to undertake the requested enquiries. Of course, depending upon the nature of those enquiries and the type of case, the requested state may be quite content for officers, investigators, and/or prosecutors from the requesting state to travel across and to play a part in the investigation.

2.155 The author of a letter of request has, to an extent, a free hand and is not constrained as to form. However, an 'international standard', gleaned from both domestic and international instruments, would include the following contents:

- an assertion of authority by the sender of the letter (in other words, that he/she is a competent judicial authority empowered to issue the letter);
- the citation of relevant treaties and conventions;
- assurances (ie as to reciprocity, dual criminality etc);
- identification of the defendant/suspect;
- the present position re the investigation/proceedings;
- charges/offences under the investigation/prosecution;
- a summary of facts and how those facts relate to the request being made;
- enquiries to be made;
- assistance required; and
- the signature of the sender.

iii. The present UK position

2.156 The C(IC)A 2003 is now the principal statutory provision in relation to mutual legal assistance. Part 1[275] has, to a large extent, replaced the mutual legal assistance provisions contained in Part 1 of the CJ(IC)A 1990 and provides for both the making of requests from the United Kingdom and the receiving by the

[275] ss 7–9 (outgoing requests) and ss 13–19 which each came into force on 26 April 2004; Crime (International Co-operation) Act (Commencement Order No 1) 2004.

United Kingdom of requests from authorities of other states. However, with an eye to the needs of practitioners, the matters set out in detail below address only the making of requests.

iv. Who may issue a letter of request?

Section 7 of C(IC)A 2003 provides that: **2.157**

> (1) If it appears to a judicial authority in the United Kingdom on an application made by a person mentioned in subsection (3)—
> (a) that an offence has been committed or that there are reasonable grounds for suspecting that an offence has been committed, and
> (b) that proceedings in respect of the offence have been instituted or that the offence is being investigated,
> the judicial authority may request assistance under this section
> (2) The assistance that may be requested under this section is assistance in obtaining outside the United Kingdom any evidence specified in the request for use in the proceedings or investigation.
> (3) The application may be made—
> (a) in relation to England and Wales and Northern Ireland, by a prosecuting authority,
> (b) in relation to Scotland, by the Lord Advocate or a procurator fiscal,
> (c) where proceedings have been instituted, by the person charged in those proceedings.
> (4) The judicial authorities are—
> (a) in relation to England and Wales, any judge or justice of the peace,
> (b) in relation to Scotland, any judge of the High Court or sheriff,
> (c) in relation to Northern Ireland, any judge or resident magistrate.
> (5) In relation to England and Wales or Northern Ireland, a designated prosecuting authority may itself request assistance under this section if—
> (a) it appears to the authority that an offence has been committed or that there are reasonable grounds for suspecting that an offence has been committed, and
> (b) the authority has instituted proceedings in respect of the offence in question or it is being investigated.
> 'Designated' means designated by an order made by the Secretary of State.
> (6) In relation to Scotland, the Lord Advocate or a procurator fiscal may himself request assistance under this section if it appears to him—
> (a) that an offence has been committed or that there are reasonable grounds for suspecting that an offence has been committed, and
> (b) that proceedings in respect of the offence have been instituted or that the offence is being investigated.
> (7) . . .

It will be seen from the above that a judicial authority, as defined in section 7(4) **2.158** of C(IC)A 2003 may issue a letter of request, as indeed may a designated prosecuting authority as long as the conditions in section 7(5) are met. It remains the case, therefore, that a formal request on behalf of the defence for evidence from abroad will have to be issued by a judge or magistrate or, of course, by the prosecutor of a designated prosecuting authority.

v. Transmission of the request

2.159 Section 8 of C(IC)A 2003 Act provides that:

> (1) A request for assistance under section 7 may be sent—
> (a) to a court exercising jurisdiction in the place where the evidence is situated, or
> (b) to any authority recognised by the government of the country in question as the appropriate authority for receiving requests of that kind.
> (2) Alternatively, if it is a request by a judicial authority or a designated prosecuting authority it may be sent to the Secretary of State (in Scotland, the Lord Advocate) for forwarding to a court or authority mentioned in subsection (1).
> (3) In cases of urgency, a request for assistance may be sent to—
> (a) the International Criminal Police Organisation, or
> (b) any body or person competent to receive it under any provisions adopted under the Treaty on European Union,
> for forwarding to any court or authority mentioned in subsection (1).

2.160 In a departure from section 3(4) and (5) of CJ(IC)A 1990, which required formal requests to be sent to the Secretary of State for transmission, except in cases of urgency; section 8(2) allows a judicial authority or designated prosecuting authority to send a request either directly to a court or to the competent authorities in the requested state, or to the Secretary of State for onward transmission.

3

MISCONDUCT IN A PUBLIC OFFICE

A. Introduction

Just like the common law offence of bribery, misconduct in a public office is confined to persons who are public office holders. Although it has existed in its present form for more than two hundred years, it has been relied upon relatively sparingly by prosecutors and almost fell into disuse during the mid-twentieth century. However, in more recent times its value as an offence has been recognized in many of the jurisdictions with a common law tradition: it has become one of the offences of choice for, *inter alia*, prosecutors with conduct of police and public official corruption cases in England and Wales; the Hong Kong Independent Commission Against Corruption; and those tasked with pursuing serious criminality amongst public servants and law enforcement personnel in Australia and some of the Caribbean states. **3.01**

Why the modern recourse to misconduct in a public office? The answer is at least fivefold: **3.02**

(1) a single charge may be used to reflect an entire course of conduct;
(2) it may be used to reflect serious misconduct which is truly 'criminal' but which cannot be satisfactorily reflected by any other offence;

(3) it may be used to reflect behaviour which would amount to perverting the course of justice in circumstances where the 'course of justice' is fictitious (ie created by those carrying out an integrity test);[1]
(4) as confidential information becomes increasingly valuable to criminals or commercial interests, it may be used to reflect the unlawful passing of such information when other offences (for example under the Data Protection Act 1998) are limited or give the court only limited sentencing options;
(5) the maximum sentence is life imprisonment (unlike the statutory corruption offences which carry a maximum of seven years' imprisonment).

3.03 Misconduct in a public office is committed when the holder of that public office acts, or omits to act, in a way which is contrary to his duty. That duty may be one imposed upon him either at common law or by statute. The offence, in the form it is known today, is often said to date back to the case of *R v Bembridge*.[2] There, the defendant was an accountant in the office of the Receiver and Paymaster-General of the Forces who was accused of corruptly concealing from his superior his knowledge that certain sums of money which should have appeared in a final account had, in fact, been omitted. Lord Mansfield CJ, giving the judgment of the Court, set out both the principles and rationale of the offence:

> The duty of the defendant is obvious; he was a trustee of the public and the Paymaster, for making every charge and every allowance he knew of;... if the defendant knew of the omission ... and if he concealed it, his motive must have been corrupt. That he did know was fully proved, and he was guilty, therefore, not of an omission or neglect, but of a gross deceit. The object could only have been to defraud the public of the whole, or part of the interest ... a man accepting an office of trust, concerning the public, especially if attended with profit, is answerable criminally to the King for misbehaviour in his office; this is true by whomever and in whatever way the officer is appointed.

3.04 However, even before *Bembridge*, the common law sought to criminalize the public officer who had the benefit of the privileged position of occupying a public office, but who failed to discharge his duties truly competently and for the public good. Thus, a constable who failed to act in accordance with his duty as an officer of the Crown was criminally liable in *Mackalley's Case*,[3] whilst in *Crouther's Case*[4] a constable was prosecuted having refused to make a 'hue and cry' after being informed of a burglary.

B. The Nature and Elements of the Offence

3.05 Courts, practitioners, and academic lawyers have struggled, and continue to struggle, to formulate the nature and elements of the offence. The learned editor

[1] See discussion re integrity testing at 4.211 below.
[2] (1783) 3 Doug 327.
[3] (1611) 9 Co Rep 656.
[4] (1600) Cro Eliz 654.

of Russell on Crime set out the common law rule thus:[5]

> Where a public officer is guilty of misbehaviour in office by neglecting a duty imposed upon him either at common-law or at statute, he commits a misdemeanour and is liable to indictment, unless another remedy is substituted by statute. The liability exists whether he is a common-law or a statutory officer; and a person holding an office of important trust and of consequence to the public, under letters patent or derivatively from such authority, is liable to indictment for not faithfully discharging the office.

A number of twentieth-century authorities also sought to formulate the essential principles and scope of the offence. In *R v Whitaker*[6] the defendant was a military officer who appealed to the Court of Criminal Appeal following his conviction for conspiring to accept bribes from the caterers who supplied his regimental canteen. In this case the key element of the offence was defined as the failure to comply with the obligation to discharge a public duty in which all the public is interested. **3.06**

In *R v Llewellyn-Jones*[7] the appellant was a county court registrar who, being heavily in debt, made an order for payment out of court of £9,000, with the intention of gaining improper personal advantage and without proper regard to the legitimate interests of others. Giving the judgment of the Court of Appeal, Lord Parker CJ stated:[8] **3.07**

> The argument has centred around what, at common-law, was embraced by the offence which can be, in general terms, described as 'misbehaviour in a public office'. [Counsel on behalf of the appellant] began his submission by saying that, quite clearly, it cannot be a criminal offence whenever there is any misbehaviour in a public office. He would say that there must be many standards of conduct which can be said to be reprehensible, which would justify his being removed from his office, but that not all of them would constitute criminal offences at common law. From that he goes on to say that, in order for there to be a criminal offence at common law in such a case as this, there must be some further ingredient [other than those set out in the counts]. He would, I think, concede that, if it was said that the misbehaviour amounted to oppression, using the powers of his office to compel someone to act in a particular way, or to extortion, causing somebody to pay him money, to corruption in the sense of bribery, to partiality, or indeed to acting fraudulently . . . if here in any of [these counts] this word fraudulently had appeared, he really could not argue that they did not describe criminal offences known to the common law.

Those, then, are some attempts at illustrating the extent of the offence (and, notwithstanding that it may be committed in one of a number of ways, the courts have accepted that it is a single offence), but what of the elements of the offence? **3.08**

5 12th Edn, 1964.
6 [1914] KB 1283; 10 Cr App R 245, CCA. See also paras 2.12, n 22 and 2.13 above.
7 [1968] 1 QB 429. See also para 2.28 above.
8 At 435.

3.09 In *R v Dytham*[9] the Court of Appeal dismissed the appeal against conviction of a police constable who, whilst on duty and in uniform, witnessed a violent assault on a man by a number of assailants who beat and kicked the man to death. The police officer had taken no steps to intervene in the assault and, when it was over, merely drove away. The indictment alleged misconduct whilst acting as an officer of justice in that he deliberately failed to carry out his duty as a police constable by wilfully omitting to take any steps to preserve the peace or to protect the man or to arrest, or otherwise bring to justice, his assailants. At his appeal, although conceding that the offence of misconduct in a public office existed at common law, the appellant contended that mere nonfeasance by a person in the discharge of his duty as the holder of a public office was insufficient to constitute the offence; rather, he averred, there had to be a finding of malfeasance or, at least, of misfeasance involving corruption or fraud.

3.10 We shall return to the issue of the nature of the misconduct required for the offence shortly.[10] But, as to the elements of criminal misconduct, the effect of Lord Widgery CJ's judgment in the *Dytham* case[11] is to distil them thus:

(1) The defendant must be a public officer who has an obligation to perform a duty.
(2) The breach of the said duty has to be by wilful neglect, not mere inadvertence. However, the breach does not have to have been deliberate.
(3) The breach has to be culpable in the sense of being without reasonable excuse or justification.
(4) The element of culpability has to be of such degree as to call for condemnation and punishment by the criminal courts.
(5) It is a question of fact for the jury to decide whether, on the evidence, there is culpability to the degree necessary to make it a criminal offence.

3.11 The judgment in the *Dytham* case was concerned primarily with misconduct on the basis of omission and did not purport to formulate a comprehensive definition. However, the Court of Appeal approved and followed it in *R v Bowden*.[12] The appellant, who was employed by a local authority as a maintenance manager, caused plumbing and electrical work to be carried out at his girlfriend's house. His appeal against conviction was dismissed,[13] and Hirst LJ, giving judgment, sought to encapsulate the extent of the offence thus:[14]

> [In the words of Lord Mansfield] . . . *R* v. *Bembridge* . . . 'that a man accepting an office of trust concerning the public is answerable criminally to the King for

[9] [1979] QB 722. [10] See 3.46 below. [11] [1979] QB 722, 725–728.
[12] [1996] 1 Cr. App R 104; [1996] 1 WLR 98.
[13] It having been argued on his behalf that the trial judge had erred in ruling that a local authority employee could be guilty of misconduct in a public office.
[14] [1996] 1 WLR 98, 103; [1996] 1 Cr App R 104, 109.

> misbehaviour in his office', and, most significantly, that '... this is true by whomever and in whatever way the officer is appointed'.

The Court in the *Bowden* case appeared to be casting the net of criminality very widely (particularly in relation to the definition of 'public officer' for the purposes of the offence)[15] without, at the same time, seeking to set out any real test to assist the practitioner in knowing where the boundaries might lie. Indeed, in his comments on the case in the *Criminal Law Review*,[16] Professor Sir John Smith QC noted that: 'The most unsatisfactory feature of common law misdemeanours is the uncertainty about their elements and limits and the boundaries between them.' **3.12**

The lack of certainty as to the elements of the offence brought the case of *Shum Kwok Sher v HKSAR*[17] to the Court of Final Appeal in Hong Kong. The question which arose was whether the common law offence of misconduct in a public office was so imprecise as to be unconstitutional under Hong Kong's Basic Law. **3.13**

The appellant was the Chief Property Manager of the Hong Kong Government Property Agency. It was the prosecution's case that he had misconducted himself in his office by exerting an improper influence over the award of contracts worth more than HK$150 million to a company in which the brothers of his sister-in-law held a financial stake. **3.14**

Giving judgment; with which all other members of the court concurred, Sir Anthony Mason NPJ, reviewed the English and Australian authorities and stated: **3.15**

> In my view, the elements of the offence of misconduct in a public office are:
>
> (1) a public official;
> (2) who in the course of, or in relation to, his public office;
> (3) wilfully and intentionally;
> (4) culpably misconducts himself.
>
> A public official culpably misconducts himself if he wilfully and intentionally neglects or fails to perform a duty to which he is subject by virtue of his office or employment without reasonable excuse or justification. A public official also culpably misconducts himself if, with an improper motive, he wilfully and intentionally exercises a power or discretion which he has by virtue of his office or employment without reasonable excuse or justification.[18]

However, in relation to the mental element required for the offence, Sir Anthony went on to express the view that the misconduct must be 'wilful' as well as 'intentional'. He held that an intention to do the act or make the omission which amounts to the breach of the duty is not enough; the public **3.16**

---

15 See 3.37–3.47 below.
16 [1996] Crim LR 57.
17 [2002] 5 HKCFAR 381.
18 ibid 409–410.

officer must also commit the act or make the omission with 'knowledge or advertence to the consequences'.[19]

3.17 The issue of whether there is a requirement for a mental element in relation to consequences is an important one to which we shall return later.[20] However, for present purposes, it is worthy of note that Sir Anthony Mason NPJ also distinguished the mental element required in a case of misconduct by an act of commission from that in relation to an act of omission. In the case of the former, it will be seen from his words, as cited above,[21] that he identified a three-pronged mental element: conduct which is intentional, wilful, and done with an improper motive. However, in relation to a case of misconduct by omission, ie non-feasence, he held that the mental element required was 'wilful intent, accompanied by absence of reasonable excuse or justification. Mere inadvertence is not enough'.[22]

3.18 The Court of Appeal in *Attorney-General's Reference (No 3 of 2003)*[23] found it difficult to understand why there was a need for conduct to be both wilful and intentional. Such an approach is, perhaps, only comprehensible if one takes 'intent' to relate to the breach, and 'wilful' to relate to consequence. However, the third element of 'improper motive' for offences of malfeasance and misfeasance only adds to the confusion.[24] In any event, such a view merits further discussion at paras 3.59 to 3.62 below.

3.19 A further requirement was also set out by Sir Anthony Mason NPJ in his judgment: a qualification to the offence and its elements is that 'the misconduct complained of must be serious misconduct. Whether it is serious misconduct in this context is to be determined having regard to the responsibilities of the office and office holder, the importance of the public objects which they serve and the nature and extent of the departure from the responsibilities'.[25] This qualification or element clearly owes something to the formulation by Lord Widgery CJ in the *Dytham* case. As in other aspects of attempts by courts to formulate a test for misconduct in a public office, an element of public policy is a significant factor here.

3.20 Following the *Shum Kwok Sher* case, the extent and elements of the misconduct offence arose for consideration in *Attorney General's Reference (No 3 of 2003)*.[26] Pill LJ, giving the judgment of the Court of Appeal, emphasized that a consistent theme from earlier cases has been that there must be 'a serious departure from proper standards before the criminal offence is committed'.[27]

[19] [2002] 5 HKCFAR 410. [20] See 3.54 to 3.69 below
[21] [2002] 5 HKCFAR 409 [22] ibid 408
[23] [2004] 3 WLR 451, 464 and see xxx below.
[24] [2002] 5 HKCFAR 409. [25] At 410, para 86. [26] [2004] 3 WLR 451.
[27] ibid 467.

Further, such a departure, to be criminal, will not be merely negligent but will be one 'amounting to an affront to the standing of the public office held'.[28] A mistake, even if it is a serious one, will not in itself suffice. In his conclusions, Pill LJ stated that:

> The elements of the offence of misconduct in a public office are:
>
> i) A public officer acting as such;
> ii) Wilfully neglects to perform his duty and/or wilfully misconducts himself;
> iii) To such a degree as to amount to abuse of the public's trust in the office holder;
> iv) Without reasonable excuse or justification.[29]

The judgment in *Attorney-General's Reference (No 3 of 2003)* also sought to give guidance on some of the issues, particularly as to state of mind, already touched on above. Pill LJ reiterated that the element of culpability must, as in Lord Widgery CJ's words in the *Dytham* case, 'be of such a degree that the misconduct impugned is calculated to injure the public interest so as to call for condemnation and punishment'.[30] In stressing such a high threshold, he emphasized that a failure to confine the test of the offence in such a manner 'would place a constraint upon the conduct of public officers in the proper performance of their duties which will be contrary to the public interest'.[31] In essence, the rationale of the test is to maintain the balance between enabling a public office holder to carry out his duties for the benefit of the public as a whole without fear of undue criminal sanction and, at the same time, being able to bring such an official to account when a serious breach occurs, on the basis that such a breach is not only a breach of the official's duty but also of the public's trust. **3.21**

As to whether the offence of misconduct in a public office is one of consequence in any respect, Pill LJ was not willing, in terms, to confine the mental element to the breach alone. Rather, he observed that: **3.22**

> . . . it will normally be necessary to consider the likely consequences of the breach in deciding whether the conduct falls so far below the standard of conduct to be expected of the officer as to constitute the offence. The conduct cannot be considered in a vacuum: the consequences likely to follow from it, viewed subjectively, will often influence the decision as to whether the conduct amounted to an abuse of the public's trust in the officer.[32]

However, as set out below, that consequence, and foresight of the same, is not an element of the offence; but is, rather, a factor going to culpability or seriousness. Thus, in the case of an obviously serious breach, such as corrupt behaviour, it may not be necessary to have regard to consequences. Certainly the view that a mental element as to consequence, on Pill LJ's formulation, is not part of the offence is one which seems to have been taken in the most recent **3.23**

---

[28] [2004] 3 WLR 467. [29] ibid 468. [30] ibid 467. [31] ibid 467.
[32] ibid 467.

appellate authority on the issue, *Sin Kam Wah and anor v HKSAR*,[33] discussed at para 3.69 below.

C. Consideration of the Individual Elements

1. Public Office Holder

3.24 Running though the discussion in the present chapter is the common law's understanding that the roles and functions of public office holders, in all their guises, are vital to the workings and order of society. Many public office holders are given extensive powers in the expectation that these will be exercised for the public good. Such privilege of power brings with it obligation: it must be exercised conscientiously, without fear or favour, and without being used as a tool for illicit gain. In the event that the position of trust is breached, the common law therefore singles out the public office holder for sanction in a way in which the holder of a non-public office or position is not.

3.25 To that theme, however, needs to be added another consideration. We now live in a world where, in many jurisdictions, traditionally public functions are often being carried out by employees of private contractors; in other words, employees in private employment, not holding 'public office' in any recognizable sense. Where, then, should public policy draw the line in rendering an individual liable for the misconduct in a public office offence? On the one hand, there is an unfairness and illogicality (as one of the submissions to the Court of Appeal in *Attorney-General's Reference (No 3 of 2003)* emphasized)[34] if public officers, such as police officers, are liable to criminal sanction not applicable to those who perform similar work, but who happen to be in private employment (such as those charged with maintaining security at courts or in transporting prisoners to and from prison). Therefore, should the test of 'public office' be a purely functional one? On the other hand, however, should public policy confine the criminal offence to individuals holding high offices of public trust who owe a duty to the Crown? Alternatively, is a 'third way' to be preferred: with a functional test being applied, but being followed by a public policy limitation to the extent that the criminal offence will be limited to those whose roles are such that a breach of trust will significantly damage or disadvantage the wider public?

3.26 At this stage, we must return to the earliest of the 'modern' authorities on the offence, the words of Lord Mansfield CJ in the *Bembridge* case. It will be recalled that he identified the principle that (a) a position which carries with it the trust of the public, particularly if it is a paid office, will render the holder liable to

[33] [2005] 2 HKLRD 375. [34] [2004] 3 WLR 451, 468.

criminal sanction for misconduct within such a position, and (b) liability in that way will exist no matter how the person comes to hold such a position (ie whether elected or appointed and whether by the Crown or otherwise).

Lord Mansfield's words set out a key feature of misconduct cases from that date to the present; namely that, for the offence to be made out, one is not confined to the holder of an 'office' in a narrow or technical sense, but, rather, one is able, in a wider sense, to encompass the person who is performing a public function. Thus, the position held need not be one for which remuneration is received; a person can be a public office holder even if he receives no payment from the public, or, indeed, no payment at all. Further, it matters not who made the appointment, nor the manner in which it was made. The key issue, then, is as to the nature and extent of the duties which the office or post requires its incumbent to perform. **3.27**

A further illustration that the early modern authorities did not feel constrained to take a narrow view of 'public office' is *Henly v Lyme Corporation*.[35] There, a civil action was brought against the Mayor and Burgesses of Lyme Regis for failing, in breach of their public duty, to repair certain sea-banks and coastal defences (in particular, the pier-quay or 'cob'). On appeal (the claim having succeeded before Littledale J at the Dorchester Spring Assizes in 1828), Best CJ, upholding the decision at first instance, stated:[36] **3.28**

> Now I take it to be perfectly clear that, if a public officer abuses his office, by an act of omission or commission, and the consequences of that is an injury to an individual, an action may be maintained against such public officer. The instances of this are so numerous, that it would be a waste of time to refer to them. Then, what constitutes a public officer? In my opinion, everyone who is appointed to discharge a public duty, and receives a compensation in whatever shape, whether from the Crown or otherwise, is constituted a public officer.

Best CJ went on to give examples of office holders and included bishops, clergymen, lords of the manor and Governers of the Bank of England. He then went on to say:[37] 'If a man takes reward, whatever be the nature of that reward, whether it be in money from the Crown, whether it be in land from the Crown, whether it be in lands or money from any individual, for the discharge of a public duty, that instant he becomes a public officer . . . ' **3.29**

Although one may doubt confining the definition to an individual who receives remuneration or reward, the breadth of the notion of 'public office holder' contained within Best CJ's words cannot be doubted. Nor is there reason to believe that there was any sort of implicit understanding in the earlier authorities that the criminal offence should be reserved for holders of high office. Indeed, mention has already been made of cases pre-dating *Bembridge* in which **3.30**

[35] (1828) 5 Bing 91. [36] ibid 107. [37] ibid 108.

a police constable was held to be a public office holder for the purposes of the offence (eg *MacKalley's Case*).[38]

3.31 Moving forwards in time, Willes J in the late nineteenth-century case of *R v Lancaster and Worrall*[39] stated that: 'The nature of the office is immaterial as long as it is for the public good.' Similarly, in *R v Hall*[40] an overseer for the poor who was charged by statute with the duty of preparing the register of voters qualified to vote in Parliamentary and council elections in Whitechapel, was implicitly held to be a public office holder for the purposes of the criminal law. On the facts, he was accused of corruptly omitting from the register persons who were qualified to vote, whilst at the same time including those who were dead or otherwise lacked entitlement. He was charged with a number of counts reflecting common law misconduct in public office, but the indictment against him was quashed on the basis that he should have been proceeded against under provisions provided by statute for election offences.

3.32 In *R v Whitaker*[41] the Court of Criminal Appeal had to consider the argument that the appellant was not a public officer in circumstances where he was an army officer, holding a commanding post, who had accepted sums of money from a firm of caterers; the sums in question having been paid to induce him to accept a representative of the firm as a tenant of the regimental canteen. The indictment described the appellant as 'a public and ministerial officer' (ie ministerial as opposed to judicial) and the court confirmed that, in its view, he was indeed a public office holder: 'A public office holder is an officer who discharges any duty in the discharge of which the public are interested, more clearly so if he is paid out of a fund provided by the public.'[42]

3.33 It is worthy of note that, although *Henly v Lyne Corporation*[43] was cited in argument, the court in the *Whitaker* case did not seek to confine its definition to the person who received remuneration. It might be easier to infer that an office holder paid by the Crown or the public is the holder of a public office, but public remuneration, or indeed the fact of any remuneration, is not in itself a key element.

3.34 The definition set out in the *Whitaker* case found favour with courts in a number of other jurisdictions in later twentieth-century cases.[44] The same test was, therefore, applied by the Court of Appeal of the Eastern Caribbean States in *Williams v R*[45] and was also applied in the South African case of *R v Sacks*

[38] (1611) 9 Co Rep 656. [39] (1890) 16 Cox CC 739. [40] [1891] 1 QB 747.
[41] [1914] 3 KB 1283; [xxx] 10 Cr App R 245, CCA and see 2.05 and 2.12, n 22 above.
[42] [1914] 3 KB 1283, 1296; [xxx] 10 Cr App R 245, 252, CCA.
[43] (1828) 5 Bing 91.
[44] The authors are grateful to Ian McWalters SC for sharing his research with them in this regard.
[45] (1986) 39 WIR 129.

and anor.[46] Shortly after the *Whitaker* decision, the question of what amounts to a 'public office' fell to be considered by the High Court of Australia in *R v Boston*.[47] The case itself concerned a conspiracy to corruptly pay moneys to a member of the Legislative Assembly of New South Wales. The Court considered whether the functions and duties of a Member of Parliament meant that he or she was a public office holder. By a majority of 4 to 2 the Court concluded that the post of MP was indeed a public office. The essence of the decision of the majority was that an MP has 'duties to perform which would constitute in law an office' and that such duties were those 'appertaining to the position that he fills, a position of no transient or temporary existence, a position forming a recognised place in the constitutional machinery of government'.[48]

Of the judges in the majority in the *Boston* case, Higgins J undertook a detailed analysis of the concept of 'public office'. Working from the *Whitaker* definition, he identified the key element in the test as whether or not there is an obligation to discharge a public duty in which the public is interested. He noted the words of Willes J in *Lancaster and Worrell*[49] and reached the conclusion that 'the application and the principle is not confined to public servants in the narrow sense, under the direct orders of the Crown'.[50] We see from the approach of the majority in the *Boston* case a desire not to be constrained by a narrow definition. As with the earlier English authorities referred to above, the focus is on the nature and extent of the duty required to be performed; in essence, a functional, not titular approach. **3.35**

The position of an MP in the criminal law was considered by Buckley J at first instance in *R v Currie and ors*.[51] The case concerned an allegation of common law bribery involving commercial contracts and an MP. One of the submissions **3.36**

---

[46] [1943] SALR 413. In addition, the *Whitaker* definition was applied by the Court of Appeal of Jamaica in *Stewart v R* (1960) 2 WIR 450. There the appellant performed public duties, but was not remunerated for his services and was not entitled to claim any payment for them. It was argued on the appellant's behalf that, in order to be a public officer, a person must be appointed under a law or regulation, or must be paid from public funds. The Court of Appeal of Jamaica rejected those contentions and held that 'the true guide to be followed is that when a person has discharged a duty in which the public is interested, he is performing a public duty and therefore is the holder of a public office' ([1960] 2 WIR 450, 453). Further, the court noted that public office holders were not confined to those who are paid from public funds and that the office the appellant occupied was a public one even through it carried with it no salary.

[47] (1923) 33 CLR 386.

[48] ibid 402. Again, the authors are indebted to Ian McWalters SC for drawing these passages to our attention.

[49] See n 40 above.

[50] (1923) 33 CLR 386, 411.

[51] (1992) unreported, Central Criminal Court. See 2.25 above.

on which Buckley J, as trial judge, was asked to rule was that bribery of an MP was not a bribe in English law as MPs are not holders of a public office. In rejecting that contention, Buckley J stated:

> To hold that the existence of a common-law crime of bribing a Member of Parliament depends on the meaning to be given to the word 'office' in this context, as opposed to looking at the principle involved, would not be calculated to commend the criminal law to the public it should serve... The undoubted common law offence of bribery is not artificially limited by reference to any particular shade of meaning of the word 'office'. The underlying reason or principle is concerned with the corruption of those who undertake a duty, in the proper discharge of which the public is interested.

3.37 Again, one has, above, the central issue seen time and again in the reported cases: does the public have an interest in the proper discharge of the duty which the individual has a duty to perform? The Court of Appeal had the opportunity to review existing case law on the issue in *R v Bowden.*[52] In giving its judgment, the court examined the existing authorities from *Bembridge* to date and concluded that the common law offence of misconduct in a public office applied generally to every person who was appointed to discharge a public duty and was paid compensation in whatever form, whether from the Crown or otherwise.

3.38 The *Bowden* case is sometimes seen as an attempt to extend the existing law. Certainly it is capable of being read in such a way as to give a particularly wide reading of what amounts to a 'public office'. At the same time, Hirst LJ, in giving judgment, was careful to indicate that the court was adopting the reasoning of Lord Mansfield CJ in *Bembridge* and of Best CJ in *Henly v Lyme Corporation*; therefore, the *Bowden* case might be regarded as an attempt to clarify the law in the context of present day arrangements for those who carry out functions on behalf of the public. In any event, the case is worthy of some detailed consideration.

3.39 Mr Bowden was employed as a miscellaneous maintenance manager by a city works department. He was, therefore, a local authority employee whose salary was paid out of public funds. Under his contract of employment he was responsible for the management and direction of subordinate employees; he was also accountable for the handling of money and was obliged to ensure that his department's activities were within budget. It was at the material time for the purposes of the offence, a statutory duty for every local authority to secure that, in respect of each financial year, its revenue for construction or maintenance work showed such positive rate of return on the capital employed for the purpose of carrying out the work as the Secretary of State might direct.

[52] [1996] 1 WLR 98; [1996] Cr App R 104.

During a six-month period Mr Bowden caused enhanced joinery, plumbing and electrical work to be carried out at residential premises within the area of his local authority by council employees. The repairs in question were not required under the repairing policy of the local authority and the particular residence was, in fact, let to Mr Bowden's girlfriend. 3.40

In his judgment, Hirst LJ quoted from Lord Mansfield CJ's words in the *Bembridge* case (referred to above), and also those of Best CJ in *Henly v Lyme Corporation* (again, as above). Having then surveyed subsequent authorities through the nineteenth and twentieth centuries, he acknowledged the argument put forward on behalf of Mr Bowden that all recent reported cases related to persons holding high offices of public trust and owing a duty to the Crown. That argument went on to assert that, at the very least, the scope of the offence was limited to offences where a breach of trust which would significantly disadvantage the public at large had taken place.[53] Further, the argument on behalf of Mr Bowden relied on the fact that in no case had a local authority employee been held to fall within the scope of the offence and that any attempt to do so based on *Henly v Lyme Corporation* was 'erroneous and fallacious' as the *Henly* case was concerned with civil and not criminal liability. 3.41

However, Hirst LJ made clear that the Court did not accept such a line of reasoning and stated that: 3.42

> In our judgement the theme which runs through all these cases over the past 200 years is, in the words of Lord Mansfield CJ in *Rex v Bembridge*, that 'a man accepting an office of trust concerning the public... is answerable criminally to the King for misbehaviour in his office,' adding, significantly, that 'this is true, by whomever and in whatever way the officer is appointed'.[54]

Tracing a line of reasoning from the *Bembridge* case to *Henly v Lyme Corporation*, Hirst LJ went on to say that: 3.43

> The same principle is to be found in *Henly v Lyme Corporation* where, in our judgment, even though it was a civil case, a public office is correctly defined, at p. 107, as embracing 'everyone who is appointed to discharge a public duty, and receives compensation in whatever shape *whether from the Crown or otherwise*' [italics reflect Hirst LJ's emphasis]. In that case, significantly, the public officers in question were not servants of the Crown, but the Mayor and Burgesses of a borough. . . .[55]

Addressing the argument that most of the cases reported are concerned with officers or agents of the Crown, Hirst LJ stated that such a fact did not establish any curtailment of the well-established principle, 'since in no case has it been laid down that the offence is limited to officers or agents of the Crown'.[56] 3.44

[53] [1996] 1 WLR 98, 102; [1996] 1 Cr App R 104, 108.
[54] [1996] 1 WLR 98, 103; [1996] 1 Cr App R 104, 109.
[55] ibid 103.
[56] ibid 103.

Indeed, as he went on to note, those cases reported during the course of the twentieth century have proceeded on the basis of the general principle as set out in *Bembridge* and *Henley v Lyme Corporation.*

3.45 As to Mr Bowden's own position, Hirst LJ found that he was responsible to his employers for the upkeep of their council housing and that, in that capacity, he was accountable for the receipt and disbursement of public money derived by the city council either from the rates or from central government grants. Moreover, Mr Bowden's salary was paid from the same public funds. Thus, in the judgment of the court, Mr Bowden fell 'fairly and squarely within the definition of "public officer" laid down in the authorities and we are unable to accept the submission that, with these responsibilities, his position was too lowly to qualify'.[57] Hirst LJ then reiterated, taking into account the words of Best CJ in *Henley v Lyme Corporation*, that Mr Bowden was appointed to discharge public duties and received compensation from the public. Such a position 'seems to us to fall fully within the public duty at common law . . . '.[58]

3.46 Despite the care taken by the Court of Appeal in the *Bowden* case to trace a line of consistent reasoning on the point from *Bembridge* onward, does the judgment of Hirst LJ actually signal any change in approach, no matter how subtle? Certainly it reflects the triumph of the functional test, in that it seems clear that the public officer may be someone who is employed or tasked to carry out a function without holding any sort of 'office' in the formal sense and that the public duty which he is under an obligation to perform is a duty in the sense that the obligation arising out of the task or function is one in which the public is interested. On that basis, would every employee of the National Health Service in performing his or her duties be liable, in the event of a breach, for prosecution for criminal misconduct? Alternatively, would the courts feel compelled, as a matter of public policy, to draw an imaginary line? Might it be said that doctors, senior administrators, and nurses fall on one side of the divide, and junior administrative staff and hospital porters on the other? In that regard, the test expounded in the *Bowden* case poses perhaps more questions than it answers.

3.47 Although the functional test to determine whether an individual is a public office holder is capable of providing a workable and practical test, it does not appear to answer the question of whether, to amount to a 'public office', the office in question has to have an existence independent of the individual who, at the material time, is occupying it. The *Bowden* judgment suggests that there has never been such a requirement of independent existence. However, the

[57] [1996] 1 WLR 98, 103; [1996] 1 Cr App R 103. [58] ibid 103.

matter has been considered more recently by the Supreme Court of India in *Rao and ors v State of India*.[59] In that case, the Supreme Court had to consider, *inter alia*, whether a member of Parliament was a 'public servant' for the purposes of the Prevention of Corruption Act 1988. The statutory definition of 'public servant' contained within that legislation provides that a public servant is 'any person who holds any office by virtue of which he is authorised or required to perform any public duty'. 'Public duty', meanwhile, is defined within the Act as: 'A duty in the discharge of which the State, the public or the community at large has an interest.' In considering these definitions, the Supreme Court was obliged to consider the concept of 'office'. In doing so, the majority of the court, following *R v Boston*,[60] held that being a Member of Parliament was an office, since it carried responsibilities of a public nature and had an existence independent of the holder of the office.[61] The first of those considerations, namely that the position carries certain responsibilities of a public character, is broad and is consistent with a functional test; however, the requirement of an independent existence suggests an attempt to narrow the otherwise broad definition. Such a limitation might have initial attraction, but it is at odds with the expansive nature of the words of both Lord Mansfield CJ and Best CJ. In addition, it does not appear to take into account the individual carrying out a public function which needs to be carried out on only a temporary basis and, perhaps most important of all, does not reflect the reality of public life in an age when privatized utilities and public private partnerships are performing tasks which, in every sense, the public has an interest in and has placed its trust in.

2. Breach of Duty

In *R v Wyat*[62] it was held that 'where an officer neglects a duty incumbent on him, either by common law or statute, he is for his default indictable'. Nearly 300 years later, in the *Dytham* case, the Court of Appeal confirmed that the misconduct in question, the breach, is not restricted: 'This involves an element of culpability which is not restricted to corruption or dishonesty, which must be of such a degree that the misconduct impugned is calculated to injure the public interest so as to call for condemnation and punishment.'[63] **3.48**

The common law has always expected public office holders to carry out duties conscientiously, and sought to punish not just the corrupt and dishonest, but also those who displayed a broader lack of integrity or who were found seriously wanting in the discharge of their duties. Dishonest behaviour was certainly capable of being reflected in a misconduct in a public office charge (for **3.49**

[59] [1999] 3 LRC 297.
[60] (1923) 33 CLR 386, and see discussion at 3.34–3.35 above.
[61] [1999] 3 LRC 297, 347.
[62] (1705) 1 Salk 380.
[63] [1979] QB 722, 727–728.

example in *Bembridge*),[64] but so was neglect and omission: 'now I take it to be perfectly clear, that if a public officer abuses his office, either by an act of omission or commission . . . an action may be maintained against such a public officer'.[65]

3.50 As late as the *Dytham* case it was argued on behalf of the appellant that misconduct in a public office required malfeasance, or, at least, misfeasance that included an element of corruption. However, Lord Widgery CJ rejected that argument, stating:[66]

> Misconduct in a public office is more vividly exhibited where dishonesty is revealed as part of the dereliction of duty. Indeed, in some cases the conduct impugned cannot be shown to have been misconduct unless it was done with a corrupt or oblique motive. This was the position, for example, in *R v Bembridge* . . . and also in the modern case of *R v Llewellyn-Jones* . . . In the present case it was not suggested that the appellant could not have summoned or sought assistance to help the victim or to arrest his assailants. The charge as framed left this answer to him. Not surprisingly he did not seek to avail himself of it, for the facts spoke strongly against any such answer. The allegation made was not of mere nonfeasance, but of deliberate failure and wilful neglect.

3.51 In the *Llewellyn-Jones* case,[67] to which Lord Widgery CJ referred, Lord Parker CJ set out a variety of activities, each of which was capable of being reflected by the offence of misconduct in a public office. These included oppression, extortion, corruption, partiality, and fraud.[68]

3.52 In a similar vein, Sir Anthony Mason NPJ in *Shum Kwok Sher v HKSAR*,[69] having reviewed existing authorities, concluded that the offence included not only acts of commission, or malfeasance, but also neglect of duty and acts of omission; that is to say, misfeasance or nonfeasance. Certainly the breadth of recent cases within the United Kingdom in which a misconduct in a public office charge has been preferred, although principally addressing acts of commission, reflects the broad applicability of the offence:

(1) *R v Barry Dickinson* (Stafford Crown Court, 2004,:[70] The defendant was a civil servant who worked as an administrator at the Driver and Vehicle Licensing Authority. He had unlawfully used his position to make checks on car registration numbers and had passed on details of owners of vehicles, etc to animal rights campaigners. As a result of his actions, individuals who were friends of the owners of a guinea pig farm were subjected to harassment and abuse. The defendant, during a single month, had made twenty-five

[64] (1783) 3 Doug KB 327.

[65] *Henly v Lyme Corporation*, Per Best CJ, (1828) 5 Bing 91, 107.

[66] [1979] QB 722, 726–727.

[67] [1968] 1 QB 429; see also 2.28 and 3.07 above.

[68] [1968] 1 QC 429, 435. See 3.07 above.

[69] [2002] 5 HKCFAR 381.

[70] [2004] EWCA Crim 3525 (appeal against unduly lenient sentence by prosecution) and additional facts of the case from, *inter alia*, the *Burton Mail*, see http:www.burtonmail.co.uk.

unauthorized vehicle checks, thirteen of which had a connection with the guinea pig farm. The defendant pleaded guilty and received a sentence of five months' imprisonment.

(2) *R v Leigh Harrington* (Central Criminal Court, November 2003, unreported):[71] The defendant was a police officer who was trained as a chaperone for complainants and victims of sexual abuse, etc. He pleaded guilty to misconduct in a public office on the basis of committing sexual acts upon an alleged victim of a sexual assault to whom he had been appointed as chaperone. The case against him was put on the basis that he had a duty to ensure that the alleged victim was treated with kindness, sensitivity, and courtesy, and to obtain the best possible evidence from her to aid the investigation of the sexual assault in respect of which she was the victim. Having admitted the offence, the defendant was sentenced to six months' imprisonment.

(3) *R v Kassim* (Central Criminal Court, September 2004, unreported):[72] The defendant was a police officer who pleaded guilty to three charges of misconduct in a public office. He had misconducted himself by misusing his position to obtain and then sell information. In particular, he accepted money to pass on information to a Saudi Arabian intelligence officer. The case against the defendant was that he used confidential databases held by the Metropolitan Police and had also been tasked by the intelligence officer to speak with and question certain individuals at their home addresses. In doing so, he did not declare that he was a police officer. It was also said that he had used the police national computer to carry out research on the registration number of a vehicle belonging to a Saudi Arabian dissident. The defendant received a total of two and a half years' imprisonment.

(4) *R v Witcher and Lang* (Winchester Crown Court, March 2005, unreported):[73] Two former police officers were found guilty of misconduct in a public office on the basis of engaging in sexual acts with a woman (who was a victim of crime) whilst on duty, lying in police communications which took place during the course of the incident and failing to report the original assault allegation which had first brought them into contact with the woman. Each was sentenced to fifteen months' imprisonment.

(5) *R v Marshall and King* (Blackfriars Crown Court, 15 April 2005, unreported):[74] The first defendant was a former civilian communications officer who had been employed by the Metropolitan Police; the second defendant was a retired police officer. At the time of the offence each was working for the

71 Various press reports, etc, including *Daily Mail*, BBC Online and *South London Press*.
72 [2005] EWCA Crim 1020, and BBC News, 7 September 2004.
73 Numerous press reports, including *The Times* and *Daily Mail*, 7 and 8 March 2005.
74 News report by *The Guardian*, 16 April 2005.

Metropolitan Police. The two defendants each pleaded guilty to conspiracy to commit misconduct in a public office. Confidential information concerning high profile figures in the public eye were accessed from the police national computer and passed through a chain to two private investigators. The two private investigators were each prosecuted for an offence under the Data Protection Act 1998. All four defendants received a conditional discharge for two years.

(6) *R v Burrows* (Middlesex Guildhall Crown Court, July 2005, unreported):[75] The defendant was a probationary police officer. He had been called to assist at a public order incident. During the course of that incident a fellow officer had assaulted a man before arresting him. That other officer, in due course, was found guilty of assault and perverting the course of public justice. Burrows had written false notes of the incident and had claimed that he had arrested one of the men involved. Both claims were shown to be false, the latter by CCTV evidence. Burrows admitted the offence of misconduct in a public office and gave evidence against the other officer. He received a sentence of six months' imprisonment in the first instance, reduced to three months on appeal.

3.53 It will be seen from the details above that prosecutors have recognized the value of the misconduct in a public office offence to cover a variety of circumstances which could not necessarily be reflected by other charges. In particular, the passing on of confidential information (in circumstances where an Official Secrets Act offence is not made out and where the non-imprisonable offence under section 55 of the Data Protection Act 1988 would be inappropriate) from police officers to private investigators or other associates; activity (such as in the case of *Harrington* above) where a gross breach of trust has taken place which would not otherwise amount to a criminal offence; and in circumstances where perverting the course of justice has occurred, but the perverting offence would not necessarily be capable of proof (for instance, where a fictitious 'course of justice' had been created for the purposes of an integrity test).[76]

3. The Mental Element Required

3.54 A great deal of confusion has arisen in relation to the required mental element for the offence of misconduct in a public office, much of it due to the words of Lord Widgery CJ in the *Dytham* case when he stated:[77] 'The neglect must be wilful and not merely inadvertent; and it must be culpable in the sense that it is without reasonable excuse or justification.'

3.55 *Dytham* was, of course, a case involving alleged neglect or omission. At common law and on general principles, 'wilful neglect' requires proof that, in the case of

[75] In various publications/websites, including http:www.newshopper.co.uk, from which the present details were obtained. [76] See discussion on integrity tests at 4.207–4.210 below. [77] [1979] QB 722, 727.

alleged omission, the defendant voluntarily omitted to perform his duty. That element would be satisfied when there was an intentional omission, and also when an accused omitted to carry out his duty, being subjectively reckless as to the existence of the duty. Further, the omission, on Lord Widgery CJ's formulation, would, of course, have to be culpable in that it occurred without reasonable excuse or justification.

Lord Widgery CJ recognized that misconduct in a public office is not a crime of consequence or a so-called 'results' crime, by making clear that, for the offence to be made out, the culpability of the public officer must be of such a degree that the misconduct[78] impugned is calculated to injure the public interest so as to call for condemnation and punishment. That question, he also affirmed is a matter for the jury. **3.56**

In order for a jury to decide whether the culpability is of such a degree that the misconduct impugned is calculated to injure the public interest, its members have to carry out an objective assessment of, *inter alia*, the likely harm which will be brought about to the public interest by the failure to perform the duty. The test for the jury is akin to that to be adopted when a jury is deciding whether a defendant is guilty of gross negligence: **3.57**

> ... the ordinary principles of the law of negligence apply to ascertain whether or not the defendant has been in breach of a duty of care towards the victim who has died. If such a breach of duty is established, the next question is whether that breach of duty caused the death of the victim. If so, the jury must go on to consider whether that breach of duty should be characterised as gross negligence and therefore as a crime. This will depend on the seriousness of the breach of duty committed by the defendant in all the circumstances in which the defendant was placed when it occurred. The jury will have to consider whether the extent to which the defendant's conduct departed from the proper standard of care incumbent upon him involving, as it must have done, a risk of death to the patient, was such that it should be judged criminal.[79]

That misconduct in a public office is indeed a conduct crime is obvious, it must be suggested, when one considers that the whole thrust of the common law offence is to prohibit certain conduct (ie a breach of duty) regardless of the consequences. Consequences will be considered, but only in relation to culpability. For the offence to be made out does not require proof of any particular result. Thus, a requirement that the defendant has to appreciate the consequences of his action would be meaningless. **3.58**

However, in his analysis of the elements of the offence in *Shum Kwok Sher*, Sir Anthony Mason NPJ asserted that misconduct in a public office is a crime of **3.59**

[78] [1979] QB 722, 727–728.

[79] *Per* Lord MacKay of Clashfern LC in *R v Adomako* [1995] 1 AC 171.

consequence. He stated:

> I consider that the misconduct must be 'wilful' as well as 'intentional'... 'wilfully' signifies knowledge or advertence to the consequences, as well as intent to do an act or refrain from doing an act. Wilfulness in this sense is the requisite mental element in the offence of misconduct in a public office, most notably in cases of non-feasance. There is no reason why the same mental element should not be requisite in cases of misfeasance and other forms of misconduct in public office. For this reason 'wilfully' and 'intentionally' are not employed disjunctively in the statement of the elements of the offence...[80]

3.60 If Sir Anthony Mason is right, the public officer must not only intend to do the act or acts which constitute the breach, but must also do so with knowledge or advertence as to the consequences which could result.

3.61 However, as referred to in para 3.17 above, not content with identifying two mental elements, Sir Anthony Mason went on to identify a third, namely improper motive, in the case of misconduct in a public office by an act or acts of commission. He discussed this requirement in relation to the fourth element of the offence on his definition, that of the defendant 'culpably misconducting himself'; however, rather than conclude that in evaluating the level of culpability of misconduct (in accordance with Lord Widgery CJ's dictum in *Dytham*) one can take into account the motive of the public officer, Sir Anthony Mason has elevated improper motive to that of an additional element of the offence in cases of malfeasance and misfeasance (but not nonfeasance). The improper motive may take one of a number of forms: it might be a dishonest or corrupt purpose, or it might be malice in the sense of a deliberate harming of another. The elevation of motive in the way envisaged by Sir Anthony Mason is troubling. If it were simply a factor to be taken into account as part of the general consideration of the culpability of the misconduct in question, there would be little conceptual difficulty. However, although not listed by him as, explicitly, a separate element of the offence, Sir Anthony Mason's words clearly point to a requirement, in any case of misconduct by an act of commission, that an improper motive be proved to have been present.

3.62 It is submitted that the better approach in relation to improper motive is to see it as a factor which will go to seriousness or culpability. Certainly, that appeared to be the view of the Court of Appeal in *Attorney-General's Reference (No 3 of 2003)*[81] where Pill LJ said that 'The threshold is a high one requiring conduct so far below acceptable standards as to amount to an abuse of the public's trust in the office holder... The motive with which a public officer acts may be relevant to the decision whether the public's trust is abused by the conduct'. If that is right, however, one has to wonder why improper motive

[80] [2002] 5 HKCFAR 381, 409–410.

[81] [2004] 3 WLR 451, 467.

should be confined only to acts of commission rather than both acts of commission and omission.

Putting 'motive' to one side, what then of the elements of 'wilful' and 'intention' which Sir Anthony Mason NPJ regarded as disjunctive? The issue of the mental element needs to be read in the light of the view reached by the Court of Appeal in *Attorney-General's Reference (No 3 of 2003)*. The head note[82] indicates that the Court of Appeal accepted that a mental element was required only in relation to the breach of duty, but that, in a given case, the issue of consequences and foresight thereof would be important to the question of seriousness: **3.63**

> Held: . . . that the elements of the offence of misconduct in a public office were . . . that he wilfully neglected to perform his duty and/or wilfully misconducted himself . . . that whether the misconduct was of a substantially serious nature would depend upon the responsibilities of the office and the office holder . . . and the seriousness of the consequences which might follow from the misconduct; that to establish the mens rea of the offence it has to be proved that the office holder was aware of the duty to act or was subjectively reckless as to the existence of the duty; that the test of recklessness applied both to the question of whether in particular circumstances a duty arose at all and to the conduct of the defendant if it did arise; . . . the subjective test applied both to reckless indifference as to the legality of the act or omission and in relation to the consequences of the act or omission . . .

However the judgment itself paints a less than clear picture. The Court of Appeal noted that the issue which had caused a difficulty at trial, namely as to whether recklessness for the purposes of 'wilful neglect' should be subjective or objective, had been resolved by the decision of the House of Lords in *R v G*[83] which had the effect of confirming that the test of recklessness is a subjective one, akin to what was once called '*Cunningham* recklessness'.[84] However, having so noted, Pill LJ went on to say:[85] **3.64**

> There must be an awareness of the duty to act or a subjective recklessness as to the existence of the duty. The recklessness test will apply to the question whether, in particular circumstances, a duty arises at all as well as to the conduct of the defendant if it does. The subjective test applies both to reckless indifference to the legality of the act or omission and in relation to the consequences of the act or omission.

These words, in themselves, seem to indicate that a mental element as to consequence is envisaged. However, later in the judgment,[86] Pill LJ commented in relation to Sir Anthony Mason's distinction between wilful and intentional: 'We share, with respect, counsels's difficulty in understanding, upon the first qualification, the need for conduct to be both wilful and intentional.' Given that Sir Anthony Mason was addressing 'wilful' in relation to **3.65**

[82] [2004] 3 WLR 451.
[83] [2004] 1 AC 1034.
[84] *R v Cunningham* [1957] 2 QB 396.
[85] [2004] 3 WLR 451, 460.
[86] ibid 464.

consequence[87] it seems that the Court of Appeal in *Attorney General's Reference (No 3 of 2003)* was not minded to follow his reasoning.

3.66 In his conclusions, however, Pill LJ appears firmly to equate consequence with the issue of seriousness of the breach, rather than seeing a mental element as to consequence as being a necessary element in order to prove the offence. In particular, his judgment states:[88]

> It will normally be necessary to consider the likely consequences of the breach in deciding whether the conduct falls so far below the standard of conduct to be expected of the officer as to constitute the offence. The conduct cannot be considered in a vacuum: the consequences likely to follow from it, viewed subjectively . . . will often influence the decision as to whether the conduct amounted to an abuse of the public's trust in the officer. A default where the consequences are likely to be trivial may not possess the criminal quality required; a similar default where the damage to the public or members of the public is likely to be great may do so . . . There will be some conduct which possesses the criminal quality even if serious consequences are unlikely, but it is always necessary to assess the conduct in the circumstances in which it occurs.

3.67 It seems, then, that the Court of Appeal was adopting a conduct rather than a 'results' or consequence formulation. However, it has formulated its approach with less clarity than would have been wished. Consequences, and recklessness or intention with regard to those consequences, will tip the balance as to whether there should be a criminal prosecution in certain instances. As Pill LJ noted:[89]

> The consequences of some conduct, such as corrupt conduct, may be obvious; the likely consequences of other conduct of public officers will be less clear, but it is impossible to gauge the seriousness of defaulting conduct without considering the circumstances in which the conduct occurs and its likely consequences. The whole should be considered in the context of the nature of the office . . . the responsibilities of the office and office holder.

3.68 Although there still remains scope for further clarification by the courts, it can be said that the offence of misconduct in a public office requires intention or recklessness in relation to the commission or omission which amounts to a breach of duty. That may be accompanied by an improper motive such as dishonesty, corruption, or malice; however, motive is not part of the mental element, rather it may go to seriousness or culpability. Further, there is no requirement that there has to be any advertence in relation to consequences, since the offence does not require proof of a consequence or result. However, consequence and advertence of it may be relevant, in a given case, as to the seriousness or culpability.

[87] See comments by I McWaters SC, 'The Common Law Offence of Misconduct in Public Office' in his book *Bribery & Corruption Law in Hong Kong* (Butterworths Asia, Hong Kong, 2002).
[88] [2004] 3 WLR 451, 467.
[89] ibid 467.

That the judgment of Pill LJ is to be read in this way is supported by the recent decision of the Hong Kong Court of Final Appeal in *Sin Kam Wah and anor v HKSAR*.[90] There the leading judgment was again given by Sir Anthony Mason NPJ, who took the opportunity to re-formulate the elements of the offence previously set out in *Shum Kwok Sher*[91] in the light of *Attorney-General's Reference (No 3 of 2003)*. His re-formulation was expressed as follows:[92] **3.69**

> (1) A public official;
> (2) In the course of, or in relation to, his public office;
> (3) Wilfully misconducts himself, by act or omission, for example, by wilfully neglecting or failing to perform his duty;
> (4) Without reasonable excuse or justification; and
> (5) Where such misconduct is serious, not trivial, having regard to the responsibilities of the office and the office-holder, the importance of the public objects which they serve and the nature and extent of the departure from those responsibilities.
>
> The misconduct must be deliberate rather than accidental in the sense that the official either knew that his conduct was unlawful or wilfully disregarded the risk that his conduct was unlawful. Wilful misconduct which is without reasonable excuse or justification is culpable.

4. The Public Office Holder Must Be Acting As Such

For the offence to be made out, the breach of duty has to be in the course of or in relation to the public office holder's position. The mischief of the offence is, after all, what is done or not done as a public office holder. Thus, there must be a causal link between the breach and the office or position. It may be that the misconduct took place during the course of duties, or it might be that it occurred as a result of the exercise of the powers, obligations, or discretion which form part of the office or position. However, there will also be a causal link when the breach occurs as a result of the abuse or misuse of rank, status, or position. Thus, a police officer may still be liable to be prosecuted for misconduct in a public office in relation to his behaviour off duty if his actions amount to misuse of his rank, or go to his capacity as a police officer. **3.70**

5. Culpability and Seriousness

i. 'The misconduct must be of such a degree as to amount to an abuse of the public's trust in the office holder'

The above formulation by the Court of Appeal in *Attorney-General's Reference (No 3 of 2003)*[93] reflects the 'culpability' test of Lord Widgery CJ in the **3.71**

[90] [2005] 2 HKLRD 375. [91] [2002] 5 HKCFAR 381.
[92] [2005] 2 HKLRD 375, 391. [93] [2004] 3 WLR 451, 467.

Dytham case (ie that there must be an element of culpability which must be of such degree that the misconduct impugned is calculated to injure the public interest so as to call for condemnation and punishment),[94] and the 'culpable misconduct' test of Sir Anthony Mason in *Shum Kwok Sher v HKSAR*.[95] The Court of Appeal in *Attorney-General's Reference (No 3 of 2003)*[96] agreed with Sir Anthony Mason that part of the test of culpability was that the misconduct complained of must be serious misconduct. Sir Anthony Mason[97] concluded that what is serious misconduct should be determined 'having regard to the responsibilities of the office and office holder, the importance of the public objects which they serve and the nature and extent of the departure from those responsibilities'. In addition, and as discussed above in relation to the mental element of the offence, the Court of Appeal in *Attorney-General's Reference (No 3 of 2003)*[98] explicitly added to this criteria the issue of consequence depending, of course, on the nature of the alleged breach. One may also add, again as discussed above, the presence or otherwise of an improper motive.

3.72 The issue of 'seriousness' will, in certain cases, tax the prosecuting authorities when deciding on charge or otherwise, and will, of course, tax the jury, given that whether or not a breach is of such seriousness and is so injurious to the public interest as to call for punishment is a question of fact. The question may well be a difficult one. Criminal courts do not want to see cases which are obviously disciplinary in nature coming before them; equally, there may be no clear dividing line on occasion. There will be some cases, for instance, where the allegation is essentially of corruption or dishonesty, where the seriousness is obvious; there will be others, perhaps, where the behaviour of the public official does not amount to any other criminal offence and where there has been no personal or financial gain, where the decision will be a much more difficult one.

ii. 'Without justification or excuse'

3.73 The Court of Appeal in *Attorney-General's Reference (No 3 of 2003)*[99] spoke of the breach of duty needing to be without justification or excuse. It was described by the Court of Appeal as 'a further requirement';[100] however, it is misleading to see it as an element of the offence. Rather, it can be seen as serving a twofold purpose: on the one hand, is there any defence which is capable of being put forward and which the prosecution will be called upon to refute? Additionally, is there a factor or aspect of the breach which in fact renders it less culpable or serious than might otherwise appear?

---

[94] [1979] 1 QB 722, 727–728.
[95] [2002] 5 HKCFAR 381, 409–410.
[96] [2004] 3 WLR 451, 467.
[97] [2002] 5 HKCFAR 381, 410.
[98] [2004] 3 WLR 451, 467.
[99] ibid 467.
[100] ibid 468.

D. The Tort of Misfeasance in Public Office

The concentration of our discussion has been in relation to the criminal offence of misconduct in a public office. However, it should not be forgotten that the tort of misfeasance in a public office also exists. Like its criminal counterpart, there has been some uncertainty as to the precise elements and ambit of tortious liability for misfeasance. However, in *Three Rivers District Council v Bank of England (No 3)*,[101] the House of Lords took the opportunity to consider in detail the elements of the tort. **3.74**

The *Three Rivers* case concerned the claim that the Bank of England was liable to former depositors with the Bank of Credit and Commerce International (BCCI) for the tort of misfeasance in public office on the basis of the Bank of England's failure in its responsibilities in supervising banking activities in the United Kingdom. **3.75**

Lord Steyn, giving the leading speech, commented that[102] 'the tort bears some resemblance to the crime of misconduct in a public office'. Although one cannot doubt the veracity of that statement, it has to be noted (as indeed Pill LJ observed in *Attorney-General's Reference (No 3 of 2003)*[103] that there are fundamental differences of approach between the criminal law and the law of tort which need to be borne in mind in the present context. In particular, and of relevance to any discussion of the respective mental elements, must be the realization that a crime, when committed, is an affront not just to a particular victim but to society and the public interest, whilst a tort, although it may well have powerful public interest considerations attached to it, may amount to a balancing of interest as between a public office holder or holders on the one hand, and an individual or a group of individuals who are seeking a remedy in relation to a specific loss. **3.76**

Lord Steyn set out the following as essential elements of the tort:[104] **3.77**

(1) the defendant is/was at material times a public officer;
(2) the defendant, at material times, was exercising power or office as a public office holder;
(3) the defendant acted, or made an omission, in subjective bad faith;
(4) the plaintiff has sufficient interest or nexus to bring an action;
(5) causation;
(6) recklessness by the defendant as to the consequences of his act. That is to say, recklessness on the basis of not caring whether the consequences come about or not.

The Court in the *Three Rivers* case examined in detail the requisite state of mind for a defendant. Lord Steyn noted that there were two separate bases for tortious **3.78**

[101] [2003] 2 AC 1. [102] ibid 191. [103] [2004] 3 WLR 451, 465.
[104] [2003] 2 AC 1, 191–194.

liability for misfeasance in a public office:[105]

> First, there is the case of targeted malice by a public officer, ie conduct specifically intended to injure a person or persons. This type of case involves bad faith in the sense of the exercise of public power for an improper or ulterior motive. The second form is where a public officer acts knowing that he has no power to do the act complained of and that the act will probably injure the plaintiff. It involves bad faith in as much as the public officer does not have an honest belief that his act is lawful.

3.79 Lord Steyn, as perhaps will be evident from the above, spoke of 'a meaningful requirement of bad faith in the exercise of public powers which is the raison d'être of the tort'[106] and described 'the unifying element of conduct amounting to an abuse of power accompanied by subjective bad faith'.[107]

3.80 In relation to what he identified as the second basis of liability, so-called 'untargeted malice', the state of mind required, on Lord Steyn's interpretation, is proof that the public officer holder acted with reckless indifference, subjectively, as to the illegality of his act. Meanwhile, in relation to the issue of damage or consequence, Lord Steyn held that what was required was knowledge by the defendant that misfeasance would probably cause damage to the plaintiff.

3.81 Lord Hutton held that dishonesty is the necessary ingredient for the tort of misfeasance and that dishonesty means acting in bad faith. He, in turn, examined the requisite elements of the tort and concluded that they comprise:

(1) an act or omission by a public officer;
(2) amounting to a breach of duty;
(3) the act or omission must be deliberate, and must be one involving an actual decision—mere inadvertence or oversight, even if injury or damage results, will not be enough;
(4) the plaintiff must prove that the public office holder foresaw that his action/omission would probably cause injury or damage to the plaintiff;
(5) in the event that the plaintiff is able to show that the public office holder knew that his unlawful conduct would probably injure or damage another person, or was reckless as to that consequence, the plaintiff will not need to prove, to establish liability, some other link, nexus, or relationship between him and the public office holder.

3.82 Specifically in relation to state of mind, Lord Hutton cited part of the judgment of Brennan J given in the High Court of Australia in *Northern Territory of Australia v Mengel*:[108]

> It is the absence of an honest attempt to perform the functions of the office that constitutes the abuse of the office. Misfeasance in public office consists of a purported exercise of some power or authority by a public officer otherwise than in

[105] [2003] 2 AC 1, 191. [106] ibid 193. [107] ibid 191.
[108] (1995) 185 CLR 307, 357.

> an honest attempt to perform the functions of his or her office, whereby loss is caused to a plaintiff. Malice, knowledge and reckless indifference are states of mind that stamp on a purported but invalid exercise of power the character of abuse of, or misfeasance, in public office.

In his analysis of the tort, Lord Hobhouse[109] found that the act of commission, or omission, must be unlawful. However, the unlawfulness may spring from, for instance, a breach of a relevant statutory provision, or from acting in excess of powers or duties granted to the office, or may arise because the act or omission is for an improper purpose. However, in any of those examples, as to state of mind, the position, in Lord Hobhouse's view is that: **3.83**

> The official concerned must be shown not to have had an honest belief that he was acting lawfully; this is sometimes referred to as not having acted in good faith . . . Another way of putting it is that he must be shown either to have known that he was acting unlawfully or to have wilfully disregarded the risk that his act was unlawful. This requirement is therefore one which applies to the state of mind of the official concerning the lawfulness of his act and covers both a conscious and subjectively reckless state of mind, either of which could be described as bad faith or dishonest.[110]

However, he went on to look at that general principle in the light of, on the one hand, targeted malice and on the other untargeted malice. He found that the state of mind of the public office holder[111] had to have regard to the effect of his act or omission upon others.

Lord Hobhouse looked separately at, in effect, three possibilities (since he divided untargeted malice into two). Turning to targeted malice he stated that:[112] **3.84**

> Here the official does the act intentionally, with the purpose of causing loss to the plaintiff, being a person who is, at the time, identified or identifiable. This limb does not call for explanation. The specific purpose of causing loss to a particular person is extremely likely to be consistent only with the official not having an honest belief that he was exercising the relevant power lawfully. If the loss is inflicted intentionally, there is no problem in allowing a remedy to the person so injured.

Then, as to the first limb of untargeted malice he stated: **3.85**

> Here the official does the act intentionally, being aware that it will in the ordinary course directly cause loss to the plaintiff or an identifiable class to which the plaintiff belongs. The element of knowledge is an actual awareness but it is not the knowledge of an existing fact or an inevitable certainty. It relates to a result which has yet to occur. It is the awareness that a certain consequence will follow as a result of the act unless something out of the ordinary intervenes. The act is not

[109] In his formulation, Lord Hobhouse referred, in this regard, to *Garrett v A-G* [1997] 2 NZLR 332, 349–350.
[110] [2003] 2 AC 1, 230.
[111] ibid 230.
[112] ibid 230.

> done with the intention or purpose of causing such a loss, but is an unlawful act which is intentionally done for a different purpose notwithstanding that the official is aware that such injury will, in the ordinary course, be one of the consequences.[113]

3.86 Finally, on the second limb or subcategory of untargeted malice, Lord Hobhouse said:[114]

> Thirdly, there is reckless untargeted malice. The official does the act intentionally being aware that it risks directly causing loss to the plaintiff or identifiable class to which the plaintiff belongs and the official wilfully disregards that risk. What the official is here aware of is that there is a risk of loss involved in the intended act. His recklessness arises because he chooses wilfully to disregard that risk.

3.87 Lord Millett identified the mischief at which the tort of misfeasance struck as being that of abuse of power. Focusing on the public office holder who had acted improperly or failed to act in respect of his duty, he stated:[115]

> This is an intentional tort. It involves deliberate or reckless wrongdoing. It cannot be committed negligently or inadvertently. Accordingly it is not enough [for the depositors] to establish negligence, or even gross negligence . . . [they] must establish some intentional or reckless impropriety . . . In the present case the depositors must prove (i) not merely that the Bank acted unlawfully, that is to say in excess of its powers or for an improper purpose, but that it did so knowingly (or recklessly not caring whether it had the necessary power or not); and (ii) that the Bank knew that its actions would probably cause loss to depositors (or was recklessly indifferent to the consequences of its actions). Such conduct in a public official is grossly improper and equates to dishonesty in a private individual.

3.88 Comparisons between the tort and the crime are perhaps of limited value, but worthy of some note. In *Attorney-General's Reference (No 3 of 2003)*[116] Pill LJ noted that 'the approach in the *Three Rivers* case appears to us to be consistent with that in the criminal cases and in our conclusions. Neither the mental element associated with the misconduct, nor the threshold of misconduct should be set lower for the crime than for the tort'.

3.89 Taking Pill LJ's comment into account, one has to recall, as already highlighted, that the criminal law and the law of torts serve different purposes. In particular, a tort gives rise to a course of action and, to be successful in that, the plaintiff needs to establish that damage has been suffered. In the case of the criminal offence of misconduct, however, it is not necessary to establish damage. Criminality, as the whole line of cases from *Bembridge* onwards makes clear, lies in the affront to the public interest and the breach of the public's trust. With that in mind, we may observe that, although subjective bad faith will equate to the formulation of 'wilful neglect', neither causation nor recklessness

---

[113] [2003] 2 AC 1, 230–231. [114] ibid 231. [115] ibid 290.
[116] [2004] 3 WLR 451, 466.

on the part of a defendant as to the consequences of his act are ingredients for the criminal offence.

E. Postscript

It is to be hoped that at least some of the confusion which has surrounded the mental element for the criminal offence has been resolved. The courts will have other questions to grapple with, though. In particular, will judges use public policy considerations in deciding who is, and who is not, a public office holder (given that the category is not confined to an 'office' at a particular level); or, will the test be applied as a purely functional one, even though such an approach might have the effect of widening the categories of those potentially liable? **3.90**

Away from the courts, and even more fundamentally, will misconduct in a public office survive as a common law offence, or might it be better reflected in statute? Continuing as the former will ensure the availability of an offence of real breadth, whilst a change to the latter might achieve greater clarity than hitherto as to its elements. The Joint Committee on the draft Corruption Bill noted that the draft Bill 'does not contain a statutory offence of "misuse of public office"'[117] and that matter had not been addressed in the Law Commission Report in 1998. **3.91**

In his evidence to the Joint Committee, the then Director of Public Prosecutions stated that he could 'see great advantage for public servants in having a misconduct offence which was statutory rather than dredged up from the Middle Ages',[118] and also noted that a statutory misconduct offence had been proposed by the Law Commission in the context of consideration of changes to the law concerning fraud.[119] Nevertheless, the Joint Committee concluded that: 'The draft Bill does not seem to us the appropriate vehicle for giving a statutory definition of misconduct in public office.'[120] **3.92**

However, whether the offence remains one at common law or gets put onto a statutory footing, it is probably fair to say that awareness, amongst practitioners, of the crime of misconduct in a public office has never been higher. **3.93**

---

[117] Joint Committee on the draft Corruption Bill, Report, para 44.

[118] Joint Committee on the draft Corruption Bill, Evidence, Q126 (Sir David Calvert-Smith).

[119] ibid Q116 (Sir David Calvert-Smith).

[120] Joint Committee on the draft Corruption Bill, Conclusions and Recommendations, Conclusion No 3.

4

THE INVESTIGATION AND PROSECUTION OF CORRUPTION

A. Criminal Investigation

1. The Police[1]

4.01 The United Kingdom does not have an all embracing national police force. Accordingly, the forty-three local police forces in England and Wales, plus their Scottish counterparts, each have a role to play in the investigation of allegations of corruption. In addition, the Serious Fraud Office (SFO) has it own investigative powers, addressed separately below.

4.02 It might be argued that the organizational structure of the police, based on separate forces, each answerable to its own authority, is heavily focused on local issues and has priorities set accordingly. Certainly recent years have seen the disbandment by some forces of dedicated fraud squads, with a consequent loss of specialization. Unsurprisingly, perhaps, concern was expressed at this by the lead examiners conducting the OECD Phase 2 review of the United Kingdom.[2] However, two forces at least, the Metropolitan Police Service (MPS) and the City of London Police (CLP), do have real specialization in corruption investigations.

4.03 The MPS has a team of about twenty-five officers within its Economic and Specialist Crimes Department (otherwise known as the Public Sector Corruption Team) based at Scotland Yard. That team investigates public sector fraud and corruption offences and can also be expected to play a part in some of the foreign bribery investigations arising from nationality, jurisdiction having been taken in relation to corruption offences. However, the MPS, despite its size, is still a local force and is limited, generally, to investigating corruption and fraud within its own police area. Certainly it still retains a national, and indeed international, role but has to answer to the Metropolitan Police Authority for its use of resources and will, accordingly, be expected to deploy those for the benefit of Londoners.

4.04 Meanwhile the CLP has also built up a specialization in economic crime and fraud (a necessity given that the City is, of course, home to much of the UK financial sector) and also plays a key role in assisting the SFO with many of its investigations.

4.05 The Ministry of Defence Police (MDP) is a civil police force and is part of the Ministry of Defence. The MDP has a jurisdiction over the investigation of foreign bribery cases which involve defence contracts.[3]

[1] The Serious and Organised Crime Agency (SOCA), once operational, will have a role to play in the investigation of some corruption allegations. However, at present, it is too early to discuss SOCA in any meaningful detail, although the reader should refer to the provisions of the Serious Organised Crime and Police Act 2005 (SOCPA 2005) and should note that some of the powers and tools provided for therein are novel.

[2] See OECD Phase 2, 29. The Phase 2 report can be found at http://www.oecd.org/corruption.

[3] See discussion on Memorandum of Understanding at 4.25ff. below.

The National Crime Squad (NCS) has, as the name suggests, a truly national role. However, its principal remit is in relation to organized crime and drug trafficking. It can, however, be expected to play a part in any proactive work which is necessary in relation to corruption offences linked to organized crime, misconduct in a public office featuring police officer suspects, and foreign bribery cases.[4] 4.06

The National Criminal Intelligence Service (NCIS) is an organization made up of permanent and seconded staff drawn from a number of agencies, including police forces. It provides strategic and tactical intelligence on serious and organized crime to all law enforcement agencies in the United Kingdom. It is home to the United Kingdom's Financial Intelligence Unit for anti-money laundering purposes. The NCIS does not have an investigative role in relation to corruption offences but, since 14 February 2002, has played a key role as 'gate keeper' in relation to foreign bribery allegations. However, as discussed below, that role has recently changed, with increased responsibility being passed to the SFO. 4.07

2. The Serious Fraud Office

The SFO was established by the Criminal Justice Act 1987, following the 1986 Fraud Trials Committee Report (the so-called Roskill Report). Under the 1987 Act, the remit of the SFO is to investigate and prosecute cases involving serious or complex fraud in England, Wales, and Northern Ireland.[5] It is also expected to contribute to deterring such fraud. Given that many typologies of corruption, particularly those in the commercial and foreign field, will involve elements of fraud and dishonesty, the SFO is also one of the natural homes for corruption investigations and prosecutions. The SFO's aims and objectives are:[6] 4.08

(1) reducing fraud and the cost of fraud;
(2) the delivery of justice and the rule of law; and
(3) maintaining confidence in the United Kingdom's business and financial institutions.

The SFO is an independent government department headed by its own director, but superintended by the Attorney-General. Its approach to criminal investigations is a multidisciplinary one: each case is allocated to a team led by an experienced lawyer, with each team comprising lawyers, accountants, financial investigators, analysts, and police officers. The SFO also makes use of private sector expertise when necessary, as in the case of specialist forensic accountancy.[7] 4.09

[4] For its anticipated role in foreign bribery investigations, see Memorandum of Understanding, discussed at 4.25ff below.
[5] CJA 1987, s 1(3) and (5).
[6] See 'Publications and Speeches', SFO website, http://www.sfo.gov.uk.
[7] ibid.

4.10 The SFO will accept a case only when the suspected offence appears to be so serious or complex that the SFO's particular expertise is required. The SFO will, *inter alia*, consider the following factors:

(1) Does the value of the alleged fraud exceed £1 million?
(2) Is there a significant international dimension?
(3) Is the case likely to be of widespread public concern?
(4) Does the case require highly specialized knowledge?
(5) Is there a need to use the SFO's special powers?[8]

4.11 Police officers, particularly those from the CLP, routinely work with SFO staff as part of a case team. The Criminal Justice Act 1987[9] provides for the conduct of investigations by the SFO in conjunction with police officers. In such circumstances, the accountability and command structure of the police remains unchanged by the deployment of police officers to an SFO case.

i. Powers of the SFO under section 2 of CJA 1987

4.12 Section 2 (Director's Investigation Powers) provides as follows:

> (1) The powers of the Director under this section shall be exercisable, but only for the purposes of an investigation under section 1 above, or, on a request made by an authority entitled to make such a request, in any case in which it appears to him that there is good reason to do so for the purpose of investigating the affairs, or any aspect of the affairs, of any person.
>
> (1A) The authorities entitled to request the Director to exercise his powers under this section are—
>
> (a) the Attorney-General of the Isle of Man, Jersey or Guernsey, acting under legislation corresponding to section 1 of this Act and having effect in the Island whose Attorney-General makes the request; and
>
> (b) the Secretary of State acting under section 4(2A) of the Criminal Justice (International Co-operation) Act 1990,[10] in response to a request received by him from an overseas court, tribunal or authority (an 'overseas authority').
>
> (1B) The Director shall not exercise his powers on a request from the Secretary of State acting in response to a request received from an overseas authority within subsection (1A)(b) above unless it appears to the Director on reasonable grounds that the offence in respect of which he has been requested to obtain evidence involves serious or complex fraud.
>
> (2) The Director may by notice in writing require the person whose affairs are to be investigated ('the person under investigation') or any other person whom he has reason to believe has relevant information to answer questions or otherwise furnish information with respect to any matter relevant to the investigation at a specified place and either at a specified time or forthwith.

---

[8] eg CJA 1987, s 2, discussed at 4.12ff below.
[9] ibid s 1(4).
[10] See now the provisions of Crime (International Co-operation) Act 2003, ss 13–19 and 2.156 above.

(3) The Director may by notice in writing require the person under investigation or any other person to produce at such place as may be specified in the notice and either forthwith or at such time as may be so specified, any specified documents which appear to the Director to relate to any matter relevant to the investigation or any documents of a specified description which appear to him so to relate; and—

(a) if any such documents are produced, the Director may—

(i) take copies or extracts from them;

(ii) require the person producing them to provide an explanation of any of them;

(b) if any such documents are not produced, the Director may require the person who was required to produce them to state, to the best of his knowledge and belief, where they are.

(4) Where, on information on oath laid by a member of the Serious Fraud Office, a justice of the peace is satisfied, in relation to any documents, that there are reasonable grounds for believing—

(a) that—

(i) a person has failed to comply with an obligation under this section to produce them;

(ii) it is not practicable to serve a notice under subsection (3) above in relation to them; or

(iii) the service of such a notice in relation to them might seriously prejudice the investigation; and

(b) that they are on premises specified in the information, he may issue such a warrant as is mentioned in subsection (5) below:

(5) The warrant referred to above is a warrant authorising any constable—

(a) to enter (using such force as is reasonably necessary for the purpose) and search the premises, and

(b) to take possession of any documents appearing to be documents of the description specified in the information or to take in relation to any documents so appearing any other steps which may appear to be necessary for preserving them and preventing interference with them.

(6) Unless it is not practicable in the circumstances, a constable executing a warrant issued under subsection (4) above shall be accompanied by an appropriate person.

(7) In subsection (6) above 'appropriate person' means—

(a) a member of the Serious Fraud Office; or

(b) some person who is not a member of that Office but whom the Director has authorised to accompany the constable.

(8) A statement by a person in response to a requirement imposed by virtue of this section may only be used in evidence against him—

(a) on a prosecution for an offence under subsection (14) below; or

(b) on a prosecution for some other offence where in giving evidence he makes a statement inconsistent with it.

(8AA) However, the statement may not be used against that person by virtue of paragraph (b) of subsection (8) unless evidence relating to it is adduced, or a question relating to it is asked, by or on behalf of that person in the proceedings arising out of the prosecution.

[(8A)–(8D) Evidence for use by overseas authority.]

(9) A person shall not under this section be required to disclose any information or produce any document which he would be entitled to refuse to disclose or produce on grounds of legal professional privilege in proceedings in the High Court, except that a lawyer may be required to furnish the name and address of his client.

(10) A person shall not under this section be required to disclose information or produce a document in respect of which he owes an obligation of confidence by virtue of carrying on any banking business unless—

(a) the person to whom the obligation of confidence is owed consents to the disclosure or production; or

(b) the Director has authorised the making of the requirement or, if it is impracticable for him to act personally, a member of the Serious Fraud Office designated by him for the purposes of that subsection has done so.

(11) Without prejudice to the power of the Director to assign functions to members of the Serious Fraud Office, the Director may authorise any competent investigator (other than a constable) who is not a member of that Office to exercise on his behalf all or any of the powers conferred by this section, but no such authority shall be granted except for the purpose of investigating the affairs, or any aspect of the affairs, of a person specified in the authority.

(12) No person shall be bound to comply with any requirement imposed by a person exercising powers by virtue of any authority granted under subsection (11) above unless he has, if required to do so, produced evidence of his authority.

(13) Any person who without reasonable excuse fails to comply with a requirement imposed on him under this section shall be guilty of an offence and liable on summary conviction to imprisonment for a term not exceeding six months or to a fine not exceeding level 5 on the standard scale or to both.

(14) A person who, in purported compliance with a requirement under this section—

(a) makes a statement which he knows to be false or misleading in a material particular; or

(b) recklessly makes a statement which is false or misleading in a material particular, shall be guilty of an offence.

(15) A person guilty of an offence under subsection (14) above shall—

(a) on conviction on indictment, be liable to imprisonment for a term not exceeding two years or to a fine or to both; and

(b) on summary conviction, be liable to imprisonment for a term not exceeding six months or to a fine not exceeding the statutory maximum, or to both.

(16) Where any person—

(a) knows or suspects that an investigation by the police or the Serious Fraud Office into serious or complex fraud is being or is likely to be carried out; and

(b) falsifies, conceals, destroys or otherwise disposes of, or causes or permits the falsification, concealment, destruction or disposal of documents which he knows or suspects are or would be relevant to such an investigation, he shall be guilty of an offence unless he proves that he had no intention of concealing the facts disclosed by the documents from persons carrying out such an investigation.

(17) A person guilty of an offence under subsection (16) above shall—
(a) on conviction on indictment, be liable to imprisonment for a term not exceeding 7 years or to a fine or to both; and
(b) on summary conviction, be liable to imprisonment for a term not exceeding 6 months or to a fine not exceeding the statutory maximum or to both.

(18) In this section, 'documents' includes information recorded in any form and, in relation to information recorded otherwise than in legible form, references to its production include references to producing a copy of the information in legible form; and 'evidence' (in relation to subsections (1A)(b),(8A), (8B) and (8C) above) includes documents and other articles.

(19) [Relates to proceedings in Scotland and Northern Ireland.]

The section 2 powers of the SFO are noticeably wide. Section 2, as set out above, contains a number of amendments from its original form. In particular, section 2(8AA) should be noted since it limits the use to which a statement obtained from a person under section 2 may be put. **4.13**

By virtue of section 2(2) and (3), SFO staff have the power to require a person, whether that person be under investigation or otherwise, to answer questions, provide information, or provide documents for the purposes of an investigation. The power is exercised by the issuing of a written notice.[11] In an urgent case, compliance with a notice may be required to be 'forthwith'.[12] **4.14**

The section 2 power gives SFO investigators the ability not just to progress an investigation without delay, but also to identify an individual or individuals who should be treated as a suspect for the purposes of the investigation. As the notice may be issued to 'any other person',[13] the SFO is able to compel information from banks, financial institutions, and accounting and other professionals. The power does, of course, override any duty of confidence,[14] but not legal professional privilege (save that a lawyer may be required to furnish the name and address of his client).[15] **4.15**

The powers under section 2 are given to the director of the SFO, but are delegated by him. They may only be exercised, however, 'for the purposes of an investigation . . . on a request made by an authority entitled to make such a request, in any case in which it appears to him [ie the Director] that there is good reason to do so for the purpose of investigating the affairs, or any aspect of the affairs, of any person'.[16] **4.16**

[11] CJA 1987, (2) and (3). [12] ibid s 2(2) and (3). [13] ibid s 2(2) and (3).

[14] In respect of any duty of confidence, regard should be had to section 2(10) which, *inter alia*, provides that a person shall not be required, under section 2, to disclose information or produce a document in respect of which he owes an obligation of confidence by virtue of carrying on any banking business unless the person to whom the obligation of confidence is owed consents to the disclosure or production, or the Director (or if he is unavailable, a designated member of the SFO staff) has authorized the making of a requirement that the disclosure or production in such circumstances should be made. [15] CJA 1987, s 2(9).

[16] ibid s 2(1).

4.17 Reference to an 'investigation' is to an investigation under section 1 of the Criminal Justice Act 1987 (CJA 1987); that is to say, an investigation involving serious or complex fraud. A corruption investigation will, however, be capable of falling under this heading provided that the element of serious or complex fraud is present. Therefore, in fulfilling the role given to it in the Memorandum of Understanding (see below) in relation to foreign bribery investigations, the SFO will be able to have recourse to its section 2 powers.

4.18 Any person who, without reasonable excuse, fails to comply with a section 2 notice shall be guilty of an offence and liable on summary conviction to imprisonment for a term not exceeding six months or to a fine not exceeding level 5 on the standard scale, or to both.[17] In addition, it is an offence under section 2(14) for a person to make a statement which he knows to be false or misleading in a material particular, or to recklessly make a statement which is false or misleading in a material particular. Such an offence is triable either way and is punishable, on conviction on indictment, by imprisonment for a term not exceeding two years or by a fine or both.[18] A further offence is created by section 2(16) which provides that where any person knows or suspects that an investigation by the police or SFO into serious or complex fraud is being or is likely to be carried out, and that person falsifies, conceals, destroys, or otherwise disposes of, or causes or permits the falsification, concealment, destruction, or disposal of documents which he knows or suspects are, or would be, relevant to such an investigation, he shall be guilty of an offence unless he proves (on the balance of probabilities) that he had no intention of concealing the facts disclosed by the documents from those carrying out the investigation. The offence is triable either way, but the penalty in the event of conviction under section 2(16) is, on indictment, imprisonment for a term not exceeding seven years or a fine or both.

4.19 The answers given by a person during a section 2 interview may only be used in evidence against him in a prosecution for the section 2(14) offence or 'on a prosecution for some other offence where, in giving evidence, he makes a statement inconsistent with it'[19] (for example in a prosecution for perjury or perverting the course of justice). However, as already noted above, section 2(8AA) has been inserted into the section to limit further the circumstances in which a statement given as a result of the exercise of a section 2 power may be used. Section 2(8AA) provides that a statement made in response to a section 2 notice may not be used against the person making that statement by virtue of section 8(b) unless evidence relating to the statement is adduced, or a question relating to it is asked, by or on behalf of the statement maker in the proceedings arising out of the SFO prosecution.

[17] CJA 1987, s 2(13). [18] ibid s 2(15). [19] ibid s 2(8)(a) and (b).

Unsurprisingly, the provisions of section 2 have become the subject of a body of case law. In *R v SFO, ex p Maxwell (Kevin)*[20] the applicant sought an order of mandamus to compel the SFO to comply with the prosecution's common law duty of disclosure prior to interview under section 2. The Divisional Court held that the effect of section 1 of the Criminal Justice Act 1987 was that the director of the SFO instigated two processes, each running concurrently, an investigative process and a judicial one. The section 2 power was, however, part of the investigative process. The Court therefore concluded that there was no obligation on the investigator to provide, to the person to be interviewed, information or disclosure. In some instances, an investigator might find it helpful to make such disclosure, but in other instances disclosure itself might be damaging. **4.20**

As to the stage at which the section 2 power can no longer be used during an investigation, the House of Lords in *R v Director of the SFO, ex p Smith*[21] concluded that the section 2 power to compel answers to questions during interview (with sanction for non-compliance) continues even after the person under investigation has been charged. Further, it has been held that the fact that a defendant has been charged does not, in itself, amount to 'reasonable excuse' for non-compliance under section 2(13).[22] **4.21**

As to the extent of the 'reasonable excuse' defence, the applicant in *R v Director of the SFO, ex p Johnson*[23] argued, in seeking leave to apply for judicial review of a section 2 notice that had been served on his wife, that his wife had a reasonable excuse for refusing to comply with the section 2 notice. It was held, however, that although section 80 of the Police and Criminal Evidence Act 1984 (PACE 1984) contains a provision preventing a person being compelled to give evidence against his or her spouse (save in certain specifically defined circumstances), CJA 1987 is a deliberately draconian piece of legislation concerned with the investigation of fraud rather than the admissibility of evidence. In addition, the Court held that it would be wrong to use judicial review to create a class of person who would have a reasonable excuse in response to a section 2 notice. **4.22**

When the SFO decides whether to prosecute a case, following investigation, it will apply the principles set out in the Code for Crown Prosecutors.[24] The SFO lawyer will therefore apply a two stage test: **4.23**

(1) On the evidence, in respect of each potential defendant, is there a realistic prospect of securing a conviction? and
(2) if so, does the public interest require a criminal prosecution?

[20] The Times, 9 October 1992. [21] [1993] AC 1.
[22] *R v Metropolitan Stipendiary Magistrate, ex p SFO* The Independent, 24 June 1994.
[23] [1993] Crown Office Digest 58.
[24] See discussion of the Code for Crown Prosecutors under 'CPS', at 4.46ff below.

4.24 Typically a case may be referred to the SFO in one of the following ways: by the police, following a report made to Crimestoppers, by a direct report made to the SFO, or (for instance, in the case of a foreign bribery allegation) via the National Criminal Intelligence Service (NCIS). In addition, government departments and regulatory bodies (such as the Department of Trade and Industry, the Bank of England, or the Financial Services Authority) may refer cases to the SFO in circumstances where a matter includes an allegation of fraud which appears serious or complex.[25]

ii. The revised Memorandum of Understanding on implementing Part 12 of ATCSA 2001

4.25 In relation to allegations of foreign bribery against UK nationals or companies, it was noted in the OECD Phase 2 Review[26] that a number of agencies and institutions have a potential role to play in the investigation of foreign bribery cases in England and Wales. Accordingly, following the coming into effect of Part 12 of the Anti-Terrorism, Crime and Security Act 2001 (ATCSA 2001), the law enforcement agencies and government departments thus affected drew up a Memorandum of Understanding (MoU). That document has gone through a number of amendments,[27] the latest being a revised MoU issued in July 2005. The MoU is not statutory, and simply provides a basis for attributing investigative and prosecutorial responsibility for foreign bribery cases.

4.26 The MoU applies to any relevant offence. A relevant offence is common law bribery or statutory corruption in circumstances where the bribery or corruption is committed overseas by a UK national or by a body incorporated under UK law. As of July 2004, (in a change that predated the latest reissue by a year) the MoU provides that the SFO will act as the focal point for receiving any allegations about offences of bribery by UK nationals or UK incorporated bodies which are alleged to have taken place overseas. Thus, even an allegation that comes to the attention of another law enforcement agency or government department should be passed to the SFO. The SFO, in fulfilling its role, will maintain a register of allegations of relevant offences. Having received information about an allegation, or the allegation itself, the SFO will undertake a vetting exercise to decide whether it, or another agency, will be best placed to run the investigation. An investigation will be led by the SFO if it falls within the SFO's remit, requires any of the SFO's special powers to be used, or is a case involving serious or complex fraud with a value above £1 million. However, even in a case being run by the SFO, the services of a police force or police forces may be utilized.

---

[25] See 'Dealing with Cases', http://www.sfo.gov.uk/cases/case_referrals.asp.

[26] OECD Phase 2 Review of the UK, 29: http://www.oecd.org/corruption.

[27] OECD Phase 2 Review of the UK, 29ff.

In a case which the SFO does not investigate, the relevant investigative bodies will be: local police forces; the Ministry of Defence police (MDP) (for cases involving Ministry of Defence employees or defence contracts where the Ministry of Defence is a party to the contract); the National Crime Squad (NCS) (in a case where there is a need for proactive/covert investigative techniques); and the MPS (in relation to any case falling within the remit of one of its specialist teams). Although the SFO is now the focal point for receiving such allegations, intelligence analysis and aspects of preparatory scoping work will be carried out by the NCIS. **4.27**

In relation to Scotland, if there is an allegation of a UK national with an address in Scotland or a UK incorporated body registered or with a principal office in Scotland having an involvement in a bribery or corruption offence overseas, then the case will be referred to the Financial Crime Unit in the Crown Office, which will oversee the investigation and prosecution of any such case. **4.28**

Any case not falling within the SFO's remit for prosecution, will fall to the CPS if a matter is linked with England and Wales. However in relation to a Northern Ireland case not falling within the remit of the SFO, the matter will be for investigation by the Police Service of Northern Ireland, with advice and prosecution by the Director of Public Prosecutions (DPP) for Northern Ireland. **4.29**

In addition to criminal investigations, the MoU also recognizes Department of Trade and Industry (DTI) investigations. Thus, where there is good reason to suspect wrongdoing by a company incorporated in the United Kingdom, but where the evidence is not such as to justify a criminal investigation, the DTI may undertake an investigation. **4.30**

The MoU does not merely address the issue of who will investigate a foreign bribery allegation, it also sets out criteria for the United Kingdom taking jurisdiction over such an offence. It recognizes that, although there is a nationality jurisdiction for corruption, the taking of such a jurisdiction does not mean that it will always be appropriate for the United Kingdom to exercise that jurisdiction. Rather, on a case-by-case basis, account will be taken of the location of the principal evidence and witnesses and any other relevant consideration which ought properly to inform that aspect of the decision-making process. **4.31**

The MoU provides that it will be 'good practice' for the SFO to report any allegation of foreign bribery worthy of investigation to the appropriate authorities in the country concerned. However, there will be exceptions to that presumption of reporting, namely: where it is apparent that such an approach would be fruitless; where the other country is able to impose the death penalty for bribery and corruption offences; or where any report might lead to the **4.32** destruction of evidence or the endangering of any individual (in particular, a witness).

3. Department of Trade and Industry (Companies Investigation Branch)

4.33 The DTI has its own Companies Investigation Branch (CIB) which forms part of its regulatory activities. Under the Companies Act 1985 the DTI has a power to investigate companies in relation to allegations of wrongdoing. However, the CIB does not carry out criminal investigations.

4.34 When an allegation is made, the CIB ascertains whether there is justification for an investigation. In effect this is a vetting process. In the event that there is sufficient reason to investigate, and assuming that it is in the public interest to do so, then investigators will be appointed. The majority of CIB investigations for the DTI are undertaken under the provisions of section 447 of the Companies Act 1985. The present form of section 447 is as substituted by section 21 of the Companies (Audit, Investigations and Community Enterprise) Act 2004.

4.35 Section 21 of the 2004 Act sets out section 447 of the Companies Act 1985 (Power to require documents and information) as follows:

> (1) The Secretary of State may act under subsections (2) and (3) in relation to a company.
> (2) The Secretary of State may give directions to the company requiring it—
> (a) to produce such documents (or documents of such description) as may be specified in the directions;
> (b) to provide such information (or information of such description) as may be so specified.
> (3) The Secretary of State may authorise a person (an investigator) to require the company or any other person—
> (a) to produce such documents (or documents of such description) as the investigator may specify;
> (b) to provide such information (or information of such description) as the investigator may specify.
> (4) A person on whom a requirement under subsection (3) is imposed may require the investigator to produce evidence of his authority.
> (5) A requirement under subsection (2) or (3) must be complied with at such time and place as may be specified in the directions or by the investigator (as the case may be).
> (6) The production of a document in pursuance of this section does not affect any lien which a person has on the document.
> (7) The Secretary of State or the investigator (as the case may be) may take copies of or extracts from a document produced in pursuance of this section.
> (8) A 'document' includes information recorded in any form.
> (9) In relation to information recorded otherwise than in legible form, the power to require production of it includes power to require the production of a copy of it in legible form or in a form from which it can readily be produced in visible and legible form.

4. Independent Police Complaints Commission

4.36 The Independent Police Complaints Commission (IPCC) is a non-departmental public body created by the Police Reform Act 2002 (PRA 2002). The IPCC is headed by a chair and deputy chair, along with (presently) sixteen other commissioners. The chair is an appointment by the Crown on the recommendation of the Home Secretary. The deputy chair and other commissioners are public appointees, appointed by the Home Secretary. Collectively known as the 'Commission', the commissioners are accountable for the work of the IPCC. Each commissioner has been appointed for a period of five years, although that period may be extended by a further five years. A commissioner must not have a police background.[28] The Commission is supported by a chief executive and staff, including (currently) 150 investigators. The general functions of the Commission are set out in section 10 of PRA 2002. The IPCC has both an overseeing and investigative role in relation to police complaints and recordable conduct matters.[29] The primary function of the IPCC is to ensure that effective and efficient arrangements are in place to address the handling of police complaints, the recording of conduct matters, and the investigation/handling of both.[30] In addition, the further functions, as set out in section 10 of the 2002 Act, provide for the IPCC's role of guardian of the police complaints system and give it a duty to raise public confidence in that system.

4.37 In relation to each complaint or recordable conduct matter referred to it, the IPCC has a duty to determine whether there should be an investigation.[31] It has no discretion in this regard; it must decide whether an investigation is called for. Having decided that a complaint or recordable conduct matter should be investigated, the IPCC has a further duty: to determine the form that such investigation should take.[32] An investigation will take one of the following forms: an investigation by the appropriate authority (ie the chief officer or police authority) on its own behalf; an investigation by the appropriate authority supervised by the IPCC; an investigation by the appropriate authority or by an external force under the management of the IPCC; or an independent investigation carried out by the IPCC.[33] In its determination as to the form of the investigation, the IPCC must have regard to the seriousness of the case and the public interest.[34]

[28] See PRA 2002, s 9: composition of the Commission and conditions, etc re the appointment of Commissioners.

[29] A recordable conduct matter is any matter which is not, and has not been, the subject of a complaint but in the case of which there is an indication (whether from the circumstances or otherwise) that a person serving with the police may have committed a criminal offence or behaved in a manner which would justify the bringing of disciplinary proceedings (s 12(2)).

[30] PRA 2002, s 10(1), (2) PRA.

[31] ibid Sch 3, para 5 and Sch 3, para 14, respectively.

[32] ibid Sch 3, para 15(1).

[33] ibid Sch 3, paras 16–19.

[34] ibid Sch 3, para 15(3).

4.38 Not all complaints or recordable conduct matters have to be referred to the IPCC. However, it is a requirement that the following shall be referred:[35]

(1) any complaint alleging conduct that has resulted in death or serious injury;
(2) a recordable conduct matter where the matter related to any incident or circumstances in, or in consequence of which, any person has died or suffered serious injury;
(3) any complaint alleging conduct which constitutes, or conduct (not being the subject of a complaint) which constitutes:
   (a) a serious assault,
   (b) a serious sexual offence,
   (c) serious corruption,
   (d) a criminal offence or behaviour which is liable to lead to disciplinary action and which, in either case, is aggravated by discriminatory action, or
   (e) a serious arrestable offence within the meaning of section 116 of PACE 1984); or
   (f) alleged conduct which arises from the same incident as one of the above.

4.39 For present purposes, it should be noted, therefore, that any case involving an allegation or matter of serious corruption and most, but perhaps not all, complaints or matters amounting to misconduct in a public office in the true sense of the offence, will fall to be notified to the IPCC for the decision-making process regarding investigations as set out above.

4.40 In addition to mandatory referrals, an appropriate authority may also refer a complaint or recordable conduct matter to the IPCC if it considers that it will be appropriate to do so by reason of either the gravity of the subject matter of the complaint/conduct matter, or any exceptional circumstance.[36]

4.41 Over and above the duties and discretions already referred to, the IPCC also has a discretion to re-determine the type of investigation, after it has initially reached a decision as to the form that the investigation should take[37] and to discontinue an investigation, having begun one, subject to certain conditions.[38]

4.42 When the IPCC was first set up, its remit was confined to matters concerning complaints and recordable conduct matters against 'persons serving with the police'. That class of persons is defined, in sections 12(7) of PRA 2002, as:

(a) a member of a police force;
(b) an employee of a police authority, who is under the direction and control of a chief officer; or

---

[35] See ibid Sch 3, paras 4(1) and 13(1) and the Police (Complaints and Misconduct) Regulations 2004.
[36] See PRA 2002, Sch 3, paras 4(2) and 13(2).
[37] ibid Sch 3, para 15(5).
[38] Sch 3, para 21 and the Police (Complaints and Misconduct) Regulations 2004.

(c) a special constable who is under the direction and control of a chief officer.

However, following the passing of the Commissioners for Revenue and Customs Act 2005, the functions of the IPCC will be extended to cover customs officials, whilst the provisions of the Serious and Organised Crime and Police Act 2005 (SOCPA 2005) extends its remit further to cover employees and agents of the new Serious and Organised Crime Agency. In relation to customs, the competence of the IPCC is effective from April 2006 (although, at the time of writing, it has already taken on oversight of at least one matter concerning a customs officer). **4.43**

It should be noted, however, that the IPCC is not a prosecuting authority. Thus, decisions as to charge, and advice as to prosecutorial issues, will be obtained from the CPS. In a supervised (and indeed an unsupervised 'local') investigation, the decision on passing the papers to the CPS will be made by the appropriate authority having considered, on all the available evidence, whether there is evidence that a criminal offence may have been committed. However, in the case of a managed or independent investigation, the IPCC will make that decision, but on the same test. **4.44**

B. The Crown Prosecution Service

The Crown Prosecution Service (CPS) was established in 1986, following the passing of the Prosecution of Offences Act 1985 (POA 1985). The Director of Public Prosecutions (DPP) is the Head of the CPS but exercises his functions under the superintendence of the Attorney-General. The duties and powers of the CPS and, indeed of the DPP, are provided by POA 1985. The CPS is the national prosecuting authority for England and Wales, responsible for about 80 percent of prosecutions. It is independent of any police force. **4.45**

Section 10 of POA 1985 requires the DPP to publish a Code for Crown Prosecutors ('the Code'), a document which must give guidance on the general principles to be applied by Crown Prosecutors in deciding: whether proceedings for an offence should be started; whether a case already started should continue; the nature of the charges; and representations to make as to the mode of trial. The importance of the Code is that a Crown Prosecutor has a wide discretion in his or her decision-making and, therefore, such discretion must be exercised responsibly, rationally, and on the basis of the application of consistent principles. **4.46**

In addressing the decision to prosecute, the Code provides that: 'In most cases, Crown Prosecutors are responsible for deciding whether a person should be charged with a criminal offence, and if so, what that offence should be. Crown Prosecutors make these decisions in accordance with this Code and the Director's guidance on charging. In those cases where the police determine **4.47** the charge, which are usually more minor and routine cases, they apply the same provisions.'

4.48 Thus, in relation to the sort of criminal offence with which the present work is concerned, it will be the case that the decision as to charge will be taken by a Crown Prosecutor. In making a charging decision, a Crown Prosecutor will apply what is referred to in the Code as the 'full Code test', save in limited circumstances where the 'threshold test' applies.[39] The full Code Test has two stages: evidential and public interest. If a case does not pass the evidential stage, it must go no further; if, however, it does pass the evidential stage, then the Crown Prosecutor will proceed to the second test, that of public interest.

4.49 The evidential stage, as set out in the Code, provides that:

> Crown Prosecutors must be satisfied that there is enough evidence to provide a 'realistic prospect of conviction' against each defendant on each charge. They must consider what the defence case may be, and how that is likely to affect the prosecution case.
>
> A realistic prospect of conviction is an objective test. It means that a jury or bench of magistrates or judge hearing a case alone, properly directed in accordance with the law, is more likely than not to convict the defendant of the charge alleged. This is a separate test from the one the criminal courts themselves must apply. A court should only convict if satisfied so that it is sure of a defendant's guilt.
>
> When deciding whether there is enough evidence to prosecute, Crown Prosecutors must consider whether the evidence can be used and is reliable. There will be many cases in which the evidence does not give any cause for concern. But there will also be cases in which the evidence may not be as strong as it first appears. Crown Prosecutors must ask themselves the following questions: can the evidence be used in court? . . . Is the evidence reliable?

4.50 In the event that the evidential stage is passed, the public interest will then be assessed. The Code provides, *inter alia*, that:

> The public interest must be considered in each case where there is enough evidence to provide a realistic prospect of conviction. Although there may be public interest factors against prosecution in a particular case, often the prosecution should go ahead and those factors should be put to the court for consideration when sentence is being passed. A prosecution will usually take place unless there are public interest factors tending against prosecution which clearly outweigh those tending in favour, or it appears more appropriate in all the circumstances of the case to divert the person from prosecution . . .
>
> Crown Prosecutors must balance factors for and against prosecution carefully and fairly. Public interest factors that can affect the decision to prosecute usually depend on the seriousness of the offence or the circumstances of the suspect. Some

[39] The threshold test will apply where the case is one in which it is proposed to keep the suspect in custody after charge, but the evidence to apply the full Code Test is not yet available. Where a decision is made in accordance with the threshold test, the case must be reviewed in accordance with the full Code Test as soon as reasonably practicable thereafter.

> factors may increase the need to prosecute, but others may suggest that another course of action may be better . . .
>
> The more serious the offence, the more likely it is that a prosecution will be needed in the public interest . . .

The Code does not provide an exhaustive list of public interest criteria; rather it seeks to set out a general framework and to identify a range of factors which are likely to be encountered. In relation to foreign bribery cases, prosecutors must be careful not to have regard to national economic interests, since the exercise of prosecutorial discretion in that manner will be likely to be in breach of the OECD Convention on the Bribery of Foreign Public Officials in International Business Transactions.[40] Although referred to as the Code for Crown Prosecutors, the Code will also form the basis for decision-making for SFO and Customs prosecutors. **4.51**

As highlighted in Chapter 2, above[41] a prosecution for a statutory corruption offence cannot be instituted save with the consent of a Law Officer of the Crown. That position may change if the UK's corruption law is rationalized in the manner envisaged by the draft Corruption Bill.[42] As to the operation of the Code in a statutory corruption case, the practice of a Crown Prosecutor will be, in the event of deciding that the evidential stage is satisfied, not to reach a decision on the public interest, but rather to submit to the Law Officers an analysis of the public interest factors (on the basis that the public interest decision will form part of the decision of the Attorney- or Solicitor-General whether or not to issue a consent). **4.52**

In relation to the CPS specifically, the following additional discretionary powers (confirmed by POA 1985) will be of relevance in corruption/misconduct in a public office case: **4.53**

(1) the ability to take over *any* criminal proceedings (ie private prosecutions);[43]
(2) the power to discontinue criminal cases in the magistrates' court and, in limited circumstances before the indictment has been preferred, in the Crown Court;[44]
(3) the power to receive documents disclosing criminal offences—this power arises not from POA 1985, but from a number of statutes of which the most important for present purposes are:
    (a) section 449 of the Companies Act 1985, which provides that the DPP is a competent authority to receive material seized from a company under the provisions in section 447 and 448 of that Act, and[45]

[40] See the discussion at 10.98ff. [41] See 2.52, 2.71 above.
[42] See 5.152 below. It should be noted that the Attorney-General, in his answers to the Joint Parliamentary Committee on the draft Corruption Bill, conceded that he would be content for the present law officers consent to become a consent from the DPP/Director of the SFO or a designated deputy for each. [43] 1985, s 6(2) POA
[44] ibid s 23. [45] See 4.34ff above.

(b) PRA 2002, in relation to reports concerning criminal offences committed by police officers. (See the discussion on the IPCC above); and

(4) the power to obtain access to documents or records, again provided for in statutes other than POA 1985—for present purposes, it should be noted that section 271 of the Companies Act 1985 provides that an application can be made by the DPP to the High Court for access to a company's books if it is believed that they contain evidence of an offence committed by an officer of the company.

4.54 The CPS is presently split into 42 'areas', each with its own Chief Crown Prosecutor. Each Chief Crown Prosecutor, in turn, reports to the DPP. The CPS areas correspond to the police force areas of England and Wales (save that London has two police forces, but only one CPS area). In addition to the CPS areas, each with their own offices, CPS headquarters has three sites: London (where the DPP is based), Birmingham, and York. Each headquarters site houses a branch or branches of the 'Casework Directorate' which, *inter alia*, deals with the most serious or sensitive of cases.

4.55 Details of the criteria governing referrals to the Casework Directorate are publicly available. Allegations of corruption or misconduct in a public office in relation to police officers, or indeed other law enforcement agents, will be dealt with by the Casework Directorate, as will matters concerning serious complaints or recordable conduct matters in respect of police officers, deaths in custody (whether in police stations or in prison), difficult corruption cases (especially those concerning public bodies), allegations of foreign bribery, and matters causing widespread public concern or involving significant international aspects. Given the relationship between corruption and fraud, it is worthy of note that any fraud involving a loss or risk valued at above £750,000 will also be referred to the Casework Directorate for consideration as to whether the matter should be conducted by the Directorate or by the relevant CPS area.

Prosecuting Authorities in Scotland

4.56 Unlike the position with the CPS, the Procurator Fiscal Service, headed and superintended by the Lord Advocate, is responsible for both the investigation and prosecution of crime, including corruption. Thus, the police are obliged to conduct investigations subject to the direction of the relevant Procurator Fiscal. Scotland is divided into eleven areas with a total of forty-eight Procurator Fiscal offices spread across them. As part of the same department as the Procurator Fiscal, the Scottish Crown Office is responsible for criminal policy matters. That, too, is headed by the Lord Advocate. In more serious cases, including allegations of bribery or corruption, the police must report the making of an allegation to the Procurator Fiscal, who will then become responsible for managing and supervising the case. In addition, the Crown Office has situated within it the International and Financial Crime Unit, the powers and remit of which are similar to those of the SFO (and which will be responsible, in Scotland, for handling foreign bribery cases).

C. The Reporting of Corruption

In the United Kingdom there is no general obligation on the public to report criminality. However, specific groups within society do have either a duty to report or, at least, a positive power to report or make disclosure. **4.57**

1. Civil Servants

UK civil servants are bound by rules set out in the Civil Service Code (which forms part of the terms and conditions of service and which is enforceable under UK employment law). The Civil Service Code sets out what the Cabinet Office describes as 'the constitutional framework within which all civil servants work and the values which they are expected to uphold'.[46] It came into force on 1 January 1996, but was revised in 1999 in response to the establishment of the Scottish and Welsh Assemblies. It provides that a civil servant *should* report any evidence of criminal or unlawful activity by others in accordance with procedures laid down in guidance or rules of conduct for his/her department. Paragraph 11 of the Civil Service Code provides that: **4.58**

> Where a civil servant believes he or she is being required to act in a way which:
>
> 1. is illegal, improper or unethical;
> 2. is in breach of constitutional convention or a professional code;
> 3. may involve possible maladministration; or,
> 4. is otherwise inconsistent with this Code;
>
> he or she should report the matter in accordance with procedures laid down in the appropriate guidance or rules of conduct for their department or administration.
>
> A civil servant should also report to the appropriate authorities evidence of criminal or unlawful activity by others and may also report in accordance with the relevant procedures if he or she becomes aware of breaches of this Code or is required to act in a way which, for him or her, raises a fundamental issue of conscience.

It will be seen that the language of the Civil Service Code, quoted above, appears to provide an authority, rather than an obligation, to report wrongdoing and does not provide specific disciplinary or criminal sanctions for failure to report. However, a failure to report, it is submitted, may be capable of amounting to gross misconduct, resulting in dismissal. At present, within the **4.59**

---

[46] See 'Propriety and Ethics' at http://www.cabinetoffice.gov.uk.

United Kingdom, the status of the Civil Service Code has been the subject of discussion and consultation. Indeed, the UK Government has published consultation proposals which would give a statutory backing to the Civil Service Code.[47] It remains to be seen, however, whether a specific disciplinary sanction for failing to report will be provided for in the future.

4.60 The United Kingdom's experience, in relation to reporting obligations for civil servants, raises a question with which a number of other jurisdictions have had to grapple—should a failure by a public official to report give rise to a specific sanction and, if so, should that sanction be disciplinary or criminal? For many, a criminal approach has an initial attraction, but one danger amongst others, is that such a sanction is introduced but is devalued by being little used even when failures do occur. It might be thought, therefore, that a specific disciplinary sanction in the case of non-compliance, when readily and appropriately enforced, is perhaps the most effective measure.

2. Posts Abroad

4.61 One particular group of UK civil servants who can expect to play an ever increasing part in the reporting process are British Embassy and High Commission staff. The United Kingdom is not alone in recognizing that diplomatic posts are well placed to play a key role in forwarding information concerning transnational or foreign bribery back to the United Kingdom. It may be that an allegation is made locally, or that a UK diplomat becomes aware of concern being expressed about the activities of a particular individual, or company, or as to the circumstances concerning a specific contract or tender process. Information received in one of these ways will be researched and analysed by the National Criminal Intelligence Service (NCIS) with a view to an evaluation of the reliability of the allegation or intelligence. Thereafter, and in accordance with the Memorandum of Understanding already detailed at paras 4.25ff above, an allegation which is credible will be forwarded to the SFO as the central vetting point.

4.62 As more states adopt a similar approach, those implementing such information flows may wish to have in mind that embassy representatives should not undertake any analysis or evaluation of information themselves in such a way as to preclude essentially valuable details being passed back to their home state. Today's idle rumour might be tomorrow's substantiated allegation. At the same time, those on the ground locally will be in a good position to inform the evaluation process by providing what is known of the level of credibility, etc. Equally, it is important that the information passed back should be recorded and, subject to any demands and restrictions in a particular state's legislation,

[47] See 'A Draft Civil Service Bill: a Consultation Document', Cm 6373.

retained. Again, this is on the basis that what is insignificant now might be of importance in the future.

3. Accountants

Effective accounting and auditing practices are pivotal to any programme which seeks to eliminate corruption and are prerequisites for the encouragement of transparency and good governance. The making of off-the-books or inadequately identified transactions is not specifically prohibited under UK legislation; rather, more general requirements are imposed by law to the effect that companies must produce true and fair accounts. Accounting records must be kept and maintained in such a way that they disclose 'with reasonable accuracy' the true financial position of the company.[48] Similarly, a company's accounts must include details of sums of money received and expended by the company from day to day and particulars of all receipts and expenditures, along with a record of the assets and liabilities accruing/owed. Those requirements apply not only to public limited companies, but also to private companies and companies limited by guarantee. A fraudulent breach of those provisions, ie fraudulent accounting, is triable in the Crown Court and carries a maximum of two years in prison and an unlimited fine. Similarly, a simple failure by a company to keep its books and accounts in the prescribed fashion carries an unlimited fine. The fraudulent accounting offence has been the subject of regular prosecutions, with on average more than 1,000 cases a year coming before the courts.[49] **4.63**

Taking a critical view, it might be said that the accounting demands described are, although well meant, too broad to be an effective detection or preventive tool in the fight against corruption. However, in reality, tax case law means that compliance with the rigorous Statements of Standard Accounting Practice and Financial Reporting Standards[50] is necessary if a company's accounts are to be regarded as true and fair. That being said, more is being done and more is to be done: as of 2005, there is a legal obligation on listed companies to provide accounts based on the International Accounting Standards. In addition, a number of changes to the law have already taken place and more are taking place, with, *inter alia*, an intention to harmonize international standards and UK standards by 2007.[51] There will be those, however, who will argue that clear and explicit accounting legislation addressing each of the matters flagged in Article 8 of the OECD Convention[52] is the only effective way of ensuring that the deterrent and detection thrust of international expectations is fully met. **4.64**

[48] Companies Act 1985, s 221. [49] OECD Phase 2 report of the UK, 21, para 65.
[50] The FRS are accounting standards issued by the Accounting Standards Board (ASB).
[51] An objective of the ASB. [52] See 10.107 below.

4.65 Turning now to the position of small and medium-sized enterprises (SMEs) in an increasingly sophisticated business world, it is fair to say that, within the United Kingdom, such enterprises enjoy more straightforward accounting requirements. As with large corporations, they are obliged to produce true and fair accounts, but are allowed to draw these up in an abbreviated form. Does that provide a cloak under which to hide the making and proceeds of bribes? Perhaps time will tell.

4.66 Of more general concern to some, neither legislation nor accounting standards in the United Kingdom specifically require the recognition, measurement, presentation, or disclosure of matters relating to any bribery offence. Arguably, though, any transaction which involves a bribe would fall within the definition of an 'exceptional item' as set out in the Financial Reporting Standards.

4. Company Internal Controls

4.67 Any discussion of reporting must also look at the presence or otherwise of company internal controls. In the United Kingdom, companies are not obliged to monitor and report upon the effectiveness of their internal control mechanisms, although it should be noted that in the financial services sector there are statutory requirements as to compliance mechanisms and internal controls which have to be adhered to. Listed companies are under a duty to explain any failure to comply with the internal controls thanks to the UK Combined Code on Corporate Governance. As to company directors in general, however, there is no obligation for a director to make a declaration of compliance with legal or regulatory regimes, nor to certify that financial information given about the company does not contain errors or irregularities. Those within other jurisdictions looking at their own legislation with a view to imposing conditions of internal control might well wish to consider the ambit and precision of such measures.

5. Auditing

4.68 External auditing often provokes debate: to what extent can it or should it be a tool of detection? Or is its value that of deterrent? Within the United Kingdom, thanks to the Companies Act 1985, all companies with a turnover exceeding an annually increasing threshold are required to submit to external audit. Similarly, those falling below the threshold, in which there is nonetheless a significant public interest (ie those working in the regulated financial sector), are required to be subject to external audit. Given that the threshold stands, at present, at a turnover of just under £6 million, one might argue that there is scope for a number of companies with substantial business interests in foreign jurisdictions to escape any scrutiny in this regard.

For completeness, the role and nature of the auditing and accounting professions now fall to be considered. Auditors are required to report without delay when they become aware of a suspected or actual instance of non-compliance with the law when there is a statutory duty on them to report (such as in the case of money laundering or terrorism financing). Where there is no statutory duty, however, but there is suspected or actual non-compliance with the law, auditors have to consider whether the matter is one which nonetheless ought to be reported to the appropriate authority in the public interest.[53] The criteria to determine the public interest will include the seriousness of the matter, the nature of the existing management, and the level of suspicion or belief which the auditor has in non-compliance. Interestingly, and importantly, UK representatives of the accounting profession told the OECD Convention lead examiners at the Phase 2 review that, in their view, bribe payments to foreign public officials would certainly constitute a matter of public interest which should be reported.[54] **4.69**

One might consider whether a specific reporting requirement should be imposed, as a matter of public policy, in relation to suspected bribery, both domestic and foreign. It is fair to say that the United Kingdom has adopted something of a middle road in relation to non-obligatory reporting by auditors. When an auditor concludes that a matter ought to be reported, it should first be brought to the attention of the board of directors in the expectation that they will then report the matter to the appropriate authority.[55] If they fail to do so, then the auditor should report.[56] Similarly, where an auditor no longer has confidence in the integrity of the board of directors, then, once again, the auditor should report directly to the authorities.[57] An auditor who fails to act in the prescribed way is him or herself liable to investigation and to regulatory action, which includes withdrawal of registration. **4.70**

There have been recent changes to strengthen the independence of auditors. Some of these changes are still in the process of being made. There will now be more frequent rotation of audit partners to avoid too close an association with the audited company, a compulsory two-year 'cooling off' period before the re-employment of an auditing firm by the same client, and the introduction of a requirement that auditor independence standards be set independently of the accounting profession. It is envisaged that these changes will be concluded by the end of 2005 or beginning of 2006. **4.71**

[53] The Auditing Practices Board (APB), in its Statements of Auditing Standards (SAS) No 120, has addressed voluntary reporting. Auditors should consider the public interest in reporting in a given case in accordance with SAS 120.13 and SAS 120.65.

[54] OECD Report of the UK, 24. [55] SAS 120.13. [56] SAS 120.14.

[57] SAS 120.15.

6. Reporting by the Tax Authorities and the Issue of Tax Non-Deductibility for Bribes

4.72 In Chapter 10 below,[58] it will seen that, as a result of the work of the OECD Working Group on Bribery and others, international attention has focused on the importance of there being an explicit prohibition on the tax deductibility of bribe payments. A closely related consideration concerns the part to be played by tax authorities in the reporting of suspected corruption. In the United Kingdom it was traditionally the case that voluntary transmission of information by the Inland Revenue to investigative/prosecuting authorities was prohibited. However, as a result of an amendment contained within section 19 of the Anti-Terrorism, Crime and Security Act 2001 (ATCSA 2001) it is now possible for the Inland Revenue to make a voluntary, unsolicited disclosure for the purposes of a criminal investigation. Such disclosures, however, although possible, are not mandatory.

4.73 To supplement the statutory power, a Memorandum of Understanding and Internal Guidelines have been drawn up to the effect that such disclosures may be made either where there is an ongoing criminal investigation and the information discovered by the tax administration may be helpful in that context, or where the tax administration considers suspicions of criminal activities may need to be brought to the attention of the appropriate law enforcement agency. It should be noted, however, that individual tax inspectors are not authorized to make reports directly to the police or the prosecuting authorities: rather, when a tax inspector becomes aware of a criminal act, for instance, he is required to report the matter to an intelligence group set up within the Inland Revenue which is responsible for deciding whether to pass such information on. It is understood that between early 2002 and July 2004, sixty-six such unsolicited disclosures were made. Five of these concerned financial crimes, but none related to bribery.[59]

7. Miscellaneous Reporting Obligations

4.74 The offences now reflected in the Proceeds of Crime Act 2002 (POCA 2002) are addressed elsewhere in the present work,[60] but should be noted. Similarly, regard should be had to the discussion of the criminal offence of misconduct in a public office[61] when considering a failure by a police officer to comply with the obligation to report a colleague if he becomes aware of corrupt behaviour by that colleague.

[58] See 10.120 below.
[59] See OECD Phase 2 Review of the UK, 20.
[60] See 2.112ff.
[61] See Ch 3 above.

D. Whistle-blower Protection

The whistle-blower has been, and is likely to continue to be, an important source of allegations of corrupt behaviour. Protection of the whistle-blower is now contained within the Public Interest Disclosure Act 1998 (PIDA 1998) which came into force on 2 July 1999. It protects those who raise concerns about malpractice, including corruption, in their place of work and seeks to give every incentive to employers and organizations to address the problem which has been exposed and to resist the temptation to engage in a 'cover-up'. Importantly, it protects the whistle-blower not just from dismissal, but also from other forms of victimization. PIDA 1998 covers all UK employees, whether in the public, private, or voluntary sector and is geared to a regime in which matters are brought to the employer's attention in order to allow, as a 'first resort', possible internal solutions to be found. Public disclosure is considered appropriate only when other avenues have failed. Therefore, the incentive to an organization is that a matter brought to its attention and remedied in the appropriate way can be managed without adverse publicity. However, such an emphasis on internal problem-solving carries with it an onus on the organization to have in place procedures which protect the employee and worker. **4.75**

PIDA 1998 brings protection to those who raise concerns in good faith about criminality, civil wrongs (such as negligence or breach of statutory duty), miscarriages of justice, and health and safety issues (both in relation to people and to the environment). Importantly, in relation to corruption, it also covers malpractice or criminality which occurs outside the United Kingdom. Equally importantly, and without restriction as to time in employment, etc, it extends protection to, amongst others, contractors, trainees, agency staff, and police officers. Again, and of note in relation to anti-corruption issues, it does not cover the self-employed, volunteers, the intelligence services, or the army. **4.76**

In the first case which came before the Court of Appeal (Civil Division) in relation to PIDA 1998, Lord Justice Mummery stated:[62] 'There are obvious tensions, public and private, between the legitimate interest in the confidentiality of the employer's affairs and the exposure of wrong.' Those words should be borne in mind when considering the provisions of the 1998 Act. **4.77**

Section 1 of PIDA 1998 inserts a new part (Part 4A) into the Employment Rights Act 1996 (ERA 1996). The provisions contained therein have the effect of making whistle-blowing law and the protection of whistle-blowers part of UK employment legislation. **4.78**

---

[62] *ALM Medical Service v Bladon* [2002] IRLR 807.

4.79 Section 43A of ERA 1996, as inserted, provides that a 'protected disclosure' means 'a qualifying disclosure (as defined in section 43B) which is made by a worker in accordance with any of sections 43C–43H'. The effect of section 43A is that for a whistle-blower to be protected the disclosure made must be in relation to one or more of the matters set out in section 43B and the disclosure made by the whistle-blower must have been made in one of the ways set out in sections 43C to 43H.

4.80 Section 43B of ERA 1996 Act provides that:

> (1) In this Part a 'qualifying disclosure' means any disclosure of information which, in the reasonable belief of the worker making the disclosure, tends to show one or more of the following—
> (a) that a criminal offence has been committed, is being committed or is likely to be committed,
> (b) that a person has failed, is failing or is likely to fail to comply with any legal obligation to which he is subject,
> (c) that a miscarriage of justice has occurred, is occurring or is likely to occur,
> (d) that the health or safety of any individual has been, is being or is likely to be endangered,
> (e) that the environment has been, is being or is likely to be damaged, or
> (f) that information tending to show any matter falling within any one of the preceding paragraphs has been, or is likely to be deliberately concealed.
> (2) For the purposes of subsection (1), it is immaterial whether the relevant failure occurred, occurs or would occur in the United Kingdom or elsewhere, and whether the law applying to it is that of the United Kingdom or of any other country or territory.
> (3) A disclosure of information is not a qualifying disclosure if the person making the disclosure commits an offence by making it.
> (4) A disclosure of information in respect of which a claim to legal professional privilege (or, in Scotland, to confidentiality as between client and professional legal adviser) could be maintained in legal proceedings is not a qualifying disclosure if it is made by a person to whom the information had been disclosed in the course of obtaining legal advice.
> (5) In this Part 'the relevant failure', in relation to a qualifying disclosure, means the matter falling within paragraphs (a) to (f) of subsection (1).

4.81 Section 43B of ERA 1996 details the type of information which will be protected; however, the disclosure must be made in accordance with the other requirements set out in PIDA 1998. It should be noted that it does not matter, for the purposes of whistle-blower protection, whether the person to whom the disclosure is made is, in fact, already aware of the information about the wrongdoing.[63]

4.82 Even if the information that is disclosed is confidential, protection will still be afforded so long as it falls within the classes of information reflected in section 43B. However, the more confidential a piece of information, the greater the

[63] ERA 1996, s 43L(3).

justification required on the part of the whistle-blower in relation to the disclosure made.[64] The effect of section 43B(1) is that the person making the disclosure must have a 'reasonable belief'. An honest but mistaken belief, if reasonable, will suffice.

As already indicated, the effect of section 43B(2) is that a disclosure can amount to a qualifying disclosure whether the offence or failure occurred in the United Kingdom or elsewhere, and whether, if elsewhere, UK law or the law of another country applied. It is also clear from the same subsection that a qualifying disclosure may be in relation to past, present, or future malpractice or misconduct. **4.83**

However, by virtue of section 43B(3), any disclosure will not amount to a qualifying disclosure if disclosure of the information is itself a criminal offence; for instance, an offence under the Official Secrets Act 1989. However, if a disclosure, which would amount to such a breach, is made formally within the government department concerned or is raised with the Civil Service Commissioners it will not amount to an offence under the Official Secrets Act. Protection under PIDA 1998 would then apply, subject to the other conditions being satisfied. **4.84**

The effect of section 43B(4) of ERA 1996 is to maintain legal professional privilege, in that if a lawyer would be bound by legal professional privilege in relation to a piece of information before a court, he will not be able to make a protected disclosure about it. **4.85**

Having seen then that, to be protected, a disclosure must be a qualifying disclosure made in the reasonable belief that it tends to show one of the matters set out in section 43B(1), section 43C limits the class of person to whom disclosure may be made by confining qualifying disclosure to disclosure made to the employer or another responsible person. Section 43C of ERA 1996 provides that: **4.86**

> (1) A qualifying disclosure is made in accordance with this section if the worker makes the disclosure in good faith—
> (a) to his employer, or
> (b) where the worker reasonably believes that the relevant failure relates solely or mainly to—
> (i) the conduct of a person other than his employer, or
> (ii) any other matter for which a person other than his employer has legal responsibility, to that other person.
>
> (2) A worker who, in accordance with a procedure whose use by him is authorised by his employer, makes a qualifying disclosure to a person other than his employer, is to be treated for the purposes of this Part as making the qualifying disclosure to his employer.

Section 43C(1) imposes a requirement that the disclosure be made in good faith. To be made in good faith, the disclosure must be made honestly, but can **4.87**

[64] See *Aspinall v MSI Mechanical Forge* [2002] EAT/891/01.

be careless and still be in good faith.[65] A disclosure made for an ulterior motive or in circumstances of dishonesty will not be a disclosure made in good faith.[66] Section 43C(1)(a) allows for disclosure to an employer. That, it is submitted, can be taken to mean disclosure to a person senior in rank or position who has been given, by the employer, line management or supervisory responsibility over the person making the disclosure. Disclosure to a colleague will not, however, be covered.

4.88 However, by virtue of section 43C(2), if an organization has a process or procedure which allows concerns to be raised with others apart from an employer (such as a union official or a confidential hotline), then such a disclosure will be treated as if it is a disclosure to the employer.

4.89 Thus, in *Brothers of Charity Services (Merseyside) v Eleady-Cole*[67] the Employment Appeals Tribunal held that a worker's concern raised through an Employee Assistance Programme (a telephone hotline) was protected as if it had been made to the employer. The worker had raised concerns about pornography and illegal drugs at a charitable hostel and had raised the matter through a telephone hotline which was run by an organization with which the charity employing the worker had entered into a contract. The essence of the contract was that the Employee Assistance Programme was bound to pass on to the charity, in anonymous form, information it had received about criminality.

4.90 As to the establishing by organizations of specific procedures for whistle-blowing, it should be noted that the absence of such procedures may make a wider disclosure more likely to be protected (see section 43G(3)(e) in para 4.98 below). One of the factors to be taken into account in determining whether a wider public disclosure should be protected is the reasonableness of the response to the concern. A worker or employee who does not have recourse to a whistle-blowing procedure, or is unaware of it, is more likely to have his wider disclosure actions regarded as reasonable and, hence, worthy of being protected.

4.91 Section 43D of ERA 1996 provides that: 'A qualifying disclosure is made in accordance with this section if it is made in the course of obtaining legal advice.' The effect of section 43D is that a worker may seek legal advice and, in doing so, will be protected in his actions. Disclosure made to a legal adviser for the purpose of obtaining legal advice does not have to be made in good faith in order to be protected under PIDA 1998. The provision does not, however, give

[65] See the explanation and details provided by the organization Public Concern At Work at its website, http://www.pcaw.co.uk/policy_pub/pida). In particular, see PCAW's explanatory note in relation to s 43C.

[66] See *Medforth v Blake* [2000] Ch 86 where the court held '. . . the breach of a duty of good faith should in this area as in all others require some dishonesty or improper motive, some element of bad faith to be established'. Although that judgment was not on the present point, as a comment on the concept it remains good law.

[67] 2002 EAT/661/00.

the legal adviser protection if he seeks to make disclosure of the information or material he has been provided with by his client. He can, though, make disclosure as instructed by the client, in which case the disclosure made will be deemed to be made by the client and will be protected insofar as it is made in accordance with the conditions set out in PIDA 1998.

As for legal advice being sought by a trade union, it has already been seen, in relation to section 43C(2), that where an organization recognizes a union or unions, then a disclosure may be made to a trade union official and be protected as if it were a disclosure made to the employer. In the case of subsequent disclosure by that trade union official to a legal adviser for the purpose of obtaining legal advice, such disclosure will, again, be protected.[68] **4.92**

Section 43E of ERA 1996 provides that: **4.93**

> A qualifying disclosure is made in accordance with this section if—
> (a) the worker's employer is—
> (i) an individual appointed under any enactment (including any enactment comprised in, or in an instrument made under, an Act of the Scottish Parliament) by a Minister of the Crown or a member of the Scottish Executive, or
> (ii) a body any of whose members are so appointed, and
> (b) the disclosure is made in good faith to a Minister of the Crown or a member of the Scottish executive.

Section 43E addresses disclosure to a Minister of the Crown. The effect of the section is that a worker in a government-appointed public body will be protected if he makes disclosure (in good faith) to the government department which sponsors the public body, rather than to the employer within the public body or the public body itself. This section will, therefore, cover non-departmental public bodies such as the Independent Police Complaints Commission (IPCC), tribunals whose members are appointed by a Minister of the Crown, NHS Trusts and, for example, bodies where an individual is appointed by a Minister of the Crown, for example to chair or head a regulator. **4.94**

Section 43F of ERA 1996 provides that: **4.95**

> (1) A qualifying disclosure is made in accordance with this section if the worker—
> (a) makes the disclosure in good faith to a person prescribed by an order made by the Secretary of State for the purposes of this section, and

[68] In this regard, see the explanation given by Public Concern at Work on its website, when specifically dealing with the provisions of PIDA 1998 (http://www.pcaw.co.uk/policy_pub/pida). Public Concern at Work highlights that when PIDA 1998 was in Bill form, Lord Borrie emphasized that a disclosure by a union member for the purpose of obtaining legal advice from a union lawyer will be protected under s 34D, *Hansard* (HL), 5 June 1998, col 624.

(b) reasonably believes—
 (i) that the relevant failure falls within any description of matters in respect of which that person is so prescribed, and
 (ii) that the information disclosed, and any allegation contained in it, are substantially true.

(2) An order prescribing persons for the purposes of this section may specify persons or descriptions of persons, and shall specify the descriptions of matters in respect of which each person, or persons of each description, is or are prescribed.

4.96 Section 43F provides protection to a worker who makes a qualifying disclosure to a person prescribed by an order made by the Secretary of State for the purposes of section 43F. The person prescribed is likely to be a regulator, non-departmental government body, or government department. To give but a few examples: the Financial Services Authority and HM Treasury have been prescribed in relation to financial services matters; the Office of Fair Trading and relevant local authorities have been prescribed for the purpose of competition and consumer issues; for utilities and private industries the Rail Regulator and OFWAT have, *inter alia*, been prescribed; and for those serving with the police, the IPCC has been prescribed.

4.97 A worker who makes a qualifying disclosure to a prescribed person in accordance with section 43F does not have to satisfy the requirement that the disclosure was reasonable, nor that the malpractice was serious, nor that he had raised the matter before and internally. At the same time, however, the effect of section 43F(b)(ii) is that the worker must satisfy the exacting requirement that he reasonably believes the information disclosed, and any allegation contained in it, are substantially true.

4.98 Section 43G of ERA 1996 provides that:

(1) A qualifying disclosure is made in accordance with this section if—
 (a) the worker makes the disclosure in good faith,
 (b) he reasonably believes that the information disclosed, and any allegation contained in it, are substantially true,
 (c) he does not make the disclosure for purposes of personal gain,
 (d) any of the conditions in subsection (2) is met, and
 (e) in all the circumstances of the case, it is reasonable for him to make the disclosure.

(2) The conditions referred to in subsection (1)(d) are—
 (a) that, at the time he makes the disclosure, the worker reasonably believes that he will be subjected to a detriment by his employer if he makes a disclosure to his employer or in accordance with section 43F,
 (b) that, in a case where no person is prescribed for the purposes of section 43F in relation to the relevant failure, the worker reasonably believes that it is likely that evidence relating to the relevant failure will be concealed or destroyed if he makes a disclosure to his employer, or
 (c) that the worker has previously made a disclosure of substantially the same information—
  (i) to his employer, or
  (ii) in accordance with section 43F.

(3) In determining for the purposes of subsection (1)(e) whether it is reasonable for the worker to make the disclosure, regard shall be had, in particular, to—
  (a) the identity of the person to whom the disclosure is made,
  (b) the seriousness of the relevant failure,
  (c) whether the relevant failure is continuing or is likely to occur in the future,
  (d) whether the disclosure is made in breach of a duty of confidentiality owed by the employer to any other person,
  (e) in a case falling within subsection (2)(c)(i) or (ii), any action which the employer or the person to whom the previous disclosure in accordance with section 43F was made has taken or might reasonably be expected to have taken as a result of the previous disclosure, and
  (f) in a case falling within subsection (2)(c)(i), whether in making the disclosure to the employer the worker complied with any procedure whose use by him was authorised by the employer.

(4) For the purposes of this section a subsequent disclosure may be regarded as a disclosure of substantially the same information as that disclosed by a previous disclosure as mentioned in subsection (2)(c) even though the subsequent disclosure extends to information about action taken or not taken by any person as a result of the previous disclosure.

Section 43G provides the circumstances in which wider disclosure may be protected. It sets out three tests or sets of criteria, each of which must be fulfilled. The first of these is that the disclosure must be made in good faith (section 43G(1)(a)); there must be a reasonable belief on the part of the worker that the information disclosed and any allegation contained within it are substantially true (section 43G(1)(b)); and the disclosure has not been made for the purpose of personal gain (section 43G(1)(c)). The second set of criteria is contained in section 43G(2), which sets out three preconditions (section 43 G)(2)(a) to (c)), one of which must be satisfied. The first is that a worker reasonably believes that, if he raises his concerns internally or with a prescribed person as provided for by section 43F, he will be subject to detriment, such as victimization. The second is when a worker reasonably believes that a cover up of the malpractice is likely to occur. The third is that the concern has previously been raised with the employer or with a prescribed regulator. Moving then to the third of the tests or set of criteria, if a disclosure is to be protected, then it must be reasonable in all the circumstances (section 43G(1)(e)). **4.99**

Section 43H of ERA 1996 provides that: **4.100**

(1) A qualifying disclosure is made in accordance with this section if—
  (a) the worker makes the disclosure in good faith,
  (b) he reasonably believes that the information disclosed, and any allegation contained in it, are substantially true,
  (c) he does not make the disclosure for purposes of personal gain,
  (d) the relevant failure is of an exceptionally serious nature, and
  (e) in all the circumstances of the case, it is reasonable for him to make the disclosure.

(2) In determining for the purposes of subsection (1)(e) whether it is reasonable for the worker to make the disclosure, regard shall be had, in particular, to the identity of the person to whom the disclosure is made.

4.101 The effect of section 43H is that a disclosure of a failure or malpractice of an exceptionally serious nature may be made to persons other than an employer, etc even though the circumstances are such that the criteria in section 43G are not met. The rationale is obvious, ie that a person should not be deterred from reporting very serious allegations. It will be noted, however, that there is a test of whether making a disclosure is reasonable in all the circumstances (section 43H(1)(e)). Thus, under section 43H, it is the view of 'Public Concern at Work' that a person working with children who wishes to report allegations of abuse, will be protected if he or she goes directly to the police, rather than his employer, etc.[69]

4.102 Section 43J of ERA 1996 provides that:

(1) Any provision in an agreement to which this section applies is void in so far as it purports to preclude the worker from making a protected disclosure.
(2) This section applies to any agreement between a worker and his employer (whether a worker's contract or not), including an agreement to refrain from instituting or continuing any proceedings under this Act or any proceedings for breach of contract.

4.103 The effect of this section is that any clause in a contract or agreement between an employer and a worker which purports to prevent the worker from making a protected disclosure is void. Furthermore, the word 'agreement' will cover settlement agreements as well as contracts of employment.

4.104 Section 2 of PIDA 1998 addresses the right not to suffer detriment and inserts s 47B, which provides that:

(1) A worker has the right not to be subjected to any detriment by any act, or any deliberate failure to act, by his employer done on the ground that the worker has made a protected disclosure.
(2) . . . this section does not apply where—
(a) the worker is an employee, and
(b) the detriment in question amounts to dismissal (within the meaning of Part X).
(3) For the purposes of this section, and of sections 48 and 49 so far as relating to this section, 'worker', 'worker's contract', 'employment' and 'employer' have the extended meaning given by section 43K.

4.105 Section 47B, as inserted, protects those who are employed from action against them by their employers short of dismissal, and protects other workers from victimization, which includes the purported termination of a contract. The sort of action which has been held to be a detriment has included: offering less work

[69] See the commentary to s 43H http://www.pcaw.co.uk/policy-pub/pida.

to a casual worker;[70] disciplining a whistle-blower;[71] and making disclosure of the whistle-blower's identity notwithstanding assurances given of anonymity.[72] It should be noted that there is an evidential presumption that there is a causal link between the disclosure and the detrimental action. Thus, it will be for an employer to rebut the suggestion that the reason for the victimization was the disclosure made.

A worker who has been subject to detriment in contravention of section 47B is able to present his complaint to an employment tribunal by virtue of section 3 of PIDA 1998. There is no limit to the award of compensation that can be made, which is assessed on the basis of loss suffered. However, an amount to reflect aggravated damages may also be awarded. **4.106**

By way of conclusion, a few general comments may be made on the above: it is no coincidence that the high-water mark of the protection for workers under PIDA 1998 is reserved for disclosure under section 43C (Disclosure to the employer). Given the implicit emphasis on internal remedies as the first port of call, it should come as no surprise that the worker who makes a disclosure anonymously is likely to face considerable difficulties, as the 1998 Act is presently framed, in bringing any action for detriment suffered. In particular, it will be difficult for a tribunal to satisfy itself that causation is present in relation to any detriment unless it can be shown that the employer knew that it was the worker who was actually responsible; and in a case of anonymity, the employer will not. Finally it should be noted that the regime of protected disclosure described above applies in relation to whistle-blowing, not to grievance procedures. The essence of whistle-blowing is the giving of information about malpractice; whilst grievance, as the name suggests, is making a complaint about one's own treatment or the behaviour of others towards one. **4.107**

E. Reactive Investigations

Traditionally, anti-corruption investigations tended to be reactive, as opposed to the increasingly important proactive investigations discussed in detail in the next section. Reactive investigations, particularly in relation to commercial corruption and corruption in relation to the obtaining of contracts, will often rely on forensic accountancy, asset tracing, and financial investigation. (A detailed discussion of those methodologies is beyond the scope of this work.) However, one of the most compelling pieces of testimony in a corruption case—but equally one of the most dangerous to all sides—is that from an **4.108**

[70] *Almond v Alphabet Children's Services* (2001), unreported ET.
[71] *Kay v Northumberland Health Care NHS Trust* (2001), unreported ET.
[72] *Carroll v Greater Manchester County Fire Service* (2001), unreported ET.

individual who was within the corrupt company or was part of the corrupt criminal network. In the case of the former, we have already explored the issues and the law concerning whistle-blowers. As for the evidence of the whistle-blower, the risk is obvious: is he or she a credible witness or has his or her evidence been distorted or even fabricated through frustration, resentment, or in the hope of some other reward? Equally, is he or she simply providing evidence because of some form of inducement? The risks around the evidence of the criminal participant, are, however, even more stark. The same concerns arise, principally those of inducement and credibility, but this time set against a background of quite possible risk to life, manipulation of the process, and, very often, a history of past and present criminality and related 'baggage'.

4.109 In a corruption or misconduct in a public office case, such a criminal associate or accomplice, perhaps faced with overwhelming evidence, may turn 'Queen's Evidence' and elect to give evidence against others. No particular difficulties of procedure arise here. It will usually be that a draft witness statement is provided by an accused who has decided to cooperate; as a matter of practice, such a witness statement will not be signed until after a plea of guilty has been entered. Sentence, meanwhile, will usually, but not invariably, be passed after he has given evidence at the trial or trials of his associates.[73]

4.110 In relation to the giving of evidence by an alleged accomplice of an accused, section 32 of the Criminal Justice and Public Order Act 1994 abrogated the requirement for a jury to be given a corroboration warning. The effect of section 32 was considered in the conjoined appeals of *R v Makanjuola; R v Easton*[74] There the Court concluded that section 32(1) abrogates the requirement to give a corroboration direction in respect of an alleged accomplice (or, as in the appeals themselves, in the case of a complainant in a sexual offence) simply because a witness happens to fall into that category. However, it is within the judge's discretion whether it is nonetheless appropriate to give a warning in relation to the evidence of such a witness. It might be appropriate for a warning

[73] The approach of judges until the end of the 1970s was that a co-accused should be sentenced before giving evidence. Lord Goddard CJ, giving judgment in *R v Payne* [1950] 1 All ER 102, stated that co-accused should generally be sentenced together but 'what I have said does not apply to the exceptional case where a man who pleads guilty is going to be called as a witness, in those circumstances it is right that he be sentenced there and then so that there can be no suspicion that his evidence is coloured by the fact that he hopes to get a lighter sentence'. However, Boreham J, giving the judgment of the Court of Appeal in *R v Weekes* (1980) 73 Cr App R 161, stated that an accused who gives evidence against his former co-accused should not be sentenced until after the co-accused's trial. He stated: 'Here are made manifest difficulties that arise when persons involved with others are sentenced before the full facts have been heard, particularly where a trial is to take place, as it was to take place here . . . There may be exceptions, but generally it is clearly right, it is clearly fairer and it is better for both the public and all the defendants concerned, that all are sentenced at the same time and at the same court whenever that is possible.' That the position remains as it was stated in the *Weekes* case was confirmed by the Court of Appeal in *R v Chan Wai-Keung* [1995] 1 WLR 251.

[74] (1995) 2 Cr App R 469.

to be given to a jury to exercise caution in relation to the unsupported evidence of an accomplice (or a complainant in respect of a sexual offence) where there was an evidential basis for the suggestion that the account given by the witness might be unreliable. An evidential basis would not, however, simply include matters put by counsel in cross-examination. Where a judge decides that it is appropriate to give a warning, there is no particular formula to be followed. It is for the judge to decide on the nature of the warning to be given.

1. Resident Informants

The same principles as regards timing of sentence and accomplice warning, etc will also be applicable in the case of a resident informant or resident source. Confusingly, the person traditionally referred to as a resident informant is called a 'protected witness' within the prison system and is often known, colloquially, as a 'supergrass'. To avoid confusion, the term resident informant will be used herein. **4.111**

The use of resident informants fell into abeyance, perhaps even disrepute, in the 1980s. Previously, resident informants had been used in trials of organized criminals and in Northern Ireland terrorist cases. However, almost insurmountable problems were encountered in relation to the preservation of credibility of the resident informant as a witness, and minimizing the risk of it being said that an individual had been induced by thought of rewards or advantage to give evidence which was unreliable or untrue. **4.112**

However, resident informants were used with real effect in some of the criminal trials arising from the MPS anti-corruption drive from the late 1990s onwards; the methodology now employed being better able to withstand challenge before a court. Given the potential importance of resident informant evidence in corruption cases where there has been a reactive investigation, the present section will focus on that relatively recently evolved 'new' approach to the handling and management of resident informants. **4.113**

There is no statutory basis for the handling of resident informants. Guidelines are, however, contained in Home Office Circular 9/1992. But, it should be noted immediately that the guidance contained therein, although useful in some respects, is generally regarded as being out of date and in need of rewriting. An attempt was made in 2001 to put together new guidance, although, at present, it is understood that the final form of any such rewrite is still being considered by the Home Office. **4.114**

There are, however, other sources of information providing detail of handling and management. The Court of Appeal considered some issues concerning resident informants in *R v Drury and ors*,[75] whilst the Court of Appeal Civil Division set **4.115**

[75] [2001] EWCA Crim 1753.

out details of the prison regime for prisoners categorized by the Prison Service as 'protected witnesses' in *Bloggs v The Secretary of State for the Home Department.*[76] In addition, in 1999, the Metropolitan Police evolved a pro forma methodology for handling and debriefing resident informants, which has subsequently been used by it and by other forces in, amongst others, corruption and organized crime prosecutions. However, it appears that, at present, the document setting out the methodology and approach has not been formally adopted by the Association of Chief Police Officers nor formally disseminated to all forces.[77]

4.116 On the basis of the Home Office Circular 9/1992, a resident informant is an active participant in a serious crime (or a number of serious crimes) who, after arrest or conviction, elects to identify, give evidence against, and provide intelligence about criminal associates involved in those or other offences.

4.117 A 'resident informant' or 'protected witness' has a formal status which is in the gift of the Prison Service (based on reports compiled by the police and the CPS). A resident informant will, therefore, be housed in a special unit within a prison.

4.118 Before any attempt is made to debrief or to take a draft witness statement from a potential resident informant, he or she should be 'cleansed' of his or her criminality; in other words, there should be an interview (in accordance with PACE 1984) as a suspect, during which all previous offending should be admitted. Those admissions will, in due course, be reflected in criminal charges sufficient to represent the level and extent of the admitted offending. It is, however, important that the potential resident informant is not misled: only two promises should be given. First, that any assistance will be brought to the attention of the sentencing judge (in a text) and that any duty of care issues arising will be properly addressed.

4.119 It is only after admissions have been obtained that the second stage, that of debriefing as a potential witness, should be undertaken. The Court of Appeal stated in *R v and Drury and ors* that the debrief process should be tape recorded (as Code E of PACE 1984 applies), even though it will usually consist of 'free recall', rather than questions and answers. Those conducting the debrief should, however, not be part of the investigative team.

4.120 Typically, the potential resident informant will have been remanded in custody by a court and will then be produced (by a production order) for the purposes of

[76] (2003) EWCA CIV 686.

[77] The new Serious and Organised Crime Agency (SOCA) will have a role to play in anti-corruption investigations in the context of organized crime, etc. The Serious Organised Crime and Police Act 2005 (SOCPA 2005) contains new specific powers in relation to assistance by offenders—in particular, ss 71 and 72 address immunities and undertakings, respectively, whilst ss 73 and 74 contain provisions concerning, in turn, reduction and review of sentence. Further, ss 82–92 deal with the protection of witnesses and other persons.

further interview and debrief. It should, therefore, be remembered that he or she will remain the prison governor's responsibility and that decisions regarding privileges and visits rest ultimately with the governor.

A resident informant who admits the full extent of his or her criminality and who remains credible to the extent that he or she gives evidence for the prosecution, can expect to receive a discount on sentence of about two-thirds (or, if not called, where the decision not to call is for reasons other than lack of credibility). **4.121**

Finally, given the twin difficulties of credibility and accusations of 'inducement', it will usually be the position that the prosecution does not seek to rely for its case on the evidence of an uncorroborated single resident informant. **4.122**

F. Proactive Investigations

1. Interception of Communications

Many jurisdictions rely heavily on the product of telephone interception to detect and, thereafter, to prosecute corruption cases. However, in the United Kingdom, there is significant restriction on the use to which such product can be put. **4.123**

Part I of the Regulation of Investigatory Powers Act 2000 (RIPA 2000) governs both interception and the acquisition of communications data. It repeals the Interception of Communications Act 1985, but replaces it with a very similar regime which, in broad terms, prohibits the interception of telecommunications, public and private (including e-mails, and items sent through the post), subject to certain exceptions. Also, and importantly, it creates a framework which has the effect of prohibiting the evidential use of the product of lawful public interception where the interception has been authorized (by warrant) by the Secretary of State. **4.124**

Section 1(1) of RIPA 2000 creates an offence for a person who intentionally and without lawful authority intercepts, within the United Kingdom, any communication which is in the course of transmission by means of a public postal service or a public telecommunication system. The definition of telecommunication system is wide and is such as to include mobile telephones and e-mail traffic.[78] **4.125**

Section 1(2) creates a further offence, that of intentionally and without lawful authority intercepting, within the United Kingdom, any communication in the course of its transmission by means of a private telecommunication system (otherwise than in circumstances in which such conduct is conducted by or on behalf of a person who has a right to control the operational use of the system.[79] **4.126**

[78] RIPA 2000, s 2(1). [79] ibid s 1 (6).

A private telecommunication system is one which is attached directly or indirectly (and whether or not for the purposes of the communication in question) to a public telecommunication system and where there is apparatus comprised in the system which is both located in the United Kingdom and used (with or without other apparatus) for making the attachment to the public communications system.[80]

4.127 With anti-corruption investigations in mind, an interception will not amount to an offence if it is done with 'lawful authority'.[81] Lawful authority may take one or a number of forms, which are set out in detail in sections 3 and 4 of RIPA 2000. Importantly, if an interception is one which is consented to by one party to the transmission (be it the sender or recipient), such an interception will be lawful, the product will be capable of being used evidentially, and will be specifically treated under the 2000 Act as amounting to directed surveillance. [82]

4.128 If an interception of a public telecommunication system is required and does not fall within the scope of lawful authority within sections 3 and 4, then a warrant will need to be sought from the Secretary of State. Such a warrant may only be sought in accordance with the criteria set out in section 5. The effect of section 5(2) and (3) is that the Secretary of State shall only issue an interception warrant if he believes that: (a) interception is necessary on one of four specified grounds (in the interests of national security, for the purpose of preventing or detecting serious crime, for the purpose of safeguarding the economic well-being of the UK, and for the purpose of giving effect to the provisions of any international mutual assistance agreement); and (ii) the conduct authorized by the warrant is proportionate to what is sought to be achieved by it. (It should be noted that 'serious crime' has a definition in section 81(3) and is discussed in detail below.)[83]

4.129 In the case of a warranted public interception, the restrictions should not be underestimated. In essence, no evidence may be adduced, questions asked, assertions or disclosures made in any legal proceedings which are likely to reveal the existence of, or absence of, an interception warrant.[84] Of such exceptions as there are,[85] the most important is that in relation to the power of a judge to order disclosure to himself, where he is satisfied that there are exceptional circumstances which make disclosure essential in the interests of justice.[86] Effectively, however, the restrictions contained within Part I of RIPA 2000 mean that it is the prosecutor's duty to secure fairness in a trial in respect of which there is, in the background, either extant interception product or where there has been an interception but the product (and the notes thereof) have been

[80] ibid s 2(1). [81] ibid s 1(1). [82] ibid s 48(4). [83] See 4.179 below.
[84] RIPA 2000, s 17(1) and (2). [85] ibid s 18. [86] ibid s 18(7), (6), and (8).

destroyed.[87] Looking at the combination of sections 17 and 18, only in circumstances where a prosecutor cannot fulfil his duty of securing fairness, should recourse be had to the trial judge, and even then only within the limitations imposed by sections 17 and 18.

2. Covert Methodologies

The nature of corrupt transactions, particularly those involving corrupt police or law enforcement officials, is such that traditionally reactive measures of investigation are fraught with difficulties. The offer or solicitation of a bribe or other advantage will often be face to face between two parties, with no independent witnesses. Where there is a willing witness, for instance a party who has been solicited by an official, he or she may be unreliable or tainted. There will be circumstances, as discussed above, where a reactive investigation, perhaps with the benefit of whistle-blower or protected witness evidence, is the only or most appropriate route. However, since the late 1990s the United Kingdom—and indeed many other jurisdictions—have recognized the value of an intelligence-led, proactive approach. Indeed, very often a proactive investigation, utilizing covert methodologies, will be the only way of progressing enquiries. Such an approach is, of course, entirely consistent with the growth of intelligence-led policing. **4.130**

Covert deployment may form the basis of intelligence gathering, obtaining evidence, or both, in the course of a corruption investigation. The proactive operation might involve information from a source, intelligence and/or evidence from the deployment of an undercover agent or participating source, and surveillance or telecommunications product. The investigation might comprise what is best described as a 'sting' operation or, more specifically, the increasingly useful intelligence-led integrity test (discussed in more detail at paras 4.211ff below). **4.131**

i. The regulation of covert investigative techniques and the impact of the ECHR

The deployment of covert, intrusive techniques is not new. However, since the early 1990s there has been an ever-increasing reliance on intelligence-led and proactive criminal investigations. The use of such techniques may well be the only way to investigate alleged corruption in any given instance, whether it is suspected on the part of a law enforcement officer with connections to organized crime or whether it is bribery within the commercial sphere. **4.132**

Traditionally the UK regulated the use of covert means by codes of practice and Home Office guidelines. The only real exception to that approach being the statutory regime for the restricted, intelligence-only use of public telecommunications interception product provided for by the Interception of Communications Act 1985 (IOCA 1985). However, with the passing of the **4.133**

[87] For disclosure to the prosecutor, see RIPA 2000, s 18(7)(a).

Human Rights Act 1998, which requires UK law to be compatible with the provisions of the European Convention on Human Rights (ECHR), a review has had to take place.

4.134 The intrusive nature of many forms of covert investigation have now to be considered in the light of Article 8 of the ECHR. Article 8 provides that:

(1) Everyone has the right to respect for his private and family life, his home and correspondence.
(2) There shall be no interference by a public authority with the exercise of this right, except such as is in accordance with the law and is necessary in a democratic society in the interests of national security, public safety or the economic well-being of the country, for the prevention of disorder or crime, for the protection of health or morals, or for the protection of the rights and freedoms of others.

4.135 Article 8, then, guarantees a right to respect for private and family life, home and correspondence. However, it is a qualified, not an absolute, right. Thus, interference with a right under Article 8(1) will amount to a breach of Article 8 unless the interference or intrusion in question can be justified on the basis of Article 8(2). From the provisions of Article 8(2), above, it can be seen that to be justified under that Article there must be a basis in law for the interference, the intrusion must have been 'necessary in a democratic society' and, in accordance with established ECHR jurisprudence, the intrusion must be proportionate. That is to say, the intrusion must correspond to a pressing social need and be proportionate to that need.[88]

4.136 In order to provide a basis in law for covert investigations which may involve interference with a subject's Article 8 rights, and to provide an authorization regime based on the key principles of necessity and proportionality, the Regulation of Investigatory Powers Act 2000 (RIPA 2000) was passed. RIPA 2000 establishes a permissive regime for a number of covert activities and powers. It has also been supplemented by subordinate legislation and by Codes of Practice. The Act provides criteria for authorization and levels of authorization which become more restrictive the greater the degree of intrusion required. RIPA 2000 consists of:

- Part I, Chapter 1: The Interception of Communications;
- Part I, Chapter 2: The Acquisition of Communications Related Data (for example telephone billing);
- Part II: The use and conduct of the 'covert human intelligence source' (ie informants, participating sources, and undercover agents), 'directed' surveillance and 'intrusive' surveillance (ie surveillance on or in residential premises and private motor vehicles);
- Part III: The power to seize electronic keys or passwords which will give access to encrypted information (ie computer material) (this part is not yet in force);

[88] See, eg, *Ludi v Switzerland* (1992) 15 EHRR 173.

- Part IV: A regime of scrutiny in relation to the use of covert powers (ie the Office of the Surveillance Commissioners); and
- Part V: Miscellaneous provisions.

Turning to the provisions of the ECHR and its jurisprudence in more detail, and with investigations into alleged corruption particularly in mind, the following should be noted: **4.137**

ii. 'In accordance with the law'

There must be a basis in domestic law or legislation which provides for the deployment of the covert technique. Such legislation must be accessible to those liable to be affected.[89] In addition, such legislation, including that which authorizes the activity liable to interfere with the Article 8(1) right, must have sufficient clarity so as to give a person an indication as to the circumstances and conditions in which covert methods by a public authority may be used.[90] **4.138**

The European Court of Human Rights (ECtHR) expects that there should be a regime of independent supervision of the use of covert, intrusive powers.[91] As to the process of authorization, the more independent the authorizing or reviewing individual/body is, the more likely it is that the ECtHR will regard the authorizing and reviewing regime to be in compliance with the requirements of Article 8(2). Indeed, in *Klass v Germany*[92] the ECtHR noted that judicial control of the authorization procedure provided 'the best guarantees of independence, impartiality and a proper procedure'. The use by the United Kingdom of domestic commissioners and tribunals (first provided for under IOCA 1985 and now found in both the Police Act 1997[93] and in RIPA 2000) is capable of satisfying the demands of Article 8.[94] **4.139**

iii. 'Necessary in a democratic society'

The interference with an individual's Article 8(1) rights must fulfil a pressing social need, be in pursuit of one of the aims set out in Article 8(2) and any deployment must be only that which is necessary to achieve the required goal, for example the detection of the particular crime. In addition, safeguards must be in place to prevent abuse by intrusive techniques, and remedies must be available in the event of such abuse. **4.140**

iv. Proportionality

The interference must be proportionate to what is sought to be achieved by it. Thus, for example, a deployment of a listening device in a target's bedroom may require much greater justification than a deployment in a living room. **4.141**

[89] eg *Silver v UK* (1983) 5 EHRR 347.
[90] *Kopp v Switzerland* (1983) 27 EHRR 91.
[91] *Malone v UK* (1984) 7 EHRR 14.
[92] (1978) 2 EHRR 214.
[93] See 4.187ff below.
[94] *Esbester v UK* (1994) 18 EHRR 72.

4.142 In considering whether a covert technique or deployment is indeed proportionate to the legitimate aim which is being pursued, consideration should be given to the following:*

(1) Have sufficient, relevant reasons been set out in support of the deployment?
(2) Could the same aim have been achieved by use of a less intrusive method?
(3) Did the authorizing/decision-making process as to the deployment take place in a way which was procedurally fair?
(4) Do adequate safeguards exist to prevent abuse?
(5) Does the interference in question destroy the very essence of the Article 8(1) right?

v. The effect of a breach of Article 8 during a proactive anti-corruption investigation

4.143 With the incorporation of the ECHR into domestic law, a breach of Article 8(1) will enable a defendant to argue that:

(1) The use by the prosecution of evidence that was obtained in breach of an Article 8(1) right, in circumstances where the breach cannot be justified under Article 8(2), has the effect of denying the defendant his right to a fair trial under Article 6 and, therefore, the proceedings in question should be stayed; or alternatively
(2) evidence obtained as a result of an unjustified Article 8(1) breach should be excluded under section 78 of the Police and Criminal Evidence Act 1984.[95]

4.144 However, in relation to either or both of the above arguments, the test is the same: what is the effect of the admission of the evidence on the fairness of the proceedings as a whole?[96] The above approach by the domestic courts has the effect of mirroring that adopted by the ECtHR, which has made it clear on a number of occasions that it is not concerned with questions of admissibility of particular evidence but rather on whether the proceedings as a whole are fair.[97]

4.145 One caveat to the above, in relation to UK criminal courts, is that heed must be had to the decision of the House of Lords in relation to entrapment, in the case of *R v Loosely; Attorney-General's Reference (No 3 of 2000)*.[98] There, it can be seen that it will be open to a court to stay proceedings as an abuse of process in circumstances where there has been a breach of an Article 8(1) right and it

* We are grateful to Kingsley Hyland of CPS for this distillation of relevant considerations.

[95] See the House of Lords decision in *R v Khan* [1997] AC 558, where the House of Lords stated that, in considering whether to exercise the discretion under PACE 1984, S 78 a judge should have regard to breaches of ECHR rights.

[96] See support for this by the Court of Appeal in *R v Bailey, Brewin and Gangai*, 15 March 2001, unreported.

[97] See, eg, *Shenck v Switzerland* (1988) 13 EHRR 242.

[98] (2002) 1 Cr App R 29.

would be unfair for the defendant to be tried, not on the basis he cannot have a fair trial, but on the basis it would be unfair to try him at all as there has been a misuse of executive power which, if allowed to go unchecked, would be 'an affront to the public conscience'.[99]

3. Covert Human Intelligence Sources

Increasingly, information from sources provides the basis for investigations into alleged corruption. Regard must therefore be had to Part II of RIPA 2000 which provides a regulatory framework for the conduct and use of the covert human intelligence source (CHIS). A CHIS is defined in section 26(8) of RIPA 2000 as a person who: 4.146

> . . . establishes or maintains a personal or other relationship with a person for the covert purpose of facilitating the doing of anything . . . [in (b) or (c) below]
> (b) he covertly uses such a relationship to obtain information or to provide access to any information to another person, or
> (c) he covertly discloses information obtained by the use of such a relationship, or as a consequence of the existence of such a relationship.

It should be noted immediately that undercover agents, test purchasers, and participating sources will fall within this definition.

Any conduct and use of a CHIS must be authorized in accordance with section 29 of RIPA 2000. The effect of section 26(7) is to define 'conduct' as: 4.147

> Any conduct of a covert human intelligence source which establishes or maintains a personal or other relationship with a person for the covert purpose of facilitating (or is incidental to) the doing of anything that:
> Covertly uses such a relationship to obtain information or to provide access to any information to another person, or
> Covertly discloses information obtained by the use of such a relationship, or as a consequence of the existence of such a relationship.

The definition of 'use' of a CHIS is, meanwhile, defined in section 26(7)(b) as: 'inducing, asking or assisting a person to engage in the conduct of such a source, or to obtain information by means of the conduct of such a source'. A key element of the above definitions is, of course, the notion of 'covert'. Covert is defined in section 26(9). It is, in effect, given its usual dictionary meaning. Thus, for example, a relationship is used covertly, for the purposes of the deployment of a CHIS, if it is used in a manner calculated to ensure that one of the parties to the relationship is unaware of the use in question.[100] 4.148

When RIPA 2000 was in Bill form, there was much discussion and concern that a large number of individuals might fall within the definition of a 'CHIS' even 4.149

[99] Lord Hoffman in *Loosely* and quoting Lord Steyn in *R v Lattif* [1996] 1 WLR 104, 112.
[100] See RIPA 2000, s 26(9)(c).

though they would not previously have been thought of as 'informants'. It is clear, however, that a restrictive definition should be applied. The 2000 Act is, after all, intended to ensure ECHR compliance; in particular, that any breach of Article 8(1) of the ECHR is justified and that deployment is authorized. The mischief which Article 8(2) seeks to prevent is an interference with an individual's Article 8(1) right by a public authority unless the qualifications contained within Article 8(2) are met. Thus, it must be that RIPA 2000 intends that an individual is a CHIS only if he or she is induced, asked, or assisted to engage in certain conduct (ie that referred to in section 26(7)(b)) and the relationship that is established or maintained is for a covert purpose. The 'good citizen' who simply reports a matter will not, therefore, fall within the definition. Although the provisions of the Act do not provide for it, it is, in fact, hard to envisage circumstances where an individual will be a CHIS if he or she had not been tasked by a public authority to obtain information, etc by establishing or maintaining a relationship for a covert purpose. That having been said, the view of the Chief Surveillance Commissioner[101] appears to be that tasking is not actually a requirement.

4.150 An application for the use and conduct of a CHIS should, unless urgent (see below), be in writing and should set out:

(1) the reasons why the authorization is necessary;
(2) the reasons why the authorization is considered proportionate to what it seeks to achieve;
(3) the purpose for which the source will be tasked or deployed;
(4) the nature of the specific operation or investigation being undertaken;
(5) the nature of what the source will be tasked to do;
(6) the level of authorization needed;
(7) details of the risks of collateral intrusion, how that has been minimized and why such intrusion as there is can be justified;
(8) in the event that confidential information is likely to be obtained, details of any such information likely to result from the authorization.[102]

4.151 Section 29(2) of RIPA 2000 sets out the criteria for authorization for the conduct or the use of a CHIS. A person shall not grant such an authorization unless he or she believes that:

> The authorisation is necessary on one or more of the following grounds:
>
> (a) In the interests of national security;
> (b) For the purpose of preventing or detecting crime or of preventing disorder;
> (c) In the interests of the economic well-being of the UK;
> (d) In the interests of public safety;

[101] See Office of the Surveillance Commissioner's website, http://www. surveillancecommissioners. gov.uk.
[102] CHIS Code of Practice, para 4.14.

(e) For the purpose of protecting public health;
(f) For the purpose of assessing or collecting any tax, duty, levy or other imposition, contribution or charge payable to a government department;
(g) For any other purpose specified by order of the Secretary of State.[103]

In addition, the authorizing officer must believe that the authorized conduct or use is proportionate to what is sought to be achieved by it and arrangements must exist in respect of the source which satisfy matters set out in section 29(5), namely provision for handling and controlling the CHIS, and for the keeping of records and maintaining confidentiality, etc. **4.152**

The Regulation of Investigatory Powers Act (Prescription of Offices, Ranks and Positions) Order 2000 requires that authorization for the conduct and use of a CHIS shall be granted by an officer of at least superintendent rank. However, in an urgent case, in the absence of an authorizing officer, authorization may be given by an officer of inspector rank. However, where the likely consequence of the conduct of the CHIS would be for a knowledge of confidential material to be acquired, then authorization must be given by the chief constable.[104] In the case of a police force, an authorization for conduct and use of a CHIS can only be granted on application from within the police force wishing to deploy the source.[105] **4.153**

Recalling that one of the mandatory referral criteria for the IPCC is serious corruption, it should be noted that the Independent Police Complaints Commission (Investigatory Powers) Order 2004 provides that an authorization for conduct or use of a CHIS may be given by an IPCC commissioner, regional director, director of investigations, or deputy director of investigations. In urgent cases, where none of the foregoing are available, an authorization may be granted by an IPCC senior investigator. **4.154**

Given the increasingly transnational nature of corruption investigations, and with foreign bribery investigation in mind, it should be noted that section 27(3) of RIPA 2000, in addressing the authorization of both the CHIS and of surveillance, provides that 'the conduct that may be authorised under this Part (ie Part II) includes conduct outside the United Kingdom'. In the case of the CHIS, the Code of Practice at para 1.6, provides that authorization may be given for the conduct and use of a source both within and outside the United Kingdom. However, it should be noted that in addition to a RIPA authorization, consideration will need to be given to authorizations and permissions in the country concerned. Such activity will usually need to be initiated via a formal letter of request.[106] **4.155**

Part II of RIPA 2000 provides detailed regulation in respect of the form, renewal, and duration of authorization, along with cancellation of the same. **4.156**

[103] RIPA 2000, 29(3).
[104] See CHIS Code of Practice, para 3.2.
[105] RIPA 2000, s 33(1).
[106] See also 2.151ff.

The detailed requirements are outside the scope of the present book, therefore reference should be made to the provisions of the Act itself.

4.157 Taking into account the nature of investigations into alleged corruption within a police force or law enforcement agency, it may well be necessary for anti-corruption investigators to deploy a participating source or undercover officer. However, RIPA 2000 makes no explicit provisions for such deployment. A 'participating source' may be defined as an individual who, with the approval of an authorizing officer, is given permission to participate in a crime which the principals have already intended to commit.

4.158 Despite the lack of provision in RIPA 2000, two passages in the CHIS Code of Practice do provide some basis for such a deployment. Paragraph 2.10 provides: 'in a very limited range of circumstances an authorisation under Part II may... render lawful, conduct which otherwise would be criminal, if it is incidental to conduct falling within section 26(8) of the 2000 Act which the source is authorised to undertake'. In addition, para 1.4 of the Code of Practice states that: 'neither Part II of the 2000 Act nor this Code of Practice is intended to affect the practices and procedures surrounding criminal participation of sources'. The Code of Practice, then, gives a basis, but it is not, of course, a basis in law as required by the ECHR jurisprudence. There is, however, common law authority for the use of a participator; in particular, *R v Birtles.*[107]

4.159 The common law, it might be said, is not a satisfactory basis in law in itself, since it is not readily accessible to persons likely to be affected and lacks the clarity which Strasbourg demands. A further difficulty is that, because RIPA 2000 makes no explicit provisions for the participator, it does not address the proportionality of the participation. It does not, for instance, confine participation to certain types of crime of particular gravamen. In addition, it does not provide for any higher level of authorization in the case of participation. Indeed, there is less provision following the introduction of RIPA 2000, than existed when participation simply purported to be regulated by guidelines. Home Office Circular 97/1969 gave more detailed guidance and required that the role played by the participator was only a peripheral one when compared to that of the principal. The Circular also provided for authorization to be granted at assistant chief constable level. Indeed, in a period just prior to the passing of the 2000 Act, the Association of Chief Police Officers and what was then HM Customs and Excise agreed a Code of Practice on the use of sources which, again, was more stringent as to participation than RIPA 2000. It, too, provided for authorization at assistant chief constable level.

[107] [1969] 1 WLR 1074, which set out two guidelines or principles: the offence for which participation is authorized must be 'already laid on' and the participator must not be used to entrap unlawfully (in other words, must not be used as an *agent provocateur*).

Those involved in anti-corruption investigations and prosecutions must, therefore, note that an Article 8 challenge may be mounted in relation to the deployment of a participating source. Indeed, the difficulties have been, in part, addressed within the Manual of Minimum Standards in the Use of Covert Human Intelligence Sources. That document, which does not give a 'basis in law' for ECHR purposes, provides that the role to be undertaken by a participator must be a minor one, that the offences under investigation must amount to serious crime (as defined in section 81(3) of RIPA 2000) and must be authorized by an officer of at least assistant chief constable rank. **4.160**

4. Surveillance

Surveillance is defined in section 48(2) of RIPA 2000 as including: **4.161**

(a) monitoring, observing or listening to persons, their movements, their conversations or their other activities or communications;
(b) recording anything monitored, recorded or listened to in the course of surveillance; and
(c) surveillance by or with the assistance of a surveillance device.

Section 48(3), meanwhile, goes on to provide that surveillance *does not* include: **4.162**

(a) Any conduct of a CHIS for obtaining or recording (whether or not using a surveillance device) any information which is disclosed in the presence of the source;
(b) The use of a CHIS for so obtaining or recording information; or
(c) Any such entry on, or interference with, property or wireless telegraphy as would be unlawful unless authorised under (i) section 5 of the Intelligence Services Act 1994 or (ii) Part III of the Police Act 1997.

The effect of section 48(3)(c) is that a covert deployment by a law enforcement agency involving an interference with real or personal property will require an authorization under Part III of the Police Act 1997 in the event that the person entitled to give permission in relation to the property has not consented to the interference. Similarly, in relation to activity by the security services, authorization of deployment in such circumstances will be under section 5 of the Intelligence Services Act 1994. **4.163**

Part II of RIPA 2000 creates two types of surveillance, directed and intrusive. Each will be of relevance to those conducting proactive investigations into allegations of corruption or misconduct in a public office. **4.164**

i. Directed surveillance

Section 26(2) of RIPA 2000 defines directed surveillance as being covert surveillance that is not intrusive and is undertaken for the purposes of a specific **4.165** investigation in such a manner as is likely to result in the obtaining of private information about a person, whether or not that person is specifically identified for the purposes of the investigation or operation in question.Intrusive surveillance is addressed, in detail, below; however, for present purposes, intrusive surveillance is covert surveillance carried out in relation to anything taking place on any residential premises or in any private vehicle.[108]

4.166 'Private information' for the purposes of directed surveillance is addressed in section 26(10) which provides that, in relation to a person, private information includes any information relating to his private or family life. In addition, para 4.3 of the Surveillance Code of Practice provides that the notion of private or family life should be interpreted broadly to include an individual's private or personal relationships with others. Such a broad definition is in line with ECtHR case law which has never favoured a restrictive interpretation.[109]

4.167 In the event of an immediate response to events or circumstances, surveillance will not amount to directed surveillance (and hence will not require an authorization) where it would not have been reasonably practicable for an authorization to have been sought.[110] It should also be noted that overt CCTV surveillance will not amount to directed surveillance unless, for example, CCTV cameras are being used in a covert manner; for instance, targeting a particular individual or group of individuals on the basis of intelligence or information received rather than by immediate response.

4.168 Conduct which amounts to directed surveillance will be lawful, for all purposes, provided that an authorization has been granted and that the surveillance activity in question is in accordance with that authorisation.[111] Authorization, as in the case of the CHIS, may be given for activities taking place in the United Kingdom or by and on behalf of UK investigators in foreign states.[112]

4.169 The criteria for authorization of directed surveillance mirrors in large part that for the CHIS. However, the usual authorization duration for directed surveillance (and indeed for surveillance activity generally) is three months, as opposed to twelve months for the CHIS. An authorizing officer or official shall not grant authorization for directed surveillance unless he or she believes that:[113]

(1) the authorization is necessary on one of the following grounds:
   (a) in the interests of national security;
   (b) for the purpose of preventing or detecting crime or of preventing disorder;
   (c) in the interests of the economic well-being of the United Kingdom;

[108] RIPA 2000, s 26(3).
[109] See, eg, *PG and JH v UK* [2002] Crim LR 308; *Neimitz v Germany* (1992) 16 EHRR 97; and *Halford v UK* (1997) 24 EHRR 523.
[110] RIPA 2000, s 26(2)(c).
[111] ibid s 27(1).
[112] ibid s 27(3).
[113] ibid s 28(2) and (3).

(d) in the interests of public safety;
(e) for the purpose of protecting the public health;
(f) for the purpose of assessing or collecting any tax, duty, levy, or other imposition, contribution, or charge payable to a government department;
(g) for any other purpose specified by order of the Secretary of State; and

(2) the authorized surveillance is proportionate to what is sought to be achieved by carrying it out.[114]

As in the case of the CHIS, the subordinate legislation[115] requires that the authorizing officer be of superintendent rank or equivalent. In urgent cases, again as with the CHIS, an authorization can be given by an inspector where no superintendent is available. However, where the likely consequence of the surveillance activity would be for any person to acquire knowledge of confidential material, authorization must be given by the chief constable. **4.170**

Urgent authorizations may be given and will last for 72 hours. If the authorizing officer is at superintendent level or above the authorization may be given orally. If at inspector rank, the authorization, even for an urgent case, must be given in writing. **4.171**

ii. Intrusive surveillance

Intrusive surveillance is covert surveillance carried out in relation to anything taking place on any residential premises or in any private motor vehicle, which involves the presence of an individual on the premises or in the vehicle, or is carried out by means of a surveillance device.[116] **4.172**

'Residential premises' for the purposes of section 26(3) refers to a premises or any part of a premises that is occupied or used, even if temporarily, for residential purposes, including those parts of hotel and prison accommodation used for residence. Common areas, such as landings, staircases, and corridors, are not, however, included.[117] From this, it will be seen that if a device is to be deployed in a police or prison cell, it will require an intrusive surveillance authorization. **4.173**

A private vehicle is one used primarily for private purposes;[118] it does not include a taxi which is plying for hire or has been hired.[119] The use of the word 'in' any private motor vehicle, will include a device being located on, under or attached to the vehicle.[120] In relation to tracking devices, in the event that the device only provides information about the location of the vehicle, the surveillance is specifically deemed to be directed and not intrusive.[121] **4.174**

[114] ibid s 28(2).
[115] The Regulation of Investigatory Powers (Prescription of Offices, Ranks and Positions) Order 2000.
[116] RIPA 2000, s 26(3).
[117] See ibid s 48(1) and (7)(b).
[118] ibid s 48(1).
[119] ibid s 48(7)(a).
[120] ibid s 26(11).
[121] ibid s 26(4).

4.175 Surveillance which is carried out by means of a surveillance device in relation to anything taking place on any residential premises or in any private vehicle without the device being present on the premises or vehicle will not be intrusive, unless the device is such that it consistently provides information of the same quality and detail that might be expected from a device actually present on the premises or in the vehicle.[122] To assist further, paragraph 5.3 of the Covert Surveillance Code of Practice indicates that an external observation post, providing only limited view and no audio, will not be considered by the Surveillance Commissioners to be intrusive.

4.176 In relation to the authorization regime, the greater *intrusion* of intrusive surveillance has dictated a much higher level of authorizing officer. The level of authorization for intrusive surveillance mirrors that for property interference under the Police Act 1997, discussed in more detail below. Section 32(1) of RIPA 2000 provides that an authorization for intrusive surveillance may only be granted by the Secretary of State or by a senior authorizing officer. 'Senior authorising officer' is defined in section 32(6) as being, for a police force, a chief constable. However, in an urgent case, an authorization may be granted by an officer of assistant chief constable rank or above.

4.177 Section 27(1) provides that conduct amounting to intrusive surveillance shall be lawful for all purposes if an authorization conferring an entitlement to engage in such conduct is conferred and that the conduct that takes place is in accordance with that authorization. The authorizing officer must believe, by virtue of section 32(2) and (3), that the authorization is necessary:

(1) in the interests of national security;
(2) for the purpose of preventing or detecting serious crime; or
(3) in the interests of the economic well-being of the United Kingdom.

4.178 Further, the authorized surveillance must be believed to be proportionate to what is sought to be achieved by carrying it out. In considering whether authorization is necessary and proportionate, the authorizing officer must take into account, *inter alia*, the question of whether the information which it is thought necessary to obtain by the authorized conduct could reasonably be obtained by other means.[123]

4.179 A 'serious crime' (see point (2) of the above list), for the purposes of RIPA 2000, is defined in section 81(3) as an offence for which a person aged 21 years or over, with no previous convictions, could reasonably be expected to receive a sentence of three years' imprisonment or more; or where the alleged conduct involves the use of violence, results in substantial financial gain, or is conducted by a large number of persons in pursuit of a common purpose.

[122] RIPA 2000, s 26(5). [123] ibid s 32(4).

An authorization for intrusive surveillance must be in writing, unless the case is urgent.[124] An urgent authorization will last for up to 72 hours; otherwise an authorization will last for up to three months. Renewal is available thereafter. The senior authorizing officer may only grant authorization in respect of an application made by a member of his or her own force.[125] Where an application for intrusive surveillance relates to residential premises, the premises in question must be in the 'area of operation' of the force making the application. **4.180**

A single authorization may, by virtue of section 33(5), combine an application for intrusive or directed surveillance under Part II of RIPA 2000 and an application for property interference under Part III of the Police Act 1997. However, the provisions and criteria of each will apply and need to be considered separately. **4.181**

Given the more intrusive nature of intrusive surveillance, and having regard to the view of the ECtHR that there should be judicial oversight, prior approval of a Surveillance Commissioner is required for an intrusive surveillance authorization to take effect (save in the case of an urgent authorization, see below). The senior authorizing officer must give written notice to a Surveillance Commissioner when a police, Customs, or IPCC authorization has been granted, renewed, or cancelled.[126] The notice must state one of two things: either that the approval of a Surveillance Commissioner is required before the authorization is able to take effect, or that the case is an urgent one.[127] If the matter is an urgent one, the grounds for that belief must be set out to the Surveillance Commissioner. Having received the notice, the Surveillance Commissioner must, as soon as practicable, consider the authorization and approve it or reject it. **4.182**

An authorization will not take effect until approval by a Surveillance Commissioner has been given and written notice of that approval has been provided to the authorizing officer.[128] The notice requirements under section 35 may, however, be transmitted electronically.[129] If the notice states that it is an urgent one, then the authorization will be effective from the time it was granted by the senior authorizing officer.[130] **4.183**

If a Surveillance Commissioner is satisfied that, at the time that the authorization was granted or renewed, there were no reasonable grounds for believing that section 32(2) criteria were fulfilled, he may quash the authorization, a decision which will be effective from the time of the authorization or from the time of the renewal (whichever is applicable).[131] Similarly where a Surveillance Commissioner is satisfied that, at any time while an authorization is extant, there are no longer any reasonable grounds for believing that the section 32(2) **4.184**

[124] ibid s 43(1).
[125] ibid s 33(3).
[126] ibid s 35(1).
[127] ibid s 35(3).
[128] ibid s 36(2).
[129] ibid s 35(9).
[130] ibid s 36(3)
[131] ibid s 37(2).

criteria are fulfilled, he may cancel the authorization. Such cancellation will take effect from the time at which it appears to the Surveillance Commissioner that the criteria ceased to be satisfied.[132]

4.185 If an urgent application has resulted in either a grant or a renewal by a senior authorizing officer, the Surveillance Commissioner may quash the authorization if he is not satisfied that, at the time of the grant or renewal as the case may be, there were reasonable grounds for believing that the case was an urgent one.[133]

4.186 In the event that a Surveillance Commissioner refuses to approve an intrusive surveillance authorization, or quashes or cancels an authorization, a senior authorizing officer may appeal to the Chief Surveillance Commissioner.[134] An appeal must be made within seven days from the day on which the decision appealed against was reported to the senior authorizing officer.[135] In the event that the Chief Surveillance Commissioner is satisfied that there were reasonable grounds for believing that the criteria in section 32(2) were fulfilled and if he is not satisfied that the authorization is not one in which the urgent application provisions have been abused, then the appeal must be allowed. Similarly, if there is an appeal against a decision to quash or cancel, the Chief Surveillance Commissioner may either reverse the decision of the Surveillance Commissioner or modify that decision (in a case where, for instance, he believes the decision should have been cancelled, but from a different time from that at which it was cancelled by the Surveillance Commissioner).

iii. Interference with Property (Part III, Police Act 1997)

4.187 In the event that, during the course of an investigation into corruption or misconduct in a public office, the investigator seeks to deploy any surveillance device in such a way as will involve an interference with property (real or personal) he must obtain an authorization under Part III of the Police Act 1997. The provisions of Part III were brought in as a result of the judgment of the House of Lords in *R v Khan*.[136]

4.188 Section 92 of the Police Act 1997 provides that no entry on or interference with property or with wireless telegraphy shall be lawful unless authorized under the Act. In addition, paragraph 6.4 of the Covert Surveillance Code of Practice provides that 'authorisations under the 1997 Act may not be necessary where the public authority is acting with the consent of a person able to give permission in respect of relevant property, although consideration should still be given to the need to obtain an authorisation under Part II of the 2000 Act'.

4.189 As already indicated, interference with property as envisaged in Part III of the Police Act 1997 relates to both real and personal property. A gloss has, however,

[132] RIPA 2000, s 37(3). [133] ibid s 37(4). [134] ibid s 38(1).
[135] ibid s 38(3). [136] [1997] AC 558.

been put on the legislation by guidance issued from the Office of the Surveillance Commissioners. This is obtainable from the Office's website.[137] That guidance indicates, *inter alia*, that a Part III authorization will not be required for entry into an area open to the public, such as in shops, public houses, restaurants, or hotel or apartment common areas and to other premises where, with an implied consent from the occupier, the public are allowed access. In essence, the mere fact that an entry into a restaurant or other establishment is for a covert purpose will not vitiate the implied consent.

The grounds for authorization for property interference are contained within section 93, which provides that: **4.190**

> (1) Where subsection (2) applies, an authorising officer may authorise—
> (a) the taking of such action, in respect of such property in the relevant area, as he may specify, or
> (b) the taking of such action in the relevant area as he may specify, in respect of wireless telegraphy.
>
> (2) This subsection applies where the authorising officer believes—
> (a) that it is necessary for the actions specified to be taken on the ground that it is likely to be of substantial value in the prevention or detection of serious crime, and
> (b) that what the action seeks to achieve cannot reasonably be achieved by other means.

Thus, the criteria of both necessity and proportionality need to be satisfied.

The definition of 'serious crime' for the purposes of Part III of the Police Act 1997 is identical to that in section 81(3) of RIPA 2000. Thus, conduct which constitutes one or more offences should only be regarded as serious crime if: **4.191**

(1) it involves the use of violence, or results in substantial financial gain, or it is conducted by a large number of persons in pursuit of a common purpose; or
(2) the offence, or one of the offences, is an offence for which a person who has attained the age of 21 years and has no previous convictions could reasonably be expected to be sentenced to imprisonment for a term of three years or more.

Just as for intrusive surveillance, the level of authorization within the police is at chief constable level. However, where it is not reasonably practicable to obtain the authorization from the authorizing officer, a designated deputy[138] may grant the authorization. In relation to the IPCC, the Independent Police Complaints Commission (Investigatory Powers) Order 2004 provides that the authorizing officers are the chair and deputy chair. In an urgent case, and in the absence of both, an IPCC commissioner may act as authorizing officer. Again, this mirrors the regime for the IPCC in relation to intrusive surveillance. **4.192**

---

[137] OSC website address: http://www.surveillancecommissioners.gov.uk/.
[138] Police Act 1997, s 94(4).

4.193 Just as for RIPA 2000 surveillance authorizations, an authorization under Part III of the Police Act 1997 must be in writing[139] and may last for up to three months.[140] Oral authorization may be given in urgent cases and will have effect for 72 hours.[141] In the event that an urgent authorization is granted by a designated deputy, that must be in writing, but will, again, last for only 72 hours.[142] At any time before an authorization ceases, the authorizing officer may renew it for a period of up to three months, beginning on the day on which the authorization would otherwise cease to have effect.[143]

4.194 A Part III authorization is only effective in the geographical area of the police force in question.[144] However, in the case of a force or authority with national responsibility, the geographical area will be construed accordingly. An authorizing officer is only able to authorize property interference on application from a member of his own force.[145] But an authorizing officer is able to authorize maintenance and retrieval of equipment outside his own force area. However, any entry on to private property outside the authorizing officer's force area will require authorization from the authorizing officer from the force in whose area the private property (ie real property) is situated.

5. Entrapment

4.195 That a person who gives or accepts a bribe will have very limited scope to avoid criminal liability on the basis that he or she was only doing so to show up the wrongdoing of the other party has already been highlighted.[146] However, the position of the 'sting' operation by law enforcement agencies must now be examined. We have seen both the ECHR framework and the domestic regime as provided for in RIPA 2000; but what of the parameters of covert operations when used to detect and gather evidence in relation to corruption and misconduct in a public office?

4.196 A proactive anti-corruption investigation might take the form of, *inter alia*, the deployment of an undercover agent to be solicited for a bribe by a suspected corrupt official, might involve participating status being afforded to a whistleblower or informant from a corporation, or might consist of an intelligence-led integrity test.[147] Yet in any of these scenarios, investigators will have to ensure that they remain investigators, not creators, of crime.

4.197 The position in domestic law has been made relatively clear following the conjoined appeal to the House of Lords in *R v Looseley* and *Attorney-General's Reference (No 3 of 2000)*.[148] Although the facts of the two cases which made

[139] Police Act 1997, s 95(1). [140] ibid s 95(2)(b). [141] ibid s 95(2)(a).
[142] ibid s 95(1) and (2)(a). [143] ibid s 95(3). [144] ibid s 93(1).
[145] ibid s 93(3). [146] See 2.20 above. [147] See the discussion at 4.211ff below.
[148] [2002] Cr App R 29.

up the appeal were, in themselves, unremarkable, the House of Lords took the opportunity to examine in detail the law on entrapment and to formulate a test which is practical, secures the balance of fairness for all interests, and is 'ECHR-centric' in approach and formulation. Moreover, the criteria for covert operations set out by their Lordships provide a test which will be applicable across the range of covert investigations from the operation against a corrupt petty official or police officer suspected of taking small bribes, to a long-term infiltration into commercial corruption, fraud/money laundering or corrupt networks centred around organized crime.

The defendant in the *Looseley* case engaged with an undercover police officer, facilitated three drug deals, and faced an indictment containing three counts of being concerned in the supply of a controlled class A drug. Having been unsuccessful at trial in arguing that the proceedings should have been stayed as an abuse of process or, alternatively, that the evidence of the undercover officer should have been excluded under section 78 of PACE 1984, the defendant pleaded guilty. An appeal against conviction on the basis of the trial judge's rulings on the legal argument was dismissed. The matter, thereafter, went to the House of Lords. **4.198**

The facts of the case which form the basis of *Attorney-General's Reference (No 3 of 2000)* were, similarly, related to an investigation concerning comparatively low-level drug dealing. In essence, the undercover officers in that case went too far in their conversations with the defendant. Accordingly, the trial judge acceded to a defence application to stay proceedings as an abuse of process. The stay was subsequently lifted in order that the prosecution could offer no evidence. **4.199**

Following that acquittal, a reference was taken by the Attorney-General to the Court of Appeal as to whether the exclusionary discretion under section 78 of PACE 1984 or the inherent jurisdiction of the court to stay proceedings as an abuse of process had been changed or modified by Article 6 of the ECHR and the incorporation into domestic law of the ECHR itself. The Court of Appeal answered that question in the negative and, again, the matter came before the House of Lords. **4.200**

Their Lordships confirmed that *R v Sang*[149] is still good law and that entrapment is not a substantive defence in English law. The basis for such a view being that even a defendant who is entrapped to commit an offence still has the necessary mental element and/or, of course, has committed the *actus reus* of the offence. **4.201**

If agents of the state, such as police officers, behave in an unacceptable and improper manner by creating crime, then the defendant will be excused, not because he is less culpable (although he may be) but because the police have **4.202**

[149] [1980] AC 402.

behaved improperly.[150] As Lord Steyn had previously noted in *R v Latif*,[151] to prosecute in such circumstances 'would be an affront to the public conscience'.

4.203 Thus, the House of Lords concluded, where a defendant has been entrapped, a stay is the appropriate remedy, not because the defendant is not guilty of the offence or because he could not receive a fair trial, but because it would be unfair to try him at all. Conversely, such an argument is not a section 78 admissibility argument: it is not being said that the admission of certain evidence renders the trial unfair; what is really being said is that there should be no trial at all.

4.204 However, the House of Lords stated in the *Looseley* case that there will be occasions when it is still appropriate for there to be a section 78 argument. But, such occasions will be limited to those set out by Potter LJ in *R v Shannon*[152] (which was quoted by Lord Hoffman and Lord Hutton in *Looseley*):

> . . . If there is good reason to question the credibility of evidence given by an agent provocateur, or which casts doubt on the reliability of other evidence procured or resulting from his actions, and that question is not capable of being properly or fairly resolved in the course of the proceedings from the available, admissible and 'untainted' evidence, then the judge may readily conclude that such evidence should be excluded.

4.205 What then amounts to 'entrapment'? The key question is as to whether the agent of the state, such as the undercover operative, has provided an opportunity to the target to commit a crime or has instigated or incited the target to commit an offence that he would not have otherwise committed. The opportunity in question must, in the words of Lord Hoffman,[153] be an 'unexceptional opportunity' and no more. As to what amounts to an unexceptional opportunity, the question will be whether the undercover agent, in his conduct, has done no more then might have been expected from someone in the role he was assuming. Thus, there will be something of a sliding scale. An undercover agent playing the role of a major organized criminal in, for instance, a police corruption investigation will most probably be able to use, in the words of the House of Lords,[154] 'a degree of persistence' in his dealings with major high-level targets. Conversely, an undercover agent assuming the role of a member of the public in relation to the investigation of a Customs officer or border guard suspected of soliciting small bribes will be expected to speak and react as a member of the public would in the circumstances.

4.206 Before the decision in the *Looseley* case, the principal considerations in any entrapment argument were the criteria set out by the Court of Appeal in *R v Smurthwaite; R v Gill*.[155] Those criteria included the question of whether

[150] Per Lord Nicholls (2002) Cr App R 29, 367.
[151] [1996] 1 WLR 104, 112.
[152] [2002] CLR 100 1.
[153] [2002] Cr App R 29, 381.
[154] ibid 381.
[155] [1994] 1 All ER 898.

the conduct of the undercover agent was active or passive. The active/passive distinction was disapproved by the House of Lords in *Looseley* as being unhelpful. Recognizing a sliding scale of what amounts to acceptable behaviour by an investigator working undercover, depending on the nature of the operation and the targets, Lord Hoffman stated that 'a good deal of active behaviour in the course of an authorised operation may therefore be acceptable without crossing the boundary between causing the offence to be committed and providing an opportunity to commit it.'[156]

However, in assessing whether an acceptable opportunity, but nothing more, has been given, there are also other considerations to be had. The more difficult an offence is to detect by conventional reactive means, the more likely that the use of a proactive covert methodology will be justified. Further, in assessing the nature of inducements given by the undercover agent, regard will have to be had to the circumstances of the defendant and, in particular, to whether the defendant is vulnerable. Again, the stronger the position of the defendant, the more likely it is that the inducement made will be regarded as acceptable. However, the predisposition of a target to offend will not be a proper basis for a covert operation and will not render acceptable that which would be unacceptable in the case of a person without previous convictions. As Lord Hoffman noted, 'since the English doctrine assumes the defendant's guilt and is concerned with the standards of behaviour for the law enforcement officers, predisposition is irrelevant to whether a stay should be granted or not'.[157] **4.207**

Given that one of the rationales for the test formulated in the *Looseley* case is what has been described[158] as a preventive or protective one (in other words a jurisdiction to prevent the abuse of executive power), and that another is the integrity principle (that is to say, a prosecution based on entrapment should be halted in order to protect the integrity of the criminal justice system), the court must be satisfied that the investigation was undertaken in good faith. As Lord Nicholls noted,[159] one way that good faith may be established is by the investigators having reasonable grounds for suspicion before the covert operation is launched. Suspicion may be as to an individual or group of individuals, but it may also be as to a location. Suspicion as to location will suffice. It might be that there is scope for future argument to the effect that, in circumstances where there is suspicion as to location, but not as to individuals, then for an investigation to be proportionate there should be intermediate steps taken (for example surveillance) to identify a target or group of targets before the more intrusive measure of introducing undercover agents is adopted. However, for the time being and on the basis of the speeches in the *Looseley* case, suspicion as to location is clearly **4.208**

156 [2002] Cr App R 29, 381.
157 [2002] Cr App R 29, 380.
158 See Andrew Ashworth (2002) in *Criminal Law Review* 2002 161.
159 *R v Looseley* [2002] Cr App R 29, 369.

enough. Nonetheless, the days of speculative, so-called 'random virtue', operations are now at an end. Not only must there be reasonable suspicion for covert activity, the deployment itself must be properly supervised with appropriate authorizations for the activities involved, in compliance with relevant Codes of Practice and with proper tasking and debriefing.

4.209 In the light of the above, what is the test that can be inferred, to judge the acceptability of a proactive operation? As encapsulated by Andrew Ashworth,[160] that test should now be seen as follows:

> There is no entrapment if:
> (i) The investigators have reasonable grounds to suspect the target or targets of involvement in a certain kind of offence, or at least the investigators have reasonable grounds to suspect people frequenting a particular location to be thus involved; and
> (ii) The investigators are duly authorised to carry out the operation in compliance with appropriate Codes of Practice etc; and
> (iii) The undercover agent (agents) do no more than provide the target or targets with an unexceptional opportunity to commit the offence.

Conversely, if the investigators do not have reasonable grounds for suspicion, or, although having reasonable grounds, go further than simply providing an exceptional opportunity, the conduct is likely to be viewed as entrapment and a stay of criminal proceedings will be likely.

4.210 Increasingly, private individuals and organizations undertake sting operations; an obvious example would be that of an investigative journalist carrying out an undercover assignment for a newspaper. In such circumstances, after a product has been obtained, material may be passed on to the police who may wish to make evidential use of it in criminal proceedings. It will be recalled, in relation to powers under RIPA 2000, that an authorization under the 2000 Act can only be granted by a designated person employed by a prescribed public authority. However, it is submitted that the test that the court should apply if an abuse or section 78 (PACE 1984) argument arises in the case of material obtained by, for instance, a journalistic sting, will be the same as for an operation carried out by a law enforcement agency. The court is a public authority for the purposes of section 6 of the Humans Rights Act 1998 and must, therefore, act compatibly with an individual's ECHR rights, even in circumstances where proceedings are taking place, ostensibly, between two private parties. Moreover, a public authority has a positive obligation, derived from Article 1 of the ECHR, to ensure that ECHR rights are properly and effectively protected. That obligation will fall to a court whether or not the rights have been infringed by a private organization or a public authority. In all the circumstances, therefore, it is difficult to see that a court could apply a different, or less demanding, test.

[160] See Ashworth (n 158 above) 161.

6. Integrity Testing

Integrity tests are becoming an increasingly used investigative tool in anti-corruption investigations. An integrity test is, however, simply one form of proactive operation and the principles on entrapment, as set out above, apply to such a test as to any other form of covert deployment. **4.211**

Integrity testing may be divided into two types. The first type is sometimes called 'random virtue' testing and is used by institutions in the United Kingdom and elsewhere to highlight the presence of issues or abuses which may not amount to criminal offences but which are of corporate concern. The second type is 'intelligence-led' tests which arise when, as the name suggests, there is information or intelligence that a particular individual or group of individuals is committing criminal or serious disciplinary offences. In anti-corruption initiatives, such tests have proved particularly valuable in cases of suspected corrupt behaviour by police officers or other public servants. A law enforcement agency may, however, be in a position to use the same techniques in responding to an allegation of corruption within the private sector. **4.212**

It should be said at once that, as an intelligence-led integrity test will inevitably involve activities which will require authorization under RIPA 2000, such authorization is not capable of being granted in order to detect disciplinary misconduct. There will need to be grounds to suspect criminal activity, therefore. (Although if, after deployment, the product obtained amounts only to a disciplinary offence, the product may, of course, be used, subject to any arguments on admissibility, in consequent disciplinary proceedings.) **4.213**

An integrity test, will involve a potential breach under Article 8 of the ECHR. There must therefore be a basis in law for any activity, as well as necessity and proportionality. In relation to an intelligence-led integrity test (our principal concern) the test, as a covert investigation, should satisfy the following criteria: **4.214**

(1) there is reliable intelligence or information;
(2) the scenario of the test seeks to replicate as closely as possible the nature of the intelligence;
(3) the test is truly a test, in the sense that it is capable of being passed or failed;
(4) there should be a complete audit trail;
(5) at all stages of the test, actions undertaken must be necessary and proportionate—thus, it might be decided that an integrity test should only be run as a final option, once other means of investigation have been discounted;
(6) the test should require the target to take action or respond in a way with which he or she is familiar through training and through the normal course of their duties;

(7) the involvement of third parties and the risk of collateral intrusion should be kept to a minimum;
(8) those responsible for the test should have in mind that an evidential product might result—therefore presentational issue for court, along with disclosure implications, should be addressed at each stage of planning and implementation;
(9) each action carried out by the investigative team should be capable of justification on established domestic and ECHR principles and it should also be remembered by them that courts do not like overly 'manufactured' incidents and that any test, therefore, should only run for as long as is necessary and should present a scenario which is both feasible and credible.

G. Extradition

4.215 Throughout the present work, we have had occasion to emphasize the increasingly transnational nature of corruption and the implications that this brings for prosecutors and investigators, particularly with regard to international cooperation. Mutual legal assistance, for restraint/confiscation requests and generally, has already been examined (in paras 2.147ff above); and so, for completeness, we now turn to extradition.

4.216 Extradition is the *sui generis* procedure for returning a person located in one country to another for the purpose of criminal proceedings or sanction. Those criminal proceedings or sanctions may take the form of a criminal trial, sentence following conviction, or the implementation of sentence already imposed. In the United Kingdom, the Extradition Act 2003 ('the 2003 Act') came into force on 1 January 2004[161] and the present discussion will, therefore, confine itself to the extradition scheme dealt with by its provisions.

4.217 Export extradition requests (ie the request for the extradition of a person from the United Kingdom) received by the Secretary of State (Home Secretary) before 1 January 2004 will continue to be subject to the Extradition Act 1989, as will any request revived post-extradition in relation to a person extradited either to or from the United Kingdom under the provisions of the 1989 Act. As to import extradition requests (that is a request by the United Kingdom to extradite a person to the United Kingdom) made before 1 January 2004, these will be made in accordance with the relevant treaty or convention then existing between the United Kingdom and the requested state.

[161] Commencement by virtue of the Extradition Act 2003 (Commencement and Savings) Order 2003, para 2.

4.218 The 2003 Act is divided into five parts. **Part 1** relates to extradition to those EU countries operating the European Arrest Warrant. They are designated as 'Category 1' Territories and comprise the 25 member states of the EU.[162]

Austria	Germany	Malta	United Kingdom
Belgium	Greece	The Netherlands	
Cyprus	Hungary	Poland	
The Czech Republic	Ireland	Portugal	
Denmark	Italy	Slovakia	
Estonia	Latvia	Slovenia	
Finland	Lithuania	Spain	
France	Luxembourg	Sweden	

4.219 All the above designated countries are now operating the European Arrest Warrant.

4.220 **Part 2** of the 2003 Act relates to extradition to Category 2 Territories. These are all other states. A list of Category 2 Territories is set out below:

Albania	Cook Islands	Kenya
Andorra	Croatia	Kiribati
Antigua and Barbuda	Cuba	Lesotho
Argentina	Dominica	Liberia
Armenia	Ecuador	Liechtenstein
Australia	El Salvador	Macedonia, FYR
Azerbaijan	Fiji	Malawi
The Bahamas	The Gambia	Malaysia
Bangladesh	Georgia	Maldives
Barbados	Ghana	Mauritius
Belize	Grenada	Mexico
Bolivia	Guatemala	Moldova
Bosnia and Herzegovina	Guyana	Monaco
Botswana	Hong Kong Special Administrative Region	Nauru
Brazil	Haiti	New Zealand
Brunei	Iceland	Nicaragua
Bulgaria	India	Nigeria
Canada	Iraq	Norway
Chile	Israel	Panama
Colombia	Jamaica	Papua New Guinea
		Paraguay
		Peru

[162] Designation by Extradition Act 2003 (Designation of Part 1 Territories) Order 2003, the Extradition Act 2003 (Amendment to Designations) Order 2004, and the Extradition Act 2003 (Amendment to Designations) Order 2005.

Romania
Russian Federation
Saint Christopher and Nevis
Saint Lucia
Saint Vincent and the Grenadines
San Marino
Serbia and Montenegro
The Seychelles
Sierra Leone
Singapore
The Solomon Islands
South Africa
Sri Lanka
Swaziland
Switzerland
Tanzania
Thailand
Tonga
Trinidad and Tobago
Turkey
Tuvalu
Uganda
Ukraine
Uruguay
The United States
Vanuatu
Western Samoa
Zambia
Zimbabwe

4.221 **Part 3** of the 2003 Act addresses import extradition and, in particular, the European Arrest Warrant for import purposes. **Part 4**, meanwhile, deals with police powers in relation to export requests, whilst **Part 5** is a 'sweep up of miscellaneous and general provisions'. Within Part 5, 5.193 addresses international conventions, which provide a legal basis for extradition. In that regard, for corruption offences, Article 44 of UNCAC provides such a basis.

1. Export Extraditions to Designated EAW Territories

4.222 The National Criminal Intelligence Service (NCIS) is the designated authority for the purposes of receiving European Arrest Warrants (EAWs) from designated territories.[163] Upon receipt of an EAW, it is for the NCIS to decide whether to certify the warrant in question. Reference should be made to the criteria for certification set out in section 2(7) of the 2003 Act. However, for present purposes, it may be noted that, to be certified, the warrant must have been issued by an appropriate authority and must contain a statement and certain specified information. In the case of an accused but not convicted person, the statement is required to say that the person named on the warrant is accused of an offence in the requesting territory and that the warrant has been issued for the purpose of securing the person's return for criminal proceedings in relation to the named offence or offences. In the case of a convicted person, the warrant must state that the person is alleged to be unlawfully at large, having been convicted in the requesting territory for the offence specified, and that the warrant has been issued to secure the person's return for the purpose of serving the sentence already imposed. In relation to a convicted person, if a person has not yet been sentenced, the warrant must contain details of any sentence or sanction which is capable of being imposed. It should also be noted, however, that Section 20 of the 2003 Act sets out specific considerations to which a Judge must direct his mind in relation to a conviction in absence.

[163] Extradition Act 2003 (Part 2 Designated Authorities) Order 2003, para 2.

The NCIS is responsible for coordinating the arrest of any person wanted in pursuance of an export extradition request, and for the arrangements for any such person to be brought a Magistrates' Court. When a person is arrested in England or Wales in relation to an EAW, the CPS will provide representation for the requesting judicial authority in any proceedings before the English courts.[164] **4.223**

Under Part 1, a person may be arrested and brought before Bow Street Magistrates' Court in one of two ways: **4.224**

(1) Under a certified Part 1 Warrant:[165] once such a warrant is certified, it may be executed by a police constable. The person arrested must then be produced at court as soon as practicable thereafter.
(2) Provisional arrest:[166] a police constable may arrest a person without a warrant if he has grounds for believing that a Part 1 Warrant either has been or will be issued in relation to that person by an appropriate authority. Having been arrested, a person subject to provisional arrest must be produced at court within 48 hours of arrest along with the fully certified Part 1 Warrant.

The arrested person, having been produced at court, an initial hearing in front of a district judge will take place. At that hearing, by virtue of sections 7 and 8 of the 2003 Act, the identity of the person (on the balance of probabilities) must be established. If identity cannot be established, the person must be discharged. Otherwise, a date must be fixed for the extradition hearing itself. The extradition hearing must take place within 21 days of arrest. The person arrested must be informed by the district judge of the contents of the warrant. The person must also be informed that he is able to consent to extradition.[167] The district judge must also decide whether the person arrested should be bailed to appear at the extradition hearing or should be remanded in custody. **4.225**

The extradition hearing itself is governed by sections 10 to 21 of the 2003 Act. Those provisions provide that the following points must be addressed at the hearing (which again takes place in front of a district judge): Firstly, is the offence an extradition offence for the purposes of Part 1 of the 2003 Act?[168] It must also be shown that the alleged offence is certified by the requesting territory to be an offence within a list of offences set out in Article 2 of the Framework Decision on the Scope of the EAW. Article 2 provides: **4.226**

> 1. A European arrest warrant may be issued for acts punishable by the law of the issuing Member State by a custodial sentence or a detention order for a maximum period of at least twelve months or, where a sentence has been passed or a detention order has been made, for sentences of at least four months.

---

[164] Extradition Act 2003, s 191.
[165] ibid ss 3 and 4.
[166] ibid ss 5 and 6.
[167] For consent, see Extradition Act 2003, ss 45 and 46.
[168] ibid s 10(2).

2. The following offences, if they are punishable in the issuing Member State by a custodial sentence or a detention order for a maximum period of at least three years and as they are defined by the law of the issuing Member State, shall, under the terms of this Framework Decision and without verification of the double criminality of the act, give rise to surrender pursuant to a European arrest warrant:

   - participation in a criminal organisation,
   - terrorism,
   - trafficking in human beings,
   - sexual exploitation of children and child pornography,
   - illicit trafficking in narcotic drugs and psychotropic substances,
   - illicit trafficking in weapons, munitions and explosives,
   - corruption,
   - fraud, including that affecting the financial interests of the European Communities within the meaning of the Convention of 26 July 1995 on the protection of the European Communities' financial interests,
   - laundering of the proceeds of crime,
   - counterfeiting currency, including of the euro,
   - computer-related crime,
   - environmental crime, including illicit trafficking in endangered animal species and in endangered plant species and varieties,
   - facilitation of unauthorised entry and residence,
   - murder, grievous bodily injury,
   - illicit trade in human organs and tissue,
   - kidnapping, illegal restraint and hostage-taking,
   - racism and xenophobia,
   - organised or armed robbery,
   - illicit trafficking in cultural goods, including antiques and works of art, swindling;
   - racketeering and extortion
   - counterfeiting and piracy of products,
   - forgery of administrative documents and trafficking therein,
   - forgery of means of payment,
   - illicit trafficking in hormonal substances and other growth promoters,
   - illicit trafficking in nuclear or radioactive materials,
   - trafficking in stolen vehicles,
   - rape,
   - arson,
   - crimes within the jurisdiction of the International Criminal Court,
   - unlawful seizure of aircraft/ships,
   - sabotage.

3. The Council may decide at any time, acting unanimously after consultation of the European Parliament under the conditions laid down in Article 39(1) of the Treaty on European Union (TEU), to add other categories of offence to the list contained in paragraph 2. The Council shall examine, in the light of the report submitted by the Commission pursuant to Article 34(3), whether the list should be extended or amended.

4. For offences other than those covered by paragraph 2, surrender may be subject to the condition that the acts for which the European arrest warrant has been issued constitute an offence under the law of the executing Member State, whatever the constituent elements or however it is described.

It will be noted that the categories of offences set out in Article 2 include both corruption and laundering the proceeds of crime. By virtue of Article 2(1) an offence must be punishable by at least a maximum period of 12 months' imprisonment or, in a case where a sentence has already been passed on a person, a sentence of at least 4 months has been given. In addition, Article 2(2) provides that if an offence falls within the category of offences specified in Article 2 and is punishable by at least 3 years imprisonment, then the requirement of dual criminality will be satisfied. In a case punishable by less than 3 years imprisonment, the court will need to consider whether the dual criminality requirement is, in fact, met. In the event that the district judge decides that the offence specified on the warrant is not, in fact, an extradition offence, then he must discharge the person. **4.227**

Secondly, do any of the bars to extradition set out in sections 11 to 19 of the 2003 Act apply? These are: double jeopardy; prejudicial treatment; passage of time; the age of a defendant (ie if the offence occurred in the United Kingdom would the defendant be below the age of responsibility? (16 years old)); hostage-taking considerations; speciality; and earlier extradition from either a Category 1 or non-Category 1 Territory. However, for full details of these bars, reference should be made to sections 11 to 19 of the 2003 Act itself. In addition, by virtue of section 25, if it appears to the district judge during the course of the extradition hearing that it would be unjust or oppressive to extradite the person arrested because of his physical or mental condition, the district judge may either order discharge or may adjourn the hearing until the physical or mental condition has improved. **4.228**

It is not possible within the confines of this chapter to address all the issues which may arise through the course of the extradition hearing. However, it should be noted that in the event of two competing warrants having been issued in relation to the same person, the district judge must choose which of the two will prevail.[169] In the event that a person has been charged with an offence in the United Kingdom, the extradition hearing must be adjourned[170] until the charge is concluded or withdrawn or dismissed. In relation to a charge in the United Kingdom resulting in a sentence of imprisonment, however, the district judge has discretion as to whether to adjourn the extradition hearing until sentence has been served.[171] **4.229**

[169] Extradition Act 2003, s 44.
[170] ibid s 22.
[171] Extradition Act 2003, s 22(3).

4.230 If, following an extradition hearing, there is no appeal, then the person must be extradited to the Category 1 Territory within ten days of the extradition order,[172] although the district judge and the requesting authority may agree that extradition should take place within ten days of a later date. However, if a person has not been extradited within the relevant period, then he or she may apply to be discharged. A discharge must be made unless reasonable cause can be shown for the delay.[173]

4.231 The Part 1 extradition procedure carries with it appeals. These are addressed in detail in sections 26 to 34 of the 2003 Act. In essence, all appeals in a Part 1 extradition case will be dealt with by the Administrative Court of the High Court. Such an appeal may be brought either by the person to be extradited or by the requesting authority. If an appellant is unsuccessful before the Administrative Court, an appeal may be made to the House of Lords.[174] Such an appeal may only be made with the leave of either the Administrative Court or of the House of Lords. Leave can only be granted if either the Administrative Court has certified that there is a point of law of general public importance involved in the decision and it appears to the court dealing with the leave of application that the point is one which ought to be considered by the House of Lords, or the House of Lords grants leave.[175] A leave application to the Administrative Court must be made within fourteen days of the decision on the appeal.[176] A leave application to the House of Lords must be made within fourteen days of the Administrative Court's refusal to grant leave.[177] An appeal to the House of Lords must, in any event, be brought within twenty-eight days of the decision to grant leave.

2. Consent (Category 1 Territories)

4.232 Section 45 to 47 of the 2003 Act contain provisions as to consent to extradition. A person may consent to extradition to a Category 1 Territory provided that: (a) he is legally represented at the time he gives consent;[178] (b) he gives his consent in front of an 'appropriate judge';[179] and (c) the consent is recorded in writing.[180] The consent, once given, is irrevocable.[181] Once a consent is given, the person giving consent must either be remanded in custody or on bail and the court must make an order for extradition within ten days of the date of consent.[182]

4.233 Extradition, meanwhile, must take place within ten days of the order for extradition being made or, if a later date has been agreed by the judge making the order and the requesting authority, within ten days of that later date.[183] However, if the person to be extradited makes an asylum claim at any time in the process

[172] ibid s 35(4). [173] ibid s 35(5). [174] ibid s 32. [175] ibid s 32(4).
[176] ibid s 33(5). [177] ibid s 32(6). [178] ibid s 45(5).
[179] ibid s 45(4)(a); the appropriate judge will, for most purposes, be a district judge at Bow Street Magistrates' Court. [180] Extradition Act 2003, s 45(4)(b).
[181] ibid s 45(4)(c). [182] ibid s 46(10). [183] ibid s 47(3).

between the EAW being certified and the extradition itself, the person must not be extradited until a determination of the asylum claim has taken place.[184]

3. Export Extradition: Category 2 Territories

The designated authority for receiving extradition requests is the Home Office. Having received a request, the Secretary of State must certify the request if it is valid. The criteria for deciding on validity are provided for in section 70 of the 2003 Act. To be valid, a request must contain a statement and must be made 'in the approved way'. If extradition is sought in relation to an accused but not convicted person, the statement must set out that the person is accused in the named Category 2 Territory of the offence or offences which are specified in the request,[185] whilst in the case of a convicted person, the statement must set out that the person is alleged to be unlawfully at large having been convicted by a court in the Category 2 Territory making the request and that the conviction was for the offence or offences specified in the request. **4.234**

In order to be made in an 'approved way', the request (for all Category 2 Territories except Hong Kong and British overseas territories) must be made by an authority of the territory believed by the Secretary of State to have the function of issuing such requests, or by someone recognized by the Secretary of State as being a diplomatic or consular representative of the Category 2 Territory concerned.[186] Once certification has taken place in relation to a Part 2 request, the Secretary of State must send the request and the certificate to the district judge at a magistrates' court. As in a Part I request, the CPS will provide legal representation for the requesting Category 2 Territory.[187] Meanwhile, the Metropolitan Police will usually be responsible for the arrest of any person sought by a Category 2 Territory under a Part 2 request. **4.235**

A person may be arrested in one of two ways: **4.236**

(1) on a warrant issued under section 73 by a magistrates' court, the court having been provided with a certified extradition request from the Secretary of State; or
(2) a provisional arrest as provided for by section 73 of the 2003 Act.

A person arrested following receipt by the court of a certified extradition request must be provided with a copy of the warrant as soon as practicable after arrest (failure to comply will give the court a power to grant an application for discharge).[188] The person must also be brought before the district judge as soon as practicable after arrest. Again, a failure to do so gives the district judge discretion to grant an application for discharge.[189] **4.237**

---

[184] ibid s 39. [185] ibid s 70(4)(a). [186] ibid s 70(7).
[187] By virtue of the Extradition Act 2003, s 190 and also the assignment made by the Attorney-General, 10 December 1996. [188] Extradition Act 2003, s 72(5).
[189] ibid s 72(6).

4.238 At the first hearing, the district judge must inform the person of the contents of the extradition request and of the procedure for consenting to extradition.[190] A date for the extradition hearing itself will be set. That must be no more than two months from the date of the first hearing. However, there is a power for the court to grant an application for a later date so long as it is in the interests of justice to do so;[191] although if a date has been fixed and not extended, the district judge must grant any application for discharge in the event that the extradition hearing fails to commence on the fixed date. At the first hearing, the district judge must also make the decision as to bail or custody.[192]

4.239 When a person has been arrested by virtue of a provisional warrant, the post-arrest procedure is governed by section 74 of the 2003 Act, which provides that a copy of the warrant must be given as soon as practicable after arrest and that a failure to comply in that regard means that an application for discharge may be granted.[193] The person must then be brought before Bow Street Magistrates' Court as soon as practicable after arrest. Again, non-compliance gives a discretion to discharge on application.[194]

4.240 At the first hearing following provisional arrest, the district judge must inform the person of the reason for arrest and the procedure for consent,[195] and must decide whether the remand should be in custody or on bail.[196] In the case of a provisional arrest, the documentation will not be with the court at the time of the first hearing. However, documents must be received by the court within 'the required period'.[197] The required period is either forty-five days from the day of arrest, or any longer period permitted by an Order in Council.[198] In the event that documents are not received within the required period, the discharge of the person whose extradition is sought must be ordered.[199] The documents required are the requests for extradition, the Secretary of State's certificate, and a copy of any relevant Order in Council.

4.241 In addition to the time constraints contained with the domestic legislation, Article 16.4 of the European Convention on Extradition Order (1990) gives a discretion to terminate the provisional arrest if the request has not been received within eighteen days of the arrest itself. In addition, a provisional arrest must be terminated if no request has been forthcoming within forty days of arrest. It may therefore be that the court will invariably take the view that, following the first appearance, there should be an adjournment for eighteen days for the request to be received; followed, if necessary, by a further adjournment up until the limit of forty days. In the event that there

[190] ibid s 72(7)(a), (b). [191] ibid s 75(3). [192] ibid s 72(7)(c). [193] ibid s 74(5).
[194] ibid s 74(6). [195] ibid s 74(7)(a)(b). [196] ibid s 72(7)(c).
[197] ibid s 74(10). [198] ibid s 74(11). [199] ibid s 74(10).

is confirmation to the court that a request has been received, the court will, of course, be able to adjourn the case up to the maximum period of forty-five days.

In the event that the documentation is received by the court within the relevant period, a date for the extradition hearing to commence will be set, to start no more than two months from the date on which the court received the documentation. However, either of the parties may apply to the district judge for a later hearing date and such an application may be granted if it is believed that it is in the interests of justice so to do.[200] **4.242**

The matters which must be addressed during the extradition hearing are set out in sections 77 to 87 of the 2003 Act. The district judge must decide the following (in order): **4.243**

(1) Does the documentation sent by the Secretary of State to the court include all required documents?[201] If the court has not been provided with those documents, then the person must be discharged.[202]
(2) The district judge must decide whether identity is satisfied: in other words that the person at court is the person in respect of whom the extradition request has been made. The decision is on the balance of probabilities. If the district judge is not satisfied, discharge must be ordered.[203]
(3) Is the offence, or are the offences, specified in the extradition request, extraditable offences?[204] In the case of a person who has not been sentenced, an extradition offence (by virtue of section 137) is an offence which is punishable in the requesting territory by a minimum of twelve months' imprisonment and the conduct which forms the basis of the offence is such as would amount to an offence in the United Kingdom punishable by at least 12 months' imprisonment in the event that it occurred within the United Kingdom. For a convicted person who has been sentenced but is unlawfully at large, an extradition offence, by virtue of section 138, is an offence for which a sentence of at least four months' imprisonment has, in fact, been imposed in the requesting country, and is an offence which, on the conduct alleged, would amount to a UK offence punishable by at least 12 months' imprisonment if it had occurred in the United Kingdom. In either case, if the district judge is not satisfied that the offence is an extradition offence, then the discharge of the person before

200 ibid s 76(4).
201 ibid s 78(2). Within the documents must be contained: the request, the certificate, a copy of any Order in Council, particulars of identity and of the offence or offences, a warrant (in the case of an unconvicted person), and a certificate of convictions/sentence (in the case of a convicted and/or sentenced person).
202 Extradition Act 2003, s. 78(3).
203 As to identity, see s 78(4)(a) and in relation to discharge see s 78(6).
204 Extradition Act 2003, s 78(4)(b).

the court must be ordered.[205] In the case of corruption offences, the offence in Category 2 Territories will invariably be an extradition offence. Similarly, the majority of offences alleging criminal misconduct by officials whilst in office will usually cross the extradition threshold as to sanction.

(4) The documents provided to the district judge by the Secretary of State must have been served on the person in respect of whom the request is made.[206] If documents have not been served, the person must be discharged.[207]

(5) The district judge has to decide whether any of the bars to extradition contained within sections 79 to 83 apply in the present case. If so, the person must be discharged.[208] The bars to extradition are:
   (a) Double jeopardy[209]—in other words if the conduct alleged had occurred in the United Kingdom would the rule against double jeopardy apply?
   (b) Is there a risk of prejudicial treatment upon extradition to the requesting country, or is there an underlying prejudicial reason behind the prosecution to take place in the requesting territory?[210]
   (c) Does the passage of time since the offence mean that it is oppressive or unjust to order extradition?[211]
   (d) Hostage-taking considerations.[212]

(6) In the case of an accused person, the district judge must decide whether there is admissible evidence amounting to a *prima facie* case.[213] If there is not, the person must be discharged.[214] However, the Secretary of State can waive this requirement in relation to particular states. Indeed, designation of a number of states has occurred by virtue of the Extradition Act 2003 (Designation of Part 2 Territories) Order 2003;[215] thus, the following states are not required to provide a *prima facie* case:

Albania	Georgia	Romania
Andorra	Iceland	Russian Federation
Armenia	Israel	Serbia and Montenegro
Australia	Liechtenstein	South Africa
Azerbaijan	Macedonia, FYR	Switzerland
Bulgaria	Moldova	Turkey
Canada	New Zealand	Ukraine
Croatia	Norway	The United States

(7) Where a person has been convicted, the district judge must decide whether the conviction was in the person's presence. If it was, then the district judge must consider whether extradition will be compatible with the person's rights under the ECHR. If conviction was in his or her absence,

[205] Extradition Act 2003, s 78(6). [206] ibid s 78(4)(c). [207] ibid s 78(6).
[208] ibid s 79(3). [209] ibid s 80. [210] ibid s 81. [211] ibid s 82.
[212] ibid s 83. [213] ibid s 84. [214] ibid s 84(5). [215] At para 3.

and the absence was not a deliberate act by the person, then a discharge must be ordered unless the district judge is satisfied that, following extradition, the person would have a right to a retrial or a full review of the evidence, being equivalent to a retrial. In the event that a person would not be entitled to a retrial or review, the district judge must decide whether there is a *prima facie* case and, if so, whether extradition would be compatible with the person's rights under the ECHR. In either of the above scenarios, if extradition would not be compatible with ECHR rights, then discharge must be ordered.[216] If, however, the district judge is satisfied that extradition would be compatible, then the matter must be sent to the Secretary of State for his decision as to whether the person is to be extradited.[217]

Where a person has been charged with an offence in the United Kingdom, the district judge must adjourn the extradition hearing until that charge has been concluded, withdrawn, or otherwise disposed of.[218] If, however, there is a conviction in relation to the UK charge and a sentence of imprisonment is imposed, there is a discretion to adjourn the extradition hearing until sentence has been served.[219] Similarly, if during the course of the extradition hearing the district judge is informed that a person is in fact serving a sentence of imprisonment in the United Kingdom, a discretion to adjourn again arises (until sentence has been served). However, if an asylum claim is made at any time between the time at which the request is certified and the time at which extradition takes place consequent on the request, the person must not be extradited until the claim has been determined by the Secretary of State (including the outcome of any appeals).[220] **4.244**

In addition to the bars to extradition it should be noted that if during the extradition hearing it appears to the district judge that it would be unjust or oppressive, by reason of the person's physical or mental condition, to extradite, then a discharge may be ordered or an adjournment granted until the person's condition improves. **4.245**

Where all criteria have been satisfied at the extradition hearing, the request for extradition is then sent to the Secretary of State for his consideration.[221] The Secretary of State has to decide whether he is prohibited from ordering extradition.[222] The grounds on which a prohibition from extradition arises are: **4.246**

(1) where the person is or could be sentenced to death for the offence for which extradition is requested in the requesting territory[223] (if at risk of the death

216 ibid s 87(2). 217 ibid s 87(3). 218 ibid s 88(2). 219 ibid s 88(3).
220 ibid s 121. 221 ibid ss 93–98 govern this aspect of the procedure.
222 Extradition Act 2003, s 93(1). 223 ibid s 94.

penalty, the Secretary of State must receive written assurance that the death penalty will not be imposed or, if imposed, will not be carried out before he can order extradition);

(2) if speciality arrangements are not in place with the requesting Category 2 Territory, no extradition shall be ordered;[224]

(3) where there has been earlier extradition to the United Kingdom or another territory.[225]

4.247 There are avenues of appeal in relation to extraditions falling within Part 2 of the Extradition Act 2003. In addition to the statutory appeals set out therein, however, there also remains the availability of other challenges such as an application for a writ of habeas corpus and judicial review. Thus, for example, although there is no power contained within the 2003 Act to dismiss an application when the request has been wrongfully certified by the Home Office, judicial review would appear to be available.[226]

4.248 As to the statutory avenues of appeal: the tribunal will be the Administrative Court. An appeal may be brought by the person who is the subject of the extradition request[227] against the decision of the district judge to send the matter to the Secretary of State. However, it cannot be heard until the Secretary of State has made his decision. It may be an appeal on either law, fact, or a combination of the two. The requesting territory may appeal against the district judge's decision to discharge a person.[228] Notice of appeal must be given within fourteen days from the date of the order for discharge. In either case, the appellant must demonstrate that (a) the district judge ought to have decided on one of the decisions he was required to make differently and that, had he done so, he would have been required to make the opposite decision on sending or discharge (as the case may be) to the decision he, in fact, made; or, (b) the appellant must raise an issue or adduce evidence not put before the court at the extradition hearing and which, had it been, would have resulted in the district judge making a different decision on sending or discharge than the one that was, in fact, made.[229]

4.249 If the appeal is allowed, the Administrative Court may order discharge and quash the order for extradition, or may remit the case to the district judge for him to decide afresh an issue on which he made a finding at the extradition hearing. Alternatively, the appeal may be dismissed. Similarly, where the requesting territory has appealed,[230] the Administrative Court may allow the appeal and quash the order for discharge or remit to the district judge for a

[224] ibid s 95. [225] ibid s 96.

[226] See *Augusto Pinto v Governor of HMP Brixton, the First Section of the First Criminal Court of Lisbon* [2004] AWHC 2986/Admin and *Nikonovs v Governor of HMP Brixton and anor* [2005] EWHC Admin 2405. [227] ibid s 103.

[228] Extradition Act 2003, s 105 [229] ibid s 103. [230] ibid s 105.

question to be decided afresh. Alternatively, once again, the appeal may be dismissed.

It should also be noted that an appeal lies to the Administrative Court against the decision of the Secretary of State. Such an appeal may either be brought by the person in respect of whom extradition is sought[231] or by the requesting territory.[232] **4.250**

In the event that either party is unsuccessful before the Administrative Court, an appeal then lies to the House of Lords. An appeal to the House of Lords may, however, only be made with the leave of the High Court or of the House of Lords.[233] Leave will only be granted if there is a point of law of general public importance and the point is one which ought to be considered by the House of Lords. An appeal to the House of Lords must be brought within twenty-eight days of the decision to grant leave.[234] **4.251**

A person who has been arrested following a request from a Category 2 Territory may consent to being returned there.[235] Consent must be given in writing and, once given, is irrevocable.[236] **4.252**

H. Import Extradition

1. Extradition Requests to EAW States

Extradition may only be sought in respect of an extradition offence. In relation to those countries operating the EAW scheme, a request by the United Kingdom will be by means of a warrant, issued under Part 3 of the Extradition Act 2003. As already seen, in relation to export extraditions, the EAW arrangements allow for provisional arrest. A Part 3 warrant will usually be drafted by a prosecuting lawyer in accordance with the contents which are required to be set out as provided for by section 142(3) to (6). **4.253**

An application for a Part 3 warrant may be made by either a constable, a crown prosecutor, or a solicitor/counsel instructed by the CPS.[237] The application may be made to a justice of the peace, a district judge, or a judge entitled to exercise jurisdiction of the crown court (ie including recorders).[238] Section 142(2) provides that, before a Part 3 warrant can be issued, a domestic warrant must already be extant and there must be reasonable grounds for believing either that the defendant has committed an extradition offence or that he is unlawfully at large after conviction for such an offence by a UK court. For the purposes of a **4.254**

[231] ibid s 108. [232] ibid s 110. [233] ibid s 114(3). [234] ibid s 114(7).
[235] See ibid ss 127–128. [236] ibid s 127(3).
[237] Extradition Act 2003, s 142(1) and (6). [238] ibid s 149(1).

Part 3 warrant application, 'extradition offence' is defined in section 148 of the 2003 Act. As already indicated, this definition is already in line with the general requirement for extraditable offence, namely that the offence must be punishable with at least twelve months' imprisonment or, in the case of a defendant unlawfully at large, a sentence of at least four months' imprisonment has already been imposed.

4.255 It should be noted that, generally, a Part 3 warrant must set out all the offences on which return to the United Kingdom is being sought. However, as to other requirements and fetters, regard should be had to the provisions of Part 3 of the Extradition Act 2003 itself.

2. Extradition Requests to Non-EAW States

4.256 A request to a state not operating the EAW will have to be made by the United Kingdom in accordance with existing extradition arrangements. It may be that there is a bilateral agreement between the United Kingdom and the state concerned, a multilateral convention to which both the United Kingdom and the requested state are parties, or a special arrangement made between the United Kingdom and the requested state in relation to the present defendant or defendants. In any of these cases, however, extradition may only be sought in relation to an extradition offence. Subject to some variation, which will not be addressed herein, the broad definition of an extradition offence should be borne in mind.[239]

4.257 Most, but not all, extradition arrangements and schemes allow for the provisional arrest of a defendant, in anticipation of receipt of a formal extradition request. As to the full request, that will invariably be required to contain one of the following: a first instance warrant (in the case of an unconvicted person) setting out the offences for which extradition is sought, a warrant issued by the court; or, in a case where a defendant has been convicted, a certified copy of the memorandum of conviction (and, if already sentenced, a certified record of the sentenced imposed). In addition, there must be sufficient material from which identification is able to be made and a statement of the UK law in respect of the offences alleged. Depending on the state from which extradition is sought, either a summary of facts or a general witness statement setting out the evidence will be required, or full statements or depositions from the prosecution witnesses sufficient to disclose a *prima facie* case against the defendant.

[239] As previously highlighted, in general, an offence punishable with at least 12 months' imprisonment in the case of an unconvicted person; or in the case of a convicted but unsentenced person, a person lawfully at large after conviction for an offence punishable by a minimum of 12 months' imprisonment; or, in the case of a sentenced defendant, an offence for which the defendant has received a sentence of at least 4 months' imprisonment.

In relation to any request for import extradition, the prosecuting lawyer must satisfy himself that the evidential and public interest tests contained in the Code for Crown Prosecutors have been met (assuming the person whose extradition is sought is unconvicted) or, in the case of a person already convicted, must satisfy himself that a person has been convicted and that return is sought for the purpose either of sentence or of imposing the sentence already given in their absence. **4.258**

The details above aim to give a general guide of the framework for extradition requests. It must be emphasized, however, that recourse needs to be had to the legislation itself and a specialist text. **4.259**

5

THE MOVEMENT FOR REFORM

> It seems to me that these kinds of troubles about malpractices . . . or mistrust of Ministers and Parliament go in cycles. From about 1860 to 1895 there was very little trouble of that sort, but from 1895 onwards there was a lot . . . From 1895 to 1930 was a period when a lot of financial scandals were going on, but it was succeeded by a period of relative quiescence . . . But something has happened more recently, and I think it may be partly connected . . . with a sort of get rich quick mentality which very much prevailed in the Edwardian era, and I think has been prevailing quite a lot in the last 20 years.[1]

A. Corruption in Public Life

1. Shifting Morality

5.01 The changes in attitude displayed by Parliament and the public in the last hundred years have been quite striking. Just before the outbreak of the First World War, the then Chancellor of the Exchequer and future Prime Minister, Lloyd George, together with another minister who went on to become Lord Chief Justice and Viceroy of India, and the Government Chief Whip all purchased shares in the American Marconi company before they went on sale to the public. They were aware that the British Government had just signed a large and lucrative contract with Marconi as a result of which the shares doubled in value as soon as they went on sale publicly. At first the ministers tried

[1] Lord Blake: quoted in Appendix 1 of the First Report of the Committee on Standards in Public Life, Cm 2850–I (May 1995): Chairman Lord Nolan (hereinafter 'Nolan').

to conceal what they had done, then, when found out, denied any wrongdoing. A Commons select committee was set up, but it divided on party lines and no action was taken. The affair received little newspaper coverage and, as Nolan says, no adverse consequences were suffered, apart from embarrassment.[2]

During the First World War, doubts were expressed about the awarding of **5.02**
wartime contracts, but it was not until the King himself, George V, expressed outrage over the offer of a peerage to a businessman recently convicted of fraud that anything was done about the sale of honours to boost party funds. Following a report from a Royal Commission set up in 1922, the Honours (Prevention of Abuses) Act was passed in 1925. A system was set up under which political candidates for honours should be vetted by three Privy Councillors, none of whom should be a member of the government of the day. That system is still in place.

Immediately after the Second World War, a junior Board of Trade Minister, **5.03**
John Belcher, who was in a position to influence the granting of government licences and permits, which were strictly controlled in a stringent post-war Britain, accepted gifts from a group of businessmen in return for 'improper official favours'. A Tribunal of Enquiry was set up under Mr Justice Lynskey, which concluded that Belcher had indeed behaved improperly and he promptly resigned as a minister, then as a member of the Commons.

The 1950s and 1960s were characterized by a number of sex and spy scandals. **5.04**
Diplomats Guy Burgess and Donald Maclean had fled to Moscow in 1951 having been tipped off by Kim Philby that they were about to be interrogated by the British Intelligence Services. In 1961 another ex-diplomat, George Blake, was given a record forty-two-year prison sentence for spying (he escaped after five years). But, even more sensationally in the eyes of the public, a Cabinet Minister, John Profumo, Secretary of State for War, lied to the House of Commons about an affair he had been having with Christine Keeler, who subsequently turned out to have slept with Eugene Ivanov, the naval attaché at the Soviet Embassy. The whole matter was referred to the Master of the Rolls, Lord Denning, who produced an official report which sold out immediately it went on sale.

Dramatic though these events were, it was not until the 1970s that a series of **5.05**
events occurred which were to change radically the perception of corruption in the United Kingdom and beyond. What became known as the Poulson Affair opened the eyes of the public and government to just how far-reaching and pernicious corruption practised on a grand scale could be. In particular, Poulson demonstrated the kind of resource that would be needed to fight large-scale corruption.

[2] Nolan (n 1 above) App 1.

5.06 John Poulson was an extremely ambitious and entrepreneurial architect. Starting out in practice in 1932, he became a Licentiate of the Royal Institute of British Architects in 1942, but by the 1960s he owned and controlled what was claimed to be the largest architectural practice in Europe, employing some 750 staff. An early exponent of 'one-stop shopping', Poulson offered a service which combined the obtaining of planning consents with surveying, engineering, and ultimately construction itself all under one roof. Much of his work was carried out in the public sector, including local authority housing, hospitals, and municipal works of all kinds. In 1961 he met T Dan Smith, at that time leader of the majority Labour group and chairman of the planning and housing committees of Newcastle-upon-Tyne City Council. During the 1960s he became chairman of the Northern Economic Planning Council, chairman of the Peterlee and Aycliffe Development Corporations, and a member of the Royal Commission on Local Government in England. His contacts were extensive and his influence considerable—important characteristics for practising corruption on a large scale.

5.07 Between 1962 and 1970, Smith incorporated fourteen public relations companies. He appointed councillors on various local authorities as paid 'consultants' to one or other of these companies. The councillors were then expected to exercise their influence on behalf of Poulson without, of course, ever declaring their interest. Local authorities were regarded as being 'under their control'—if they were not, Poulson would resort to direct bribery, often of Tory interests. By 1970, the financial strains of running this complex, corrupt, empire became too great and Poulson filed for bankruptcy in 1972. Poulson was cross-examined by Muir Hunter QC, the leading insolvency practitioner of the day, and within a month the Fraud Squad became involved.

5.08 Poulson proved to have been a meticulous record-keeper and the Attorney-General appointed two QCs full time to handle the prosecutions arising in the case. There were over 300 contemplated cases under the Prevention of Corruption Acts. Apart from Poulson himself and T Dan Smith, the Secretary of the Department of Agriculture and Fisheries for Scotland, the divisional chief engineer of the National Coal Board, the secretary of the South West Metropolitan Regional Hospital Board, an estate and rating surveyor of the British Transport Commission, the chairman of Durham Police Authority, a principal at the Ministry of Health, and the former Lord Mayor of Newcastle-upon-Tyne, to name but a few, were all found to be on the Poulson payroll and were convicted of corruption and conspiracy offences.

5.09 While the Poulson Affair was still unfolding, the Prime Minister of the day[3] appointed Lord Redcliffe-Maud to head a Committee to examine local

[3] Edward Heath MP.

government law and practice in response to widespread public disquiet. When the Committee was appointed in 1973, prosecutions were still taking place and the whole affair was still being investigated. Possibly as a result of this, there is no direct reference to Poulson in the Committee's Report. Indeed the whole Poulson affair was light years beyond the type of rather parochial corruption considered by Redcliffe-Maud, whose Report now has a rather complacent tone, but none of his Committee could have imagined at the time just how deeply corruption could become embedded in both local and national government without being detected, or acted upon.

B. The Redcliffe-Maud Committee

The Redcliffe-Maud Committee reported in 1974: its terms of reference were to examine local government law and practice and how it might affect (a) the conduct of members and officers in situations involving a conflict of interest between their public functions and private interests, and (b) qualification or disqualification for service as a member of a local authority or any of its committees.[4] **5.10**

Reading the Report thirty years after it was written, it is striking how few prosecutions had actually taken place before Poulson—widespread press coverage had clearly excited public interest but corruption seems not to have been nearly as widespread as the public seemed to fear. In the period 1964 to 1972 there were 48,000 councillors and over two million employees of local authorities. A total of ten councillors and twenty-two employees had been convicted of offences under the Prevention of Corruption Acts, and sixteen Councillors were convicted of failure to disclose a pecuniary interest under the Local Government Acts.[5] The maximum sentence imposed was three years for a local authority contracts manager who was bribed to pass false claims made by contractors, there were a couple of prosecutions for bribes taken in granting contracts and influencing the granting of planning permission, all of which resulted in jail sentences. A works supervisor of a River Drainage Board was fined £60 for demanding money to grant contracts for clearing weeds, and there were two cases of local authority housing officers demanding sexual intercourse from women to provide council flats—one received a suspended sentence, the other was imprisoned for nine months.[6] The predominant flavour of the prosecutions is one of petty, localized, corruption. **5.11**

[4] *Conduct in Local Government: Vol 1, Report of the Committee*, HMSO Cmnd 5636 (hereinafter 'Redcliffe-Maud Report'), Introduction, para 2.

[5] ibid para 14.

[6] Redcliff-Maud Report, App C.

5.12 The Committee nevertheless felt that the perceived need to deal firmly with corruption justified strengthening the Prevention of Corruption Acts in two respects:

(1) The presumption of corruption under section 2 of the Prevention of Corruption Act 1916, which arises where it is proved that anyone holding or seeking a contract with a public body has made a payment to an employee of that body, should be extended to apply not only to contracts, but also to other exercises of discretion such as the grant of planning permission or the allocation of a council house, and to apply also to elected members as well as employees of local authorities.[7]

(2) Persons who were convicted of an offence of corruption were liable to be disqualified for election to a public body for a period of five years on a first offence, and for life on a second offence.[8] The Committee recommended that the law should be amended to allow the court a discretion to disqualify for life on a first offence.

5.13 The Report made various perceptive comments about the nature of corruption generally and, in particular, recognized the practical issues arising with regard to the reporting of corruption by members of the public, whom the Committee felt had a shared responsibility for standards in local government.[9] It was noted that a general reluctance existed to go to the police in cases of dishonest or corrupt behaviour, in contrast with the readiness to report crimes of violence. In part, the Committee attributed this to a reluctance to become involved, but, tellingly, they also felt that this reluctance might arise from the belief that it was no concern of the individual if no personal loss had been suffered, as in the case of violence, theft, or fraud. As the Committee stated: 'In corruption the loss is suffered by the public, and it is a public responsibility to report it.'[10]

5.14 It was not, however, in the field of legislative change that the Redcliffe-Maud Committee made its mark, it was in recognizing that the time had come for 'correct behaviour' to be codified in order to provide rules of conduct for those in public life at this level.[11] The Committee incorporated in its Report a draft document entitled 'The National Code of Local Government Conduct'. This represented an important step forward in the fight against corruption and, it could be said, was the foundation stone for all the codes which have subsequently been written in the United Kingdom and overseas, both within government and

[7] ibid para 162.

[8] Under the Public Bodies Corrupt Practices Act 1889, s 2(c) and (d) as amended by the Representation of the People Act 1948, s 52(7).

[9] Redcliffe-Maud Report, para 164.

[10] ibid para 168.

[11] Government Ministers already had a form of code, dating from 1945, entitled 'Questions of Procedure for Ministers' (QPM). Although added to over the years, it remained (almost unbelievably) a confidential document until 1992.

without.[12] The draft code in the Report was subsequently adopted with little alteration and reproduced as a joint circular from the Department of the Environment, the Scottish Development Department, and the Welsh Office.[13]

The Code was subsequently criticized in a number of respects by Lord Nolan in his Third Report[14] as being too complex and difficult to provide useful daily guidance for local government officers, and he advocated a new set of principles which could form the basis of codes to be adopted by individual councils. However, as the original 'bible' of good practice in public office, practitioners having to deal with corruption cases may find that it still provides a useful set of guidelines when having to deal with such issues as conflicts of interest, gifts and hospitality, confidentiality, membership of committees, and what has come to be known in modern parlance as cronyism. **5.15**

The government of the time welcomed the the Redcliffe-Maud Report,[15] but, apart from encouraging local authorities to adopt the Code, which did not require legislation, very little action was taken to implement its recommendations. Perhaps, also, this was because by the time it was published, the Salmon Report was already anticipated.[16] **5.16**

C. The Salmon Report

In contrast to the Redcliffe-Maud Committee, the Salmon Commission had the advantage of knowing a great deal more about the Poulson affair and the Report opens with a detailed summary of it. There had been local press articles and '*Private Eye*' had published a series of articles on the 'Slicker of Wakefield'[17] but, as Lord Salmon says in his introduction, what was really disturbing was that, had it not been for Poulson's bankruptcy and his habit of preserving everything he ever wrote or which was written to him, he and T Dan Smith could have continued their corrupt practices unmolested. Lord Salmon hoped that the adoption of the recommendations in the Report, 'should make it much more difficult for anything resembling the Poulson affair to occur in the future'.[18] **5.17**

[12] See, eg, Public Sector Codes of Conduct listed on the website of Transparency International www.transparency.org.

[13] DOE Circular 94/75, SDD Circular 95/75, and WO Circular 166/75. It is reproduced in App 4 of the Salmon Report (see 5.17ff and n 18 below): the original Redcliffe-Maud version of the Code appears in App 26 below.

[14] As to which, see further below.

[15] See Written Answer, *Hansard* HC vol 874, cols 236–237 (23 May 1974).

[16] ibid.

[17] Mrs Ward-Jackson, a member of the Commission, in a separate 'Addendum' to the Report, observed that almost all the investigations that had led to prosecutions had been sparked off either by *Private Eye* or by commercial television or by other branches of the media or other unofficial bodies or individuals.

[18] *Report of the Royal Commission on Standards of Conduct in Public Life 1974–1976* (hereinafter 'Salmon Report') Chairman, The Rt Hon Lord Salmon, HMSO, Cmnd 5624: a full account of the Poulson Affair is given at paras 11–24.

5.18 The Royal Commission on Standards of Conduct in Public Life, to give the Salmon Commission its full title, had terms of reference which went beyond those of the Redcliffe-Maud Committee's local government remit, but many of that Committee's conclusions were reinforced. Salmon's terms of reference confined the Commission to the public sector, causing him to observe that most of the serious crime in this sector seemed to revolve around planning decisions and local government housing and development contracts, ie the areas where the most money was to be made.

5.19 The Commission felt that elected members of local councils often entered public life with little preparation and found themselves handling matters on a financial scale quite beyond anything they experienced in private life: the power to make decisions which lead to large capital gains or business profits gave rise to obvious temptations on both sides. The Commission also observed that the local authorities most vulnerable to corruption were those in which one party or the other had virtually unchallenged dominance. The Commission therefore saw its role as recommending measures which would not only discourage corruption but also make it easier for those who suspected corruption (whistle-blowers) to get a hearing and to ensure that swift and effective remedial action could be taken.

5.20 The first chapter in the section of the Commission's Report dealing with 'Laws, Rules and Codes affecting individuals' is entitled 'Bribery'. The Commission examined the law of corruption and recommended that the Corruption Acts 1889–1916, insofar as they applied to the public sector, ought to be consolidated and amended. The Commission considered that, so far as transactions involving Crown servants and members or employees of public bodies were concerned, 'the essence of the offence should remain the corrupt offering, giving, soliciting or accepting of considerations as an inducement or reward in respect of the affairs of the organisation in question'.[19] The Commission's analysis of the offence of corruption in the 1889 and 1906 Acts was that it contained three main ingredients. It had to be shown:

(i) that a gift or consideration was given or offered by one party to another;
(ii) that the gift or consideration was given, or received, as an *inducement* or *reward* for services to be rendered or already rendered in relation to official duties; and
(iii) that the transaction took place *corruptly*.[20]

5.21 The Commission's view of these ingredients is contained in paragraphs 52ff of the Report:

> The first of these ingredients is objective, and is the basic fact which the prosecution have to prove to get a case on its feet. The definitions of relevant gifts and considerations in the Acts are broad, and no great problems have arisen in

[19] ibid para 88. [20] ibid para 51 (emphasis in original).

> interpreting them in the courts. Bribes need not actually pass hands for an offence to be committed; soliciting or agreeing to accept them are offences just as much as their acceptance, and offering to give them is an offence just as much as actually giving them.[21]

In contrast to the first element, the Commission expressed the view that: **5.22**

> The second and third ingredients involve a mental element or *mens rea*. The prosecution have to establish a particular intention on the part of the person giving or receiving a gift—namely that matters relevant to the affairs of a third party (the public body or principal) should be improperly influenced. It is an offence corruptly to accept a gift offered as an inducement even if the recipient has no intention of letting the gift influence his conduct: it is the recipient's perception of the gift as an intended inducement that counts. A state of mind is something to be inferred from the facts proved. Normally in cases of this kind, the giving or receipt of a gift—certainly if it is substantial—would leave no jury in any doubt as to the state of mind of the giver or receiver.[22]

After this succinct analysis of the ingredients of the offence, the Commission went **5.23** on to examine the use of the word 'corruptly' in defining the offence, observing that its inclusion had exercised Parliament during the passage of the 1906 Act and that it had subsequently 'attracted judicial attention'. The question posed was whether the inclusion of the word added anything to the requirements in respect of inducement or reward and, if so, what was its precise effect? The Commission considered that just as the word 'dishonestly' had, so far as it was aware, never been defined 'and the criminal law has got along very well without such a definition', so they did not 'believe that it would be possible to construct a satisfactory definition of corrupt intent that would meet all the cases that might arise'. The Commission's conclusion was therefore that 'the law should continue to rely on the ordinary English word "corruptly" to speak for itself'.[23]

Two further points considered by the Commission under the 'bribery' heading **5.24** are of particular interest in the light of the further attention they have received from the Law Commission. In a section entitled 'The Guilty Parties', Salmon looked at the position of intermediaries and third parties. The concern was first whether the existing legislation caught the main parties in a transaction where the corrupt gift or consideration is made to a third party (Salmon cites the examples of a friend or relative) rather than to the public servant himself. Secondly, were intermediaries who arrange corrupt transactions (or attempt to arrange them without the knowledge of both the other parties) caught? Salmon's conclusion was that the 1889 Act was sufficiently broadly drafted to cover all these situations, but that the 1906 Act was substantially different. 'On the first point, the 1906 Act catches an agent in respect of a corrupt gift or consideration given by a third party, but it does not specifically prohibit the

[21] ibid para 52. [22] ibid para 53. [23] ibid paras 54–56.

actual giving of a corrupt gift to anyone other than the agent himself.' On the second point, Salmon felt that the 1906 Act caught an intermediary 'only to the extent that he actually gives or offers a corrupt gift or consideration to the agent'.[24] Salmon preferred the wider drafting of the 1889 Act, but felt that it was unsatisfactory that identifiable offences of this type should be left, in practice, to be dealt with by framing indictments for conspiracy. The Commission therefore recommended 'that the broad drafting of the 1889 Act be adopted to apply to all offences of corruption in the public sector'.

5.25 However, again, no further action was taken at the time by the Government. The Salmon Report was not even discussed in the Commons, but it was fully debated in the House of Lords, where it received a mixed response.[25] Lord Pannell felt that it dealt with the 'small change' of local government, and went on: 'The amount of paper work and the number of civil servants needed to put the thing on the statute book simply would not be worthwhile.'[26]

D. Post-Salmon

5.26 It took nearly twenty years for Parliament to return to the question of standards in public life, with the appointment of a new Committee, chaired by Lord Nolan. Nolan's Committee had a much wider remit than Redcliffe-Maud or Salmon, being called upon not only to revisit corruption and standards in local government, which he did in his Third Report, but also education (in the Second Report). Nolan's First Report, however, dealt with the 'large change' of parliamentary standards. In it, Nolan recalled the work of the Salmon Commission and expressed the view that the Law Commission should take forward the work on clarifying the law relating to bribery in relation in particular to bribing Members of Parliament, where there was constitutional uncertainty as to whether Parliament itself had jurisdiction or whether MPs could be tried by the courts. Nolan's view was that the Law Commission could at the same time usefully take forward the question of consolidating the statute law on bribery, as Salmon had recommended and the government had accepted, but had done nothing about,[27] the topic having no doubt got lost in the general inertia which seemed to spread in relation to standards in local government following the House of Lords debate on Salmon.

5.27 Thirty years on, two Law Commission Reports and a consultation process later, Parliament is moving cautiously towards legislating on these difficult issues. In the

[24] Salmon Report, para 57.
[25] *Hansard* HL vol 378, cols 585–604 and 611–674 (8 December 1976).
[26] ibid col 645—cited in the Law Commission's Consultation Paper No 145, para 3.15.
[27] Nolan (n 1 above) paras 2.103, 2.104.

meantime the Poulson Affair, a great scandal in its time, had been overtaken by other large financial scandals involving ever greater sums of money—the PCW Affair at Lloyd's, Guinness, Barlow Clowes, Maxwell, and BCCI. Insofar as these raised issues relating to governance, the questions raised related more to the various regulatory regimes in place and led, ultimately, to the creation of the Financial Services Authority (FSA). It is perhaps not surprising that these cases shifted the attention of Parliament away from corruption issues: individual cases of corruption do not tend to cause direct loss to the taxpayer; large-scale regulatory failure can prove extremely expensive, as Barlow Clowes in particular (where the government ended up paying over £100 million in compensation to defrauded investors) demonstrated. Alleged misfeasance in public office by officials of the Bank of England in respect of failure to regulate BCCI might also have led to a huge liability if the liquidators had succeeded on behalf of former depositors in the *Three Rivers District Council* litigation.[28] However, the difficulties of showing bad faith on the part of the Bank of England officials finally proved insurmountable, and the liquidators dropped their case nearly two years into the trial. The Bank had freely admitted negligence in exercising its supervisory role, but enjoys statutory protection under section 1(4) of the Banking Act 1987.[29]

None of these affairs involved large-scale corruption of public officials in the **5.28** United Kingdom in the same way that Poulson did. Perhaps the rewards to be gained from Poulson-type activities are no longer so great, but perhaps, also, the establishment of clear guidelines for public servants in the United Kingdom, following Redcliffe-Maud, has played its part. This can be seen as an encouraging precedent for governments facing similar problems, particularly in the developing world. To a large extent nowadays, corruption has moved 'offshore'—the big bribery cases involve arms dealing, the energy industry and, in this respect like Poulson, the construction industry. This is particularly the case insofar as all these activities involve developing countries. But it still takes two to bribe, and the regrettable fact is that, in the majority of the modern cases, the bribers are from the developed world. Both Redcliffe-Maud and Salmon identified the difficulty of getting the public to report corruption: it is hard enough in a society in which the rule of law prevails, nigh on impossible in less developed societies. It behoves the United Kingdom to ensure that its domestic legislation gives as little comfort as possible to the perpetrators of corruption worldwide.[30]

[28] The House of Lords established the test to be applied in determining whether there had been misfeasance in public office in *Three Rivers District Council v Bank of England (No 3)* [2000] 2 WLR 1220, and in [2001] 2 All ER 513 the House of Lords, by a majority (Lords Hobhouse and Millett dissenting), determined that this claim should proceed to trial.

[29] *The Times*, 3 November 2005.

[30] In this respect, the news that the SFO is investigating four cases in which British companies have allegedly bribed public officials in multi-million pound transactions in the Middle East, Asia, and Africa using powers under ATCSA 2001 is especially welcome: *The Times*, 1 August 2005.

5.29 Overall, the conclusions reached in Nolan and by the Law Commission have been that the two fronts on which action is needed are the consolidation of the law relating to bribery and the misuse of public office. As far as the latter is concerned, the Nolan Committee was in favour of legislation being prepared, again in consultation with the Law Commission, and a public consultation process was put in hand in 1997 which is dealt with at para 5.40 below.

E. The Committee on Standards in Public Life

5.30 Growing public disquiet over the conduct of Members of Parliament on such issues as 'cash for questions',[31] declarations of Members' interests, acceptance on leaving office of positions on the boards of companies with which ministers had had official dealings whilst in office, and appointments to serve on 'quangos' led to the establishment of the Committee on Standards in Public Life (CSPL) in October 1994.[32]

5.31 A Gallup survey carried out in November 1994 revealed that 67 percent of those polled felt that 'the ethical and moral standards of British politicians have been declining in recent years'. In response to specific questions on acceptable behaviour by MPs, 95 percent said it was not right to accept cash for asking questions in Parliament, 92 percent that it was not right to accept free holidays abroad, 69 percent that it was not right to accept free Wimbledon or other sporting event tickets, 47 percent that it was not right to accept a free lunch at a restaurant, and 45 percent did not think it right for MPs to be given bottles of wine or whisky at Christmas.[33] It was apparent that the general public expected the highest standards of their MPs.

5.32 The First Nolan Report was published in May 1995, concentrating on Members of Parliament, the Executive: ministers and civil servants, and quangos. As noted in Chapter 8 below, the Committee was unable to state conclusively that standards in public life had declined but it was able to say that conduct in public life was subject to more rigorous scrutiny than ever before and that the great majority of people in public life met the high standards the public expected of them.

5.33 In making its recommendations, the Committee thought it important that the general principles of conduct underpinning public life should be restated. The Report sets out what it termed The Seven Principles of Public Life.[34] These

[31] At the heart of this concern was the revelation that two Government Ministers, Neil Hamilton and Tim Smith, had accepted cash from Mohamed Al Fayed, owner of Harrods department store, for asking questions in Parliament. What had made matters worse was that the Government had been accused of an attempted cover-up of the whole affair, *The Guardian*, 13 November 1996.

[32] See 8.05ff below.

[33] Nolan (n 1 above) Table 3, p 108.

[34] ibid 14: they are set out in full at the beginning of Ch 8 below.

principles, said the Committee, should be incorporated in Codes of Conduct to be drawn up by all public bodies.[35] Independent scrutiny of internal systems was recommended for maintenance of standards and the need for education to promote and reinforce standards of conduct is identified, particularly through induction training. The specific recommendations relating to the three sectors of public life examined by Nolan in the First Report are dealt with in Chapter 8 below. The inquiry encompassed the whole spectrum of public life in the United Kingdom including Parliament, central government (ministers and civil servants), various types of appointed bodies, local government, special advisers, and others. Since the First Report of the Committee a further nine Reports have been produced. The further Reports are also dealt with in Chapter 8 below.

F. The Home Office Initiatives

1. Bribery of MPs

Independently of the work being undertaken by the Law Commission, the Government did take steps to clarify the law relating to bribery of, or receipt of bribes by, Members of Parliament. In December 1996 the Home Office published a document addressing this issue. The document, entitled *Clarification of the Law Relating to Bribery of Members of Parliament*, was addressed to the Select Committee on Standards and Privileges in the House of Commons and the Committee for Privileges in the House of Lords. The Government accepted there was ambiguity in the existing situation regarding MPs committing corrupt acts. It seemed likely that such acts would constitute the common law offence of Misuse of Public Office, but the effect of article 9 of the Bill of Rights, 1688, was likely to be that some of the evidence necessary to establish guilt or innocence might not be available. Article 9 provides that the freedom of speech in debates or proceedings in Parliament ought not to be impeached or questioned in any court or place outside Parliament. The Committees were invited to consider four broad options:[36] **5.34**

(1) to rely solely on parliamentary privilege to deal with the accusations of bribery of MPs;
(2) to subject MPs to the present corruption statutes in full;
(3) to distinguish between conduct which should be dealt with by criminal law and that which should be left to Parliament itself; and
(4) to make criminal proceedings subject to the approval of the relevant House of Parliament.

[35] Nolan thus maintains the approach first advocated by Redcliffe-Maud: his Seven Principles are concisely stated and, as previously observed, intended as guidelines for the drafting of Codes appropriate to individual bodies.

[36] Set out in para 9.

5.35 It was recognized that an approach which relied purely on parliamentary privilege had several drawbacks. There was the question of sanctions—misconduct by an MP could be punished by suspension or expulsion; conviction under the Prevention of Corruption Acts could mean prison for up to seven years or an unlimited fine. The investigative machinery available to Parliament could not be compared to that of the police. Importantly, if the conduct of the MP was not covered by the criminal law, then the conduct of the person bribing the Member (or being bribed by him or her) would also be immune from criminal investigation and proceedings. Finally, Parliament would be without an effective sanction if the corrupt conduct only came to light after the individual had ceased to be a Member of the House.[37]

5.36 In June 1997, the Home Secretary announced his intention to take forward the Law Commission's proposals on the new offence of corruption and to legislate to bring bribery of MPs in respect of their official parliamentary duties within the scope of statute law once the reports of the parliamentary committees had been received and considered. At the same time, the Home Office produced its own consultation document on the prevention of corruption.[38] It contained a number of interesting and useful statements on the Government's approach. It also stated that there might be some justification for having a single offence of corruption[39] and that there was a case for extending the existing statutes to cover trustees and all situations where a person has a duty, express or implied, to use his or her impartial judgment on an issue.[40] It suggested that it was right to consider carefully an extension to the presumption of corruption.[41] It also suggested that a corruption offence should be a serious arrestable offence.[42]

5.37 The Statement recognized that there was work under way in international fora on corruption and made specific reference to work in the Council of Europe on a criminal law convention on corruption[43] and that of the OECD on the bribery of foreign public officials.[44] It recognized that this work raised the question of the adequacy of existing UK laws in dealing with corruption outside the jurisdiction. In the section of the Statement dealing with jurisdiction it was pointed out that provided one element of the corrupt transaction took place in England or Wales (offer, acceptance, or agreement to accept) the courts would have jurisdiction, but noted that there were proposals under discussion to make acts preparatory to corrupt activity abroad, which amounted to conspiracy or incitement, an offence. Thus, as the Statement says, the board or senior management of a UK based company authorizing the use of bribes abroad in order

---

[37] See para 12 of the Discussion Paper.

[38] *The Prevention of Corruption: Consolidation and Amendment of the Prevention of Corruption Acts 1899–1916*, A Government Statement, June 1997 (hereinafter 'Statement').

[39] ibid para 3.6. [40] ibid para 3.10. [41] ibid para 3.12

[42] ibid para 3.14 [43] See Ch 9 below. [44] See Ch 10 below.

to secure business could, if the proposals were eventually enacted, attract criminal liability in the United Kingdom, provided the bribe in question was unlawful in the country in which it was to be made.[45]. This has now been addressed in the Anti-Terrorism, Crime and Security Act 2001.[46]

Consideration was given to various possible definitions of corrupt behaviour, in particular one formulated by the Council of Europe, but it was noted that whilst it covered bribery it did not extend to the creation of false documentation (said to be covered by the 1906 Act) and suggested some separate definitions.[47] On the question of misuse of office, the Statement noted that this was a concept known to several continental jurisdictions as 'trading in influence' and suggested that it could constitute an offence 'for a person to influence intentionally, directly or indirectly, a decision, in order to gain undue advantage for himself, or any other person'.[48] **5.38**

The Statement concluded by inviting views on the creation of a single offence of corruption to cover both the public and private sectors and the need to cover trustees and misuse of public office. It expressed the hope that responses to the Statement, taken with the Law Commission Consultation Paper on corruption offences and emerging conclusions on work in international fora should put the Government 'in a better position early next year [1998] to determine whether and how to amend the law of corruption'.[49] Seven years on, the Government has yet to amend the law of corruption, whilst hardly a day goes by without reports in the newspapers of fresh stories of bribery and corruption, both internationally and in the United Kingdom.[50] The need for reform seems to be greater than ever. **5.39**

G. The Law Commission

1. Legislating the Criminal Code: Corruption, a Consultation Paper

As has been seen above, the Salmon Commission had recommended the rationalization of the statute law on bribery. The Nolan Committee had pointed out that since the Government had accepted but not implemented the recommendation, it might be a task which the Law Commission could take **5.40**

---

[45] Statement (n 38 above) section d, para 3.19. [46] See 5.159 below.

[47] Statement (n 38 above) para 4.7. [48] ibid para 4.8.

[49] Statement (n 38 above) para 5.3.

[50] In the first two weeks of August 2005, the first report of the Volcker Committee appointed to investigate allegations of bribery at the United Nations in the Iraqi Oil for Food programme found extensive evidence of bribe taking and corruption, *The Times* 9 August 2005; the SFO announced its investigation into allegations of bribery by British companies in the Middle East, Asia and Africa, *The Times* 1 August 2005; on 10 August the *International Herald Tribune* front page headline was 'In Russia, bribery is the cost of business' and President Lula of Brazil was having to apologize to the people for a bribery scandal involving his party which he said he had not known about, *International Herald Tribune*, 13–14 August 2005.

forward. On 15 January 1997, The Law Commission published a Consultation Paper,[51] inviting comments by 30 June 1997. In answer to a Parliamentary question as to what action he proposed to take on reform and consolidation of the law of corruption, with particular reference to the bribery of Members of Parliament, the Home Secretary stated on 9 June 1997 that the Government was committed to tackling corruption in all areas of public and private life, including the bribery of MPs.[52] He announced that he was publicizing on that day the Statement on reform of the corruption statutes considered above.

5.41 On 27 October 1997, the Minister of State for the Home Office said, in answer to a written parliamentary question, that the Home Secretary was expected to make a further statement on reform in early 1998.[53] The Law Commission's Report was laid before Parliament and published on 2 March 1998.[54]

5.42 As has been noted above, the Law Commission adhered to the view that it was not for it to look into the position of MPs and that the same applied to Ministers of the Crown. They considered the position would be clarified by the Home Office Review. The result was that the Law Commission's Report does not expressly refer to ministers or MPs. The Law Commission stated that they expected the draft Bill to be amended in accordance with the conclusions of the current Home Office Review and express provision made. The remit of the Law Commission only covered England and Wales. The Prevention of Corruption Acts apply in Scotland as in England and Wales, with only minor differences. However, there are major differences between the relevant rules of evidence and procedure in the two jurisdictions and the common law is different.

5.43 The Law Commission's Consultation Paper represents the most comprehensive review there has been of the nature of corruption and how it can be tackled through legislation making it a criminal offence. Flaws in the existing legislation are exposed and comprehensive proposals are set out, together with the invitation to comment. Part I of the Consultation Paper considers the meaning of corruption, corruption and breach of duty, and the interrelationship of corruption with theft, fraud, and dishonesty. These considerations are followed by the Commission's Conclusions and Proposals. The remainder of the Consultation Paper looks at various issues in depth, for example the Agency Relationship,[55] Formulating a Modern Bribery Offence,[56] and Territorial Jurisdiction.[57] It also appends summaries of the laws of Australia, Canada, South Africa, Hong Kong, and Sweden, as well as taking a look at Australia's

51 *Legislating the Criminal Code: Corruption*, A Consultation Paper, Law Com No 145 (hereinafter 'Consultation Paper').

52 Written Answers, *Hansard* HC vol 295, col 346 (9 June 1997).

53 Written Answers, *Hansard* HC vol 299, col 739 (27 October 1997).

54 *Legislating the Criminal Code: Corruption*, Law Com No 248 (hereinafter 'Report').

55 Consultation Paper (n 51 above) part VII.

56 ibid Part VIII.

57 ibid Part IX.

Law Reform Proposals.[58] The full text of the Commission's Proposals is set out below, following a brief resumé of the Commission's initial considerations in Part I.

2. The Meaning of Corruption

The Commission selects the following meanings of the verb 'to corrupt' from the *Oxford English Dictionary*: 'To destroy or pervert the integrity or fidelity of (a person) in his discharge of duty; to induce to act dishonestly or unfaithfully; to make venal; to bribe.' The adjective 'corrupt' it quotes as meaning, amongst other things: 'Perverted from uprightness and fidelity in the discharge of duty; influenced by bribery or the like; venal.' **5.44**

3. Corruption and Breach of Duty

The Commission describes a corrupt transaction in its simplest form as involving three parties: A, the donor of the bribe (the briber); B, the agent of C and recipient of the bribe (the bribee), and C, the principal of B. It goes on to set out the interplay of interests of these three actors thus: **5.45**

(1) A and C both act in self-interest, and their interests potentially conflict with each other.
(2) B, as agent of C, is not entitled to act in self-interest, but is under a duty to act in the interests of C.
(3) By bribing B, A (acting in self-interest) tempts B to breach the duty owed by B to C, by appealing to B's self-interest.

Thus, says the Commission, the essential 'purpose of a bribe by A is to cause B to act contrary to the interests of C and in the interests of A. A does this, not by requiring B to act in the interests of A rather than C, but by *tempting* B to act in self-interest, the result of which will coincide with a result desired by A, also acting in self-interest'.[59] As the Commission goes on to say: 'The paradigm set out above casts A as the wrongdoer: *but for* A, B would have discharged his or her duty on behalf of C. A variant of the corrupt transaction, however, is one in which it is B who is the initiator: B *offers* to breach his or her duty to C, to the advantage of A, in exchange for a bribe from A.'[60] **5.46**

The Commission concludes that, given the consensual nature of bribery, the moral reprehensibility of A and B in the paradigm and its variant is fairly **5.47**

[58] ibid Apps B and C.

[59] Consultation Paper (n 51) para 1.12. The Commission refers to a dictum of Lawton LJ, identifying the purpose of the Prevention of Corruption Acts 1889–1916 as being 'to prevent agents and public servants being put in positions of temptation': *Wellburn* (1979) 69 Cr App R 254, 265.

[60] The Commission notes that under the 1889 Act, s 1, it is an offence corruptly to 'solicit' a bribe; under the 1906 Act, s 1(1), it is an offence for any agent corruptly to 'attempt to obtain' a bribe.

evenly balanced: the only distinction is in the identity of the instigator. In the Commission's view, therefore, the existing law of corruption could be said to address two mischiefs:

(1) the *fundamental mischief* (B's breach of duty); and
(2) the *mischief of temptation* (A's temptation of B, by bribery, to breach his or her duty).[61]

5.48 Thus, said the Commission, 'in focusing on the mischief of temptation, the Prevention of Corruption Acts do not criminalise corruption in the *fundamental* sense of criminalising breaches of duty: rather, they seek to prevent it by criminalising a particular kind of conduct—bribery—which is *likely to encourage* breaches of duty'.[62]

4. Corruption, Theft, Fraud, and Dishonesty

5.49 The Law Commission originally intended to carry out a comprehensive review of the law of dishonesty and saw the corruption project as part of that exercise.[63] However, when it looked further into the matter, the Commission began to see corruption as a distinct and independent kind of crime which, as it states, had certain implications for the issues addressed in the Consultation Paper and the proposals made.

5. Corruption and Theft

5.50 The Commission recognized that it is arguable that the acceptance of a bribe by a fiduciary amounts to theft.[64] However, they also recognized that there is uncertainty about the legal status of the appropriated property which arises from a consideration of the civil cases on the subject, particularly *Lister v Stubbs*[65] and *Attorney-General for Hong Kong v Reid*.[66] Both of these cases will be discussed below.[67] The essential question for the Commission was whether the principal could be said to have a proprietary interest in the bribe such that subsequent dishonest dealing with the proceeds would amount to an act of theft: the Privy Council's decision in the *Reid* case would open up that possibility. The Commission points out however that, strictly speaking, the Court of Appeal's decision in *Lister* was binding on the courts below, whilst in theory that of the Privy Council in *Reid* is only persuasive. At the same time, as it notes, there are instances when a Privy Council decision has been consistently preferred to a Court of Appeal decision which has never been overruled.[68]

[61] Consultation Paper (n 51 above) para 1.15. [62] ibid para 1.16.
[63] ibid para 1.17.! [64] Theft Act 1968, s 1(1). [65] (1890) 45 ChD 1.
[66] [1994] 1 AC 324 PC. [67] See 6.33–6.35 below.
[68] *Worcester Works Finance Ltd v Cooden Engineering Co Ltd* [1972] 1 QB 210, 217, 219 is authority for saying that if the Privy Council declines to follow a Court of Appeal decision, an

But, according to the Commission, even if the *Reid* decision is right, its implications for the law of theft are as yet unclear. In *Attorney-General's Reference (No 1 of 1985)*[69] the Court of Appeal held that the receipt by an agent of a secret profit was not theft. This was before the *Reid* decision so the Court did not think there was a proprietary interest, but said, even if the principal had had such an interest, it was not the sort of proprietary interest with which the Theft Act was concerned. In other words, as the Commission says, the Court appears to have taken the view that, even if the taking of a secret profit (or bribe) could be squeezed within the wording of the Act, it was not within its spirit.[70] The Commission did not form a view, but for other reasons felt that this was outside the scope of this project.[71] **5.51**

6. Corruption and Fraud

The concept of fraud is wider than theft, in that it includes any dishonest conduct intended to result in loss (or the risk of loss) to another.[72] An agreement between two or more persons to engage in such conduct is a conspiracy to defraud at common law, even if the course of conduct agreed upon does not involve appropriation of property belonging to another.[73] In the majority of corruption cases the corrupt agent will be defrauding his or her principal, for example the principal may be paying more for goods or services because the agent has corruptly accepted a higher tender, or arranged for overpriced invoices to be rendered. Corruption is therefore often charged as conspiracy to defraud, which is frequently easier to prove than an offence under the Prevention of Corruption Acts, which require proof that a bribe has been offered, solicited, or provided.[74] In addition, the consent of the Attorney-General is not required in order to bring a prosecution—in contrast to the requirement in both the 1889 and 1906 Acts. **5.52**

The difficulty with classifying corruption under fraud is that fraud offences presuppose the existence of a victim. As noted below,[75] corruption is often thought of as a victimless crime. Under the civil law this does not matter—an agent has to account for a bribe even if the principal has suffered no loss, because the agent has been unjustly enriched.[76] For criminal law, however, the element of loss to another person is crucial—no loss (or risk of loss), no fraud. **5.53**

English court is thereafter at liberty to follow the Privy Council decision. *Reid* has been applied in *A-G v Blake* [1997] Ch 84, *Tesco Stores Ltd v Pook* [2003] EWHC 823 and *Corporacion Nacional del Cobre de Chile v Interglobal Inc* [2002–03] 5I TELR 744 (a Cayman Islands case)

[69] [1986] QB 491.
[70] Consultation Paper (n 51 above) para 1.21.
[71] ibid para 1.22.
[72] *Scott v Metropolitan Police Commissioner* [1975] AC 819.
[73] *Criminal Law: Conspiracy to Defraud* (1994) Law Com No 228.
[74] ibid para 4.56.
[75] See 6.19 below.
[76] *Parker v McKenna* (1875) 10 Ch App 96, 124–125, *per* Williams LJ.

The Law Commission's view, however, was that loss is not central to a crime of corruption: the criminal element consists in its being contrary to the public interest and the damaging consequences, all too apparent in some countries, if such conduct becomes widespread. It is therefore in the public interest, says the Commission, that people should refrain from conduct which encourages agents to act in breach of duty, *whether or not anyone would be defrauded by such conduct.*[77] The Commission also recognized that a second criminal element is the fraud on the principal, because the principal's private interests are improperly put at risk.

7. Corruption and Dishonesty

5.54 Dishonesty is an element in offences of theft and conspiracy to defraud and has been defined as including whatever the jury or magistrates believe 'ordinary and honest people' would find dishonest—provided the defendant is shown to have realized that ordinary and honest people would take that view.[78] Ordinary people would almost certainly take the view that giving or receiving a bribe involves acting dishonestly, even if the act was not a fraud (in the absence of loss). However, the Law Commission takes the view that it is not necessarily helpful to use the concept of dishonesty in such a broad sense for the purpose of classifying and defining criminal offences generally, or law reform projects. It feels that it is preferable to confine 'offences of dishonesty' to those involving a *victim*, ie in effect, offences involving fraud and, as it remarks, 'just as there can be fraud without corruption, so there can be corruption without fraud'.[79]

5.55 The Law Commission's provisional conclusion was, therefore, that 'corruption is not in essence, and should not be treated as, an offence of dishonesty or fraud'. It took the view that corruption is a crime in its own right, independent of the law of fraud, and should not therefore conform to the structure or conventions of that law, for example by introducing the notion of dishonesty, which the Commission regarded as being incidental to the *essence* of corruption.[80]

H. Provisional Conclusions and Proposals

1. The New Offence

5.56 The Law Commission's provisional conclusion was that the law of corruption was in an unsatisfactory condition, and should be re-stated in a modern statute

[77] Consultation Paper (n 51 above) para 1.25 (Original emphasis).
[78] *Ghosh* [1982] QB 1053.
[79] Consultation Paper (n 51 above) para 1.25.
[80] ibid para 1.30.

creating a new offence of bribery.[81] The Commission provisionally proposed[82] that the new offence should be committed where:

(1) an agent corruptly accepts, solicits, or agrees to accept an advantage in connection with the performance of his or her duty;
(2) any person corruptly accepts, solicits, or agrees to accept an advantage in connection with the performance by an agent of his or her duty;
(3) any person corruptly confers, or offers, or promises to confer, an advantage on an agent in connection with the performance of his or her duty; or
(4) any person corruptly confers, or offers, or promises to confer, an advantage on any person in connection with the performance by an agent of his or her duty.

2. The Agency Relationship

For the purpose of the new offence, the Commission proposed that the term 'agent' should be defined as: **5.57**

(1) any person who, by virtue of his or her status, falls within one or more of certain specified categories;
(2) subject to any express exclusion, any person who has undertaken (expressly or impliedly) to act on behalf of another, where that undertaking involves one or some of the following features:
    (a) that person exercising a discretion on the other's behalf,
    (b) that person having access to the other's assets (irrespective of whether he or she has been given a discretion to act in regard to those assets),
    (c) that person having influence over the other's decisions (as regards the other's assets or any other interest); or
(3) subject to any express exclusion, any person who has undertaken to discharge a public duty (whether appointed as a public office holder or to perform a specified public function).

'The Agency Relationship' is considered in depth in Part VII of the Consultation Paper. The Commission used the definition to be found in *Halsbury's Laws of England*[83] to define an 'agency relationship' in its strict technical sense: 'the relation which exists where one person has an authority or capacity to create legal relations between a person occupying the position of principal and third parties'. However, although in the Consultation Paper the Commission refers to the relationship between B and C as an agency relationship, it says that it is not intended that the proposed offence of bribery should be confined to cases of agency in the strict sense,[84] rather, it provisionally proposes that the terms 'agent' and 'principal' should simply be used to describe the parties to the core relationship required by a modern offence of bribery.[85] **5.58**

[81] ibid para 1.35
[82] The proposals are set out in paras 1.36–1.44 of the Consultation Paper: they are reproduced below and in following pages.
[83] D Hay (ed) (4th edn, London: Butterworths, 1990) vol 1(2), p 4, para 1.
[84] Consultation Paper (n 51 above) para 7.4.
[85] ibid para 7.6.

5.59 In considering the scope of the agency relationship, the Commission recognizes that it is necessary to take into account the fact that an individual may owe a duty of loyalty to another individual, or he or she may be the holder of a public office and be charged with public duties so that the duty of loyalty is owed not to another individual but to an abstraction, ie the public or the public interest.[86] The Commission then goes on to consider how the 'agency relationship' can be best defined and turns to the essential fiduciary nature of the relationship, embodying both loyalty and trust. This 'obligation of loyalty' was described judicially in the following terms: 'someone who has undertaken to act for or on behalf of another in a particular matter in circumstances which give rise to a relationship of trust and confidence. The distinguishing obligation of a fiduciary is the obligation of loyalty. The principal is entitled to the single-minded loyalty of his fiduciary'.[87]

5.60 After considering status-based fiduciaries, such as trustee and beneficiary; agent and principal in the strict sense; partner and co-partner; director and company; employee and employer; and legal practitioner and client, all of whom, it says, offer classic examples of the agency relationship in bribery, the Commission turns to fact-based fiduciaries, ie those who do not fall within the status-based relationship, but are nevertheless regarded as fiduciaries because of 'the factual situation of the particular relationship'. The Commission sets out factors to be taken into account to test the relationship[88] and then offers a preliminary definition of the agency relationship, based on the fiduciary model, on which the Proposal set out in (2)(a) to (c) at para 5.57 above is based.

5.61 The Commission then goes on to introduce the concept of the quasi-fiduciary. It makes the point that, historically, the corruption laws were at first concerned only with public officers[89] and were only later extended to private agency relationships,[90] whereas in its Consultation Paper, the starting point of the Commission's analysis is the private law concept of fiduciary, extended to incorporate a public law analogue—the *quasi-fiduciary*. The distinguishing feature of the quasi-fiduciary is that he or she owes duties to the particular authority under which he or she holds office, for example the Crown. The Commission quotes PD Finn[91] on the interrelationship between the two sets of duties owed by a public officer:

> . . . quite apart from th[e] 'employment' relationship the public nature of his position subjects him to additional duties and liabilities. The public is, in the eyes

86 ibid para 7.7.

87 *per* Lord Ellenborough CJ in *Thompson v Havelock* (1808) 1 Camp 527.

88 Consultation Paper (n 51 above) para 7.13.

89 Under the common law and the Public Bodies Corrupt Practices Act 1889.

90 The Prevention of Corruption Act 1906.

91 PD Finn *Fiduciary Obligations* (Sydney: Law Book Company, 1977).

of the law, regarded as reposing 'trust and confidence' in him, and the common law—on grounds of public policy—and equity—through the rules of fiduciary obligation—have combined to ensure that that trust and confidence is not ignored or abused.[92]

Rather than simply substituting 'the public' for 'C' in the preliminary definition given in para 5.45 above, the Commission thought it preferable to provide a separate definition, as expressed in para 5.57 (3) above.

The Commission then introduces its 'List' concept, having perceived that there would be individuals who fell within the agency relationship test based on the fiduciary model who nevertheless should not be subject to the criminal law of corruption. Classes of persons who *should* be on the list in the Commission's view include: judges, local councilors, and police officers. Excluded from the list should be witnesses, jurors, and electors. Also excluded, but mainly because the Commission did not consider it appropriate for itself to be dealing with them, are Members of Parliament, members of the House of Lords and government ministers.[93] The Commission asks for views on whether the List-based approach is of practical assistance.[94] **5.62**

3. Tripartite Relationships: Liability of the Agent

Reverting to its paradigm cited at para 5.45 above, the Commission introduces a more complex form of transaction in which: **5.63**

(1) A confers an advantage on a *third party*, D, with a view to tempting B; or
(2) D acts as *intermediary* between A, the briber, and B, the bribee.

Where a person, D, other than an agent corruptly accepts a bribe in connection with the performance by an agent of his or her duty, the Commission proposed that the offence should also be committed by that agent if he or she receives some or all of: **5.64**

(1) the bribe itself;
(2) the proceeds of the bribe; or
(3) a benefit resulting from the bribe.

The reasoning behind this proposal was as follows: under the 1889 Act, so long as B did not solicit, receive, or agree to receive any payment, B would not be a principal in the commission of the offence. However, B might incur liability under other legislation if he aids, abets, counsels, or procures the receipt of a **5.65**

[92] 'Public Officers: Some Personal Liabilities' (1977) 51 ALJ 313, 315.

[93] The Home Office had, as has been mentioned in 5.34 above, in December 1996, published its own document: *Clarification of the law relating to the Bribery of Members of Parliament: a Discussion Paper.*

[94] Consultation Paper (n 51 above) para 7.52.

bribe by the third party, D,[95] or if he conspires with D with a view to D receiving the bribe.[96]

5.66 B might also incur liability if D passes on some or all of the bribe to him—something it could be quite difficult to define. B might receive some or all of the bribe payment itself, but he could also receive a payment which might be said to be the *proceeds* of the bribe, not necessarily financial—for example sexual favours, or financial, but only indirectly so—for example remission of a debt. Hence the proposal above to include a benefit.

4. Tripartite Relationships: Liability of Third Parties

5.67 The Commission went on provisionally to propose that:

> . . . the offence should be committed by any person who corruptly accepts, solicits or agrees to accept an advantage in connection with the performance by an agent of his or her duty.

5.68 The 1889 Act does not require B, the person being tempted to act in breach of duty, to be the recipient of the bribe. Thus, in a transaction in which the third party, D, is the recipient and distinct from B (the member, officer, or servant of a public body whose conduct is sought to be influenced), D may be guilty of an offence if the receipt can be shown to have been an 'inducement to' or 'reward for' or 'otherwise on account of' B's acting (or refraining from acting) in his or her capacity as a member, officer, or servant of a public body.[97]

5.69 The 1906 Act, however, unlike the 1889 Act, does not allow for such a separation of roles. In the circumstance where A pays a third party, D, with a view to influencing or rewarding an agent, B, neither B nor D would be guilty of an offence under the first paragraph of section 1(1) of the 1906 Act and A would not be guilty under the second paragraph.[98] In this respect the 1906 Act is more limited than the 1899 Act, and, as a result, although third-party transactions involving those associated with public bodies fall foul of the 1889 Act, the 1906 Act will not bite on similar transactions in the private sector.[99]

5.70 As has been seen above,[100] Salmon preferred the wider scope of the 1889 Act, and the Commission agrees, stating that it can see no justification for requiring, by law, that the recipient of a bribe and the agent involved be one and the same person. Accordingly, the Commission took the view that the modern law of bribery should recognize a separation of the role of recipient and agent.

---

[95] Accessories and Abettors Act 1861, s 8. [96] Criminal Law Act 1977, s 1.

[97] Consultation Paper (n 51 above) para 8.70.

[98] If, however, D passed A's 'bribe' to B, both B and D would be guilty under the 1906 Act, since D would then be an offeror and B the recipient agent.

[99] Consultation Paper (n 51 above) para 8.71. [100] See 5.24 above.

5. The Nature of the Benefit

For the purpose of the new offence, the Commission proposed that a person (A) should be regarded as conferring an advantage on another (B) if: **5.71**

(1) A does something that B wants A to do, or that is otherwise of benefit to B; or
(2) A has a right to act to B's disadvantage, and forbears to exercise that right.

The use of the word 'advantage' is derived from the 1889 Act which refers to a 'gift, loan, fee, reward or advantage': section 7 of the Act defines 'advantage' as including: **5.72**

> . . . any office or dignity, and any forbearance to demand any money or money's worth or valuable thing, and includes any aid, vote, consent, or influence, or pretended aid, vote, consent, or influence and also includes any promise or procurement of or agreement or endeavour to procure, or the holding out of any expectation of any gift, loan, fee, reward, or advantage, as before defined.

The Commission took the view that with or without this definition, the word 'advantage' seemed wide enough to cover the doing by one person of any act which is either desired by, or in the interests of, another. In the case of forbearing to act, which is also covered by the definition, the Commission's provisional view was that 'where A has a right to act to B's disadvantage, and forbears to exercise that right, that forbearance should be regarded, for the purpose of [the] proposed new offence, as the conferring of an advantage on B'.[101] **5.73**

6. Corrupt and Non-Corrupt Conduct

The provisional view of the Commission was that an advantage is accepted and conferred 'corruptly' if: **5.74**

(1) it is an inducement to an agent to act or refrain from acting in breach of duty, or a reward for an agent's so acting or refraining from so acting; or
(2) it is an inducement to an agent to act or refrain from acting in any way, or a reward for an agent's so acting or refraining, provided that the transaction has a substantial tendency to encourage that agent, or others in comparable positions, to act in breach of duty.

The Commission considered the distinction between 'inducement' and 'reward'. Inducement is more readily associated with bribery than reward, and in Australia it was proposed that there should be two separate offences—a more serious one involving inducement and a less serious one where rewards were concerned. Despite there being some English authority supporting such a view, the Commission decided on balance to recommend that both be treated equally.[102] The question of whether or not the act procured or rewarded is itself a breach of duty was also considered but the Commission provisionally proposed that it should not be. **5.75**

[101] Consultation Paper (n 51 above) paras 8.61–8.64.

[102] ibid para 8.11.

5.76 The Commission gave thought to the question of whether to define 'corruptly' or to leave the offences to speak for themselves. It was mindful of the view expressed by the Australian Committee[103] which studied the issue, that the quest for certainty in the criminal law can be 'counterproductive if the definitions of concepts like "corruptly" become too complex'.[104]

5.77 The Commission decided in the circumstances to ask for views on (a) whether its analysis of the meaning of the word 'corruptly' is correct (and if not, what it does mean); and (b) whether its meaning should be set out in a statutory definition.

7. Persons Who Have Been, or Are About to Become, Agents

5.78 The Commission provisionally proposed that:

> where a person corruptly accepts, solicits or agrees to accept, or confers or offers or promises to confer, an advantage in connection with the performance by an agent of his or her duty, that person should be guilty of the offence even if the agent in question is no longer an agent, or is not yet an agent, at the material time.

5.79 The Commission took the view that limiting criminality on the basis of *when* a bribe is offered or received was unnecessarily restrictive and artificial. The Model Criminal Code Officers Committee (MCCOC) had reached a similar conclusion: 'Obviously, a person should not be able to avoid liability for these offences . . . simply because he or she sought the benefit just before being appointed to a position, or was paid a reward just after resignation'.[105]

8. Jurisdiction

5.80 It was provisionally proposed that 'the new offence should be included among the offences in respect of which Part I of the Criminal Justice Act 1993, when it is brought into force, will extend the territorial jurisdiction of the English courts'.

5.81 The 1993 Act extended the jurisdiction of the English courts with regard to the inchoate offences of conspiracy, attempt and incitement—by adding bribery to the list of those offences it would, as the Commission states, make it an offence indictable in England and Wales to conspire, outside the jurisdiction, to make a corrupt payment within it. Similarly, a contractor based in England effecting a bribe payment to an agent overseas should also be caught, although the Commission does not say that in terms.[106] What it does say, however, is that, in

[103] The MCCOC, or Model Criminal Code Officers Committee, which produced a Report in December 1995, *Theft, Fraud, and Bribery and Related Offences*.

[104] MCCOC Report, 291.

[105] MCCOC Report, 297–299.

[106] The question of territorial jurisdiction is considered in the Consultation Paper (n 51 above) part IX.

its view, the corrupt activities of foreign quasi-fiduciaries who are not fiduciaries proper should not be subject to UK jurisdiction, on the basis that it is not necessarily appropriate for one country's criminal law to uphold the public interest of another.[107] Whilst there is ever-increasing international cooperation in fighting corruption, such an extension of jurisdiction could be fraught with difficulty if the view is taken that in some jurisdictions vast commission payments, which might be regarded in the United Kingdom as bribes, may be legal in the country of receipt.[108]

9. Distinction between Public Bodies and Others

The Commission provisionally proposed that 'the distinction currently drawn between public bodies and others should be abandoned. In particular, [it provisionally proposed] the abolition of the presumption of corruption created by section 2 of the 1916 Act, which applies only where the alleged bribe has been paid to a person in the employment of the Crown, a government department or a public body.' **5.82**

This proposal was especially welcome in that it recognizes that in the modern world of privatization many functions formerly carried out by public bodies are now carried out by private contractors subject to regulation.[109] **5.83**

I. The Law Commission's Report

Legislating the Criminal Code: Corruption

1. Introduction

The Law Commission's Report[110] was published in March 1998, its terms having been agreed by mid-January, just six months after the closure of the consultation period allowed under the Consultation Paper,[111] which had itself been agreed exactly a year earlier. The Commission acknowledges receipt of **5.84**

[107] Paper (n 51 above) para 7.57.

[108] GR Sullivan, in his interesting article, 'Reformulating the Corruption Laws—the Law Commission Proposals' [1997] Crim LR 730–739, cites the example of the Al Yamahah arms deals with Saudi Arabia where it is obligatory to appoint a local agent as a pre-requisite of doing certain forms of business and 'grotesque' 'commissions' were paid, and refers to ED Herlihy and TA Levine, 'Corporate Crisis: The Overseas Payment Problem' (1976) 8 *Law and Policy in International Business* 547, an article on the Congressional and Senate Hearings into the Lockheed Corporation's extensive bribery of Japanese politicians, which revealed certain British companies 'to be aggressive in paying bribes'. These examples raise interesting questions regarding 'legitimate' levels of commission payments in these jurisdictions.

[109] The Distinction between public bodies and others is the subject of the Consultation Paper (n 51 above) Part VI.

[110] Report (n 54 above).

[111] Consultation Paper (n 51 above).

many and helpful comments from persons and organizations listed in Appendix C of the Report. Annexed to the Report, in Appendix A, is a Draft Corruption Bill,[112] which gives formal expression to the matters considered in the Consultation Paper and taken forward in the Report. Once again, consideration of issues relating to the bribery of ministers and members of both Houses of Parliament are left to the select committees.

5.85 In the summary of the Report which follows, the Commission's Recommendations are considered in detail,[113] followed by a summary of the reasoning behind them.

2. The Present Law and the Need for Change

5.86 The Commission's basic recommendation was that: 'The common law offence of bribery and statutory offences of corruption should be replaced by a modern statute.' This recommendation reflects the Commission's conclusion in the Consultation Paper. The Commission had identified four major defects in the present law. Firstly, there was the multiplicity of sources, including many overlapping common law offences[114] and at least eleven statutes.[115] Much of the legislation was what would now be termed 'knee-jerk' and was thus neither consistent, nor comprehensive.

5.87 The second problem had to do with the distinction between public and private bodies referred to above.[116] Thirdly, there was the difficulty of being sure about exactly to whom the current legislation applies—is a judge an agent for corruption purposes? There were also the questions of timing, and third-party recipients.[117] Fourthly, there was the question of the rebuttable presumption of corruption in the case of public officers, considered by Redcliffe-Maud and by Salmon,[118] and considered further below.

5.88 These defects, together with statements setting out the Government's approach[119] and international initiatives being taken by, amongst others, the European Union, the Council of Europe, the Organization for Economic Co-operation and Development (OECD), the Commonwealth Law Ministers, the G7, the United Nations, the World Trade Organization, the International Monetary Fund, and the Organization of American States,[120] all pointed towards the necessity for having a modern law of bribery.

[112] Reproduced as App 33 below.
[113] They appear in the Report (n 54 above) Part IX.
[114] Considered in Ch 2 above.
[115] Listed in the Consultation Paper (n 51 above) see para 1.3.
[116] See 5.82 above.
[117] Considered at 5.63–5.70 and 5.78–5.79 above.
[118] See 5.12 above and the Salmon Report (n 18 above) paras 59–62, which endorsed Redcliffe Maud's views.
[119] See, eg, 5.36–5.39 above.
[120] See, generally, Ch 9 below.

In the consultation process few disagreed with this conclusion. Such dissent as there was expressed the view that the present laws had not in fact led to many difficulties and questioned whether the introduction of new legislation would make very much difference in an already heavily regulated financial services sector.[121] **5.89**

3. The Presumption of Corruption and the Distinction between Public Bodies and Others

The Commission recommended that: **5.90**

> The new law of corruption
>
> 1) should not include a presumption comparable to that created by section 2 of the 1916 Act (under which a transaction is in certain circumstances presumed to be corrupt unless the contrary is proved), and
> 2) should not draw a distinction between public bodies and others.

These issues are considered in Parts III and IV of the Report. Part III deals with the distinction between public bodies and others. The arguments for and against retaining the distinction had been examined in Part VI of the Consultation Paper. The statutory anomaly that is raised by the rebuttable presumption of corruption of public officials introduced by section 2 of the 1916 Act—which has the effect of making any money, gift, or consideration *deemed* to have been paid or given and received corruptly as an inducement or reward *unless the contrary is proved*—is that it applies only where the employer of the putative bribee or the body with which the putative briber holds or seeks to gain a contract is the Crown, a Government Department, or a public body. The presumption applies to the 1889 Act, which is confined to public bodies but is anomalous in applying also to the 1906 Act, which is concerned with the private sector.[122] **5.91**

One of the difficulties caused by the distinction is in defining what constitutes a public body: in the case of *DPP v Holly and Manners*[123] it was held that the North Thames Gas Board was a public body and that that expression included 'bodies which have public or statutory duties to perform and which perform those duties and carry out their transactions for the benefit of the public and not for private profit'. **5.92**

As the Commission recognized, the public/private distinction had become increasingly anomalous, as more and more functions previously performed by national or local government entities were subcontracted to private companies, and joint ventures between local and central government and private companies increased. The Consultation drew attention to the position of an agent of a **5.93**

[121] These views were submitted by, respectively, the Securities and Investments Board (SIB) and the Financial Law Panel.
[122] Report (n 54 above) para 3.8.
[123] [1978] AC 43, HL.

nationalized industry who accepted a bribe being prosecuted under the 1889 Act and having to prove that the transaction was not corrupt, whilst an agent doing the same thing after privatization would only be committing an offence under the 1906 Act, so that the burden of proof would rest entirely on the prosecution.[124]

5.94 The Commission also considered the question of whether there was some kind of 'higher duty' owed by public employees than by those in the private sector which would justify retaining the distinction. The provisional view expressed in the Consultation Paper[125] was that the point was irrelevant. The MCCOC had taken a similar view, pointing out that when large bribes hit the headlines in the private sector it can be just as damaging to public confidence in the general commerce and financial sectors of the community, which in turn can have an effect on the economy as a whole. The MCCOC were of the view that the amount of damage in a particular case should be a matter for sentencing rather than the subject of a separate offence.[126]

5.95 Consultation respondents, including the CPS, mostly supported the Commission's proposal to discard the distinction—the minority who disagreed were those who believed that a higher standard should be applied to the public sector. The proposal was, however, subject to dealing with the question of the presumption and burden of proof, which was considered in Part IV of the Report.

5.96 Two pieces of legislation that had a direct bearing on the question had come into being just before the Commission published its Consultation Paper, the Criminal Justice and Public Order Act 1994 (CJPOA 1994) and the European Convention on Human Rights (ECHR),[127] Article 6 (2) of which provides that a person charged with a criminal offence must be presumed innocent until proved guilty. The significance of CJPOA 1994 lies in sections 34 and 35. Under section 34, where the defendant relies on a fact in his or her defence at trial which was not put forward when he or she was questioned or charged, or informed that he or she might be prosecuted, the court or jury 'may draw such inferences . . . as appear proper' in determining whether there is a case to answer or whether the defendant is guilty of the offence charged. Section 35 is potentially even more relevant as far as the presumption was concerned, as it allows the jury to 'draw such inferences as appear proper' from a defendant's failure to testify or to answer any particular question.

5.97 The essential question examined by the Commission was whether, with the assistance of CJPOA 1994, the withdrawal of the presumption would make it

---

124 Consultation Paper (n 51 above) para 6. 28.

125 ibid para 6.25.

126 MCCOC Report (n 102 above) 271–273.

127 Convention for the Protection of Human Rights and Fundamental Freedoms (the European Human Rights Convention) Rome, 4 November 1950; TS71 (1953); Cmd 8969.

more difficult for the prosecution (a) to establish a case to answer and, (b) to gain convictions? These matters are given detailed consideration at paragraphs 4.37 to 4.48 of the Report, using different scenarios, with and without the presumption and relying on CJPOA 1994. The outcome was, so far as the Commission could predict, that it would not be significantly more difficult to succeed without the presumption than with it. In this it was supported by the views of the Bar Council, the Criminal Bar Association and the Serious Fraud Office who wrote to say: 'We agree that the case for the retention of the presumption falls, once a case can no longer be made for regarding corruption in the public sector as inherently more difficult to investigate. Corruption of itself is no more or less difficult to investigate than other forms of financial crime.'[128]

Both the Salmon Commission and the Redcliffe-Maud Committee had taken the view that there was a case for extending the presumption and, interestingly, both the Association of Chief Police Officers (ACPO) and the Metropolitan Police Company Fraud Department were in favour, expressing the view that there can be no more serious offence than corruption as 'it erodes and finally destroys public confidence in individuals and institutions' and concluding that 'corruption is an exceptional offence and requires exceptional measures to deal with it'.[129] **5.98**

The Commission concluded, however, that there was no evidence that it was harder to obtain convictions for those corruption offences to which the presumption did not apply than to those to which it did and that, therefore, no special reasons existed to justify the continued existence of the presumption in relation to corruption offences.[130] **5.99**

4. The Agency Relationship: the Law Commission's Recommendations

The Commission recommended that: **5.100**

(1) a person should be regarded as an agent, and another as a principal for whom he or she performs functions, if
  (a) the first is a trustee and the second is a beneficiary under the same trust;
  (b) the first is a director of a company and the second is the company;
  (c) each is a partner in the same partnership;
  (d) the first is a professional person (such as lawyer or accountant) and the second is his or her client;
  (e) the first is an agent and the second is his or her principal (taking agent and principal in the sense normally understood by lawyers); or
  (f) the first is the employee of the second;

(2) a person who does not fall within any of the categories above should be regarded as an agent, and another as a principal for whom he or she performs functions, if there is an agreement or understanding between them (express or implied) that the first is to perform the functions for the second; and

[128] Report (n 54 above) para 4.71. [129] ibid para 4.54. [130] ibid para 4.77.

(3) a person should be regarded as an agent performing functions for the public if the functions he or she performs are of a public nature (whether or not in relation to the United Kingdom).

5.101 The Commission further recommended that: 'Consideration should be given to extending the scope of the corruption offences to include officials of international intergovernmental organisations.' The Commission's consideration of these issues falls within Part V of the Report, which is entitled: *Formulating a Modern Law of Corruption*. The modern statute, the Commission recommended, should create four offences, namely:

(1) corruptly conferring, or offering or agreeing to confer, an advantage;
(2) corruptly obtaining, soliciting or agreeing to obtain an advantage;
(3) corrupt performance by an agent of his or her functions as an agent; and
(4) receipt by an agent of a benefit which consists of, or is derived from, an advantage which the agent knows or believes to have been corruptly obtained.[131]

5.102 As the Commission goes on to say,[132] there are certain concepts which are crucial to these offences:

(1) the relationship of 'agency'
(2) 'conferring an advantage/obtaining an advantage' and
(3) conferring an advantage *corruptly*

5.103 At the heart of the Commission's conception of corruption was the notion of 'breach of duty' by agents. This was heavily criticized because of the potential difficulties it might raise in relation to analysing precisely what duty it was that the agent was supposed to have breached. The Commission therefore altered its stance on this and adopted, with qualifications, a suggestion made by Professor Sir John Smith,[133] that corrupt conduct should be defined in terms of an intention to influence the agent's conduct as agent. This is considered further at paras 5.114 ff below in the section dealing with the conferring of an advantage.[134]

5.104 The Consultation Paper took as its starting point for its analysis of bribery that it was essentially conduct which threatened the relationship of trust which exists between an agent and principal.[135] The traditional concept of an agency relationship was then extended in various ways, for example taking it out of the 'private' context into the idea that the agent could have 'the public' as a principal. The essential quality of the relationship was a fiduciary one, extended to encompass the concept of 'loyalty' in the public sector. The Commission suggested a two-part definition of the agency relationship: private, and quasi-fiduciary.

---

[131] ibid para 5.2. [132] ibid para 5.3.
[133] Emeritus Professor of Law at the University of Nottingham, who assisted the Law Commission throughout the project. [134] See, in particular 5.126 ff below.
[135] Consultation Paper (n 51 above) Parts I and V.

i. Private agency relationships

The Commission reconsidered its definition of private agency relationships and decided it was too complex because it had tried to identify a comprehensive set of circumstances which would give rise to the sort of relationships it envisaged. The Commission accepted that the danger of trying to envisage every situation, whilst useful for illustrative purposes, was that it would be under-inclusive. The Commission therefore adopts an alternative approach, by endeavouring to describe the *essential character* of the agency relationship in terms of *trust*.[136] **5.105**

ii. Quasi-fiduciary relationships

In the Consultation Paper, the Commission defined a quasi-fiduciary agent as one who 'has undertaken to discharge a public duty (whether appointed as public office holder or to perform a specified public function)'. Apparently, very few correspondents expressed a view about the lack of a definition of 'public duty' or 'public function'. The Commission considered whether to try to supply definitions, but had regard to a view expressed by Lord Woolf that the question of whether an issue involves public law depends not on the body concerned being described as a public body but upon the function being performed—furthermore, according to Lord Woolf, the boundaries between public and private functions are 'indistinct and evolving'.[137] The Commission therefore took the view that it should not attempt to define the concept of 'public function' other than in the general terms used in its Recommendation.[138] **5.106**

iii. The list of examples

The Commission continues to maintain in the Report that it is useful to have a list to illustrate those categories of relationship which would invariably fall within the terms of the offence in order to provide a short cut and avoid legal argument over whether a particular kind of relationship would be caught. Others argued that the list approach might cause confusion if a relationship was not within the list. The Commission, however, felt it was still more useful than not to have the illustrations, particularly where the labels 'principal' and 'agent' have more restrictive meanings in other areas of the law. The Commission did, however, accept that there was little point in having a list for those discharging **5.107**

---

[136] Report (n 54 above) paras 5.21–5.24.

[137] The Rt Hon Lord Woolf of Barnes, 'Droit Public-English Style' (1995) *Public Law* 57, 64.

[138] An approach, the Commission notes, adopted in the Human Rights Bill when it was introduced in the House of Lords the previous year, giving effect to the European Human Rights Convention by requiring public authorities to exercise their powers in a manner compatible with the Convention—where 'public authority' is not defined and is said to include 'any person certain of whose functions are functions of a public nature'. Report (n 54 above) para 5.27.

public functions, as there would be no risk of the restricted meaning being applied in those cases.[139]

5. Transnational agency relationships

i. Agents with private foreign principals

5.108 The Consultation Paper provisionally concluded that an agent of a private foreign principal should be regarded as covered by the offence. This was uncontroversial and in tune with efforts being made on the international scene to fight international corruption.

ii. Agents acting for the public interest of another country

5.109 In the Consultation Paper the view was taken that agents acting solely on behalf of the public interest of another country should be exempted from the scope of the new offence. This was met with a barrage of criticism. The Commission took another look at all the international activity taking place and took particular note of the preamble of a draft[140] of the Council of Europe Convention on Corruption which stated that 'corruption threatens the rule of law, democracy and human rights, undermines good governance, fairness and social justice, distorts competition, hinders economic development, and endangers the stability of democratic institutions and the moral foundations of society'. The Commission agreed that exempting those who are required to act in the public interest of other countries would undermine those efforts. It therefore stated that it would be recommending that 'agent' should include a person acting on behalf of the public, not only of the United Kingdom, but also of another country.

iii. Agents acting on behalf of international intergovernmental organizations

5.110 The Commission would not go so far as to recommend the inclusion of an agent who acts on behalf of an international intergovernmental institution, such as the European Union, because it did not feel that it was a matter for the Law Commission. However, it did recommend that consideration be given to including such officials in the future.

6. The Concept of Advantage

5.111 The Law Commission recommended that:

> (1) a person should be regarded as conferring an advantage if
>
> (a) he or she does something or omits to do something which he or she has a right to do, and

---

[139] ibid paras 5.29, 5.30.

[140] As approved by the Working Group on Criminal Law after a second reading of the draft at its 10th meeting, 4–6 November 1997.

(b) the act or omission is done or made in consequence of another's request (express or implied) or with the result (direct or indirect) that another benefits; and

(2) a person should be regarded as obtaining an advantage if

(a) another does something or omits to do something which he or she has a right to do, and

(b) the act or omission is done or made in consequence of the first person's request (express or implied) or with the result (direct or indirect) that the first person benefits.

The choice of the word 'advantage' for the purpose of describing the benefit corruptly conferred, obtained, offered, or solicited was explained in the Consultation Paper.[141] The Commission's provisional view was that the new legislation should apply to anything done by one person (A) which another (B) wants A to do, or which is of benefit to B, and also to an omission by A to exercise a right to act to B's disadvantage. Both kinds of benefit were described as the conferring of an 'advantage' by A on B, and this approach apparently won general approval.[142] The Commission felt, however, that the concept could be improved upon by adding further examples of circumstances in which benefits could be conferred: the additional circumstances are set out at paragraphs 5.40 to 5.42 of the Report—the wording of the Commission's Recommendation reflects the different circumstances envisaged by the Commission. **5.112**

7. The Offences

The Commission sets out its Recommendations regarding the kinds of conduct in relation to an 'advantage' that should be prohibited in the form of the proposed offences set out below. **5.113**

8. Corruptly Conferring, or Offering or Agreeing to Confer, an Advantage

The Commission's Recommendation was that a person should commit an offence if he or she '(1) corruptly confers an advantage, or (2) corruptly offers or agrees to confer an advantage'. The existing legislation uses both the words 'promise' (1889 Act) and 'agree' (1906 Act) to confer an advantage. In the Consultation Paper the Commission marginally preferred 'promise', on the ground it seemed a simpler term. On reflection they preferred 'agree' because it implies the need for agreement by the prospective bribee, which is more consistent with the proposal that it should also be an offence to agree to *accept* a corrupt advantage.[143] **5.114**

[141] See 5.72, 5.73 above.
[142] Report (n 54 above) para 5.39.
[143] ibid paras 5.45, 5.46.

i. Advantage conferred on a person other than the agent

5.115 The omission of the word 'agent' from the definition arises from the Commission's view that conferring the advantage on a person other than the agent should be caught. In this respect the Commission follows the 1889, rather than the 1906 Act, and the views expressed by Salmon. The thinking behind this is to prevent the briber from avoiding the offence by, for example, paying the bribe to the agent's wife.[144]

ii. Intermediaries

5.116 In the Consultation Paper, the Commission provisionally proposed that an intermediary should not commit the offence as a principal offender,[145] perceiving his or her role to be less criminal and open to prosecution for aiding and abetting. Several correspondents made the point, however, that, since the law makes no distinction between an accessory and a principal in the formulation of a charge, the proposed distinction was unnecessary and artificial, if not positively undesirable. Certainly intermediaries frequently play a major role in bringing about corrupt transactions.[146]

9. Corruptly Obtaining, Soliciting, or Agreeing to Obtain an Advantage

5.117 The Commission recommended that a person should commit an offence if he or she '(1) corruptly obtains an advantage, or (2) corruptly solicits or agrees to obtain an advantage'. Under the 1889 Act a person may commit an offence by soliciting, receiving, or agreeing to receive an advantage; under the 1906 Act by accepting it or agreeing to do so, obtaining it or attempting to do so. In the Consultation Paper the words were thought to be interchangeable and 'accept' was provisionally suggested. On further reflection the Commission felt that 'obtain' would be more appropriate to express willing acquiescence in the corrupt conferment of an advantage, for example having moneys paid into a bank account.[147]

10. Corruptly Performing Functions as an Agent

5.118 The Commission recommended that: 'A person should commit an offence if he or she performs his or her functions as an agent corruptly.' Although succinctly expressed, the scope of this offence is intended to be wide. The intention is to catch not only corrupt inducements to show favour in the future, but also corrupt rewards for favour shown in the past. It is also intended to cover the situation where the agent has not actually received the reward, on the basis that the real criminality of the agent's conduct lies in the fact that he or she has allowed his or her judgment to be affected by the *hope* of obtaining a reward,

[144] ibid para 5.47. [145] Consultation Paper (n 51 above) para 8.79.
[146] See 6.25, 6.91 and 10.143 below. [147] Report (n 54 above) para 5.51.

not in the fact that he or she has actually obtained one. The Commission recognized that the conduct of the agent in such a case could be prosecuted as a conspiracy to defraud, but found it inherently unsatisfactory that such an offence should have to be prosecuted in that way when the conduct was essentially corrupt, and should be prosecuted as such under corruption legislation.[148]

11. Agent Receiving Benefit from Corruption

The Commission's Recommendation was that: **5.119**

If

(1) an advantage is obtained corruptly by a person other than the agent concerned,
(2) the agent receives a benefit (in any form) which consists of or is derived (directly or indirectly) from all or part of the advantage,
(3) the agent knows or believes that the advantage was obtained corruptly and that the benefit consists of or is derived from all or part of the advantage, and
(4) the agent gives his or her express or implied consent to receiving the benefit,
the agent should commit an offence.

This Recommendation is designed to deal with the situation where an advantage is initially conferred on someone other than the agent whose conduct it is sought to influence, and the agent later corruptly receives some of the proceeds or some other consequential benefit (for example the remission of a debt); in that situation it is debatable whether the agent committed an offence.[149] However, as the Commission points out, it could not be an offence for an agent merely to receive the benefit in the knowledge that it is derived from an advantage corruptly obtained, because the receipt of the benefit (like the obtaining of the advantage) need not involve the cooperation or consent of the receiver. The Commission therefore recommends that the offence should only be committed if the agent gives consent (express or implied) to the receipt of the benefit.[150] **5.120**

12. 'Corruptly'

The Commission's Recommendation was: **5.121**

(1) that a person who confers an advantage, or offers or agrees to confer an advantage, should be regarded as doing so corruptly if he or she
  (a) intends a person, in performing his or her functions as an agent, to do an act or make an omission, and
  (b) believes that, if the person did so, it would probably be primarily in return for the conferring of the advantage (or the advantage when conferred), whoever obtains it,[151]

[148] Report (n 54 above) para 5.55.
[149] Consultation Paper (n 51 above) para 8.75.
[150] Report (n 54 above) paras 5.59, 5.60.
[151] See Recommendation 10 and the Commission's draft Corruption Bill, cl 6(1).

unless

(i) the advantage is conferred (or to be conferred) by or on behalf of the agent's principal (or, in the case of functions performed for the public, on behalf of the public) as remuneration or reimbursement in respect of the performance of the functions,[152] or

(ii) the functions concerned are performed only for one or more principals (not the public), and each principal is aware of all the material circumstances and consents to the conferring of the advantage or the making of the offer or agreement;

(2) a person should be treated as if he or she were aware of all the material circumstances, and consented to the conferring of the advantage or the making of the offer or agreement, if the defendant believes that that person

(a) is aware of those circumstances and so consents, or

(b) would so consent if aware of those circumstances; and

(3) consent should count for these purposes if given on a principal's behalf by any agent of the principal, unless in giving it the agent performs his or her functions as an agent corruptly.[153]

5.122 This Recommendation is made in response to the necessity perceived by the Commission for defining what is meant by 'corruptly', the word at the heart of all the offences as formulated by the Commission.

13. Is a Definition Necessary?

5.123 It will be recalled that the Salmon Commission thought that it was not necessary to define 'corruptly'.[154] The Law Commission felt that it could not take understanding of the meaning for granted. They had two empirical sources for ascertaining whether there was a consensus on the meaning of the word. One was the interpretative history in the cases, the other was the comments received on the definition provisionally put forward by them.

5.124 In the Consultation Paper two strands of judicial interpretation of 'corruptly' were put forward: on the one hand, an act which the law forbids as tending to corrupt,[155] and on the other, a dishonest intention to weaken the loyalty of an agent to his or her principal.[156] Lanham's conclusion was that the authorities are in 'impressive disarray'.[157] According to the Commission, the responses to the Consultation Paper 'ranged far and wide' and there was little consensus; the clear implication for the Commission was that it was right to identify in the Consultation Paper the uncertainty of the meaning of the word 'corruptly' as one of the most important defects in the present law. Its conclusion was therefore that a definition was most definitely required.[158]

---

[152] ibid cl 10. [153] ibid cl 11. [154] See 5.23 above.

[155] *Cooper v Slade* (1857) 6 HL Cas 746; 10 ER 1488, and *Wellburn* (1979) 69 Cr App R 254.

[156] *Lindley* [1957] Crim LR 321 and *Callard* [1967] Crim LR 236.

[157] D Lanham, 'Bribery and Corruption' in P Smith (ed) *Criminal Law, Essays in Honour of JC Smith* (London: Butterworths, 1987) 92, 104. [158] Report (n 54 above) paras 5.62–5.65.

The Commission approached the task of definition down two routes: the first, devising a workable test of a corrupt *inducement* to an agent to act (or omit to act) in a particular way in the future, and the second how that test might be adapted for corrupt *rewards* to agents for having acted (or omitted to act) in a certain way in the past.[159] **5.125**

14. Corruptly Conferring an Advantage as an Inducement

As has been noted above,[160] the Commission abandoned the approach taken in the Consultation Paper of defining a corrupt inducement in terms of a breach of duty, which the Commission termed 'the first limb' of its definition. 'The second limb' was expressed in terms of a transaction which had 'a substantial tendency to encourage that agent, or others in comparable positions, to act in breach of duty'.[161] After consultation, the Commission came to the view that the second limb was too vague, and too difficult to prove, as well as probably having little practical application.[162] The Commission therefore reformulated the definition, following Professor Sir John Smith's suggestion, as follows: 'An advantage is a corrupt inducement if it is intended to influence an agent in the performance of his or her functions as an agent.' **5.126**

However, as indicated previously, the Commission's feeling was that such a definition, without more, was too wide. The difficulty that it perceived related especially to the practice of the majority of commercial enterprises being caught by the definition when trying to bring in business in a whole variety of ways which involve 'influencing' the agents of other firms whose job it is to decide where their firms' business should go. Some of the methods used, such as advertising, do not involve the 'conferring of advantage', others most certainly do. **5.127**

i. Corporate hospitality

The Commission (rightly in the view of most) recognized the need to exempt advantages bestowed by way of entertainment. The example it cited was of A Ltd, a company hoping to get business from B Ltd, which invites B Ltd's managing director to attend an important football match as the guest of A Ltd's directors. The match is preceded by drinks and lunch, during which, amongst other things, A Ltd's current and future activities are discussed. It is intended that the managing director shall enjoy the event—it is an 'advantage'—and be influenced by it; yet most people would hesitate to conclude that the whole exercise is corrupt. Why should this be? the Commission asked itself.[163] **5.128**

[159] ibid para 5.66. [160] See 5.103 above.
[161] Consultation Paper (n 51 above) para 8.19.
[162] Professor Sir John Smith commented: 'It seems too uncertain—a question which might be the subject of elaborate sociological research but which will be decided by a jury or a magistrate on a hunch.' [163] Report (n 54 above) para 5.77.

5.129 Its answer involved an analysis of the *way* in which A Ltd hoped to influence B Ltd's managing director. The Commission suggested the following possibilities:

(1) the agent may acquire information about the host company which militates in that company's favour when the agent comes to compare it with its rivals; or
(2) the agent's existing relationships with employees of the host company may be cemented, and new ones formed, and the agent may have a natural preference for doing business with people he or she knows; or
(3) the agent may simply decide to favour the host company in return for an enjoyable occasion.[164]

5.130 In the Commission's view, the first and second of the above possibilities are acceptable, the third is not. This is because the first and second methods do not involve *solely* an intent to influence; A Ltd will not much care about the reasons for receiving the business from B Ltd, even if it is awarded. In the third scenario however, if A Ltd knows that B Ltd would not give it the business unless the managing director was invited to the match then it intends the agent to be corruptly influenced.[165]

5.131 The Commission recognizes that there will inevitably be issues as to which of the reasons A Ltd believes there might be for obtaining the work from B Ltd and concludes that the crucial question is whether the provider of the alleged inducement thinks it *probable* (ie more likely than not) that the agent acted in the manner desired *primarily* in return for the advantage conferred. The Commission accepts that this may be a difficult test to apply in practice, but is of the view that this type of question is likely *only* to arise in corporate hospitality and similar situations, where there is a legitimate interaction between the agent and donor. Corporate hospitality would only be likely to be the subject of prosecution where it is blatantly corrupt on any view, the Commission believed.[166]

ii. 'Sweeteners'

5.132 It was always the intention of the Commission to ensure that situations in which A conferred an advantage on B not in order to cause any *specific* breach of duty but to influence the agent's conduct at some indeterminate future time should be caught by the new offences. For this reason the Commission avoids defining the conduct desired of the agent as having to take place *in a particular way*. Instead, it is sufficient if the conferring of the advantage causes the agent to *do an act or make an omission* in performing his or her functions as an agent, without the briber knowing when it is intended they should be done or made.[167]

---

164 ibid para 5.78. 165 ibid, para 5.79. 166 ibid, para 5.82.
167 Report (n 54 above) paras 5.83, 5.84, and see draft Bill, cl 6(3), also in the Report, App A (see App 33 below).

iii. Bribee unaware of corrupt purpose

In the view of the Commission it should make no difference to the culpability of the briber that the bribee is, unknown to the briber, unaware of the briber's corrupt purpose—nearly all respondents agreed.[168] **5.133**

iv. Proper remuneration or reimbursement

These clearly have to be excluded from the definition of 'corruptly' conferring an advantage: this would not be the case if the corrupt intention consisted *solely* of an intention to induce an agent to perform his or her functions as agent in return for the promise of an advantage, in this case, payment of remuneration and reimbursement of expenses legitimately incurred. The formulation of the exception specifically takes into account both the private agent's functions and those of a 'public' agent, as well as those whose functions are mixed private and public.[169] **5.134**

v. Things done with the consent of the principal

This is an important and difficult area. What is the situation where an employee, an agent for the purposes of the Commission's definition, accepts bribes with the full knowledge of the management, and possibly with their active connivance—will this afford a complete defence to the briber? A number of the Commission's respondents, including Professor Sir John Smith, took the view that the principal's consent should provide a complete defence. In the Consultation Paper, however, the Commission had rejected this view, for three main reasons. **5.135**

First, the Commission argued that because corruption is not an offence of fraud or dishonesty (in the sense used by the Commission),[170] the principal's consent should not be a complete defence: whilst acceptance of a bribe with the principal's consent could not amount to a fraud on the principal, it could contribute to a climate in which bribery is common.[171] One has only to look at practices in certain developing countries to realize that this is so. Nevertheless, as a result of abandoning its 'second limb' of the definition,[172] the Commission felt that its argument had become unconvincing.[173] **5.136**

Secondly, the Commission pointed out that such a defence could have no application in relation to a duty owed to the *public*, rather than any particular person. The way around this, the Commission suggested, would be for the law to say that the defence would be available if any *person* to whom the agent owed a duty consented. Thus an advocate who owes a professional duty to the court would not be able to invoke the defence simply because his *client* consented to his being bribed.[174] **5.137**

[168] Report (n 54 above) para 5.85. [169] ibid paras 5.86, 5.87.
[170] See 5.54, 5.55 above. [171] Consultation Paper (n 51 above) para 8.43.
[172] See 5.126 above. [173] Report (n 54 above) para 5.90. [174] ibid, para 5.91.

5.138 Thirdly, the Commission looked at the situation in a corporate body, where the agent clearly owes a duty to the corporate body, but it is not clear who in that body has authority to consent on its behalf. It is likely that the consent will actually have to be given by another 'agent', perhaps the original agent's manager, who may of course also have been bribed, or hope to be. Difficult issues of authority under company law may arise, which, as the Commission acknowledges, would be unsuitable for determination in a criminal court. The Commission therefore recommends that consent may be given by another agent, but that consent will not provide a defence if it is given corruptly.

5.139 If the agent is mistaken about the facts, the law will treat him as if the facts were as he or she believed them to be,[175] thus an agent's conduct will not be corrupt if he or she mistakenly believes that the relevant principal knows all the material circumstances and consents to what is done. The more difficult case, as the Commission acknowledges, is that of the agent who knows that his or her principal has not consented, but believes that if the principal had known the full facts, he or she would have consented. This is similar to the defence that can be raised in theft cases where an appropriation of another's property is not theft if the defendant believes that the owner would have consented if he or she had known of the appropriation and the circumstances of it. Whilst not wishing to condone the conduct of an agent who assumes consent would be forthcoming without making further enquiry, the Commission recommends following the example of the Theft Act, thus not making the agent guilty of a corruption offence in such circumstances.[176]

15. Corruptly Conferring an Advantage as a Reward

5.140 The Commission recommended that:

> A person who confers an advantage, or offers or agrees to confer an advantage, should be regarded as doing so corruptly if he or she
>
> (1) knows or believes that, in performing his or her functions as an agent, a person has done an act or made an omission,
> (2) knows or believes that that person has done an act or made the omission primarily in order to secure that a person obtains an advantage (whoever obtains it), and
> (3) intends the person known or believed to have done the act or made the omission to regard the advantage (or the advantage when conferred) as conferred primarily in return for the act or omission.[177]

5.141 The Consultation Paper looked at the question of characterizing inducements and rewards as corrupt and recommended that both should be offences.[178]

---

[175] *Williams (Gladstone)* [1987] 3 All ER 411, *Beckford* [1988] AC 130.
[176] Report (n 54 above) paras 5.97, 5.98.
[177] See Report (n54 above) para 5.109 above and draft Bill, cl 6(2).
[178] See Report (n 54 above) para 5.101.

All respondents who expressed a view on the provisional definition agreed with it, thus the Commission had no doubt that the new offences should, *in some circumstances*, extend to rewards as well as inducements. The Commission then had to define the circumstances in which a reward could be classified as corrupt. It did this by extending the analysis referred to above[179] to cover the following four situations:

(1) A leads B to believe that, if B acts in a particular way, A will reward B for doing so. B therefore acts in that way, and A does reward B.
(2) Without any encouragement from A, B nevertheless believes that, if B acts in a particular way, A will reward B for doing so—for example, because B believes that A has rewarded other agents for acting in that way. B therefore acts in that way, and A does reward B.
(3) B acts in a particular way, not as a result of a corrupt inducement and not (or not primarily) with a view to reward. A rewards B for acting in that way, hoping that the reward will influence B to act in a similar way in the future.
(4) B acts in a particular way, not as a result of a corrupt inducement and not (or not primarily) with a view to reward. A rewards B for acting in that way, with no thought of influencing B to act in a similar way in the future.[180]

The Commission took the view that cases (1) and (3) above are really forms of inducement, and therefore fall within the principles set out in the previous Recommendation.[181] The Commission also thought that case (2) was corrupt if the hope of reward is B's *primary purpose* in acting in that way and that, if that is the case, and A rewards B in the knowledge that it is the case, A is implicated in B's corrupt purpose, and the reward is therefore corrupt.[182] **5.142**

Thus, it is only case (4) which is not, in the view of the Commission, corrupt at all. The act rewarded was not a corrupt act, because it was not illegitimately influenced by inducements or the hope of reward. The reward for it is therefore not a corrupt reward: there is no mischief in rewarding an agent for the way he or she performs his or her functions, provided the agent does not do so corruptly and that the reward is not also an inducement for the future.[183] In this way, tipping and the gift to the agent of a bottle of whisky at Christmas escape being labelled as either corrupt inducements or corrupt rewards. **5.143**

16. Former and Future Agents

The provisional proposals in the Consultation Paper regarding the timing of the bribe taking by the agent, whereby the offence is committed even if the agent in question is no longer an agent or is not yet an agent,[184] were agreed by all respondents who commented on them.[185] **5.144**

[179] See 5.118 above. [180] The situations are set out in para 5.104 of the Report.
[181] Report (n 54 above) para 5.105. [182] ibid para 5.108.
[183] ibid para 5.106. [184] See 5.78 above. [185] Report (n 54 above) para 5.110.

17. Corruptly Obtaining or Agreeing to Obtain an Advantage

5.145 The Commission recommended that:

(1) a person who obtains an advantage should be regarded as obtaining it corruptly if he or she
   (a) knows or believes that the person conferring it confers it corruptly, and
   (b) gives his or her implied consent to obtaining it (in a case where he or she does not request it);[186] and

(2) a person who agrees to obtain an advantage should be regarded as agreeing to obtain it corruptly if he or she knows or believes that the person agreeing to confer it agrees corruptly.[187]

5.146 In most corruption cases both parties will know each other and each other's motives, and both are corrupt. There may, however, be cases where the potential bribee, the agent, knows that the briber is endeavouring to confer an advantage, for example by sending round lavish gifts or paying money into the agent's account, but the agent has no intention of being influenced or acting in the way the briber wants. No offence should be committed unless the agent consents to keep it or act upon it.

18. Corruptly Soliciting an Advantage

5.147 The Commission's Recommendation was that: 'A person who solicits an advantage should be regarded as soliciting it corruptly if he or she (1) intends a person to confer it or agree to confer it, and (2) believes that, if the person did so, he or she would probably do so corruptly.'[188]

5.148 A person soliciting an advantage will probably not be concerned with whether or not it is conferred corruptly or otherwise, as long as it is conferred. Likewise, the person conferring a solicited advantage will probably not care why the agent does the act or makes the omission, as long as he or she does so. Accordingly the Commission took the view that such a person should be regarded as acting corruptly if he or she believes that the act or omission would *probably* be primarily done or made in return for the inducement.[189]

19. Corruptly Performing Functions as an Agent

5.149 The Commission's Recommendation was that:

A person who performs his or her functions as an agent should be regarded as performing them corruptly if he or she

(1) does an act or makes an omission primarily in order to secure that a person confers an advantage (whoever obtains it), and believes that if a person did so he or she would probably do so corruptly, or

---

[186] See ibid para 5.118 and draft Bill, cl 7 (1). [187] See ibid cl 7(2).
[188] See Report (n54) para 5.120 and draft Bill, cl 7(3).
[189] Report (n 54 above) para 5.119.

(2) does an act or makes an omission when he or she knows or believes that a person has corruptly conferred an advantage (whoever obtained it), and regards the act or omission as done or made primarily in return for the conferring of the advantage.[190]

The Commission was of the view that an agent should be guilty of an offence not only if he or she corruptly obtains an advantage, or solicits one or agrees to obtain one, but also if he or she corruptly performs his or her functions as an agent, whether in the hope of reward or in return for a previous inducement.[191] **5.150**

20. Territorial Jurisdiction

The Commission recommended that: 'The new offences should be Group A offences for the purposes of the Criminal Justice Act 1993.' Jurisdiction was considered in Part IX of the Consultation Paper[192] and the respondents did not disagree with the Commission's proposal, which remains unchanged in the Report.[193] **5.151**

21. Requirement of the Attorney-General's Consent

The Commission's Recommendation was that: 'Prosecutions for the new offences should not require the Attorney-General's consent.' The 1889 and 1906 Acts had consent provisions: 'the original reasons for introducing the requirement of the Attorney-General's consent were to avoid bribery, collusion, blackmail and other improper practices which frequently surrounded the private prosecution'.[194] **5.152**

'The basic reason for including in a statute a restriction on bringing of prosecutions is that otherwise there would be a risk of prosecutions being brought in inappropriate circumstances': this was stated in a Home Office Memorandum[195] to the Departmental Committee on section 2 of the Official Secrets Act 1911 (the Franks Committee). Five overlapping reasons were given for considering the inclusion of a consent requirement: none was thought by the Commission to be relevant for the proposed corruption offences.[196] **5.153**

In the Consultation Paper the Commission took the provisional view that the requirement of consent should only be used for those offences: **5.154**

(1) which directly affect freedom of expression;
(2) which may involve the national security or have some international element; or
(3) in respect of which it is particularly likely, given the availability of civil proceedings in respect of the same conduct, that the public interest would not require a prosecution.[197]

[190] See ibid page 122 and draft Bill, cl 8. [191] Report (n 54 above) para 5.121.
[192] See 5.80 ff above. [193] Report (n 54 above) paras 7.12–7.15, dealing with jurisdiction.
[194] P Fennell and PA Thomas, *Corruption in England and Wales: An Historical Analysis* (1983) 11 International Journal of the Sociology of Law 167, 173.
[195] Further memorandum by the Home Office on the control of prosecutions by the Attorney-General and the Director of Public Prosecutions (April 1972).
[196] Report (n 54 above) paras 7.18, 7.19. [197] ibid para 7.20.

5.155 Since none of the new offences would fall within any of these exceptions, the Commission did not believe that consent should be needed for any of them. The majority of the respondents did not want a consent provision, accordingly the Commission made the Recommendation above.

22. Mode of Trial

5.156 Existing offences under the Prevention of Corruption Acts are triable either way. Although two respondents thought that corruption cases were too serious to be tried summarily, the Commission felt that it could not be said that *all* instances of corrupt behaviour were sufficiently serious to be tried only on indictment, so they recommended that they continue to be triable either way.[198]

23. Retrospectivity

5.157 The Commission's recommendation was that the new law should not be retrospective in effect: this was uncontroversial.[199]

J. The Government Response

1. The Government White Paper

5.158 The Government's Response to The Law Commission's Report was a White Paper entitled *Raising Standards and Upholding Integrity: The Prevention of Corruption* containing 'The Government's Proposals for the Reform of the Criminal Law of Corruption in England and Wales', published in June 2000[200] with a Foreword by the Rt Hon Jack Straw, then the Home Secretary, stating:

> Corruption is like a deadly virus. Left unchecked it weakens economies, creates huge inequalities and undermines the very foundations of democratic government. The international business community is increasingly coming to realise that a culture of corruption is a disincentive to investment and trade.
>
> We are committed to the the fight against corruption wherever it is found. Corruption knows no boundaries. And the development of e-commerce makes it increasingly difficult to pin down the physical location at which a corrupt transaction has taken place. The law has to catch up with these realities. So along with a reform of the corruption offences themselves, the Government proposes two key changes in the jurisdiction of UK courts:
>
> - UK citizens to be triable in the UK for corruption offences committed abroad;
> - Citizens of any country to be triable here even though the offences did not occur wholly in the UK.

[198] ibid paras 7.27, 7.28. [199] ibid paras 7.31, 7.32. [200] Cm 4759.

i. Scope of the Government's proposals

The first of these objectives was realized with astonishing speed. Later in 2001, the Anti-Terrorism, Crime and Security Act was passed, in response to the events of 11 September in New York[201] into which was inserted a clause[202] making it an offence for a UK citizen (including corporate entities) to commit acts abroad which, if they had been committed in England and Wales, would have been prosecuted under the Acts of 1889, 1906, and 1916. This new legislation became effective on 14 February 2002 and, as has been seen, in 2005 the Serious Fraud Office announced that it was investigating commercial bribery cases in the Middle East, Asia, and Africa.[203] **5.159**

The Government went on largely to accept the Law Commission's recommendations and proposed to bring forward legislation modelled on the draft Bill contained in its Report. Specifically, by reference to the paragraphs in the White Paper: **5.160**

(1) The Government accepted the Commission's recommendations that there should be an express exception in respect of remuneration, tips, and gratuities (para 2.6).
(2) A further exception would be made where the principal's consent had been obtained (para 2.7).
(3) A single definition of 'acting corruptly' was accepted, which would concentrate on the agent/principal relationship rather than on the status of the person concerned (para 2.9).
(4) As a result of the distinction between public and private sectors being removed, the presumption of corruption introduced by the 1916 Act would be abolished (para 2.9).
(5) The relationship between agent and principal was acknowledged as being of key importance, and the Government proposed to provide a statutory definition of the agent and principal relationship (paras 2.10 and 2.11).
(6) The Government proposed to introduce a new offence of 'trading in influence' (para 2.14). This proposal stemmed from the Government's having signed, in December 1999, the Council of Europe Criminal Law Convention on Corruption in which there was a requirement to criminalize trading in influence which was not covered in existing legislation.
(7) Trading in influence' is defined in the White Paper as

> intentionally, the promising, giving or offering, directly or indirectly, of any undue advantage to anyone who asserts or confirms that he or she is able to exert an improper influence over the decision-making of [domestic public officials, members of domestic public assemblies, foreign public officials, members of foreign public assemblies, officials of international organisations,

[201] the so-called '9/11 attacks'. [202] ATCSA 2001, s 109.
[203] *The Times*, 1 August 2005, see 5.28, n 30 above.

members of international parliamentary assemblies, and judges and officials of international courts] in consideration thereof, whether the undue advantage is for himself or herself or for anyone else, as well as the request, receipt or the acceptance of the offer or the promise of such an advantage, in consideration of that influence, whether or not the influence is exerted or whether or not the supposed influence leads to the intended result.(2.13)

(8) On territorial jurisdiction, the Government proposed to ensure that offences that occur 'wholly or in part' within the United Kingdom could be prosecuted, in line with 'the requirements of many international instruments' (para 2.19).

(9) On nationality jurisdiction, the Government proposed to assume jurisdiction over offences committed by UK nationals abroad, putting 'beyond doubt the UK's commitment to join forces with the international community in the fight against corruption' (para 2.23).[204]

(10) The Government agreed that the new offences should continue to be triable either in the Magistrate's Courts or in the Crown Court. It also believed that the current maximum sentence of seven years, imprisonment should remain unchanged (para 5.1).

(11) The Government declined to accept the Law Commission's Recommendation to abandon law officer consent to bringing a prosecution, taking the view that one of the categories for requiring consent was relevant to corruption offences, namely 'offences which create a high risk that the right of private prosecutions will be abused and the institution of proceedings will cause the defendant irreparable harm' (paras 5.2 and 5.3).

(12) The Government believed that its proposals to amend the law of corruption met in full its obligations under the international agreements on tackling corruption to which it was a party (para 4.1).[205]

2. Bribery and Members of Parliament

5.161 The Government proposed to refer specifically to Members of both Houses in a future Bill on corruption and to proceed to amend the criminal law on corruption in the way recommended by the Joint Committee on Parliamentary Privilege. In fact the draft Corruption Bill included MPs.[206] The Joint Committee had accepted that corruption could only be dealt with effectively by using the police and the courts. The Committee accepted that this would involve an encroachment upon the freedom of speech guaranteed by Article 9 of the Bill of Rights 1688: 'freedom of speech and debates or proceedings in Parliament ought not to be impeached or questioned in any court or place out of Parliament'. The

[204] As stated in 5.159 above, this was the first of the Government's commitments to be realised.

[205] The Instruments in question are listed in the Annex to the White Paper (Cm 4759).

[206] Draft corruption Bill, cl 12.

Committee recommended that 'Members of both Houses should be brought within the criminal law of bribery by legislation containing a provision to the effect that evidence relating to an offence committed or alleged to be committed under the relevant sections shall be admissible notwithstanding Article 9' (para 3.2).

The White Paper also deals (para 3.5) with the question of sponsorship of MPs. **5.162** The government believed that sponsorship of MP's should continue to be acceptable 'provided that the Members in question do not accept money or other considerations in respect of specific acts designed to favour the organisation sponsoring them'. This mirrored the position under the rules of the House and took into account Recommendations 9 and 10 of the Sixth Report of the Neill Committee on Standards in Public Life,[207] which related to the guidelines on paid advocacy. Recommendation 9 supported the retention of the ban and Recommendation 10 proposed to amend the guidelines to make it possible for an MP who has a personal interest to initiate proceedings which relate in a general way (and not exclusively) to that interest, subject to the following safeguards:

- The MP is prohibited from engaging in 'paid advocacy' on behalf of that interest;
- He or she is required to register and declare the interest in accordance with the guidelines;
- He or she must identify his or her interest on the Order Paper (or Notice Paper) by way of an agreed symbol when initiating a debate.

3. Comments on Main Proposals in the White Paper

The Government published its response to the comments made in consultations **5.163** in April 2001.[208] There was nothing in any of the comments which caused the Government to change its stated view on any of the Law Commission's proposals, but the following points may be noted (references are to paragraph numbers in the Response):

(1) In response to a suggestion that there should be a 'criminal law of markets', the Government noted that abuse of markets is generally dealt with by civil proceedings, under the Fair Trading Act 1973, the Competition Act 1998, and Articles 81 and 82 of the EC Treaty. (para 3).
(2) The proposed legislation was to cover England, Wales, and Northern Ireland—changes to the law in other jurisdictions would be a matter for the authorities in those jurisdictions—the Scottish Executive recognized the advantages of a consistent approach (para 10).
(3) Jurisdiction of the Serious Fraud Office: in response to a suggestion that the SFO's powers should be extended to cover offences of corruption, the

[207] Cm 4557, 1 January 2000.
[208] Home Office, Raising Standards and Upholding Integrity : The Prevention of Corruption (M4759, June 2000): Government Response to the Comments made in Consultations, published by the Home Office in April 2001.

Government felt that the SFO had already demonstrated its ability to prosecute corruption cases and that therefore no further extension was needed (para 11).

(4) Inland Revenue Confidentiality Rules: it was suggested that these should be relaxed to facilitate prosecution of corruption. In response, the Government referred to the Criminal Justice and Police Bill introduced before the House of Commons in January 2001, which would permit both the Inland Revenue and HM Customs and Excise to disclose information:
   (a) for any criminal investigation or criminal proceedings being carried out, or which may be carried out, in the United Kingdom or elsewhere;
   (b) for initiating or bringing to an end any such investigation or proceedings, or helping to determine whether the investigation or proceedings should be initiated or brought to an end (para 12).[209]

(5) Locus of prosecutions: there was a proposal by the CBI that corruption should be prosecuted where possible 'in the place of payment'. The Government recognized that there were merits in prosecuting where the bulk of the evidence and witnesses were likely to be available and stated that that should be the preferred option wherever possible, but at the same time recognised that 'in practice some developing countries may not always be in a position to handle such prosecutions, which may be of a complex and international nature. That is why the government proposes to extend jurisdiction over UK nationals and employees of UK companies abroad' (para 15).

4. The Government's Draft Corruption Bill

5.164 The draft Corruption Bill was published on 24 March 2003.[210] It largely follows the model contained in the Law Commission's Report. Clauses 1 to 3 set out the offences. The meaning of conferring an advantage is contained in clause 4 and obtaining an advantage in clause 8. The meaning of 'corruptly' is addressed in terms of 'conferring an advantage' (clause 5), 'obtaining an advantage' (clause 9), and 'performing functions' (clause 10).

5.165 The concept of principal and agent being central to defining the relationships involved is adhered to, together with a (more limited) list of illustrative situations (clause 11): the public/private distinction is abolished in the same clause. Clause 6 is the first of the exemption clauses and covers remuneration of an agent working in both the private and public sector, as well as a mixture of both. Clause 7 deals with the exemption for the principal's consent.

5.166 New to the draft is the provision dealing with proceedings in Parliament vitiating the effect of Article 9 of the Bill of Rights in corruption proceedings (clause 12).

---

209 The Act received Royal Assent on 11 May 2001.

210 Cm 5777. The text is set out in App 35 below.

Also new is clause 13, dealing with corruption offences committed outside the United Kingdom. Both of these matters were foreshadowed in the White Paper.[211]

Trading in influence is not included. Clause 14 adopts the Law Commission's recommendation to classify corruption as a Class A offence, and extends it to Northern Ireland. Clauses 15 and 16 deal with authorizations specific to the Intelligence Services, basically providing further exceptions as far as their activities are concerned, a reflection of life in modern Britain. The Government also remains true to its determination set out in the White Paper, requiring consent from the Attorney-General before a prosecution can be brought (clause 17). Seven years is retained as the maximum penalty (clause 18). **5.167**

Clause 19 abolishes the common law offence of bribery and repeals the 1889 Act. The 1906 and 1916 Acts are amended to remove references to agency and public bodies. It is not proposed that the legislation should be retrospective. **5.168**

5. The Joint Committee on the Draft Corruption Bill and the Government Reply

The Joint Committee was appointed on 24 March 2003 to consider the draft Bill published on that day. Its Report was published on 31 July 2003.[212] Its Conclusions and Recommendations criticized the draft Bill on almost every count. The Government Reply to the Joint Committee Report was published in December 2003.[213] The Joint Committee's criticisms and the Government's response to them will be dealt with together below, in the format adopted in the Government Reply (references are to paragraph numbers in the Joint Committee's Report). **5.169**

(1) The Committee was not persuaded that UK companies should be made explicitly liable for the actions of non-resident foreign subsidiaries and agents because the individuals—in many cases nationals of the countries concerned-will be subject to national law in that jurisdiction. (Para 78)
(2) The case for a separate offence of trading in influence is not, in our view, convincing. (Para 79)
(3) The draft Bill does not seem to us the appropriate vehicle for giving a statutory definition of misconduct in public office. (Para 80)

The Government fully agreed with the Joint Committee on these points, although none of them are in fact in the draft Bill, despite all having been canvassed at various times: **5.170**

(4) Our overall conclusion, however, is that by adopting only the agent/principal approach the Bill does not proceed on the right basis and that corrupt acts outside that relationship ought to be included in the Bill. (Para 81)
(5) The Committee has therefore concluded that the only way to address the problems which are inherent in the Bill (which arise from [the] agent/

[211] See 5.159ff above. [212] HL Paper 157, HC 705. See App 34. [213] Cm 6086.

principal model) is to move away from the definition of 'corruptly' in clause 5. (Para 89)

(6) Having examined all these different models, we consider that (leaving aside related offences) the essence of corruption could be better expressed in the following terms:

A person acts corruptly if he gives, offers or agrees to give an improper advantage with the intention of influencing the recipient in the performance of his duties or functions;

A person acts corruptly if he receives, asks for or agrees to receive an improper advantage with the intention that it will influence him in the performance of his duties or functions. (Para 92)

(7) As we have already indicated, it could be possible to substitute for 'improper advantage' the words 'advantage to which a person is not legally entitled'. (Para 93)

(8) In the light of the criticisms which have been made of it, we do not consider that the draft Bill should be left as it stands on the essential issue . . . We conclude that the Bill would still be obscure and [un]satisfactory if the offences remain based on the concept of agency. (Para 98)

(9) We believe that a Bill centred on a simple definition such as ours would be clearer and would work better. We also believe it would be more likely to receive general approval. (Para 99)

5.171 The Government, in a reasoned response to these suggestions, rejects them on several grounds, accepting that while the Bill might appear visually daunting to the layman, it is necessary to set out within the Bill the elements which make a transaction corrupt. It points out that the agent/principal concept is not unique to the United Kingdom, having been adopted in Ireland, Canada, and Australia.[214] It felt that the Committee's suggestions would have the effect of narrowing the scope of the law in several respects:[215]

(10) We consider it would be better if the Joint Committee recommendations were followed and a Parliamentary Privilege Bill dealing with all these matters were brought forward. (Para 114)

5.172 The Government notes the views of the Joint Committee and states that discussions are taking place between officials in the Cabinet Office and the House authorities about the case for a Parliamentary Privilege Bill.

(11) We therefore recommend that clause 12 be narrowed. This would apply only to the words or actions of an MP or peer in the case where he is the defendant . . . We also recommend that, to the extent that the words or actions of an MP or peer are admissible for or against him, they should also be admissible for or against all co-defendants in respect of corruption offences based on the same facts. (Para 134)

(12) We recommend that Clause 12 be redrafted on the lines set out in paragraph 135 [of the full Report].

---

[214] Although none of these jurisdictions have as wide a definition of the principal/agency relationship as is proposed in the Bill.

[215] See the Government Response (n 207 above) paras 2–16.

Clause 12 is the one affecting proceedings in Parliament and freedom of speech under Article 9 of the Bill of Rights. The Government's response is to take note and say that as this is a matter which affects the working practices of Parliament, they would like to hear further from both Houses before coming to a firm view: **5.173**

(13) We recommend that Clause 17 be replaced by a requirement for the consent to be given by [the] Director of Public Prosecutions or one nominated deputy. (Para 139)

The Government concurs: **5.174**

(14) We recommend that the Government gives further consideration to the question of whether the Clause 15 exemption for intelligence agencies is so wide that Clause 15 risks non-compliance with the UK's international obligations. (Para 153)

The Government states, rather cryptically, that it has acted on this recommendation and met the Committee's concerns in this regard: **5.175**

(15) We also recommend that the Government considers whether Clause 15 should be amended so that the exemption for activities of the intelligence agencies applies only to acts or omissions done or made in the interests of national security or preventing or detecting serious crime. (Para 154)

The Government states that it is making the necessary change in the Bill.

6. Current Status of the Draft Legislation

On 8 December 2005 the Home Office issued a further Consultation Paper entitled 'Bribery: Reform of the Prevention of Corruption Acts and SFO Powers in Cases of Bribery of Foreign Officials'. The text of the Consultation Paper can be found on the Home Office website[216], unfortunately this has been received too late for detailed consideration in this Chapter. Reference to it will, however, shows that the Government wishes to consult further on a variety of issues raised by the proposed legislation, including: **5.176**

- the use of the word 'bribery' instead of 'corruption';
- the definition of 'corruptly'.
- separating out public sector offences from those which apply in the private sector; and
- whether the Bill should be introduced as it stands, subject to the recommendations of the Joint Committee which were accepted.

There is also a practical proposal to enhance the powers of the SFO in foreign bribery cases. Responses are requested by 1 March 2006. No indication is given regarding a timetable for legislation.

[216] Home Office (2005). *Bribery—Reform of the Prevention of Corruption Acts and SFO Powers in Cases of Bribery of Foreign Officials, A Consultation Paper.* http://www.homeoffice.gov.uk/documents/Bribery-Consultation-Paper.pdf [accessed 29/12/2005]

6

CIVIL REMEDIES

A. Introduction

1. The Importance of Civil Remedies

The purpose of the criminal law in cases of corruption is to mark society's disapproval of an offender's conduct by convicting and punishing him for the offences he has committed, and in the case of a public official, by disqualifying him from office. Although in earlier times offenders' assets were forfeit to the Crown, it is only in very recent years that states have begun to establish comprehensive procedures for the restraint and confiscation of assets obtained as a result of criminal conduct. These procedures are primarily designed to deprive offenders of the proceeds of their crimes, not to compensate persons who have lost their property as a result of crime. **6.01**

6.02 The criminal courts do now have power to order a person convicted of an offence to compensate a victim for loss suffered as a result of an offence (including loss suffered as a result of other offences taken into consideration in determining sentence), and such compensation orders take precedence over confiscation by the Crown. As described later,[1] the Proceeds of Crime Act 2002 (POCA 2002) also provides a mechanism for forfeited cash to be paid to its rightful owner, and the Assets Recovery Agency (ARA) (or, in Scotland, the Civil Recovery Unit of the Crown Office) has power to bring civil proceedings *in rem* to recover moneys or other assets as the proceeds of crime. Although these latter proceedings are not dependent on a successful criminal conviction in the United Kingdom of the wrongdoer or his associates, it is unlikely that action would be taken unless there is good reason why a prosecution cannot take place.

6.03 Foreign governments have the option of requesting mutual legal assistance but experience has shown that in the United Kingdom the process can be slow, cumbersome, and uncertain in outcome. Mutual legal assistance does not of itself result in foreign prosecutions and, whilst in theory it might be possible for the ARA to take action, governments are generally not that keen on spending their own taxpayers' money pursuing claims on behalf of foreign governments which have little chance of winning votes at home. This may now change with the growing realization that corruption is genuinely a global problem: as we shall see,[2] the United Nations Convention Against Corruption[3] has the potential to produce a significant shift in the attitude of governments to providing international assistance.

6.04 Often the only practical redress for a victim of corruption, particularly an overseas party, will therefore be to bring its own civil action to recover the property of which it has been deprived. For the foreseeable future, the civil courts will continue to be central to the fight against corruption when it comes to recovery of corrupt payments. Civil action can take many forms. A principal who has been deceived by an agent who has accepted a bribe can recover the bribe moneys from the agent by making a claim in the civil courts. The principal can also claim against the payer of the bribe. Similarly, a company which has tendered for a contract, but failed to procure it because of bribery, can make a civil claim against the briber and the person bribed, if it wants to be compensated for the loss it has suffered by losing the contract, and a state which has suffered loss through embezzlement of state funds which have been salted away abroad, can pursue civil procedures to obtain their repatriation from the state to which they have been sent.

6.05 This chapter will examine the civil remedies available in England for persons who have suffered loss as a result of corrupt acts, and touch on the procedures

[1] See 7.69ff below. [2] See 9.10ff below.
[3] See App 29 below for the text of the Convention.

adopted in foreign jurisdictions, where relevant. It will also consider some of the avenues which have been well trodden by liquidators and receivers dealing with large international corporate collapses involving the tracing of misappropriated assets, but which have yet to be travelled extensively by governments in pursuit of funds purloined from their citizens. A liquidator acting at the behest of a committee of creditors is in a very different position from a government which has to summon the political will to take effective action, with or without the support of those of its members who may have gained the most from years of corrupt rule.

2. Bribery and Corruption

Just as English criminal law was initially concerned only with the bribery of public officials[4] and except in the case of election offences, the word 'corrupt' was not employed until the Corruption Acts 1889–1916, so also in civil law the emphasis was on 'bribery'. The word 'corruption' does not even appear in the indices of the traditional civil law textbooks. Instead, reference has to be made to entries under 'bribes', 'bribery', and 'secret profits'. The most comprehensive treatment of these subjects is to be found in the leading work on agency, *Bowstead and Reynolds*;[5] *Chitty on Contracts*[6] has a one-line entry under 'Bribes'–'restitution'; and Goff and Jones' '*Law of Restitution*'[7] refers to the agent's and briber's liability under the heading 'Fiduciary Relationships'.[8] Of the tort textbooks, *Winfield & Jolocwicz*[9] has no reference either to corruption or to bribery as a tort and *Clerk & Lindsell*[10] refers only to contributory negligence and deceit under 'bribery'. **6.06**

Whilst references to corruption and corrupt activity will be found in the case law, these will invariably translate into cases dealing specifically with bribery and secret commissions, which focus on breaches of fiduciary duty. The courts use strong words which reflect the desire to condemn bribery as a matter of public policy: 'Bribery is an evil practice which threatens the foundation of any civilized society' said the Privy Council in 1994.[11] 'It corrupts not only the recipient but the giver of the bribe.'[12] **6.07**

Definitions of bribery in civil cases have tended to concentrate on the principal/agent relationship; for example: **6.08**

> For the purposes of the civil law a bribe means the payment of a secret commission, which only means (i) that the person making the payment makes it to the

[4] See Ch 2 above.
[5] FMB Reynolds, *Bowstead and Reynolds on Agency* (17th edn, London: Sweet & Maxwell, 2001).
[6] *Chitty on Contracts* (29th edn, London: Sweet & Maxwell, 2004) 2 vols, 29–156.
[7] R Goff and G Jones, *Law of Restitution* (6th edn, London: Sweet & Maxwell, 2002).
[8] ibid Ch 33.
[9] WVH Rogers, *Winfield & Jolowicz on Tort* (16th edn, London: Sweet & Maxwell, 2002).
[10] *Clerk & Lindsell on Torts* (18th edn, London: Sweet & Maxwell, 2000).
[11] *A-G for Hong Kong v Reid* [1994] 1 AC 324 (PC) *per* Lord Templeman, 330.
[12] *Daraydan Holdings Ltd v Solland International Ltd* [2005] Ch 119 *per* Collins J, 122.

> agent of the other person with whom he is dealing; (ii) that he makes it to that person knowing that that person is acting as the agent of the other person with whom he is dealing; and (iii) that he fails to disclose to the other person with whom he is dealing that he has made that payment to the person whom he knows to be the other person's agent.[13]

Or, as Steel J said in *Petrotrade v Smith*:[14]

> The key distinguishing feature of a corrupt payment [is that] the making of it gives rise to a conflict of interest on the part of the agent . . . An agent should not put himself in a position where his duty and interest may conflict, and if bribes are taken by an agent, the principal is deprived of the disinterested advice of the agent, to which the principal is entitled. Any surreptitious dealing between one principal to a transaction and the agent of the other is a fraud on the other principal.

3. Principal and Agent

6.09 The common feature of the definitions given above is that they refer to the relationship of principal and agent. This is because it is primarily around the principal/agency relationship and the concept of fiduciary duty that the civil case law has built up, and it is still true to say that it is in that context that many bribery cases will arise. There is now, however, a widespread appreciation that this is too narrow a basis on which to proceed. The UK Government's draft Bill,[15] produced in March 2003, is (as has been seen in Chapter 5 above) built around the principal/agency relationship.[16] In the consultation process it was said: 'The concept of agency, although well developed in common law, has been stretched unreasonably in this Bill.'[17] This and other representations led the Parliamentary Joint Committee considering the Bill to state that: 'Our overall conclusion . . . is that by adopting the agent/principal approach the Bill does not proceed on the right basis and that corrupt acts outside that relationship ought to be included in the Bill.'[18] This criticism was, however, rejected by the Government in its response to the Joint Committee.[19]

6.10 One of the main concerns over the limitations of the definition in the Bill which emerged during the consultation process was that misconduct in public office was not covered. Another was that trading in influence would not be caught. The Joint Committee was negative in its attitude to the inclusion of these areas,[20] but the fact that they were raised in the consultation process on the

---

13 *Industries and General Mortgage Co Ltd v Lewis* [1949] 2 All ER 573 *per* Slade J, 575.

14 [2000] 1 Lloyd's Rep 486, 490.

15 Draft Corruption Bill: Cm 5777.

16 See, eg, draft Corruption Bill, cl 5 and 5.100ff above.

17 Evidence to the Joint Committee on the Draft Corruption Bill: Report [HL Paper 157, HC705] published 31 July 2003, para 28, citing evidence given by Transparency International (UK).

18 ibid para 81.

19 See 5.169ff above.

20 Evidence to the Joint Committee (n 17 above) paras 79 and 80.

criminal Bill is also an indication of the kinds of issues now raised in civil corruption cases. Bribery nowadays is very likely to be concerned with corruption on the part of public officials and payments made to influence governmental conduct. The 'victims' of such conduct are persons who are the least likely to be able to bring the malefactors to justice. In the aftermath of the tsunami disaster of 26 December 2004 it became apparent that many of those who lost their lives in Banda Aceh did so because their houses were inadequately built and the roads which would have assisted the rescue efforts did not exist: the funds which should have been spent on providing proper housing and roads had been siphoned off by corrupt officials. The disaster provoked the largest-ever aid response: the problem then became corrupt embezzlement of aid payments.[21]

Examples of international infrastructure contracts involving corrupt payments abound.[22] One of the questions to be addressed in this chapter is what action may be taken through the civil courts to redress these wrongs? Before considering this question, however, it is helpful to review the development of the civil law relating to bribery and corruption in order both to see how it has developed and whom it can assist. **6.11**

B. Who May Be a Claimant?

1. The Principal

The most obvious class of potential claimant is the principal who is the victim of the corrupt transaction. Thus, where bribery is involved, the principal whose agent has in some way cheated him will be the claimant. Bribery occurs most often when there is a business transaction involving contractual relationships and the principal is represented by an agent, who may or may not be an employee, but who, under the general law of agency, owes a fiduciary duty to the principal.[23] That duty is breached when the agent accepts a bribe from a briber: 'a bribe consists in a commission or other inducement, which is given by a third party to an agent as such, and which is secret from his principal'.[24] The principal can suffer in a variety of ways as the result of the bribe having been **6.12**

---

[21] See, eg A Hill and M Bright, 'Poorest get Worst Deal in Tsunami Aid Handout' *The Observer*, 26 June 2005 and R Taylor, 'Asia: Millions Missing in Indonesia Tsunami Aid says Watchdog' *Australia Associated Press*, 1 July 2005.

[22] See, eg The Corner House Briefing: Susan Hawley, *Turning a Blind Eye: Corruption and the UK Export Credits Guarantee Department*, June 2003, available at http://www.thecornerhouse.org.uk.

[23] Reynolds (n 5 above) para 1-001.

[24] *Anangel Atlas Compania Naviera SA v Ishikawama-Harima Heavy Industries Co Ltd* [1990] 1 Lloyd's Rep 167, 171.

taken by his agent: he may be paying more, often substantially more,[25] or he may be deprived of a bargain.[26]

6.13 Claimant-principals are a disparate class. The early cases reflect a bygone age, but they are the building blocks from which the modern claimant's rights arise. The Indian army widow who had had her son, a young cornet, kitted out by an army agent who added up to 15 per cent to the cost of the boy's uniform and each item of equipment purchased on his behalf was horrified to receive a bill for 700*l*, a significant amount in 1869. When challenged about the mark-up, the agent claimed that he was 'authorised to do all this by the custom of my trade or profession of army agent'. Not so, said the Vice-Chancellor of the day, 'a person dealing with another man's money . . . ought not to receive anything in the nature of a present or allowance without the full knowledge of the principal that he is so acting'.[27] Bowstead[28] comments that in a case such as this, where the payment is not for a corrupt purpose, it is more appropriate to refer to the arrangement simply as a secret commission rather than a bribe, but it is still a breach of fiduciary duty.

6.14 'Secrecy is a badge of fraud' is a well-known judicial pronouncement, but it can be difficult sometimes in bribery cases to distinguish between legitimate commissions and secret commissions—certainly judges have not always been at one with juries on this. In the seminal bribery case of *Hovenden v Millhoff*[29] the jury awarded the wholesale perfumer and hairdressers' sundrymen plaintiffs just one farthing against the bribing tobacconist Millhoff, who gave seasonal 'gifts' to Hovenden's buyers to ensure that they chose Millhoff cigars and cigarettes—gifts which only amounted to two and a half per cent of the total value of the goods sold. But the Court of Appeal said that result was 'absurd' and then, as will be seen below, found some difficulty in characterizing the exact legal nature of the claim. It was an early indication of the difficulties of categorization that have been a feature of bribery cases over the years.

6.15 Other early examples of defrauded principal-claimants include the horse purchaser who relied on the advice of a vet who shared the price paid for the horse with the vendor,[30] the city corporation whose servant received one shilling per ton of coal purchased from the merchant supplying the local gasworks,[31] and

[25] In *Dubai Aluminium Co Ltd v Salaam* [2003] 2 AC 366, HL two of the agents had collected US$20.3 m and $16.5 m respectively by adding those amounts to the invoices they caused to be raised.

[26] In *Mahesan S/O Thambiah v Malaysia Government Officers' Co-operative Housing Society* [1979] AC 374, PC the Housing Society bought for US$944,000 land which had been acquired by the vendor for US $456,000 thanks to their agent having been bribed: see further 6.38ff.

[27] *Turnbull v Garden* (1869) 38 LJ Ch 331, 334.

[28] Reynolds (n 5 above) para 6-083.

[29] *Hovenden & Sons v Millhoff* (1900) 83 LT 41.

[30] *Shipway v Broadwood* [1899] 1 QB 369.

[31] *The Mayor of Salford v Lever* [1891] 1 QB 168.

the underwater cable-laying company whose consultant engineer turned out not only to have given biased advice but also to have hired his own company as subcontractor, thus apparently achieving the dubious double feat of being effectively both agent and briber.[32]

In modern times the cases are bigger and the transactions more complex, but the Arab Monetary Fund, whose first President received 10 per cent ($1.85 m) of the construction cost of its new headquarters building;[33] Fyffes, the banana importers, who paid the shippers of their Caribbean bananas an inflated price which included a secret commission being paid to Fyffes's agent by the shippers;[34] and Sheikh Mohammed, Deputy Prime Minister of Qatar, whose interior designers had his agent virtually on their payroll[35] are just some of the more high-profile, but readily identifiable, victims. **6.16**

2. Extending the Concept of 'Principal'

As has been seen in Chapter 5 above, The Law Commission has given extensive consideration to the concept of agency as it relates to corruption. The situations envisaged in its Consultation Paper and Report and the conclusions expressed are no less valid in a civil context than in the criminal one. Classic examples of the agency relationship, in addition to agent and principal in the strict sense, are given as trustee and beneficiary, partner and co-partner, director and company, employee and employer, legal practitioner and client.[36] It was additionally suggested that a person was an agent if he or she 'has undertaken to discharge a public duty (whether appointed as a public office-holder or to perform a specified public function)':[37] this concept is of considerable practical value when a government is considering, for example, bringing an action against a corrupt former head of state. It will also cover corrupt ministers, but might not extend to 'advisers'. **6.17**

As has been seen, the term 'quasi-fiduciary' was proposed by The Law Commission to encompass relationships which fall outside the traditional concept of principal and agent and, in the Consultation Paper,[38] The Law Commission produced a list intended to provide a short-cut to the definition of 'agent'. References to the 'status-based fiduciary' and the 'fact-based fiduciary' and a test **6.18**

---

[32] *Panama and South Pacific Telegraph Company v India Rubber, Gutta Percha, and Telegraph Works Company* (1874–1875) LR 10 Ch App 515, Div Ct, but, see 6.48 below, as to whether this was in reality a bribery case.

[33] *Arab Monetary Fund v Hashim* [1996] 1 Lloyd's Rep 589.

[34] *Fyffes Group Ltd v Templeman* [2000] 2 Lloyd's Rep 643.

[35] *Daraydan Holdings Ltd v Solland International Ltd* [2004] 3 WLR 1106.

[36] Law Com Consultation Paper No 145 (1997) para 7.31.

[37] Law Com No 248, para 5.25.

[38] Law Com Consultation Paper, paras 7.26ff. See also 5.57ff above.

for ascertaining the relationship: 'Broadly speaking, a fiduciary relationship is one in which a person undertakes to act on behalf of or for the benefit of another, often as an intermediary with a discretion or power which affects the interests of the other who depends on the fiduciary for information and advice'[39] could be highly apposite in civil proceedings for establishing the fiduciary liability of a ministerial 'adviser', whether official or unofficial.

6.19 Bribery is sometimes characterized as a victimless crime; taken literally, this would mean that the real victims of corrupt transactions would never be in a position to bring claims directly themselves. As has been seen above, the effects of bribery are most pernicious in the developing world. Where a large infrastructure contract has been procured by bribery in a developing country, the people of that country are further impoverished by the actions of their leaders or corrupt officials. Action to prosecute these individuals may deprive them of their liberty, and may be accompanied by confiscation or forfeiture action, but prosecution may not always be feasible, for example when the individual dies.[40] In such situations it is very often the intermediaries against whom claims for breach of fiduciary duty need to be made.

6.20 However, the main problem will then be, who should bring the claims? The reality for people in developing countries will generally be that they have to await a change of government before any action is taken and they will then be dependent on the will of that government to pursue the officials and, more importantly, the bribing contractors. Such actions are, however, beginning to be brought—the series of actions commenced by the Attorney-General of Lesotho is an outstanding example.[41] In those Commonwealth countries where the rule of law is properly upheld, and in the United Kingdom, the Attorney-General may bring claims in the name of the Crown or the people, but clearly this will only be possible when the government is itself prepared to take action.[42]

6.21 A further category of potential claimant not directly involved in the relationship between principal and agent is the rival bidder—the company which fails to obtain a valuable contract through the corrupt activity of a competitor.[43] Cases

---

[39] Law Com Consultation Paper, para 7.14.

[40] The Abacha case is a classic example—see 7.51ff below.

[41] See case study in Ch 10 below. A critique entitled 'The Lesotho Highland Water Development Project-What Went Wrong?' is on the website of the NGO The Corner House-http://www.thecornerhouse.org.uk.

[42] *A-G for Hong Kong v Reid* [1994] 1 AC 324 (PC) (see 6.34ff below) is a famous example of this happening in a corruption case. The citizens of Kenya have not been so fortunate: the Attorney-General there apparently proved to be so reluctant to bring anti-corruption cases against fellow members of the government that the Bar Association of Kenya commenced proceedings against him (see eg AP Report 4 March 2005: 'Bar Association charges Kenya's Attorney General with corruption')

[43] Speculation on the possibility of an 'illegal means' conspiracy action by the unsuccessful tenderer against the successful tenderer and the principal's employee who has taken the bribe, is to

brought by such claimants are understandably thin on the ground; however, in a recent South African case, the Supreme Court affirmed a substantial damages award based on the loss of profits suffered by a tenderer. A printing business was being sold by a para-statal; the tenderer lost the bid to a competitor company which had bribed an official in the para-statal. The para-statal admitted being party to the fraud in the lower court and had to pay nearly 60 million Rand in damages.[44]

An unsuccessful bidder losing a contract to a bribing competitor may also be able to bring proceedings for breach of statutory duty against its competitor (and potentially the recipient of the bribe) for infringement of European or English law, which prohibits agreements and other collusive practices distorting or restricting competition, and also abuse of a dominant position.[45] Such proceedings can be brought in the Competition Appeal Tribunal or the High Court, although the former first requires a decision of the Office of Fair Trading or European Commission establishing the infringement. **6.22**

Claimant principals often only learn of the corruption which has taken place at the trial stage,[46] or after dismissing an employee on other grounds.[47] The burden of proof for a third party where all transactions are shrouded in secrecy is bound to be even heavier. The case may have to be brought as a claim alleging conspiracy between the briber and the principal or his executive.[48] **6.23**

C. Who May Be a Defendant?

1. Agents and Bribers

The persons who may be defendants in claims arising from corruption are principally the dishonest agent and the person paying the bribe. In addition to these are those who have assisted in the corrupt acts and those who have handled property which has passed as a result of those acts. **6.24**

The agent may be an agent, properly so-called, or an executive or employee of the principal. Similarly, the payer of the bribe may be a contractor retained by the principal or his agent, or a third party retained by the contractor, in which case he may be the contractor's agent, or he may go under the soubriquet **6.25**

be found in the excellent article by Alan Berg, 'Bribery-transaction validity and other civil law implications' [2001] LMCLQ 27, 62.

[44] *Transnet Ltd v Sechaba Photoscan (Pty) Ltd* [2004] Reportable Case No 98.

[45] EC Treaty, Art 81 or 82 (if trade between member states is affected) or under the Competition Act 1998, Ch I or II (if trade within the UK is affected), provided jurisdiction is established.

[46] See, eg, *Shipway v Broadwood* [1829] 1 QB 369.

[47] *Boston Deep Sea Fishing & Ice Co v Ansell* (1888) 39 ChD 339.

[48] *Lonrho plc v Fayed* [1992] AC 448, HL.

'intervener' or 'intermediary'. Any of these persons may be dishonestly assisted by others, either directly or indirectly, in effecting the corruption. An involved party may not even be directly connected with the principal, he may simply be a recipient of a share of the corrupt payment, usually by virtue of the position he holds. Frequently, but not always, that position will be an official one. He may not have any direct connection with the transaction in respect of which the payment is being made, he may simply be 'owed a favour' from past transactions, or transactions still to come. A common method of giving spurious respectability to recipients is to label them 'Consultants' and to draw up a 'Consultancy Agreement' under which the obligations are minimal, such as providing 'secretarial services'—often in return for the payment of millions of dollars.

6.26 Invariably there will then be persons or institutions who handle the proceeds of the corrupt payments, possibly innocently.[49] Parties to a fraud holding corrupt property or funds will commonly be described as 'constructive trustees'.[50] The doctrines of vicarious liability and joint and several liability can be invoked to spread the net still wider.[51]

6.27 However, the law does not now allow multiple or even double recovery of the corrupt amounts paid or received and the claimant will be put to an election, which he need not exercise until after judgment has been given, thus giving him the chance to maximize his return.[52]

6.28 The categories of potential defendant mentioned above can probably never be exhaustive, and the legal relationship to claimants will be a consideration in deciding what action can be taken against them, but always the most important consideration will be what remedies are available: these will be the subject of succeeding sections. However, such is the multifarious nature of this trillion dollar per annum business,[53] it is inevitable that the law will have difficulty in categorizing every variation. What can be said is that civil law remedies, particularly in common law jurisdictions with the ability to make new law through the courts, almost certainly offer the best chance for defrauded principals to effect meaningful recoveries.[54]

---

[49] See, eg, the references to 'the bankers, the lawyers and the accountants' in the Commission for Africa Report, *Our Common Interest* para 4.5.1, available at http://www.commissionforafrica.org; see also 1.48 above.

[50] Millett LJ in *Paragon Finance plc v DB Thackerah & Co* [1999] 1 AER 400, 409, AC doubted that this was an appropriate term where assets have been acquired by fraud but it continues to be in general use. See further 6.35 below.

[51] See, eg, *Dubai Aluminium Co Ltd v Salaam* [2003] 2 AC 366, HL.

[52] *Mahesan S/O Thambiah v Malaysia Government Officers' Co-operative Housing Society* [1979] AC 374, PC, but see further discussion of this question below at 6.37ff.

[53] See 1.46 above.

[54] That said, there is no doubt, that in the UK particularly, a little assistance from legislators would be welcome. In the US triple damages are available to defrauded principals under the

D. Remedies Against a Dishonest Agent

1. Dismissal

No principal, having discovered that his agent has taken a bribe, is likely to keep his agent on and he will be fully justified in dismissing him summarily once the agent's breach of fiduciary duty becomes apparent.[55] This will still be so even if the bribe is not discovered until after dismissal.[56] 6.29

2. Restitution of the Amount of the Bribe

There is a long line of authorities going back to the early part of the nineteenth century which demonstrates that the courts have been unanimous in the view that the principal is entitled to recover from his agent all of the money the agent has received by way of bribes: 'when a [principal] finds out this state of things, he may call upon his agent... to disgorge'.[57] It should be noted, however, that this does not necessarily mean that the agent has to give up the entirety of his secret commission. In the early case of *Fawcett v Whitehouse*[58] which was treated by the Court as a case of equitable fraud, one of the three partners to a land transaction, who had been paid £12,000 by the vendor, was allowed to keep £4,000 for himself: the Court only ordered him to pay over £4,000 each to his two other partners—on the basis that he was a trustee who had received moneys for his partners' use. 6.30

In *Salford v Lever*[59] the Corporation's agent retained the money he had been paid in bribes, despite the Court having taken the view that he was liable in damages for fraud—this being the alternative approach to money had and received. The reason was that the court also found the coal merchant, the briber, liable for his part in the conspiracy to defraud the Corporation. The mechanics of the fraud were the same as those frequently deployed today—the coal merchant's invoices were inflated by the one shilling 'commission': 'commissions sometimes cover a multitude of sins' said the Court.[60] The Court held that 6.31

Racketeer Influenced and Corrupt Organisations Act (RICO) legislation. In the UK the Law Commission published a Consultation Paper on *Illegal Transactions*; LCCP No 154 (October 1998) which addressed the complexity, injustice, and uncertainty of the law on illegal transactions and the need for legislative reform. Previously, in December 1997, the Law Commission published a report recommending legislation to widen the power of the courts to award exemplary and restitutionary damages (Law Com No 247). As with the Corruption Bill itself, law reform in this area seems to be endlessly bogged down—to the detriment of victims of corruption everywhere. See generally, Ch 5 above.

[55] *Bulfield v Fournier* (1895) 11 TLR 282; *Swale v Ipswich Tannery Ltd* (1906) 11 Com Cas 88; *Temperley v Blackrod Manufacturing Co Ltd* (1907) 71 JP 341; *Federal Supply and Cold Storage Co of South Africa v Angehrn & Piel* (1910) 80 LJPC 1.

[56] *Boston Deep Sea Fishing & Ice Co v Ansell* (1888) 39 ChD 339.

[57] *Hovenden v Milhoff* (1900) 83 LT 41, CA, 42.

[58] (1829) 1 Russ & My 132, 39 ER 51.

[59] [1891] 1 QB 168.

[60] ibid at 175. Lord Esher had preceded this remark by saying 'They call this a commission, a term very well known, at all events in the North of England...'.

the Corporation could proceed against either *or both* the agent and the briber, but the agent had struck a deal with the Corporation under which he lodged securities to the value of the funds he had received in a trust account and pledged to assist in recovering from Lever the sums paid out in bribes—any shortfall in the recoveries was to be made up from the sale of the lodged securities. The Court recognized that unless the Corporation had struck the deal that it did with its agent it would have recovered nothing, but it did not regard the agent as having been released by the Corporation or exonerated at law. Moreover, the fact that the Corporation chose not to sue its agent, but the coal merchant, did not afford the merchant a defence; both remained liable as joint tortfeasors. In this case the result allowed the recipient of the bribes to retain them, whilst the briber had, in effect, to pay out again, which caused Lord Esher to remark 'I am sorry for it; but such, in my opinion, is the law'.[61]

6.32 By 1900, money paid as a secret commission to the agent of a vendor of land was being regarded as money had and received by the agent to the vendor's use, for which he had to account—the price received by the vendor having been reduced by the amount of the secret commission. As only part of the commission had been received by the agent, the unpaid balance, still in the hands of the purchaser, also became due as money received to the use of the vendor—on the basis that although this was no longer contractually due to the agent, it represented a reduction in the price the purchaser had been prepared to pay, the benefit of which should go to the vendor. It was no defence for the purchaser to say that he thought or would have thought that the agent would have disclosed the commission to the vendor.[62]

3. Recovering Profits in Addition to the Bribe (1)

6.33 One problem with the restitution[63] approach to recovery was that it limited the claimant to recovering only what had been received by the agent: what if the agent had in the meantime put the money to good use and profited from his ill-gotten gains? The first time this had to be considered by the courts was in 1891.[64] The recipient of the bribes had invested the proceeds on the stockmarket and had made a profit. The plaintiff claimed not only the amount of the bribes but also the profit. The Court took the view that this was essentially an action in debt for the amount of the bribes. It was fearful that if it ruled that the agent held the bribe

[61] [1891] 1 QB 178.

[62] *Grant v The Gold Exploration and Development Syndicate Ltd* [1900] 1 QB 233, CA, following *Salford Corporation v Lever (No 2)* [1891] 1 QB 168, CA: the court in *Hovenden* (n 57 above, decided in the same year) also approved this approach. Money had and received became a common law remedy following the passing of the Judicature Act in 1875—the right to recover on this basis was described in these terms for the first time in *Boston Deep Sea Fishing* (n 56 above).

[63] In *Fyffes Group Ltd v Templeman* [2000] 2 Lloyd's Rep 643 Toulson J stated: 'The archaic notion of money had and received has now become part of the law of restitution.'

[64] *Lister & Co v Stubbs* (1890) 45 ChD 1.

money on trust for his principal, the profits would also be impressed with the trust. The result of this would have been that, if the agent became bankrupt, the additional monies would not be available to his creditors. The principal's recovery was thus limited to the amount of the bribe in the *Lister* case.

It took over one hundred years for this notion to be overturned. In *Attorney-General for Hong Kong v Reid*,[65] the Privy Council held that the greater evil was that the agent should profit from his misdeeds. Reid was a New Zealand solicitor who became for a while acting Director of Public Prosecutions in Hong Kong. Misusing his office, he habitually blocked prosecutions for which he received bribes from grateful criminals. When he retired to New Zealand he invested the proceeds in real estate which increased in value: was the claimant entitled to those profits? The Court said: 'the fiduciary should account for the bribe as soon as he receives it . . . equity regards as done that which ought to be done'. As a result, the Court held that the moneys were all held on constructive trust for the claimant, allowing him to benefit from Reid's profitable investments. The court also said that if there had proved to be a shortfall, the defendant as constructive trustee would be liable to make it good and the full amount of the original bribes would have had to be paid over. **6.34**

There is, however, judicial disagreement on the question of regarding the agent as a constructive trustee in these circumstances, and this was highlighted by Lord Templeman in his judgment in *Reid*. He made reference to an article by Sir Peter Millett (as he then was)[66] which stated that equity would not allow the fiduciary to say that he had obtained the bribe for himself and not his principal. If he does so, said Millett, 'equity insists on treating it as a legitimate payment intended for the benefit of the principal'. The consequence of this is that the moneys would not in fact be held on constructive trust by the agent. Six years later, as Lord Justice Millett, there was an opportunity to spell this out in a case:[67] 'such a person is not in fact a trustee at all, even though he may be liable to account as if he were . . . In such a case the expressions "constructive trust" and "constructive trustee" are misleading, for there is no trust and usually no possibility of a proprietary remedy; they are "nothing more than a formula for equitable relief"'.[68] The practical consequences of the distinction are considered below.[69] **6.35**

4. Remedies Against the Briber

The case of *Hovenden* confirmed the view expressed in the *Salford* and *Grant* cases that the briber could be liable as well as the agent and the Court said that **6.36**

[65] [1994] 1 AC 324, PC.
[66] 'Bribes and Secret Commissions' [1993] 3 *Restitution Law Review* 20–21.
[67] *Paragon Finance plc v DB Thackerah & Co* [1999]1 AER 400, 409.
[68] See *Selangor United Rubber Estates Ltd v Cradock (No 3)* [1968] 1 WLR 1555, 1582 *per* Ungoed-Thomas J.
[69] In 'Recovering profits in addition to the bribe (2)', 6.43ff below.

it made 'little difference . . . which view is the right one' as to the cause of action: in modern parlance, damages for the tort of fraud, or restitution.[70] The *Hovenden* case is important, however, for the dicta of Romer LJ. These established that in bribery cases the motive for giving the bribe is irrelevant and that an irrebuttable presumption arises that the agent was influenced by the bribe. He also felt that there should be an irrebuttable presumption that, as against the briber, the true price of the goods sold to the purchaser should be the sale price less the bribe.[71]

6.37 It took nearly a hundred years for the courts to revise their views of the law concerning double recovery, and then it was by way of appeal from the Federal Court of Malaysia to the Privy Council. In the *Mahesan* case[72] their Lordships decided that it was not, after all, right for the defrauded principal to have the ability to recover twice over—he must make an election. However, the election was not so much between recovery from his agent and the payer of the bribe, rather, it was between the two measures of loss flowing from the election.

6.38 In the *Mahesan* case the lesser recoverable sum was the actual amount of the bribe, ie US$122,000. The greater sum was the loss sustained by the Housing Society in purchasing land for US$944,000 which had just been purchased by one Manickam ('M') for $456,000. M had connived with the Housing Society's agent to set up the onward sale, making a profit of US$488,000, which he agreed to split 75/25 with the agent, who thus received the bribe of US$122,000. M's share was US$366,000 but he then spent $45,000 evicting squatters from the land so that his net profit was $321,000. As soon as the sale was completed, M disappeared and was never seen again. The agent was arrested and imprisoned under Malaysia's 1961 Prevention of Corruption Act. A few days later the Housing Society issued a civil suit against the agent claiming both his US$122,000 share (the bribe) and the whole $488,000 difference in prices. At first instance the judge awarded the amount of the bribe, but not the profit made on the purchase. He reasoned that property prices were rising fast in Malaysia at the time and the Housing Society had failed to prove that they had paid more than the open market price at the time of their purchase.

6.39 On appeal the Federal Court of Malaysia took a truly punitive view of the transaction. They upheld the judgment on the bribe, US$122,000. Then they awarded as damages the difference between the two prices, $488,000, deducting the $45,000 paid to evict the squatters, giving a net sum of $443,000. The Housing Society was thereby recovering the amount of the bribe twice over, but then, in addition to the $565,000 already awarded, it also stood to receive the statutory penalty handed down by the criminal court which was, again, the

[70] But see Toulson J's analysis in the *Fyffes* case, 6.44ff below.

[71] *Hovenden* (n 29 above) 43.

[72] [1979] AC 374.

amount of the bribe. So the Housing Society stood to make $687,000 in all if the criminal confiscation proceedings were successful (they were not, only $13,000 was recovered from the agent).

The Privy Council considered the judgments in *Salford* and in *Hovenden* and observed that those cases concerned recovery from the bribers, not the agents concerned. Although remarks made by the judges in those cases indicated that they thought that recovery against the bribers would not be a bar to recovery against the agents, those comments were made obiter. In fact, in neither case did the principals exercise their supposed option to make a double recovery and the plaintiffs were unable to point to any other case in which this had ever happened. The Judicial Committee then proceeded to carry out an exhaustive analysis of the state of the law relating to bribery, focusing on the nature of the causes of action available and the remedies that flowed from them. In reaching its judgment, the Privy Council did not take into account the penalty raised in the criminal proceedings which, by section 30 of the Prevention of Corruption Act, did not affect the principal's right of recovery in the civil proceedings. **6.40**

Lord Diplock delivered the judgment, which can be summarized thus: **6.41**

- By the early nineteenth century it was established in equity that an agent who received a secret advantage for himself from the other party to a transaction had to account to his principal for it.[73]
- There was no reported case before the Judicature Act 1875 of recovery by a principal from his agent of a bribe at common law but by 1888 Bowen LJ was able to say that such recovery *could* take place at common law as money had and received.[74]
- This right of recovery at common law was not dependent on the principal having to show any loss as the result of his agent's conduct,[75] but the giving of the bribe was treated in equity as constructive fraud on the part of the giver with the consequence that the principal was entitled to the equitable remedy of rescission where there was a contract between the briber and the principal.
- If the principal chooses not to exercise his right of rescission he is not prevented from recovering the amount of the bribe from his agent.[76] The decision in the *Bagnall* case was followed in *Salford*, but rescission was not

[73] *Fawcett v Whitehouse* (1829) 1 Russ & Mg 132.

[74] *Boston Deep Sea Fishing and Ice Co v Ansell* (1888) 39 ChD 339, 367.

[75] *Reading v A-G* [1949] 2 KB 232; [1951] AC 507. This was a case in which an army sergeant in Cairo made large sums of money escorting lorries carrying illicit goods through checkpoints—his uniform ensuring they were not inspected. The money was confiscated by the military authorities and he petitioned the Crown for its return. He was not allowed to keep it—although he had obtained the money by reason of his employment, it was in dereliction of his duty. The Crown thus kept the proceeds, even though they were earned through criminal activity.

[76] *Bagnall v Carlton* (1877) 6 ChD 371.

available to the Corporation because all the coal had been consumed. The price of the coal had been inflated by the amount of the bribes and that was the measure of the damage suffered by the Corporation.

- In the *Salford* case, however, the Court of Appeal held that the principal's cause of action for recovery of the bribe from the agent was a separate and different cause of action from his cause of action against the briber for damages for fraud. This led the three judges to state that the principal's remedies were separate and cumulative, with the result that damages could be recovered against both agent and briber without making allowance for any recovery made against either one of them, ie a double recovery was possible.
- The cause of action against the briber in the *Salford* case was said by two of the judges to be fraud: from this it followed that the agent was a party to the fraud, ie a joint tortfeasor, enabling either or both of the agent and/or briber to be sued but, as Lord Diplock pointed out, fraud is a tort for which damages are limited to the actual loss sustained. If the principal has already recovered from one of the parties, the actual loss he has sustained is reduced by that amount. He cannot therefore then go on to make a double recovery.
- Whilst it was accurate to say that the principal had two distinct remedies against the agent, one for money had and received, the other for damages for the tort of fraud, it was wrong to say that the remedies were not alternative but cumulative. The principal must elect which remedy to pursue—this was well established by the House of Lords:[77] where two causes of action lie against the same defendant on the same facts the plaintiff must elect, but the election is not irrevocable until judgment is recovered on one cause of action or the other.
- In the same case[78] the House of Lords held that two defendants can be pursued by means of separate causes of action—money had and received against one, damages in tort against the other, but a judgment satisfied in part against one operates *pro tanto* against the other.
- Damage is the gist of an action in fraud and, to the extent that it may be possible to show a loss greater than the amount of the bribe, the principal may be expected to elect the remedy giving the greater return.
- After the *Salford* case differences of opinion arose between members of the Court of Appeal as to whether or not the principal had an alternative cause of action against the briber as well as against the agent for money had and received. In *Grant v Gold Exploration and Development Syndicate Ltd*[79] Collins LJ thought there was such a case against the briber: Smith and Vaughan Williams LLJ, however, had doubts and preferred to give judgments

[77] *United Australia Ltd v Barclays Bank Ltd* [1941] AC 1. [78] ibid.
[79] [1900] 1 QB 233 CA.

for damages for fraud, holding that the principal had proved a loss up to the amount of the bribe. In the *Hovenden* case Smith and Vaughan Williams LLJ changed tack and a new remedy became available to the defrauded principal.

- The three rules laid down by Romer LJ in *Hovenden* were such as to make bribery a wrong which is *sui generis* and defies classification. The irrebuttable presumption of the loss or damage being in the amount of the bribe means that, unlike in the tort of fraud, loss or damage is no longer the gist of the action. However, going on to say that an amount greater than the bribe can be recovered if the loss can be proved is to produce a hybrid form of legal wrong in which actual damage is the gist of a part only of a single cause of action.
- In fact, however, these rules amount to no more than allowing the principal to recover against the briber the amount of the bribe as money had and received or, as damages in tort, the actual amount of the loss incurred as a result of entering in to the tainted transaction. And, as the House of Lords decided in the *United Australia* case, the principal must elect.

In the *Mahesan* case itself Lord Diplock found that the Housing Society was bound to elect between recovering the amount of the bribe, US$122,000, and $443,000, the value of their claim for fraud. Since it was obvious which one they would choose, judgment was entered in the larger sum, with, presumably, little hope of recovery of such a sum against the agent. But, as M had disappeared, that was the best the Housing Society could hope to do beyond the US$13,000 recovered from the agent through the criminal confiscation procedure. Of course, if they had ever managed to bring M before the court, they would have been able to claim the balance of US$430,000 (assuming they had got no more from Mahesan, the agent), but one suspects that they might have had some difficulty locating the assets against which to execute their hard-won judgment. **6.42**

5. Recovering Profits in Addition to the Bribe (2)

The practical importance of the distinction referred to in the *Reid* case[80] is considerable. A restitutionary remedy confines the claimant to recovering the bribe and any profit accruing from it, as in *Reid*. However, because of the restrictions inherent in treating these moneys as being subject to a constructive trust, it would not permit a claimant to recover the profits made from the contract obtained by the bribe. The hybrid nature of the relief claimed in bribery cases had been specifically identified by Lord Diplock in the *Mahesan* case[81] and this was the aspect closely considered by Toulson J in the *Fyffes* case.[82] **6.43**

There, the agent, Templeman, had received bribes from Seatrade, the shipping company transporting Fyffes's bananas from the Caribbean back to **6.44**

[80] See 6.34 above.

[81] *Mahesan S/O Thambiah v Malaysia Government Officers' Co-operative Housing Society* [1979] AC 374, PC.

[82] *Fyffes Group Ltd v Templeman* [2000] 2 Lloyd's Rep 643.

the United Kingdom. There was no doubt about Templeman's liability. A restitutionary claim against him was stated to be in the alternative to the claim against the briber, seemingly affirming that double recovery was not considered a feasible option,[83] but in this case, as in *Salford v Lever*,[84] the agent, Templeman, had agreed to assist the claimants.[85] However, the judge said that the question raised in this case was whether an account of the profits made from the transaction was available against the briber, and how the jurisdiction should be exercised, there being no previous direct English authority on the point. He referred to an Australian case[86] in which it had been found that, just as it was inequitable that a fiduciary should benefit from his fraudulent conduct, so also it was 'equally inequitable that one who knowingly took part in the breach should retain the benefit that resulted therefrom'. The cases of *Reading v Attorney-General*,[87] the Spycatcher case,[88] and George Blake[89] provided useful parallels. The similarity with the liability of a person who procures a breach of contract or knowingly interferes with its due performance was also noted.

6.45 The ability of the defrauded principal to recover from the briber the profits made from the illegally induced contract not only enhances recovery but also 'serves the dual purpose of making good the beneficiary's loss should the trustee lack financial means and imposing a liability which will discourage others from behaving in a similar fashion'.[90]

6.46 The judge found that it was likely that Fyffes would have contracted with these shippers in any event, with or without the bribes being paid to Templeman; accordingly he did not order that Seatrade account to Fyffes for the whole profit earned from dishonestly assisting Templeman in his breaches of duty. Instead, he assessed as damages the additional profits earned over and above what would have constituted a reasonable profit. Toulson J was mindful of a further Australian case, heard in the High Court,[91] which had warned of the dangers of 'the liability of the fiduciary [being] transformed into a vehicle for the unjust enrichment of the plaintiff'.

---

[83] But as in *Mahesan* the choice will generally be governed by the amount recoverable.

[84] *The Mayor of Salford v Lever* [1891] 1 QB 168.

[85] There is, however, no indication that Templeman had put up security for Fyffes' claims in the same way as Salford Corporation's agent did.

[86] *Consul Developments Pty Ltd v DPC Estates Pty Ltd* [1975] 132 CLR 373.

[87] [1951] AC 507, see para 6.41, n 75 above.

[88] *A-G v Guardian Newspapers (No 2)* [1990] 1 AC 109 in which Peter Wright, the MI5 Agent, was knowingly assisted by *The Sunday Times* to breach his duty of confidentiality and had to give an account of its profits to the Crown.

[89] *A-G v Blake* [2001] 1 AC 268 HL.

[90] Lord Nicholls in *Royal Brunei Airlines v Tan* [1995] 2 AC 378, 386–387. Mr Tan's liability arose from his being an accessory to the breach of trust committed by the airline, which had gone into liquidation.

[91] *Warman International Ltd v Dwyer* [1995] 182 CLR.

6. Rescission, Voidability, and Termination

Where a principal has been induced to enter into a contract by fraudulent conduct on the part of his agent, he is entitled to set the contract aside and treat it as having been void *ab initio*. Goff states that the principal must be able to restore the *status quo ante*.[92] As Berg[93] remarks, this tends to overstate the requirement so far as the equitable right to rescind is concerned. Berg goes on to suggest that a contract obtained by bribery may, in the alternative, be: **6.47**

(1) non-existent as a matter of agency law, unless ratified by the principal; or
(2) unenforceable by the briber as a matter of public policy; or
(3) capable of being terminated by the principal pursuant to an express term in the contract itself or in a side agreement between the briber and the principal; or
(4) capable of being rescinded by the principal on the ground that it was induced by a misrepresentation by a person making the misrepresentation with the briber's authority or knowledge.[94]

Rescission as a remedy was established in the *Pacific Telegraph* case.[95] Although it is usually cited as a bribery case, the conduct of Sir Charles Bright, the consultant engineer, was not in fact influenced by payment of bribes so much as the payments he stood to receive as the result of having manoeuvred himself into a position between the respective telegraph and cable-laying companies whereby he was, in effect, to certify his own remuneration. The court regarded this as a case of *res ipsa loquitur* and held that the company which had employed him as a consultant, not actually as their agent, was, as of right, entitled to rescission of the contracts he had persuaded them to enter into. In this case nothing had, in fact, been paid under the cable-laying contract and rescission ensured that nothing did get paid. **6.48**

Where the principal has already paid a price which is inflated by the amount of the secret commission, as in the *Salford, Grant*, and *Hovenden* cases, rescission is a remedy which is unlikely to bring any additional benefit. In *Logicrose v Southend Football Club*,[96] however, it resulted in a windfall gain for the club. Logicrose negotiated a deal with the chairman of Southend FC which permitted them to hold a twice-weekly market in the car park of the Club. This deal was not only against the advice of the Club's solicitor, it was achieved by paying **6.49**

[92] R Goff and G Jones, *The Law of Restitution* (15th edn, London: Sweet & Maxwell, 1998) para 33-023.

[93] [2001] LMCLQ 27, 34.

[94] Berg also speculates interestingly on possible remedies under insolvency law. Specifically, the briber (if a company) carrying on business for a fraudulent purpose, Insolvency Act 1986, s 213; transaction at an undervalue, ibid s 238; and disqualification of a director of the bribing company, Company Directors Disqualification Act 1986, s 6.

[95] *Panama and South Pacific Telegraph Co. v India Rubber, Gutter Percha, and Telegraph Works Co* (1875) LR 10 Ch App 96.

[96] [1988] 1 WLR 1256.

£70,000 into the account of an Isle of Man company controlled by the chairman. Millett J, after a marathon hearing,[97] handed down a judgment which, in its full version, ran to 366 pages. In it, he held that where an agent received a bribe, the principal was entitled to recover it from the agent whether he elected to confirm or rescind the contract—there was no implication that the principal adopted the contract by seeking recovery from the agent. Although rescission normally required the principal to return all the benefits received under the contract to the other party, a bribe paid to the principal's agent was not to be treated as a benefit under the contract, and was therefore not returnable. Thus Southend FC did not have to allow the markets to be held and was able to retain the £70,000 which the chairman had surrendered early on in the whole saga.

7. Rescission in Other Situations

6.50 What happens when a principal's agent bribes a third party in order to induce the third party to enter into a contract with the principal? Robert Goff LJ expressed the opinion,[98] on which he noted that there is a remarkable dearth of English authority, that in those circumstances the principal is vicariously liable for his agent's actions and, if the third party suffers loss as a result, he is entitled both to claim damages and rescission, or, if it is too late to rescind the original contract, to bring it to an end. The judge reserved his position on the question of whether a principal, induced to enter into a contract by his agent who has been bribed by a stranger, can, when the bribery is discovered, rescind the contract in circumstances where the other party to it is innocent.[99]

6.51 The 'stranger' in this last scenario envisaged by Goff LJ will usually, in fact, have a considerable interest in the transaction in question: that interest will frequently be given pseudo-respectability by means of a so-called 'consultancy' contract. The 'stranger' may be a person of influence within a government, a minister for example, who requires the government official responsible for negotiating the contract on behalf of the government to arrange the separate 'consultancy' contract as a condition for obtaining the main contract. The contractor, if it wants the main contract, has then to increase the price to the government to take into account the 'consultancy' fee. Rescission of the whole contract will be one option for the government, if it finds out what has happened, but that may be a very expensive option if it has to get in another contractor to complete the contract: such expense might form part of a claim for damages, but the outcome, as well as the ability of the defendants to pay, could

[97] It lasted 57 days.

[98] *Armagas Ltd v Mundogas SA* [1986] AC 717, AC, 741ff; see also *Barry v Stoney Point Canning Co* (1917) 55 SCR 51, a case decided by the Supreme Court of Canada, cited by Goff LJ at 744.

[99] *Armagas* (n 98 above) 745.

be uncertain. The government may therefore prefer (as did the government of Lesotho)[100] to confine itself to recovery of the surplus monies it paid out to cover the 'consultancy fee'.

The contractor, who did not offer the bribe in the first place, but was rather induced to give it, may not itself benefit from the 'consultancy fee', unless, as is often in fact the case, the contractor, or one of its employees, is also receiving a percentage of the fee for 'facilitating' the payment on to the 'consultant'. That percentage could be the subject of a restitutionary claim by the government, but it is suggested that the 'consultancy fee' itself would, as against the contractor, probably be treated as a claim in damages for fraud, on the basis that the contractor was a co-conspirator with the government official. Such an action would certainly be punitive as against a contractor which had already paid over the fee and might act as a deterrent to others entering into these kinds of arrangement, but the real 'villain' is the minister or official who engineered the whole deal and is usually the one who reaps the major part of the benefit, either for himself or those in higher authority. Part of the deal will very often also be that the contractor will pay the 'consultancy fee' into an offshore account, compounding the difficulties that will face a government trying to retrieve its money. **6.52**

E. Remedies Against Third Parties

Remedies are available against third parties that have wrongfully assisted in the misappropriation of the funds, or that have received misappropriated trust funds. These remedies have been given the labels of 'knowing assistance' and 'knowing receipt' in some quarters. These claims are the subject of a separate group of cases which do not have bribery at their centre, but the principles which have emerged, which have mostly to do with constructive trusts and restitution, are likely to be applicable as much to scenarios of the type outlined above as to assisting in any other form of dishonest activity. **6.53**

1. Remedies Against Persons who Dishonestly Assist in Corruption

A stranger to a trust will be liable to account as a constructive trustee if he knowingly assists in the furtherance of a fraudulent and dishonest breach of trust. He does not have to have received any part of the trust property, but must have been a dishonest accessory to a breach of trust. That breach is often fraudulent, and invariably so in the situations considered in this chapter, but is not necessarily so. Knowing assistance is made out by dishonest assistance in an honest breach of trust,[101] though such situations may be rare in practice. **6.54**

[100] See Lesotho case study at 10.131ff below.

[101] *Royal Brunei Airlines v Phillip Tan Kok Ming* [1995] 2 AC 378, PC.

6.55 After the case of *Baden v Société Générale*[102] it was thought there was no difference between 'knowing receipt' and 'knowing assistance'. In *Agip (Africa) Ltd v Jackson,*[103] however, a distinction was drawn, and 'knowing receipt' and tracing claims were said to be concerned with rights of priority over property taken by a legal owner for his own benefit. 'Knowing assistance', on the other hand, was specifically concerned with the furtherance of fraud. The *Baden* case famously set out six tests for establishing 'knowledge':[104] in the *Agip* case it was said 'that the true distinction is between honesty and dishonesty'.[105]

6.56 In *Royal Brunei Airlines*[106] it was said that 'the *Baden* scale of knowledge is best forgotten'.[107] The Privy Council gave close consideration to the ingredients of 'dishonesty', ingredients which are readily transferable to participation in a bribery operation. In particular, the Court said that individuals are not free to set their own standards of honesty in particular circumstances: 'Honesty is not an optional scale, with higher or lower values according to the moral standards of each individual.'[108] Honesty is not a subjective, but an objective standard—in a business setting, a dishonest person has been described as 'guilty of commercially unacceptable conduct in the particular context involved'.[109] In a bribery context it is also significant that the defendant, Tan, was held to be the company for the purposes of the judgment and his state of mind was imputed to the company.

6.57 Despite the seemingly clear establishment of what constitutes dishonesty in the *Royal Brunei Airlines* case the concept was subjected to further scrutiny in *Grupo Torras v Al-Sabah.*[110] In that case the issue of law for decision was whether it is necessary in a claim for dishonest assistance to establish that the defendant had knowledge of the facts giving rise to the breach of trust or fiduciary duty.[111] The court distinguished between two types of dishonesty: so-called 'Robin Hood' dishonesty, where the defendant falls below an objective standard of honesty (the *Royal Brunei* test); and 'blind eye dishonesty'. The latter category requires conscious impropriety in the sense that the defendant closes his eyes and asks no

102 [1993] 1 WLR 509.
103 [1990] Ch 265.
104 *Baden v Société Générale* [1993] 1 WLR 509, 575ff.
105 *Agip (Africa) Ltd v Jackson* [1990] Ch 265, 293.
106 *Royal Brunei Airlines v Philip Tan Kok Ming* [1995] 2 AC 378.
107 ibid 392.
108 ibid 389.
109 *Cowan de Groot Properties Ltd v Eagle Trust plc* [1992] 4 All ER 700, 761.
110 [2001] 1 Lloyd's Rep 117, AC . The court in reaching its decision considered four cases which had been decided since *Royal Brunei*; the Court of Appeal decision in *Twinsectra Ltd v Yardley* [2000] Lloyd's Rep PN 239, which then went to the House of Lords [2002] 2 AC 164, HL, considered in 6.58ff below; *Heinl v Jyske Bank (Gibraltar) Ltd* [1999] Lloyd's Rep Bank 511; *Mortgage Express v S Newman & Co* [2000] Lloyd's Rep PN 745 and *Walker v Stones* [2000] 4 All ER 412. None of these were bribery cases, but the court observed that 'all the cases show that in this area of the law the nature of the transaction, and whether it would appear to an honest observer as an ordinary commercial transaction, is always a most important factor.'
111 *Grupo Torras v Al-Sabah* [2001] Lloyd's Rep 117, 127ff.

questions, not because (as in the *Grupo Torras* case itself) it was negligent not to ask those questions, but because any honest person (in that case, a Spanish lawyer) would have asked them. Not asking the questions was characterized by counsel as a 'suppression of the moral antennae', caused by a desire for personal gain, but also as a result of the influence wielded by one of the malefactors. This last feature can be particularly significant in the type of hierarchical society often found in developing countries where corruption is rife.

The meaning of dishonesty in the context of 'knowing assistance' was not settled by the string of cases referred to above. The issue reached the House of Lords in *Twinsectra v Yardley*.[112] Mr Leach, a solicitor, had acted for a client in a transaction which involved the negotiation of a loan of £1 million from Twinsectra. The loan was subject to an undertaking that it would be used solely for the acquisition of property. Mr Leach paid the money out on his client's instructions, without taking steps to ensure that it was used in this way. His client used the money for other purposes and the loan was not repaid. The trial judge found that Mr Leach had, in the words of Lord Hoffman, 'shut his eyes to the problems or implications of what happened, yet he acquitted him of dishonesty'. Was that correct? **6.58**

Lord Hutton noted that the question of whether Mr Leach had acted dishonestly depended on the meaning to be given to that term in the *Royal Brunei Airlines* case. Their Lordships, with Lord Millet dissenting, held that the test for liability as an accessory to a breach of trust consisted of two limbs. First, the defendant must have acted dishonestly by the ordinary standards of reasonable and honest people. Secondly, the defendant must have been aware himself that by those standards he was acting dishonestly.[113] Applying this test, the House of Lords upheld the trial judge's decision, after the benefit of cross-examination, that Mr Leach was misguided but not dishonest in carrying out his client's instructions. He had not deliberately closed his eyes to the obvious but had a blinkered approach to his professional duties as a solicitor and had honestly believed that the loan was at the disposal of his client. **6.59**

Liability therefore depends on recognition that particular conduct would be regarded as dishonest by objective standards. Stupidity is insufficient. Of course, as Lord Steyn recognized in his judgment, shutting one's eyes to obvious problems or implications may well indicate dishonesty. Many potential accessories will plead honest error to a charge of dishonesty, and the difficult task for the court is to decide, in all the circumstances, whether that can really be a true explanation of their conduct. **6.60**

---

[112] [2002] AC 164 HL.

[113] It is instructive to compare this test with that in *Ghosh* [1982] QB 1053; see 5.54 above.

2. Remedies Against Persons Who Receive the Proceeds of Corruption

6.61 The term 'knowing receipt' is often used to describe the cause of action which arises when a claimant can demonstrate that a third party (such as a bank or other financial institution) beneficially received proceeds in the knowledge that they were corruptly obtained. Such a situation could arise, for example, where funds are used to pay off an overdraft or are paid as fees. 'Constructive' knowledge will suffice, and such claims are likely to be assessed in accordance with the guidelines which have been developed in dealing with cases of dishonest assistance (see above). It is necessary to demonstrate that the recipient's state of knowledge makes it unconscionable for it to retain the funds.[114] It is possible that third parties innocently receive the illicit funds, and subsequently acquire actual or constructive knowledge that they are the proceeds of corruption, but pay them away on the wrongdoer's instructions. Such cases should probably be treated as dishonest assistance, or akin to it, and be dealt with by the principles in the preceding section (paras 6.54ff). It has been suggested that the law in this area should be changed in order to impose strict liability in respect of receipt of moneys which have been disposed of in breach of trust, subject to defences of bona fide purchaser in good faith and change of position.[115]

6.62 It seems now to be well established that a claimant can successfully recover not only the amount of a bribe, but also any additional sum that may have accrued as a result of investment of the illicit funds.[116] Equally, a defendant would have to make good any shortfall that may have arisen as the result of spending the money or investing it unwisely, since he is liable in the first instance for the whole amount of the bribe. What is far less certain is the outcome in a situation where, say, an innocent bank has the proceeds of a corrupt transaction frozen in its hands. It has no interest in or claim to the money but, with the leave of the court and knowledge of the claimant, continues to invest the money on instructions from the defendant pending a decision from the court as to ownership. As a result, substantial losses are incurred. Is the claimant still entitled to be made whole?[117]

6.63 In the majority of cases, corruption involves the payment of money—these days, very often, very large sums of money. The money may be the proceeds of a bribe, or it may be receipts from over-invoicing; it can comprise misappropriated aid payments, or it may be straightforward theft of state funds. Whatever the source, the 'beneficiary' of these payments has a problem: how to

---

[114] *Bank of Credit and Commerce International (Overseas) Ltd v Akindele* [2001] Ch 437.

[115] Lord Nicholls: 'Restitution, Past, Present and Future' in WR Cornish (ed) *Essays in honour of Gareth Jones* (Oxford: Hart, 1998).

[116] *A-G for Hong Kong v Reid* [1994] 1 AC 324, PC; see 6.34ff above, but also 5.50ff.

[117] This situation could easily arise in litigation such as that conducted by Nigeria to recover funds looted by ex-President Abacha where huge sums of money were frozen in Switzerland, Liechtenstein, and Luxembourg at a time when markets were falling.

put the money to some form of use? Most commonly, the money will go into a bank account, preferably one where the true identity of the recipient can be obscured; numbered accounts in Switzerland used to be ideal for this purpose. The setting up of dummy 'trust' companies in offshore jurisdictions which do not demand to know the identity of the true beneficial owner is another favourite method.

Investment in financial securities, real property, works of art, and gold bullion have also all been popular for those who have the knowledge and confidence to operate in those markets. Sometimes the proceeds are simply dissipated: President Sese Seko Mobutu, President of the Congo for thirty-two years, not only spent lavishly on vainglorious building projects at home but also had to pay out huge sums to those whose political manoeuvring kept him in power (the 'mouvanciers'). It was estimated that over US$12 billion in aid was siphoned off by Mobutu—when he was toppled in May 1997, just $4 million was found. He claimed that in his lifetime he was never worth more than $50 million.[118] **6.64**

The common feature of all these forms of disposal is the requirement for assistance by bankers, accountants, financial advisers, lawyers, estate agents, art dealers—anyone who can conveniently handle, or launder, large sums of illegally acquired money in a 'discreet' way. The problem for the victim of the corrupt activity is how to get the money (or property) back. Until recent changes in the law, criminal confiscation did not provide a satisfactory answer because the prosecuting state usually kept the proceeds; the Proceeds of Crime Act 2002 has improved the position to an extent by providing a means for victims of crime to recover funds confiscated as a result of civil proceedings by the Assets Recovery Agency, although such proceedings may prove to be rare.[119] **6.65**

3. Heads of Claim

Claims may be brought in a variety of forms against a variety of wrongdoers. The most frequent in practice are likely to be those named in freezing orders[120] for restitution of funds which represent the proceeds of corruption, against whom there may or may not also be dishonest assistance and knowing receipt claims. However, where a fraudulent recipient receives the proceeds of corruption and pays them on to third parties, the recipient is treated as a fiduciary and the claimant can trace into the hands of the third parties.[121] **6.66**

In addition to, or as an alternative to, any proprietary claims a victim may have, he may be able to claim damages against those assisting in a breach of fiduciary **6.67**

[118] A fascinating account of the Mobutu kleptocracy is to be found in Michelle Wrong's book *In the Footsteps of Mr Kurtz* (London: Fourth Estate, 2000).

[119] Proceeds of Crime Act 2002; see 7.69ff below.

[120] See, further, Ch 7 below.

[121] *Twinsectra v Yardley* [2002] 2AC 164, *Westdeutsche LBG v Islington LBC* [1996] AC 669.

duty[122] or bring a claim for wrongful interference with the proceeds of corruption in the form of movable property.[123] Participation in a tortious conspiracy against the claimant[124] is another possible head of action. Against advisers, claims for damages for negligence and/or breach of contract or breach of a duty of care in performance of services for the claimant are also possibilities.[125] If loss occurs as a result of a breach of duty of care, liability will arise without the need for proof of dishonesty.

6.68 In bringing any of these claims, however, there may be formidable difficulties of proof to be surmounted, particularly when the claim is proprietary and the defendant has mixed the proceeds of lawful activity with unlawful. The claimant will have to provide particulars sufficient for the court to be satisfied that the account or assets in question do indeed contain tainted proceeds.[126] This can also be particularly difficult if an account is suspected of containing the proceeds of more than one corrupt transaction but insufficient details are available to the claimant to identify any of them with certainty. The courts have, however, developed following and tracing rules to identify misappropriated property and its proceeds as it passes through different accounts and hands.[127]

F. International Arbitration and Corruption

1. Arbitration Awards

6.69 There can be no doubt as to the importance of this topic in modern times. The majority of major infrastructure contracts these days contain arbitration clauses and it is in the realm of public procurement, as remarked above, that major corruption takes place. It is not so long ago that the activities of arbitrators and their tribunals were a closed book. The confidentiality of arbitration proceedings ensured not only that the parties' secrets were preserved, but also that the practice followed in arbitrations remained largely unknown. This is no longer the case. Many arbitrations involve such huge sums and matters of such widespread, often political, interest, that publicity has become inevitable. Many

122 *Agip v Jackson* [1991] Ch 547, and see 'Dishonest Assistance', 6.54ff above.

123 Such claims would lie against, eg fine art dealers, auctioneers, yacht brokers, bloodstock dealers.

124 *Kuwait Oil Tanker Co v Al Bader* [2000] 2 All ER (Comm) 271; *Grupo Torras SA v Al-Sabah* [2001] I Lloyd's Rep 117, AC.

125 Banks and intermediaries owe a duty of care (and now have statutory obligations also) to, eg, ask proper questions of those opening accounts with them: *Grupo Torras* (n 122 above).

126 A clear example of this difficulty is demonstrated in the Abacha Swiss proceedings, where the Swiss Supreme Court, in its judgment given on 7 February 2005, refused to order payment of all the moneys held in frozen accounts to Nigeria; see, further 7.55 below.

127 See, eg, J McGhee, *Snell's Equity* (31st edn, London: Sweet & Maxwell, 2004) paras 28-32 to 28-44 and the cases cited.

of the awards made in arbitrations conducted under the rules of the International Chamber of Commerce (ICC), based in Paris, are now available—albeit identified by reference numbers only, in order to preserve the parties' anonymity. The International Centre for the Settlement of Investment Disputes (ICSID), based in Washington, makes awards available on line when they are published.[128]

The awards themselves attract considerable comment amongst practitioners and the jurisprudence has become very much more significant with parties being encouraged, particularly in a jurisdiction such as England, actively to seek methods of alternative dispute resolution (ADR). The result in England has been a dramatic falling off in the number of cases being brought before the civil courts.[129] In addition, since the passing of the Arbitration Act 1996 in England, the likelihood of court intervention has been greatly reduced. This has been part of a general jurisdictional trend internationally, as the general undesirability of having national courts as *de facto* courts of appeal in arbitration proceedings where the parties have often opted for arbitration precisely because they do want (or think they want) finality in dispute resolution has become widely recognized. **6.70**

2. Arbitrability

Dealing with issues arising out of corruption presents a whole set of considerations which need to be looked at.[130] It has already been noted above that the English courts have traditionally expressed themselves in strong terms when dealing with bribery issues. The judges would say that 'public policy' demands that they should do so, in order that no one should be in any doubt that bribery is not an activity which will, under any circumstances, be justified: a zero tolerance approach. The judges represent an important part of our civil society and have traditionally seen themselves as guardians of our moral welfare. But what of arbitrators? Should they also inhabit such high moral ground? Judges are, at the end of the day, servants of the public, who pay their salaries. Arbitrators are creatures of contract—their appointment is enshrined in terms agreed between two freely contracting parties—to whom do they owe a duty, beyond those who have appointed them? Sayed, having analysed large numbers of awards, concludes that arbitrators fall broadly into two categories in their attitudes towards dealing with corruption issues. On the one hand, there is a 'repressive' tendency, which is characterized by arbitrators with strong **6.71**

[128] See http://www.worldbank.org/icsid/cases/cases.htm.

[129] In 1998 120,000 cases were commenced in the Queen's Bench Division of the High Court. By 2003 the number was down to 14,000, *The Times*, 12 October 2004.

[130] A comprehensive attempt to do precisely this is contained in Abdulhay Sayed's book *Corruption in International Trade and Commercial Arbitration* (London: Kluwer Law International, 2004), which has provided much valuable material for this section.

(personal) views on the general undesirability of corruption. On the other, there are those whom Sayed categorizes as 'indifferent': these arbitrators will avoid making moral judgments, taking the parties as they find them and resolving their differences without sitting in judgment on their commercial behaviour.[131]

6.72 The doctrine of separability of arbitration clauses in contracts from the issues which fall to be decided has come to be widely accepted in most jurisdictions. This makes it less easy for a party to challenge the setting up of the arbitral panel on the ground that the underlying contract is void *ab initio*. It also avoids situations in which arbitrators do not feel they can proceed with the arbitration. There is a distinction to be made, however, between cases in which it is apparent that corruption played a part in procuring the contract and cases in which the subject matter of the arbitration is a dispute over the terms of the corruption deal itself.

6.73 The most celebrated example of the latter type of dispute is probably an ICC case which led to the so-called 'Lagergren Award' named after the distinguished Swedish jurist who acted as arbitrator, Judge Gunnar Lagergren.[132] The claimant was an Argentinian businessman and engineer who claimed that he was due certain commissions from an English company which had been awarded a series of contracts to supply electrical stations and substations around Buenos Aires. There was no written agreement, only a series of letters written in 1950 in which payment of a commission of 5 per cent was promised, to be paid by instalments following receipt by the respondent company of payments under the public procurement contract the claimant had assisted the respondent in obtaining. There had been a further oral agreement for payment of a 10 per cent commission if the respondent's parent company was successful in bidding for a further major power station project. Following refusal by the respondent to pay the commissions, the parties agreed in a separate *compromis* to arbitrate the matter under ICC rules in Paris. At the heart of these agreements was the claimant's ability to influence key decision-makers, including President Peron. The respondent took no point on voidability of the underlying agreements by reason of their inherently corrupt nature—it was, after all, a party to the arrangements in question. Instead its defences went to merits, including questions of which contracts were actually awarded as a result of the claimant's influence. It was Judge Lagergren himself who took the corruption point, asking whether it could be right for an arbitrator to adjudicate an agreement to pay

[131] Sayed (n 130 above) has a passage at the beginning of his book (pp 9–25) in which he summarizes the contrasting attitudes and sets out the competing rationales where bribery is concerned. It refers to further literature on the subject and is highly recommended for those interested in seeing both sides of the argument.

[132] ICC Case No 1110 (1994) 10(3), *Arbitration International* 282–294. Also a good example of the new openness regarding the publication of awards: the actual award was made 30 years previously.

secret commissions. In his view the contract violated what he termed 'public decency and morality', and justified his rejection of the parties' *compromis*.

In reaching his decision, Judge Lagergren relied on Article V-2-b of the New York Convention,[133] which states that a national judge has the power '*ex officio*' to refuse enforcement of an award on the ground that it would be deemed contrary to public policy in the country concerned. According to Judge Lagergren, this power given to the national judge at the enforcement stage meant that *a fortiori* the arbitrator could decide whether to exercise his jurisdiction over the matter on an *ex officio* basis. In deciding that jurisdiction should be declined, Judge Lagergren also carried out his own analysis of the laws of the countries connected with the parties and the arbitration. **6.74**

In looking at French law on the law of the place of arbitration, he took the view that cases involving public policy were reserved for the French courts. He was probably wrong about this, but in his evaluation of the position under French law he carried out an exercise of a type which, thirty years later, was to commend itself to an English Commercial Court Judge.[134] He recognized that there were laws which might be termed 'state specific', for example anti-smuggling laws. On the other hand there were also matters which would be contrary to public policy in a foreign state which would also be deemed such under the laws of France: thus smuggling accompanied by the use of violence or corruption would in his view fall into such a category. Judge Lagergren was also much attracted by the English distinction between acts which were *malum prohibitum* and *malum in se*. A case involving corruption would clearly fall within the latter category and the French courts would not be able, he said, to enforce a contract based on grave offence to *bonos mores*. He also noted that, under Argentine law, article 768:5 of the Code of Procedure provided that 'all questions which affect good morals are excluded from arbitration'. His conclusion was expressed thus: **6.75**

> After weighing all the evidence I am convinced a case such as this, involving such gross violations of good morals and international public policy, can have no countenance in any Court whether in the Argentine or in France, or for that matter, in any other civilised country, nor in any arbitral Tribunal. Thus, jurisdiction must be declined in this case.

In reaching this conclusion, Judge Lagergren was undoubtedly influenced by his own abhorrence at the idea of being asked to adjudicate upon a corrupt agreement—his task would have been made easier if the respondent had taken the nullity point. It is not at all clear to what extent Judge Lagergren had attempted to examine the facts, but it was certainly clear from the witness statements that the payments were required not only to obtain Presidential approval of the contracts, **6.76**

[133] New York Convention on the Recognition and Enforcement of Foreign Arbitral Awards, 1958.

[134] Colman J in the *Westacre* case, as to which, see further below.

but also to pay off lower officials—interestingly there is considerable discussion as to what was a 'safe' going rate in order not to arouse the suspicions of the Ministry of Finance. If the collaborators were caught they could face imprisonment apparently, which presumably might have required further bribes to be paid.[135] No attempt was made by Judge Lagergren to examine the legal or moral system which prevailed in Argentina at the time. The commissions were built into the tender price and clearly had to be paid by anyone wishing to do business with Peronist Argentina. The amounts involved were not outrageously high—many would regard 10 per cent to a bona fide agent obtaining business as a 'commercial' rate. Whilst there may appear to be something inherently unsatisfactory in the way Judge Lagergren seemingly comes to an intuitive conclusion of his own motion (the point not having been raised by the parties) in order to declare the matter 'non-arbitrable', many commentators have applauded the stand which he took. It is also worth noting that when the award was finally published it turned out that there had not in fact been a contractual arbitration clause. Judge Lagergren's decision was, however, based simply on non-arbitrability.

3. The Approach of Foreign Courts

6.77 There is no doubt that the existence of bribery in public procurement contracts which are submitted to arbitration does raise very difficult issues—particularly in countries where there is seemingly no other way of obtaining the contracts which, in themselves, may be extremely important for a developing country's infrastructure. Sayed examines the problem both from the perspective of the national judge and that of the arbitrator.[136] The Supreme Court of Pakistan found that where there is *prima facie* evidence of corruption and/or misuse of public office, the matter is non-arbitrable;[137] indeed, it went further and said that such matters have to be decided in a court of law. In ICC Case No 6474, objections to the arbitrator's jurisdiction were raised by the defendant state in a case tainted by corruption, which the state said would not be arbitrable under its own laws on the basis that the award would not be enforceable in the state concerned. The arbitrator was unimpressed, as he believed that the award could be enforced in other states and, in any event, under the doctrine of separability, the arbitrator held that the corruption would only be a factor if it had directly affected the arbitration clause itself.[138]

6.78 One of the largest and best known cases involving bribery and a head of state was the *Westinghouse* case in which Westinghouse were alleged to have paid

[135] A summary of the content of the witness statements is to be found in Sayed (n 130 above) 111–113.

[136] Sayed (n 130 above) 70 ff.

[137] *Hub Power Co Ltd (HUBCO) v Pakistan WAPDA and Federation of Pakistan* (2000) 15(7) *Mealey's International Arbitration Report*, Section A.1, pp A-15 to A-16.

[138] Partial Award in ICC Case No 6474 of 1992 (2000) XXV *Yearbook of Commercial Arbitration* 279–311.

bribes to President Marcos to secure contracts for the design and construction of a nuclear power plant in the Philippines. The case involved numerous arbitral and judicial proceedings in Switzerland, all of which are publicly available.[139] The Tribunal spent a great deal of time and effort in determining the bribery allegations at the preliminary stage of the proceedings in order to determine whether the doctrine of separability had itself been vitiated. The allegation was that one effect of the bribes was that Marcos himself had intervened to force officials in the Philippine National Power Corporation (PNPC) to agree to the inclusion of an arbitration clause in the construction contract, this following the award of the consultancy contract to Burns & Roe in circumstances which clearly smacked of bribery.[140] The issue had particular importance in the light of the fact that PNPC had specifically pleaded clear breaches of the Philippine Anti-Graft Act. The Tribunal found, however, that the PNPC had failed to prove the bribery allegations so that it did not have to consider the separability point—although it did concede that there might be circumstances, for example if the arbitration clause was inserted as the result of duress, where the clause itself might be invalid. As Sayed observes,[141] it is curious that the Tribunal conducted the comprehensive review that it did of the bribery allegations for the purposes of a preliminary award restricted to jurisdiction issues. In concluding that bribery had not affected the validity of the arbitration clause it seems almost as though the Tribunal based its decision on a finding that the main contracts themselves were unaffected by bribery.

The decision of the Tribunal did not go unchallenged. PNPC took the case **6.79**
before the Swiss *Tribunal Fédéral* alleging that the arbitrators had erred in assuming jurisdiction and that public policy had been violated. It was asserted that both the consultancy and the construction contracts were null and void as a result of the Marcos corruption. The case was rejected by the Swiss Court. It regarded the application as an attempted appeal on the facts—the thorough way in which the arbitral tribunal had investigated the bribery allegations could not, said the *Tribunal Fédéral*, give grounds under the relevant provision of the Swiss Private International Law Act[142] to challenge the decision of the arbitrators. The Act specifically limited the grounds on which challenges could be invoked in order to ensure the maximum effectiveness of arbitral proceedings in Switzerland; that objective would be compromised if the

[139] The most relevant report for present purposes is ICC Case No 6401 *Westinghouse International Projects Co, Westinghouse Electric SA, Westinghouse Electric Corp, and Burns & Roe Enterprises, Inc v National Power Corp, The Republic of the Philippines*, Preliminary Award, 19 December 1991 (1992) 7(1) *Mealey's International Arbitration Report*, Section B.

[140] The purpose of the consultancy contract was to advise the PNPC on the bidding process: the contract was awarded to another company before being awarded to Burns & Roe following intervention by an 'intermediary', one Mr Disini, who was known to have extensive common business interests with the President—see Preliminary Award, 40.

[141] Sayed (n 130 above) 79–80.

[142] Art 190, para 2.

Tribunal appeared to have the power freely to review the factual findings of Arbitrators.[143]

6.80 The Swiss courts have been consistent in their refusal to go behind arbitrators' findings on corruption. *Frontier AG v Thomson CSF* was a case involving the sale of sixteen frigates by Thomson to the Taiwanese navy. It is a celebrated case, which was at the heart of many of the allegations in the Elf corruption scandal in France in the late 1990s. Thomson, the French engineering giant, retained the services of Frontier, a Swiss company, to assist it in overcoming French Government resistance to the sale—the resistance being based on Chinese opposition to its taking place.[144] Frontier, under a letter-contract, the only copy of which was secreted away in a Swiss bank vault, was to receive one per cent of the US$160 million price tag if the deal went through. It did, and Thomson then refused to pay on the grounds, *inter alia*, that it offended against article 178 of the old French penal code which outlawed influence peddlling.

6.81 The Tribunal found that article 178 did not apply to influencing Chinese officials—a conclusion which Thomson challenged in the Swiss Court as being contrary to international public policy. The Swiss Supreme Court was unimpressed. It regarded the challenge as being limited to an assertion that the arbitrators had made an error in applying the law, which, without demonstrating that the failure went to the root of the award, was not in itself sufficient to justify setting aside the award—only if the arbitrators themselves had transgressed public policy in making the award would a fundamental principle have been violated, said the Court.[145] Thomson was ordered to pay the whole amount of the commission. Frontier AG sought to enforce the award in France. Thomson then took the matter before the French courts, filing a criminal complaint alleging that part of the commission payable was used to bribe French officials. The matter went before the Paris Court of Appeal, where Thomson made a further allegation to the effect that Frontier had conducted the whole arbitration fraudulently, using fictitious evidence, thus contravening public policy. The Court ordered a total review of all the facts, moving away from its previous policy of interfering as little as possible with arbitration awards.

6.82 The *Thomson* case does, however, give rise to a different perspective regarding the mechanics of corrupt payments and the actual evil that public policy is addressing. The assumption made by Thomson was that payments had to be made to

[143] *National Power Corporation v Westinghouse*, Swiss *Tribunal Fédéral*, 2 September 1993 (1994) 5 *Bulletin de l'Association Suisse de l'arbitrage* 244–247, 245.

[144] Thomson, however, only made vague allegations concerning bribery of French officials—in particular the role played by Alfred Sirven, a senior executive at Elf Aquitaine, who had allegedly set up a whole scheme to bribe the French Foreign Minister of the time, Roland Dumas.

[145] *Thomson v Frontier AG*, Judgment of 28 January 1997 (1998) 16 *Bulletin de l'Association Suisse de l'arbitrage* 118–131.

intermediaries in China in order to lift the Chinese opposition to the deal. The terms of the letter-contract appear in the Award[146]—as with all such agreements, the wording is innocent enough, providing for the consultant to provide services in connection with obtaining the sale. However, the Tribunal noted that it was not a question in this case of simply bribing Taiwanese or French officials, but exercising influence in a third state, China, which was not party to the contract. No Chinese state assets were involved, nor was any Chinese 'decision' purchased—the payments had been made to get China to drop the objections it had been expressing to the French Government. This did not translate, according to the Tribunal, into corruption. Yet the uncomfortable fact remains that Chinese public officials benefited. There was no pecuniary loss to China, but its foreign (or, in the case of Taiwan, China would say, its domestic) policy was compromised—impossible to put a price on that, particularly when that policy was perceived by many in the West as being obnoxious in any event.

It can be seen that 'public policy' in this instance moves into very grey areas indeed. At the end of the day, the Tribunal clearly felt that the service provided for under the agreement had been performed and should be remunerated. In this way it might be thought that the Tribunal was sanctioning corruption, but, in truth, the application of the legal principles examined in this chapter becomes extraordinarily unclear in a case of this kind. If action was to have been taken, it would have had to have been on the part of the Chinese authorities who were, in the circumstances, those probably least likely to take such action. **6.83**

4. The Approach of the English Courts

Failure by the governments of states which are the victims of corruption to take action against those accepting bribes is, regrettably, all too common, particularly in developing countries. What is even more regrettable, however, is the attitude sometimes displayed in the developed world—tax relief on bribes being one of the most blatant examples. The ambivalence towards the treatment of corruption sometimes demonstrated in arbitration proceedings can permeate into the English courts as well, particularly when it comes to enforcement of arbitration awards. Three cases decided in the last two years of the twentieth century demonstrate a worrying relaxation of the strict view of corruption which had been built up by the English courts in the previous 200 years. The decisions are all the more surprising in the light of the growing awareness of the damage large-scale commercial corruption can do—an awareness that was specifically recognized in the first case, but dismissed in the interest of having finality in arbitration awards. That case was *Westacre Investment Inc v Jugoimport-SPDR Holding Co Ltd and ors.*[147] **6.84**

[146] ICC Case No 7664 *Frontier AG & Brunner Sociedade v Thomson CSF*, 31 July 1996, para 57.
[147] [1998] 2 Lloyd's Law Reps 65.

6.85 Westacre had a 'Consultancy Agreement' with the Federal Directorate of Supply and Procurement of Yugoslavia (which subsequently became Jugoimport-SPDR Holding Co Ltd—'Jugoimport') and a Yugoslav Bank under which it was to receive 15 per cent of the sale price of military equipment, including M-84 tanks sold to the Kuwait Ministry of Defence by Jugoimport—the payments being guaranteed by the bank. A dispute having arisen as to whether sales worth in excess of US$500 million were 'conclusively and irrebuttably' due to the efforts of Westacre, the matter was referred to ICC Arbitration in Switzerland, with Swiss law governing the contract. An award[148] was rendered in February 1994 which was confirmed by the Swiss *Tribunal Fédéral* in December 1994. Under it, Jugoimport were to pay 'fees' in excess of US$50 million. The issue of bribery was raised before the arbitrators, who recognized that it would be fatal to the claimants' case, but it was not apparently pleaded with any particularity: 'The word "bribery" is clear and unmistakable. If the defendant does not use it in his presentation of facts an arbitral tribunal does not have to investigate' said the arbitrators.

6.86 When the matter went before the Swiss *Tribunal Fédéral*, the defendants alleged that Westacre was in fact a vehicle for receiving bribes on behalf of a Mr Al-Otaibi, a member of the Kuwaiti Government. However, it was only when Westacre commenced proceedings on the award in England that the full strength of the allegations emerged, in an affidavit. The purpose of the 'commission' was to ensure that Jugoimport not only got the supply contract but would also get 20 per cent of the value of all spares contracts for the next twenty years. As the deponent said, these percentages were unusually high—it must have been appreciated that additional money was needed to pay bribes. It also emerged that there was a Kuwaiti law which expressly forbade the payment of commissions on military supply contracts and indeed excluded the use of intermediaries such as Westacre. All of this Mr Al-Otaibi had apparently been able to circumvent.

6.87 The case came before Colman J in the Commercial Court at first instance. He did not give the defendants leave to amend and took the view that they had had ample opportunity to make their points in Switzerland. Whilst he accepted that an agreement to procure a contract by payment of bribes is void *ab initio*, the point that he had to decide was whether the English court should intervene on the basis of new, convincing, but untested, evidence to refuse enforcement on the ground that the Swiss award offended English public policy: this had to be balanced against the desirability of having finality in arbitration awards. Colman J considered the gravity of commercial corruption, as compared with offences such as drug trafficking, paedophilia, prostitution, and terrorism; all of

148 Published in (1995) 2 *Bulletin de l'Association Suisse de l'arbitrage* 301–357 and in (1996) XXI *Yearbook of Commercial Arbitration* 79–98.

these would, he felt, clearly be against public policy. In the case of corruption however, notwithstanding an express reference by him to the newly introduced OECD Convention on Combating the Bribery of Foreign Officials, he did not think that public policy considerations outweighed the importance of upholding the arbitration award.

Two judges in the Court of Appeal, in judgments which total less than one page, agreed with Colman J. The third judge in the Court of Appeal, Waller LJ, in a judgment running to twenty-two pages, disagreed. In his view the bribery issue had not been properly ventilated before the Swiss arbitrators. He could quite understand how the defendants might have been reluctant at that stage to acknowledge that they or their employees were involved in a corrupt scheme but, as he said, the English court is concerned with the integrity of its own system, and concerned that its executive power is not abused: 'If the agreement represented a contract to pay a bribe, Westacre should not be entitled to enforce the agreement before an English court and should not be entitled to enforce an award based on it.'[149] Waller LJ specifically disagreed with Colman J on the level of opprobrium at which to place commercial corruption. He found that it was within a bracket already recognized in two previous cases[150] 'as being based on public policy of the greatest importance and almost certainly recognised in most jurisdictions throughout the world.[151] I believe it important that the English court is not seen to be turning a blind eye to corruption on this scale'.[152] Sadly, it is not only the courts which, on occasion, seemingly turn a blind eye.[153] **6.88**

Between Colman J's judgment at first instance in *Westacre* and that case coming before the Court of Appeal, Waller LJ, with a different court, had the opportunity to consider another case involving enforcement of an arbitration award where the underlying contract was tainted with illegality.[154] The corruption was not on the same scale as in the *Westacre* case; this was a dispute between father and son, involving the illegal export of Persian carpets from Iran. The son had devised an (extremely risky) method of bribing diplomats to take the carpets out as part of their diplomatic baggage. The father, resident in England, had sold **6.89**

[149] *Westacre Investments Inc v Jugoimport-SPDR Ltd* (CA) [2000] 1 QB 288, 316.

[150] *Lemenda Trading Co Ltd v African Middle East Petroleum Co Ltd* [1988] QB 448 *per* Phillips J, and *ED & F Man (Sugar) Ltd v YaniHaryanto (No 2)* [1991] 1 Lloyd's Rep 429 *per* Neill LJ.

[151] Waller LJ also had no doubt that if the case had been tried in England the court would have required the papers to be sent to the DPP; as it was, despite being in a minority, he suggested that the facts of the case be transmitted to the Ministry of Defence in Kuwait for investigation and possible prosecution: *Westacre* (n 149 above) 316.

[152] *Westacre* (n 149 above) 315.

[153] See, eg Dr Susan Hawley, 'Turning a Blind Eye—Corruption and the Export Credits Guarantee Department', The Corner House, June 2003.

[154] *Soleimany v Soleimany* (CA) [1999] QB 785. The court comprised Morritt LJ and Sir Christopher Staughton sitting with Waller LJ.

the carpets on at a handsome profit, but, instead of remitting to his son a share of the sales, he used the money to invest in inferior carpets and ended up making losses with the result that the son received virtually nothing for his efforts. By agreement, the case came before the Chief Rabbi's court, the *Beth Din*, which applied Jewish law. The *Dayan* (judge) took no point on the illegality of the underlying operation, which was only in any event referred to in passing, and awarded the son 50 per cent of the profits from the sale of the illegally exported carpets.

6.90 Once again, the case came before the Court of Appeal at the enforcement stage. The question was once more whether the English courts would allow an arbitration award made in respect of an illegal contract to be enforced. There was the difference that in this case the illegality was recognized on all sides, but, it was argued, under the doctrine of separability, the court could not intervene to upset the decision of the *Beth Din*. Waller LJ accepted that the *Dayan* was entitled to make his award as he did but stated that the court would not enforce it: 'In an appropriate case [the court] may inquire . . . into an issue of illegality even if an arbitrator had jurisdiction and found that there was no illegality.'[155] Making matters quite clear, Waller LJ went on to say that the English court would no more enforce a foreign law contract where performance under that country's laws would be illegal than it would enforce an award based on a contract governed by English law, or to be performed in England, which was illegal under English law. Waller LJ did not on this occasion state that *Westacre* was wrongly decided, accepting that the Swiss arbitrators were a highly sophisticated tribunal and that, on the facts put before them, they were entitled to come to the conclusion that they did; but Waller LJ clearly felt, even at this stage, that more enquiry might have been made by the court below.[156]

6.91 Unsurprisingly in the circumstances, the contrast between the decisions in the *Westacre* and *Soleimany* cases, especially coming so close to one another, excited a considerable amount of extra-judicial comment at the time.[157] There was, however, yet a third case to be considered by the English Courts at this time: *OTV v Hilmarton.*[158] The result was even more startling. Hilmarton was an English company retained by OTV in the capacity of 'legal and fiscal consultant' (in reality, intermediary) in the negotiation of a construction contract to

[155] *Soleimany v Soleimany* (CA) [1999] QB 803. [156] ibid 803.

[157] See, eg S Wade, 'Westacre v. Soleimany: What Policy? Which Public?' (1999) 2 *International Arbitration Law Review* 97–102: A Sheppard and J Delaney, 'The Effect of Allegations of Corruption of International Arbitration Proceedings, in Particular in Relation to the Jurisdiction of the Tribunal and the Enforcement of Awards' paper presented at the 10th International Anti-Corruption Conference, held in Prague in October 2001.

[158] More fully, *Omnium de Traitement et de Valorisation SA v Hilmarton Ltd* QB (Com Ct) 24 May 1999 (1999) 2 Lloyd's Law Reps, Part 4, 222–226, also published in (1999) 14(6) *Mealey's Arbitration Report* Section A.

provide a drainage system for the city of Algiers. Fees were payable by way of commission at a rate of 4 per cent of the total value of the contract, on an instalment basis. 50 per cent of the fees due were paid by OTV, who then stopped payments, and the matter went to ICC arbitration in Switzerland, the law of the contract also being Swiss. Before the first (Swiss) arbitrator appointed in the case, OTV raised the illegality point, stating that there was in fact an Algerian law which prohibited the use of intermediaries in placing government procurement contracts, which law, said OTV, was compatible with the Swiss concept of good morals.

The arbitrator decided to take the illegality point first and decided on the basis of the available evidence that the real nature of Hilmarton's activities was the obtaining of confidential commercial information and 'the use of personal influence on some Algerian authorities, *against payment*, in order to have the Defendant's bid preferred to bids from other companies'[159] (emphasis added). However, the arbitrator had to concede that 'bribery has not been proved beyond doubt'.[160] Unsurprisingly, no direct evidence was available, although he clearly considered he could make a strong inference. The arbitrator then considered the question of violation of a foreign law as an infringement of Swiss law. To qualify as an offence against Swiss 'good morals', the foreign law had to 'protect individual and community interests generally acknowledged to be fundamental, or else judicial interests which are, from an ethical point of view, more important than contractual freedom' in accordance with Article 20(1) of the Swiss *Code des Obligations*. In the arbitrator's view, the law in question, Algerian Law No 78-02, was aimed at 'guaranteeing healthy and fair commercial practices and at fighting against corruption in general'[161] as well as at 'avoiding all trading in influence'.[162] The arbitrator conducted a lengthy examination of international law materials relating to the fight against corruption, looking at many scholarly texts,[163] abundant US authorities,[164] and the work of the ICC itself[165] on corruption in international trade, before concluding that Swiss law took a common stance on what might be described as international public policy. This being the case, the arbitrator concluded that the original agreement between OTV and Hilmarton was null and void under Swiss law. **6.92**

[159] ICC Case 5622, *Hilmarton Ltd v Omnium de Traitement et de Valorisation* (1994) XIX *Yearbook of Commercial Arbitration* 105, 107, para 6.

[160] ibid 112, para 23.

[161] ibid 115, para 34.

[162] ibid 114, para 31; it is to be noted that Swiss law appears to condone this practice, as the *Westacre* case showed.

[163] Including: P Lalive, 'Ordre Public transnational (ou réellement international) et arbitrage international' (1986) *Revue de l'arbitrage* 339; P Leboulanger and AS El-Kosherie, 'L'arbitre face à la corruption et aux traffics d'influence' (1984) *Revue de l'arbitrage* 3–19.

[164] Including *Northrop v Triad* 593 F Supp 928; 811 F 2d 1265; *Mohamed Habib and Middle East Services v Raytheon Company & Raytheon Services Co* 616 F 2d 1204; *Lockheed Aircraft Corporation v Ora E Gaines* 645 F 2d 761.

[165] *L'exaction et la corruption dans les transactions commerciales*, ICC, Paris, 1978.

6.93 The award did not survive, despite the arbitrator's valiant efforts. Hilmarton sought annulment before the Geneva Court of Justice, and it was granted. The Court did not share the arbitrator's view of the effect of breaking Algerian law in the absence of proof that actual bribes had been paid. In fact, far from being against Swiss public policy, the Court found that the activities undertaken by Hilmarton fell within Swiss laws permitting intermediaries to 'follow the file within a [foreign] administration'.[166] The Court professed to be 'shocked' at the idea that OTV, having entered into this agreement in knowing defiance of Algerian law, should then purport to avoid its liabilities relying on its own breach—especially when it had already made part payment.[167]

6.94 The case went on up to the Swiss *Tribunal Fédéral.* Whilst accepting that 'a contract violating a foreign legal provision can be considered, under certain conditions, an affront to morality according to Swiss law',[168] this was certainly not one of those cases. This was particularly so because the Algerian law in question purported to breach that most treasured right—contractual freedom. The *Tribunal Fédéral* found that, far from protecting against corruption, Law 78-02 clearly sought to provide the state with a monopoly of international trade activity in Algeria; it was protectionist and too widely drawn, prohibiting, as it appeared to, any activity by intermediaries, not being confined to payment of bribes, influence trafficking and other dubious activities.[169]

6.95 Following the annulment, a second round of arbitral proceedings was held. The first arbitrator, M Dagon, resigned and a Professor Jolidon was appointed. No new evidence was taken. He also found that although the Algerian Law 78-02 had been violated, the contract was valid and enforceable in Switzerland. The balance of fees due, FFr2.5 million, was ordered to be paid. It was at this stage that the case came to England, for enforcement of the second award under section 103 of the Arbitration Act 1996.[170] OTV argued that enforcement would be contrary to public policy in England. The Commercial Court had no doubt that, if the case had been tried in England, under English law violation of a foreign law would have been fatal, whether or not the law of the contract had been English.[171] However, the Court said, this was a Swiss award, decided in

[166] Judgment of the Geneva Court of Justice in the matter of *Hilmarton v OTV*, dated 17 November 1989 (1994) XIX *Yearbook of Commercial Arbitration* 216–219, 219, para 11.

[167] ibid 219, paras 12–13.

[168] *OTV v Hilmarton*, Judgment of 17 April 1990 (1994) XIX *Yearbook of Commercial Arbitration* 220–222, 221, para 24.

[169] ibid 222, para 25.

[170] *OTV v Hilmarton*, QB [1999] 2 Lloyd's Rep 222.

[171] *Regazzoni v KC Sethia (1944) Ltd.*, [1957] 2 Lloyd's Rep 289, 294, where it is stated: 'Whether or not the proper law of the contract is English law, an English Court will not enforce a contract, or award damages for its breach if its performance will involve the doing of an act in a foreign and friendly state which violates the law of that state.' cf the comments made by Waller LJ in *Westacre.*

accordance with the chosen law of the parties, Swiss law, and in the absence of a finding of actual corruption, which would have given rise to public policy considerations, the award must be enforced as a matter of the policy of upholding the enforceability of foreign awards in England. The fact that an English court would have reached a different conclusion on the facts was held to be immaterial.

5. The Extent of the Arbitral Tribunal's Duties

One lesson is very clear from these decisions: parties to contracts involving the payment of commissions to intermediaries for 'influence peddling' are well advised to have Swiss arbitration clauses and to make their contracts subject to Swiss law, especially if violation of foreign laws is involved. Switzerland, with its banking secrecy laws, was of course also a favourite haven for the actual commission payments. That is changing, however, as Switzerland takes an ever-tougher view of money laundering activity. The proceeds of the Hilmarton contract, being received in breach of what is presumably a criminal statute in Algeria, might, on one view, be regarded as proceeds of crime, and subject to Swiss anti-money laundering legislation. It is possible that, in the future, Swiss civil courts will not take such a sanguine view of these awards. **6.96**

The major arbitration cases undoubtedly highlight some of the very difficult situations that arise in big public procurement contracts. The reality is that probably none of these contracts have historically been free of the involvement of intermediaries. Evidence given by M Sirven in the *Thomson* case, reported in *Le Monde*[172] described the situation well enough: **6.97**

> A corporation has a project in Beijing or Taiwan. Beyond official contacts, official delegations, there is a host of actions of persuasion, of 'under the table' negotiations. Large groups all maintain networks in France and overseas. We do not talk about the question of remuneration. Very often we are confronted with another form of political or other interests in the country. There is a lot of fantasy seen from the outside. Interests are material, but they are not necessarily pecuniary.

It is always going to be well nigh impossible for courts to monitor or curb activity which, many would argue, quite reasonably, is at the heart of doing business successfully overseas. At the same time it is to be remembered that M Sirven was himself responsible for disbursing huge sums of money from what came to be known as the Elf 'slush fund' (in reality a fund used by the French Government for peddling influence on a global scale, particularly in the developing world). That activity landed him in jail, but the scale of the corruption problem always escalates hugely when sovereign states are involved. It is to the credit of the French legal system that so many of those involved were **6.98**

[172] 4–5 February 2001; the authors are, again, indebted to Sayed for noting and translating this extract from his book (n 130 above) 315.

brought to justice, albeit largely thanks to the efforts of a Norwegian-born French examining magistrate, Mme Eva Joly.

6.99 From the point of view of English law, one of the most extraordinary features of all three of these cases is that in each one of them it is the intermediary who is bringing the action against his own principal in respect of agreements which, in each case, violate the laws of the countries in which the intermediary was operating. Not only that, but the principals in each case are trying to avoid their obligations under the agreements by virtue of their own participation in illegal activities. It is not difficult to understand why the principals find it difficult to produce evidence of bribes having been paid—the burden of proof being on them to do so—the independent evidence they need would presumably have to come from the officials or politicians whom the intermediary has bribed, which is hardly likely when the bribe takers are likely to lay themselves open to the possibility of prosecution in their home countries. There have been attempts by unpaid intermediaries to obtain payments under agreements of this kind in the English courts but they have generally received short shrift. It is, however, noteworthy that there is no indication that in any of these cases has there been any attempt by the 'victim' states concerned to take action either against the bribe takers or the intermediaries or their principals in order to recover any bribes paid or to terminate the contracts in question. The cases all received a fair amount of publicity. The conclusion, regrettably, must be that those who might bring the cases have more to lose by doing so than by not doing so—a circumstance that emphasizes the difficulties faced by those who endeavour to fight against corruption around the world.

6.100 The doctrine of separability has now achieved widespread national and international recognition. Thus, an allegation of illegality does not, in itself, deprive the arbitral tribunal of jurisdiction; the tribunal will hear the arguments and receive evidence in order to determine for itself the question of illegality. However, in arbitration as in court proceedings involving allegations of corruption, the more difficult questions frequently relate to proof and, if the allegations are proved, the consequences of the impropriety under the relevant law. An ad hoc arbitral tribunal acting under the UNCITRAL Arbitration Rules recently addressed allegations of corruption put before it in this way:

> The members of the Arbitral Tribunal do not live in any ivory tower. Nor do they view the arbitral process as one which operates in a vacuum divorced from reality. The arbitrators are well aware of the allegations that commitments by public-sector entities have been made with respect to major projects in Indonesia without adequate heed to their economic contribution to public welfare, simply because they benefited a few influential people. The arbitrators believe that cronyism and other forms of abuse of public trust do indeed exist in many countries, causing great harm to untold millions of ordinary people in a myriad of insidious ways.

> They would rigorously oppose any attempt to use the arbitral process to give effect to contracts contaminated by corruption. But such grave accusations must be proven . . . Rumours or innuendo will not do.[173]

The heart of the problem for an arbitration tribunal is still the question of whether or not it should carry out its own investigation and publish the results of that investigation as part of its award. Such a step might result in the tribunal being accused of exceeding its remit but, on the other hand, if it does not address the illegality issue, the enforceability of the award might be threatened. This would not be in keeping with the tribunal's duty to use its best endeavours to ensure that its award is enforceable.[174] **6.101**

[173] *Himpurna California Energy Ltd v PT (Persero) Perusahaan Listruik Negara*, Final Award dated 4 May 1999, extracts of which are published in (2000) XXV *Yearbook of Commercial Arbitration*. This perceptive passage is quoted in A Redfern, M Hunter, N Blackaby, and C Partasides, *Law & Practice of International Commercial Arbitration* (4th edn, London: Sweet & Maxwell, 2004).

[174] Redfern, ibid 144.

7

CIVIL RECOVERIES

A. Interim Relief

1. Freezing and Disclosure

There are two priorities for claimants pursuing the proceeds of corruption in the civil courts. The first is to trap the funds before they can be removed to jurisdictions where pursuit not only becomes difficult and expensive, but may also become subject itself to the forces of corruption.[1] The second is the gathering of information. The order of these two priorities will vary according to the circumstances of the claimant. The two objectives are closely intertwined in English civil procedure, and applications to the courts, which must be made to a judge, frequently embody elements of both types of relief: as soon as information about assets is revealed, generally through third parties, the 7.01

[1] See further 7.48ff below.

claimant needs to be certain that those assets are preserved pending judgment or further orders of the court.

7.02 In England, the development of the jurisdiction to freeze assets has gone hand in hand with great strides forward in obtaining pre-action disclosure of documents and 'search and seize' orders.[2] The armoury of relief available in the civil courts to the victims of corruption is formidable; its primary purpose is recovery of the assets, not punishment of the wrongdoer, and the courts are generally disposed to make the orders requested where the liberty of the individual is not the immediate issue. Orders for interim remedies are governed by rule 25.1 of the Civil Procedure Rules (CPR). A short survey of the types of relief available, requirements, and possible results achievable, follows.[3]

2. Search and Seize Orders

7.03 The jurisdiction to make search and seize orders (known as Anton Piller orders prior to the introduction of the CPR) now derives from statute.[4] Applications are invariably made without notice, surprise being of the essence. The search process must be supervised by an independent solicitor appointed by the court, but the claimant's solicitor will attend as well. Categories of documents relating to the location of assets will be stipulated in the order—precedents for which are to be found in Part 25 of the CPR. The ability to search premises under the control of or connected with the defendant puts the operation of the civil law in this regard on a similar footing to the criminal law where the issue of search warrants to the police performs a similar function of gathering evidence for a contemplated prosecution.

3. Pre-action Disclosure

7.04 In addition, under the civil law, there are other pre-action disclosure orders that can be obtained against a defendant, subject to the privilege against self-incrimination.[5] When a claimant is reasonably sure that a defendant has been involved in corrupt activity but is uncertain as to the extent of it and also wants

---

[2] The jurisdiction was first developed to assist in intellectual property cases where prompt action was needed on an *ex parte* basis to preserve not only evidence but often also the infringing articles themselves. The first reported case was *EMI Ltd v Pandit* [1976] Ch 75, but the Court's jurisdiction to make such orders was first upheld by the Court of Appeal in *Anton Piller KG v Manufacturing Processes* [1975] 1 WLR 302, CA.

[3] Comprehensive guidance to all forms of interim relief is to be found in Stephen Gee QC's *Commercial Injunctions* (5th edn, London: Sweet & Maxwell, 2004).

[4] Civil Procedure Act 1997, s 7; CPR, r 25.1(1)(h) governs the procedure.

[5] This privilege is not circumvented by ordering disclosure to the defendant's solicitor. In the case of *Den Norske Bank v Antonatos* [1999] QB 271 the claimant bank suspected that one of its former managers had been taking bribes and wanted to find out what had happened to the proceeds. Disclosure by the defendant to his solicitor would still have exposed him to the risk of self-incrimination and should not have been made.

to know where the proceeds have gone, the request to the judge must be carefully drafted and the timing needs to be right. If it is not, there is a danger that a judge will say that the claimant is on a 'fishing expedition' and simply trying to find out if there are further claims which can be brought, rather than asking for relief which is ancillary to the claims before the court. In such cases the better course is often to make the application on the basis that there is a proprietary claim in respect of moneys which are held on trust. Once a course of conduct has been established the questions become: how much has been taken and where is it now?

Pre-action disclosure in order to establish whether there is a case to be brought, to identify wrongdoers and to assist in tracing assets can be obtained also against third parties under the principles established in *Norwich Pharmacal v Customs & Excise Commissioners*.[6] In that case those holding the relevant information, HM Customs & Excise, were innocent parties who, through no fault of their own, had got 'mixed up' in the tortious acts of others and unwittingly facilitated their wrongdoing—they did not incur any liability themselves but were held to be under an obligation to assist the wronged party by giving 'full information', which included disclosing the identity of the wrongdoers. **7.05**

The application of *Norwich Pharmacal* principles to obtain information about assets from third parties without the knowledge of the defendant was first made in the case of *Bankers Trust v Shapira*.[7] An application for such disclosure would now be made under rule 31.17 of the CPR.[8] The claimant does not necessarily have to demonstrate that he has sufficient information to establish a tracing claim, but he will generally be able to produce in his supporting affidavit strong, if unparticularized, evidence of wrongdoing. The usual principles regarding full and frank disclosure and not misleading the court apply, and undertakings in damages and for costs will also be needed. The practitioner must ensure that the client claimant fully understands these requirements and will be in a position to honour them if the need arises.[9] **7.06**

4. Bankers' Books

When making a *Bankers Trust v Shapira*-type application, it would be usual to combine it with an application under section 7 of the Bankers' Books Evidence **7.07**

[6] [1974] AC 175. For a full discussion of the *Norwich Pharmacal* principles, their applicability, and accompanying procedures, see Gee (n 3 above) paras 22.048ff.

[7] [1980] 1 WLR 1274.

[8] Certain requirements have to be satisfied under CPR, T 31.17: see, now, *Three Rivers District Council v Governor and Company of the Bank of England (No 4)* [2003] 1 WLR 210 which examined the threshold test for whether documents disclosed by a third party were 'likely' to support the applicant's case or adversely affect that of another.

[9] The position on costs when a *Norwich Pharmacal* order is made was considered in some depth in the case of *Totalise plc v The Motley Fool Ltd* [2002] EMLR 20, 358.

Act 1879. 'Bankers' Books' are defined in section 9 as including 'ledgers, day books, cash books, account books, and all other books used in the ordinary business of the bank, whether those records are in written form or are kept on microfilm, magnetic tape or any other form of mechanical or electronic data retrieval mechanism'. The idea is that these records are open to inspection at the bank by the claimant's legal advisers in order to avoid the inconvenience for the bank of bringing the records to court.

7.08 The order will normally be restricted to inspection of records relating to the affairs of a defendant but it can be made at any time during the proceedings. It is quite common for additional defendants to be added to the proceedings as more information becomes available and indeed some of those defendants may well be added mainly for the purpose of obtaining additional information, rather than in the hope of making recoveries from them.

7.09 The courts will not, however, permit Bankers' Books orders to be used for gathering information on non-parties. Equally, information obtained as part of the disclosure process should not be passed on to other potential claimants. When the banks themselves are made defendants, it may not be just for information gathering purposes, but because the claimant may be contemplating a claim for dishonest assistance and/or knowing receipt. Joining the banks as parties should secure full discovery of their own internal records, in particular compliance and credit level decisions. The existence and sources of customer references when opening the accounts may be of particular interest.

5. Preservation of Evidence

7.10 In certain cases it may also be appropriate to apply for an injunction under section 37(1) of the Supreme Court Act 1981. Section 37 can be used to preserve not only assets within the jurisdiction, but also evidence. The section allows the court to grant an injunction in any case in which it appears to the court just and convenient to do so. This wide discretion can be directed against non-parties as well as parties to proceedings and is exercisable regardless of presence, residence, or domicile within the jurisdiction. It can also be used to appoint a receiver over assets, which can be of considerable assistance in piercing the corporate veil of recalcitrant defendant companies.

6. Foreign Banks

7.11 Whilst *Bankers Trust v Shapira* orders are commonly made against English banks and branches of foreign banks operating within the English jurisdiction, the court will not force disclosure by the foreign branch of an English bank by means of an order obtained against the English branch. The principle is that the foreign branch should be subject to the jurisdiction of the courts of the country in which it is situated in the same way as the English courts exercise jurisdiction over the branches of foreign banks situated within the English jurisdiction.[10]

In order to obtain information concerning assets held in foreign bank accounts for use in proceedings in England, the claimant will need to issue a Letter of Request to the judicial authorities of the foreign country under rule 34.13 of the CPR. Alternatively, the claimant may commence proceedings directly in the foreign jurisdiction, which may be a better option in terms of speed in obtaining the information: Letters of Request are generally served through diplomatic channels and can take a long time to process. If the substantive proceedings are in England, there may be reluctance on the part of the foreign court to assist, but there is generally no such reluctance on the part of the English courts to assist courts in foreign jurisdictions where the substantive proceedings are taking place, whether those proceedings concern the merits or relate to a tracing or proprietary claim.[11] **7.12**

7. Witness Summonses

Sometimes a witness summons may also be issued under rule 34.2 of the CPR. The extent of the ancillary relief that can be granted under this rule is not free from doubt: it may be that the court can only make such an order in support of a proprietary claim. The difficulty arises in connection with the documents that a third party can be required to produce, as the wording of rule 34.2(5) of the CPR limits production to the documents a person could be required to produce at a hearing, which could be interpreted as trial. On balance, Gee concludes that a wide interpretation should be given to the rules, enabling the court to grant such an application.[12] **7.13**

8. Secrecy

A *Bankers Trust v Shapira*-type order permits the applicant to have access to the defendant's bank accounts for copying purposes and to obtain information generally about the accounts from the defendant's bankers. This can be done without the defendant's knowledge; it is important therefore that the defendant can continue to operate his account normally at this information-gathering stage. Typically the applicant's solicitors will agree transaction limits on the account. These will be designed to allow everyday transactions to take place unimpeded, but will require the bank to give notice if the defendant is putting through a large or unusual transaction. The applicant's lawyers thus effectively monitor the defendant's accounts until such time as they have completed their **7.14**

---

[10] *Mackinnon v Donaldson, Lufkin and Jeanrette Securities* [1986] Ch 482—see in particular Hoffmann J at 493.
[11] *Republic of Haiti v Duvalier* [1990] 1 QB 202.
[12] Gee (n 3 above) para 22.042.

investigations, a large transaction has to be stopped, or the time set by the court expires. Clearly such orders represent a considerable erosion of the defendant's freedoms and the courts are reluctant to allow them to continue for too long on a without notice basis—much depends on the particular facts, but more than two months would be exceptional.

7.15 At the end of the monitoring period the defendant will be served with the proceedings. The defendant may want to challenge what has been done, but such a challenge will be dependent upon his being able to demonstrate that the provenance of funds is not tainted by corruption. It is likely that lengthy affidavits will be required within fixed time limits to give explanations regarding sources of funds, consideration for payments made and received, the role of persons involved, and a host of other matters. If such explanations are forthcoming, the corrupt defendant will very often try to limit his responses to what he thinks the claimant already knows. There will generally be a host of further questions which will also need to be answered under oath on affidavit. In these ways very considerable pressure can be brought to bear on defendants and it will frequently be at that point that a defendant will offer to cut a deal with the claimant.

7.16 For a claimant whose primary objective in bringing the proceedings was recovery of assets, this may be a good result. Frequently, however, the civil proceedings will be running in tandem with criminal proceedings, in which case plea bargain considerations may arise as the defendant is unlikely to reach a deal unless he can obtain releases. If the criminal authorities are not amenable to plea bargaining the almost inevitable result will be that the criminal proceedings will have to be fought through to their conclusion before the civil proceedings can be finalized, with all the implications for costs and delay that that entails. This will of course also mean that the defendant is unlikely to give voluntary disclosure of the whereabouts of further assets not located through the tracing process. Identifying and securing the release of those assets, particularly in foreign jurisdictions, may thus become that much more difficult and expensive to achieve.

9. Materials Obtained in Criminal Proceedings

7.17 Documents and information obtained in mutual legal assistance proceedings are invariably restricted in the use that can be made of them. Their use will usually be confined to the criminal authorities in the requesting state: they cannot be used in civil recovery proceedings without the permission of the state providing assistance. This is why in Switzerland, for example, the requesting state may be permitted to become a civil party to the proceedings, thus allowing much wider access to and use of the materials. The bar on use of documents obtained through mutual legal assistance is similar to the undertaking given by a claimant in the *Norwich Pharmacal* proceedings to use the information disclosed only for the purpose of the civil proceedings in which it is obtained. The permission of the court is likely to be forthcoming where the intention is to pursue civil proceedings elsewhere.[13] Likewise, requests for permission to use documents transmitted through mutual legal assistance proceedings to pursue civil recoveries are likely to be granted.

Cases of corruption may of course give rise both to criminal investigations and prosecutions, and to civil proceedings commenced by the victim of wrongdoing. During the course of criminal investigations, the police or other investigatory bodies may seize or obtain documents and take statements, whether or not under caution. This material may be very usefully deployed by the victim in civil proceedings, for example a Government seeking to recover stolen assets or recoup bribes paid to corrupt officials. Typically, a civil trial will not proceed until criminal proceedings have concluded. In these circumstances, the relevant material should have entered the public domain and can be deployed in civil proceedings. However, this will not always be the case: criminal trials may not proceed for a variety of reasons or there may be compelling reasons, particularly in fraud cases, requiring urgent civil action. It is open to a claimant in civil proceedings to apply for an order against the police or other relevant body for disclosure of the material.[14] Assuming that the documents are relevant,[15] disclosure may be ordered if the public interest in the civil claim being tried on the basis of all relevant evidence outweighs the public interest in maintaining the confidentiality of the documents.[16] Strict and specific conditions on the use of the documents are likely. Evidence obtained from overseas through mutual legal assistance/letters of request cannot be used for any purpose other than that for which it was obtained without the permission of the sending state.[17] This would preclude disclosure to a victim for use in civil proceedings, in the absence of the necessary permission. **7.18**

10. Freezing Orders

The freezing order is probably the single most potent weapon in the 'civil' arsenal available to the claimant in the fight against corruption. In this electronic age, when vast sums can flit through jurisdictions at the press of a button, it is vital first of all to secure the target's assets. Not only does a freezing order ensure the close attention of the defendant, it will, in the majority of cases, secure jurisdiction on home territory, although the effect of the injunction would usually be declared to be worldwide in large-scale corruption cases. **7.19**

[13] See, eg *Omar v Omar* [1995] 1 WLR 1428

[14] CPR 1998, r 31.17.

[15] See ibid r 31.6.

[16] See, eg *Marcel v Commissioner of Police of the Metropolis* [1992] Ch 225, CA and *Frankson v Home Office* [2003] EWCA Civ 655 CA.

[17] Crime (International Co-operation) Act 2003, s 9.

7.20 Rule 25.1(1)(f) of the CPR states that the court may grant:

> ... an order (referred to as a 'freezing injunction')—
>
> (i) restraining a party removing from the jurisdiction assets located there; or
> (ii) restraining a party from dealing with any assets whether located within the jurisdiction or not.

7.21 This terminology, which puts the relief sought in jargon-free language, should not be allowed to obscure the essential flexibility of the freezing order (also widely known by its previous name of 'Mareva' injunction,[18] a term now understood worldwide as describing this relief). Such an order does not freeze particular assets, it imposes a restraint on the person injuncted. It does not operate *in rem* against the individual assets, but has an ambulatory effect on assets, similar to that of a floating charge, leaving a person free to organize his affairs so that only so much as is required to be preserved under the order is affected. In cases where the claimant is unclear as to the total value of the assets in the defendant's hands, the order will be phrased in such a way as to ensure that, for example, all monies standing to the account of the defendant in accounts held at a bank are not to be disposed of. This is because those assets are, in the case of proprietary claims, regarded as being held on trust for the claimant. When applying for a freezing order it is usual to apply simultaneously for other forms of ancillary relief under rule 25 of the CPR.

7.22 The banks, on which the orders are served as soon as possible after the order is made, not only face potentially heavy penalties for non-cooperation[19] but are also put under a positive obligation to assist the claimant. The typical freezing order is combined with the disclosure order which requires a bank to conduct a rigorous search for all accounts that might conceivably have any connection with the target defendant. The claimant will generally have to meet the bank's reasonable costs of carrying the orders into effect, but that is usually a small price to pay for securing the defendant's assets and the valuable information that can be obtained. This is particularly so these days when stringent 'know your customer' (KYC) requirements imposed by anti-money laundering legislation

[18] The first case in which an order was made on a without notice application against a defendant resident outside the jurisdiction restraining it from moving money out of a bank account was *Nippon Yusen Kaisha v Karageorgis* [1975] 1 WLR 1093 in which the Court of Appeal made the order, and for a time they were known as Karageorgis orders, a fitting tribute in the minds of some lawyers to the contribution made to the development of English commercial law by the Greek shipping community. That case was however swiftly followed by *Mareva Compania Naviera SA v International Bulkcarriers Ltd* [1975] 2 Lloyd's Rep 509, and it was the Mareva name that stuck.

[19] Including civil liability to the claimant if frozen funds are paid away in error following service of a freezing injunction: see *Customs & Excise Commissioners v Barclays Bank* [2004] EWCA Civ 1555, CA where it was confirmed that banks owe a duty of care to claimants to take care that frozen funds are not dissipated in breach of an injunction.

should ensure that the beneficial ownership of all UK-based accounts is known to the financial institutions,[20] thus enabling them to give even wider effect to the orders.

In cases where there has been widespread corruption it is possible, as has been seen above, to have the court impose an absolute embargo on information about the proceedings for a fixed period of time, renewable on notice. This will include such matters as ensuring that the names of the parties do not appear in the daily court lists in order to ensure that the defendant is not tipped off about the existence of the proceedings. **7.23**

The draconian nature of 'freezing injunctions' meant that, in the early days, the defendant could be bereft of funds with which to pay legal fees, or even to live. It is therefore now common practice for the courts to permit stipulated sums to be drawn down from frozen accounts for living expenses and for legal costs to be paid out, subject to the supervision of the claimant's solicitors. This jurisdiction has to be exercised with considerable care where proprietary claims are made because it could lead to the defendant effectively being allowed to use the claimant's money to live and to defend himself, a situation which can give rise to strong emotions on the part of the claimant.[21] The court may refuse to allow funds to be released, in which case the defendant will have to represent himself, unless he can obtain legal aid as Mr Hashim (the first President of the Arab Monetary Fund) did—in highly controversial circumstances.[22] **7.24**

11. 'Free standing' Freezing Injunctions

Freezing orders are frequently made now in support of foreign judgments. Such orders are sometimes referred to as 'free standing' freezing injunctions: they are applied for solely in order to ensnare assets, whilst the substantive decision on the merits of the case may be made abroad. The Civil Jurisdiction and **7.25**

---

[20] The KYC requirements are set out exhaustively in *The Money Laundering Guidance Notes for the Financial Sector*, published and regularly updated by The Joint Money Laundering Steering Group (JMLSG) since 1990, initially as a self-regulatory exercise by banks in conjunction with the Bank of England. The revised version, dated December 2003, incorporates new guidance to reflect the provisions of POCA 2002 and the Money Laundering Regulations 2003 which implement the 2nd European Directive on the Prevention of Money Laundering and the Financial Services Authority Rules. They contain real-life examples drawn from experience of situations that have arisen which should have given rise to suspicion. JMLSG updates are on their website at http://www.jmlsg.org.uk.

[21] For a case in which the court had to make a difficult decision of this kind, see *Fitzgerald v Williams* [1996] QB 657, 669. For an example of the kind of order that may be made see *PCW (Underwriting Agencies) Ltd v Dixon* [1983] 2 All ER 697.

[22] Mr Hashim, who was also a close associate of Saddam Hussein, was being sued for sums in excess of US$133m taken from the accounts of the Arab Monetary Fund and lived in considerable style in Arizona. For reasons now hard to comprehend, he received over £4m in legal aid payments. See further, 7.43ff below.

Judgments Act 1982 (Interim Relief) Order 1997[23] gives the High Court power under section 25 of the Civil Jurisdiction and Judgments Act 1982 to grant interim relief in relation to 'proceedings' regardless of where they are commenced. The Civil Procedure Rules specifically deal with applications for interim relief not only in cases where the proceedings are already taking place outside the jurisdiction but also, potentially very valuably, where proceedings *will* be instituted beyond the jurisdiction.[24] The relief is also available as an aid to execution where judgment has already been given.[25]

7.26 The ability to seek interim relief in a relatively straightforward manner before the English civil courts is one of the main reasons why a foreign claimant in a corruption case, particularly a state, may find it preferable to go down the civil route rather than seeking mutual legal assistance from the Home Office (this is examined further below in the section on recovery of State Assets).[26]

B. Jurisdiction and Choice of Law

1. In England

7.27 In the older cases where the parties were both resident within the jurisdiction and the bribes were paid in pounds sterling, jurisdiction or choice of law clearly was not an issue. Likewise, cases coming on appeal to the Privy Council presented no problem. Nowadays it would probably be true to say that it would be extremely rare for a bribery case to come before the English courts without a foreign element, thus requiring the court to answer two questions: does the English court have jurisdiction to hear the case? If so, the law of which country should be applied?

7.28 Under the civil law the High Court has jurisdiction *in personam* if the defendant can be served with due process in England, or abroad in certain specified cases. Members of the European Community and the European Free Trade Area (EFTA) have agreed regimes intended to determine questions of jurisdiction in disputes between entities 'domiciled' within them.[27] The general rule is that a defendant should be sued in the courts of the state in which it is domiciled.[28] However, that rule is subject to a number of exceptions, including matters relating to 'tort, delict or quasi-delict' where a defendant may be sued in the

[23] SI 1997/392. [24] CPR, r 25.4. [25] ibid, r 25.2. [26] See 7.50ff.

[27] Council Regulation (EC) 44/2001 (the 'Judgment Regulation') applies to all members of the European Community, bar Denmark; the 1968 Brussels Convention applies between European Community Member States and Denmark; the 1988 Lugano Convention applies between European Community Member States and Iceland, Norway, and Switzerland, the EFTA countries.

[28] 'Domicile' is not defined in the Judgment Regulation or other conventions, it being left to domestic courts to determine what constitutes domicile in accordance with their domestic law. For a full explanation and discussion of the Judgment Regulation and the Conventions, see AV

courts of the place where the harmful event took place. That exception could, for example, capture cases involving constructive trusts[29] which involve either a breach of fiduciary duty or dishonest assistance in that breach. It may not, however, capture a claim for restitution.[30]

A defendant who is not present in England may submit to the jurisdiction of the English court. This puts the defendant on the same footing as one who is served in England, ie the claimant can require the court to exercise jurisdiction, which it must do, subject to a discretion to stay the action to prevent injustice—the court can also strike out or dismiss an action in appropriate circumstances. The court may, however, assume jurisdiction in cases where the defendant is not present within the jurisdiction, provided an action can be brought under one of the 'gateways' contained in rule 6.20 of the CPR. The gateways contain the tests by which the court will determine whether a corruption case is sufficiently closely connected to the United Kingdom for the English court to assume jurisdiction. **7.29**

The exercise by the courts of jurisdiction under the gateways in rule 6.20 of the CPR is discretionary and is exercised with considerable care. Historically this was because the English courts were wary of usurping the jurisdiction of courts in foreign states lest that be interpreted as an interference with their sovereignty—it is, however, now much more common for all states to exercise jurisdiction over foreign nationals. Further factors to be borne in mind are that any doubts on the part of the court concerning construction of the gateways in rule 6.20 will be exercised in favour of the defendant, and full and frank disclosure of all relevant circumstances to the court must be made by the applicant: failure to do so may lead to the action being struck out at the request of the defendant. Lastly, it should be noted that the court will not permit service out of the jurisdiction if the case is within the letter but not the spirit of the order. The relevant case law is cited under Rule 27 in Dicey and Morris.[31] Having made those points, it should be noted that there is at least anecdotal evidence that the courts are willing to strain what are perhaps the natural meanings of the 'gateways' to ensure, in the absence of practical alternative jurisdictions, that proceedings can be taken against flagrant fraudsters. **7.30**

Gateways likely to be of particular interest in pursuing corruption cases include claims in tort under rule 6.20(8) of the CPR, where damage was sustained **7.31**

Dicey and JHC Morris, *The Conflict of Laws* (4th Supplement to 13th edn, London: Sweet & Maxwell, 1996) commentary under paras 11-006–007.

29 *Casio Computer Co Ltd v Sayo (No 3)* [2001] EWCA Civ 661 and *Dexter Limited (In Administrative Receivership) v Harley* The Times, 2 April 2001; *Cronos Containers NV v Palatin* [2003] EWHC 2819 (Comm).

30 *Kleinwort Benson v Glasgow City Council* [1999] 1 AC 153.

31 Dicey and Morris (n 28 above). The cited passages currently analyse the position in relation to RSC Ord 11, the predecessor of CPR, r 6.20, although the principles are the same.

within the jurisdiction or resulted from an act committed within the jurisdiction; under rule 6.20(1), where the whole subject matter of a claim relates to property within the jurisdiction; and under rule 6.20(14) and (15), for constructive trust and restitutionary claims respectively, where the defendant's alleged liability arises out of acts committed within the jurisdiction.

7.32 As Dicey and Morris state, this latter category was added in 1990 after it had been held that a claim based on constructive trust was not founded on a tort for the purposes of the old RSC order 11.[32] Dicey and Morris go on to cite subsequent interpretations by the courts, which started out on a very narrow basis,[33] confining the application of what is now rule 6.20(14) of the CPR to acts committed in England, which would have excluded an action based on knowing receipt of the proceeds of fraud abroad, thus depriving the clause of much of its usefulness. Now it is only necessary for some of the acts to have been committed in England. This enables a claimant to pursue a foreign entity which has been used as a receptacle for the proceeds of fraud but which might not have participated in the fraud itself (ie the typical foreign bank account scenario).[34]

7.33 It is open to an English court to decline jurisdiction to hear a case falling within the gateways described above on the ground of *forum non conveniens*, ie a foreign court is a more appropriate forum for the trial of the proceedings. The key test is which jurisdiction has the most real and substantial connection with the dispute. The relevant principles are described in detail in Dicey and Morris.[35] Experience suggests that, in corruption cases, the English courts will be reluctant to refuse jurisdiction on the ground of *forum non conveniens* unless satisfied that a foreign court is able and willing properly to adjudicate upon the dispute.

2. Restitution and the Conflict of Laws

7.34 In cases involving a foreign element, the court may also have to determine the governing law. The English courts may, of course, have jurisdiction over disputes governed by foreign law. As a general rule the governing law is that which has the closest and most real connection with the claim. Dicey and Morris state a general rule that in restitution cases, which for these purposes probably includes constructive trusts, the governing law is that of the country where the enrichment occurs.[36]

[32] *Metall und Rohstoff AG v Donaldson Lufkin & Jenrette Inc* [1990] 1 QB 391, 473–474, CA.

[33] This was the view taken by Millett J in the unreported case of *ISC Technologies Ltd v Guerin* 1990—the wider view was taken at a later stage in the same litigation by Hoffmann J-reported in [1992] 2 Lloyd's Rep 430.

[34] Knox J affirmed Hoffmann J's view in *Polly Peck Ltd v Nadir* as reported in *The Independent*, 2 September 1992.

[35] See Dicey and Morris (n 28 above) ch 12.

[36] ibid ch 34 and para 29–26.

As has been seen from the bribery cases mentioned earlier, the courts have always endeavoured under English law to try to ensure that the recipient does not keep the proceeds of the bribe or of any profits derived therefrom.[37] In *Fibrosa Spolka Akcyjna v Fairbairn Lawson Combe Barbour Ltd*[38] remedies in unjust enrichment cases were recognized as being 'generically different from remedies in contract or in tort, and are now recognized to fall within a third category of the common law which has been called quasi-contract or restitution'.[39] This is recognized as an independent obligation in domestic law[40] and when it comes to conflict of laws.[41] **7.35**

It is stated in the 13th edition[42] of Dicey and Morris that cases in which the courts had had to deal with conflict of law questions in matters involving restitution and unjust enrichment were rare until comparatively recently. This has no doubt been a factor of the increased turnover in bribes which seems to have taken place in the last fifteen years, their size and the increased likelihood of foreign involvement, particularly when it comes to hiding the proceeds. *Arab Monetary Fund v Hashim*[43] was a landmark case in this regard also. **7.36**

Rule 200 in Dicey and Morris states: **7.37**

> (1) The obligation to restore the benefit of an enrichment obtained at another person's expense is governed by the proper law of the obligation.
> (2) The proper law of the obligation is (*semble*) determined as follows:
> (a) If the obligation arises in connection with a contract, its proper law is the law applicable to the contract;
> (b) If it arises in connection with a transaction concerning an immovable (land), its proper law is the law of the country where the immovable is situated (*lex situs*);
> (c) If it arises under any other circumstances, its proper law is the law of the country where the enrichment occurs.[44]

It is this latter case which is of most interest in corruption cases. In the Fourth Supplement to the 13th edition, Dicey and Morris deal with two more recent cases where these issues fell to be considered. In *Kuwait Oil Tanker SAK v Al Bader*[45] the Court of Appeal cited rule 200(2)(c) with approval when dealing with the questions of fiduciary duty and constructive trust, and adopted a **7.38**

[37] *A-G for Hong-Kong v Reid* [1994] 1 AC 324, PC; see 6.34 above.
[38] [1943] AC 32 (HL).
[39] ibid 61.
[40] See R Goff and G Jones, *The Law of Restitution* (5th edn, London: Sweet & Maxwell, 1998), 14–15.
[41] Dicey and Morris cite J Blaikie, 'Unjust Enrichment in the Conflict of Law' (1984) *The Judicial Review* 112.
[42] Dicey and Morris (n 28 above) para 34-003.
[43] [1993] 1 Lloyd's Rep 543.
[44] Dicey and Morris (n 28 above) para 34R-001.
[45] [2000] 2 All ER (Comm) 271, CA.

passage from Chadwick J's judgment in the *Hashim* Chancery proceedings, which ran as follows:

> . . . in cases involving a foreign element in which an English court is asked to treat a defendant as a constructive trustee of assets which he has acquired through misuse of his powers, the relevant questions are: (i) what is the proper law which governs the relationship between the defendant and the person for whose benefit those powers have been conferred, (ii) what, under that law, are the duties to which the defendant is subject in relation to those powers, (iii) is the nature of those duties such that they would be regarded by an English court as fiduciary duties and (iv), if so, is it unconscionable for the defendant to retain those assets?[46]

7.39 In the *Kuwait Oil Tanker* case Kuwaiti law was found to be applicable, under which, although the concept of trusts was unknown, two articles of the 1980 Civil Code (264 and 267) were agreed by the experts to impose an obligation on each of the defendants to make restitution of funds which had been misapplied by them.[47] Those provisions, the court said, were the equivalent of fiduciary duties found under English law and it would have been unconscionable for the defendants to retain the funds.

7.40 The court then went on to consider the question of interest payable on the misappropriated funds. The judge at first instance had awarded compound interest in accordance with precepts of Lord Browne-Wilkinson set down by him in *Westdeutsche Landesbank Girozentrale v Islington London Borough Council*[48] to the effect that compound interest can be awarded in all cases where a fiduciary has improperly profited from his trust, such an award being made in accordance with equitable principles to ensure that the wrongdoer makes full restitution. Such an award could not have been made under Kuwaiti law, but the court of appeal upheld the judge's view that it was in accordance with the procedural law of the *lex fori*. This exercise of the court's equitable jurisdiction goes some way towards introducing a punitive element which could usefully be deployed in bribery cases.

7.41 The second case considered by Dicey and Morris in the Supplement[49] is *Grupo Torras SA v Al Sabah*,[50] already referred to above in the context of dishonest assistance. In dealing with the conflict of laws question, a differently constituted court of appeal from the one which heard the *Kuwait Oil Tankers* appeal held that neither the choice of law rules for restitutionary claims nor the common law rules for tort claims were applicable. Thus, rather than considering whether Spanish law had provisions which accorded with English notions of fiduciary

---

[46] *Arab Monetary Fund v Hashim* (Chadwick J) (unreported, 15 June 1994).

[47] In this case the funds were not bribes but huge secret profits and commissions the defendants had been retaining from Kuwait Oil Tankers' chartering operations.

[48] [1996] AC 669, 702.

[49] Dicey and Morris (n 28 above) para 34–032.

[50] [2001] CLC 221, CA.

duties, the court simply went ahead and applied Spanish law, which gave rise to a liability on the part of the defendant. This, the court said, confirmed and established the defendant's liability under English law.

Rule 201 in Dicey and Morris states that issues in tort are now governed by the provisions of Part III of the Private International Law (Miscellaneous Provisions) Act 1995,[51] and Rule 202 states that the general rule is that the law applicable to issues of tort is the law of the country in which the events constituting the tort in question occur.[52] The 1995 Act was not applicable in the cases mentioned above because the events giving rise to the claims took place before the Act came into force. **7.42**

The Court of Appeal had occasion to consider the import of rule 202 in a bribery case when giving their decision in *Arab Monetary Fund v Hashim (No 9)*.[53] It will be recalled that when Dr Hashim was the first President (from 1977 to 1982) of the Arab Monetary Fund (AMF), he received a sum which represented almost exactly 10 per cent of the contract price for the construction of the Fund's headquarters building in Abu Dhabi.[54] He had had a sum of US $1.8 million paid into a Swiss bank account by the UK contractors, Bernard Sunley.[55] The AMF submitted that they had the following rights under Abu Dhabi law: **7.43**

(1) to recover damages from the contractor in what English law would describe as tort;
(2) to recover the amount of the bribe from Dr Hashim on principles of unjust enrichment; and
(3) to recover damages from Dr Hashim both in tort and for breach of contract.

The Court of Appeal held that all of these matters were governed by the law of Abu Dhabi, citing and approving Rules 201 and 202 in the 12th edition of Dicey & Morris.[56] Saville LJ had this to say on the law relating to bribery: **7.44**

> As a matter of English law, it seems to me that in the context of bribes, the obligation arises, not so much from the making of the bribe agreement or the payment of the bribe as from the fact that such an agreement and the payment

[51] Dicey and Morris (n 28 above) para 35R-001.
[52] ibid para 35R-078. [53] [1996] 1 Lloyd's Rep 589, CA. [54] See 6.16 above.
[55] The action to recover the bribe in the Commercial Court was separate from the contemporaneous proceedings taking place in the Chancery Division relating to the diversion by Mr Hashim of some US$133 m from AMF accounts for his own personal use.
[56] Rule 201 is Rule 200, and Rule 202 is Rule 201 in the 13th edition. The Court referred to the 'double actionability' rule for tort cases under which the English courts would have jurisdiction if the actions were both contrary to the law of the foreign state and constituted a tort in England, referring to *Metall und Rohstoff AG v Donaldson Lufkin & Jenrette Inc* [1990] 1 QB 391 (see *AMF/Hashim* judgment at 597).

under it constitute a dishonest abuse by the briber and the recipient of the bribe of their relationships with the third party concerned. It is that dishonest abuse which creates the right in the third party to recover the unjust enrichment and thus the correlative obligation on the bribe giver and receiver to disgorge the ill-gotten gains.

7.45 In support of this statement, Saville LJ cited the *Mahesan* case.[57] He then went on to find that in this case all the relevant factors, including the place where the dishonest abuse took place, led to the governing law being that of Abu Dhabi, and agreed with the judgment of Evans J at first instance that restitutionary claims would also be governed by the law of Abu Dhabi. It was accepted by the AMF that Abu Dhabi law did not recognize the restitutionary right existing in English law to recover the amount of the bribe from the bribe giver.

7.46 Regrettably the Court of Appeal found that it did not have to consider the tort and unjust enrichment claims as these were time-barred under Abu Dhabi law. Under Shari'a law, however, the limitation period in respect of contractual claims is fifteen years, so the claim which arose under Dr Hashim's contract of employment was allowed.[58]

7.47 Well-funded defendants in corruption cases, very often resident overseas, litigating over bribes paid under foreign procurement contracts or the proceeds of state looting, are likely to take these sorts of complex and difficult points. As the number of instruments promoting international cooperation in the fight against corruption proliferate, it is to be hoped that issues raised by conflict of laws problems will recede. It remains to be seen whether the UN Convention Against Corruption (UNCAC) will make a difference, as states introduce legislation to make themselves compliant.[59]

3. Bringing Claims Abroad

7.48 Claimants may be able to bring proceedings with relative ease in European jurisdictions and even the traditional offshore havens, such as the Channel Islands, the Isle of Man, the Cayman Islands, Gibraltar, the British Virgin Islands, and Vanuatu. With the advent of internationally recognized anti-money laundering compliance mechanisms designed to isolate non-compliant

[57] *Mahesan v Malaysia Government Officers' Co-operative Housing Society Ltd* [1979] AC 374.

[58] *AMF v Hashim* (n 46 above) 601. It is also interesting to note that one of the defences attempted by Bernard Sunley was to plead that the payment to Dr Hashim was *ultra vires*. Evans J found that a lawful commission paid to an agent for the purpose of procuring business was within the scope of the memorandum of association and went on to find that the bribe paid was within the scope of para 3(j) of the memorandum being 'remuneration or other compensation or reward for services rendered or to be rendered . . . in or about the conduct of . . . the business' of Bernard Sunley and thus was not *ultra vires*.

[59] The provisions of the UNCAC are considered at 9.10ff below.

regimes,[60] these centres have all had to look carefully at their regulatory regimes in order to preserve their status as refuges for legitimate financial activity. As a result, also, there has been a noticeably increased willingness to cooperate both in the field of mutual legal assistance and civil suits dealing with corruption. In all of these centres it is possible to have reasonable confidence in the integrity of legal practitioners, law officers, and law enforcement agencies, as well as in the court system and the judiciary—historical links with the United Kingdom and the common law system also allow UK practitioners to feel reasonably confident that they know what they are dealing with.

The real problems for claimants and practitioners begin when funds make their way to jurisdictions whose legal systems are something of an unknown quantity—Saudi Arabia, Indonesia, and the Russian Federation are examples of states where particular difficulties may be encountered. There are other states, particularly within the Commonwealth, which have familiar legal systems and in many cases laws similar to those in the United Kingdom, but levels of corruption, often within the judiciary itself, are very high, resulting in systems where justice is available to the highest bidder.[61] Where state looting has taken place and a successor government needed to obtain domestic court orders to satisfy international mutual legal assistance requirements, this has caused particular problems in the past but, again, one of the main ideas behind the UNCAC has been to lessen reliance on the findings of domestic courts as a component of mutual legal assistance. **7.49**

C. Recovery and Repatriation of State Assets

1. Looting by Heads of States

Reference was made at the beginning of this book[62] to the huge scale of bribery transactions in the world. Attention was also drawn to the billions stolen by the world's dictators and those in their immediate circle. It was only as the twentieth century drew towards its close that serious efforts began to be made to recover some of these looted assets. The demise of Sese Seke Mobutu in 1997 **7.50**

[60] See the 40 Recommendations (supplemented by the 8 Anti-Terrorist Financing recommendations) of the Financial Action Task Force (FATF), http://www.FATF.org, the proliferation of Financial Intelligence Units (FIUs) linked by the workings of the Egmont Group, and the List of Non-Cooperative Countries and Territories (NCCTs)–all dealt with in more detail in Ch 9 below.

[61] See, generally, Transparency International's Corruption Perceptions Index: http://www.transparency.org. Some states, such as Nigeria and Pakistan, are making real efforts to clamp down on corruption and pursue malefactors. Others, such as Kenya, where members of the Bar demonstrate on a regular basis with slogans such as 'Why Hire a Lawyer when you can Buy a Judge?', accompanied by (no doubt facetious) tables setting out 'going rates' according to the seniority of the judge, appear to be slipping backwards.

[62] See Ch 1 above.

did not produce much of a result. Efforts by Indonesia to recover Suharto's riches have been continuously and effectively blocked by his family and supporters. In Pakistan every attempt to recover assets stolen by Benazir Bhutto and her husband, Asif Ali Zardari, has been characterized by the political party that still regards her as its spiritual head as politically motivated victimization. Ex-President Fujimori of Peru has been sheltered by Japan and efforts to extradite him to Peru have met with the objection, upheld by the courts in Japan, that he is a Japanese citizen, despite having ruled and looted Peru for a decade, between 1990 and 2000. However, he ended his self-imposed exile in November 2005, traveled to Chile, and was promptly arrested, pending the outcome of further extradition proceedings.[63]

2. The Case of Abacha

7.51 The death of General Sani Abacha in Nigeria, in June 1998, marked a turning point in state asset recovery. Nigeria's Head of State had seized power in a military coup in November 1993, discarding the results of democratic elections which had just swept Chief MKO Abiola, reputedly Nigeria's richest man, to victory. Abacha imprisoned Abiola (who himself died less than a month after Abacha, never regaining his freedom) and set about making himself and his family the wealthiest group in Nigeria. Estimates vary of the extent of that wealth but it is unlikely to have been less than US$3 billion and may have been in excess of US$5 billion. Accumulating money at a rate of about US$1 billion per annum requires theft on a huge scale and the term 'grand corruption' is certainly appropriate to describe Abacha's efforts.

7.52 Over US$2.2 billion was looted straight out of the Central Bank of Nigeria. This money was extracted by raising a series of demands for funds to meet completely spurious national security needs. Letters from Abacha's National Security Adviser, countersigned by Abacha, and then presented to the Central Bank, were about all that was required. Over half the proceeds were laundered through the City of London and then went on to accounts in Jersey, Switzerland, Luxembourg, and Liechtenstein. Other monies were received from illegal trading in oil and massive kickbacks from contractors. One huge scam, which came posthumously before the Commercial Court in London, involved the purchase and resale by the Abacha family of bonds in the giant (and so far entirely unproductive) Ajaokuta steel plant in south-central Nigeria. The bonds had been issued to secure the debt owed by Nigeria to the Russian Government for the construction of the plant. They were purchased for 26 per cent of their face value by an Abacha-controlled company and then sold back to the

[63] This appears to have been a deliberate tactic by Mr Fujimori, who hopes to fight the next Peruvian election *Financial Times*, 10 November 2005.

Government a fortnight later for 53 per cent of their face value—a 100% profit, worth nearly DM500 million. The purchase and sale of vaccines and ballot boxes by companies run by the President's wife and sons to the Government, with 100% mark-ups, were other examples of revenue-raising schemes, worth about $100 million.[64]

The speed with which the Abacha family built up their fortune combined with the General's premature demise meant that there was not much opportunity to disperse assets as widely as might otherwise have been the case. Mobutu had had over thirty years in power in the Congo—he looted more (mainly from development aid) but distributed it quickly, leaving the coffers pretty well empty by the time he died. Almost as swift was the response of the Nigerian Government once Abacha had gone. The interim military administration, headed by General Abdulsalami Abubakar, immediately set about recovery of the stolen assets and within a couple of months had received over $700 million voluntarily handed over by family members who claimed that that was all there was. Unsurprisingly, it was only the tip of the iceberg. **7.53**

Shortly after the democratic election of former general Olusegun Obasanjo as President of Nigeria in May 1999, the Government set about trying to recover the rest of the looted assets. Letters requesting mutual assistance were delivered to a number of states. The most productive in terms of assets located and frozen were Switzerland, Luxembourg, and Liechtenstein. In Switzerland, which was fresh from the hubris of returning Holocaust funds to Jewish families, the dynamic investigating Magistrate Zechin of the Canton of Geneva immediately set about gathering evidence to ascertain the ownership of the moneys trapped in Swiss banks. **7.54**

3. Repatriation of State Assets

In February 2005, nearly six years after Magistrate Zechin commenced his investigation, the Federal Supreme Court in Switzerland ruled that sums totalling $480 million be returned to Nigeria. A further $70 million was to stay in Switzerland awaiting determination of its ownership and $10 million was to be paid into an escrow account, one of the signatories to which will be the Nigerian Government.[65] **7.55**

One of the matters that preoccupied the Swiss was to ensure that the repatriated moneys would be used for proper purposes on behalf of the Nigerian people. Undertakings to that effect have been given by the Obasanjo Government, but, **7.56**

[64] Much of the history of the Ajaokuta matter is contained in the 218-page judgment given by Rix J in *Compagnie Noga d'Importation et d'Exportation SA v Australia and New Zealand Banking Group and ors* (unreported) QBD (Comm) 27 Feb 2001.

[65] Swiss Federal Court Decision (1A.215/2004 /col), 7 February 2005.

in the interests of transparency, Switzerland has requested that payment of the moneys and their distribution should be overseen by the World Bank, thus causing further delay in their return.[66]

7.57 This has not been the first time that the Swiss authorities have faced this issue. President Marcos of the Philippines was estimated to have looted about US$27 billion between 1965 and 1986. After his death the relatively paltry sum of US$657 million was found in Swiss accounts. After protracted legal battles to secure the assistance of the Swiss authorities, the moneys were returned to Manila but paid into an escrow account under the control of the Zurich District Attorney at the Philippine National Bank. Certain conditions were imposed by the Swiss Supreme Court before the moneys could be released, including a requirement that a final judgment be obtained in a Philippines court complying with the procedural requirements of due process and rights of the accused under the *Swiss* constitution. The moneys were deposited in 1998, nine years after Marcos's death in Hawaii in 1989 and only released in 2003 after a Philippines court found that the Marcos family had 'failed to justify the lawful nature of the their acquisition of the Swiss funds'.[67] Repatriation of state assets is no easy matter if the paying state imposes these kinds of conditions. Under UNCAC it will not be possible for them to do so (see below).

7.58 There is no doubt that the publicity given to the Abacha debt and the professed determination of President Obasanjo to recover the stolen moneys together with raised public awareness of the devastating damage the activities of corrupt leaders can do to their countries' economies, particularly in Africa, have been a major trigger for the introduction of UNCAC.

4. The Role of UNCAC

7.59 Chapter V of the Convention deals with Asset Recovery.[68] Article 57 concerns the return and disposal of assets: it provides that States Parties which have received requests for assistance from other States Parties (respectively 'requested' and 'requesting' States Parties) shall return confiscated property representing embezzled public funds. The requested state can waive the requirement that there should be a final judgment in the courts of the requesting state before remitting funds.[69] This is clearly a very important provision, given the ability of

[66] See, eg Reuters Report, 'Nigeria accuses Swiss of blackmail over looted funds', 29 May 2005.

[67] Reported in the *Sunday Mail* (Australia), 6 August 2003.

[68] The Convention is dealt with in detail at 9.10ff below.

[69] UNCAC, Art 57.3(a): it is also important to note that under Art 57.4 there is provision for a requested state to deduct reasonable expenses incurred in the investigation and any prosecutions or judicial proceedings, thus, potentially, overcoming the reluctance of states to expend their taxpayers' money assisting the citizens of foreign states. Nevertheless it has to be recognized that this has to be in the nature of a 'success fee', involving all the risks commonly associated with such methods of remuneration.

malefactors to delay matters and obtain perverse judgments in their domestic courts.[70]

UNCAC came into force on 14 December 2005.[71] Whilst it is inevitable that it will take time for States Parties to introduce the necessary domestic legislation, the fact of having ratified the Convention should assist the passage of such legislation and the principles enunciated in the Convention may in the interim assist pleaders before domestic courts in persuading judges that assistance should in principle be given. **7.60**

5. The Effectiveness of Mutual Legal Assistance

Reference has been made above to the initial speed and effectiveness of the Swiss investigating magistrate in the Abacha proceedings.[72] This is in great contrast to the rendering of Mutual Legal Assistance in England.[73] It took over three years from the initial request made by the Government of Pakistan for assistance in recovering assets acquired in the United Kingdom by Benazir Bhutto and her husband, Asif Ali Zardari, before relevant papers were handed over by the Home Office. In the case of Abacha it took four years. One of the main reasons for these delays is the ability of well-funded malefactors[74] to bring judicial review proceedings not only in the initial stages when the Home Secretary has to exercise discretion in deciding whether to grant the request, but also at the 'transmission' stage when the Home Secretary has to give the malefactors notice of his intention to transmit the documents to the requesting state. It is very much to be hoped that ways will be found of streamlining this process in the future.[75] **7.61**

The alternative, civil court, route was eventually used by Nigeria in England. By bringing a tracing action in the Chancery Division of the High Court, using the powers given by the freezing jurisdiction and, in particular, the type of order **7.62**

[70] The Abacha family obtained judgments in Nigeria's Federal High Court to the effect that it was 'unconstitutional' for the Federal Government to issue Letters of Request for mutual legal assistance, despite Nigeria being a party to the Harare Convention. They then attempted to utilize those judgments in Judicial Review proceedings before the Divisional Court, challenging the Home Secretary's decision to give assistance: *Abacha v The Secretary of State for the Home Department* [2001] EWHC Admin 787.

[71] 123 states signed UNCAC, it came into force 90 days after the 30th ratification, which took place on 15 September 2005 when Ecuador ratified.

[72] Evidence obtained by the Magistrate, Zechin, was admitted in the Commercial Court Ajaokuta proceedings: *Compagnie Noga d'Importation et d'Exportation SA v ANZ* (see n 64 above).

[73] For comprehensive coverage of the workings of Mutual Legal Assistance in England, see L Harris and C Murray, *Mutual Assistance in Criminal Matters, international co-operation in the investigation and prosecution of crime* (London: Sweet & Maxwell, 2000).

[74] Uncertainty over the sources of funds trapped in frozen accounts gives the English courts the opportunity to exercise their discretion in favour of allowing reasonable living expenses and legal fees to be paid out of the trapped funds, see *PCW (Underwriting Agencies) Ltd v Dixon* [1983] 2 All ER 697. See 7.24 above.

[75] This is a matter under review by the House of Commons International Development Committee on Corruption: see Fourth Report, HC 39-II, 29 March 2001.

that was made in *Bankers' Trust v Shapira*,[76] virtually all the information that the Home Office had taken four years to provide was obtained in less than four months. This was in part despite, or perhaps because of, the fact that, as typically happens, the forces of the Serious Fraud Office (SFO), the Financial Services Authority (FSA) and the National Criminal Investigation Service (NCIS) were all utilized in assisting with the implementation of the letter of request.

7.63 One reason why civil proceedings can be a very effective course of action is the result of the jurisdiction of the civil courts to grant interim relief.[77] Even more importantly, if the applicant state is able and willing to pay for them, the services of forensic accountants and, frequently, competent enquiry agents, can be retained to marshall all of the information gathered with a view not only to effecting recoveries but also obtaining more information to enable further applications to be made to courts both within the United Kingdom and abroad. With the permission of the court, evidence obtained in civil proceedings can be deployed in other jurisdictions. Permission will usually be forthcoming when civil action is intended. However, the court will be reluctant to allow evidence to be deployed in criminal proceedings.

6. Bearing the Cost of Recovery

7.64 Probably the most comprehensive and far-reaching asset tracing exercise ever carried out has been that conducted by the liquidators of the Bank of Credit and Commerce International (BCCI). The costs incurred have been enormous, but the results obtained for the creditors of the Bank have shown how worthwhile such expenditure can be. The Bank's deficit is currently estimated to be US$9 billion. A dividend of less than 15 per cent was originally forecast—after fourteen years returns to creditors are 75 per cent.[78] It is fantasy to imagine that foreign states will be prepared to make the kind of investment required to achieve such results; claimant states will also invariably face huge political difficulties at home raising budgets for this type of exercise. One way forward may be the provision of significant donor aid, but even that remains only a possibility at the present time. As the BCCI experience shows, the sums involved may run into many millions—this is a huge burden on the economy of a developing economy already impoverished by the looters' activities.

7.65 Governments who find themselves in this position fall easy prey to so-called 'booty-hunters'. These operators offer to collect the looted assets for a percentage (generally 40 per cent or thereabouts) of the recoveries on a 'no-win, no-fee' basis. Their resources are generally sparse, although that is not the impression they will give, and they will generally have one or two lawyers among their number who may or may not be qualified to practise in the appropriate

---

[76] [1980] 1 WLR 1274. [77] See 7.1ff above.

[78] For further details, visit http://www.deloitte.com.

jurisdictions. Typically, they will concentrate on the 'easy pickings', having persuaded the government agencies to open up their books. They will then collect that money, deduct a substantial fee and disappear, possibly leaving the state with insurmountable limitation problems.

There is undoubtedly a feeling in developing countries that the recovery bills should be picked up by the developed economies to whose shores the funds have often fled and from whose shores often emanate the bribes and kickbacks which enriched the kleptocrats in the first place. Whilst it seems extremely unlikely that the governments of the developed countries are prepared to commit the required resources, the possibility of being able to deduct reasonable expenses from recoveries, as envisaged in the UNCAC, may help in this regard, but a requested government would essentially be being asked to act on a contingency basis. **7.66**

In England the obvious route would be to use the Asset Recovery Agency (ARA)[79] but there is simply no precedent for any government anywhere in the world being prepared to take on commitments of this kind[80] and the current budget of the ARA makes such action impossible even to contemplate at the present time. The possibility of contingency fees being utilized in England to provide assistance from the private sector is not feasible for as long as they are not permitted, and while it is now possible to act on a 'success fee' basis[81] the outlays and risks involved are such that even the least risk-averse practitioner is unlikely to be attracted to this area of business. **7.67**

It is, finally, worth recalling the Recommendation contained in the Commission for Africa Report mentioned at the beginning of this book.[82] It remains to be seen what, if anything, the G8 countries are prepared to do to make progress in this enormously important area but it is submitted that financial assistance to states for bringing civil proceedings may offer the most promising way forward. **7.68**

D. Civil Recovery and the Proceeds of Crime Act 2002

1. The Assets Recovery Agency

Nowadays, the recovery of the proceeds of crime is facilitated in the United Kingdom by the Proceeds of Crime Act of 2002 (POCA 2002). An important part of that Act, as has been seen in Chapter 2 above, when it comes to the **7.69**

[79] Set up under the POCA 2002: see further, 7.69ff below.

[80] For the steps taken to date to resource asset recovery under POCA 2002 see the Joint Review entitled 'Payback Time' available on www.hmcpsi.gov.uk/reports/jointins.shtml. The likelihood is that, if the ARA is ever to take on large actions such as state asset recovery, funding will have to be provided by one of the interested government departments, such as the Foreign Office or the Department for International Development (DFID).

[81] A useful discussion of costs funding options is contained in The Society for Advanced Legal Studies' Anti-Corruption Working Group paper, of February 2000, 'Banking on Corruption', ch4.

[82] See 1.48 above; the Recommendation is at para 4.5.3 of the Report.

prosecution of those who handle funds or property obtained by crime, which may include corruption, contains the provisions which deal with money laundering.[83] Especially important are the reporting requirements which are designed precisely to catch those attempting to assist in the conversion of the proceeds of corruption into 'clean' money. Proceedings under POCA 2002, however, whether criminal or civil under the auspices of the ARA are all instigated by the state, and the ARA will not normally take action without a referral from the law enforcement or prosecution authorities. The ability of the UK authorities to assist in the process of such recoveries,[84] whether because of a lack of political will or a simple reluctance to expend UK taxpayers' money on effecting recoveries that do not directly benefit British citizens has hitherto seemed limited. During 2005, however, cases involving seizure of assets brought into the UK by corrupt Nigerian state governors and the ensuing prosecutions indicate the emergence of a far more pro-active stance by both police and prosecutors.

7.70 Part 2 of POCA 2002 contains statutory powers to confiscate the assets of convicted criminals.[85] The amount of the confiscation order is intended to equal the defendant's benefit from criminal conduct.[86] Confiscated assets are forfeit to the Crown.[87] A victim of crime cannot intervene in confiscation hearings to seek, for example, the return of stolen funds. In practice, however, prosecutors will have in mind the possibility of asking the count to make a compensation order in appropriate cases. The amount of compensation payable will depend on the court's view of the defendant's means: the compensation can be paid out of the sums confiscated.[88] However, a court has discretion not to make a confiscation order, or to reduce its amount, if the victim of the criminal conduct has started or intends to start proceedings against the defendant.[89]

7.71 Part 5 of POCA 2002 introduces for the first time under both English and Scottish law the possibility of recovery by a government agency of property that is, or represents, property obtained through unlawful conduct by means of civil proceedings. In England this is to be done by the Director of the ARA. The scheme is set out in sections 243 to 288 of the 2002 Act. This entirely new right of action is reserved to the ARA. Cash may be forfeited by bringing civil proceedings in a magistrates court (sections 289 to 303).

7.72 It is not necessary for criminal proceedings to have been brought in respect of the property. The procedure is envisaged as being particularly useful where there are insufficient grounds for a prosecution, where the person suspected of having committed an offence is dead, or, potentially, in state asset recoveries, where the

[83] POCA 2002, ss 327–340, and see 2.112ff above.

[84] The experience of the governments of Nigeria in trying to recover looted Abacha assets and of Pakistan in attempting to recover assets stolen by the Bhutto regime are cases in point.

[85] See 2.121ff above.

[86] POCA 2002, s 7.

[87] See 2.118ff above.

[88] POCA 2002, s 13(5) and (6).

[89] POCA 2002, s 6(6).

person is outside the jurisdiction. It seems, however, that it will be rare for the ARA to bring civil proceedings to confiscate or forfeit assets in the absence of a conviction, and the preferred course of action is to seek confiscation of assets following conviction. It will be interesting to see if, in time, the ARA expands the circumstances in which it is prepared to use its civil powers.

Section 241 of POCA 2002 defines 'unlawful conduct', which may be unlawful under the criminal law of the part of the United Kingdom in which it occurred, but also includes conduct which occurs outside the United Kingdom and is unlawful under the laws of the foreign state, and those of the United Kingdom. Cash intended for use abroad in pursuit of unlawful conduct may also be forfeited. The standard of proof to be applied is the civil standard of a balance of probabilities—proving beyond reasonable doubt in such cases is often immensely difficult. **7.73**

The meaning of obtaining property through unlawful conduct is set out in section 242. The definition is wide enough to cover taking bribes corruptly to award a contract.[90] Section 242 also provides that it is not necessary to show that property or cash was obtained through a *particular kind* of unlawful conduct. It will thus be sufficient to show, for example, that funds are attributable to money laundering activity.[91] Again, this has considerable potential value when it comes to forfeiting looted state assets. **7.74**

Stolen property, or other property held on constructive trust, obtained through unlawful conduct is recoverable by the ARA. Section 281,[92] however, allows the true owner of the property to obtain a declaration that he has a valid claim to it and that he was deprived of it by unlawful conduct. The victim's claim has precedence. The section can, of course, be deployed only at the successful conclusion of recovery proceedings brought by the ARA. **7.75**

One of the first actions brought by the ARA concerned illegally acquired funds in Northern Ireland; the defendant challenged the nature of the proceedings, effectively saying that although they were labelled civil, they were more in the nature of criminal proceedings.[93] Such a challenge would have important implications as it would effectively entitle defendants to all the normal rights of accused persons, such as the right to silence, thus making the procedure virtually unworkable. The court held that whilst civil forfeiture proceedings required a finding that a person had acted contrary to the criminal law, that did not take place in a criminal setting. The defendant was not required to plead to a criminal charge 'and all the trappings of the proceedings are those normally associated with a civil claim'. The purpose of civil recovery proceedings was to recover from a person that which he should not have had in the first place, ie the **7.76**

[90] The example is specifically cited in para 294 of the Explanatory Notes which accompany POCA 2002.
[91] POCA 2002, Part 7 deals with money laundering offences.
[92] POCA 2002, 301 applies to cash, see 2.134 above.
[93] *Walsh v Director of Assets Recovery Agency* [2005] NICA 6.

proceeds of crime, by proceedings *in rem*. The Constitutional Court in South Africa, where civil forfeiture proceedings have been pioneered, has found that one of the most useful purposes of civil forfeiture is to remove the incentive for crime, not punish offenders.[94]

2. Know Your Customer and Money Laundering

7.77 Until comparatively recently, banks could shelter behind the provisions of the Banking Acts to preserve their anonymity when forced to disclose the existence of accounts held in the names of malefactors, claiming that customer confidentiality was paramount. This was particularly frustrating for civil claimants who might see the SFO swing into action at the behest of the FSA, discover the existence of a host of accounts, and then be unable to disclose the identity of the account-holding institutions to the claimant.[95]

7.78 Nowadays, banks run the serious risk of being found in default of the know your customer (KYC) requirements and being named and shamed, with supposedly serious consequences for their reputations.[96] The whole business of KYC took on new significance as the result of the Abacha case and questions were raised before the House of Commons Committee on Corruption.[97] Particularly welcome has been the requirement to identify and report on the existence of accounts held by Politically Exposed Persons (PEPs). However, as with much else in recent history, it was the events of 11 September 2001 that changed the face of compliance. Tracking down potential sources of terrorist financing became a major pre-occupation of the Bush Government and had a major impact also on the United Kingdom. The great irony is that it is now widely appreciated that the sorts of sums used by terrorists to finance their operations would be unlikely, even in these days of stringent reporting requirements, to attract reports of suspicious activity by virtue of their size

---

[94] *NDPP v Mohamed* NO 2002 (4) SA 843, CC.

[95] On 8 March 2001, the FSA issued a Press Release announcing that they had investigated 23 banks in connection with the laundering of US$1.3bn through 42 accounts linked to Abacha, over a space of 4 years; 98% of the money went through 15 banks which were found to have significant control weaknesses. The majority of the banks were in the City of London and included UK banks and banks both inside and outside the EU. See FSA website: http://www.fsa.gov.uk.

[96] Naming and shaming has yet to be seen to have a serious impact on shareholder confidence, as banks continue to turn in record profits, almost year on year. To date, only on three occasions have fines have been imposed by the FSA in respect of breaches of the money laundering rules. The largest, £2.32m, was against Abbey National Asset Managers in 2003 (£300,000 was paid as compensation to a small number of clients), the other two fines were £1.25m each against the Bank of Scotland and Northern Bank (no compensation was payable): see FSA website (n 95 above). There has yet to be a hefty fine levied in respect of a high-profile corruption case—arguably it becomes less and less likely that this will happen as compliance measures become ever more stringent.

[97] International Development Committee on Corruption 4th Report (HC (2001) 39-I and 39-II). Vol II, containing Minutes of Evidence, is of particular interest.

alone. The reporting requirements are much more likely to be of real value in assisting the tracking down of corrupt funds—arguably also the existence of those funds is likely to prove a longer-term threat to the lives of many more in the developing world than those who lost their lives in the Twin Towers.

There is little doubt that claimants seeking civil relief could benefit enormously from the facilitation of flows of information from the regulatory and investigative authorities. This is particularly so when government authorities are unable or unwilling to expend resources on pursuing targets of foreign investigations. There is nothing, except cost, to stop foreign claimants, usually governments, from seeking relief in the civil courts, and if they really want to effect recoveries, that is still the route down which they have to go unless the ARA is prepared to take on the role that many, including many foreign governments, would like to see it assume. **7.79**

E. The Tax Treatment of Bribe Payments

1. UK Taxation Legislation

The tax treatment of bribes is currently governed by section 577A of the Income and Corporation Taxes Act 1988 (ICTA 1988). Until 2002, bribes paid abroad were tax deductible. By section 68(2) of the Finance Act 2002 on or after 1 April 2002 'no deduction shall be made for any expenditure incurred ... in making a payment outside the United Kingdom where the making of a corresponding payment in any part of the United Kingdom would constitute a criminal offence there'.[98] **7.80**

However, since the coming into force of Part 12 of ATCSA 2001 extending UK jurisdiction under the Corruption Acts to foreign bribery transactions, it is likely that section 577A(1)(a) of ICTA 1988, which covers expenditure constituting the commission of a criminal offence, would apply to make payments made under such a transaction non-deductible. **7.81**

Inland Revenue Guidance Notes BIM 43145 and 43150 explain the position regarding expenditure involving crime further, with particular regard to territoriality, jurisdiction, and nationality. Thus, for example, the payment of a bribe by a UK resident trader into a foreign official's bank account in London would make both parties guilty of a corruption offence.[99] If the offer and payment were made abroad by foreign entities, corruption jurisdiction would not generally be available under the law as it stands. However, preparatory **7.82**

---

[98] The relevant section in ICTA 1988 now becomes s 577A(1)(b).

[99] Prevention of Corruption Act 1916 (see Ch 2 above).

actions might be caught since it is now an offence to conspire to commit offences abroad.[100]

7.83 Where a non-UK national in an overseas branch of a UK company pays a bribe and does not report it to head office, that would previously have been tax-deductible because there was no 'knowing mind' in the United Kingdom nor any UK national directly involved in the payment. Now, however, section 577A(1)(b) catches that type of payment because 'a corresponding payment in any part of the United Kingdom' would be a criminal offence. Whilst these changes to the tax treatment of corrupt payments are welcome, they do not lessen the need for the contemplated primary legislation.

[100] Criminal Justice (Terrorism and Conspiracy) Act 1998, ss 5–7.

8

THE REGULATION OF CONDUCT IN PUBLIC LIFE

The Seven Principles of Public Life

Selflessness

Holders of public office should take decisions solely in terms of the public interest. They should not do so in order to gain financial or other material benefits for themselves, their family, or their friends.

Integrity

Holders of public office should not place themselves under any financial or other obligation to outside individuals or organisations that might influence them in the performance of their official duties.

Objectivity

In carrying out public business, including making public appointments, awarding contracts, or recommending individuals for rewards and benefits, holders of public office should make choices on merit.

Accountability

Holders of public office are accountable for their decisions and actions to the public and must submit themselves to whatever scrutiny is appropriate to their office.

Openness

Holders of public office should be as open as possible about all the decisions and actions that they take. They should give reasons for their decisions and restrict information only when the wider public interest clearly demands.

Honesty

Holders of public office have a duty to declare any private interests relating to their public duties and to take steps to resolve any conflicts arising in a way that protects the public interest.

Leadership

Holders of public office should promote and support these principles by leadership and example[1]

A. Introduction

1. The Seven Principles of Public Life

8.01 Ten years ago it would have appeared strange that a book on the law of corruption and misuse of public office should include a chapter on the regulation of conduct in public life. Corruption has always been treated by lawyers as a discrete topic to be dealt with by the courts, whereas the regulation of conduct outside the criminal law has been regarded as a matter for internal discipline to be dealt with on an ad hoc basis by disciplinary bodies. For many years, however, it has been accepted that the prevalence of corruption in society and its institutions can be reduced by the development of effective codes of conduct

[1] CSPL, First Report (also known as the Nolan Report), Cm 2850-1 (1955).

regulating those who are involved not only in public life, but also in commercial institutions.[2] Moreover, in jurisdictions where it is difficult to establish proof of corruption, the non-observance of codes of practice is a powerful weapon in the armoury of investigators and prosecutors.

Some of the codes which have been developed contain restatements of core principles, for example the Code of Conduct for Members of Parliament contains the Seven Principles of Public Life, set out above.[3] All of them contain detailed rules of conduct tailored to the requirements of the office holders concerned and the risks they are likely to encounter. The rules include requirements to declare and register interests and to avoid conflicts of interest and situations which may create a perception of conflict of interest. In many codes, including the codes of conduct for judges,[4] they specifically prohibit the soliciting and receipt of gifts. **8.02**

A substantial part of this chapter is focused on the work of the Committee on Standards in Public Life (CSPL) which was established in the United Kingdom in 1995, and the extent to which its recommendations have been embodied in legislation and codes of conduct affecting the three organs of government: the legislature, the executive, and the judiciary. In the case of the judiciary, the recent reforms in the United Kingdom introduced by the Constitutional Reform Act 2005, are set against the background of the international development of codes of judicial ethics. The CSPL's recommendations relating to the improvement of the honours system; electoral reform and the funding of political parties have already been considered in Chapter 2 above.[5] **8.03**

The result of the CSPL's recommendations is that codes of conduct and systems of self-regulation have been introduced and, where they already existed, have been strengthened, thereby ensuring the transparency and accountability without which corrupt practices are likely to thrive. As a standing committee the CSPL, is able to monitor and review the implementation of its recommendations and conduct inquiries into new subjects according to the focus of public concern at any particular time. **8.04**

2. The Committee on Standards in Public Life

In the mid-1990s, allegations of 'sleaze' against Members of Parliament led to serious public concern about standards in public life in the United Kingdom. **8.05**

---

[2] P Fennell and PA Thomas, 'The Law Relating to Corruption, an historical analysis' (1983) 11 *International Journal of Social Law* 167.

[3] HC 24 July 1996, 688; HCC 688 (1995–6); and HC Debates, 24 July 1996, col 392. A revised form of the Code was issued on 14 July 2005. It can be viewed at http://www.publications.parliament.ukpa/cm/cmcode.htm.

[4] See 8.91 and 8.108, below.

[5] See 2.94, 2.98, 2.108 above.

The immediate cause was the 'cash for questions' scandal, involving a small number of MPs, alleged to have accepted payment to raise questions in the House of Commons. This was exacerbated by the Government's failure to respond generally to charges about MPs' financial conflicts, former ministers obtaining employment with firms they had connections with whilst in office, methods of financing of political parties, and a general perception that appointments to public bodies were being unduly influenced by party political considerations.[6] The normal political processes were not providing solutions to ethical problems in the public sector and the time had come for the Government to adopt a comprehensive approach to the problem.[7]

8.06 On 25 October 1994, the then Prime Minister, John Major, announced in the House of Commons the setting up of a Committee on Standards in Public Life:

> . . . to examine current concerns about standards of conduct of all office holders of public office, including arrangements relating to financial and commercial activities, and to make recommendations as to any changes in present arrangements which might be required to ensure the highest standards of propriety in public life . . . For these purposes public office should include: Ministers, civil servants and advisers; Members of Parliament and UK Members of the European Parliament; Members and senior officers of all non-departmental public bodies and of national health service bodies; non-ministerial office holders; members and other senior officers of other bodies discharging publicly-funded functions; and elected members and senior officers of local authorities.[8]

8.07 When the CSPL was established, Mr Major said: 'If the rules governing conduct in public life are vague or unsatisfactory, [the CSPL] will clarify them. But [its] task is not just to meet immediate questions. It is to act as a running authority of reference—almost, you might say, an ethical workshop called in to do running repairs.'[9]

8.08 The CSPL was constituted as an advisory non-departmental standing public body with accommodation in the Cabinet Office and a secretariat of eight to nine members. It was subject to review by its sponsoring body, the Cabinet Office, every five years. The first such review was in 2001.[10] Lord Nolan was the

[6] Specifically, Executive Non-Departmental Public Bodies (NDPBs) and National Health Service (NHS) bodies (see 8.77 below). See also the Sixth Report of the CSPL, 'Reinforcing Standards', Summary of List of Recommendations, para 1.

[7] 'The First Ten Years' by Peter Riddell, Chief Political Commentator of *The Times*, Committee on Standards, Annual Report 2004, published March 2005. Riddell says it has survived the era of 'spin' and now he worries about 'cronyism'.

[8] *Hansard* (HC) vol XX, col 758, (25 October 1994).

[9] Speech at Lord Mayor's banquet, 14 November 1994.

[10] Report of the Quinquennial Review of the CSPL, Central Secretariat, Cabinet Office, January 2001.

Committee's first Chairman.[11] On 12 November 1997 the Prime Minister, Tony Blair, extended the CSPL's terms of reference 'to review issues in relation to the funding of political parties, and to make recommendations as to any changes in present arrangements'.[12]

In its First Report,[13] published in May 1995, the CSPL stated that it aimed 'to rebuild public confidence' in holders of public office and 'to restore some clarity and direction wherever moral uncertainty had crept in'. It said that it: **8.09**

> . . . could not say that standards of behaviour in public life had declined, but it could say that conduct in public life is more rigorously scrutinised than it was in the past, that the standards which the public demands remain high,[14] and that the great majority of people in public life meet those standards, but there are weaknesses in the procedures for maintaining and enforcing those standards. As a result people in public life are not always as clear as they should be about where the boundaries of acceptable conduct lie. This we regard as the principal reason for public disquiet. It calls for urgent remedial action.[15]

The CSPL's recommendations were radical and far-reaching. The first general recommendation was that the principles underpinning standards in public life should be restated. These principles, as formulated by the CSPL, have become known as *The Seven Principles of Public Life*: selflessness, integrity, objectivity, accountability, openness, honesty, and leadership, and have come to be regarded as 'the touchstone for ethical standards across the public sector generally'.[16] The CSPL's second recommendation was that all public bodies should draw up codes of conduct incorporating the seven principles of public life. The third was that internal systems for maintaining standards should be supported by independent scrutiny; and the fourth, that more should be done to promote and reinforce standards of conduct in public bodies, particularly through guidance and training, including induction training. **8.10**

The CSPL has published ten reports, the most recent being entitled *Getting the Balance Right*, published on 15 January 2005. They have covered every aspect of public life, including Parliament; the Prime Minister; ministers; the civil service and special advisers; public bodies and quangos, and local government; as well as the funding of political parties and the honours system under its extended terms of reference. In some cases, such as the bribery of MPs and the administration of the civil service, they have recommended legislation. In others they have recommended systems for self-regulation by the introduction and **8.11**

[11] Members of the CSPL are appointed by the Prime Minister for a period of three years. Lord Nolan was succeeded by Lord Neill of Bladon QC, in November 1997; Sir Nigel Wicks, on 1 March 2001; and Sir Alistair Graham, in 26 April 2004. Sir Alistair Graham is due to retire as Chairman on 30 September 2006.

[12] See 2.108 above on elections and honours.

[13] Cm 2850-1.

[14] See 5.31 above.

[15] CSPL, First Report Summary para 2.

[16] CSPL, Sixth Report, 8, Cm 4557-1.

strengthening of codes of conduct, and by the establishment of organs for their enforcement with rights of representation and appeal. As noted below, many of the Committee's recommendations have been adopted.

8.12 In January 2001, under the Chairmanship of Lord Neill of Bladon QC, the CSPL published a Quinquennial Review. The Review confirmed there was a need for the CSPL's continued existence. It concluded that the first five years had seen significant developments in standards in public life, that the mapping out of the ethical framework was complete, except for the House of Lords, but there remained a continuing need to monitor the ethical environment and to respond to issues of concern as they arise.[17]

8.13 In September 2001, the CSPL published a report entitled *The First Seven Reports—A Review of Progress*, in which it reviewed the scope of the Committee's work up to that date coupled with changes in public life over the previous seven years and the outcome of action taken in response to its recommendations. As it put it, it was a 'snapshot' of the position at the end of August 2001.

8.14 The specific recommendations relating to the sectors of public life examined by the CSPL, the government responses, and the extent to which the recommendations have been implemented are set out below.

B. The Legislature

1. The House of Commons

i. The liability of Members of Parliament for offences of bribery and corruption

8.15 Bribery of or by a member of either House of Parliament in connection with his parliamentary duties is a contempt of Parliament and the person offering the bribe and the member can be punished for contempt. It is likely it is also a common law offence of bribery, but the position is considered far from clear.[18]

8.16 Instances of Parliament considering cases of bribery are not common. There were only a limited number of cases in the 20th century. The footnotes in Erskine May's Parliamentary Practice record a number of instances in which MPs have been punished by the House for bribery offences, but there appears to be no record of the punishment of a person who offered a bribe to an MP. Since

[17] Report of the Quinquennial Review of the CSPL, Central Secretariat, Cabinet Office, January 2001, para 13.

[18] Erskine May, Parliamentary Practice, 23rd Ed (2004) (Butterworths Lexis Nexis), p 132–134, see paras 2.24, 5.84 above.

1940, such cases have been treated as raising issues relating to the observation of standards which the House is entitled to expect from its members.[19]

In 1991 a prosecution for common law bribery was commenced against defendants who were alleged to have bribed an MP in relation to his responsibilities to his constituents. The trial judge ruled that it would be a common law offence for a person to bribe an MP and for an MP to accept a bribe in such circumstances, and that no privilege under Article IX of the Bill of Rights could be claimed. Later, after hearing the evidence, the judge directed the jury to acquit the defendants charged with offering the bribe and the Prosecution offered no evidence against the MP.[20] **8.17**

In 1976, the Salmon Commission recommended that the subject of bribery of MP's should be considered by Parliament with the consolidation of the statute law of bribery.[21] In December 1991, the Home Office published a discussion paper, entitled *Clarification of the Law Relating to the Bribery of Members of Parliament*, setting out a number of options for developing the criminal law to cover bribery of MPs. In 1995 the CSPL repeated the Salmon Commission's recommendations and suggested that the task should be taken forward by the Law Commission.[22] **8.18**

ii. The Code of Conduct, appointment of a Parliamentary Commissioner for Standards and the investigation of complaints

In its First Report, the CSPL recommended that the House of Commons should introduce a new Code of Conduct for Members and appoint a Parliamentary Commissioner for Standards to advise and give expanded guidance on the Code, having particular regard to the work of Standing Committees.[23] It recommended that the Commissioner should be a person of independent standing; should have power to initiate and investigate complaints; that the Commissioner's findings should be made public; and in those cases where further action is recommended, a complaint should be referred to a subcommittee of the Committee of Privileges. The subcommittee should consist of up to seven MPs and normally sit in public and should have power to impose penalties and to report to the Full Privileges Committee of the House. MPs who were the subject of a complaint should be entitled to be accompanied by advisers.[24] **8.19**

---

[19] Ibid See AW Bradley and KD Ewing, *Constitutional and Administrative Law* (13th edn, (London), Longman, 2003), paras 2.15, 2.30.

[20] *R v Greenaway*, (1992) *The Times*, 8, 15, and 22 December. Erskine May 134–5; *Public Law*, April 1998; Report of the Joint Committee on the draft Corruption Bill, para 104 (Session 2002–3, HC705).

[21] The Royal Commission on Standards in Public Life. HMSO, Cmnd 6524, 1976, p 24, para 87.

[22] CSPL First Report, para 2.104.

[23] CSPL, First Report, paras 2.59, 2.85, 2.89.

[24] ibid para 2.11.

iii. The Register of Members' Interests and the ban on paid advocacy

8.20 The House of Commons established a compulsory register of MPs' interests following the Poulson affair in 1975.[25] The Register is maintained by a senior clerk of the House and supervised by a select committee.[26]

8.21 The CSPL noted in its First Report that a fall in public confidence in the probity of Members had coincided with an increase in the number of MPs holding paid consultancies relating to their Parliamentary role.[27] It considered that MPs should remain free to have paid employment unrelated to that role, but recommended that the House should re-state its 1947 resolution,[28] which places an absolute ban on MPs entering into agreements which in any way restrict their freedom to act and speak as they wish, or require them to act in Parliament as representatives of outside bodies. It recommended that MPs selling their services to firms engaged in lobbying on behalf of clients should be banned;[29] that full disclosure of consultancy agreements and payments and trade union sponsorship agreements and payments should be introduced immediately; and that Parliament should review the merits of allowing MPs to hold such consultancies, taking into account their wider implications.[30]

8.22 The CSPL also recommended a Parliamentary Commissioner for Standards should be appointed and that the Register should be more informative; and that the rules on declaring such interests and avoiding conflicts of interest should be set out in more detail.[31]

iv. Implementation of the CSPL's recommendations

8.23 The Government's response to the CSPL's First Report was published in July 1995.[32] It reaffirmed the Government's commitment to consolidate the laws on corruption, and welcomed the opportunity to clarify the law relating to bribery, but stated that the review of the law relating to MPs would be considered in the light of the House of Commons' debate on the Report of the CSPL.[33] In December 1996 the Government published its own document on the topic,[34] with the result that the Law Commission decided it would be inappropriate to look into the matter at that stage.[35] In March 1999, the Joint Committee on

[25] ibid para 2.58. [26] Bradley and Ewing 228 (n 19 above).

[27] Some 30% of backbench MPs had such consultancies: CSPL First Report para 2.8.

[28] Ibid paras 2.21, 2.59. HC Debates, 15 July 1947, vol XX, col 284; HC 118 (1946–7).

[29] CSPL, First Report, para 2.59. [30] ibid paras 2.59, 2.85.

[31] ibid, paras 2.59, 2.70.

[32] *The Government's Response to the First Report from the Committee on Standards in Public Life* (1995) Cm 2931, debated in Parliament on 18 July 1995. See *Hansard* HC, vol 263, cols 1473–1484 (18 July 1995) and *Hansard* HL, vol 566, cols 157–168 (18 July 1995).

[33] *Report on Standards in Public Life* (HC 637), published on 7 July 1995.

[34] Home Office, A Discussion Paper, *Clarification of the law relating to the Bribery of Members of Parliament.*

[35] *Legislating the Criminal Code: Corruption, a Consultation Paper*, No 145, paras 7.49 to 7.58. The Law Commission's Report is considered in detail in Chapter 5.

Parliamentary Privilege, under the Chairmanship of Lord Nicholls of Birkenhead, recommended that members of both Houses of Parliament should be brought within the criminal law of bribery.[36]

The Joint Committee recommended that Members of both Houses should be brought within the criminal law of bribery by legislation containing a provision to the effect that evidence relating to an offence committed or alleged to be committed under the relevant sections should be admissible notwithstanding Article IX.[37] It stated that Parliament should be vigilant to retain necessary rights and immunities, and equally rigorous in discarding all others, but pointed out that the problems raised by parliamentary privilege in the prosecution of bribery of MP's are purely evidential. The Joint Committee accepted that its recommendation would involve an encroachment on the guarantee by Article IX of the Bill of Rights 1689 that freedom of speech and debates or proceedings in Parliament ought not to be impeached or questioned in any court or place out of Parliament. It stated, however, that corruption, as a serious and insidious offence, could only be dealt with effectively by using the police and the courts. **8.24**

The draft Corruption Bill intended that MP's and peers should be subject to the same corruption law as everyone else. The Joint Committee on the Draft Corruption Bill supported the proposal. No witness before the Joint Committee argued against it. The Standards and Privileges Committee of the House of Commons, the Constitution Committee of the House of Lords and the CSPL (Wickes Committee) also supported it. The result is that in spite of general agreement that MPs should be brought within the criminal law of bribery, pending a comprehensive statutory reform of the law relating to bribery and corruption, no action will be taken.[38] **8.25**

Following the CSPL's First Report the House of Commons approved a Code of Conduct with a guide to the Rules,[39] appointed a Parliamentary Commissioner for Standards, and provided for the Committee on Standards and Privileges to oversee the Commissioner's work and consider complaints against MPs which the Commissioner referred to it. The House re-stated the 1947 resolution on MPs' interests; with amendments; adopted stricter rules for the Register of Interests; and required a member, who has entered into an employment agreement to provide services as an MP, to register a full copy of the agreement **8.26**

---

[36] The *Nicholls Report* 1999. The Nicholls Committee is the Joint Committee on Parliamentary Privilege. It was chaired by Lord Nicholls of Birkenhead. The Nicholls Report was published in March 1999 (HL Paper 43-1 and HC 214-1 (1998–99). The '*minimum standards of fairness*' are set out on p 75, para 281. See 8.28, n 43 below.

[37] Report of the Joint Committee on the Draft Corruption Bill, Report and Evidence, Session 2002–3, HL Paper 157, HC 705, Report, Clause 12. HL Paper 43-11 and HC 214-11 (1998–9) para 135.

[38] Ibid para 101.

[39] *The Code of Conduct together with the Rules relating to the Conduct of Members*, See n.3.

with the Commissioner. Schedule 7 to the Political Parties, Elections and Referendums Act 2000, provided that MPs must also disclose certain donations received to the Electoral Commission and donations must not be received from impermissible sources.[40]

8.27 Between 1997 and 2001, the Committee on Standards and Privileges issued some seventy reports, many concerning failure to register relevant interests. The most serious led to a recommendation for suspension by the House for a stated period. The most substantial inquiry related to allegations, which were established, that while an MP, Neil Hamilton, had received undisclosed cash payments from Mr Al Fayed for lobbying services and undisclosed hospitality.[41]

8.28 In its Sixth Report,[42] in January 2000, entitled *Reinforcing the Standards, a Review of the First Report*, the CSPL recommended that the Government should introduce its proposed legislation on the criminal law of bribery as soon as possible and continued to support the self-regulation of Parliament for allegations of misconduct, except those involving allegations of crime. It recommended that where a complaint of criminal conduct is made to the Commissioner and the complaint is neither malicious nor frivolous, the Commissioner should report to the Committee on Standards and Privileges with a recommendation that the complaint should be referred to the police for further investigation. In cases where the Commissioner finds a *prima facie* case of serious misconduct, it recommended that the Commissioner should report the finding to the Committee on Standards and Privileges and recommended that the Committee should refer it to an investigative tribunal composed of an independent lawyer of substantial seniority as chairman, sitting with two to four experienced members; the tribunal to be governed by procedures which satisfy the 'minimum standards of fairness' as defined by the Nicholls Committee,[43] with a right of appeal to an ad hoc appellate tribunal. The CSPL stated that it was troubled by a widely held view that the Guidelines inhibit contributions in the House by MPs who have substantial expertise and experience, but said that it was committed to the ban on paid advocacy, although it proposed amendments to the guidelines to ease the restrictions governing initiation of proceedings.[44]

---

[40] See 2.110 above.

[41] HC 30, 261 (1997–98); and HC Debates, 17 November 1997, cols 81–121. see also Bradley and Ewing (n 19 above) 231. The Commissioner's findings are not subject to judicial review; *R v Parliamentary Commissioner for Standards, ex p Al Fayed* [1998] 1 All ER 93.

[42] Cm 4557–1.

[43] CSPL Sixth Report, Recommendations 3–10 and n 36 above.

[44] CSPL, Sixth Report, Recommendation 9.

In its Eighth Report,[45] published in November 2002, the CSPL reported that the system put in place after 1996 had largely eradicated the problem of paid advocacy, but it believed the system for regulating standards of conduct had fallen short in delivering confidence in certain respects.[46] It recommended that the Commissioner's independence should be underpinned by clearly identifying the Commissioner as an office holder, appointed and paid for, but not employed, by the House, and that the Investigatory Panel should have an independent chair external to the House. It recommended that the Chairman of the Committee of Standards and Privileges should continue to be drawn from the opposition parties, but that no party should have an overall majority on the Committee; that the Committee should draw on external legal advice in more serious cases; take evidence in public; give reasons for its decisions; and seek the views of relevant external organizations when it reviews the Code of Conduct for Members. Although it was concerned that the Committee was vulnerable to the charge that 'to the observer, the emphasis is still upon defending the ancient traditions of the House, defending the rights of members, defending the principle of self-regulation', it considered that the development of a clearer, demonstrably fair and impartial system, combined with the ready cooperation of all those regulated by it, would both create and reinforce the right cultural outlook. The CSPL rejected putting the system for regulating standards of conduct in the House of Commons on a statutory basis and introducing MPs into the decision-making process. It stated that the changes it recommended would introduce an external element at every stage: the development of standards of conduct, investigation, and the adjudication of complaints. **8.29**

2. The House of Lords

In 1995, the House of Lords passed a resolution that its peers should always act on their own personal honour, should never accept a financial benefit in return for exercising parliamentary influence; and that peers who have a direct interest in lobbying ought not to speak, vote, or otherwise use their office on behalf of **8.30**

[45] Cm 5663. In September 2001, the Committee announced that it would review, in due course, the implementation of all its reports and stated its intention to begin its promised review by turning first to the system for regulating standards of conduct in the House of Commons.

[46] The Committee quoted Baroness Boothroyd, a former Speaker of the House, as putting the point strongly: 'I am concerned about the public's perception of members of Parliament. One only has to have one or two rotten apples in and the public think that everybody is tainted with that same disease' (Eighth Report, Summary, para 4). It also referred to the direction in which the systems for regulating standards of conduct in organizations outside the House were going and the evidence of Lord Nicholls of Birkenhead to the Committee on 28 May 2002, when he referred to public differences expressed by a former Commissioner for Standards, Elizabeth Filkin, and the house authorities that the latter were not always as rigorous and thorough as they might be. The result was that he had changed his views about self-regulation. He referred to the 'ongoing march of outside participation in disciplinary and regulatory processes' and concluded that 'the public feels that self-regulation is not 100 per cent reliable'.

clients. The House created a register of peers' consultancies and similar financial interests in lobbying for clients. The register was limited in scope, but peers might register other matters 'which they consider may affect public perception of the way in which they discharge their parliamentary duties'.[47]

8.31 The CSPL reported on issues relating to standards of conduct in the House of Lords in its Seventh Report, published in November 2000. By that time the compositional changes brought about by the House of Lords Act 1999, which excluded all but ninety-two of the hereditary peers from the House, had been passed and the House of Lords Appointments Commission, had been established to make recommendations for non-party-political peerages.[48]

8.32 The CSPL noted that its inquiry was not prompted by any scandal or crisis and in framing its recommendations it had regard to the changes in membership of the House and the possibility that it would have a higher profile following those changes. It also had regard to the importance of 'proportionality' (a course of action should be proportionate to the problem or deficiency it seeks to remedy). It recommended that the House of Lords should adopt a Code of Conduct, incorporating the Seven Principles of Public Life and the principles adopted by the House of Lords in its 1995 resolution.[49] The proposed code included the basic rules on the regulation of interests requiring the declaration of a wider range of interests and continuing to restrict members in parliamentary lobbying; mandatory regulation of all peers' relevant interests; a tightening up of the present guidance on lobbying to ensure public confidence in its propriety; a review of the House of Lords induction process with a view to providing more detailed guidance about the operation and scope of the relevant rules; the appointment, where appropriate, of an ad hoc independent investigator to assist the Sub-Committee on Lords' Interests in cases involving a serious allegation of misconduct.

8.33 The CSPL recommended mandatory registration of all three categories of the then Lords Register, ie: (1) consultancies or similar arrangements, involving payment or other incentive or reward for providing parliamentary advice or services; (2) financial interests in businesses involved in parliamentary lobbying on behalf of clients; and (3) particulars relating to matters which peers consider may affect the public perception of the way in which they discharge their parliamentary duties. It recommended that Category (3) should cover financial and non-financial interests and that the test of 'relevant interest' under that

[47] HL 90 and 98 (1994–95; HL Debates, 1 November 1995, col 1428, and 7 November 1995, col 1631. Bradley and Ewing (n 19 above) 232.

[48] Cm 4903–1. The CSPL had delayed its inquiry pending the report of the Griffiths Committee on the declaration and registration of interests in the House of Lords, The Griffiths Report, HL Paper 90 (1994–1995).

[49] CSPL Seventh Report, para 1.7 and Recommendation 1.3.

category should be whether the interest may reasonably be thought to affect the public perception of the way in which a peer discharges his or her parliamentary duties. The CSPL said that peers should continue to be allowed to hold parliamentary consultancies, subject to the existing prohibition on paid advocacy.

The CSPL recommended that peers should be encouraged in the first instance to raise any allegation of a breach of the rules in a private communication with the peer against whom the complaint is made. Thereafter, the complaining peer should, in accordance with the Griffiths Committee's recommendation,[50] refer the allegation to the Sub-Committee on Lords' Interests. The CSPL saw no reason for a Commissioner of Standards for the House of Lords, but recommended that the Sub-Committee of Lords' Interests should continue to be responsible for the adjudication of allegations relating to the conduct of peers and should be able to appoint an ad hoc investigator. It repeated the need for procedures with 'minimum requirements of fairness', set out by the Nicholls Committee and recommended that a peer who receives an adverse ruling should have a right of appeal to the Committee of Privileges. **8.34**

i. Implementation of the CSPL's recommendations

On 17 January 2001, the Leader of the House of Lords announced the setting up of a working group to assist the House in deciding how to proceed with the recommendations contained in the Report. The Working Group reported on 1 May 2001,[51] and accepted unanimously the CSPL's recommendations. On 2 July 2001, the House passed a resolution to adopt a new code. Minor amendments to the text were agreed on 24 July 2001[52] and The House of Lords Code of Conduct came into force on 31 March 2002.[53] **8.35**

C. The Executive

1. Introduction

The organization and regulation of the Executive is set out in Orders in Council which are an exercise of the Royal Prerogative. They have the force of law but are not normally scrutinized by Parliament and can be changed by the Council without reference to it. The CSPL concluded that in practice, Orders in Council allow the Executive to exercise authority largely without direct constraint, **8.36**

---

[50] See n 48 above.
[51] Working Group Report on Standards of Conduct in the House of Lords, HL 68 (2000–01).
[52] *Hansard*, HL, vol 688 col 630 (2 July 2001).
[53] It can be found at http://www.publications.parliament.uk/pa/ld/ldcond/ldcond.htm.

especially so far as the civil service is concerned. Accordingly, it recommended there should be a Civil Service Act, although debate on this continues.[54]

2. Ministers

8.37 'Ministers are at the heart of the Executive. They are accountable to Parliament and responsible for driving forward the Government's programme. Public confidence in their standards of conduct is crucial to delivering confidence in the Executive.[55] Ministers are not only leaders of the Executive, but regarded as leaders in public life. In order to maintain public trust and public confidence, they must lead by example.' The importance of this issue is illustrated by the fact that the CSPL considered the position of ministers in its First, Sixth, Ninth, and Tenth Reports.[56]

8.38 Although instances of misconduct by ministers are rare, they excite intense public interest when they occur. They are damaging to the government in which they arise and to the perception of government in general. Memories of them tend to linger long after the life of the Parliament in which they occur.[57] This highlights the need to develop mechanisms to regulate ministerial conduct.

i. The Ministerial Code

8.39 The conduct of ministers is governed by the Ministerial Code. The Code was first compiled in 1945, although some of its provisions are older.[58] Prior to 1997, it was known as the *Questions of Procedure for Ministers* (QPM). It is issued by the Prime Minister to ministerial colleagues at the start of every administration or on their appointment into office. The growth of ethical material in the QPM had grown largely as a result of specific incidents in much the same way as the statutory law of corruption. The QPM was first made public in 1992.

8.40 In its First Report,[59] the CSPL considered the existing guidance contained in the QPM was sound, but that it failed to provide a coherent set of principles of practical guidance. It recommended that the Prime Minister should

---

[54] CSPL, First Report, para 3.55 and Recommendation 30; CSPL, Ninth Report, *Defining the Boundaries within the Executive: Ministers, Special Advisers and the Permanent Civil Service*, Cm 5775, para 29. See 8.60 below.

[55] CSPL, Ninth Report, ch 5.1.

[56] CSPL, First Report, Cm 2850-1, ch.3; CSPL, Sixth Report, Cmd 4557-1, ch 4; CSPL, Ninth Report, Cm 5775, ch 5; Tenth Report, p 15.

[57] The CSPL's First Report referred to the number of instances of ministers having to resign following errors of judgment since the First World War (para 17). Well-known instances include the use of secret information in the Marconi affair in 1912; bribery in the Belcher scandal, which led to the Lynskey Tribunal in 1948; the Poulson affair, which led to the resignation of the Home Secretary, Reginald Maudling in 1976; and the acceptance of hospitality from Mohammed Al Fayed in the Neil Hamilton affair in 2000. See also 5.03 above.

[58] CSPL, First Report, para 3.8. Bradley and Ewing (n 18 above) 270.

[59] ibid.

commission a document extracting the ethical principles and rules it contained, or produce a free standing code.[60] It recommended that certain principles should be spelt out in the code, including the duty of ministers to ensure no conflict arises or appears to arise between their public duties and private interests, that they must not mislead Parliament or the public, and that they should avoid accepting gifts or hospitality which might, or might appear to, compromise their judgment or place them under an improper obligation.[61] It recommended that careful consideration be given to the means of investigating breaches of the Code, that the means should depend on the circumstances, and that advice from civil servants to ministers should not be made public. The Report also recommended that the first paragraph of the QPM should be amended to reflect the role of the Prime Minister in deciding whether a minister retains his or her confidence.[62]

ii. Acceptance of gifts and hospitality

The CSPL considered that the rule set out in the QPM stating that 'that no **8.41** Minister or public servant should accept gifts, hospitality or services from anyone which would, or might appear to, place him or her under an obligation', was an important one.[63] It considered recent cases in which ministers had accepted hospitality or had their travel costs paid, and recommended that departmental records of hospitality accepted by ministers in their official capacity should be maintained and that they should be made available on request. It also considered that ministers who accept hospitality on the basis of personal friendship, involving accommodation or holidays, 'or other significant cost' would be well advised to record that they had done so 'if they think that the failure to do so might otherwise be misunderstood or misrepresented'.[64] Such a record would supplement the requirement for ministers to declare in the Register of Members' Interests gifts above £125 in value, and hospitality if above £160 in value.[65]

iii. The Business Appointments Rules

The CSPL recommended that ministers should obtain leave from an Advisory **8.42** Board on Business Appointments before taking up business appointments after leaving office and that a system similar to the Civil Service Business Appointment Rules,[66] should apply to them. It recommended that an automatic waiting period of three months should apply for cabinet ministers, in line with permanent secretaries, after leaving office, but this should not apply to other ministers and whips. In cases where a further waiting period was recommended,

[60] ibid para 3.15. [61] ibid para 3.16.
[62] ibid, para 3.13: 'It will be for individual members to judge how best to act in order to uphold the highest standards. It will be for the Prime Minister to determine whether or not they have done so in any particular circumstance.' [63] ibid para 3.16.
[64] ibid para 3.40–41. [65] ibid, para 3.42. [66] ibid para 3.31.

it should be a maximum of two years. The CSPL recommended that the Advisory Board should act on an advisory basis and be administered by the existing Advisory Committee on Business Appointments.[67] The recommendation was made in an attempt to meet public concerns over, say, a minister accepting a board position with an enterprise over whose privatization he or she had presided during office. It was not intended as a punishment, but to allay public fears.[68]

iv. Implementation of recommendations in the First Report

8.43 The Government accepted the recommendations in the CSPL's First Report, in its formal response, entitled *The Government's Response to the First Report from the Committee for Standards in Public Life,*[69] published in July 1995. The existing code was revised and reissued by the Prime Minister, Tony Blair, in 1997 and entitled 'the Ministerial Code'. The Prime Minister provided a Foreword, thereby underlining its status as his document.[70] The Government did not accept the CSPL's text on the role of the Prime Minister and inserted a different formulation: 'It will be for individual ministers to judge how best to act in order to uphold the highest standards. They are responsible for justifying their conduct to Parliament and they can only remain in office for so long as they retain the Prime Minister's confidence'.[71]

8.44 Section 1 of the Code reminds ministers that they are expected to behave according to the highest standards of constitutional and personal conduct and are required to observe the nine principles of ministerial conduct set out in the Code. Under the current rules they must, on taking up office, resign from all company directorships and dispose of controlling interests in any company which could give rise to conflict.[72] In case of doubt, the Prime Minister must be informed and he is the final judge on the issue. Ministers are also reminded of their legal obligations, including their obligation under the Part V of the Criminal Justice Act 1993 against the use of unpublished price-sensitive information acquired by virtue of their office.

3. Investigating Allegations of Misconduct

8.45 In its Sixth Report,[73] the CSPL considered how the Prime Minister should investigate allegations of misconduct by ministers.[74] It decided against the

[67] ibid para 3.29.

[68] CSPL, First Report, paras 3.12–32. Para 52 of the Ministerial Code requires ministers to seek advice from the Advisory Committee on Business Appointments about any appointments they may wish to take up within two years of leaving office. On 30 October 2005, David Blunkett resigned as Works and Pensions Secretary after acknowledging that he had failed to consult the Committee before becoming an executive director of DNA Bioscience.

[69] Cm 2931.

[70] The Code is set out in full at http://www.Cabinet office.gov.uk/central/1997/mcode.

[71] CSPL, Sixth Report, para 4.7 (See also CSPL, First Report, paras 4.74–4.78).

[72] Ministerial Code para 1.1.

[73] CSPL, Sixth Report, Cm 4557-1.

[74] ibid paras 4.59–71.

appointment of an external adjudicator such as an ethics commissioner. It recommended that the Ministerial Code should be amended to make it clear that a minister, having had the advice of his or her Permanent Secretary on potential conflicts of interest, must take full responsibility for any subsequent decision.[75] However, it also recommended that the Prime Minister's formulation of his role should be amended to indicate that he is the ultimate judge of the requirements of the Code and the consequences for breach of it.[76]

Following a number of high profile cases, the CSPL reconsidered in its Ninth Report[77] the manner in which ministers were given guidance on conflicts of interest and how breaches were investigated. It considered that the Cabinet Secretary and Private Secretaries should no longer have the responsibility of giving such advice,[78] but that they should be advised by an Adviser on Ministerial Interests, who should be appointed by open competition. A minister, on taking office, would provide the adviser with a full list in writing of all his or her interests and the adviser would be responsible for maintaining a record of them and they would be published.[79] The CSPL considered that the ad hoc approach to investigating breaches of the Code should cease and should be replaced by the appointment of two or three individuals of senior standing at the beginning of each Parliament to carry out an investigation, should the Prime Minister consider one necessary. The findings of any investigation would be reported to the Prime Minister.[80] **8.46**

i. The Prime Minister's Office

In its Ninth Report, the CSPL also considered the organization of the Prime Minister's Office, having regard to its relevance to the boundaries between ministers, special advisers and the civil service, which it was investigating at that time.[81] Although the wider constitutional issues are outside the CSPL's terms of reference and the confines of this book, it is worthy of note that the CSPL did not consider that issues relating to standards of conduct should, in principle, prevent a Prime Minister from adapting his or her office to suit his or her own individual approach, provided it is done in a way that safeguards the boundaries between the three arms of government identified in its report. It considered that it should be for the government to decide on the overall distribution between departments of the number of special advisers approved by Parliament, but that **8.47**

[75] ibid Recommendation 11, para 4.58.

[76] ibid Recommendation 13, paras 4.74–4.79.

[77] CSPL, Ninth Report, Cm 5775, ch 9. [78] ibid, para 5.22.

[79] ibid 5.23–31. On 16 November 2005, Tony Blair, although not required to do so, declared in the Register of Members' Interests a record of his wife, Cherie Booth QC's earnings from a book on life at No 10, and from lecturing, 'to err on the side of caution and to be open and transparent', *The Times*, 17 November 2005.

[80] CSPL, Ninth Report, Cm 5775, paras 42–44. [81] ibid ch 9.

the Ministerial Code should be amended to make clear that the Prime Minister is personally accountable to Parliament for the management and discipline of his or her special advisers.[82] It also recommended that the most senior special adviser in the Prime Minister's Office should be responsible to the Prime Minister for ensuring that the day-to-day activities of special advisers appointed by the Prime Minister should comply with the Code of Conduct for Special Advisers[83] and that the existence of two special adviser posts in the Prime Minister's Office with executive powers should be a matter for Parliamentary debate and agreement.[84] It considered that special advisers with executive powers should not ask civil servants to do anything improper or illegal, or anything which might undermine the role and duties of permanent civil servants; undermine the political impartiality of civil servants or the duty of civil servants to give honest and impartial advice to Ministers; or have any role in the appraisal, reward, discipline, or promotion of permanent civil servants.

D. The Civil Service

1. Introduction

8.48 The departments of central government are staffed by administrative, professional, technical, and other officials, who constitute the civil service. They can serve successive governments and the requirement of political impartiality is an important part of their code of conduct.[85] Traditionally, they are regarded as appointed by the Royal Prerogative, although their terms of employment are regarded as legally enforceable.[86]

8.49 By the mid-nineteenth century, the civil service was well provided with codes of behaviour and detailed rules of conduct. From 1854 to the late 1960s, it developed greater uniformity and tighter control. In the 1980s the position was reversed with the establishment of executive agencies and the delegation of many management responsibilities. The question of standards was not much considered and pre-eminence was given to the need for efficiency and effectiveness.[87] In 1994, the Report of the Treasury and Civil Service Select Committee and the Government's White Paper, *Taking Forward Continuity and Change*,[88] endorsed the core values of the service but indicated that greater

[82] ibid Recommendation 29. [83] CSPL, Ninth Report, Recommendation 30.
[84] ibid Recommendation 31.
[85] AW Bradley and KD Ewing, *Constitutional and Administrative Law* (13th edn, London: Longman, 2003) 272.
[86] See *R v Civil Service Appeal Board, ex p Bruce* [1988] 3 All ER 686, 690.
[87] CSPL, First Report, 5.43.
[88] Treasury and Civil Service Committee, Fifth Report, House of Commons, Cmnd 2748, 199527, 1993–94.

vigilance was called for due to delegation and more movement in and out of the service. The White Paper recommended the establishment of a new senior civil service; a new handbook for agency chief executives; a new civil service code; and independent line of appeal for civil servants to the Civil Service Commissioners.[89]

2. The First Report

In its First Report in 1995, the CSPL concluded that standards of behaviour in the service remained high and that cases of outright corruption and fraud are rare.[90] It welcomed the introduction of a new Civil Service Code and recommended that it should be brought into immediate effect, subject to it being revised to cover the conduct of civil servants, who though not personally involved, are aware of wrongdoing or maladministration taking place. It also recommended changes to make appeals to the Civil Service Commissioners relating to the Code more effective and open, including a requirement that the Commissioners should report all successful appeals to Parliament. It recommended that the Cabinet Office should continue to survey and disseminate best practice on maintaining standards of conduct to ensure that the basic principles of conduct are being properly observed.[91] **8.50**

3. Implementation of the CSPL's Recommendations

The new Civil Service Code was published under the authority of the Civil Service Order in Council 1995, and formally incorporated in the Civil Servant Management Code as Chapter 4, Annex A. It was brought into operation in 1996.[92] **8.51**

The Code is a concise statement of the role and responsibilities of civil servants and includes a direct line of appeal to the Civil Service Commissioners, who are independent of government and responsible for the conduct and discipline of civil servants. Observance of the Code is monitored by the Cabinet Office. The Prime Minister is Minister for the Civil Service and is supported by the Head of the Home Civil Service. **8.52**

Chapter 4.1.1, Annex A of the Code declares that 'the constitutional and practical role of the Civil Service is with integrity, honesty, impartiality, and objectivity' to assist the government in formulating policies, carrying out decisions, and in administering the public services for which they are **8.53**

[89] See CSPL, First Report, para 3.47.

[90] Sir Richard Scott's Report on the sale of arms to Iraq was published in 1996.

[91] CSPL, First Report, paras 43–62.

[92] It was revised in 1999 and can be found on the Cabinet Office website http://www.cabinet-office.gov.uk/central/1999/cscode.htm.

responsible. Civil servants are required to give honest and impartial advice to ministers, to act according to law and to the principles set out in the Code, recognizing ethical standards governing particular professions.[93] They must not misuse their official position or information acquired in the course of their official duties to further their private interests or those of others, and they should not receive benefits of any kind from a third party which might reasonably be seen to compromise their personal judgment or integrity.[94] Where a civil servant believes he or she is being required to act in a way which is illegal, improper, or unethical, he or she should report the matter in accordance with procedures laid down in appropriate guidance or rules of conduct for his or her department or administration and must report evidence of criminal or unlawful activity by others. In the event of not receiving a reasonable response he or she may report the matter to the Civil Service Commissioners.[95]

i. Conduct: Standards of Propriety

8.54 Chapter 4.3, Annex A provides that departments and agencies must require their staff to report relevant business interests, and that unless the civil servant has fully disclosed the measure of his/her interest in the contract and senior management has given permission, they must not let contracts to:

(1) any civil servant in the department or agency;
(2) any partnership of which a civil servant in the department or agency is a member; or
(3) any company where a civil servant in the department or agency is a director, except as a nominee of the department or agency.

8.55 Chapter 4.3.3, Annex A provides that departments and agencies must not sell surplus government property to civil servants who have been able to get special knowledge about the condition of the goods because of their official duties; or have been officially associated with the disposal arrangements; or at a discount that would not otherwise be available. Departments and agencies must require staff to seek permission before accepting any outside employment which might affect their work either directly or indirectly and must make appropriate arrangements, which reflect the Business Appointments Rules and any local needs, for the handling of such requests.[96] Departments and agencies must inform staff of the circumstances in which they need to report offers of gifts, hospitality, awards, decorations or other benefits and of the circumstances in which they need to seek permission before accepting them. In drawing up such rules departments and agencies must draw attention of staff to the provisions of

[93] Civil Service Management Code, ch 4.1.4, Annex A.
[94] ibid ch 4.1.8, Annex A. See also Bradley and Ewing (n 85 above) 277.
[95] ibid ch 4.1.11, and 4.1.12, Annex A.
[96] ibid ch 4.3.4, Annex A.

the Prevention of Corruption Acts 1906 and 1916.[97] Breaches of the established procedures for the awarding of contracts and the disposal of surplus property are subject to investigation by the Comptroller and Auditor General who, if not satisfied with them, may report them to the Public Accounts Committee of the House of Commons.[98]

ii. The Business Appointments Rules

The Civil Service Management Code requires civil servants to seek advice from the Advisory Committee of Business Appointments before taking up a business appointment after leaving office.[98] The Committee is appointed by the Prime Minister and comprises persons with experience of the relationships between the civil service and the private sector.[100] Applications for approval must be made by civil servants: **8.56**

- if they are in the Senior Civil Service in salary band 4 or above and in a post attracting a minimum job evaluation for senior posts score of 13; or if they are specialists or special advisers of equivalent standing; or
- if they have had any official dealings with their respective employer during the last two years of Crown employment; or
- if they have had official dealings of a continued or repeated nature with their prospective employer at any time during their period of Crown employment; or
- if they have had access to commercially sensitive information of competitors of their prospective employer in the course of their official duties; or
- if their official duties during the last two years of Crown employment have involved advice or decisions benefiting the prospective employer, for which the offer of employment could be interpreted as a reward, or have involved developing policy, knowledge of which might be of benefit to the prospective employer; or
- if they are employed on a consultancy basis either for a firm of consultants or as an independent or self-employed consultant and they have had any dealings of a commercial nature with outside bodies or organizations in the last two years of Crown employment.[101]

Approval is required for the initial appointment; and any further appointment within two years of leaving Crown employment.[102] The rules do not apply to unpaid appointments in non-commercial organizations, appointments in the **8.57**

[97] ibid ch 4.3.5, Annex A. [98] The Government Resources and Accounts Act 2000, s 6.
[99] Civil Service Management Code, chs 4.3.7–4.3.12, Annex A.
[100] ibid ch 4.3.2, Annex A. [101] ibid, ch 4.3.7, Annex A.
[102] ibid ch 4.3.9, Annex A.

gift of ministers; or in the case of part-time staff, appointments held with the department's or agency's agreement while they were civil servants.[103]

8.58 Staff on secondment from the civil service to other organizations, are subject to the rules in the same way as other civil servants. Staff on secondment to the civil service from other organizations, are also subject to the rules, unless they return to their seconding organization at the end of the secondment and remain there for two years. Special advisers are subject to the rules in the same way as other civil servants unless they are offered a post by the same employer which they left on being appointed as advisers and remain there for two years.[104] The rules do not apply to special advisers appointed before 1 April 1996 on terms exempting them from the rules, unless they have volunteered to be subject to them.[105]

iii. Civil servants and lobbyists

8.59 In 1998, following the 'cash for questions' affair, new guidelines were issued relating to civil servants' contacts with lobbyists. Before that, there were no rules governing civil servants' contact with lobbyists. The guidelines adopt the approach adopted by the CSPL in its First Report, that lobbyists are a feature of our democratic system and access should be permitted, but controlled.[106] The CSPL's First Report recommended the rules be strengthened.[107]

iv. The CSPL's Sixth and Ninth Reports

8.60 In March 1999, the Government published a White Paper entitled *Modernising Government*, and in December 1999, Sir Richard Wilson, Cabinet Secretary and Head of the Home Civil Service, reported to the Prime Minister on civil service reform. In its Sixth Report the CSPL recognized that the report demonstrated the Government's commitment to changing the civil service, but it considered that the Government should give greater priority to putting the Civil Service Code on a statutory footing. It stated that a Civil Service Act had for too long been heralded and a timetable should be produced as soon as possible.

8.61 The CSPL was concerned that more recruitment from outside the civil service by using short-term contracts might affect the public service ethos and recommended that those coming in from outside the service should be given training and induction opportunities at which ethical issues within the public sector are examined and explained. It recommended that a central or local record of invitations and offers of hospitality should be kept in all departments and agencies and clear rules of when to accept hospitality. It also recommended that the Business Appointment Rules should be amended so that when an appointment had been taken up the Advisory Committee on Business

[103] ibid ch 4.3.8, Annex A. [104] Civil Service Management Code, ch 4.12, Annex A.
[105] ibid. [106] Cm 280-1, 1995, para 72.
[107] CSPL, First Report, Recommendation 28.

Appointments should give reasons for its decision. It also suggested that special advisers should be subject to the business appointment rules.[108]

In its Ninth Report, the CSPL repeated its call to the Government to put the civil service on a statutory footing and recommended reinforcement of independent scrutiny of the maintenance of the core values, by giving the Civil Service Commissioners power to investigate on their own initiative. It recommended that the Government should actively establish a register of departmental nominated officers to whom civil servants may go if they believe that they are being required to act in a way which is inconsistent with the Civil Service Code, and that the Commissioners should establish and maintain contacts with the departmental nominated officers. It stated that departments should report the number of appeals they handle under the Code to the Civil Service Commissioners so that the Commissioners can publish figures in their annual report. **8.62**

The CSPL made a further call for a Civil Service Act in its 2004 Annual Report. In response the Government reaffirmed its acceptance in principle of the case for a Civil Service Act and undertook to publish a draft Bill for consultation. On 5 January 2004, the Public Administration Select Committee published a draft Bill reflecting many of the recommendations in the Ninth Report. Shortly after this, Lord Lester introduced a similar draft Bill in the House of Lords. On 15 November 2004, the Government published its own draft Civil Service Bill for consultation, which included many, if not all the Committee's recommendations.[109] **8.63**

4. Special Advisers

Special advisers are appointed on the authority of Article 3 of the Civil Service Order in Council 1995. They are temporary civil servants and are appointed personally by ministers to advise and assist them mainly on party political matters, but also on other matters where their exceptional skills and experience are of value. They are required to act in conformity with the Civil Service Code[110] and the Seven Principles of Public Life.[111] They are not subject to the general civil service obligation to be objective and impartial and they are able to represent ministers' views on government policy to the media with a degree of political commitment.[112] Their employment ceases when the administration ends. **8.64**

Article 3.3 of the Civil Service Order in Council 1995, allows the Prime Minister to appoint up to three special advisers at No 10. By means of a 1997 amendment to the Civil Service Order in Council 1995, three special advisers in the Prime **8.65**

[108] CSPL, Sixth Report, para 69.
[109] *A Draft Civil Service Bill: A Consultation Document*, November 2004, Cm 6373.
[110] Civil Service Management Code, ch 4, Annex A.
[111] See 8.01 above
[112] Code of Conduct for Special Advisers, para 8.

Minister's Office are permitted to have executive powers.[113] The increase in numbers of them since 1995 and the high public profile of some of them have generated a debate about their function, about whether they should be paid out of public funds, and about how they should be regulated.[114]

8.66 There is a Model Contract for special advisers, as required by the Employment Rights Act 1991. This provides that special advisers must not ask a civil servant to do anything inconsistent with the Code and that the Business Appointment Rules apply to them. Responsibility for their conduct rests with the minister who appoints them. The CSPL considered the position of special advisers in its Sixth and Ninth Reports. In its Sixth Report, the CSPL acknowledged the valuable function of special advisers, but considered that the increase in their numbers should be subject to public scrutiny, that there should be a statutory limit on their numbers, and that a Special Advisers Code should be issued, replacing the Civil Service Code and the Model Contract.[115]

8.67 In its Ninth Report, the CSPL recommended that special advisers should be separated out as a category of government servant distinct from the civil service.[116] It recommended the use of statute to set out what special advisers can do, including that they should not undermine the impartiality of civil servants or have any role in their appraisal, reward, discipline or promotion. The CSPL recommended that a Code of Conduct for Special Advisers should continue to list the type of work special advisers may do if their ministers request it and that the Ministerial Code should make clear that ministers are personally accountable for the management and discipline of their special advisers

E. Local Government, Quangos, and Local Spending Bodies

1. Local Government in England, Scotland, and Wales

i. The CSPL's Third Report

8.68 In July 1997, the CSPL published its Third Report, in which it considered the rules regulating local government.[117] At that time the conduct of councillors was subject to the National Code of Local Government Conduct, which was first proposed and drafted in the 1970s by the Redcliffe-Maude Committee on Local Government Rules of Conduct[118] and was revised in 1990, following the Widdicombe Committee of Inquiry into Local Authority Business. The

[113] ibid para 15. [114] ibid para 16.
[115] Code of Conduct for Special Advisers, para 17.
[116] CSPL, Ninth Report, Recommendation 15.
[117] CM 3702-1. *Standards of Conduct in Local Government in England, Scotland and Wales.*
[118] See para 5.10 above.

Code has statutory status, and was approved by resolution of each House of Parliament.

The Code laid down standards of conduct for councillors and included such matters as when to declare pecuniary and non-pecuniary interests, when to seek advice from officers, and related issues. Every councillor had to sign the Code and confirm that he understood its contents. Failure to observe the Code's requirements could result in criminal prosecution and in most cases a surcharge imposed by the District Auditor with or without disqualification from office. The Code of Conduct for Officers was issued by the Local Government Management Board, together with the local authority associations. In addition, in recent years auditors have been given additional powers to issue prohibition notices, preventing councils from undertaking activities which they consider to be unlawful, and to seek judicial review of decisions with financial implications which they consider may be unlawful. **8.69**

The CSPL said that it had found local government to be far more constrained by rules than any other part of the public sector and warned that attempting to enforce good conduct through detailed rules could itself contribute to wrongdoing.[119] Over the years, statutory and non-statutory arrangements for codes, registers, and declaration of interests, as well as the punishment of misconduct had grown into a confused, and confusing, mixture where lack of clarity could easily lead to wrongdoing. As a result, the CSPL stated, it was unsurprising that a lack of clarity over standards of conduct persisted in local government. Despite some instances of corruption and impropriety, it concluded that the vast majority of councillors observed high standards of conduct. **8.70**

The CSPL called for 'a radical change in the way in which local government operates'. It recommended a fundamental restructuring of the framework of standards of discipline for councillors and officers by replacing the National Code of Local Government Conduct with individual codes tailored to the needs of each council; abolition of the surcharge; and new rules on registration and declaration of interests. Its object was to achieve clarity about standards of conduct at the same time as giving greater responsibility to local government itself for devising and regulating those standards in local government. **8.71**

The CSPL recommended: **8.72**

(1) a clearer framework for developing and enforcing ethical behaviour within local government;
(2) involvement of the courts in imposing penalties for misconduct;
(3) following consultation, a new statutory offence of misuse of public office;

[119] 'A lack of clarity can easily lead to wrongdoing'; Lord Nolan's letter to the Prime Minister, accompanying the CSPL's Third Report.

(4) in the longer term, the abolition of surcharge;
(5) greater clarity in the rules relating to planning, with special focus on planning gain and councils granting themselves planning permission; and
(6) improved rules on whistle-blowing, and wider access to council complaints and whistle-blowing procedures.

8.73 The CSPL also recommended:

(1) that representatives of local government should prepare a Model Code of Conduct for Local Councillors, to be approved by Parliament;
(2) that each local authority should adopt a local code of conduct which incorporates and reflects the general principles and achieves at least the same effect as the approved model code;
(3) that there should be a public register of interests covering the pecuniary interests of councillors, close family members, and members of their households, and non-pecuniary interests which relate to their service on bodies with which the council is associated;
(4) that each council should have a Standards Committee to deal with matters of propriety and to have powers to recommend to the full council that errant members should be disciplined;
(5) that new Local Government Tribunals should be created to act as independent arbiters on matters relating to the codes and to hear appeals from councillors and others;
(6) that the courts should be involved in imposing penalties for misconduct; and
(7) that following consultation, the surcharge should be replaced by a new statutory offence of misuse of public office.

8.74 The CSPL found it particularly unsatisfactory that the District Auditor should not only formulate and prosecute the case against individual councillors but should also determine guilt or innocence and determine the penalty on the basis of his own calculation of financial loss. The inequity of such a system, and the hardship it could produce, unique to local councillors, had been pointed out to the CSPL from the beginning of its deliberations; not the least of its shortcomings being the disincentive it provided for people to volunteer to serve as local councillors. In the CSPL's view, the courts should be involved in imposing penalties for misconduct.

ii. Implementation of the CSPL's recommendations

8.75 In 1998, the Government published a Green Paper entitled *Modernising Local Government—A New Ethical Framework*,[120] setting out measures for taking forward the proposals. In July 1998, it was followed by a White Paper entitled

[120] A publication of the then Department of the Environment, Transport and the Regions.

Modern Local Government, in Touch with the People.[121] Draft legislation was published by consultation in March 1999, in a document entitled *Local Leadership, Local Choice.*[122] The Local Government Act 2000 finally received Royal Assent in July 2000.

As responsibility for local government in Scotland and Wales had been devolved since the CSPL Report, the Local Government Act 2000 only covers local government in England. However, it empowers the Welsh administration to regulate its authorities along similar lines to those in England. The Scottish Parliament has passed the Ethical Standards in Public Life etc (Scotland) Act 2000, which also received Royal Assent in July 2000. **8.76**

2. Quangos[123](Executive NDPBs and NHS bodies)

In its First Report, the CSPL recommended that the ultimate responsibility for appointments to Executive Non-Departmental Public Bodies and National Health Service Bodies should remain with ministers[124] and that all appointments should be governed by the overriding principle of appointment on merit.[125] In order to meet public concerns as to whether appointments were being unduly influenced by party political considerations; whether there was sufficient openness in appointments and the proceedings of quangos; and whether enough was being done to maintain standards of propriety,[126] it recommended that a new independent Commissioner for Public Appointments should be appointed and that this unit should be taken out of the Cabinet Office.[127] **8.77**

It also recommended that the Government should undertake a review in order to produce a more consistent legal framework governing propriety and accountability in public bodies; in other words, a complete overhaul.[128] It recommended that the Treasury should review the arrangements for external audit of public bodies[129] and that the Audit Commission should be authorized to publish public interest reports on NHS bodies at its own discretion.[130] **8.78**

3. Local Spending Public Bodies

The CSPL's Second Report published in May 1996 considered the position of local spending public bodies (LSPBs).[131] Their common characteristics are the use of taxpayers' money to provide public services, mainly to local communities, and that they are subject to special regulation. The Report made fifty detailed **8.79**

[121] Cm 4014. [122] Cm 4298.
[123] Quasi-autonomous non-governmental organizations.
[124] CSPL, First Report, para 4.29. [125] ibid para 4.35. [126] ibid para 4.1.
[127] ibid paras 4.53, 4.57. [128] ibid para 4.81. [128] ibid para 4.109.
[130] ibid para 4.105.
[131] CSPL, Second Report, *Local Public Spending Bodies*, Cm 3270-1.

recommendations about standards of governance, accountability, and propriety in them: It recommended that the principles of good practice in the First Report should be applied to them with modifications. It dealt with Further and Higher Education Bodies (including universities), Grant Maintained Schools, Training and Enterprise Councils, Local Enterprise Companies and Registered Housing Associations, all of which are 'not for profit' organizations whose members are rarely elected, or appointed by ministers. They provide public services usually delivered at a local level, and are largely or wholly publicly funded.

8.80 Consideration of issues relating to corruption do not form a direct part of the Second Report, but it does contain recommendations on the adoption of codes of conduct based on the Seven Principles of Public Life,[132] appointments procedures, openness, training, and whistle-blowing, all of which were included in the First Report. The Second Report states that the standards set out in the First Report should be applied in full to the bodies covered in the study, recognizing that 'practice needs to be proportional to the size and adapted to the nature of these bodies.'[133]

8.81 In February 1997 the Government published a White Paper entitled *The Governance of Public Bodies: a Progress Report*[134] in response to the Report. The main body of the White Paper picked up some of the recommendations, others were left to be dealt with by sectoral responses. In 1997, the CSPL received the implementation of the recommendations in its Fourth Report. Since the Second Report had been published, responsibility for the local spending bodies in Scotland and Wales had been devolved, training and enterprise councils had ceased to exist, and housing associations are now known as registered social landlords. The Committee may revisit the recommendations when the new organizations have become established.

8.82 The Committee made it clear that it would review the effect of its recommendations from each of its reports from time to time. The first of these reviews, published in November 1997, covered national executive quangos, NHS bodies, and local public spending bodies. The review noted that all of the substantial recommendations relating to these bodies in its first two reports had been accepted and that the funding and regulatory bodies had worked to implement them.[135]

8.83 But there were a number of areas where considerably more work needed to be done. There were a number of points of weakness, primarily relating to the way in which standards of conduct and whistle blowing procedures were communicated to staff, and understood by them and there was evidence that

[132] CSPL, Second Report, *Local Public Spending Bodies* Cm 3270–1 paras 29–44.
[133] ibid Introduction, para 5. [134] Cm 3557.
[135] http://www.archive.official-dcuments.co.uk/document/caboff/nolan4/nolan/htm.

some sectors or individual organisations were implementing the recommendations slowly. The Committee was also concerned about the way its recommendations on appointment on merit had been interpreted by some departments. It stressed the importance of the principle of 'proportionality'—procedure appropriate to the nature of the post and the size and weight of its responsibilities.[136]

F. The Judiciary

1. Introduction

It is an essential element of a democratic society that its judiciary should be, and be seen to be, institutionally and individually independent of the legislative and executive arms of government and that judges should be impartial, in that they are free from bias, whether arising by conflict of interest or otherwise. Although in the United Kingdom, the public tend to accept that judges are independent and impartial subject to any inherent prejudices, the separation of powers has not been formally observed. The executive, that is the government, is drawn exclusively from members of the legislature, the Lord Chancellor sits in Parliament, is a government minister, and until recently also sat as a judge.[137] Similarly, until recently, there had been no move towards the adoption of any code or guide of ethics for judges. **8.84**

Corrupt judges were not uncommon in England in the thirteenth century and there were some examples as late as the eighteenth century,[138] but there have been no reported cases of judicial corruption in the United Kingdom in modern times. The reason is probably because in the United Kingdom judges are recruited from a strong and independent legal profession, they are properly remunerated and not exposed to temptation. The position is different in developing countries, where judicial corruption remains a serious problem. **8.85**

2. International Initiatives

i. The UN Basic Principles on the Independence of the Judiciary

The importance of judicial independence was recognized in 1985 when the UN General Assembly endorsed *The UN Basic Principles on the Independence of the Judiciary*, which require the independence of the judiciary to be guaranteed by the State and enshrined in a country's Constitution or law, and impose a duty **8.86**

[136] Cm 4413.

[137] See J Hatchard, M Ndulo, and P Slinn, *Comparative Constitutionalism and Good Governance in the Commonwealth: An Eastern and Southern African Perspective*, Cambridge, Cambridge University Press, 2004, Ch 1.

[138] See para 2.13 above.

on all governmental institutions and other institutions to respect and observe the judiciary's independence.[139]

8.87 The Principles require the judiciary to decide matters before them impartially. There must no interference with the judicial process, and judicial decisions must not be subject to revision other than by judicial review, or mitigation, or computation by competent authorities of sentences imposed by the judiciary, in accordance with law. It is also the duty of each Member State to provide adequate resources to enable the judiciary to properly perform its functions. Yet judicial independence does not mean that members of the judiciary are unaccountable for their actions, and increasingly attention is being given to the development and adoption by judiciaries of codes of ethics and conduct as a means of ensuring the accountability of judges.[140]

ii. The Bangalore Principles

8.88 In February 2000, the International Commission of Jurists Centre for the Independence of Judges and Lawyers convened an Expert Group in Geneva, drawn from fourteen countries, to address the issue of judicial corruption. The Group agreed on *The Policy Framework for Preventing and Eliminating Corruption and Ensuring the Impartiality of the Judicial System*. A principal element of the *Policy Framework* was an enforceable statement of judicial ethics.

8.89 In the same year, following discussions initiated by Transparency International, eight chief justices responded positively to a suggestion that a small 'Leadership Group' should be established to address the issue of judicial accountability. In April 2000, the UN Centre for International Crime Prevention invited chief justices from eight countries in Asia and Africa to formulate a concept of judicial accountability which would be of practical effect and have the potential to impact positively on the standard of judicial conduct and raise the level of public confidence in the rule of law. The Leadership Group, has ever since been referred to as *The Judicial Group on Strengthening Judicial Integrity*.[141]

8.90 At its first meeting, *The Judicial Group* agreed that national judiciaries need to assume an active role in strengthening judicial integrity by effecting systemic

[139] The Principles on the Judiciary were adopted by the Seventh UN Congress on the Prevention of Crime and the Treatment of Offenders, held in Milan from 26 August to 6 October 1985 and endorsed by General Assembly Resolutions 40/32 of 29 November 1985 and 40/146 of 13 December 1985.

[140] *Parliamentary Supremacy and Judicial Independence: A Commonwealth Approach*. J Hatchard and P Slinn (eds) (London: Cavendish Publishing Ltd, 1999); *Commonwealth (Latimer House) Principles on the Accountability of and Relationship between the Three Branches of Government*, Commonwealth Secretariat, CPA, CLEA, CMJA, and CLA, April 2004.

[141] The Group included the chief justices of Australia, Bangladesch, Canada, India, Nepal, Nigeria, South Africa, Sri Lanka, Tanzania, and Uganda under the chairmanship of Judge Weeramantry, Vice-President of the International Court of Justice. Justice Michael Kirby of the High Court of Australia, was rapporteur.

reform. It acknowledged the need for a universally acceptable statement of judicial standards, capable of being enforced by the judiciary without the intervention of the legislature or the executive branches of government, and requested that existing codes of conduct should be analysed and a report prepared to consider whether the codes were suitable for adoption elsewhere.

At its second meeting in Bangalore in February 2001, *The Judicial Group* adopted the text of a statement of judicial standards, *The Bangalore Draft of a Code of Judicial Conduct*. The draft identified seven core values: propriety, independence, integrity, impartiality, equality, competence, and diligence, and accountability. Like many of the codes *The Judicial Group* examined,[142] the Draft included detailed provisions relating to judges and their families receiving gifts or favours in connection with the performance of the judges' official duties and other conduct which might give rise to an appearance of partiality. *The Judicial Group* also agreed that a national plan of action to combat corruption in the judiciary should be adopted in each of the participating countries by diagnosing systemic weaknesses in judicial systems, through the use of surveys and case audits and with the assistance of court users and other stakeholders. When the *Bangalore Principles of Judicial Conduct*, as they are now known, were adopted at the Round Table Meeting of Chief Justices held at the Peace Palace in the Hague, Judge Weeramantry described it as 'a significant step towards making judges accountable for their conduct'.[143] On 25 April 2003, the member states of the UN Commission on Human Rights endorsed the *Bangalore Principles of Judicial Conduct* at its Fifty-Ninth Session in Geneva. **8.91**

iii. The Limassol Colloquium

In June 2002, Commonwealth judicial officers, including heads of judiciary representing twenty-three jurisdictions, held a colloquium in Limassol, Cyprus, sponsored by the Commonwealth Secretariat and Commonwealth Magistrates and Judges Association, to consider how best the judiciary could contribute to the goals of eliminating corruption and promoting high ethical standards in the court system. The Colloquium welcomed the Heads of Government commitment to the Commonwealth Framework and recommended the adoption of guidelines on judicial ethics as a means of underpinning the integrity of the formulation of national strategies aimed at eliminating conflicts of interest and corrupt practices. It urged all national and international legal professional organizations within the Commonwealth to promote anti-corruption programmes for the legal profession. It called for sufficient resources for the courts; and for the process of appointment of judges to respect the principle of separation of powers and reflect the principles of transparency, competitiveness, **8.92**

[142] See, eg, the codes for Canada, East Caribbean Supreme Court, Guyana, Nigeria, and Uganda.

[143] Transparency International, Press Release, 25 April 2003.

and merit; and expressed the view that judicial training programmes should be available on ethical and corruption issues.[144]

3. Constitutional Reform in the United Kingdom

8.93 In a speech to the Labour Party Conference on 4 October 1994, Tony Blair stated that his Party's programme of constitutional reform was 'the biggest programme of change to democracy ever proposed'. The programme included the modernisation of political institutions, particularly the Houses of Parliament, civil service and local government.

i. The Constitutional Reform Act 2005

8.94 In July 2003, the Government announced radical plans to reform the judicial system. These included abolishing the office of Lord Chancellor and transferring his powers to a Secretary of State for Constitutional Affairs, making the Lord Chief Justice head of the judiciary,[145] abolishing the system of Law Lords sitting in the House of Lords, and replacing it by a separate Supreme Court. A Judicial Appointments Commission was to be established which would make appointments itself or nominate candidates to a responsible minister.

8.95 The newly formed Department for Constitutional Affairs issued consultation papers on 14 July 2003.[146] The Constitutional Reform Bill was unveiled in the Queen's Speech in November 2003. The following month Lord Falconer, the Lord Chancellor, in a speech to the Institute for Public Policy Research, announced that judges were to have their independence enshrined in law and that the statutory right to judicial independence was likely to be enforced by the Secretary of State for Constitutional Affairs. He said judicial independence is 'too important to this country to be left unspecified, un-codified and unwritten', 'we want to guarantee judicial independence and that is what we are going to do explicitly'. His proposal was supported by the judiciary and the legal profession.

---

[144] The Colloquium also recorded its support in principle for the *Latimer House Guidelines on Parliamentary Supremacy and Judicial Independence* and their footnotes as they relate to the judiciary, which have since been endorsed in distilled form by Commonwealth Heads of Government at their Meeting in Abuja, Nigeria, in December 2003, as the *Commonwealth (Latimer House) Principles on the Accountability of and Relationship between the Three Branches of Government.*

[145] It had been agreed that irrespective of the outcome of the Bill, the arrangements agreed in January 2004 between the Government and the Lord Chief Justice, which have become known as the 'Concordat' and by which the Lord Chief Justice becomes head of the judiciary, should be implemented by legislation. Several amendments were made to the Bill to ensure that the terms of the Concordat are fulfilled.

[146] Constitutional Reform: CP10/03, a new way of appointing judges and CP11/03, a Supreme Court for the United Kingdom, published by the Department for Constitutional Affairs, July 2003, setting out the options for achieving this to which the Committee responded (The Chair's letter to the DCA November 2003 available at www.public-standards.gov.uk.)

The Bill was introduced to the House of Lords on 24 February 2004.[147] Some of its provisions, particularly the proposal to abolish the office of Lord Chancellor, were controversial and the House of Lords made amendments to it. The House accepted the provisions relating to the Judicial Appointments Commission and the end of the Lord Chancellor's active judicial role in judicial appointments. **8.96**

The Bill was introduced to the House of Commons on 21 December 2004 and received the Royal Assent on 24 March 2005. As at 1 October 2005, no commencement orders have been made. The final Act retains the office of Lord Chancellor, although the Lord Chancellor's role in relation to the judiciary is greatly reduced. **8.97**

ii. The rule of law

The 2005 Act expressly provides that its provisions do not adversely affect (a) the existing constitutional principle of the rule of law, or (b) the Lord Chancellor's existing constitutional role in relation to that principle.[148] It reforms the office of Lord Chancellor, transferring his judicial functions to a President of the Courts of England and Wales. The Lord Chief Justice becomes President of the Courts of England and Wales. He is responsible for the training, guidance and deployment of judges and it is his duty to represent the views of the judiciary of England and Wales to Parliament and ministers.[149] **8.98**

iii. Judicial independence

The 2005 Act enshrines in law a duty on government ministers to uphold the independence of the judiciary. Ministers are expressly barred from trying to influence judicial decisions through any special access to judges.[150] The Lord Chancellor is required to have regard to (a) the need to defend that independence; (b) the need for members of the judiciary to have the support necessary for them to be able to exercise their functions; and (c) the need for the public interest in regard to matters relating to the judiciary or otherwise to the administration of justice to be properly represented in decisions affecting those matters. Section 4 guarantees the continued independence of the judiciary of Northern Ireland. **8.99**

iv. The Supreme Court

The 2005 Act establishes a new, independent Supreme Court, separate from the House of Lords, with a President, Deputy President, and Justices. The Court will have its own independent appointments system, its own staff and budget, and, ultimately, its own building.[151] **8.100**

147 *Hansard* HL, vol 658, col 120 (24 February 2004).
148 Constitutional Reform Act 2005, Pt 2, ss 2–22.
149 ibid Pt 1, s 1.
150 ibid Pt 2, ss 3–7.
151 ibid Pt 3, ss 23–30.

8.101 The first members of the Court are to be the present members of the Judicial Committee of the House of Lords. In the case of a vacancy, the Lord Chancellor convenes a selection commission which makes a selection and reports to the Lord Chancellor, who notifies the Prime Minister, who recommends the appointment to The Queen.[152] Provision is made for acting judges and a supplementary panel.[153] A justice of the Supreme Court holds office during good behaviour but may be removed on the address of both Houses of Parliament.[154] A chief executive, who is appointed by the Lord Chancellor after consulting the President, must ensure the Court's resources are used to provide an efficient and effective system to support the Court in carrying out its business.[155] The existing Supreme Court of England and Wales is re-named the Senior Courts of England and Wales.[156]

v. The Judicial Appointments Commission

8.102 The Act establishes an independent Judicial Appointments Commission responsible for selecting candidates to be recommended for judicial appointment to the Secretary of State for Constitutional Affairs.[157] It contains detailed provisions for the appointment of the Commission and its functions,[158] the appointment and disciplining of judges,[159] and for a Judicial Appointments and Conduct Ombudsman.[160] Appointments are required to be made solely on merit[161] and the Judicial Appointments Commission is required to have regard to diversity.[162] Since 2003, the Department for Constitutional Affairs has been striving to boost the representation of women, ethnic minorities, and the disabled amongst judges and to widen the pool of condidates in order to obtain a judiciary that more visibly reflects contemporary society.

4. The Guide to Judicial Conduct in England and Wales

8.103 The adoption of written codes of judicial ethics throughout the world and the endorsement of the *Bangalore Principles* in April 2003 by the UN Human Rights Commission in Geneva, indicated that a written code for judges in England and Wales was overdue. In November 2002, a paper entitled 'Guidelines on Judicial Ethics', drafted under the auspices of the Judicial Studies Board, was placed before the Judges' Council. The Council set up a working group under Lord Justice Pill, then senior presiding judge, which after consultation produced Guidelines to Judicial Conduct. The final draft was presented to the Lord Chancellor and was published by the Council. Lord Woolf, the Lord Chief Justice, in his Foreword to the Guide emphasized that

[152] ibid s 26 and Sch 8. [153] Constitutional Reform Act 2005, Pt 3, ss 38 and 39.
[154] ibid s 33. [155] ibid s 51. [156] ibid s 59(1). [157] ibid Pt 4, ss 61–122.
[158] ibid ss 63–107 and Sch 12. [159] ibid ss 61–122. [160] ibid s 62 and Sch 13.
[161] ibid s 63. [162] ibid s 64.

the Guidelines recognized that the responsibilites and perception to which judges should adhere were continuously evolving and that they would have to evolve to keep up with the changes. He added that although the Guide was primarily aimed at professional full- and part-time judges, it would be a valuable tool in assisting judges to deal with difficult ethical problems. He hoped that although important requirements as to conduct were set out in each member of the judiciary's terms of appointment, the Guide would be of assistance to all the judiciary, including lay magistrates and members of tribunals.

The Guide acknowledges the efforts of Commonwealth countries to produce **8.104**
guides to judicial conduct, particularly a seminal study by Mr Justice Thomas, a judge of the Supreme Court of Queensland, *Judicial Ethics in Australia* (1988); the Canadian Judicial Council's *Ethical Principles for Judges* (1988); *A Guide to Judicial Conduct*, published for the Council of Chief Justices of Australia (2002); and *A Code for Judicial Officers* of the Federal Republic of Nigeria.

The Guide is designed to provide guidance to judges and to afford the judiciary **8.105**
a framework for regulating judicial conduct and to assist members of the executive and the legislature, lawyers, and the public in general to better understand and support the judiciary. It states that judicial independence is a prerequisite to the rule of law and a fundamental guarantee of a fair trial. A judge shall therefore uphold and exemplify judicial independence in both its individual and institutional aspects.

The Guide acknowledges and gives due weight to the six values set out the **8.106**
Bangalore Principles of Judicial Conduct, namely:

(1) Judicial independence is a prerequisite to the rule of law and a fundamental guarantee of a fair trial. A judge shall therefore uphold and exemplify judicial independence in both its individual and institutional aspects.
(2) Impartiality is essential to the proper discharge of the judicial office. It applies not only to the decision itself but also to the process by which the decision is made.
(3) Integrity is essential to the proper discharge of the judicial office.
(4) Propriety, and the appearance of propriety, are essential to the performance of the judicial office.
(5) Ensuring equality of treatment to all before the courts is essential to the due performance of the judicial office
(6) Competence and diligence are prerequisites to the due performance of the judicial office.

The Guide states that the concept of judicial independence is another aspect of **8.107**
judicial integrity and judicial impartiality and that there is substantial overlap between the principles relevant to the values. It emphasizes that it must be read

against the background of the memorandums and conditions of appointment accepted by the judge on taking up office and that the primary responsibility for deciding whether an activity is appropriate rests with the individual judge.

8.108 Sections 1 to 6 consider the general principles (1) to (6) listed above with some discussion as to their effect including, in section 2 (Judicial Independence) and section 3 (Impartiality) issues relating to the interests of a judge or his family in the outcome of a case in which the judge may be involved as a judge, including his abstention from any kind of political activity. Section 5 (Propriety) considers the need for a judge not to allow the his family, social, or other relationships to influence his judicial conduct, nor to use or allow confidential information acquired by him in his judicial capacity to be used for any purpose not related to his judicial duties. It also includes guidance on the receipt of gifts or favours by a judge in connection with the performance of his judicial duties and his obligation not knowingly to permit court staff to receive gifts or favours in contravention of the guidance.

8.109 Sections 7 to 9 of the Guide consider a number of specific problems that a judge may have to consider including personal relations and perceived bias; activities outside court; gifts, hospitality, and social activities; and conduct after retirement including return to practice and appointment as an arbitrator.

8.110 The Guide as a whole and the sections specifying the ethical problems likely to be encountered by judges are yet another illustration of the manner in which guides and codes of practice are being employed to support legislation relating to the conduct of persons in public life.

9

INTERNATIONAL AND REGIONAL INITIATIVES

A. Introduction

9.01 The last ten years have seen a plethora of international and regional anti-corruption initiatives that culminated in the United Nations Convention Against Corruption (UNCAC). This came into force on 14 December 2005. The Convention seeks to build upon the earlier multilateral anti-corruption instruments and in its Preamble notes these instruments 'with appreciation'.[1] The purpose of this chapter is to provide an overview of UNCAC and other international and regional initiatives and to consider the main threads making up the international response to corruption.

1. The Importance of International and Regional Initiatives

9.02 Corruption is a problem that, particularly in its most serious manifestation, often contains a transnational element. International and regional initiatives can help to encourage countries to harmonize their anti-corruption measures and policies, and are potentially more politically acceptable in that it may be reassuring to know that neighbouring states are experiencing similar problems and that joint action is therefore appropriate. Because of its transnational nature, it is also important that the fight against corruption involves the strengthening of international and regional cooperation as well as the sharing of experiences and resources.

2. Developing Appropriate Strategies

9.03 Corruption is a multifaceted problem that requires a range of legal and non-legal strategies. This is reflected in the international and regional instruments which offer a comprehensive set of standards designed to make corrupt practices

[1] Those specifically noted are: the Inter-American Convention against Corruption, the Convention on the Fight against Corruption involving Officials of the European Union, the OECD Convention on the Bribery of Foreign Public Officials in International Business Transactions, the Council of Europe Criminal Law Convention on Corruption and Civil Law, and the African Union Convention on Preventing and Combating Corruption.

more difficult and costly. As one might expect, there is considerable overlap between the instruments as to the strategies to be employed, although points of detail vary in some cases.[2] In the case of the European initiatives there has been a deliberate attempt to harmonize strategies.

In essence, the instruments recognise five main pillars in the fight against corruption: **9.04**

(1) prevention;
(2) criminalization;
(3) international cooperation;
(4) asset recovery; and
(5) establishing effective monitoring procedures.

One further characteristic is that some instruments, and most notably the United Nations Convention Against Corruption, contain a mixture of legally binding obligations and non-binding provisions, a point emphasizing that work is still required to produce an international consensus on the effective implementation of all the strategies. In doing so, countries are left with the discretion to determine how best to adapt the international standards in their own domestic situation. **9.05**

B. The United Nations

1. Early Initiatives

During the 1970s, the United Nations addressed the issue of corruption on several occasions. In 1975 the UN General Assembly adopted Resolution 3514 which condemned all corrupt practices, including bribery. Of particular interest was the fact that the resolution emphasized the right of states to take legal action within their jurisdictions against transnational corporations and urged states to prosecute offenders within the scope of their national jurisdictions. The Resolution also requested the Economic and Social Council (ECOSOC) to include the issue of foreign illicit payments in its work programme. **9.06**

In 1974, ECOSOC established the Commission on Transnational Corporations (CTC). The main objective of this intergovernmental body was to prepare a Code of Conduct on Transnational Corporations for adoption by the United Nations. The aim was essentially to provide for stability, confidence, and transparency in international transactions, including tackling corrupt practices. At this point the Ad Hoc Intergovernmental Working Group on the Problem of Corrupt Practices was established in 1976[3] to draft an article on the proposed **9.07**

[2] Where there is any such conflict, it is advisable for State Parties to adhere to the provisions of the stricter agreement, in order to give effect to each of these treaties' principles and goals.
[3] See GA Resolution 3514 (XXX) of 15 December 1975.

code of conduct. In 1978 the Working Group was replaced by the Committee on an International Agreement on Illicit Payments. A draft text was agreed and this was sent to the CTC for inclusion in the code. The principal provision required states to criminalize a range of conduct including: (a) The offering, promising, or giving of any payment, gift or other advantage by any natural person, on his own behalf or on behalf of any enterprise or any other person whether juridical or natural, to or for the benefit of a public official, as undue consideration for performing or refraining from the performance of his duties in connection with an international commercial transaction; (b) The soliciting, demanding, accepting, or receiving, directly or indirectly, by a public official of any payment, gift, or other advantage, as undue consideration for performing or refraining from the performance of his duties pertaining to an international commercial transaction. The draft Code was not adopted but the approach of the Working Group is reflected in later international and regional anti-corruption instruments.

9.08 The next major development came in 1996 with the adoption by the UN General Assembly of a Declaration against Corruption and Bribery in International Commercial Transactions.[4] Despite its non-binding nature, the Declaration again reflected the issues dealt with by the Working Group. Work then commenced on the UN Convention against Transnational Organised Crime (the Palermo Convention), which was adopted in 2000 and came into force on 29 September 2003. The UK has signed, but at 5 October 2005 had not ratified the convention. This contains two Articles dealing with corruption relating to public officials, as follows:

> *Article 8: Criminalization of corruption:*
> 1. Each State Party shall adopt such legislative and other measures as may be necessary to establish as criminal offences, when committed intentionally:
>   (a) The promise, offering or giving to a public official, directly or indirectly, of an undue advantage, for the official himself or herself or another person or entity, in order that the official act or refrain from acting in the exercise of his or her official duties;
>   (b) The solicitation or acceptance by a public official, directly or indirectly, of an undue advantage, for the official himself or herself or another person or entity, in order that the official act or refrain from acting in the exercise of his or her official duties.
> 2. Each State Party shall consider adopting such legislative and other measures as may be necessary to establish as criminal offences conduct referred to in paragraph 1 of this article involving a foreign public official or international civil servant. Likewise, each State Party shall consider establishing as criminal offences other forms of corruption.

[4] The various initiatives leading up to the 1996 Declaration are usefully set out by A Posadas (1996) 10 *Duke Journal of Comparative and International Law* 345, 370–372.

3. Each State Party shall also adopt such measures as may be necessary to establish as a criminal offence participation as an accomplice in an offence established in accordance with this article.
4. For the purposes of paragraph 1 of this article and article 9 of this Convention, 'public official' shall mean a public official or a person who provides a public service as defined in the domestic law and as applied in the criminal law of the State Party in which the person in question performs that function.

Article 9: Measures against corruption

1. In addition to the measures set forth in article 8 of this Convention, each State Party shall, to the extent appropriate and consistent with its legal system, adopt legislative, administrative or other effective measures to promote integrity and to prevent, detect and punish the corruption of public officials.
2. Each State Party shall take measures to ensure effective action by its authorities in the prevention, detection and punishment of the corruption of public officials, including providing such authorities with adequate independence to deter the exertion of inappropriate influence on their actions.

However, the need for another convention devoted specifically to corruption **9.09** emerged from the deliberations on the draft convention. This was reflected in Resolution 55/61 of 4 December 2000, in which the General Assembly recognized that an effective international legal instrument against corruption, independent of the Palermo Convention, was desirable and decided to establish an Ad Hoc Committee for the negotiation of such an instrument.

2. UN Convention Against Corruption

The text of UNCAC was negotiated during seven sessions of the Ad Hoc **9.10** Committee for the Negotiation of the Convention Against Corruption, held between 21 January 2002 and 1 October 2003, with participation from over 120 states. The Convention was approved by the Ad Hoc Committee and adopted by the General Assembly by Resolution 58/4 of 31 October 2003. The General Assembly, in Resolution 57/169, accepted the offer of the Government of Mexico to host a high-level signing conference in Merida, Mexico, for the purpose of signing the Convention and this took place in December 2003. On 15 September 2005, Ecuador became the thirtieth state to ratify the Convention and, in accordance with Article 68, the Convention entered into force on 14 December 2005.[5] UNCAC is a significant initiative and its worldwide support demonstrates the necessity for a systematic, global effort to combat corruption in both the public and private sectors.

[5] For the current status on ratifications see http://www.unodc.org/unodc/en/crime_signatures_corruption.html. As at 15 September 2005, a total of 133 states had signed the Convention. The text of the UNCAC is in App 29 below.

3. Purposes of the Convention

9.11 UNCAC has three purposes: (a) to promote and strengthen measures to prevent and combat corruption more efficiently and effectively; (b) to promote, facilitate, and support international cooperation and technical assistance in the prevention of, and fight against, corruption, including asset recovery; and (c) to promote integrity, accountability, and proper management of public affairs and public property (Article 1). 'Corruption' is not defined in the Convention.

4. Structure of the Convention

9.12 UNCAC is similar to other international and regional instruments in that it deals with: Prevention (Chapter II, Articles 5 to 14); Criminalization and law enforcement (Chapter III, Articles 15 to 42); International cooperation (Chapter IV, Articles 43 to 50); and Asset recovery (Chapter V Articles 51 to 62). It also sets out mechanisms for its implementation (Chapter VII).

9.13 Each State Party undertakes to take the necessary measures, including legislative and administrative measures, in accordance with the fundamental principles of its domestic law, to ensure the implementation of its obligations under the Convention (Article 65(1)). However, UNCAC negotiators were unable to agree on a set of mandatory requirements and thus the Convention is a mixture of both mandatory and non-binding provisions. This is unfortunate in that it inhibits the development of consistent international rules and means that a patchwork of differing laws and regulations may well result. It is also a curious mixture of approaches, with some Articles providing a detailed set of provisions (for example on the measures needed to prevent corruption in the private sector and mutual legal assistance) whilst others receive minimal comment (for example measures to counter corruption in the prosecution service).

5. The Convention Provisions

i. Chapter II: Preventative measures

9.14 The Articles in this Chapter generally contain a mandatory requirement for action by States Parties whilst giving them flexibility in determining the appropriate measures to be adopted in domestic law in order to achieve the overall objectives of the Chapter. The Convention mandates State Parties to develop a coordinated approach to corruption, which includes developing and maintaining effective policies for dealing with corruption and for implementing the various measures identified in it. State Parties must also have in place institutions responsible for the implementation of these measures.

9.15 Article 5 requires each State Party, in accordance with the fundamental principles of its legal system, to develop and implement or maintain effective, coordinated anti-corruption policies. Curiously, the establishment and promotion of practices aimed at the prevention of corruption and the periodic evaluation of their anti-corruption laws and procedures are merely discretionary. States are further required to ensure the existence of an independent anti-corruption body or bodies designed to oversee and coordinate the state's anti-corruption policies (Article 6). Many states will be able to use existing bodies to fulfil this obligation and the size and nature of the body will depend upon national circumstances. In practice, there is an increasing trend towards establishing anti-corruption commissions with a mandate to both investigate and prevent corruption. Such bodies are considered in Chapter 11 below.

Addressing probity in the public service is widely seen as a key area in the fight against corruption, and Article 7 sets out a series of fundamental requirements in this regard. Yet disagreement between negotiators means that the Article contains no mandatory provisions. Thus Article 7(1) merely calls on states to endeavour to adopt, maintain, and strengthen systems for the 'recruitment, hiring, retention, promotion and retirement of civil servants and, where applicable, other non-elected public officials'.[6] These should (a) be based on principles of efficiency, transparency, and objective criteria such as merit, equity, and aptitude; (b) include adequate procedures for selection and training; and (c) provide adequate remuneration, taking into account the level of economic development of each country. The development of anti-corruption education and training programmes for members of the public service is particularly weak, with State Parties merely being asked to promote such programmes which 'may make reference to codes or standards of conduct in applicable areas'. **9.16**

One issue that is not addressed is the position of senior public servants on fixed-term contracts. This raises issues similar to those concerning contract judges, ie reconciling such appointments with security of tenure. Here concern over a future renewal of contract might influence decision-making. The aim must be to ensure that those at the most senior level should enjoy security of tenure, for it is at this level, in particular, that political influence is more readily felt. The approach to the selection to public office also failed to produce agreement at the Convention negotiations and resulted in each state being left to determine the criteria for candidature.[7] In practice, it is common to find that individual states have their own constitutional and/or legislative restrictions on the holding of public office and it may well be that these will adequately address the issue. **9.17**

[6] The Convention provides no definition of a 'civil servant' but defines a 'public official' as including 'any person holding a legislative, executive, administrative or judicial office, as well as foreign public officials and officials of public international organisations', Art 2.

[7] See Art 7(2).

9.18 Article 7(3) deals with the sensitive issue of political funding. Its importance is illustrated by the results from the TI Global Corruption Barometer 2004, which found that in thirty-six of the sixty-two countries surveyed on corruption in institutions, political parties were rated by the general public as the institution most affected by corruption.[8] The Framework for Commonwealth Principles on Promoting Good Governance and Combating Corruption (see para 9.147 below) recognizes that the funding of political parties has the potential to become a major source of corruption as well as a vehicle for hiding corruption and that clear links can be drawn between inappropriate or inadequate controls on such funding and the prevalence of corruption.[9] Further, the need for corporate responsibility in this area is highlighted in the Rules of Conduct and Recommendations: Combating Extortion and Bribery (2005 edition) developed by the International Chamber of Commerce. Article 4 states:

(a) Enterprises should only make contributions to political parties, party officials and candidates in accordance with applicable laws and all requirements for public disclosure should be fully complied with. The amount and timing of political contributions should be reviewed to ensure that they are not used as a subterfuge for bribery.
(b) Enterprises should take measures within their powers to ensure that their charitable contributions and sponsorships are not used as a subterfuge for bribery. Charitable contributions and sponsorships should be transparent and in accordance with applicable law.
(c) Enterprises should establish reasonable controls and procedures to ensure that improper political and charitable contributions are not made. Special care should be exercised in reviewing contributions to organizations in which prominent political figures, or their relatives, friends or business associates are involved.

9.19 Yet the issue proved contentious during negotiations on the Convention, with the result that the sub-Article provides that states 'shall also consider taking appropriate . . . measures' to enhance transparency in funding candidates for elected office and political party funding. It may well be that attention will be diverted to those regional instruments that address the issue in a more robust manner. The work of the Commonwealth in this area is particularly helpful here and this is discussed below.[10]

9.20 Article 8 reflects, in particular, the growing attention being paid to the development of codes or standards of conduct for specific groups of public officials. It requires State Parties to promote integrity, honesty, and responsibility among their public officials. How this is done is left to individual states to decide, the

---

[8] On a scale of 1 (not at all corrupt) to 5 (extremely corrupt), political parties scored 4.0.
[9] Framework for Commonwealth Principles, para 8.
[10] This is an issue that will also be addressed in the Third GRECO evaluation: see below.

Convention merely requiring them to or 'consider' a series of possibilities including:

(1) applying codes or standards of conduct for the correct, honourable, and proper performance of public functions, taking note of, for example, the UN International Code of Conduct for Public Officials;[11]
(2) facilitating whistleblowing by public officials; and
(3) requiring public officials to make declarations relating to assets and conflicts of interest.

ii. Public procurement and management of public finances

Article 9(1) requires State Parties to 'establish appropriate systems of procurement based on transparency, competition and objective criteria in decision-making . . . that are effective . . . in preventing corruption'. These may include (a) the public distribution of information relating to procurement procedures and contracts; (b) the establishment, in advance, of conditions for participation; (c) the use of objective and predetermined criteria for public procurement decisions; (d) an effective system of domestic review, including an effective system of appeal, to ensure legal recourse and remedies in the event that the rules or procedures are not followed; and (e) where appropriate, measures to regulate matters regarding personnel responsible for procurement. State Parties are also required to take appropriate measures to promote transparency and accountability in the management of public finances. Such measures shall encompass, amongst other things: '(a) procedures for the adoption of the national budget; (b) timely reporting on revenue and expenditure; (c) a system of accounting and auditing standards and related oversight; (d) effective and efficient systems of risk management and internal control; and (e) where appropriate, corrective action in the case of failure to comply with the requirements established in this paragraph' (Article 9(2)). State Parties must also take appropriate measures to enhance transparency in their public administration (Article 10). **9.21**

Article 11 requires States Parties to take measures to strengthen integrity and to prevent opportunities for corruption amongst members of their judiciaries and prosecution services. Such measures should be seen in the light of Article 60, which requires State Parties, amongst other things, to put in place training programmes for their personnel responsible for preventing and combating corruption. The independence of the judiciary is entrenched in most national constitutions but it is the need to take steps to protect and strengthen judicial **9.22**

[11] The text of the code is contained in App 30.

integrity in practice that is equally important. This must also include the administrative staff of judiciaries as well as prosecutors. The Article is particularly lacking in detail and should be augmented by reference to a range of other initiatives.[12]

9.23 Article 12 provides the most detailed treatment of private-private corruption in any international instrument to date. It requires State Parties to develop anti-corruption strategies for the private sector and lists a range of detailed measures that might be utilized. In particular it emphasizes the duty of states to have appropriate accounting and auditing standards and to disallow the tax deductibility of expenses that constitute bribes (and other expenses incurred in furtherance of corrupt conduct). Where appropriate, State Parties must provide effective, proportionate, and dissuasive civil, administrative, or criminal penalties for failure to comply with such measures.

9.24 The importance of the participation of society[13] in combating corruption is recognized in Article 13. State Parties must take appropriate steps to promote the active participation of individuals and groups outside the public sector such as civil society, non-governmental organizations and community-based organizations. Such steps may include ensuring effective public access to information and undertaking public anti-corruption education programmes, with perhaps the underlying theme being the recognition that government and society must work together to combat corruption.[14]

9.25 Overall, these provisions highlight the need for a coordinated approach to tackling corruption and the need for states to have in place bodies/authorities responsible for the implementation of these policies. How this is achieved is a matter for each individual state and much will depend upon the available staffing and resources. Perhaps the key concern is to ensure that there are a number of different channels open to address corruption, so that a matter is not stopped by one channel, and that there are sufficient legislative provisions and powers available to implement the preventive measures.

iii. Chapter III: Criminalization and law enforcement

9.26 The Convention provides for several mandatory criminal offences. Article 15 requires each State Party to adopt such measures as may be necessary to establish offences relating to the bribery of national public officials when committed intentionally. These cover both 'active bribery', ie 'The promise, offering or

[12] These include the Commonwealth Framework Principles, which set standards by which Commonwealth judiciaries must operate (see 9.147 below) as well as the Limassol Recommendations on Combating Corruption Within the Judiciary (see 8.92 above).

[13] A word that covers groups and individuals outside the public sector.

[14] The contribution that civil society organizations (CSOs) can make towards combating corruption is examined in Ch 12 below.

giving, to a public official, directly or indirectly, of an undue advantage, for the official himself or herself or another person or entity, in order that the official act or refrain from acting in the exercise of his or her official duties'; and 'passive bribery', ie 'The solicitation or acceptance by a public official, directly or indirectly, of an undue advantage, for the official himself or herself or another person or entity, in order that the official act or refrain from acting in the exercise of his or her official duties'.

Article 16 addresses the bribery of foreign public officials and officials of public international organizations with the elements of the offences essentially following those in Article 15. Indeed, it has been suggested that the offence could be removed by expanding the definition of 'public official' in Article 15 to cover foreign public officials or by applying the section to 'all persons'.[15] However, one significant difference from other international instruments, and particularly from the OECD Convention on Combating Bribery of Foreign Public Officials in International Business Transactions (the OECD Convention), is that under Article 16(2) State Parties under UNCAC are not required to criminalize 'passive bribery' by a foreign public official. In view of the fact that the UNCAC provisions largely replicate those in the OECD Convention, an analysis of these provisions is deferred until Chapter 10.[16] The offences of 'Embezzlement, misappropriation or other diversion of property by a public official' contained in Article 17 appear to cover the same ground, at least in common law jurisdictions and are likely to be found in some form in existing criminal laws. Similarly, the offence of the obstruction of justice in Article 25 is likely to be covered by the general criminal law. **9.27**

The Convention also includes several discretionary offences. One such offence is trading in influence. Article 18 provides that State Parties shall consider adopting such legislative and other measures as may be necessary to establish as criminal offences, when committed intentionally: **9.28**

> (a) The promise, offering or giving to a public official or any other person, directly or indirectly, of an undue advantage in order that the public official or the person abuse his or her real or supposed influence with a view to obtaining from an administration or public authority of the State Party an undue advantage for the original instigator of the act or for any other person; (b) The solicitation or acceptance by a public official or any other person, directly or indirectly, of an undue advantage for himself or herself or for another person in order that the public official or the person abuse his or her real or supposed influence with a view to obtaining from an administration or public authority of the State Party an undue advantage.

[15] Report of the Commonwealth Expert Group on Legislative and Related Measures to Combat Corruption, Commonwealth Secretariat, 2004, para 40 (the Commonwealth Expert Group Report).

[16] See especially para 10.22ff below.

9.29 This is a potentially useful offence that seeks to tackle the 'background corruption' that can adversely affect public confidence in public administration. What constitutes an 'undue advantage' is clearly a key issue, although UNCAC does not offer any guidance as to its meaning. The scope of the phrase is explored in paras 10.42ff below. The importance of the offence is highlighted by it being mandatory for State Parties to the Council of Europe Criminal Law Convention on Corruption to establish such an offence in their domestic law and an opportunity to ensure it is extended further afield has seemingly been lost by the more cautious approach in UNCAC.

Similarly, the 'abuse of functions' by a public officer is a discretionary offence. This goes further than the bribery provisions in that it could apply (in addition to an attempt) where a public official seeks to use his or her position to gain an undue advantage, even when no such advantage is actually obtained. In practice, such conduct would probably fall within the common law offence of 'misuse of public office'. Article 21 deals with bribery in the private sector, in much the same terms as Article 15, whilst Article 22 covers embezzlement of property in the private sector.

9.30 The offence of illicit enrichment in Article 20, applies where there is a 'significant increase in the assets of a public official that he or she cannot reasonably explain in relation to his or her income'. This provision was the subject of considerable debate during negotiations and, despite its proven effectiveness in tackling corruption,[17] perceived constitutional difficulties for some countries mean that it is not a mandatory provision. This could prove problematic because, as a Commonwealth Expert Group has pointed out, the divergent views between states may adversely affect international cooperation. For example, in a situation where one state has such an offence and another does not, there can be a problem of lack of dual criminality, making extradition and, for some states, mutual legal assistance unavailable.[18]

9.31 Article 14 deals with measures to prevent money laundering. In doing so, State Parties are called upon to use as a guideline the relevant initiatives of the regional, interregional, and multilateral organizations against money laundering (Article 14(4)). Here the work of the Financial Action Task Force and its Forty Recommendations will, in particular, play a key role in helping to shape anti-money laundering policy. Article 14(1) requires State Parties to institute a comprehensive domestic regulatory and supervisory regime in order to detect

[17] See, eg, the position in Hong Kong, see 11.77 below.

[18] Commonwealth Expert Group on Legislative and Related Measures to Combat Corruption, Report, para 45. A possible solution appears in Art IX of the OAS Convention which provides that: 'Any State Party that has not established illicit enrichment as an offence shall, insofar as its laws permit, provide assistance and cooperation with respect to this offence as provided in this Convention.'

and deter all forms of money laundering through banks and 'non-bank financial institutions, including natural or legal persons, that provide formal or informal services for the transmission of money or value and, where appropriate, other bodies particularly susceptible to money laundering. In doing so, State Parties must have in place appropriate measures to facilitate cooperation and information exchange at both the national and international levels. Strangely, State Parties are only to consider establishing a financial intelligence unit (Article 58) and the implementation of measures on cross-border financial transactions. Yet, given the influence of the Financial Action Task Force on the development of anti-money laundering laws worldwide, it is likely that most states will already have in place adequate legislation in this regard. As regards the difficult issue of tackling the cross-border movement of cash and negotiable instruments, Article 14(2) provides that State Parties shall 'consider implementing feasible measures to detect and monitor' such activity, including a requirement that individuals and businesses report the cross-border transfer of substantial quantities of cash and negotiable instruments.

As regards the criminalization of money laundering, Article 23 requires each State Party to adopt, in accordance with fundamental principles of its domestic law, such legislative and other measures as may be necessary to establish as criminal offences, when committed intentionally, the following offences: **9.32**

(a) (i) the conversion or transfer of property, knowing that such property is the proceeds of crime, for the purpose of concealing or disguising the illicit origin of the property or of helping any person who is involved in the commission of the predicate offence to evade the legal consequences of his or her action;
   (ii) the concealment or disguise of the true nature, source, location, disposition, movement, or ownership of, or rights with respect to property, knowing that such property is the proceeds of crime;

(b) Subject to the basic concepts of its legal system:
   (i) the acquisition, possession or use of property, knowing, at the time of receipt, that such property is the proceeds of crime;
   (ii) participation in, association with or conspiracy to commit, attempts to commit and aiding, abetting, facilitating, and counselling the commission of any of the offences established in accordance with this article.

As regards predicate offences, each State Party is required, subject to the fundamental principles of its domestic law, to include, at a minimum, the criminal offences established in accordance with the Convention, including offences committed both within and, subject to the limitations set out in Article 23(2)(c), outside the jurisdiction. **9.33**

The Convention also contains the most detailed provisions of any anti-corruption instrument regarding procedure and sanctions. These include the need for State Parties to (a) establish, where appropriate, a long statute of **9.34** limitations period in which to commence proceedings; (b) establish the liability of legal persons for Convention offences;[19] (c) ensure that sanctions for Convention offences take into account the gravity of the offence; and (d) ensure that victims of corruption have the right to initiate legal proceedings against those responsible in order to obtain compensation.

9.35 **Immunities** Article 30(2) requires State Parties to take necessary measures to ensure an appropriate balance between any immunities or jurisdictional privileges accorded to public officials and the need for the effective investigation and prosecution of corruption offences.

9.36 Of particular concern during negotiations was parliamentary immunity that can be used as a cloak for bribery.[20] As discussed in Chapter 8 above, in the United Kingdom, this is a matter that has raised considerable interest having been considered by both the Salmon Committee and Nolan Committee, but it has a wider significance in that many Commonwealth countries uphold the same privileges for parliamentarians as are available to members of the House of Commons at Westminster.

9.37 **Addressing the needs of victims** The Convention recognizes that a key component in any anti-corruption strategy is addressing the needs of victims of corruption and/or whistleblowers. The difficulty of proving corruption makes it all the more important to implement effective protection provisions for those reporting corruption or giving evidence at a corruption trial. Article 32 requires each State Party to take appropriate measures 'within its means' to provide effective protection from potential retaliation or intimidation of witnesses and experts who give testimony and, as appropriate, for their relatives and other persons close to them. The measures envisaged might include witness protection programmes, including relocation and the use of video evidence. The issue of relocation, in particular, raises practical problems, especially for small states, where it may be impossible to relocate the witness locally. The Convention thus envisages the development of inter-state agreements for the relocation of such persons.

9.38 Similar problems may face whistleblowers: defined in Article 33 as 'any person who reports in good faith and on reasonable grounds to the competent authorities' any facts concerning a corruption offence under UNCAC. Even if they do not become witnesses at any subsequent trial, such persons may need

[19] For a full discussion of this issue, see 10.69 below.

[20] A situation particularly well illustrated by the Indian case of *P V Narasimha Rao v State* 1998 SC 626. For a discussion, see K M N Rao, 'Parliamentary Privilege versus the Courts' in J Hatchard and P Slinn (eds) *Parliamentary Supremacy and Judicial Independence* (London: Cavendish Publishing, 1999), 65–72.

protection and the Convention invites State Parties to consider taking the necessary measures.

State Parties may also consider corruption as a relevant factor in proceedings to rescind or annul a contract or withdraw a concession. In addition, they must ensure that victims of corruption have the right to seek compensation through the courts. **9.39**

Law enforcement Article 36 requires State Parties to have in place a law enforcement body or bodies specialized in combating corruption. This might be a separate body or a specialized police unit. Whilst this provision is distinct from the Article 6 requirement to establish 'preventive' anti-corruption agencies, a combined function along the lines of the Independent Commission Against Corruption in Hong Kong is becoming increasingly popular.[21] **9.40**

Again, in recognition of the problems of prosecuting corruption, Article 37 requires State Parties to take measures to encourage cooperation with law enforcement agencies such as mitigation of punishment or granting immunity from prosecution. Cooperation between law enforcement agencies and between such agencies and the private sector, and in particular with financial institutions, is also encouraged. In this respect, State Parties must ensure that bank secrecy laws do not obstruct the investigation and prosecution of corruption offences.[22] **9.41**

Jurisdiction[23] The Convention requires that each State Party adopt such measures as may be necessary to establish its jurisdiction over the Convention offences when the offence is committed in its territory. Subject to the need to protect its sovereignty, the Convention also recognises that a State party may establish jurisdiction over an UNCAC offence when the offence is: **9.42**

(1) committed against a national of that State Party; or
(2) committed by a national of that State Party or a stateless person who has his or her habitual residence in its territory; or
(3) One of those established in accordance with Article 23(1) (G) (ii) and is commited outside its territory with a view to the commision of an offence under Article 23(1) (b) (i) within its territory (See 9.32 above) or;
(4) committed against the State Party.

Given their often international dimensions, encouraging states to establish a wider jurisdiction in corruption cases is extremely useful, particularly as this can assist in the prosecution of corporations from developed countries and relieve the burden on the victim developing countries.[24] **9.43**

[21] See 11.82 below for further details. [22] Arts 38–40. [23] Art 42.
[24] See 9.77 below on the approach of the African Convention and also the discussion at 10.140 below.

iv. Chapter IV: International cooperation

9.44 State Parties are required to cooperate in criminal matters relating to provisions contained in Chapter IV. They are also asked to consider assisting each other in relation to investigations and proceedings of a non-criminal nature (Article 43). Dual criminality is deemed fulfilled if the underlying conduct is a criminal offence under the laws of both State Parties.

9.45 **Extradition** In relation to extradition, State Parties are to ensure that all convention offences are extraditable in terms of their domestic law. Article 44 deals in detail with extradition in very similar terms to other international instruments and it is not intended to analyse its provisions here.[25]

9.46 **Mutual legal assistance** State Parties are required to afford one another the widest measure of mutual legal assistance in investigations, prosecutions, and judicial proceedings in relation to Convention offences. Section 46 contains the most detailed provisions relating to mutual legal assistance amongst all the anti-corruption instruments, albeit in very similar form to those in the Scheme Relating to Mutual Assistance in Criminal Matters within the commonwealth (the Harare scheme) and in the 40 Recommendations of the Financial Action Task Force. The Article emphasizes the fundamental features of mutual assistance, such as the requirement to establish a central authority to receive, execute, and transmit requests; the need for confidentiality as to the fact and substance of the request; the need for flexibility in dealing with the request; and the fact that a request for mutual assistance cannot be refused solely on the grounds either that the offence is considered to involve fiscal matters or of bank secrecy.[26]

9.47 **Other forms of cooperation** Article 48 of the Convention also requires State Parties to cooperate closely with each other to enhance effective law enforcement, in particular to establish effective channels of communication and information exchange. Each State Party is also required to take measures to allow for the 'appropriate use by its competent authorities' of controlled delivery and other special investigative techniques such as electronic or other forms of surveillance and undercover operations within its territory.[27] State Parties may also provide for joint investigations.[28]

v. Chapter V: Asset recovery

9.48 The Convention represents an important breakthrough as regards the return of assets. With the aim of helping to remove the profit from corruption, Article 51 states that a fundamental principle of the Convention is the return of assets and

[25] For the position in the UK, see 4.215ff above.
[26] For the position in the UK see 2.143ff above
[27] Art 50.
[28] Art 49.

that State Parties are required to afford each other the widest measure of cooperation and assistance in this regard.

Under Article 52, State Parties are required to take appropriate measures to prevent and detect transfers of proceeds of crime, including requiring financial institutions to implement 'know your customer' measures and, perhaps with a view to preventing the looting of state coffers by the likes of Mobuto, Marcos, and Abacha, to 'conduct enhanced security of accounts sought or maintained by or on behalf of individuals who are, or have been, entrusted with prominent public functions and their family members and close associates'. **9.49**

The Convention also includes some familiar anti-money laundering provisions. For example, State Parties are required to implement 'appropriate and effective measures' to prevent the establishment of banks that have no physical presence and that are not affiliated with any regulated financial group, and may consider requiring their financial institutions to refuse to enter into or continue a correspondent banking relationship with such institutions.[29] **9.50**

Articles 54 to 57 set out the mechanisms for asset recovery through international cooperation. With respect to instrumentalities involved in or property acquired through the commission of a Convention offence, State Parties are required to take the necessary measures to permit their competent authorities to: **9.51**

(1) handle mutual legal assistance requests for the purposes of the confiscation of proceeds or instrumentalities;
(2) issue a freezing or seizure order at the request of another State Party;
(3) give effect to a confiscation order issued by a court of another State Party and consider establishing a civil forfeiture system.

State Parties are required to adopt the necessary legislative or other measures to enable the return of confiscated property at the request of another State Party, taking into account the rights of bona fide third parties. This is a particularly important provision that is designed to prevent repatriating countries from imposing conditions on those repatriations.[30] **9.52**

vi. Chapter VII: Mechanisms for implementation

With the Convention now in force, much will depend upon whether an effective monitoring process is established. Under Article 63, a Conference of the States Parties to the Convention (COSP) must be established within one year following the entry into force of the convention. This will seek to 'improve the capacity of and cooperation between States Parties to achieve the objectives set forth in this Convention and to promote and review its implementation'. **9.53**

[29] Art 52(4). [30] Art 57. See also 7.55ff

Efforts were made by a number of countries to have monitoring mechanisms built into the Convention itself. However, these foundered, partly because of existing monitoring mechanisms in other international instruments, such as the OECD Convention and the two Council of Europe Conventions against Corruption, and the duplication of effort such a provision might entail. Now that UNCAC is in force, the work of COSP may well be instrumental in determining the effectiveness (or otherwise) of the Convention.

6. Related United Nations Intitatives

9.54 The Global Programme against Corruption (GPAC) was launched in 1999 by what is now the United Nations Office on Drugs and Crime (UNODC). GPAC has been active in four main areas, namely:

(1) providing technical assistance to Member States in strengthening their legal and institutional anti-corruption frameworks;
(2) supporting and servicing international groups of Chief Justices in strengthening judicial integrity;
(3) the development and dissemination of anti-corruption policies and tools; and
(4) enhancing interagency anti-corruption coordination.

9.55 UNODC has produced a range of important anti-corruption materials for practitioners and policy-makers. These include: the *Handbook on Practical Corruption Measures for Prosecutors and Investigators*;[31] the *UN Anti-Corruption Toolkit*, which provides detailed coverage of anti-corruption prevention and enforcement strategies (particularly useful are the sections on international cooperation, money laundering and recovery, and return of proceeds of corruption);[32] and a *Compendium of International Legal Instruments on Corruption*, which contains many of the international and regional anti-corruption documents.[33] The United Nations has also commenced a series of country assessments designed to document trends within public administration and 'street-level' corruption (the experience of citizens with public administration agencies); private sector corruption (especially in medium-sized businesses); and high-level financial and political corruption. Reports on assessments in Colombia, Hungary, Iran, Iraq, Kenya, Lebanon, Nigeria, Romania, and South Africa are available.[34]

---

[31] The Handbook is available at www.undoc.org/pdf/crime/corruption/Handbook.pdf.

[32] The 3rd edn (2004) is available at www.undoc.org/undoc/en/corruption_toolkit.html.

[33] The 2nd edn (2005) is available at www.undoc.org/undoc/en/corruption/compendium_e.pdf.

[34] These are available at www.undoc.org/undoc/en/corruption_projects.html#summaries.

C. The Organization for Economic Co-operation and Development

The Convention on the Organization for Economic Co-operation and Development was signed by twenty countries on 14 December 1960. Since then, a further ten countries have become members of the organization. The UK ratified the Convention on 2 May 1961. The role of the OECD is to promote policies designed to (a) achieve the highest sustainable economic growth and employment and a rising standard of living in member countries, whilst maintaining financial stability, and thus to contribute to the development of the world economy; (b) contribute to sound economic expansion in member as well as non-member countries in the process of economic development; and (c) contribute to the expansion of world trade on a multilateral, non-discriminatory basis in accordance with international obligations. **9.56**

The most high-profile aspect of OECD work in the anti-corruption field is the Convention on Combating Bribery of Foreign Public Officials in International Business Transactions to which the UK is a party. This Convention is examined in detail in Chapter 10 below. Other OECD work on international standard setting is illustrated by the Guidelines for Multinational Enterprises. These constitute a set of voluntary recommendations to multinational enterprises on business ethics, including human rights, information disclosure, combating bribery, and taxation issues. Adhering governments have committed to promoting them among multinational enterprises operating in or from their territories. The text of the Guidelines is found in App 25 below **9.57**

The instrument's distinctive implementation mechanisms include the operation of National Contact Points (NCPs), which are government offices charged with promoting the Guidelines and handling enquiries in the national context. Adhering countries comprise all thirty OECD member countries, and nine non-member countries (Argentina, Brazil, Chile, Estonia, Israel, Latvia, Lithuania, Romania, and Slovenia). In addition, the Guidelines are complemented by commentaries which provide information on and explanation of the Guidelines text and implementation procedures. **9.58**

D. Africa

With the majority of the fifty-three countries of the African Union towards the bottom of the Transparency International Bribery Perception Index, the need to develop effective anti-corruption strategies has become a priority. This led to the development of important regional and pan-African instruments. **9.59**

1. Southern African Development Community Protocol Against Corruption

9.60 The Southern African Development Community (SADC)[35] was established in 1992 as the successor body to the Southern African Development Co-ordination Conference (SADCC).[36] In August 2000, at a regional round-table on ethics and governance held at Victoria Falls, Zimbabwe, SADC Ministers of Justice, Attorneys-General, and heads of anti-corruption agencies agreed on initiatives to fight corruption in the region. Amongst other things, the meeting recommended the development of a SADC regional anti-corruption instrument. This work was undertaken by the SADC Legal Sector and by a non-governmental organization, the Human Rights Trust of Southern Africa (SAHRIT). Progress was rapid, and in August 2001 the SADC Protocol Against Corruption was signed by the heads of state and government of the SADC Community at their summit in Blantyre, Malawi.

9.61 The purposes of the Protocol are to promote and strengthen the development, by each of the State Parties, of mechanisms to fight against corruption; to promote international cooperation and to 'foster the development and harmonization of policies and domestic legislation' to combat corruption.[37] The Protocol applies to both the public and private sectors. The document is clearly influenced by other regional instruments and seeks to embrace good practice from other parts of the world. Its twenty-two articles cover: (i) preventative measures; (ii) criminalization; (iii) international cooperation; (iv) proceeds of crime, and (v) monitoring.

i. Preventative measures

9.62 State Parties undertake to adopt a range of preventative measures, including the development of standards of conduct for the 'correct, honourable and proper fulfilment of public functions as well as mechanisms to enforce those standards'; the development of government revenue collection and control systems that deter corruption; laws that deny favourable tax treatment for any individual or corporation of expenditures made in violation of the anti-corruption laws of the State Parties; and public anti-corruption education programmes and mechanisms to promote access to information. State Parties are required to establish a 'whistleblowing' system. Anti-corruption measures to prevent and combat corruption in the private sector are also required.

---

[35] Comprising Angola, Botswana, the Democratic Republic of Congo, Lesotho, Malawi, Mozambique, Namibia, the Seychelles, South Africa, Swaziland, Tanzania, Zambia, and Zimbabwe. The text of the protocol is found in App 27 below.

[36] SADCC was formed in Lusaka, Zambia, on 1 April 1980, following the adoption of the Lusaka Declaration. The Declaration and Treaty establishing the SADC was signed at the Summit of Heads of State or Government on 17 August 1992, in Windhoek, Namibia.

[37] Art 2. The text of the protocol is found in App 27 below.

ii. Criminalization

The wide-ranging provisions on the criminalization of corruption cover passive and active corruption in relation to a public official; an act by a public official or other employee for the purpose of obtaining undue benefit; the diversion of property by a public official; active or passive corruption by a person working in the private sector; improper influencing of any person in the public or private sector relating to such person's decision-making functions; and the fraudulent use or concealment of property derived from acts of corruption (money laundering). These cover participation as a principal, co-principal, agent, instigator, accomplice, or accessory after the fact. Whilst seeking to provide for comprehensive provisions, the Article also allows two or more State Parties to agree to criminalize between or amongst themselves other acts of corruption not covered by the Protocol. States are also required to criminalize the bribery of foreign public officials: this in much the same terms as in the OECD Convention.[38] **9.63**

Jurisdiction can be established over the Protocol offences on grounds of territoriality, nationality, or where the alleged criminal is present in the territory of the State Party and it decides not to extradite that person to another country.[39] The Protocol does not exclude any criminal jurisdiction exercised by a State Party in accordance with its domestic law. This would cover, for example, the approach of Lesotho, where the courts have taken jurisdiction in corruption cases through the adoption of the harmful effects doctrine.[40] **9.64**

iii. International cooperation and asset recovery

Articles 8 to 10 address the issues of international cooperation, extradition, and recovery of assets. Whilst lacking in detail, the provisions emphasize the need for State Parties to provide the widest measure of assistance to each other. **9.65**

iv. Monitoring

The development of effective monitoring arrangements is seen as crucial to the success of the Protocol. Thus the Protocol provides for the establishment of a Committee of State Parties to oversee the implementation of the Protocol. State Parties will be required to report regularly to the Committee on progress made in the implementation of the Protocol. The Committee is then responsible for information gathering, organizing training programmes, and other assistance. Unlike some other instruments, there is no provision for a mutual evaluation system. **9.66**

One noteworthy aspect is that the Protocol does not allow for reservations. The Protocol requires ratification by two-thirds of the SADC members. To date (April 2005) there have been eight ratifications. **9.67**

[38] Art 6. See 10.22ff below. [39] Art 5. [40] See 10.140 below.

2. The Economic Community of West African States Protocol on the Fight Against Corruption

9.68 The Economic Community of West African States (ECOWAS) has also adopted a Protocol on the fight against corruption.[41] This is in similar terms to the SADC Protocol.[42]

3. African Union Convention on Preventing and Combating Corruption

9.69 The African Union (AU) was established in 2002 as the successor body to the Organization of African Unity. It objectives are to help promote democracy, human rights, and development across Africa, especially by increasing foreign investment through the New Partnership for Africa's Development (NEPAD) programme. The AU Convention was adopted in July 2001 and its negotiation process is notable for the fact that representatives of civil society were able to participate in its drafting.[43]

9.70 The Objectives of the Convention are similar to those of the SADC Protocol, namely to: promote and strengthen the development of anti-corruption mechanisms in the public and private sectors; promote cooperation among the State Parties; coordinate and harmonize the anti-corruption policies and legislation between State Parties; promote socio-economic development by removing obstacles to the enjoyment of economic, social, and cultural rights, as well as civil and political rights; and establish the necessary conditions to foster transparency and accountability in the management of public affairs. In essence, the State Parties undertake to combat corruption through just and honest government.[44]

9.71 In structure, the African Union Convention follows the approach of other anti-corruption instruments. Thus there are sections on prevention, criminalization, international cooperation, proceeds of crime, and monitoring. Particularly noteworthy is the fact that all the substantive provisions of the Convention are mandatory, in contrast to, for example, the provisions of UNCAC.

---

[41] The member states are: Benin, Burkina Faso, Cape Verde, Côte d'Ivoire, The Gambia, Ghana, Guinea, Guinea-Bissau, Liberia, Mali, Niger, Nigeria, Senegal, Sierra Leone, and Togo.

[42] The text of the protocol is found in App 31 below.

[43] The Convention has four equally authentic versions in Arabic, English, French, and Portuguese (Art 28). Yet, as Schroth has pointed out, the four texts often say different things and this may well be a cause of considerable confusion as State Parties move to comply with their obligations under the Convention: see PW Schroth 'The African Union Convention on Preventing and Combating Corruption' (2005) 49 *Journal of African Law* 24–38.

[44] eg State Parties undertake to 'respect democratic principles and institutions, popular participation, the rule of law and good governance', Art 3.1.

i. Preventative measures

State Parties undertake to adopt legislative and other measures, including strengthening national control measures on the setting up and operation of foreign companies and legislation to strengthen internal accounting and auditing systems. The need to protect whistle-blowers is also addressed, with Article 5(5) and (6) requiring State Parties to adopt legislation and other measures to protect informants and witnesses, including protection of their identities. Yet Article 5(7) then provides that State Parties shall: 'Adopt national legislative measures in order to punish those who make false and malicious reports against innocent persons in corruption and related offences' This may well act as a significant deterrent to potential whistle-blowers as even truthful allegations may be difficult to prove, particularly if they are made against politically powerful individuals or large corporations. Further, State Parties are required to provide for the declaration of assets of public officials, create an internal committee mandated to establish a code of conduct, and to monitor its implementation and sensitize and train public officials on matters of ethics. State Parties also undertake to take steps to promote anti-corruption public education programmes. As in other instruments, State Parties undertake to establish, maintain and strengthen independent national anti-corruption authorities or agencies. Such institutions are widely seen as a useful addition to anti-corruption efforts and increasing numbers of African states are introducing them.[45] **9.72**

The important area of access to information is recognized, although somewhat opaquely, in Article 9, which provides that each State Party 'shall adopt such legislative and other measures to give effect to the right of access to any information that is required to assist in the fight against corruption and related offences'. The Article is reinforced by an undertaking by State Parties to ensure that the media are given access to information in cases of corruption and related offences.[46] **9.73**

Particularly noteworthy is Article 10, which addresses the funding of political parties and provides that State Parties 'shall adopt legislative and other measures to (a) proscribe the use of funds acquired through illegal and corrupt practices to finance political parties; and (b) incorporate the principle of transparency into funding of political parties'. This means that the AU Convention is the only international anti-corruption instrument to have mandatory provisions on this topic. **9.74**

[45] In Africa, specialized anti-corruption commissions operate in Botswana, Kenya, Malawi, Nigeria, and Zambia. Offices of the ombudsman and human rights commissions perform similar functions in several other countries. See 11.97ff.

[46] Article 12(4). This is on condition that the 'dissemination of such information does not adversely affect the investigation process and the right to a fair trial'.

9.75 Article 12 is also noteworthy for setting out the role of civil society and the media. Here State Parties, amongst other things, must undertake to create an environment 'that will enable civil society and the media to hold governments to the highest levels of transparency and accountability in the management of public affairs' and 'ensure and provide for the participation of Civil Society' in the implementation of the Convention.

ii. Criminalization

9.76 The Convention does not define 'corruption' but rather extends it to cover 'the acts and practices including related offences proscribed in this Convention'.[47] State Parties are required to criminalize a range of 'acts of corruption' and related offences. These are broadly similar to those covered in the SADC Protocol. There is no specific reference to the bribery of foreign public officials, although the Convention offences extend to a 'public official or any other person' and this is arguably wide enough to cover such cases as well as those in the private sector. The Convention also requires State Parties to establish an offence of illicit enrichment, an offence that, unusually, is not limited to the public sector, ie the significant increase in the assets of a public official or any other person which he or she cannot reasonably explain in relation to his or her income.[48] Aside from the constitutional issues raised concerning the presumption of innocence, the inclusion of the phrase 'or any other person' is puzzling. It may be that the intention of the drafters was to extend the offence to cover private-private corruption, as Article 11(1) requires State Parties to criminalize the same conduct in the private sector as in the public sector. Yet the effect of the current wording is to make the offence exceedingly wide-ranging.

9.77 The provisions relating to jurisdiction in Article 13 are similar to those in the SADC Protocol. However, Article 13 goes further by providing for jurisdiction over an offence which, although committed outside its territory, is one that affects, in the view of the state concerned, its vital interests or when the 'deleterious or harmful consequences or effects of such offences impact on the State Party'. This follows the approach of the Supreme Court of Zimbabwe in *S v Mharapara*.[49]

9.78 Article 14 is unusual in that it asserts the right of persons accused of corruption offences of the minimum guarantees of a fair trial, as contained in the African Charter on Human and Peoples' Rights, and any other relevant international human rights instrument recognized by the concerned State Parties. This seems designed to address the needs of non-Commonwealth African states, as detailed

---

[47] Art 1. [48] Art 8.

[49] 1985 (4) SA 42 (HC); 1986 (1) SA 556 (ZSC); [1986] LRC (Const) 235. See the discussion at 10.140 below.

safeguards relating to fair trial are already found in the constitutions of Anglophone African states.

iii. International cooperation and proceeds of corruption

The provisions on international cooperation, extradition, and proceeds of corruption are similar to those elsewhere. There are also familiar provisions that deal with the laundering of the proceeds of corruption. **9.79**

iv. Monitoring

The Convention envisages the establishment of an Advisory Board on Corruption within the African Union, comprising eleven suitably representative and qualified members elected by the Executive Council, who serve in their individual capacity.[50] This is an innovative measure and should enable members of civil society to be actively involved in the monitoring process. The functions of the Board are limited to promoting anti-corruption measures, collecting and analysing information on corruption, and providing advice to governments on anti-corruption strategies. **9.80**

State Parties are required to inform the Board within one year of the coming into force of the Convention on the progress made in its implementation. An annual report must then be made to the Board (Article 22(7)). These functions are similar to those of the SADC Protocol, although it remains to be seen whether the Advisory Board proves more effective than the Committee of State Parties. In particular, there is no provision for sanctions and it is not clear what resources will be available for any follow-up work by the Board. **9.81**

The Convention will enter into force thirty days after the fifteenth ratification. As at 29 September 2005, there had been ten ratifications. **9.82**

v. Overview

On the face of it, the SADC and ECOWAS Protocols and AU Convention demonstrate the commitment of African states to tackling corruption in a comprehensive and meaningful manner. Given the poor record of African states, these represent a positive step forward. Indeed they go further in some important respects than other international and regional instruments. However, to date, none of the instruments has come into force. Some of the delay is attributable, at least in part, to the need for some states to adopt the new legislation and procedures required under the Convention. Thus the effectiveness of the instruments in practice remains a matter of conjecture. **9.83**

[50] These will be from a list of experts 'of the highest integrity, impartiality, and recognised competence' in the prevention and combating of corruption and related offences. The Executive Council must ensure adequate gender representation and equitable geographical representation (Art 22).

E. The Organization of American States

9.84 The Organization of American States (OAS) was founded in 1948 when twenty-one states signed the OAS Charter. In the Declaration of Principles and Plan of Action signed at the First Summit of the Americas in 1995, the now thirty-four State Parties to the Charter recognized that 'effective democracy requires a comprehensive attack on corruption as a factor of social disintegration and distortion of the economic system that undermines the legitimacy of political institutions'.[51] The Plan of Action included an agreement to develop within the OAS: 'a hemispheric approach to acts of corruption in both the public and private sectors that would include extradition and prosecution of individuals so charged, through a new hemispheric agreement or new arrangements within existing frameworks for international cooperation'.

1. The Inter-American Convention Against Corruption

9.85 The rapid progress made by the OAS meant that in March 1996, the Inter-American Convention Against Corruption was adopted and opened for signature. It entered into force in March 1997,[52] making the OAS the first regional body to address directly the issue of corruption by means of a binding treaty. The Preamble to the Convention recognizes that corruption has international dimensions which requires coordinated action by states to fight it effectively and notes the deep concern caused 'by the steadily increasing links between corruption and the proceeds generated by illicit narcotics trafficking which undermine and threaten legitimate commercial and financial activities, and society, at all levels'.

9.86 The Convention has twin purposes. First, to promote and strengthen the development of mechanisms needed to prevent, detect, punish, and eradicate corruption; and secondly, to promote, facilitate, and regulate cooperation amongst the States Parties to effect these goals.[53] The Convention suggests a series of measures that states may take to prevent corruption. These include establishing and maintaining codes of ethics and protecting whistleblowers ie public servants and private citizens who, in good faith, report acts of corruption, including protection of their identities. It also supports the development of mechanisms to encourage participation by civil society and

[51] The Declaration was signed by Antigua and Barbuda, Argentina, The Bahamas, Barbados, Belize, Bolivia, Brazil, Canada, Chile, Colombia, Costa Rica, Dominica, The Dominican Republic, Ecuador, El Salvador, Grenada, Guatemala, Guyana, Haiti, Honduras, Jamaica, Mexico, Nicaragua, Panama, Paraguay, Peru, St Kitts and Nevis, St Lucia, St Vincent and the Grenadines, Suriname, Trinidad and Tobago, the US, Uruguay, and Venezuela.

[52] As at August 2005, all the states mentioned in the previous note had ratified the Convention, with the exception of The Bahamas. The text of the convention is found in App 24 below.

[53] Art II.

non-governmental organizations in efforts to prevent corruption. The Convention adopts the same multi-strand strategy as elsewhere to tackling corruption, although not all provisions are mandatory.

i. Preventive measures

The Convention contains a range of preventive measures that State Parties 'agree to consider' applying. These cover the development of standards of conduct in the proper fulfilment of public functions and mechanisms to enforce them. These can be reinforced by non-governmental organizations and professional associations, in particular activities such as public awareness campaigns, public hearings, opinion surveys and conferences. **9.87**

ii. Criminalization

State Parties are required to criminalize 'Acts of Corruption'. These cover (a) the solicitation or acceptance by a government official[54], or offering or granting of any benefit to a government official, in exchange for any act or omission in the performance of his/her public functions; (b) any act or omission in the discharge of his/her duties by a government official for the purpose of illicitly obtaining benefits for him/herself or for a third party; or (c) the fraudulent use or concealment of property derived from any such acts. States are also required to provide for the offence of illicit enrichment, ie a significant increase in the assets of a government official that he or she cannot reasonably explain in relation to their lawful earnings during the performance of his or her functions (Article IX). States Parties are also required to criminalize the bribery of foreign public officials (Article VIII). **9.88**

The Convention also lists a series of offences that states 'undertake to consider establishing as offences': **9.89**

(1) the improper use by a government official or a person who performs public functions, for his own benefit or that of a third party, of any kind of classified or confidential information which that official or person who performs public functions has obtained because of, or in the performance of, his functions;
(2) the improper use by a government official or a person who performs public functions, for his own benefit or that of a third party, of any kind of property belonging to the State or to any firm or institution in which the State has a proprietary interest, to which that official or person who performs public functions has access because of, or in the performance of, his functions;

[54] Including a person who performs public functions (see Art I).

(3) any act or omission by any person who, personally or through a third party, or acting as an intermediary, seeks to obtain a decision from a public authority whereby he illicitly obtains for himself or for another person any benefit or gain, whether or not such act or omission harms State property; and

(4) the diversion by a government official, for purposes unrelated to those for which they were intended, for his own benefit or that of a third party, of any movable or immovable property, monies or securities belonging to the State, to an independent agency, or to an individual, that such official has received by virtue of his position for purposes of administration, custody or for other reasons (Article XI).

9.90 Jurisdiction is based on territoriality, nationality, or habitual residence. A State Party must also establish jurisdiction when the alleged criminal is present in its territory and it does not extradite such person to another country on the ground of the nationality of the alleged criminal. The Convention does not preclude the application of any other rule of criminal jurisdiction established by a State Party under its domestic law.[55]

iii. International cooperation and proceeds of corruption

9.91 States Parties are required to afford one another the widest measure of mutual assistance by processing requests from authorities that, in conformity with their domestic laws, have the power to investigate or prosecute the acts of corruption described in the Convention, to obtain evidence and take other necessary action to facilitate legal proceedings and measures regarding the investigation or prosecution of acts of corruption. The States Parties also undertake to provide each other with the widest measure of mutual technical cooperation on the most effective ways and means of preventing, detecting, investigating, and punishing acts of corruption. To this end, they must foster exchanges of experiences by way of agreements and meetings between competent bodies and institutions, and shall pay special attention to methods and procedures of citizen participation in the fight against corruption.

9.92 The Convention requires States Parties to take appropriate steps to facilitate extradition for any of the corruption offences and to implement effective proceeds of crime laws. Article XV also requires State Parties to provide for the identification, tracing, freezing, seizure, and forfeiture of proceeds and instrumentalities. Provision is made for the sharing of such property or proceeds with other State Parties that assisted in the investigation or proceedings.

---

[55] Art V.

iv. Monitoring

The Convention did not contain a monitoring process to evaluate its implementation. In 2000, a follow-up mechanism was established (MESICIC) conducted by a Committee of Experts consisting of government appointees. The system is based on self-evaluation, with each State Party responding to a questionnaire concerning its implementation of the Convention. The Committee then reviews the responses and issues a report including recommendations for action. The rules of the follow-up mechanism also allow for civil society organizations to submit parallel responses. **9.93**

F. Council of Europe

The Council of Europe (COE) was founded in 1949 and, as at October 2005, has forty-six member states. The United Kingdom has been a member since 1949. Whilst it is probably best known as a human rights protection organization, especially through the judgments of the European Court of Human Rights, the COE also works actively on anti-corruption matters. In 1994, at their 19th Conference in Malta, European Ministers of Justice recognized corruption as a serious threat to democracy, the rule of law, and human rights and launched their own anti-corruption initiative. On the recommendation of the Ministers of Justice, the Committee of Ministers agreed to establish the Multidisciplinary Group on Corruption (GMC) whose terms of reference were as follows: **9.94**

> Under the responsibility of the European Committee on Crime Problems (CDPC) and the European Committee on Legal Co-operation (CDCJ),
>
> - to elaborate as a matter of priority one or more international conventions to combat corruption, and a follow-up mechanism to implement undertakings contained in such instruments, or any other legal instrument in this area;
> - to elaborate as a matter of priority a draft European Code of Conduct for Public Officials;
> - after consultation of the appropriate Steering Committee(s) to initiate, organise or promote research projects, training programmes and the exchange at national and international level of practical experiences of corruption and the fight against it;
> - to implement the other parts of the Programme of Action against Corruption, taking into account the priorities set therein;
> - to take into account the work of other international organisations and bodies with a view to ensuring a coherent and co-ordinated approach;
> - to consult the CDCJ and/or CDPC on any draft legal text relating to corruption and take into account its/their views.

As part of this mandate, in February 1996, the Criminal Law Working Group of the GMC began drafting a criminal law convention. In November 1997, it **9.95** sent a draft text to the GMC and a final draft was submitted to the Committee of Ministers in November 1998, at which time the Ministers adopted the COE Convention. This was opened for signature on January 27 1999 and entered into force on 1 July 2002. It applies to members of the Council of Europe as well as other non-signatories.[56] The United Kingdom ratified the Convention on 9 December 2003 and it entered into force on 1 April 2004.

9.96 A related COE initiative contained in Resolution (97)24 of the Committee of Ministers of 6 November 1997 are the Twenty Guiding Principles for the Fight against Corruption (the Guiding Principles).[57] These provide an excellent blueprint for the development of a comprehensive and multidisciplinary anti-corruption strategy and include: developing effective prevention measures; raising public awareness and promoting ethical behaviour; ensuring coordinated criminalization of national and international corruption; developing effective international cooperation and measures to seize and forfeit proceeds of crime; developing transparent procedures for public procurement; and developing appropriate codes of conduct for public officials. In order to promote a dynamic process for effectively preventing and combating corruption, the Committee of Ministers invited national authorities to apply these Principles in their domestic legislation and practice.

1. Criminal Law Convention on Corruption[58]

9.97 The Preamble to the Criminal Law Convention reflects the concern that member States of the Council of Europe and other signatory States pursue a common criminal policy aimed at the protection of society against corruption and recognizes that an effective fight against corruption requires increased, rapid and well-functioning international cooperation in criminal matters. The Convention addresses three main areas: Measures to be taken at the national level (Chapter II); Monitoring of implementation: this is to be undertaken by the Group of States against Corruption (GRECO) (Chapter III); and International co-operation (Chapter IV).

9.98 The wide scope of the Convention is reflected in Chapter II, which requires Parties to criminalize, on the basis of a set of common elements, both active and passive bribery of domestic, foreign, and international public servants, members of legislatures and judges, including prosecutors and holders of judicial office.

---

[56] It is also open to the non-Member States that participated in its drawing up: Canada, Japan, Mexico, and the US.

[57] These are set out in full in App 10 below.

[58] The text of the convention is found in App 9 below. For a useful overview of the Convention, see P Csonka, 'The Council of Europe's Anti-Corruption Treaties' a paper given at the 9th International Anti-Corruption Conference, Durban, 1999.

As regards domestic public officials, the active bribery offence covers, when committed intentionally, 'the promising, offering or giving by any person, directly or indirectly, of any undue advantage to any of [the State's] public officials, for himself or herself or for anyone else, for him or her to act or refrain from acting in the exercise of his or her functions' (Article 2). The passive bribery offence is in similar terms save that it covers a domestic public official requesting or receiving any undue advantage (Article 3). It is immaterial whether the request was actually acted upon or whether the advantage was for the public servant personally or for someone else.

Whilst the undue advantage will generally be of an economic nature, the essence of the offence is that a person is, or would be, placed in a better position than that prior to the offence and that the public official was not entitled to the benefit. Such advantages might consist of, for example, holidays, loans, food and drink or better career prospects. The meaning of 'undue' is of considerable importance in that it appears in several international instruments, including UNCAC. In the context of the Criminal Law Convention, the Council of Europe Explanatory Report (the Explanatory Report) suggests that the word should be interpreted as something that the recipient is not lawfully entitled to accept or receive.[59] The meaning of the word 'undue' is further considered in para 10.42 below. **9.99**

Articles 4 and 6 extend the provisions of Articles 2 and 3 to members of domestic and foreign public assemblies when exercising legislative or administrative powers. Given the breadth of the term 'public official' in Article 1, this offence also extends to members of local and regional assemblies and members of any other public body whose members are elected or appointed and who exercise legislative or administrative powers. Under Article 10, a similar position pertains to members of international parliamentary assemblies of international organizations (such as the Parliamentary Assembly of the Council of Europe) or supranational organizations (such as the European Parliament) of which the State Party is a member. **9.100**

Article 9 extends the provisions of Articles 2 and 3 to officials of international organizations. This covers conduct 'involving any official or other contracted employee, within the meaning of the staff regulations, of any public international or supranational organisation or body of which the Party is a member, and any person, whether seconded or not, carrying out functions corresponding to those performed by such officials or agents'. **9.101**

Article 5 extends the conduct referred to in Articles 2 and 3 to the bribery of foreign public officials of any other State Party. The Article is particularly **9.102**

59 See Council of Europe Explanatory Report on the Criminal Law Convention on Corruption, para 38, http://conventions.coe.int/treaty/en/Reports/Html/173.htm.

significant in that it addresses both the active and passive side of bribery. Article 11 does likewise in respect of any 'holders of judicial office or officials of any international court whose jurisdiction is accepted by the Party'.

9.103 Another feature of the Convention is that Articles 7 and 8 extend criminal responsibility for bribery to the private sector. This reflects the need to limit the differences in rules applicable to the private and public spheres, which is especially important given the transfer of so many major public functions to the private sector. Thus the Convention requires State Parties to establish as criminal offences, when committed intentionally in the course of business activity, both active bribery, ie 'the promising, offering or giving, directly or indirectly, of any undue advantage to any persons who direct or work for, in any capacity, private sector entities, for themselves or for anyone else, for them to act, or refrain from acting, in breach of their duties' and passive bribery, ie 'the request or receipt, directly or indirectly, by any persons who direct or work for, in any capacity, private sector entities, of any undue advantage or the promise thereof for themselves or for anyone else, or the acceptance of an offer or a promise of such an advantage, to act or refrain from acting in breach of their duties'. Articles 7 and 8 extend to persons who 'direct or work for, *in any capacity*, private sector entities'[60] (emphasis added). This is also designed to cover business relationships where there is no contract of employment, such as partnerships. It would also cover members of the board of an enterprise, its consultants, and agents who can engage the responsibility of the company. One significant difference between the public bribery and private bribery offences is that, as regards the latter, the breach of duty is one of the essential elements of the offence. Arguably, the term 'breach of duty' extends beyond a breach of contract to include a general breach of loyalty owed to one's principal.

9.104 The Convention includes several other mandatory offences. Trading in influence in Article 12 addresses both active and passive aspects of the offence. This comprises intentionally

> the promising, giving or offering, directly or indirectly, of any undue . . . advantage to anyone who asserts or confirms that he or she is able to exert an improper influence over the decision making of any person referred to in Articles 2, 4 to 6 and 9 to 11 in consideration thereof, whether the undue advantage is for himself or herself or for anyone else, as well as the request, receipt or the acceptance of the offer or the promise of such an advantage, in consideration of that influence, whether or not the influence is exerted or whether or not the supposed influence leads to the intended result.

9.105 As paragraph 64 of the Explanatory Report puts it, 'criminalising trading in influence seeks to reach the close circle of the official or the political party to

[60] 'Private sector entities' refers to companies, enterprises, trusts, and other entities which are entirely, or to a determining extent, owned by private persons.

which s/he belongs and to tackle the corrupt behaviour of those persons who are in the neighbourhood of power and try to obtain advantages from their situation, contributing to the atmosphere of corruption'. Thus, unlike bribery, the influence peddlers are 'outsiders' who cannot take decisions themselves but misuse their real or alleged influence on other persons. Article 13 addresses money laundering of the proceeds of corruption. It requires Parties to criminalize the laundering offences in Article 6(1) and (2) of the Council of Europe Convention on Laundering, Search, Seizure and Confiscation of the Proceeds from Crime (ETS No 141) in respect of offences contained in Articles 2–12. The laundering offences in Article 6 are as follows:

> 1. Each Party shall adopt such legislative and other measures as may be necessary to establish as offences under its domestic law, when committed intentionally:
>   a. the conversion or transfer of property, knowing that such property is proceeds of an offence, for the purpose of concealing or disguising the illicit origin of the property or of assisting any person who is involved in the commission of the predicate offence to evade the legal consequences of his actions;
>   b. the concealment or disguise of the true nature, source, location, disposition, movement, rights with respect to, or ownership of, property, knowing that such property is proceeds; and, subject to its constitutional principles and the basic concepts of its legal system;
>   c. the acquisition, possession or use of property, knowing, at the time of receipt, that such property was proceeds;
>   d. participation in, association or conspiracy to commit, attempts to commit and aiding, abetting, facilitating and counselling the commission of any of the offences established in accordance with this article.
> 2. For the purposes of implementing or applying paragraph 1 of this article:
>   a. it shall not matter whether the predicate offence was subject to the criminal jurisdiction of the Party;
>   b. it may be provided that the offences set forth in that paragraph do not apply to the persons who committed the predicate offence;
>   c. knowledge, intent or purpose required as an element of an offence set forth in that paragraph may be inferred from objective, factual circumstances.

Article 13 contains two exceptions: firstly where the State Party has made a **9.106**
reservation or declaration with respect to those offences; and secondly where the Party 'does not consider such offences as serious ones for the purpose of their money laundering legislation'.

To complement efforts to tackle the convention offences, Article 14 contains **9.107**
two 'Account Offences'. It requires each Party to adopt such legislative and other measures as may be necessary to establish as offences liable to criminal or other sanctions under its domestic law the following acts or omissions, when committed intentionally, in order to commit, conceal or disguise the offences referred to in Articles 2 to 12, to the extent the Party has not made a reservation or a declaration: (a) creating or using an invoice or any other accounting

document or record containing false or incomplete information; and (b) unlawfully omitting to make a record of a payment.

9.108 With regard to corporate liability, Article 18 requires Parties to adopt measures to ensure that legal persons (corporations or organizations) can be held liable for active bribery, trading in influence, and money laundering where those offences were committed for the corporation's benefit by a natural person with a 'leading position' within the organization. This should extend to a failure to supervise or control an employee or other person under the authority of the corporation who engages in the prohibited offences for the benefit of the corporation. For a detailed discussion of this area, see para 10.69 below.

9.109 Parties are required to enact the necessary legislation and other measures to establish jurisdiction over the Convention offences where:

(1) the offence is committed in whole or in part in its territory;
(2) the offender is one of its nationals or public officials or a member of one of its domestic public assemblies; or
(3) the offence involves one of its public officials, a member of a domestic public assembly, or a national who is a member of an international organization or court.

9.110 Article 19 provides that each Party shall provide, in respect of the Convention offences 'effective, proportionate and dissuasive sanctions and measures, including, when committed by natural persons, penalties involving deprivation of liberty which can give rise to extradition'. It further requires that legal persons held liable under Article 18 shall be subject to 'effective, proportionate and dissuasive criminal or non-criminal sanctions, including monetary sanctions'. There is also a general obligation upon State Parties to provide for an adequate legal framework enabling them to confiscate the instrumentalities and the proceeds of Convention offences, or property the value of which corresponds to such proceeds.

9.111 The Additional Protocol to the Criminal Law Convention on Corruption was opened for signature in May 2003. This extends the scope of the Convention to arbitrators in commercial, civil, and other matters, as well as to jurors, thus complementing the Criminal Law Convention's provisions aimed at protecting judicial authorities from corruption. The Protocol entered into force on 1 February 2005 and has been ratified by the UK.

9.112 Monitoring the implementation of the Convention and the Additional Protocol is the responsibility of the Group of States Against Corruption (GRECO) (see para 9.118 below).

2. Civil Law Convention on Corruption

One weakness of many international instruments is the absence of provisions on the rights of victims of corruption. One document that specifically addresses this point is the Civil Law Convention on Corruption. This was adopted on 4 November 1999, and is the first attempt to define common international rules for civil litigation in corruption cases. The text of the convention is found in App 8 below. It requires Parties to ensure that those affected by corruption can sue the perpetrators and obtain compensation for damage as a result of acts of corruption. However, it must be noted that this approach may be appropriate for well-functioning states, but it can impose unrealistic burdens on countries whose governments are struggling with systemic corruption, particularly in the field of procurement, if the state itself, rather than the individuals involved, is to be held liable for losses and loss of profits. **9.113**

The Convention requires the enactment of civil law provisions which ensure that anyone who has suffered damage resulting from corruption can recover for 'material damage, loss of profits and non-pecuniary loss'. Damages can be recovered against anyone who has committed a corrupt act, authorized someone else to do so, or failed to take reasonable steps to prevent the act, including the state itself, provided that a causal link between the act and the damages claimed can be proved. Where appropriate, courts also have the power to declare contractual obligations resulting from corruption to be null and void, where the consent of any party to the contract has been 'undermined' by corruption. **9.114**

The Civil Law Convention is narrower that its criminal law counterpart in the forms of corruption to which it applies, extending only to bribery and similar acts, although it applies to such acts in both private and public sector circumstances. Other useful requirements in the Convention concern whistleblower protection for employees, the need to establish international cooperation procedures, and the fact that no reservation may be made in respect of any provision in the Convention. As with the Criminal Law Convention, monitoring will be undertaken by GRECO. The Convention came into force on 1 November 2003 and thus it is too early to establish its impact. The United Kingdom signed the Convention on 8 June 2000 but has yet to ratify it. **9.115**

3. Model Code of Conduct for Public Officials

Principle 10 of the Twenty Guiding Principles provides that states should 'ensure that the rules relating to the rights and duties of public officials take into account the requirements of the fight against corruption and provide for appropriate and effective disciplinary measures; and promote further specification of the behaviour expected from public officials by appropriate means, such as codes of conduct'. Based on this, the GMC proceeded to draft a code of **9.116** conduct. The Committee of Ministers at its 106th Session in May 2000 then adopted Recommendation R(2000)10, inviting member states to promote 'the adoption of national codes of conduct for public officials' based on a Model Code of Conduct for Public Officials.[61]

9.117 The object of the Model Code is to specify the 'standards of integrity and conduct to be observed by public officials,[62] to help them meet those standards and to inform the public of the conduct it is entitled to expect of public officials'.[63] The Model Code then addresses a wide range of issues including conflicts of interest, declaration of assets, whistleblowing, and political or public activity. It also includes provisions as to the observance of the Code and provides that the Code forms part of the terms of employment of the public official and that breach of them may result in disciplinary action. The Group of States against Corruption is tasked with monitoring the implementation of the Recommendation.[64]

4. Group of States Against Corruption

9.118 In its Programme of Action against Corruption, the Committee of Ministers directed the GMC to develop a follow-up mechanism that would monitor the implementation of the Guiding Principles. In response, the Committee proposed the creation of the Group of States against Corruption (GRECO). On 5 May 1998, the Committee of Ministers adopted Resolution (98) 7, which authorized the establishment of GRECO, with participation open to member and non-member states that had adopted the Guiding Principles, or acceded to the COE Convention.[65]

9.119 The aim of GRECO is to 'improve the capacity of its members to fight corruption by following up, through a dynamic process of mutual evaluation and peer pressure, compliance with their undertakings' in the fight against corruption.[66] In order to do so, GRECO is to monitor the observance of the Guiding Principles and monitor the implementation of the international legal instruments to be adopted in pursuance of the Programme of Action against Corruption.[67] This is done through a system of evaluations of GRECO

[61] The text is set out in App 11 below. For the Recommendation on common rules against corruption in the funding of political parties and electoral campaigns see App 12.

[62] Defined as 'a person employed by a public authority', Art 1(2).

[63] Art 3.

[64] For a detailed analysis of the Code, see Council of Europe, Committee of Ministers Explanatory Memorandum to Recommendation R (2000) 10 on Codes of conduct for public officials available at http://cm.coe.int/stat/E/Public/2000/ExpRec(00)10.htm.

[65] Full membership of GRECO is limited to those countries that participate fully in the mutual evaluation process and agree to be evaluated.

[66] Statute of GRECO, Art 1.

[67] To date these comprise the Criminal Law Convention on Corruption, the Additional protocol, the Civil Law Convention on Corruption and Recommendation R (2000) 10 on codes of conduct for public officials.

members.[68] Each state is required to answer a questionnaire which provides the framework for the evaluation process. Its reply to the questionnaire is then evaluated by a team of experts appointed by GRECO and drawn from other member states. The team may also undertake a country visit. It then prepares a preliminary draft evaluation report which is submitted to the evaluated country for comment. A draft report is then submitted to GRECO where it is debated in plenary and then put to the vote for adoption, with or without amendments. The report then designates measures to be taken by the member state in areas found not to be in compliance with the recommendations.

The first evaluation round took place between 1 January 2000 and 31 December 2002 and concerned Guiding Principles 3 (independence of investigation and prosecutorial bodies), 6 (limits on immunity from investigation and prosecution), and 7 (promoting the specialisation of persons or bodies in charge of fighting corruption). Virtually all GRECO member states have now been subject to such evaluation and the reports made public.[69] GRECO has also launched a compliance procedure which aims at assessing whether the recommendations adopted during the first evaluation have been satisfactorily implemented. The Compliance Report on the United Kingdom was made public in July 2005.[70] **9.120**

On 1 January 2003, GRECO launched a second evaluation round dealing with the confiscation of corruption proceeds, liability of legal persons, public administration, tax measures to curb corruption, and accounting offences relating to corruption. The third evaluation round will be devoted to the transparency of political party funding and the implementation of the criminal law provisions in the Criminal Law Convention on Corruption. **9.121**

i. The OCTOPUS Programme

This Programme began as a joint initiative between the Council of Europe and the European Commission aimed at fighting corruption and organized crime in sixteen countries in transition.[71] It is now continued by the Council of Europe. In June 1996, the European Commission and the Council of Europe launched the first phase of the OCTOPUS Programme. **9.122**

Problems related to corruption and organized crime, as well as measures undertaken by governments, were analysed in the sixteen states. For each **9.123**

[68] The evaluation procedures are set out in the Statute of GRECO Arts 10–16 and in Title II of its Rules of Procedure.

[69] A listing of evaluation reports and compliance reports adopted by GRECO is available at http://www.greco.coe.int/evaluations/cycle1/Eval1Reports.htm.

[70] See 2.138 above.

[71] Albania, Bulgaria, Croatia, the Czech Republic, Estonia, Hungary, Latvia, Lithuania, Moldova, Poland, Romania, the Russian Federation, Slovakia, Slovenia, the former Yugoslav Republic of Macedonia, and Ukraine.

country, a set of recommendations was prepared. OCTOPUS II (1999–2000) aimed at strengthening capacities, policies, and cooperation (national and international) for the control of corruption and organized crime in Europe. With ten of the sixteen programme countries of central and eastern Europe being candidates for membership in the European Union, OCTOPUS II helped them to put in place the legislation, standards, and practices of the European Union needed in the fight against organized crime and corruption. Since then, the Council of Europe has continued to support a range of anti-corruption activities, the most recent addressing the strengthening of public ethics in local government.

G. The European Union

9.124 The European Union (EU) has made the fight against corruption one of its priorities. Article 29 of the EU Treaty lists the preventing and combating of corruption as one objective towards creating a European area of freedom, security, and justice through: (a) closer cooperation between police forces, customs authorities and other competent authorities in the Member States, both directly and through the European Police Office (Europol); (b) closer cooperation between judicial and other competent authorities of the Member States; and (c) the 'approximation' of criminal laws of the Member States in order to fight corruption.

9.125 There are now a series of EU instruments addressing the issue. Starting with the 1995 Convention on the Protection of the European Communities' Financial Interests, recognition of the significance of corruption then led to the drawing up of two Protocols and thence to the Convention on the fight against corruption involving officials of the European Communities or officials of Member States of the European Union.[72]

1. EU Convention on the Protection of the Financial Interests of the Communities and Protocols

9.126 The first significant move to address corruption came in 1995 as part of an effort to protect the financial interests of the European Union. The Convention on the Protection of the European Union's Financial Interests[73] which was drawn up on the basis of Article K.3 of the Treaty on European Union, requires

[72] See generally S White, *The Protection of the Financial Interests of the European Communities: The Fight Against Fraud and Corruption* (Kluwer, 1998).

[73] Adopted by the Council on 26 July 1995 (95/C316/03). The text of the convention is in App 14 below.

Member States to criminalize fraud affecting the EU's financial interests. Article 1(1) provides that such fraud consists of:

(a) In respect of expenditure, any intentional act or omission relating to:
- —The use or presentation of false, incorrect or incomplete statements or documents, which has as its effect the misappropriation or wrongful retention of funds from the general budget of the European Communities or budgets managed by, or on behalf of, the European Communities,
- —Non-disclosure of information in violation of a specific obligation, with the same effect,
- —The misapplication of such funds for purposes other than those for which they were originally granted;

(a) In respect of revenue, any intentional act or omission relating to:
- —The use or presentation of false, incorrect or incomplete statements or documents, which has as its effect the illegal diminution of the resources of the general budget of the European Communities or budgets managed by, or on behalf of, the European Communities,
- —Non-disclosure of information in violation of a specific obligation, with the same effect,
- —Misapplication of a legally obtained benefit, with the same effect.

With the exception of cases of minor fraud, each Member State is also required **9.127** to criminalize 'the intentional preparation or supply of false, incorrect or incomplete statements or documents having the effect described in Article 1(1)' which 'constitutes a criminal offence if it is not already punishable as a principal offence or as participation in, instigation of, or attempt to commit, fraud' as defined in that paragraph (Article 1(3)).

Member States are required to ensure that offences under Article 1(1) are **9.128** punishable by 'effective, proportionate and dissuasive criminal penalties', including, at least in cases of serious fraud, penalties involving deprivation of liberty which can give rise to extradition (Article 2(1)) and apply to heads of businesses or any persons having power to take decisions or exercise control within a business.

The Convention also requires Member States to establish its jurisdiction over **9.129** the offences it has established in accordance with Article 1 and 2(1) when:

(1) fraud, participation in fraud or attempted fraud affecting the European Communities' financial interests is committed in whole or in part within its territory, including fraud for which the benefit was obtained in that territory;
(2) a person within its territory knowingly assists or induces the commission of such fraud within the territory of any other State; or
(3) the offender is a national of the Member State concerned, provided that the law of that Member State may require the conduct to be punishable also in the country where it occurred.

The Convention also deals with extradition and mutual assistance and requires Member States to apply the *ne bis in idem* rule in their domestic law.

9.130 The Convention entered into force on 17 October 2002, having been ratified by all Member States.

i. The First Protocol

9.131 The First Protocol to the 1995 Convention specifically addresses corruption by or against national and Community officials 'which damages or is likely to damage the European Communities' financial interests'. Member States are required to criminalize both passive and active bribery. Article 2 provides that:

> For the purposes of this Protocol, the deliberate action of an official, who, directly or through an intermediary, requests or receives advantages of any kind whatsoever, for himself or for a third party, or accepts a promise of such an advantage, to act or refrain from acting in accordance with his duty or in the exercise of his functions in breach of his official duties in a way which damages or is likely to damage the European Communities' financial interests shall constitute passive corruption.

9.132 As regards active corruption, Article 3 provides:

> For the purposes of this Protocol, the deliberate action of whosoever promises or gives, directly or through an intermediary, an advantage of any kind whatsoever to an official for himself or for a third party for him to act or refrain from acting in accordance with his duty or in the exercise of his functions in breach of his official duties in a way which damages or is likely to damage the European Communities' financial interests shall constitute active corruption.

9.133 Member States are required to take the necessary measures to ensure that such acts are punishable by 'effective, proportionate and dissuasive criminal penalties, including in serious cases, penalties involving deprivation of liberty which can give rise to extradition' (Article 5). The Protocol entered into force on 17 October 2002 after having been ratified by all Member States. The text of the Protocol is in App 17 below.

ii. The Second Protocol

9.134 The Second Protocol to the 1995 Convention supplements the earlier instruments in four main respects. First, it requires Member States to establish money laundering as a criminal offence (Article 2). Secondly, Article 3 addresses the issue of the liability of legal persons and provides that Each Member State shall take the necessary measures to ensure that legal persons can be held liable for fraud, active corruption and money laundering committed for their benefit by any person, acting either individually or as part of an organ of the legal person, who has a leading position within the legal person, based on any of the following: (a) a power of representation of the legal person, or (b) an authority to take decisions on behalf of the legal person, or (c) an authority to exercise control within the legal person, as well as for involvement as accessories or instigators in such fraud, active corruption or money laundering or the attempted commission of such fraud. Thirdly, Member States are required to take measures to enable the seizure and confiscation of the proceeds of corruption and money laundering as well as instrumentalities (Article 5). Finally, there is a requirement for Member States to cooperate with the European Commission in the fight against fraud, corruption, and money laundering (Articles 6 and 7). The text of the Protocol is in App 16 below.

2. Convention on the Fight against Corruption involving Officials of the European Communities or Officials of Member States of the European Union

This 1997 Convention criminalises corrupt conduct involving officials of both **9.135**
the Community and Member States. It fills a significant gap in that previously the criminal law in most Member States did not apply to officials of other Member States even if the conduct took place in their own territory or was instigated by one of their own nationals. In addition, the offences of passive and active bribery are no longer limited to the damage or likely damage to the EU's financial interests. The Convention also contains provisions relating to extradition, co-operation and *ne bis in idem* that reflect the approach in the 1995 Convention. The text of the Convention is found in App 13 below.

3. Framework Decision on Combating Corruption in the Private Sector

On 22 December 1998, the Council of the European Union adopted a 'Joint **9.136**
Action' (98/742/JHA) on corruption in the private sector, ie the giving or receiving of an undue advantage in the course of business activities leading to acts in breach of a person's duty. It was envisaged that Member States would make this a criminal offence within two years. This did not occur and it was then proposed by the Danish presidency that the Joint Action be replaced by a binding framework decision. This led to the adoption by the Council of the EU Framework Decision of 22 July 2003, the principal aims of which are to ensure that both active and passive corruption in the private sector are criminalized in all Member States, that legal persons may also be held responsible for such offences, and that these offences incur 'effective, proportionate and dissuasive penalties'.[74] Thus Member States are required to ensure that the following conduct constitutes a criminal offence, when committed intentionally and when carried out in the course of business activities both within profit and non-profit

[74] Council Framework Decision 2003/568/JHA, Preamble Point 10. The text of the Framework Decision is in App 17 below.

making entities:[75]

(1) promising, offering or giving, directly or through an intermediary, to a person who in any capacity directs or works for a private-sector entity an undue advantage of any kind, for that person or for a third party, in order that that person should perform or refrain from performing any act, in breach of that person's duties; or

(2) directly or through an intermediary, requesting or receiving an undue advantage of any kind, or accepting the promise of such an advantage, for oneself or for a third party, while in any capacity directing or working for a private-sector entity, in order to perform or refrain from performing any act, in breach of one's duties.

9.137 Each Member State is required to take the necessary measures to ensure that these offences are punishable by 'effective, proportionate and dissuasive criminal penalties' with a penalty of a maximum of at least one to three years' imprisonment. Member States were required to take the necessary measures to comply with the provisions of the Framework Decision before 22 July 2005, although this has not occurred in all cases.

9.138 At present there is no monitoring and evaluation process envisaged regarding these instruments, the EU Commission taking the view that, given the existing mechanisms under the OECD Convention and Council of Europe (GRECO), a separate EU initiative is currently inappropriate as being an unnecessary duplication of efforts.[76]

9.139 At the political level, in 1997 the Council, in its Action Plan against organized crime, advocated the development of a comprehensive policy against corruption focusing primarily on preventive measures. In doing so, and this is a continuing feature of the EU action on corruption, it emphasized the need to take into account the work being carried out in other international fora. This has ensured a consistent approach, particularly in respect of the work of the Council of Europe. In response to the Action Plan, a Communication from the European Commission suggested the development of a range of measures designed to help to formulate an appropriate strategy both within and outside the EU. Measures suggested included banning the tax deductibility of bribes, rules on public procurement, and blacklisting of companies involved in corruption.[77] Further,

---

[75] The Framework Decision covers any person who directs or works for a private-sector entity. This very broad definition, modelled on that contained in the Council of Europe Criminal Law Convention, covers all types of contractual relations—relations between employer and employee, between partners and so on.

[76] Commission of the European Communities, Communication from the Commission to the Council, the European Parliament and the European Economic and Social Committee on the comprehensive EU policy against corruption, COM(2003)317 final, 28 May 2003, 9.

[77] Commission of the European Communities, Communication from the Commission to the Council and the European Parliament on a Union policy against corruption, COM(97) 192 final, 21 May 1997.

at the 1999 Tampere European Council, EU heads of state or government, endorsed the 1998 Council of Vienna Action Plan, by identifying corruption, in the context of financial crime, as one of the sectors of particular relevance where common definitions, 'incriminations', and sanctions should be agreed upon. This led to the so-called Millennium Strategy on the Prevention and Control of Organised Crime, which reiterated the need for the harmonization of national legislation and the development of a more multidisciplinary EU policy towards corruption, again taking into account work being carried out in other international fora. In addition, Member States were urged to ratify the relevant EU and Council of Europe anti-corruption instruments within a given timetable.[78] This has still not taken place and remains a matter of concern to the Commission.

Looking ahead, the European Commission has stated, in its May 2003 Communication on a comprehensive EU policy against corruption, that the future EU policy on corruption should consist of the following core elements: **9.140**

- A strong political commitment against all forms of corruption should come from the highest level of EU institutions.
- The implementation of existing anti-corruption instruments should be closely monitored and strengthened for the time being through the adherence of the European Community to one or both Conventions on Corruption of the Council of Europe and the participation in its monitoring mechanism, GRECO.
- EU Member States should develop and improve investigative tools and allocate more specialized staff to the fight against corruption.
- Member States and EU institutions and bodies should enhance efforts to combat corruption damaging the financial interests of the European Community.
- Common integrity standards in public administrations across the EU, such as the Common Assessment Framework of EU Heads of Civil Service and Public Administration, should be further developed at EU level.
- Member States and the Commission should support the private sector in its efforts to raise integrity and corporate responsibility.
- The fight against political corruption and illicit financing of social partner entities and other interest groups needs to be strengthened at EU and Member State level.
- The EU should continue making the fight against corruption an integral part of its external and trade policy.
- In their permanent dialogue with acceding, candidate, and other third countries, the Member States and the Commission should systematically

[78] This section is drawn largely from the Commission's document COM(2003) 317 final (above).

include corruption-related issues and further assist these countries in their efforts to set up and implement national anti-corruption policies.

The Communication was approved by the European Parliament in December 2003 and the Justice and Home Affairs Council in April 2005.

9.141 Working with acceding, candidate, and other third countries to develop anti-corruption measures is a key part of the current EU agenda. For example, during negotiations for entry for those candidate states which joined in 2004, the adequacy of the steps taken by them to counter corruption was high on the agenda. This remains the case as regards the next set of countries seeking entry. Here the European Commission has highlighted the need for countries such as Serbia and Montenegro, Croatia, and Albania to take action to tackle corruption.[79] Further, as part of the ACP-EU Partnership Agreement, signed in Cotonou in June 2000 between the EU and 77 African, Caribbean, and Pacific states, the importance of good governance was recognized and it was agreed that this includes 'capacity building for elaborating and implementing measures aiming in particular to preventing and combating corruption'. Article 97 then provides that where the EU is a significant partner in terms of financial support to economic and sectoral policies and programmes, serious cases of corruption should give rise to a consultation procedure between the parties. If the consultations do not lead to a solution acceptable to both parties or if consultation is refused, the parties 'shall take the appropriate measures' which must be 'proportional to the seriousness of the situation'.

9.142 In a further effort to encourage and improve the fight against corruption in the acceding, candidate and other third countries, the EU Commission has developed the following ten principles:

1. To ensure credibility, a clear stance against corruption is essential from leaders and decision-makers. Bearing in mind that no universally applicable recipes exist, *national* anti-corruption strategies or programmes, covering both preventive and repressive measures, should be drawn up and implemented. These strategies should be subject to broad consultation at all levels.
2. Current and future EU Members shall fully align with the EU *acquis* and ratify and implement all main international anti-corruption instruments they are party to (UN, Council of Europe and OECD Conventions). Third countries should sign and ratify as well as implement relevant international anti-corruption instruments.
3. Anti-corruption laws are important, but more important is their implementation by competent and visible anti-corruption bodies (ie well trained and specialized services such as anti-corruption prosecutors). Targeted investigative techniques, statistics and indicators should be developed. The role of law enforcement bodies should be strengthened concerning not only corruption but also fraud, tax offences and money laundering.

[79] See *Europa-Enlargement Newsletter*, November 2005, European Commission.

4. Access to public office must be open to every citizen. Recruitment and promotion should be regulated by objective and merit-based criteria. Salaries and social rights must be adequate. Civil servants should be required to disclose their assets. Sensitive posts should be subject to rotation.
5. Integrity, accountability and transparency in public administration (judiciary, police, customs, tax administration, health sector, public procurement) should be raised through employing quality management tools and auditing and monitoring standards, such as the Common Assessment Framework of EU Heads of Public Administrations and the Strasbourg Resolution. Increased transparency is important in view of developing confidence between the citizens and public administration.
6. Codes of Conduct in the public sector should be established and monitored.
7. Clear rules should be established in both the public and private sector on whistle blowing (given that corruption is an offence without direct victims who could witness and report it) and reporting.
8. Public intolerance of corruption should be increased, through awareness-raising campaigns in the media and training. The central message must be that corruption is not a tolerable phenomenon, but a criminal offence. Civil society has an important role to play in preventing and fighting the problem.
9. Clear and transparent rules of party financing, and external financial control of political parties, should be introduced to avoid covert links between politicians and (illicit) business interests. Political parties evidently have strong influence on decision-makers, but are often immune to anti-bribery laws.
10. Incentives should be developed for the private sector to refrain from corrupt practices, such as codes of conduct or 'white lists' for integer companies.

H. The Commonwealth

The modern Commonwealth dates from a 1949 meeting in London at which Commonwealth prime ministers of the, then, eight countries of the Commonwealth, Australia, Britain, Canada, Ceylon (as Sri Lanka was then known), India, New Zealand, Pakistan, and South Africa agreed the London Declaration. This transformed the whole character of the Commonwealth from a relic of Empire into a cooperative association based on the voluntary membership of free and sovereign states working to promote their mutual interests. The association thus formally became 'the Commonwealth' and ceased to be the 'British' Commonwealth. Today, the Commonwealth comprises fifty-three independent member countries, with a total population estimated at over 1.7 billion. It spans all major political groupings, regions, and economic zones and includes some of the largest (eg India) and smallest (eg Nauru) countries in the world, as well as some of poorest and some of the richest. It embraces major parts of Africa and Asia, almost all of the Caribbean and much of the Pacific and Australasia, as well as having members in Europe and America. It also contains a high proportion of small states.[80] **9.143**

[80] The 1971 Declaration of Commonwealth Principles puts it as follows: 'The Commonwealth of Nations is a voluntary association of independent sovereign States . . . Members of the

9.144 The Commonwealth is remarkable in that it has neither a charter nor any formal constitutional structure. Its members voluntarily cooperate with each other in furtherance of their common interests and seek to reach decisions by consensus. As a result, it has gone through a gradual evolution over time as its membership has expanded and issues of joint concern have changed. The principles and aims of the organization are set out in the form of Declarations or Statements which have been issued at the biennial meetings of Commonwealth Heads of Government (CHOGM).

1. The Legal Legacy

9.145 In terms of the fight against corruption, Commonwealth member states have much in common:

(1) Common language: Whilst the people of the Commonwealth speak many languages, they communicate with each other through the shared language of English (due to their shared colonial administrative history). As a result, their written laws and the decisions of their superior courts are almost invariably available in English.
(2) Common legal heritage: The laws and legal system of the vast majority of Commonwealth states are based on the English common law. Countries with an Islamic Law or Roman-Dutch law tradition also make extensive use of common law principles in areas such as administrative law and criminal procedure.
(3) Common constitutional principles: The Westminster model constitution was used as the basis for the independence constitutions of many Commonwealth member states. This commonality has encouraged courts to share jurisprudence on constitutional matters and to develop common principles of constitutional interpretation.
(4) Common legal challenges: There is an enormous amount of cooperation between Commonwealth countries, for example through the use of the various Commonwealth schemes.[81]

2. Developing the Just and Honest Government Agenda

9.146 Over the years, Commonwealth Heads of Government have adopted a series of documents which enshrine the Association's core beliefs. In 1991, Commonwealth Heads of Government, at their Meeting in Zimbabwe, adopted the Harare Commonwealth Declaration. This set out the Association's priorities, one of which is the promotion of the Commonwealth's fundamental political values—democracy, the rule of law, and human rights.

Commonwealth come from territories in the six continents and five oceans, include people of different races, languages and religions, and display every stage of economic development, from poor developing nations to wealthy industrialised nations'.

[81] In particular, the Harare Scheme on Mutual Legal Assistance in Criminal Matters and the London Scheme on Extradition of Fugitive Offenders.

Concern over the deleterious effect of corruption on these values led to the Commonwealth Secretary-General convening an Expert Group on Good Governance to analyse and examine ways of promoting good governance and reducing corruption in economic management. Its final Report contained a Framework for Commonwealth Principles on Promoting Good Governance and Combating Corruption ('the Framework Principles').[82] These called for national action in five areas: 1. Ethics and Integrity in the Public and Private Sectors; 2. Economic and Fiscal Policies; 3. Management of Services Provided in the Public Interest; 4. The Judiciary and Legal System; 5. Civil Society. In November 1999, Commonwealth Heads of Government endorsed the Framework Principles as a basis for pursuing concerted strategies to tackle all types of corruption at both national and global levels. They requested the Secretary-General to formulate strategies to facilitate the implementation of the Framework Principles, and for reviews of its progress to be reported at regular intervals. They also emphasized that 'corruption has become global in reach and that it must be tackled comprehensively through action at both national and international levels' and, somewhat ambitiously, committed themselves to a policy of 'zero tolerance', recognizing that any strategy to promote good governance and eliminate corruption required strong political will at the highest levels of government. Finally, the Heads of Government adopted a declaration embodying a call for action on the five areas covered by the Framework Principles. **9.147**

The first area addresses the need to promote ethics and integrity in the public and private sectors. This emphasizes the threat posed by corruption to the stability and well-being of society and recognizes that the implementation of effective anti-corruption strategies is of the highest priority. Of particular interest is the attention paid by the Framework Principles to the funding of political parties for this 'has the potential to become a major source of corruption as well as a vehicle for hiding corruption'.[83] It is noted that clear links can be drawn between inappropriate or inadequate controls on such funding and the prevalence of corruption but also recognized that different approaches to the issue may be necessary, depending upon the prevailing political and social norms. Several factors that are relevant in tackling the problems associated with money and politics are highlighted. These include: (a) whether or not there are established political parties; (b) the capacity of the state to finance political parties and/or election campaigns, and levels of expenditure on political campaigns; (c) limits on financial contributions and the integrity of their sources; (d) the role of national and international companies in providing funds to political parties; and (e) the national interest in ensuring that foreign interests do not influence domestic political priorities and decisions. **9.148**

[82] For the full texts see App 5 and 6 below. [83] para 8.

9.149 Paragraph 9 then notes that, although rules on funding for political parties will vary depending upon national circumstances, in general it is important that these rules should serve to (i) prevent conflicts of interest and the exercise of improper influence; (ii) preserve the integrity of democratic political structures and processes; (iii) proscribe the use of funds acquired through illegal and corrupt practices to finance political parties; and (iv) enshrine the concept of transparency in the funding of political parties by requiring the declaration of donations exceeding a specified limit.

9.150 The second area focuses on the need to adopt economic and fiscal reforms designed to maximize transparency and certainty and minimize administrative discretion. Such policy reforms might include: (a) liberalizing trade regimes through the progressive removal of inefficient quantitative restrictions and import/export licences; (b) reducing foreign exchange controls and increasing transparency in foreign exchange allocation processes; and (c) eliminating price controls.[84]

9.151 The third area addresses the need to improve the management, efficiency, and delivery of public services. As the Framework Principles note, when 'services are provided in an efficient manner, fewer opportunities for corruption arise as citizens are no longer required to compete, often by way of paying bribes, for scarce and inefficient services'.[85]

9.152 The fourth area considers the need to establish an independent, competent and accountable judiciary and to strengthen the legal system. A particularly important element here is the need for states to ensure that their criminal laws provide a 'meaningful deterrent' and that the 'vigorous application and enforcement of existing laws and prosecution of offenders is essential if the rule of law is to be respected'.[86] The Principles go on to note that whilst most countries have at their disposal a wide range of laws that can be used to combat corruption, 'these laws are often under-utilised and, at times, even ignored'. The final area highlights the need for regular consultation and collaboration with civil society on the development of anti-corruption strategies.

9.153 Perhaps the most visible work of the Commonwealth in this area comes through technical assistance designed to assist member countries to implement the Framework Principles into domestic law. This is particularly relevant given that that small and developing states make up the vast majority of Commonwealth members, and most have serious resource and staffing constraints. Three examples are helpful.

9.154 First, the convening of Expert Groups to examine key areas affecting Commonwealth member states. The use of expert groups has several advantages:

[84] para 10. [85] para 11. [86] para 20.

(a) it enhances the objective of seeking a pan-Commonwealth approach to legal issues; (b) it enables smaller Commonwealth jurisdictions to be fully involved in the discussions on and development of new principles; and (c) it assists those member states with resource and/or personnel constraints to develop their laws through the use of the Expert Group reports and subsequent development of model laws. This is well illustrated by the Commonwealth response to the UN Convention Against Corruption.

At their meeting in Abuja, in December 2003, the Heads of Government issued the Aso Rock Commonwealth Declaration, in which they welcomed the adoption of the Convention and urged the early signature, ratification, and implementation of it by member states. An Expert Working Group on Legislative and Related Measures to Combat Corruption, comprising government and non-government experts drawn from across the Commonwealth, was then established to assist member countries with the domestic implementation of UNCAC. The Group was asked to look at the provisions of UNCAC and make recommendations on the content of model legislation that could be used to introduce the relevant measures under domestic law. If the particular measure was not suitable for model legislation, the Group was asked to make recommendations as for how states could most effectively implement the measure in domestic law; what the content of domestic action should be; whether there are administrative measures or executive action that can be taken; and, where possible, to give examples of best practice. The resulting Model Law is now available for use by Commonwealth member states.[87] **9.155**

Secondly, a thread running through the international anti-corruption instruments is the need for states to develop effective mutual legal assistance and extradition procedures. In practice, most Commonwealth states already have some legislation based on the two Commonwealth schemes: the Harare Scheme on Mutual Assistance in Criminal Matters and the London Scheme for Extradition Within the Commonwealth. These Schemes (which pioneered global cooperation in both these areas and whose provisions are now reflected in the global instruments) are kept under active review by Commonwealth Law Ministers at their regular biennial meetings, in order, amongst other things, to enhance the ability of member countries to combat corrupt practices. **9.156**

Particularly significant here is the work of the Commonwealth Working Group on Asset Repatriation which reported in 2005. Its Report provides a blueprint for 'seeking the recovery and repatriation of assets of illicit origin focusing on maximising co-operation and assistance between governments'. The Group **9.157**

[87] Report and Recommendations of the Expert Working Group on Legislative and Related Measures to Combat Corruption, Commonwealth Secretariat, London, 2004.

examined the issues in much the same way as they would develop in practice and recommended as follows:

(1) Immunities: There is a need to ensure that heads of state and government and other officials do not enjoy immunities from criminal prosecution, which can preclude effective prosecution and pursuit of illicit assets in corruption cases.
(2) Preventing the Movement of Funds: Countries need to implement fully the international standards and measures designed to prevent money laundering.
(3) Serving Heads of State: The Group recognized that delicate problems can arise where assets believed to have been obtained through corruption by a serving head of state are located in another state. It recommended the utilization, to the greatest extent possible, of existing legislation and procedures for the reporting of suspicious transactions and the sharing of that information, and that Commonwealth Heads of Government should give consideration to an ad hoc Commonwealth peer review mechanism for such situations.
(4) Mechanisms for Asset Confiscation: The Group recommended that Commonwealth countries that have not already done so, should promptly put in place strong and comprehensive legislation for both conviction and non-conviction based asset confiscation, and establish and properly fund agencies dealing with asset confiscation and management.
(5) Tracing and Tracking of Assets: The Group emphasized the need for training, dedicated resources, and coordinated efforts to enhance the strength of the relevant investigative agencies.
(6) Mutual Legal Assistance: It was recommended that member states address the obstacles to effective mutual assistance, including allowing legal assistance without a requirement for a bilateral treaty and in the absence of dual criminality. Further, the establishment of a Commonwealth Network similar to the European Judicial Network/Eurojust was supported. With regard to the availability of mutual assistance, the need for mutual assistance to be available in respect of investigations and proceedings for non-conviction based asset confiscation was emphasized and, significantly, the Group urged Commonwealth countries to permit the use of evidence gathered through mutual legal assistance in civil proceedings related to corruption matters. Further examination of the possible use of mutual legal assistance to gather evidence for proceedings brought by a victim country for the purpose of asset recovery in corruption cases was also recommended.
(7) Mutual Assistance for Freezing/Restraint/Confiscation of Assets: Noting the practical advantages of the direct enforcement of foreign orders for freezing/restraint and confiscation, the Group recommended the adoption

of legislation establishing a direct enforcement system, covering both conviction and non-conviction based orders.

(8) Restraint of Assets: Bearing in mind the fact that delay is a major problem in effective restraint action, it was recommended that Commonwealth countries ensure their legislative schemes for restraint and forfeiture permit early applications for a restraint order.

(9) Effective Repatriation of Assets: Delay was again identified as a significant problem and Commonwealth countries are encouraged to 'fast track' corruption cases. The need to implement the asset recovery provisions in Chapter V of the United Nations Convention Against Corruption was also highlighted.[88]

Given the active support of the Commonwealth Heads of Government, Commonwealth Secretariat, and Commonwealth Law Ministers, the Commonwealth can play, and is playing, a significant role in the development of effective anti-corruption strategies. This is especially important in that so many of the major offshore banking centres are situated in Commonwealth member states and territories. **9.158**

I. ADB/OECD Anti-Corruption Action Plan for Asia and the Pacific

The Asia-Pacific region, unlike virtually all the other major regional groupings, has no regional anti-corruption instrument. However, an initiative by the Asian Development Bank (ADB) and the OECD saw the development, in 2000, of an Action Plan for the region. Twenty-three countries have formally endorsed the Action Plan and committed themselves to its goals. As with the international and regional anti-corruption instruments, the Action Plan also contains a monitoring process.[89] The Action Plan contains a series of non-binding principles and standards based on three pillars of action. **9.159**

Pillar 1 addresses the need to develop effective and transparent systems for the public service. It recognizes that a major factor in developing integrity in the public service is the establishment of codes of conduct that proscribe conflicts of interest, ensure the proper use of public resources, and promote the highest levels of professionalism and integrity. These are backed up by measures that encourage whistleblowers, including taking measures to protect the safety and professional status of whistleblowers, and the regular education, training, and supervision of officials to ensure that they have a proper understanding of their responsibilities. The prevention of corruption is addressed through the **9.160**

[88] The Summary of Recommendations of the Working Group is set out in App 7 below.
[89] The Action Plan is set out in App 1 below.

endorsing states taking a series of accountability and transparency measures, particularly addressing fiscal matters and public procurement, backed up by appropriate auditing procedures and supervision of financial institutions.

9.161 Pillar 2 addresses the strengthening of anti-bribery actions and the promotion of integrity in business operations. Here the endorsing states agree to take effective measures 'to actively combat bribery' through the development of effective anti-corruption laws, including anti-money laundering legislation; effective investigation and prosecutorial capacities; and the development of effective international cooperation arrangements. Endorsing states also agree to take effective measures to promote corporate responsibility and accountability on the basis of existing relevant international standards.[90] These include developing legislation designed both to eliminate indirect support of bribery, such as tax deductibility of bribes, and to require transparent company accounts. A potentially useful strategy is to ensure that access to bidding for public sector contacts can be denied as a sanction for the bribery of public officials.

9.162 Pillar 3 addresses the need to develop active public participation. Here the role of civil society is emphasized through the development of anti-corruption education and awareness campaigns as well as the need to provide public access to information.

9.163 The implementation of the Action Plan is based on two core principles: (a) a review mechanism based on self-assessment reports, and (b) the provision of specific and practical assistance to governments on key reform issues. Given the very different political and economic circumstances of the endorsing countries, each is given the opportunity of identifying, in consultation with the Secretariat of the Initiative, up to three priority areas for reform that fall under the three pillars of action. To date, two implementation cycles have been completed, although not all the endorsing states have completed the process.

J. Other International and Regional Initiatives

9.164 The need for the private sector to play its part in combating corruption is reflected in a number of significant international initiatives. The OECD Convention is the most visible sign of this development,[91] but the work of the International Chamber of Commerce, the World Bank, and the International Monetary Fund should also be noted.

1. International Chamber of Commerce

9.165 In 1977, the International Chamber of Commerce (ICC) published its *Report on Extortion and Bribery in Business Transactions*, which called for

[90] These might include, eg, the Rules of Conduct of the International Chamber of Commerce and 'Business and the Principles for Countering Bribery' noted at 9.165 below.

[91] See Ch 10 below.

complementary and mutually supportive action by governments, intergovernmental bodies, and the business community to combat extortion and bribery in international trade. It also included non-binding Rules of Conduct to Combat Extortion and Bribery for enterprises which, amongst other things, prohibited extortion and bribery in connection with obtaining or retaining business. The liberalization of world trade achieved as a result of the Uruguay Round and the need for fair competition were factors which later led the ICC to seek a review of its original report.

In 1994, an ad hoc committee produced an updated report which contained revised ICC Rules. These are 'intended as a method of self-regulation by international business . . . Their voluntary acceptance by business enterprises will not only promote high standards of integrity in business transactions . . . but will also form a valuable defensive protection to those enterprises which are subjected to attempts at extortion'.[92] The Basic Principle of the Rules is that: 'All enterprises should conform to the relevant laws and regulations of the countries in which they are established and in which they operate, and should observe both the letter and spirit of these Rules of Conduct'. The Rules themselves[93] constitute what is considered as good commercial practice. These are: **9.166**

- No one may, directly or indirectly, demand or accept a bribe and no enterprise may, directly or indirectly, offer or give a bribe and any demands for such a bribe must be rejected (articles 1 and 2). This is a significant strengthening of the 1977 Rules.
- Enterprises should take measures reasonably within their power to prevent the use of agents to facilitate bribery.
- Financial transactions should be properly and fairly recorded in appropriate books of account. There must be no 'off the books' or secret accounts.
- Those with ultimate authority for the enterprise should take reasonable steps to prevent any payments being made by the enterprise in contravention of the Rules of Conduct.
- Enterprises should draw up their own codes of conduct applicable to their own circumstances but consistent with the ICC Rules.

The Rules reflect a concern regarding a 'zero tolerance' approach to corruption and state, perhaps realistically, that there is a need to prioritize anti-corruption efforts. Thus the 'highest priority should be directed to ending large-scale extortion and bribery involving politicians and senior officials' as these 'represent the greatest threat to democratic institutions and cause the gravest economic distortions'.[94] Somewhat more problematic is the view that 'under current conditions in some parts of the world, an effective programme against **9.167**

[92] ICC Rules, Introduction. The rules were updated in 2005.
[93] These appear in full in App 19 below.
[94] Rules of Conduct, Introduction.

extortion and bribery may have to be implemented in stages'. The ICC has also established a follow-up procedure by means of the Standing Committee on Extortion and Bribery in support of the Rules.[95]

9.168 Similar Business Principles (*The Business Principles for Countering Bribery*[96]) have been developed by Transparency International and Social Accountability International which have recently been adopted by the World Economic Forum. These are discussed at 12.03 below.

2. The World Bank and International Monetary Fund

9.169 The World Bank is not specifically mandated to tackle corruption. However, its Articles of Agreement require that loan proceeds be used for the specific purposes for which they were granted and it has insisted on a transparent and competitive loan procurement process. This has led to the development of a four-pronged strategy to combat corruption:

(1) preventing fraud and corruption within Bank-financed projects;
(2) providing assistance to countries seeking to reduce corruption;
(3) taking corruption into account in lending and in formulating country assistance strategies; and
(4) supporting international and national efforts against corruption.[97]

9.170 In 1996, Procurement Guidelines were issued which state that in the event of fraudulent or corrupt conduct by a bidder or, once financing has been granted, by a borrower, the Bank will (a) reject the bidder's proposals for awards; (b) cancel the remaining portions of loans already granted to the borrower; and (c) ban the borrower from future World Bank financing for a period of time that is subject to the Bank's discretion. The Bank is also empowered to inspect the books and records of any suppliers and contractors involved in any Bank-financed contract and to submit the records to outside auditors.

9.171 In 1997 the World Bank issued the Guidelines: Selection and Employment of Consultants by World Bank Borrowers.[98] These provide that in the event of fraudulent or corrupt conduct by the consultant, or, once the contract has been granted, by a borrower, the Bank will: (a) reject the consultant's proposal for contract; (b) cancel the portion of the loan allocated to the consultant's contract; (c) declare the consultant ineligible, either indefinitely or for a stated period of time, for a Bank-financed contract; (d) have the right to inspect the consultant's accounts and records relating to the performance of a Bank-financed contract and have them audited.

[95] See generally B Zagaris and S Lakhani, 'The Emergence of an International Enforcement Regime on Transnational Corruption in the Americas' (1999) 30 *Law and Policy in International Business* 53.
[96] http://www.transparency.org/building_coalitions/private_sector/business_principles.html.
[97] See *Helping Countries Combat Corruption: The Role of the World Bank*, World Bank, 1997.
[98] The most recent edition being issued in May 2004.

The World Bank's policy on 'Fraud and Corruption' is set out in its Procurement Guidelines as follows: **9.172**

> 1.14 It is the Bank's policy to require that Borrowers (including beneficiaries of Bank loans), as well as bidders, suppliers, and contractors under Bank-financed contracts, observe the highest standard of ethics during the procurement and execution of such contracts. In pursuance of this policy, the Bank:
>
> (a) defines, for the purposes of this provision, the terms set forth below as follows:
>   (i) 'corrupt practice' means the offering, giving, receiving, or soliciting, directly or indirectly, of anything of value to influence the action of a public official in the procurement process or in contract execution;
>   (ii) 'fraudulent practice' means a misrepresentation or omission of facts in order to influence a procurement process or the execution of a contract;
>   (iii) 'collusive practices' means a scheme or arrangement between two or more bidders, with or without the knowledge of the Borrower, designed to establish bid prices at artificial, non-competitive levels;
>   (iv) 'coercive practices' means harming or threatening to harm, directly or indirectly, persons, or their property to influence their participation in a procurement process, or affect the execution of a contract.
>
> (b) will reject a proposal for award if it determines that the bidder recommended for award has, directly or through an agent, engaged in corrupt, fraudulent, collusive, or coercive practices in competing for the contract in question;
>
> (c) will cancel the portion of the loan allocated to a contract if it determines at any time that representatives of the Borrower or of a beneficiary of the loan engaged in corrupt, fraudulent, collusive, or coercive practices during the procurement or the execution of that contract, without the Borrower having taken timely and appropriate action satisfactory to the Bank to remedy the situation;
>
> (d) will sanction a firm or individual, including declaring ineligible, either indefinitely or for a stated period of time, to be awarded a Bank-financed contract if it at any time determines that the firm has, directly or through an agent, engaged in corrupt, fraudulent, collusive, or coercive practices in competing for, or in executing, a Bank-financed contract; and
>
> (e) will have the right to require that a provision be included in bidding documents and in contracts financed by a Bank loan, requiring bidders, suppliers and contractors to permit the Bank to inspect their accounts and records and other documents relating to the bid submission and contract performance and to have them audited by auditors appointed by the Bank.[99]

In recent years the International Monetary Fund (IMF) has lent its support to international anti-corruption efforts, especially through activities aimed at the promotion of good governance and the prevention of public sector corruption. This has been built upon the Interim Committee's 1996 Declaration on Partnership for Sustainable Global Growth, which placed great emphasis on 'promoting good governance in all its aspects, including by ensuring the rule of law, improving the efficiency and accountability of the public sector, and tackling corruption, as essential elements of a framework within which **9.173**

[99] See also *Helping Countries Combat Corruption: Progress at the World Bank since 1997*, World Bank, 2000 (http://www1.worldbank.org).

economies can prosper'. In consequence, the IMF has developed two codes of good practice: the Code of Good Practices on Fiscal Transparency (the Fiscal Transparency Code) and the Code of Good Practices on Transparency in Monetary and Financial Policies: Declaration of Principles.

9.174 In 1998 the IMF adopted the Fiscal Transparency Code which was the 'first attempt to set a framework of international standards for the conduct of fiscal policy . . . and to make governments more accountable for the way in which they raise and spend public funds'.[100] Updated in 2001, the Code is divided into four main principles and identifies a range of good practices based on the experience of countries worldwide. The main principles and elements of the Code of particular relevance to anti-corruption issues are as follows:

> *I Clarity of Roles and Responsibilities*
>
> 1.1 The government sector should be distinguished from the rest of the public sector and from the rest of the economy, and policy and management roles within the public sector should be clear and publicly disclosed.
>
> 1.1.5 Government involvement in the rest of the economy (eg through regulation and equity ownership) should be conducted in an open and public manner, and on the basis of clear rules and procedures that are applied in a non-discriminatory way.
>
> 1.2 There should be a clear legal and administrative framework for fiscal management.
>
> 1.2.1 Any commitment or expenditure of public funds should be governed by comprehensive budget laws and openly available administrative rules.
>
> 1.2.2 Taxes, duties, fees and charges should have an explicit legal basis. Tax laws and regulations should be easily accessible and understandable, and clear criteria should guide any administrative discretion in their application.
>
> 1.2.3 Ethical standards of behaviour for public servants should be clear and well publicized.
>
> *II Public Availability of Information*
>
> 2.1 The public should be provided with full information on the past, current, and projected fiscal activity of government.
>
> 2.1.3 Statements should be published with the annual budget giving a description of the nature and fiscal significance of contingent liabilities, tax expenditures, and quasi-fiscal activities.
>
> 2.1.4 The central government should regularly publish information on the level and composition of its debt and financial assets.
>
> 2.2 A commitment should be made to the timely publication of fiscal information.
>
> *III Open Budget Preparation, Execution, and Reporting*
>
> 3.1 The budget documentation should specify fiscal policy objectives, the macroeconomic framework, the policy basis for the budget, and the identifiable fiscal risks.

[100] M Petrie, 'The IMF Fiscal Transparency Code: A Potentially Powerful New Anti-Corruption Tool', paper delivered at the 9th International Anti-Corruption Conference, Durban 1999, p 2. See also W Allan, 'Implementing the Fiscal Transparency Code', IMF Fiscal Affairs Department, 2001.

3.2 Budget information should be presented in a way that facilitates policy analysis and promotes accountability.
3.3 Procedures for the execution and monitoring of approved expenditure and for collecting revenues should be clearly specified.
3.4 There should be regular fiscal reporting to the legislature and the public.

IV Assurances of Integrity
4.1 Fiscal data should meet accepted data quality standards.
4.2 Fiscal information should be subjected to independent scrutiny.
4.2.1 A national audit body, or equivalent organisation, which is independent of the executive, should provide timely reports for the legislature and public on the financial integrity of government accounts.

The Code places no obligation on countries to adhere to it but is a powerful statement of principle and international best practice. It is complemented by a *Manual on Fiscal Transparency*, which provides detailed guidance on the implementation of the Code.[101]

9.175 The Code of Good Practices on Transparency in Monetary and Financial Policies: Declaration of Principles was adopted by the IMF Interim Committee in 1999, with its primary purpose being to develop the capacity of domestic institutions—legislatures, auditors—general, financial markets, press—as well as the public and civil society organizations, to hold their monetary and financial authorities accountable for monetary policy and management, and the supervision of, and any interventions in, financial institutions. As such, the Code can be a useful tool in preventing corruption.[102] The Code is in two parts. The first sets out 'Good Transparency Practices for Monetary Policy by Central Banks' (sections I–IV) whilst the second sets out 'Good Transparency Practices for Financial Policies by Financial Agencies'(sections V–VIII). In this context, financial agencies refer to 'the institutional arrangements for the regulation, supervision, and oversight of the financial and payment systems, including markets and institutions, with the view to promoting financial stability, market efficiency, and client-asset and consumer protection'. The main points from the Declaration are as follows:

I Clarity of Roles, Responsibilities and Objectives of Central Banks for Monetary Policy
1.1 The ultimate objective(s) and institutional framework of monetary policy should be clearly defined in relevant legislation or regulation, including, where appropriate, a central bank law.
1.2 The institutional relationship between monetary and fiscal operations should be clearly defined [and consistent with the IMF's Code of Good Practices on Fiscal Transparency].

[101] Available at http://www.imf.org/external/np/fad/trans/manual/index.htm.
[102] See IMF, 'The IMF's Approach to Promoting Good Governance and Combating Corruption' 2005, 8–9. Available at http://www.imf.org/external/np/gov/guide/eng/index.htm. The code is in App 20 below.

1.3 Agency roles performed by the central bank on behalf of the government should be clearly defined.

II Open Process for Formulating and Reporting Monetary Policy Decisions

2.1 The framework, instruments, and any targets that are used to pursue the objectives of monetary policy should be publicly disclosed and explained.

2.2 Where a permanent monetary policy-making body meets to assess underlying economic developments, monitor progress towards achieving its monetary policy objective(s), and formulate policy for the period ahead, information on the composition, structure and functions of that body should be publicly disclosed.

2.3 Changes in setting of monetary policy instruments (other than fine-tuning measures) should be publicly announced and explained in a timely manner.

2.4 The central bank should issue public statements on progress toward achieving its monetary policy objective(s) as well as prospects for achieving them. The arrangements could differ depending on the monetary policy framework, including the exchange rate regime.

2.5 For substantive technical changes to the structure of monetary regulations, there should be a presumption in favour of public consultations, within an appropriate period.

2.6 The regulations on data reporting by financial institutions to the central bank for monetary policy purposes should be publicly disclosed.

III Public Availability of Information on Monetary Policy

3.1 Presentations and releases of central bank data should meet the standards related to coverage, periodicity, timeliness of data and access by the public that are consistent with the International Monetary Fund's data dissemination standards.

3.2 The central bank should publicly disclose its balance sheet on a pre-announced schedule and, after a predetermined interval, publicly disclose selected information on its aggregate market transactions.

3.3 The central bank should establish and maintain public information services.

3.4 Texts of regulations issued by the central bank should be readily available to the public.

IV Accountability and Assurances of Integrity by the Central Bank

4.1 Officials of the central bank should be available to appear before a designated public authority to report on the conduct of monetary policy, explain the policy objective(s) of their institution, describe their performance in achieving their objective(s), and, as appropriate, exchange views on the state of the economy and the financial system.

4.2 The central bank should publicly disclose audited financial statements of its operations on a pre-announced schedule.

4.3 Information on the expenses and revenues in operating the central bank should be publicly disclosed annually.

4.4 Standards for the conduct of personal financial affairs of officials and staff of the central bank and rules to prevent exploitation of conflicts of interest, including any general fiduciary obligation, should be publicly disclosed.

Good Transparency Practices for Financial Policies by Financial Agencies

V *Clarity of Roles, Responsibilities and Objectives of Financial Agencies Responsible for Financial Policies*

5.1 The broad objective(s) and institutional framework of financial agencies should be clearly defined, preferably in relevant legislation or regulation.

5.2 The relationship between financial agencies should be publicly disclosed.
5.3 The role of oversight agencies with regard to payments systems should be publicly disclosed.
5.4 Where financial agencies have oversight responsibilities for self-regulatory organizations (eg payment systems), the relationship between them should be publicly disclosed.
5.5 Where self-regulatory organizations are authorized to perform part of the regulatory and supervisory process, they should be guided by the same good transparency practices specified for financial agencies.

VI Open Process for Formulating and Reporting of Financial Policies

6.1 The conduct of policies by financial agencies should be transparent, compatible with confidentiality considerations and the need to preserve the effectiveness of actions by regulatory and oversight agencies.
6.2 Significant changes in financial policies should be publicly announced and explained in a timely manner.
6.3 Financial agencies should issue periodic public reports on how their overall policy objectives are being pursued.
6.4 For proposed substantive technical changes to the structure of financial regulations, there should be a presumption in favour of public consultations, within an appropriate period.

VII Public Availability of Information on Financial Policies

7.1 Financial agencies should issue a periodic public report on the major developments of the sector(s) of the financial system for which they carry designated responsibility.
7.2 Financial agencies should seek to ensure that, consistent with confidentiality requirements, there is public reporting of aggregate data related to their jurisdictional responsibilities on a timely and regular basis.
7.3 Where applicable, financial agencies should publicly disclose their balance sheets on a pre-announced schedule and, after a predetermined interval, publicly disclose information on aggregate market transactions.
7.4 Financial agencies should establish and maintain public information services.
7.5 Texts of regulations and any other generally applicable directives and guidelines issued by financial agencies should be readily available to the public.
7.6 Where there are deposit insurance guarantees, policy-holder guarantees, and any other client asset protection schemes, information on the nature and form of such protections, on the operating procedures, on how the guarantee is financed, and on the performance of the arrangement, should be publicly disclosed.
7.7 Where financial agencies oversee consumer protection arrangements (such as dispute settlement processes), information on such arrangements should be publicly disclosed.

VIII Accountability and Assurances of Integrity by Financial Agencies

8.1 Officials of financial agencies should be available to appear before a designated public authority to report on the conduct of financial policies, explain the policy objective(s) of their institution, describe their performance in pursuing their objective(s), and, as appropriate, exchange views on the state of the financial system.
8.2 Where applicable, financial agencies should publicly disclose audited financial statements of their operations on a pre-announced schedule.
8.3 Where applicable, information on the operating expenses and revenues of financial agencies should be publicly disclosed annually.

8.4 Standards for the conduct of personal financial affairs of officials and staff of financial agencies and rules to prevent exploitation of conflicts of interest, including any general fiduciary obligation, should be publicly disclosed.

In 2000 the IMF published a *Supporting Document to the Code of Good Practices on Transparency in Monetary and Financial Policies* which, drawing on transparency practices around the world, is a very useful guide on how to implement the code.[103]

K. Overview

9.176 The last decade has seen remarkable success in the development of international and regional instruments that provide a framework of rules and standards for addressing corruption. Together they represent an expression of a high level of political commitment to developing effective anti-corruption strategies and they provide internationally agreed reference points for governments and the private sector to follow. In doing so, they can create peer pressure on governments through, for example, the mutual evaluation exercises. They can also encourage transparency and accountability in the private sector and further support the efforts of civil society. The next task is to encourage states to become parties to the relevant instruments so as to ensure that they come into force as quickly as possible. Certainly the swift coming into force of the United Nations Convention Against Corruption in December 2005 is a major step forward.

9.177 As noted earlier, in essence, the instruments address five main themes: prevention; criminalization; developing international cooperation; recovering the proceeds of corruption; and establishing effective monitoring procedures. It might be helpful therefore to examine some of these strategies further at this stage.

1. Prevention

9.178 Preventative measures play a key role in any anti-corruption strategy and the instruments place a considerable responsibility on State Parties to develop effective anti-corruption strategies and to ensure that public officials receive appropriate 'good governance' education and training. Here the provision of appropriate technical assistance is also regarded as an essential part of any prevention strategy. The establishment and maintenance of independent anti-corruption agencies is also widely supported, as is the contribution that civil society bodies can make.

9.179 Several instruments also recognize that codes or standards of conduct for public officials, parliamentarians, and judicial officers are important corruption

[103] Available at http://www.imf.org/external/np/mae/mft/sup/index.htm.

prevention tools. Here the Council of Europe Model Code of Conduct for Public Officials and the International Code of Conduct for Public Officials provide a useful reference point. Codes of conduct are also becoming more common in private enterprises, particularly through the work of the International Chamber of Commerce.

Codes of judicial ethics and the like are also becoming popular, particularly in common law jurisdictions. They are useful as a means of establishing the parameters for public expectation and criticism of judicial conduct, both in the exercise of judicial duties and extra-judicial activities. An excellent example of the development and adoption of a model code of conduct in this respect is found in the *Bangalore Principles of Judicial Conduct*, which was drafted by the Judicial Group on Strengthening Judicial Integrity.[104] The Principles recognize seven values and principles that are prerequisites to the due performance of judicial office and which, if adhered to, provide an important anti-corruption mechanism: **9.180**

(1) judicial independence is a prerequisite to the rule of law and a fundamental guarantee of a fair trial, a judge shall therefore uphold and exemplify judicial independence in both its individual and institutional aspects;
(2) impartiality is essential to the proper discharge of judicial office, it applies not only to the decision itself but also to the process by which the decision is made;
(3) integrity is essential to the proper discharge of the judicial office;
(4) propriety, and the appearance of propriety, are essential to the performance of all of the activities of a judge;
(5) ensuring equality of treatment to all before the courts;
(6) competence; and
(7) diligence.[105]

Given the difficulties of proof in corruption cases, the need for states to provide for a whistle-blowing system is now a feature of several instruments. They also recognize that those who report corruption require effective protection from possible retaliation or intimidation. **9.181**

2. Criminalization

A comprehensive set of criminal offences is seen as fundamental to the success of anti-corruption strategies and, rather than attempt the sometimes tortuous process of providing a definition of 'corruption', the instruments seek rather to identify the type of conduct to be criminalized. There is considerable agreement **9.182**

[104] This comprised the Chief Justices of Bangladesh, Karnataka State, India, Nepal, Nigeria, South Africa, Sri Lanka, Tanzania, and Uganda under the chairmanship of Judge Weeramantry, Vice-President of the International Court of Justice.

[105] The Principles are set out in full in App 4 below.

as to the 'core' corruption offences, although the unsatisfactory division between 'mandatory' and 'non-mandatory' offences in the instruments remains. The meaning of 'public official' also varies to some extent between instruments[106] and this might cause some practical difficulties as regards joint criminality in respect of extradition proceedings and (possibly) mutual assistance requests.

9.183 A key feature of the instruments is the criminalizing of corruption in the private sector, although not all the instruments make this mandatory. Finally, there is now an increasing recognition of the rights of victims of bribery, both as regards their protection in criminal cases and their right to seek compensation.

3. International Cooperation

9.184 Tackling serious forms of corruption, in particular, almost invariably involves transnational elements. Thus all the instruments, albeit in varying detail, require states to cooperate with one another in the investigation and prosecution of such offences, including the provision of mutual legal assistance and extradition. This is an area that has developed considerably in recent years due, in no small part, to the work of the Commonwealth and Financial Action Task Force. The challenge remains to ensure the effectiveness of such cooperation.

4. Asset Recovery

9.185 The need to take the profit out of corruption is reflected in the detailed provisions relating to asset recovery. This is a particularly complex issue and many states have yet to enact the appropriate legislation or acquire the necessary institutional arrangements for doing so. This is an area where technical assistance from the United Nations and the Commonwealth will remain invaluable. In this respect, the 2005 Report of the Commonwealth Working Group on Asset Repatriation demands particular attention.

5. Monitoring

9.186 The credibility of the efforts to combat corruption depends to a considerable extent upon whether governments can be held to their commitments. Experience shows that it is important to have an effective institutionalized monitoring system and, here, a process of mutual evaluation is potentially most effective.[107]

[106] eg UNCAC, Art 1 does not cover officials of state-owned enterprises, persons serving in quasi-official capacities, or those who perform other public functions. By contrast, both the Inter-American and OECD Conventions prohibit the bribery of those who perform public functions, and of officials of state-owned enterprises.

[107] See, eg, the discussion on GRECO at 9.118.

10

THE BRIBERY OF FOREIGN PUBLIC OFFICIALS

A. Introduction

Bribery within the setting of international business raises issues not just of law, but of politics, morality, good governance and, of course, economics. The first 10.01

truly concerted international attempt to confront such bribery came about in 1989,[1] with the setting up by the OECD of an ad hoc working group which sought to explore, in a comparative way, the approach of different jurisdictions and their laws to bribery and corruption and to offences committed wholly or partially abroad. Within its remit the working group was also able to examine the preventive and detection roles being played by civil and administrative—as well as criminal—law and, importantly, by financial and banking provisions and regulations.[2]

10.02 The efforts of the working group revealed that some jurisdictions already had laws in place which applied, at least in principle, to the bribery of foreign public officials.[3] However, it became apparent that a more focused response was required; a need emphasized by a recognition that only the United States (with its Foreign Corrupt Practices Act of 1977) had, at the time, legislation which provided for criminal sanctions for individuals and companies bribing anywhere abroad.

10.03 The setting up of the working group had been in response to calls from a number of interests: the United States business community were unhappy at a perceived trade disadvantage; the United States government called for action; the end of the Cold War meant that reformers turned their attention to corruption; and the 'crashes' of financial and money markets had heightened the awareness of many to the susceptibility of developing countries to the 'skewing' of their economies.

10.04 To move matters forward, a so-called 'soft law' approach was initially taken[4] with the adoption by the OECD Ministerial Council of the 1994 'Recommendation of the Council on Bribery in International Business Transactions',[5] which invited OECD members to take 'effective measures to detect, prevent and combat bribery of foreign public officials in international business'. To that end, member countries were urged to take 'concrete and meaningful steps' to achieve that aim by amending their anti-bribery laws, tax and accounting systems, and public procurement procedures as appropriate.

10.05 Following the Recommendation, the existing working group was given a formal standing as the 'Working Group on Bribery' (WGB) in International Business Transactions. That development was followed in 1997 by the adoption by the OECD Ministerial Council of the Revised Recommendation of the Council on

[1] An earlier attempt in the late 1970s by the UN to put in place an anti-corruption convention had been dogged by political problems.

[2] See 'No Longer Business as Usual: Fighting Bribery and Corruption', OECD Publication, 2000; and 'OECD Convention on Combating Bribery in International Business Transactions', an IMF paper, 18 Sept 2001.

[3] See, eg, Sweden.

[4] In other words, a recommendation urging that OECD members take certain action, rather than a formal instrument containing mandatory provisions.

[5] OECD: C(94)75/Final.

Combating Bribery in International Business Transactions.[6] The Revised Recommendation was more far-reaching and, in particular, addressed the tax deductibility of bribes.

Thereafter, there was much debate within the WGB on the most expedient approach to criminalization of bribery of foreign public officials. Those favouring a formal instrument prevailed, and the OECD Convention on Combating Bribery of Foreign Public Officials in International Business Transactions was adopted by the negotiating conference on 21 November and signed on 17 December 1997. The requirements of the OECD Convention are addressed in detail below. **10.06**

The criminalization provisions contained within the OECD Convention are replicated within the United Nations Convention Against Corruption 2003 (UNCAC);[7] therefore, the issues surrounding criminalization, which are dealt with below, are equally applicable to UNCAC. **10.07**

B. The OECD Convention on Combating Bribery of Foreign Public Officials in International Business Transactions 1977

1. Background

The OECD Convention on Combating Bribery of Foreign Public Officials in International Business Transactions ('the OECD Convention') entered into force on 15 February 1999. There are thirty-six signatory countries, with the most recent Party to the Convention being Estonia, which deposited its instrument on 23 November 2004. The thirty-six countries include all thirty OECD members (each of whom has ratified) and six non-members: Argentina, Brazil, Bulgaria, Chile, Estonia, and Slovenia.[8] **10.08**

One of the strengths of the OECD Convention is its programme of systematic monitoring which takes the form of evaluation by peer review. Such follow-up is in the hands of the WGB, which was mandated by the OECD in 1997 to have responsibility for monitoring and ensuring Convention implementation.[9] The WGB meets five times a year at the OECD Headquarters in Paris. Its central function is to ensure Convention compliance. The system of peer review, already referred to, is key to that. **10.09**

---

[6] DAFFE/IME/BR (97) 20. [7] See 9.10ff above.

[8] See fact sheet in 'The OECD Anti-Bribery Convention: Does it work?', OECD publication, updated 13 July 2005.

[9] The OECD Anti-Bribery Convention: Does it work?, OECD publication.

10.10 The monitoring process is divided into two 'phases'. Phase 1 examines the anti-corruption laws and legislation of the country concerned and is, essentially, a paper exercise. However, Phase 2, which focuses on implementation and enforcement of the Convention, comprises a comprehensive questionnaire which the examined country has to complete and a one-week onsite visit which involves question and answer meetings in the examined country with a range of panels comprising representatives from relevant government departments, prosecution and investigative authorities, the legal profession, business and commerce, trade organizations and trade unions, and civil society. The aim of that visit is to make a detailed assessment of implementation and Convention compliance. The Phase 1 process is nearing completion, and, at the time of writing, fifteen countries (including all G7) have been subject to the Phase 2 review. It is anticipated by the WGB that the remaining Phase 2 reviews will be completed by 2007.[10]At the conclusion of the Phase 2 round, the WGB will have to decide whether, by way of further work, there should be a Phase 3.

10.11 The Phase 1 and Phase 2 evaluations are each carried out by lead examiners from two different countries, assisted by members of the OECD Secretariat. The size of the evaluation teams varies, according to the country being examined and the volume of work which is likely to be generated; however, for a Phase 2 review it is common to have a team of lead examiners comprising seven or eight experts (drawn from two countries) complemented by a secretariat team of three or four.

10.12 Following both a Phase 1 and a Phase 2 evaluation, the lead examiners present their report to the WGB in plenary. The report is then discussed and further questions may be asked of the lead examiners and/or the examined country by any member of the WGB. The report will also contain recommendations for action to be taken by the examined country or for follow-up by the WGB. Those recommendations have to be discussed and agreed upon by the WGB in plenary. At the conclusion of such discussions, both the report and recommendations are adopted in a final form by the WGB and are then made public.[11] The value of recommendations by international organizations is always open to debate; nevertheless, Parties to the OECD Convention have on several occasions enacted amending legislation following the making of recommendations by the WGB.

10.13 Added value is brought to the peer review process by a system of 'follow-up' which has become increasingly formalized. Twelve months after the approval of a country's Phase 2 report, the examined country is subject to an oral follow-up

---

[10] The OECD Anti-Bribery Convention: Does it work?, OECD publication.

[11] Phase 1 and Phase 2 evaluation reports can be found on the OECD's website, http://www.oecd.org/bribery.

report, which takes place in the plenary and addresses both actions taken as to the recommendations and issues of 'follow-up' as set out in the Phase 2 report. That consists of a 30-minute session divided into two: a presentation by the examined country and a question and answer session led by, but not confined to, the lead examiners. After a further twelve months, the examined country is required to present a written follow-up report and, again, is subject to questioning in plenary.

There are aspects of the peer review process, and indeed of the WGB itself, which raise issues and concerns. The reviews, in both Phase 1 and 2, are drafted by members of the secretariat, with the lead examiners playing a greater or lesser role in adding with and amending the draft, depending on the composition and ability of those making up the lead examining team. Such an approach may be contrasted with that of GRECO, where the genesis of a report is a draft by the examiners themselves. Of course, it might be argued that a conscientious examiner for the OECD is able to rewrite a draft by the secretariat and that, equally, an indifferent GRECO examiner can quite easily compile a superficial report or, indeed, avoid making any real contribution However, even accepting such arguments, some will say that, vesting the responsibility for the draft in it, has undoubtedly produced an 'issue aggressive' secretariat, which takes it upon itself to pursue certain topics at the expense of others, and which fails to recognize the wider practicalities, and sometimes difficulties, with which State Parties to the Convention are faced in countering bribery in the transnational setting. **10.14**

Any consideration of the OECD Convention has to have regard to the following OECD Anti-Corruption instruments: **10.15**

(1) the OECD Convention on Combating Bribery of Foreign Public Officials in International Business Transactions 1997;
(2) the 1997 Revised Recommendation of the Council on Combating Bribery in International Business Transactions;
(3) the 1996 Recommendation of the Council on the Tax Deductibility of Bribes to Foreign Public Officials;
(4) the OECD Guidelines for Multinational Enterprises; and
(5) the 2003 Action Statement on Bribery and Officially Supported Export Credits.

2. Scope of the Convention

As Commentary 1 to the OECD Convention makes clear, the Convention addresses what is sometimes called 'active corruption' or 'active bribery'; that is to say, bribery on the supply side. It is concerned, then, with the offence committed by the person who offers, promises, or gives the bribe as opposed to **10.16** the official who solicits or receives the bribe. Almost as a misnomer, the latter is often referred to as 'passive bribery'.[12]

10.17 The OECD Convention is seemingly of narrow scope and specific application, addressing, as it does, the bribery of foreign public officials within the context of international trade. However, its importance belies its apparent ambit. Indeed, one might mount a sustainable argument that, until the advent of UNCAC, the OECD Convention was in practice the most far-reaching and important anti-corruption instrument of all. An argument perhaps reinforced by the way in which it has influenced the form and words of the bribery and related offences criminalization provisions within UNCAC. The OECD Convention has, on its own, helped to shape anti-corruption legislation and criminalization both within and outside the OECD for the reasons set out below.

10.18 To ensure compliance with the Convention, the thirty-six states which have ratified are required to have in place a wide range of preventive, implementation, and enforcement measures.[13] Inevitably such provisions, when put in place by the State Parties, have had an effect far beyond the 'foreign bribery' offence; indeed, in some instances, State Parties have reshaped domestic corruption law entirely.[14]

10.19 Article 12 provides for a systemic monitoring and follow-up procedure, the State Parties being required to 'co-operate in carrying out a programme of systemic follow-up to monitor and promote the full implementation of this Convention'.[15] The effect has been that assessment by peer review within the framework of the WGB has set demanding compliance standards for State Parties. Both Phase 1[16] and Phase 2[17] evaluations have tended to interpret issues relevant to the Convention robustly and broadly. As a result, examined countries have found most, if not all, of their anti-corruption measures and legislation subject to rigorous and legalistic assessment.

10.20 All thirty of the OECD member states have ratified the Convention. Those State Parties are home to just about all major multinational/international companies. The steps taken by them to counter foreign bribery have had a direct effect on international trade generally and on specific trading partners in

[12] Commentary 1 of the 'Official Commentaries to the OECD Convention of Combating Bribery of Officials in International Business Transactions', adopted by the OECD Negotiating Conference on 21 November 1997.

[13] These encompass, *inter alia*, criminalization requirements (Art 1); provision for the liability of legal persons (Art 2); effective sanctioning (Art 3); and a fetter on the improper exercise of prosecutorial discretion (Art 5).

[14] eg the extension of nationality jurisdiction in the case of the UK.

[15] Art 12; see also Commentaries 34–36.

[16] Examining compliance or otherwise of national laws of the parties.

[17] Evaluating implementation and enforcement of the Convention, and including a one-week on-site visit.

particular. Moreover OECD has undertaken a number of 'outreach' programmes and activities focusing on preventive and enforcement anti-corruption issues. Such programmes have embraced much of the 'non-OECD' world.[18]

The OECD Convention does not seek to impose a uniformity of approach as between State Parties in the criminalization of foreign bribery. It does not set out to change the fundamental principles of national legal systems;[19] rather, the main thrust is to 'assure a functional equivalence'[20] among the measures taken. Thus, for example, a State Party in which prosecutors enjoy a discretion whether or not to bring a case would be Convention non-compliant if it allowed its prosecution authorities to apply a different test, or different criteria, to the foreign bribery offence from the domestic counterpart. **10.21**

C. Criminalization (Article 1)

Article 1 requires each State Party to take such measures as may be necessary to establish the criminal offence of bribery of a foreign public official. The elements which such criminalization must encompass are as follows: **10.22**

- intentionally,
- offering, promising, or giving,
- any undue pecuniary or other advantage,
- directly or through intermediaries,
- to a foreign public official,
- for the official him/herself or for a third party,
- in order that the official act or refrain from acting in relation to the performance of official duties,
- in order to obtain or retain business or other improper advantage in the conduct of international business.

There is no requirement that the precise terms of Article 1 need to be incorporated within the offence; indeed, any approach may be used so long as the obligations are fulfilled. However, an offence will not be Convention compliant **10.23**

[18] Programmes include the Asian-Pacific initiative, outreach activities with Romania and Russia, and anti-corruption activities in Central and Latin America. See further 11.89ff.

[19] Commentary 2.

[20] ibid. As Professor Mark Pieth pointed out in his paper, 'Making the OECD Initiative Work', presented at the 9th International Anti-Corruption Conference, Durban, South Africa, October 1999: 'The Convention borrows a principle developed in comparative law. According to the functional approach of comparison, attention is drawn to the overall working of systems, rather than individual institutions. The assumption is that each legal system has its own logic and is not necessarily determined by the legal texts alone. Practices and formal rules are part of this approach as well as other aspects of the legal system taking over ancillary functions. Therefore the focus of comparison would lie on overall effects produced by a country's legal system rather than the individual rules.'

if it requires proof of elements beyond those which would be required to be proved if the offence were simply defined as in Article 1's form of words.[21] Nor is it a requirement that each Party to the OECD Convention must have a specific offence of bribery of a foreign public official. A State Party may choose to comply either by, for instance, 'prohibiting the bribery of agents generally'[22] or by an offence specifically limited to the foreign public official.

1. 'Foreign Public Official'

10.24 'Foreign Public Official', for the purpose the OECD Convention, is defined in Article 1, paragraph 4;[23] however, that definition and its scope is addressed in much more detail in Commentaries 12 to 19.[24] In the light of the range of activities caught within the Convention definition, there are advantages to a State Party in adopting an autonomous definition which follows these provisions and which, importantly, will not require a prosecuting authority to obtain proof of how a foreign country actually defines a particular individual's role. The objectives of the OECD Convention might otherwise be thwarted if it was open to a defendant charged with the foreign bribery offence to show that in the public official's own country, by quirk or design and notwithstanding that the official in question was performing a public function, he was not in fact regarded as a public official.

10.25 In highlighting the potential benefit provided by an autonomous definition, it is worth highlighting some of the comments made by lead examiners during the Phase 2 reviews to date. In the review of the United Kingdom, for instance, it was queried whether in fact all the categories of officials set out in the OECD Convention and Commentary as being required to be covered within the definition are in fact provided for by the existing criminalization.[25] It is clear from the Phase 2 report that the United Kingdom maintained that all manifestations of foreign public official are covered and that there is Convention compliance; however, the lead examiners (from Canada and France) were less than fully satisfied as, when UK corruption law was extended in 2001[26] to criminalize the bribery of foreign public officials (on the basis of nationality jurisdiction), the new legislation, in effect, simply added what might be described as a 'foreign' element to existing definitions of 'public office', 'public body', and 'public authorities', as well as 'agent' and 'principal'.

10.26 Given that there is an increasing blurring of public and private activities, it is axiomatic that a Party to the OECD Convention must take great care to ensure that anyone carrying out a public function is in fact regarded as being a public

[21] Commentary 3. [22] ibid 3. [23] See App 22 below.

[24] Ibid. [25] See UK Phase 2 review, p 58, paras 183ff.

[26] By the Anti-Terrorism Crime and Security Act 2001, Pt 12, which came into force on 14 February 2002.

official for the purposes of the foreign bribery offence, particularly in circumstances where domestic law or practice does not accommodate an autonomous definition. Certainly, with an eye to the breadth of the OECD Convention definition, some countries have seen fit to insert specific provisions into existing legislation. For instance, within the Swiss Criminal Code a new provision, Article 322 *Octies*, paragraph 3 was inserted to provide that 'individuals who carry out public functions are deemed to be public officials'.

Some jurisdictions find that there is a bar within the domestic criminal code or criminal legal theory to the adoption of an autonomous interpretation. Slovenia, for instance, as the first country to accede to the OECD since its adoption in 1997 (Estonia, of course, has subsequently been added), has encountered such difficulties. The issue was raised as part of the Phase 1 evaluation when it was noted that the definition of 'foreign public official' is not autonomous.[27] Indeed the position in Slovenian law at the time of writing is that, to ascertain whether a person is a foreign public official, it is first necessary to determine whether the person would conform to the definition of a Slovenian public official. It may well be that the substantive criteria in place in Slovenia for deciding who is a domestic public official is sufficiently wide to cover all conceivable types of public function in the foreign context; certainly the need to have reference to the domestic definition is not in any sense indicative of Convention non-compliance. Nevertheless, the absence of an autonomous definition will always prompt a long, hard look by the WGB. **10.27**

Those Parties to the Convention, and indeed, non-OECD members, seeking to address the point will inevitably look around the world for workable definitions. In South Africa, for instance, the Prevention and Combating of Corrupt Activities Act 2004 arrived at a definition of a foreign public official as being any person 'holding a legislative, administrative or judicial office of a foreign state'.[28] Although the definition does not address all the issues raised within the OECD Convention and the Commentaries in terms, it appears to be wide enough to cover all officials in a foreign state who have been either appointed or elected to carry out functions or to hold office on behalf of that state. However, some might query whether it extends to officials of international organizations. **10.28**

2. 'Offering, Promising or Giving'

The offering, promising or giving of a bribe to a foreign public official must be criminalized.[29] Legislators should, therefore, consider incorporating those three key words of 'offering', 'promising', or 'giving', into the foreign bribery offence. However, such an approach will not be appropriate in every jurisdiction. As any **10.29**

[27] See Slovenia, Phase 1 rewiew, p 7, paras 25ff.

[28] Prevention and Combating of Corrupt Activities Act 2004, s 1(v).

[29] Art 1.

'promise' must surely involve an 'offer', it may be that the word 'promise' need not appear within the offence created. Thus, in the United Kingdom, section 1 of the Prevention of Corruption Act 1906 refers to any person who 'Corruptly gives or agrees to give or offers', and would seem to cover all aspects of the OECD Convention even though 'promise' is not specifically mentioned. It is to be noted, though, that at both the Phase 1 and Phase 1 *bis* reviews of the United Kingdom by the WGB, a recommendation was made that any future amendment to the UK corruption law should cover the notions of 'offering', 'promising', or 'giving' specifically.

10.30 Given that the majority of State Parties to the OECD Convention, and hence the preponderance of lead examiners, are from civil code jurisdictions where definitions are expected to be thorough and capable of standing alone, any criminalization under the OECD Convention which does not include the three components explicitly is liable to comment and query during any monitoring or review process. Difficulties on the point are not, however, confined to common law countries. The Phase 1 and Phase 2 evaluations have highlighted the difficulties which a number of countries have had in creating a substantive bribery offence which is completed when just a promise or offer is made. For instance, under Italian law, acceptance of a bribe by an official is an essential element of the substantive offence of bribery (including foreign bribery).[30] The expectation of the OECD Convention is, of course, broader and anticipates that substantive criminality will reflect not just the giving of a bribe, but the offer or a promise even where there has been no acceptance.

10.31 Such problems in themselves do not, without more, mean non-compliance, since the criminality might in fact be reflected by complicity, participation, or attempt offences.[31] Real difficulties will arise, however, when a complicity or attempt offence is the only one available (for example to reflect an offer) and, in the event of conviction, the sanctions provided for are much lower than those for a substantive offence and are arguably not dissuasive. In such circumstances, there is likely to be a breach of Article 3 (Sanctions) which, *inter alia*, states that 'the bribery of a foreign public official should be punishable by effective, proportionate and dissuasive criminal penalties'. If a higher penalty is provided for in a particular jurisdiction for the substantive bribery offence, and if that offence is only made out by the giving of a bribe or at least the acceptance of an offer, whilst offering or promising attracts a lower penalty (as, for instance, an incitement offence), then those evaluating are bound to query effectiveness and proportionality.

[30] See Phase 2 review of Italy, p 31, paras 113ff.

[31] Art 1, para 2: 'Each Party shall take any measures necessary to establish that complicity in, including incitement, aiding and abetting, or authorisation of, an act of bribery of a foreign public official, shall be a criminal offence. Attempt and conspiracy to bribe a foreign public official shall be criminal offences to the same extent as attempt and conspiracy to bribe a public official of that Party.'

The difficulties on the point do not end there. Returning to the Italian example, the offence of incitement (*istigazione alla corruzione*) will be available where a public official does not accept an offer or promise of a bribe, whilst the offence of attempted bribery may be used where the offer or promise was, in effect, impossible to carry through.[32] However, domestic law in Italy provides that, in relation to the *istigazione* offence, the court must consider whether the advantage offered, was minimal or persuasive, and the means, circumstances, and the position of the public official involved. This does not sit happily with either Article 5 (Enforcement), dealt with below, which provides, *inter alia*, that the prosecution of a bribery offence should 'not be influenced by considerations of... the identity of a natural or legal persons involved', or Commentary 7 which provides that foreign bribery is an offence 'irrespective of, inter alia, the value of the advantage, its results...'. **10.32**

The notion of the substantive bribery offence requiring some sort of meeting of minds between briber and public official is not unique to Italy. Another of the strengths of the OECD Convention to date has been a focus on difficulties caused in enforcement, in relation to both foreign and domestic bribery, when a particular law requires the existence of what is sometimes called a 'corruption pact'. The prior existence of such a pact has, for instance, traditionally been a requirement in Luxembourg, where the bribery offence was only capable of being made out if the pact had been concluded before the official performed or abstained from the act he was being bribed to undertake or otherwise.[33] Thus, any steps taken unsuccessfully by a briber in order to create such a pact were capable only of prosecution as an attempt. On that traditional approach within Luxembourg, even the giving of a bribe might not amount to the substantive offence! However, Luxembourg has now addressed the problem. A new offence of 'Bribery ex post facto' has been introduced by virtue of Article 249 of the Luxembourg Criminal Code. A substantive offence is now completed where an unlawful corruption pact has been concluded after a public official has performed or abstained from doing an act. Thus, payment of a bribe alone will establish the bribery offence, even in the absence of a prior agreement between the parties. **10.33**

French law displays a similar requirement for a corruption pact. On the face of it, in France, active bribery is made out by an offer or a promise, whether that offer or promise has been accepted or not.[34] However, in examining the offence of bribery of a French public official (ie the domestic offence), the courts have evolved the notion of a corruption pact by demanding evidence of a meeting of **10.34**

32 See Italian Phase 2 review, p 31, paras 116ff.

33 See Luxemburg, Phase 1 Evaluation, p 3, paras 1.1.3–1.1.4.

34 See France Phase 1 Report, pp 4 and 5, para 1.1.3 and Phase 2 Report, p 43, para 113.

minds between briber and recipient. What is required is not proof of a contract, but rather that the briber knows that the purpose of his proposal is to obtain an act or omission and that, similarly, the bribed party is aware that he will receive an undue advantage in doing that act or making the omission. The principle has evolved from case law and practice, rather than statutory provision, and is equally applicable to the foreign bribery offence.[35] However, it seems that the existence of a pact can be established and inferred from a range of evidence: direct, circumstantial, or by way of explanation from the parties involved.[36]

10.35 The difficulty posed by the requirement of a meeting of minds is not one unique to continental European jurisdictions. Other State Parties to the OECD Convention have also experienced, and continue to experience, this same problem in the context of Article 1. Thus, it was ascertained during the Phase 2 evaluation of the Republic of Korea that an offer, promise, or gift that does not result in the provision of a benefit to a public official or is not accepted by the public official (or does not come to his attention) may not constitute the full offence. Moreover, in Korean law, attempts to bribe a foreign public official are not criminalized. Such lacunae have sometimes emerged during OECD evaluations. Sticking with the Korean example, domestically, article 133(1) of the Criminal Act does, in fact, establish the offence of promising, delivering, or manifesting a will to deliver a bribe to a domestic public official. There is, however, no equivalent in the foreign bribery context. Moreover, it seems that even the domestic offence is not intended to cover attempts.[37] Therefore, both for domestic and foreign bribery, an offer not accepted, or at least, not received by the public official, and a bribe sent, but not received, may not amount to criminal offences.

3. 'Directly or Through Intermediaries'

10.36 The offer, promise, or giving must be criminalized, whether made directly to the foreign public official or through an intermediary or intermediaries. In that regard, the OECD Convention recognizes that, as corruption in international business transactions becomes more sophisticated and as bribery in general is increasingly transnational, the use of intermediaries is not only a reality but a norm which has to be addressed if anti-corruption measures and legislation are to have any teeth. Indeed, the same message is apparent from UNCAC, which, in its criminalization provisions,[38] requires that the bribery offences in both active and passive forms cover direct and indirect offering of an undue advantage.

10.37 The WGB evaluations, at both Phase 1 and Phase 2, have generally sought to apply a strict test. The message is that enforcement and implementation may be

[35] See France Phase 2 Review, pp 39–40.
[36] See France Phase 2 Review, p 43, para 114.
[37] See Korea Phase 2 Review, p 31, paras 98–100.
[38] Art 15 and 16.

problematic if the wording of the foreign bribery offence (and, by implication, the domestic equivalent as well) is couched in terms which do not reflect explicitly 'directly or through intermediaries', or, alternatively, in the words of the UNCAC, 'directly or indirectly'. Thus, both the Phase 1 and Phase 2 reviews of the United Kingdom drew attention to what appeared to the lead examiners to be a shortcoming in the Prevention of Corruption Act 1906[39] Certainly the provisions of the 1906 Act, and indeed the body of case law creating the common law offence, do not expressly refer to an offer, etc being made through an intermediary. Nevertheless, common law practitioners will no doubt argue, and have argued,[40] that the 1906 Act does in fact criminalize bribery through an intermediary on two bases: first, that Section 1 talks of 'gives or agrees to give or offers any gift or consideration to *any agent . . .*'; secondly, in respect of both the statutory and common law offence, a bribe passing through an intermediary, or indeed an offer of a bribe, is likely to be caught since, on general principles, the use of an agent (whether innocent or a knowing accomplice) will not allow the principal offender to escape criminal liability. Further, although outside the scope of supply side bribery, it is worthy of note that, under the 1906 Act, any agent who corruptly accepts, or obtains, a gift or consideration, etc '*from any person*' will fall prey to the passive bribery offence.

On the point overall, the lessons to be learnt from the WGB's approach to the issue of Convention compliance, as gleaned from the evaluations it has carried out, is that where bribery through an intermediary is not to be specifically provided for within the stated elements of the offence, those State Parties to the Convention who require there to be an agreement between the briber and the official for the substantive offence of bribery run the risk of the accusation of non-compliance. Secondly, where there is an offence of complicity which can be used, such as incitement, the OECD Convention is capable of being satisfied. However, in that regard, any fetter on the use of incitement, etc[41] will, quite properly, draw criticism; whilst, further, in evaluating complicity offences, the WGB is bound to have regard to the sufficiency or otherwise of available sanctions.[42] **10.38**

4. Third-party Beneficiaries

In recognizing the use of other participants, apart from the briber and bribee, in transnational corrupt practices, the Convention goes further than simply addressing the use of intermediaries. Criminalization, to be Convention **10.39**

[39] See UK Phase 1 Review, p 5, para 1.1.5 and Phase 2 Review, p 60, para 187.

[40] See UK Phase 2 Review, p 60, para 187.

[41] As, for instance, in the Italian example: pp 31–32, paras 113–120 of the Phase 2 Review of Italy.

[42] Taking into account the provisions of Art 3, para 1: 'the bribery of a foreign public official shall be punishable by effective, proportionate, and dissuasive criminal penalties'.

compliant, must encompass the circumstance where an undue advantage is offered, promised, or given not to the foreign public official himself, but to a third party. Again, as sophistication grows, the expectation is that an advantage will not even go through the hands of a foreign public official, but will rather go or be paid directly to the spouse or an associate.

10.40 In fact, those who are charged with the task of criminalizing, must take into account two scenarios which need to be addressed:

(i) The advantage which goes to the third party beneficiary without passing through the hands of the foreign public official;
(ii) The advantage which goes through the hands of the foreign public official but to, and for the benefit of, the third party beneficiary.

10.41 The use of a complicity offence such as incitement has already been referred to in the context of those countries which are unable to reflect an offer of a bribe in a substantive offence. However, all State Parties to the Convention are required to address and criminalize complicity. Article 1, paragraph 2 requires countries to take any measures necessary to establish as a criminal offence complicity in the bribing of a foreign public official. Complicity, for these purposes, is expressly stated to include incitement, aiding, and abetting, and the authorization of an act of bribery. As to attempted bribery and conspiracy to bribe, those must be criminalized in relation to foreign bribery 'to the same extent as attempt and conspiracy to bribe a public official of that Party'.[43] Similarly, within UNCAC, there is a requirement that participation/secondary party involvement must be criminalized, but an offence of attempt or 'preparation' in relation to an act of bribery is not mandatory.[44]

5. The 'Advantage'

10.42 The 'advantage' for the purposes of the OECD Convention includes 'any undue pecuniary or other advantage'.[45] Some jurisdictions may have the difficulty of imprecision in using the term 'undue'. Interestingly, although UNCAC also talks of 'undue advantage',[46] the EU Convention and Protocol (both of which require the criminalization of the giving or receiving of advantages to or by EU and Member State officials) refer instead to 'advantages of any kind whatsoever'.[47] Neither the OECD Convention nor UNCAC offer guidance on the meaning of 'undue'. Conversely, the Council of Europe's Convention states that 'undue' for the purposes of the COE Convention should be interpreted as something the recipient is not lawfully entitled to accept or receive.

10.43 In relation to both the OECD and UNCAC it may be asked whether 'undue' is simply a reference to something to which the recipient was not entitled or

[43] Art 1, para 2. [44] UNCAC, Art 27. [45] Art 1. [46] eg in Art 15 and 16.
[47] See EU Convention, Art 3.1.

whether its aim is to qualify 'advantage' to the extent of not just excluding advantages permitted by law or by administrative rules, but also gifts which are of low value or are socially acceptable. The dangers of the latter interpretation are obvious: one of the mischiefs at which the OECD Convention seeks to strike is the using of the 'I was operating in a gift giving culture' excuse and the dressing up of a bribe as a gift.

Within the United Kingdom, the term 'undue' has an imprecise meaning. The same difficulty is experienced in other parts of the English-speaking world to a greater or lesser extent. It is worthy of note that the 2003 draft Corruption Bill did not seek to qualify the word 'advantage' by the use of either 'undue' or 'improper'.[48] There certainly seems to be no definition of either word in English which has sufficient precision. The dictionary definition and general understanding (bearing in mind that a jury would be considering the issue) of either word ranges from 'incorrect', 'unsuitable', 'unbecoming', 'unlawful' (civil or criminal), or 'criminal'. **10.44**

The risk is not simply one of arriving at a definition which is equivocal, rather it is that the use of 'undue', or indeed 'improper' might result in a position where any form of agreement or contract between corrupt parties precludes a corruption charge (on the premise that there was in existence a legal basis for the advantage). Within the United Kingdom, at least, the difficulty does not stop there, since no true definition of what is meant by 'corruptly' has evolved; therefore, 'corrupt advantage' is probably not the smoothest path to Convention compliance by an English-speaking party in the absence of an ability to define what 'corrupt' actually is. The common law has been better at saying what corruption is not (for instance, it does not have to involve an element of dishonesty),[49] than at saying what it actually is. **10.45**

Those State Parties which do not have such a linguistic difficulty will want to consider incorporating the precise words of the OECD Convention in this regard into the foreign bribery offence. In any event, given the nature of corrupt transactions, it is important that any definition encompasses both the pecuniary and non-pecuniary. With the realities of commerce, the offering, etc of the intangible and non-monetary are eventualities which do, and will, all too frequently arise. **10.46**

The OECD evaluations have forced a number of examined State Parties to consider afresh the breadth of their definition of 'advantage'. Prior to the Phase 1 Review of Bulgaria, for instance, that country's Penal Code described an advantage as 'a gift or any other material benefits'.[50] However, following **10.47**

[48] See draft Corruption Bill clauses 1, 2, and 4.
[49] See, eg *R v Harvey* [1999] Crim LR 70.
[50] Bulgaria Penal Code, Art 304(1).

criticism in the Phase 1 Review,[51] that definition was amended to 'gift or any other kind of advantage'; the change making it clear that both non-pecuniary and intangible benefits were covered, as well as the pecuniary advantage. The Phase 1 Review of Chile found a similar weakness when faced with the term 'an economic advantage' within the Chilean offence.[52] Although such a definition will cover both tangible and intangible pecuniary advantages, it will not reflect a non-pecuniary advantage, such as providing admission to a school or university which the official's child might not otherwise have secured.

10.48 As to arriving at a Convention compliant definition, regard must also be had to the underlying notion of 'functional equivalence'. Conversely, there may be occasions when the definition within the foreign bribery offence needs to be fuller. Thus, in Mexico the domestic active bribery offence[53] encompasses 'money or any other advantage', whilst, in relation to the foreign equivalent, the definition is 'money or any other advantage, whether in assets or services'.

6. 'In order that the official act or refrain from acting . . .'

10.49 For the purposes of the OECD Convention, the criminalization requirement is in relation to bribes offered, etc 'in order that the official act or refrain from acting in the exercise of his or her official duties'.[54] In other words, the expected act or omission must be in the public official's official capacity. In seeking to adhere to the broad wording of Article 1 in this regard, legislators must take care to ensure that the construction they use to reflect 'in order that the official act or refrain from acting' covers all situations, including that of an official being given money in order to do/not do something he or she would/would not have done anyway. Given that the OECD Convention (and indeed UNCAC) is therefore phrased so as to encompass acts which would have been proper for the official to do/not do had there been no offer or giving of a bribe, care must be taken if legislation is phrased along the lines of 'to induce a breach of the official's duty'. This wording, and wording like it, will cause difficulties in relation to both domestic and foreign bribery offences. For present purposes, in relation to the foreign offence and as Commentary 3 makes clear, an offence defined in those terms is capable of being Convention compliant so long as it is understood that every public official has a duty to exercise judgment or discretion impartially and that the phrase 'to induce etc', if used, is therefore an autonomous definition which does not require proof of, for instance, the law governing 'duty' in the particular official's own country. Similarly, it may be noted in passing that, for domestic bribery cases, such a wording will also cause difficulties unless it

---

[51] See Bulgaria Phase 1 Review, p 3, para 1.1.4 and p 18, para 1.1.

[52] See Chile Phase 1 Review, p 5, para 14.

[53] Mexico Criminal Code, Art 222.

[54] Art 1, para 1.

is understood that the breach of duty is the failure to exercise an impartial discretion unaffected by the giving or offering of an advantage; after all, the domestic official may, similarly, be being bribed to do what he or she would have done in his/her duty in any event.

This causative element also carries with it, for common law jurisdictions and for some others, the notion of intention as to consequence. To date, however, there is little in any of the evaluation reports to suggest that the WGB has focused on this aspect of the bribery offence. As will be seen elsewhere in this work,[55] in the United Kingdom, case law on corruption cases has tended to shy away from a thorough discussion of intent as to consequence. It remains to be seen whether the WGB will regard this aspect of the mental element of the offence as being worthy of attention in any detail. **10.50**

The purposive element of the offence must be wide enough to incorporate the second causative element: 'in order to obtain or retain business or other undue advantage in relation to the conduct of international business'. Under the OECD Convention, a jurisdiction may choose to limit the foreign bribery offence in accordance with this, whilst another may choose to leave the offence broader in scope. Whatever the approach, the phrase 'other undue advantage' should be noted. The requirement is that the criminalization must include an advantage such as that which accrues to a company which obtains an operating permit for a factory in circumstances where it clearly fails to meet the statutory requirements usually required for such a grant—in short, obtaining an advantage to which there is clearly no entitlement. **10.51**

7. 'Intentionally'

The requirement of 'intentionally' prefaces the offence established under Article 1. Unsurprisingly, the evaluations have revealed differences of approach between various legal systems in the way that 'intentionally' is reflected in any statute which brings about criminalization. For those with a common law tradition, peer review has revealed an established approach to intent in relation to corruption which amounts to an intent as to the giving of the advantage and an intent as to the consequence of the giving (ie that the official does an act or makes an omission as a result of the advantage being given). In the reviews of New Zealand and the United Kingdom,[56] the two terms used to reflect intent in corruption legislation have been either 'corruptly' or 'with intent'. Thus, in the case of New Zealand, the foreign bribery offence includes the requirement 'with the intent to influence a foreign public official'.[57] An alternative approach which **10.52**

[55] See 2.16ff above.
[56] See New Zealand Phase 1 Review, p 4, para 1.1.2 and UK Phase 2 at p 61, para 191.
[57] Section 105C of the Crimes Amendment Act 2001, s 105C.

may be taken in a common law country is reflected within the provisions of the UK draft Corruption Bill.[58]

10.53 The process of evaluation under the OECD Convention has, however, shown that some jurisdictions regard 'intentionally' as covering both direct intention and recklessness. Thus, the Slovenian authorities were able to indicate, during their Phase 1 Review, that the Slovenian offence of foreign bribery would encompass the case where a company representative directed an intermediary to obtain a contract from a foreign government 'through any means', without expressly directing the intermediary to offer any bribe. For Slovenia, such recklessness in those circumstances amounts to a form of intent.

10.54 How may one, then, articulate the minimum international standard for criminalization in this regard? It appears to be the offering, giving, etc of an advantage with the direct intent that the foreign public official will do an act or make an omission as a result.

D. The Consequent Debate: The Scope of Criminalization

10.55 A wide range of issues are engaged by any debate on foreign bribery, from competition or due diligence (on the part of business and commerce), to questions of good governance, poverty reduction and political stability (on the part of civil society and non-governmental organizations (NGOs)). As a result of the interests of, and debate between, so many stakeholders, the OECD Convention has highlighted a fundamental concern: what should be the scope of a bribery offence?

10.56 Most jurisdictions will seek to define corruption by adopting a transactional approach; in other words, providing for a criminal offence which is made out when, in broad terms, the offering or giving of an advantage in return for a gain takes place. However, should the definition of the corruption offence be further limited by reference to the agent/principal relationship (as in the UK Prevention of Corruption Act 1906) or by the notion of breach of trust? For instance, Australia, Canada, and Ireland, in addition to United Kingdom, have each adopted an agent/principal approach to some of their corruption offences, whilst several other countries, including Germany and Austria, have a concept of private sector corruption based on breach of duty which is conceptually very similar to agent/principal. Certainly breach of duty lies at the heart of the approach to private section corruption found in international instruments: for example, the Council of Europe Criminal Law Convention; the EU Joint Action and Framework Decision on Private Sector Corruption; and, more recently, UNCAC itself. However, as well as engendering the debate, the

[58] Draft Corruption Bill, clauses 5, 9, and 10; see App 33 below.

OECD Convention does not seek to constrain Parties on the point; as Commentary 3 (in relation to Article 1) states: 'a statute prohibiting the bribery of agents generally which does not specifically address bribery of a foreign public official, and a statute specifically limited to this case, could both comply with this Article'. Thus, criminalization on the basis of agent/principal is acceptable, as is a general bribery offence which is not confined to the foreign public official, but rather includes him amongst a wider range of officials or bribees (since public and private sector bribery may be reflected within the same offence and still be Convention compliant).

The rigours and the breadth of evaluations under the OECD Convention and **10.57** the nature of peer review itself have engendered wider debates. Is criminalization best served by a generic offence, (like the one traditionally favoured by the United Kingdom), or by a number of different corruption offences reflecting different types of corrupt transactions and relationships (as, for instance, adopted by South Africa)? Perhaps even more fundamentally, should a State Party seek to formulate a free standing definition of what amounts to corruption or should one avoid a definition of what amounts to the term 'corruptly' and simply define the offence in relation to a breach of the agent/principal relationship or, at least, the notion of breach of trust? In the sphere of corrupt activity with which the OECD Convention is particularly concerned, such considerations arise from a very basic difficulty: how to differentiate a corrupt act from the various kinds of legitimate giving and receiving of advantages that make up ordinary transactions of both business and social life.

Article 1 compliance necessarily requires a jurisdiction to consider the nature **10.58** of corruption: should the offence be confined to activity which is essentially the subversion of loyalty to a principal, such as an employer or, indeed, the public at large? Is the essence of corrupt activity 'cheating' on the person or entity whom you should be safeguarding or is it the wider notion of criminalizing those activities within business/commerce and government which are morally reprehensible and which are not perhaps presently capable of being reflected by other existing offences? To some extent the debate strays beyond the topic of foreign bribery, but it is central to those questions of principle which have arisen as a result of the Phase 1 and Phase 2 reviews. Many NGOs will certainly argue that, in the modern business world, corrupt activity needs to be understood in a much wider context than is presently provided for many corruption offences. Thus, in the United Kingdom, what of the situation where the owner of one business gives money to the owner of another in order to induce him not to tender for a particular contract? Should such activity be understood as corruption or should it, as presently in UK law, be understood as an anti-competition offence?[59]

---

[59] eg as reflected by the criminal offence of bid-rigging under the Enterprise Act 2002.

E. Defences

1. General Defences

10.59 In most jurisdictions there will, of course, be general defences which a defendant may rely on when facing an allegation of foreign (or indeed domestic) bribery. However, what is capable of undermining the thrust of the OECD Convention is any defence which strikes at the matters addressed in Commentary 7, which states 'it is also an offence irrespective of, inter alia, the value of the advantage, its results, perceptions of local custom, the tolerance of such payments by local authorities, or the alleged necessity of the payment in order to obtain or retain business or other improper advantage'. Further, the Revised Recommendation of 1997, in Annex 3, supplements the words of the Commentary with the following: 'bribery of foreign public officials in order to obtain or retain business is an offence irrespective of the value or the outcome of the bribe, of perceptions of local custom or of the tolerance of the bribery by local authorities'.

2. Pressure, Effective Regret, and Cooperation

10.60 The WGB has shown itself ready to highlight the existence of any defence which contravenes the above provisions. Perhaps a striking example, highlighted by the Phase 2 evaluation of Italy, is the defence of *concussione* in Italian law, which may be pleaded in either a domestic or foreign bribery case.[60] Under the Italian criminal provisions, an individual is not guilty of bribery if a public official abuses his functions or power and obliges or induces that individual to unduly give or promise money or other assets either to the official or to a third party. Instead, the official himself is guilty of *concussione*,[61] whilst the bribe payer is regarded as a victim and potential witness.

10.61 The rationale in Italian domestic cases for such a provision is obvious: if one is trying to eradicate corruption amongst officials, then the prospect of being able to call as a witness the payer who is, indeed, in many senses a victim, will be an attractive one. However, transpose that rationale to the increasingly sophisticated context of transnational bribery and the defence of *concussione*, with its threshold set much lower than duress or extortion as understood as a defence by many jurisdictions, becomes a cause for some concern. The very attraction within domestic law, namely that the bribe payer will be a witness, is unlikely to be capable of being brought about in the context of foreign bribery, particularly where a public official is from a state where corruption is endemic.

[60] See Phase 2 Review of Italy, pp 33–34, para 128–140.
[61] See Italian Criminal Code, art 317.

As a cautionary tale to other jurisdictions which have, or contemplate having, such a defence, one may go further: the concept of *concussione* is further complicated by the notion of *concussione ambientale*, which was developed by Italian jurisprudence in the 1990s.[62] This form of *concussione* may be said to occur when an individual is in a place or an environment which leads him to believe that he must provide a public official with an advantage, either to avoid harm or to obtain something to which he is entitled. Compelled by the environment itself and without any express demands from the official, the individual then obliges. Within the context of foreign bribery, it would therefore seem that an individual or a company operating in a country in which payment of a bribe is a prerequisite for being part of a tendering process, will be able to avail him/itself of the defence, even where there has been no express solicitation by a public official. **10.62**

It will be entirely acceptable and within the spirit of the OECD Convention for a court to weigh in the balance the pressure or persuasion exerted by a public official over the active briber, and there may be circumstances where the sanction against the briber should be reduced accordingly. However, the extinguishing of criminal liability at such a low threshold as is envisaged by *concussione* will, if adopted any more widely, run the risk of undermining the very process of foreign bribery criminalization which the OECD Convention has brought about. Nevertheless, amongst the State Parties to the OECD Convention, the Italian example is not an isolated one. For instance, Chile has a defence of 'necessity' which seems capable of being drawn widely,[63] whilst Bulgaria has a defence of blackmail, the extent of which, at present, seems uncertain.[64] **10.63**

In relation to Bulgaria, pursuant to article 306 of the Bulgarian Penal Code, a person who is given a bribe shall not be punished if he is being blackmailed by the official and if he has informed the authorities without delay and voluntarily.[65] It has to be accepted that the latter requirement has a limiting effect on the ambit of the defence. But, given that if the crime of blackmail is made out, then no offence of bribery will have been committed, one has to at least question whether the article 306 defence of blackmail is still unduly wide and presents the same difficulties as *concussione*. The key question, of course, will be the level of threat needed to found the defence. Will Bulgarian courts, faced with a bribery case, regard a threat by a public official that a company will be excluded from bidding for a contract unless a bribe is paid, as blackmail? **10.64**

Given that crimes of corruption are notoriously difficult to prosecute, or even to detect, there will be occasions for all State Parties to the OECD Convention **10.65**

62 See Phase 2 Review of Italy, p 34, para 134.
63 See Phase 1 Review of Chile, p 3, para 7.
64 See Phase 1 and Phase 2 Reports of Bulgaria, p 2 and p 30, respectively.
65 See Phase 2 Review of Bulgaria, p 30.

when cooperating defendant programmes, etc are valuable. However, the lesson from the WGB's evaluations is that care must be taken if a jurisdiction is providing an absolute defence to those who voluntarily come forward to the authorities. By way of illustration, the Slovenian bribery offence[66] is framed in such a way that, in the event that the public official solicited the bribe, the briber may escape conviction if he reports the act to the Slovenian authorities. Domestically, the argument for the defence of so-called 'effective regret' is a powerful one, since very often the real mischief to be confronted is that of the solicitation or passive bribery offence committed by the official. However, in relation to the foreign bribery setting, such policy considerations lose their force. Just as with *concussione*, it may well be that the passive party, the public official, will never in fact be brought before a court. In addition, for the purposes of the OECD Convention, it must be remembered that such a defence is not within its contemplation.

10.66 The fact that the OECD Convention places limitations on the availability of certain defences does not mean that regard cannot be had to the position in law in the foreign public official's own country. Thus, Commentary 8 provides that 'it is not an offence, however, if the advantage was permitted or required by the written law or regulation of the foreign public official's country, including case law'.

3. Facilitation Payments

10.67 Whilst considering defences, it is apposite to consider the issue of 'facilitation' payments. For the purposes of the OECD Convention, it is perfectly acceptable for a State Party to exclude facilitation payments from bribery criminalization and/or to provide a specific defence if an alleged bribe can be shown to be a facilitation payment. Commentary 9 makes clear that 'small facilitation payments do not constitute payments made "to obtain or retain business or other improper advantage" within the meaning of paragraph 1 [of Article 1] and, accordingly, are not an offence'. Some jurisdictions do not recognize in their law the concept of a facilitation payment; thus, in the United Kingdom, the question is whether a payment is corrupt, whether it is a bribe, irrespective of its size.[67] However, in other jurisdictions, such as the United States,[68] the notion of the facilitation payment is provided for and excluded from criminalization.

---

[66] Slovenian Penal Code, art 268.

[67] Although the exercise of prosecutorial discretion may result in a decision being made not to prosecute on the basis of a public statement (see http://www.ukti.gov.uk) to the effect that it is difficult to envisage circumstances in which a prosecution will be brought where a small payment was made to a public official in circumstances of extortion.

[68] See Foreign Corrupt Practices Act 1977, §78dd-1(b) and (c)

It is timely to ask whether the WGB will in the future carry out a meaningful re-examination of the whole issue of facilitation payments. It might be argued that the OECD Convention itself needs revisiting on the point. Certainly Commentary 9 goes on to reflect the underlying unease that some State Parties to the Convention have: **10.68**

> ...such payments, which, in some countries, are made to induce public officials to perform their functions, such as issuing licences or permits, are generally illegal in the foreign country concerned. Other countries can and should address this corrosive phenomenon by such means as support of programmes of good governance. However, criminalisation by other countries does not seem practical or effective complementary action.

F. Liability of Legal Persons (Article 2)

Article 2 provides that a Party 'shall take such measures as may be necessary, in accordance with its legal principles, to establish the liability of legal persons for the bribery of a foreign public official'. Commentary 20 supplements that provision by stating that 'in the event that, under the legal system of a Party, criminal responsibility is not applicable to legal persons, that Party shall not be required to establish such criminal responsibility'. As one would expect from the OECD Convention as a whole, Article 2 does not seek to get State Parties to change the whole basis of their domestic law, rather it requires them to establish liability for foreign bribery on the basis of a functional equivalence and in accordance with the approach in existing domestic provisions (insofar as those will provide for a basis of liability). However, that principle of functional equivalence only applies where a state already has criminal, civil, or administrative liability for legal persons. To be compliant with the OECD Convention, one of those three forms of liability must be introduced. **10.69**

The issue of the liability of the legal person is a crucial, yet vexed, one. In all jurisdictions, the criminal law evolved as the response of society and the State to the actions of individuals. In the modern world, in relation to corruption cases in particular, it is, however, very often the legal person (typically the company or corporation) which drives, and benefits from, corrupt activity. With that in mind, jurisdictions which traditionally have or have introduced criminal liability for legal persons have had to consider how to make that liability workable and, in particular, how to attribute corrupt acts to the legal entity. Meanwhile, those with no liability for legal persons or with only administrative or civil liability available have had to consider whether to go down the path of criminalization. Whichever basis of liability is chosen, no anti-corruption strategy will have a real chance of success unless the liability of legal persons is capable of enforcement. Whilst it is not the intention of this chapter to engage in a full **10.70** discussion of legal person liability and all the issues it raises, the topic is so central to implementation and enforcement of the OECD Convention that some consideration is required.

10.71 A State Party is likely to seek to criminalize not just the offering, etc of a bribe by a company, but also the directing or authorizing by a parent company of a bribe to be paid by a domestic or foreign subsidiary. Although, in relation to the last of those, there have long been understood to be difficulties of principle and practice which need to be addressed, liability for such activities raises a host of additional general issues, including jurisdiction, complicity, and participation and the nature of the responsibility had for the acts of an agent. For present purposes, however, the focus will be on the extent to which the various bases for the liability of a legal person favoured by the State Parties to the OECD Convention are consistent with its enforcement and implementation. Given that the business transaction is at the heart of the activities addressed by the OECD Convention, a basis of liability which is unlikely in practice to give rise to the possibility of mounting a prosecution will be hugely problematic.

10.72 The Phase 1 and Phase 2 evaluations of the United Kingdom[69] have drawn attention to the difficulties in the traditional common law model for establishing criminal liability, namely 'attribution'. The concept of criminal liability for a legal person or corporation grew up in the nineteenth century when, of course, it was relatively straightforward to identify who in fact ran a company. With some additional gloss, that test remains in place today. As the United Kingdom's WGB evaluations[70] made clear, in the United Kingdom, where an offence involves a mental element such as intent, the finding of liability in relation to a legal person depends on identifying someone within the corporation with an appropriate level of authority who can be said to possess the state of mind of the corporation itself: in other words, the so-called 'directing' or 'controlling' mind. The traditional test for identifying the controlling mind, has been the aptly named 'identification theory'. That works on the premise that certain officers within a corporation are the embodiment of it when it acts in the course of its business. The acts and states of mind of such company officers are deemed to be those of the company. The leading case in modern case law is that of *Tesco Supermarkets Ltd v Nattress*,[71] which restricts such liability to the acts of 'the board of directors, managing director, and perhaps other superior managers of the company who carry out functions of management, and speak and act as "the company" '. When conducting that test, one needs to consider, *inter alia*, the constitution of the company, its memorandum and articles of association, the actions of directors in general meetings, etc and the extent, if any, of delegation.

[69] See Phase 1 Evaluation, p 8 and Phase 2 Evaluation, p 63, paras 197–199.

[70] See Phase 1 Review, p 8 and Phase 2, p 63, paras 197–199.

[71] [1972] AC 153.

In its Phase 2 evaluation, the United Kingdom drew the attention of the lead examiners to the more recent attribution test propounded by the Privy Council in *Meridian Global Funds Management Asia Ltd v Securities Commission*,[72] a case which envisages a broader test which depends on the purpose of the provisions that create the relevant offence rather than simply focusing on a search for a directing mind. But the lead examiners tasked with evaluating the United Kingdom had doubts as to the wider applicability of the *Meridian Test*, as it had been put to them, since it related to securities law disclosure rather than to crime in the conventional sense.[73] **10.73**

It is clear from the tenor of the Phase 2 Report of the United Kingdom and on the report's recommendations[74] that the lead examiners and the WGB are troubled by the traditional common law stance. They are, of course, not alone. There has been a history of disquiet as to the directing/controlling mind test, and ongoing requests for government to come up with an alternative. In the context of transnational bribery, in particular, it has to be recognized that the common law test does not permit the creation of a corporate intent by simply aggrregating the states of mind of more than one person within the corporation. Even on the *Meridian Test*, one individual has to be 'the company' for the purpose of the mental element. The Phase 2 Report,[75] with some force, questions enforcement capacity under the OECD Convention in circumstances where the criminal liability of a legal person depends on proving both the culpable act/omission and the required mental element by a single person within the corporation, even though, of course, a criminal conviction of that particular individual is not a prerequisite. **10.74**

With an eye to likely future work by the WGB, the United Kingdom, and indeed other jurisdictions, need to have one further issue in mind: in the event of a wholly-owned foreign subsidiary of a UK parent company paying a bribe, the parent company will only be liable if it can be shown to have directed or authorized the bribe. Moreover, on the principle of attribution just discussed, any such direction or authorization will have to be shown to be carried out by the directing or controlling mind. Given that position, to what extent in the future will there be pressure to introduce some form of liability, deemed or otherwise, for a parent company in such circumstances, even if this is by the introduction of regulatory, accounts, or 'books' offences? **10.75**

Phase 2 evaluations of other common law jurisdictions have, however, highlighted the potential for introducing a new, more workable, test of attribution. Thus, in the Phase 2 Review of Canada[76] it was noted that, although Canada **10.76**

[72] [1995] 2 AC 500. [73] See Phase 2 Review of the UK, p 63, paras 197–199.
[74] See Phase 2 Review of the UK, p 81, para 255(c).
[75] See Phase 2 Review of the UK, p 64, paras 201–202.
[76] See Phase 2 Review of Canada, pp 30–32.

had been subject to the same restrictions inherent in the 'directing mind' test, it was in the process of taking legislative steps to move away from the traditional identification theory. It noted that the Supreme Court of Canada case of *Canadian Dredge and Dock Co v The Queen*[77] had formulated an attribution test on the basis of the directing mind or 'ego' of the corporation, but that the Government of Canada, in 2002, accepted the findings of a Standing Committee and decided to introduce legislation on the liability of legal persons. The Commentary by the lead examiners on Canada illustrates the WGB's view on the approach which common law jurisdictions should take: 'the lead examiners welcome the most recent initiative of the Government of Canada to reform the law on corporate criminal liability by clarifying (through codification) and expanding its scope, and believe that the revised law would significantly improve the effectiveness of the liability of legal persons for the bribery of a foreign public official'.

10.77 Since the Phase 2 Review, the initiative of the Canadian Government is now reflected in Bill C45, an 'Act to Amend the Criminal Code (Criminal Liability of Organizations)', which came into force on 31 March 2004. It has established new rules for attributing to organizations, including corporations, criminal liability. In essence, it criminalizes on the basis that: when a senior person with policy or operational authority commits an offence personally; or has the necessary intent and directs the affairs of the corporation in order that lower level employees carry out the illegal act; or fails to take action to stop criminal conduct of which he/she is aware or wilfully blind; towards then criminal liability will be attributed to the corporation.

10.78 Canada is not alone amongst State Parties to the OECD Convention in seeking a workable reformulation of the test of attribution. New Zealand has also moved away from the strict identification theory as generally understood.[78] Although criminal responsibility of a corporation under New Zealand law still depends upon assigning responsibility on the basis of a culpable act and of the requisite state of mind of the representative of the corporation, the position of that representative does not have to be that of a 'directing mind'; rather, the test is whether the director or employee of the corporation had actual authority within it in relation to the area of alleged conduct. In essence, does the natural person in question have real control on behalf of the legal person over the activities which relate to the alleged offence? As in the United Kingdom, the position in New Zealand remains that the conviction of the natural person is not needed as a precondition to the prosecution of the legal person.

10.79 Those minded to create a (new) test of attribution either for the purposes of OECD Convention enforcement or pursuant to UNCAC, might wish to

[77] [1985] 1 SCR 662.

[78] See Phase 1 Report of New Zealand, p 11, paras 2.1.1–2.1.2.

consider the alternative model described in the Phase 2 report of the United States. The US position might be described as vicarious, or even strict, liability on the part of the legal person. As the Phase 2 Report makes clear,[79] a company is criminally liable for the acts of its directors, officials, or employees, whenever they act within the scope of their duties and for the benefit of the company. Importantly, those elements are interpreted broadly to the extent that an argument cannot be advanced on behalf of a company that the act of giving or authorizing a bribe is itself outside the scope of duties when the company is the beneficiary of the unlawful conduct.

In a real sense, indeed, the basis for legal person liability on that test is almost strict, since there is no requirement for any imputed 'mental element' by the 'mind' of the company. Thus, it is irrelevant whether the conduct has been allowed, condoned, or even condemned by the management at a particular level. Such liability is applicable not just to domestic bribery and to offences under the Foreign Corrupt Practices Act 1977, but generally. In the field of anti-corruption, however, the advantage of the US approach is obvious: companies will react to the legal threat and seek to protect themselves by introducing stringent due diligence practices. Moreover, since the Foreign Corrupt Practices Act 1977 takes the principle further, and also imposes criminal liability on legal persons for foreign bribery committed by third parties acting as agents, such due diligence safeguards will also be put in place in dealing with intermediaries and sales representatives and will not just be confined to codes of conduct and employment contracts for company employees. **10.80**

A similar approach by the Republic of Korea was highlighted by its Phase 2 Review.[80] Article 4 of the Foreign Bribery Prevention Act 1998 creates what is, in essence, a vicarious liability and provides that: **10.81**

> ... in the event that a representative, agent, employee or other individual working for a legal person has committed the offence as set out in Article 3.1 [Foreign Bribery] in relation to its business, the legal person shall also be subject to a fine of 1 billion won in addition to the imposition of sanctions on the actual performer... if the legal person has paid due attention or has exercised proper supervision to prevent the offence against this Act, it shall not be subject to the above sanctions.

The above provision does, however, beg the question: what amounts to due attention or proper supervision? In addition, it seems unclear whether the natural person has to be prosecuted and/or convicted for the legal person to be liable. However, the Phase 2 Review[81] indicates that the lead examiners were informed that the natural person who is the perpetrator must be identified but, **10.82**

[79] Phase 2 Report of the US, p 7.
[80] Phase 2 Report of Korea, pp 35–38.
[81] Phase 2 Report on Korea, p 38.

if he is not proceeded against, the court is able to make a finding of fact that he bribed a foreign public official. However, in the event that the natural person is proceeded against under the Act, then the legal person may only be found guilty if the natural person perpetrator is himself convicted and sanctioned.

10.83 The notion of a legal entity possessing a 'mind' will be alien to civil code jurisdictions; accordingly, a number have chosen to criminalize on the basis of an imputed or deemed liability. Thus, since 1994, the Criminal Code in France[82] has allowed a judge, in respect of active bribery as well as other prescribed offences, to assign criminal responsibility to a legal person. The prosecution of a natural person or persons does not preclude the concomitant prosecution of the legal person.[83]

10.84 In Finland, criminal liability of legal persons was introduced in 1995, and initially required that a person belonging to the management must have been an accomplice or must have allowed, authorized or directed the offence. However, following an amendment to the Penal Code in 2001, liability was extended to include a natural person exercising a *de facto* management function, regardless of whether that natural person was formally a part of the management.[84]

10.85 Norway introduced criminal liability for legal persons in 1991. However, it is governed by a special set of discretionary criteria. Section 48a(1) of the Penal Code provides that when a penal provision is contravened by a person who has acted on behalf of an enterprise, the enterprise may be liable for a penalty: 'this applies even if no individual person may be punished for the contravention'. Here, the Penal Code goes on to provide that the word 'enterprise' includes 'a company, society or other association, one-man enterprise, foundation, and state or public activity'. However, in deciding whether the legal person will be liable for a penalty, the Norwegian court will consider, in its discretion, the following matters:

(1) the preventive effect of the penalty;
(2) the seriousness of the offence;
(3) whether the enterprise could have prevented the offence by guidelines, instruction, training, or control;
(4) whether the offence had been committed in order to promote the interests of the enterprise;
(5) whether the enterprise has obtained an advantage by the offence;
(6) the economic capacity of the enterprise; and
(7) whether any penalty has been imposed on an individual person.

[82] French Criminal Code, arts 435–436 and 121–122.
[83] French Criminal Code, arts 121–122, and see Phase 2 Review of France, p 46.
[84] See Phase 2 Review of Finland, p 18.

In principle, Norwegian law does not require the involvement of a leading person within the company or enterprise; thus, liability may be triggered by the acts of a single employee who is not part of the management structure. However, one of the discretionary criteria is whether the enterprise could have prevented the offence by guidelines, training, control, etc. Thus, depending on the weight a particular court gives to that criterion, the level within the company of the employee who has, for instance, paid the bribe may be of some importance and may, in theory, become a determining factor.[85] **10.86**

The Phase 2 evaluation process has also provided the opportunity to evaluate countries in which administrative (rather than criminal) liability is imposed and to make an assessment of the enforcement and implementation issues which arise from this. Thus, in the Phase 2 review of Germany[86] it was noted that, under the Administrative Offences Act, a fine may be imposed on the legal person in the course of criminal proceedings against the natural person. However, if a natural person is not prosecuted because he cannot be identified, or has died, it is then possible to sanction the legal person in separate proceedings. However, the lead examiners formed the view that[87] the liability of the legal person is regarded in Germany as an 'incidental consequence' of an offence committed by the natural person and that it was in fact very unusual to proceed against the legal person where the natural person had not also been proceeded against. **10.87**

Similarly, in Italy, the theory of administrative liability is that it is attributed to a legal person for certain criminal offences (including bribery) committed by the natural person.[88] Italian law[89] imposes liability on the legal person for offences committed by two categories of natural person: (a) those in senior positions, and (b) those subject to the management or control of those in category (a). A person is in a senior position if he/she carries out activities of representation, administration, or management of the corporate body or of one of its autonomous units. **10.88**

However, under the Italian Decree, the legal person is liable only for offences 'committed in its interest and its advantage' and therefore will not be liable where the natural person acts exclusively in his/her own interests or for a third party. In that regard, the WGB will, no doubt, wish to consider in the future whether the Italian courts will interpret widely the notion of a natural person committing an offence in the interest of the legal person and also whether non-liability on the basis that a natural person has acted for a third party would include, as a third party, a subsidiary of the legal person. **10.89**

[85] See Phase 2 Review of Norway, pp 32–35.
[86] See Phase 2 Review of Germany, pp 28–32.
[87] Phase 2 Review of Germany, p 30.
[88] Decree 231/2001.
[89] See ibid.

G. Sanctions (Article 3)

10.90 Article 3 provides that sanctions for the bribery of a foreign public official must be effective, proportionate, and dissuasive. There must be functional equivalence in the sense that the range of penalties available for the foreign offence must be comparable to those applicable to the bribery of a domestic public official. Furthermore, in the case of a natural person, the available sanction must include deprivation of liberty sufficient to enable effective mutual legal assistance and extradition.[90]

10.91 If a State Party has civil or administrative liability, rather than criminal, for the legal person, then that State Party must ensure that the non-criminal sanctions are, similarly, effective, proportionate, and dissuasive. Those administrative sanctions must include the availability of monetary sanctions.

10.92 Whatever the basis of liability for the legal person, each State Party to the OECD Convention 'shall consider' the imposition of additional civil or administrative sanctions upon a person who has been subject to sanction for the foreign bribery offence.[91] That consideration applies to both natural and legal persons. However, in the case of the legal person, Commentary 24 gives illustrations of the range of civil or administrative sanctions which may be imposed. These include exclusion from entitlement to public benefits or aid, temporary or permanent disqualification from participation in public procurement, temporary or permanent disqualification from the practice of other commercial activities, placing under judicial supervision, and a judicial winding up order.

10.93 In addition, and of particular practical and preventative importance, Article 3, paragraph 3 provides that each State Party to the OECD Convention 'shall take such measures as may be necessary to provide that the bribe and the proceeds of the bribery of a foreign public official, or property the value of which corresponds to that of such proceeds, are subject to seizure and confiscation or that monetary sanctions of comparable effect are applicable'. As a gloss to paragraph 3, Commentary 21 goes on to makes clear that the 'proceeds' of bribery are the profits or other benefits derived by the briber from the transaction, or other improper advantage obtained or retained through bribery. Thus, there is certainly an argument, subject to considerations of 'remoteness', that the profits of a company under a contract in circumstances where the contract was obtained by giving a bribe to, for instance, a contract officer (perhaps to secure a place in the tendering process) should be liable for confiscation if a state is to be convention compliant in this regard. At the same time, though, Commentary 23 explains that Article 3, paragraph 3 does not preclude setting appropriate limits to monetary sanctions; such limits must, however, be at a level that does not

[90] See Art 3, para 1. [91] Art 3, para 4.

defeat any of the mandatory provisions of Article 3 and must allow for available sanctions to be effective, proportionate, and dissuasive.

It will be appreciated that there is no one level of sanctions for either a natural or legal person which is 'right'. Rather, each State Party to the OECD Convention has to strike a balance between meeting international expectations and requirements on the one hand, and reflecting domestic law and practice on the other. **10.94**

H. Jurisdiction (Article 4)

Given the nature of international business transactions, there is a powerful argument that State Parties to the Convention should seek to take a nationality jurisdiction in relation to their nationals, whether they be natural persons or corporations. Although a nationality jurisdiction has found favour amongst the State Parties, there are notable exceptions.[92] It should be stressed that the OECD Convention does not require that nationality jurisdiction be taken. Rather it requires that a State Party shall take 'such measures as may be necessary to establish its jurisdiction over the bribery of a foreign public official when an offence is committed in whole or in part in its territory'.[93] It does, however, go on to encourage a broad interpretation of the territorial requirement, by stating, at Commentary 25, that 'the territorial basis for jurisdiction shall be interpreted broadly so that an extensive physical connection to the bribery act is not required'. **10.95**

Where a State Party has nationality jurisdiction and is therefore able to prosecute its nationals for offences committed abroad, Article 4, paragraph 2 provides that such a Party 'shall take such measures as may be necessary to establish its jurisdiction to do so in respect of the bribery of a foreign public official, according to the same principles'. Once again, the OECD Convention is striving at functional equivalence. Thus, if, on general principles, nationality jurisdiction is taken for only certain categories of offences and one of those categories includes domestic bribery, then the effect of Article 4 and of the related Commentaries will be that nationality jurisdiction must be taken for the foreign bribery offence as well. Similarly, insofar as general principles and conditions in a Party's legal system require consideration of 'dual criminality', the requirement of dual criminality must be given a broad interpretation.[94] **10.96**

It may well be, in the case of a prosecution for foreign bribery, that more than one Party to the OECD Convention has jurisdiction over the offence. In such **10.97**

92 eg Canada has territorial, not nationality, jurisdiction.

93 See Art 4, para 1.

94 See Commentary 26.

circumstances Article 4, paragraph 3 provides that 'the Parties involved shall, at the request of one of them, consult with a view to determining the most appropriate jurisdiction for prosecution'. Practitioners may well feel that the particular topic of competing jurisdictions is one which the WGB might choose to look at in the future, particularly if prosecutions for foreign bribery become more frequent than hitherto.[95]

10.98 Traditionally, international lawyers have been adept at describing jurisdiction and its underlying principles (for example 'protective', 'passive personality', etc), but less certain at determining how the best jurisdiction for the criminal process should be arrived at. Perhaps the WGB might take it upon itself to address when and how the issue of jurisdiction should be considered (ie at the start of investigation or enquiry? Before assessing aspects of conviction? After the nature of the case has been shaped and possible admissibility issues have been dealt with?) and also whether there can be a practical set of criteria developed to resolve jurisdictional issues. For instance, should one ask: Where are most of the witnesses located? Which of the countries involved has the most effective laws? Which has the most effective confiscation laws in the event of conviction? Where would there be less chance of delay?

10.99 At present, no satisfactory model exists to assist practitioners in such decision-making, even though cases where there is parallel jurisdiction are becoming increasingly commonplace. In transnational corruption, especially, a real potential exists for no one initiating a prosecution (because each believes the other is considering the issue), the 'wrong' country prosecuting, or for two or more countries to each initiate a prosecution with inadvertent obstruction of one by the other.

I. Enforcement and Prosecutorial Discretion (Article 5)

10.100 Article 5 addresses enforcement and recognizes that a legal system may involve either mandatory prosecution or prosecutorial discretion. Either approach is capable of being Convention compliant.[96] However, although investigation and prosecution of the foreign bribery offence 'shall be subject to the applicable rules and principles of each Party',[97] the exercise of prosecutorial discretion where provided for by domestic law must not be subject to improper influence by concerns of a political nature.[98] Thus, Article 5 states that investigation and prosecution 'shall not be influenced by considerations of national economic

[95] At the time of writing, apart from prosecutions in the US under FCPA 1977, only Korea and Sweden have secured convictions for the foreign bribery offence.
[96] See Commentary 27. [97] Art 5. [98] Commentary 27.

interest, the potential effect upon relations with another state, or the identity of the national or legal person involved'.

Article 5 is complemented by paragraph 6 of the Annex to the 1997 Revised Recommendation, which stresses that 'public prosecutors should exercise their discretion independently, based on professional motives'. The decision of whether or not to prosecute should not be based on, *inter alia*, fostering good political relations. In addition, and fundamentally, paragraph 6 of the Annex states that 'national governments should provide adequate resources to prosecuting authorities so as to permit effective prosecution of bribery of foreign public officials'. **10.101**

Prosecutorial discretion may include the application of a public interest test by the prosecutor. The taking into account of public interest criteria will not offend against the OECD Convention, so long as the discretion is exercised in a way which is Article 5 compliant (taking into account Commentary 27 and paragraph 6 of the Annex to the 1997 Revised Recommendation); one way of helping to ensure compliance might be by means of a published code for prosecutors as, for example, the 'Code for Crown Prosecutors' in the United Kingdom. **10.102**

Care must be exercised by a State Party, however, if domestic law provides for different approaches depending on whether the defendant is a natural or legal person, or whether the offence is committed within the jurisdiction or outside it. Thus, the lead examiners drew the attention of the WGB to the position in Germany,[99] where the principle of mandatory prosecution applies to natural persons, but discretionary prosecution applies to legal persons. In their Commentary,[100] the lead examiners recommended that 'Germany take measures to ensure the effectiveness of the liability of legal persons, which could include providing guidelines on the use of prosecutorial discretion for legal persons'. **10.103**

Similarly, in circumstances where either prosecutorial discretion is to be exercised or a prosecutor has the sole authority to allow a prosecution to proceed, the WGB will have firmly in mind the underlying notion of functional equivalence. Thus, in the case of France, the lead examiners stated in one of their Commentaries that: **10.104**

> . . . the lead examiners noted the assurances given by the Ministry of Justice that, in accordance with the law, no instruction not to prosecute is given in specific cases. However, given the current exceptional regime assigning to the public prosecutor sole authority for offences of bribery involving public officials of states that are not members of the European Union, and given the hierarchical structure of the public prosecutor's office which is by law subject to the executive, they recommend that the French authorities facilitate prosecutions based on complaints lodged by victims in cases involving bribery of public officials of any

[99] See Phase 2 Review of Germany, p 31.

[100] ibid pp 36–37.

foreign state, on the same basis as that provided for in cases of bribery of French public officials.[101]

J. Statute of Limitations (Article 6)

10.105 Some countries impose a limitation on the time that an investigation may take and/or on the time during which a case may be brought to court. A State Party to the OECD Convention may have in place a statute of limitations in relation to either investigation or prosecution, but any such limitation 'shall allow an adequate period of time for the investigation and prosecution of this [ie the foreign bribery] offence'.[102] A Party must bear in mind that, by their very nature, investigations into and prosecutions of transnational corruption may take a protracted time, particularly if requests for mutual legal assistance have to be made and executed. In any evaluation, the lead examiners and the WGB will ask themselves whether, as a matter of fact, a particular jurisdiction allows sufficient time for what are, inevitably, complicated cases. However, a statute of limitations which seems to impose very tight limits, may nonetheless be Convention compliant if there is scope for the time running to be suspended in circumstances where, for instance, letters of request have been issued.

K. Money Laundering (Article 7)

10.106 The OECD Convention does not make it a mandatory requirement that a State Party shall make foreign bribery a predicate offence for the purposes of anti-money laundering legislation, unless such a Party has made bribery of its own public officials a predicate offence for the same purpose. Where the domestic offence is a predicate, then a Party must do likewise for the foreign bribery offence on identical terms. In this context, a State Party shall not have regard to 'the place where the bribery occurred'.[103]

10.107 In relation to money laundering, the notion of functional equivalence is to be construed widely. Thus, Commentary 28 provides that the foreign bribery offence is to be made a predicate offence where a Party has made *either* active or passive bribery of its own public officials predicate. Moreover, the effect of Article 7, as outlined by Commentary 28, is that where a State Party has made only passive bribery of its domestic public officials a predicate offence, then any laundering of the foreign bribe payment must similarly be subject to money laundering legislation. In short, Article 7 'is intended broadly'.[104]

10.108 It should be noted that the issue of the foreign bribery offence being a predicate offence for the purposes of anti-money laundering legislation is one of those

[101] See Phase 2 Report of France, p 31. [102] Art 6. [103] Art 7.
[104] See Commentary 28.

issues which has been earmarked for future work by the OECD Council.[105] Such future issues are discussed more fully below.

L. Accounting (Article 8)

Each WGB evaluation has paid full and particular attention to accounting and auditing practices in the examined country. Article 8 recognizes that, to combat foreign bribery effectively, a number of accounting books and records measures need to be in place. Thus, it is a mandatory requirement that such measures as may be necessary, within the framework of domestic law and regulations, must be taken in relation to the maintenance of books and records, financial statement disclosures, and accounting and auditing standards, in order to prohibit: the establishment of off-the-books accounts; the making of off-the-books transactions; the recording of non-existent expenditures; the entry of liabilities with incorrect identification of their object; and the use of false documents. That prohibition is aimed, of course, at attempts by companies to facilitate or to hide the carrying out of corrupt activities in transnational commerce. The provisions of Article 8 are complemented by further detailed provisions on accounting and auditing requirements, which are contained in section IV of the 1997 Revised Recommendation. **10.109**

The accounting provisions seek to add to the overall effectiveness of prevention, enforcement, and detection. However, as Commentary 29 makes clear, there are certain immediate consequences which implementation of this aspect of the OECD Convention brings about: in particular, 'companies which are required to issue financial statements disclosing their material contingent liabilities will need to take into account the full potential liabilities under this Convention, in particular its Articles 3 and 8, as well as other losses which might flow from conviction of the company or its agents for bribery'. Further, each State Party will need to consider the implications under its own laws and regulations for auditors who come across indications of foreign bribery taking place/having taken place. **10.110**

Article 8 goes on to impose a mandatory requirement as to sanctioning those who falsify books and records, etc: Parties to the OECD Convention shall provide 'effective, proportionate, and dissuasive civil, administrative or criminal penalties for such omissions and falsifications in respect of the books, records, accounts and financial statements of such companies'.[106] **10.111**

[105] See 'Battling International Bribery 2004', published by the US Department of State (Bureau of Economic and Business Affairs) 33.

[106] Art 8, para 2. Mention of 'such omissions', etc refers back to those matters set out in Art 8, para 1.

M. Mutual Legal Assistance (Article 9)

10.112 Annex A to the 1997 Revised Recommendation[107] states that 'effective mutual legal assistance is critical to be able to investigate and obtain evidence in order to prosecute cases of bribery of foreign public officials'. Moreover, pointing the way to possible future work by the WGB, it states that 'means should be explored and undertaken to improve the efficiency of mutual legal assistance'.

10.113 By virtue of Article 9, it is a mandatory requirement of the OECD Convention that each State Party shall provide prompt and effective legal assistance to another State Party for the purpose of any criminal investigation and proceedings concerning a Convention offence and, indeed, for any non-criminal proceedings within the scope of the OECD Convention which has been brought by a Party against a legal person. The mandatory requirement is, however, qualified to the extent that the requested Party needs to comply 'to the fullest extent possible under its laws and relevant treaties and arrangements'.[108]

10.114 For those State Parties who make mutual legal assistance conditional upon the existence of dual criminality, dual criminality shall be deemed to exist if the offence for which the assistance is sought is 'within the scope of this Convention'.[109] Further assistance in relation to dual criminality is provided by Commentary 32, which provides that 'Parties with statutes as diverse as the statute prohibiting the bribery of agents generally and a statute directed specifically at bribery of foreign public officials should be able to cooperate fully regarding cases whose facts fall within the scope of the offences described in this Convention'. Thus, Parties are being urged by the Commentary to adopt a wide interpretation of dual criminality.

10.115 Inevitably many requests for mutual legal assistance issued pursuant to the OECD Convention will be requests for financial and banking details. In order that the effectiveness of the OECD Convention in that regard is not thwarted, Article 9, paragraph 3 provides that 'a Party shall not decline to render mutual legal assistance for criminal matters within the scope of this Convention on the ground of bank secrecy'.

10.116 On another practical enforcement note, Commentary 31 states that Parties should, on a request being made, 'facilitate or encourage the presence or availability of persons, including persons in custody, who consent to assist in investigations or participate in proceedings'. It goes on to provide that measures should be put in place to effect the temporary transfer of such a person to the requesting Party. In such circumstances, the time spent in custody in the

[107] At para 8. [108] Art 9, para 1. [109] Art 9, para 2.

requesting State Party should be credited to the transferred person's sentence and return to the requested State Party should be capable of taking place without the necessity of extradition proceedings.

N. Extradition (Article 10)

Article 10 provides that foreign bribery 'shall be deemed to be included as an extraditable offence under the laws of the Parties and the extradition treaties between them'.[110] Further, as a result of Article 10, paragraph 2, a State Party may consider the OECD Convention to be a legal basis for extradition, if such a Party requires an extradition treaty. **10.117**

There is an element of overlap between the jurisdiction provisions in Article 4 and those relating to extradition in Article 10. Thus, by virtue of Article 10, paragraph 3, a State Party which is not able to extradite its nationals, must take any measures necessary to ensure that it can prosecute its nationals for the foreign bribery offence. Further, a Party which declines an extradition request solely on the ground that the request relates to one of its nationals, must submit the case to its competent authorities for the purpose of prosecution within its own territory. **10.118**

Continuing its demand for a broad interpretation of dual criminality requirements, Article 10, paragraph 4 provides that where extradition is made conditional upon the existence of dual criminality, that condition 'shall be deemed to be fulfilled if the offence for which extradition is sought is within the scope of Article 1 of this Convention'. **10.119**

O. Tax Deductibility

Although not specifically provided for by any Article within the OECD Convention, the issue of the prohibition of tax deductibility for bribes is addressed in the 1997 Revised Recommendation. Indeed, in advance of the OECD Convention itself, the OECD Council recommended in 1996 that OECD member states which had not yet disallowed the tax deductibility of bribes to foreign public officials should re-examine such treatment with the intention of denying deductibility.[111] That recommendation was given added weight by its inclusion within section IV of the 1997 Revised Recommendations. Although by signing and ratifying the OECD Convention **10.120**

[110] Art 10, para 1.

[111] Taken from 'Battling International Bribery 2004' published by US Department of State (Bureau of Economic and Business Affairs) 31.

the Parties have confirmed that bribes of foreign public officials are not tax deductible, only some have specifically and explicitly denied the tax deductibility of bribes in their domestic laws.

10.121 During WGB evaluations, the implementation of the Revised Recommendation and its requirements on the prohibition of tax deductibility, in particular, are examined. Indeed, the Phase 2 reviews have identified certain recurring weaknesses in the denial of tax liability by State Parties. There have, for instance, been numerous examples of tax inspectors not being fully conversant with the law or tax policy, as the case may be, which requires them to deny tax deductibility for foreign bribes, particularly in circumstances where there is no specific prohibition in domestic law for a foreign bribery payment. Similarly, a lack of training in detecting deductions relating to the payment of foreign bribes has been highlighted, as have the detection problems which arise when domestic law protects the confidentiality of taxpayer information and/or allows the taxpayer to exercise the privilege against self-incrimination.[112]

10.122 In answer to such difficulties, the WGB has proposed that State Parties work to introduce an explicit denial of deductibility of foreign bribes, a programme aimed at increasing the awareness of tax authorities and officials on the point, and provisions requiring tax officials to report suspected bribery of a foreign public official to investigative/prosecuting authorities. In addition, the WGB has recommended that auditors and/or accountants who are responsible for a corporation's books should be required to report suspicious transactions—which point to foreign bribery taking, or having taken, place—to the corporation's management or to the investigative/prosecuting authorities as may be appropriate.[113]

P. Future Work and Convention Amendment (Article 16)

10.123 Looking ahead, it may be that the scope of the OECD Convention is revisited. In particular, there remain the so-called five 'unresolved issues'.[114] These were identified in 1997 by the OECD Council and were thought worthy of further examination and consideration in the future. The five are:

(1) bribes in relation to the funding, etc of foreign political parties;
(2) bribes or advantages offered, etc to a person in anticipation of him/her becoming a foreign public official;

[112] As set out and referred to in 'Battling International Bribery 2004' (n 111 above) ch 4.
[113] ibid 32.
[114] See, for instance, the discussion in F. Heimann, 'Defining bribery and four critical issues' in Vincke, François, Heimann, Fritz (eds) *Fighting Corruption: A Corporate Practices Manual* (Paris: ICC, 1999).

(3) the foreign bribery offence as a predicate for anti-money laundering legislation;
(4) the role of foreign subsidiaries in transnational bribery; and
(5) the part played by offshore centres/tax havens in foreign bribery.

There has been discussion of the five issues within the WGB at various times since 1997. However, little seems to have emerged. The most recent work of substance was the calling together of a group of WGB experts in October 2003, at the suggestion of the United States, to discuss the issue of foreign subsidiaries. To assist those discussions, State Parties were asked to provide up-to-date information on their capacity to respond to bribery involving a foreign subsidiary. The answers provided suggested that Parties would have no difficulty (on general principles) when an act took place within their territories. However, no Party to the OECD Convention imposes a strict liability on a parent company for criminality by its subsidiaries. Nonetheless, taking into account differences in domestic law and legal principle, Parties were able to confirm that a parent company would be capable of being held liable for the acts of a subsidiary where it could be proved that there was authorization, direction, or active conniving by the parent company. The conclusion of the WGB was that the OECD Convention, in its present form, adequately addresses the issue. In reality, one suspects that many practitioners will probably disagree. In any event, it remains to be seen whether the topic will be revisited. **10.124**

As to other likely future developments, one issue that may achieve greater prominence is that of the role and functions for diplomatic posts and missions. At various times, the EWG has had consultations with business, trade union, and civil society representatives in this regard. In addition, the Business Industry Advisory Council (BIAC) has requested that State Parties to the Convention help companies doing business in other states in confronting the solicitation of bribes by public officials. In that regard, there is the potential for an enhanced role for, for instance, commercial attachés. Any reader of the WGB's Phase 2 reports will see that there is an increasing emphasis on the part that embassies and High Commissions might play. Those in diplomatic posts will, of course, receive information concerning tenders and contracts, the activities of particular companies, and the approach taken by contract officials. In addition, however, such post holders should be able to play an even greater role than at present in raising awareness; reporting back any suspicions they may have of bribery; and, perhaps, even a more formalized role in monitoring the commercial practice and behaviour of their own countries, and even of neighbouring countries. **10.125**

In addition to the many activities undertaken by the WGB in relation to State Parties to the Convention, one awaits to see whether its outreach strategy in relation to other states achieves an even greater prominence than hitherto. **10.126**

Certainly, the WGB faces challenges: should outreach target those states seen as future members of the WGB in the short term, or should there be a more long-term view taken of the need to enhance capacity building in the developing world? Perhaps even more fundamentally, should outreach focus on particular, selected states, or should the WGB's work consist of more regional initiatives, given the success and high profile of the Asia-Pacific Initiative?[115]

1. Accession (Article 13): Looking Ahead

10.127 The OECD Convention is open to non-OECD member countries on the basis that expansion of membership, albeit in a gradual and conservative manner, will assist in the fight against transnational bribery. Since the coming into force of the OECD Convention, two countries, Slovenia and Estonia, have joined. Of the two, only Estonia joined on the basis of fulfilling the new criteria and procedures for accession, which were agreed on by the WGB in December 2003 (those changes having been agreed by the OECD Council in February 2004).

10.128 Given the nature and extent of the WGB's outreach work, it may well be that major exporters and regional forces such as China, Russia and, on the Pacific Rim, Malaysia and Singapore, will in due course seek and obtain membership. It is clear, though, from the new criteria, that the WGB will be focusing its efforts on attracting states whose membership of the WGB will bring mutual benefit and whose corporations have a substantial and meaningful presence either regionally or globally. Given the cost of the peer review programme and the views of key WGB members such as the United States,[116] a rapid enlargement of membership is, at present, unlikely. The revised enlargement considerations[117] require that requests for accession be measured and thoroughly examined against two criteria: 'willing and able' and 'mutual benefit'.

10.129 Those two criteria may be broken down into the following key factors which will fall to be considered in respect of each application:

> A country applying for accession to the Convention and participation in the WGB must show:

- that its existing legal framework for combating bribery on a domestic level, including legislation relating to the criminalisation of passive bribery, is satisfactory,
- that it can meet the standards laid down in the 1997 Revised Recommendation, including criminalisation of bribery of foreign public officials (Article III),

[115] See 9.159 above.

[116] As set out and referred to in 'Battling International Bribery 2004' (n 111 above) ch 6.

[117] See the criteria for accession set out in document c (2004) 1 at http://www.oils.oecd.org.

- that it already disallows the tax deductibility of bribes (Article IV),
- that it has accounting requirements, external audit and internal company controls compatible with the Revised Recommendation (Article V), and
- that it is able to cooperate with other Parties to the Convention as concerns mutual legal assistance (Article VII),
- that it has a satisfactory enforcement capacity, particularly for investigation and prosecution of bribery cases,
- that it is ready and able to submit to the same vigorous monitoring mechanism as the other Parties in the Convention, and
- that it is prepared and able to participate as a lead examiner in peer reviews of other parties to the Convention,
- whether its companies engaged in international business are involved in transactions where solicitations of bribes by/for foreign public officials could occur,
- that it is a significant economic factor in its geographical region or sub-region, or in particularly important or sensitive economic sectors,
- the extent of its GDP derived from international trade and investment activities.

2. Export Credits, Credit Guarantees, and Bribery

The OECD Trade Committee's Working Party on Export Credits and Credit Guarantees recognized that many of those international business transactions to which the Convention is addressed benefit from official export support credit. Thus, from January 1998 it began an ongoing process of information exchange, using a survey procedure to obtain details of the processes and practices employed in relation to deterring and combating bribery by the OECD member states within the context of export credits support. As a result of that work, the OECD issued an 'Action Statement on Bribery and Officially Supported Export Credits' on 17 November 2000. That document, essentially, called for OECD members to take appropriate measures and action to deter corruption before granting export credit in relation to overseas contracts. **10.130**

The activity of that Working Party has been ongoing and, in November 2001, the survey was reformulated and further responses collated. The initiative continued and on 20 February 2003 a new 'Action Statement on Bribery and Officially Supported Export' was issued. That document[118] provides, *inter alia*, **10.131**

[118] Available on the OECD website at www.olis.oecd.org, and also from the OECD as document TD/ECG(2000)15[unclassified].

that the members of the OECD Working Party on Export Credits and Credit Guarantees (ECG) agree:

- Combating bribery in international business transactions is a priority issue and the ECG is the appropriate forum to ensure the implementation of the Convention and the 1997 Revised Recommendation in respect of international business transactions benefiting from official export credit support.
- To take appropriate measures to deter bribery in officially supported export credits and, in the case that bribery, as defined by the Convention, was involved with the award of the export contract, to take appropriate action including:
  (i) All official export credit and export credit insurance providers shall inform applicants requesting support about the legal consequences of bribery in international business transactions under its national legal system, including its national laws prohibiting such bribery.
  (ii) The applicant and/or the exporter, in accordance with the practices followed in each ECG member's export credit system, shall be invited to provide an undertaking/declaration that neither they, nor anyone acting on their behalf, have been engaged or will engage in bribery in the transaction.
- The applicant and other parties receiving or benefiting from support remain fully responsible for the proper description of international business transactions and the transparency of relevant payments.
- The applicant and other parties involved in the transaction remain fully responsible for compliance with all applicable laws and regulations, including national provisions for combating bribery of foreign public officials in international business transactions.
- If there is sufficient evidence that such bribery was involved in the award of the export contract, the official export credit or export credit insurance provider shall refuse to approve credit, cover or other support.
- If, after credit, cover or other support has been approved, an involvement of a beneficiary in such bribery is proved, the official export credit or export credit insurance provider shall take appropriate action, such as denial of payment or indemnification, refund of sums provided and/or referral of evidence of such bribery to the appropriate national authorities.
- These actions are not prejudicial to the rights of other parties not responsible for the legal payments.
- To continue to exchange views with appropriate stakeholders.
- To review periodically actions taken pursuant to this Action Statement . . .

10.132 There is little doubt that export credits and surrounding issues will become increasingly high profile. NGOs will be paying particular attention to the response of governments and export credit agencies. Those on all sides in the debate will, more and more, have to undertake the difficult balancing exercise between ensuring that effective anti-bribery measures are in place and yet legitimate commercial concerns and sensitivities are not overlooked.[119]

Q. Some Lessons from the Lesotho Highlands Water Project

Whilst the OECD Convention is a landmark achievement, the fact remains that there have been few prosecutions in member states. For those developing countries that are the 'victims' of the bribery of their public officials by foreign corporations, the decision of Lesotho to prosecute those corporations and their agents who were allegedly involved in the Lesotho Highlands Water Project (LHWP) corruption scandal raises interesting possibilities. **10.133**

The Lesotho Highlands Water Project is one of the world's largest dam projects. It was set up under a 1986 Treaty between Lesotho and South Africa with the twin aims of providing hydro-electric power for Lesotho and delivering water to South Africa. A statutory body, the Lesotho Highlands Development Authority (LHDA), was established in 1986 to oversee the project and its first chief executive was a local engineer, Masupha Sole. Part funded by the World Bank, the project attracted many major Western construction companies, all from countries that are parties to the OECD Convention. These included Acres International, a Canadian construction firm that was to be the first to be tried and convicted on bribery charges.[120] **10.134**

Concern over the running of the LHDA led to an audit in 1994 which uncovered serious financial irregularities on the part of Sole. This led to his dismissal in 1995 and the LHDA then began a civil action against him to recover the misappropriated funds. Despite his claims to the contrary, the case eventually revealed that Sole had bank accounts in South Africa and Switzerland. A Swiss investigation undertaken at the request of the Lesotho authorities revealed that Sole had several accounts in Switzerland totalling well **10.135**

---

[119] See the discussion as to recent developments in the UK at para 12.19.

[120] The Crown's summary of substantial facts to the charges stated that the contractors and/or consultants who were awarded contracts by the LHDA in the building of the LHWP in respect of the project were as follows: 'The consortium/partnership Highlands Water Venture (HWV), Sogreah, Spie Batignolles, the Lesotho Highlands Project Contractors (LHPC), Asea Brown Boveri Schaltanglagen GmbH, Germany (ABB, Germany), Asea Brown Boveri Generation AG, Sweden (ABB, Sweden), Lahmeyer International GmbH (Lahmeyer), Acres International Limited (Acres), Dumez International (Dumez), Sir Alexander Gibb & Partners Ltd (Gibb), Cegelec and Coyne et Bellier (Coyne)'. See *R v Sole* (High Court of Lesotho, unreported, 18 May 2001) 7 and 8.

over US$1 million. Further, whilst the payments had been received via so-called intermediaries, the origin of these payments was the contractors and consultants on the LHWP.

10.136 Sole himself was later charged and convicted of bribery and fraud. However, for present purposes, the most significant aspect of the affair was the decision of the Lesotho authorities to prosecute the alleged bribers as well.[121] This led to a plethora of preliminary issues being raised by the various contractors/ consultants and, in the event, a total of over one hundred such applications were made before the first trial even began. These applications fell for decision in the High Court of Lesotho by an experienced expatriate judge, Cullinan AJ.[122] Several applications are of particular interest.

1. Joinder

10.137 In view of the cost and time implications, the prosecution intended to proceed with the matter in one big trial. However, an application was made for a separation of trials and, given the number of potential defendants each with their own different interests, this was eventually granted. On the issue of whether the charges related to the 'same offence', Cullinan AJ rejected the argument that this should be construed as meaning the 'same species of offence', as this would open the door to the possibility of an unlimited joinder of unconnected offences.[123] Further, whilst the Crown argued that the joinder before the court was in the interests of justice, Cullinan AJ held that this would not be favourable to, or in the interests of, the accused.[124] The effect of the ruling was to require the holding of a series of long and costly trials,[125] which imposed a considerable financial burden upon Lesotho. As noted below, this has been exacerbated by the fact that the promised financial assistance towards the prosecution costs from the international community has not materialized.

2. Whose Name Should Appear on the Indictment?

10.138 An application by Acres International and Lahmeyer International was concerned with whether it was appropriate to cite them as the accused rather than their representatives. In his ruling[126] Cullinan AJ, after undertaking a detailed

[121] A helpful analysis of the affair is provided by F Darroch, 'The Lesotho Corruption Trials—A Case Study' (2003) 29 *Commonwealth Law Bulletin* 901.

[122] In addition to the numerous preliminary applications, a constitutional challenge was made to the appointment of Cullinan AJ, who was a former appeal court judge in Zambia and Chief Justice of Lesotho. This was swiftly was rejected by the Court of Appeal in *Sole v Cullinan and ors* [2004] LRC 550.

[123] *R v Sole and ors* (High Court of Lesotho, unreported, 26 February 2001) 63.

[124] ibid 66.

[125] These were still in progress as at September 2005.

[126] *R v Sole, Du Plooy, Bam, Lahmeyer International GmbH and Acres International* (High Court of Lesotho, unreported, 6 March 2001).

review of the relevant legislation and case law, rejected the application and concluded that the practice of citing the company has 'the advantages (a) that the name of the case remains constant irrespective of the identity of the representative; and (b) what is even more important, that a clear distinction is drawn between the citation of the natural person . . . *qua* representative, and his personal citation . . . The risk of imperfect citations, as in *S v Freeman*[127] or irregular substitutions, as in *R v Erasmus*[128] is thereby diminished'.[129]

3. Proving the Fact of Bribery

It was argued in *R v Sole*[130] that in order to prove bribery the Crown had to prove 'action or inaction' by the alleged bribee. However, Cullinan AJ, held that the common law crime of bribery is complete, by the briber, when the corrupt offer is made to (or consideration is agreed with) the bribee, and the offence by the bribee is complete when the latter agrees to take the consideration. The action or inaction sought may actually be in accordance with the bribee's duty. It may even be in the public interest. In fact, it is immaterial whether or not the briber's goal is achieved. Where the Crown does know of the proposed action or inaction, or whether or not the bribee did what he or she was supposed to do, it should detail this. However, this is not essential. **10.139**

4. Jurisdiction

The Crown only had evidence that the moneys were paid secretly into Swiss accounts belonging to Sole. The inability of the Crown to prove where the alleged corrupt agreement(s) was made then led to a particularly important ruling on jurisdiction.[131] It was argued on behalf of Sole that a court in Lesotho did not have jurisdiction in a case in which the alleged bribes were paid in another country and no money changed hands in Lesotho. In a ruling delivered on 18 May 2001, Cullinan AJ, after undertaking a wide-ranging review of the authorities,[132] adopted the 'harmful effects' test as propounded by Gubbay JA (as he then was) in the Zimbabwean case of *S v Mharapara*.[133] Here a Zimbabwean citizen was charged with theft, it being alleged that in the course of his employment as a diplomat at the Embassy of Zimbabwe in Brussels, he had **10.140**

[127] 1970 (3) SA 700 (N). [128] 1970 (4) SA 378 (R). [129] ibid 60.

[130] *R v Sole* (High Court of Lesotho, unreported, 20 May 2002).

[131] *R v Sole* (High Court of Lesotho, unreported, 18 May 2001).

[132] This judgment is a veritable *tour de force* on the development of the rules relating to jurisdiction. As the Court of Appeal in *R v Sole* noted: 'The separate judgment of the court in relation to this issue ranged far and wide: as regards different legal systems, different periods of legal history, and disparate offences. These extend from actions of debt for penalties under old English statutes against usury, to deaths at sea from blows struck on shore, to cheques forged in one country and uttered in another, to bigamy.'

[133] 1985 (4) SA 42 (HC); 1986 (1) SA 556 (ZSC); [1986] LRC (Const) 235.

stolen a sum of money. At his trial in Zimbabwe, the issue of jurisdiction was raised. The trial judge ruled the court had jurisdiction on the basis of the nationality or active personality principle. Gubbay JA, giving the judgment of the Supreme Court of Zimbabwe, held:

> . . . I can see no justification for a rigid adherence to the principle that, with the exception of treason, only those common law crimes perpetrated within our borders are punishable. That principle is becoming decreasingly appropriate to the facts of international life. The facility of communication and of movement from country to country is no longer restricted or difficult. Both may be taken expeditiously and at short notice. Past is the era when almost invariably the preparation and completion of a crime and the presence of the criminal would coincide in one place, with that place being the one most harmed by its commission. The inevitable consequence of the development of society along sophisticated lines and the growth of technology have led crimes to become more and more complex and their capacity for harming victims even greater. They are no longer as simple in nature or as limited in their effect as they used to be. Thus a strict interpretation of the principle of territoriality could create injustice where the constituent elements of the crime occur in more than one State or where the *locus commissi* is fortuitous so far as the harm flowing from the crime is concerned. Any reluctance to liberalise the principle and adopt Anglo-American thinking could well result in the negation of the object of criminal law in protecting the public and punishing the wrongdoer. A more flexible and realistic approach based on the place of impact, or of intended impact, of the crime must be favoured. Accordingly, I am satisfied that although all the constituent elements of the theft occurred in Belgium, in particular the obtaining of the money there, the State is nonetheless entitled to proceed upon the present indictment and adduce evidence at the trial, if such is available, to establish that the harmful effect of the appellant's crime was felt by the Zimbabwean Government within this country.

10.141 A similar approach has also been taken by the Supreme Court of Canada in the *Libman* case[134] where La Forest J observed that while it may remain true that the 'primary basis of criminal jurisdiction is territorial . . . as well, along with other types of protective measures, States increasingly exercise jurisdiction over criminal behaviour in other States that has harmful consequences within their own territory or jurisdiction . . .'.[135]

10.142 Based on these authorities, Cullinan AJ concluded that in the instant case, the only country affected by the bribes was Lesotho. It was a state official from Lesotho who was involved in the bribes and the harm that resulted from them related to Lesotho, and this gave Lesotho jurisdiction. The decision was upheld on appeal, the Court of Appeal noting that:

> The Crown argued that [jurisdiction] was sufficiently established by the harmful consequence immediately inflicted upon the integrity of public administration in

[134] (1985) 21 DLR (4th) 174; (1986) LRC (Crim) 86.

[135] At 90. See also the Court of Appeal of Hong Kong in *Yeung Sun-shun* [1987] LRC (Crim) 94; [1989] LRC (Crim) 1 and in the *Liangsiriprasert v Government of the United States* [1991] Ac 225.

> Lesotho by the conclusion of the corrupt agreements. We agree. The development scheme administered by the LHDA is . . . of great importance to Lesotho, and indeed, to the Southern African Development Community. It involves Lesotho's international relations and is central to its economic future. Its success and integrity matter vitally to this country. Corrupt agreements by its chief executive with its international contractors, if established, would be a cancer at its heart. Since it is not a requirement for the *actus reus* of bribery that loss be suffered, it is not in our view necessary to consider whether, in addition to harm of this kind, specific harmful effects arose in relation to each count for the State of Lesotho.[136]

5. The Use of Agents, Representatives, and Intermediaries

A key issue in the whole affair concerned the role of 'agents', 'representatives', and 'intermediaries'. In practice, an agency agreement or representation agreement in which a local person agrees to act as the agent of a corporation is not unusual and may well be essential to assist a corporation where, for example, it is entering a new field/country and is reliant on local advice and influence. As Scherer puts it: 'Only a foolish principal would retain an agent *without* influence. Agents may have acquired influence as a result of longstanding professional experience, through the force of their personality, by their standing in society or through their respected expertise.'[137] **10.143**

However, the LHWP case illustrates that such agreements are potentially already a mechanism for bribes. In 2002, the first of the international contractors, Acres International, was charged with two counts of bribery in relation to the obtaining of a major construction contract on the LHWP (Contract 65). Count 1 alleged that the company had paid into the Swiss bank account of Zalisiwonga Bam (Bam), the company's representative in Lesotho,[138] almost C$500, 000 and that part of this sum was then transferred to Sole. Count 2 alleged that the company had paid almost C$200, 000 into a Swiss bank account held by Bam's wife and that part of this money was transferred, or supposedly transferred, to Sole. It was the Crown case that the only reasonable inference to be drawn from the facts was that Acres International knew it was paying Bam to use its money to bribe Sole and that it used Bam as a conduit to camouflage the fact. The Crown argued that this was evidenced (a) by the use of the intermediaries through whose offices payments were made by the contractors/consultants; and (b) by the use of representation agreements, which reflected the contractual or allegedly corrupt nature of the relationships between the intermediaries, Sole, and the contractors/consultants. Bam had died in 1999 and Sole had remained silent throughout the entire criminal and related proceedings and thus conviction **10.144**

136 *Sole v R* (unreported, 14 April 2003). Para 21.

137 M Scherer, 'Circumstantial Evidence in Corruption Cases before International Arbitral Tribunals' [2002] Int ALR 29, 30 (emphasis in original).

138 In fact for much of the time, Bam was working in Botswana.

hinged on the weight of the accumulated circumstantial evidence. Consequently, the argument in *R v Acres*[139] revolved around whether Bam and his wife had been used as a conduit to pay bribes to Sole.

10.145 Many of the main facts were uncontested. Acres had made a series of secret payments to Bam and his wife through numbered Swiss bank accounts, amounting to the equivalent of 25 per cent of Acres' profit. Bam had then passed on some 60 per cent of the money received to Sole, the person who was in a *position* to secure the construction contracts for Acres. The key question was whether the company was buying 'political intelligence' from Bam (as it asserted) or whether it had known that Bam was passing the money on to Sole. The case emphasizes that the terms of a contract are not necessarily a trustworthy guide to the real intent of the parties. In a detailed 250-page judgment, Lehohla CJ examined the evidence and concluded that Acres International was guilty on both counts. The court's findings were as follows and provide a fascinating insight into the abuse of representative arrangements:

1. The court's findings are that the representative agreement is not what it purports to be but a mere sham.
2. The court rejects the theory that Acres did not know that Bam was paying Sole with the money obtained from Acres.
3. Acres had an interest in ensuring that Sole was kept happy in order for Acres to derive the benefit of a favourable disposition by the LHDA towards it. For this it was prepared to pay Sole.
4. In order to pay Sole, Bam's accounts were used as a conduit. Again this was done with Acres' full knowledge.
5. All the monies that Bam paid in the ratio of 60% to Sole while Bam retained 40% or thereabouts were bribe monies paid to ensure that Acres' interests in the LHDA were secured to the detriment of other competitors who were under the false belief that Acres had won [Contract 65] by fair means over them:–
   (1) Bam could hardly have squeezed so much money out of Acres without persuading Acres that it was worth its while. That he was paid 25% of Acres' mark-up is a clear indication that he achieved this by letting Acres know that Sole was in on the deal.
   (2) Because of my acceptance of this on reasonable grounds, now everything falls into place. *Anomalies in the Acres' version* like (i) wanting to use Bam as an agent even though he was in Botswana; (ii) paying so much money allegedly for political intelligence; (iii) why it is that most of the services in the representation agreement were not necessary; (iv) the fact that no one knew Bam was Acres' agent; (v) the fact he was paid in Switzerland *begin to make sense.*
   (3) Acres' reliance on the representative agreement pronounced a sham in (1) above establishes *mens rea* in the sense that by relying on this document Acres, as in the case of an alibi, put all its eggs in one basket. Thus because of the crack suffered by the defence in an instance where their denial of criminal liability was proved to be false the whole proverbial edifice was destined to come tumbling down.

[139] *R v Acres International Ltd* (High Court of Lesotho, unreported, 13 September 2002).

6. The court further finds that the reason why Acres would want to hide its true agreement or understanding with Bam is that it has guilty knowledge of what the real situation involved here is (much akin to a man intending to murder his wife carefully plans his alibi in advance so that it is in place if and when he becomes a suspect).
7. The court further relies in making the above findings on the concession by the defence that the representation agreement does not reflect the true agreement.
8. The incontrovertible facts before this court are a negation of the validity of the representative agreement, thus leaving the credibility of Acres in tatters in this case. (There is no reason for the court to believe Acres about the need to provide 'political intelligence' when, if this was true, Acres could and would easily have drawn the agreement in those terms).
9. . . . various amendments were made to the agreement for over one and a half years yet at no stage were the services provided for in Schedule 1 ever amended, thus showing they were not required. Thus the court makes a finding that they could only have been intended as 'window dressing' or just as an 'eye-wash'.
10. The 40/60% split of Acres money between Bam and Sole and the very amounts conceded to be 'huge' by the defence, connote the existence of a specific and compelling reason why Bam made these payments to Sole. The reason was the promotion of corruption. Payment of these monies into and out of Swiss bank accounts held by Bam and in turn to Sole betokens corrupt motives as these accounts were operated in breach of foreign exchange regulations and were secret.
11. The court finds that it makes no difference that Acres thought payments they made to Mrs Bam's and Bam's accounts were in the ACPM account[140] for as long as it established, as indeed has been the case, payments were made with the intention to bribe.
12. The court also finds that not all the monies can be traced through to Sole. However it does not change the fact that all monies involved were used in order to facilitate bribery. Thus the fact that a portion thereof remained with Bam for his part in the scheme does not affect the situation.
13. Because the Crown has discharged its onus in respect of both counts of which Acres stands charged, the court accordingly finds Acres guilty on both counts of bribery. My Assessors agree.

In August 2003, the Court of Appeal of Lesotho, comprising three senior South **10.146**
African judges, heard the appeal by Acres International against conviction and sentence. Here counsel for Acres made some crucial concessions, namely that:

(a) the payments made by Bam to Sole were funded by payments made by the appellants to Bam and were made unlawfully;
(b) the Crown evidence, particularly as to the flow of payments, placed an obligation on the appellants to explain the payments to Bam;
(c) there was an evidential burden on the appellants to explain such payments; and
(d) without an acceptable explanation, the inference could properly be drawn that the appellant was guilty of bribery.

[140] See 10.147 below as regards the background to ACPM.

10.147 The judgment of the Court of Appeal of Lesotho[141] sheds further light on the abuse of representation agreements:

> [22] We now come to deal with the circumstances in which the relevant representation agreement was concluded between the appellant and ACPM. We will examine this document with reference to the description of the agent; how the parties themselves evidenced the document; the nature of the obligations undertaken by the representative and to what extent Bam or ACPM discharged those obligations. We will also consider the arrangements concerning where and how the payments were made and what the relationship was between the amounts paid to Bam and the services he was to render as well as the changes that were made after Sole's term of office finally came to an end.
>
> [23] It is common cause that the fifth and final draft of the representation agreement was concluded on the 23rd November 1990. However negotiations in regard to its terms—particularly as to whom, how and where payments had to be made—were conducted over a period of some months. In so far as the identity of the payee under the representation agreement was concerned it is also an admitted fact that the first draft submitted by DW1—a Mr. Hare (appellant's principal witness)—to Bam, provided for the appointment of Lescon as the representative... However at Bam's request the identity of the representative was altered to ACPM—an entity that was never formally constituted and was unknown to anyone other than to Bam and the appellant. A further observation to be made is that during the negotiations changes were made only to the clauses relating to payments, the amounts thereof and their structure. This despite material developments in the relationship between appellant and LHDA in so far as the conclusion of Contract 65 was concerned.
>
> [24] The use of the name ACPM in the representation agreement did of course have the effect of disguising the true identity of the person the appellant wished to use as a representative and the fact that money was being paid to Bam. Indeed the appellant knew that it was paying Bam and not ACPM. The witness Hare said so and the documentation disclosed by the appellant demonstrates that the appellant knew the true identity of the payee when it made payments to Bam. Despite Hare's protestations to the contrary, it is certainly a reasonable inference to be drawn from these facts that the change from identifying Lescon—known to be Bam's firm—as the appellant's representative—to ACPM was deliberately designed to obscure the true identity of the person to whom the appellant was making payments. Indeed had it not been for the discovery of Sole's Swiss banking records, the link between the payments made by the appellant to Bam and thence to Sole would never have been discovered.
>
> [25] Counsel for the appellant contended that the Court should not draw the inference that this substitution was a deliberate effort at concealment on the part of the appellant and Bam. However, Hare's evidence that the fact of the concealment of Bam's identity did not arouse his suspicion was correctly in our view rejected by the trial court.

[141] *Acres International Ltd v The Crown* (unreported, 2003). Judgment available at www.odiousdebts.org.

> [26] This inference is buttressed by other facts. At the time this contract was negotiated it was a notorious fact that the records of Swiss banks were secret and were regarded as a safe haven for 'hot' money. Whilst reasons could be advanced why payment in a foreign currency, such as the then dominant currency—the US dollar—should be nominated as the monetary unit for payments under the contractual obligations, no acceptable reason was advanced why the payments should have been made to a non-existent agency called ACPM, in a nominated Swiss bank account number. The objective of this device could certainly sustain the inference that it was intended to hide the true identity of the recipient. It is therefore a reasonable inference to be drawn in the absence of an acceptable explanation that the underpinning of these payments was an illegal and not a regular or transparent transaction. Hare, who was involved in the structuring of the RA, must have been aware that Bam, who was insistent on the concealment of his identity and who required that he be paid into numbered accounts in Switzerland, was making the appellant a party to an unlawful transaction.
>
> [27] There is also evidence that the parties themselves viewed the transaction as one that had to be recorded in communications between them in obscure or opaque terminology.

In the event, the Court of Appeal dismissed the appeal on Count 1 holding that 'looking at the mosaic as a whole', Acres International had not provided a satisfactory explanation for the body of evidence pointing to the conclusion that it had bribed Sole. However, adopting a similar approach to the second count, they considered that there was a reasonable doubt that Acres intended to bribe Sole with this money, and accordingly upheld the appeal on this count. A fine of M15 million (US$1 million) was imposed. **10.148**

The *Acres* case and subsequent cases where other contractors/consultants were convicted on similar evidence,[142] highlights the obligation on corporations to refrain from (and to guard against) the abuse of agents/representatives agreements in international business contracts. Here so-called 'red flags' provide a useful mechanism for indicating situations where a high risk of bribery exists. These are situations where an intermediary: **10.149**

- requests payment in cash or to a numbered account or the account of a third party
- requests payment in a country other than the intermediary's country of residence or the territory of the sales activity, and especially if it is a country with little banking transparency
- requests payment in advance or partial-payment immediately prior to a procurement decision

[142] In June 2003, the Lesotho High Court convicted a German firm, Lahmeyer International, of paying bribes to Sole totalling some US$150,000 and fined it US$1.5m, whilst in February 2004, a French-based company, Schneider International, pleaded guilty on 16 counts of bribery relating to the LHWP. In September 2003, one Jacobus du Plooy pleaded guilty to acting as an intermediary in bribing Sole on behalf of an Italian company. He was given a suspended prison sentence of three years and fined 500,000 South African rand.

- requests reimbursement for extraordinary, ill-defined or last minute expenses
- has a family member in a government position, especially if the family member works in a procurement or decision-making position or is a high-ranking official in the department that is the target of the intermediary's efforts
- refuses to disclose owners, partners or principals
- uses shell or holding companies that obscure ownership without credible explanation
- is specifically requested by a customer
- is recommended by an employee with enthusiasm out of proportion to qualifications
- has a business that seems understaffed, ill-equipped or inconveniently located to support the proposed undertaking
- has little or no expertise in the industry in which she seeks to represent the company
- is insolvent or has significant financial difficulties
- is ignorant of or indifferent to the local laws and regulations governing the region in question and the intermediary's proposed activities in particular
- identifies a business reference who declines to respond to questions or who provides an evasive response
- is the subject of credible rumours or media reports of inappropriate payments.[143]

10.150 The Acres case also emphasizes the importance of the recent work on developing international best practice on the use of agents. The Business Principles for Countering Bribery, developed by Transparency International, and Social Accountability International in conjunction with several international corporations, provide as follows:

> 6.2.2.1 The enterprise should not channel improper payments through an agent
> 6.2.2.2 The enterprise should undertake due diligence before appointing an agent
> 6.2.2.3 Compensation paid to agents should be appropriate and justifiable remuneration for legitimate services rendered
> 6.2.2.4 The relationship should be documented
> 6.2.2.5 The agent should contractually agree to comply with the enterprise's anti-bribery Programme
> 6.2.2.6 The enterprise should monitor the conduct of its agents and should have a right of termination in the event that they pay bribes.

10.151 The above Business Principles are reinforced by the 'Partnering against Corruption Principles for Countering Bribery' that have been endorsed by more than sixty countries worldwide under the auspices of the Partnering against Corruption Initiative, led by the World Economic Forum in partnership with Transparency International and the Basle Institute of Governance. The Partnering

[143] This is a list developed by TRACE International, an NGO that specializes in working with companies and intermediaries to reduce the risks of corruption in international business transactions.

against Corruption Principles commit signatory companies to two basic actions: the adoption of a zero tolerance policy on bribery and the development of a practical and effective internal 'programme' for implementing that policy. In relation to agents, advisers and other intermediaries, the Principles state:

> 5.2.3.1 The enterprise should undertake due diligence before appointing an agent, advisor or other intermediary, and on an on-going basis as circumstances warrant.
>
> 5.2.3.2 The Programme should provide guidance for conducting due diligence, entering into contractual relationships, and supervising the conduct of an agent, advisor or other intermediary.
>
> 5.2.3.2.1 Due diligence review and other material aspects of the relationship with the agent, advisor or other intermediary should be documented
>
> 5.2.3.2.2 All agreements with agents, advisors and other intermediaries should require prior approval of senior management
>
> 5.2.3.2.3 The agent, advisor or other intermediary should contractually agree in writing to comply with the enterprise's Programme and should be provided with materials explaining this obligation
>
> 5.2.3.2.4 Provision should be included in all contracts with agents, advisors and other intermediaries relating to access to records, co-operation in investigations and similar matters pertaining to the contract
>
> 5.2.3.2.5 Compensation paid to agents, advisors and other intermediaries should be appropriate and justifiable remuneration for legitimate services rendered and should be paid through bona fide channels
>
> 5.2.3.2.6 The enterprise should monitor the conduct of its agents, advisors and other intermediaries and should have a contractual right of termination in case of conduct inconsistent with the Programme.

The OECD Guidelines for Multinational Enterprises, in Section VI(2), also state **10.152** that enterprises should: 'Ensure that remuneration of agents is appropriate and for legitimate services only. Where relevant, a list of agents employed in connection with transactions with public bodies and state owned enterprises should be kept and made available to competent authorities.' Further, Article 3 of the ICC Rules of Conduct to Combat Corruption, Extortion and Bribery states that:

> Enterprises should take measures reasonably within their power to ensure
>
> (a) that any payment made to an agent represents no more than an appropriate remuneration for legitimate services rendered by such agent;
>
> (b) that no part of any such payment is passed on by the agent as a bribe or otherwise in contravention of these Rules of Conduct; and
>
> (c) that they maintain a record of the names and terms of employment of all agents who are retained by them in connection with transactions with public bodies or State enterprises. This record should be available for inspection by auditors and, upon specific request, by appropriate duly authorised governmental authorities under conditions of confidentiality.

10.153 Increasingly companies are expressly stating their compliance with such principles and they provide a useful marker as to the corporate commitment to develop effective anti-corruption strategies and at the same time provide protection for reputable agents and representatives.

6. Overview

10.154 The possibilities offered to developing countries by the Lesotho Highlands Water Project cases are considerable. In particular, the cases demonstrate that developing countries can now take effective action against those from outside the country who seek to bribe their public officials and will no longer have to wait (indefinitely, it would appear) for Western countries to prosecute the bribers. Further, in July 2004, the World Bank was galvanized into declaring that Acres International was ineligible to receive any World Bank financed contracts for a period of three years.[144] Hitting corporations financially in this way is potentially an effective way of combating the bribery of foreign public officials.

10.155 Two other points must be noted. First, the need for the political will to embark on such a process is fundamental. In the case of Lesotho, the catalyst for the investigation was the return of the country to civilian rule in 1993, together with a strong government commitment to tackling corruption, and skilled and dedicated law officers. It remains to be seen whether such political will is present in other developing countries. Secondly, developing countries may find the prosecution of such cases an expensive business. As the Attorney General of Lesotho has noted, when you prosecute international bribery 'you are on your own'. As he noted in 2003:

> Various offers of financial assistance have been made to Lesotho. To date none has been forthcoming. Here mention is made of a meeting held on 17 November 1999 in Pretoria, South Africa. This meeting was called as a result of this bribery scandal breaking in Lesotho and the declaration by the Lesotho Government to prosecute those involved. This meeting was called by the World Bank and was attended by representatives of various role players concerned with the Highlands Water Project, including representatives from South Africa, Britain, the European Union, the European Investment Bank, individual banks in Europe and so on. At this meeting the actions of the Lesotho Government were praised. More importantly, from various quarters, promises were made of assistance in these

[144] The World Bank has been the subject of considerable international criticism over its failure to act more promptly: see, eg F Darroch, 'Lesotho Highlands Water Project: Corruption and Debarment' (2004) Available from the Tiri website: www.tiri.org/papers-research/Lesotho/pdf. It remains to be seen whether the other enterprises convicted of bribery will suffer the same fate.

prosecutions. This was after the representatives from Lesotho had pointed out to those present that these prosecutions would constitute a considerable drain on Lesotho's financial resources. Unfortunately none of this help has been forthcoming.[145]

[145] L F Maema, 'Prosecuting bribery in Lesotho', paper delivered at the 11th International Anti-Corruption Conference, Seoul, May 2003. Text available from www.odiousdebts.org.

11

THE CORRUPTION LAWS OF OTHER JURISDICTIONS

This chapter provides an overview of the criminal laws relating to corruption in a number of key jurisdictions. In view of their increasing importance, the chapter then examines the role of specialized anti-corruption agencies. **11.01**

A. The United States

11.02 The principle of double sovereignty in the United States means that the federal system and the state systems are separate and independent of each other. Each state has sovereignty with respect to its own laws with the federal state being sovereign with respect to federal laws. In practice there are a plethora of corruption laws at both the federal and state levels with the result that there is often an overlap between them. This section is limited to a discussion of the federal law.

i. Corruption offences

11.03 The US Criminal Code divides corruption laws into general and specific offences. §201(b)(1) of the US Criminal Code (18 USC) addresses 'active bribery'. This applies to:

> ... whoever directly or indirectly, corruptly gives, offers or promises anything of value to any public official or person who has been selected to be a public official, or offers or promises any public official or any person who has been selected to be a public official to give anything of value to any other person or entity, with intent (A) to influence any official act; or (B) to influence such public official or person who has been selected to be a public official to commit or aid in committing, or collude in, or allow, any fraud or make opportunity for the commission of any fraud on the United States; or (C) to induce such public official or such person who has been selected to be a public official to do or omit to do any act in violation of the lawful duty of such official or person.

11.04 §201(a)(2) addresses 'passive bribery'. This applies to:

> ... whoever being a public servant or person selected to be a public official, directly or indirectly, corruptly demands, seeks, receives, accepts, or agrees to receive or accept anything of value personally or for any other person or entity, in return for (A) being influenced in the performance of any official act; (B) being influenced to commit or aid in committing, or to collude in, or allow, any fraud, or make opportunity for the commission of any fraud on the United States; or (C) being induced to do or omit to do any act in violation of the official duty of such official or person.

11.05 In this context a 'public official' is defined in §201(a) to include 'an officer or employee or person acting for or on behalf of the United States, or any department, agency or branch of Government thereof, including the District of Columbia, in any official function, under or by authority of any such department, agency or branch of Government, or a juror'.

11.06 Other provisions of 18 USC deal with corruption or conflicts of interest committed by specific groups:

- Members of Congress, federal officers and employees or federal judges, acting in a representational capacity in any proceeding in which the United States is a party or has a direct and substantial interest (§§203 and 205);

- any officer or employee of the executive branch of ther United States Government or of an independent agency of the United States, participating in any matter in which she or he or a member of that person's family or business or organization with which she or he is associated has a financial interest (§208);
- any officer or employee of the executive branch of the United States Government or of an independent agency of the United States, receiving, and any person paying such officer or employee, any supplementation of his/her official salary in respect of his/her official duties (§209);
- any person paying another to use his or her influence to procure any appointive office or place under the United States for any person (§210);
- any candidate for public office promising to use his/her influence or to appoint any person to a public or private office in exchange for their support in the election (§599); and
- any person promising any public post or governmental contract in exchange for political activity in connection with any election to any political office (§600).

In addition, the Racketeer Influenced and Corrupt Organizations Act (RICO) prohibits any person receiving any income derived from a racketeering activity, including bribery under §201, from investing in, acquiring, or establishing any enterprise which is engaged in, or the activities of which affect, interstate or foreign commerce.[1] RICO marked an important break with the past, as the law was used not simply to punish individuals but as a weapon to break the power of complex criminal organizations. Its use has expanded well beyond the confines of organized crime and variations of the law have been enacted in various states. The extremely broad language used has made it possible for individuals to be charged if they are members of an enterprise that has embarked on a concerted pattern of lawbreaking. It has been used, among other things, to prosecute a mayor in Rhode Island for corruption in City Hall.[2] **11.07**

Other federal laws relating to corruption include 18 USC §1952, Interstate and Foreign Travel or Transportation in Aid of Racketeering Enterprises, which prohibits any interstate or foreign travel or the use of any facility in interstate or foreign commerce in furtherance of the violation of state or US bribery laws, whilst 18 USC §666 prohibits theft or bribery in programmes receiving federal funding. There are no specific federal corruption offences dealing with the private sector but such provisions appear in many state anti-corruption laws. **11.08**

There are a large number of federal and state bodies charged with investigating and prosecuting corruption. At the federal level, responsibility rests largely with the US Department of Justice, usually through the Public Integrity Section **11.09**

[1] 18 USC §§1961–1963.

[2] The case is described in J O'Brien, *Wall Street on Trial* (London: John Wiley & Sons, 2003) 115–139.

of the Criminal Division. Other bodies have responsibility for dealing with specific aspects of corruption and these include the Securities and Exchange Commission (SEC) which may bring enforcement actions involving bribery of foreign public officials.

ii. Bribery of foreign public officials[3]

11.10 The impetus for a law on the bribery of foreign public officials dates back to the mid-1970s when, during an SEC investigation, over 400 US companies admitted to making questionable or illegal payments in excess of US$300 million to foreign government officials, politicians, and political parties.[4] This led to the passing of the Foreign Corrupt Practices Act 1977 (FCPA) that sought to halt the practice and to restore public confidence in the integrity of the American business system.[5] The FCPA makes it unlawful for US citizens and companies to make a corrupt payment to a foreign official for the purpose of obtaining or retaining business for or with, or directing business to, any person.[6] The FCPA also requires companies whose securities are listed in the United States to meet strict accounting and reporting requirements.[7] These require corporations covered by the provisions to make and keep books and records that accurately and fairly reflect the transactions of the corporation and to devise and maintain an adequate system of internal accounting controls.

11.11 The impact of the Act soon led to concern that it was placing US companies at a comparative disadvantage to foreign companies which routinely paid bribes and which, in some countries, were permitted to deduct the cost of such bribes as business expenses.[8] Successive US administrations resisted pressure from corporate America to repeal the Act in its entirety, and instead adopted a policy of internationalizing a measure which President Jimmy Carter had (inaccurately) expected others would follow in any event, simply because of its moral force. Thus, US pressure for an international agreement on the issue was decisive in the moves towards the development of the OECD Convention on Combating Bribery of Foreign Public Officials in International Business Transactions.[9] In 1998 the United States ratified the Convention and the International

[3] See generally D Zarin, *Doing Business under the Foreign Corrupt Practices Act*, Practising Law Institute, 2002

[4] HR Rep No 95–640, 4; S Rep No 95–114, 3

[5] For a useful background on the debate see TC Sorensen, 'Improper Payments Abroad: Perspectives and Proposals' (1976) *Foreign Affairs* 719.

[6] For a discussion on the scope of the phrase see the important decision of the US Court of Appeals, Fifth Circuit in *US v Kay and Murphy* 359 F 3d 738. (the bribery of foreign public officials in order to reduce a company's tax burden or customs duties could constitute an offence under the FCPA). For detail of recent criminal enforcement actions, see the OECD *United States: Phase 2 Follow-up Report*, 2005, Annex 1.

[7] See 15 USC §78m.

[8] For the period of May 1994 to April 2000, the US government received information that 353 contracts valued at US$165 bn might have been affected by the bribery of foreign firms. US companies allegedly lost 92 of these contracts at an estimated value of US$26 bn: Second Annual Report to Congress on the OECD Convention, at v.

[9] See Ch 10 above.

Anti-Bribery and Fair Competition Act 1998 amended the FCPA to bring it into line with the Convention.

The Act applies to any individual, firm, officer, director, employee, or agent of a firm, and any stockholder acting on behalf of a firm. Individuals and firms may also be liable if they order, authorize, or assist someone else to breach the Act or if they conspire to do so. **11.12**

The Act imposes liability for foreign bribery committed by third parties acting as agents. As a GRECO Report notes, it is this ever-present threat of vicarious liability which has prompted the introduction of stringent 'due diligence' practices among many larger multinationals in selecting their local agents, business partners, and sales representatives, and in screening potential joint venture partners who might bring with them the risk of possible hidden exposures.[10] **11.13**

A US parent company is potentially liable for the acts of its foreign subsidiary if it is proved that it authorized, directed, or controlled that subsidiary in committing the corrupt act, with wilful blindness or 'reckless disregard' sufficing to trigger liability. **11.14**

The 1988 amendment to the FCPA excludes payments made to facilitate or expedite the performance of a 'routine governmental action'. These include payments to obtain permits and visas, provide police protection, or protect perishable products. The 1998 Act also incorporates an 'affirmative' defence for payments that are lawful under the written laws of the relevant foreign country or are bona fide expenditures directly relating to the promotion of products or services, or to the execution or performance of a contract with a foreign government or agency.[11] **11.15**

iii. Penalties

Upon conviction, corporations and other business entities are subject to a fine of up to US$2,000,000, whilst officers, directors, stockholders, employees, and agents are subject to a fine of up to US$100,000 and imprisonment for up to five years.[12] The Attorney-General or SEC may also bring a civil action against such persons. The Civil Asset Forfeiture Reform Act 2000 expands the grounds for civil and criminal forfeiture, making forfeitable the proceeds of a contravention of the FCPA. Under guidelines issued by the Office of **11.16**

[10] See GRECO, 'Evaluation Report on the United States of America', 2004, para 39.

[11] Inserted into the FCPA as Article 104A.

[12] A fine may also be based on gain or loss under 18 USC Ch 227. Sub-Ch C §3571 provides that if any person derives pecuniary gain from the offence, or if the offence results in pecuniary loss to a person other than the defendant, the defendant may be fined not more than the greater of twice the gross gain or twice the gross loss, unless imposition of a fine under the subsection would unduly complicate or prolong the sentencing process.

Management and Budget, a person or firm found in violation of the FCPA may also be barred from doing business with the federal government.

11.17 The United States does not allow deductions for bribes paid to foreign public officials if that bribe is a criminal offence under the FCPA. With respect to US tax provisions for Controlled Foreign Corporations, any payment of a bribe by a foreign subsidiary is treated as taxable income to the US parent.

B. Selected Commonwealth Countries

1. Australia

11.18 The eights states and territories of Australia have power to enact their own criminal laws. The Commonwealth has power to enact criminal laws in relation to its responsibilities under the Constitution. At Commonwealth level, the provisions of the Criminal Code dealing with fraud and corruption have a wide application and cover most persons working for or on behalf of the Commonwealth. The Crimes Act 1914 provisions were repealed and were re-enacted in the Criminal Code Act 1995 ('the Code').

i. Corruption offences

11.19 Chapter 7, Part 7.6 of the Commonwealth Criminal Code covers bribery and related offences. Subsection 141.1 makes the giving to, or receiving of a bribe by, a Commonwealth public official an offence punishable by up to five years' imprisonment. Unlike other jurisdictions, such as the United Kingdom, the giving or receipt must be done dishonestly.[13]

11.20 At the state level, bribery remains a common law offence in New South Wales and Victoria whilst elsewhere the state codes have broadly similar provisions.[14] Some states also have secret commission offences which apply to the making of payments for the purpose of influencing anyone in the private or public sector. The effect of section 70.6 of the Code is that an offence may be prosecuted under state legislation, provided that the relevant law is not excluded or limited by the Commonwealth legislation.

11.21 The Commonwealth Fraud Control Guidelines 2002[15] require that all budget-funded agencies and relevant Commonwealth Authorities and Companies Act 1997 funded bodies put in place practices and procedures for

---

[13] A similar provision relating to influencing a Commonwealth public official in the exercise of that person's duties is found in art 142.1.

[14] The Queensland Criminal Code 1995, 'Bribery' also specifically covers bribery relating to the administration of justice (Division 2).

[15] Made under the Financial Management and Accountability Regulations 1997, reg 19.

effective fraud control. In this context, 'fraud' includes 'bribery, corruption or the abuse of office'. Amongst other things, the Guidelines state that agencies should consider prosecution in appropriate cases and should be committed to recovering losses caused by illegal activity through proceeds of crime and civil recovery processes and, in the absence of criminal prosecution, to applying appropriate civil, administrative, or disciplinary penalties.[16]

ii. Bribery of foreign public officials

In 1999, Australia ratified the OECD Convention on the Bribery of Foreign Public Officials and gave effect to it in the Criminal Code Amendment (Bribery of Foreign Public Officials) Act 1999.[17] Tax deductibility for bribes paid overseas in the course of doing business was removed in the Taxation Laws Amendment Act (No 2) 2000. **11.22**

Section 70.2(1) of the Criminal Code Act provides that a person is guilty of an offence if: **11.23**

(a) the person
  (i) provides a benefit to another person; or
  (ii) causes a benefit to be provided to another person; or
  (iii) offers to provide, or promises to provide, a benefit to another person; or
  (iv) causes an offer of the provision of a benefit, or a promise of the provision of a benefit, to be made to another person; and
(b) the benefit is not legitimately due to the other person; and
(c) the first-mentioned person does so with the intention of influencing a foreign public official (who may be the other person) in the exercise of the official's duties as a foreign public official in order to:
  (i) obtain or retain business; or
  (ii) obtain or retain a business advantage that is not legitimately due to the recipient, or intended recipient, of the business advantage (who may be the first-mentioned person).

An Australian in another country who bribes or attempts to bribe an official of that country can be prosecuted for bribery in an Australian court. 'Bribery' includes providing or promising to provide a benefit (including non-monetary and non-tangible inducements) to another person where that benefit is not legitimately due. The benefit must be provided or promised with the intention of influencing a foreign public official in the exercise of the official's duties in order to obtain or retain business or a business advantage. It is not necessary to prove that any business advantage was obtained in fact. **11.24**

The definition of 'foreign public official' includes: an employee, or official of a foreign government body; a person performing the duties of an appointment, **11.25**

[16] Guideline 1(4).

[17] The Act amended the Criminal Code Act 1995. See now Chapter 4, Division 70—Bribery of foreign public officials. The full text is available at http://scaleplus.law.gov.au/html/pasteact/1/686/0/PA001000.htm.

office, or position under a law of a foreign country; a person holding or performing the duties of an appointment, office, or position created by custom or convention of a foreign country; a person in the service of a foreign government body (including service as a member of a military force or police force); a member of the executive, judiciary, or magistracy of a foreign country; an employee or contractor of a public international organization; a member or officer of the legislature of a foreign country, or an individual who is or who holds himself or herself out to be an authorized intermediary of a foreign public official.

11.26 The corruption laws apply to both individuals and companies. Companies can be held to be criminally responsible for the conduct of a corporate agent in a range of situations, including where the corporate culture exist that directs, encourages, tolerates, or leads to breaches of the legislation, or where the company fails to create and maintain a corporate culture that requires compliance with the law.

11.27 Companies must ensure they have in place a corporate policy of compliance with the law. Further, companies must exercise due diligence and take reasonable precautions to ensure that their employees do not commit foreign bribery offences.

iii. Defences

11.28 There are two specific defences to a charge of bribing a foreign public official. The first applies where the conduct is legal in the country where the conduct takes place.[18] However, domestic bribery is unlawful in almost every country in the world, and it is irrelevant that the conduct is customary or officially tolerated.

11.29 The second defence applies to the making of 'facilitation payments' where the benefit provided is minor (an amount left undefined) and the conduct was for the sole or dominant purpose of expediting or securing the performance of a routine governmental action of a minor nature (such as the issuing of a visa or licence).[19] Such governmental action cannot involve a decision about (or encourage a decision about) whether to award new business or continue business with a particular party. Persons intending to rely on this defence must show a record of the transaction, including their own identity, the date, benefit provided, the identity of the foreign public official, and the action that the benefit was provided to achieve. The defence is rarely (if ever) available in circumstances where the payment was made to facilitate making a decision to award business to a company.

11.30 Defences of mistake or duress may also apply.[20] In the case of duress, the scope is wider than in most other common law jurisdictions, being available where

[18] s 70.3. [19] s 70.4. [20] Criminal Code, s 10.2 (2).

(a) a threat has been made that will be carried out unless an offence is committed; (b) there is no reasonable way that the threat can be rendered ineffective; and (c) the conduct is a reasonable response to the threat. A specific defence of due diligence is available to a corporation for conduct engaged in by a 'high managerial agent'. A high managerial agent of a company is an employee, agent, or officer of the company with such responsibility that his or her conduct may fairly be assumed to represent the company's policy.

iv. Penalties

The bribery of a domestic public official carries a maximum of two years' imprisonment and/or a fine of A$13,200, whilst a 'body corporate' can be fined a maximum of A$66 000. Penalties are greatly increased for the bribery of foreign public officials. Natural persons are liable to imprisonment for up to ten years and/or a fine.[21] Bodies corporate face considerably stiffer fines than for domestic bribery (up to A$330 000). **11.31**

v. Anti-corruption agencies

There is no specific anti-corruption agency at the federal level. However, New South Wales (Independent Commission Against Corruption (ICAC)), Queensland (Crime and Misconduct Commission), and Western Australia (the Corruption and Crime Commission of Western Australia formerly the Anti-Corruption Commission) have established specific anti-corruption bodies with special powers to investigate corruption, including a power to question similar to the section 2 power of the Serious Fraud Office in England and Wales.[22] In respect of the Western Australia Anti-Corruption Commission, the Supreme Court of Western Australia has emphasized that it is not empowered to make decisions with reference to the commencement or conduct of criminal prosecutions. Its function is 'to receive or initiate allegations of criminal conduct, [to] investigate them and to assemble evidence obtained in the course of its functions and furnish, to an appropriate authority, evidence which may be admissible in the prosecution of a person for a criminal offence, or which may be relevant to the functions of an agency or authority'.[23] **11.32**

---

[21] According to the Australian authorities, given the maximum term of imprisonment, it is very unlikely that a person convicted of bribing a foreign public official would not be imprisoned: OECD, *Australia: Review of the Implementation of the Convention and 1997 Recommendation*, 34.

[22] For the scope of these powers see *Western Australian Police Union of Workers v Anti-Corruption Commission and ors* [1998] WASC 226.

[23] *Per* Malcolm CJ in *Parker and Five Others v Miller and* [1998] WASCA 148. See also *Parker and ors v Anti-Corruption Commission* [1998] WASC 267. This is the position of the ICAC in New South Wales: see *Balog v Independent Commission Against Corruption* (1990) 169 CLR 625.

2. Canada

11.33 Canada is a federal state with power divided between the federal and the ten provincial governments. Corruption and related offences are found in Part IV of the nationally applicable Canadian Criminal Code under the title 'Offences against the Administration of Law and Justice'.

i. Corruption Offences

11.34 Section 119 creates two offences relating to judicial officers and parliamentarians. Subsection 1(a) addresses the acceptance of a bribe. Here the offence is complete where any such person 'corruptly (i) accepts or obtains; (ii) agrees to accept, or (iii) attempts to obtain any money, valuable consideration, office, place or employment from himself or another person in respect of anything done or omitted or to be done or omitted by him in his official capacity'.[24]

11.35 Subsection 1(b) provides that the giving or offering corruptly to such persons of '(a) any money, valuable consideration, office, place or employment in respect of anything done or omitted or to be done or omitted by him in his official capacity for himself or another person' constitutes an offence. In both cases, the act must be done corruptly and in order to influence the office holder in his or her official capacity. In each case the penalty is imprisonment for up to fourteen years.

11.36 The word 'corruptly' is not defined in section 119, although in *R v Brown*,[25] a case involving a secret commission offence, the word was held to refer to an act done *mala fides* 'designed wholly or partially for bringing about the effect forbidden by the section' and did not import any concept of wickedness or dishonesty.[26]

11.37 Section 121 creates a series of offences that cover, in part, peddling in influence by officials. An 'official' means a person who (a) holds an office, or (b) is appointed to discharge a public duty. An 'office' includes (a) an office or appointment under the government, (b) a civil or military commission, or (c) a position or an employment in a public department.[27] In most cases the offences are widely drawn to cover the situation where the intended beneficiary is a family member of the official. Any person committing an offence under section 121 is liable to up to five years' imprisonment. Section 122 creates the offence of fraud or breach of trust by an official in connection with the duties of his office. 'Trust' in this context relates to 'public trust'.[28] Section 123 provides that any municipal

[24] The offence can relate to an act of a member of Parliament when undertaking an administrative act of government: *Bruneau* [1964] 1 CCC 97 (Ontario CA).

[25] (1956) 116 CCC 287 (Ontario CA).

[26] Canadian Criminal Code, s 120 is in similar terms to s 119 but covers a person 'being a justice, police commisioner, peace officer, public officer or officer of a juvenile court or those employed in the administration of criminal law'. The maximum penalty is also 14 years' imprisonment.

[27] Canadian Criminal Code, s 118.

[28] Thus it has no reference to the law of trusts: *R v Campbell* [1967] 3 CCC 250.

official[29] who demands or accepts a benefit in return for using their influence in relation to their responsibilities and those who offer such benefits commit a criminal offence punishable by imprisonment for up to five years. The prohibited act must be in connection with job-related responsibilities.

Section 426 creates the offence of secret commissions with an agent[30] concerning the affairs of his or her principal. The offence is not limited to the public sector. Subsection (1)(a) states that every one commits an offence who corruptly (i) gives, offers or agrees to give or offer to an agent, or (ii) being an agent, demands, accepts or offers or agrees to accept from a person: **11.38**

> any reward, advantage or benefit of any kind as consideration for doing or forbearing to do, or for having done or forborne to do, any act relating to the affairs or business of his principal or for showing or forbearing to show favour or disfavour to any person with relation to the affairs or business of his principal; . . .[31]

In this context, 'corruptly' means secretly or without requisite disclosure and there is no requirement for any corrupt bargain.[32]

ii. Bribery of foreign public officials

Canada ratified the OECD Convention in December 1998 and implemented it through the Corruption of Foreign Public Officials Act (CFPOA) which came into force in February 1999. Section 3(1) of the CFPOA provides that: **11.39**

> Every person commits an offence who, in order to obtain or retain an advantage in the course of business, directly or indirectly gives,[33] offers or agrees to give or offer a loan, reward, advantage or benefit of any kind to a foreign public official or to any person for the benefit of a foreign public official (a) as consideration for an act or omission by the official in connection with the performance of the official's duties or functions; or (b) to induce the official to use his or her position to influence any acts or decisions of the foreign state or public international organisation for which the official performs duties or functions.

The term 'foreign public official' covers persons holding legislative, administrative or judicial positions in a foreign state; those performing public duties or functions for a foreign state, and officials of a public international organization.[34] Section 5 contains money laundering provisions relating to the bribery of a foreign public official. **11.40**

---

[29] A 'municipal officer' means a member of a municipal council or a person who hold an office under a municipal government: section 123(3)

[30] For the scope of an 'agent' see *R v Wile* (1990) 58 CCC (3d) 85.

[31] s 426(2) further states that 'Every one commits an offence who is knowingly privy to the commission of an offence under subsection (1)'.

[32] *R v Kelly* [1992] 2 SCR 170 and *R v Arnold* [1992] 2 SCR 208.

[33] This would appear to cover bribes paid through intermediaries: see 10. 144 above for a useful example of such action by a Canadian company.

[34] CFPOA, s 2.

iii. Defences

11.41 The CFPOA does not apply to a 'loan, reward, advantage or benefit . . . made to expedite or secure the performance by a foreign public official of any act of a routine nature that is part of the foreign official's duties or functions'.[35] A list of actions of a routine nature is included and is similar to that in the US FCPA. These include the processing of official documents, such as visas and work permits, and the provision of police protection and the protection of perishable commodities.

11.42 Further, no person is guilty of an offence under section 3(1) where the loan, reward, advantage, or benefit 'is permitted or required under the laws of the relevant foreign state or public international organisation'[36] or 'was made to pay the reasonable expenses incurred in good faith by or on behalf of the foreign public official' that relate directly to (a) the promotion, demonstration, or explanation of the person's products and services, or (b) the execution or performance of a contract between the person and the foreign state for which the official performs the duties or functions.[37] Unlike the US FCPA, in the case of the CFPOA the burden of proof remains on the prosecution. No tax deduction is permissible in relation to bribes paid to foreign public officials.

iv. Jurisdiction

11.43 Canada adopts territorial jurisdiction unless required by treaty to do otherwise. In practice, territorial jurisdiction has received a wide interpretation. Thus in *R v Libman*[38] the Supreme Court of Canada held that an offence was subject to the jurisdiction of the Canadian courts if 'a significant portion of the activities constituting the offence took place in Canada', and that it was sufficient if there was a 'real and substantial link' between the offence and Canada. Even so, an OECD Report has expressed concern as to whether this is broad enough and has recommended that the Government of Canada should reconsider the position.[39]

v. Penalties

11.44 The maximum sentence for a natural person is five years' imprisonment and/or a fine. A corporation is liable to an unlimited fine.

3. New Zealand

11.45 In New Zealand the criminal law has been codified since 1893, with the main statute governing the more serious crimes now being the Crimes Act 1961. However, many general principles of criminal liability, general defences, and procedure and evidential rules are still derived from the common law.

---

[35] CFPOA, s 3(4). [36] ibid s 3(3)(a). [37] ibid s 3(3)(b).
[38] [1985] SCR 178. [39] OECD Canada: Phase 2 Report, 2004, p 33.

i. Corruption Offences

Bribery and corruption offences are found in Part 6 of the Crimes Act 1961 (as amended) under the heading 'Crimes Affecting the Administration of Law and Justice'. A bribe means 'any money, valuable consideration, office, or employment, or any benefit, whether direct or indirect' (section 99). Section 105 provides for a general offence of the bribery of an 'official', ie 'any person in the service of Her Majesty in right of New Zealand (whether that service is honorary or not, and whether it is within or outside New Zealand), or any member or employee of any local authority or public body, or any person employed in the Education service . . . '. Section 15 provides as follows: **11.46**

(1) Every official is liable to imprisonment for a team not exceeding 7 years who, whether within New Zealand or elsewhere, corruptly accepts or obtains or agrees or offers to accept or attempts to obtain, any bribe for himself or any other person in respect of any act done or omitted, or to be done or omitted, by him in his official capacity.
(2) Every one is liable to imprisonment for a term not exceeding [7 years] who corruptly gives or offers or agrees to give any bribe to any person with intent to influence any official in respect of any act or omission by him in his official capacity.

There are further provisions addressing corruption in relation to specific groups: Judicial officers and senior court officials (sections 100 and 101); Ministers of the Crown or member of the Executive Council (section 102); Members of parliament (section 103); and law enforcement officers (section 104). Section 105A also sets out the offence of the corrupt use or disclosure of information by an official acquired by him or her in his or her official capacity to obtain an advantage or pecuniary gain. **11.47**

ii. Bribery of foreign public officials

New Zealand has implemented the OECD Convention via the Crimes (Bribery of Foreign Public Officials) Act 2001 which added sections 105C to 105E to the Crimes Act 1961. Section 105C(2) creates the offence of corruptly giving or offering or agreeing to give a bribe to a person with intent to influence a foreign public official in respect of any act or omission by that official in his or her official capacity (whether or not the act or omission is within the scope of the official's authority) in order to (a) obtain or retain business or (b) obtain any improper advantage in the conduct of business. **11.48**

Under section 105C, foreign public officials are defined as a member or officer of the executive, judiciary, or legislature of a foreign country; a person who is employed by a foreign government, foreign public agency, foreign public enterprise, or public international organization; or a person, while acting in the service of or purporting to act in the service of a foreign government, foreign public agency, foreign public enterprise, or public international organization. **11.49**

Legislation adopted in October 2002 makes bribes paid to foreign and domestic public officials in the conduct of business non tax deductible.

11.50 The offence is not complete where the act was committed for the sole or primary purpose of ensuring or expediting the performance by a foreign public official of a routine government action and the value of the benefit was small (section 105C(3)). 'Routine government action' is defined by way of a negative list and no thresholds are set as to what constitutes a small benefit.[40]

iii. Jurisdiction

11.51 New Zealand has established nationality jurisdiction over the foreign bribery cases, although the act must constitute an offence under the law of the country where the foreign public official's 'principal office' is located.

iv. Penalties

11.52 Similar penalties exist for the bribery of both domestic officials and foreign public officials. The maximum sentence is up to seven years' imprisonment and/or an unlimited fine. A 'body corporate' is liable to an unlimited fine.

v. Investigation and prosecution

11.53 The New Zealand Police operates nationally and is responsible for investigating criminal offences. The Serious Fraud Office may investigate cases of serious or complex fraud and operates in much the same manner as the Serious Fraud Office in England and Wales. The National Prosecutions Service is responsible for the prosecution of all summary offences. Crown Counsel have the responsibility for prosecuting indictable offences.

4. South Africa

i. Corruption offences

11.54 The law on corruption in South Africa was originally a mixture of common law and statute. This was replaced by the Corruption Act 1992 which, in turn, was replaced by Prevention and Combating of Corrupt Activities Act 2004 (No 12 of 2004). The 2004 statute was drafted by the Parliamentary Portfolio Committee on Justice. State anti-corruption agencies, civil society, and private sector representatives all made public submissions to the Committee ensuring broad consultation in the drafting process. In doing so, the drafters also sought to realize the objectives of the South African Development Community (SADC) Protocol Against Corruption.[41] The result is a wide-ranging piece of legislation that, in part, provides an international example of good practice.

---

[40] For the OECD review of the legislation and generally on the implementation of the convention in New Zealand see: http://www.oecd.org.dataoecd/51/62/2088257.pdf.

[41] See 9.60 above.

Amongst other things, the Act:

(1) includes a list of codified corruption offences relating to specific persons (including public officials, agents, members of the legislature, judicial officers, members of the prosecuting authority);
(2) reinstates the common law crime of bribery—corruption is no longer only the domain of public sector officials but is recognized as emanating from within the private sector as well;
(3) includes provisions governing the bribery of foreign public officials by South African citizens (including SA companies);
(4) contains a list of codified corruption offences related to specific matters (including witness and evidential material, contracts, the procuring and withdrawal of contracts, auctions, sporting events, gambling games or games of chance);
(5) provides that certain designated officials (in the private or public sector) have a duty to report corruption or face stiff penalties;
(6) empowers the National Director of Public Prosecutions to investigate 'unexplained wealth';
(7) requires the National Treasury to establish a register of tender defaulters for corrupt individuals or firms in order to both name and shame bribe payers; and
(8) imposes heavy penalties for individuals found guilty of certain corruption–related offences—including life imprisonment in some instances.

Chapter 2 of the 2004 Act creates a range of corruption offences. Section 3 creates a general offence of corruption, although 'corruption' itself is not defined in the Act.[42] The section is in the following terms: **11.55**

Any person who, directly or indirectly—

(a) accepts or agrees or offers to accept any gratification from any other person, whether for the benefit of himself or herself or for the benefit of another person; or
(b) gives or agrees or offers to give to any other person any gratification, whether for the benefit of that other person or for the benefit of another person,

in order to act, personally or by influencing another person so to act, in a manner—

(i) that amounts to the—
(aa) illegal, dishonest, unauthorised, incomplete or biased; or
(bb) misuse or selling of information or material acquired in the course of the exercise, carrying out or performance of any powers, duties or functions arising out of a constitutional, statutory, contractual or any other legal obligation;
(ii) that amounts to—
(aa) the abuse of a position of authority;

[42] This reflects the approach taken in the 1992 statute where the avoidance of a definition was an express policy of the drafters: see Report of the South African Law Commission, *Bribery* (Report No 116) para 5.9.

(bb) a breach of trust; or
(cc) the violation of a legal duty or a set of rules;
(iii) designed to achieve an unjustified result; or
(iv) that amounts to any other unauthorised or improper inducement to do or not to do anything,

is guilty of the offence of corruption.

11.56 Part 2 of Chapter 2 creates a series of corruption offences in respect of specific groups and the offences parallel, in many respects, the section 3 offence.[43] Sections 4 and 5 create offences relating to the offering to, or acceptance of bribes by, public officers and foreign public officials,[44] respectively.

11.57 Part 3 deals with offences in respect of corrupt activities concerning the 'receiving or offering of unauthorised gratification'. Section 10 states as follows:

Any person—

(a) who is party to an employment relationship and who, directly or indirectly, accepts or agrees or offers to accept from any other person any unauthorised gratification, whether for the benefit of that person or for the benefit of another person; or
(b) who, directly or indirectly, gives or agrees or offers to give to any person who is party to an employment relationship any unauthorised gratification, whether for the benefit of that party or for the benefit of another person, in respect of that party doing any act in relation to the exercise, carrying out or performance of that party's powers, duties or functions within the scope of that party's employment relationship, is guilty of the offence of receiving or offering an unauthorised gratification.

11.58 Part 4 creates a series of offences in respect of corrupt activities relating to: witnesses and evidential material, contracts, procuring and withdrawal of tenders, auctions, sporting events, and gambling games and games of chance.

11.59 Part 5 creates a series of miscellaneous offences relating to 'possible conflict of interest and other unacceptable conduct'. Section 17 provides that any public officer who acquires or holds a private interest in any contract, agreement, or investment emanating from or connected with the public body in which he or she is employed or which is made on account of that public body, is guilty of an offence. This does not apply where a public official acquires or holds such interest as a shareholder of a listed company or one whose conditions of employment do not prohibit him or her from acquiring or holding such interest. It also does not apply where, in the case of a tender process, a public officer acquires a contract, agreement, or investment through a tender process and whose conditions of employment do not prohibit him or her from acquiring or holding such interest and who acquires or holds such interest through an independent tender process (section 17(2)).

[43] With the exception of corruption offences relating to agents, each section includes specific instances of corrupt acts relating to the specified persons.

[44] Including officials or agents of public international organisations (s 1(v)).

The 2004 Act also contains important provisions regarding whistleblowing. Section 34 imposes a duty on any person who holds a 'position of authority',[45] and who 'knows or ought reasonably to have known or suspected that any other person' has committed a corruption offence involving sums in excess of R100,000,[46] to report the fact to any police official. Failure to do so can result in a fine or up to ten years' imprisonment. **11.60**

The 2004 Act provides for a 'blacklisting' process through the establishment of a Register of Tender Defaulters. A court can order the names of companies or individuals found guilty of corruption relating to contracts, procurement, or the withdrawal of tenders to be placed on the Register for a period of between five and ten years. Any name on the list is then excluded from any government business, including tendering, for the same period. South Africa is seemingly the first country to establish such a nationwide system and this may well become an international model of good practice. **11.61**

The 2004 Act includes some of the most severe penalties in the world. Thus, for the majority of offences, the High Court can impose a fine and/or sentences up to life imprisonment.[47] **11.62**

ii. Anti-corruption agencies[48]

There are a series of state bodies entrusted with dealing with corruption. These include the Public Protector, who has the power to 'investigate any conduct in state affairs, or in the public administration in any sphere of government, that is alleged or suspected to be improper or to result in any impropriety or prejudice'[49] and the Office of the Auditor General.[50] Other bodies include the Directorate of Special Operations (the Scorpions), Special Investigative Units created by the Special Investigative Units and Special Tribunals Act 1996 and the Anti-Corruption Unit based in the South African Revenue Authority.[51] The South African National Prosecuting Authority Act 1998 provides for a single national prosecuting authority. Within it are three investigating Directorates, two of which deal with the investigation of serious economic crime and corruption respectively, and have extensive search and seizure powers. These survived a constitutional challenge in *Investigating Directorate: Serious Economic Crimes and Others v Hyundai Motor Distibutors (Pty) Ltd.*[52] **11.63**

[45] These are persons referred to in s 34(4), which covers both the public and private sectors.
[46] £900 approx as at September 2005.
[47] In the case of regional courts the maximum sentence is 10 years' imprisonment.
[48] See generally L Van Tonder and P Goss, 'Effective Use of Legal Remedies for Corruption: A South African Perspective' available at http://www.transparency.org/iacc/9th_iacc/papers/day3/ws1/d3ws1_pricewaterhouse.html.
[49] Constitution of South Africa 1996, s 182(1).
[50] ibid s 188
[51] For a discussion on the scope of the investigation powers of Special Investigation Units, see *Special Investigation Unit v Nadasen* [2001] ZASCA 97.
[52] 2000 (10) BCLR; [2000] ZACC 12.

11.64 Civil asset forfeiture was introduced in South Africa in the Prevention of Organised Crime Act 1998. On an application by the National Director of Public Prosecutions, the High Court can make an order forfeiting property to the state which the court finds to be an instrumentality of a crime or the 'proceeds of unlawful activities'. The Asset Forfeiture Unit was established in 1999 and is a specialist multi-disciplinary body based in the Office of the National Director of Public Prosecutions, with a remit to facilitate the forfeiture provisions.[53]

11.65 The National Anti-corruption Forum was established to bring the public, business, and civil society sectors together as equal partners in the fight against corruption. The Forum is working towards the creation of a national consensus on the fight against corruption; is a vehicle for business and civil society to advise government; is an exchange for view on good practise and general information; and, lastly, serves as a mechanism for the three sectors to advise each other on improving their sectoral anti-corruption strategies.[54]

C. Other Jurisdictions

1. Ireland

11.66 The law in Ireland is based on the English prevention of corruption legislation as amended by the Adoption Order 1928 and the Electoral Act 1963. Section 38 of the Ethics in Public Office Act 1995 extends the application of the legislation to special advisers personally appointed by ministers, directors, and persons employed in public bodies. The Prevention of Corruption (Amendment) Act 2001, *inter alia*, implements the OECD Convention, as well as expanding the scope of corporate liability.[55]

11.67 The Prevention of Corruption (Amendment) Act 2001 enabled Ireland to ratify the OECD Convention[56] by extending the definition of an agent in the 1906 Act to a wide range of office holders and officials not previously covered. This includes 'a judge of a court in any other state' which seems to extend the scope of the statute beyond exclusively protecting a fiduciary relationship.[57] Section 43 of the Criminal Justice (Theft and Fraud) Act 2001 establishes a specific offence of 'active bribery' which covers the bribery of an official of the European

[53] A useful in-depth study on corruption in South Africa is the 2005 TI Country Study Report that is available at http://www.transparency.org.

[54] See further http://www.tisa.org.za.

[55] Prevention of Corruption (Amendment) Act 2001, s 10(2) provides that the legislation may be cited as the Prevention of Corruption Acts 1889 to 2001 'and shall be construed together as one'.

[56] The Act also addresses Ireland's obligations under the Council of Europe Criminal Law Convention on Corruption.

[57] These also include a member of the European Parliament, member of the government or member of Parliament of any other state and public prosecutors in any other state: see the 2001 Act, s 2(5).

Union (or EU Member State official) in a case where damage to the European Union's financial interests is concerned.[58]

Section 9 of the Prevention of Corruption (Amendment) Act 2001 also expands the scope of corporate liability in the following terms: **11.68**

> (1) Where an offence under the Prevention of Corruption Acts 1889 to 2001, has been committed by a body corporate and is proved to have been committed with the consent or connivance of or to be attributable to any wilful neglect on the part of the person being a director, manager, secretary or other officer of the body corporate, or a person who was purporting to act in any such capacity, that person as well as the body corporate shall be guilty of an offence. . . .
>
> (2) Where the affairs of a body corporate are managed by its members, subsection (1) shall apply in relation to the acts and defaults of a member in connection with his or her functions of management as if he or she were a director or manager of the body corporate.

Bribes paid to foreign public officials are not tax deductible on public policy grounds.[59] All prosecutions of corruption require the consent of the Director of Public Prosecutions. The penalties for the bribery of both national and foreign public officials are the same, providing a maximum sentence of ten years' imprisonment on indictment. **11.69**

The Ethics in Public Office Act 1995 is a useful example of legislation designed to prevent corruption. This provides for disclosure of interests by the holders of designated positions of employment in the public service and the directors of designated public bodies. It establishes the Public Offices Commission to provide guidelines and advice, and to undertake investigations and report on any possible contravention. The Act also established Select Committees in both Houses of the *Oireachtas*, which publish guidelines, provide assistance and advice to members in relation to compliance, and are empowered to investigate and report on possible contraventions of the Act. **11.70**

The key provisions of the Act are requirements that annual written statements be made by persons holding public employment in respect of certain personal interests (and those interests of a spouse, child, or step-child of which they are aware) which could materially influence them in the performance of their official duties. These interests include: gifts from one source exceeding £500 in value; salaried positions; large shareholdings in a company (above £10,000 value); directorships; ownership of land (valued at £10,000 or more) other than personal dwellings; and public service contracts. Further, an ad hoc declaration **11.71**

---

[58] This incorporates the definition in the First Protocol to the Convention on the Protection of the European Communities' Financial Interests, Art 3.1. See App 17 below.

[59] See Update on the Implementation of the OECD Recommendation on Tax Deductibility to Foreign Public Officials, March 2003.

is required where a potential conflict of interests could directly arise in the performance of official duties between the public interest and the interests of the individual concerned or those of connected persons, for example close relatives or business partners.[60]

2. Hong Kong

11.72 Since 1 July 1997, Hong Kong has been a special administrative region of the People's Republic of China. Its Basic Law provides for the continuation of the common law system, legal profession, and system of courts. The only significant change effected by the Basic Law concerning the courts system is the creation of the Hong Kong Court of Final Appeal, to take the place of the Judicial Committee of the Privy Council.

i. Corruption law and related offences

11.73 The main anti-corruption laws are found in two Ordinances. The first of these, the Elections (Corrupt and Illegal Conduct) Ordinance (Cap 554), prohibits corrupt conduct and illegal conduct at elections, regulates electoral advertising, and imposes requirements with respect to the receipt of donations and the expenditure of money at or in connection with elections.

11.74 The second major anti-corruption Ordinance, the Prevention of Bribery Ordinance (Cap 201), provides a range of offences:

(1) soliciting or accepting any advantage by a prescribed officer (section 3);
(2) bribery of a public servant (section 4(1));
(3) soliciting a bribe by a public servant (section 4(2));
(4) bribery in relation to the obtaining or giving of contracts (section 5);
(5) bribery in relation to tenders (section 6);
(6) bribery in relation to auctions (section 7);
(7) bribery of public servants by persons having dealings with public bodies (section 8);
(8) corrupt transactions with agents (section 9); and
(9) the possession of unexplained wealth (section 10). This is discussed below.

11.75 Sentences range from one to ten years' imprisonment depending upon the offence charged. In addition, a court may order a person convicted under section 3 to pay to the government the whole or part of the amount or value of the advantage received by him. Further, a court may order a person convicted under section 10 to pay to the government (a) a sum not exceeding the amount

[60] See Second Schedule The positions and directorships in the civil and broader public service which have been designated for the purposes of the Act are contained in the Ethics in Public Office (Designated Positions in Public Bodies) Regulations 1996 and the Ethics in Public Office (Prescribed Public Body, Designated Directorships and Designated Positions in Public Bodies) Regulations 1997.

of the pecuniary resources; or (b) a sum not exceeding the value of the property, the acquisition of which was not explained by him or her to the satisfaction of the court. The Ordinance also empowers the Independent Commission Against Corruption to seize travel documents and seek the freezing of assets.

In *Shum Kwok Sher v Hong Kong Special Administrative Region*[61] the Court of **11.76** Appeal examined the common law offence of misconduct in public office. Here Sir Anthony Mason NPJ held the following to accurately represent the object of the offence: 'Official Misconduct is not concerned primarily with the abuse of official position for pecuniary gain, i.e. with corruption in the popular sense. Its object is simply to ensure that an official does not, by any wilful act or omission, act contrary to the duties of his (or her) office and does not abuse intentionally the trust reposed in him (or her)'.[62] He went on to hold that the elements of the offence are: (1) A public official; (2) who in the course of or in relation to his public office; (3) wilfully and intentionally;[63] (4) culpably misconducts himself. He added that:

> A public official culpably misconducts himself if he wilfully and intentionally neglects or fails to perform a duty to which he is subject by virtue of his office or employment without reasonable excuse or justification. A public official also culpably misconducts himself if, with an improper motive, he wilfully and intentionally exercises a power or discretion which he has by virtue of his office or employment without reasonable excuse or justification . . . the misconduct complained of must be serious misconduct. Whether it is serious misconduct in this context is to be determined having regard to the responsibilities of the office and the officeholder, the importance of the public objects which they serve and the nature and extent of the departure from those responsibilities.[64]

ii. Possession of unexplained wealth

Given the 'notorious evidential difficulty' of proving bribery,[65] the offence of **11.77** possession of unexplained wealth under section 10 is said to have proved its effectiveness in the fight against corruption.[66] Section 10(1) provides that any person who, being or having been a prescribed officer (a) maintains a standard of living above that which is commensurate with his present or past official emoluments; or (b) is in control of pecuniary resources or property disproportionate to his present or past official emoluments shall, unless he gives a satisfactory explanation to the court as to how he was able to maintain such a standard of living or how such pecuniary resources or property came under his

[61] [2002] 5 HKCFAR 381

[62] Adopting the words of PD Finn, 'Official Misconduct' (1978) 2 *Criminal Law Journal* LJ 307, 308. See also PD Finn, 'Public Officers: Some Personal Liabilities' (1977) 51 *Australian Law Journal* 313.

[63] Referring to *R v Shepherd* [1981] AC 394.

[64] Noting that this underlies the concluding observations of Lord Widgery CJ in *R v Dytham* [1979] QB 722. The Court of Appeal also held that the offence was not imprecise, vague, or arbitrary so as to offend the Basic Law. For a critique of the judgment, see 3.14 above and for a recent re-statement see 3.69 above.

[65] *Mok Wei Tak v The Queen* [1990] 2 AC 333, 343.

[66] See Bokhary JA in *A-G v Hui Kin-hong* [1995] 1 HKCLR 227, 229, CA.

control, be guilty of an offence. Section 10(2) further provides that where a court is satisfied in proceedings under subsection (1)(b) that, having regard to the closeness of his relationship to the accused and to other circumstances, there is reason to believe that any person was holding pecuniary resources or property in trust for or otherwise on behalf of the accused or acquired such resources or property as a gift from the accused, such property or resources shall, in the absence of evidence to the contrary, be presumed to have been in the control of the accused.

11.78 The section 10 provisions have been heavily criticized as adversely affecting the rights of innocent government officials[67] and, in the view of the Law Commission, a similar provision in England would be 'doomed to failure' in the European Court of Human Rights on the ground that it was unreasonable or out of proportion to the mischief prevented.[68] Indeed, the section has spawned a number of cases on its relationship with the presumption of innocence that is protected by article 11(i) of the Hong Kong Bill of Rights. Here the courts have held that the presumption can be limited, provided such limitation is rational and proportional.[69] In *Attorney-General v Hui Kin-hong*[70] the Court of Appeal found the provision to be consistent with the presumption of innocence and emphasized the importance of finding an acceptable balance between the presumption of innocence and the need of society to combat corruption, the latter being characterized as a cancerous activity and an evil practice. The Court of Appeal noted that under section 10, the prosecution was not simply required to prove that expenditure was greater than income but also: (a) the amount of pecuniary resources and other assets in the accused's control at the charge date; (b) the accused's total official emoluments up to the same date; and a disproportion between (a) and (b), ie that the acquisition of the total assets under the accused's control could not reasonably, in all the circumstances, have been afforded out of the total official emoluments up to that date. In other words, the disproportionality must be significant enough to call for an explanation.

11.79 The Court of Appeal noted the notorious evidential difficulty in proving that a government servant had solicited or accepted a bribe. The primary facts on which the accused's explanation would be based, such as the existence of any capital or income of his, independent of his official emoluments, would be peculiarly within his own knowledge. The standard was described as the mere balance of probabilities. Only at that stage would a court be asked to decide whether the factual matters on which the accused based his or her explanation might reasonably account for the incommensurate standard of living. The Court of Appeal pointed out that once the expenditure had reached a

[67] See B Downey, 'Combating Corruption: the Hong Kong Solution' (1976) 6 HKLJ 33.

[68] See *Legislating the Criminal Code: Corruption*, para 11.56. This is reinforced in para 4.58 of the final report.

[69] See, eg, *Sin Yau Min* (1991) 1 HKPLR 88.

[70] [1995] 1 HKCLR 227.

threshold level of 'incommensurateness' or disparity, the smaller the disproportion the easier it would be to give an explanation.

The *Hui Kin-hong* case is an application of the Privy Council's decision in *Attorney-General v Lee Kwong Kut*. It involved a balancing exercise between individual rights and the wider needs of society—to combat corruption. It also confirms the legal principles applicable in assessing the validity of reverse onus clauses and sends a clear message to the government and the public that the judiciary is prepared to accept some limitation of rights where wider public interests so warrant. With this provision, law enforcement officers, such as the Independent Commission Against Corruption (ICAC), will be able to continue to combat corruption. **11.80**

The use of third parties to conceal corruption has also been subject to judicial attention. In *Attorney-General v Hui Kin-hong* the Hong Kong Court of Appeal noted that: **11.81**

> Before the prosecution can rely on the presumption that pecuniary resources or property were in the accused's control, it has, of course, to prove beyond reasonable doubt the facts which give rise to it. The presumption must receive a restrictive construction so that those facts must make it more likely than not that the pecuniary resources or property . . . were held . . . on behalf of the accused or were acquired as a gift from him. And construed restrictively in that way, the presumption is consistent with the accused's fundamental right, being a measured response to devices by which the unscrupulous could easily make a mockery of the whole section.[71]

This approach has proved effective in that it avoids the need to prove specific acts of corruption.

iii. Investigation and prosecution

Hong Kong is the home to the ICAC, perhaps the best known of all anti-corruption agencies and definitely the best resourced. Established in 1974 under the Independent Commission Against Corruption Ordinance, it has adopted a three-pronged approach to combat corruption. Its aims are: **11.82**

(1) to pursue the corrupt through effective detection and investigation;
(2) to eliminate opportunities for corruption by introducing corruption resistant practices; and
(3) to educate the public on the evils of corruption and foster their support in fighting corruption.

The Commission is headed by a Commissioner who is directly accountable to the Chief Executive. The Commission has a staff of over 1,300 and an annual **11.83**

[71] [1995] HKCA 127 For a useful discussion on the issue see B de Speville 'Reversing the Onus of Proof: Is it Compatible with Respect for Human Rights?', http://www.transparency.org/iacc/8th_iacc/papers/despeville.html.

budget of nearly US$100 million. In an effort to ensure integrity within the organization, the majority of staff are appointed on short-term contracts, renewable upon satisfactory performance and conduct.

11.84 Reports of corruption are made in confidence and the Commission has established a witness protection programme. The Commission has extensive powers of arrest, detention, and granting of bail. It also has wide powers of search and seizure, and is authorized to take non-intimate samples from a suspect.[72] Under the Prevention of Bribery Ordinance the ICAC has powers enabling it to: (a) search bank accounts; (b) hold and examine business and private documents; (c) require suspects to provide details of their assets, both income and expenditure;[73] and (d) search for and seize of documents. The Commission is also empowered to seize travel documents and to freeze property. It does not prosecute cases; the decision to prosecute and the prosecution itself is left to the normal prosecution authorities.

11.85 In practice, the Commission has proved very effective in tackling corruption. Much of this is due to the development of a sound legal framework backed up by access to adequate funding and an ability to attract and keep well-trained staff. A further important factor has been the placing of the Commission in the office of the Governor and having it report to the legislature. This has kept it largely separate from the public service and given it autonomy of operation. The power to prosecute 'illicit enrichment' without having to prove specific acts of corruption has also added to its effectiveness. There is also an oversight board, including members of the private sector and civil society, whose consent is required before an investigation can be discontinued.

11.86 The effectiveness of ICAC has led to its being used as model in a number of other countries. Yet, as noted below, much of its success is due to factors that cannot be replicated elsewhere, in particular, political support, a strong judiciary committed to the Rule of Law, a strong organizational structure, and adequate staffing and resources.

D. Other Regions

11.87 In a book of this nature, it is not possible to deal with a wide range of countries. However, the following entries provide information on accessing corruption-related legal materials in other countries and regions.

---

[72] See *Commissioner of the Independent Commission Against Corruption v Ch'ng Poh* A [1996] HKCA 414.

[73] This power supercedes the privilege against self-incrimination as the legislature had clearly intended to abrogate this common law privilege: see *Chan Sze Ting and Lee Chin Ming v Hong Kong Special Administrative Region* (unreported, 2000).

1. The GRECO Countries

Evaluation Reports and/or Compliance Reports are available, providing invaluable and up-to-date information and analysis on the anti-corruption laws and mechanisms for the following member states of GRECO: Albania, Belgium, Bosnia and Herzegovina, Bulgaria, Croatia, Cyprus, Czech Republic, Denmark, Estonia, Finland, France, Georgia, Germany, Greece, Hungary, Iceland, Ireland, Latvia, Lithuania, Luxembourg, Malta, Moldova, the Netherlands, Norway, Poland, Portugal, Romania, Slovakia, Slovenia, Spain, Sweden, the former Yugoslav Republic of Macedonia, the United Kingdom, and the United States.[74] **11.88**

2. Russia, Eastern Europe, and Eurasia

The Anti-Corruption Gateway for Europe and Eurasia provides primary materials and direct links to major information sources on Russia, the countries of Eastern Europe and of the former Soviet Union. The Gateway provides a readily accessible repository of anti-corruption project documentation, legislation, regional and international agreements, news, survey results, reports, and research.[75] **11.89**

3. Baltic Anti-Corruption Initiative

In 2001, Estonia, Latvia, and Lithuania launched the Baltic Anti-Corruption Initiative. This is designed to develop anti-corruption programmes and legislation and to institutionalize a consultation process on anti-corruption issues between government and civil society. This builds upon the first phase which comprised, in particular, a peer review process that assessed the adequacy of anti-corruption laws and practice in the three states. Current issues being addressed are: **11.90**

(1) public procurement reform;
(2) the role of tax administrations in the fight against corruption;
(3) developing effective monitoring of anti-bribery measures, including the involvement of the business community, trade unions, and civil society; and
(4) developing ethical standards in public administration and business, including the use of codes of conduct.[76]

4. South-Eastern Europe

The Stability Pact Anti-Corruption Initiative for South Eastern-Europe (SPAI) is the result of the 1999 Stability Pact for South-Eastern Europe, which was **11.91**

[74] The Reports are available from http://www.greco.coe.int.
[75] The Gateway can be accessed through http://www.nobribes.org.
[76] The information can be accessed at http://www.oecd.org.

adopted by the then fifteen European Union Member States, several countries in the region,[77] the Council of Europe and the OECD. Its objective is to help and support the countries of the region to adopt effective legislation, establish institutions, and develop appropriate practices in the fight against corruption.

11.92 The overall objectives and principles for implementing the Initiative are set out in the Compact and Action Plan which calls on the SPAI countries to take measures identified in five pillars of the Initiative:

(1) the adoption and implementation of international anti-corruption instruments;
(2) the promotion of good governance and reliable public administration;
(3) the strengthening of national legislation and the rule of law;
(4) the promotion of integrity in business operations; and
(5) the promotion of an active civil society.

11.93 A booklet entitled *Anti-Corruption Measures in South Eastern Europe: Country Reviews and Priorities for Reform*, detailing current anti-corruption measures in the region, has been published by the SPAI Steering Group.[78] Information on anti-corruption and related legislation is available for Macedonia, Montenegro, Romania, and Serbia.[79] The Regional Secretariat Liaison Office, based in Sarajevo, Bosnia Herzegovina, was established in 2002 and serves as a regional resource and information centre and as a primary point of contact with members of SPAI. The OECD and the Council of Europe remain partners with SPAI in their capacity as members of the Steering Group.

5. Asia-Pacific

11.94 In 2000, thirty-six member states of the Asian Development Bank and the OECD launched the ADB/OECD Anti-Corruption Initiative for Asia Pacific.[80] An extensive database of anti-corruption laws and other materials on thirty-seven Asia-Pacific countries and territories is available from http://www1.oecd.org/daf/asiacom/countries/index.htm.

11.95 The establishment of a self-assessment exercise by the member states encourages them to evaluate the adequacy of their national legal and institutional anti-corruption framework. As a result, the Initiative has published *Anti-Corruption Policies in Asia and the Pacific: The Legal and Institutional Frameworks for Fighting Corruption in Twenty-one Asian and Pacific Countries*, which contains much useful information about anti-corruption laws and law enforcement in the region.[81]

[77] These are Albania, Bosnia and Herzegovina, Croatia, Macedonia, Moldova, Romania, Serbia, and Montenegro.

[78] The Information can be accessed at http://www.nobribes.org.

[79] The information can be accessed at http://www.spai-rslo.org.

[80] For details of the Initiative see 9.159 above.

[81] Available from http://www1.oecd.org/daf/asiacom/stocktaking.htm#stocktaking.

Based on the results of the stocktaking exercise, in 2004, the ADB-OECD Steering Group launched a series of in-depth thematic studies, the first of which examines national systems to curb corruption in public procurement.[82]

6. The Arab States

The UNDP Programme on Governance in the Arab Region (POGAR) was launched in 2000, with the objectives being the promotion and development of good governance practices and related reforms in the Arab states. Rule of law and transparency and accountability are two of the three main aspects of the Programme. The website, www.pogar.org, contains useful resources and information on governance reform in the Arab states, including general and country-specific essays on the themes pertaining to each concept, related publications, empirical studies, statistics, searchable databases, and valuable web links, in addition to information on POGAR's activities and collaborating institutions. **11.96**

E. Anti-Corruption Commissions and Related Institutions

The UN Convention Against Corruption requires State Parties to establish and maintain an anti-corruption body or bodies designed to combat corruption. These are to enjoy the necessary independence and appropriate resources to enable them to carry out their functions effectively and free from any undue influence.[83] In practice, donor pressure, amongst other things, has already seen an increasing number of developing countries introducing anti-corruption agencies, many enjoying powers and responsibilities based on the Hong Kong ICAC model but meeting with varying degrees of success. This section provides an overview of the contribution that such agencies can make in the prevention and investigation of corruption. **11.97**

There are a number of different types of agencies dealing with corruption. Some states have established separate anti-corruption commissions. These have proved particularly popular in Africa where they operate in Botswana (Directorate on Corruption and Economic Crime); Kenya (Kenyan Anti-Corruption Commission); Mauritius (Independent Commission Against Corruption); Malawi (Anti-Corruption Bureau); Nigeria (Independent Corrupt Practices and Other Related Offences Commission); Sierra Leone (Anti-Corruption Commission); Swaziland (Anti-Corruption Commission); Tanzania (Prevention of Corruption Bureau); and Zambia (Anti-Corruption Commission). **11.98**

In the Asia-Pacific region they operate in countries such as Australia (see above); Bangladesh (Anti-Corruption Commission); Brunei (Anti-Corruption **11.99**

[82] Full details are available from http://www.adb.org.

[83] Arts 6 and 36.

Bureau[84]; the Hong Kong Special Administrative Region of China;[85] India (Central Vigilance Commission);[86] Indonesia (Independent Commission of Anti-Corruption); Malaysia (Anti-Corruption Agency); Pakistan (National Accountability Bureau);[87] Singapore (Corrupt Practices Investigation Bureau);[88] and South Korea (Korea Independent Commission Against Corruption). Several Eastern European countries have recently established such commissions, including Bulgaria (Anti-Corruption Coordination Commission); Lithuania (Special Investigations Service); Romania (Independent Agency for Combating Corruption); and Slovenia (Office for the Prevention of Corruption).

11.100 Other countries have preferred to include anti-corruption as a specific function of an office of the ombudsman or human rights commission: for example Ghana (Commission for Human Rights and Administrative Justice); Namibia (Office of the Ombudsman); Papua New Guinea (Office of the Ombudsman); The Philippines (Office of the Ombudsman); South Africa (Public Protector); Uganda (Inspector-General of Government); and Vanuatu (Office of the Ombudsman). Yet others have a specialist unit established within an existing law enforcement agency that deals with corruption-related cases, such as a Serious Fraud Office.

1. An Integrated Body?

11.101 For many developing countries, in particular, the issue of whether or not to establish a separate anti-corruption agency is a very real one. Although national circumstances may dictate the most appropriate or politically acceptable institutional structure, there are a number of factors which lend support for an integrated approach. First, administrative costs are likely to be reduced. Secondly, focusing attention on a single body can raise its public profile and better counter executive attempts to weaken or undermine its operation. In particular, it cannot be assumed that government is fully committed to the establishment of a powerful and effective national institution and one way to dissipate its strength is to ensure that its functions are fragmented. Thirdly, expertise can be concentrated in a single institution. Finally, it avoids both uncertainty as to which institution or institutions have jurisdiction and the possible duplication of powers and work.

11.102 Even so, in reality each of these institutions has a distinct function: that of a human rights commission is to promote and protect human rights; that of an office of the ombudsman is to promote administrative justice in the public

[84] See http://www.anti-corruption.gov.bn.

[85] See http://www.icac.org.hk.

[86] See http://cvc.nic.in.

[87] See http://www.nab.gov.pk.

[88] See http://www.cpib.gov.sg.

sector, with a key to success being the need to gain the support of both the public and public officials. However, an agency that is charged with investigating (and prosecuting) public officials is more likely to be regarded with suspicion rather than being trusted and, arguably, is thus better left as a separate institution.

2. Role and Powers of Anti-Corruption Agencies

The role of anti-corruption agencies is reflected in the three-pronged approach of the Hong Kong ICAC that involves investigation, prevention, and community education. However, the remit of such institutions varies considerably and two examples neatly illustrate the point. **11.103**

The functions of the former Kenya Anti-Corruption Commission were: **11.104**

- to take necessary measures for the prevention of corruption in the public, parastatal, and private sectors;
- to investigate and, subject to the directions of the Attorney-General, to prosecute for offences under this Act and other offences involving corrupt transactions;
- to advise the Government and the parastatal organizations on ways and means of preventing corruption;
- to inquire into and investigate the extent of the liability of any public officer in the loss of any public funds and to institute civil proceedings against the officer and any other person involved in the transaction which resulted in the loss, for the recovery of such loss;
- to investigate any conduct of a public officer which is connected with or conducive to corrupt practices and to make suitable recommendation thereon;
- to undertake such further or other investigations as may be directed by the Attorney-General; and
- to enlist members of the public in fighting corruption by the use of education and outreach programmes.

An example of a commission with a much narrower remit is that of the former Anti-Corruption Commission of Western Australia whose functions were as follows:[89] **11.105**

(1) The functions of the Commission are—
  (a) to receive or initiate allegations of corrupt conduct, criminal conduct, criminal involvement or serious improper conduct about—
    (i) police officers; and
    (ii) other public officers;

[89] Anti-Corruption Commission Act 1988, s 12 (as amended).

(b) to consider whether further action is needed in relation to an allegation and, if so, by whom that further action should be carried out;
(c) to carry out further action in relation to allegations itself, if it is appropriate for it to do so, or to refer allegations to other authorities so that they can carry out further action;
(d) to furnish reports and make recommendations on the outcome of further action taken in relation to allegations;
(e) to furnish general reports and make general recommendations about matters relating to its functions;
(f) to consult, co-operate and exchange information with independent agencies, appropriate authorities and—
  (i) the Commissioner of the Australian Federal Police;
  (ii) the Commissioner (however designated) of the police force of another State or a Territory;
  (iii) the Chairman of the National Crime Authority established by the National Crime Authority Act 1984 of the Commonwealth; and
  (iv) any authority or body of this State, the Commonwealth, another State or a Territory that is authorised to conduct inquiries or investigations in relation to conduct in the nature of corrupt conduct, criminal conduct, criminal involvement or serious improper conduct and is declared by the Minister to be an authority or body to which this paragraph applies;
(g) to assemble evidence obtained in the course of its functions and—
  (i) furnish to an independent agency or an appropriate authority, evidence which may be admissible in the prosecution of a person for a criminal offence against a written law or which may otherwise be relevant to the functions of the agency or authority; and
  (ii) furnish to the Attorney General or a suitable authority of another State, a Territory, the Commonwealth or another country, evidence which may be admissible in the prosecution of a person for a criminal offence against a law of the jurisdiction concerned or which may otherwise be relevant to that jurisdiction;
(h) to disseminate information to the public about matters relating to its functions; and
  (i) to do anything else that it is required or authorised to do under this Act or any other written law.

Yet whatever their remit, experience has shown that for such agencies to be effective, a series of six key 'building blocks' are required:

i. Firm legal foundation

11.106 An anti-corruption agency must enjoy a legal framework that explicitly protects its independence and must be supported by an independent judiciary committed to the rule of law. Entrenching it in the national constitution is the ideal, as this provides a measure of protection against any attempt to weaken it or even to legislate it out of existence. If this is not done, establishing it through an Act of Parliament is acceptable, although this makes the agency more susceptible to political interference through amendments to its founding statute.

ii. Independence

Ideally such an agency should enjoy support from a government that is fully committed to its success and which has provided it with sufficient resources and legal powers. Yet there is no guarantee of such support and the effectiveness of an anti-corruption agency can be hampered, deliberately or otherwise, by a lack of independence, funding constraints, and capacity limitations.[90] This reflects the reality that a government may wish to give the impression that it is committed to tackling corruption whilst lacking the political will to ensure that the agency is effective. In fact the commitment may be confined to exposing the corruption of previous regimes—not necessarily a bad thing in itself but one that must go hand in hand with a commitment to tackling corruption within the current administration. **11.107**

Fundamental to establishing an independent body is the need to provide for a demonstrably fair and open appointment procedure. This is essentially a confidence-building exercise for government, citizens, civil society, and donors alike in the integrity, independence, and competence of the agency. Furthermore, the agency must be separate from the public service and enjoy autonomy in its operations. It follows that care must be taken when dealing with an agency where there is apparently undue executive influence over the appointment process or an agency that is directly responsible to the head of state/government. **11.108**

There is no consensus as to the qualifications needed for appointment to an anti-corruption agency. In some cases legal qualifications or experience in the civil service is required.[91] However, the appointment of a serving judge to head such a body has been held invalid as being in contravention of the separation of powers.[92] It is questionable whether specific qualifications for appointment are **11.109**

[90] See P Dale, 'Southern Africa' in R Hodess (ed) *Global Corruption Report 2001* (Berlin: Transparency International, 2001) 58–59. See generally C Kunaka, N Mashumba, and P Matsheza, *The SADC Protocol Against Corruption*, Human Rights Research and Documentation Trust of Southern Africa, Harare, 2002.

[91] eg in Uganda the Inspector-General of Government must have served in a discipline relevant to the work of the office for not less than 7 years.

[92] *South African Association of Personal Injury Lawyers v Heath and ors* [2001] 4 LRC 99. This did not affect the operation of the Commission and a later statute remedied the problem. See also J Sarkin, 'Evaluating the Constitutional Court's decision in *Heath* in the context of crime and corruption in South Africa' (2002) 118(4) *South African Law Journal* 747. cf Kenya, where the High Court ruled the Anti-Corruption Commission unconstitutional in similar circumstances: see *Gachiengo and Kahura v Republic* (unreported, 2000), available at http://www.lawafrica.com.

either necessary or desirable. Certainly, ready access to legal expertise within the institution is essential, but the real need is to appoint demonstrably independent, able persons who possess public credibility.

iii. Security of tenure for commissioners

11.110 By the very nature of the work, an anti-corruption agency may well gain access to politically and commercially sensitive information and at the same time come into conflict with powerful political and economic interests. Thus it is vital that commissioners enjoy security of tenure. This can be achieved, for example, by affording them the same status as a senior judge: thus removal can only be in accordance with the formal constitutional procedure.

iv. Adequate funding and resources

11.111 Operational independence is a prerequisite for an anti-corruption agency. This includes enjoying financial autonomy and access to adequate and secure funding so as to retain appropriate staffing levels, operational structure, premises, and resources.

11.112 In practice, donor support has played a major part in funding the establishment and operation of anti-corruption agencies in many developing countries. Such funding may well raise concerns, particularly on the part of government, over its possible effect on the independence of the recipient institution. Equally, donor expectations for such agencies may be unrealistic given the political and economic realities of the country. Indeed one recent study on Africa has concluded that anti-corruption commissions have been donor led in developing their priorities and plans, with funding going to front-line activities and a resultant neglect of organizational infrastructure.[93]

v. Adequate investigative powers

11.113 Anti-corruption commissions usually investigate allegations of corruption as a result of receiving information or complaints. Here a key test for judging political support for an agency is whether it is able to investigate allegations against officials at the highest levels of government and the military.

11.114 A key feature of most anti-corruption agencies is their extensive investigative powers. These normally include the power of a court to: (a) issue summons or other orders requiring any person to appear before it; (b) compel any person to answer questions in connection with an investigation; (c) hold a formal public hearing into the allegation; (d) compel the production of relevant documents or records; and (e) enter and search buildings and compel the giving of

[93] A Doig, *et al*, 'Measuring "success" in five African Anti-Corruption Commissions' U4, 2005, available at http://www.u4.no/document/showdoc.cfm?id = 100.

information.[94] In this connection many agencies have the power to commit for contempt for failure to comply with their orders. Other common powers are the setting of specific time limits within which agencies are required to respond and the seizure of travel documents.

Given the common difficulty of procuring evidence in corruption cases, it is also usual for anti-corruption commissions to develop witness protection programmes. In some cases this enables witnesses to change their identities and relocate. **11.115**

The power to prosecute corruption by an anti-corruption agency varies from state to state. In common law countries, such powers are often subject to the consent of the Attorney-General. Given the often political nature of the office, this is a position that can cause difficulties. Even where this is not the case, the role of the Director of Public Prosecutions can be decisive in the decision whether or not to prosecute and, again, much depends upon the independence of the office holder. **11.116**

vi. Accountability of an anti-corruption agency

Protecting the independence of an anti-corruption agency does not mean insulating it from regular review (although not *supervision*) of its performance. This is needed in order to maintain both public confidence in the institution, which is an absolute prerequisite for an effective body, and high operational standards. Indeed, it should serve as a vehicle to prevent the agency itself becoming corrupt. **11.117**

[94] As noted above, the powers of anti-corruption commissions have been challenged in a number of cases. To these may be added the important decision of the Supreme Court of Pakistan regarding the powers of the National Accountability Bureau: see *Khan Asfandyar Wali and ors v Federation of Pakistan and ors* PLD 2001 SC 607.

12

THE ROLE OF CIVIL SOCIETY ORGANISATIONS IN COMBATING CORRUPTION

There are numerous civil society organizations (CSOs) operating at the international, regional, and national levels that are involved in an array of anti-corruption issues. This short chapter provides an overview of the work of some of the major CSOs in this area, focusing particularly upon the assistance and information that they can provide for legal practitioners in both the government and private sector, policy-makers, parliamentarians, donors, and the like. A background note on some of these key organizations is included at the end of the chapter. **12.01**

A. Promoting Standard Setting in the Corporate Sector

Civil society organizations are at the forefront in the development of principles of good practice, particularly in the corporate sector. This reflects the increasing expectation that enterprises will develop new policies or review existing ones **12.02** aimed at combating corruption. Certainly, global investors are increasingly concerned about the potential reputation and litigation risks to which a company exposes itself by having insufficient systems to address and avoid instances of bribery and corruption within its operations and this is reinforced by increased public expectations of accountability and probity in the corporate sector. This has led to a number of initiatives spearheaded by CSOs designed to assist the corporate sector to address this issue.

12.03 In 2002, the Business Principles for Countering Bribery were launched. These were developed by Transparency International (TI) and Social Accountability International in partnership with a Steering Committee drawn from international companies (including General Electric, Norsk Hydro, Rio Tinto, and Shell), academia, trade unions and other CSOs. The two principal tenets of the Business Principles are that:

- The enterprise shall prohibit bribery in any form whether direct or indirect;
- The enterprise shall commit to the implementation of a programme to counter bribery.[1]

12.04 The aims of the Business Principles are 'to provide a framework for good business practices and risk management strategies for countering bribery'. In doing so, the intention is to assist enterprises to '(a) eliminate bribery; (b) demonstrate their commitment to countering bribery; and (c) make a positive contribution to improving business standards of integrity, transparency and accountability wherever they operate'.[2] The Principles therefore represent a practical tool to which enterprises can look for a comprehensive reference to good practice to counter bribery and which can be used as a starting point for developing their own anti-bribery systems or as a benchmark.[3] TI has also produced a Guidance Document to complement the Guidelines.[4]

12.05 In July 2005, the TI Six-Step Implementation Process was launched and is designed to support the Business Principles for Countering Bribery.[5] It offers practical assistance on establishing a corporate anti-corruption programme and is designed particularly for companies that have no systematic anti-bribery policy or process for countering bribery. However, it can also be of use for

[1] The working definition adopted for the purposes of the Business Principles cover abuse of office, breach of trust, or illegal acts by an employee or a third party on behalf of the enterprise.

[2] Business Principles section 3.

[3] See, eg, the principles relating to the use of representatives/agents discussed in 10.150 above.

[4] The full text of the Guidelines and the Guidance Document are available on the TI website, http://www.transparency.org.

[5] TI 'Business Principles for Countering Bribery: TI Six-Step Process: A practical guide for companies implementing anti-bribery policies and programmes' 2005, available at http://www.transparency.org.

companies that already have elements of a system in place allowing them to enter the TI Six-Step Process at a stage of their choice.[6] The TI Six-Step Process is flexible and can be modified to take into account the size of a company and its ability to complete the steps within the suggested timeframe.

Another important initiative was launched in July 2005 with the publication of the FTSE4Good criteria for Countering Bribery & Corruption. FTSE4Good, a social responsibility index, draws substantially on the advice of TI in developing the criteria and uses the Business Principles for Countering Bribery as a key reference code. The FTSE4Good criteria seek to encourage those 'high impact companies' who have not yet achieved best practice standards in the management of bribery and corruption to take action and put into place quality management systems to address these issues. This recognizes the fact that there are certain business activities within the high-risk sectors that are more likely to be subject to the potential for bribery. These are generally considered to be those with a direct interface with government activities (for example construction projects, hospitals, schools, etc where large tenders are involved). For the purposes of the criteria, any companies that are involved in any way with government/public contracts, or which must have a government licence to operate their businesses (for example a gaming licence or mining exploration), are considered to be at high risk of involvement in bribery. Once applied, the new criteria will ensure that all FTSE4Good constituent companies that are assessed as having a higher potential risk of exposure to bribery and corrupt practices, are managing these risks appropriately.[7] **12.06**

B. Providing Access to Legal Materials

1. Legislation and Case Law

Whilst much material is readily available from commercial publishers, the service provided by the World Legal Information Institute (WorldLII) (www.worldlii.org) is noteworthy. WorldLII is a free, independent, and non-profit making global legal research facility developed collaboratively by the **12.07**

[6] The Six-Step Process comprises: Step 1: Decide on a no-bribes policy and on implementing a programme; Step 2: Plan the implementation; Step 3: Develop the programme content; Step 4: Implement the programme; Step 5: Monitor; Step 6: Evaluate the Programme.

[7] See further http://www.ftse.com. See also the Partnering Against Corruption Initiative led by the World Economic Forum, TI, and the Basle Institute of Governance, which has developed the 'Partnering against Corruption Principles for Countering Bribery': see http://www.weforum.org. An example of the principles regarding the use of representatives/agent is discussed in 10.151 above.

following Legal Information Institutes:

- Australasian Legal Information Institute (AustLII) (www.austlii.edu.au);
- British and Irish Legal Information Institute (BAILII) (www.bailii.org);
- Canadian Legal Information Institute (CanLII) (www.canlii.org);
- Commonwealth Legal Information Institute (CommonLII) (www.commonlii.org);
- Hong Kong Legal Information Institute (HKLII) (www.hklii.org);
- Legal Information Institute (LII) (www.cornell.edu);
- Pacific Islands Legal Information Institute (PacLII) (www.paclii.org);
- Southern African Legal Information Institute (SALII) (www.saflii.org).

12.08 WorldLII comprises three main facilities, Databases, Catalog, and Websearch, and provides a single search facility for databases located on the other Legal Information Institutes websites. These include databases of decisions of international courts and tribunals, databases from a number of Asian countries, and databases from South Africa. Over 270 databases from forty-eight jurisdictions in twenty countries are included in the initial release of WorldLII. Databases of case law, legislation, treaties, law reform reports, law journals, and other materials are included. These are particularly helpful in locating comparative materials on corruption and bribery, as well as legislation that may not be readily available elsewhere.

12.09 A range of cases and materials on corruption from around the common law world can be found in the *Corruption Case Law Reporter*. This is a quarterly series published under the auspices of Tiri and is supported by the Commonwealth Legal Education Association and the Commonwealth Secretariat. The reports are freely available at http://www.tiri.org/implementation/case-law-project.html.

2. Articles and Research Materials

12.10 Several CSOs provide access to a wide range of articles and research materials relating to corruption. These include the TI Corruption Online Research & Information System (CORIS) which includes access to the TI Source Book, Global Corruption Report and Anti-Corruption Toolkit (see www.coriweb.org). The annual TI Global Corruption Report, in particular, provides an invaluable analysis of current corruption issues, including trends and regional perspectives, an analysis of global issues relating to corruption, and comparative research on corruption from a range of sources—international organisations, CSOs, and the private sector, as well as a number of academic contributions.

12.11 Other organizations, such as Probe International and the U4 Anti-Corruption Resource Centre, also provide access to a range of other materials. Information on these is provided below.

C. Involvement in the Development of International and Regional Anti-Corruption Instruments

The accumulated expertise of CSOs, has led to their active involvement in the development of several anti-corruption instruments, including the United Nations Convention Against Corruption and the AU Convention. In the case of the SADC Protocol Against Corruption,[8] for instance, the Human Rights Trust of Southern Africa (SAHRIT) essentially spearheaded its development by organizing a series of roundtables of representatives from the SADC region to raise awareness of the problems of corruption in the region and to press for a regional initiative to address the problem. This led to SADC requesting SAHRIT to facilitate the development and adoption of the Protocol by bringing together experts from six SADC countries to develop a draft document that was later adopted by the SADC Heads of State and Government in 2001.[9] In addition, CSOs continue to press for the ratification and implementation of international and regional anti-corruption instruments. **12.12**

D. Providing Education and Training

The need to provide education and training in order to prevent and combat corruption is an accepted part of any anti-corruption effort. This is epitomized by Article 60 of UNCAC which provides that 'Each State Party shall, to the extent necessary, initiate, develop or improve specific training programmes for its personnel responsible for preventing and combating corruption'. Much has already been done in this context with anti-corruption training materials being developed by TI, the United Nations, and the World Bank. **12.13**

The development of the Public Integrity Education Network (PIEN) takes the matter still further. PIEN is a network of universities brought together by Tiri (the Governance-Access-Learning Network) and the Center for Policy Studies at the Central European University. The development of the Network is based on the recognition that 'a critical ingredient to the success and sustainability of the anti-corruption movement is the integration of public and organisational integrity and anti-corruption courses into the curriculum of major universities and civil service training institutions'. This process of integration has played an important part in the 'mainstreaming' of the human rights and environmental movements. Major universities in Europe and North America have, in recent years, begun teaching courses on corruption and development. Executive **12.14**

[8] The Protocol is discussed at paras 8.64ff.

[9] See C Kunaka, N Mashumba, and P Matsheza, *The SADC Protocol Against Corruption: A Regional Framework to Combat Corruption* Human Rights Trust of Southern Africa, 2002, Ch 4.

training programmes for senior civil servants and officials of international agencies are now being developed in a wide range of countries. Major corporations have also introduced training and compliance programmes. What is missing from these efforts is:

(i) Access to these courses for the overwhelming majority of young to mid-career professionals in developing and transition countries in particular—those regions where such programmes are most urgently needed;
(ii) The considerable benefits that accrue from sharing case studies, syllabi, teaching methods, etc. No forum or Network currently exists that brings these institutions together; and
(iii) Critical and independent case studies and direct access to the wide range of good practice that is emerging around the world in recent years.[10]

12.15 The basic objective of the Network is to develop, and facilitate the introduction of, effective, policy-oriented training and teaching programmes on corruption control and organizational integrity at universities around the world. Of particular importance is the still-unfulfilled need to develop a course and materials on combating corruption aimed at law schools, professional legal training courses, and continuing legal education. PIEN also aims to build regional research networks that will offer frameworks for joint research projects and facilitate the compilation of critical and independent case studies of reforms.

12.16 Tiri has developed a *Corruption Prosecutor's Handbook* that is designed to assist in the training of investigators and prosecutors of corruption cases. Developed for the United Nation's Global Programme Against Corruption in a network involving the International Association of Prosecutors, the Handbook is available from the United Nations Office of Drugs and Crime, in Vienna.

E. Seeking to Quantify Corruption

12.17 Assumptions that corruption is non-quantifiable have changed markedly in recent years. Much of this change is due to the development of TI's *Corruption Perception Index* (CPI) and *Bribe Payers Index*. Given the fact that, by its very nature, hard data on actual levels of corruption are unavailable, the CPI seeks to provide a composite view of corruption in an individual country largely from the perspective of decision-makers in the areas of trade and investment. In doing so it aims to 'create change towards a world free of corruption'.[11] The CPI annually ranks countries in terms of experts' perception of corruption. As regards the 2004 Index, this revealed that 106 out of 146 countries scored less than 5 against a clean score of 10, whilst sixty countries scored less than

[10] Tiri, 'Aims of PIEN', Available at http://www.tiri.org.
[11] From TI's mission statement.

3 out of 10, indicating rampant corruption. Corruption was perceived to be most acute in Bangladesh, Haiti, Nigeria, Chad, Myanmar, Azerbaijan, and Paraguay, all of which have a score of less than 2. Angola, Azerbaijan, Chad, Ecuador, Indonesia, Iran, Iraq, Kazakhstan, Libya, Nigeria, Russia, Sudan, Venezuela, and Yemen also all had extremely low scores. Countries with a score higher than 9, ie those with very low levels of perceived corruption, were predominantly Western countries, namely Finland, New Zealand, Denmark, Iceland, Singapore, Sweden, and Switzerland.

In practice, the CPI is widely used as a basis for assessing the record of a country as regards corruption and provides a mechanism for pressurizing governments into taking measures that seek to reduce the level of corruption. As Galtung has put it 'it has spurred a determination to shed the label of being "one of the world's most corrupt countries" '.[12] Whilst the influence of the CPI on changing perceptions and policies is not in doubt, the fact is that the Index concentrates on bribees (almost invariably developing countries) whilst neglecting the bribers and their associates. The TI *Bribe Payers Index* (BPI) seeks to address this point by measuring the supply side of corruption. First published in 1999, the 2002 BPI is based on surveys conducted in: Argentina, Brazil, Colombia, Hungary, India, Indonesia, Mexico, Morocco, Nigeria, the Philippines, Poland, Russia, South Africa, South Korea, and Thailand—which are among the largest involved in trade and investment with multinational firms. The questions related to the propensity of companies from twenty-one leading exporting countries to pay bribes to senior public officials in the surveyed emerging market countries. The survey placed the United Kingdom as the eighth least likely country to pay or offer bribes to win or retain business in these countries. Not unexpectedly, the business sectors most susceptible to bribery were found to be public works/construction, followed by arms/defence, and oil and gas. Perhaps the next challenge is to develop a mechanism that measures or ranks the willingness of countries to provide a safe haven for the proceeds of corruption.[13] **12.18**

F. Scrutinizing and Contributing to the Development of Anti-Corruption Laws and Procedures

An example of the work of CSOs here concerns the development by the UK Export Credits Guarantee Department (ECGD) of its anti-bribery and corruption procedures. The ECGD is a Department of State that is governed by **12.19**

[12] Galtung, 'Measuring the Immeasurable: Boundaries and Functions of (Macro) Corruption Indices' in F Galtung and C Sampford (eds) *Measuring Corruption* (Aldershot: Ashgate, 2005), p 1.

[13] See, eg, the views of Galtung (n 12 above).

the Export and Investment Guarantees Act 1991. It provides a range of assistance to UK businesses trading overseas, especially in developing countries. In particular it provides insurance to protect exporters who do not receive the contractual payments owing to them. It also provides guarantees to banks, in particular to secure finance provided to exporting businesses in connection with overseas projects. The ECGD normally guarantees the bank loan to the exporter so that, if the business defaults, the ECGD pays the bank. In doing so, it is the policy of the UK government that the ECGD should seek to deter corrupt practices in international contracts.

12.20 In 2000, anti-bribery and corruption procedures were introduced designed to minimize the chances of the ECGD supporting corrupt activity with taxpayers' money. These were periodically revised. In May 2004, one such revision took place following which representations were made to the ECGD from some exporters and banks to the effect that they could not comply with the new provisions. This led to the Revised ECGD Procedures to Combat Bribery and Corruption being issued on 5 November 2004 and introduced in December 2004.

12.21 The response of The Corner House and Transparency International to the revised document neatly illustrates the oversight role that CSOs can play in such matters. Following publication of the revised Guidelines, The Corner House instituted proceedings against the Secretary of State for Trade and Industry, claiming that the December 2004 revisions had been undertaken without consulting The Corner House or other interested CSOs—although the ECGD had 'carried out extensive and detailed consultation with its corporate customers and their representatives', who had lobbied the ECGD intensively on the rules. It was argued that the one-sided nature of the consultation led to a result biased in favour of the ECGD's commercial customers. The Corner House's claim was that the ECGD's failure to consult with other interested organisations 'was a serious breach of basic public law standards of fairness and the ECGD's own published consultation policy'. On 13 January 2005, just as a two-day hearing in the High Court was to begin, the UK government settled out of court. It agreed to instigate a full public consultation on its changes to its anti-corruption rules, and to pay The Corner House's legal costs. It also agreed to make public some 380 pages of documents relating to the court case.[14] Particularly significant for CSOs was the fact that The Corner House was awarded an

[14] The documents themselves can be found at http://www.ecgd.gov.uk/20050121_webdocs_lowres.pdf. These consist largely of correspondence between three British companies (Airbus, BAe Systems, and Rolls Royce) and the Confederation of British Industry with the ECGD. They include the initial complaints these exporters made to the ECGD about the department's rules aimed at reducing corruption and the subsequent detailed exchanges and negotiations on the revisions that the exporters were seeking.

unprecedented full 'protective costs order' for a judicial review.[15] This may well encourage others to bring similar types of cases.

This was followed in June 2005, by TI (UK) making a detailed submission on the December 2004 amendments following the invitation of the UK Government to comment thereon. The summary response of TI (UK) was that the changes 'materially increase the risk that (a) bribery will occur in relation to projects covered by an ECGD guarantee; (b) ECGD will suffer unnecessary loss; and (c) ECGD managers may be prosecuted for aiding and abetting bribery'. It concluded that the December changes did not 'have the effect of ensuring that, so far as practicable, taxpayers' money is not used to support transactions tainted with bribery and/or corruption'.[16] **12.22**

To complement the CPI, BPI, and Global Corruption Barometer,[17] TI has also developed the concept of the National Integrity System (NIS). The NIS is the sum total of the laws, institutions, and practices in a country that maintain the accountability and integrity of public, private, and the civil society organizations. The NIS is concerned with combating corruption as part of the larger struggle against misconduct and misappropriation, and with creating an efficient and effective government working in the public interest, supported by a vital, transparent civil society and private sector. The NIS country study report includes an executive summary and a country overview. In more recent country studies, this is followed by a corruption profile, assessing the nature and extent of corruption in that country. The country study report then covers core laws, rules, and practices that contribute to the strength of National Integrity Systems. The report then addresses the anti-corruption activities in the country in the last five to ten years, including the government's anti-corruption strategy (where such a strategy exists); provides a review of the anti-corruption activities of donors, including an evaluation of the coordination of these activities; and offers suggestions for future research and donor action, areas within the NIS that the study author believes are in greatest need of increased attention. A final section of the report addresses the effectiveness of the NIS in that country, particularly the way the NIS pillars interact and the strength of the anti-corruption efforts undertaken in the country. Each report ends with a discussion of policy priorities and recommendations, based on the findings of the study.[18] **12.23**

[15] See *R (on the application of Corner House Research) v Secretary of State for Trade and Industry* [2005] EWCA Civ 192 (1 March 2005). See also 'Corner House Double Victory on UK Government Department's Anti-Bribery Rules and Public Interest Litigation' 2005, The Corner House, available at http://www.thecornerhouse.org.uk.

[16] Transparency International (UK) 'Consultation on Changes to ECGD's Anti-Bribery and Corruption Procedures Introduced in December 2004: TI(UK)'s Submission' June 2005, 2.

[17] This is a survey that assesses general public attitudes towards and experience of corruption is selected countries worldwide.

[18] See further http://www.transparency.org.

G. A Note on Selected Anti-Corruption Organizations

12.24 This section provides a brief overview of the background and work of a number of leading anti-corruption CSOs noted in this chapter.

1. Transparency International

12.25 Launched in 1993, Transparency International is 'devoted to combating corruption by bringing civil society, business, and governments together in a powerful global coalition'. Its 'Vision Statement' demands 'a world in which government, politics, business, civil society and the daily lives of people are free of corruption' and seven core values guide its work: transparency, accountability, integrity, solidarity, courage, justice, and democracy. The scope and importance of its work is reflected not only in this chapter, but also throughout the book. A considerable amount of information, as well as materials, is available from the TI website: at http://www.transparency.org.

2. The Corner House

12.26 Founded in 1997, The Corner House aims to support democratic and community movements for environmental and social justice, in part by carrying out analyses, research, and advocacy. As well as its advocacy work, epitomized by the ECGD case noted earlier, the organization has produced a series of excellent discussion and other papers on a range of corruption issues. These are available at http://www.thecornerhouse.org.uk/subject/corruption.

3. Unicorn

12.27 UNICORN is a 'Global Unions Anti-Corruption Network' whose overall mission is to mobilize workers to share information and coordinate action to combat international bribery. Located within the School of Social Sciences at the University of Cardiff, the organization collects empirical evidence on international bribery and publishes research on related policy issues. 'Cracking Down on Corporate Corruption: The UK' is a current major research project based on the perceived need for trade unions and civil society to work together to hold corporations to account. The project focuses on the public-private interface and tracks incidences of bribery and other (legal) types of corporate corruption, and provides details of legal, administrative, and voluntary measures aimed at deterring and sanctioning corporate corruption in all its forms. The website http://www.againstcorruption.org, contains details of corruption cases involving UK enterprises, reports on key contemporary corruption issues,[19] and provides details of 'whistle-blower' cases.

[19] See, eg, K Drew, 'The OECD Report on the UK's Implementation of the OECD Anti-Bribery Convention: Key Points and Recommendations', 2005, Unicorn, http://www.againstcorruption.org.

4. Tiri—the Governance-Access-Learning Network

The objectives of Tiri are to build and empower networks of professionals, activists, policy-makers, and constitutional office holders with the long-term goal of helping to counter corruption by assisting in the building and remodelling of institutions and practices. At the heart of Tiri's mission lie the core objectives: to improve governance in both public and private institutions; to deepen access; and to increase learning for effective corruption control. Tiri emphasizes the processes and strategies required to attain just, responsive, and open institutions that deliver just and honest government to all citizens. This is reflected, for example, in its work on judicial integrity, and especially in its role in the development of the Judicial Integrity Group. **12.28**

The Judicial Integrity Group is an autonomous entity, (facilitated by Tiri in partnership with the United Nations Office on Drugs and Crime), owned and driven by its members, all of whom are heads of the judiciary in their respective countries. Consistent with the principle of judicial independence, the Group seeks to strengthen the integrity of the judicial system through self-regulation (for example by the application of an effective code of judicial conduct drafted and enforced by the judiciary), and through reform measures, formulated in consultation with court users and other stakeholders, which the judiciary is competent to undertake on its own through the exercise of its own powers (such as oversight and/or disciplining of judges, reorganization of the court registry, reform of trial and appellate procedures, and the training of judicial officers). **12.29**

The Group formulates and promotes principles, standards, and instruments relating to vital aspects of the judicial system (such as independence and accountability) based on its own experience. The Group facilitates critical peer review by senior judges of other countries and other legal systems in a unique, two-way interactive learning process. The Group's Programme Goals are the strengthening of judicial independence, competence, and integrity, thereby strengthening the Rule of Law, protecting human rights, and promoting development and the alleviation of poverty. Its Programme Objectives are to strengthen the rule of law and the independence of the judiciary in sustainable ways by advancing the application and implementation within developing countries and countries in transition of the values identified in the Bangalore Principles. (see 8.88ff and 8.106 above). Other examples of the work of Tiri, noted earlier, are the production of the *Corruption Case Law Reporter* and the *Corruption Prosecutors' Handbook.*[20] **12.30**

5. U4—Utstein Anti-Corruption Resource Centre

U4 is a 'web based knowledge bank' designed to strengthen anti-corruption efforts. The website, http://www.u4.no, contains four main parts: (i) *Themes*: This **12.31**

[20] Full details of the organization and work of Tiri is available at http://www.tiri.org.

section contains reports and research material on a range of corruption issues. These include (a) Public Sector Management—this provides a discussion forum and issues papers on topics such as revenue administration and budget reform; (b) Debarment—this contains a particularly useful study focusing on the effectiveness of a formal debarment (or blacklisting) process as a means to challenge corruption openly, and in particular debarment as a means of reducing levels of corruption in public procurement processes.[21] (ii) *Resources*: This section includes links to a wide range of anti-corruption literature and materials and guides to research papers and best practice provisions. (iii) *Projects*: This section contains information about anti-corruption projects worldwide categorized by agency, area, and keywords. (iv) *Expert Answers*: This is a helpdesk which seeks to answer queries from anti-corruption practitioners.

6. Probe International

12.32 Probe International's Odious Debts website (http://www.odiousdebts.org) contains a range of corruption-related information and materials including a selection of the judgments from the Lesotho Highlands Water Project. It also provides a news service on recent anti-corruption developments from around the world.

12.33 Overall, CSOs are extremely active and influential in the international fight to prevent and combat corruption and, as demonstrated throughout this book, are now indispensable to national and international anti-corruption efforts. They bring with them a unique range and depth of expertise and therefore represent an outstanding resource for practitioners and others.

[21] J Pope, A Doig, and J Moran, 'Debarment as an Anti-Corruption Means: A Review Report' 2004, available at http://www.u4.no/themes/debarment/main.cfm.

APPENDICES

APPENDIX 1

ADB OECD Anti-Corruption Initiative for Asia-Pacific Anti-Corruption Action Plan for Asia and the Pacific

PREAMBLE[1]

We, governments of the Asia-Pacific region, building on objectives identified at the Manila Conference in October 1999 and subsequently at the Seoul Conference in December 2000;

Convinced that corruption is a widespread phenomenon which undermines good governance, erodes the rule of law, hampers economic growth and efforts for poverty reduction and distorts competitive conditions in business transactions;

Acknowledging that corruption raises serious moral and political concerns and that fighting corruption is a complex undertaking and requires the involvement of all elements of society;

Considering that regional co-operation is critical to the effective fight against corruption;

Recognizing that national anti-corruption measures can benefit from existing relevant regional and international instruments and good practices such as those developed by the countries in the region, the Asian Development Bank (ADB), the Asia-Pacific Economic Co-operation (APEC), the Financial Action Task Force on Money Laundering (FATF), the Organisation for Economic Co-operation and Development (OECD), the Pacific Basin Economic Council (PBEC), the United Nations and the World Trade Organisation (WTO).[2]

Concur, as governments of the region, in taking concrete and meaningful priority steps to deter, prevent and combat corruption at all levels, without prejudice to existing international commitments and in accordance with our jurisdictional and other basic legal principles;

Welcome the pledge of representatives of the civil society and the business sector to promote integrity in business and in civil society activities and to support the governments of the region in their anti-corruption effort;

Welcome the pledge made by donor countries and international organisations from outside and within the region to support the countries of the region in their fight against corruption through technical co-operation programmes.

---

[1] The Action Plan, together with its implementation plan, is a legally non-binding document which contains a number of principles and standards towards policy reform which interested governments of the region politically commit to implement on a voluntary basis.

[2] In particular: the 40 Recommendations of the FATF as supported by the Asia/Pacific Group on Money Laundering, the Anti-Corruption Policy of the ADB, the APEC Public Procurement Principles, the Basel Capital Accord of the Basel Committee on Banking Supervision, the OECD Convention on Combating Bribery of Foreign Public Officials in International Business Transactions and the Revised Recommendation, the OECD Council Recommendation on Improving Ethical Conduct in the Public Service, the OECD Principles on Corporate Governance, the PBEC Charter on Standards for Transactions between Business and Government, the United Nations Convention on Transnational Organised Crime and the WTO Agreement on Government Procurement.

Pillars of Action

In order to meet the above objectives, participating governments in the region endeavour to take concrete steps under the following three pillars of action with the support, as appropriate, of ADB, OECD and other donor organisations and countries:

Pillar 1—Developing effective and transparent systems for public service

Integrity in Public Service

Establish systems of government hiring of public officials that assure openness, equity and efficiency and promote hiring of individuals of the highest levels of competence and integrity through:

- Development of systems for compensation adequate to sustain appropriate livelihood and according to the level of the economy of the country in question;
- Development of systems for transparent hiring and promotion to help avoid abuses of patronage, nepotism and favouritism, help foster the creation of an independent civil service, and help promote a proper balance between political and career appointments;
- Development of systems to provide appropriate oversight of discretionary decisions and of personnel with authority to make discretionary decisions;
- Development of personnel systems that include regular and timely rotation of assignments to reduce insularity that would foster corruption;

Establish ethical and administrative codes of conduct that proscribe conflicts of interest, ensure the proper use of public resources, and promote the highest levels of professionalism and integrity through:

- Prohibitions or restrictions governing conflicts of interest;
- Systems to promote transparency through disclosure and/or monitoring of, for example, personal assets and liabilities;
- Sound administration systems which ensure that contacts between government officials and business services users, notably in the area of taxation, customs and other corruption-prone areas, are free from undue and improper influence.
- Promotion of codes of conduct taking due account of the existing relevant international standards as well as each country's traditional cultural standards, and regular education, training and supervision of officials to ensure proper understanding of their responsibilities;
- Measures which ensure that officials report acts of corruption and which protect the safety and professional status of those who do.

Accountability and Transparency

Safeguard accountability of public service through effective legal frameworks, management practices and auditing procedures through:

- Measures and systems to promote fiscal transparency;
- Adoption of existing relevant international standards and practices for regulation and supervision of financial institutions;
- Appropriate auditing procedures applicable to public administration and the public sector, and measures and systems to provide timely public reporting on performance and decision making;
- Appropriate transparent procedures for public procurement that promote fair competition and deter corrupt activity, and adequate simplified administration procedures.
- Enhancing institutions for public scrutiny and oversight;
- Systems for information availability including on issues such as application processing procedures, funding of political parties and electoral campaigns and expenditure;
- Simplification of the regulatory environment by abolishing overlapping, ambiguous or excessive regulations that burden business.

Pillar 2—Strengthening Anti-Bribery Actions and Promoting Integrity in Business Operations

Effective Prevention, Investigation and Prosecution

Take effective measures to actively combat bribery by:

- Ensuring the existence of legislation with dissuasive sanctions which effectively and actively combat the offence of bribery of public officials;
- Ensuring the existence and effective enforcement of anti-money laundering legislation that provide for substantial criminal penalties for the laundering of the proceeds of corruption and crime consistent with the law of each country;
- Ensuring the existence and enforcement of rules to ensure that bribery offences are thoroughly investigated and prosecuted by competent authorities; these authorities should be empowered to order that bank, financial or commercial records be made available or be seized and that bank secrecy be lifted.
- Strengthening of investigative and prosecutorial capacities by fostering inter-agency co-operation, by ensuring that investigation and prosecution are free from improper influence and have effective means for gathering evidence, by protecting those persons helping the authorities in combating corruption, and by providing appropriate training and financial resources.
- Strengthening bi- and multilateral co-operation in investigations and other legal proceedings by developing systems which—in accordance with domestic legislation—enhance (i) effective exchange of information and evidence, (ii) extradition where expedient, and (iii) co-operation in searching and discovering of forfeitable assets as well as prompt international seizure and repatriation of these forfeitable assets.

Corporate Responsibility and Accountability

Take effective measures to promote corporate responsibility and accountability on the basis of existing relevant international standards through:

- Promotion of good corporate governance which would provide for adequate internal company controls such as codes of conduct, the establishment of channels for communication, the protection of employees reporting corruption, and staff training;
- The existence and the effective enforcement of legislation to eliminate any indirect support of bribery such as tax deductibility of bribes;
- The existence and thorough implementation of legislation requiring transparent company accounts and providing for effective, proportionate and dissuasive penalties for omissions and falsifications for the purpose of bribing a public official, or hiding such bribery, in respect of the books, records, accounts and financial statements of companies;
- Review of laws and regulations governing public licenses, government procurement contracts or other public undertakings, so that access to public sector contracts could be denied as a sanction for bribery of public officials.

Pillar 3—Supporting Active Public Involvement

Public discussion of corruption

Take effective measures to encourage public discussion of the issue of corruption through:

- Initiation of public awareness campaigns at different levels;
- Support of non-governmental organisations that promote integrity and combat corruption by, for example, raising awareness of corruption and its costs, mobilising citizen support for clean government, and documenting and reporting cases of corruption;
- Preparation and/or implementation of education programs aimed at creating an anti-corruption culture.

Access to information

Ensure that the general public and the media have freedom to receive and impart public information and in particular information on corruption matters in accordance with domestic law and in a manner that would not compromise the operational effectiveness of the administration or, in any other way, be detrimental to the interest of governmental agencies and individuals, through:

- Establishment of public reporting requirements for justice and other governmental agencies that include disclosure about efforts to promote integrity and accountability and combat corruption;
- Implementation of measures providing for a meaningful public right of access to appropriate information.

Public participation

Encourage public participation in anti-corruption activities, in particular through:

- Co-operative relationships with civil society groups such as chambers of commerce, professional associations, NGOs, labor unions, housing associations, the media, and other organisations;
- Protection of whistleblowers;
- Involvement of NGOs in monitoring of public sector programmes and activities.

Implementation

In order to implement these three pillars of action, participating governments of the region concur with the attached Implementation Plan and will endeavour to comply with its terms.

Participating governments of the region further commit to widely publicise the Action Plan throughout government agencies and the media and, in the framework of the Steering Group Meetings, to meet and to assess progress in the implementation of the actions contained in the Action Plan.

Implementation Plan

1 Introduction

The Action Plan contains legally non-binding principles and standards towards policy reform which participating governments of the Asia-Pacific region (hereinafter: participating governments) voluntarily commit to implement in order to combat corruption and bribery in a co-ordinated and comprehensive manner and thus contribute to development, economic growth and social stability. Although the Action Plan describes policy objectives that are currently relevant to the fight against corruption in Asia and the Pacific, it remains open to ideas and partners. Updates of the Action Plan will be the responsibility of the Steering Group.

This section describes the implementation of the Action Plan. Taking into account national conditions, implementation will draw upon existing instruments and good practices developed by countries of the region and international organisations such as the Asian Development Bank (ADB), the Asia-Pacific Economic Co-operation (APEC), the Organisation for Economic Co-operation and Development (OECD) and the United Nations.

2 Core principles of Implementation

The implementation of the Action Plan will be based upon two core principles: i) establishing a mechanism by which overall reform progress can be promoted and assessed; ii) providing specific and practical assistance to governments of participating countries on key reform issues.

The implementation of the Action Plan will thus aim at offering participating countries regional and country-specific policy and institution-building support. This strategy will be tailored to policy priorities identified by participating countries and provide means by which participating countries and partners can assess progress and measure the achieved results.

Identifying Country priorities

While the Action Plan recalls the need to fight corruption and lays out overall policy objectives, it acknowledges that the situation in each country of the region may be specific.

To address these differences and target country-specific technical assistance, each participating country will endeavour, in consultation with the Secretariat of the Initiative, to identify priority reform areas which would fall under any of the three pillars, and aim to implement these in a workable timeframe.

The first consultation on these priorities will take place in the framework of the Tokyo Conference, immediately after the formal endorsement of the Action Plan. Subsequent identification of target areas will be done in the framework of the periodical meetings of the Steering Group that will be set up to review progress in the implementation of the Action Plan's three pillars.

Reviewing progress in the reform process

Real progress will primarily come from the efforts of the governments of each participating country supported by the business sector and civil society. In order to promote emulation, increase country responsibilities and target bilateral and international technical assistance, a mechanism will be established by which overall progress can be promoted and reviewed.

The review process will focus on the priority reform areas selected by participating countries. In addition, there will be a thematic discussion dealing with issues of specific, cross-regional importance as identified by the Steering Group.

Review of progress will be based on self-assessment reports by participating countries. The review process will use a procedure of plenary review by the Steering Group to take stock of each country's implementation progress.

Providing assistance to the reform process

While governments of participating countries have primary responsibility for addressing corruption related problems, the regional and international community as well as civil society and the business sector have a key role to play in supporting countries' reform efforts.

Donor countries and other assistance providers supporting the Action Plan will endeavour to provide the assistance required to enhance the capacity of participating countries to achieve progress in the priority areas and to meet the overall policy objectives of the Action Plan.

Participating governments of the region will endeavour, in consultation with the Initiative's Secretariat, to make known their specific assistance requirements in each of the selected priority areas and will co-operate with the assistance providers in the elaboration, organisation and implementation of programmes.

Providers of technical assistance will support participating governments' anti-corruption efforts by building upon programmes and initiatives already in place, avoiding duplications and facilitating, whenever possible, joint ventures. The Secretariat will continue to support this process through the Initiative's web site (www.oecd.org/daf/ASIAcom) which provides information on existing and planned assistance programmes and initiatives.

3 Mechanisms

Country Representatives

To facilitate the implementation of the Action Plan, each participating government in the region will designate a contact person. This government representative will have sufficient authority as well as adequate staff support and resources to oversee the fulfilment of the policy objectives of the Action Plan on behalf of his/her government.

Regional Steering Group

A Steering Group will be established and meet back-to-back with the Initiative's annual conferences to review progress achieved by participating countries in implementing the Action Plan. It will be composed of the government representatives and national experts on the technical issues discussed during the respective meeting as well as representatives of the Initiative's Secretariat and Advisory Group (see below).

The Steering Group will meet on an annual basis and serve three main purposes: (i) to review progress achieved in implementing each country's priorities; (ii) to serve as a forum for the exchange of experience and for addressing cross-regional issues that arise in connection with the implementation of the policy objectives laid out in the Action Plan; and (iii) to promote a dialogue with representatives of the international community, civil society and the business sector in order to mobilise donor support.

Consultations in the Steering Group will take place on the day preceding the Initiative's annual meeting. This shall allow the Steering Group to report on progress achieved in the implementation of the policy objectives laid out in the Action Plan, present regional good practices and enlarge support for anti-corruption efforts among ADB regional member countries.

Secretariat

The ADB and the OECD will act as the Secretariat of the Initiative and, as such, carry out day-to-day management. The role of the Secretariat also includes to assist participating governments in preparing their self-review reports. For this purpose, in-country missions by the Secretariat will be organised when necessary.

Advisory Group

The Secretariat will be assisted by an informal Advisory Group whose responsibility will be to help mobilise resources for technical assistance programmes and advise on priorities for the implementation of the Action Plan. The Group will be composed of donor countries and international donor organisations as well as representatives of civil society and the business sector, such as the Pacific Basin Economic Council (PBEC) and Transparency International (TI), actively involved in the implementation of the Action Plan.

Funding

Technical assistance programmes and policy advice in support of government reforms as well as capacity building in the business sector and civil society aiming at implementing the Action Plan will be financially supported by international organisations, governments and other parties from inside and outside the region actively supporting the Action Plan.

(http://www1.oecd.org/daf/asiacom/ActionPlan.htm#actionplan)

APPENDIX 2

The Arusha Declaration

Declaration of the Customs Co-operation Council Concerning Integrity in Customs

The Customs Co-operation Council

Noting that Customs is an essential instrument for the effective management of an economy and that it performs simultaneously the vital roles of combating smuggling and facilitating the flow of legitimate trade.

Acknowledging that:

- corruption can destroy the efficient functioning of any society and diminish the ability of the Customs to accomplish its mission;
- a corrupt Customs
  —will not deliver the revenue that is properly due to the State,
  —will not be effective in the fight against illicit trafficking, and
  —will obstruct the growth of legitimate international trade and hinder economic development;
- the Customs has no right to public recognition or trust if its staff break the law habitually.

Considering that corruption can be combated effectively only as part of a comprehensive national effort;

Declares that a top priority for all Governments should be to ensure that Customs is free of corruption. This requires a firm commitment at the highest political and administrative levels to maintaining a high standard of integrity throughout the civil service and particularly in the Customs.

Declares that a national Customs integrity programme must take account of the following key factors:

1. Customs legislation should be clear and precise. Import tariffs should be moderated where possible. The number of rates should be limited. Administrative regulation of trade should be reduced to the absolute minimum. There should be as few exemptions to the standard rules as possible.

2. Customs procedures should be simple, consistent, and easily accessible, and should include a procedure for appealing against decisions of the Customs, with the possibility of recourse to independent adjudication in the final instance. They could be based on the Kyoto Convention and should be so framed as to reduce to a minimum the inappropriate exercise of discretion.

3. Automation (including EDI) is a powerful tool against corruption, and its utilization should have priority.

4. In order to reduce the opportunities for malpractice, Customs managers should employ such measures as strategic segregation of functions, rotation of assignments and random allocation of examinations among Customs officers and, in certain circumstances, regular relocation of staff.

5. Line managers should have prime responsibility for identifying weaknesses in working methods and in the integrity of their staff, and for taking steps to rectify such weaknesses.
6. Internal and external auditing are essential, effective internal auditing being a particularly useful means of ensuring that Customs procedures are appropriate and are being implemented correctly. The internal auditing arrangements should be complemented by an internal affairs unit that has the specific task of investigating all cases of suspected malpractice.
7. The management should instil in its officers loyalty and pride in their service, an 'esprit de corps' and a desire to co-operate in measures to reduce their exposure to the possibility of corruption.
8. The processes for the recruitment and advancement of Customs officers should be objective and immune from interference. They should include a means of identifying applicants who have, and are likely to maintain, a high standard of personal ethics.
9. Customs officers should be issued with a Code of Conduct, the implications of which should be fully explained to them. There should be effective disciplinary measures, which should include the possibility of dismissal.
10. Customs officers should receive adequate professional training throughout their careers, which should include coverage of ethics and integrity issues.
11. The remuneration received by Customs officers should be sufficient to afford them a decent standard of living, and may in certain circumstances include social benefits such as health care and housing facilities, and/or incentive payments (bonuses, rewards, etc.).
12. Customs administrations should foster an open and transparent relationship with Customs brokers and with the relevant sectors of the business community. Liaison committees are useful in this respect.

Made at Arusha, Tanzania on the 7th day of July, 1993 (81st/82nd Council Sessions)

For more info on the World Customs Organisation's Integrity related efforts please contact the Secretariat, Human Resources Development Services: 30, rue du Marché, B-1210 Bruxelles, Belgique Tel: +32-2-2099444, Fax: +32-2-2099496, or by e-mail: hrds@wcoomd.org.

APPENDIX 3

African Union Convention on Preventing and Combating Corruption[1]

PREAMBLE

The Member States of the African Union:

Considering that the Constitutive Act of the African Union recognizes that freedom, equality, justice, peace and dignity are essential objectives for the achievement of the legitimate aspiration of the African peoples;

Further Considering that Article 3 of the said Constitutive Act enjoins Member States to coordinate and intensify their cooperation, unity, cohesion and efforts to achieve a better life for the peoples of Africa;

Cognizant of the fact that the Constitutive Act of the African Union, *inter alia*, calls for the need to promote and protect human and peoples' rights, consolidate democratic institutions and foster a culture of democracy and ensure good governance and the rule of law;

Aware of the need to respect human dignity and to foster the promotion of economic, social, and political rights in conformity with the provisions of the African Charter on Human and People's Rights and other relevant human rights instruments;

Bearing in mind the 1990 Declaration on the Fundamental Changes Taking Place in the World and their Implications for Africa; the 1994 Cairo Agenda for Action Relaunching Africa's Socio-economic Transformation; and the Plan of Action Against Impunity adopted by the Nineteenth Ordinary Session of the African Commission on Human and Peoples Rights in 1996 as subsequently endorsed by the Sixty fourth Ordinary Session of the Council of Ministers held in Yaounde, Cameroon in 1996 which, among others, underlined the need to observe principles of good governance, the primacy of law, human rights, democratization and popular participation by the African peoples in the processes of governance.

Concerned about the negative effects of corruption and impunity on the political, economic, social and cultural stability of African States and its devastating effects on the economic and social development of the African peoples;

Acknowledging that corruption undermines accountability and transparency in the management of public affairs as well as socio-economic development on the continent;

Recognizing the need to address the root causes of corruption on the continent;

Convinced of the need to formulate and pursue, as a matter of priority, a common penal policy aimed at protecting the society against corruption, including the adoption of appropriate legislative and adequate preventive measures;

Determined to build partnerships between governments and all segments of civil society, in particular, women, youth, media and the private sector in order to fight the scourge of corruption;

---

[1] The Convention was adopted in Maputo on 11 July 2003. As at 10 January 2005, the Convention had been signed by 34 States and ratified by 6: Comoros, Lesotho, Libyan Arab Jamahiriya, Namibia, Rwanda and Uganda. The Convention shall enter into force 30 days after the deposit of the fifteenth instrument of ratification.

Recalling resolution AHG-Dec 126(XXXIV) adopted by the Thirty-fourth Ordinary Session of the Assembly of Heads of State and Government in June 1998 in Ouagadougou, Burkina Faso, requesting the Secretary General to convene, in cooperation with the African Commission on Human and Peoples' Rights, a high level meeting of experts to consider ways and means of removing obstacles to the enjoyment of economic, social and cultural rights, including the fight against corruption and impunity and propose appropriate legislative and other measures;

Further Recalling the decision of the 37th ordinary session of the Assembly of Heads of State and Government of the OAU held in Lusaka, Zambia, in July 2001 as well as the Declaration adopted by the first session of the Assembly of the Union held in Durban, South Africa in July 2002, relating to the New Partnership for Africa's Development (NEPAD) which calls for the setting up of a coordinated mechanism to combat corruption effectively.

Have agreed as follows:

Article 1
Definitions

1. For the purposes of this Convention;

'Chairperson of the Commission' means Chairperson of the Commission of the African Union;

'Confiscation' means any penalty or measure resulting in a final deprivation of property, proceeds or instrumentalities ordered by a court of law following proceedings in relation to a criminal offence or offences connected with or related to corruption;

'Corruption' means the acts and practices including related offences proscribed in this Convention;

'Court of Law' means a court duly established by a domestic law;

'Executive Council' means the Executive Council of the African Union;

'Illicit enrichment' means the significant increase in the assets of a public official or any other person which he or she cannot reasonably explain in relation to his or her income.

'Private Sector' means the sector of a national economy under private ownership in which the allocation of productive resources is controlled by market forces, rather than public authorities and other sectors of the economy not under the public sector or government;

'Proceeds of Corruption' means assets of any kind corporeal or incorporeal, movable or immovable, tangible or intangible and any document or legal instrument evidencing title to or interests in such assets acquired as a result of an act of corruption;

'Public official' means any official or employee of the State or its agencies including those who have been selected, appointed or elected to perform activities or functions in the name of the State or in the service of the State at any level of its hierarchy;

'Requested State Party' means a State Party requested to extradite or to provide assistance under this Convention;

'Requesting State Party' means a State Party making a request for extradition or assistance in terms of this Convention;

'State Party' means any Member State of the African Union which has ratified or acceded to this Convention and has deposited its instruments of ratification or accession with the Chairperson of the Commission of the African Union.

2. In this Convention, the singular shall include the plural and vice versa.

Article 2
Objectives

The objectives of this Convention are to:

1. Promote and strengthen the development in Africa by each State Party, of mechanisms required to prevent, detect, punish and eradicate corruption and related offences in the public and private sectors.

2. Promote, facilitate and regulate cooperation among the State Parties to ensure the effectiveness of measures and actions to prevent, detect, punish and eradicate corruption and related offences in Africa.
3. Coordinate and harmonize the policies and legislation between State Parties for the purposes of prevention, detection, punishment and eradication of corruption on the continent.
4. Promote socio-economic development by removing obstacles to the enjoyment of economic, social and cultural rights as well as civil and political rights.
5. Establish the necessary conditions to foster transparency and accountability in the management of public affairs.

Article 3

Principles

The State Parties to this Convention undertake to abide by the following principles:

1. Respect for democratic principles and institutions, popular participation, the rule of law and good governance.
2. Respect for human and peoples' rights in accordance with the African Charter on Human and Peoples Rights and other relevant human rights instruments.
3. Transparency and accountability in the management of public affairs.
4. Promotion of social justice to ensure balanced socio-economic development.
5. Condemnation and rejection of acts of corruption, related offences and impunity.

Article 4

Scope of Application

1. This Convention is applicable to the following acts of corruption and related offences:
   (a) the solicitation or acceptance, directly or indirectly, by a public official or any other person, of any goods of monetary value, or other benefit, such as a gift, favour, promise or advantage for himself or herself or for another person or entity, in exchange for any act or omission in the performance of his or her public functions;
   (b) the offering or granting, directly or indirectly, to a public official or any other person, of any goods of monetary value, or other benefit, such as a gift, favour, promise or advantage for himself or herself or for another person or entity, in exchange for any act or omission in the performance of his or her public functions;
   (c) any act or omission in the discharge of his or her duties by a public official or any other person for the purpose of illicitly obtaining benefits for himself or herself or for a third party;
   (d) the diversion by a public official or any other person, for purposes unrelated to those for which they were intended, for his or her own benefit or that of a third party, of any property belonging to the State or its agencies, to an independent agency, or to an individual, that such official has received by virtue of his or her position;
   (e) the offering or giving, promising, solicitation or acceptance, directly or indirectly, of any undue advantage to or by any person who directs or works for, in any capacity, a private sector entity, for himself or herself or for anyone else, for him or her to act, or refrain from acting, in breach of his or her duties;
   (f) the offering, giving, solicitation or acceptance directly or indirectly, or promising of any undue advantage to or by any person who asserts or confirms that he or she is able to exert any improper influence over the decision making of any person performing functions in the public or private sector in consideration thereof, whether the undue advantage is for himself or herself or for anyone else, as well as the request, receipt or the acceptance of the offer or the promise of such an advantage, in consideration of that influence, whether or not the influence is exerted or whether or not the supposed influence leads to the intended result;

(g) illicit enrichment;
(h) the use or concealment of proceeds derived from any of the acts referred to in this Article; and
(i) participation as a principal, co-principal, agent, instigator, accomplice or accessory after the fact, or on any other manner in the commission or attempted commission of, in any collaboration or conspiracy to commit, any of the acts referred to in this article.

2. This Convention shall also be applicable by mutual agreement between or among two or more State Parties with respect to any other act or practice of corruption and related offences not described in this Convention.

Article 5

Legislative and other Measures

For the purposes set-forth in Article 2 of this Convention, State Parties undertake to:

1. Adopt legislative and other measures that are required to establish as offences, the acts mentioned in Article 4 paragraph 1 of the present Convention.
2. Strengthen national control measures to ensure that the setting up and operations of foreign companies in the territory of a State Party shall be subject to the respect of the national legislation in force.
3. Establish, maintain and strengthen independent national anticorruption authorities or agencies.
4. Adopt legislative and other measures to create, maintain and strengthen internal accounting, auditing and follow-up systems, in particular, in the public income, custom and tax receipts, expenditures and procedures for hiring, procurement and management of public goods and services.
5. Adopt legislative and other measures to protect informants and witnesses in corruption and related offences, including protection of their identities.
6. Adopt measures that ensure citizens report instances of corruption without fear of consequent reprisals.
7. Adopt national legislative measures in order to punish those who make false and malicious reports against innocent persons in corruption and related offences.
8. Adopt and strengthen mechanisms for promoting the education of populations to respect the public good and public interest, and awareness in the fight against corruption and related offences, including school educational programmes and sensitization of the media, and the promotion of an enabling environment for the respect of ethics.

Article 6

Laundering of the Proceeds of Corruption

States Parties shall adopt such legislative and other measures as may be necessary to establish as criminal offences:

(a) The conversion, transfer or disposal of property, knowing that such property is the proceeds of corruption or related offences for the purpose of concealing or disguising the illicit origin of the property or of helping any person who is involved in the commission of the offence to evade the legal consequences of his or her action.
(b) The concealment or disguise of the true nature, source, location, disposition, movement or ownership of or rights with respect to property which is the proceeds of corruption or related offences;
(c) The acquisition, possession or use of property with the knowledge at the time of receipt, that such property is the proceeds of corruption or related offences;

Article 7

Fight Against Corruption and Related Offences in the Public Service

In order to combat corruption and related offences in the public service, State Parties commit themselves to:

1. Require all or designated public officials to declare their assets at the time of assumption of office during and after their term of office in the public service.
2. Create an internal committee or a similar body mandated to establish a code of conduct and to monitor its implementation, and sensitize and train public officials on matters of ethics.
3. Develop disciplinary measures and investigation procedures in corruption and related offences with a view to keeping up with technology and increase the efficiency of those responsible in this regard.
4. Ensure transparency, equity and efficiency in the management of tendering and hiring procedures in the public service.
5. Subject to the provisions of domestic legislation, any immunity granted to public officials shall not be an obstacle to the investigation of allegations against and the prosecution of such officials.

Article 8

Illicit Enrichment

1. Subject to the provisions of their domestic law, State Parties undertake to adopt necessary measures to establish under their laws an offence of illicit enrichment.
2. For State Parties that have established illicit enrichment as an offence under their domestic law, such offence shall be considered an act of corruption or a related offence for the purposes of this Convention.
3. Any State Party that has not established illicit enrichment as an offence shall, in so far as its laws permit, provide assistance and cooperation to the requesting State with respect to the offence as provided in this Convention.

Article 9

Access to Information

Each State Party shall adopt such legislative and other measures to give effect to the right of access to any information that is required to assist in the fight against corruption and related offences.

Article 10

Funding of Political Parties

Each State Party shall adopt legislative and other measures to:

(a) Proscribe the use of funds acquired through illegal and corrupt practices to finance political parties; and
(b) Incorporate the principle of transparency into funding of political parties.

Article 11

Private Sector

State Parties undertake to:

1. Adopt legislative and other measures to prevent and combat acts of corruption and related offences committed in and by agents of the private sector.
2. Establish mechanisms to encourage participation by the private sector in the fight against unfair competition, respect of the tender procedures and property rights.
3. Adopt such other measures as may be necessary to prevent companies from paying bribes to win tenders.

Article 12

Civil Society and Media

State Parties undertake to:

1. Be fully engaged in the fight against corruption and related offences and the popularisation of this Convention with the full participation of the Media and Civil Society at large;
2. Create an enabling environment that will enable civil society and the media to hold governments to the highest levels of transparency and accountability in the management of public affairs;
3. Ensure and provide for the participation of Civil Society in the monitoring process and consult Civil Society in the implementation of this Convention;
4. Ensure that the Media is given access to information in cases of corruption and related offences on condition that the dissemination of such information does not adversely affect the investigation process and the right to a fair trial.

Article 13

Jurisdiction

1. Each State Party has jurisdiction over acts of corruption and related offences when:
   (a) the breach is committed wholly or partially inside its territory;
   (b) the offence is committed by one of its nationals outside its territory or by a person who resides in its territory; and
   (c) the alleged criminal is present in its territory and it does not extradite such person to another country;
   (d) when the offence, although committed outside its jurisdiction, affects, in the view of the State concerned, its vital interests or the deleterious or harmful consequences or effects of such offences impact on the State Party.
2. This Convention does not exclude any criminal jurisdiction exercised by a State Party in accordance with its domestic law.
3. Notwithstanding the provision of paragraph I of this Article, a person shall not be tried twice for the same offence.

Article 14

Minimum Guarantees of a Fair Trial

Subject to domestic law, any person alleged to have committed acts of corruption and related offences shall receive a fair trial in criminal proceedings in accordance with the minimum guarantees contained in the African Charter on Human and Peoples' Rights and any other relevant international human rights instrument recognized by the concerned States Parties.

Article 15

Extradition

1. This Article shall apply to the offences established by the State Parties in accordance with this Convention.
2. Offences falling within the jurisdiction of this Convention shall be deemed to be included in the internal laws of State Parties as crimes requiring extradition. State Parties shall include such offences as extraditable offences in extradition treaties existing between or among them.
3. If a State Party that makes extradition conditional on the existence of a treaty receives a request for extradition from a State Party with which it does not have such treaty, it shall consider this Convention as a legal basis for all offences covered by this Convention.
4. A State Party that does not make extradition conditional on the existence of a treaty shall recognize offences to which this Convention applies as extraditable offences among themselves.

5. Each State Party undertakes to extradite any person charged with or convicted of offences of corruption and related offences, carried out on the territory of another State Party and whose extradition is requested by that State Party, in conformity with their domestic law, any applicable extradition treaties, or extradition agreements or arrangements existing between or among the State Parties.
6. Where a State Party in whose territory any person charged with or convicted of offences is present and has refused to extradite that person on the basis that it has jurisdiction over offences, the Requested State Party shall be obliged to submit the case without undue delay to its competent authorities for the purpose of prosecution, unless otherwise agreed with the Requesting State Party, and shall report the final outcome to the Requesting State Party.
7. Subject to the provisions of its domestic law and any applicable extradition treaties, a Requested State Party may, upon being satisfied that the circumstances so warrant and are urgent and at the request of the Requesting State Party, take into custody a person whose extradition is sought and who is present in its territory, or take other appropriate measures to ensure that the person is present at the extradition proceedings.

Article 16
Confiscation and Seizure of the Proceeds and Instrumentalities of Corruption

1. Each State Party shall adopt such legislative measures as may be necessary to enable:
   (a) its competent authorities to search, identify, trace, administer and freeze or seize the instrumentalities and proceeds of corruption pending a final judgement;
   (b) confiscation of proceeds or property, the value of which corresponds to that of such proceeds, derived, from offences established in accordance with this convention;
   (c) repatriation of proceeds of corruption.
2. The Requested State Party shall, in so far as its law permits and at the request of the Requesting State Party, seize and remit any object:
   (a) which may be required as evidence of the offence in question; or
   (b) which has been acquired as a result of the offence for which extradition is requested and which, at the time of arrest is found in possession of the persons claimed or is discovered subsequently.
3. The objects referred to in clause 2 of this Article may, if the Requesting State so requests, be handed over to that State even if the extradition is refused or cannot be carried out due to death, disappearance or escape of the person sought.
4. When the said object is liable for seizure or confiscation in the territory of the Requested State Party the latter may, in connection with pending or ongoing criminal proceedings, temporarily retain it or hand it over to the Requesting State Party, on condition that it is returned to the Requested State Party.

Article 17
Bank Secrecy

1. Each State Party shall adopt such measures necessary to empower its courts or other competent authorities to order the confiscation or seizure of banking, financial or commercial documents with a view to implementing this Convention.
2. The Requesting State shall not use any information received that is protected by bank secrecy for any purpose other than the proceedings for which that information was requested, unless with the consent of the Requested State Party.
3. State Parties shall not invoke banking secrecy to justify their refusal to cooperate with regard to acts of corruption and related offences by virtue of this Convention.
4. State Parties commit themselves to enter into bilateral agreements to waive banking secrecy on doubtful accounts and allow competent authorities the right to obtain from banks and financial institutions, under judicial cover, any evidence in their possession.

Article 18

Cooperation and Mutual Legal Assistance

1. In accordance with their domestic laws and applicable treaties, State Parties shall provide each other with the greatest possible technical cooperation and assistance in dealing immediately with requests from authorities that are empowered by virtue of their national laws to prevent, detect, investigate and punish acts of corruption and related offences.
2. If two or several State Parties have established relations on the basis of uniform legislation or a particular regime, they may have the option to regulate such mutual relations without prejudice to the provisions of this Convention.
3. State Parties shall co-operate among themselves in conducting and exchanging studies and researches on how to combat corruption and related offences and to exchange expertise relating to preventing and combating corruption and related offences.
4. State Parties shall co-operate among themselves, where possible, in providing any available technical assistance in drawing up programmes, codes of ethics or organizing, where necessary and for the benefit of their personnel, joint training courses involving one or several states in the area of combating corruption and related offences.
5. The provisions of this Article shall not affect the obligations under any other bilateral or multilateral treaty which governs, in whole or in part, mutual legal assistance in criminal matters.
6. Nothing in this Article shall prevent State Parties from according one another more favourable forms of mutual legal assistance allowed under their respective domestic law.

Article 19

International Cooperation

In the spirit of international cooperation, State Parties shall:

1. Collaborate with countries of origin of multi-nationals to criminalise and punish the practice of secret commissions and other forms of corrupt practices during international trade transactions.
2. Foster regional, continental and international cooperation to prevent corrupt practices in international trade transactions.
3. Encourage all countries to take legislative measures to prevent corrupt public officials from enjoying ill-acquired assets by freezing their foreign accounts and facilitating the repatriation of stolen or illegally acquired monies to the countries of origin.
4. Work closely with international, regional and sub regional financial organizations to eradicate corruption in development aid and cooperation programmes by defining strict regulations for eligibility and good governance of candidates within the general framework of their development policy.
5. Cooperate in conformity with relevant international instruments on international cooperation on criminal matters for purposes of investigations and procedures in offences within the jurisdiction of this Convention.

Article 20

National Authorities

1. For the purposes of cooperation and mutual legal assistance provided under this Convention, each State Party shall communicate to the Chairperson of the Commission at the time of signing or depositing its instrument of ratification, the designation of a national authority or agency in application of offences established under Article 4(1) of this Convention.
2. The national authorities or agencies shall be responsible for making and receiving the requests for assistance and cooperation referred to in this Convention.

3. The national authorities or agencies shall communicate with each other directly for the purposes of this Convention.
4. The national authorities or agencies shall be allowed the necessary independence and autonomy, to be able to carry out their duties effectively.
5. State Parties undertake to adopt necessary measures to ensure that national authorities or agencies are specialized in combating corruption and related offences by, among others, ensuring that the staff are trained and motivated to effectively carry out their duties.

Article 21

Relationship with other Agreements

Subject to the provisions of Article 4 paragraph 2, this Convention shall in respect to those State Parties to which it applies, supersede the provisions of any treaty or bilateral agreement governing corruption and related offences between any two or more State Parties.

Article 22

Follow up Mechanism

1. There shall be an Advisory Board on Corruption within the African Union.
2. The Board shall comprise 11 members elected by the Executive Council from among a list of experts of the highest integrity, impartiality, and recognized competence in matters relating to preventing and combating corruption and related offences, proposed by the State Parties. In the election of the members of the board, the Executive Council shall ensure adequate gender representation, and equitable geographical representation.
3. The members of the Board shall serve in their personal capacity.
4. Members of the Board shall be appointed for a period of two years, renewable once.
5. The functions of the Board shall be to:
   (a) promote and encourage adoption and application of anticorruption measures on the continent;
   (b) collect and document information on the nature and scope of corruption and related offences in Africa;
   (c) develop methodologies for analyzing the nature and extent of corruption in Africa, and disseminate information and sensitize the public on the negative effects of corruption and related offences;
   (d) advise governments on how to deal with the scourge of corruption and related offences in their domestic jurisdictions;
   (e) collect information and analyze the conduct and behaviour of multi-national corporations operating in Africa and disseminate such information to national authorities designated under Article 18 (1) hereof;
   (f) develop and promote the adoption of harmonized codes of conduct of public officials;
   (g) build partnerships with the African Commission on Human and Peoples' Rights, African civil society, governmental. Intergovernmental and non-governmental organizations to facilitate dialogue in the fight against corruption and related offences;
   (h) submit a report to the Executive Council on a regular basis on the progress made by each State Party in complying with the provisions of this Convention;
   (i) perform any other task relating to corruption and related offences that may be assigned to it by the policy organs of the African Union.
6. The Board shall adopt its own rules of procedure.
7. States Parties shall communicate to the Board within a year after the coming into force of the instrument, on the progress made in the implementation of this Convention. Thereafter, each State Party, through their relevant procedures, shall ensure that the national anticorruption authorities or agencies report to the Board at least once a year before the ordinary sessions of the policy organs of the AU.

Final Clauses

Article 23

Signature, ratification, accession and Entry into Force

1. The present Convention shall be open for signature, ratification or accession by the Member States of the African Union.
2. The Convention shall enter into force thirty (30) days after the date of the deposit of the fifteenth instrument of ratification or accession.
3. For each State Party ratifying or acceding to the Convention after the date of the deposit of the fifteenth Instrument of Ratification, the Convention shall enter into force thirty (30) days after the date of the deposit by that State of its instrument of ratification or accession.

Article 24

Reservations

1. Any State Party may, at the time of adoption, signature, ratification or accession, make reservation to this Convention provided that each reservation concerns one or more specific provisions and is not incompatible with the object and purposes of this Convention.
2. Any State Party which has made any reservation shall withdraw it as soon as circumstances permit. Such withdrawal shall be made by notification to the Chairperson of the Commission.

Article 25

Amendment

1. This Convention may be amended if any State Party makes a written request to the Chairperson of the Commission.
2. The Chairperson of the Commission shall circulate the proposed amendments to all State Parties. The proposed amendments shall not be considered by the State Parties until a period of six (6) months from the date of circulation of the amendment has elapsed.
3. The amendments shall enter into force when approved by a two-thirds majority of the Member States of the AU.

Article 26

Denunciation

1. Any state Party may denounce the present Convention by sending notification to the Chairperson of the Commission. This denunciation shall take effect six (6) months following the date of receipt of notification by the Chairperson of the Commission.
2. After denunciation, cooperation shall continue between State Parties and the State Party that has withdrawn on all requests for assistance or extradition made before the effective date of withdrawal.

Article 27

Depository

1. The Chairperson of the Commission shall be the depository of this Convention and the amendments thereto.
2. The Chairperson of the Commission shall inform all State Parties of the signatures, ratifications, accessions, entry into force, requests for amendments submitted by States and approvals thereof and denunciations.
3. Upon entry into force of this Convention, the Chairperson of the Commission shall register it with the Secretary General of the United Nations in accordance with Article 102 of the Charter of the United Nations.

Article 28

Authentic Texts

The original of this Convention, of which the Arabic, English, French and Portuguese texts are equally authentic, shall be deposited with the Chairperson of the Commission.

APPENDIX 4

The Bangalore Principles of Judicial Conduct

Preamble

Whereas the Universal Declaration of Human Rights recognizes as fundamental the principle that everyone is entitled in full equality to a fair and public hearing by an independent and impartial tribunal, in the determination of rights and obligations and of any criminal charge.

Whereas the International Covenant on Civil and Political Rights guarantees that all persons shall be equal before the courts, and that in the determination of any criminal charge or of rights and obligations in a suit at law, everyone shall be entitled, without undue delay, to a fair and public hearing by a competent, independent and impartial tribunal established by law.

Whereas the foregoing fundamental principles and rights are also recognized or reflected in regional human rights instruments, in domestic constitutional, statutory and common law, and in judicial conventions and traditions.

Whereas the importance of a competent, independent and impartial judiciary to the protection of human rights is given emphasis by the fact that the implementation of all the other rights ultimately depends upon the proper administration of justice.

Whereas a competent, independent and impartial judiciary is likewise essential if the courts are to fulfil their role in upholding constitutionalism and the rule of law.

Whereas public confidence in the judicial system and in the moral authority and integrity of the judiciary is of the utmost importance in a modern democratic society.

Whereas it is essential that judges, individually and collectively, respect and honour judicial office as a public trust and strive to enhance and maintain confidence in the judicial system.

Whereas the primary responsibility for the promotion and maintenance of high standards of judicial conduct lies with the judiciary in each country.

And Whereas the United Nations Basic Principles on the Independence of the Judiciary are designed to secure and promote the independence of the judiciary, and are addressed primarily to States.

The Following Principles are intended to establish standards for ethical conduct of judges. They are designed to provide guidance to judges and to afford the judiciary a framework for regulating judicial conduct. They are also intended to assist members of the executive and the legislature, and lawyers and the public in general, to better understand and support the judiciary. These principles presuppose that judges are accountable for their conduct to appropriate institutions established to maintain judicial standards, which are themselves independent and impartial, and are intended to supplement and not to derogate from existing rules of law and conduct which bind the judge.

Value 1: Independence

Principle

Judicial independence is a pre-requisite to the rule of law and a fundamental guarantee of a fair trial. A judge shall therefore uphold and exemplify judicial independence in both its individual and institutional aspects.

Application

1.1 A judge shall exercise the judicial function independently on the basis of the judge's assessment of the facts and in accordance with a conscientious understanding of the law, free of any extraneous influences, inducements, pressures, threats or interference, direct or indirect, from any quarter or for any reason.

1.2 A judge shall be independent in relation to society in general and in relation to the particular parties to a dispute which the judge has to adjudicate.

1.3 A judge shall not only be free from inappropriate connections with, and influence by, the executive and legislative branches of government, but must also appear to a reasonable observer to be free therefrom.

1.4 In performing judicial duties, a judge shall be independent of judicial colleagues in respect of decisions which the judge is obliged to make independently.

1.5 A judge shall encourage and uphold safeguards for the discharge of judicial duties in order to maintain and enhance the institutional and operational independence of the judiciary.

1.6 A judge shall exhibit and promote high standards of judicial conduct in order to reinforce public confidence in the judiciary which is fundamental to the maintenance of judicial independence.

Value 2: Impartiality

Principle

Impartiality is essential to the proper discharge of the judicial office. It applies not only to the decision itself but also to the process by which the decision is made.

Application

2.1 A judge shall perform his or her judicial duties without favour, bias or prejudice.

2.2 A judge shall ensure that his or her conduct, both in and out of court, maintains and enhances the confidence of the public, the legal profession and litigants in the impartiality of the judge and of the judiciary.

2.3 A judge shall, so far as is reasonable, so conduct himself or herself as to minimise the occasions on which it will be necessary for the judge to be disqualified from hearing or deciding cases.

2.4 A judge shall not knowingly, while a proceeding is before, or could come before, the judge, make any comment that might reasonably be expected to affect the outcome of such proceeding or impair the manifest fairness of the process. Nor shall the judge make any comment in public or otherwise that might affect the fair trial of any person or issue.

2.5 A judge shall disqualify himself or herself from participating in any proceedings in which the judge is unable to decide the matter impartially or in which it may appear to a reasonable observer that the judge is unable to decide the matter impartially. Such proceedings include, but are not limited to, instances where

2.5.1 the judge has actual bias or prejudice concerning a party or personal knowledge of disputed evidentiary facts concerning the proceedings;

2.5.2 the judge previously served as a lawyer or was a material witness in the matter in controversy; or

2.5.3 the judge, or a member of the judge's family, has an economic interest in the outcome of the matter in controversy:
Provided that disqualification of a judge shall not be required if no other tribunal can be constituted to deal with the case or, because of urgent circumstances, failure to act could lead to a serious miscarriage of justice.

Value 3: Integrity

Principle

Integrity is essential to the proper discharge of the judicial office.

Application

3.1 A judge shall ensure that his or her conduct is above reproach in the view of a reasonable observer.

3.2 The behaviour and conduct of a judge must reaffirm the people's faith in the integrity of the judiciary. Justice must not merely be done but must also be seen to be done.

Value 4: Propriety

Principle

Propriety, and the appearance of propriety, are essential to the performance of all of the activities of a judge.

Application

4.1 A judge shall avoid impropriety and the appearance of impropriety in all of the judge's activities.

4.2 As a subject of constant public scrutiny, a judge must accept personal restrictions that might be viewed as burdensome by the ordinary citizen and should do so freely and willingly. In particular, a judge shall conduct himself or herself in a way that is consistent with the dignity of the judicial office.

4.3 A judge shall, in his or her personal relations with individual members of the legal profession who practise regularly in the judge's court, avoid situations which might reasonably give rise to the suspicion or appearance of favouritism or partiality.

4.4 A judge shall not participate in the determination of a case in which any member of the judge's family represents a litigant or is associated in any manner with the case.

4.5 A judge shall not allow the use of the judge's residence by a member of the legal profession to receive clients or other members of the legal profession.

4.6 A judge, like any other citizen, is entitled to freedom of expression, belief, association and assembly, but in exercising such rights, a judge shall always conduct himself or herself in such a manner as to preserve the dignity of the judicial office and the impartiality and independence of the judiciary.

4.7 A judge shall inform himself or herself about the judge's personal and fiduciary financial interests and shall make reasonable efforts to be informed about the financial interests of members of the judge's family.

4.8 A judge shall not allow the judge's family, social or other relationships improperly to influence the judge's judicial conduct and judgment as a judge.

4.9 A judge shall not use or lend the prestige of the judicial office to advance the private interests of the judge, a member of the judge's family or of anyone else, nor shall a judge convey or permit others to convey the impression that anyone is in a special position improperly to influence the judge in the performance of judicial duties.

4.10 Confidential information acquired by a judge in the judge's judicial capacity shall not be used or disclosed by the judge for any other purpose not related to the judge's judicial duties.

4.11 Subject to the proper performance of judicial duties, a judge may:

4.11.1 write, lecture, teach and participate in activities concerning the law, the legal system, the administration of justice or related matters;

4.11.2 appear at a public hearing before an official body concerned with matters relating to the law, the legal system, the administration of justice or related matters;

4.11.3 serve as a member of an official body, or other government commission, committee or advisory body, if such membership is not inconsistent with the perceived impartiality and political neutrality of a judge; or

4.11.4 engage in other activities if such activities do not detract from the dignity of the judicial office or otherwise interfere with the performance of judicial duties.

4.12 A judge shall not practise law whilst the holder of judicial office.

4.13 A judge may form or join associations of judges or participate in other organisations representing the interests of judges.

4.14 A judge and members of the judge's family, shall neither ask for, nor accept, any gift, bequest, loan or favour in relation to anything done or to be done or omitted to be done by the judge in connection with the performance of judicial duties.

4.15 A judge shall not knowingly permit court staff or others subject to the judge's influence, direction or authority, to ask for, or accept, any gift, bequest, loan or favour in relation to anything done or to be done or omitted to be done in connection with his or her duties or functions.

4.16 Subject to law and to any legal requirements of public disclosure, a judge may receive a token gift, award or benefit as appropriate to the occasion on which it is made provided that such gift, award or benefit might not reasonably be perceived as intended to influence the judge in the performance of judicial duties or otherwise give rise to an appearance of partiality.

Value 5: Equality

Principle

Ensuring equality of treatment to all before the courts is essential to the due performance of the judicial office.

Application

5.1 A judge shall be aware of, and understand, diversity in society and differences arising from various sources, including but not limited to race, colour, sex, religion, national origin, caste, disability, age, marital status, sexual orientation, social and economic status and other like causes ('irrelevant grounds').

5.2 A judge shall not, in the performance of judicial duties, by words or conduct, manifest bias or prejudice towards any person or group on irrelevant grounds.

5.3 A judge shall carry out judicial duties with appropriate consideration for all persons, such as the parties, witnesses, lawyers, court staff and judicial colleagues, without differentiation on any irrelevant ground, immaterial to the proper performance of such duties.

5.4 A judge shall not knowingly permit court staff or others subject to the judge's influence, direction or control to differentiate between persons concerned, in a matter before the judge, on any irrelevant ground.

5.5 A judge shall require lawyers in proceedings before the court to refrain from manifesting, by words or conduct, bias or prejudice based on irrelevant grounds, except such as are legally relevant to an issue in proceedings and may be the subject of legitimate advocacy.

Value 6: Competence and Diligence

Principle

Competence and diligence are prerequisites to the due performance of judicial office.

Application

6.1 The judicial duties of a judge take precedence over all other activities.

6.2 A judge shall devote the judge's professional activity to judicial duties, which include not only the performance of judicial functions and responsibilities in court and the making of decisions, but also other tasks relevant to the judicial office or the court's operations.

6.3 A judge shall take reasonable steps to maintain and enhance the judge's knowledge, skills and personal qualities necessary for the proper performance of judicial duties, taking advantage for this purpose of the training and other facilities which should be made available, under judicial control, to judges.

6.4 A judge shall keep himself or herself informed about relevant developments of international law, including international conventions and other instruments establishing human rights norms.

6.5 A judge shall perform all judicial duties, including the delivery of reserved decisions, efficiently, fairly and with reasonable promptness.

6.6 A judge shall maintain order and decorum in all proceedings before the court and be patient, dignified and courteous in relation to litigants, jurors, witnesses, lawyers and others with whom the judge deals in an official capacity. The judge shall require similar conduct of legal representatives, court staff and others subject to the judge's influence, direction or control.

6.7 A judge shall not engage in conduct incompatible with the diligent discharge of judicial duties.

Implementation

By reason of the nature of judicial office, effective measures shall be adopted by national judiciaries to provide mechanisms to implement these principles if such mechanisms are not already in existence in their jurisdictions.

Definitions

In this statement of principles, unless the context otherwise permits or requires, the following meanings shall be attributed to the words used:

'Court staff' includes the personal staff of the judge including law clerks. 'Judge' means any person exercising judicial power, however designated.

'Judge's family' includes a judge's spouse, son, daughter, son-in-law, daughter-in-law, and any other close relative or person who is a companion or employee of the judge and who lives in the judge's household.

'Judge's spouse' includes a domestic partner of the judge or any other person of either sex in a close personal relationship with the judge.

Explanatory Note

1. At its first meeting held in Vienna in April 2000 on the invitation of the United Nations Centre for International Crime Prevention, and in conjunction with the 10th United Nations Congress on the Prevention of Crime and the Treatment of Offenders, the Judicial Group on Strengthening Judicial Integrity (comprising Chief Justice Latifur Rahman of Bangladesh, Chief Justice Y. Bhaskar Rao of Karnataka State in India, Justice Govind Bahadur Shrestha of Nepal, Chief Justice M.L. Uwais of Nigeria, Deputy President Pius Langa of the Constitutional Court of South Africa, Chief Justice F.L. Nyalali of Tanzania, and Justice B.J. Odoki of

Uganda, meeting under the chairmanship of Judge Christopher Weeramantry, Vice-President of the International Court of Justice, with Justice Michael Kirby of the High Court of Australia as Rapporteur, and with the participation of Dato' Param Cumaraswamy, UN Special Rapporteur on the Independence of Judges and Lawyers) recognized the need for a code against which the conduct of judicial officers may be measured. Accordingly, the Judicial Group requested that codes of judicial conduct which had been adopted in some jurisdictions be analyzed, and a report be prepared by the Co-ordinator of the Judicial Integrity Programme, Dr Nihal Jayawickrama, concerning:

(a) the core considerations which recur in such codes; and
(b) the optional or additional considerations which occur in some, but not all, such codes and which may or may not be suitable for adoption in particular countries.

2. In preparing a draft code of judicial conduct in accordance with the directions set out above, reference was made to several existing codes and international instruments including, in particular, the following:
   (a) The Code of Judicial Conduct adopted by the House of Delegates of the American Bar Association, August 1972.
   (b) Declaration of Principles of Judicial Independence issued by the Chief Justices of the Australian States and Territories, April 1997.
   (c) Code of Conduct for the Judges of the Supreme Court of Bangladesh, prescribed by the Supreme Judicial Council in the exercise of power under Article 96(4)(a) of the Constitution of the People's Republic of Bangladesh, May 2000.
   (d) Ethical Principles for Judges, drafted with the cooperation of the Canadian Judges Conference and endorsed by the Canadian Judicial Council, 1998.
   (e) The European Charter on the Statute for Judges, Council of Europe, July 1998.
   (f) The Idaho Code of Judicial Conduct 1976.
   (g) Restatement of Values of Judicial Life adopted by the Chief Justices Conference of India, 1999.
   (h) The Iowa Code of Judicial Conduct.
   (i) Code of Conduct for Judicial Officers of Kenya, July 1999.
   (j) The Judges' Code of Ethics of Malaysia, prescribed by the Yang di-Pertuan Agong on the recommendation of the Chief Justice, the President of the Court of Appeal and the Chief Judges of the High Courts, in the exercise of powers conferred by Article 125(3A) of the Federal Constitution of Malaysia, 1994.
   (k) The Code of Conduct for Magistrates in Namibia.
   (l) Rules Governing Judicial Conduct, New York State, USA.
   (m) Code of Conduct for Judicial Officers of the Federal Republic of Nigeria.
   (n) Code of Conduct to be observed by Judges of the Supreme Court and of the High Courts of Pakistan.
   (o) The Code of Judicial Conduct of the Philippines, September 1989.
   (p) The Canons of Judicial Ethics of the Philippines, proposed by the Philippines Bar Association, approved by the Judges of First Instance of Manila, and adopted for the guidance of and observance by the judges under the administrative supervision of the Supreme Court, including municipal judges and city judges.
   (q) Yandina Statement: Principles of Independence of the Judiciary in Solomon Islands, November 2000.
   (r) Guidelines for Judges of South Africa, issued by the Chief Justice, the President of the Constitutional Court, and the Presidents of High Courts, the Labour Appeal Court, and the Land Claims Court, March 2000.
   (s) Code of Conduct for Judicial Officers of Tanzania, adopted by the Judges and Magistrates Conference, 1984.
   (t) The Texas Code of Judicial Conduct.

(u) Code of Conduct for Judges, Magistrates and Other Judicial Officers of Uganda, adopted by the Judges of the Supreme Court and the High Court, July 1989.
(v) The Code of Conduct of the Judicial Conference of the United States.
(w) The Canons of Judicial Conduct for the Commonwealth of Virginia, adopted and promulgated by the Supreme Court of Virginia, 1998.
(x) The Code of Judicial Conduct adopted by the Supreme Court of the State of Washington, USA, October 1995.
(y) The Judicial (Code of Conduct) Act, enacted by the Parliament of Zambia, December 1999.
(z) Draft Principles on the Independence of the Judiciary ('Siracusa Principles'), prepared by a committee of experts convened by the International Association of Penal Law, the International Commission of Jurists, and the Centre for the Independence of Judges and Lawyers, 1981.
(aa) Minimum Standards of Judicial Independence adopted by the International Bar Association, 1982.
(bb) United Nations Basic Principles on the Independence of the Judiciary, endorsed by the UN General Assembly, 1985.
(cc) Draft Universal Declaration on the Independence of Justice ('Singhvi Declaration') prepared by Mr L.V. Singhvi, UN Special Rapporteur on the Study on the Independence of the Judiciary, 1989.
(dd) The Beijing Statement of Principles of the Independence of the Judiciary in the Lawasia Region, adopted by the 6th Conference of Chief Justices, August 1997.
(ee) The Latimer House Guidelines for the Commonwealth on good practice governing relations between the Executive, Parliament and the Judiciary in the promotion of good governance, the rule of law and human rights to ensure the effective implementation of the Harare Principles, 1998.
(ff) The Policy Framework for Preventing and Eliminating Corruption and Ensuring the Impartiality of the Judicial System, adopted by the expert group convened by the Centre for the Independence of Judges and Lawyers, February 2000.

3. At its second meeting held in Bangalore in February 2001, the Judicial Group (comprising Chief Justice Mainur Reza Chowdhury of Bangladesh, Justice Claire L'Heureux Dube of Canada, Chief Justice P.V. Reddi of Karnataka State in India, Chief Justice Keshav Prasad Upadhyay of Nepal, Chief Justice M.L. Uwais of Nigeria, Deputy Chief Justice Pius Langa of South Africa, Chief Justice S.N. Silva of Sri Lanka, Chief Justice B.A. Samatta of Tanzania, and Chief Justice B.J. Odoki of Uganda, meeting under the chairmanship of Judge Weeramantry, with Justice Kirby as Rapporteur, and with the participation of the UN Special Rapporteur and Justice P.N. Bhagwati, Chairman of the UN Human Rights Committee, representing the UN High Commissioner for Human Rights) proceeding by way of examination of the draft placed before it, identified the core values, formulated the relevant principles, and agreed on the Bangalore Draft Code of Judicial Conduct. The Judicial Group recognized, however, that since the Bangalore Draft had been developed by judges drawn principally from common law countries, it was essential that it be scrutinized by judges of other legal traditions to enable it to assume the status of a duly authenticated international code of judicial conduct.

4. The Bangalore Draft was widely disseminated among judges of both common law and civil law systems and discussed at several judicial conferences. In June 2002, it was reviewed by the Working Party of the Consultative Council of European Judges (CCJE-GT), comprising Vice-President Gerhard Reissner of the Austrian Association of Judges, Judge Robert Fremr of the High Court in the Czech Republic, President Alain Lacabarats of the Cour d'Appel de Paris in France, Judge Otto Mallmann of the Federal Administrative Court of Germany, Magistrate Raffaele Sabato of Italy, Judge Virgilijus of the Lithuanian Court of Appeal,

Premier Conseiller Jean-Claude Wiwinius of the Cour d'Appel of Luxembourg, Juge Conseiller Orlando Afonso of the Court of Appeal of Portugal, Justice Dusan Ogrizek of the Supreme Court of Slovenia, President Johan Hirschfeldt of the Svea Court of Appeal in Sweden, and Lord Justice Mance of the United Kingdom. On the initiative of the American Bar Association, the Bangalore Draft was translated into the national languages, and reviewed by judges, of the Central and Eastern European countries; in particular, of Bosnia-Herzegovina, Bulgaria, Croatia, Kosovo, Romania, Serbia and Slovakia.

5. The Bangalore Draft was revised in the light of the comments received from CCJE-GT and others referred to above; Opinion no.1 (2001) of CCJE on standards concerning the independence of the judiciary; the draft Opinion of CCJE on the principles and rules governing judges' professional conduct, in particular ethics, incompatible behaviour and impartiality; and by reference to more recent codes of judicial conduct including the Guide to Judicial Conduct published by the Council of Chief Justices of Australia in June 2002, the Model Rules of Conduct for Judges of the Baltic States, the Code of Judicial Ethics for Judges of the People's Republic of China, and the Code of Judicial Ethics of the Macedonian Judges Association.
6. The revised Bangalore Draft was placed before a Round-Table Meeting of Chief Justices (or their representatives) from the civil law system, held in the Peace Palace in The Hague, Netherlands, in November 2002, with Judge Weeramantry presiding. Those participating were Judge Vladimir de Freitas of the Federal Court of Appeal of Brazil, Chief Justice Iva Brozova of the Supreme Court of the Czech Republic, Chief Justice Mohammad Fathy Naguib of the Supreme Constitutional Court of Egypt (assisted by Justice Dr Adel Omar Sherif), Conseillere Christine Chanet of the Cour de Cassation of France, President Genaro David Gongora Pimentel of the Suprema Corte de Justicia de la Nacion of Mexico, President Mario Mangaze of the Supreme Court of Mozambique, President Pim Haak of the Hoge Raad der Nederlanden, Justice Trond Dolva of the Supreme Court of Norway, and Chief Justice Hilario Davide of the Supreme Court of the Philippines (assisted by Justice Reynato S. Puno). Also participating in one session were the following Judges of the International Court of Justice: Judge Raymond Ranjeva (Madagascar), Judge Geza Herczegh (Hungary), Judge Carl-August Fleischhauer (Germany), Judge Abdul G. Koroma (Sierra Leone), Judge Rosalyn Higgins (United Kingdom), Judge Francisco Rezek (Brazil), Judge Nabil Elaraby (Egypt), and Ad-Hoc Judge Thomas Frank (USA). The UN Special Rapporteur was in attendance. The Bangalore Principles of Judicial Conduct was the product of this meeting.

APPENDIX 5

Framework for Commonwealth Principles On Promoting Good Governance and Combating Corruption

Preamble

1. Good governance is not a luxury but a basic requirement for development. Corruption, which undermines development, is generally an outcome and a symptom of poor governance. It has reached global proportions and needs to be attacked directly and explicitly.

2. Corruption is always a two-way transaction with a supply and a demand side. It occurs in poor, emerging, and developed nations, regardless of the level of social and economic development and in countries with varying forms of government ranging from dictatorships to established democracies.

3. Corruption, which is multi-dimensional, generally occurs at the nexus between the public and private sectors, with actors in the private sector interacting with holders of offices of trust in the public sector. Some aspects of corruption such as fraud and the misappropriation of assets or funds can occur entirely within the private or public sectors. However, with increasing privatisation of public utilities and services, the distinction between the public and private sectors is becoming less relevant in some areas.

4. Corruption is generally defined as the abuse of public office for private gain. As the scope of corruption has widened, this definition has been enlarged to cover the abuse of all offices of trust[1] for private gain. There are many types and levels of corruption including 'grand corruption', which involves huge sums paid by major businesses to high-level politicians and/or government officials; widespread systemic corruption which may take the form of substantial bribes to public officials to obtain, for example, licences/permits or to by-pass regulations; and petty corruption which involves modest but recurring payments to avoid delays, jump queues or to obtain goods in controlled markets. All forms of corruption entail high economic and social costs: transaction costs are increased; public revenues are reduced; resource allocation is distorted; investment and economic growth is retarded; and the rule of law is weakened.

5. The Commonwealth should firmly commit itself to the policy of 'zero tolerance' of all types of corruption. This policy must permeate national political cultures, governance, legal systems and administration. Where corruption is ingrained and pervasive, especially at the highest political levels, its eradication may require a sustained effort over a protracted period of time. However, the policy of 'zero tolerance' should be adopted from the outset, demonstrating a serious commitment to pursue the fight against corruption. The Commonwealth should remain firm in its determination that the high standards and goals enunciated in the 1991 Harare Declaration are upheld and enhanced. Creating an environment which is corruption-free will require vigorous actions at the national and international levels, and within the Commonwealth itself. These

[1] The term 'holders of offices of trust', that is used hereafter in this document, covers the following: politicians (elected and appointed), public/civil servants, judges, officers of the armed forces, officials of bodies providing services (including privatised services) for or on behalf of the government and executive officers of private corporations.

actions should encompass the prevention of corruption, the enforcement of laws against it and the mobilisation of public support for anti-corruption strategies.

National Actions

6. All Commonwealth countries which have not done so should develop their own national strategies to promote good governance and eliminate corruption. These strategies will require strong political will at the highest levels of government if they are to succeed. Furthermore, they cannot be externally imposed: they must be internally driven and domestically owned, based on the specific concerns and circumstances in each country. National strategies need to be comprehensive in engendering transparency and accountability in all sectors, and in covering all the active and passive actors involved in corruption. To be effective, they should be implemented in a timely manner and include principles from the five inter-related platforms described below.

A. Ethics and Integrity in the Public and Private Sectors

(i) High-level Corruption

7. Corruption at the highest level poses perhaps the greatest threat to the stability and well-being of societies. Its elimination must therefore be given the highest priority in the implementation of effective anti-corruption strategies. Failure to root out high-level political corruption undermines anti-corruption measures at other levels. It perpetuates double standards inimical to the development of an anti-corruption culture.

(ii) Funding of Political Parties

8. The funding of political parties has the potential to become a major source of corruption as well as a vehicle for hiding corruption. Clear links can be drawn between inappropriate or inadequate controls on such funding and the prevalence of corruption. Among those countries which have sought to address the issue of transparency in political funding and the maintenance of the integrity of the political system, there is divergence and the different approaches adopted are largely the result of prevailing political and societal norms. Several factors are relevant in tackling the problems associated with money and politics. They include:

- whether or not there are established political parties;
- the capacity of the state to finance political parties and/or election campaigns, and levels of expenditure on political campaigns;
- limits on financial contributions and the integrity of their sources;
- the role of national and international companies in providing funds to political parties; and
- the national interest in ensuring that foreign interests do not influence domestic political priorities and decisions.

9. Although rules on funding for political parties will vary depending upon national circumstances, in general, it is important that these rules should serve to:

- prevent conflicts of interest and the exercise of improper influence;
- preserve the integrity of democratic political structures and processes;
- proscribe the use of funds acquired through illegal and corrupt practices to finance political parties; and
- enshrine the concept of transparency in the funding of political parties by requiring the declaration of donations exceeding a specified limit.

B. Economic and Fiscal Policies

10. Opportunities for seeking economic rents are a major cause of corruption. These opportunities are greater when there is a lack of transparency and undue administrative discretion. Policy reforms that can help to maximise transparency and certainty and minimise administrative

discretion will reduce rent-seeking as well as eliminate incentives which generate corrupt practices. They will help to improve foreign investors' perceptions of the investment environment in many countries. Such policy reforms include:

- Liberalising trade regimes through the progressive removal of inefficient quantitative restrictions and import/export licences, as well as high tariffs that shield industries from competition and create artificial monopolies.
- Reducing foreign exchange controls and increasing transparency in foreign exchange allocation processes.
- Eliminating price controls and poorly targeted subsidies which, by lowering the price of goods below their market values, create artificial scarcities and parallel markets.
- Simplifying regulations in order to reduce the scope for bureaucratic discretion (e.g. in customs administration).
- Increasing transparency in the allocation of land-use permits and in the zoning of land.
- Reducing excessive levels of taxation where they create incentives for tax evasion and fraud and eliminating the use of discretionary authority in tax administration and enforcement which encourages corrupt practices.
- Ensuring that fiscal and tax rules do not permit bribes or other illicit payments to be treated as deductible expenses for tax purposes.

C. Management of Services Provided in the Public Interest

11. Improving the management, efficiency and delivery of public services should be an essential element of any national strategy to enhance governance and reduce corruption. When services are provided in an efficient manner, fewer opportunities for corruption arise as citizens are no longer required to compete, often by way of paying bribes, for scarce and inefficient services. In view of the increasing trend towards contracting out and/or privatising services previously provided by the State, measures to improve management and efficiency should encompass all those who have responsibilities for providing goods and services in the public interest.

The main areas to be covered are:

The Public Service and Providers of Public Services

12. A merit-based, professional and non-partisan civil service which is appropriately sized and well-motivated is of critical importance. Over-sized public administration systems, with bloated and poorly paid bureaucracies, engender corruption. Down-sizing alone is not enough but should be complemented with merit-based recruitment and promotion, career growth policies and incentives to retain the better performers within the civil service. Civil servants need to be adequately paid if they are to maintain the probity, professionalism and integrity that should be required of the public service. They should also be free from political interference.

13. The rule of law should apply to all those involved in the administration and provision of services in the public interest, as it does to the whole of civil society. Those holding offices of trust need to be bound by well publicised Codes of Conduct with appropriate sanctions for breaches that are enforced consistently and vigorously. These Codes should, *inter alia*, cover: standards of integrity, potential conflicts of interest, acceptance of gifts, misuse of information for personal gain, and disclosure of assets and financial interests. Ethical standards should be promoted—through education and training where necessary—which instil pride in the virtues of integrity, professionalism, efficiency, transparency and impartiality in the public service.

Financial Management

14. Sound financial management systems are essential tools of good governance, which enable governments to set macroeconomic targets, to allocate resources and to implement programmes and projects efficiently. Processes for budget preparation, execution and monitoring need to be

open and transparent. Clear procedures and criteria should be used for developing public investment programmes and projects, including those by public enterprises, and for allocating recurrent expenditure budgets. There should be rigorous accounting, financial reporting and auditing systems covering all public programmes and investments. Public accounts should be subject to scrutiny by appropriate bodies such as parliamentary committees and Auditors-General. Timely compliance with auditing requirements is important to ensure the legitimacy of public expenditures. Where audits indicate deficiencies or are themselves unsatisfactory, prompt remedial action should be taken. Auditors-General, or other supreme auditing authorities, should be sufficiently independent to allow open criticism of government finances. Countries should be encouraged to adopt codes of fiscal transparency based on the model provided by the 'The Code of Good Practices on Fiscal Transparency—Declaration of Principles', adopted by the IMF's Interim Committee in April 1998.

15. It is also important for countries to have effective regulations for their financial sectors (including private financial institutions and parastatals), that reduce opportunities for corrupt practices. The key aspects of a sound financial system include transparency of the financial system; competent management; effective risk control systems; adequate capital requirements; prudential regulation; supervisory authorities with sufficient autonomy, authority and capacity; and effective supervision of cross-border banking, which is also important in combating money laundering.

Public Procurement

16. Transparency in government procurement practices is not an established norm in many countries. Corruption is widespread, both in the award of contracts and during their implementation. Governments should be encouraged to review their procurement practices and to develop comprehensive guidelines of their own, with transparent processes to cover contracts for goods, civil works and services, and criteria for using all types of procedures ranging from prudent shopping to national and international competitive bidding. In order to increase efficiency, probity and economy in public procurement, governments should adopt standard bidding documents, establish processes for public bid opening, set objective criteria for bid evaluation, and institute a system for the review of awards. The collection and dissemination of data on public procurement prices of goods and services of similar specifications, which are procured by different agencies regularly in large quantities, can have substantial and prompt effects in reducing corruption. An accountable and reviewable process for the black-listing of contractors guilty of resorting to corrupt practices can be a particularly effective anti-corruption weapon.

D. The Judiciary and the Legal System

17. Countries need effective institutional arrangements to resolve disputes between citizens, corporations and governments; to clarify ambiguities in laws and regulations; and to enforce compliance. The rule of law in a country is of vital importance for economic, social and political development. Inherent in the concept of the rule of law are the notions of impartiality, fairness and equality. Strengthening the rule of law will, *inter alia*, require the following actions:

The Judiciary

(i) Entrenching an independent judiciary

18. An independent and competent judiciary, which is impartial, efficient and reliable, is of paramount importance. This requires objective criteria for the selection and removal of judges, adequate remuneration, security of tenure, and independence from the executive and legislative branches of government.

19. However, judicial independence does not imply a lack of accountability. Judges should act properly in accordance with their office and should be subject to the ordinary criminal laws of the

land. There should be procedures to discipline or dismiss them if they act improperly or otherwise fail in the performance of their duties to society. These procedures should be transparent and administered by institutions which are themselves independent and impartial.

Strengthening the legal system

(ii) Compliance

20. Vigorous application and enforcement of existing laws and prosecution of offenders is essential if the rule of law is to be respected. Although most countries have at their disposal a wide range of laws which can be used to combat corruption, these laws are often under-utilised and, at times, even ignored. Governments should seek to make effective use of existing criminal and civil laws to obtain the appropriate remedy in each case.

21. Investigative, policing and prosecutorial services which remain weak in many countries, need to be enhanced to ensure compliance with the law. Independent anticorruption agencies such as ombudsman offices, inspectors-general, and anti-corruption commissions can be effective if they are genuinely free from being influenced by the executive branch of government and where there is a strong judiciary in place.

(iii) Enforcing Criminal Law

22. As the nature and prevalence of corruption has grown, laws against corruption may need to be strengthened to provide a meaningful deterrent, and complemented in several ways:

(a) Both active and passive corruption should be made criminal offences, comprehensively covering the holders of all offices of trust.
(b) Criminal law should provide for the seizure and forfeiture of the proceeds of corruption.
(c) There should be legal provisions to protect witnesses and whistle-blowers in cases involving corruption.
(d) Statutes which permit investigators and prosecutors to base criminal proceedings on the discovery of significant increases in the assets of the holder of an office of trust, which cannot be reasonably attributed to lawful sources of income, can be of great assistance.
(e) The laundering of the proceeds of corruption must be criminalised and laws which provide for the granting of assistance (either extradition or mutual assistance in criminal matters) to other countries investigating or prosecuting money laundering offences must be available to ensure effective international co-operation to combat money laundering.

(iv) Civil, administrative and regulatory laws

(a) The civil law is the source of many remedies which can be used to combat corruption. For example, the use of damages awards and the facility to void contracts may be appropriate in many cases.
(b) Administrative action, such as the use of disciplinary procedures, can contribute to the battle against corruption and ease over-burdened court systems by dispensing appropriate sanctions. Relatively minor offences can be dealt with effectively through disciplinary bodies such as public service commissions.
(c) Regulations requiring declarations of assets and financial interests by holders of offices of trust, which might give rise to potential conflicts of interest, can enhance the integrity of service providers and reduce the opportunities for corruption.
(d) Non-criminal laws such as those providing for disqualification of directors guilty of improper conduct in the management of corporations, and the regulation of financial institutions to prevent money laundering, can be useful.

E. Civil Society

23. Civil society should be seen as an independent and creative partner in the development of effective coalitions to improve governance and combat corruption. Beyond periodic electoral

processes, governments that can regularly consult, collaborate with, and listen to their citizens are better able to develop national ownership of policies and the political will required to pursue anti-corruption programmes. Important factors that enable civil society to play an effective role are:

- Freedom of association: Citizens should enjoy the right to establish organisations around particular interests (e.g. professional and business associations, labour unions) to pursue general or specific social, economic or political objectives. Such associations can often act as critical watchdogs of the integrity of service providers. At the local level, grassroots community organisations, co-operatives and local NGOs can help the poor and marginalised to get their voices heard in the corridors of power.
- Freedom of the press and media: Transparency in any society requires information to be available freely in the public domain. A free and competent press is essential in this process, and is critical to the success of anti-corruption strategies. Freedom of the press and media calls for access to information; the absence of government controls or censorship (except where national security issues are involved); the liberty to express views; and sufficient financial independence to resist control of editorial policy and news coverage. Civil society should promote genuine competition in the media market-place to ensure diversity of ownership, so that alternative outlets can provide a broad range of views on public policy issues. In situations where the media itself may be corrupt or susceptible to corruption, adherence to high standards of integrity in journalism should be promoted, along with the development of professional well-informed media, through self-regulation and training.
- Information technology: advances in information technology help to increase civil society's access to new sources of information and channels of communication, including foreign publications and broadcasts.
- Research and analysis: The development by civil society of independent public policy research institutes and think-tanks can provide increased domestic capacity to analyse deficiencies in the system of governance. Such bodies can help to study the particular types of corruption in a country, and identify country-specific remedial options.

International Actions

24. With the increasing globalisation of corruption, several international fora and agencies including the UN General Assembly, the OECD, the IMF, the World Bank, the OAS, the European Union, the Council of Europe and the International Chamber of Commerce, have mounted initiatives to improve governance and combat corruption. These include conventions to limit corruption in transnational business and stronger anticorruption programmes by international financial institutions and aid agencies. These efforts are important and have the potential to lead to significant results. There are, however, gaps in their coverage, and continuing weaknesses in policies and practices, which need to be addressed. In addition there are some special areas that require further international action.

A. International Initiatives Against Corruption

25. At present, there are three international legally binding conventions against corruption: (i) The 1996 Inter-American Convention Against Corruption, a regional OAS initiative, that covers active and passive corruption as well as illicit enrichment. (ii) The 1997 OECD Convention on Combating Bribery of Foreign Public Officials in International Business Transactions, which focuses on active bribery of foreign public officials. (iii) The 1999 Council of Europe's Criminal Law Convention on Corruption, which covers active and passive bribery of domestic and foreign public and private sector officials, as well as judges and members of public assemblies.

26. Except for the OAS Convention, these initiatives have been promoted by the major developed countries and do not correspond fully to the needs of developing countries. The battle

against cross-border corruption should be joined by all nations, both developed and developing, from all parts of the world. This calls for the mobilisation of international support for a global compact against corruption, negotiated under the auspices of the United Nations with universal participation, which builds on the positive elements of existing conventions and other regional and international initiatives.

B. Programmes of International Financial Institutions and Aid Agencies

27. The IMF, the World Bank, the regional development banks and bilateral aid agencies have for many years been aiding countries in improving governance through policy advice, technical assistance, institutional reform and capacity building. As corruption has become increasingly a part of the debate on aid effectiveness, aid agencies have taken on stronger anti-corruption programmes. The World Bank has adopted new anti-fraud/corruption procurement guidelines, and improved disbursement and financial auditing procedures. The IMF is taking a more pro-active stance and has adopted guidelines for promoting good governance (A Guidance Note on The Role of the IMF in Governance Issues was approved by the IMF's Executive Board in July 1998). Both the Bretton Woods institutions are beginning to take corruption explicitly into account in defining their country assistance programmes. Several bilateral donors are designing programmes to assist nations in their anti-corruption efforts. Areas in development assistance that need added scrutiny and further action include greater transparency and accountability, conditionality, procurement, and bilateral aid practices.

(i) Transparency and accountability

- International financial institutions need to be more transparent in their operations, objectives and decision-making processes. There has been greater openness in the past few years and the recent discussions on a new international financial architecture may lead to further progress. To increase national ownership and public participation in reform programmes, key documents such as Policy Framework Papers, Letters of Development Policy and Letters of Intent should be more systematically released by borrowing countries and widely disseminated via the Bretton Woods institutions, unless there are valid reasons for non-disclosure.
- There should be a more open acknowledgement by donors and international financial institutions of their share in the responsibility for the outcomes of the country programmes they help design and for the policy advice they give. When these outcomes are not satisfactory because of flaws in programme design and policy advice, these deficiencies should be rectified and additional financial assistance should be provided.
- The staff of lending agencies should be subjected to greater scrutiny and internal accountability.

(ii) Conditionality

- Domestic ownership and political will to implement measures to improve governance and reduce corruption are paramount. Measures imposed externally as conditions of financial assistance are rarely effective. However, the availability of external funding (both project and non-project related) has the potential to encourage corrupt practices. Hence, the levels of corruption in recipient countries should be taken into account in determining the quantum and direction of external funding/assistance. Where it is necessary for international financial institutions to take up issues related to governance and corruption in their policy dialogue with countries and in the development of country assistance strategies, this should be done in a manner that is consistent with their mandates. Reforms agreed with the IMF and the World Bank to improve governance and reduce corruption should take account of a country's capacity to implement them within realistic time-frames.
- 'Floating Tranches', which have been adopted recently in several World Bank structural adjustment loans, should be used more widely to enable governments to sequence reform measures in the light of local circumstances without holding up entire programmes.

- To promote local ownership of reforms, foreign donors should agree with governments on the objectives to be achieved, identify alternative paths for meeting these ends, but leave the route to be selected to the government concerned.
- The IMF should be even-handed by raising issues related to transparency, governance and corruption in developed countries when exercising its surveillance function, as it does in developing countries when it is financing programmes.

(iii) Procurement

- All international financial institutions, multilateral development banks and multilateral agencies providing development assistance should be encouraged to strengthen their procurement guidelines along the lines of the anti-fraud/corruption provisions of the World Bank's 1996 guidelines on procurement. These provide strong sanctions against borrowing countries and firms that engage in corrupt practices, including rejection of contract awards or cancellation of loan funds, and making corporations judged to have engaged in fraudulent or corrupt practices ineligible for future Bank-financed projects (i.e. blacklisting). They also require bidders to disclose commissions made to agents.

(iv) Practices of Agencies Providing Bilateral Development Assistance

- Bilateral development assistance agencies should be encouraged to adopt the antifraud/corruption provisions of the World Bank's 1996 procurement guidelines and to utilise similar standard bidding documents.
- Since the tying of aid to procurement from a donor country reduces the scope for competitive bidding and increases the incentives for corrupt practices, tied aid should be reduced.
- Supplier credits should be carefully monitored as they often involve projects with little equity by the promoters, which increases the scope for corrupt payments.
- As part of the negotiations on the OECD Convention, a separate resolution was adopted in 1996 calling on member countries which allow the tax deductibility of bribes to foreign public officials to re-examine their tax laws with a view to denying this deductibility. All donor countries that have not already done so should amend their tax laws accordingly.

C. Special Areas Requiring Further Action

(i) Monitoring of Corruption

28. The monitoring of corruption and the ranking of countries based on perceptions of levels of corruption prevailing in them by some NGOs (e.g. Transparency International), has raised awareness of the problem of corruption globally. However, it is important to improve the methodological basis for such quantitative assessments. Moreover, bearing in mind the 'supply/demand' dimension of corruption in international business transactions, it would be useful to rank multinational corporations and their subsidiaries in terms of their track records on corruption, thus providing exposure of those known to be engaging in corrupt practices.

(ii) The Arms Trade

29. It is difficult to determine how the arms trade is financed, e.g. through military aid, debt creation, compensatory trade offsets, or cash transactions. The secrecy that surrounds the international arms trade often encourages corruption in these transactions. There should be much more transparency in the trade. This could be achieved through:

- wider and more detailed reporting of arms trade transactions in the UN arms register;
- a new international code of conduct for the arms trade, requiring the disclosure of far greater information than is currently provided by all the parties involved; and
- the inclusion of specific clauses in arms sales contracts that reduce the role of middlemen and ban illegal commissions.

(iii) Money Laundering

30. The endorsement by Commonwealth Heads of Government of the 40 Recommendations of the Financial Action Task Force of the OECD, which are designed to combat money laundering through the use of the criminal law and effective regulation of the financial sector, should be replicated globally to ensure that money laundering is tackled on the broadest possible front. As money laundering becomes a global phenomenon, the formation of multi-disciplinary regional groups, such as the Caribbean Financial Action Task Force and the Eastern and Southern African Money Laundering Group should be encouraged in order to strengthen anti-money laundering measures.

- Additional international efforts are required to pursue illicit funds to numerous off shore financial centres, located in developed and developing countries, which make corruption less risky since the proceeds can be hidden overseas.
- Stronger mechanisms are required to enable the expeditious repatriation of the proceeds of corruption.
- The extent to which countries with large parallel economies are vulnerable to money laundering should be the subject of studies in order to determine appropriate countermeasures.
- Global efforts to assess the effectiveness of anti-money laundering strategies should be enhanced.

Commonwealth Actions

31. In addition to actions taken at national levels, the Commonwealth can also act collectively to improve governance and combat corruption in several ways.

(i) The Commonwealth's commitment to promote good governance and fight corruption should be credible, tangible and visible. As a first step, Heads of Government should consider adopting a Declaration that commits the Commonwealth to specific principles, standards and goals. In order to ensure that the momentum of such a high-level political initiative is maintained, the Declaration could provide for the establishment of a mechanism/process to facilitate its implementation as well as periodic reviews of progress (say, biennially, coinciding with Meetings of Commonwealth Heads of Government CHOGMs).

(ii) At the same time, the Commonwealth should also support the development of a truly global compact against corruption that would fill gaps in existing instruments and be universal in its scope, thus creating a level playing field for all countries. For this purpose, in consultation with other interested parties, it could work for the initiation, under the auspices of the United Nations General Assembly, of timebound negotiations for a universal, legally binding inter-governmental convention against corruption. Such a convention would require all signatories to abide with minimum standards and rules (in the case of non-state actors these would apply through legislative and other measures adopted by governments) to foster good governance and fight corruption. These standards and rules should be general enough to accommodate diversity in political, economic, socio-cultural and legal systems, but without compromising the basic policy objective of zero-tolerance for all types of corruption. Pending the adoption of a global convention, countries should be encouraged to become parties to existing anti-corruption conventions that are appropriate to their needs and circumstances.

(iii) The Commonwealth should ensure that maximum use is made by member countries of its existing and proposed Schemes of Co-operation in the Administration of Justice, and that these Schemes are kept under active review in order to meet the needs of countries seeking to combat corrupt practices.

(iv) The Commonwealth should work with other international agencies to develop effective standards to ensure that all off-shore financial centres in all parts of the world are not used to launder the proceeds of corrupt practices.

(v) Given the economic, social, and political benefits to be gained through Commonwealth co-operation, the Commonwealth Secretariat should be given additional resources to enable it to:

- assist member countries, when requested, with policy advice and technical support to design their own anti-corruption strategies; and
- compile and disseminate information on emerging good practice in combating corruption and improving governance in key areas such as the funding of political parties, economic reforms and judicial reforms.

APPENDIX 6

Commonwealth Report of Expert Group on Good Governance

I Introduction

1. The main focus of this Report is on corruption in economic management. Section II provides an overview of the nature of corruption, its different dimensions and appropriate responses to deal with the problems it poses. Sections III and IV set out the actions that are necessary at the national and international level, respectively, to combat corruption. The role of the Commonwealth is examined in Section V.

II Corruption: Causes, Costs and Responses

2. Corruption manifests itself in various ways and it is useful to distinguish between personal corruption (motivated by personal gain) and political corruption (motivated by political gain). A further distinction can be made between individual corruption and organisational or institutional corruption. In the context of the State, corruption most often refers to criminal or otherwise unlawful conduct by government agencies, or by officials of these organisations acting in the course of their employment.

3. The significance of institutional corruption can be understood only if it is clearly distinguished from individual corruption. There are tendencies in all cases of corruption to individualise misconduct, and at the same time to institutionalise it. These two tendencies may appear to be opposites, but the latter tendency is also perpetrated by those accused of misconduct, either by excusing misconduct or by justifying it as an institutional privilege.

4. Corruption has become global in its scope, impact, and possible solutions. It is an increasing threat to the fabric of global society. As with drug trafficking, pollution, international terrorism and other serious crimes, the fight against corruption requires international co-operation.

5. While the problem of corruption is global, many actions to combat it have to be taken at the national level. There cannot be any effective action against corruption without a clear sense of national ownership of anti-corruption strategies. A new culture must evolve which is intolerant of corruption. Greater information, education, empowerment of people, and above all, strong political leadership committed to effective action are essential to create and sustain such a culture. Smaller and more efficient government, fewer discretionary powers in administration, greater reliance on diversity and private initiative, a free press and other media, well-paid civil servants appointed by merit, democratic processes in political parties and supremacy of the rule of law, are all important factors that serve to promote good governance and reduce corruption.

6. Forceful national action to combat corruption is possible in all countries. The objective should be to attain '*zero tolerance*' for all types of corruption. This attitude must permeate value systems, current policies and legislative frameworks. While it may be unrealistic to expect an immediate or total elimination of corruption, the principle of 'zero tolerance' should be adopted from the outset, demonstrating a serious political commitment to pursue the fight against corruption. The implications of such a commitment are spelt out in this Report. National efforts should be

reinforced with appropriate support at the international level. Corruption originating within national boundaries and that resulting from international transactions should be fought with equal vigour.

7. Actions taken should focus not only on corrupt activities but also address their underlying causes. Since these differ from country to country, national circumstances should be taken into account in combating corruption. It is also important to recognise that corruption is not necessarily associated with any particular type of political/social system, form of government, or level of economic development.

8. Although the political barriers to change may sometimes seem formidable, governments can often be expected to respond to public concerns and to reasoned argument. However, in extreme cases, where corruption is so pervasive and deeply entrenched, the adoption of a vigorous 'zero tolerance' approach will be difficult. In such situations, the achievement of any progress may depend upon fundamental political change brought about by internal democratic forces.

9. Political commitment is not primarily a matter of the personal character of leaders. It is more an outcome of political culture and the effectiveness of political institutions. In some cases, corruption has become the primary means of funding political parties, as well as the personal enrichment of political leaders. This is particularly pernicious when there is a failure to differentiate between the wealth of leaders and the funds of political parties. In such cases, major reforms will be needed including the reform of elections, controls over party spending and full disclosure of financial contributions to political parties. This would require political parties to maintain and publish proper accounts and to clearly designate the officials responsible for these accounts.

10. **The costs of poor governance and corruption** Poor governance and corruption are major constraints to the pursuit of economic development:

- bribery increases the costs of government development programmes and spawns projects of little economic merit;
- corruption undermines revenue collection capacity, contributing to fiscal weaknesses and macro-economic difficulties;
- perceptions of high levels of corruption and rent-seeking[1] act as a strong disincentive to genuine foreign investors, while attracting more dubious enterprises
- diversion of resources from their intended purposes distorts the formulation of public policy;
- the use of bribes to gain access to public services undermines stated allocation priorities, benefiting the few at the expense of the many;
- bribery can subvert essential public regulatory systems; and
- widespread corruption brings government into disrepute and encourages cynicism about politics and public policy.

11. One area of special concern is the impact of widespread petty corruption on the poor. The intention of public programmes to provide the poor with access to land, education, health, and the legal system will be thwarted if bribery determines the allocation of these resources and services in practice. Petty corruption reinforces existing economic and .social inequalities at the local level. Such corruption is politically costly because it undermines the credibility of government and public institutions.

12. The costs of corruption are particularly high for those poor countries in great need of inflows of productive foreign capital. Widespread corruption provides a poor environment in which to attract foreign investment, discouraging those investors most likely to make a long-term contribution to development, and encouraging those who seek quick profits through dubious

[1] The term 'rent-seeking' is used in the Report in the context of corruption and does not mean that all forms of rent-seeking are corrupt, e.g. competitive positioning by businesses in order to gain a temporary source of above-normal profits (or economic rents).

ventures. Corruption in aid programmes reduces their benefits to recipients and undermines public support in donor countries for their continued funding. Where programmes are funded through loans, the burden of external debt may be increased without a commensurate social return. There is a strong case for a co-operative international effort to improve the investment environment, thus increasing both the quantity and productivity of resource transfers.

13. **The systemic causes of corruption** While corruption has many causes, it is strongly interrelated to poor governance. Failures in economic policy create rent opportunities and weaknesses in public administration result in a decline in the probity of public servants and inadequate legislative oversight of government. All of these factors contribute to an environment favourable to the growth of corruption. In turn, corruption erodes the authority and effectiveness of public institutions. It becomes a prime cause of weaknesses in governance and sustains rent-seeking vested interests which act as a barrier to reform. Improvements in the effectiveness and transparency of economic policies and administrative reform can contribute powerfully to the fight against corruption as well as enhance governance. More generally, it is vital to achieve greater transparency and accountability in conducting all government business in order to instill public confidence in public institutions.

14. Inappropriate controls that encourage the exercise of undue political or administrative discretion create rent-seeking opportunities as do inappropriate pricing policies which encourage the development of parallel markets. Excessive levels of taxation increase the incentive for tax fraud and the bribing of tax authorities. Poor fiscal management and inadequate government personnel policies (in areas such as recruitment, promotion and remuneration) result in declining efficiency in the public sector. Improvements in economic and fiscal management as well as in personnel management policies are therefore key components of a strategy to enhance government capacity.

15. However, even when inefficient economic controls are eliminated and excessive tax rates are reduced, governments will still engage in a large number of economic activities involving transactions with the private sector. These range from taxation, government procurement of goods and services and delivery of public services, to transport, health and environmental regulations. Even if the reduction of rent-seeking opportunities reduces the scope for corruption, the normal range of government business leaves ample scope for the bribery of public servants. Furthermore, the transition to reform may itself pose difficult challenges to governments and create new incentives for corrupt behaviour. The process of privatisation, for example, creates opportunities for illicit gains, if the transfer of assets takes place in a non-transparent fashion. In designing and implementing economic policy reforms, it is also important to encourage transparency in business practices and establish level playing fields for domestic and foreign investors. Corruption in the private sector can cause as much harm to the health of the economy as corruption in the public sector. It must also be recognised that the distinction between the two sectors is becoming increasingly blurred.

16. **The diversity of corruption** In some societies, corruption exists but is not pervasive enough to significantly affect resource allocation decisions. In other societies, corruption has greatly distorted government programmes and undermined the effectiveness of public interventions. Corruption can occur at all levels, from pay-offs at the top of the system, to 'petty corruption' by way of bribes to local officials for the delivery of services and to evade regulations. In some cases, the gains from corruption may be siphoned off to foreign bank accounts, while in other cases proceeds are 'recycled' in the local economy. However, despite its diversity, corruption always involves social and economic costs, erodes the credibility of public institutions and engenders public cynicism.

17. **Corruption and political systems** While the inter-relationship between corruption and the broader governance agenda must be recognised, any facile conclusions regarding the relationship between corruption and any particular set of political institutions should be avoided. There are

many examples of corrupt practices that feed upon multi-party political processes, just as there are authoritarian regimes which have relatively 'clean' records of economic management.

18. **The need for national anti-corruption measures** The fight against corruption should go hand in hand with more general efforts to improve economic governance. However, success in more general reform efforts should be seen as neither a necessary nor sufficient condition for eliminating corruption, nor should the difficulties to be overcome in implementing broad-based reforms be used as an excuse for delay in tackling corruption. Furthermore, even in an otherwise well ordered system of governance, corruption can thrive in the absence of effective vigilance and enforcement. Sustained action is required at two levels to address the root causes of corruption and tackle all its manifestations:

- systemic reforms, which target the underlying weaknesses in policy, administration and politics, and create an environment conducive to the elimination of corruption; and
- specific, focused national anti-corruption strategies.

19. In mounting a serious national anti-corruption programme, the first step of securing a strong commitment at the highest political level to fight corruption is often the most difficult hurdle. When corruption is widespread, particularly where it involves the political establishment, this may involve serious political risks, despite popular support for cleaner government. One solution may be an amnesty for corrupt acts committed in the past, combined with an explicit code of conduct, spelling out minimum standards of universal applicability, which will be enforced vigorously from the start of the new anti-corruption programme.

20. **Popular mobilisation against corruption** The most potent force in the fight against corruption is the widespread resentment of corrupt practices and popular support for firm action. Anti-corruption programmes need to be designed to meet the expectations of citizens and with public participation. They are likely to be more effective when they are built on the foundation of popular empowerment, nationally owned and designed to meet national circumstances.

21. **The private sector and civil society** The concept of good governance extends beyond government. Although an anti-corruption strategy usually focuses initially on preventing the use of public office for private gain, support could be enhanced if the dangers of unethical practices in the private sector and non-governmental institutions are more widely appreciated. Corrupt behaviour (e.g. by corporate purchasing agents, or in job recruitment) can be as destructive of the performance of businesses or of non-governmental organisations (NGOs) as it is of government. Private businesses, co-operatives and NGOs all have a stake in combating a culture of corruption. Moreover, even where governments are less than enthusiastic in tackling corruption, popular support and the agencies of civil society can still be mobilised in support of an anti-corruption agenda.

22. **The need for an international response** There is a strong case on a number of grounds for international co-operation in fighting corruption:

- countries embarking on an anti-corruption strategy can learn from the experience of those that have already had some success in reducing corruption; furthermore, international cooperation can reinforce national efforts to combat corruption;
- in a globalised economy, transactions across borders are of increasing importance, but are often difficult to monitor by national authorities acting alone;
- international transactions may sometimes provide a conducive environment for corrupt practices, where actors are willing to engage in dubious practices abroad that would be unacceptable at home; and
- international financial transactions provide opportunities for the laundering of financial gains from corrupt practices.

23. Given the global nature of corruption, there should be no double standards. Anti-corruption measures should apply equally to rich and poor countries. They should target those who are

directly guilty of corrupt behaviour as well as those who facilitate corruption (e.g. by providing money laundering opportunities). They should penalise both bribers and bribees (i.e. those who offer, as well as those who accept, bribes).

III National Actions

24. Under the over-arching principle of 'zero tolerance', specific measures are required to *prevent* corruption, *enforce* laws against it and *mobilise public support*. These should be the sinews of coherent national programmes to achieve good governance and combat corruption.

A general approach to the formulation of such programmes is set out below, but specific programmes reflecting national realities and circumstances will be required to translate such a general approach into practice. The Expert Group therefore proposes that each Commonwealth government should develop its own national good governance and anti-corruption strategy, which should identify clear objectives, effective instruments, realistic timetables and credible implementation and monitoring mechanisms.

25. The Commonwealth should render technical assistance in the development of such strategies and promote exchange of experience in close collaboration with UN programmes, the Bretton Woods Institutions, the Organisation for Economic Co-operation and Development (OECD), Transparency International and other relevant agencies. In designing national strategies, care should be taken to respect different cultural, moral, political and social environments, provided these are not inconsistent with the objective of achieving 'zero tolerance'. The initiative for strategy development and the choice of goals should lie with national authorities and not be externally imposed.

26. National strategies should encompass both the public and private sectors. Corruption in the private sector (e.g. in the operation of financial markets) can be as corrosive to economic performance as public sector corruption. Moreover, public sector corruption typically involves actors from the private sector. A national culture opposed to corruption requires high standards of behaviour from all sections of society, but especially from political leaders.

27. Effective national campaigns against corruption need support from the highest levels of government and implementation of the strategy requires high-level co-ordination. Hence, an important first step in developing national strategies is for the political leadership to recognise that corruption in both the public and private sectors has heavy economic and political costs and that, no matter how deeply embedded it is, it is possible to adopt effective measures against it, provided there is sufficient political will.

The Main Building Blocks

28. While the content of national strategies will vary, depending on national circumstances, there are three main building blocks for effective strategies: prevention, enforcement and the engagement of civil society.

29. **Prevention** should address underlying causes of corruption, particularly those arising from failures of public policy and weaknesses in political and administrative institutions. Economic policy reform to reduce rent-seeking opportunities; civil service reform to improve the effectiveness and probity of the public service; reforms in tax policy and administration; tightening of controls over public expenditure; and reforms in the political system, are all important ingredients of a prevention strategy.

30. An important contribution to prevention can be made by strengthening transparency in economic management, through:

- full disclosure and examination of government finances, especially by parliamentary scrutiny;
- strengthening of parliamentary public accounts committees;

- the use of open competitive bidding for government contracts;
- publication of full information on the reports of government auditors and evaluations of development projects;
- media access to information on government finances;
- full disclosure of assets by government leaders and their families;
- setting international financial agreements before the legislature (including arms procurement) and establishing clear guidelines for fiscal discipline; and
- establishment of mechanisms for public exposure where the above do not occur.

31. Prevention should concentrate not only on the behaviour of public officials, but also aim to affect the behaviour of those who offer bribes. A code of practice for private business should spell out what is a corrupt practice, and what is legitimate business promotion. Acceptable practices in relation to business sponsorship of public activities (e.g. sports and social events) and to the employment of public officials as consultants or in other capacities, while in office and after retirement, need to be spelt out. As with all regulation, prevention is more likely if lawful behaviour is widely accepted as the norm.

32. **Enforcement** involves firm action against corrupt behaviour at all levels. Since effective enforcement is dependent upon the competence and honesty of investigators, prosecutors and the judiciary, it is important to allocate sufficient resources to ensure the probity and effectiveness of these agents. The rule of law should apply to economic transactions, with equality and impartiality in the application of the law and in access to legal remedies. Any ambiguities in laws and regulations that create incentives for corrupt behaviour should be removed. Where the integrity of legal institutions has eroded, action to restore their credibility must come early in the implementation of a national anti-corruption strategy.

33. **Mobilisation of popular support** through the engagement of civil society and popular opinion is important in changing public mores, as well as in exerting pressure on governments (at both national and local levels) to take the necessary actions to prepare and implement anti-corruption programmes. Perhaps the greatest potential force for reforms to combat corruption stems from public resentment of corruption and the burdens it places on citizens. This can provide an important basis of political support for anti-corruption actions, and challenge vested interests. Popular pressures can ensure accountability for the management of public resources, including accountability through the appropriate legislative bodies to the general public and, where external resources are concerned, to the international community.

34. Popular opinion can be activated and focused through the educational impact of the media and through the activities of NGOs; in particular:

- the freedom of the press and of other media contributes to public awareness of corruption and its consequences;
- the commitment of governments to freedom of expression and association is therefore a critical factor in creating conditions which are conducive for improving governance and eliminating corruption; and
- in situations where the media itself may be corrupt or susceptible to corruption, adherence to high standards of integrity in journalism should be promoted, along with the development of professional well-informed media, through self-regulation and training.

35. NGOs concerned with governance and corruption (e.g. Transparency International) should be encouraged in their efforts to create a presence and raise awareness at the national level. Governments should be encouraged to recognise and respect the positive contribution of national NGOs which campaign on corruption issues.

Key Reforms in Governance and the Fight Against Corruption

36. While action against corruption should not await the implementation of other complex reforms, parallel actions to improve economic management, administration and the political process could greatly improve the prospects of success in combating corruption. Key reforms which would contribute to the fight against corruption include:

- Economic reforms, which reduce rent-seeking opportunities, through the reduction of bureaucratic controls, simplification of economic regulations, and the removal of policy-induced scarcities (which create parallel markets and incentives to bribe to gain access to scarce goods and amenities).
- Fiscal reforms, which increase the efficiency of the public sector, thus permitting adequate funding of public services.
- Reform of subsidised public lending programmes which readily become a vehicle for corruption. This may be achieved by greater transparency in the operation of the programmes, by changing and strengthening the criteria for entitlement and reducing reliance on political/ administrative discretion in their operation.
- Civil service reform, which restores the morale and integrity of the public service through merit-based recruitment and promotion, and reduces the size and tasks of public administration to levels consistent with available fiscal resources, thus making it easier to enhance emoluments and reward good performance.
- Legal reform, which commits sufficient resources to the judiciary, investigative and prosecution services, ensures the autonomy of the judiciary from political interference, and demands high standards of honesty and commitment in recompense.
- Local government reforms, for the purpose of empowering people to combat corruption; ownership of national action would not be complete without the empowerment of people and strengthening of civil society.
- Monitoring of privatisation to ensure that the transfer of public assets does not create opportunities for the illicit accumulation of wealth.
- Opening up the administrative and political systems to greater public scrutiny through parliamentary enquiries and freedom of information provisions, with the aim of bringing public pressure to bear on political and economic decision-makers to maintain high standards in public service.
- Reforms to reduce the need for political parties to be dependent on contributions from commercial sources, special interest groups and international sources which can distort these parties' domestic concerns; and to limit the size of private contributions as well as make public the sources of party funding.
- Capacity building to enhance the capacity of core economic management institutions (e.g. ministries of finance, revenue collection agencies and auditor- generals' departments).

37. Some aspects of economic reform, while ultimately having the potential to reduce corruption, can create additional opportunities for misappropriation of public resources during the implementation phase. Thus, privatisation programmes, intended to reduce the scope for public sector rents, have themselves provided opportunities for corrupt public servants to illicitly transfer public assets. Fiscal stabilisation, aimed at reducing disequilibrium in the economy, has often resulted in reductions of the real income of civil servants, consequently increasing pressures on them to seek illicit incomes. The introduction of multi-party politics, intended to promote pluralism and place governments under tighter public scrutiny, also increases the need for politicians to seek funds.

38. National anti-corruption strategies should define a longer-term programme, with some decisive short-term time-bound actions to ensure that there is credibility and continuity in the

process of change. There is a need to move on a number of fronts simultaneously, but at varying speeds, as some reforms are easier to implement than others. In cases where corruption has fed on poor economic policies and fiscal imbalances, progress will be easier when certain basic economic reforms have been put in place, as a prelude to administrative reforms and the launching of an anti-corruption campaign. In other cases, political reform may have to be the first step in order to increase the likelihood of the political leadership finding the political will to sustain a national strategy.

39. Although the speed with which a meaningful programme can be formulated and implemented will vary, all governments should be encouraged to commit themselves to the principle of 'zero tolerance' and to institute the first steps to formulate comprehensive and realistic programmes.

Role of the Judiciary and Legal System

40. The legal system is central to the effective implementation of a national anti-corruption strategy. The rule of law implies that legally defined procedures govern public economic management, rather than political favouritism or personal connections. The independence and integrity of the judiciary is of vital importance. Most Commonwealth countries formally guarantee the independence of the judiciary from political control, but a key factor is the integrity of the members of the judiciary. Where the judiciary is corrupt, a crucial first step in a national strategy is reform which restores its efficiency and integrity. This may require restructuring, training and committing sufficient funds to compensate members of the judiciary adequately and to provide them with the means of operating effectively. Similarly, the quality and integrity of those public agencies responsible for investigating corruption and prosecuting offenders needs to be ensured. Public prosecution should be supplemented by broadening access to the courts, with individuals and community groups being given the right to take legal action in the public interest.

41. Critical components of a strategy of legal reform should include:

- *Entrenching an independent judiciary:* Commonwealth Law Ministers, at their 1996 meeting, recognised that the protections enjoyed by judges, including financial independence and security of tenure, were an important defence against improper interference. However, judicial independence does not imply a lack of accountability, as judges should act properly and in accordance with their office, and there should be procedures to discipline or dismiss them if they do not. Such procedures should be transparent and publicly administered by institutions which are themselves independent and impartial.
- *Court systems:* An efficient court system is an essential component of an effective governance and anti-corruption strategy. The courts of all countries are, however, overburdened. A court system which is able to dispense unbiased and corruption-free justice requires the implementation of proper case management systems to minimise delay and ensure equal access to justice. Access to justice ought not to be for sale. Hence, it is important to ensure that court lists are not influenced by payments made to court staff, who should be rigorous in their adherence to anti-corruption codes of conduct.
- *Detecting and dealing with corrupt conduct:* Many countries have enacted laws which permit the investigation of persons whose apparent assets exceed their known lawful sources of income. This permits relevant authorities (often anti-corruption commissions) to require persons to explain the sources of their assets and where the assets cannot be attributed to lawful acquisition, the person can be charged with a corruption offence. In addition to laws which criminalise corrupt conduct, laws which permit the confiscation of the proceeds of corruption are an essential weapon in the fight against corruption. It is also important to have legal provisions to protect witnesses and whistle-blowers in cases involving corruption.

- *Corporate liability:* Increasingly, Commonwealth countries are introducing the concept of corporate criminal liability, where corporations are involved in particular forms of criminal conduct or are used to facilitate or disguise criminal conduct.
- *Non-criminal legal remedies in corruption Cases:* Effective anti-corruption legal strategies cannot rely on the criminal law alone. Civil, administrative and regulatory laws all have a place in a comprehensive strategy:
  - —Civil law can provide effective remedies, but the civil law must be accessible and provide adequate protection to citizens' interests. Also, to permit the bringing of a civil law action there must be an identifiable victim or plaintiff.[2] The civil law can also be used, to supplement the criminal law, to facilitate recovery of assets from a public official who has benefited from the wrongful exercise of a public function (e.g. in cases where public officials purchase land in the knowledge of prospective re-zoning proposals which would increase the value of land).
  - —In the sphere of regulatory law reform, laws relating to unfair competition and to the control of monopoly trading could be useful to fight corruption. Provisions which incorporate proper processes including the application of the rules of natural justice could permit: the exclusion of persons (natural and legal) from public tenders (blacklisting); withdrawal of licences to conduct business; prohibition of anti-competitive acts; and disqualification of company directors.
  - —The Commonwealth principles (adopted by Law Ministers) on Co-operation between Business Regulatory Agencies have the potential to assist in the resolution of cases involving corruption which are dealt with under the laws relating to business regulation (rather than under the criminal laws).
  - —In cases involving petty corrupt practices, an appropriate remedy (certainly in 'first offence' cases) could lie with disciplinary bodies such as public service commissions, rather than action through the courts. The rights of employees could be protected by appropriate appeals procedures. Administrative tribunals with jurisdiction to review decisions made by public officials and to order rectification in appropriate cases could also offer redress in cases involving abuse of office. Their mere existence places moral and professional pressure on public officials to act transparently and in good faith.

IV. International Actions

42. In many instances, especially where corruption transcends national boundaries, national anti-corruption measures need to be reinforced with support at an international level, including co-operative law-enforcement initiatives against corruption (e.g. in the area of money laundering). There is a need for greater consultation on the international aspects of corruption on a genuinely multilateral basis, involving developed and developing countries, and a careful assessment of the degree to which international anti-corruption conventions designed to meet the needs of developed economies, also correspond to the requirements of developing economies. Most developing countries, with the exceptions of those who are members of the Organisation of American States (OAS), are not parties to the existing conventions. All developing countries should be able to participate effectively in the international campaign against corruption. This is particularly important in view of the increasing proportion of procurement under multilateral

[2] Citizens can suffer injury where they: (1) are unjustly excluded from public tendering procedures; (2) lose legitimate earnings; or (3) are forced to pay higher prices as a result of corruption. Among the victims of corruption are unsuccessful competitors and state agencies. Members of associations could also be victims and, hence, class actions may be available in certain cases such as consumer or environmental protection organisations. The damages which may be claimed in an action based on corruption could relate to pecuniary and non-pecuniary loss and may include punitive or exemplary damages in certain cases.

assistance which is sourced in developing countries, and the growing volumes of South-South trade and investment.

43. A number of international agencies have launched initiatives to address corruption and governance issues. In 1996, the United Nations (UN) General Assembly adopted a resolution on corruption, together with a Code of Conduct for Public Officials, which was intended to guide member states in their efforts against corruption. The following year, the OECD Convention on Combating Bribery of Foreign Public Officials in International Business Transactions (the OECD Convention) was signed. It has since entered into force in 12 of the 34 countries that have signed it. Other important initiatives include the Inter-American Convention against Corruption, the Council of Europe's recent Criminal Law Convention on Corruption, and the programmes for combating corruption adopted by the Bretton Woods institutions.

44. The World Bank has heightened its defences against corruption in its operations through new anti-fraud and corruption provisions in its procurement guidelines, improved disbursement provisions and strengthened financial auditing arrangements. The International Monetary Fund (IMF) is taking a more proactive approach to eliminate the opportunity for fraudulent activity and in 1997 adopted new guidelines for promoting good governance. In addition, both the World Bank and the IMF are providing assistance to national authorities in designing measures to strengthen the financial integrity of government institutions. Initiatives have also been taken in the private sector. For example, in 1996, the International Chamber of Commerce adopted a report that proposed strict rules of conduct for corporate self-regulation.

45. One of the major goals of existing international instruments on corruption has been to ensure a 'level playing field' for international businesses competing for business in developing countries (e.g. through the OECD Convention). There are gaps in the coverage of these initiatives and some continuing weaknesses in the practices of international and national financial institutions which fund aid and trade. Areas in which further effort is required include:

- *Funding of political parties:* the OECD Convention does not cover acts of bribery in relation to foreign political parties and it is not clear to what extent it might cover bribery of political party officials.
- *Laundering of the proceeds of corruption:* provisions relating to the laundering of the proceeds of corruption could be strengthened.
- *Offshore financial centres* safeguards are needed to prevent them from being used to harbour the proceeds of corruption.
- *Balance in accountability* aid and international lending agencies need to strengthen their procedures and rules in order to increase the internal scrutiny and accountability of their staff.
- *Shared responsibility for outcomes* there should be a more open acknowledgement by donors and international financial institutions for their share in the responsibility for programmes which they help design and for the policy advice they provide.
- *Lack of balance in exposure* at present, the main efforts (e.g. Transparency International's corruption index) to rank performance in relation to corruption seek to rank countries. There is no comparable effort to rank international corporations. In general, there is a need to direct the spotlight on the behaviour of these corporations.

46. It should be noted that developments currently underway may fill some of these gaps. The OECD's work on money laundering is at an advanced stage. The IMF and the World Bank are moving towards greater openness in their negotiations with their members. Both institutions and other donors have strengthened their financial and technical assistance in support of national efforts to improve governance and combat corruption.

47. Further movement in the direction of publishing the details of key international financial negotiations and mission reports by the international financial institutions would be welcome, as part of a process of increasing transparency that generates greater public information about policy issues and programme formulation. Governments should take advantage of the new openness to make maximum public disclosure of the contents of international financial negotiations and agreements. To increase public participation and national ownership of reform programmes, key documents such as Policy Framework Papers, Letters of Intent, and Letters of Development Policy should be published by the borrowing countries and widely disseminated, unless there are valid reasons for non-disclosure.

48. The results of monitoring and of operational evaluation by aid agencies and national governments should get maximum public exposure. The wider public dissemination of national and international reports on corruption should be encouraged, to increase public knowledge of the extent of corrupt practices and possible avenues for reform.

49. In line with its 1997 guidelines, the IMF should be even-handed by raising governance and corruption issues in developed countries when exercising its surveillance function, as it does in developing countries when it is financing programmes. Measures to improve governance and reduce corruption should be domestically owned and rarely imposed externally as conditions for financial support. When such conditionality is introduced by international financial institutions in exceptional cases, this should be consistent with their mandates. In designing conditionality on governance and corruption issues, the IMIIF and the World Bank should take full account of a country's capability to implement reforms and define realistic time schedules. 'Floating tranches', which have been recently adopted in several World Bank structural adjustment loans, could be used more widely to achieve more effective timing and sequencing of reform measures without holding up entire programmes. To promote national ownership of reforms, donors should agree with governments on the objectives to be achieved, identify alternative paths to those ends, but leave the route to be selected to the government.

50. The work of Transparency International in monitoring global corruption is to be welcomed. Working with national governments, Transparency International is promoting 'integrity workshops' which will help raise consciousness about corruption issues. Its proposals to collect data on public procurement costs of selected generic items also warrant support. However, the Expert Group does not believe that Transparency International's Corruption Perception Index presently provides a reliable and comprehensive guide to relative country performance. The Index should be improved by increasing its comprehensiveness, extending the data sources on which it is based, and providing some indication of trends over time. Monitoring should also be extended to include multinational corporations. Other credible international NGOs which are involved in monitoring corruption and campaigning against it also deserve international support.

51. The international arms trade is a potent source of corruption, surrounded by secrecy and fuelled by illicit payments to middlemen. In addition to the need to control the arms trade in furtherance of international peace and security, much greater efforts are required to reduce corruption in this sphere.

52. Two actions would help to achieve this:

- a new code of conduct covering the international trade in arms, requiring full disclosure by the parties involved (the recipient government, the arms suppliers and their governments)[3] and
- strengthening support for the UN arms register.

[3] This should take account of recent initiatives which include the Code of Conduct on Arms Exports adopted by the European Union's Council in May 1998 (the Code is to be reviewed annually and may be progressively strengthened); and the draft International Code of Conduct for the arms trade which has been drafted by a group of former Nobel Peace Prize Laureates headed by Dr Arias. former President of Costa Rica.

53. There is also a need to reform aid policies by reducing tied-aid, and by monitoring suppliers credits. The tying of aid to procurement from the donor country not only increases costs but also reduces the scope for competitive bidding. This increases the incentive for corrupt practices on the part of the suppliers, both in relation to the recipient and the donor agency. Likewise, supplier credits can be used to fund projects with little equity involvement on the part of the promoter, thus generating quick returns which increases the scope for payoffs. There is also a need for transparency to expose conflicts of interest among those involved in project formulation, appraisal and implementation (e.g. where firms involved in project formulation and appraisal are also contracted to undertake project implementation).

54. Stronger conditions attached to aid projects which ensure that procurement and disbursement related to the project are shielded from corruption, and blacklisting contractors who engage in corrupt practices, are desirable. Regional financial institutions and bilateral donors who have not already done so should adopt anti-fraud and corruption provisions in their procurement guidelines similar to those adopted by the World Bank in 1996.

55. International support for basic harmonisation of national laws on corruption will facilitate international co-operation in the investigation and prosecution of these offences, particularly in the areas of extradition and mutual assistance in criminal matters. In this regard, the European Criminal Law Convention on Corruption is a good model.

V. A Role for the Commonwealth

56. Commonwealth governments should lend support to the international initiatives outlined in the previous section of this Report. In parallel with formal international conventions of the kind being promoted by the OECD, there is an equally important role for less formal co-operation between countries. Given its voluntary and informal nature, its democratic ethos and the common legal traditions shared by its diverse membership (which includes both developed and developing countries), the Commonwealth is particularly well adapted to provide channels of communication and mutual aid in tackling the delicate and controversial political issues which must be confronted in combating corruption.

57. The Commonwealth can reinforce efforts in some areas which are not susceptible to formal legal compacts or are not the primary concern of the other multilateral organisations which have taken initiatives in this area. In particular, the Commonwealth is in a good position to promote dialogue on the political aspects of reform, and to sponsor initiatives for the strengthening of legal institutions required for effective enforcement of anti-corruption measures. There is a rich and varied experience among Commonwealth countries in efforts to improve governance and combat corruption. This has included notable successes in uprooting deeply entrenched corrupt practices. Although the diversity among Commonwealth countries (e.g. in relation to income levels) may mean that some approaches will need to be carefully adapted to be transferable, the legal and political traditions shared by many Commonwealth countries suggest that there are many useful lessons to be learnt by sharing experiences.

58. The Expert Group considered the advantages and disadvantages of different instruments through which the Commonwealth's commitment to promote good governance and combat corruption might be best expressed in tangible terms. One approach would be for the association to have its own legally binding instrument or convention on governance and corruption. Such an instrument would reflect the Commonwealth's specific concerns, values and aspirations and its effectiveness would be subject to Commonwealth control. Because of its legally binding nature, a convention would give 'teeth' to the Commonwealth's commitment and greatly strengthen the enforcement of anti-corruption measures at national levels. It would also help to improve foreign investors' perceptions of the investment environment in many Commonwealth countries.

59. On the other hand, many Commonwealth members might have strong reservations about the negotiation of a legally binding instrument, as this would be historically unprecedented and constitute a radical departure from the Commonwealth's tradition of articulating collective commitments of the association through morally, but not legally, binding declarations adopted by consensus. Furthermore, the process of negotiating, signing and ratifying a Commonwealth convention could prove to be a protracted as well as a costly enterprise. In addition, in some regions of the Commonwealth, a legal instrument confined exclusively to the Commonwealth might not be effective when the co-operation of neighbouring non-Commonwealth countries is needed to tackle trans-border problems of corruption.

60. An alternative approach, more consistent with Commonwealth practice, would be for Heads of Government to adopt a morally binding declaration of principles which would provide the foundation for concerted action by the association to promote good governance and combat corruption. Drawing on the analysis and discussion of issues in this Report, the Expert Group has proposed a possible draft framework for such principles in the accompanying document entitled 'Promoting Good Governance and Combating Corruption: Framework for Commonwealth Principles'. This could be supplemented by a Commonwealth scheme for the implementation of national and international measures to combat corruption.

61. Recognising the need for a broader, global campaign against corruption in which it should play an active role the Commonwealth could also agree to promote, in consultation with other interested parties, an initiative to launch, under the auspices of the United Nations, negotiations on a global, legally binding intergovernmental compact against corruption. Details of such a possible initiative are elaborated in Annex 2.

62. Another option for consideration is whether Commonwealth governments might become parties to existing international, but not universal, conventions against corruption such as the OECD and OAS Conventions and the Council of Europe's Criminal Law Convention on Corruption. This would appear to be a relatively simpler way of improving the enforcement of anti-corruption measures in Commonwealth countries. It is likely that Commonwealth countries which wish to join these Conventions would be able to do so, provided they are able to meet membership criteria and related obligations. However, the scope of some of these conventions (e.g. the OECD Convention) might be considered to be too narrow by some Commonwealth governments.[4]

63. The Group believes the Commonwealth's commitment to fight corruption and promote good governance should be credible, tangible and visible. It needs to be articulated at the highest level, which is by Heads of Government. Their meeting in South Africa towards the end of 1999 provides a unique opportunity for the Commonwealth to act sooner rather than later. Commonwealth governments should therefore consider carefully the most appropriate means of evidencing and advancing the Commonwealth's commitment to effective action to combat corruption. The Group hopes that, in the first instance, Commonwealth Law Ministers will be able to offer guidance on this subject at their meeting in May 1999.

64. There are a number of important practical ways a specific Commonwealth contribution can also be made to improve governance and combat corruption. The Group agreed on the following specific proposals for action:

- The Commonwealth Secretariat should assist member countries that request help in designing and implementing their own national strategies to promote good governance and eliminate corruption. Such assistance could take the form of technical assistance and training for capacity building in countries that face serious human resource and institutional constraints. The

[4] A Note by the Commonwealth Secretariat on existing multilateral conventions on corruption and their membership criteria is at Annex 3.

Secretariat should also compile and disseminate information on emerging good practice in combating corruption and improving governance, and gather information on a regular basis from members on their progress in implementing national strategies.

- The Commonwealth should finalise and adopt its draft Code of Conduct on Integrity in Public Office; and the Commonwealth Code for Good Corporate Governance should be finalised, taking account of the work on similar codes undertaken by the World Bank and the OECD, and disseminated widely.
- The Commonwealth and the international financial institutions should support the implementation of standards that have been agreed to ensure that off-shore financial centres (many of which fall within jurisdictions of developed and developing Commonwealth countries) are not used to launder bribes.

65. The Commonwealth should also offer encouragement and support for the further development of the international initiatives described in Section IV. Areas where further developments should be encouraged include:

- further work by the OECD to tackle the issues of contributions to political parties and to strengthen measures against the laundering of bribes;
- the extension of the scope of the work of Transparency International to report on the behaviour of international business, along with improved reporting on perceptions of national corruption;
- further work by the IMF related to its Code of Good Practices on Fiscal Transparency in developing, together with other institutions including the Bank for International Settlements and the World Bank, a Code of Good Practices on Transparency in Monetary and Financial Policies; and on the proposed Transparency Reports which would indicate country performance in these areas;
- support for the work of the Council of Europe on corruption;
- encouragement of other international agencies, including Transparency International, to focus attention on corruption associated with the international arms trade; and
- sponsoring more work on the specific needs of developing economies in relation to international agreements to combat corruption.

66. As resources at the disposal of the Commonwealth are limited, the Commonwealth Secretariat should seek to help members states in accessing other sources of funding to support national anti-corruption strategies and should identify actions which are additional and complementary to existing national and international initiatives.

67. The Expert Group believes that, if the Commonwealth is to make a serious contribution to the promotion of good governance and the fight against corruption, there will be a need to commit additional resources to enable the Secretariat to undertake the tasks outlined above. Given the potential economic, social and political gains, there is justification for the commitment of sufficient resources to support this venture.

APPENDIX 7

Commonwealth Working Group on Asset Repatriation

Recommendations

General

1. Commonwealth countries should sign, ratify and implement the United Nations Convention against Corruption as a matter of urgency.

Misappropriation of Assets

2. Commonwealth countries should have regard to the Commonwealth Framework and Chapter II of the UNCAC on Preventive Measures and adopt a comprehensive regime under domestic law.

3. Having regard to the criminal offence provisions of the UNCAC, Commonwealth countries should ensure that there are a broad range of criminal offences under domestic law for use in corruption cases, including an offence of bribery of foreign officials abroad.

4. Commonwealth countries should ensure that the law clearly describes how public funds may be used including by Heads of State/Government and that there are criminal offences applicable to any misuse of those funds.

5. Commonwealth countries should introduce an offence of unjust enrichment if it does not already exist.

6. Commonwealth Heads of State/Government and other public officials should not have immunity from prosecution in domestic courts for alleged criminal activity.

7. Heads of Government should commit themselves to take active steps to ensure the removal of these immunities.

8. The Commonwealth Secretariat should prepare periodic reports for consideration by Heads of Government on progressive action towards reaching the optimum goal of no immunities at all for criminal prosecutions throughout the Commonwealth.

9. The Commonwealth as an organisation of sovereign states should advance a position for the inclusion of corruption offences within the Rome Statute of the International Criminal Court at the Review Conference for the Statute in 2009.

10. The law in Commonwealth countries should provide for

(a) a judicial review mechanism for claims of public interest immunity
(b) exceptions to the privilege where it can be established that the information or evidence sought is relevant to the investigation of (serious) criminal activity, with appropriate safeguards on any disclosure as may be necessary.

Preventing the Movement of Funds

11. Commonwealth countries which have not already done so should implement the broad range of international initiatives directed at preventing the movement of illicit assets and combating

money laundering. This should include adopting and enforcing anti-money laundering and proceeds of crime laws with relevant structures and administrative procedures. The Commonwealth Secretariat should continue to support member countries with these efforts.

12. The Commonwealth Secretariat should develop programmes to assist countries with the development and implementation of early warning systems to raise awareness about political situations particularly vulnerable to corruption.

13. Commonwealth countries should enact laws to allow for expedited cash seizures at the border and generally throughout the country in respect of cash which exceeds a specified threshold.

14. Enhanced scrutiny regimes should be applied to Politically Exposed Persons (PEPs) as defined by the Financial Action Task Force but extending to both domestic and foreign PEPs.

15. The Commonwealth Secretariat should continue to support countries in the implementation of international initiatives to combat money laundering and to gather and disseminate information regarding anti-money laundering and corruption legislation within the Commonwealth.

Serving Heads of State

16. Commonwealth countries should have in place independent and effective mechanisms by which allegations of corruption with respect to a current Head of State/Government can be investigated and prosecuted and the relevant assets can be frozen and confiscated.

17. The procedures relating to suspicious transaction reporting should apply where suspect funds belong to a current Head of State/Government of another country are identified. Where possible and appropriate, the FIU or other appropriate body or authority in the receiving state should communicate the information about suspect funds to the FIU or other appropriate body or authority in the home state for action to be taken.

18. Where there is sufficient evidence, the receiving state should use the methods available under domestic law to obtain the restraint and confiscation of the relevant assets.

19. In cases involving allegations of corruption by serving Heads of State/Government the Commonwealth should have an ad hoc peer review mechanism in place.

Mechanisms for Asset Confiscation

20. Commonwealth countries that have yet to do so should promptly put in place strong and comprehensive legislation and procedures for criminal conviction based asset confiscation. This should include a power to confiscate in circumstances where the accused has absconded or died.

21. Commonwealth countries should also put in place comprehensive laws and procedures for non-conviction based asset confiscation.

22. Commonwealth countries should allocate sufficient resources to establish and properly fund law enforcement and other agencies dealing with asset confiscation and management.

Tracing and Tracking of Assets

23. For asset confiscation legislation to be effectively implemented law enforcement authorities need to have the requisite knowledge and skills. Commonwealth countries, with support from the Commonwealth Secretariat, should develop and implement programmes for training/capacity building for police, prosecutors and judicial officers in relation to asset confiscation laws and practice.

24. The Commonwealth Secretariat should continue with and enhance its programme for placement of prosecution and law enforcement mentors within Commonwealth countries and regions to assist with ongoing asset confiscation and money laundering cases and contribute to capacity building.

25. Commonwealth countries should adopt best practices for asset confiscation investigations and proceedings including:

- establishing dedicated, law enforcement teams to investigate proceeds of crime matters which are multidisciplinary in composition or have support from experts in various relevant disciplines;
- establishing where possible joint investigative teams on a domestic and/or international level;
- providing sufficient funds for the investigation and prosecution of confiscation cases including funding specialist support;
- adoption or review and amendment of laws to provide for a range of investigative powers of particular relevance to these investigations including for compelled interviews, production orders, account monitoring and interception of communications.

26. Adoption or review and amendment of laws which allow for investigators to access tax information for their investigations.

Mutual Legal Assistance—General

27. Mutual legal assistance between Commonwealth countries should be available on the basis of the Commonwealth Scheme for Mutual Assistance in Criminal Matters (the Harare Scheme) without a requirement for a bilateral treaty. Commonwealth countries that currently require a treaty for mutual legal assistance should consider removing such a requirement. Optimally domestic law should allow for assistance to be rendered to all countries on the basis of national law without the requirement for a treaty.

28. Commonwealth countries which have yet to do so should promptly establish a central authority as required under the Harare Scheme.

29. Consultation between central and other relevant authorities (e.g. law enforcement) regarding mutual legal assistance requests should be strongly encouraged.

30. Central authorities and the mutual legal assistance execution process should be properly resourced and funded and Commonwealth countries should allocate sufficient resources for this purpose.

31. The Commonwealth Secretariat should establish a webpage which would include practical information on mutual legal assistance laws (including restraint and confiscation requirements) and systems within member countries and provide some guidance on how to make requests to different countries.

32. Creation of a Commonwealth Network similar to the European Judicial Network/Eurojust adapted to the particular circumstances of the Commonwealth. This could include setting up both regional bodies as well as a Commonwealth entity.

33. The Commonwealth Secretariat should continue and enhance its assistance programmes to Commonwealth countries relating to capacity building and training. The Secretariat should also continue to facilitate co-operation by maintaining lists of central authorities and providing contact particulars for central authorities and other relevant officials to member countries in response to requests.

34. Commonwealth countries should have the legal capacity to render mutual legal assistance in the absence of dual criminality.

35. Commonwealth countries should adopt best practices for effective mutual legal assistance including:

(a) encouraging the development of personal contacts between central authorities and other relevant officials;
(b) where appropriate develop MOUs to enhance working relationships;
(c) to the extent possible consulting with authorities in the requested state about applicable laws and the content of a request prior to submitting any formal documentation;

(d) ensuring that requests for assistance are kept confidential and that the requesting state is consulted when circumstances arise where disclosure of the request is sought;
(e) implementing the Best Practice Recommendations of the UNODC Expert Working Group (2001).

Availability of Mutual Legal Assistance

36. Commonwealth countries should have the legal capacity to provide mutual legal assistance with respect to investigations and proceedings relating to non-conviction based asset confiscation. Similarly, the Harare Scheme should be amended to cover such types of assistance.

37. The mutual legal assistance regimes in Commonwealth countries should permit evidence gathered from a criminal proceeding to be subsequently used in civil proceedings and requests for such use should be granted in corruption cases.

38. Commonwealth Law Ministers should examine further the issue of the possible use of mutual legal assistance to gather evidence for use in civil proceedings brought by a victim country for the recovery of assets in corruption cases.

Mutual Assistance for Freezing/Restraint/Confiscation of Assets

39. Commonwealth countries which have yet to provide for restraint and confiscation of assets in response to a foreign request should promptly adopt legislation which establishes a direct enforcement system. The direct enforcement system should

(i) allow for all foreign orders to be enforced but subject to an executive discretion to grant or refuse requests in particular cases;
(ii) provide for the enforcement of conviction based and non-conviction based orders;
(iii) allow for innocent third parties to challenge a restraint order or the enforcement of a confiscation order in both the requesting and requested state;
(iv) permit the accused to challenge a restraint order in the requested state on a limited basis related to procedural questions or fundamental human rights but not to challenge the underlying criminal offences or orders issued in the requesting state.

40. Commonwealth countries which have an existing law for enforcing foreign requests for restraint and confiscation should review their legislation and procedures and amend them as necessary to ensure that foreign requests for restraint and confiscation can be effectively and speedily enforced. If the current law does not provide for the enforcement of non-conviction based orders, it should be amended to do so.

41. Commonwealth countries should ensure proper co-ordination of cross border restraint and confiscation efforts and the management of assets.

42. Commonwealth countries should have the legal capacity to render legal assistance in relation to requests for restraint and confiscation from another country in the absence of dual criminality.

Mutual Assistance—The Harare Scheme

43. Commonwealth countries that have yet to do so should promptly enact mutual legal assistance legislation.

44. National legislation for mutual legal assistance in Commonwealth countries should implement the provisions of the Harare Scheme.

45. The Harare Scheme should be amended to

- extend the application of the Scheme to non-conviction based asset confiscation;
- ensure the Scheme applies to the various models for asset confiscation within the Commonwealth and incorporates comprehensive definitions;

- makes the Scheme more effective in asset confiscation cases by providing for the production of documents, the presence of representatives of the requesting state in the execution process and providing that requests shall not be refused on the ground of bank secrecy;
- enhance the provisions of the Scheme relating to asset sharing.

Restraint of Assets

46. Commonwealth countries should ensure that the legislative scheme for restraint and confiscation is flexible and permits early application for a restraint order.

47. Commonwealth countries should ensure that the legislative scheme contains appropriate mechanisms for asset management.

48. FIU's or other appropriate authorities within each country should have the power to issue short term administrative freezing orders.

Effective Repatriation of Assets

49. Where the relevant countries agree the Commonwealth should assist in reaching an agreement on the final disposition of confiscated assets.

50. Commonwealth countries that require a bilateral treaty or memorandum of understanding for asset sharing or the return of assets should eliminate this requirement.

51. Clause 28 of the Harare Scheme should be amended . . . to ensure that the Scheme can be used as a basis for the sharing of assets and to provide for the repatriation of assets.

52. Commonwealth countries should provide by law, either through a judicial process or executive decision, for the return of funds minus reasonable expenses to a requesting country:

(a) in cases of misappropriation or other unlawful taking of public funds or the laundering thereof;

(b) where the requesting country reasonably establishes its prior ownership of confiscated property; or

(c) when the requested country recognises damage to the requesting country.

53. The law for the return of funds should be distinct from any existing laws or provisions relating to asset sharing. Where possible, Commonwealth countries returning the funds should give consideration to waiving the deduction of reasonable costs.

54. Commonwealth countries are encouraged to implement 'fast track' priority systems for corruption cases to reduce the amount of delay in repatriation to a minimum.

55. The Commonwealth Secretariat should liaise with the G8 presidency in relation to the identification of suitable cases for the establishment of case co-ordination teams and asset recovery task forces to assist member countries as appropriate.

Recommendations for Implementation

56. Commonwealth countries should give priority attention to the implementation of the recommendations in this Report, particularly the key recommendations.

57. Commonwealth Heads of Government should commit increased resources for the Commonwealth Secretariat to assist Commonwealth countries with the implementation of these recommendations.

58. Commonwealth Heads of Government should keep asset repatriation on the agenda for their meetings and commit themselves to periodic review and discussion (by Heads of Government/Law and Finance Ministers) of the progress on implementation of the recommendations in the Report.

London, 2005

APPENDIX 8

Civil Law Convention on Corruption

Strasbourg, 4 November 1999

Preamble

The member States of the Council of Europe, the other States and the European Community, signatories hereto,

Considering that the aim of the Council of Europe is to achieve a greater unity between its members;

Conscious of the importance of strengthening international co-operation in the fight against corruption;

Emphasising that corruption represents a major threat to the rule of law, democracy and human rights, fairness and social justice, hinders economic development and endangers the proper and fair functioning of market economies;

Recognising the adverse financial consequences of corruption to individuals, companies and States, as well as international institutions;

Convinced of the importance for civil law to contribute to the fight against corruption, in particular by enabling persons who have suffered damage to receive fair compensation;

Recalling the conclusions and resolutions of the 19th (Malta, 1994), 21st (Czech Republic, 1997) and 22nd (Moldova, 1999) Conferences of the European Ministers of Justice;

Taking into account the Programme of Action against Corruption adopted by the Committee of Ministers in November 1996;

Taking also into account the feasibility study on the drawing up of a convention on civil remedies for compensation for damage resulting from acts of corruption, approved by the Committee of Ministers in February 1997;

Having regard to Resolution (97) 24 on the 20 Guiding Principles for the Fight against Corruption, adopted by the Committee of Ministers in November 1997, at its 101st Session, to Resolution (98) 7 authorising the adoption of the Partial and Enlarged Agreement establishing the 'Group of States against Corruption (GRECO)', adopted by the Committee of Ministers in May 1998, at its 102nd Session, and to Resolution (99) 5 establishing the GRECO, adopted on 1st May 1999;

Recalling the Final Declaration and the Action Plan adopted by the Heads of State and Government of the member States of the Council of Europe at their 2nd summit in Strasbourg, in October 1997,

Have agreed as follows:

Chapter I Measures to be taken at National Level

Article 1
Purpose

Each Party shall provide in its internal law for effective remedies for persons who have suffered damage as a result of acts of corruption, to enable them to defend their rights and interests, including the possibility of obtaining compensation for damage.

Article 2
Definition of corruption

For the purpose of this Convention, 'corruption' means requesting, offering, giving or accepting, directly or indirectly, a bribe or any other undue advantage or prospect thereof, which distorts the proper performance of any duty or behaviour required of the recipient of the bribe, the undue advantage or the prospect thereof.

Article 3
Compensation for damage

1 Each Party shall provide in its internal law for persons who have suffered damage as a result of corruption to have the right to initiate an action in order to obtain full compensation for such damage.
2 Such compensation may cover material damage, loss of profits and non-pecuniary loss.

Article 4
Liability

1 Each Party shall provide in its internal law for the following conditions to be fulfilled in order for the damage to be compensated:
   i the defendant has committed or authorised the act of corruption, or failed to take reasonable steps to prevent the act of corruption;
   ii the plaintiff has suffered damage; and
   iii there is a causal link between the act of corruption and the damage.
2 Each Party shall provide in its internal law that, if several defendants are liable for damage for the same corrupt activity, they shall be jointly and severally liable.

Article 5
State responsibility

Each Party shall provide in its internal law for appropriate procedures for persons who have suffered damage as a result of an act of corruption by its public officials in the exercise of their functions to claim for compensation from the State or, in the case of a non-state Party, from that Party's appropriate authorities.

Article 6
Contributory negligence

Each Party shall provide in its internal law for the compensation to be reduced or disallowed having regard to all the circumstances, if the plaintiff has by his or her own fault contributed to the damage or to its aggravation.

Article 7

Limitation periods

1 Each Party shall provide in its internal law for proceedings for the recovery of damages to be subject to a limitation period of not less than three years from the day the person who has suffered damage became aware or should reasonably have been aware, that damage has occurred or that an act of corruption has taken place, and of the identity of the responsible person. However, such proceedings shall not be commenced after the end of a limitation period of not less than ten years from the date of the act of corruption.

2 The laws of the Parties regulating suspension or interruption of limitation periods shall, if appropriate, apply to the periods prescribed in paragraph 1.

Article 8

Validity of contracts

1 Each Party shall provide in its internal law for any contract or clause of a contract providing for corruption to be null and void.

2 Each Party shall provide in its internal law for the possibility for all parties to a contract whose consent has been undermined by an act of corruption to be able to apply to the court for the contract to be declared void, notwithstanding their right to claim for damages.

Article 9

Protection of employees

Each Party shall provide in its internal law for appropriate protection against any unjustified sanction for employees who have reasonable grounds to suspect corruption and who report in good faith their suspicion to responsible persons or authorities.

Article 10

Accounts and audits

1 Each Party shall, in its internal law, take any necessary measures for the annual accounts of companies to be drawn up clearly and give a true and fair view of the company's financial position.

2 With a view to preventing acts of corruption, each Party shall provide in its internal law for auditors to confirm that the annual accounts present a true and fair view of the company's financial position.

Article 11

Acquisition of evidence

Each Party shall provide in its internal law for effective procedures for the acquisition of evidence in civil proceedings arising from an act of corruption.

Article 12

Interim measures

Each Party shall provide in its internal law for such court orders as are necessary to preserve the rights and interests of the parties during civil proceedings arising from an act of corruption.

Chapter II International Co-operation and Monitoring of Implementation

Article 13

International co-operation

The Parties shall co-operate effectively in matters relating to civil proceedings in cases of corruption, especially concerning the service of documents, obtaining evidence abroad, jurisdiction, recognition and enforcement of foreign judgements and litigation costs, in accordance with the provisions of relevant international instruments on international co-operation in civil and commercial matters to which they are Party, as well as with their internal law.

Article 14
Monitoring

The Group of States against Corruption (GRECO) shall monitor the implementation of this Convention by the Parties.

Chapter III Final Clauses

Article 15
Signature and entry into force

1 This Convention shall be open for signature by the member States of the Council of Europe, by non-member States that have participated in its elaboration and by the European Community.
2 This Convention is subject to ratification, acceptance or approval. Instruments of ratification, acceptance or approval shall be deposited with the Secretary General of the Council of Europe.
3 This Convention shall enter into force on the first day of the month following the expiration of a period of three months after the date on which fourteen signatories have expressed their consent to be bound by the Convention in accordance with the provisions of paragraph 2. Any such signatory, which is not a member of the Group of States against Corruption (GRECO) at the time of ratification, acceptance or approval, shall automatically become a member on the date the Convention enters into force.
4 In respect of any signatory which subsequently expresses its consent to be bound by it, the Convention shall enter into force on the first day of the month following the expiration of a period of three months after the date of the expression of their consent to be bound by the Convention in accordance with the provisions of paragraph 2. Any signatory, which is not a member of the Group of States against Corruption (GRECO) at the time of ratification, acceptance or approval, shall automatically become a member on the date the Convention enters into force in its respect.
5 Any particular modalities for the participation of the European Community in the Group of States against Corruption (GRECO) shall be determined as far as necessary by a common agreement with the European Community.

Article 16
Accession to the Convention

1 After the entry into force of this Convention, the Committee of Ministers of the Council of Europe, after consulting the Parties to the Convention, may invite any State not a member of the Council and not having participated in its elaboration to accede to this Convention, by a decision taken by the majority provided for in Article 20.*d.* of the Statute of the Council of Europe and by the unanimous vote of the representatives of the Parties entitled to sit on the Committee.
2 In respect of any State acceding to it, the Convention shall enter into force on the first day of the month following the expiration of a period of three months after the date of deposit of the instrument of accession with the Secretary General of the Council of Europe. Any State acceding to this Convention shall automatically become a member of the GRECO, if it is not already a member at the time of accession, on the date the Convention enters into force in its respect.

Article 17

Reservations

No reservation may be made in respect of any provision of this Convention.

Article 18

Territorial application

1 Any State or the European Community may, at the time of signature or when depositing its instrument of ratification, acceptance, approval or accession, specify the territory or territories to which this Convention shall apply.

2 Any Party may, at any later date, by a declaration addressed to the Secretary General of the Council of Europe, extend the application of this Convention to any other territory specified in the declaration. In respect of such territory the Convention shall enter into force on the first day of the month following the expiration of a period of three months after the date of receipt of such declaration by the Secretary General.

3 Any declaration made under the two preceding paragraphs may, in respect of any territory specified in such declaration, be withdrawn by a notification addressed to the Secretary General. The withdrawal shall become effective on the first day of the month following the expiration of a period of three months after the date of receipt of such notification by the Secretary General.

Article 19

Relationship to other instruments and agreements

1 This Convention does not affect the rights and undertakings derived from international multilateral instruments concerning special matters.

2 The Parties to the Convention may conclude bilateral or multilateral agreements with one another on the matters dealt with in this Convention, for purposes of supplementing or strengthening its provisions or facilitating the application of the principles embodied in it or, without prejudice to the objectives and principles of this Convention, submit themselves to rules on this matter within the framework of a special system which is binding at the moment of the opening for signature of this Convention.

3 If two or more Parties have already concluded an agreement or treaty in respect of a subject which is dealt with in this Convention or otherwise have established their relations in respect of that subject, they shall be entitled to apply that agreement or treaty or to regulate these relations accordingly, in lieu of the present Convention.

Article 20

Amendments

1 Amendments to this Convention may be proposed by any Party, and shall be communicated by the Secretary General of the Council of Europe to the member States of the Council of Europe, to the non member States which have participated in the elaboration of this Convention, to the European Community, as well as to any State which has acceded to or has been invited to accede to this Convention in accordance with the provisions of Article 16.

2 Any amendment proposed by a Party shall be communicated to the European Committee on Legal Co-operation (CDCJ) which shall submit to the Committee of Ministers its opinion on that proposed amendment.

3 The Committee of Ministers shall consider the proposed amendment and the opinion submitted by the European Committee on Legal Co-operation (CDCJ) and, following consultation of the Parties to the Convention which are not members of the Council of Europe, may adopt the amendment.

4 The text of any amendment adopted by the Committee of Ministers in accordance with paragraph 3 of this article shall be forwarded to the Parties for acceptance.

5 Any amendment adopted in accordance with paragraph 3 of this article shall come into force on the thirtieth day after all Parties have informed the Secretary General of their acceptance thereof.

Article 21

Settlement of disputes

1 The European Committee on Legal Co-operation (CDCJ) of the Council of Europe shall be kept informed regarding the interpretation and application of this Convention.

2 In case of a dispute between Parties as to the interpretation or application of this Convention, they shall seek a settlement of the dispute through negotiation or any other peaceful means of their choice, including submission of the dispute to the European Committee on Legal Co-operation (CDCJ), to an arbitral tribunal whose decisions shall be binding upon the Parties, or to the International Court of Justice, as agreed upon by the Parties concerned.

Article 22

Denunciation

1 Any Party may, at any time, denounce this Convention by means of a notification addressed to the Secretary General of the Council of Europe.

2 Such denunciation shall become effective on the first day of the month following the expiration of a period of three months after the date of receipt of the notification by the Secretary General.

Article 23

Notification

The Secretary General of the Council of Europe shall notify the member States of the Council and any other signatories and Parties to this Convention of:

a any signature;

b the deposit of any instrument of ratification, acceptance, approval or accession;

c any date of entry into force of this Convention, in accordance with Articles 15 and 16;

d any other act, notification or communication relating to this Convention.

In witness whereof the undersigned, being duly authorised thereto, have signed this Convention.

Done at Strasbourg, the 4th day of November 1999, in English and in French, both texts being equally authentic, in a single copy which shall be deposited in the archives of the Council of Europe. The Secretary General of the Council of Europe shall transmit certified copies to each member State of the Council of Europe, to the non-member States which have participated in the elaboration of this Convention, to the European Community, as well as to any State invited to accede to it.

APPENDIX 9

Criminal Law Convention on Corruption

Strasbourg, 27 January 1999

PREAMBLE

The member States of the Council of Europe and the other States signatory hereto,

Considering that the aim of the Council of Europe is to achieve a greater unity between its members;

Recognising the value of fostering co-operation with the other States signatories to this Convention;

Convinced of the need to pursue, as a matter of priority, a common criminal policy aimed at the protection of society against corruption, including the adoption of appropriate legislation and preventive measures;

Emphasising that corruption threatens the rule of law, democracy and human rights, undermines good governance, fairness and social justice, distorts competition, hinders economic development and endangers the stability of democratic institutions and the moral foundations of society;

Believing that an effective fight against corruption requires increased, rapid and well-functioning international co-operation in criminal matters;

Welcoming recent developments which further advance international understanding and co-operation in combating corruption, including actions of the United Nations, the World Bank, the International Monetary Fund, the World Trade Organisation, the Organisation of American States, the OECD and the European Union;

Having regard to the Programme of Action against Corruption adopted by the Committee of Ministers of the Council of Europe in November 1996 following the recommendations of the 19th Conference of European Ministers of Justice (Valletta, 1994);

Recalling in this respect the importance of the participation of non-member States in the Council of Europe's activities against corruption and welcoming their valuable contribution to the implementation of the Programme of Action against Corruption;

Further recalling that Resolution No. 1 adopted by the European Ministers of Justice at their 21st Conference (Prague, 1997) recommended the speedy implementation of the Programme of Action against Corruption, and called, in particular, for the early adoption of a criminal law convention providing for the co-ordinated incrimination of corruption offences, enhanced co-operation for the prosecution of such offences as well as an effective follow-up mechanism open to member States and non-member States on an equal footing;

Bearing in mind that the Heads of State and Government of the Council of Europe decided, on the occasion of their Second Summit held in Strasbourg on 10 and 11 October 1997, to seek common responses to the challenges posed by the growth in corruption and adopted an Action Plan which, in order to promote co-operation in the fight against corruption, including its links with organised crime and money laundering, instructed the Committee of Ministers, *inter alia*, to secure the rapid completion of international legal instruments pursuant to the Programme of Action against Corruption;

Considering moreover that Resolution (97) 24 on the 20 Guiding Principles for the Fight against Corruption, adopted on 6 November 1997 by the Committee of Ministers at its 101st Session, stresses the need rapidly to complete the elaboration of international legal instruments pursuant to the Programme of Action against Corruption;

In view of the adoption by the Committee of Ministers, at its 102nd Session on 4 May 1998, of Resolution (98) 7 authorising the partial and enlarged agreement establishing the 'Group of States against Corruption—GRECO', which aims at improving the capacity of its members to fight corruption by following up compliance with their undertakings in this field,

Have agreed as follows:

Chapter I Use of Terms

Article 1
Use of terms

For the purposes of this Convention:

a 'public official' shall be understood by reference to the definition of 'official', 'public officer', 'mayor', 'minister' or 'judge' in the national law of the State in which the person in question performs that function and as applied in its criminal law;

b the term 'judge' referred to in sub-paragraph a above shall include prosecutors and holders of judicial offices;

c in the case of proceedings involving a public official of another State, the prosecuting State may apply the definition of public official only insofar as that definition is compatible with its national law;

d 'legal person' shall mean any entity having such status under the applicable national law, except for States or other public bodies in the exercise of State authority and for public international organisations.

Chapter II Measures to be Taken at National Level

Article 2
Active bribery of domestic public officials

Each Party shall adopt such legislative and other measures as may be necessary to establish as criminal offences under its domestic law, when committed intentionally, the promising, offering or giving by any person, directly or indirectly, of any undue advantage to any of its public officials, for himself or herself or for anyone else, for him or her to act or refrain from acting in the exercise of his or her functions.

Article 3
Passive bribery of domestic public officials

Each Party shall adopt such legislative and other measures as may be necessary to establish as criminal offences under its domestic law, when committed intentionally, the request or receipt by any of its public officials, directly or indirectly, of any undue advantage, for himself or herself or for anyone else, or the acceptance of an offer or a promise of such an advantage, to act or refrain from acting in the exercise of his or her functions.

Article 4
Bribery of members of domestic public assemblies

Each Party shall adopt such legislative and other measures as may be necessary to establish as criminal offences under its domestic law the conduct referred to in Articles 2 and 3, when involving any person who is a member of any domestic public assembly exercising legislative or administrative powers.

Article 5

Bribery of foreign public officials

Each Party shall adopt such legislative and other measures as may be necessary to establish as criminal offences under its domestic law the conduct referred to in Articles 2 and 3, when involving a public official of any other State.

Article 6

Bribery of members of foreign public assemblies

Each Party shall adopt such legislative and other measures as may be necessary to establish as criminal offences under its domestic law the conduct referred to in Articles 2 and 3, when involving any person who is a member of any public assembly exercising legislative or administrative powers in any other State.

Article 7

bribery in the private sector

Each Party shall adopt such legislative and other measures as may be necessary to establish as criminal offences under its domestic law, when committed intentionally in the course of business activity, the promising, offering or giving, directly or indirectly, of any undue advantage to any persons who direct or work for, in any capacity, private sector entities, for themselves or for anyone else, for them to act, or refrain from acting, in breach of their duties.

Article 8

Passive bribery in the private sector

Each Party shall adopt such legislative and other measures as may be necessary to establish as criminal offences under its domestic law, when committed intentionally, in the course of business activity, the request or receipt, directly or indirectly, by any persons who direct or work for, in any capacity, private sector entities, of any undue advantage or the promise thereof for themselves or for anyone else, or the acceptance of an offer or a promise of such an advantage, to act or refrain from acting in breach of their duties.

Article 9

Bribery of officials of international organisations

Each Party shall adopt such legislative and other measures as may be necessary to establish as criminal offences under its domestic law the conduct referred to in Articles 2 and 3, when involving any official or other contracted employee, within the meaning of the staff regulations, of any public international or supranational organisation or body of which the Party is a member, and any person, whether seconded or not, carrying out functions corresponding to those performed by such officials or agents.

Article 10

Bribery of members of international parliamentary assemblies

Each Party shall adopt such legislative and other measures as may be necessary to establish as criminal offences under its domestic law the conduct referred to in Article 4 when involving any members of parliamentary assemblies of international or supranational organisations of which the Party is a member.

Article 11

Bribery of judges and officials of international courts

Each Party shall adopt such legislative and other measures as may be necessary to establish as criminal offences under its domestic law the conduct referred to in Articles 2 and 3 involving any holders of judicial office or officials of any international court whose jurisdiction is accepted by the Party.

Article 12
Trading in influence

Each Party shall adopt such legislative and other measures as may be necessary to establish as criminal offences under its domestic law, when committed intentionally, the promising, giving or offering, directly or indirectly, of any undue advantage to anyone who asserts or confirms that he or she is able to exert an improper influence over the decision-making of any person referred to in Articles 2, 4 to 6 and 9 to 11 in consideration thereof, whether the undue advantage is for himself or herself or for anyone else, as well as the request, receipt or the acceptance of the offer or the promise of such an advantage, in consideration of that influence, whether or not the influence is exerted or whether or not the supposed influence leads to the intended result.

Article 13
laundering of proceeds from corruption offences

Each Party shall adopt such legislative and other measures as may be necessary to establish as criminal offences under its domestic law the conduct referred to in the Council of Europe Convention on Laundering, Search, Seizure and Confiscation of the Products from Crime (ETS No. 141), Article 6, paragraphs 1 and 2, under the conditions referred to therein, when the predicate offence consists of any of the criminal offences established in accordance with Articles 2 to 12 of this Convention, to the extent that the Party has not made a reservation or a declaration with respect to these offences or does not consider such offences as serious ones for the purpose of their money laundering legislation.

Article 14
Account offences

Each Party shall adopt such legislative and other measures as may be necessary to establish as offences liable to criminal or other sanctions under its domestic law the following acts or omissions, when committed intentionally, in order to commit, conceal or disguise the offences referred to in Articles 2 to 12, to the extent the Party has not made a reservation or a declaration:

a creating or using an invoice or any other accounting document or record containing false or incomplete information;

b unlawfully omitting to make a record of a payment.

Article 15
Participatory acts

Each Party shall adopt such legislative and other measures as may be necessary to establish as criminal offences under its domestic law aiding or abetting the commission of any of the criminal offences established in accordance with this Convention.

Article 16
Immunity

The provisions of this Convention shall be without prejudice to the provisions of any Treaty, Protocol or Statute, as well as their implementing texts, as regards the withdrawal of immunity.

Article 17
Jurisdiction

1 Each Party shall adopt such legislative and other measures as may be necessary to establish jurisdiction over a criminal offence established in accordance with Articles 2 to 14 of this Convention where:

a the offence is committed in whole or in part in its territory;

b the offender is one of its nationals, one of its public officials, or a member of one of its domestic public assemblies;

c the offence involves one of its public officials or members of its domestic public assemblies or any person referred to in Articles 9 to 11 who is at the same time one of its nationals.

2 Each State may, at the time of signature or when depositing its instrument of ratification, acceptance, approval or accession, by a declaration addressed to the Secretary General of the Council of Europe, declare that it reserves the right not to apply or to apply only in specific cases or conditions the jurisdiction rules laid down in paragraphs 1 b and c of this article or any part thereof.

3 If a Party has made use of the reservation possibility provided for in paragraph 2 of this article, it shall adopt such measures as may be necessary to establish jurisdiction over a criminal offence established in accordance with this Convention, in cases where an alleged offender is present in its territory and it does not extradite him to another Party, solely on the basis of his nationality, after a request for extradition.

4 This Convention does not exclude any criminal jurisdiction exercised by a Party in accordance with national law.

Article 18

Corporate liability

1 Each Party shall adopt such legislative and other measures as may be necessary to ensure that legal persons can be held liable for the criminal offences of active bribery, trading in influence and money laundering established in accordance with this Convention, committed for their benefit by any natural person, acting either individually or as part of an organ of the legal person, who has a leading position within the legal person, based on:

— a power of representation of the legal person; or

— an authority to take decisions on behalf of the legal person; or

— an authority to exercise control within the legal person;

— as well as for involvement of such a natural person as accessory or instigator in the above-mentioned offences.

2 Apart from the cases already provided for in paragraph 1, each Party shall take the necessary measures to ensure that a legal person can be held liable where the lack of supervision or control by a natural person referred to in paragraph 1 has made possible the commission of the criminal offences mentioned in paragraph 1 for the benefit of that legal person by a natural person under its authority.

3 Liability of a legal person under paragraphs 1 and 2 shall not exclude criminal proceedings against natural persons who are perpetrators, instigators of, or accessories to, the criminal offences mentioned in paragraph 1.

Article 19

Sanctions and measures

1 Having regard to the serious nature of the criminal offences established in accordance with this Convention, each Party shall provide, in respect of those criminal offences established in accordance with Articles 2 to 14, effective, proportionate and dissuasive sanctions and measures, including, when committed by natural persons, penalties involving deprivation of liberty which can give rise to extradition.

2 Each Party shall ensure that legal persons held liable in accordance with Article 18, paragraphs 1 and 2, shall be subject to effective, proportionate and dissuasive criminal or non-criminal sanctions, including monetary sanctions.

3 Each Party shall adopt such legislative and other measures as may be necessary to enable it to confiscate or otherwise deprive the instrumentalities and proceeds of criminal offences established in accordance with this Convention, or property the value of which corresponds to such proceeds.

Article 20

Specialised authorities

Each Party shall adopt such measures as may be necessary to ensure that persons or entities are specialised in the fight against corruption. They shall have the necessary independence in accordance with the fundamental principles of the legal system of the Party, in order for them to be able to carry out their functions effectively and free from any undue pressure. The Party shall ensure that the staff of such entities has adequate training and financial resources for their tasks.

Article 21

Co-operation with and between national authorities

Each Party shall adopt such measures as may be necessary to ensure that public authorities, as well as any public official, co-operate, in accordance with national law, with those of its authorities responsible for investigating and prosecuting criminal offences:

a by informing the latter authorities, on their own initiative, where there are reasonable grounds to believe that any of the criminal offences established in accordance with Articles 2 to 14 has been committed, or

b by providing, upon request, to the latter authorities all necessary information.

Article 22

Protection of collaborators of justice and witnesses

Each Party shall adopt such measures as may be necessary to provide effective and appropriate protection for:

a those who report the criminal offences established in accordance with Articles 2 to 14 or otherwise co-operate with the investigating or prosecuting authorities;

b witnesses who give testimony concerning these offences.

Article 23

Measures to facilitate the gathering of evidence and the confiscation of proceeds

1 Each Party shall adopt such legislative and other measures as may be necessary, including those permitting the use of special investigative techniques, in accordance with national law, to enable it to facilitate the gathering of evidence related to criminal offences established in accordance with Article 2 to 14 of this Convention and to identify, trace, freeze and seize instrumentalities and proceeds of corruption, or property the value of which corresponds to such proceeds, liable to measures set out in accordance with paragraph 3 of Article 19 of this Convention.

2 Each Party shall adopt such legislative and other measures as may be necessary to empower its courts or other competent authorities to order that bank, financial or commercial records be made available or be seized in order to carry out the actions referred to in paragraph 1 of this article.

3 Bank secrecy shall not be an obstacle to measures provided for in paragraphs 1 and 2 of this article.

Chapter III Monitoring of Implementation

Article 24

Monitoring

The Group of States against Corruption (GRECO) shall monitor the implementation of this Convention by the Parties.

Chapter IV International Co-operation

Article 25

General principles and measures for international co-operation

1 The Parties shall co-operate with each other, in accordance with the provisions of relevant international instruments on international co-operation in criminal matters, or arrangements agreed on the basis of uniform or reciprocal legislation, and in accordance with their national law, to the widest extent possible for the purposes of investigations and proceedings concerning criminal offences established in accordance with this Convention.

2 Where no international instrument or arrangement referred to in paragraph 1 is in force between Parties, Articles 26 to 31 of this chapter shall apply.

3 Articles 26 to 31 of this chapter shall also apply where they are more favourable than those of the international instruments or arrangements referred to in paragraph 1.

Article 26

Mutual assistance

1 The Parties shall afford one another the widest measure of mutual assistance by promptly processing requests from authorities that, in conformity with their domestic laws, have the power to investigate or prosecute criminal offences established in accordance with this Convention.

2 Mutual legal assistance under paragraph 1 of this article may be refused if the requested Party believes that compliance with the request would undermine its fundamental interests, national sovereignty, national security or *ordre public*.

3 Parties shall not invoke bank secrecy as a ground to refuse any co-operation under this chapter. Where its domestic law so requires, a Party may require that a request for co-operation which would involve the lifting of bank secrecy be authorised by either a judge or another judicial authority, including public prosecutors, any of these authorities acting in relation to criminal offences.

Article 27

Extradition

1 The criminal offences established in accordance with this Convention shall be deemed to be included as extraditable offences in any extradition treaty existing between or among the Parties. The Parties undertake to include such offences as extraditable offences in any extradition treaty to be concluded between or among them.

2 If a Party that makes extradition conditional on the existence of a treaty receives a request for extradition from another Party with which it does not have an extradition treaty, it may consider this Convention as the legal basis for extradition with respect to any criminal offence established in accordance with this Convention.

3 Parties that do not make extradition conditional on the existence of a treaty shall recognise criminal offences established in accordance with this Convention as extraditable offences between themselves.

4 Extradition shall be subject to the conditions provided for by the law of the requested Party or by applicable extradition treaties, including the grounds on which the requested Party may refuse extradition.

5 If extradition for a criminal offence established in accordance with this Convention is refused solely on the basis of the nationality of the person sought, or because the requested Party deems that it has jurisdiction over the offence, the requested Party shall submit the case to its competent authorities for the purpose of prosecution unless otherwise agreed with the requesting Party, and shall report the final outcome to the requesting Party in due course.

Article 28

Spontaneous information

Without prejudice to its own investigations or proceedings, a Party may without prior request forward to another Party information on facts when it considers that the disclosure of such information might assist the receiving Party in initiating or carrying out investigations or proceedings concerning criminal offences established in accordance with this Convention or might lead to a request by that Party under this chapter.

Article 29

Central authority

1 The Parties shall designate a central authority or, if appropriate, several central authorities, which shall be responsible for sending and answering requests made under this chapter, the execution of such requests or the transmission of them to the authorities competent for their execution.

2 Each Party shall, at the time of signature or when depositing its instrument of ratification, acceptance, approval or accession, communicate to the Secretary General of the Council of Europe the names and addresses of the authorities designated in pursuance of paragraph 1 of this article.

Article 30

Direct communication

1 The central authorities shall communicate directly with one another.

2 In the event of urgency, requests for mutual assistance or communications related thereto may be sent directly by the judicial authorities, including public prosecutors, of the requesting Party to such authorities of the requested Party. In such cases a copy shall be sent at the same time to the central authority of the requested Party through the central authority of the requesting Party.

3 Any request or communication under paragraphs 1 and 2 of this article may be made through the International Criminal Police Organisation (Interpol).

4 Where a request is made pursuant to paragraph 2 of this article and the authority is not competent to deal with the request, it shall refer the request to the competent national authority and inform directly the requesting Party that it has done so.

5 Requests or communications under paragraph 2 of this article, which do not involve coercive action, may be directly transmitted by the competent authorities of the requesting Party to the competent authorities of the requested Party.

6 Each State may, at the time of signature or when depositing its instrument of ratification, acceptance, approval or accession, inform the Secretary General of the Council of Europe that, for reasons of efficiency, requests made under this chapter are to be addressed to its central authority.

Article 31

Information

The requested Party shall promptly inform the requesting Party of the action taken on a request under this chapter and the final result of that action. The requested Party shall also promptly inform the requesting Party of any circumstances which render impossible the carrying out of the action sought or are likely to delay it significantly.

Chapter V Final Provisions

Article 32
Signature and entry into force

1 This Convention shall be open for signature by the member States of the Council of Europe and by non-member States which have participated in its elaboration. Such States may express their consent to be bound by:

a signature without reservation as to ratification, acceptance or approval; or

b signature subject to ratification, acceptance or approval, followed by ratification, acceptance or approval.

2 Instruments of ratification, acceptance or approval shall be deposited with the Secretary General of the Council of Europe.

3 This Convention shall enter into force on the first day of the month following the expiration of a period of three months after the date on which fourteenth States have expressed their consent to be bound by the Convention in accordance with the provisions of paragraph 1. Any such State, which is not a member of the Group of States against Corruption (GRECO) at the time of ratification, shall automatically become a member on the date the Convention enters into force.

4 In respect of any signatory State which subsequently expresses its consent to be bound by it, the Convention shall enter into force on the first day of the month following the expiration of a period of three months after the date of the expression of their consent to be bound by the Convention in accordance with the provisions of paragraph 1. Any signatory State, which is not a member of the Group of States against Corruption (GRECO) at the time of ratification, shall automatically become a member on the date the Convention enters into force in its respect.

Article 33
Accession to the Convention

1 After the entry into force of this Convention, the Committee of Ministers of the Council of Europe, after consulting the Contracting States to the Convention, may invite the European Community as well as any State not a member of the Council and not having participated in its elaboration to accede to this Convention, by a decision taken by the majority provided for in Article 20d of the Statute of the Council of Europe and by the unanimous vote of the representatives of the Contracting States entitled to sit on the Committee of Ministers.

2 In respect of the European Community and any State acceding to it under paragraph 1 above, the Convention shall enter into force on the first day of the month following the expiration of a period of three months after the date of deposit of the instrument of accession with the Secretary General of the Council of Europe. The European Community and any State acceding to this Convention shall automatically become a member of GRECO, if it is not already a member at the time of accession, on the date the Convention enters into force in its respect.

Article 34
Territorial application

1 Any State may, at the time of signature or when depositing its instrument of ratification, acceptance, approval or accession, specify the territory or territories to which this Convention shall apply.

2 Any Party may, at any later date, by a declaration addressed to the Secretary General of the Council of Europe, extend the application of this Convention to any other territory specified in the declaration. In respect of such territory the Convention shall enter into force on the first

day of the month following the expiration of a period of three months after the date of receipt of such declaration by the Secretary General.

3 Any declaration made under the two preceding paragraphs may, in respect of any territory specified in such declaration, be withdrawn by a notification addressed to the Secretary General of the Council of Europe. The withdrawal shall become effective on the first day of the month following the expiration of a period of three months after the date of receipt of such notification by the Secretary General.

Article 35

Relationship to other conventions and agreements

1 This Convention does not affect the rights and undertakings derived from international multilateral conventions concerning special matters.

2 The Parties to the Convention may conclude bilateral or multilateral agreements with one another on the matters dealt with in this Convention, for purposes of supplementing or strengthening its provisions or facilitating the application of the principles embodied in it.

3 If two or more Parties have already concluded an agreement or treaty in respect of a subject which is dealt with in this Convention or otherwise have established their relations in respect of that subject, they shall be entitled to apply that agreement or treaty or to regulate those relations accordingly, in lieu of the present Convention, if it facilitates international co-operation.

Article 36

Declarations

Any State may, at the time of signature or when depositing its instrument of ratification, acceptance, approval or accession, declare that it will establish as criminal offences the active and passive bribery of foreign public officials under Article 5, of officials of international organisations under Article 9 or of judges and officials of international courts under Article 11, only to the extent that the public official or judge acts or refrains from acting in breach of his duties.

Article 37

Reservations

1 Any State may, at the time of signature or when depositing its instrument of ratification, acceptance, approval or accession, reserve its right not to establish as a criminal offence under its domestic law, in part or in whole, the conduct referred to in Articles 4, 6 to 8, 10 and 12 or the passive bribery offences defined in Article 5.

2 Any State may, at the time of signature or when depositing its instrument of ratification, acceptance, approval or accession declare that it avails itself of the reservation provided for in Article 17, paragraph 2.

3 Any State may, at the time of signature or when depositing its instrument of ratification, acceptance, approval or accession declare that it may refuse mutual legal assistance under Article 26, paragraph 1, if the request concerns an offence which the requested Party considers a political offence.

4 No State may, by application of paragraphs 1, 2 and 3 of this article, enter reservations to more than five of the provisions mentioned thereon. No other reservation may be made. Reservations of the same nature with respect to Articles 4, 6 and 10 shall be considered as one reservation.

Article 38

Validity and review of declarations and reservations

1 Declarations referred to in Article 36 and reservations referred to in Article 37 shall be valid for a period of three years from the day of the entry into force of this Convention in respect of the State concerned. However, such declarations and reservations may be renewed for periods of the same duration.

2 Twelve months before the date of expiry of the declaration or reservation, the Secretariat General of the Council of Europe shall give notice of that expiry to the State concerned. No later than three months before the expiry, the State shall notify the Secretary General that it is upholding, amending or withdrawing its declaration or reservation. In the absence of a notification by the State concerned, the Secretariat General shall inform that State that its declaration or reservation is considered to have been extended automatically for a period of six months. Failure by the State concerned to notify its intention to uphold or modify its declaration or reservation before the expiry of that period shall cause the declaration or reservation to lapse.
3 If a Party makes a declaration or a reservation in conformity with Articles 36 and 37, it shall provide, before its renewal or upon request, an explanation to GRECO, on the grounds justifying its continuance.

Article 39
Amendments

1 Amendments to this Convention may be proposed by any Party, and shall be communicated by the Secretary General of the Council of Europe to the member States of the Council of Europe and to every non-member State which has acceded to, or has been invited to accede to, this Convention in accordance with the provisions of Article 33.
2 Any amendment proposed by a Party shall be communicated to the European Committee on Crime Problems (CDPC), which shall submit to the Committee of Ministers its opinion on that proposed amendment.
3 The Committee of Ministers shall consider the proposed amendment and the opinion submitted by the CDPC and, following consultation of the non-member States Parties to this Convention, may adopt the amendment.
4 The text of any amendment adopted by the Committee of Ministers in accordance with paragraph 3 of this article shall be forwarded to the Parties for acceptance.
5 Any amendment adopted in accordance with paragraph 3 of this article shall come into force on the thirtieth day after all Parties have informed the Secretary General of their acceptance thereof.

Article 40
Settlement of disputes

1 The European Committee on Crime Problems of the Council of Europe shall be kept informed regarding the interpretation and application of this Convention.
2 In case of a dispute between Parties as to the interpretation or application of this Convention, they shall seek a settlement of the dispute through negotiation or any other peaceful means of their choice, including submission of the dispute to the European Committee on Crime Problems, to an arbitral tribunal whose decisions shall be binding upon the Parties, or to the International Court of Justice, as agreed upon by the Parties concerned.

Article 41
Denunciation

1 Any Party may, at any time, denounce this Convention by means of a notification addressed to the Secretary General of the Council of Europe.
2 Such denunciation shall become effective on the first day of the month following the expiration of a period of three months after the date of receipt of the notification by the Secretary General.

Article 42
Notification

The Secretary General of the Council of Europe shall notify the member States of the Council of Europe and any State which has acceded to this Convention of:

a any signature;
b the deposit of any instrument of ratification, acceptance, approval or accession;
c any date of entry into force of this Convention in accordance with Articles 32 and 33;
d any declaration or reservation made under Article 36 or Article 37;
e any other act, notification or communication relating to this Convention.

In witness whereof the undersigned, being duly authorised thereto, have signed this Convention.

Done at Strasbourg, this 27th day of January 1999, in English and in French, both texts being equally authentic, in a single copy which shall be deposited in the archives of the Council of Europe. The Secretary General of the Council of Europe shall transmit certified copies to each member State of the Council of Europe, to the non-member States which have participated in the elaboration of this Convention, and to any State invited to accede to it.

APPENDIX 10

Resolution (97) 24 on the Twenty Guiding Principles for the Fight Against Corruption

Adopted by
the Committee of Ministers on 6 November 1997, at its 101st session of the Committee of Ministers

The Committee of Ministers,

Considering the Declaration adopted at the Second Summit of Heads of State and Government, which took place in Strasbourg on 10 and 11 October 1997 and in pursuance of the Action Plan, in particular section III, paragraph 2 'Fighting corruption and organised crime';

Aware that corruption represents a serious threat to the basic principles and values of the Council of Europe, undermines the confidence of citizens in democracy, erodes the rule of law, constitutes a denial of human rights and hinders social and economic development;

Convinced that the fight against corruption needs to be multi-disciplinary and, in this respect having regard to Programme of Action against Corruption as well as to the resolutions adopted by the European Ministers of Justice at their 19th and 21st Conferences held in Valletta and Prague respectively;

Having received the draft 20 guiding principles for the fight against corruption, elaborated by the Multidisciplinary Group on Corruption (GMC);

Firmly resolved to fight corruption by joining the efforts of our countries,

Agrees to adopt the 20 Guiding principles for the Fight Against Corruption, set out below:

1. To take effective measures for the prevention of corruption and, in this connection, to raise public awareness and promoting ethical behaviour;

2. To ensure co-ordinated criminalisation of national and international corruption;

3. To ensure that those in charge of the prevention, investigation, prosecution and adjudication of corruption offences enjoy the independence and autonomy appropriate to their functions, are free from improper influence and have effective means for gathering evidence, protecting the persons who help the authorities in combating corruption and preserving the confidentiality of investigations;

4. To provide appropriate measures for the seizure and deprivation of the proceeds of corruption offences;

5. To provide appropriate measures to prevent legal persons being used to shield corruption offences;

6. To limit immunity from investigation, prosecution or adjudication of corruption offences to the degree necessary in a democratic society;

7. To promote the specialisation of persons or bodies in charge of fighting corruption and to provide them with appropriate means and training to perform their tasks;

8. To ensure that the fiscal legislation and the authorities in charge of implementing it contribute to combating corruption in an effective and co-ordinated manner, in particular by denying tax deductibility, under the law or in practice, for bribes or other expenses linked to corruption offences;

9. To ensure that the organisation, functioning and decision-making processes of public administrations take into account the need to combat corruption, in particular by ensuring as much transparency as is consistent with the need to achieve effectiveness;

10. To ensure that the rules relating to the rights and duties of public officials take into account the requirements of the fight against corruption and provide for appropriate and effective disciplinary measures; promote further specification of the behaviour expected from public officials by appropriate means, such as codes of conduct;

11. To ensure that appropriate auditing procedures apply to the activities of public administration and the public sector;

12. To endorse the role that audit procedures can play in preventing and detecting corruption outside public administrations;

13. To ensure that the system of public liability or accountability takes account of the consequences of corrupt behaviour of public officials;

14. To adopt appropriately transparent procedures for public procurement that promote fair competition and deter corruptors;

15. To encourage the adoption, by elected representatives, of codes of conduct and promote rules for the financing of political parties and election campaigns which deter corruption;

16. To ensure that the media have freedom to receive and impart information on corruption matters, subject only to limitations or restrictions which are necessary in a democratic society;

17. To ensure that civil law takes into account the need to fight corruption and in particular provides for effective remedies for those whose rights and interests are affected by corruption;

18. To encourage research on corruption;

19. To ensure that in every aspect of the fight against corruption, the possible connections with organised crime and money laundering are taken into account;

20. To develop to the widest extent possible international co-operation in all areas of the fight against corruption.

And, in Order to Promote a Dynamic Process for Effectively Preventing and Combating Corruption

The Committee of Ministers

1. Invites national authorities to apply these Principles in their domestic legislation and practice;

2. Instructs the Multidisciplinary Group on Corruption (GMC) rapidly to complete the elaboration of international legal instruments pursuant to the Programme of Action against Corruption;

3. Instructs the Multidisciplinary Group on Corruption (GMC) to submit without delay a draft text proposing the establishment of an appropriate and efficient mechanism, under the auspices of the Council of Europe, for monitoring observance of these Principles and the implementation of the international legal instruments to be adopted.

APPENDIX 11

GMC (2000) 26 Multidisciplinary Group on Corruption (GMC) Recommendation No. R (2000) 10 of the Committee of Ministers to Member States On Codes of Conducts for Public Officials

Adopted by
the Committee of Ministers at its
106th Session on 11 May 2000

Directorate General I (Legal Affairs) 26 May 2000

The Committee of Ministers, under the terms of Article 15.*b* of the Statute of the Council of Europe,

Considering that the aim of the Council of Europe is to achieve a greater unity between its members;

Considering that public administrations play an essential role in democratic societies and that they must have at their disposal suitable personnel to carry out properly the tasks which are assigned to them;

Considering that public officials are the key element of a public administration, that they have specific duties and obligations, and that they should have the necessary qualifications and an appropriate legal and material environment in order to carry out their tasks effectively;

Convinced that corruption represents a serious threat to the rule of law, democracy, human rights, equity and social justice, that it hinders economic development and endangers the stability of democratic institutions and the moral foundations of society;

Having regard to the recommendations adopted at the 19th and 21st Conferences of European Ministers of Justice (Valletta, 1994 and Prague, 1997 respectively);

Having regard to the Programme of Action against Corruption adopted by the Committee of Ministers in 1996;

Having regard to Recommendation No. R (81) 19 of the Committee of Ministers of the Council of Europe on the access to information held by public authorities;

Having regard to Recommendation No. R (2000) 6 of the Committee of Ministers of the Council of Europe on the status of public officials in Europe;

In accordance with the Final Declaration and the Plan of Action adopted by the heads of state and government of the Council of Europe at their Second Summit, held in Strasbourg, on 10 and 11 October 1997;

Recalling in this respect the importance of the participation of non-member states in the Council of Europe's activities against corruption and welcoming their valuable contribution to the implementation of the Programme of Action against Corruption;

Having regard to Resolution (97) 24 on the twenty guiding principles for the fight against corruption;

Having regard to Resolutions (98) 7 and (99) 5 authorising and respectively adopting the Enlarged Partial Agreement establishing the Group of States against Corruption (GRECO), which aims at improving the capacity of its members to fight corruption by following up compliance with their undertakings in this field;

Convinced that raising public awareness and promoting ethical values are valuable as means to prevent corruption,

Recommends that the governments of member states promote, subject to national law and the principles of public administration, the adoption of national codes of conduct for public officials based on the model code of conduct for public officials annexed to this Recommendation; and

Instructs the Group of States against Corruption (GRECO) to monitor the implementation of this Recommendation.

Appendix to Recommendation No. R (2000) 10 Model code of conduct for public officials

Interpretation and application

Article 1

1. This Code applies to all public officials.
2. For the purpose of this Code 'public official' means a person employed by a public authority.
3. The provisions of this Code may also be applied to persons employed by private organisations performing public services.
4. The provisions of this Code do not apply to publicly elected representatives, members of the government and holders of judicial office.

Article 2

1. On the coming into effect of this Code, the public administration has a duty to inform public officials about its provisions.
2. This Code shall form part of the provisions governing the employment of public officials from the moment they certify that they have been informed about it.
3. Every public official has the duty to take all necessary action to comply with the provisions of this Code.

Article 3

Object of the Code

The purpose of this Code is to specify the standards of integrity and conduct to be observed by public officials, to help them meet those standards and to inform the public of the conduct it is entitled to expect of public officials.

General principles

Article 4

1. The public official should carry out his or her duties in accordance with the law, and with those lawful instructions and ethical standards which relate to his or her functions.
2. The public official should act in a politically neutral manner and should not attempt to frustrate the lawful policies, decisions or actions of the public authorities.

Article 5

1. The public official has the duty to serve loyally the lawfully constituted national, local or regional authority.
2. The public official is expected to be honest, impartial and efficient and to perform his or her duties to the best of his or her ability with skill, fairness and understanding, having regard only for the public interest and the relevant circumstances of the case.

3. The public official should be courteous both in his or her relations with the citizens he or she serves, as well as in his or her relations with his or her superiors, colleagues and subordinate staff.

Article 6

In the performance of his or her duties, the public official should not act arbitrarily to the detriment of any person, group or body and should have due regard for the rights, duties and proper interests of all others.

Article 7

In decision making the public official should act lawfully and exercise his or her discretionary powers impartially, taking into account only relevant matters.

Article 8

1. The public official should not allow his or her private interest to conflict with his or her public position. It is his or her responsibility to avoid such conflicts of interest, whether real, potential or apparent.
2. The public official should never take undue advantage of his or her position for his or her private interest.

Article 9

The public official has a duty always to conduct himself or herself in a way that the public's confidence and trust in the integrity, impartiality and effectiveness of the public service are preserved and enhanced.

Article 10

The public official is accountable to his or her immediate hierarchical superior unless otherwise prescribed by law.

Article 11

Having due regard for the right of access to official information, the public official has a duty to treat appropriately, with all necessary confidentiality, all information and documents acquired by him or her in the course of, or as a result of, his or her employment.

Article 12

Reporting

1. The public official who believes he or she is being required to act in a way which is unlawful, improper or unethical, which involves maladministration, or which is otherwise inconsistent with this Code, should report the matter in accordance with the law.
2. The public official should, in accordance with the law, report to the competent authorities if he or she becomes aware of breaches of this Code by other public officials.
3. The public official who has reported any of the above in accordance with the law and believes that the response does not meet his or her concern may report the matter in writing to the relevant head of the public service.
4. Where a matter cannot be resolved by the procedures and appeals set out in the legislation on the public service on a basis acceptable to the public official concerned, the public official should carry out the lawful instructions he or she has been given.
5. The public official should report to the competent authorities any evidence, allegation or suspicion of unlawful or criminal activity relating to the public service coming to his or her knowledge in the course of, or arising from, his or her employment. The investigation of the reported facts shall be carried out by the competent authorities.

6. The public administration should ensure that no prejudice is caused to a public official who reports any of the above on reasonable grounds and in good faith.

Article 13

Conflict of interest

1. Conflict of interest arises from a situation in which the public official has a private interest which is such as to influence, or appear to influence, the impartial and objective performance of his or her official duties.
2. The public official's private interest includes any advantage to himself or herself, to his or her family, close relatives, friends and persons or organisations with whom he or she has or has had business or political relations. It includes also any liability, whether financial or civil, relating thereto.
3. Since the public official is usually the only person who knows whether he or she is in that situation, the public official has a personal responsibility to:
   — be alert to any actual or potential conflict of interest;
   — take steps to avoid such conflict;
   — disclose to his or her supervisor any such conflict as soon as he or she becomes aware of it;
   — comply with any final decision to withdraw from the situation or to divest himself or herself of the advantage causing the conflict.
4. Whenever required to do so, the public official should declare whether or not he or she has a conflict of interest.
5. Any conflict of interest declared by a candidate to the public service or to a new post in the public service should be resolved before appointment.

Article 14

Declaration of interests

The public official who occupies a position in which his or her personal or private interests are likely to be affected by his or her official duties should, as lawfully required, declare upon appointment, at regular intervals thereafter and whenever any changes occur the nature and extent of those interests.

Article 15

Incompatible outside interests

1. The public official should not engage in any activity or transaction or acquire any position or function, whether paid or unpaid, that is incompatible with or detracts from the proper performance of his or her duties as a public official. Where it is not clear whether an activity is compatible, he or she should seek advice from his or her superior.
2. Subject to the provisions of the law, the public official should be required to notify and seek the approval of his or her public service employer to carry out certain activities, whether paid or unpaid, or to accept certain positions or functions outside his or her public service employment.
3. The public official should comply with any lawful requirement to declare membership of, or association with, organisations that could detract from his or her position or proper performance of his or her duties as a public official.

Article 16

Political or public activity

1. Subject to respect for fundamental and constitutional rights, the public official should take care that none of his or her political activities or involvement on political or public debates impairs the confidence of the public and his or her employers in his or her ability to perform his or her duties impartially and loyally.

2. In the exercise of his or her duties, the public official should not allow himself or herself to be used for partisan political purposes.
3. The public official should comply with any restrictions on political activity lawfully imposed on certain categories of public officials by reason of their position or the nature of their duties.

Article 17
Protection of the public official's privacy

All necessary steps should be taken to ensure that the public official's privacy is appropriately respected; accordingly, declarations provided for in this Code are to be kept confidential unless otherwise provided for by law.

Article 18
Gifts

1. The public official should not demand or accept gifts, favours, hospitality or any other benefit for himself or his or her family, close relatives and friends, or persons or organisations with whom he or she has or has had business or political relations which may influence or appear to influence the impartiality with which he or she carries out his or her duties or may be or appear to be a reward relating to his or her duties. This does not include conventional hospitality or minor gifts.
2. Where the public official is in doubt whether he or she can accept a gift or hospitality, he or she should seek the advice of his or her superior.

Article 19
Reaction to improper offers

If the public official is offered an undue advantage he or she should take the following steps to protect himself or herself:
— refuse the undue advantage; there is no need to accept it for use as evidence;
— try to identify the person who made the offer;
— avoid lengthy contacts, but knowing the reason for the offer could be useful in evidence;
— if the gift cannot be refused or returned to the sender, it should be preserved, but handled as little as possible;
— obtain witnesses if possible, such as colleagues working nearby;
— prepare as soon as possible a written record of the attempt, preferably in an official notebook;
— report the attempt as soon as possible to his or her supervisor or directly to the appropriate law enforcement authority;
— continue to work normally, particularly on the matter in relation to which the undue advantage was offered.

Article 20
Susceptibility to influence by others

The public official should not allow himself or herself to be put, or appear to be put, in a position of obligation to return a favour to any person or body. Nor should his or her conduct in his or her official capacity or in his or her private life make him or her susceptible to the improper influence of others.

Article 21
Misuse of official position

1. The public official should not offer or give any advantage in any way connected with his or her position as a public official, unless lawfully authorised to do so.

2. The public official should not seek to influence for private purposes any person or body, including other public officials, by using his or her official position or by offering them personal advantages.

Article 22

Information held by public authorities

1. Having regard to the framework provided by domestic law for access to information held by public authorities, a public official should only disclose information in accordance with the rules and requirements applying to the authority by which he or she is employed.
2. The public official should take appropriate steps to protect the security and confidentiality of information for which he or she is responsible or of which he or she becomes aware.
3. The public official should not seek access to information which it is inappropriate for him or her to have. The public official should not make improper use of information which he or she may acquire in the course of, or arising from, his or her employment.
4. Equally the public official has a duty not to withhold official information that should properly be released and a duty not to provide information which he or she knows or has reasonable ground to believe is false or misleading.

Article 23

Public and official resources

In the exercise of his or her discretionary powers, the public official should ensure that on the one hand the staff, and on the other hand the public property, facilities, services and financial resources with which he or she is entrusted are managed and used effectively, efficiently and economically. They should not be used for private purposes except when permission is lawfully given.

Article 24

Integrity checking

1. The public official who has responsibilities for recruitment, promotion or posting should ensure that appropriate checks on the integrity of the candidate are carried out as lawfully required.
2. If the result of any such check makes him or her uncertain as to how to proceed, he or she should seek appropriate advice.

Article 25

Supervisory accountability

1. The public official who supervises or manages other public officials should do so in accordance with the policies and purposes of the public authority for which he or she works. He or she should be answerable for acts or omissions by his or her staff which are not consistent with those policies and purposes if he or she has not taken those reasonable steps required from a person in his or her position to prevent such acts or omissions.
2. The public official who supervises or manages other public officials should take reasonable steps to prevent corruption by his or her staff in relation to his or her office. These steps may include emphasising and enforcing rules and regulations, providing appropriate education or training, being alert to signs of financial or other difficulties of his or her staff, and providing by his or her personal conduct an example of propriety and integrity.

Article 26

Leaving the public service

1. The public official should not take improper advantage of his or her public office to obtain the opportunity of employment outside the public service.

2. The public official should not allow the prospect of other employment to create for him or her an actual, potential or apparent conflict of interest. He or she should immediately disclose to his or her supervisor any concrete offer of employment that could create a conflict of interest. He or she should also disclose to his or her superior his or her acceptance of any offer of employment.
3. In accordance with the law, for an appropriate period of time, the former public official should not act for any person or body in respect of any matter on which he or she acted for, or advised, the public service and which would result in a particular benefit to that person or body.
4. The former public official should not use or disclose confidential information acquired by him or her as a public official unless lawfully authorised to do so.
5. The public official should comply with any lawful rules that apply to him or her regarding the acceptance of appointments on leaving the public service.

Article 27

Dealing with former public officials

The public official should not give preferential treatment or privileged access to the public service to former public officials.

Article 28

Observance of this Code and sanctions

1. This Code is issued under the authority of the minister or of the head of the public service. The public official has a duty to conduct himself or herself in accordance with this Code and therefore to keep himself or herself informed of its provisions and any amendments. He or she should seek advice from an appropriate source when he or she is unsure of how to proceed.
2. Subject to Article 2, paragraph 2, the provisions of this Code form part of the terms of employment of the public official. Breach of them may result in disciplinary action.
3. The public official who negotiates terms of employment should include in them a provision to the effect that this Code is to be observed and forms part of such terms.
4. The public official who supervises or manages other public officials has the responsibility to see that they observe this Code and to take or propose appropriate disciplinary action for breaches of it.
5. The public administration will regularly review the provisions of this Code.

Explanatory Memorandum

To the Recommendation No. R(2000) 10 of the Committee of Ministers to member States on Codes of Conduct for Public Officials

Adopted by
the Committee of Ministers on 11 May 2000 at its 106th Session

Explanatory Memorandum

Introduction

1. The Council of Europe became strongly interested in the international fight against corruption because of the obvious threat corruption poses to the basic principles this organisation stand for: the rule of law, the stability of democratic institutions, human rights and economic progress. Corruption is also a subject well-suited for international co-operation: it is a problem shared by most, if not all, member States and it often conyains trans-national elements. However, the

specificity of the Council of Europe lies in it multidisciplinary approach, meaning that it deals with corruption from a criminal, civil; administrative law point of view.

2. At the 1994 Malta Conference of the European Ministers of Justice, the Council of Europe launched its intiative against corruption. The Ministers considered that corruption was to democracy, the rule of law and human rights and that the Council of the pre-eminent European institution defending these fundamental val ond to that threat.

3. The Reslution adopted at this Conference endorsed the need for a multidisciplinary approach, and recommended the setting up of a Multidisciplinary Group on Corruption with the task of examining what measures could be included in a programme of a action at international level, and the possibility of drafting model laws or codes of conduct, including international conventions, on this subject. The importance of elaborating a follow-up mechanism to implement the undertakings contained in such instruments was alsounderlined.

4. In the light of these recommendations, the Committee of Ministers agreed, in September 199 Multidisciplinary Group on Corruption (GMC) under the joint responsibility of the European Committee on Crime Problems (CDPC) and the European Committee on Legal Co-operation (CDCJ) and invited it to examine what measures would be suitable for a programme of action at international level against corruption, to make proposals on priorities and working structures, taking due account of the work of other international organisations and to examine the possibility of drafting model laws or codes of conduct in selected areas, including the elaboration of an international convention on this subject and a follow-up mechanism to implement undertakings contained in such instruments. The GMC started operating in March 1995.

5. The Programme of Action against Corruption (PAC), prepared by the GMC in the course of 1995 and adopted by the Committee of Ministers at the end of 1996, is an ambitious document, which attempts to cover all aspects of the international fight against this phenomenon. It defines the areas in which action is necessary and provides for a number of measures to be followed in order to realise a global, multidisciplinary and comprehensive approach to tackling corruption. The Committee of Ministers instructed the GMC to implement this programme before the end of the year 2000.

6. At theire 21st Conference (Prague 1997), the European Ministers of Justice adopted Resolution No 1 on the links between corruption and organised crime. The Ministers emphasised that corruption represents a major threat to the rule of law, democracy and human right, of democratic institutions and the moral foundations of society. They further underlined that a successful strategy to combat corruption and organised crime requires a firm commitment by States to join their efforts, share their experience and take common actions. The European Ministers of Justice specifically recommended speeding up the implementation of the Programme of Action against corruption and to pursue the work concerning the elaboration of a model code of conduct for public officials.

7. On 10 and 11 October 1997, the 2nd Summit of the Heads of State and Government of the member States of the Council of Europe took place in Strasbourg. The Heads of state and Government, in order to seek common responses to the challenges posed by corruption throughout Europe and to promote co-operation among Council of Europe member States in the fight against corruption, instructed, *inter alia*, the Committee of Ministers to secure the rapid completion of international legal instruments pursuant to Council of Europe's Programme of Action against Corruption.

8. The Committee of Ministers, at its 101st Session on 6 November 1997, adopted Resolution (97) 24 on the 20 Guiding Principles for the fight against Corruption. Principle 10 specifically indicates that States should 'ensure that the rules relating to the rights and duties of public officials take into account the requirements of the fight against corruption and provide for appropriate

and effective disciplinary measures; and to promote further specification of the behaviour expected from public officials by appropriate means, such as codes of conduct'.

9. Consequently, following the adoption of the Criminal Law Convention on Corruption (European Treaty Series No 173), of Resolutions (98) 7 and (99) 5, authorising and establishing, respectively, the 'Group of States against Corruption (GRECO)' and of the Civil Law Convention on Corruption (European Treaty Series No 174), the Council of Europe adopted a recommendation inviting the Governments of member State to promote, subject to national law and principles of public administration, the adoption of national codes of conduct for public officials based on the Model Code of Conduct for Public Officials annexed to the recommendation.

Preparatory work

10. In January 1996 the Committee of Ministers at the 554th meeting of the Ministers' Deputies required the GMC to elaborate a draft [European] Code of Conduct for Public Officials.

11. However, in the course of the preparation of this text, the GMC agreed to delete the term 'European' in the title of the Model Code in order to acknowledge the contribution of non-member States to the implementation of the Programme of action against corruption and to account the fact that some non-European States may wish to draw inspiration from this code.

12. The GMC's Working Group on Administrative and Constitutional Law (GMCA) met 6 times from 1997 to 1999 to consider and finalise a draft recommendation of the Committee of Ministers including in appendix a model code of conduct. The GMC examined this text at its 18th meeting (Strasbourg, 8–10 September 1999), approved it in second reading at its 19th meeting (Strasbourg, 8–10 December 1999) and submitted it to the European Committee on Legal Co-operation (CDCJ) for its opinion. The GMC considered the CDCJ opinion and approved the draft recommendation at its 20th plenary meeting (Strasbourg, 11–13 April 2000). The Committee of Ministers of the Council of Europe adopted the Recommendation at its 106 session (Strasbourg, 11 May 2000) and authorised the publication of the explanatory report.

Public service codes of conduct in general

Context

13. A successful strategy for fighting corruption should be global and supported by all parties concerned, especially by those with the highest responsibilities. It should be based on prevention, education and enforcement. Each of these elements is essential, equally important and complementary. In this context codes of conduct play a part in all three elements of the strategy. Their main contribution is educational and preventive, but they also have enforcement aspects. They can be effective in changing the ethical climate in both the public private sectors.

Common considerations

14. In the discussion concerning corruption over the past years, the adoption and implementation of codes of conduct has been considered to be of crucial importance. However, voluntary regulation of behaviour by codes of conduct cannot replace legal norms and external control (by authorities or business auditors). Corruption can in fact occur despite subscription to a code of conduct. Accordingly, the public sometimes suspects that companies use much publicised codes of conduct mainly as a means for marketing. An effective implementation of the codes is therefore of utmost importance.

15. Codes of conduct have many names and purposes. They may, for instance, be called 'codes of ethics' or 'codes of business practice' or they may take the form of administrative regulations. Usually, codes of conduct describe guidelines binding employees to act in a certain manner whereas codes of practice are often addressed to clients rather than to of the institution for whom the code is drafted. Codes of practice lay down standards that clients have a right to expect, rather than standards that members of the profession are instructed to uphold.

16. Here the generic term 'code of conduct' is used although it should be emphasised that certain distinctions sometimes need to be made, depending on the purpose of the code. For instance, a code of good practice may be drafted for the purpose of giving detailed guidelines to employees on how to act in certain situations related to the work. Such a code may be of a totally different character from a normal code of conduct.

17. Codes may be adopted for various reasons and for various categories of public persons, such as public officials, judges, prosecutors, business people, auditors, members of other professions as well as elected representatives and members of government, both at the national and local level.

18. Codes of conduct dealing with issues of corruption may be very detailed. For instance, in one member Sate examples may be found where the codes deal with such issues as acceptance of flowers or boxes of chocolate and the exact value of gifts which may be accepted.

19. The legs basis for the adoption of codes may vary. Some are adopted on the basis of legislation whereas others are adopted on a voluntary basis. Some codes of conduct have the status of a semi-public instrument, although drawn up by private entities. An example may be found in the banking field where a due diligence code has been elaborated. Other such codes have been drafted for accountants and lawyers. Most codes are drafted to protect the interests of the company or the profession but some may be elaborated with a view to introducing clean practices in entire sectors of the industry. Examples may be found where entire employer's associations or larger companies in a specific sector undertake to abstain from corrupt practices.

20. As regards both public officials and the business community, the code may be seen as part of the employment contract and may in such cases be signed by the employee. A subsequent breach of the code can be a breach of the contract of employment. On the other hand, codes for independent professions and codes for elected representatives or members government may be of a different character: breach would not amount to a breach of contract but may nevertheless result in disciplinary proceedings.

21. The codes may be applicable only to active and form part of the employment contract as such, but some codes may contain provisions that apply when the employed person or the elected representative has left his work or has left his work or his post. Such codes may, for instance contain provisions restricting a person from taking a post in a company with which he had dealings in his previous position ('pantouflage'). Such provisions may be codes for public officials and for politicians.

22. The sanctions for disobedience of the codes vary as well, ranging from administrative sanctions such as reprimands to dismissal and other disciplinary measures. Some codes may not provide for any sanctions but may simply make reference to corruption offences in existing criminal codes. To a great extent the effectiveness of a code may depend on the sanctions which are provided. The scope for taking disciplinary measures is of course wider than the scope for criminal law measures. For certain categories of persons, for instance members of Parliament or the government, special types of sanctions apply. The codes may be used in administrative, civil and criminal decision-making as a reference document, in particular in assessment of what may be fair or appropriate in a given situation.

23. For a code of conduct to be widely accepted and complied with by those who are to be bound by it, it is advisable that they should be consulted during its preparation.

24. A model code of conduct for public officials could be of great benefit in the fight against corruption, in particular in the emerging democracies of Central and Eastern Europe. Codes of conduct for other categories of persons, such as members of government or elected representatives, can be of importance in setting minimum standards in ethics.

Public officials

25. Given the variety of tasks undertaken by a modern public administration, with staff from differ is and from non-homogenous social groups, the need to codify rules of conduct is now greater than in the past, when a more homogenous staff carried out similar activities and shared similar values.

26. The specific statutes of the civil service need to be taken into account when codes of conduct are considered, in particular when the codes are to be used, inter alia, as a means of combating corruption. Public service requires integrity from public officials. They are not only in the service of the government, taken in a narrow sense, but should also carry out their duties as a service to society at large. The responsibilities of the public official are therefore to a certain extent different from those of an employee in the private sector.

27. Special consideration needs to be given to the senior civil service and to members of the government who may be at the same time elected representatives. These categories may require special rules.

28. It should be noted, however, that a code of conduct cannot replace a statutory law on the status of public officials.

Elected representatives

29. Elected representatives are usually responsible to their electorate and/or to their party. At the same time, the public interest requires from them accountability, transparency and integrity. Tradition plays a great role in the evolution of the situation in member States. In the context of combating corruption, special attention needs to be given to questions of immunity, relation with the party, sanctions and conflicts of interest, and changes to the current situation require careful consideration.

Other persons

30. Codes of conduct differ depending on which category of persons is addressed. The aims of codes for judges or prosecutors necessarily differ from those drafted for auditors or private business. As the aims and legal situation differ, so do the sanctions which may apply in a particular case.

Purpose

31. Codes of conduct should be clear and concise statements of the guiding principles of conduct by which an organisation expects its members to behave and the values for which it stands.

32. The purpose of a code of conduct for public servants is threefold:

- it is a statement of the ethical climate that prevails in the public service;
- it spells out the standards of ethical conduct expected of public servants;
- it tells members of the public what to expect of public servants in conduct and attitude when dealing with them.

33. It is both a public document and a message addressed to every individual public servant. It cannot be assumed that a public servant knows what standards of conduct are expected of him if he has never been told what they are. Reliance on some unwritten process of absorption of standards in the working environment is haphazard and insufficient. If the public servant is to be called to account for his conduct, it is essential that he should have been informed of what was expected of him and that he should know in what respects his conduct has fallen short of those expectations. A clear, concise and accessible written statement of the standards by which his working life is to be conducted is a basic requirement.

Features

34. A model code should be capable of being adopted, with or without modification, for the generality of public officials. Its provisions should state the guiding principles and, at the same

time, provide advice sufficiently specific to be of use in any given situation. As a model of general application, it might not provide detailed guidance necessary to certain categories of officials or employees whose functions or professions require specific rules.

Content

35. Codes of conduct should not be limited to addressing corruption. They should go further and promote high standards of ethical behaviour. They should state general principles covering lawfulness, diligence, efficiency and thrift, transparency, confidentiality and the handling of classified information, personal responsibility and independent judgement, fair dealing and integrity, and professional training.

36. Their guidance can also be broadly divided into provisions dealing with personal integrity and those dealing with managerial responsibilities for upholding the integrity of the public service or the company, such as devising and putting in place appropriate systems of operation, ensuring that subordinates are informed and aware of their duties, applying systems of supervision and accountability, applying proper selection procedures, enforcing the code of conduct and maintaining discipline.

Application

37. To whom should a code apply? Should a code designed for the general public service apply to government ministers, to judges or to elected representatives? Should that code apply also to short term employees (perhaps seconded from the private sector), or to agents or independent consultants? To what extent can and should the code continue to apply to those who have left the organisation? These are questions that should be addressed when proposing a code for any organisation.

38. A general code may be insufficient for those doing certain kinds of work or in certain professions. Additional provisions or additional emphasis or even separate, special codes may be necessary. The 'Leadership Code' adopted in some countries is an example of a special code applying to a limited number of people in public service.

Preparation and promulgation

39. Consulting those to whom the code will apply is essential in its preparation since it must be accepted by those who are to lead their working lives in accordance with its guidance. It must be pragmatic and practical so as to foster compliance and to allow those to whom it applies to exercise their responsibility. The code must address the ethical issues people have to face every day.

40. Not only must every member of staff receive his or her own copy, everyone must be given practical instruction about its provisions and how to comply with them. Everyone must understand the importance of compliance and the consequences of not complying.

Implementation

41. It is the responsibility of management to ensure that the practices of the organisation are consistent with the code, that there is no contradiction between the standards required of staff and the goals or targets they are expected to meet.

42. It must also be the responsibility of every manager and supervisor to make sure that those for whom they are responsible are constantly aware of the standards set by the code and in practice carry out their work in conformity with them.

Enforcement

43. Deliberate failure to comply with the standards required must be met by appropriate disciplinary action. In deciding on appropriate disciplinary sanction, management should consider whether the breach results from ignorance or from deliberate self-serving wrongdoing of which

the management would disapprove or from wrongdoing done in the mistaken belief that the organisation would benefit.

Relationship to law

44. The law shapes the code and provides a strong reason for putting a code in place, and the code in turn articulates the rules of conduct which govern the working lives of those to whom it is addressed. Codes of conduct should reflect at a minimum the standards of the criminal law relating to dishonesty and corruption. Moreover, there should always be a relationship between codes of conduct and the laws and regulations concerned with disciplinary action.

The Recommendation of the Committee of Ministers on Codes of Conduct for Public Officials

The Recommendation

45. The Recommendation of the Committee of Ministers makes clear that the recommended adoption of codes of conduct for public officials should be subject to national law and to national principles of public administration. In recommending that such codes should be based on the annexed Model Code of Conduct, the recommendation also makes clear that the model should be adapted to meet the circumstances of the particular public service.

46. The Recommendation instructs GRECO to follow up on the implementation of the recommendation.

The Model Code of Conduct for Public Officials

Structure

47. The Model Code is so structured that it states a number of general principles before setting out more specific guidance. It starts with application and interpretation provisions, states the object of the code and sets out the general principles. It then deals with the following specific matters: reporting breaches of the code, conflict of interest, declaration of interests, incompatible outside interests, political or public activity, protection of official's privacy, gifts, reaction to improper offers, susceptibility to influence by others, misuse of official position, information held by public authorities, public and official resources, integrity checking, supervisory accountability, leaving the public service, dealing with former public officials and, finally, observance of the code and sanctions.

Style

48. The code offers guidance. It addresses public officials and members of the public. It is intended to be frequently referred to and read. It is therefore not drafted in the style of a law or regulation. Rather it offers practical advice and explanations to readers who are not necessarily learned nor legally trained. It nevertheless tries to be reasonably precise since breach of its provision could result in disciplinary proceedings.

Provisions

49. In adopting the provisions of the code, a State may need to adapt its provisions to meet the particular requirements of the State's public service.

Interpretation and application

Article 1

50. This article says the code applies to all public officials and defines 'public official' as a person employed by a public authority.

51. The term 'public official' is drawn widely. However the provisions of this article and the code as a whole do not cover the exercise of private functions or services, whether done by public

officials or not. Thus, private contractors remunerated from public revenues would not be covered, but the code is intended to cover the exercise of public functions on a private basis, such as, in some countries: notaries, public registers, etc. States themselves will have to decide the extent of the term 'public authority'.

52. In accordance with paragraph 4, the provisions of the Model Code do not apply to publicly elected representatives, members of governments and holders of judicial office given the particular nature of the functions they perform.

53. The GMC considered that it was necessary to draw a clear distinction between public officials who exercise functions within public administration or a public sector entity on the one hand, and ministers and elected representatives who are political figures responsible before parliament and ultimately to the voters. Thus, for instance, the principle of political neutrality recognised in paragraph 2 of Article 4 could not be applied to the latter.

54. Similarly, holders of judicial office are also excluded from the scope of this code. In certain countries prosecutors, on account of the nature of the functions that they perform may also be considered as holders of judicial office. Indeed the principle of judicial independence is incompatible with some of the principles stated in this code such as for instance the principle of accountability to the immediate hierarchical superior enshrined in Article 10.

55. Notwithstanding the exclusion of these categories of persons from the application of this code, it would be desirable for States to adopt ethical standards appropriate for the functions performed by these persons. With this in mind, States can decide to draw inspiration from the present code.

56. Moreover, States may decide to apply or adapt the provisions of this Code, totally or in part, to other categories of persons not included in Article 1.

Article 2

57. The code applies to a public official from the time he or she is informed of its provisions and certifies he has been so informed.

58. The application of this provision shall be adapted in the case of civil services based on the career system where conditions of service are governed by a civil service statute, where the code is enacted by the competent authority (responsible for public officials), for example the Minister for Public Administration or the Minister of the Interior, and the code would thus be an integral part of the regulations that apply to public officials.

Object of the Code

Article 3

59. The article states the aims of the code, i.e.: to specify standards of integrity and conduct, help public officials meet those standards and tell the public what it is entitled to expect from its public officials.

60. Given that public administrations play an essential role in democratic societies, that public officials are the key element thereof and since corruption undermines the citizens' trust in their administration, the code aims at eliminating any ambiguity about the general attitude of the administration towards corruption and clearly expresses what is expected from every employee in that respect.

61. The Code of conduct fills the gap between on the one hand often abstract legal regulations as to the principles of behaviour and, on the other hand the requirement of guidance in numerous difficult situations of an employed person's day-to-day life. It seeks to eliminate areas of uncertainty by offering either directly applicable instructions on how to cope with a given situation, or indications on where and how to receive such instructions. The Code can offer

specific guidance in situations where the employed person may feel that he has to deal with a conflict of interest.

62. In addition, the Code contributes to greater transparency in the functioning of public administration by clearly informing citizens of what they are entitled to expect from public officials.

General Principles

Articles 4–11

63. These articles set out the public official's general obligations to act lawfully, obediently, ethically and loyally. He or she is expected to be honest, impartial, conscientious, fair and just, and to act politically neutral, only in the public interest and with courtesy to all with whom he or she has contact.

64. He or she must not allow his or her private interests to affect, or appear to affect, his or her public position nor take undue advantage of that position. The term 'private interest' is explained in Article 13. It is for States to define the expression 'undue advantage'. However, it should be understood in a broad sense, as including not only advantages offered or given to the public official but also the avoidance of any disadvantages or burdens imposed upon him or her. Undue advantages are usually of an economic nature but may also be of a non-material nature.

65. What is important for the purposes of Article 8 is that a public official or a third person, for example a relative, should not be placed in a better position or acquire that benefit. Examples of undue advantage are money, holidays, loans, food and drink, a case handled more quickly than others or better career prospects.

66. The public official's behavior should enhance the public's regard for the public service and he or she should be accountable for his or her conduct. Thus, Article 6 forbids him to act arbitrarily to the detriment of any person, group of persons or body. In the course of the discussions, the GMC examined whether this Article should also forbid acting for the benefit of a person, group or body without any advantage for the public official or ensuring prejudice for a third party. However, in the light of the principles of impartiality and lawfulness stated respectively in Articles 5 and 7, the GMC did not consider it necessary to include expressly such a prohibition.

67. His or her handling of information must respect both the right to official information and the need for appropriate confidentiality. The expression 'necessary confidentiality' should be understood in a flexible manner, as allowing adaptation to the context of each member State, and in the light of the legal rules concerning the use of confidential information. Transparency is a key element in the fight against corruption. The principle contained in Article 11 does not aim at restricting unnecessarily the access of the public to official documents.

Reporting

Article 12

68. This article requires the public official to report, in accordance with the law, whenever he or she believes he or she is being required to act inconsistently with the code.

69. If, having reported the matter in accordance with the law, he or she is not satisfied with the response, he or she may take the matter up in writing with the relevant head of the public service, namely the person ultimately responsible for the public service. This will obviously vary from country to country, for example the Minister for Public Administration or the Minister of the Interior. When the matter has been taken as far as procedures allow, the article makes clear that the public official must then comply with lawful instructions.

70. Moreover, paragraph 2 requires public officials to report to the competent authorities in accordance with the law any breach of the code by another public official of which he or she

becomes aware. The GMC was aware of the practical difficulties that the application of this provision in public administration could entail in certain cases since it could create tensions among public officials. However, it considered that the passive or tolerant attitude of public officials. However, it considered that the passive or tolerant attitude of public officials regarding those breaches would be more harmful for public administration and society as a whole.

71. Unlawful or criminal activities are to be reported to the appropriate authorities. Once reported, the investigation will be the responsibility of the competent authorities and not of the public official.

72. For its part the public administration must ensure that no prejudice is caused to a public official who makes such a report on reasonable grounds and in good faith.

Conflict of interest

Article 13

73. This article explains what is a private interest and how a conflict can arise between a public official's public duties and his or her private interest. He or she must be aware of the possibility of a conflict arising, take steps to avoid it, disclose it to his supervisor at the earliest opportunity and comply with any proper instruction to resolve it. Whenever required to do so, he or she should state whether or not a conflict arises.

Declaration of interests

Article 14

74. The article explains that certain public officials may be lawfully required periodically to declare their personal or private interests. This obligation has a preventive character. It is generally imposed upon officials holding high level posts. However, the main criterion should be the nature of the functions performed and the responsibilities relating thereto. This may lead States to impose such obligations upon certain officials even if they hold posts of a modest hierarchical level.

75. Periodic declarations of interest are essential for the effectiveness of this measure. Keeping this in mind, the code provides that the declaration will be made not only upon appointment but also at regular intervals thereafter determined by national legislation. Any change in the situation affecting the public official's interests will imply the obligation for him or her to submit a new declaration.

76. Since this obligation represents an interference in private life it needs to be always justified. It is the duty of public administration to ensure the confidentiality of such declarations which in turn is guaranteed by Article 17.

Incompatible outside interest

Article 15

77. The article states that public officials are not to engage in any activities incompatible with the proper performance of official functions. If unsure, they should seek the advice of their superiors.

78. Subject to the law, the public official should seek his or her employer's approval to undertake certain activities, positions or functions outside the public service. This requirement is made subject to law because some countries have regulations governing the taking of outside or second jobs. It should be noted that this principle does not prohibit a public official from having a second job outside the public service.

79. The ariticle also requires the public official to comply with any lawful requirement to declare his or her affiliation to organisations that could detract from his or her position or the proper performance as a public official.

Political or public activity

Article 16

80. This article enjoins the public official to be careful firstly not to allow his or her political activities to impair his or her impartiality or loyalty and secondly not to let himself or herself be used for partisan political purposes. He or she should comply with any restriction on political activity lawfully imposed by reason of his or her duties as a public official.

Protection of the public official's privacy

Article 17

81. Like other citizens, public officials have a right to privacy and have a duty to respect the privacy of other public officials. This article makes that clear and specifically requires declarations made in accordance with the code to be kept confidential unless otherwise required by law.

82. The right to respect for private life is not an absolute one. It might be necessary to interfere or restrict the exercise of this right in order to attain certain legitimate objectives such as the prevention of crime and the protection of the rights of others. Consequently, the general principle of confidentiality of declarations recognised in this Article could be lifted for instance in the framework of criminal investigations or disciplinary procedures affecting the public official.

Gifts

Article 18

83. This article makes clear that the public official should not seek or accept any gift or benefit for himself or anyone else that could influence, or appear to influence, the carrying out of his or her duties. The public official should never accept either gifts that constitute a real or apparent reward for actions or omissions in the exercise of his or her functions. It is essential to preserve the citizens' trust in the impartiality of public administration. Such trust would be undermined if the citizen observes or is under the impression that the public official, whose salary should be paid in principle out of the public budget, receives compensation from private individuals in exchange for the performance of his or her duties.

84. The Code allows for some exceptions to the general prohibition of gifts, in respect of conventional hospitality or minor gifts. This expression comprises for instance, modest invitations to food and drinks, calendars, low price pens, advertising materials, small stationary . . . It is for each country to establish the criteria to differentiate between what is acceptable and the gifts which fall within the general prohibition rule. Often the value of the gift or invitation is used as a criterion, it being understood that whenever the value is lower than the threshold, the gift or invitation could be acceptable. However, low value may not always be a proper criterion. He or she should be alert however to the possibility of even a generally permitted advantage giving rise to a conflict of interest in particular circumstances. Thus, gifts or invitations offered repeatedly, even if low value could affect the public official's imparitiality in the exercise of his or her functions.

85. During discussions, the GMC considered the possibility of introducing a general obligation of declaring all gifts, even those of low value. Once the gifts are declared, the hierarchical superior or other competent authority would decide which gifts the public official was authorised to accept. The GMC preferred however, not to include such a general system in a model code, it being understood that each country is free to adopt more restrictive provisions than those contained in the code.

86. When social circumstances prevent him or her refusing an advantage, the public official should promptly report the fact and circumstances of his acceptance to his immediate superior and comply with any direction for disposal.

87. When in doubt, the public official should seek advice from his or her superior.

88. Elementary prudence would require that the request and the advice should be made in writing.

Reaction to improper offers

Article 19

89. Public officials need to know how to react appropriately when improperly offered a gift or benefit. This article gives specific guidance on what he or she should do in such circumstances.

Susceptibility to influence by others

Article 20

90. Public officials can become the targets of attempts to compromise them. The purpose of this article is to alert them to the danger by advising them that they should not put themselves in a position of obligation to return a favour, nor conduct themselves in their official or private lives in such a way that they become susceptible to the improper influence of others.

Misuse of official position

Article 21

91. The public official is enjoyed firstly not to offer any advantage connected with his position as an official unless lawfully authorised to do so, and secondly not to try to influence anyone for his or her own private benefit by using his or her official position or by offering personal advantages. These advantages can be offered directly or indirectly.

Information held by public authorities

Article 22

92. In the course of serving the common good, the public service creates, acquires and holds a great deal of information, the value or significance of which may not always be obvious. The handling of information held by public authorities is a frequent cause of difficulty. This article provides guidance in four distinct aspects.

93. First, the public official should disclose information only in accordance with applicable rules and requirements.

94. Second, he or she must protect the security and confidentiality of information, not only for which he or she is responsible but also of which he or she becomes aware.

95. Third, the public official should not seek official information to which he or she should not have access, nor should he or she make improper use of information come by in his or her employment.

96. Fourth, he or she has an equally strong duty not to withhold official information that may or should be released nor to provide false or misleading information.

Public and official resources

Article 23

97. This article requires the public official to manage and make use of personnel resources on one hand and of public property, facilities, services and financial resources on the other effectively, efficiently and economically. Unauthorised use for private purposes is forbidden, when authorisation is given according to the law. Thus, for instance, the public official should not, without proper authorisation, use the official car for private travel, of the office telephone for private calls, or ask his or her secretary to do work unrelated to his or her official duties.

98. In this connection, the GMC considered the use by public officials of fidelity programmes organised by airlines, hotel chains, and by other service providers. Thus, for instance, whenever the public official enjoys a margin of discretion in the choice of the airline for an official journey, this article requires the public official to be careful to choose without being influenced by personal considerations to the detriment of the economic interest of the public administration as defined above.

Integrity checking

Article 24

99. Experience shows the importance of carrying out integrity checks or acting on them in order to avoid long-term integrity problems in the public service. This article therefore requires the public official responsible for recruitment, promotion or posting to make sure that appropriate integrity checks are carried out as lawfully required.

100. Again, he or she is enjoined to seek appropriate advice if the results of the checks make it unclear how to proceed.

Supervisory accountability

Article 25

101. The notion that every person in a supervisory position should be responsible and accountable for the conduct of those he or she supervises has a significant effect on the integrity of the public service.

102. This article lays a dual responsibility on the supervisor or manager. He or she should manage or supervise in accordance with the policies and purposes of the public service and he or she should be answerable for the failings of his staff if he or she has not taken reasonable steps to prevent them.

103. The article goes on to give specific guidance. The supervisor or manager should take steps to prevent corruption by enforcing the rules, providing education or training, being alert to signs of financial or other difficulties and setting a personal example.

Leaving the public service

Article 26

104. If it is in the public interest that people with experience of public administration should be able to take up appointment outside the public service, it is equally important that the taking up of appointment elsewhere should not cause suspicion of impropriety. The guidance provided in this article therefore aims to allay suspicion:

- that the advice, decisions or actions of the public official could be influenced by the hope or expectation of future employment with a particular employer; or
- that the employer might be gaining an unfair advantage over competitors by employing a public official who had access to information that competitors regard as their own commercial secrets or that relates to proposed developments in government policy affecting them.

105. Accordingly, the public official should not take improper advantage of his official position to obtain a job outside the public service. He or she should be careful to avoid the possibility of conflict of interest arising from the prospect of future employment. For and appropriate period he or she should avoid acting or advising in matters in which he or she was involved as a public official. Nor should he use or disclose confidential information acquired as an official. Finally he or she should comply with any rules that apply to accepting appointments after leaving the public service.

Dealing with former public officials

Article 27

106. This Article forbids public officials to grant former public officials preferential treatment or privileged access to the public service as this would be contrary to the principles stated in this code such as, for instance, those in Article 5, paragraphs 2, 7 and 9.

107. This provision does not concern the cases where national legislation grants former public officials certain advantages such as, for instance, the use of public facilities like holiday camps, preferential or free fares awarded to public administration, etc.

Observance of the Code and sanctions

Article 28

108. This article first states the authority under which it is issued, a matter that will vary from country to country. It then reminds the official of the duty to conduct himself or herself in accordance with the code and therefore to become and remain familiar with, its provisions. He or she urged to seek advice when unsure of how to proceed.

109. The article then points out that subject to Article2, paragraph2, the code forms part of the official's terms of employment and that failure to comply with it may lead to disciplinary action.

110. The official who has responsibilities for negotiating terms of employment is reminded of his or her duty to include in them a provision that the code forms part of those terms.

111. The supervisor or manager is made responsible for ensuring that those under him or her observe the code and for initiating disciplinary action for failure to comply with it.

112. The public administration is under the obligation to review at regular intervals the provisions of this code so as to ensure that they are still appropriate.

APPENDIX 12

Recommendation Rec (2003) 4 of the Committee of Ministers to Member States on Common Rules Against Corruption in the Funding of Political Parties and Electoral Campaigns

Adopted by
the Committee of Ministers on 8 April 2003 at
the 835th meeting of the Ministers' Deputies

The Committee of Ministers, under the terms of Article 15.*b* of the Statute of the Council of Europe,

Considering that the aim of the Council of Europe is to achieve a greater unity between its members;

Considering that political parties are a fundamental element of the democratic systems of states and are an essential tool of expression of the political will of citizens;

Considering that political parties and electoral campaigns funding in all states should be subject to standards in order to prevent and fight against the phenomenon of corruption;

Convinced that corruption represents a serious threat to the rule of law, democracy, human rights, equity and social justice, that it hinders economic development, endangers the stability of democratic institutions and undermines the moral foundations of society;

Having regard to the recommendations adopted at the 19th and 21st Conferences of European Ministers of Justice (Valetta, 1994 and Prague, 1997 respectively);

Having regard to the Programme of Action against Corruption adopted by the Committee of Ministers in 1996;

In accordance with the Final Declaration and the Plan of Action adopted by the Heads of State and Government of the Council of Europe at their Second Summit, held in Strasbourg on 10 and 11 October 1997;

Having regard to Resolution (97) 24 on the twenty guiding principles for the fight against corruption, adopted by the Committee of Ministers on 6 November 1997 and in particular Principle 15, which promotes rules for the financing of political parties and election campaigns which deter corruption;

Having regard to Recommendation 1516 (2001) on the financing of political parties, adopted on 22 May 2001 by the Council of Europe's Parliamentary Assembly;

In the light of the conclusions of the 3rd European Conference of Specialised Services in the Fight against Corruption on the subject of Trading in Influence and Illegal Financing of Political Parties held in Madrid from 28 to 30 October 1998;

Recalling in this respect the importance of the participation of non-member states in the Council of Europe's activities against corruption and welcoming their valuable contribution to the implementation of the Programme of Action against Corruption;

Having regard to Resolution (98) 7 authorising the Partial and Enlarged Agreement establishing the Group of States against Corruption (GRECO) and Resolution (99) 5 establishing the Group of States against Corruption (GRECO), which aims at improving the capacity of its members to fight corruption by following up compliance with their undertakings in this field;

Convinced that raising public awareness on the issues of prevention and fight against corruption in the field of funding of political parties is essential to the good functioning of democratic institutions,

Recommends that the governments of member states adopt, in their national legal systems, rules against corruption in the funding of political parties and electoral campaigns which are inspired by the common rules reproduced in the appendix to this recommendation,—in so far as states do not already have particular laws, procedures or systems that provide effective and well-functioning alternatives, and instructs the 'Group of States against Corruption—GRECO' to monitor the implementation of this recommendation.

Appendix

Common Rules Against Corruption in the Funding of Political Parties and Electoral Campaigns

I. External sources of funding of political parties

Article 1

Public and private support to political parties

The state and its citizens are both entitled to support political parties.

The state should provide support to political parties. State support should be limited to reasonable contributions. State support may be financial.

Objective, fair and reasonable criteria should be applied regarding the distribution of state support.

States should ensure that any support from the state and/or citizens does not interfere with the independence of political parties.

Article 2

Definition of donation to a political party

Donation means any deliberate act to bestow advantage, economic or otherwise, on a political party.

Article 3

General principles on donations

a. Measures taken by states governing donations to political parties should provide specific rules to:
   - — avoid conflicts of interests;
   - — ensure transparency of donations and avoid secret donations;
   - — avoid prejudice to the activities of political parties;
   - — ensure the independence of political parties.

b. States should:
   - i provide that donations to political parties are made public, in particular, donations exceeding a fixed ceiling;
   - ii consider the possibility of introducing rules limiting the value of donations to political parties;
   - iii adopt measures to prevent established ceilings from being circumvented.

Article 4

Tax deductibility of donations

Fiscal legislation may allow tax deductibility of donations to political parties. Such tax deductibility should be limited.

Article 5

Donations by legal entities

a. In addition to the general principles on donations, states should provide:
   i that donations from legal entities to political parties are registered in the books and accounts of the legal entities; and
   ii that shareholders or any other individual member of the legal entity be informed of donations.
b. States should take measures aimed at limiting, prohibiting or otherwise strictly regulating donations from legal entities which provide goods or services for any public administration.
c. States should prohibit legal entities under the control of the state or of other public authorities from making donations to political parties.

Article 6

Donations to entities connected with a political party

Rules concerning donations to political parties, with the exception of those concerning tax deductibility referred to in Article 4, should also apply, as appropriate, to all entities which are related, directly or indirectly, to a political party or are otherwise under the control of a political party.

Article 7

Donations from foreign donors

States should specifically limit, prohibit or otherwise regulate donations from foreign donors.

II. Sources of funding of candidates for elections and elected officials

Article 8

Application of funding rules to candidates for elections and elected representatives

The rules regarding funding of political parties should apply *mutatis mutandis* to:

— the funding of electoral campaigns of candidates for elections;
— the funding of political activities of elected representatives.

III. Electoral campaign expenditure

Article 9

Limits on expenditure

States should consider adopting measures to prevent excessive funding needs of political parties, such as, establishing limits on expenditure on electoral campaigns.

Article 10

Records of expenditure

States should require particular records to be kept of all expenditure, direct and indirect, on electoral campaigns in respect of each political party, each list of candidates and each candidate.

IV. Transparency

Article 11

Accounts

States should require political parties and the entities connected with political parties mentioned in Article 6 to keep proper books and accounts. The accounts of political parties should be consolidated to include, as appropriate, the accounts of the entities mentioned in Article 6.

Article 12
Records of donations

a. States should require the accounts of a political party to specify all donations received by the party, including the nature and value of each donation.
b. In case of donations over a certain value, donors should be identified in the records.

Article 13
Obligation to present and make public accounts

a. States should require political parties to present the accounts referred to in Article 11 regularly, and at least annually, to the independent authority referred to in Article 14.
b. States should require political parties regularly, and at least annually, to make public the accounts referred to in Article 11 or as a minimum a summary of those accounts, including the information required in Article 10, as appropriate, and in Article 12.

V. Supervision

Article 14
Independent monitoring

a. States should provide for independent monitoring in respect of the funding of political parties and electoral campaigns.
b. The independent monitoring should include supervision over the accounts of political parties and the expenses involved in election campaigns as well as their presentation and publication.

Article 15
Specialised personnel

States should promote the specialisation of the judiciary, police or other personnel in the fight against illegal funding of political parties and electoral campaigns.

VI. Sanctions

Article 16
Sanctions

States should require the infringement of rules concerning the funding of political parties and electoral campaigns to be subject to effective, proportionate and dissuasive sanctions.

APPENDIX 13

Council of the European Union: Convention On the Fight Against Corruption involving Officials of the European Communities or Officials of Member States of the European Union[1]

Council Act of 26 May 1997 drawing up, on the basis of Article K.3(2)(c) of the Treaty on European Union,

Referring to the Act of the Council of the European Union of 26 May 1997,

Whereas the Member States consider the improvement of judicial cooperation in the fight against corruption to be a matter of common interest, coming under the cooperation provided for in Title VI of the Treaty;

Whereas by its Act of 27 September 1996 the Council drew up a Protocol directed in particular at acts of corruption involving national or Community officials and damaging or likely to damage the European Communities' financial interests;

Whereas, for the purpose of improving judicial cooperation in criminal matters between Member States, it is necessary to go further than the said Protocol and to draw up a Convention directed at acts of corruption involving officials of the European Communities or officials of the Member States in general;

Desirous of ensuring consistent and effective application of this Convention throughout the European Union;

Have agreed on the following provisions:

Article 1
Definitions

For the purposes of this Convention:

(a) 'official' shall mean any Community or national official, including any national official of another Member State;

(b) 'Community official' shall mean:

— any person who is an official or other contracted employee within the meaning of the Staff Regulations of officials of the European Communities or the Conditions of Employment of other servants of the European Communities,

— any person seconded to the European Communities by the Member States or by any public or private body, who carries out functions equivalent to those performed by European Community officials or other servants.

Members of bodies set up in accordance with the Treaties establishing the European Communities and the staff of such bodies shall be treated as Community officials, inasmuch as the Staff Regulations of officials of the European Communities or the Conditions of Employment of other servants of the European Communities do not apply to them;

[1] The Convention was adopted by the Council of the European Union on 26 May 1997.

(c) 'National official' shall be understood by reference to the definition of 'official' or 'public officer' in the national law of the Member State in which the person in question performs that function for the purposes of application of the criminal law of that Member State.

Nevertheless, in the case of proceedings involving a Member State's official initiated by another Member State, the latter shall not be bound to apply the definition of 'national official' except insofar as that definition is compatible with its national law.

Article 2

Passive corruption

1 For the purposes of this Convention, the deliberate action of an official, who, directly or through an intermediary, requests or receives advantages of any kind whatsoever, for himself or for a third party, or accepts a promise of such an advantage, to act or refrain from acting in accordance with his duty or in the exercise of his functions in breach of his official duties shall constitute passive corruption.

2 Each Member State shall take the necessary measures to ensure that conduct of the type referred to in paragraph 1 is made a criminal offence.

Article 3

Active corruption

1 For the purposes of this Convention, the deliberate action of whosoever promises or gives, directly or through an intermediary, an advantage of any kind whatsoever to an official for himself or for a third party for him to act or refrain from acting in accordance with his duty or in the exercise of his functions in breach of his official duties shall constitute active corruption.

2 Each Member State shall take the necessary measures to ensure that conduct of the type referred to in paragraph 1 is made a criminal offence.

Article 4

Assimilation

1 Each Member State shall take the necessary measures to ensure that in its criminal law the descriptions of the offences referred to in Articles 2 and 3 committed by or against its Government Ministers, elected members of its parliamentary chambers, the members of its highest Courts or the members of its Court of Auditors in the exercise of their functions apply similarly in cases where such offences are committed by or against Members of the Commission of the European Communities, the European Parliament, the Court of Justice and the Court of Auditors of the European Communities respectively in the exercise of their duties.

2 Where a Member State has enacted special legislation concerning acts or omissions for which Government Ministers are responsible by reason of their special political position in that Member State, paragraph 1 may not apply to such legislation, provided that the Member State ensures that Members of the Commission of the European Communities are also covered by the criminal legislation implementing Articles 2 and 3.

3 Paragraphs 1 and 2 shall be without prejudice to the provisions applicable in each Member State concerning criminal proceedings and the determination of the competent court.

4 This Convention shall apply in full accordance with the relevant provisions of the Treaties establishing the European Communities, the Protocol on the Privileges and Immunities of the European Communities, the Statutes of the Court of Justice and the texts adopted for the purpose of their implementation, as regards the withdrawal of immunity.

Article 5
Penalties

1 Each Member State shall take the necessary measures to ensure that the conduct referred to in Articles 2 and 3, and participating in and instigating the conduct in question, is punishable by effective, proportionate and dissuasive criminal penalties, including, at least in serious cases, penalties involving deprivation of liberty which can give rise to extradition.
2 Paragraph 1 shall be without prejudice to the exercise of disciplinary powers by the competent authorities against national officials or Community officials. In determining the penalty to be imposed, the national criminal courts may, in accordance with the principles of their national law, take into account any disciplinary penalty already imposed on the same person for the same conduct.

Article 6
Criminal liability of heads of businesses

Each Member State shall take the necessary measures to allow heads of businesses or any persons having power to take decisions or exercise control within a business to be declared criminally liable in accordance with the principles defined by its national law in cases of corruption, as referred to in Article 3, by a person under their authority acting on behalf of the business.

Article 7
Jurisdiction

1 Each Member State shall take the measures necessary to establish its jurisdiction over the offences it has established in accordance with the obligations arising out of Articles 2, 3 and 4 where:
   (a) the offence is committed in whole or in part within its territory;
   (b) the offender is one of its nationals or one of its officials;
   (c) the offence is committed against one of the persons referred to in Article 1 or a member of one of the European Community institutions referred to in Article 4(1) who is at the same time one of its nationals;
   (d) the offender is a Community official working for a European Community institution or a body set up in accordance with the Treaties establishing the European Communities which has its headquarters in the Member State in question.
2 Each Member State may declare, when giving the notification provided for in Article 13 (2), that it will not apply or will apply only in specific cases or conditions one or more of the jurisdiction rules laid down in paragraph 1(b), (c) and (d).

Article 8
Extradition and prosecution

1 Any Member State which, under its law, does not extradite its own nationals shall take the necessary measures to establish its jurisdiction over the offences it has established in accordance with the obligations arising out of Articles 2, 3 and 4, when committed by its own nationals outside its territory.
2 Each Member State shall, when one of its nationals is alleged to have committed in another Member State an offence established in accordance with the obligations arising out of Articles 2, 3 and 4 and it does not extradite that person to that other Member State solely on the ground of his nationality, submit the case to its competent authorities for the purpose of prosecution if appropriate. In order to enable prosecution to take place, the files, information and exhibits relating to the offence shall be transmitted in accordance with the procedures laid down in Article 6 of the European Convention on Extradition of 13 December 1957. The requesting Member State shall be informed of the prosecution initiated and of its outcome.

3 For the purposes of this Article, the term 'national' of a Member State shall be construed in accordance with any declaration made by that State under Article 6(1)(b) of the European Convention on Extradition and with paragraph 1(c) of that Article.

Article 9

Cooperation

1 If any procedure in connection with an offence established in accordance with the obligations arising out of Articles 2, 3 and 4 concerns at least two Member States, those States shall cooperate effectively in the investigation, the prosecution and in carrying out the punishment imposed by means, for example, of mutual legal assistance, extradition, transfer of proceedings or enforcement of sentences passed in another Member State.

2 Where more than one Member State has jurisdiction and has the possibility of viable prosecution of an offence based on the same facts, the Member States involved shall cooperate in deciding which shall prosecute the offender or offenders with a view to centralizing the prosecution in a single Member State where possible.

Article 10

Ne bis in idem

1 Member States shall apply, in their national criminal laws, the ne bis in idem rule, under which a person whose trial has been finally disposed of in a Member State may not be prosecuted in another Member State in respect of the same facts, provided that if a penalty was imposed, it has been enforced, is actually in the process of being enforced or can no longer be enforced under the laws of the sentencing State.

2 A Member State may, when giving the notification referred to in Article 13(2), declare that it shall not be bound by paragraph 1 of this Article in one or more of the following cases:

(a) if the facts which were the subject of the judgment rendered abroad took place in its own territory either in whole or in part; in the latter case this exception shall not apply if those facts took place partly in the territory of the Member State where the judgment was rendered;

(b) if the facts which were the subject of the judgment rendered abroad constitute an offence directed against the security or other equally essential interests of that Member State;

(c) if the facts which were the subject of the judgment rendered abroad were committed by an official of that Member State contrary to the duties of his office.

3 If a further prosecution is brought in a Member State against a person whose trial, in respect of the same facts, has been finally disposed of in another Member State, any period of deprivation of liberty served in the latter Member State arising from those facts shall be deducted from any sanction imposed. To the extent permitted by national law, sanctions not involving deprivation of liberty shall also be taken into account insofar as they have been enforced.

4 The exceptions which may be the subject of a declaration under paragraph 2 shall not apply if the Member State concerned in respect of the same facts requested the other Member State to bring the prosecution or granted extradition of the person concerned.

5 Relevant bilateral or multilateral agreements concluded between Member States and relevant declarations shall remain unaffected by this Article.

Article 11

Internal provisions

No provision in this Convention shall prevent Member States from adopting internal legal provisions which go beyond the obligations deriving from this Convention.

Article 12
Court of Justice

1 Any dispute between Member States on the interpretation or application of this Convention which it has proved impossible to resolve bilaterally must in an initial stage be examined by the Council in accordance with the procedure set out in Title VI of the Treaty on European Union with a view to reaching a solution. If no solution has been found within six months, the matter may be referred to the Court of Justice of the European Communities by one of the parties to the dispute.
2 Any dispute between one or more Member States and the Commission of the European Communities concerning Article 1, with the exception of point (c), or Articles 2, 3 and 4, insofar as it concerns a question of Community law or the Communities' financial interests, or involves members of officials of Community institutions of bodies set up in accordance with the Treaties establishing the European Communities, which it has proved impossible to settle through negotiation, may be submitted to the Court of Justice by one of the parties to the dispute.
3 Any court in a Member State may ask the Court of Justice to give a preliminary ruling on a matter concerning the interpretation of Articles 1 to 4 and 12 to 16 raised in a case pending before it and involving members or officials of Community institutions or bodies set up in accordance with the Treaties establishing the European Communities, acting in the exercise of their functions, if it considers that a decision on that matter is necessary to enable it to give judgment.
4 The competence of the Court of Justice provided for in paragraph 3 shall be subject to its acceptance by the Member State concerned in a declaration to that effect made at the time of the notification referred to in Article 13(2) or at any subsequent time.
5 A Member State making a declaration under paragraph 4 may restrict the possibility of asking the Court of Justice to give a preliminary ruling to those of its courts against the decisions of which there is no judicial remedy under national law
6 The Statute of the Court of Justice of the European Community and its Rules of Procedure shall apply. In accordance with those Statutes, any Member State, or the Commission, whether or not it has made a declaration pursuant to paragraph 4, shall be entitled to submit statements of case or written observations to the Court of Justice in cases which arise under paragraph 3.

Article 13
Entry into force

1 This Convention shall be subject to adoption by the Member States in accordance with their respective constitutional requirements.
2 Member States shall notify the Secretary-General of the Council of the European Union of the completion of the procedures laid down by their respective constitutional requirements for adopting this Convention.
3 This Convention shall enter into force ninety days after the notification, referred to in paragraph 2, by the last Member State to fulfil that formality.
4 Until the entry into force of this Convention, any Member State may, when giving the notification referred to in paragraph 2 or at any time thereafter, declare that this Convention, with the exception of Article 12 thereof, shall apply to it in its relationships with those Member States which have made the same declaration. This Convention shall become applicable in respect of the Member State that makes such a declaration on the first day of the month following the expiry of a period of ninety days after the date of deposit of its declaration.
5 A Member State that has not made any declaration as referred to in paragraph 4 may apply this Convention with respect to the other contracting Member States on the basis of bilateral agreements.

Article 14

Accession of new Member States

1 This Convention shall be open to accession by any State that becomes a member of the European Union.
2 The text of this Convention in the language of the acceding State, drawn up by the Council of the European Union, shall be authentic.
3 Instruments of accession shall be deposited with the depositary.
4 This Convention shall enter into force with respect to any State acceding to it ninety days after the date of deposit of its instrument of accession or on the date of entry into force of the Convention if it has not already entered into force at the time of expiry of the said period of ninety days.
5 If this Convention has not yet entered into force when the instrument of accession is deposited, Article 13(4) shall apply to acceding States.

Article 15

Reservations

1 No reservation shall be authorized with the exception of those provided for in Articles 7(2) and 10(2).
2 Any Member State which has entered a reservation may withdraw it at any time in whole or in part by notifying the depositary. Withdrawal shall take effect on the date on which the depositary receives the notification.

Article 16

Depositary

1 The Secretary-General of the Council of the European Union shall act as depositary of this Convention.
2 The depositary shall publish in the Official Journal of the European Communities information on the progress of adoptions and accessions, declarations and reservations and any other notification concerning this Convention.

APPENDIX 14

COUNCIL OF THE EUROPEAN UNION: CONVENTION ON THE PROTECTION OF THE EUROPEAN COMMUNITIES' FINANCIAL INTERESTS[1]

CONVENTION DRAWN UP ON THE BASIS OF ARTICLE K.3 OF THE TREATY ON EUROPEAN UNION, ON THE PROTECTION OF THE EUROPEAN COMMUNITIES' FINANCIAL INTERESTS

The high contracting parties to this Convention, Member States of the European Union,

Referring to the Act of the Council of the European Union of 26 July 1995;

Desiring to ensure that their criminal laws contribute effectively to the protection of the financial interests of the European Communities;

Noting that fraud affecting Community revenue and expenditure in many cases is not confined to a single country and is often committed by organized criminal networks;

Convinced that protection of the European Communities' financial interests calls for the criminal prosecution of fraudulent conduct injuring those interests and requires, for that purpose, the adoption of a common definition;

Convinced of the need to make such conduct punishable with effective, proportionate and dissuasive criminal penalties, without prejudice to the possibility of applying other penalties in appropriate cases, and of the need, at least in serious cases, to make such conduct punishable with deprivation of liberty which can give rise to extradition;

Recognizing that businesses play an important role in the areas financed by the European Communities and that those with decision-making powers in business should not escape criminal responsibility in appropriate circumstances;

Determined to combat together fraud affecting the European Communities' financial interests by undertaking obligations concerning jurisdiction, extradition, and mutual cooperation,

Have agreed on the following provisions:

Article 1
General provisions

1. For the purposes of this Convention, fraud affecting the European Communities' financial interests shall consist of:
   (a) In respect of expenditure, any intentional act or omission relating to:
      —The use or presentation of false, incorrect or incomplete statements or documents, which has as its effect the misappropriation or wrongful retention of funds from the general budget of the European Communities or budgets managed by, or on behalf of, the European Communities,
      —Non-disclosure of information in violation of a specific obligation, with the same effect,
      —The misapplication of such funds for purposes other than those for which they were originally granted;

[1] The Convention entered into force on 17 October 2002.

(b) In respect of revenue, any intentional act or omission relating to:
   — The use or presentation of false, incorrect or incomplete statements or documents, which has as its effect the illegal diminution of the resources of the general budget of the European Communities or budgets managed by, or on behalf of, the European Communities,
   — Non-disclosure of information in violation of a specific obligation, with the same effect,
   — Misapplication of a legally obtained benefit, with the same effect.

2. Subject to Article 2(2), each Member State shall take the necessary and appropriate measures to transpose paragraph 1 into their national criminal law in such a way that the conduct referred to therein constitutes criminal offences.
3. Subject to Article 2(2), each Member State shall also take the necessary measures to ensure that the intentional preparation or supply of false, incorrect or incomplete statements or documents having the effect described in paragraph 1 constitutes a criminal offence if it is not already punishable as a principal offence or as participation in, instigation of, or attempt to commit, fraud as defined in paragraph 1.
4. The intentional nature of an act or omission as referred to in paragraphs 1 and 3 may be inferred from objective, factual circumstances.

Article 2
Penalties

1. Each Member State shall take the necessary measures to ensure that the conduct referred to in Article 1, and participating in, instigating, or attempting the conduct referred to in Article 1(1), are punishable by effective, proportionate and dissuasive criminal penalties, including, at least in cases of serious fraud, penalties involving deprivation of liberty which can give rise to extradition, it being understood that serious fraud shall be considered to be fraud involving a minimum amount to be set in each Member State. This minimum amount may not be set at a sum exceeding ECU 50 000.
2. However in cases of minor fraud involving a total amount of less than ECU 4 000 and not involving particularly serious circumstances under its laws, a Member State may provide for penalties of a different type from those laid down in paragraph 1.
3. The Council of the European Union, acting unanimously, may alter the amount referred to in paragraph 2.

Article 3
Criminal liability of heads of businesses

Each Member State shall take the necessary measures to allow heads of businesses or any persons having power to take decisions or exercise control within a business to be declared criminally liable in accordance with the principles defined by its national law in cases of fraud affecting the European Community's financial interests, as referred to in Article 1, by a person under their authority acting on behalf of the business.

Article 4
Jurisdiction

1. Each Member State shall take the necessary measures to establish its jurisdiction over the offences it has established in accordance with Article 1 and 2(1) when:
   — fraud, participation in fraud or attempted fraud affecting the European Communities' financial interests is committed in whole or in part within its territory, including fraud for which the benefit was obtained in that territory,
   — a person within its territory knowingly assists or induces the commission of such fraud within the territory of any other State,

— the offender is a national of the Member State concerned, provided that the law of that Member State may require the conduct to be punishable also in the country where it occurred.

2. Each Member State may declare, when giving the notification referred to in Article 11 (2), that it will not apply the rule laid down in the third indent of paragraph 1 of this Article.

Article 5

Extradition and prosecution

1. Any Member State which, under its law, does not extradite its own nationals shall take the necessary measures to establish its jurisdiction over the offences it has established in accordance with Articles 1 and 2(1), when committed by its own nationals outside its territory.
2. Each Member State shall, when one of its nationals is alleged to have committed in another Member State a criminal offence involving the conduct described in Articles 1 and 2(1), and it does not extradite that person to that other Member State solely on the ground of his or her nationality, submit the case to its competent authorities for the purpose of prosecution if appropriate. In order to enable prosecution to take place, the files, information and exhibits relating to the offence shall be transmitted in accordance with the procedures laid down in Article 6 of the European Convention on Extradition. The requesting Member State shall be informed of the prosecution initiated and of its outcome.
3. A Member State may not refuse extradition in the event of fraud affecting the European Communities' financial interests for the sole reason that it concerns a tax or customs duty offence.
4. For the purposes of this Article, a Member State's own nationals shall be construed in accordance with any declaration made by it under Article 6(1)(b) of the European Convention on Extradition and with paragraph 1(c) of the Article.

Article 6

Cooperation

1. If a fraud as defined in Article 1 constitutes a criminal offence and concerns at least two Member States, those States shall cooperate effectively in the investigation, the prosecution and in carrying out the punishment imposed by means, for example, of mutual legal assistance, extradition, transfer of proceedings or enforcement of sentences passed in another Member State.
2. Where more than one Member State has jurisdiction and has the possibility of viable prosecution of an offence based on the same facts, the Member States involved shall cooperate in deciding which shall prosecute the offender or offenders with a view to centralizing the prosecution in a single Member State where possible.

Article 7

Ne bis in idem

1. Member States shall apply in their national criminal laws the 'ne bis in idem' rule, under which a person whose trial has been finally disposed of in a Member State may not be prosecuted in another Member State in respect of the same facts, provided that if a penalty was imposed, it has been enforced, is actually in the process of being enforced or can no longer be enforced under the laws of the sentencing State.
2. A Member State may, when giving the notification referred to in Article 11 (2), declare that it shall not be bound by paragraph 1 of this Article in one or more of the following cases:
   (a) if the facts which were the subject of the judgement rendered abroad took place on its own territory either in whole or in part; in the latter case this exception shall not apply if those facts took place partly on the territory of the Member State where the judgement was rendered;
   (b) if the facts which were the subject of the judgment rendered abroad constitute an offence directed against the security or other equally essential interests of that Member State;

(c) if the facts which were the subject of the judgment rendered abroad were committed by an official of the Member State contrary to the duties of his office.

3. The exceptions which may be the subject of a declaration under paragraph 2 shall not apply if the Member State concerned in respect of the same facts requested the other Member State to bring the prosecution or granted extradition of the person concerned.
4. Relevant bilateral or multilateral agreements concluded between Member States and relevant declarations shall remain unaffected by this Article.

Article 8

Court of Justice

1. Any dispute between Member States on the interpretation or application of this Convention must in an initial stage be examined by the Council in accordance with the procedure set out in Title VI of the Treaty on European Union with a view to reaching a solution.

   If no solution is found within six months, the matter may be referred to the Court of Justice of the European Communities by a party to the dispute.
2. Any dispute between one or more Member States and the Commission of the European Communities concerning the application of Article 1 or 10 of this Convention which it has proved impossible to settle through negotiation may be submitted to the Court of Justice.

Article 9

Internal provisions

No provision in this Convention shall prevent Member States from adopting internal legal provisions which go beyond the obligations deriving from this Convention.

Article 10

Transmission

1. Member States shall transmit to the Commission of the European Communities the text of the provisions transposing into their domestic law the obligations imposed on them under the provisions of this Convention.
2. For the purposes of implementing this Convention, the High Contracting Parties shall determine, within the Council of the European Union, the information to be communicated or exchanged between the Member States or between the Member States and the Commission, and also the arrangements for doing so.

Article 11

Entry into force

1. This Convention shall be subject to adoption by the Member States in accordance with their respective constitutional requirements.
2. Member States shall notify the Secretary-General of the Council of the European Union of the completion of their constitutional requirements for adopting this Convention.
3. This Convention shall enter into force 90 days after the notification, referred to in paragraph 2, by the last Member State to fulfil that formality.

Article 12

Accession

1. This Convention shall be open to accession by any State that becomes a member of the European Union.
2. The text of this Convention in the language of the acceding State, drawn up by the Council of the European Union, shall be authentic.
3. Instruments of accession shall be deposited with the depositary.

4. This Convention shall enter into force with respect to any State that accedes to it 90 days after the deposit of its instrument of accession or on the date of entry into force of the Convention if it has not already entered into force at the time of expiry of the said period 90 days.

Article 13

Depositary

1. The Secretary-General of the Council of the European Union shall act as depositary of this Convention.
2. The depositary shall publish in the Official Journal of the European Communities information on the progress of adoptions and accessions, declarations and reservations, and also any other notification concerning this Convention.

APPENDIX 15

Second Protocol to the Convention on the Protection of the European Communities' Financial Interests[1]

Second Protocol, Drawn up on the Basis of Article K.3 of the treaty on European Union, to the Convention on the Protection of the European Communities' Financial Interests

The high contracting parties to this Protocol, Member States of the European Union,

Referring to the Act of the Council of the European Union of 19 June 1997;

Desiring to ensure that their criminal laws contribute effectively to the protection of the financial interests of the European Communities;

Recognizing the importance of the Convention on the protection of the European Communities' financial interests of 26 July 1995 in combating fraud affecting Community revenue and expenditure;

Recognizing the importance of the Protocol of 27 September 1996 to the said Convention in the fight against corruption damaging or likely to damage the European Communities' financial interests;

Aware that the financial interests of the European Communities may be damaged or threatened by acts committed on behalf of legal persons and acts involving money laundering;

Convinced of the need for national law to be adapted, where necessary, to provide that legal persons can be held liable in cases of fraud or active corruption and money laundering committed for their benefit that damage or are likely to damage the European Communities' financial interests;

Convinced of the need for national law to be adapted, where necessary, to penalize acts of laundering of proceeds of fraud or corruption that damage or are likely to damage the European Communities' financial interests and to make it possible to confiscate proceeds of such fraud and corruption;

Convinced of the need for national law to be adapted, where necessary, in order to prevent the refusal of mutual assistance solely because offences covered by this Protocol concern or are considered as tax or customs duty offences.

Noting that cooperation between Member States is already covered by the Convention on the protection of the European Communities' financial interests of 26 July 1995, but that there is a need, without prejudice to obligations under Community law, for appropriate provision also to be made for cooperation between member States and the Commission to ensure effective action against fraud, active and passive corruption and related money laundering damaging or likely to damage the European Communities' financial interests, including exchange of information between the Member States and the Commission.

Considering that, in order to encourage and facilitate the exchange of information, it is necessary to ensure adequate protection of personal data.

---

[1] The Protocol was adopted by the Council of the European Union on 19 June 1997.

Considering that the exchange of information should not hinder ongoing investigations and that it is therefore necessary to provide for the protection of investigation secrecy;

Considering that appropriate provisions have to be drawn up on the competence of the Court of Justice of the European Communities;

Considering finally that the relevant provisions of the Convention on the protection of the European Communities' financial interests of 26 July 1995 should be made applicable to certain acts covered by this Protocol,

Have agreed on the following provisions:

Article 1
Definitions

For the purposes of this Protocol:

(a) 'Convention' shall mean the Convention drawn up on the basis of Article K.3 of the Treaty on European Union on the protection of the European Communities' financial interests, of 26 July 1995;
(b) 'fraud' shall mean the conduct referred to in Article 1 of the Convention;
(c) 'passive corruption' shall mean the conduct referred to in Article 2 of the Protocol drawn up on the basis of Article K.3 of the Treaty on European Union to the convention on the protection of the European Communities' financial interests, of 27 September 1996,—'active corruption' shall mean the conduct referred to in Article 3 of the same Protocol;
(d) 'legal person' shall mean any entity having such status under the applicable national law, except for States or other public bodies in the exercise of State authority and for public international organizations;
(e) 'money laundering' shall mean the conduct as defined in the third indent of Article 1 of Council Directive 91/308/EEC of 10 June 1991 on the prevention of the use of the financial system for the purpose of money laundering, related to the proceeds of fraud, at least in serious cases, and of active and passive corruption.

Article 2
Money laundering

Each Member State shall take the necessary measures to establish money laundering as a criminal offence.

Article 3
Liability of legal persons

1. Each Member State shall take the necessary measures to ensure that legal persons can be held liable for fraud, active corruption and money laundering committed for their benefit by any person, acting either individually or as part of an organ of the legal person, who has a leading position within the legal person, based on
   — a power of representation of the legal person, or
   — an authority to take decisions on behalf of the legal person, or
   — an authority to exercise control within the legal person, as well as for involvement as accessories or instigators in such fraud, active corruption or money laundering or the attempted commission of such fraud.
2. Apart from the cases already provided for in paragraph 1, each Member State shall take the necessary measures to ensure that a legal person can be held liable where the lack of supervision or control by a person referred to in paragraph 1 has made possible the commission of a fraud or an act of active corruption or money laundering for the benefit of that legal person by a person under its authority.

3. Liability of a legal person under paragraphs 1 and 2 shall not exclude criminal proceedings against natural persons who are perpetrators, instigators or accessories in the fraud, active corruption or money laundering.

Article 4

Sanctions for legal persons

1. Each Member State shall take the necessary measures to ensure that a legal person held liable pursuant to Article 3(1) is punishable by effective, proportionate and dissuasive sanctions, which shall include criminal or non-criminal fines and may include other sanctions such as:
   (a) exclusion from entitlement to public benefits or aid;
   (b) temporary or permanent disqualification from the practice of commercial activities;
   (c) placing under judicial supervision;
   (d) a judicial winding-up order.
2. Each Member State shall take the necessary measures to ensure that a legal person held liable pursuant to Article 3(2) is punishable by effective, proportionate and dissuasive sanctions or measures.

Article 5

Confiscation

Each Member State shall take the necessary measures to enable the seizure and, without prejudice to the rights of bona fide third parties, the confiscation or removal of the instruments and proceeds of fraud, active and passive corruption and money laundering, or property the value of which corresponds to such proceeds. Any instruments, proceeds or other property seized or confiscated shall be dealt with by the Member State in accordance with its national law.

Article 6

Cooperation with the Commission of the European Communities

A Member State may not refuse to provide mutual assistance in respect of fraud, active and passive corruption and money laundering for the sole reason that it concerns or is considered as a tax or customs duty offence.

Article 7

Cooperation with the Commission of the European Communities

1. The Member States and the Commission shall cooperate with each other in the fight against fraud, active and passive corruption and money laundering.
   To that end, the Commission shall lend such technical and operational assistance as the competent national authorities may need to facilitate coordination of their investigations.
2. The competent authorities in the Member States may exchange information with the Commission so as to make it easier to establish the facts and to ensure effective action against fraud, active and passive corruption and money laundering. The Commission and the competent national authorities shall take account, in each specific case, of the requirements of investigation secrecy and data protection. To that end, a Member State, when supplying information to the Commission, may set specific conditions covering the use of information, whether by the Commission or by another Member State to which that information may be passed.

Article 8

Data protection responsibility for the Commission

The Commission shall ensure that, in the context of the exchange of information under Article 7(2), it shall observe, as regards the processing of personal data, a level of protection equivalent to the level of protection set out in Directive 95/46/EC of the European Parliament and of the Council of 24 October 1995 on the protection of individuals with regard to the processing of personal data and on the free movement of such data.

Article 9

Publication of data protection rules

The rules adopted concerning the obligations under Article 8 shall be published in the Official Journal of the European Communities.

Article 10

Transfer of data to other Member States and third countries

1. Subject to any conditions referred to in Article 7 (2), the Commission may transfer personal data obtained from a Member State in the performance of its functions under Article 7 to any other Member State. The Commission shall inform the Member State which supplied the information of its intention to make such as transfer.
2. The Commission may, under the same conditions, transfer personal data obtained from a Member State in the performance of its functions under Article 7 to any third country provided that the Member State which supplied the information has agreed to such transfer.

Article 11

Supervisory authority

Any authority designated or created for the purpose of exercising the function of independent data protection supervision over personal data held by the Commission pursuant to its functions under the Treaty establishing the European Community, shall be competent to exercise the same function with respect to personal data held by the Commission by virtue of this Protocol.

Article 12

Relation to the Convention

1. The provisions of Articles 3, 5 and 6 of the Convention shall also apply to the conduct referred to in Article 2 of this Protocol.
2. The following provisions of the Convention shall also apply to this Protocol:
   —Article 4, on the understanding that, unless otherwise indicated at the time of the notification provided for in Article 16(2) of this Protocol, any declaration within the meaning of Article 4(2) of the Convention, shall also apply to this Protocol,
   —Article 7, on the understanding that the ne bis in idem principle also applies to legal persons, and that, unless otherwise indicated at the time the notification provided for in Article 16(2) of this Protocol is being given, any declaration within the meaning of Article 7(2), of the Convention shall also apply to this Protocol,
   —Article 9,
   —Article 10.

Article 13

Court of Justice

1. Any dispute between Member States on the interpretation or application of this Protocol must in an initial stage be examined by the Council in accordance with the procedure set out in Title VI of the Treaty on European Union with a view to reaching a solution. If no solution is found within six months, the matter may be referred to the Court of Justice by a party to the dispute.
2. Any dispute between one or more Member States and the Commission concerning the application of Article 2 in relation to Article 1 (e), and Article 7, 8, 10 and 12(2), fourth indent of this Protocol which it has proved impossible to settle through negotiation may be submitted to the Court of Justice, after the expiry of a period of six months from the date on which one of the parties has notified the other of the existence of a dispute.
3. The Protocol drawn up on the basis of Article K.3 of the Treaty on European Union, on the interpretation, by way of preliminary rulings, by the Court of Justice of the European Communities of the Convention on the protection of the European Communities' financial

interests, of 29 November 1996, shall apply to this Protocol, on the understanding that a declaration made by a Member State pursuant to Article 2 of that Protocol is also valid regarding this Protocol unless the Member State concerned makes a declaration to the contrary when giving the notification provided for in Article 16(2) of this Protocol.

Article 14

Non-contractual liability

For the purposes of this Protocol, the non-contractual liability of the Community shall be governed by the second paragraph of Article 215 of the Treaty establishing the European Community. Article 178 of the same Treaty shall apply.

Article 15

Judicial control

1. The Court of Justice shall have jurisdiction in proceedings instituted by any natural or legal person against a decision of the Commission addressed to that person or which is of direct and individual concern to that person, on ground of infringement of Article 8 or any rule adopted pursuant thereto, or misuse of powers.
2. Articles 168a(1) and (2), 173, fifth paragraph, 174, first paragraph, 176, first and second paragraphs, 185 and 186 of the Treaty establishing the European Community, as well as the Statute of the Court of Justice of the European Community, shall apply, mutatis mutandis.

Article 16

Entry into force

1. This Protocol shall be subject to adoption by the Member States in accordance with their respective constitutional requirements.
2. Member States shall notify the Secretary-General of the Council of the European Union of the completion of the procedures required under their respective constitutional rules for adopting this Protocol.
3. This Protocol shall enter into force ninety days after the notification provided for in paragraph 2, by the State which, being a member of the European Union on the date of the adoption by the Council of the act drawing up this Protocol, is the last to fulfil that formality. If, however, the Convention has not entered into force on that date, this Protocol shall enter into force on the date on which the Convention enters into force.
4. However, the application of Article 7(2) shall be suspended if, and for so long as, the relevant institution of the European Communities has not complied with its obligation to publish the data protection rules pursuant to Article 9 or the terms of Article 11 concerning the supervisory authority have not been complied with.

Article 17

Accession of new Member States

1. This Protocol shall be open to accession by any State that becomes a member of the European Union.
2. The text of this Protocol in the language of the acceding State, drawn up by the Council of the European Union, shall be authentic.
3. Instruments of accession shall be deposited with the depositary.
4. This Protocol shall enter into force with respect to any State that accedes to it ninety days after the deposit of its instrument of accession or on the date of entry into force of this Protocol if it has not yet entered into force at the time of expiry of the said period of ninety days.

Article 18

Reservations

1. Each Member State may reserve the right to establish the money laundering related to the proceeds of active and passive corruption as a criminal offence only in serious cases of active and passive corruption. Any Member State making such a reservation shall inform the depositary, giving details of the scope of the reservation, when giving the notification provided for in Article 16(2). Such a reservation shall be valid for a period of five years after the said notification. It may be renewed once for a further period of five years.
2. The Republic of Austria may, when giving its notification referred to in Article 16(2), declare that it will not be bound by Articles 3 and 4. Such a declaration shall cease to have effect five years after the date of the adoption of the act drawing up this Protocol.
3. No other reservations shall be authorized, with the exception of those provided for in Article 12 (2), first and second indent.

Article 19

Depositary

1. The Secretary-General of the Council of the European Union shall act as depositary of this Protocol.
2. The depositary shall publish in the Official Journal of the European Communities information on the progress of adoptions and accessions, declarations and reservations and any other notification concerning this Protocol.

APPENDIX 16

Council of The European Union Framework Decision on Combating Corruption in The Private Sector[1]

The Council of the European Union,

Having regard to the Treaty on European Union, and in particular Article 29, Article 31(1)(e) and Article 34(2)(b) thereof,

Having regard to the initiative of the Kingdom of Denmark,

Having regard to the opinion of the European Parliament,

Whereas:

(1) Along with globalisation, recent years have brought an increase in cross-border trade in goods and services. Any corruption in the private sector within a Member State is thus not just a domestic problem but also a transnational problem, most effectively tackled by means of a European Union joint action.

(2) On 27 September 1996 the Council adopted the Act drawing up a Protocol to the Convention on the Protection of the European Communities' Financial Interests. The Protocol, which entered into force on 17 October 2002, contains definitions of and harmonised penalties for offences of corruption.

(3) On 26 May 1997 the Council approved a Convention on the fight against corruption involving officials of the European Communities or officials of Member States of the European Union.

(4) On 22 December 1998, the Council also adopted Joint Action 98/742/JHA on corruption in the private sector. In connection with the adoption of that Joint Action, the Council issued a statement to the effect that it agreed that the Joint Action represents the first step at European Union level towards combating such corruption, and that additional measures will be implemented at a later stage in the light of the outcome of the assessment which is to take place pursuant to Article 8(2) of the Joint Action. A report on Member States' transposition of that Joint Action into national law is not yet available.

(5) On 13 June 2002 the Council adopted Framework Decision 2002/584/JHA on the European arrest warrant and the surrender procedures between the Member States, in which corruption is included in the list of offences falling within the scope of the European arrest warrant, in respect of which prior verification of double criminality is not required.

(6) Under Article 29 of the Treaty on European Union, it is the Union's objective to provide citizens with a high level of safety within an area of freedom, security and justice, an objective to be achieved by preventing and combating crime, organised or otherwise, including corruption.

(7) According to point 48 of the conclusions of the European Council meeting in Tampere on 15 and 16 October 1999, corruption is an area of particular relevance in establishing minimum rules on what constitutes a criminal offence in Member States and the penalties applicable.

(8) An OECD Convention on Combating Bribery of Foreign Public Officials in International Business Transactions was approved at a negotiating conference on 21 November 1997, and

[1] The framework decision entered into force on 31 July 2003, in accordance with article 11.

the Council of Europe has also approved a Criminal Law Convention on Corruption, which opened for signature on 27 January 1999. That Convention is accompanied by an Agreement establishing the Group of States against Corruption (GRECO). Negotiations have also been opened for a UN Convention on combating corruption.

(9) Member States attach particular importance to combating corruption in both the public and the private sector, in the belief that in both those sectors it poses a threat to a law-abiding society as well as distorting competition in relation to the purchase of goods or commercial services and impeding sound economic development. In that context the Member States which have not yet ratified the European Union Convention of 26 May 1997 and the Council of Europe Convention of 27 January 1999 will consider how to do so as soon as possible.

(10) The aim of this Framework Decision is in particular to ensure that both active and passive corruption in the private sector are criminal offences in all Member States, that legal persons may also be held responsible for such offences, and that these offences incur effective, proportionate and dissuasive penalties,

Has adopted this Framework decision

Article 1
Definitions

For the purposes of this Framework Decision:

— 'legal person' means any entity having such status under the applicable national law, except for States or other public bodies acting in the exercise of State authority and for public international organisations,

— 'breach of duty' shall be understood in accordance with national law. The concept of breach of duty in national law should cover as a minimum any disloyal behaviour constituting a breach of a statutory duty, or, as the case may be, a breach of professional regulations or instructions, which apply within the business of a person who in any capacity directs or works for a private sector entity.

Article 2
Active and passive corruption in the private sector

1. Member States shall take the necessary measures to ensure that the following intentional conduct constitutes a criminal offence, when it is carried out in the course of business activities:
   (a) promising, offering or giving, directly or through an intermediary, to a person who in any capacity directs or works for a private-sector entity an undue advantage of any kind, for that person or for a third party, in order that that person should perform or refrain from performing any act, in breach of that person's duties;
   (b) directly or through an intermediary, requesting or receiving an undue advantage of any kind, or accepting the promise of such an advantage, for oneself or for a third party, while in any capacity directing or working for a private-sector entity, in order to perform or refrain from performing any act, in breach of one's duties.
2. Paragraph 1 applies to business activities within profit and non-profit entities.
3. A Member State may declare that it will limit the scope of paragraph 1 to such conduct which involves, or could involve, a distortion of competition in relation to the purchase of goods or commercial services.
4. Declarations referred to in paragraph 3 shall be communicated to the Council at the time of the adoption of this Framework Decision and shall be valid for five years as from 22 July 2005.
5. The Council shall review this Article in due time before 22 July 2010 with a view to considering whether it shall be possible to renew declarations made under paragraph 3.

Article 3

Instigation, aiding and abetting

Member States shall take the necessary measures to ensure that instigating, aiding and abetting the conduct referred to in Article 2 constitute criminal offences.

Article 4

Penalties and other sanctions

1. Each Member State shall take the necessary measures to ensure that the conduct referred to in Articles 2 and 3 is punishable by effective, proportionate and dissuasive criminal penalties.
2. Each Member State shall take the necessary measures to ensure that the conduct referred to in Article 2 is punishable by a penalty of a maximum of at least one to three years of imprisonment.
3. Each Member State shall take the necessary measures in accordance with its constitutional rules and principles to ensure that where a natural person in relation to a certain business activity has been convicted of the conduct referred to in Article 2, that person may, where appropriate, at least in cases where he or she had a leading position in a company within the business concerned, be temporarily prohibited from carrying on this particular or comparable business activity in a similar position or capacity, if the facts established give reason to believe there to be a clear risk of abuse of position or of office by active or passive corruption.

Article 5

Liability of legal persons

1. Each Member State shall take the necessary measures to ensure that legal persons can be held liable for offences referred to in Articles 2 and 3 committed for their benefit by any person, acting either individually or as part of an organ of the legal person, who has a leading position within the legal person, based on:
   (a) a power of representation of the legal person;
   (b) an authority to take decisions on behalf of the legal person; or
   (c) an authority to exercise control within the legal person.
2. Apart from the cases provided for in paragraph 1, each Member State shall take the necessary measures to ensure that a legal person can be held liable where the lack of supervision or control by a person referred to in paragraph 1 has made possible the commission of an offence of the type referred to in Articles 2 and 3 for the benefit of that legal person by a person under its authority.
3. Liability of a legal person under paragraphs 1 and 2 shall not exclude criminal proceedings against natural persons who are involved as perpetrators, instigators or accessories in an offence of the type referred to in Articles 2 and 3.

Article 6

Penalties for legal persons

1. Each Member State shall take the necessary measures to ensure that a legal person held liable pursuant to Article 5(1) is punishable by effective, proportionate and dissuasive penalties, which shall include criminal or non-criminal fines and may include other penalties such as:
   (a) exclusion from entitlement to public benefits or aid;
   (b) temporary or permanent disqualification from the practice of commercial activities;
   (c) placing under judicial supervision; or
   (d) a judicial winding-up order.
2. Each Member State shall take the necessary measures to ensure that a legal person held liable pursuant to Article 5(2) is punishable by penalties or measures which are effective, proportionate and dissuasive.

Article 7

Jurisdiction

1. Each Member State shall take the necessary measures to establish its jurisdiction with regard to the offences referred to in Articles 2 and 3, where the offence has been committed:
   (a) in whole or in part within its territory;
   (b) by one of its nationals; or
   (c) for the benefit of a legal person that has its head office in the territory of that Member State.
2. Any Member State may decide that it will not apply the jurisdiction rules in paragraph 1(b) and (c), or will apply them only in specific cases or circumstances, where the offence has been committed outside its territory.
3. Any Member State which, under its domestic law, does not as yet surrender its own nationals shall take the necessary measures to establish its jurisdiction with regard to the offences referred to in Articles 2 and 3, when committed by its own nationals outside its territory.
4. Member States which decide to apply paragraph 2 shall inform the General Secretariat of the Council and the Commission accordingly, where appropriate with an indication of the specific cases or circumstances in which the decision applies.

Article 8

Repeal

Joint Action 98/742/JHA shall be repealed.

Article 9

Implementation

1. Member States shall take the necessary measures to comply with the provisions of this Framework Decision before 22 July 2005.
2. By the same date, Member States shall transmit to the General Secretariat of the Council and the Commission the text of the provisions transposing into their national law the obligations imposed on them under this Framework Decision. On the basis of a report established using this information and a written report from the Commission, the Council shall before 22 October 2005 assess the extent to which Member States have complied with the provisions of this Framework Decision.

Article 10

Territorial application

This Framework Decision shall apply to Gibraltar.

Article 11

Entry into force

This Framework Decision shall enter into force on the day of its publication in the Official Journal of the European Union.

APPENDIX 17

Council of the European Union: Protocol to the Convention On the Protection of the European Communities' Financial Interests[1]

Protocol drawn up on the basis of Article K.3 of the Treaty on European Union to the Convention on the protection of the European Communities' financial interests

The high contracting parties to this Protocol, Member States of the European Union,

Referring to the Act of the Council of the European Union of 27 September 1996,

Desiring to ensure that their criminal laws contribute effectively to the protection of the financial interests of the European Communities;

Recognizing the importance of the Convention on the protection of the European Communities' financial interests of 26 July 1995 for combating fraud affecting Community revenue and expenditure;

Aware that the financial interests of the European Communities may be damaged or threatened by other criminal offences, particularly acts of corruption by or against national and Community officials, responsible for the collection, management or disbursement of Community funds under their control;

Considering that people of different nationalities, employed by different public agencies or bodies, may be involved in such corruption and that, in the interests of effective action against such corruption with international ramifications, it is important for their reprehensible nature to be perceived in a similar manner under Member States' criminal laws;

Noting that several Member States' criminal law on crime linked to the exercise of public duties in general and concerning corruption in particular covers only acts committed by or against their national officials and does not cover, or covers only in exceptional cases, conduct involving Community officials or officials of other Member States;

Convinced of the need for national law to be adapted where it does not penalize acts of corruption that damage or are likely to damage the financial interests of the European Communities involving Community officials or officials of other Member States;

Convinced also that such adaptation of national law should not be confined, in respect of Community officials, to acts of active or passive corruption, but should be extended to other crimes affecting or likely to affect the revenue or expenditure of the European Communities, including crimes committed by or against persons in whom the highest responsibilities are vested;

Considering that appropriate rules should also be laid down on jurisdiction and mutual cooperation, without prejudice to the legal conditions under which they are to apply in specific cases, including waiver of immunity where appropriate;

---

[1] The Protocol was adopted by the Council of the European Union on 27 September 1996.

Considering finally that the relevant provisions of the Convention on the protection of the European Communities' financial interests of 26 July 1995 should be made applicable to the criminal acts covered by this Protocol,

Have agreed on the following provisions:

Article 1

Definitions

For the purposes of this Protocol:

1. (a) 'official' shall mean any 'Community' or 'national' official, including any national official of another Member State;
   (b) the term 'community official' shall mean:
      — any person who is an official or other contracted employee within the meaning of the Staff Regulations of officials of the European Communities or the Conditions of employment of other servants of the European Communities,
      — any person seconded to the European Communities by the Member States or by any public or private body, who carries out functions equivalent to those performed by European Community officials or other servants. Members of bodies set up in accordance with the Treaties establishing the European Communities and the staff of such bodies shall be treated as Community officials, inasmuch as the Staff Regulations of the European Communities or the Conditions of employment of other servants of the European Communities do not apply to them;
   (c) the term 'national official' shall be understood by reference to the definition of 'official' or 'public officer' in the national law of the Member State in which the person in question performs that function for the purposes of application of the criminal law of that Member State. Nevertheless, in the case of proceedings involving a Member State's official initiated by another Member State the latter shall not be bound to apply the definition of 'national official' except in so far as that definition is compatible with its national law;
2. 'Convention' shall mean the Convention drawn up on the basis of Article K.3 of the Treaty on European Union, on the protection of the European Communities' financial interests, of 26 July 1995.

Article 2

Passive corruption

1. For the purposes of this Protocol, the deliberate action of an official, who, directly or through an intermediary, requests or receives advantages of any kind whatsoever, for himself or for a third party, or accepts a promise of such an advantage, to act or refrain from acting in accordance with his duty or in the exercise of his functions in breach of his official duties in a way which damages or is likely to damage the European Communities' financial interests shall constitute passive corruption.
2. Each Member State shall take the necessary measures to ensure that conduct of the type referred to in paragraph 1 is made a criminal offence.

Article 3

Active corruption

1. For the purposes of this Protocol, the deliberate action of whosoever promises or gives, directly or through an intermediary, an advantage of any kind whatsoever to an official for himself or for a third party for him to act or refrain from acting in accordance with his duty or in the exercise of his functions in breach of his official duties in a way which damages or is likely to damage the European Communities' financial interests shall constitute active corruption.

2. Each Member State shall take the necessary measures to ensure that conduct of the type referred to in paragraph 1 is made a criminal offence.

Article 4

Assimilation

1. Each Member State shall take the necessary measures to ensure that in its criminal law the descriptions of the offences constituting conduct of the type referred to in Article 1 of the Convention committed by its national officials in the exercise of their functions apply similarly in cases where such offences are committed by Community officials in the exercise of their duties.
2. Each Member State shall take the necessary measures to ensure that in its criminal law the descriptions of the offences referred to in paragraph 1 of this Article and in Articles 2 and 3 committed by or against its Government Ministers, elected members of its parliamentary chambers, the members of its highest Courts or the members of its Court of Auditors in the exercise of their functions apply similarly in cases where such offences are committed by or against members of the Commission of the European Communities, the European Parliament, the Court of Justice and the Court of Auditors of the European Communities respectively in the exercise of their duties.
3. Where a Member State has enacted special legislation concerning acts or omissions for which Government Ministers are responsible by reason of their special political position in that Member State, paragraph 2 of this Article may not apply to such legislation, provided that the Member State ensures that Members of the Commission of the European Community are covered by the criminal legislation implementing Articles 2 and 3 and paragraph 1 of this Article.
4. Paragraphs 1, 2 and 3 shall be without prejudice to the provisions applicable in each Member State concerning criminal proceedings and the determination of the competent court.
5. This Protocol shall apply in full accordance with the relevant provisions of the Treaties establishing the European Communities, the Protocol on the Privileges and Immunities of the European Communities, the Statutes of the Court of Justice and the texts adopted for the purpose of their implementation, as regards the withdrawal of immunity.

Article 5

Penalties

1. Each Member State shall take the necessary measures to ensure that the conduct referred to in Articles 2 and 3, and participating in and instigating the conduct in question, are punishable by effective, proportionate and dissuasive criminal penalties, including, at least in serious cases, penalties involving deprivation of liberty which can give rise to extradition.
2. Paragraph 1 shall be without prejudice to the exercise of disciplinary powers by the competent authorities against national officials or Community officials. In determining the penalty to be imposed, the national criminal courts may, in accordance with the principles of their national law, take into account any disciplinary penalty already imposed on the same person for the same conduct.

Article 6

Jurisdiction

1. Each Member State shall take the measures necessary to establish its jurisdiction over the offences it has established in accordance with Articles 2, 3 and 4 where:
   (a) the offence is committed in whole or in part within its territory;
   (b) the offender is one of its nationals or one of its officials;
   (c) the offence is committed against one of the persons referred to in Article 1 or a member of one of the institutions referred to in Article 4(2) who is one of its nationals;

(d) the offender is a Community official working for a European Community institution or a body set up in accordance with the Treaties establishing the European Communities which has its headquarters in the Member State concerned.

2. Each Member State may declare when giving the notification provided for in Article 9(2) that it will not apply or will apply only in specific cases or conditions one or more of the jurisdiction rules laid down in paragraph 1(b), (c), and (d).

Article 7

Relation to the Convention

1. Articles 3, 5(1), (2) and (4) and Article 6 of the Convention shall apply as if there were a reference to the conduct referred to in Articles 2, 3 and 4 of this Protocol.
2. The following provisions of the Convention shall also apply to this Protocol:
   —Article 7, on the understanding that, unless otherwise indicated at the time of the notification provided for in Article 9(2) of this Protocol, any declaration within the meaning of Article 7(2) of the Convention shall also apply to this Protocol,
   —Article 9,
   —Article 10.

Article 8

Court of Justice

1. Any dispute between Member States on the interpretation or application of this Protocol must in an initial stage be examined by the Council in accordance with the procedure set out in Title VI of the Treaty on European Union with a view to reaching a solution. If no solution is found within six months, the matter may be referred to the Court of Justice of the European Communities by a party to the dispute.
2. Any dispute between one or more Member States and the Commission of the European Communities concerning Article 1, with the exception of point 1(c), or Articles 2, 3 and 4, or the third indent of Article 7(2) of this Protocol which it has proved impossible to settle through negotiation may be submitted to the Court of Justice of the European Communities.

Article 9

Entry into force

1. This Protocol shall be subject to adoption by the Member States in accordance with their respective constitutional requirements.
2. Member States shall notify the Secretary-General of the Council of the European Union of the completion of the procedures required under their respective constitutional rules for adopting this Protocol.
3. This Protocol shall enter into force 90 days after the notification provided for in paragraph 2 has been given by the State which, being a Member of the European Union at the time of adoption by the Council of the Act drawing up this Protocol, is the last to fulfil that formality. If, however, the Convention has not entered into force on that date, this Protocol shall enter into force on the date on which the Convention enters into force.

Article 10

Accession of new Member States

1. This Protocol shall be open to accession by any State that becomes a member of the European Union.
2. The text of this Protocol in the language of the acceding State, drawn up by the Council of the European Union, shall be authentic.
3. Instruments of accession shall be deposited with the depositary.

4. This Protocol shall enter into force with respect to any State that accedes to it 90 days after the deposit of its instrument of accession or on the date of entry into force of this Protocol if it has not yet entered into force at the time of expiry of the said period of 90 days.

Article 11
Reservations

1. No reservation shall be authorized with the exception of those provided for in Article 6 (2).
2. Any Member State which has entered a reservation may withdraw it at any time in whole or in part by notifying the depositary. Withdrawal shall take effect on the date on which the depositary receives the notification.

Article 12
Depositary

1. The Secretary-General of the Council of the European Union shall act as depositary of this Protocol.
2. The depositary shall publish in the Official Journal of the European Communities information on the progress of adoptions and accessions, declarations and reservations and any other notification concerning this Protocol.

In witness whereof, the undersigned Plenipotentiaries have hereunto set their hands. Done in a single original, in the Danish, Dutch, English, Finnish, French, German, Greek, Irish, Italian, Portuguese, Spanish and Swedish languages, each text being equally authentic, such original remaining deposited in the archives of the General Secretariat of the Council of the European Union.

APPENDIX 18

Statute of the GRECO Appendix to Resolution (99) 5

Article 1

Aim of the GRECO

The aim of the Group of States against Corruption (hereinafter referred to as the 'GRECO') is to improve the capacity of its members to fight corruption by following up, through a dynamic process of mutual evaluation and peer pressure, compliance with their undertakings in this field.

Article 2

Functions of the GRECO

In order to achieve the aim laid down in Article 1, the GRECO shall:

i. monitor the observance of the Guiding Principles for the Fight against Corruption as adopted by the Committee of Ministers of the Council of Europe on 6 November 1997;
ii. monitor the implementation of international legal instruments to be adopted in pursuance of the Programme of Action against Corruption, in conformity with the provisions contained in such instruments;

Article 3

Seat

The GRECO's seat shall be in Strasbourg.

Article 4

Procedure for membership of the GRECO

1. Any Member States of the Council of Europe, other than those mentioned in the Resolution establishing the GRECO, may join the GRECO at any time by so notifying the Secretary General of the Council of Europe.
2. Any non-Member States having participated in the elaboration of this Enlarged Partial Agreement[1] may join the GRECO at any time by so notifying the Secretary General of the Council of Europe. The notification shall be accompanied by a declaration to the effect that the non-Member States undertakes to apply the Guiding Principles for the Fight against Corruption, adopted by the Committee of Ministers of the Council of Europe on 6 November 1997.
3. States which become Parties to international legal instruments adopted by the Committee of Ministers of the Council of Europe in pursuance of the Programme of Action against Corruption providing for compulsory membership of the GRECO shall become members of the GRECO ipso facto in conformity with the provisions contained in these instruments.
4. The Committee of Ministers of the Council of Europe in its composition restricted to the States members of the Enlarged Partial Agreement, following consultation of the non-Member States already participating, may invite non-Member States, other than those covered by

[1] These States are the following: Belarus (10), Canada (11), Holy See (10), Japan (10), Mexico (10) and United States of America (11). Bosnia and Herzegovina has participated twice in GMC meetings.

paragraph 2 above, to join the GRECO. The non-Member States having received such an invitation, shall notify to the Secretary General its intention to join the GRECO, accompanied by a declaration to the effect that it undertakes to apply the Guiding Principles for the Fight against Corruption.

Article 5
Participation of the European Community

The European Community may be invited by the Committee of Ministers to participate in the work of the GRECO. The modalities of its participation shall be determined in the resolution inviting it to participate.

Article 6
Composition of the GRECO

1. Each member shall appoint a delegation to the GRECO consisting of not more than two representatives. One representative shall be appointed as head of the delegation.
2. The budget of the Enlarged Partial Agreement shall bear the travel and subsistence expenses of one of the representatives of the delegation.
3. The representatives appointed to the GRECO shall enjoy the privileges and immunities applicable under Article 2 of the Protocol to the General Agreement on Privileges and Immunities of the Council of Europe.

Article 7
Other Representatives

1. The European Committee on Legal Co-operation (CDCJ) and the European Committee on Crime Problems (CDPC) shall each appoint a representative to the GRECO.
2. The Committee of Ministers may invite other Council of Europe bodies to appoint a representative to the GRECO after consulting the latter.
3. The Statutory Committee, set up under Article 18 below, shall appoint a representative to the GRECO.
4. Representatives appointed under paragraphs 1 to 3 above shall participate in plenary meetings of the GRECO without the right to vote. Their travel and subsistence expenses shall not be borne by the budget of the Enlarged Partial Agreement.

Article 8
Operation of the GRECO

1. The GRECO shall take the necessary decisions for its operation. In particular, it shall:
   i. adopt evaluation reports in accordance with Article 15;
   ii. approve its draft annual programme of activities and submit, in conformity with the Financial Regulations, proposals to the Secretary General of the Council of Europe relating to the elaboration of the draft annual budget, prior to its transmission to the Statutory Committee set up under Article 18 below;
   iii. approve its annual activity report, including its annual accounts, prior to its submission to the Statutory Committee and to the Committee of Ministers;
2. The GRECO shall hold at least two plenary meetings a year and may decide to set up working parties whenever necessary and in accordance with its Rules of Procedure.
3. The GRECO will publish every year its annual report of activities including its annual accounts, once approved by the relevant bodies pursuant to Article 18 below.
4. The GRECO shall draw up its own Rules of Procedure. Any State or the European Community, when becoming a member of the GRECO, shall be deemed to have accepted the Statute and the Rules of Procedures of the GRECO.
5. The GRECO shall hold its meetings in camera.

6. Members of the GRECO participating in the mutual evaluation shall have the right to vote. Each of them shall be entitled to cast one vote. However, unless otherwise decided by the Statutory Committee, a member which has failed to pay all or a substantial part of its compulsory contribution to the budget of the enlarged partial agreement for a period of two years, shall no longer take part in the decision-making process.
7. Decisions of the GRECO shall be taken by two-thirds of the votes cast[2] and the majority of those entitled to vote. However, procedural decisions shall be taken by a majority of the votes cast.
8. The GRECO shall elect its President and Vice-President among the representatives of the members entitled to vote.

Article 9
Bureau

1. There shall be a Bureau composed of the President and the Vice-President referred to in Article 8 paragraph 8 above and five other persons elected by the GRECO, among the representatives of the members entitled to vote which are, as far as possible, Parties to at least one of the international legal instruments adopted in pursuance of the Programme of action against corruption.
2. The Bureau shall carry out the following functions:
   — prepare the preliminary draft annual programme of activities and the draft annual activity report;
   — make proposals to the GRECO concerning the preliminary draft budget;
   — organise country visits on the basis of the decisions taken by the GRECO;
   — make proposals to the GRECO on the composition of the ad hoc evaluation teams;
   — prepare the agenda for the meetings of the GRECO including those at which evaluation reports will be discussed;
   — make proposals to the GRECO as regards the provisions to be selected for evaluation procedures in pursuance of Article 10 paragraph 3 below;
   — make proposals to the GRECO concerning the appointment of scientific experts and consultants.
3. The Bureau shall carry out any other function assigned to it by the GRECO.
4. The Bureau shall exercise its functions under the general supervision of the GRECO.

Article 10
Evaluation procedure

1. The GRECO shall conduct evaluation procedures in respect of each of its members in pursuance of Article 2.
2. The evaluation shall be divided in rounds. An evaluation round is a period of time determined by the GRECO, during which an evaluation procedure shall be conducted to assess the compliance of members with selected provisions contained in the Guiding Principles and in other international legal instruments adopted in pursuance of the Programme of Action against Corruption.
3. At the beginning of each round the GRECO shall select the specific provisions on which the evaluation procedure shall be based.
4. Each member shall identify a maximum of 5 experts who would be able to undertake the tasks set out in Articles 12–14.
5. Each member shall ensure that its authorities co-operate, to the fullest possible extent, in the evaluation procedure, within the limits of its national legislation.

[2] Only votes 'in favour' or 'against' are taken into account when counting the number of votes cast (Article 10 paragraph 5 of the Rules of Procedure of the Ministers' Deputies).

Article 11

Questionnaire

1. The GRECO shall adopt a questionnaire for each evaluation round, which shall be addressed to all members concerned by the evaluation.
2. The questionnaire shall provide the framework of the evaluation procedure.
3. Members shall address their replies to the Secretariat within the time limits fixed by the GRECO.

Article 12

Evaluation teams

1. The GRECO shall appoint, from the experts referred to in paragraph 4 of Article 10, a team for the evaluation of each member (hereinafter referred to as 'the team'). When the evaluation concerns the implementation of one of the international legal instruments adopted in pursuance of the Programme of Action against Corruption, the GRECO shall appoint teams composed exclusively of experts proposed by members who are Parties to the instrument concerned.
2. The team shall examine the replies given to the questionnaire and may request, where appropriate, additional information from the member undergoing the evaluation, to be submitted either orally or in writing.
3. The budget of the Enlarged and Partial Agreement shall bear the travel and subsistence expenses of the experts participating in the teams.

Article 13

Country visits

1. The GRECO may instruct the team to visit a member, for the purpose of seeking additional information concerning its law or practice, which is useful for the evaluation.
2. ECO shall give a minimum of two months notice to the member concerned of its intention to carry out the visit.
3. The visit shall be carried out in accordance with a programme arranged by the member concerned, taking into account the wishes expressed by the team.
4. The members of the team shall enjoy the privileges and immunities applicable under Article 2 of the Protocol to the General Agreement on Privileges and Immunities of the Council of Europe.
5. The budget of the Enlarged Partial Agreement shall bear the travel and subsistence expenses necessary for the carrying out country visits.

Article 14

Evaluation reports

1. On the basis of the information gathered, the team shall prepare a preliminary draft evaluation report on the state of the law and the practice in relation to the provisions selected for the evaluation round.
2. The preliminary draft report shall be transmitted to the member undergoing the evaluation for comments. These comments shall be taken into account by the team when finalising the draft report.
3. The draft report shall be submitted to the GRECO.

Article 15

Discussion and adoption of reports

1. The GRECO shall debate in Plenary the draft report submitted by the team.
2. The member undergoing the evaluation shall be entitled to submit observations orally and/or in writing to the Plenary.
3. At the close of the debate, the GRECO shall adopt, with or without amendments, the report in respect of the member undergoing the evaluation.

4. All members shall be entitled to participate in the vote leading to the adoption of evaluation reports relating to the application of the Guiding Principles. Only members which are Parties to an international legal instrument adopted in pursuance of the Programme of Action against Corruption shall be entitled to participate in the vote leading to the adoption of evaluation reports on the implementation of the instrument concerned.
5. Evaluation reports shall be confidential. Unless otherwise decided, access to these reports shall be restricted to members of the team which has carried out the evaluation, in addition to members of the GRECO, of the Statutory Committee and of the Secretariat of these bodies.
6. The GRECO's report may contain recommendations addressed to the member undergoing the evaluation in order to improve its domestic laws and practices to combat corruption. The GRECO shall invite the member to report on the measures taken to follow these recommendations.

Article 16

Public Statements

1. The Statutory Committee may issue a public statement when it believes that a member remains passive or takes insufficient action in respect of the recommendations addressed to it as regards the application of the Guiding Principles.
2. The Statutory Committee, in its composition restricted to the members who are parties to the instruments concerned, may issue a public statement when it believes that a member remains passive or takes insufficient action in respect of the recommendations addressed to it as regards the implementation of an instrument adopted in pursuance of the Programme of Action against Corruption.
3. The Statutory Committee shall inform the member concerned and provide an opportunity for the member to submit further comments before confirming its decision to issue a public statement referred to in paragraphs 1 and/or 2 above.

Article 17

The GRECO's financial resources

1. The budget of the GRECO shall be financed through the annual compulsory contributions of its members;
2. The GRECO may receive additional voluntary contributions from its members;
3. The GRECO may also receive voluntary contributions from interested international institutions;
4. Financial resources covered by paragraph 3 above shall be subject to the authorisation of the Statutory Committee prior to their acceptance.
5. The GRECO's assets shall be acquired and held on behalf of the Council of Europe and shall benefit as such from the privileges and immunities applicable to the Council's assets under existing agreements.

Article 18

Statutory Committee

1. The Statutory Committee shall be composed of the representatives on the Committee of Ministers of the Member States of the Council of Europe which are also members of the GRECO and of representatives specifically designated to that effect by the other members of the GRECO.
2. The Statutory Committee shall determine every year the members' compulsory contributions to the GRECO. The scale according to which the contributions of non-members of the Council of Europe are calculated shall be decided in agreement with the latter; as a general rule, that scale shall conform to the criteria for the determination of the scale of contributions to the general budget of the Council of Europe.

3. The Statutory Committee shall adopt every year the GRECO's budget on expenditure relating to the implementation of the programme of activities and common secretariat expenditure.
4. The Statutory Committee shall approve every year the GRECO's annual accounts which shall be drawn up by the Secretary General of the Council of Europe in accordance with the Financial Regulations of the Council of Europe and submitted to the Statutory Committee accompanied by the report of the Board of Auditors. In order to discharge the Secretary General from responsibility for the management of the financial year in question, the Statutory Committee shall transmit to the Committee of Ministers the annual accounts, together with its approval or any comments, and the report drawn up by the Board of Auditors.
5. The Financial Regulations of the Council of Europe shall apply, mutatis mutandis, to the adoption and management of the budget.

Article 19
Secretariat

1. The GRECO shall be assisted by a Secretariat provided by the Secretary General of the Council of Europe.
2. The GRECO's Secretariat shall be headed by an Executive Secretary appointed by the Secretary General of the Council of Europe.

Article 20
Amendments

1. The GRECO or any of its members may propose amendments to this Statute to the Statutory Committee.
2. This Statute may be amended by Statutory Committee by unanimous decision. If the amendment has not been proposed by the GRECO, the latter shall be consulted by the Statutory Committee.

Article 21
Withdrawal

1. Subject to the applicable provisions of international legal instruments mentioned in Article 2, paragraph 2 above, any member may withdraw from the GRECO by means of a declaration addressed to the Secretary General of the Council of Europe by the Minister for Foreign Affairs or a diplomatic representative who shall be given specific powers to this effect.
2. The Secretary General shall acknowledge receipt of the declaration and inform the member concerned that it will be submitted to the Statutory Committee.
3. By analogy with Article 7 of the Statute of the Council of Europe, the withdrawal shall take effect:
   — at the end of the financial year in which it is notified, if the notification is given during the first nine months of that financial year;
   — at the end of the next financial year, if the notification is given in the last three months of the financial year.
4. In accordance with Article 18 of the Financial Regulations of the Council of Europe, the Statutory Committee shall examine the financial consequences of the withdrawal and make the appropriate arrangements.
5. The Secretary General shall immediately inform the member concerned of the consequences for it of its withdrawal and keep the Statutory Committee informed of the outcome.

APPENDIX 19

PART II—Rules of Conduct to Combat Extortion and Bribery

Introduction

These Rules of Conduct are intended as a method of self-regulation by international business, and they should also be supported by governments. Their voluntary acceptance by business enterprises will not only promote high standards of integrity in business transactions, whether between enterprises and public bodies or between enterprises themselves, but will also form a valuable defensive protection to those enterprises which are subjected to attempts at extortion.

These Rules of Conduct are of a general nature constituting what is considered good commercial practice in the matters to which they relate but are without direct legal effect. They do not derogate from applicable local laws, and since national legal systems are by no means uniform, they must be read *mutatis mutandis* subject to such systems.

The business community objects to all forms of extortion and bribery. It is recognized, however, that under current conditions in some parts of the world, an effective programme against extortion and bribery may have to be implemented in stages. The highest priority should be directed to ending large-scale extortion and bribery involving politicians and senior officials. These represent the greatest threat to democratic institutions and cause the gravest economic distortions. Small payments to low-level officials to expedite routine approvals are not condoned. However, they represent a lesser problem. When extortion and bribery at the top levels is curbed, government leaders can be expected to take steps to clean up petty corruption.

Basic Principle

All enterprises should conform to the relevant laws and regulations of the countries in which they are established and in which they operate, and should observe both the letter and the spirit of these Rules of Conduct.

For the purposes of these Rules of Conduct, the term 'enterprise' refers to any person or entity engaged in business, whether or not organized for profit, including any entity controlled by a State or a territorial subdivision thereof; it includes, where the context so indicates, a parent or a subsidiary.

Basic Rules

Article 1
Extortion

No one may, directly or indirectly, demand or accept a bribe.

Article 2
Bribery and 'Kickbacks'

a) No enterprise may, directly or indirectly, offer or give a bribe and any demands for such a bribe must be rejected.
b) Enterprises should not (i) kick back any portion of a contract payment to employees of the other contracting party, or (ii) utilize other techniques, such as subcontracts, purchase orders

or consulting agreements, to channel payments to government officials, to employees of the other contracting party, their relatives or business associates.

Article 3

Agents

Enterprises should take measures reasonably within their power to ensure:

a) that any payment made to any agent represents no more than an appropriate remuneration for legitimate services rendered by such agent;
b) that no part of any such payment is passed on by the agent as a bribe or otherwise in contravention of these Rules of Conduct; and
c) that they maintain a record of the names and terms of employment of all agents who are retained by them in connection with transactions with public bodies or State enterprises. This record should be available for inspection by auditors and, upon specific request, by appropriate, duly authorized governmental authorities under conditions of confidentiality.

Article 4

Financial Recording and Auditing

a) All financial transactions must be properly and fairly recorded in appropriate books of account available for inspection by boards of directors, if applicable, or a corresponding body, as well as auditors.
b) There must be no 'off the books' or secret accounts, nor may any documents be issued which do not properly and fairly record the transactions to which they relate.
c) Enterprises should take all necessary measures to establish independent systems of auditing in order to bring to light any transactions which contravene the present Rules of Conduct. Appropriate corrective action must then be taken.

Article 5

Responsibilities of Enterprises

The board of directors or other body with ultimate responsibility for the enterprise should:

a) take reasonable steps, including the establishment and maintenance of proper systems of control aimed at preventing any payments being made by or on behalf of the enterprise which contravene these Rules of Conduct;
b) periodically review compliance with these Rules of Conduct and establish procedures for obtaining appropriate reports for the purposes of such review; and
c) take appropriate action against any director or employee contravening these Rules of Conduct.

Article 6

Political Contributions

Contributions to political parties or committees or to individual politicians may only be made in accordance with the applicable law, and all requirements for public disclosure of such contributions shall be fully complied with. All such contributions must be reported to senior corporate management.

Article 7

Company Codes

These Rules of Conduct being of a general nature, enterprises should, where appropriate, draw up their own codes consistent with the ICC Rules and apply them to the particular circumstances in which their business is carried out. Such codes may usefully include examples and should enjoin employees or agents who find themselves subjected to any form of extortion or bribery immediately to report the same to senior corporate management. Companies should develop clear policies, guidelines, and training programmes for implementing and enforcing the provisions of their codes.

APPENDIX 20

Revised Code of Good Practices on Fiscal Transparency (Updated on February 28, 2001)

I. Clarity of Roles and Responsibilities

1.1 The government sector should be distinguished from the rest of the public sector and from the rest of the economy, and policy and management roles within the public sector should be clear and publicly disclosed

1.1.1 The structure and functions of government should be clearly specified.

1.1.2 The responsibilities of different levels of government, and of the executive branch, the legislative branch, and the judiciary, should be well defined.

1.1.3 Clear mechanisms for the coordination and management of budgetary and extra-budgetary activities should be established.

1.1.4 Relations between the government and non-government public sector agencies (i.e., the central bank, public financial institutions, and non-financial public enterprises) should be based on clear arrangements.

1.1.5 Government involvement in the private sector (e.g., through regulation and equity ownership) should be conducted in an open and public manner, and on the basis of clear rules and procedures that are applied in a non-discriminatory way.

1.2 There should be a clear legal and administrative framework for fiscal management

1.2.1 Any commitment or expenditure of public funds should be governed by comprehensive budget laws and openly available administrative rules.

1.2.2 Taxes, duties, fees, and charges should have an explicit legal basis. Tax laws and regulations should be easily accessible and understandable, and clear criteria should guide any administrative discretion in their application.

1.2.3 Ethical standards of behavior for public servants should be clear and well publicized.

II. Public Availability of Information

2.1 The public should be provided with full information on the past, current, and projected fiscal activity of government

2.1.1 The budget documentation, final accounts, and other fiscal reports for the public should cover all budgetary and extra-budgetary activities of the central government, and the consolidated fiscal position of the central government should be published.

2.1.2 Information comparable to that in the annual budget should be provided for the outturns of the two preceding fiscal years, together with forecasts of the main budget aggregates for two years following the budget.

2.1.3 Statements describing the nature and fiscal significance of central government contingent liabilities and tax expenditures, and of quasi-fiscal activities, should be part of the budget documentation.

2.1.4 The central government should publish full information on the level and composition of its debt and financial assets.

2.1.5 Where sub-national levels of government are significant, their combined fiscal position and the consolidated fiscal position of the general government should be published.

2.2 A commitment should be made to the timely publication of fiscal information

2.2.1 publication of fiscal information should be a legal obligation of government.

2.2.2 Advance release date calendars for fiscal information should be announced.

III. Open Budget Preparation, Execution, and Reporting

3.1 The budget documentation should specify fiscal policy objectives, the macroeconomic framework, the policy basis for the budget, and identifiable major fiscal risks

3.1.1 A statement of fiscal policy objectives and an assessment of fiscal sustainability should provide the framework for the annual budget.

3.1.2 Any fiscal rules that have been adopted (e.g., a balanced budget requirement or borrowing limits for sub-national levels of government) should be clearly specified.

3.1.3 The annual budget should be prepared and presented within a comprehensive and consistent quantitative macroeconomic framework, and the main assumptions underlying the budget should be provided.

3.1.4 New policies being introduced in the annual budget should be clearly described.

3.1.5 Major fiscal risks should be identified and quantified where possible, including variations in economic assumptions and the uncertain costs of specific expenditure commitments (e.g., financial restructuring).

3.2 Budget information should be presented in a way that facilitates policy analysis and promotes accountability

3.2.1 Budget data should be reported on a gross basis, distinguishing revenue, expenditure, and financing, with expenditure classified by economic, functional, and administrative category. Data on extra-budgetary activities should be reported on the same basis.

3.2.2 A statement of objectives to be achieved by major budget programs (e.g., improvement in relevant social indicators) should be provided.

3.2.3 The overall balance of the general government should be a standard summary indicator of the government's fiscal position. It should be supplemented where appropriate by other fiscal indicators for the general government (e.g., the operational balance, the structural balance, or the primary balance).

3.2.4 The public sector balance should be reported when non-government public sector agencies undertake significant quasi-fiscal activities.

3.3 Procedures for the execution and monitoring of approved expenditure and for collecting revenue should be clearly specified

3.3.1 There should be a comprehensive, integrated accounting system which provides a reliable basis for assessing payment arrears.

3.3.2 Procurement and employment regulations should be standardized and accessible to all interested parties.

3.3.3 Budget execution should be internally audited, and audit procedures should be open to review.

3.3.4 The national tax administration should be legally protected from political direction and should report regularly to the public on its activities.

3.4 There should be regular fiscal reporting to the legislature and the public

3.4.1 A mid-year report on budget developments should be presented to the legislature. More frequent (at least quarterly) reports should also be published.

3.4.2 Final accounts should be presented to the legislature within a year of the end of the fiscal year.

3.4.3 Results achieved relative to the objectives of major budget programs should be presented to the legislature annually.

IV. Assurances of Integrity

4.1 Fiscal data should meet accepted data quality standards

4.1.1 Budget data should reflect recent revenue and expenditure trends, underlying macroeconomic developments, and well-defined policy commitments.

4.1.2 The annual budget and final accounts should indicate the accounting basis (e.g., cash or accrual) and standards used in the compilation and presentation of budget data.

4.1.3 Specific assurances should be provided as to the quality of fiscal data. In particular, it should be indicated whether data in fiscal reports are internally consistent and have been reconciled with relevant data from other sources.

4.2 Fiscal information should be subjected to independent scrutiny

4.2.1 A national audit body or equivalent organization, which is independent of the executive, should provide timely reports for the legislature and public on the financial integrity of government accounts.

4.2.2 Independent experts should be invited to assess fiscal forecasts, the macroeconomic forecasts on which they are based, and all underlying assumptions.

4.2.3 A national statistics agency should be provided with the institutional independence to verify the quality of fiscal data.

APPENDIX 21

Joint Action of 22 December 1998

Adopted by the Council on the Basis of Article K.3 of the Treaty on European Union, on Corruption in the Private Sector

(98/742/JHA)

The Council of The European Union,

Having regard to the Treaty on European Union, and in particular Articles K.1(7) and K.3(2)(b) thereof,

Having regard to the report of the High-level Group on Organised Crime, which was approved by the European Council meeting in Amsterdam on 16 and 17 June 1997, and more particularly Recommendation No 6 of the Action Plan to combat organised crime of 28 April 1997,[1] which provides for the development of a comprehensive policy against corruption,

Whereas the Member States attach particular importance to combating corruption in the private sector on an international level;

Having regard to the conclusions of the Conference on achieving a corruption free environment—the EU Contribution (Brussels, April 1998),

Having regard to the Council Resolution of 21 December 1998 on the prevention of organised crime with reference to the establishment of a comprehensive strategy for combating it,[2]

Whereas the Member States stress the fact that prevention is no less important than repression in an integrated approach to corruption in the private sector;

Having regard to the Protocol, adopted by the Council on 27 September 1996, to the Convention on the protection of the European Communities' financial interests, to[3] the Second Protocol, adopted by the Council on 19 June 1997, to the Convention on the protection of the European Communities' financial interests[4] and to the Convention on the fight against corruption involving officials of the European Communities or officials of Member States of the European Union, adopted by the Council on 26 May 1997;[5]

Whereas this Joint Action is not aimed at corruption already covered by the instruments referred to;

Having regard to the communication of 21 May 1997 from the Commission to the European Parliament and the Council on a Union policy against corruption,

Whereas corruption distorts fair competition and undermines the principles of openness and freedom of markets, and in particular the smooth functioning of the internal market, and also militates against transparency and openness in international trade;

Whereas, for the purpose of this Joint Action, it is of importance that the concept of 'breach of duties' is covered in a sufficiently broad way by national law of Member States;

---

[1] OJ C 251, 15.8.1997, p.1.
[2] OJ C 408, 29.12.1998, p.1.
[3] OJ C 313, 23.10.1996, p.2.
[4] OJ C 221, 19.7.1997, p.11.
[5] OJ C 195, 25.6.1997, p.2.

Having examined the views of the European Parliament,[6] following consultation carried out by the Presidency in accordance with Article K.6 of the Treaty,

Has Adopted This Joint Action:

Article 1

Definitions

For the purposes of this Joint Action:

— 'person' means any employee or other person when directing or working in any capacity for or on behalf of a natural or legal person operating in the private sector,

— 'legal person' means any entity having such status under the applicable national law, except for States or other public bodies acting in the exercise of State authority and for public international organisations,

— 'breach of duty' shall be understood in accordance with national law. The concept of breach of duty in national law should cover as a minimum any disloyal behaviour constituting a breach of a statutory duty, or, as the case may be, a breach of professional regulations or instructions, which apply within the business of a 'person' as defined in the first indent.

Article 2

Passive corruption in the private sector

1. For the purposes of this Joint Action, the deliberate action of a person who, in the course of his business activities, directly or through an intermediary, requests or receives an undue advantage of any kind whatsoever, or accepts the promise of such an advantage, for himself or for a third party, for him to perform or refrain from performing an act, in breach of his duties, shall constitute passive corruption in the private sector.
2. Subject to Article 4(2), each Member State shall take the necessary measures to ensure that conduct of the type referred to in paragraph 1 is made a criminal offence. These measures shall at least cover such conduct which involves, or could involve, the distortion of competition, as a minimum within the common market, and which results, or might result, in economic damage to others by the improper award or improper execution of a contract.

Article 3

Active corruption in the private sector

1. For the purposes of this Joint Action, the deliberate action of whosoever promises, offers or gives, directly or through an intermediary, an undue advantage of any kind whatsoever to a person, for himself or for a third party, in the course of the business activities of that person in order that the person should perform or refrain from performing an act, in breach of his duties, shall constitute active corruption in the private sector.
2. Subject to Article 4(2), each Member State shall take the necessary measures to ensure that conduct of the type referred to in paragraph 1 is made a criminal offence. These measures shall at least cover such conduct which involves, or could involve, the distortion of competition, as a minimum within the common market, and which results, or might result, in economic damage to others by the improper award or improper execution of a contract.

Article 4

Penalties

1. Each Member State shall take the necessary measures to ensure that the conduct referred to in Articles 2 and 3, and the acting as an accessory in or instigator of such conduct, are punishable by effective, proportionate and dissuasive criminal penalties, including, at least in serious cases, penalties involving deprivation of liberty which can give rise to extradition.

[6] OJ C 371, 8.12.1997, p.193.

2. However, for minor cases of active or passive corruption, in the private sector, a Member State may provide for penalties of a different kind from those referred to in paragraph 1.

Article 5
Liability of legal persons

1. Each Member State shall take the necessary measures to ensure that legal persons can be held liable for active corruption of the type referred to in Article 3 committed for their benefit by any person, acting either individually or as part of an organ of the legal person, who has a leading position within the legal person, based on:
   — a power of representation of the legal person, or
   — an authority to take decisions on behalf of the legal person, or
   — an authority to exercise control within the legal person,

   as well as for involvement as accessories or instigators in the commission of such an offence.
2. Apart from the cases already provided for in paragraph 1, each Member State shall take the necessary measures to ensure that a legal person can be held liable where the lack of supervision or control by a person referred to in paragraph 1 has made possible the commission of an act of active corruption of the type referred to in Article 3 for the benefit of that legal person by a person under its authority.
3. Liability of a legal person under paragraphs 1 and 2 shall not exclude criminal proceedings against natural persons who are involved as perpetrators, instigators or accessories in the active corruption.

Article 6
Sanctions for legal persons

1. Each Member State shall take the necessary measures to ensure that a legal person held liable pursuant to Article 5(1) is punishable by effective, proportionate and dissuasive sanctions, which shall include criminal or non-criminal fines and may include other sanctions such as:
   (a) exclusion from entitlement to public benefits or aid;
   (b) temporary or permanent disqualification from the practice of commercial activities;
   (c) placing under judicial supervision;
   (d) a judicial winding-up order.
2. Each Member State shall take the necessary measures to ensure that a legal person held liable pursuant to Article 5(2) is punishable by effective, proportionate and dissuasive sanctions or measures.

Article 7
Jurisdiction

1. Each Member State shall take the necessary measures to establish its jurisdiction with regard to the offences referred to in Articles 2 and 3 where the offence has been committed:
   (a) in whole or in part within its territory; or
   (b) by one of its nationals, provided that the law of that Member State may require the conduct to be punishable also in the country where it occurred; or
   (c) for the benefit of a legal person operating in the private sector that has its head office in the territory of that Member State.
2. Any Member State may decide that it will not apply, or will apply only in specific cases or circumstances, the jurisdiction rule set out in:
   — paragraph 1(b),
   — paragraph 1(c).
3. Member States shall inform the General Secretariat of the Council accordingly where they decide to apply paragraph 2, where appropriate with an indication of the specific cases or circumstances in which the decision applies.

4. Any Member State which, under its law, does not extradite its own nationals shall take the necessary measures to establish its jurisdiction with regard to the offences referred to in Articles 2 and 3, when committed by its own nationals outside its territory.

Article 8

Implementation of the Joint Action

1. Each Member State shall, within two years after the entry into force of this Joint Action, bring forward appropriate proposals to implement this Joint Action for consideration by the competent authorities with a view to their adoption.
2. The Council will assess, on the basis of appropriate information, the fulfilment by Member States of their obligations under this Joint Action within three years after its entry into force.

Article 9

This Joint Action shall be published in the Official Journal.

Article 10

This Joint Action shall enter into force on the date of its publication in the Official Journal.

Done at Brussels, 22 December 1998.

For the Council

The President

C. EINEM

APPENDIX 22

Organisation for Economic Cooperation and Development: Convention on Combating Bribery of Foreign Public Officials in International Business Transactions[1]

Preamble

The Parties,

Considering that bribery is a widespread phenomenon in international business transactions, including trade and investment, which raises serious moral and political concerns, undermines good governance and economic development, and distorts international competitive conditions;

Considering that all countries share a responsibility to combat bribery in international business transactions;

Having regard to the Revised Recommendation on Combating Bribery in International Business Transactions, adopted by the Council of the Organisation for Economic Co-operation and Development (OECD) on 23 May 1997, C(97)123/FINAL, which, *inter alia*, called for effective measures to deter, prevent and combat the bribery of foreign public officials in connection with international business transactions, in particular the prompt criminalisation of such bribery in an effective and co-ordinated manner and in conformity with the agreed common elements set out in that Recommendation and with the jurisdictional and other basic legal principles of each country;

Welcoming other recent developments which further advance international understanding and co-operation in combating bribery of public officials, including actions of the United Nations, the World Bank, the International Monetary Fund, the World Trade Organisation, the Organisation of American States, the Council of Europe and the European Union;

Welcoming the efforts of companies, business organisations and trade unions as well as other non-governmental organisations to combat bribery;

Recognising the role of governments in the prevention of solicitation of bribes from individuals and enterprises in international business transactions;

Recognising that achieving progress in this field requires not only efforts on a national level but also multilateral co-operation, monitoring and follow-up;

Recognising that achieving equivalence among the measures to be taken by the Parties is an essential object and purpose of the Convention, which requires that the Convention be ratified without derogations affecting this equivalence;

[1] The Convention was adopted on 17 December 1997. It entered into force on 15 February 1999. As at 10 March 2004, the Convention had been ratified by the following States: Argentina, Australia, Austria, Belgium, Brazil, Bulgaria, Canada, Chile, Czech Republic, Denmark, Finland, France, Germany, Greece, Hungary, Iceland, Ireland, Italy, Japan, Luxembourg, Mexico, Netherlands, New Zealand, Norway, Poland, Portugal, Republic of Korea, Slovakia, Slovenia, Spain, Sweden, Switzerland, Turkey, United Kingdom of Great Britain and Northern Ireland and United States of America.

Have agreed as follows:

Article 1
The Offence of Bribery of Foreign Public Officials

1. Each Party shall take such measures as may be necessary to establish that it is a criminal offence under its law for any person intentionally to offer, promise or give any undue pecuniary or other advantage, whether directly or through intermediaries, to a foreign public official, for that official or for a third party, in order that the official act or refrain from acting in relation to the performance of official duties, in order to obtain or retain business or other improper advantage in the conduct of international business.
2. Each Party shall take any measures necessary to establish that complicity in, including incitement, aiding and abetting, or authorisation of an act of bribery of a foreign public official shall be a criminal offence. Attempt and conspiracy to bribe a foreign public official shall be criminal offences to the same extent as attempt and conspiracy to bribe a public official of that Party.
3. The offences set out in paragraphs 1 and 2 above are hereinafter referred to as 'bribery of a foreign public official'.
4. For the purpose of this Convention:
   a. 'foreign public official' means any person holding a legislative, administrative or judicial office of a foreign country, whether appointed or elected; any person exercising a public function for a foreign country, including for a public agency or public enterprise; and any official or agent of a public international organisation;
   b. 'foreign country' includes all levels and subdivisions of government, from national to local;
   c. 'act or refrain from acting in relation to the performance of official duties' includes any use of the public official's position, whether or not within the official's authorised competence.

Article 2
Responsibility of Legal Persons

Each Party shall take such measures as may be necessary, in accordance with its legal principles, to establish the liability of legal persons for the bribery of a foreign public official.

Article 3
Sanctions

1. The bribery of a foreign public official shall be punishable by effective, proportionate and dissuasive criminal penalties. The range of penalties shall be comparable to that applicable to the bribery of the Party's own public officials and shall, in the case of natural persons, include deprivation of liberty sufficient to enable effective mutual legal assistance and extradition.
2. In the event that, under the legal system of a Party, criminal responsibility is not applicable to legal persons, that Party shall ensure that legal persons shall be subject to effective, proportionate and dissuasive non-criminal sanctions, including monetary sanctions, for bribery of foreign public officials.
3. Each Party shall take such measures as may be necessary to provide that the bribe and the proceeds of the bribery of a foreign public official, or property the value of which corresponds to that of such proceeds, are subject to seizure and confiscation or that monetary sanctions of comparable effect are applicable.
4. Each Party shall consider the imposition of additional civil or administrative sanctions upon a person subject to sanctions for the bribery of a foreign public official.

Article 4
Jurisdiction

1. Each Party shall take such measures as may be necessary to establish its jurisdiction over the bribery of a foreign public official when the offence is committed in whole or in part in its territory.
2. Each Party which has jurisdiction to prosecute its nationals for offences committed abroad shall take such measures as may be necessary to establish its jurisdiction to do so in respect of the bribery of a foreign public official, according to the same principles.
3. When more than one Party has jurisdiction over an alleged offence described in this Convention, the Parties involved shall, at the request of one of them, consult with a view to determining the most appropriate jurisdiction for prosecution.
4. Each Party shall review whether its current basis for jurisdiction is effective in the fight against the bribery of foreign public officials and, if it is not, shall take remedial steps.

Article 5
Enforcement

Investigation and prosecution of the bribery of a foreign public official shall be subject to the applicable rules and principles of each Party. They shall not be influenced by considerations of national economic interest, the potential effect upon relations with another State or the identity of the natural or legal persons involved.

Article 6
Statute of Limitations

Any statute of limitations applicable to the offence of bribery of a foreign public official shall allow an adequate period of time for the investigation and prosecution of this offence.

Article 7
Money Laundering

Each Party which has made bribery of its own public official a predicate offence for the purpose of the application of its money laundering legislation shall do so on the same terms for the bribery of a foreign public official, without regard to the place where the bribery occurred.

Article 8
Accounting

1. In order to combat bribery of foreign public officials effectively, each Party shall take such measures as may be necessary, within the framework of its laws and regulations regarding the maintenance of books and records, financial statement disclosures, and accounting and auditing standards, to prohibit the establishment of off-the-books accounts, the making of off-the-books or inadequately identified transactions, the recording of non-existent expenditures, the entry of liabilities with incorrect identification of their object, as well as the use of false documents, by companies subject to those laws and regulations, for the purpose of bribing foreign public officials or of hiding such bribery.
2. Each Party shall provide effective, proportionate and dissuasive civil, administrative or criminal penalties for such omissions and falsifications in respect of the books, records, accounts and financial statements of such companies.

Article 9
Mutual Legal Assistance

1. Each Party shall, to the fullest extent possible under its laws and relevant treaties and arrangements, provide prompt and effective legal assistance to another Party for the purpose of criminal investigations and proceedings brought by a Party concerning offences within the

scope of this Convention and for non-criminal proceedings within the scope of this Convention brought by a Party against a legal person. The requested Party shall inform the requesting Party, without delay, of any additional information or documents needed to support the request for assistance and, where requested, of the status and outcome of the request for assistance.

2. Where a Party makes mutual legal assistance conditional upon the existence of dual criminality, dual criminality shall be deemed to exist if the offence for which the assistance is sought is within the scope of this Convention.
3. A Party shall not decline to render mutual legal assistance for criminal matters within the scope of this Convention on the ground of bank secrecy.

Article 10
Extradition

1. Bribery of a foreign public official shall be deemed to be included as an extraditable offence under the laws of the Parties and the extradition treaties between them.
2. If a Party which makes extradition conditional on the existence of an extradition treaty receives a request for extradition from another Party with which it has no extradition treaty, it may consider this Convention to be the legal basis for extradition in respect of the offence of bribery of a foreign public official.
3. Each Party shall take any measures necessary to assure either that it can extradite its nationals or that it can prosecute its nationals for the offence of bribery of a foreign public official. A Party which declines a request to extradite a person for bribery of a foreign public official solely on the ground that the person is its national shall submit the case to its competent authorities for the purpose of prosecution.
4. Extradition for bribery of a foreign public official is subject to the conditions set out in the domestic law and applicable treaties and arrangements of each Party. Where a Party makes extradition conditional upon the existence of dual criminality, that condition shall be deemed to be fulfilled if the offence for which extradition is sought is within the scope of Article 1 of this Convention.

Article 11
Responsible Authorities

For the purposes of Article 4, paragraph 3, on consultation, Article 9, on mutual legal assistance and Article 10, on extradition, each Party shall notify to the Secretary-General of the OECD an authority or authorities responsible for making and receiving requests, which shall serve as channel of communication for these matters for that Party, without prejudice to other arrangements between Parties.

Article 12
Monitoring and Follow-up

The Parties shall co-operate in carrying out a programme of systematic follow-up to monitor and promote the full implementation of this Convention. Unless otherwise decided by consensus of the Parties, this shall be done in the framework of the OECD Working Group on Bribery in International Business Transactions and according to its terms of reference, or within the framework and terms of reference of any successor to its functions, and Parties shall bear the costs of the programme in accordance with the rules applicable to that body.

Article 13
Signature and Accession

1. Until its entry into force, this Convention shall be open for signature by OECD members and by non-members which have been invited to become full participants in its Working Group on Bribery in International Business Transactions.
2. Subsequent to its entry into force, this Convention shall be open to accession by any non-signatory which is a member of the OECD or has become a full participant in the Working Group on Bribery in International Business Transactions or any successor to its functions. For each such non-signatory, the Convention shall enter into force on the sixtieth day following the date of deposit of its instrument of accession.

Article 14
Ratification and Depositary

1. This Convention is subject to acceptance, approval or ratification by the Signatories, in accordance with their respective laws.
2. Instruments of acceptance, approval, ratification or accession shall be deposited with the Secretary-General of the OECD, who shall serve as Depositary of this Convention.

Article 15
Entry into Force

1. This Convention shall enter into force on the sixtieth day following the date upon which five of the ten countries which have the ten largest export shares set out in DAFFE/IME/BR(97)18/FINAL and which represent by themselves at least sixty per cent of the combined total exports of those ten countries, have deposited their instruments of acceptance, approval, or ratification. For each signatory depositing its instrument after such entry into force, the Convention shall enter into force on the sixtieth day after deposit of its instrument.
2. If, after 31 December 1998, the Convention has not entered into force under paragraph 1 above, any signatory which has deposited its instrument of acceptance, approval or ratification may declare in writing to the Depositary its readiness to accept entry into force of this Convention under this paragraph 2. The Convention shall enter into force for such a signatory on the sixtieth day following the date upon which such declarations have been deposited by at least two signatories. For each signatory depositing its declaration after such entry into force, the Convention shall enter into force on the sixtieth day following the date of deposit.

Article 16
Amendment

Any Party may propose the amendment of this Convention. A proposed amendment shall be submitted to the Depositary which shall communicate it to the other Parties at least sixty days before convening a meeting of the Parties to consider the proposed amendment. An amendment adopted by consensus of the Parties, or by such other means as the Parties may determine by consensus, shall enter into force sixty days after the deposit of an instrument of ratification, acceptance or approval by all of the Parties, or in such other circumstances as may be specified by the Parties at the time of adoption of the amendment.

Article 17
Withdrawal

A Party may withdraw from this Convention by submitting written notification to the Depositary. Such withdrawal shall be effective one year after the date of the receipt of the notification. After withdrawal, co-operation shall continue between the Parties and the Party which has withdrawn on all requests for assistance or extradition made before the effective date of withdrawal which remain pending.

APPENDIX 23

Revised Recommendation of the Council of the Organisation for Economic Cooperation and Development on Combating Bribery in International Business Transactions[1]

a. Preamble
b. General
c. Criminalisation of bribery of public officials
d. Tax deductibility
e. Accounting requirements, external audit and internal company controls
f. Public procurement
g. International co-operation
h. Follow-up and institutional arrangements
i. Co-operation with non-OECD members
j. Relations with international govermnetal and non-governmental organizations
k. Annex: Agreed common elements of criminal legislation and related action.

The Council

Having regard to Articles 3, 5 a) and 5 b) of the Convention on the Organisation for Economic Co-operation and Development of 14 December 1960;

Considering that bribery is a widespread phenomenon in international business transactions, including trade and investment, raising serious moral and political concerns and distorting international competitive conditions;

Considering that all countries share a responsibility to combat bribery in international business transactions;

Considering that enterprises should refrain from bribery of public servants and holders of public office, as stated in the OECD Guidelines for Multinational Enterprises;

Considering the progress which has been made in the implementation of the initial Recommendation of the Council on Bribery in International Business Transactions adopted on 27 May 1994, C(94)75/FINAL and the related Recommendation on the tax deductibility of bribes of foreign public officials adopted on 11 April 1996, C(96)27/FINAL; as well as the Recommendation concerning Anti-corruption Proposals for Bilateral Aid Procurement, endorsed by the High Level Meeting of the Development Assistance Committee on 7 May 1996;

Welcoming other recent developments which further advance international understanding and co-operation regarding bribery in business transactions, including actions of the United Nations, the Council of Europe, the European Union and the Organisation of American States;

Having regard to the commitment made at the meeting of the Council at Ministerial level in May 1996, to criminalise the bribery of foreign public officials in an effective and co-ordinated manner;

---

[1] The Revised Recommendation on Combating Bribery in International Business Transactions was adopted by the Council on 23 May 1997.

Noting that an international convention in conformity with the agreed common elements set forth in the Annex, is an appropriate instrument to attain such criminalisation rapidly;

Considering the consensus which has developed on the measures which should be taken to implement the 1994 Recommendation, in particular, with respect to the modalities and international instruments to facilitate criminalisation of bribery of foreign public officials; tax deductibility of bribes to foreign public officials; accounting requirements, external audit and internal company controls; and rules and regulations on public procurement;

Recognising that achieving progress in this field requires not only efforts by individual countries but multilateral co-operation, monitoring and follow-up;

General

I. *Recommends* that Member countries take effective measures to deter, prevent and combat the bribery of foreign public officials in connection with international business transactions.

II. *Recommends* that each Member country examine the following areas and, in conformity with its jurisdictional and other basic legal principles, take concrete and meaningful steps to meet this goal:

i) criminal laws and their application, in accordance with section III and the Annex to this Recommendation;
ii) tax legislation, regulations and practice, to eliminate any indirect support of bribery, in accordance with section IV;
iii) company and business accounting, external audit and internal control requirements and practices, in accordance with section V;
iv) banking, financial and other relevant provisions, to ensure that adequate records would be kept and made available for inspection and investigation; and
v) public subsidies, licences, government procurement contracts or other public advantages, so that advantages could be denied as a sanction for bribery in appropriate cases, and in accordance with section VI for procurement contracts and aid procurement; and
vi) civil, commercial, and administrative laws and regulations, so that such bribery would be illegal;
vii) international co-operation in investigations and other legal proceedings, in accordance with section VII.

Criminalisation of Bribery of Foreign Public Officials

III. *Recommends* that Member countries should criminalise the bribery of foreign public officials in an effective and co-ordinated manner by submitting proposals to their legislative bodies by 1 April 1998, in conformity with the agreed common elements set forth in the Annex, and seeking their enactment by the end of 1998.

Decides, to this end, to open negotiations promptly on an international convention to criminalise bribery in conformity with the agreed common elements, the treaty to be open for signature by the end of 1997, with a view to its entry into force twelve months thereafter.

Tax Deductibility

IV. *Urges* the prompt implementation by Member countries of the 1996 Recommendation which reads as follows: 'that those Member countries which do not disallow the deductibility of bribes to foreign public officials re-examine such treatment with the intention of denying this deductibility. Such action may be facilitated by the trend to treat bribes to foreign officials as illegal.'

Accounting Requirements, External Audit and Internal Company Controls

V. *Recommends* that Member countries take the steps necessary so that laws, rules and practices with respect to accounting requirements, external audit and internal company controls are in line with the following principles and are fully used in order to prevent and detect bribery of foreign public officials in international business.

A. Adequate accounting requirements

i) Member countries should require companies to maintain adequate records of the sums of money received and expended by the company, identifying the matters in respect of which the receipt and expenditure takes place. Companies should be prohibited from making off-the-books transactions or keeping off-the-books accounts.
ii) Member countries should require companies to disclose in their financial statements the full range of material contingent liabilities.
iii) Member countries should adequately sanction accounting omissions, falsifications and fraud.

B. Independent external audit

i) Member countries should consider whether requirements to submit to external audit are adequate.
ii) Member countries and professional associations should maintain adequate standards to ensure the independence of external auditors which permits them to provide an objective assessment of company accounts, financial statements and internal controls.
iii) Member countries should require the auditor who discovers indications of a possible illegal act of bribery to report this discovery to management and, as appropriate, to corporate monitoring bodies.
iv) Member countries should consider requiring the auditor to report indications of a possible illegal act of bribery to competent authorities.

C. Internal company controls

i) Member countries should encourage the development and adoption of adequate internal company controls, including standards of conduct.
ii) Member countries should encourage company management to make statements in their annual reports about their internal control mechanisms, including those which contribute to preventing bribery.
iii) Member countries should encourage the creation of monitoring bodies, independent of management, such as audit committees of boards of directors or of supervisory boards.
iv) Member countries should encourage companies to provide channels for communication by, and protection for, persons not willing to violate professional standards or ethics under instructions or pressure from hierarchical superiors.

Public procurement

VI. *Recommends*:

i) Member countries should support the efforts in the World Trade Organisation to pursue an agreement on transparency in government procurement;
ii) Member countries' laws and regulations should permit authorities to suspend from competition for public contracts enterprises determined to have bribed foreign public officials in contravention of that Member's national laws and, to the extent a Member applies procurement sanctions to enterprises that are determined to have bribed domestic public

officials, such sanctions should be applied equally in case of bribery of foreign public officials.[2]

iii) In accordance with the Recommendation of the Development Assistance Committee, Member countries should require anti-corruption provisions in bilateral aid-funded procurement, promote the proper implementation of anti-corruption provisions in international development institutions, and work closely with development partners to combat corruption in all development co-operation efforts.[3]

International co-operation

VII. *Recommends* that Member countries, in order to combat bribery in international business transactions, in conformity with their jurisdictional and other basic legal principles, take the following actions:

i) consult and otherwise co-operate with appropriate authorities in other countries in investigations and other legal proceedings concerning specific cases of such bribery through such means as sharing of information (spontaneously or upon request), provision of evidence and extradition;

ii) make full use of existing agreements and arrangements for mutual international legal assistance and where necessary, enter into new agreements or arrangements for this purpose;

iii) ensure that their national laws afford an adequate basis for this co-operation and, in particular, in accordance with paragraph 8 of the Annex.

Follow-up and institutional arrangements

VIII. *Instructs* the Committee on International Investment and Multinational Enterprises, through its Working Group on Bribery in International Business Transactions, to carry out a programme of systematic follow-up to monitor and promote the full implementation of this Recommendation, in co-operation with the Committee for Fiscal Affairs, the Development Assistance Committee and other OECD bodies, as appropriate. This follow-up will include, in particular:

i) receipt of notifications and other information submitted to it by the Member countries;

ii) regular reviews of steps taken by Member countries to implement the Recommendation and to make proposals, as appropriate, to assist Member countries in its implementation; these reviews will be based on the following complementary systems:

   a. a system of self-evaluation, where Member countries' responses on the basis of a questionnaire will provide a basis for assessing the implementation of the Recommendation;

   b. a system of mutual evaluation, where each Member country will be examined in turn by the Working Group on Bribery, on the basis of a report which will provide an objective assessment of the progress of the Member country in implementing the Recommendation.

iii) examination of specific issues relating to bribery in international business transactions;

iv) examination of the feasibility of broadening the scope of the work of the OECD to combat international bribery to include private sector bribery and bribery of foreign officials for reasons other than to obtain or retain business;

v) provision of regular information to the public on its work and activities and on implementation of the Recommendation.

---

[2] Member countries' systems for applying sanctions for bribery of domestic officials differ as to whether the determination of bribery is based on a criminal conviction, indictment or administrative procedure, but in all cases it is based on substantial evidence.

[3] This paragraph summarises the DAC recommendation which is addressed to DAC members only, and addresses it to all OECD Members and eventually non-member countries which adhere to the Recommendation.

IX. *Notes* the obligation of Member countries to co-operate closely in this follow-up programme, pursuant to Article 3 of the OECD Convention.

X. *Instructs* the Committee on International Investment and Multinational Enterprises to review the implementation of Sections III and, in co-operation with the Committee on Fiscal Affairs, Section IV of this Recommendation and report to Ministers in Spring 1998, to report to the Council after the first regular review and as appropriate there after, and to review this Revised Recommendation within three years after its adoption.

Co-operation with non-members

XI. *Appeals* to non-member countries to adhere to the Recommendation and participate in any institutional follow-up or implementation mechanism.

XII. *Instructs* the Committee on International Investment and Multinational Enterprises through its Working Group on Bribery, to provide a forum for consultations with countries which have not yet adhered, in order to promote wider participation in the Recommendation and its follow-up.

Relations with international governmental and non-governmental organisations

XIII. *Invites* the Committee on International Investment and Multinational Enterprises through its Working Group on Bribery, to consult and co-operate with the international organisations and international financial institutions active in the combat against bribery in international business transactions and consult regularly with the non-governmental organisations and representatives of the business community active in this field.

Annex

Agreed common elements of criminal legislation and related action

1) Elements of the offence of active bribery

i) Bribery is understood as the promise or giving of any undue payment or other advantages, whether directly or through intermediaries to a public official, for himself or for a third party, to influence the official to act or refrain from acting in the performance of his or her official duties in order to obtain or retain business.

ii) Foreign public official means any person holding a legislative, administrative or judicial office of a foreign country or in an international organisation, whether appointed or elected or, any person exercising a public function or task in a foreign country.

iii) The offeror is any person, on his own behalf or on the behalf of any other natural person or legal entity.

2) Ancillary elements or offences

The general criminal law concepts of attempt, complicity and/or conspiracy of the law of the prosecuting state are recognised as applicable to the offence of bribery of a foreign public official.

3) Excuses and defences

Bribery of foreign public officials in order to obtain or retain business is an offence irrespective of the value or the outcome of the bribe, of perceptions of local custom or of the tolerance of bribery by local authorities.

4) Jurisdiction

Jurisdiction over the offence of bribery of foreign public officials should in any case be established when the offence is committed in whole or in part in the prosecuting State's territory. The territorial basis for jurisdiction should be interpreted broadly so that an extensive physical connection to the bribery act is not required.

States which prosecute their nationals for offences committed abroad should do so in respect of the bribery of foreign public officials according to the same principles.

States which do not prosecute on the basis of the nationality principle should be prepared to extradite their nationals in respect of the bribery of foreign public officials.

All countries should review whether their current basis for jurisdiction is effective in the fight against bribery of foreign public officials and, if not, should take appropriate remedial steps.

5) Sanctions

The offence of bribery of foreign public officials should be sanctioned/punishable by effective, proportionate and dissuasive criminal penalties, sufficient to secure effective mutual legal assistance and extradition, comparable to those applicable to the bribers in cases of corruption of domestic public officials.

Monetary or other civil, administrative or criminal penalties on any legal person involved, should be provided, taking into account the amounts of the bribe and of the profits derived from the transaction obtained through the bribe.

Forfeiture or confiscation of instrumentalities and of the bribe benefits and the profits derived from the transactions obtained through the bribe should be provided, or comparable fines or damages imposed.

6) Enforcement

In view of the seriousness of the offence of bribery of foreign public officials, public prosecutors should exercise their discretion independently, based on professional motives. They should not be influenced by considerations of national economic interest, fostering good political relations or the identity of the victim.

Complaints of victims should be seriously investigated by the competent authorities.

The statute of limitations should allow adequate time to address this complex offence.

National governments should provide adequate resources to prosecuting authorities so as to permit effective prosecution of bribery of foreign public officials.

7) Connected provisions (criminal and non-criminal)

a. Accounting, record keeping and disclosure requirements

In order to combat bribery of foreign public officials effectively, states should also adequately sanction accounting omissions, falsifications and fraud.

b. Money laundering

The bribery of foreign public officials should be made a predicate offence for purposes of money laundering legislation where bribery of a domestic public official is a money laundering predicate offence, without regard to the place where the bribery occurs.

8) International co-operation

Effective mutual legal assistance is critical to be able to investigate and obtain evidence in order to prosecute cases of bribery of foreign public officials.

Adoption of laws criminalising the bribery of foreign public officials would remove obstacles to mutual legal assistance created by dual criminality requirements.

Countries should tailor their laws on mutual legal assistance to permit co-operation with countries investigating cases of bribery of foreign public officials even including third countries (country of the offeror; country where the act occurred) and countries applying different types of criminalisation legislation to reach such cases.

Means should be explored and undertaken to improve the efficiency of mutual legal assistance.

Recommendation of the council on the tax deductibility of bribes to foreign public officials (adopted by the OECD Council on 11 April 1996)

The Council

I. *Recommends* that those Member countries which do not disallow the deductibility of bribes to foreign public officials re-examine such treatment with the intention of denying this deductibility. Such action may be facilitated by the trend to treat bribes to foreign officials as illegal.

II. *Instructs* the Committee on Fical Affairs, in co-operation with the Committee on International Investment and Multinational Enterprises, to monitor the implementation of this Recommendation, to promote the Recommendation in the context of contacts with non-member countries and to report to the Council as appropriate.

APPENDIX 24

Organization of American States: Inter-American Convention Against Corruption[1]

Preamble

The Member States of the Organization of American States,

Convinced that corruption undermines the legitimacy of public institutions and strikes at society, moral order and justice, as well as at the comprehensive development of peoples;

Considering that representative democracy, an essential condition for stability, peace and development of the region, requires, by its nature, the combating of every form of corruption in the performance of public functions, as well as acts of corruption specifically related to such performance;

Persuaded that fighting corruption strengthens democratic institutions and prevents distortions in the economy, improprieties in public administration and damage to a society's moral fiber;

Recognizing that corruption is often a tool used by organized crime for the accomplishment of its purposes;

Convinced of the importance of making people in the countries of the region aware of this problem and its gravity, and of the need to strengthen participation by civil society in preventing and fighting corruption;

Recognizing that, in some cases, corruption has international dimensions, which requires coordinated action by States to fight it effectively;

Convinced of the need for prompt adoption of an international instrument to promote and facilitate international cooperation in fighting corruption and, especially, in taking appropriate action against persons who commit acts of corruption in the performance of public functions, or acts specifically related to such performance, as well as appropriate measures with respect to the proceeds of such acts;

Deeply Concerned by the steadily increasing links between corruption and the proceeds generated by illicit narcotics trafficking which undermine and threaten legitimate commercial and financial activities, and society, at all levels;

Bearing in Mind the responsibility of States to hold corrupt persons accountable in order to combat corruption and to cooperate with one another for their efforts in this area to be effective; and

Determined to make every effort to prevent, detect, punish and eradicate corruption in the performance of public functions and acts of corruption specifically related to such performance,

---

[1] The Convention was adopted in Caracas on 29 March 1996. It entered into force on 6 March 1997. The Convention has been ratified by the following States: Argentina, Antigua and Barbuda, Bahamas, Belize, Bolivia, Brazil, Canada, Chile, Colombia, Costa Rica, Dominica, Dominican Republic, Ecuador, El Salvador, Grenada, Guatemala, Guyana, Haiti, Honduras, Jamaica, Mexico, Nicaragua, Panama, Paraguay, Peru, Saint Kitts and Nevis, Saint Lucia, Saint Vincent and the Grenadines, Suriname, Trinidad and Tobago, United States of America, Uruguay and Venezuela.

Have agreed to adopt the following:

Article I
Definitions

For the purposes of this Convention:

'Public function' means any temporary or permanent, paid or honorary activity, performed by a natural person in the name of the State or in the service of the State or its institutions, at any level of its hierarchy.

'Public official', 'government official', or 'public servant' means any official or employee of the State or its agencies, including those who have been selected, appointed, or elected to perform activities or functions in the name of the State or in the service of the State, at any level of its hierarchy.

'Property' means assets of any kind, whether movable or immovable, tangible or intangible, and any document or legal instrument demonstrating, purporting to demonstrate, or relating to ownership or other rights pertaining to such assets.

Article II
Purposes

The purposes of this Convention are:

1. To promote and strengthen the development by each of the States Parties of the mechanisms needed to prevent, detect, punish and eradicate corruption; and
2. To promote, facilitate and regulate cooperation among the States Parties to ensure the effectiveness of measures and actions to prevent, detect, punish and eradicate corruption in the performance of public functions and acts of corruption specifically related to such performance.

Article III
Preventive Measures

For the purposes set forth in Article II of this Convention, the States Parties agree to consider the applicability of measures within their own institutional systems to create, maintain and strengthen:

1. Standards of conduct for the correct, honorable, and proper fulfillment of public functions. These standards shall be intended to prevent conflicts of interest and mandate the proper conservation and use of resources entrusted to government officials in the performance of their functions. These standards shall also establish measures and systems requiring government officials to report to appropriate authorities acts of corruption in the performance of public functions. Such measures should help preserve the public's confidence in the integrity of public servants and government processes.
2. Mechanisms to enforce these standards of conduct.
3. Instruction to government personnel to ensure proper understanding of their responsibilities and the ethical rules governing their activities.
4. Systems for registering the income, assets and liabilities of persons who perform public functions in certain posts as specified by law and, where appropriate, for making such registrations public.
5. Systems of government hiring and procurement of goods and services that assure the openness, equity and efficiency of such systems.
6. Government revenue collection and control systems that deter corruption.
7. Laws that deny favorable tax treatment for any individual or corporation for expenditures made in violation of the anticorruption laws of the States Parties.
8. Systems for protecting public servants and private citizens who, in good faith, report acts of corruption, including protection of their identities, in accordance with their Constitutions and the basic principles of their domestic legal systems.

9. Oversight bodies with a view to implementing modern mechanisms for preventing, detecting, punishing and eradicating corrupt acts.
10. Deterrents to the bribery of domestic and foreign government officials, such as mechanisms to ensure that publicly held companies and other types of associations maintain books and records which, in reasonable detail, accurately reflect the acquisition and disposition of assets, and have sufficient internal accounting controls to enable their officers to detect corrupt acts.
11. Mechanisms to encourage participation by civil society and nongovernmental organizations in efforts to prevent corruption.
12. The study of further preventive measures that take into account the relationship between equitable compensation and probity in public service.

Article IV

Scope

This Convention is applicable provided that the alleged act of corruption has been committed or has effects in a State Party.

Article V

Jurisdiction

1. Each State Party shall adopt such measures as may be necessary to establish its jurisdiction over the offenses it has established in accordance with this Convention when the offense in question is committed in its territory.
2. Each State Party may adopt such measures as may be necessary to establish its jurisdiction over the offenses it has established in accordance with this Convention when the offense is committed by one of its nationals or by a person who habitually resides in its territory.
3. Each State Party shall adopt such measures as may be necessary to establish its jurisdiction over the offenses it has established in accordance with this Convention when the alleged criminal is present in its territory and it does not extradite such person to another country on the ground of the nationality of the alleged criminal.
4. This Convention does not preclude the application of any other rule of criminal jurisdiction established by a State Party under its domestic law.

Article VI

Acts of Corruption

1. This Convention is applicable to the following acts of corruption:
   a. The solicitation or acceptance, directly or indirectly, by a government official or a person who performs public functions, of any article of monetary value, or other benefit, such as a gift, favor, promise or advantage for himself or for another person or entity, in exchange for any act or omission in the performance of his public functions;
   b. The offering or granting, directly or indirectly, to a government official or a person who performs public functions, of any article of monetary value, or other benefit, such as a gift, favor, promise or advantage for himself or for another person or entity, in exchange for any act or omission in the performance of his public functions;
   c. Any act or omission in the discharge of his duties by a government official or a person who performs public functions for the purpose of illicitly obtaining benefits for himself or for a third party;
   d. The fraudulent use or concealment of property derived from any of the acts referred to in this article; and
   e. Participation as a principal, co-principal, instigator, accomplice or accessory after the fact, or in any other manner, in the commission or attempted commission of, or in any collaboration or conspiracy to commit, any of the acts referred to in this article.

2. This Convention shall also be applicable by mutual agreement between or among two or more States Parties with respect to any other act of corruption not described herein.

Article VII

Domestic Law

The States Parties that have not yet done so shall adopt the necessary legislative or other measures to establish as criminal offenses under their domestic law the acts of corruption described in Article VI(1) and to facilitate cooperation among themselves pursuant to this Convention.

Article VIII

Transnational Bribery

Subject to its Constitution and the fundamental principles of its legal system, each State Party shall prohibit and punish the offering or granting, directly or indirectly, by its nationals, persons having their habitual residence in its territory, and businesses domiciled there, to a government official of another State, of any article of monetary value, or other benefit, such as a gift, favor, promise or advantage, in connection with any economic or commercial transaction in exchange for any act or omission in the performance of that official's public functions.

Among those States Parties that have established transnational bribery as an offense, such offense shall be considered an act of corruption for the purposes of this Convention.

Any State Party that has not established transnational bribery as an offense shall, insofar as its laws permit, provide assistance and cooperation with respect to this offense as provided in this Convention.

Article IX

Illicit Enrichment

Subject to its Constitution and the fundamental principles of its legal system, each State Party that has not yet done so shall take the necessary measures to establish under its laws as an offense a significant increase in the assets of a government official that he cannot reasonably explain in relation to his lawful earnings during the performance of his functions.

Among those States Parties that have established illicit enrichment as an offense, such offense shall be considered an act of corruption for the purposes of this Convention.

Any State Party that has not established illicit enrichment as an offense shall, insofar as its laws permit, provide assistance and cooperation with respect to this offense as provided in this Convention.

Article X

Notification

When a State Party adopts the legislation referred to in paragraph 1 of articles VIII and IX, it shall notify the Secretary General of the Organization of American States, who shall in turn notify the other States Parties. For the purposes of this Convention, the crimes of transnational bribery and illicit enrichment shall be considered acts of corruption for that State Party thirty days following the date of such notification.

Article XI

Progressive Development

1. In order to foster the development and harmonization of their domestic legislation and the attainment of the purposes of this Convention, the States Parties view as desirable, and undertake to consider, establishing as offenses under their laws the following acts:
   a. The improper use by a government official or a person who performs public functions, for his own benefit or that of a third party, of any kind of classified or confidential information which that official or person who performs public functions has obtained because of, or in the performance of, his functions;

b. The improper use by a government official or a person who performs public functions, for his own benefit or that of a third party, of any kind of property belonging to the State or to any firm or institution in which the State has a proprietary interest, to which that official or person who performs public functions has access because of, or in the performance of, his functions;
c. Any act or omission by any person who, personally or through a third party, or acting as an intermediary, seeks to obtain a decision from a public authority whereby he illicitly obtains for himself or for another person any benefit or gain, whether or not such act or omission harms State property; and
d. The diversion by a government official, for purposes unrelated to those for which they were intended, for his own benefit or that of a third party, of any movable or immovable property, monies or securities belonging to the State, to an independent agency, or to an individual, that such official has received by virtue of his position for purposes of administration, custody or for other reasons.

2. Among those States Parties that have established these offenses, such offenses shall be considered acts of corruption for the purposes of this Convention.
3. Any State Party that has not established these offenses shall, insofar as its laws permit, provide assistance and cooperation with respect to these offenses as provided in this Convention.

Article XII
Effect on State Property

For application of this Convention, it shall not be necessary that the acts of corruption harm State property.

Article XIII
Extradition

1. This article shall apply to the offenses established by the States Parties in accordance with this Convention.
2. Each of the offenses to which this article applies shall be deemed to be included as an extraditable offense in any extradition treaty existing between or among the States Parties. The States Parties undertake to include such offenses as extraditable offenses in every extradition treaty to be concluded between or among them.
3. If a State Party that makes extradition conditional on the existence of a treaty receives a request for extradition from another State Party with which it does not have an extradition treaty, it may consider this Convention as the legal basis for extradition with respect to any offense to which this article applies.
4. States Parties that do not make extradition conditional on the existence of a treaty shall recognize offenses to which this article applies as extraditable offenses between themselves.
5. Extradition shall be subject to the conditions provided for by the law of the Requested State or by applicable extradition treaties, including the grounds on which the Requested State may refuse extradition.
6. If extradition for an offense to which this article applies is refused solely on the basis of the nationality of the person sought, or because the Requested State deems that it has jurisdiction over the offense, the Requested State shall submit the case to its competent authorities for the purpose of prosecution unless otherwise agreed with the Requesting State, and shall report the final outcome to the Requesting State in due course.
7. Subject to the provisions of its domestic law and its extradition treaties, the Requested State may, upon being satisfied that the circumstances so warrant and are urgent, and at the request of the Requesting State, take into custody a person whose extradition is sought and who is present in its territory, or take other appropriate measures to ensure his presence at extradition proceedings.

Article XIV
Assistance and Cooperation

1. In accordance with their domestic laws and applicable treaties, the States Parties shall afford one another the widest measure of mutual assistance by processing requests from authorities that, in conformity with their domestic laws, have the power to investigate or prosecute the acts of corruption described in this Convention, to obtain evidence and take other necessary action to facilitate legal proceedings and measures regarding the investigation or prosecution of acts of corruption.
2. The States Parties shall also provide each other with the widest measure of mutual technical cooperation on the most effective ways and means of preventing, detecting, investigating and punishing acts of corruption. To that end, they shall foster exchanges of experiences by way of agreements and meetings between competent bodies and institutions, and shall pay special attention to methods and procedures of citizen participation in the fight against corruption.

Article XV
Measures Regarding Property

1. In accordance with their applicable domestic laws and relevant treaties or other agreements that may be in force between or among them, the States Parties shall provide each other the broadest possible measure of assistance in the identification, tracing, freezing, seizure and forfeiture of property or proceeds obtained, derived from or used in the commission of offenses established in accordance with this Convention.
2. A State Party that enforces its own or another State Party's forfeiture judgment against property or proceeds described in paragraph 1 of this article shall dispose of the property or proceeds in accordance with its laws. To the extent permitted by a State Party's laws and upon such terms as it deems appropriate, it may transfer all or part of such property or proceeds to another State Party that assisted in the underlying investigation or proceedings.

Article XVI
Bank Secrecy

1. The Requested State shall not invoke bank secrecy as a basis for refusal to provide the assistance sought by the Requesting State. The Requested State shall apply this article in accordance with its domestic law, its procedural provisions, or bilateral or multilateral agreements with the Requesting State.
2. The Requesting State shall be obligated not to use any information received that is protected by bank secrecy for any purpose other than the proceeding for which that information was requested, unless authorized by the Requested State.

Article XVII
Nature of the Act

For the purposes of articles XIII, XIV, XV and XVI of this Convention, the fact that the property obtained or derived from an act of corruption was intended for political purposes, or that it is alleged that an act of corruption was committed for political motives or purposes, shall not suffice in and of itself to qualify the act as a political offense or as a common offense related to a political offense.

Article XVIII
Central Authorities

1. For the purposes of international assistance and cooperation provided under this Convention, each State Party may designate a central authority or may rely upon such central authorities as are provided for in any relevant treaties or other agreements.

2. The central authorities shall be responsible for making and receiving the requests for assistance and cooperation referred to in this Convention.
3. The central authorities shall communicate with each other directly for the purposes of this Convention.

Article XIX

Temporal Application

Subject to the constitutional principles and the domestic laws of each State and existing treaties between the States Parties, the fact that the alleged act of corruption was committed before this Convention entered into force shall not preclude procedural cooperation in criminal matters between the States Parties. This provision shall in no case affect the principle of non-retroactivity in criminal law, nor shall application of this provision interrupt existing statutes of limitations relating to crimes committed prior to the date of the entry into force of this Convention.

Article XX

Other Agreements or Practices

No provision of this Convention shall be construed as preventing the States Parties from engaging in mutual cooperation within the framework of other international agreements, bilateral or multilateral, currently in force or concluded in the future, or pursuant to any other applicable arrangement or practice.

Article XXI

Signature

This Convention is open for signature by the Member States of the Organization of American States.

Article XXII

Ratification

This Convention is subject to ratification. The instruments of ratification shall be deposited with the General Secretariat of the Organization of American States.

Article XXIII

Accession

This Convention shall remain open for accession by any other State. The instruments of accession shall be deposited with the General Secretariat of the Organization of American States.

Article XXIV

Reservations

The States Parties may, at the time of adoption, signature, ratification, or accession, make reservations to this Convention, provided that each reservation concerns one or more specific provisions and is not incompatible with the object and purpose of the Convention.

Article XXV

Entry Into Force

This Convention shall enter into force on the thirtieth day following the date of deposit of the second instrument of ratification. For each State ratifying or acceding to the Convention after the deposit of the second instrument of ratification, the Convention shall enter into force on the thirtieth day after deposit by such State of its instrument of ratification or accession.

Article XXVI

Denunciation

This Convention shall remain in force indefinitely, but any of the States Parties may denounce it. The instrument of denunciation shall be deposited with the General Secretariat of the

Organization of American States. One year from the date of deposit of the instrument of denunciation, the Convention shall cease to be in force for the denouncing State, but shall remain in force for the other States Parties.

Article XXVII
Additional Protocols

Any State Party may submit for the consideration of other States Parties meeting at a General Assembly of the Organization of American States draft additional protocols to this Convention to contribute to the attainment of the purposes set forth in Article II thereof.

Each additional protocol shall establish the terms for its entry into force and shall apply only to those States that become Parties to it.

Article XXVIII
Deposit of Original Instrument

The original instrument of this Convention, the English, French, Portuguese, and Spanish texts of which are equally authentic, shall be deposited with the General Secretariat of the Organization of American States, which shall forward an authenticated copy of its text to the Secretariat of the United Nations for registration and publication in accordance with Article 102 of the United Nations Charter. The General Secretariat of the Organization of American States shall notify its Member States and the States that have acceded to the Convention of signatures, of the deposit of instruments of ratification, accession, or denunciation, and of reservations, if any.

APPENDIX 25

The OECD Guidelines for Multinational Enterprises, Revision 2000

Pursuant to Article 1 of the Convention signed in Paris on 14th December 1960, and which came into force on 30th September 1961, the Organisation for Economic Co-operation and Development (OECD) shall promote policies designed:

— to achieve the highest sustainable economic growth and employment and a rising standard of living in Member countries, while maintaining financial stability, and thus to contribute to the development of the world economy;

— to contribute to sound economic expansion in Member as well as non-member countries in the process of economic development; and

— to contribute to the expansion of world trade on a multilateral, non-discriminatory basis in accordance with international obligations.

The original Member countries of the OECD are Austria, Belgium, Canada, Denmark, France, Germany, Greece, Iceland, Ireland, Italy, Luxembourg, the Netherlands, Norway, Portugal, Spain, Sweden, Switzerland, Turkey, the United Kingdom and the United States. The following countries became Members subsequently through accession at the dates indicated hereafter: Japan (28th April 1964), Finland (28th January 1969), Australia (7th June 1971), New Zealand (29th May 1973), Mexico (18th May 1994), the Czech Republic (21st December 1995), Hungary (7th May 1996), Poland (22nd November 1996) and Korea (12th December 1996). The Commission of the European Communities takes part in the work of the OECD (Article 13 of the OECD Convention).

Foreword

I want to express my gratitude for the efforts of all those who have contributed over the past two years to the important work of revising the OECD Guidelines for Multinational Enterprises: the government delegates to the OECD Committee on International Investment and Multinational Enterprises and its Working Group on the Guidelines; the OECD Business and Industry Advisory Committee (BIAC) and the OECD Trade Union Advisory Committee (TUAC), who worked with their constituencies to ensure that the review benefited fully from the views of business and labour; the non-governmental organisations (NGOs) who participated in our process so it would better reflect the concerns of the citizens who are especially interested in our work. All of these participants have demonstrated their commitment to forge a forward-looking set of Guidelines that will be broadly supported in the years and decades ahead.

The theme of the OECD Ministerial level meeting that approved the revised Guidelines was 'Shaping Globalisation'. The integration of national economies into one global economy is accelerating and intensifying, driven by new technologies and new opportunities. These new opportunities are not only to reap profit, but also to stimulate development and improved social conditions around the world. The revised Guidelines will be an important instrument for shaping globalisation. They provide a government-backed standard of good corporate conduct that will help to level the playing field between competitors in the international market place. They will also be a standard that corporations themselves can use to demonstrate that they are indeed important agents of positive change throughout the developing as well as the developed world.

I also believe that the revised Guidelines for Multinational Enterprises are an example of the type of multilateral instrument that will be used more and more to set a rules-based, values-based framework for globalisation. It is true that the Guidelines are not legally binding. But they enjoy a number of important advantages over multilateral conventions: notably, the Guidelines were negotiated relatively quickly and they set a high standard, reflecting our values and aspirations. At the same time, they are meant to work and include procedures for implementation, follow-up and monitoring. Through such serious political commitments governments, working with business, labour and other representatives of civil society, can chart the directions that the global community wishes for global economic development.

I am very gratified that four countries that are not Members of OECD—Argentina, Brazil, Chile and the Slovak Republic—have declared their adherence to the Guidelines as part of the OECD Declaration on International Investment and Multinational Enterprises. All adhering governments look forward to seeing other countries join with them to reap the benefits of international co-operation in this field.

Donald J. Johnston
Secretary-General of the OECD

Statement by the Chair of the Ministerial, June 2000

Over the past two years, OECD has conducted a major review of its *Guidelines for Multinational Enterprises* to ensure their continued relevance and effectiveness in the rapidly changing global economy. I am pleased to announce that, today, the governments of 29 member countries and four non-members—Argentina, Brazil, Chile and the Slovak Republic—have adopted a new set of *Guidelines* and enhanced implementation procedures.

The *Guidelines* are recommendations on responsible business conduct addressed by governments to multinational enterprises operating in or from the 33 adhering countries. While many businesses have developed their own codes of conduct in recent years, the OECD *Guidelines* are the only multilaterally endorsed and comprehensive code that governments are committed to promoting. The *Guidelines* express the shared values of the governments of countries that are the source of most of the world's direct investment flows and home to most multinational enterprises. They apply to business operations world-wide.

This initiative is very timely. It is widely recognised that foreign investment is important for economic growth and that multinational enterprises contribute to economic, social and environmental progress. At the same time, public concerns remain about the impact of their activities on home and host countries. The new *Guidelines* represent an important step in responding to some of these concerns while improving the climate for international investment. The basic premise of the *Guidelines* is that principles agreed internationally can help prevent conflict and to build an atmosphere of confidence between multinational enterprises and the societies in which they operate.

The *Guidelines* are not a substitute for, nor do they override, applicable law. They represent standards of behaviour supplemental to applicable law and, as such, do not create conflicting requirements.

The new text of the *Guidelines* contains far-reaching changes that reinforce the economic, social and environmental elements of the sustainable development agenda. Recommendations have been added on the elimination of child labour and forced labour, so they now cover all internationally recognised core labour standards. A recommendation on human rights has been introduced, and new chapters on combating corruption and consumer protection have been added. The environment section now encourages multinational enterprises to raise their environmental performance through improved internal environmental management and better contingency planning for environmental impacts. The chapter on disclosure and transparency has been updated to reflect the OECD *Principles on Corporate Governance* and to encourage social and environmental accountability.

Implementation procedures have been significantly improved. While the *Guidelines*' recommendations are addressed to business, governments through their network of National Contact Points are responsible for promoting the *Guidelines*, handling enquiries and helping to resolve issues that arise in specific instances. The Review has provided considerable guidance to help National Contact Points to carry out their duties and it has established mechanisms for promoting transparency, accountability and best practice. The OECD Committee on International Investment and Multinational Enterprises (CIME) remains the responsible body for clarifying the meaning of the Guidelines and overseeing their effectiveness.

The review process itself deserves special mention. The CIME conducted an extensive series of consultations with the business community, labour representatives, non-governmental organisations and non-member countries. Opportunities for public comment were offered via the Internet. This effort towards increased ransparency and openness provided essential inputs for the Review and reflects in important evolution in the way OECD goes about its business.

For decades, the OECD has promoted co-operation on international investment through its Declaration on International Investment and Multinational Enterprises. The Declaration sets forth non-binding principles and standards addressed both to governments and to enterprises. The *Guidelines*, which are addressed to enterprises, remain an important part of this balanced package and contribute to a favourable investment climate. The other elements of the package contain commitments by governments to provide national treatment for foreign-controlled enterprises, to avoid imposing conflicting requirements on enterprises and to co-operate regarding investment incentives and disincentives. Non-OECD members are encouraged to adhere to this Declaration.

As a final point, I would like to emphasise that the task of making the *Guidelines* a meaningful instrument for the international business community has only just begun. The ongoing support and involvement of thc business community, labour representatives and non-governmental organisations will be crucial if the revised *Guidelines* are to be a useful reference point and tool for promoting corporate social responsibility. Nonadhering governments too have an important contribution to make. Ultimately, the success and effectiveness of the *Guidelines* will depend on the responsibility and good faith of all parties involved with their promotion and implementation.

The Honourable Peter Costello, M.P.,
Treasurer of the Commonwealth of Australia

Extract from the final news release at the Ministerial, June 2000

26. Ministers welcomed the updated Guidelines for Multinational Enterprises adopted by OECD governments together with those of Argentina, Brazil, Chile and the Slovak Republic. The Guidelines provide a robust set of recommendations for responsible corporate behaviour worldwide consistent with existing legislation. They are part of the OECD Declaration on International Investment and Multinational Enterprises which provides a balanced framework to improve the international investment climate and encourage the positive contributions multinational enterprises can make to economic, social and environmental goals. The Guidelines have been developed in constructive dialogue with the business community, labour representatives and non-governmental organisations and represent an important step in addressing some of the public concerns over globalisation. Effective implementation will depend upon the responsibility and good faith of all concerned: governments, business and labour organisations and other interested parties all have a role to play.

27. OECD will continue its analytical work in the field of investment policy, including work on maximising the benefits of investment liberalisation, its social and environmental dimensions and on harmful forms of policy-based competition to attract investment. OECD will encourage non-members to adhere to the Declaration on International Investment and Multinational Enterprises.

TABLE OF CONTENTS

DECLARATION ON INTERNATIONAL INVESTMENT AND MULTINATIONAL ENTERPRISES

27 June 2000

Adhering Governments[1]

Considering:

That international investment is of major importance to the world economy, and has considerably contributed to the development of their countries;

That multinational enterprises play an important role in this investment process;

That international co-operation can improve the foreign investment climate, encourage the positive contribution which multinational enterprises can make to economic, social and environmental progress, and minimise and resolve difficulties which may arise from their operations;

[1] As at 27 June 2000 adhering governments are those of all OECD Members, as well as Argentina, Brazil, Chile and the Slovak Republic. The European Community has been invited to associate itself with the section on National Treatment on matters falling within its competence.

That the benefits of international co-operation are enhanced by addressing issues relating to international investment and multinational enterprises through a balanced framework of inter-related instruments;

Declare:

I. Guidelines for Multinational Enterprises

That they jointly recommend to multinational enterprises operating in or from their territories the observance of the Guidelines, set forth in Annex I hereto,[2] having regard to the considerations and understandings that are set out in the Preface and are an integral part of them;

II. National Treatment

1. That adhering governments should, consistent with their needs to maintain public order, to protect their essential security interests and to fulfil commitments relating to international peace and security, accord to enterprises operating in their territories and owned or controlled directly or indirectly by nationals of another adhering government (hereinafter referred to as 'Foreign-Controlled Enterprises') treatment under their laws, regulations and administrative practices, consistent with international law and no less favourable than that accorded in like situations to domestic enterprises (hereinafter referred to as 'National Treatment');

2. That adhering governments will consider applying 'National Treatment' in respect of countries other than adhering governments;

3. That adhering governments will endeavour to ensure that their territorial subdivisions apply 'National Treatment';

4. That this Declaration does not deal with the right of adhering governments to regulate the entry of foreign investment or the conditions of establishment of foreign enterprises;

III. Conflicting Requirements

That they will co-operate with a view to avoiding or minimizing the imposition of conflicting requirements on multinational enterprises and that they will take into account the general considerations and practical approaches.[3]

IV. International Investment Incentives and Disincentives

1. That they recognise the need to strengthen their co-operation in the field of international direct investment;

2. That they thus recognise the need to give due weight to the interests of adhering governments affected by specific laws, regulations and administrative practices in this field (hereinafter called 'measures') providing official incentives and disincentives to international direct investment;

3. That adhering governments will endeavour to make such measures as transparent as possible, so that their importance and purpose can be ascertained and that information on them can be readily available;

V. Consultation Procedures

That they are prepared to consult one another on the above matters in conformity with the relevant Decisions of the Council;

---

[2] The text of the Guidelines for Multinational Enterprises is reproduced in Part I of this Booklet.

[3] The text of General considerations and Practical Approaches concerning Conflicting Requirements Imposed on Multinational Enterprises is available from the OECD Website http://www.oecd.org/daf/investment/guidelines/conflict.htm.

VI. Review

That they will review the above matters periodically with a view to improving the effectiveness of international economic co-operation among adhering governments on issues relating to international investment and multinational enterprises.

Part 1 The OECD Guidelines for Multinational Enterprises

Preface

1. The OECD *Guidelines for Multinational Enterprises* (the *Guidelines*) are recommendations addressed by governments to multinational enterprises. They provide voluntary principles and standards for responsible business conduct consistent with applicable laws. The *Guidelines* aim to ensure that the operations of these enterprises are in harmony with government policies, to strengthen the basis of mutual confidence between enterprises and the societies in which they operate, to help improve the foreign investment climate and to enhance the contribution to sustainable development made by multinational enterprises. The *Guidelines* are part of the OECD *Declaration on International Investment and Multinational Enterprises* the other elements of which relate to national treatment, conflicting requirements on enterprises, and international investment incentives and disincentives.

2. International business has experienced far-reaching structural change and the *Guidelines* themselves have evolved to reflect these changes. With the rise of service and knowledge-intensive industries, service and technology enterprises have entered the international marketplace. Large enterprises still account for a major share of international investment, and there is a trend toward large-scale international mergers. At the same time, foreign investment by small- and medium-sized enterprises has also increased and these enterprises now play a significant role on the international scene. Multinational enterprises, like their domestic counterparts, have evolved to encompass a broader range of business arrangements and organizational forms. Strategic alliances and closer relations with suppliers and contractors tend to blur the boundaries of the enterprise.

3. The rapid evolution in the structure of multinational enterprises is also reflected in their operations in the developing world, where foreign direct investment has grown rapidly. In developing countries, multinational enterprises have diversified beyond primary production and extractive industries into manufacturing, assembly, domestic market development and services.

4. The activities of multinational enterprises, through international trade and investment, have strengthened and deepened the ties that join OECD economies to each other and to the rest of the world. These activities bring substantial benefits to home and host countries. These benefits accrue when multinational enterprises supply the products and services that consumers want to buy at competitive prices and when they provide fair returns to suppliers of capital. Their trade and investment activities contribute to the efficient use of capital, technology and human and natural resources. They facilitate the transfer of technology among the regions of the world and the development of technologies that reflect local conditions. Through both formal training and on-the-job learning enterprises also promote the development of human capital in host countries.

5. The nature, scope and speed of economic changes have presented new strategic challenges for enterprises and their stakeholders. Multinational enterprises have the opportunity to implement best practice policies for sustainable development that seek to ensure coherence between social, economic and environmental objectives. The ability of multinational enterprises to promote sustainable development is greatly enhanced when trade and investment are conducted in a context of open, competitive and appropriately regulated markets.

6. Many multinational enterprises have demonstrated that respect for high standards of business conduct can enhance growth. Today's competitive forces are intense and multinational enterprises face a variety of legal, social and regulatory settings. In this context, some enterprises may be

tempted to neglect appropriate standards and principles of conduct in an attempt to gain undue competitive advantage. Such practices by the few may call into question the reputation of the many and may give rise to public concerns.

7. Many enterprises have responded to these public concerns by developing internal programmes, guidance and management systems that underpin their commitment to good corporate citizenship, good practices and good business and employee conduct. Some of them have called upon consulting, auditing and certification services, contributing to the accumulation of expertise in these areas. These efforts have also promoted social dialogue on what constitutes good business conduct. The *Guidelines* clarify the shared expectations for business conduct of the governments adhering to them and provide a point of reference for enterprises. Thus, the *Guidelines* both complement and reinforce private efforts to define and implement responsible business conduct.

8. Governments are co-operating with each other and with other actors to strengthen the international legal and policy framework in which business is conducted. The post-war period has seen the development of this framework, starting with the adoption in 1948 of the Universal Declaration of Human Rights. Recent instruments include the ILO Declaration on Fundamental Principles and Rights at Work, the Rio Declaration on Environment and Development and Agenda 21 and the Copenhagen Declaration for Social Development.

9. The OECD has also been contributing to the international policy framework. Recent developments include the adoption of the Convention on Combating Bribery of Foreign Public Officials in International Business Transactions and of the OECD Principles of Corporate Governance, the OECD Guidelines for Consumer Protection in the Context of Electronic Commerce, and ongoing work on the OECD Guidelines on Transfer Pricing for Multinational Enterprises and Tax Administrations.

10. The common aim of the governments adhering to the *Guidelines* is to encourage the positive contributions that multinational enterprises can make to economic, environmental and social progress and to minimise the difficulties to which their various operations may give rise. In working towards this goal, governments find themselves in partnership with the many businesses, trade unions and other non-governmental organisations that are working in their own ways toward the same end. Governments can help by providing effective domestic policy frameworks that include stable macroeconomic policy, non-discriminator treatment of firms, appropriate regulation and prudential supervision, an impartial system of courts and law enforcement and efficient and honest public administration. Governments can also help by maintaining and promoting appropriate standards and policies in support of sustainable development and by engaging in ongoing reforms to ensure that public sector activity is efficient and effective. Governments adhering to the *Guidelines* are committed to continual improvement of both domestic and international policies with a view to improving the welfare and living standards of all people.

I. Concepts and Principles

1. The *Guidelines* are recommendations jointly addressed by governments to multinational enterprises. They provide principles and standards of good practice consistent with applicable laws. Observance of the *Guidelines* by enterprises is voluntary and not legally enforceable.

2. Since the operations of multinational enterprises extend throughout the world, international co-operation in this field should extend to all countries. Governments adhering to the *Guidelines* encourage the enterprises operating on their territories to observe the *Guidelines* wherever they operate, while taking into account the particular circumstances of each host country.

3. A precise definition of multinational enterprises is not required for the purposes of the *Guidelines*. These usually comprise companies or other entities established in more than one country and so linked that they may co-ordinate their operations in various ways. While one or

more of these entities may be able to exercise a significant influence over the activities of others, their degree of autonomy within the enterprise may vary widely from one multinational enterprise to another. Ownership may be private, state or mixed. The *Guidelines* are addressed to all the entities within the multinational enterprise (parent companies and/or local entities). According to the actual distribution of responsibilities among them, the different entities are expected to co-operate and to assist one another to facilitate observance of the *Guidelines.*

4. The *Guidelines* are not aimed at introducing differences of treatment between multinational and domestic enterprises; they reflect good practice for all. Accordingly, multinational and domestic enterprises are subject to the same expectations in respect of their conduct wherever the *Guidelines* are relevant to both.

5. Governments wish to encourage the widest possible observance of the *Guidelines.* While it is acknowledged that small- and medium-sized enterprises may not have the same capacities as larger enterprises, governments adhering to the *Guidelines* nevertheless encourage them to observe the *Guidelines* recommendations to the fullest extent possible.

6. Governments adhering to the *Guidelines* should not use them for protectionist purposes nor use them in a way that calls into question the comparative advantage of any country where multinational enterprises invest.

7. Governments have the right to prescribe the conditions under which multinational enterprises operate within their jurisdictions, subject to international law. The entities of a multinational enterprise located in various countries are subject to the laws applicable in these countries. When multinational enterprises are subject to conflicting requirements by adhering countries, the governments concerned will co-operate in good faith with a view to resolving problems that may arise.

8. Governments adhering to the *Guidelines* set them forth with the understanding that they will fulfil their responsibilities to treat enterprises equitably and in accordance with international law and with their contractual obligations.

9. The use of appropriate international dispute settlement mechanisms, including arbitration, is encouraged as a means of facilitating the resolution of legal problems arising between enterprises and host country governments.

10. Governments adhering to the *Guidelines* will promote them and encourage their use. They will establish National Contact Points that promote the *Guidelines* and act as a forum for discussion of all matters relating to the *Guidelines.* The adhering Government will also participate in appropriate review and consultation procedures to address issues concerning interpretation of the *Guidelines* in a changing world.

II. General Policies

Enterprises should take fully into account established policies in the countries in which they operate, and consider the views of other stakeholders. In this regard, enterprises should:

1. Contribute to economic, social and environmental progress with a view to achieving sustainable development.

2. Respect the human rights of those affected by their activities consistent with the host government's international obligations and commitments.

3. Encourage local capacity building through close co-operation with the local community, including business interests, as well as developing the enterprise's activities in domestic and foreign markets, consistent with the need for sound commercial practice.

4. Encourage human capital formation, in particular by creating employment opportunities and facilitating training opportunities for employees.

5. Refrain from seeking or accepting exemptions not contemplated in the statutory or regulatory framework related to environmental, health, safety, labour, taxation, financial incentives, or other issues.

6. Support and uphold good corporate governance principles and develop and apply good corporate governance practices.

7. Develop and apply effective self-regulatory practices and management systems that foster a relationship of confidence and mutual trust between enterprises and the societies in which they operate.

8. Promote employee awareness of, and compliance with, company policies through appropriate dissemination of these policies, including through training programmes.

9. Refrain from discriminatory or disciplinary action against employees who make *bona fide* reports to management or, as appropriate, to the competent public authorities, on practices that contravene the law, the *Guidelines* or the enterprise's policies.

10. Encourage, where practicable, business partners, including suppliers and subcontractors, to apply principles of corporate conduct compatible with the *Guidelines*.

11. Abstain from any improper involvement in local political activities.

III. Disclosure

1. Enterprises should ensure that timely, regular, reliable and relevant information is disclosed regarding their activities, structure, financial situation and performance. This information should be disclosed for the enterprise as a whole and, where appropriate, along business lines or geographic areas. Disclosure policies of enterprises should be tailored to the nature, size and location of the enterprise, with due regard taken of costs, business confidentiality and other competitive concerns.

2. Enterprises should apply high quality standards for disclosure, accounting, and audit. Enterprises are also encouraged to apply high quality standards for nonfinancial information including environmental and social reporting where they exist. The standards or policies under which both financial and non-financial information are compiled and published should be reported.

3. Enterprises should disclose basic information showing their name, location, and structure, the name, address and telephone number of the parent enterprise and its main affiliates, its percentage ownership, direct and indirect in these affiliates, including shareholdings between them.

4. Enterprises should also disclose material information on:
a) The financial and operating results of the company.
b) Company objectives.
c) Major share ownership and voting right.
d) Members of the board and key executives, and their remuneration.
e) Material foreseeable risk factors.
f) Material issues regarding employees and other stakeholders.
g) Governance structures and policies.

5. Enterprises are encouraged to communicate additional information that could include:
a) Value statements or statements of business conduct intended for public disclosure including information on the social, ethical and environmental policies of the enterprise and other codes of conduct to which the company subscribes. In addition, the date of adoption, the countries and entities to which such statements apply and its performance in relation to these statements may be communicated.

b) Information on systems for managing risks and complying with laws, and on statements or codes of business conduct.
c) Information on relationships with employees and other stakeholders.

IV. Employment and Industrial Relations

Enterprises should, within the framework of applicable law, regulations and prevailing labour relations and employment practices:

1. a) Respect the right of their employees to be represented by trade unions and other bona fide representatives of employees, and engage in constructive negotiations, either individually or through employers' associations, with such representatives with a view to reaching agreements on employment conditions;
   b) Contribute to the effective abolition of child labour.
   c) Contribute to the elimination of all forms of forced or compulsory labour.
   d) Not discriminate against their employees with respect to employment or occupation on such grounds as race, colour, sex, religion, political opinion, national extraction or social origin, unless selectivity concerning employee characteristics furthers established governmental policies which specifically promote greater equality of employment opportunity or relates to the inherent requirements of a job.

2. a) Provide facilities to employee representatives as may be necessary to assist in the development of effective collective agreements.
   b) Provide information to employee representatives which is needed for meaningful negotiations on conditions of employment.
   c) Promote consultation and co-operation between employers and employees and their representatives on matters of mutual concern.

3. Provide information to employees and their representatives which enables them to obtain a true and fair view of the performance of the entity or, where appropriate, the enterprise as a whole.

4. a) Observe standards of employment and industrial relations not less favourable than those observed by comparable employers in the host country.
   b) Take adequate steps to ensure occupational health and safety in their operations.

5. In their operations, to the greatest extent practicable, employ local personnel and provide training with a view to improving skill levels, in co-operation with employee representatives and, where appropriate, relevant governmental authorities.

6. In considering changes in their operations which would have major effects upon the livelihood of their employees, in particular in the case of the closure of an entity involving collective lay-offs or dismissals, provide reasonable notice of such changes to representatives of their employees, and, where appropriate, to the relevant governmental authorities, and co-operate with the employee representatives and appropriate governmental authorities so as to mitigate to the maximum extent practicable adverse effects. In light of the specific circumstances of each case, it would be appropriate if management were able to give such notice prior to the final decision being taken. Other means may also be employed to provide meaningful co-operation to mitigate the effects of such decisions.

7. In the context of bona fide negotiations with representatives of employees on conditions of employment, or while employees are exercising a right to organise, not threaten to transfer the whole or part of an operating unit from the country concerned nor transfer employees from the enterprises' component entities in other countries in order to influence unfairly those negotiations or to hinder the exercise of a right to organise.

8. Enable authorised representatives of their employees to negotiate on collective bargaining or labour-management relations issues and allow the parties to consult on matters of mutual

concern with representatives of management who are authorised to take decisions on these matters.

V. Environment

Enterprises should, within the framework of laws, regulations and administrative practices in the countries in which they operate, and in consideration of relevant international agreements, principles, objectives, and standards, take due account of the need to protect the environment, public health and safety, and generally to conduct their activities in a manner contributing to the wider goal of sustainable development. In particular, enterprises should:

1. Establish and maintain a system of environmental management appropriate to the enterprise, including:

a) Collection and evaluation of adequate and timely information regarding the environmental, health, and safety impacts of their activities.
b) Establishment of measurable objectives and, where appropriate, targets for improved environmental performance, including periodically reviewing the continuing relevance of these objectives; and
c) Regular monitoring and verification of progress toward environmental, health, and safety objectives or targets.

2. Taking into account concerns about cost, business confidentiality, and the protection of intellectual property rights:

a) Provide the public and employees with adequate and timely information on the potential environment, health and safety impacts of the activities of the enterprise, which could include reporting on progress in improving environmental performance; and
b) Engage in adequate and timely communication and consultation with the communities directly affected by the environmental, health and safety policies of the enterprise and by their implementation.

3. Assess, and address in decision-making, the foreseeable environmental, health, and safety-related impacts associated with the processes, goods and services of the enterprise over their full life cycle. Where these proposed activities may have significant environmental, health, or safety impacts, and where they are subject to a decision of a competent authority, prepare an appropriate environmental impact assessment.

4. Consistent with the scientific and technical understanding of the risks, where there are threats of serious damage to the environment, taking also into account human health and safety, not use the lack of full scientific certainty as a reason for postponing cost-effective measures to prevent or minimise such damage.

5. Maintain contingency plans for preventing, mitigating, and controlling serious environmental and health damage from their operations, including accidents and emergencies; and mechanisms for immediate reporting to the competent authorities.

6. Continually seek to improve corporate environmental performance, by encouraging, where appropriate, such activities as:

a) Adoption of technologies and operating procedures in all parts of the enterprise that reflect standards concerning environmental performance in the best performing part of the enterprise.
b) Development and provision of products or services that have no undue environmental impacts; are safe in their intended use; are efficient in their consumption of energy and natural resources; can be reused, recycled, or disposed of safely.
c) Promoting higher levels of awareness among customers of the environmental implications of using the products and services of the enterprise; and

d) Research on ways of improving the environmental performance of the enterprise over the longer term.

7. Provide adequate education and training to employees in environmental health and safety matters, including the handling of hazardous materials and the prevention of environmental accidents, as well as more general environmental management areas, such as environmental impact assessment procedures, public relations, and environmental technologies.

8. Contribute to the development of environmentally meaningful and economically efficient public policy, for example, by means of partnerships or initiatives that will enhance environmental awareness and protection.

VI. Combating Bribery

Enterprises should not, directly or indirectly, offer, promise, give, or demand a bribe or other undue advantage to obtain or retain business or other improper advantage. Nor should enterprises be solicited or expected to render a bribe or other undue advantage. In particular, enterprises should:

1. Not offer, nor give in to demands, to pay public officials or the employees of business partners any portion of a contract payment. They should not use subcontracts, purchase orders or consulting agreements as means of channeling payments to public officials, to employees of business partners or to their relatives or business associates.

2. Ensure that remuneration of agents is appropriate and for legitimate services only. Where relevant, a list of agents employed in connection with transactions with public bodies and state-owned enterprises should be kept and made available to competent authorities.

3. Enhance the transparency of their activities in the fight against bribery and extortion. Measures could include making public commitments against bribery and extortion and disclosing the management systems the company has adopted in order to honour these commitments. The enterprise should also foster openness and dialogue with the public so as to promote its awareness of and co-operation with the fight against bribery and extortion.

4. Promote employee awareness of and compliance with company policies against bribery and extortion through appropriate dissemination of these policies and through training programmes and disciplinary procedures.

5. Adopt management control systems that discourage bribery and corrupt practices, and adopt financial and tax accounting and auditing practices that prevent the establishment of 'off the books' or secret accounts or the creation of documents which do not properly and fairly record the transactions to which they relate.

6. Not make illegal contributions to candidates for public office or to political parties or to other political organisations. Contributions should fully comply with public disclosure requirements and should be reported to senior management.

VII. Consumer Interests

When dealing with consumers, enterprises should act in accordance with fair business, marketing and advertising practices and should take all reasonable steps to ensure the safety and quality of the goods or services they provide. In particular, they should:

1. Ensure that the goods or services they provide meet all agreed or legally required standards for consumer health and safety, including health warnings and product safety and information labels.

2. As appropriate to the goods or services, provide accurate and clear information regarding their content, safe use, maintenance, storage, and disposal sufficient to enable consumers to make informed decisions.

3. Provide transparent and effective procedures that address consumer complaints and contribute to fair and timely resolution of consumer disputes without undue cost or burden.

4. Not make representations or omissions, nor engage in any other practices, that are deceptive, misleading, fraudulent, or unfair.

5. Respect consumer privacy and provide protection for personal data.

6. Co-operate fully and in a transparent manner with public authorities in the prevention or removal of serious threats to public health and safety deriving from the consumption or use of their products.

VIII. Science and Technology

Enterprises should:

1. Endeavour to ensure that their activities are compatible with the science and technology (S&T) policies and plans of the countries in which they operate and as appropriate contribute to the development of local and national innovative capacity.

2. Adopt, where practicable in the course of their business activities, practices that permit the transfer and rapid diffusion of technologies and know-how, with due regard to the protection of intellectual property rights.

3. When appropriate, perform science and technology development work in host countries to address local market needs, as well as employ host country personnel in an S&T capacity and encourage their training, taking into account commercial needs.

4. When granting licenses for the use of intellectual property rights or when otherwise transferring technology, do so on reasonable terms and conditions and in a manner that contributes to the long term development prospects of the host country.

5. Where relevant to commercial objectives, develop ties with local universities, public research institutions, and participate in co-operative research projects with local industry or industry associations.

IX. Competition

Enterprises should, within the framework of applicable laws and regulations, conduct their activities in a competitive manner. In particular, enterprises should:

1. Refrain from entering into or carrying out anti-competitive agreements among competitors:
   a) To fix prices.
   b) To make rigged bids (collusive tenders).
   c) To establish output restrictions or quotas; or
   d) To share or divide markets by allocating customers, suppliers, territories or lines of commerce.

2. Conduct all of their activities in a manner consistent with all applicable competition laws, taking into account the applicability of the competition laws of jurisdictions whose economies would be likely to be harmed by anti-competitive activity on their part.

3. Co-operate with the competition authorities of such jurisdictions by, among other things and subject to applicable law and appropriate safeguards, providing as prompt and complete responses as practicable to requests for information.

4. Promote employee awareness of the importance of compliance with all applicable competition laws and policies.

X. Taxation

It is important that enterprises contribute to the public finances of host countries by making timely payment of their tax liabilities. In particular, enterprises should comply with the tax laws and regulations in all countries in which they operateand should exert every effort to act in accordance with both the letter and spirit of those laws and regulations. This would include such measures as providing to the relevant authorities the information necessary for the correct determination of taxes to be assessed in connection with their operations and conforming transfer pricing practices to the arm's length principle.

Part 2 Implementation Procedures of the OECD Guidelines for Multinational Enterprises

Decision of the OECD Council

June 2000

The Council,

Having regard to the Convention on the Organisation for Economic Co-operation and Development of 14th December 1960;

Having regard to the OECD Declaration on International Investment and Multinational Enterprises (the 'Declaration'), in which the Governments of adhering countries ('adhering countries') jointly recommend to multinational enterprises operating in or from their territories the observance of Guidelines for Multinational Enterprises (the 'Guidelines');

Recognising that, since operations of multinational enterprises extend throughout the world, international co-operation on issues relating to the Declaration should extend to all countries;

Having regard to the Terms of Reference of the Committee on International Investment and Multinational Enterprises, in particular with respect to its responsibilities for the Declaration [C(84)171(Final), renewed in C/M(95)21];

Considering the Report on the First Review of the 1976 Declaration [C(79)102(Final)], the Report on the Second Review of the Declaration [C/MIN(84)5(Final)], the Report on the 1991 Review of the Declaration [DAFFE/IME(91)23], and the Report on the 2000 Review of the Guidelines [C(2000)96];

Having regard to the Second Revised Decision of the Council of June 1984 [C(84)90], amended June 1991 [C/MIN(91)7/ANN1];

Considering it desirable to enhance procedures by which consultations may take place on matters covered by these Guidelines and to promote the effectiveness of the Guidelines;

On the proposal of the Committee on International Investment and Multinational Enterprises:

Decides:

To repeal the Second Revised Decision of the Council of June 1984 [C(84)90], amended June 1991 [C/MIN(91)7/ANN1], and replace it with the following:

I. National Contact Points

1. Adhering countries shall set up National Contact Points for undertaking promotional activities, handling inquiries and for discussions with the parties concerned on all matters covered by the Guidelines so that they can contribute to the solution of problems which may arise in this connection, taking due account of the attached Procedural Guidance. The business community, employee organisations, and other interested parties shall be informed of the availability of such facilities.

2. National Contact Points in different countries shall co-operate if such need arises, on any matter covered by the Guidelines relevant to their activities. As a general procedure, discussions at the national level should be initiated before contacts with other National Contact Points are undertaken.

3. National Contact Points shall meet annually to share experiences and report to the Committee on International Investment and Multinational Enterprises.

II. The Committee on International Investment and Multinational Enterprises

1. The Committee on International Investment and Multinational Enterprises ('CIME' or 'the Committee') shall periodically or at the request of an adhering country hold exchanges of views on matters covered by the Guidelines and the experience gained in their application.

2. The Committee shall periodically invite the Business and Industry Advisory Committee to the OECD (BIAC), and the Trade Union Advisory Committee to the OECD (TUAC) (the 'advisory bodies'), as well as other non-governmental organizations to express their views on matters covered by the Guidelines. In addition, exchanges of views with the advisory bodies on these matters may be held at their request.

3. The Committee may decide to hold exchanges of views on matters covered by the Guidelines with representatives of non-adhering countries.

4. The Committee shall be responsible for clarification of the Guidelines. Clarification will be provided as required. If it so wishes, an individual enterprise will be given the opportunity to express its views either orally or in writing on issues concerning the Guidelines involving its interests. The Committee shall not reach conclusions on the conduct of individual enterprises.

5. The Committee shall hold exchanges of views on the activities of National Contact Points with a view to enhancing the effectiveness of the Guidelines.

6. In fulfilling its responsibilities for the effective functioning of the Guidelines, the Committee shall take due account of the attached Procedural Guidance.

7. The Committee shall periodically report to the Council on matters covered by the Guidelines. In its reports, the Committee shall take account of reports by National Contact Points, the views expressed by the advisory bodies, and the views of other non-governmental organisations and non-adhering countries as appropriate.

III. Review of the Decision

This Decision shall be periodically reviewed. The Committee shall make proposals for this purpose.

Procedural Guidance

I. National Contact Points

The role of National Contact Points (NCP) is to further the effectiveness of the Guidelines. NCPs will operate in accordance with core criteria of visibility, accessibility, transparency and accountability to further the objective of functional equivalence.

A. Institutional Arrangements

Consistent with the objective of functional equivalence, adhering countries have flexibility in organising their NCPs, seeking the active support of social partners, including the business community, employee organisations, and other interested parties, which includes non-governmental organisations.

Accordingly, the National Contact Point:

1. May be a senior government official or a government office headed by a senior official. Alternatively, the National Contact Point may be organised as a co-operative body, including representatives of other government agencies. Representatives of the business community, employee organisations and other interested parties may also be included.

2. Will develop and maintain relations with representatives of the business community, employee organisations and other interested parties that are able to contribute to the effective functioning of the Guidelines.

B. Information and Promotion

National Contact Points will:

1. Make the Guidelines known and available by appropriate means, including through on-line information, and in national languages. Prospective investors (inward and outward) should be informed about the Guidelines, as appropriate.

2. Raise awareness of the Guidelines, including through co-operation, as appropriate, with the business community, employee organisations, other nongovernmental organisations, and the interested public.

3. Respond to enquiries about the Guidelines from:
   a) Other National Contact Points.
   b) The business community, employee organisations, other non-governmental organisations and the public; and
   c) Governments of non-adhering countries.

C. Implementation in Specific Instances

The NCP will contribute to the resolution of issues that arise relating to implementation of the Guidelines in specific instances. The NCP will offer a forum for discussion and assist the business community, employee organisations and other parties concerned to deal with the issues raised in an efficient and timely manner and in accordance with applicable law. In providing this assistance, the NCP will:

1. Make an initial assessment of whether the issues raised merit further examination and respond to the party or parties raising them.

2. Where the issues raised merit further examination, offer good offices to help the parties involved to resolve the issues. For this purpose, the NCP will consult with these parties and where relevant:
   a) Seek advice from relevant authorities, and/or representatives of the business community, employee organisations, other non-governmental organisations, and relevant experts.
   b) Consult the National Contact Point in the other country or countries concerned.
   c) Seek the guidance of the CIME if it has doubt about the interpretation of the Guidelines in particular circumstances.
   d) Offer, and with the agreement of the parties involved, facilitate access to consensual and non-adversarial means, such as conciliation or mediation, to assist in dealing with the issues.

3. If the parties involved do not reach agreement on the issues raised, issue a statement, and make recommendations as appropriate, on the implementation of the Guidelines.

4. a) In order to facilitate resolution of the issues raised, take appropriate steps to protect sensitive business and other information. While the procedures under paragraph 2 are underway, confidentiality of the proceedings will be maintained. At the conclusion of the procedures, if the parties involved have not agreed on a resolution of the issues raised, they are free to communicate about and discuss these issues. However, information and views

provided during the proceedings by another party involved will remain confidential, unless that other party agrees to their disclosure.

b) After consultation with the parties involved, make publicly available the results of these procedures unless preserving confidentiality would be in the best interests of effective implementation of the Guidelines.

5. If issues arise in non-adhering countries, take steps to develop an understanding of the issues involved, and follow these procedures where relevant and practicable.

D. Reporting

1. Each National Contact Point will report annually to the Committee.

2. Reports should contain information on the nature and results of the activities of the National Contact Point, including implementation activities in specific instances.

II. Committee on International Investment and Multinational Enterprises

1. The Committee will discharge its responsibilities in an efficient and timely manner.

2. The Committee will consider requests from NCPs for assistance in carrying out their activities, including in the event of doubt about the interpretation of the Guidelines in particular circumstances.

3. The Committee will:

a) Consider the reports of NCPs.

b) Consider a substantiated submission by an adhering country or an advisory body on whether an NCP is fulfilling its responsibilities with regard to its handling of specific instances.

c) Consider issuing a clarification where an adhering country or an advisory body makes a substantiated submission on whether an NCP has correctly interpreted the Guidelines in specific instances.

d) Make recommendations, as necessary, to improve the functioning of NCPs and the effective implementation of the Guidelines.

4. The Committee may seek and consider advice from experts on any matters relating to the Guidelines. For this purpose, the Committee will decide on suitable procedures.

Part 3 Commentaries

Note by the Secretariat: These commentaries have been prepared by the Committee on International Investment and Multinational Enterprises to provide information on and explanation of the *Guidelines* text and of the Council Decision on Implementation of the *Guidelines.* They are not part of the Declaration on International Investment and Multinational Enterprises or of the Council Decision on the *Guidelines for Multinational Enterprises.*

Commentary on the OECD Guidelines for Multinational Enterprises

Commentary on General Policies

1. The General Policies chapter of the *Guidelines* is the first to contain specific recommendations to enterprises. As such it is important for setting the tone and establishing common fundamental principles for the specific recommendations in subsequent chapters.

2. Obeying domestic law is the first obligation of business. The *Guidelines* are not a substitute for nor should they be considered to override local law and regulation. They represent supplementary principles and standards of behaviour of a non-legal character, particularly concerning the international operations of these enterprises. While the *Guidelines* extend beyond the law in many cases, they should not and are not intended to place an enterprise in a situation where it faces conflicting requirements.

3. Enterprises are encouraged to co-operate with governments in the development and implementation of policies and laws. Considering the views of other stakeholders in society, which includes the local community as well as business interests, can enrich this process. It is also recognised that governments should be transparent in their dealings with enterprises, and consult with business on these same issues. Enterprises should be viewed as partners with government in the development and use of both voluntary and regulatory approaches (of which the *Guidelines* are one element) to policies affecting them.

4. There should not be any contradiction between the activity of multinational enterprises (MNEs) and sustainable development, and the *Guidelines* are meant to foster complementarities in this regard. Indeed, links among economic, social, and environmental progress are a key means for furthering the goal of sustainable development.[4] On a related issue, while promoting and upholding human rights is primarily the responsibility of governments, where corporate conduct and human rights intersect enterprises do play a role, and thus MNEs are encouraged to respect human rights, not only in their dealings with employees, but also with respect to others affected by their activities, in a manner that is consistent with host governments' international obligations and commitments. The Universal Declaration of Human Rights and other human rights obligations of the government concerned are of particular relevance in this regard.

5. The *Guidelines* also acknowledge and encourage the contribution that MNEs can make to local capacity building as a result of their activities in local communities. Similarly, the recommendation on human capital formation is an explicit and forwardlooking recognition of the contribution to individual human development that MNEs can offer their employees, and encompasses not only hiring practices, but training and other employee development as well. Human capital formation also incorporates the notion of non-discrimination in hiring practices as well as promotion practices, life-long learning and other on-the-job training.

6. Governments recommend that, in general, enterprises avoid efforts to secure exemptions not contemplated in the statutory or regulatory framework related to environmental, health, safety, labour, taxation and financial incentives among other issues, without infringing on an enterprise's right to seek changes in the statutory or regulatory framework. The words 'or accepting' also draw attention to the role of the state in offering these exemptions. While this sort of provision has been traditionally directed at governments, it is also of direct relevance to MNEs. Importantly, however, there are instances where specific exemptions from laws or other policies can be consistent with these laws for legitimate public policy reasons. The environment and competition policy chapters are examples.

7. The paragraph devoted to the role of MNEs in corporate governance gives further impetus to the recently adopted OECD Principles of Corporate Governance. Although primary responsibility for improving the legal and institutional regulatory framework lies with governments, enterprises also have an interest in good governance.

8. An increasing network of non-governmental self-regulatory instruments and actions address aspects of corporate behaviour and the relationships between business and society. Enterprises recognise that their activities often have social and environmental implications. The institution of self-regulatory practices and management systems by enterprises sensitive to reaching these goals—thereby contributing to sustainable development—is an illustration of this. In turn, developing such practices can further constructive relationships between enterprises and the societies in which they operate.

9. Following from effective self-regulatory practices, as a matter of course, enterprises are expected to promote employee awareness of company policies. Safeguards to protect *bona fide*

[4] One of the most broadly accepted definitions of sustainable development is in the 1987 World Commission on Environment and Development (the Brundtland Commission): 'Development that meets the needs of the present without compromising the ability of future generations to meet their own needs'.

'whistle-blowing' activities are also recommended, including protection of employees who, in the absence of timely remedial action or in the face of reasonable risk of negative employment action, report practices that contravene the law to the competent public authorities. While of particular relevance to anti-bribery and environmental initiatives, such protection is also relevant to other recommendations in the *Guidelines*.

10. Encouraging, where practicable, compatible principles of corporate responsibility among business partners serves to combine a re-affirmation of the standards and principles embodied in the *Guidelines* with an acknowledgement of their importance to suppliers, contractors, sub-contractors, licensees and other entities with which MNEs enjoy a working relationship. It is recognised that there are practical limitations to the ability of enterprises to influence the conduct of their business partners. The extent of these limitations depends on sectoral, enterprise and product characteristics such as the number of suppliers or other business partners, the structure and complexity of the supply chain and the market position of the enterprise *vis-à-vis* its suppliers or other business partners. The influence enterprises may have on their suppliers or business partners is normally restricted to the category of products or services they are sourcing, rather than to the full range of activities of suppliers or business partners. Thus, the scope for influencing business partners and the supply chain is greater in some instances than in others. Established or direct business relationships are the major object of this recommendation rather than all individual or ad hoc contracts or transactions that are based solely on open market operations or client relationships. In cases where direct influence of business partners is not possible, the objective could be met by means of dissemination of general policy statements of the enterprise or membership in business federations that encourage business partners to apply principles of corporate conduct compatible with the Guidelines.

11. Finally, it is important to note that self-regulation and other initiatives in a similar vein, including the *Guidelines,* should not unlawfully restrict competition, nor should they be considered a substitute for effective law and regulation by governments. It is understood that MNEs should avoid potential trade or investment distorting effects of codes and self-regulatory practices when they are being developed.

Commentary on Disclosure

12. The purpose of this chapter is to encourage improved understanding of the operations of multinational enterprises. Clear and complete information on enterprises is important to a variety of users ranging from shareholders and the financial community to other constituencies such as employees, local communities, special interest groups, governments and society at large. To improve public understanding of enterprises and their interaction with society and the environment, enterprises should be transparent in their operations and responsive to the public's increasingly sophisticated demands for information. The information highlighted in this chapter may be a supplement to disclosure required under the national laws of the countries in which the enterprise operates.

13. This chapter addresses disclosure in two areas. The first set of disclosure recommendations is identical to disclosure items outlined in the *OECD Principles of Corporate Governance*. The *Principles* call for timely and accurate disclosure on all material matters regarding the corporation, including the financial situation, performance, ownership, and governance of the company. Companies are also expected to disclose sufficient information on the remuneration of board members and key executives (either individually or in the aggregate) for investors to properly assess the costs and benefits of remuneration plans and the contribution of incentive schemes, such as stock option schemes, to performance. The *Principles* contain annotations that provide further guidance on the required disclosures and the recommendations in the *Guidelines* should be construed in relation to these annotations. They focus on publicly traded companies. To the extent that they are deemed applicable, they should also be a useful tool to improve corporate governance in non-traded enterprises; for example, privately held and state owned enterprises.

14. The *Guidelines* also encourage a second set of disclosure or communication practices in areas where reporting standards are still emerging such as, for example, social, environmental, and risk reporting. Many enterprises provide information on a broader set of topics than financial performance and consider disclosure of such information a method by which they can demonstrate a commitment to socially acceptable practices. In some cases, this second type of disclosure—or communication with the public and with other parties directly affected by the firms' activities—may pertain to entities that extend beyond those covered in the enterprises' financial accounts. For example, it may also cover information on the activities of subcontractors and suppliers or of joint venture partners.

15. Many enterprises have adopted measures designed to help them comply with the law and standards of business conduct, and to enhance the transparency of their operations. A growing number of firms have issued voluntary codes of corporate conduct, which are expressions of commitments to ethical values in such areas as environment, labour standards or consumer protection. Specialised management systems are being developed with the aim of helping them respect these commitments—these involve information systems, operating procedures and training requirements. Enterprises are co-operating with NGOs and intergovernmental organisations in developing reporting standards that enhance enterprises' ability to communicate how their activities influence sustainable development outcomes (*e.g.* the Global Reporting Initiative).

16. The OECD *Principles of Corporate Governance* support the development of high quality internationally recognised standards of accounting, financial and non-financial disclosure, and audit, which can serve to improve the comparability of information among countries. Financial audits conducted by independent auditors provide external and objective assurance on the way in which financial statements have been pre pared and presented. The transparency and effectiveness of non-financial disclosure may be enhanced by independent verification. Techniques for independent verification of non-financial disclosure are emerging.

17. Enterprises are encouraged to provide easy and economical access to published information and to consider making use of information technologies to meet this goal. Information that is made available to users in home markets should also be available to all interested users. Enterprises may take special steps to make information available to communities that do not have access to printed media (*e.g.* poorer communities that are directly affected by the enterprise's activities).

18. Disclosure requirements are not expected to place unreasonable administrative or cost burdens on enterprises. Nor are enterprises expected to disclose information that may endanger their competitive position unless disclosure is necessary to fully inform the investment decision and to avoid misleading the investor.

Commentary on Employment and Industrial Relations

19. This chapter opens with a chapeau that includes a reference to 'applicable' law and regulations, which is meant to acknowledge the fact that multinational enterprises, while operating within the jurisdiction of particular countries, may be subject to *national, sub-national*, as well as *supra-national* levels of regulation of employment and industrial relations matters. The terms 'prevailing labour relations' and 'employment practices' are sufficiently broad to permit a variety of interpretations in light of different national circumstances—for example, different bargaining options provided for employees under national laws and regulations.

20. The International Labour Organisation (ILO) is the competent body to set and deal with international labour standards, and to promote fundamental rights at work as recognised in its 1998 Declaration on Fundamental Principles and Rights at Work. The *Guidelines*, as a non-binding instrument, have a role to play in promoting observance of these standards and principles among multinational enterprises. The provisions of the *Guidelines* chapter echo relevant provisions of the 1998 Declaration, as well as the ILO's 1977 Tripartite Declaration of Principles

concerning Multinational Enterprises and Social Policy. The Tripartite Declaration sets out principles in the fields of employment, training, working conditions, and industrial relations, while the OECD Guidelines cover all major aspects of corporate behaviour. The OECD Guidelines and the ILO Tripartite Declaration refer to the behaviour expected from enterprises and are intended to parallel and not conflict with each other. The ILO Tripartite Declaration can therefore be of use in understanding the *Guidelines* to the extent that it is of a greater degree of elaboration. However, the responsibilities for the follow-up procedures under the Tripartite Declaration and the *Guidelines* are institutionally separate.

21. The first paragraph of this chapter is designed to echo all four fundamental principles and rights at work which are contained in the ILO's 1998 Declaration, namely the freedom of association and right to collective bargaining, the effective abolition of child labour, the elimination of all forms of forced or compulsory labour, and non-discrimination in employment and occupation. These principles and rights have been developed in the form of specific rights and obligations in ILO Conventions recognised as fundamental.

22. The chapter recommends that multinational enterprises contribute to the effective abolition of child labour in the sense of the ILO 1998 Declaration and ILO Convention 182 concerning the worst forms of child labour. Long-standing ILO instruments on child labour are Convention 138 and Recommendation 146 (both adopted in 1973) concerning minimum ages for employment. Through their labour management practices, their creation of high quality, well paid jobs and their contribution to economic growth, multinational enterprises can play a positive role in helping to address the root causes of poverty in general and of child labour in particular. It is important to acknowledge and encourage the role of multinational enterprises in contributing to the search for a lasting solution to the problem of child labour. In this regard, raising the standards of education of children living in host countries is especially noteworthy.

23. The chapter also recommends that enterprises contribute to the elimination of all forms of compulsory labour, another principle derived from the 1998 ILO Declaration. The reference to this core labour right is based on the ILO Conventions 29 of 1930 and 105 of 1957. C. 29 requests that governments 'suppress the use of forced or compulsory labour in all its forms within the shortest possible period', while C. 105 requests of them to 'suppress and not to make use of any form of forced or compulsory labour' for certain enumerated purposes (*e.g.* as a means of political coercion or labour discipline), and 'to take effective measures to secure [its] immediate and complete abolition'. At the same time, it is understood that the ILO is the competent body to deal with the difficult issue of prison labour, in particular when it comes to the hiring-out of prisoners to (or their placing at the disposal of) private individuals, companies or associations.

24. The principle of non-discrimination with respect to employment and occupation is considered to apply to such terms and conditions as hiring, discharge, pay, promotion, training and retirement. The list of non-permissible grounds for discrimination which is taken from ILO Convention 111 of 1958 considers that any distinction, exclusion or preference on these grounds is in violation of the Convention. At the same time, the text makes clear that the terms do not constitute an exhaustive list. Consistent with the provisions in paragraph 1d), enterprises are expected to promote equal opportunities for women and men with special emphasis on equal criteria for selection, remuneration, and promotion, and equal application of those criteria, and prevent discrimination or dismissals on the grounds of marriage, pregnancy or parenthood.

25. The reference to consultative forms of employee participation in paragraph two of the *Guidelines* is taken from ILO Recommendation 94 of 1952 concerning Consultation and Co-operation between Employers and Workers at the Level of the Undertaking. It also conforms to a provision contained in the 1977 ILO Tripartite Declaration of Principles concerning Multinational Enterprises and Social Policy. Such consultative arrangements should not substitute for employees' right to bargain over terms and conditions of employment. A recommendation on

consultative arrangements with respect to employment arrangements is also part of paragraph eight.

26. In paragraph three of this chapter, information provided by companies to their employees is expected to provide a 'true and fair view' of performance. It relates to the following: the structure of the enterprise, its economic and financial situation and prospects, employment trends, and expected substantial changes in operations, taking into account legitimate requirements of business confidentiality. Considerations of business confidentiality may mean that information on certain points may not be provided, or may not be provided without safeguards.

27. In paragraph four, employment and industrial relations standards are understood to include compensation and working-time arrangements. The reference to occupational health and safety implies that MNEs are expected to follow prevailing regulatory standards and industry norms to minimise the risk of accidents and injury to health arising out of, linked with, or occurring in, the course of employment. This encourages enterprises to work to raise the level of performance with respect to occupational health and safety in all parts of their operation even where this may not be formally required by existing regulations in countries in which they operate. It also encourages enterprises to respect employees' ability to remove themselves from a work situation when there is reasonable justification to believe that it presents an imminent and serious risk to health or safety. Reflecting their importance and complementarities among related recommendations, health and safety concerns are echoed elsewhere in the *Guidelines*, most notably in chapters on Consumer Interests and the Environment.

28. The recommendation in paragraph five of the chapter encourages MNEs to recruit an adequate workforce share locally, including managerial personnel, and to provide training to them. Language in this paragraph on training and skill levels complements the text in paragraph four of the General Policies chapter on encouraging human capital formation. The reference to local personnel complements the text encouraging local capacity building in paragraph three of the General Policies chapter.

29. Paragraph six recommends that enterprises provide reasonable notice to the representatives of employees and relevant government authorities, of changes in their operations which would have major effects upon the livelihood of their employees, in particular the closure of an entity involving collective layoffs or dismissals. As stated therein, the purpose of this provision is to afford an opportunity for co-operation to mitigate the effects of such changes. This is an important principle that is widely reflected in the industrial relations laws and practices of adhering countries, although the approaches taken to ensuring an opportunity for meaningful co-operation are not identical in all adhering countries. The paragraph also notes that it would be appropriate if, in light of specific circumstances, management were able to give such notice prior to the final decision. Indeed, notice prior to the final decision is a feature of industrial relations laws and practices in a number of adhering countries. However, it is not the only means to ensure an opportunity for meaningful co-operation to mitigate the effects of such decisions, and the laws and practices of other adhering countries provide for other means such as defined periods during which consultations must be undertaken before decisions may be implemented.

Commentary on the Environment

30. The text of the Environment Chapter broadly reflects the *principles* and objectives contained in the Rio Declaration on Environment and Development, in Agenda 21 (within the Rio Declaration). It also takes into account the (Aarhus) Convention on Access to Information, Public Participation in Decision-making, and Access to Justice in Environmental Matters and reflects *standards* contained in such instruments as the ISO Standard on Environmental Management Systems.

31. Sound environmental management is an important part of sustainable development, and is increasingly being seen as both a business responsibility and a business *opportunity*. Multinational enterprises have a role to play in both respects. Managers of these enterprises should therefore give appropriate attention to environmental issues within their business strategies. Improving environmental performance requires a commitment to a systematic approach and to continual improvement of the system. An environmental management system provides the internal framework necessary to control an enterprise's environmental impacts and to integrate environmental considerations into business operations. Having such a system in place should help to assure stockholders, employees and the community that the enterprise is actively working to protect the environment from the impacts of its activities.

32. In addition to improving environmental performance, instituting an environmental management system can provide economic benefits to companies through reduced operating and insurance costs, improved energy and resource conservation, reduced compliance and liability charges, improved access to capital, improved customer satisfaction, and improved community and public relations.

33. In the context of these *Guidelines,* 'sound environmental management' should be interpreted in its broadest sense, embodying activities aimed at controlling both direct and indirect environmental impacts of enterprise activities over the long-term, and involving both pollution control and resource management elements.

34. In most enterprises, an internal control system is needed to manage the enterprise's activities. The environmental part of this system may include such elements as targets for improved performance and regular monitoring of progress towards these targets.

35. Information about the activities of enterprises and associated environmental impacts is an important vehicle for building confidence with the public. This vehicle is most effective when information is provided in a transparent manner and when it encourages active consultation with stakeholders such as employees, customers, suppliers, contractors, local communities and with the public-at-large so as to promote a climate of long-term trust and understanding on environmental issues of mutual interest.

36. Normal business activity can involve the ex ante assessment of the potential environmental impacts associated with the enterprise's activities. Enterprises often carry out appropriate environmental impact assessments, even if they are not required by law. Environmental assessments made by the enterprise may contain a broad and forward-looking view of the potential impacts of an enterprise's activities, addressing relevant impacts and examining alternatives and mitigation measures to avoid or redress adverse impacts. The *Guidelines* also recognise that multinational enterprises have certain responsibilities in other parts of the product life cycle.

37. Several instruments already adopted by countries adhering to the *Guidelines*, including Principle 15 of the Rio Declaration on Environment and Development, enunciate a 'precautionary approach'. None of these instruments is explicitly addressed to enterprises, although enterprise contributions are implicit in all of them.

38. The basic premise of the *Guidelines* is that enterprises should act as soon as possible, and in a proactive way, to avoid, for instance, serious or irreversible environmental damages resulting from their activities. However, the fact that the *Guidelines* are addressed to enterprises means that no existing instrument is completely adequate for expressing this recommendation. The *Guidelines* therefore draw upon, but do not completely mirror, any existing instrument.

39. The *Guidelines* are not intended to reinterpret any existing instruments or to create new commitments or precedents on the part of governments—they are intended only to recommend how the precautionary approach should be implemented at the level of enterprises. Given the early stage of this process, it is recognised that some flexibility is needed in its application, based

on the specific context in which it is carried out. It is also recognised that governments determine the basic framework in this field, and have the responsibility to periodically consult with stakeholders on the most appropriate ways forward.

40. The *Guidelines* also encourage enterprises to work to raise the level of environmental performance in all parts of their operations, even where this may not be formally required by existing practice in the countries in which they operate.

41. For example, multinational enterprises often have access to technologies or operating procedures which could, if applied, help raise environmental performance overall. Multinational enterprises are frequently regarded as leaders in their respective fields, so the potential for a 'demonstration effect' on other enterprises should not be overlooked. Ensuring that the environment of the countries in which multinational enterprises operate also benefits from available technologies is an important way of building support for international investment activities more generally.

42. Enterprises have an important role to play in the training and education of their employees with regard to environmental matters. They are encouraged to discharge this responsibility in as broad a manner as possible, especially in areas directly related to human health and safety.

Commentary on Combating Bribery

43. Bribery and corruption are not only damaging to democratic institutions and the governance of corporations, but they also impede efforts to reduce poverty. In particular, the diversion of funds through corrupt practices undermines attempts by citizens to achieve higher levels of economic, social and environmental welfare. Enterprises have an important role to play in combating these practices.

44. Progress in improving the policy framework and in heightening enterprises' awareness of bribery as a management issue has been significant. The OECD *Convention of Combating Bribery of Foreign Public Officials* (the *Convention*) has been signed by 34 countries and entered into force on 15 February 1999. The *Convention*, along with the 1997 revised *Recommendation on Combating Bribery in International Business Transactions* and the 1996 *Recommendation on the Tax Deductibility of Bribes to Foreign Public Officials*, are the core instruments through which members of the anti bribery group co-operate to stop the flow of bribes for the purpose of obtaining or retaining international business. The three instruments target the offering side of the bribery transaction. They aim to eliminate the 'supply' of bribes to foreign public officials, with each country taking responsibility for the activities of its companies and what happens on its own territory.[5] A monitoring programme has been established to assure effective and consistent implementation and enforcement of the Convention.

45. To address the demand side of bribery, good governance practices are important elements to prevent companies from being asked to pay bribes. In addition, governments should assist companies confronted with solicitation of bribes.

46. Another important development has been the International Chamber of Commerce's recent update of its *Report on Extortion and Bribery in Business Transactions*. The *Report* contains

[5] For the purposes of the Convention, a 'bribe' is defined as an '. . . offer, promise, or giv(ing) of any undue pecuniary or other advantage, whether directly or through intermediaries, to a foreign public official, for that official or for a third party, in order that the official act or refrain from acting in relation to the performance of official duties, in order to obtain or retain business or other improper advantage in the conduct of international business.' The Commentaries to the Convention (paragraph 9) clarify that '(s)mall "facilitation" payments do not constitute payments made "to obtain or retain business or other improper advantage" within the meaning of paragraph 1 and, accordingly, are also not an offence. Such payments, which, in some countries, are made to induce public officials to perform their functions, such as issuing licenses or permits, are generally illegal in the foreign country concerned. Other countries can and should address this corrosive phenomenon by such means as support for programmes of good governance. . . .'

recommendations to governments and international organizations on combating extortion and bribery as well as a code of conduct for enterprises that focuses on these issues.

47. Transparency in both the public and private domains is a key concept in the fight against bribery and extortion. The business community, non-governmental organizations and governments and inter-governmental organisations have all co-operated to strengthen public support for anti-corruption measures and to enhance transparency and public awareness of the problems of corruption and bribery. The adoption of appropriate corporate governance practices is a complementary element in fostering a culture of ethics within the enterprise.

Commentary on Consumer Interests

48. A brief reference to 'consumer interests' was first introduced into the *Guidelines* in 1984, to reflect increasingly international aspects of consumer policies and the impact that the expansion of international trade, product packaging, marketing and sales and product safety can have on those policies. Since that time, the development of electronic commerce and the increased globalisation of the marketplace have substantially increased the reach of MNEs and consumer access to their goods and services. In recognition of the increasing importance of consumer issues, a substantial percentage of enterprises, in their management systems and codes of conduct include references to consumer interests and protections.

49. In light of these changes, and with an eye to helping enhance consumer safety and health, a chapter on *consumer interests* has been added to the *Guidelines* as a result of the current Review. Language in this chapter draws on the work of the OECD Committee on Consumer Policy, as well as that embodied in various individual and international corporate codes (such as those of the ICC), the UN Guidelines on Consumer Policy, and the OECD Guidelines for Consumer Protection in the Context of Electronic Commerce.

50. A variety of consumer protection laws exist that govern business practices. The emerging framework is intended to both protect consumer interests and foster economic growth and places a growing emphasis on the use of self-regulatory mechanisms. As noted, many existing national and international corporate codes of conduct include a reference to some aspect of consumer protection and amplify the commitment of industry to help protect health and safety and build consumer confidence in the marketplace. Ensuring that these sorts of practices provide consumers with effective and transparent protection is essential to help build trust that encourages consumer participation and market growth.

51. The emphasis on alternative dispute resolution in paragraph 3 of the chapter is an attempt to focus on what may in many cases be a more practicable solution to complaints than legal action which can be expensive, difficult and time consuming for everyone involved. It is particularly important that complaints relating to the consumption or use of a particular product that results in serious risks or damages to public health should be resolved in a fair and timely manner without undue cost or burden to the consumer.

52. Regarding paragraph 5, enterprises could look to the OECD Guidelines Governing the Protection of Privacy and Transborder Flows of Personal Data as a helpful basis for protecting personal data.

Commentary on Science and Technology

53. In a knowledge-based and globalised economy where national borders matter less, even for small or domestically oriented enterprises, the ability to access and utilise technology and know-how is essential for improving firm performance. Such access is also important for the realisation of the economy-wide effects of technological progress, including productivity growth and job creation, within the context of sustainable development. Multinational enterprises are the main conduit of technology transfer across borders. They contribute to the national innovative capacity of their host countries by generating, diffusing, and even enabling the use of new technologies by

domestic enterprises and institutions. The R&D activities of MNEs, when well connected to the national innovation system, can help enhance the economic and social progress in their host countries. In turn, the development of a dynamic innovation system in the host country expands commercial opportunities for MNEs.

54. The chapter thus aims to promote, within the limits of economic feasibility, competitiveness concerns and other considerations, the diffusion by multinational enterprises of the fruits of research and development activities among the countries where they operate, contributing thereby to the innovative capacities of host countries. In this regard, fostering technology diffusion can include the commercialisation of products which imbed new technologies, licensing of process innovations, hiring and training of S&T personnel and development of R&D co-operative ventures. When selling or licensing technologies, not only should the terms and conditions negotiated be reasonable, but MNEs may want to consider the long-term developmental, environmental and other impacts of technologies for the home and host country. In their activities, multinational enterprises can establish and improve the innovative capacity of their international subsidiaries and subcontractors. In addition, MNEs can call attention to the importance of local scientific and technological infrastructure, both physical and institutional. In this regard, MNEs can usefully contribute to the formulation by host country governments of policy frameworks conducive to the development of dynamic innovation systems.

Commentary on Competition

55. These *Guidelines* are intended to emphasise the importance of competition laws and policies to the efficient operation of both domestic and international markets, to reaffirm the importance of compliance with those laws and policies by domestic and multinational enterprises, and to ensure that all enterprises are aware of developments concerning the number, scope, and severity of competition laws and in the extent of co-operation among competition authorities. The term 'competition' law is used to refer to laws, including both 'antitrust' and 'antimonopoly' laws, that prohibit collective or unilateral action to (a) abuse market power or dominance, (b) acquire market power or dominance by means other than efficient performance, or (c) engage in anti-competitive agreements.

56. In general, competition laws and policies prohibit (a) hard core cartels; (b) other agreements that are deemed to be anti-competitive; (c) conduct that exploits or extends market dominance or market power; and (d) anti-competitive mergers and acquisitions. Under the 1998 Recommendation of the OECD Council Concerning Effective Action Against Hard Core Cartels, C(98)35/Final, the anticompetitive agreements referred to in sub (a) constitute hard core cartels, but the Recommendation incorporates differences in Member countries' laws, including differences in the laws' exemptions or provisions allowing for an exception or authorisation for activity that might otherwise be prohibited. These guidelines should not be interpreted as suggesting that enterprises should not avail themselves of such exemptions or provisions. The categories sub (b) and (c) are more general because the effects of other kinds of agreements and of unilateral conduct are more ambiguous, and there is less consensus on what should be considered anti-competitive.

57. The goal of competition policy is to contribute to overall social welfare and economic growth by creating and maintaining market conditions in which the nature, quality, and price of goods and services are determined by market forces except to the extent a jurisdiction considers necessary to achieve other goals. In addition to benefiting consumers and a jurisdiction's economy as a whole, such a competitive environment rewards enterprises that respond efficiently to consumer demand, and enterprises should provide information and advice when governments are considering laws and policies that might reduce their efficiency or otherwise affect the competitiveness of markets.

58. Enterprises should be aware that competition laws are being enacted in a rapidly increasing number of jurisdictions, and that it is increasingly common for those laws to prohibit

anti-competitive activities that occur abroad if they have a harmful impact on domestic consumers. Moreover, the growth of cross-border trade and investment makes it more likely that anti-competitive conduct taking place in one jurisdiction will have harmful effects in other jurisdictions. As a result, anti-competitive unilateral or concerted conduct that is or may be legal where it occurs is increasingly likely to be illegal in another jurisdiction. Enterprises should therefore take into account both the law of the country in which they are operating and the laws of all countries in which the effects of their conduct are likely to be felt.

59. Finally, enterprises should understand that competition authorities are engaging in more and deeper co-operation in investigating and challenging anti-competitive activity. *See generally*: Recommendation of the Council Concerning Co-operation between Member Countries on Anticompetitive Practices Affecting International Trade, C(95)130/Final; *Making International Markets More Efficient Through 'Positive Comity' in Competition Law Enforcement*, Report of the OECD Committee on Competition Law and Policy, DAFFE/CLP(99)19. When the competition authorities of various jurisdictions are reviewing the same conduct, enterprises' facilitation of co-operation among the authorities promotes consistent and sound decision-making while also permitting cost savings for governments and enterprises.

Commentary on Taxation

60. Corporate citizenship in the area of taxation implies that enterprises should comply with the taxation laws and regulations in all countries in which they operate, co-operate with authorities and make certain kinds of information available to them. However, this commitment to provide information is not without limitation. In particular, the *Guidelines* make a link between the information that should be provided and its relevance to the enforcement of applicable tax laws. This recognises the need to balance the burden on business in complying with applicable tax laws and the need for tax authorities to have the complete, timely and accurate information to enable them to enforce their tax laws.

61. A member of an MNE group in one country may have extensive economic relationships with members of the same MNE group in other countries. Such relationships may affect the tax liability of each of the parties. Accordingly, tax authorities may need information from outside their jurisdiction in order to be able to evaluate those relationships and determine the tax liability of the member of the MNE group in their jurisdiction. Again, the information to be provided is limited to that which is relevant to the proposed evaluation of those economic relationships for the purpose of determining the correct tax liability of the member of the MNE group. MNEs should co-operate in providing that information.

62. Transfer pricing is another important issue for corporate citizenship and taxation. The dramatic increase in global trade and cross-border direct investment (and the important role played in such trade and investment by MNEs) has meant that transfer pricing tends now to be a significant determinant of the tax liabilities of members of an MNE group. It is recognised that determining whether transfer pricing respects the arm's length standard (or principle) is often difficult both for MNEs and for tax administrations.

63. The Committee on Fiscal Affairs (CFA) of the OECD undertakes ongoing work to develop recommendations for ensuring transfer pricing reflects the arm's length principle. Its work resulted in the publication in 1995 of the OECD Transfer Pricing Guidelines for Multinational Enterprises and Tax Administrations (OECD Transfer Pricing Guidelines) which was the subject of the Recommendation of the OECD Council on the Determination of Transfer Pricing between Associated Enterprises (members of an MNE group would normally fall within the definition of Associated Enterprises).

64. The OECD Transfer Pricing Guidelines focus on the application of the arm's length principle to evaluate the transfer pricing of associated enterprises. The Transfer Pricing Guidelines aim to help tax administrations (of both OECD Member countries and non-member

countries) and MNEs by indicating mutually satisfactory solutions to transfer pricing cases, thereby minimising conflict among tax administrations and between tax administrations and MNEs and avoiding costly litigation. MNEs are encouraged to follow the guidance in the OECD Transfer Pricing Guidelines, as amended and supplemented, in order to ensure that their transfer prices reflect the arm's length principle.

Commentary on the Implementation Procedures of the OECD Guidelines for Multinational Enterprises

1. The Council Decision represents the commitment of adhering countries to further the implementation of the recommendations contained in the text of the *Guidelines*. Procedural guidance for both NCPs and the CIME is attached to the Council Decision.

2. The Council Decision sets out key adhering country responsibilities for the *Guidelines* with respect to NCPs, summarised as follows:

- Setting up NCPs (which will take due account of the procedural guidance attached to the Decision), and informing interested parties of the availability of *Guidelines*-related facilities.
- NCPs in different countries to co-operate with each other as necessary.
- NCPs to meet annually and report to the CIME.

3. The Council Decision also establishes CIME's responsibilities for the *Guidelines*, including:

- Organising exchanges of views on matters relating to the *Guidelines*
- Issuing clarifications as necessary
- Holding exchanges of views on the activities of NCPs
- Reporting to the OECD Council on the *Guidelines*

4. CIME is the OECD body responsible for overseeing the functioning of the *Guidelines*. This responsibility applies not only to the *Guidelines*, but to all elements of the Declaration (National Treatment Instrument, and the instruments on International Investment Incentives and Disincentives, and Conflicting Requirements). In the Declaration, CIME seeks to ensure that each element is respected and understood, and that they all complement and operate in harmony with each other.

5. Reflecting the increasing relevance of the *Guidelines* to countries outside the OECD, the Decision provides for consultations with non-adhering countries on matters covered by the *Guidelines*. This provision allows CIME to arrange periodic meetings with groups of countries interested in *Guidelines* issues, or to arrange contacts with individual countries if the need arises. These meetings and contacts could deal with experiences in the overall functioning of the *Guidelines* or with specific issues. Further guidance concerning CIME and NCP interaction with non-adhering countries is provided in the Procedural Guidance attached to the Decision.

I. Procedural Guidance for NCPs

6. National Contact Points have an important role in enhancing the profile and effectiveness of the *Guidelines*. While it is enterprises that are responsible for observing the *Guidelines* in their day-to-day behaviour, governments can contribute to improving the effectiveness of the implementation procedures. To this end, they have agreed that better guidance for the conduct and activities of NCPs is warranted, including through annual meetings and CIME oversight.

7. Many of the functions in the Procedural Guidance of the Decision are not new, but reflect experience and recommendations developed over the years (*e.g.* the 1984 Review Report C/MIN(84)5(Final)). By making them explicit the expected functioning of the implementation mechanisms of the *Guidelines* is made more transparent. All functions are now outlined in four parts of the Procedural Guidance pertaining to NCPs: institutional arrangements, information and promotion, implementation in specific instances, and reporting.

8. These four parts are preceded by an introductory paragraph that sets out the basic purpose of NCPs, together with core criteria to promote the concept of 'functional equivalence'. Since governments are accorded flexibility in the way they organise NCPs, NCPs should function in a visible, accessible, transparent, and accountable manner. These criteria will guide NCPs in carrying out their activities and will also assist the CIME in discussing the conduct of NCPs.

Core Criteria for Functional Equivalence in the Activities of NCPs

Visibility. In conformity with the Decision, adhering governments agree to nominate National Contact Points, and also to inform the business community, employee organisations and other interested parties, including NGOs, about the availability of facilities associated with NCPs in the implementation of the *Guidelines*. Governments are expected to publish information about their contact points and to take an active role in promoting the *Guidelines*, which could include hosting seminars and meetings on the instrument. These events could be arranged in co-operation with business, labour, NGOs, and other interested parties, though not necessarily with all groups on each occasion.

Accessibility. Easy access to NCPs is important to their effective functioning. This includes facilitating access by business, labour, NGOs, and other members of the public. Electronic communications can also assist in this regard. NCPs would respond to all legitimate requests for information, and also undertake to deal with specific issues raised by parties concerned in an efficient and timely manner.

Transparency. Transparency is an important criterion with respect to its contribution to the accountability of the NCP and in gaining the confidence of the general public. Thus most of the activities of the NCP will be transparent. Nonetheless when the NCP offers its 'good offices' in implementing the *Guidelines* in specific instances, it will be in the interests of their effectiveness to take appropriate steps to establish confidentiality of the proceedings. Outcomes will be transparent unless preserving confidentiality is in the best interests of effective implementation of the *Guidelines*.

Accountability. A more active role with respect to enhancing the profile of the *Guidelines*—and their potential to aid in the management of difficult issues between enterprises and the societies in which they operate—will also put the activities of NCPs in the public eye. Nationally, parliaments could have a role to play. Annual reports and annual meetings of NCPs will provide an opportunity to share experiences and encourage 'best practices' with respect to NCPs. CIME will also hold exchanges of views, where experiences would be exchanged and the effectiveness of the activities of NCPs could be assessed.

Institutional Arrangements

9. The composition of NCPs should be such that they provide an effective basis for dealing with the broad range of issues covered by the *Guidelines*. Different forms of organisation (*e.g.* representatives from one Ministry, an interagency group, or one that contained representatives from non-governmental bodies) are possible. It may be helpful for the NCP to be headed by a senior official. NCP leadership should be such that it retains the confidence of social partners and fosters the public profile of the *Guidelines*. NCPs, whatever their composition, are expected to develop and maintain relations with representatives of the business community, employee organisations, and other interested parties.

Information and Promotion

10. The NCP functions associated with information and promotion are fundamentally important to enhancing the profile of the *Guidelines*. These functions also help to put an accent on 'pro-active' responsibilities of NCPs.

11. NCPs are required to make the *Guidelines* better known and available by appropriate means, including in national languages. On-line information may be a cost-effective means of doing this,

although it should be noted that universal access to this means of information delivery cannot be assured. English and French language versions will be available from the OECD, and website links to the OECD *Guidelines* website are encouraged. As appropriate, NCPs will also provide prospective investors, both inward and outward, with information about the *Guidelines*. A separate provision also stipulates that in their efforts to raise awareness of the *Guidelines*, NCPs will co-operate with a wide variety of organisations and individuals, including, as appropriate, the business community, employee organisations, other non-governmental organisations, and the interested public.

12. Another basic activity expected of NCPs is responding to legitimate enquiries. Three groups have been singled out for attention in this regard: (i) other National Contact Points (reflecting a provision in the Decision); (ii) the business community, employee organisations, other non-governmental organisations and the public; and (iii) governments of non-adhering countries.

Implementation in Specific Instances

13. When issues arise relating to implementation of the *Guidelines* in specific instances, the NCP is expected to help resolve them. Generally, issues will be dealt with by the NCP in whose country the issue has arisen. Among adhering countries, such issues will first be discussed on the national level and, where appropriate, pursued at the bilateral level. This section of the Procedural Guidance provides guidance to NCPs on how to handle such situations. The NCP may also take other steps to further the effective implementation of the *Guidelines*.

14. In making an initial assessment of whether the issue raised merits further examination, the NCP will need to determine whether the issue is *bona fide* and relevant to the implementation of the *Guidelines*. In this context, the NCP will take into account:.

- the identity of the party concerned and its interest in the matter;
- whether the issue is material and substantiated;
- the relevance of applicable law and procedures;
- how similar issues have been, or are being, treated in other domestic or international proceedings;
- whether the consideration of the specific issue would contribute to the purposes and effectiveness of the *Guidelines*.

15. Following its initial assessment, the NCP is expected to respond to the party or parties having raised the issue. If the NCP decides that the issue does not merit further consideration, it will give reasons for its decision.

16. Where the issues raised merit further consideration, the NCP would discuss the issue further with parties involved and offer 'good offices' in an effort to contribute informally to the resolution of issues. Where relevant, NCPs will follow the procedures set out in paragraph 2a) through 2d). This could include seeking the advice of relevant authorities, as well as representatives of the business community, labour organisations, other non-governmental organisations, and experts. Consultations with NCPs in other countries, or seeking guidance on issues related to the interpretation of the *Guidelines* may also help to resolve the issue.

17. As part of making available good offices, and where relevant to the issues at hand, NCPs will offer, or facilitate access to, consensual and non-adversarial procedures, such as conciliation or mediation, to assist in dealing with the issues at hand, such as conciliation or mediation. In common with accepted practices on conciliation and mediation procedures, these procedures would be used only upon agreement of the parties concerned.

18. If the parties involved fail to reach agreement on the issues raised, the NCP will issue a statement, and make recommendations as appropriate, on the implementation of the *Guidelines*. This procedure makes it clear that an NCP will issue a statement, even when it feels that a specific recommendation is not called for.

19. Transparency is recognised as a general principle for the conduct of NCPs in their dealings with the public (see para. 8 in 'Core Criteria' section, above). However, paragraph C-4 recognises that there are specific circumstances where confidentiality is important. The NCP will take appropriate steps to protect sensitive business information. Equally, other information, such as the identity of individuals involved in the procedures, should be kept confidential in the interests of the effective implementation of the *Guidelines*. It is understood that proceedings include the facts and arguments brought forward by the parties. Nonetheless, it remains important to strike a balance between transparency and confidentiality in order to build confidence in the *Guidelines* procedures and to promote their effective implementation. Thus, while para. C-4 broadly outlines that the proceedings associated with implementation will normally be confidential, the results will normally be transparent.

20. As noted in para. 2 of the 'Concepts and Principles' chapter, enterprises are encouraged to observe the *Guidelines* wherever they operate, taking into account the particular circumstances of each host country.

- In the event *Guidelines*-related issues arise in a non-adhering country, NCPs will take steps to develop an understanding of the issues involved. While it may not always be practicable to obtain access to all pertinent information, or to bring all the parties involved together, the NCP may still be in a position to pursue enquiries and engage in other fact finding activities. Examples of such steps could include contacting the management of the firm in the home country, and, as appropriate, government officials in the non-adhering country.
- Conflicts with host country laws, regulations, rules and policies may make effective implementation of the *Guidelines* in specific instances more difficult than in adhering countries. As noted in the commentary to the General Policies chapter, while the *Guidelines* extend beyond the law in many cases, they should not and are not intended to place an enterprise in a situation where it faces conflicting requirements.
- The parties involved will have to be advised of the limitations inherent in implementing the *Guidelines* in non-adhering countries.
- Issues relating to the *Guidelines* in non-adhering countries could also be discussed at NCP annual meetings with a view to building expertise in handling issues arising in non-adhering countries.

Reporting

21. Reporting would be an important responsibility of NCPs that would also help to build up a knowledge base and core competencies in furthering the effectiveness of the *Guidelines*. In reporting on implementation activities in specific instances, NCPs will comply with transparency and confidentiality considerations as set out in para. C 4.

II. Procedural Guidance for the CIME

22. The Procedural Guidance to the Council Decision provides additional guidance to the Committee in carrying out its responsibilities, including:

- Discharging its responsibilities in an efficient and timely manner
- Considering requests from NCPs for assistance
- Holding exchanges of views on the activities of NCPs
- Providing for the possibility of seeking advice from experts

23. The non-binding nature of the *Guidelines* precludes the Committee from acting as a judicial or quasi-judicial body. Nor should the findings and statements made by the NCP (other than interpretations of the *Guidelines*) be questioned by a referral to CIME. The provision that CIME shall not reach conclusions on the conduct of individual enterprises has been maintained in the Decision itself.

24. CIME will consider requests from NCPs for assistance, including in the event of doubt about the interpretation of the *Guidelines* in particular circumstances. This paragraph reflects paragraph C-2c) of the Procedural Guidance to the Council Decision pertaining to NCPs, where NCPs are invited to seek the guidance of the CIME if they have doubt about the interpretation of the *Guidelines* in these circumstances.

25. When discussing NCP activities, it is not intended that CIME conduct annual reviews of each individual NCP, although the CIME will make recommendations, as necessary, to improve their functioning, including with respect to the effective implementation of the *Guidelines.*

26. A substantiated submission by an adhering country or an advisory body that an NCP was not fulfilling its procedural responsibilities in the implementation of the *Guidelines* in specific instances will also be considered by the CIME. This complements provisions in the section of the Procedural Guidance pertaining to NCPs reporting on their activities.

27. Clarifications of the meaning of the *Guidelines* at the multilateral level would remain a key responsibility of the CIME to ensure that the meaning of the *Guidelines* would not vary from country to country. A substantiated submission by an adhering country or advisory body with respect to whether an NCP interpretation of the *Guidelines* is consistent with CIME interpretations will also be considered. This may not be needed very often, but would provide a vehicle to ensure consistent interpretation of the *Guidelines.*

28. Finally, the Committee may wish to call on experts to address and report on broader issues (*e.g.* child labour, human rights) or individual issues, or to improve the effectiveness of procedures. For this purpose, CIME could call on OECD inhouse expertise, international organisations, the advisory bodies, NGOs, academics and others. It is understood that this will not become a panel to settle individual issues.

APPENDIX 26

Report of the Committee on Conduct in Local Government Cmnd 5636, May 1974

The National Code of Local Government Conduct

This Code is an authoritative guide for all councillors elected or co-opted to local authorities in England, Wales and Scotland. It supplements both the law enacted by Parliament and the standing orders made by individual councils.

Contents

1. Law, Standing Orders and National Code
2. Public duty and private interest
3. Disclosure of pecuniary and other interests
4. Membership and chairmanship of committees and sub-committees
5. Councillors and officers
6. Use of confidential information
7. Gifts and hospitality
8. Use of allowances
9. Use of council facilities

1. Law, Standing Orders and National Code

Make sure that you fully understand the rules of conduct which the law, standing orders and the national code require you to follow. It is your personal responsibility to apply their requirements on every relevant occasion. Seek any advice about them that you need from your council's senior officer.

2. Public duty and private interest

(i) Your over-riding duty as a councillor is to the whole local community

(ii) You have a special duty to your own constituents, including those who did not vote for you

(iii) Whenever you have a private or personal interest in any question which councillors have to decide, you must not do anything to let that interest influence the decision

(iv) Do nothing as a councillor which you could not justify if it became public

(v) The reputation of your council and of your party if you belong to one, depends on your conduct and what the public believes about your conduct.

3. Disclosure of pecuniary and other interests

(i) The law makes specific provision requiring you to disclose pecuniary interests, direct and indirect. But interests which are not pecuniary can be just as important. Kinship, friendship, membership of an association, society, or trade union, trusteeship and many other kinds of relationship can sometimes influence your judgment or give the impression that they might do so. A good test is to ask yourself whether others would think the interest close enough to influence someone in your position. If you think they would, or if you are in doubt, treat the interest as if it were a pecuniary one, disclose it and withdraw from the meeting.

(ii) You must follow the principles about disclosure of interest in your unofficial relations with other councillors—at party group meetings, or other informal occasions and in casual conversation—no less scrupulously that at formal meetings of the council, its committees and sub-committees.

4. Membership and Chairmanship of Council Committees and Sub-committees

(i) You, or some firm or body with which you are personally connected, may have professional business or personal interests within the area for which the council is responsible, and such interests may be closely related to the work of one or more of the council's committees or sub-committees, concerned (say) with planning or developing land, council housing or the letting of contracts for supplies, services or works. Before seeking or accepting membership of any such committee or sub-committee, you should seriously consider whether your membership would involve you (a) in disclosing an interest so often that you could be of little value to the committee or sub-committee, or (b) in weakening public confidence in the impartiality of the committee or sub-committee.

(ii) You should not seek or accept the chairmanship of a committee or sub-committee whose business is closely related to a personal interest of yourself or any other body with which you are associated.

5. Councillors and officers

(i) Both councillors and officers are servants of the public, and they are indispensable to each other. But their responsibilities are distinct. Councillors are responsible to the electorate and serve only so long as their term of office lasts. Officers are responsible to the council and are permanently appointed. An officer's job is to give advice to councillors and to carry out the council's work under the direction and control of councillors.

(ii) Mutual respect between councillors and officers is essential to good local government. Close personal familiarity between individual councillor and officer can damage this relationship and prove embarrassing to other councillors and officers.

(iii) If you are called upon to take part in appointing an officer, the only question you should consider is which candidate would best serve the whole council. You should not let your personal or political preferences influence your judgment. You should not canvass the support of colleagues for any candidate and you should resist any attempt by others to canvass yours.

6. Use of confidential information

As a councillor you necessarily acquire much information that has not yet been made public. You should not normally reveal such information to anyone outside the council's membership or staff. It is a grave betrayal of trust to use confidential information for the personal advantage of yourself or of anyone known to you.

7. Gifts and hospitality

Treat with extreme caution any offer or gift, favour or hospitality that is made to you personally by any person or organisation that is doing or seeking to do business with the council or is applying to the council for any planning or other kind of decision. Working lunches and other social occasions arranged or authorised by the council or by one of its committees or sub-committees may be a proper way of doing business, provided that no extravagance is involved. Nor can there be any hard and fast rule about acceptance or refusal of tokens of good will on special occasions. But you are personally responsible for all such decisions and for avoiding the risk of damage to public confidence in local government.

8. Use of allowances

Observe scrupulously the rules entitling you to claim

(a) allowances for performing 'approved duty' as a councillor and
(b) repayment of expenses incurred for travel and subsistence while doing business on the council's behalf.

9. Use of council facilities

Make sure that any facilities—such as transport, stationery, or secretarial services—provided by the council for your use in your official duties are used strictly for those duties and for no other purpose.

APPENDIX 27

Southern African Development Community Protocol Against Corruption[1]

Preamble

We, the Heads of State or Government of:

The Republic of Angola
The Republic of Botswana
The Democratic Republic of Congo
The Kingdom of Lesotho
The Republic of Malawi
The Republic of Mauritius
The Republic of Mozambique
The Republic of Namibia
The Republic of Seychelles
The Republic of South Africa
The Kingdom of Swaziland
The United Republic of Tanzania
The Republic of Zambia
The Republic of Zimbabwe

Mindful of Article 21 of the Treaty establishing the Southern African Development Community which enjoins Member States to cooperate in all areas necessary to foster regional development, integration and cooperation and Article 22 of the Treaty which mandates Member states to conclude Protocols as may be necessary in each are of cooperation;

Concerned about the adverse and destabilizing effects of corruption throughout the world on the culture, economic, social and political foundations of society;

Noting that corruption is a serious international problem which is presently the subject of concerted action in other parts of the world and one which countries in every stage of development should tackle as a matter of urgency;

Welcoming initiatives of the United Nations General Assembly (UNGA) and collective regional efforts to combat corruption;

Taking cognizance of the Resolutions adopted by Ministers of Justice and Attorneys-General of the Southern African Development Community at the 3rd Regional Roundtable on Ethics and Governance held at Victoria Falls, Zimbabwe in August, 2000 in which they agreed on initiatives to fight corruption in the Region;

Aware of the inter-relationships between corruption and other criminal activities;

Acknowledging that corruption undermines good governance which includes the principles of accountability and transparency;

---

[1] The Protocol was signed on 114 August 2001. It has not yet entered into force.

Recognising that demonstrable political will and leadership are essential ingredients to wage an effective war against the scourge of corruption;

Reaffirming the need to eliminate the scourge of corruption through the adoption of effective preventative and deterrent measures and by strictly enforcing legislation against all types of corruption and fostering public support for these initiatives;

Bearing in Mind the responsibility of Member States to hold corrupt persons in the public and private sectors accountable and to take appropriate action against persons who commit acts of corruption in the performance of their functions and duties;

Convinced of the need for a joint and concerted effort as well as the prompt adoption of a regional instrument to promote and facilitate cooperation in fighting corruption;

Hereby agree as follows:

Article 1

Definitions

In this Protocol, unless the context otherwise requires:

'confiscation' means any penalty or measure resulting in a final deprivation of property, proceeds or instrumentalities ordered by a court of law following proceedings in relation to a criminal offence or offences connected with or related to corruption;

'Corruption' means any act referred to in Article 3 and includes bribery or any other behaviour in relation to persons entrusted with responsibilities in the public and private sectors which violates their duties as public officials, private employees, independent agents or other relationships of that kind and aimed at obtaining undue advantage of any kind for themselves or others;

'Council' means the Council of Ministers of the Southern African Development Community established by Article 9 of the Treaty;

'Executive Secretary' means the chief executive officer of the Southern African Development Community appointed under Article 10(7) of the Treaty;

'Member State' means a Member of the Southern African Development Community;

'Property' includes assets of any kind, whether corporeal or incorporeal, moveable or immovable, tangible or intangible and any document or legal instrument evidencing title to, or interest in such assets;

'Public Official' means any person in the employment of the State, its agencies, local authorities or parastatals and includes any person holding office in the legislative, executive or judicial branch of a State or exercising a public function or duty in any of its agencies or enterprises;

'Requested State Party' means a State Party being requested to extradite or to provide assistance in terms of this Protocol;

'Requesting State Party' means a State Party making a request for extradition or assistance in terms of this Protocol;

'State Parties' means Member States who have ratified or acceded to this Protocol;

'Treaty' means the Treaty establishing the Southern African Development Community;

'Tribunal' means the Tribunal of the Community established by Article 9 of the Treaty.

Article 2

Purposes

The purposes of this Protocol are:

a) to promote and strengthen the development, by each of the State Parties, of mechanisms needed to prevent, detect, punish and eradicate corruption in the public and private sector,
b) to promote, facilitate and regulate cooperation among the State Parties to ensure the effectiveness of measures and actions to prevent, detect, punish and eradicate corruption in the public and private sectors.

c) to foster the development and harmonization of policies and domestic legislation of the State Parties relating to the prevention, detection, punishment and eradication of corruption in the public and private sectors.

Article 3

Acts of Corruption

1. This Protocol is applicable to the following acts of corruption:
   a) the solicitation or acceptance, directly or indirectly, by a public official, of any article of monetary value, or other benefit, such as a gift, favour, promise or advantage for himself or herself or for another person or entity, in exchange for any act or omission in the performance of his or her public functions;
   b) the offering or granting, directly or indirectly, by a public official, of any article of monetary value, or other benefit, such as a gift, favour, promise or advantage for himself or herself or for another person or entity, in exchange for any act or omission in the performance of his or her public functions;
   c) any act or omission in the discharge of his or her duties by a public official for the purpose of illicitly obtaining benefits for himself or herself or for a third party;
   d) the diversion by a public official, for purposes unrelated to those for which they were intended, for his or her own benefit or that of a third party of any movable or immovable property, monies or securities belonging to the State, to an independent agency, or to an individual, that such official received by virtue of his or her position for purposes of administration, custody or for other reasons;
   e) the offering or giving, promising, solicitation or acceptance, directly or indirectly, of any undue advantage to or by any person who directs or works for, in any capacity, a private sector entity, for himself or herself or for anyone else, for him or her to act, or refrain from acting, in breach of his or her duties;
   f) the offering, giving, solicitation or acceptance directly or indirectly, or promising of any undue advantage to or by any person who asserts or confirms that he or she is able to exert any improper influence over the decision making of any person performing functions in the public or private sector in consideration thereof, whether the undue advantage is for himself or herself or for anyone else, as well as the request, receipt or the acceptance of the offer or the promise of such an advantage, in consideration of the influence, whether or not the influence is exerted or whether or not the supposed influence leads to the intended result;
   g) the fraudulent use or concealment of property derived from any of the acts referred to in this Article; and
   h) participation as a principal, co-principal, agent, instigator, accomplice or accessory after the fact, or in any other manner, in the commission or attempted commission of, in any collaboration or conspiracy to commit, any of the acts referred to in this Article.
2. This Protocol shall also be applicable by mutual agreement between or among two or more State Parties with respect to any other act of corruption not described in this Protocol.

Article 4

Preventative Measures

1. For the purposes set forth in Article 2 of this Protocol, each State Party undertakes to adopt measures, which will create, maintain and strengthen:
   a) standards of conduct for the correct, honourable and proper fulfillment of public functions as well as mechanisms to enforce those standards;
   b) systems of government hiring and procurement of goods and services that ensure the transparency, equity and efficiency of such systems;

c) government revenue collection and control systems that deter corruption as well as laws that deny favourable tax treatment for any individual or corporation for expenditures made in violation of the anti-corruption laws of the State Parties;
d) mechanisms to promote access to information to facilitate eradication and elimination of opportunities for corruption;
e) systems for protecting individuals who, in good faith, report acts of corruption;
f) laws that punish those who make false and malicious reports against innocent persons;
g) institutions responsible for implementing mechanisms for preventing, detecting, punishing and eradicating corruption;
h) deterrents to the bribery of domestic public officials, and officials of foreign States, such as mechanisms to ensure that publicly held companies and other types of associations maintain books and records which, in reasonable details, accurately reflect the acquisition and disposition of assets, and have sufficient internal accounting controls to enable the law enforcement agencies to detect acts of corruption;
i) mechanisms to encourage participation by the media, civil society and non governmental organizations in efforts to prevent corruption; and
j) mechanisms for promoting public education and awareness in the fight against corruption.

2. Each State Party shall adopt such legislative and other measures under its domestic law to prevent and combat acts of corruption committed in and by private sector entities.

Article 5
Jurisdiction

1. Each State Party shall adopt measures necessary to establish its jurisdiction over the offences established in accordance with this Protocol when:
   a) the offence in question is committed in its territory;
   b) the offence is committed by one of its nationals or by a person who habitually resides in its territory; and
   c) the alleged criminal is present in its territory and it does not extradite such person to another country.
2. This Protocol does not exclude any criminal jurisdiction exercised by a State Party in accordance with its domestic law.
3. Paragraph 1 of this Article shall be subject to the principle that a person shall not be tried twice for the same offence.

Article 6
Acts of Corruption Relating to an Official of a Foreign State

1. Subject to its domestic law, each State Party shall prohibit and punish the offering or granting, directly or indirectly, by its own nationals, persons having their habitual residence in its territory, and businesses domiciled there, to an official of a foreign State, of any article of monetary value, or other benefit, such as a gift, favour, promise or advantage, in connection with any economic or commercial transaction in exchange for any act or omission in the performance of that official's public functions.
2. Among those State Parties that have established the offence referred to in paragraph 1, such offence shall be considered an act of corruption for the purposes of this Protocol and any State Party that has not established such an offence shall, insofar as its laws permit, provide assistance and cooperation with respect to this offence as provided in this Protocol.

Article 7

Development and Harmonization of Policies and Domestic Legislation

1. State Parties undertake, to the extent possible, to develop and harmonise their policies and domestic legislation for the attainment of the purpose of this Protocol.
2. Each State Party shall adopt the necessary legislative or other measures to establish as criminal offences under its domestic law the acts of corruption described in Article 3.

Article 8

Confiscation and Seizure

1. Each State Party shall adopt such measures as may be necessary to enable:
   a) confiscation of proceeds derived from offences established in accordance with this Protocol, or property the value of which corresponds to that of such proceeds; and
   b) its competent authorities to identify, trace and freeze or seize proceeds, property or instrumentalities for the purpose of eventual confiscation.
2. In order to carry out measures referred to in this Article, each State Party shall empower its courts or other competent authorities to order that bank, financial or commercial records be made available or be seized and shall not invoke bank secrecy as a basis for refusal to provide assistance.
3. The Requesting State Party shall not use any information received that is protected by bank secrecy for any purpose other than the proceedings for which that information was requested, unless with the consent of the Requested State Party.
4. In accordance with their applicable domestic law and the relevant treaties or other agreements that may be in force between or among them, State Parties shall provide each other the broadest possible measure of assistance in the identification, tracing, freezing, seizure and confiscation of property, instrumentalities or proceeds obtained, derived from or used in the commission of offences established in accordance with this Protocol.
5. A State Party that enforces its own or another State Party's judgment against property or proceeds described in paragraph 1 of this Article shall dispose of the property or proceeds in accordance with its laws.
6. To the extent permitted by a State Party's laws and upon such terms, as it deems appropriate, it may transfer all or part of property referred to in paragraph 1 of this Article to another State Party that assisted in the underlying investigation or proceedings.

Article 9

Extradition

1. This Article shall apply to the offences established by the State Parties in accordance with this Protocol.
2. Each of the offences to which this Article applies shall be deemed to be included as an extraditable offence in any extradition treaty existing between or among the State Parties.
3. State Parties undertake to include offences referred to in this Protocol as extraditable offences in every extradition treaty to be concluded between or among them.
4. If a State Party that makes extradition conditional on the existence of a treaty receives a request for extradition from another State Party with which it does not have an extradition treaty, it may consider this Protocol as the legal basis for extradition with respect to any offence to which this Protocol applies.
5. State Parties that do not make extradition conditional on the existence of a treaty shall recognise offences to which this Article applies as extraditable offences among themselves.
6. Extradition shall be subject to the conditions provided for by the law of the Requested State Party or by applicable extradition treaties, including the grounds on which the Requested State Party may refuse extradition.

7. If extradition for any offence to which this Article applies is refused because the Requested State Party deems that it has jurisdiction over the offence, the Requested State Party shall within a reasonable time, submit the case to its competent authorities for the purpose of prosecution unless otherwise agreed with the Requesting State Party, and shall report the final outcome to the Requesting State Party.
8. Subject to the provisions of its domestic law and its extradition treaties, a Requested State Party may, upon being satisfied that the circumstances so warrant and are urgent, and at the request of the Requesting State Party, take into custody a person whose extradition is sought and who is present in its territory, or take other appropriate measures to ensure that the person is present at the extradition proceedings.
9. State Parties shall endeavour to conclude bilateral and multilateral agreements to carry out or enhance the effectiveness of extradition.

Article 10

Judicial Cooperation and Legal Assistance

1. In accordance with their domestic law and applicable treaties, State Parties shall afford one another the widest measure of mutual assistance by processing requests from authorities that, in conformity with their domestic law, have the power to investigate or prosecute the acts of corruption described in this Protocol, to obtain evidence and take other necessary action to facilitate legal proceedings and measures regarding the investigation or prosecution of acts of corruption.
2. State Parties shall provide each other with the widest measure of mutual technical cooperation on the most effective ways and means of preventing, detecting, investigating and punishing acts of corruption.
3. The provision of this Article shall not affect the obligations under any other bilateral or multilateral treaty which governs, in whole or in part, mutual legal assistance in criminal matters.
4. Nothing in this Article shall prevent State Parties from affording one another more favourable forms of mutual legal assistance allowed under their respective domestic law.

Article 11

Institutional Arrangements for Implementation

1. A Committee consisting of State Parties is hereby established to oversee the implementation of this Protocol.
2. Each State Party shall report to the Committee within one year of becoming a Party, on the progress made in the implementation of this Protocol. Thereafter, each State Party shall report to the Committee every two years.
3. The Committee shall, *inter-alia*, be responsible for the following:
   a) gathering and disseminating information amongst State Parties;
   b) organising training programmes as and when appropriate;
   c) evaluating programmes to be put in place and a programme of cooperation for the implementation of this Protocol; and
   d) providing any other related assistance to State Parties as and when appropriate;
   e) reporting to Council on a regular basis on the progress made by each State Party in complying with the provisions of this Protocol.

Article 12

Authority

1. For the purposes of cooperation and assistance under this Protocol, each State Party shall designate an Authority.

2. The Authority shall be responsible for making and receiving the requests for assistance and cooperation referred to in this Protocol.
3. The Authority shall communicate with each other directly for the purpose of this Protocol.

Article 13
Transitional Provisions

1. Subject to the domestic law of each State Party and existing treaties between State Parties, nothing shall prevent a State Party from providing procedural cooperation in criminal matters solely on the basis that the alleged act of corruption was committed before this Protocol entered into force.
2. The provision of this Article shall not affect the principle of non-retroactivity in criminal law, nor shall application of this provision interrupt existing statutes of limitations relating to crimes committed prior to the date of the entry into force of this Protocol.

Article 14
Relationship with Other Treaties

Subject to the provisions of Article 3 paragraph 2, this Protocol shall in respect of those countries to which it applies, supercede the provisions of any treaty or bilateral agreement governing corruption between any two State Parties.

Article 15
Notification

Any State Party which has or enacts any legislation pursuant to Articles 3, 6 or 7 shall notify the Executive Secretary who shall in turn notify the other State Parties.

Article 16
Signature

This Protocol shall be signed by duly authorized representatives of Member States.

Article 17
Ratification

This Protocol shall be ratified by the Signatory States in accordance with their constitutional or other procedures.

Article 18
Entry into Force

1. This Protocol shall enter into force 30 days after the deposit of the instruments of ratification by two thirds of the Member States.
2. In respect of each Member State ratifying or acceding to the Protocol after the deposit of the ninth instrument of ratification, this Protocol shall enter into force in respect of that Member State, 30 days after the date of deposit of its instrument of ratification or accession.

Article 19
Accession

This Protocol shall remain open for accession by any Member State.

Article 20
Depositary

1. This Protocol and all instruments of ratification or accession shall be deposited with the Executive Secretary, who shall transmit certified copies thereof to all Member States.
2. The Executive Secretary shall notify Member States of the dates of deposit of instruments of ratification and accession.

3. The Executive Secretary shall register this Protocol with the United Nations, and the Organisation of African Unity.

Article 21

Amendment

1. An amendment to this Protocol shall be adopted by a decision of three quarters of Members of the Summit.
2. A proposal for the amendment of this Protocol may be made to the Executive Secretary by any State Party for preliminary consideration by the Council, provided however, that the proposed amendment shall not be submitted to the Council for preliminary consideration until all Member States have been duly notified of it, and a period of three months has elapsed after such notification.

Article 22

Settlement of Disputes

Any dispute arising from the interpretation or application of this Protocol which cannot be settled amicably shall be referred to the Tribunal.

APPENDIX 28

Prevention of Corruption Acts 1889 to 1916

Public Bodies Corrupt Practices Act 1889

1. Corruption in office a misdemeanour

(1) Every person who shall by himself or by or in conjunction with any other person, corruptly solicit or receive, or agree to receive, for himself, or for any other person, any gift, loan, fee, reward, or advantage whatever as an inducement to, or reward for, or otherwise on account of any member, officer, or servant of a public body as in this Act defined, doing or forbearing to do anything in respect of any matter of transaction whatsoever, actual or proposed, in which the said public body is concerned, shall be guilty of a misdemeanour.

(2) Every person who shall by himself or by or in conjunction with any other person corruptly give, promise, or offer any gift, loan, fee, reward, or advantage whatsoever to any person, whether for the benefit of that person or of another person, as an inducement to or reward for or otherwise on account of any member, officer, or servant of any public body as in this Act defined, doing or forbearing to do anything in respect of any matter or transaction whatsoever, actual or proposed, in which such public body as aforesaid is concerned, shall be guilty of a misdemeanour.

2. Penalty for offences

(1) Any person on conviction for offending as aforesaid shall, at the discretion of the court before which he is convicted,

(a) be liable

(i) on summary conviction, to imprisonment for a term not exceeding 6 months or to a fine not exceeding the statutory maximum, or to both; and

(ii) on conviction on indictment, to imprisonment for a term not exceeding 7 years or to a fine, or to both, and

(b) in addition be liable to be ordered to pay to such body, and in such manner as the court directs, the amount or value of any gift, loan, fee, or reward received by him or any part thereof; and

(c) be liable to be adjudged incapable of being elected or appointed to any public office for five years from the date of his conviction, and to forfeit any such office held by him at the date of his conviction; and

(d) in the event of a second conviction for a like offence he shall, in addition to the foregoing penalties, be liable to be adjudged to be for ever incapable of holding any public office, and to be incapable for five years of being registered as an elector, or voting at an election either of members to serve in Parliament or of members of any public body, and the enactments for preventing the voting and registration of persons declared by reason of corrupt practices to be incapable of voting shall apply to a person adjudged in pursuance of this section to be incapable of voting; and

(e) if such person is an officer or servant in the employ of any public body upon such conviction he shall, at the discretion of the court, be liable to forfeit his right and claim to any compensation or pension to which he would otherwise have been entitled.

3. Savings

(1) [Repealed]
(2) A person shall not be exempt from punishment under this Act by reason of the invalidity of the appointment or election of a person to a public office.

4. Restriction on prosecution

(1) A prosecution for an offence under this Act shall not be instituted except by or with the consent of the Attorney-General.
(2) In this section the expression 'Attorney-General' means the Attorney or Solicitor General for England, and as respect Scotland means the Lord Advocate . . .

5. [Repealed]

6. [Repealed]

7. Interpretation

In this Act—

The expression 'public body' means any council of a county or county of a city or town, any council of a municipal borough, also any board, commissioners, select vestry, or other body which has power to act under and for the purposes of any Act relating to local government, or the public health, or to poor law or otherwise to administer money raised by rates in pursuance of any public general Act, but does not include any public body as above defined existing elsewhere than in the United Kingdom:

The expression 'public office' means any office or employment of a person as a member, officer, or servant of such public body:

The expression 'person' includes a body of persons, corporate or unincorporated:

The expression 'advantage' includes any office or dignity, and any forbearance to demand any money or money's worth or valuable thing, and includes any aid, vote, consent, or influence, or pretended aid, vote, consent, or influence, and also includes any promise or procurement of or agreement or endeavour to procure, or the holding out of any expectation of any gift, loan, fee, reward, or advantage, as before defined.

8. [Applies only to Scotland]

9. [Repealed]

10. Short title

This Act may be cited as the Public Bodies Corrupt Practices Act 1889.

Prevention Of Corruption Act 1906

1. Punishment of corrupt transactions with agents

(1) If any agent corruptly accepts or obtains, or agrees to accept or attempts to obtain, from any person, for himself or for any other person, any gift or consideration as an inducement or reward for doing or forbearing to do, or for having after the passing of this Act done or forborne to do, any act in relation to his principal's affairs or business, or for showing or forbearing to show favour or disfavour to any person in relation to his principal's affairs or business; or

If any person corruptly gives or agrees to give or offers any gift or consideration to any agent as an inducement or reward for doing or forbearing to do, or for having after the passing of this Act done or forborne to do, any act in relation to his principal's affairs or business, or for showing or forbearing to show favour or disfavour to any person in relation to his principal's affairs or business; or

If any person knowingly gives to any agent, or if any agent knowingly uses with intent to deceive his principal, any receipt, account, or other document in respect of which the principal is interested, and which contains any statement which is false or erroneous or defective in any material particular, and which to his knowledge is intended to mislead the principal;

he shall be guilty of a misdemeanour, and shall be liable—

(a) on summary conviction, to imprisonment for a term not exceeding 6 months or to a fine not exceeding the statutory maximum, or to both; and

(b) on conviction on indictment, to imprisonment for a term not exceeding 7 years or to a fine, or to both.

(2) For the purposes of this Act the expression 'consideration' includes valuable consideration of any kind; the expression 'agent' includes any person employed by or acting for another; and the expression 'principal' includes an employer.

(3) A person serving under the Crown or under any corporation or any . . . borough, county, or district council, or any board of guardians, is an agent within the meaning of this Act.

2. Prosecution of offences

(1) A prosecution for an offence under this Act shall not be instituted without the consent, in England of the Attorney-General or Solicitor-General, and in Ireland of the Attorney-General or Solicitor-General for Ireland.

(2) [Repealed]

(3) Every information for any offence under this Act shall be upon oath.

(4) [Repealed]

(5) [Repealed]

(6) Any person aggrieved by a summary conviction under this Act may appeal to the Crown Court.

3. [Applies to Scotland only]

4. Short title and commencement

(1) This Act may be cited as the Prevention of Corruption Act 1906

(2) [Repealed]

Prevention of Corruption Act 1916

1. [Repealed]

2. Presumption of corruption in certain cases

Where in any proceedings against a person for an offence under the Prevention of Corruption Act 1906, or the Public Bodies Corrupt Practices Act 1889, it is proved that any money, gift, or other consideration has been paid or given to or received by a person in the employment of Her Majesty or any Government Department or a public body by or from a person, or agent of a person, holding or seeking to obtain a contract from Her Majesty or any Government Department or public body, the money, gift, or consideration shall be deemed to have been paid or given and received corruptly as such inducement or reward as is mentioned in such Act unless the contrary is proved.

3. [Repealed]

4. Short title and interpretation

(1) This Act may be cited as the Prevention of Corruption Act 1916, and the Public Bodies Corrupt Practices Act 1889, the Prevention of Corruption Act 1906, and this Act may be cited together as the Prevention of Corruption Acts 1889 to 1916.

(2) In this Act and in the Public Bodies Corrupt Practices Act 1889, the expression 'public body' includes, in addition to the bodies mentioned in the last-mentioned Act, local and public authorities of all descriptions.

(3) A person serving under such public body is an agent within the meaning of the Prevention of Corruption Act 1906, and the expression 'agent' and 'consideration' in this Act have the same meaning as in the Prevention of Corruption Act 1906, as amended by this Act.

Anti-Terrorism, Crime and Security Act 2001

Part 12

Bribery and Corruption

108 Bribery and corruption: foreign officers etc.

(1) For the purposes of any common law offence of bribery it is immaterial if the functions of the person who receives or is offered a reward have no connection with the United Kingdom and are carried out in a country or territory outside the United Kingdom.

(2) In section 1 of the Prevention of Corruption Act 1906 (c. 34) (corrupt transactions with agents) insert this subsection after subsection (3)—

(4) For the purposes of this Act it is immaterial if—

(a) the principal's affairs or business have no connection with the United Kingdom and are conducted in a country or territory outside the United Kingdom;

(b) the agent's functions have no connection with the United Kingdom and are carried out in a country or territory outside the United Kingdom.

(3) In section 7 of the Public Bodies Corrupt Practices Act 1889 (c. 69) (interpretation relating to corruption in office) in the definition of 'public body' for 'but does not include any public body as above defined existing elsewhere than in the United Kingdom' substitute 'and includes any body which exists in a country or territory outside the United Kingdom and is equivalent to any body described above'.

(4) In section 4(2) of the Prevention of Corruption Act 1916 (c. 64) (in the 1889 and 1916 Acts public body includes local and public authorities of all descriptions) after 'descriptions' insert '(including authorities existing in a country or territory outside the United Kingdom)'.

109 Bribery and corruption committed outside the UK

(1) This section applies if—

(a) a national of the United Kingdom or a body incorporated under the law of any part of the United Kingdom does anything in a country or territory outside the United Kingdom, and

(b) the act would, if done in the United Kingdom, constitute a corruption offence (as defined below).

(2) In such a case—

(a) the act constitutes the offence concerned, and

(b) proceedings for the offence may be taken in the United Kingdom.

(3) These are corruption offences—

(a) any common law offence of bribery;

(b) the offences under section 1 of the Public Bodies Corrupt Practices Act 1889 (c. 69) (corruption in office);

(c) the first two offences under section 1 of the Prevention of Corruption Act 1906 (c. 34) (bribes obtained by or given to agents).

(4) A national of the United Kingdom is an individual who is—

(a) a British citizen, [a British Dependent Territories citizen], a British National (Overseas) or a British Overseas citizen,

(b) a person who under the British Nationality Act 1981 (c. 61) is a British subject, or
(c) a British protected person within the meaning of that Act.

110 Presumption of corruption not to apply

Section 2 of the Prevention of Corruption Act 1916 (c. 64) (presumption of corruption in certain cases) is not to apply in relation to anything which would not be an offence apart from section 108 or section 109.

APPENDIX 29

United Nations Convention Against Corruption

Preamble

The States Parties to this Convention,

Concerned about the seriousness of problems and threats posed by corruption to the stability and security of societies, undermining the institutions and values of democracy, ethical values and justice and jeopardizing sustainable development and the rule of law,

Concerned also about the links between corruption and other forms of crime, in particular organized crime and economic crime, including money-laundering,

Concerned further about cases of corruption that involve vast quantities of assets, which may constitute a substantial proportion of the resources of States, and that threaten the political stability and sustainable development of those States,

Convinced that corruption is no longer a local matter but a transnational phenomenon that affects all societies and economies, making international cooperation to prevent and control it essential,

Convinced also that a comprehensive and multidisciplinary approach is required to prevent and combat corruption effectively,

Convinced further that the availability of technical assistance can play an important role in enhancing the ability of States, including by strengthening capacity and by institution-building, to prevent and combat corruption effectively,

Convinced that the illicit acquisition of personal wealth can be particularly damaging to democratic institutions, national economies and the rule of law,

Determined to prevent, detect and deter in a more effective manner international transfers of illicitly acquired assets and to strengthen international cooperation in asset recovery,

Acknowledging the fundamental principles of due process of law in criminal proceedings and in civil or administrative proceedings to adjudicate property rights,

Bearing in mind that the prevention and eradication of corruption is a responsibility of all States and that they must cooperate with one another, with the support and involvement of individuals and groups outside the public sector, such as civil society, non-governmental organizations and community-based organizations, if their efforts in this area are to be effective,

Bearing also in mind the principles of proper management of public affairs and public property, fairness, responsibility and equality before the law and the need to safeguard integrity and to foster a culture of rejection of corruption,

Commending the work of the Commission on Crime Prevention and Criminal Justice and the United Nations Office on Drugs and Crime in preventing and combating corruption,

Recalling the work carried out by other international and regional organizations in this field, including the activities of the African Union, the Council of Europe, the Customs Cooperation Council (also known as the World Customs Organization), the European Union, the League of Arab States, the Organisation for Economic Cooperation and Development and the Organization of American States,

Taking note with appreciation of multilateral instruments to prevent and combat corruption, including, inter alia, the Inter-American Convention against Corruption, adopted by the Organization of American States on 29 March 1996,[1] the Convention on the Fight against Corruption involving Officials of the European Communities or Officials of Member States of the European Union, adopted by the Council of the European Union on 26 May 1997,[2] the Convention on Combating Bribery of Foreign Public Officials in International Business Transactions, adopted by the Organisation for Economic Cooperation and Development on 21 November 1997,[3] the Criminal Law Convention on Corruption, adopted by the Committee of Ministers of the Council of Europe on 27 January 1999,[4] the Civil Law Convention on Corruption, adopted by the Committee of Ministers of the Council of Europe on 4 November 1999,[5] and the African Union Convention on Preventing and Combating Corruption, adopted by the Heads of State and Government of the African Union on 12 July 2003,

Welcoming the entry into force on 29 September 2003 of the United Nations Convention against Transnational Organized Crime,[6]

Have agreed as follows:

Chapter I General Provisions

Article 1
Statement of purpose

The purposes of this Convention are:

(a) To promote and strengthen measures to prevent and combat corruption more efficiently and effectively;

(b) To promote, facilitate and support international cooperation and technical assistance in the prevention of and fight against corruption, including in asset recovery;

(c) To promote integrity, accountability and proper management of public affairs and public property.

Article 2
Use of terms

For the purposes of this Convention:

(a) 'Public official' shall mean: (i) any person holding a legislative, executive, administrative or judicial office of a State Party, whether appointed or elected, whether permanent or temporary, whether paid or unpaid, irrespective of that person's seniority; (ii) any other person who performs a public function, including for a public agency or public enterprise, or provides a public service, as defined in the domestic law of the State Party and as applied in the pertinent area of law of that State Party; (iii) any other person defined as a 'public official' in the domestic law of a State Party. However, for the purpose of some specific measures contained in chapter II of this Convention, 'public official' may mean any person who performs a public function or provides a public service as defined in the domestic law of the State Party and as applied in the pertinent area of law of that State Party;

(b) 'Foreign public official' shall mean any person holding a legislative, executive, administrative or judicial office of a foreign country, whether appointed or elected; and any person exercising a public function for a foreign country, including for a public agency or public enterprise;

---

[1] See E/1996/99.
[2] *Official Journal of the European Communities*, C 195, 25 June 1997.
[3] See *Corruption and Integrity Improvement Initiatives in Developing Countries* (United Nations publication, Sales No. E.98.III.B.18).
[4] Council of Europe, *European Treaty Series*, No. 173.
[5] Ibid., No. 174.
[6] General Assembly resolution 55/25, annex I.

(c) 'Official of a public international organization' shall mean an international civil servant or any person who is authorized by such an organization to act on behalf of that organization;
(d) 'Property' shall mean assets of every kind, whether corporeal or incorporeal, movable or immovable, tangible or intangible, and legal documents or instruments evidencing title to or interest in such assets;
(e) 'Proceeds of crime' shall mean any property derived from or obtained, directly or indirectly, through the commission of an offence;
(f) 'Freezing' or 'seizure' shall mean temporarily prohibiting the transfer, conversion, disposition or movement of property or temporarily assuming custody or control of property on the basis of an order issued by a court or other competent authority;
(g) 'Confiscation', which includes forfeiture where applicable, shall mean the permanent deprivation of property by order of a court or other competent authority;
(h) 'Predicate offence' shall mean any offence as a result of which proceeds have been generated that may become the subject of an offence as defined in article 23 of this Convention;
(i) 'Controlled delivery' shall mean the technique of allowing illicit or suspect consignments to pass out of, through or into the territory of one or more States, with the knowledge and under the supervision of their competent authorities, with a view to the investigation of an offence and the identification of persons involved in the commission of the offence.

Article 3
Scope of application

1. This Convention shall apply, in accordance with its terms, to the prevention, investigation and prosecution of corruption and to the freezing, seizure, confiscation and return of the proceeds of offences established in accordance with this Convention.
2. For the purposes of implementing this Convention, it shall not be necessary, except as otherwise stated herein, for the offences set forth in it to result in damage or harm to state property.

Article 4
Protection of sovereignty

1. States Parties shall carry out their obligations under this Convention in a manner consistent with the principles of sovereign equality and territorial integrity of States and that of non-intervention in the domestic affairs of other States.
2. Nothing in this Convention shall entitle a State Party to undertake in the territory of another State the exercise of jurisdiction and performance of functions that are reserved exclusively for the authorities of that other State by its domestic law.

Chapter II Preventive Measures

Article 5
Preventive anti-corruption policies and practices

1. Each State Party shall, in accordance with the fundamental principles of its legal system, develop and implement or maintain effective, coordinated anti-corruption policies that promote the participation of society and reflect the principles of the rule of law, proper management of public affairs and public property, integrity, transparency and accountability.
2. Each State Party shall endeavour to establish and promote effective practices aimed at the prevention of corruption.
3. Each State Party shall endeavour to periodically evaluate relevant legal instruments and administrative measures with a view to determining their adequacy to prevent and fight corruption.

4. States Parties shall, as appropriate and in accordance with the fundamental principles of their legal system, collaborate with each other and with relevant international and regional organizations in promoting and developing the measures referred to in this article. That collaboration may include participation in international programmes and projects aimed at the prevention of corruption.

Article 6

Preventive anti-corruption body or bodies

1. Each State Party shall, in accordance with the fundamental principles of its legal system, ensure the existence of a body or bodies, as appropriate, that prevent corruption by such means as:
   (a) Implementing the policies referred to in article 5 of this Convention and, where appropriate, overseeing and coordinating the implementation of those policies;
   (b) Increasing and disseminating knowledge about the prevention of corruption.
2. Each State Party shall grant the body or bodies referred to in paragraph 1 of this article the necessary independence, in accordance with the fundamental principles of its legal system, to enable the body or bodies to carry out its or their functions effectively and free from any undue influence. The necessary material resources and specialized staff, as well as the training that such staff may require to carry out their functions, should be provided.
3. Each State Party shall inform the Secretary-General of the United Nations of the name and address of the authority or authorities that may assist other States Parties in developing and implementing specific measures for the prevention of corruption.

Article 7

Public sector

1. Each State Party shall, where appropriate and in accordance with the fundamental principles of its legal system, endeavour to adopt, maintain and strengthen systems for the recruitment, hiring, retention, promotion and retirement of civil servants and, where appropriate, other non-elected public officials:
   (a) That are based on principles of efficiency, transparency and objective criteria such as merit, equity and aptitude;
   (b) That include adequate procedures for the selection and training of individuals for public positions considered especially vulnerable to corruption and the rotation, where appropriate, of such individuals to other positions;
   (c) That promote adequate remuneration and equitable pay scales, taking into account the level of economic development of the State Party;
   (d) That promote education and training programmes to enable them to meet the requirements for the correct, honourable and proper performance of public functions and that provide them with specialized and appropriate training to enhance their awareness of the risks of corruption inherent in the performance of their functions. Such programmes may make reference to codes or standards of conduct in applicable areas.
2. Each State Party shall also consider adopting appropriate legislative and administrative measures, consistent with the objectives of this Convention and in accordance with the fundamental principles of its domestic law, to prescribe criteria concerning candidature for and election to public office.
3. Each State Party shall also consider taking appropriate legislative and administrative measures, consistent with the objectives of this Convention and in accordance with the fundamental principles of its domestic law, to enhance transparency in the funding of candidatures for elected public office and, where applicable, the funding of political parties.
4. Each State Party shall, in accordance with the fundamental principles of its domestic law, endeavour to adopt, maintain and strengthen systems that promote transparency and prevent conflicts of interest.

Article 8

Codes of conduct for public officials

1. In order to fight corruption, each State Party shall promote, inter alia, integrity, honesty and responsibility among its public officials, in accordance with the fundamental principles of its legal system.
2. In particular, each State Party shall endeavour to apply, within its own institutional and legal systems, codes or standards of conduct for the correct, honourable and proper performance of public functions.
3. For the purposes of implementing the provisions of this article, each State Party shall, where appropriate and in accordance with the fundamental principles of its legal system, take note of the relevant initiatives of regional, interregional and multilateral organizations, such as the International Code of Conduct for Public Officials contained in the annex to General Assembly resolution 51/59 of 12 December 1996.
4. Each State Party shall also consider, in accordance with the fundamental principles of its domestic law, establishing measures and systems to facilitate the reporting by public officials of acts of corruption to appropriate authorities, when such acts come to their notice in the performance of their functions.
5. Each State Party shall endeavour, where appropriate and in accordance with the fundamental principles of its domestic law, to establish measures and systems requiring public officials to make declarations to appropriate authorities regarding, inter alia, their outside activities, employment, investments, assets and substantial gifts or benefits from which a conflict of interest may result with respect to their functions as public officials.
6. Each State Party shall consider taking, in accordance with the fundamental principles of its domestic law, disciplinary or other measures against public officials who violate the codes or standards established in accordance with this article.

Article 9

Public procurement and management of public finances

1. Each State Party shall, in accordance with the fundamental principles of its legal system, take the necessary steps to establish appropriate systems of procurement, based on transparency, competition and objective criteria in decision-making, that are effective, inter alia, in preventing corruption. Such systems, which may take into account appropriate threshold values in their application, shall address, inter alia:
   (a) The public distribution of information relating to procurement procedures and contracts, including information on invitations to tender and relevant or pertinent information on the award of contracts, allowing potential tenderers sufficient time to prepare and submit their tenders;
   (b) The establishment, in advance, of conditions for participation, including selection and award criteria and tendering rules, and their publication;
   (c) The use of objective and predetermined criteria for public procurement decisions, in order to facilitate the subsequent verification of the correct application of the rules or procedures;
   (d) An effective system of domestic review, including an effective system of appeal, to ensure legal recourse and remedies in the event that the rules or procedures established pursuant to this paragraph are not followed;
   (e) Where appropriate, measures to regulate matters regarding personnel responsible for procurement, such as declaration of interest in particular public procurements, screening procedures and training requirements.

2. Each State Party shall, in accordance with the fundamental principles of its legal system, take appropriate measures to promote transparency and accountability in the management of public finances. Such measures shall encompass, inter alia:
   (a) Procedures for the adoption of the national budget;
   (b) Timely reporting on revenue and expenditure;
   (c) A system of accounting and auditing standards and related oversight;
   (d) Effective and efficient systems of risk management and internal control; and
   (e) Where appropriate, corrective action in the case of failure to comply with the requirements established in this paragraph.
3. Each State Party shall take such civil and administrative measures as may be necessary, in accordance with the fundamental principles of its domestic law, to preserve the integrity of accounting books, records, financial statements or other documents related to public expenditure and revenue and to prevent the falsification of such documents.

Article 10

Public reporting

Taking into account the need to combat corruption, each State Party shall, in accordance with the fundamental principles of its domestic law, take such measures as may be necessary to enhance transparency in its public administration, including with regard to its organization, functioning and decision-making processes, where appropriate. Such measures may include, inter alia:

(a) Adopting procedures or regulations allowing members of the general public to obtain, where appropriate, information on the organization, functioning and decision-making processes of its public administration and, with due regard for the protection of privacy and personal data, on decisions and legal acts that concern members of the public;
(b) Simplifying administrative procedures, where appropriate, in order to facilitate public access to the competent decision-making authorities; and
(c) Publishing information, which may include periodic reports on the risks of corruption in its public administration.

Article 11

Measures relating to the judiciary and prosecution services

1. Bearing in mind the independence of the judiciary and its crucial role in combating corruption, each State Party shall, in accordance with the fundamental principles of its legal system and without prejudice to judicial independence, take measures to strengthen integrity and to prevent opportunities for corruption among members of the judiciary. Such measures may include rules with respect to the conduct of members of the judiciary.
2. Measures to the same effect as those taken pursuant to paragraph 1 of this article may be introduced and applied within the prosecution service in those States Parties where it does not form part of the judiciary but enjoys independence similar to that of the judicial service.

Article 12

Private sector

1. Each State Party shall take measures, in accordance with the fundamental principles of its domestic law, to prevent corruption involving the private sector, enhance accounting and auditing standards in the private sector and, where appropriate, provide effective, proportionate and dissuasive civil, administrative or criminal penalties for failure to comply with such measures.
2. Measures to achieve these ends may include, inter alia:
   (a) Promoting cooperation between law enforcement agencies and relevant private entities;
   (b) Promoting the development of standards and procedures designed to safeguard the integrity of relevant private entities, including codes of conduct for the correct, honourable and

proper performance of the activities of business and all relevant professions and the prevention of conflicts of interest, and for the promotion of the use of good commercial practices among businesses and in the contractual relations of businesses with the State;

(c) Promoting transparency among private entities, including, where appropriate, measures regarding the identity of legal and natural persons involved in the establishment and management of corporate entities;

(d) Preventing the misuse of procedures regulating private entities, including procedures regarding subsidies and licences granted by public authorities for commercial activities;

(e) Preventing conflicts of interest by imposing restrictions, as appropriate and for a reasonable period of time, on the professional activities of former public officials or on the employment of public officials by the private sector after their resignation or retirement, where such activities or employment relate directly to the functions held or supervised by those public officials during their tenure;

(f) Ensuring that private enterprises, taking into account their structure and size, have sufficient internal auditing controls to assist in preventing and detecting acts of corruption and that the accounts and required financial statements of such private enterprises are subject to appropriate auditing and certification procedures.

3. In order to prevent corruption, each State Party shall take such measures as may be necessary, in accordance with its domestic laws and regulations regarding the maintenance of books and records, financial statement disclosures and accounting and auditing standards, to prohibit the following acts carried out for the purpose of committing any of the offences established in accordance with this Convention:

(a) The establishment of off-the-books accounts;

(b) The making of off-the-books or inadequately identified transactions;

(c) The recording of non-existent expenditure;

(d) The entry of liabilities with incorrect identification of their objects;

(e) The use of false documents; and

(f) The intentional destruction of bookkeeping documents earlier than foreseen by the law.

4. Each State Party shall disallow the tax deductibility of expenses that constitute bribes, the latter being one of the constituent elements of the offences established in accordance with articles 15 and 16 of this Convention and, where appropriate, other expenses incurred in furtherance of corrupt conduct.

Article 13
Participation of society

1. Each State Party shall take appropriate measures, within its means and in accordance with fundamental principles of its domestic law, to promote the active participation of individuals and groups outside the public sector, such as civil society, non-governmental organizations and community-based organizations, in the prevention of and the fight against corruption and to raise public awareness regarding the existence, causes and gravity of and the threat posed by corruption. This participation should be strengthened by such measures as:

(a) Enhancing the transparency of and promoting the contribution of the public to decision-making processes;

(b) Ensuring that the public has effective access to information;

(c) Undertaking public information activities that contribute to non-tolerance of corruption, as well as public education programmes, including school and university curricula;

(d) Respecting, promoting and protecting the freedom to seek, receive, publish and disseminate information concerning corruption. That freedom may be subject to certain restrictions, but these shall only be such as are provided for by law and are necessary:

(i) For respect of the rights or reputations of others;

(ii) For the protection of national security or *ordre public* or of public health or morals.

2. Each State Party shall take appropriate measures to ensure that the relevant anti-corruption bodies referred to in this Convention are known to the public and shall provide access to such bodies, where appropriate, for the reporting, including anonymously, of any incidents that may be considered to constitute an offence established in accordance with this Convention.

Article 14

Measures to prevent money-laundering

1. Each State Party shall:
   (a) Institute a comprehensive domestic regulatory and supervisory regime for banks and non-bank financial institutions, including natural or legal persons that provide formal or informal services for the transmission of money or value and, where appropriate, other bodies particularly susceptible to money-laundering, within its competence, in order to deter and detect all forms of money-laundering, which regime shall emphasize requirements for customer and, where appropriate, beneficial owner identification, record-keeping and the reporting of suspicious transactions;
   (b) Without prejudice to article 46 of this Convention, ensure that administrative, regulatory, law enforcement and other authorities dedicated to combating money-laundering (including, where appropriate under domestic law, judicial authorities) have the ability to cooperate and exchange information at the national and international levels within the conditions prescribed by its domestic law and, to that end, shall consider the establishment of a financial intelligence unit to serve as a national centre for the collection, analysis and dissemination of information regarding potential money-laundering.
2. States Parties shall consider implementing feasible measures to detect and monitor the movement of cash and appropriate negotiable instruments across their borders, subject to safeguards to ensure proper use of information and without impeding in any way the movement of legitimate capital. Such measures may include a requirement that individuals and businesses report the cross-border transfer of substantial quantities of cash and appropriate negotiable instruments.
3. States Parties shall consider implementing appropriate and feasible measures to require financial institutions, including money remitters:
   (a) To include on forms for the electronic transfer of funds and related messages accurate and meaningful information on the originator;
   (b) To maintain such information throughout the payment chain; and
   (c) To apply enhanced scrutiny to transfers of funds that do not contain complete information on the originator.
4. In establishing a domestic regulatory and supervisory regime under the terms of this article, and without prejudice to any other article of this Convention, States Parties are called upon to use as a guideline the relevant initiatives of regional, interregional and multilateral organizations against money-laundering.
5. States Parties shall endeavour to develop and promote global, regional, subregional and bilateral cooperation among judicial, law enforcement and financial regulatory authorities in order to combat money-laundering.

Chapter III Criminalization and Law Enforcement

Article 15

Bribery of national public officials

Each State Party shall adopt such legislative and other measures as may be necessary to establish as criminal offences, when committed intentionally:

(a) The promise, offering or giving, to a public official, directly or indirectly, of an undue advantage, for the official himself or herself or another person or entity, in order that the official act or refrain from acting in the exercise of his or her official duties;

(b) The solicitation or acceptance by a public official, directly or indirectly, of an undue advantage, for the official himself or herself or another person or entity, in order that the official act or refrain from acting in the exercise of his or her official duties.

Article 16

Bribery of foreign public officials and officials of public international organizations

1. Each State Party shall adopt such legislative and other measures as may be necessary to establish as a criminal offence, when committed intentionally, the promise, offering or giving to a foreign public official or an official of a public international organization, directly or indirectly, of an undue advantage, for the official himself or herself or another person or entity, in order that the official act or refrain from acting in the exercise of his or her official duties, in order to obtain or retain business or other undue advantage in relation to the conduct of international business.
2. Each State Party shall consider adopting such legislative and other measures as may be necessary to establish as a criminal offence, when committed intentionally, the solicitation or acceptance by a foreign public official or an official of a public international organization, directly or indirectly, of an undue advantage, for the official himself or herself or another person or entity, in order that the official act or refrain from acting in the exercise of his or her official duties.

Article 17

Embezzlement, misappropriation or other diversion of property by a public official

Each State Party shall adopt such legislative and other measures as may be necessary to establish as criminal offences, when committed intentionally, the embezzlement, misappropriation or other diversion by a public official for his or her benefit or for the benefit of another person or entity, of any property, public or private funds or securities or any other thing of value entrusted to the public official by virtue of his or her position.

Article 18

Trading in influence

Each State Party shall consider adopting such legislative and other measures as may be necessary to establish as criminal offences, when committed intentionally:

(a) The promise, offering or giving to a public official or any other person, directly or indirectly, of an undue advantage in order that the public official or the person abuse his or her real or supposed influence with a view to obtaining from an administration or public authority of the State Party an undue advantage for the original instigator of the act or for any other person;

(b) The solicitation or acceptance by a public official or any other person, directly or indirectly, of an undue advantage for himself or herself or for another person in order that the public official or the person abuse his or her real or supposed influence with a view to obtaining from an administration or public authority of the State Party an undue advantage.

Article 19

Abuse of functions

Each State Party shall consider adopting such legislative and other measures as may be necessary to establish as a criminal offence, when committed intentionally, the abuse of functions or position, that is, the performance of or failure to perform an act, in violation of laws, by a public official in the discharge of his or her functions, for the purpose of obtaining an undue advantage for himself or herself or for another person or entity.

Article 20

Illicit enrichment

Subject to its constitution and the fundamental principles of its legal system, each State Party shall consider adopting such legislative and other measures as may be necessary to establish as a criminal offence, when committed intentionally, illicit enrichment, that is, a significant increase in the assets of a public official that he or she cannot reasonably explain in relation to his or her lawful income.

Article 21

Bribery in the private sector

Each State Party shall consider adopting such legislative and other measures as may be necessary to establish as criminal offences, when committed intentionally in the course of economic, financial or commercial activities:

(a) The promise, offering or giving, directly or indirectly, of an undue advantage to any person who directs or works, in any capacity, for a private sector entity, for the person himself or herself or for another person, in order that he or she, in breach of his or her duties, act or refrain from acting;

(b) The solicitation or acceptance, directly or indirectly, of an undue advantage by any person who directs or works, in any capacity, for a private sector entity, for the person himself or herself or for another person, in order that he or she, in breach of his or her duties, act or refrain from acting.

Article 22

Embezzlement of property in the private sector

Each State Party shall consider adopting such legislative and other measures as may be necessary to establish as a criminal offence, when committed intentionally in the course of economic, financial or commercial activities, embezzlement by a person who directs or works, in any capacity, in a private sector entity of any property, private funds or securities or any other thing of value entrusted to him or her by virtue of his or her position.

Article 23

Laundering of proceeds of crime

1. Each State Party shall adopt, in accordance with fundamental principles of its domestic law, such legislative and other measures as may be necessary to establish as criminal offences, when committed intentionally:
   (a) (i) The conversion or transfer of property, knowing that such property is the proceeds of crime, for the purpose of concealing or disguising the illicit origin of the property or of helping any person who is involved in the commission of the predicate offence to evade the legal consequences of his or her action;
   (ii) The concealment or disguise of the true nature, source, location, disposition, movement or ownership of or rights with respect to property, knowing that such property is the proceeds of crime;
   (b) Subject to the basic concepts of its legal system:
   (i) The acquisition, possession or use of property, knowing, at the time of receipt, that such property is the proceeds of crime;
   (ii) Participation in, association with or conspiracy to commit, attempts to commit and aiding, abetting, facilitating and counselling the commission of any of the offences established in accordance with this article.
2. For purposes of implementing or applying paragraph 1 of this article:
   (a) Each State Party shall seek to apply paragraph 1 of this article to the widest range of predicate offences;

(b) Each State Party shall include as predicate offences at a minimum a comprehensive range of criminal offences established in accordance with this Convention;
(c) For the purposes of subparagraph (b) above, predicate offences shall include offences committed both within and outside the jurisdiction of the State Party in question. However, offences committed outside the jurisdiction of a State Party shall constitute predicate offences only when the relevant conduct is a criminal offence under the domestic law of the State where it is committed and would be a criminal offence under the domestic law of the State Party implementing or applying this article had it been committed there;
(d) Each State Party shall furnish copies of its laws that give effect to this article and of any subsequent changes to such laws or a description thereof to the Secretary-General of the United Nations;
(e) If required by fundamental principles of the domestic law of a State Party, it may be provided that the offences set forth in paragraph 1 of this article do not apply to the persons who committed the predicate offence.

Article 24

Concealment

Without prejudice to the provisions of article 23 of this Convention, each State Party shall consider adopting such legislative and other measures as may be necessary to establish as a criminal offence, when committed intentionally after the commission of any of the offences established in accordance with this Convention without having participated in such offences, the concealment or continued retention of property when the person involved knows that such property is the result of any of the offences established in accordance with this Convention.

Article 25

Obstruction of justice

Each State Party shall adopt such legislative and other measures as may be necessary to establish as criminal offences, when committed intentionally:

(a) The use of physical force, threats or intimidation or the promise, offering or giving of an undue advantage to induce false testimony or to interfere in the giving of testimony or the production of evidence in a proceeding in relation to the commission of offences established in accordance with this Convention;
(b) The use of physical force, threats or intimidation to interfere with the exercise of official duties by a justice or law enforcement official in relation to the commission of offences established in accordance with this Convention. Nothing in this subparagraph shall prejudice the right of States Parties to have legislation that protects other categories of public official.

Article 26

Liability of legal persons

1. Each State Party shall adopt such measures as may be necessary, consistent with its legal principles, to establish the liability of legal persons for participation in the offences established in accordance with this Convention.
2. Subject to the legal principles of the State Party, the liability of legal persons may be criminal, civil or administrative.
3. Such liability shall be without prejudice to the criminal liability of the natural persons who have committed the offences.
4. Each State Party shall, in particular, ensure that legal persons held liable in accordance with this article are subject to effective, proportionate and dissuasive criminal or non-criminal sanctions, including monetary sanctions.

Article 27

Participation and attempt

1. Each State Party shall adopt such legislative and other measures as may be necessary to establish as a criminal offence, in accordance with its domestic law, participation in any capacity such as an accomplice, assistant or instigator in an offence established in accordance with this Convention.
2. Each State Party may adopt such legislative and other measures as may be necessary to establish as a criminal offence, in accordance with its domestic law, any attempt to commit an offence established in accordance with this Convention.
3. Each State Party may adopt such legislative and other measures as may be necessary to establish as a criminal offence, in accordance with its domestic law, the preparation for an offence established in accordance with this Convention.

Article 28

Knowledge, intent and purpose as elements of an offence

Knowledge, intent or purpose required as an element of an offence established in accordance with this Convention may be inferred from objective factual circumstances.

Article 29

Statute of limitations

Each State Party shall, where appropriate, establish under its domestic law a long statute of limitations period in which to commence proceedings for any offence established in accordance with this Convention and establish a longer statute of limitations period or provide for the suspension of the statute of limitations where the alleged offender has evaded the administration of justice.

Article 30

Prosecution, adjudication and sanctions

1. Each State Party shall make the commission of an offence established in accordance with this Convention liable to sanctions that take into account the gravity of that offence.
2. Each State Party shall take such measures as may be necessary to establish or maintain, in accordance with its legal system and constitutional principles, an appropriate balance between any immunities or jurisdictional privileges accorded to its public officials for the performance of their functions and the possibility, when necessary, of effectively investigating, prosecuting and adjudicating offences established in accordance with this Convention.
3. Each State Party shall endeavour to ensure that any discretionary legal powers under its domestic law relating to the prosecution of persons for offences established in accordance with this Convention are exercised to maximize the effectiveness of law enforcement measures in respect of those offences and with due regard to the need to deter the commission of such offences.
4. In the case of offences established in accordance with this Convention, each State Party shall take appropriate measures, in accordance with its domestic law and with due regard to the rights of the defence, to seek to ensure that conditions imposed in connection with decisions on release pending trial or appeal take into consideration the need to ensure the presence of the defendant at subsequent criminal proceedings.
5. Each State Party shall take into account the gravity of the offences concerned when considering the eventuality of early release or parole of persons convicted of such offences.
6. Each State Party, to the extent consistent with the fundamental principles of its legal system, shall consider establishing procedures through which a public official accused of an offence established in accordance with this Convention may, where appropriate, be removed,

suspended or reassigned by the appropriate authority, bearing in mind respect for the principle of the presumption of innocence.

7. Where warranted by the gravity of the offence, each State Party, to the extent consistent with the fundamental principles of its legal system, shall consider establishing procedures for the disqualification, by court order or any other appropriate means, for a period of time determined by its domestic law, of persons convicted of offences established in accordance with this Convention from:
   (a) Holding public office; and
   (b) Holding office in an enterprise owned in whole or in part by the State.
8. Paragraph 1 of this article shall be without prejudice to the exercise of disciplinary powers by the competent authorities against civil servants.
9. Nothing contained in this Convention shall affect the principle that the description of the offences established in accordance with this Convention and of the applicable legal defences or other legal principles controlling the lawfulness of conduct is reserved to the domestic law of a State Party and that such offences shall be prosecuted and punished in accordance with that law.
10. States Parties shall endeavour to promote the reintegration into society of persons convicted of offences established in accordance with this Convention.

Article 31

Freezing, seizure and confiscation

1. Each State Party shall take, to the greatest extent possible within its domestic legal system, such measures as may be necessary to enable confiscation of:
   (a) Proceeds of crime derived from offences established in accordance with this Convention or property the value of which corresponds to that of such proceeds;
   (b) Property, equipment or other instrumentalities used in or destined for use in offences established in accordance with this Convention.
2. Each State Party shall take such measures as may be necessary to enable the identification, tracing, freezing or seizure of any item referred to in paragraph 1 of this article for the purpose of eventual confiscation.
3. Each State Party shall adopt, in accordance with its domestic law, such legislative and other measures as may be necessary to regulate the administration by the competent authorities of frozen, seized or confiscated property covered in paragraphs 1 and 2 of this article.
4. If such proceeds of crime have been transformed or converted, in part or in full, into other property, such property shall be liable to the measures referred to in this article instead of the proceeds.
5. If such proceeds of crime have been intermingled with property acquired from legitimate sources, such property shall, without prejudice to any powers relating to freezing or seizure, be liable to confiscation up to the assessed value of the intermingled proceeds.
6. Income or other benefits derived from such proceeds of crime, from property into which such proceeds of crime have been transformed or converted or from property with which such proceeds of crime have been intermingled shall also be liable to the measures referred to in this article, in the same manner and to the same extent as proceeds of crime.
7. For the purpose of this article and article 55 of this Convention, each State Party shall empower its courts or other competent authorities to order that bank, financial or commercial records be made available or seized. A State Party shall not decline to act under the provisions of this paragraph on the ground of bank secrecy.
8. States Parties may consider the possibility of requiring that an offender demonstrate the lawful origin of such alleged proceeds of crime or other property liable to confiscation, to the extent that such a requirement is consistent with the fundamental principles of their domestic law and with the nature of judicial and other proceedings.

9. The provisions of this article shall not be so construed as to prejudice the rights of bona fide third parties.
10. Nothing contained in this article shall affect the principle that the measures to which it refers shall be defined and implemented in accordance with and subject to the provisions of the domestic law of a State Party.

Article 32

Protection of witnesses, experts and victims

1. Each State Party shall take appropriate measures in accordance with its domestic legal system and within its means to provide effective protection from potential retaliation or intimidation for witnesses and experts who give testimony concerning offences established in accordance with this Convention and, as appropriate, for their relatives and other persons close to them.
2. The measures envisaged in paragraph 1 of this article may include, inter alia, without prejudice to the rights of the defendant, including the right to due process:
   (a) Establishing procedures for the physical protection of such persons, such as, to the extent necessary and feasible, relocating them and permitting, where appropriate, non-disclosure or limitations on the disclosure of information concerning the identity and whereabouts of such persons;
   (b) Providing evidentiary rules to permit witnesses and experts to give testimony in a manner that ensures the safety of such persons, such as permitting testimony to be given through the use of communications technology such as video or other adequate means.
3. States Parties shall consider entering into agreements or arrangements with other States for the relocation of persons referred to in paragraph 1 of this article.
4. The provisions of this article shall also apply to victims insofar as they are witnesses.
5. Each State Party shall, subject to its domestic law, enable the views and concerns of victims to be presented and considered at appropriate stages of criminal proceedings against offenders in a manner not prejudicial to the rights of the defence.

Article 33

Protection of reporting persons

Each State Party shall consider incorporating into its domestic legal system appropriate measures to provide protection against any unjustified treatment for any person who reports in good faith and on reasonable grounds to the competent authorities any facts concerning offences established in accordance with this Convention

Article 34

Consequences of acts of corruption

With due regard to the rights of third parties acquired in good faith, each State Party shall take measures, in accordance with the fundamental principles of its domestic law, to address consequences of corruption. In this context, States Parties may consider corruption a relevant factor in legal proceedings to annul or rescind a contract, withdraw a concession or other similar instrument or take any other remedial action.

Article 35

Compensation for damage

Each State Party shall take such measures as may be necessary, in accordance with principles of its domestic law, to ensure that entities or persons who have suffered damage as a result of an act of corruption have the right to initiate legal proceedings against those responsible for that damage in order to obtain compensation.

Article 36

Specialized authorities

Each State Party shall, in accordance with the fundamental principles of its legal system, ensure the existence of a body or bodies or persons specialized in combating corruption through law enforcement. Such body or bodies or persons shall be granted the necessary independence, in accordance with the fundamental principles of the legal system of the State Party, to be able to carry out their functions effectively and without any undue influence. Such persons or staff of such body or bodies should have the appropriate training and resources to carry out their tasks.

Article 37

Cooperation with law enforcement authorities

1. Each State Party shall take appropriate measures to encourage persons who participate or who have participated in the commission of an offence established in accordance with this Convention to supply information useful to competent authorities for investigative and evidentiary purposes and to provide factual, specific help to competent authorities that may contribute to depriving offenders of the proceeds of crime and to recovering such proceeds.
2. Each State Party shall consider providing for the possibility, in appropriate cases, of mitigating punishment of an accused person who provides substantial cooperation in the investigation or prosecution of an offence established in accordance with this Convention.
3. Each State Party shall consider providing for the possibility, in accordance with fundamental principles of its domestic law, of granting immunity from prosecution to a person who provides substantial cooperation in the investigation or prosecution of an offence established in accordance with this Convention.
4. Protection of such persons shall be, mutatis mutandis, as provided for in article 32 of this Convention.
5. Where a person referred to in paragraph 1 of this article located in one State Party can provide substantial cooperation to the competent authorities of another State Party, the States Parties concerned may consider entering into agreements or arrangements, in accordance with their domestic law, concerning the potential provision by the other State Party of the treatment set forth in paragraphs 2 and 3 of this article.

Article 38

Cooperation between national authorities

Each State Party shall take such measures as may be necessary to encourage, in accordance with its domestic law, cooperation between, on the one hand, its public authorities, as well as its public officials, and, on the other hand, its authorities responsible for investigating and prosecuting criminal offences. Such cooperation may include:

(a) Informing the latter authorities, on their own initiative, where there are reasonable grounds to believe that any of the offences established in accordance with articles 15, 21 and 23 of this Convention has been committed; or

(b) Providing, upon request, to the latter authorities all necessary information.

Article 39

Cooperation between national authorities and the private sector

1. Each State Party shall take such measures as may be necessary to encourage, in accordance with its domestic law, cooperation between national investigating and prosecuting authorities and entities of the private sector, in particular financial institutions, relating to matters involving the commission of offences established in accordance with this Convention.
2. Each State Party shall consider encouraging its nationals and other persons with a habitual residence in its territory to report to the national investigating and prosecuting authorities the commission of an offence established in accordance with this Convention.

Article 40
Bank secrecy

Each State Party shall ensure that, in the case of domestic criminal investigations of offences established in accordance with this Convention, there are appropriate mechanisms available within its domestic legal system to overcome obstacles that may arise out of the application of bank secrecy laws.

Article 41
Criminal record

Each State Party may adopt such legislative or other measures as may be necessary to take into consideration, under such terms as and for the purpose that it deems appropriate, any previous conviction in another State of an alleged offender for the purpose of using such information in criminal proceedings relating to an offence established in accordance with this Convention.

Article 42
Jurisdiction

1. Each State Party shall adopt such measures as may be necessary to establish its jurisdiction over the offences established in accordance with this Convention when:
   (a) The offence is committed in the territory of that State Party; or
   (b) The offence is committed on board a vessel that is flying the flag of that State Party or an aircraft that is registered under the laws of that State Party at the time that the offence is committed.
2. Subject to article 4 of this Convention, a State Party may also establish its jurisdiction over any such offence when:
   (a) The offence is committed against a national of that State Party; or
   (b) The offence is committed by a national of that State Party or a stateless person who has his or her habitual residence in its territory; or
   (c) The offence is one of those established in accordance with article 23, paragraph 1 (b)(ii), of this Convention and is committed outside its territory with a view to the commission of an offence established in accordance with article 23, paragraph 1(a)(i) or (ii) or (b)(i), of this Convention within its territory; or
   (d) The offence is committed against the State Party.
3. For the purposes of article 44 of this Convention, each State Party shall take such measures as may be necessary to establish its jurisdiction over the offences established in accordance with this Convention when the alleged offender is present in its territory and it does not extradite such person solely on the ground that he or she is one of its nationals.
4. Each State Party may also take such measures as may be necessary to establish its jurisdiction over the offences established in accordance with this Convention when the alleged offender is present in its territory and it does not extradite him or her.
5. If a State Party exercising its jurisdiction under paragraph 1 or 2 of this article has been notified, or has otherwise learned, that any other States Parties are conducting an investigation, prosecution or judicial proceeding in respect of the same conduct, the competent authorities of those States Parties shall, as appropriate, consult one another with a view to coordinating their actions.
6. Without prejudice to norms of general international law, this Convention shall not exclude the exercise of any criminal jurisdiction established by a State Party in accordance with its domestic law.

Chapter IV International Cooperation

Article 43

International cooperation

1. States Parties shall cooperate in criminal matters in accordance with articles 44 to 50 of this Convention. Where appropriate and consistent with their domestic legal system, States Parties shall consider assisting each other in investigations of and proceedings in civil and administrative matters relating to corruption.
2. In matters of international cooperation, whenever dual criminality is considered a requirement, it shall be deemed fulfilled irrespective of whether the laws of the requested State Party place the offence within the same category of offence or denominate the offence by the same terminology as the requesting State Party, if the conduct underlying the offence for which assistance is sought is a criminal offence under the laws of both States Parties.

Article 44

Extradition

1. This article shall apply to the offences established in accordance with this Convention where the person who is the subject of the request for extradition is present in the territory of the requested State Party, provided that the offence for which extradition is sought is punishable under the domestic law of both the requesting State Party and the requested State Party.
2. Notwithstanding the provisions of paragraph 1 of this article, a State Party whose law so permits may grant the extradition of a person for any of the offences covered by this Convention that are not punishable under its own domestic law.
3. If the request for extradition includes several separate offences, at least one of which is extraditable under this article and some of which are not extraditable by reason of their period of imprisonment but are related to offences established in accordance with this Convention, the requested State Party may apply this article also in respect of those offences.
4. Each of the offences to which this article applies shall be deemed to be included as an extraditable offence in any extradition treaty existing between States Parties. States Parties undertake to include such offences as extraditable offences in every extradition treaty to be concluded between them. A State Party whose law so permits, in case it uses this Convention as the basis for extradition, shall not consider any of the offences established in accordance with this Convention to be a political offence.
5. If a State Party that makes extradition conditional on the existence of a treaty receives a request for extradition from another State Party with which it has no extradition treaty, it may consider this Convention the legal basis for extradition in respect of any offence to which this article applies.
6. A State Party that makes extradition conditional on the existence of a treaty shall:
   (a) At the time of deposit of its instrument of ratification, acceptance or approval of or accession to this Convention, inform the Secretary-General of the United Nations whether it will take this Convention as the legal basis for cooperation on extradition with other States Parties to this Convention; and
   (b) If it does not take this Convention as the legal basis for cooperation on extradition, seek, where appropriate, to conclude treaties on extradition with other States Parties to this Convention in order to implement this article.
7. States Parties that do not make extradition conditional on the existence of a treaty shall recognize offences to which this article applies as extraditable offences between themselves.
8. Extradition shall be subject to the conditions provided for by the domestic law of the requested State Party or by applicable extradition treaties, including, inter alia, conditions in relation to the minimum penalty requirement for extradition and the grounds upon which the requested State Party may refuse extradition.

9. States Parties shall, subject to their domestic law, endeavour to expedite extradition procedures and to simplify evidentiary requirements relating thereto in respect of any offence to which this article applies.
10. Subject to the provisions of its domestic law and its extradition treaties, the requested State Party may, upon being satisfied that the circumstances so warrant and are urgent and at the request of the requesting State Party, take a person whose extradition is sought and who is present in its territory into custody or take other appropriate measures to ensure his or her presence at extradition proceedings.
11. A State Party in whose territory an alleged offender is found, if it does not extradite such person in respect of an offence to which this article applies solely on the ground that he or she is one of its nationals, shall, at the request of the State Party seeking extradition, be obliged to submit the case without undue delay to its competent authorities for the purpose of prosecution. Those authorities shall take their decision and conduct their proceedings in the same manner as in the case of any other offence of a grave nature under the domestic law of that State Party. The States Parties concerned shall cooperate with each other, in particular on procedural and evidentiary aspects, to ensure the efficiency of such prosecution.
12. Whenever a State Party is permitted under its domestic law to extradite or otherwise surrender one of its nationals only upon the condition that the person will be returned to that State Party to serve the sentence imposed as a result of the trial or proceedings for which the extradition or surrender of the person was sought and that State Party and the State Party seeking the extradition of the person agree with this option and other terms that they may deem appropriate, such conditional extradition or surrender shall be sufficient to discharge the obligation set forth in paragraph 11 of this article.
13. If extradition, sought for purposes of enforcing a sentence, is refused because the person sought is a national of the requested State Party, the requested State Party shall, if its domestic law so permits and in conformity with the requirements of such law, upon application of the requesting State Party, consider the enforcement of the sentence imposed under the domestic law of the requesting State Party or the remainder thereof.
14. Any person regarding whom proceedings are being carried out in connection with any of the offences to which this article applies shall be guaranteed fair treatment at all stages of the proceedings, including enjoyment of all the rights and guarantees provided by the domestic law of the State Party in the territory of which that person is present.
15. Nothing in this Convention shall be interpreted as imposing an obligation to extradite if the requested State Party has substantial grounds for believing that the request has been made for the purpose of prosecuting or punishing a person on account of that person's sex, race, religion, nationality, ethnic origin or political opinions or that compliance with the request would cause prejudice to that person's position for any one of these reasons.
16. States Parties may not refuse a request for extradition on the sole ground that the offence is also considered to involve fiscal matters.
17. Before refusing extradition, the requested State Party shall, where appropriate, consult with the requesting State Party to provide it with ample opportunity to present its opinions and to provide information relevant to its allegation.
18. States Parties shall seek to conclude bilateral and multilateral agreements or arrangements to carry out or to enhance the effectiveness of extradition.

Article 45
Transfer of sentenced persons

States Parties may consider entering into bilateral or multilateral agreements or arrangements on the transfer to their territory of persons sentenced to imprisonment or other forms of deprivation of liberty for offences established in accordance with this Convention in order that they may complete their sentences there.

Article 46

Mutual legal assistance

1. States Parties shall afford one another the widest measure of mutual legal assistance in investigations, prosecutions and judicial proceedings in relation to the offences covered by this Convention.
2. Mutual legal assistance shall be afforded to the fullest extent possible under relevant laws, treaties, agreements and arrangements of the requested State Party with respect to investigations, prosecutions and judicial proceedings in relation to the offences for which a legal person may be held liable in accordance with article 26 of this Convention in the requesting State Party.
3. Mutual legal assistance to be afforded in accordance with this article may be requested for any of the following purposes:
   (a) Taking evidence or statements from persons;
   (b) Effecting service of judicial documents;
   (c) Executing searches and seizures, and freezing;
   (d) Examining objects and sites;
   (e) Providing information, evidentiary items and expert evaluations;
   (f) Providing originals or certified copies of relevant documents and records, including government, bank, financial, corporate or business records;
   (g) Identifying or tracing proceeds of crime, property, instrumentalities or other things for evidentiary purposes;
   (h) Facilitating the voluntary appearance of persons in the requesting State Party;
   (i) Any other type of assistance that is not contrary to the domestic law of the requested State Party;
   (j) Identifying, freezing and tracing proceeds of crime in accordance with the provisions of chapter V of this Convention;
   (k) The recovery of assets, in accordance with the provisions of chapter V of this Convention.
4. Without prejudice to domestic law, the competent authorities of a State Party may, without prior request, transmit information relating to criminal matters to a competent authority in another State Party where they believe that such information could assist the authority in undertaking or successfully concluding inquiries and criminal proceedings or could result in a request formulated by the latter State Party pursuant to this Convention.
5. The transmission of information pursuant to paragraph 4 of this article shall be without prejudice to inquiries and criminal proceedings in the State of the competent authorities providing the information. The competent authorities receiving the information shall comply with a request that said information remain confidential, even temporarily, or with restrictions on its use. However, this shall not prevent the receiving State Party from disclosing in its proceedings information that is exculpatory to an accused person. In such a case, the receiving State Party shall notify the transmitting State Party prior to the disclosure and, if so requested, consult with the transmitting State Party. If, in an exceptional case, advance notice is not possible, the receiving State Party shall inform the transmitting State Party of the disclosure without delay.
6. The provisions of this article shall not affect the obligations under any other treaty, bilateral or multilateral, that governs or will govern, in whole or in part, mutual legal assistance.
7. Paragraphs 9 to 29 of this article shall apply to requests made pursuant to this article if the States Parties in question are not bound by a treaty of mutual legal assistance. If those States Parties are bound by such a treaty, the corresponding provisions of that treaty shall apply unless the States Parties agree to apply paragraphs 9 to 29 of this article in lieu thereof. States Parties are strongly encouraged to apply those paragraphs if they facilitate cooperation.
8. States Parties shall not decline to render mutual legal assistance pursuant to this article on the ground of bank secrecy.

9. (a) A requested State Party, in responding to a request for assistance pursuant to this article in the absence of dual criminality, shall take into account the purposes of this Convention, as set forth in article 1;
   (b) States Parties may decline to render assistance pursuant to this article on the ground of absence of dual criminality. However, a requested State Party shall, where consistent with the basic concepts of its legal system, render assistance that does not involve coercive action. Such assistance may be refused when requests involve matters of a *de minimis* nature or matters for which the cooperation or assistance sought is available under other provisions of this Convention;
   (c) Each State Party may consider adopting such measures as may be necessary to enable it to provide a wider scope of assistance pursuant to this article in the absence of dual criminality.
10. A person who is being detained or is serving a sentence in the territory of one State Party whose presence in another State Party is requested for purposes of identification, testimony or otherwise providing assistance in obtaining evidence for investigations, prosecutions or judicial proceedings in relation to offences covered by this Convention may be transferred if the following conditions are met:
    (a) The person freely gives his or her informed consent;
    (b) The competent authorities of both States Parties agree, subject to such conditions as those States Parties may deem appropriate.
11. For the purposes of paragraph 10 of this article:
    (a) The State Party to which the person is transferred shall have the authority and obligation to keep the person transferred in custody, unless otherwise requested or authorized by the State Party from which the person was transferred;
    (b) The State Party to which the person is transferred shall without delay implement its obligation to return the person to the custody of the State Party from which the person was transferred as agreed beforehand, or as otherwise agreed, by the competent authorities of both States Parties;
    (c) The State Party to which the person is transferred shall not require the State Party from which the person was transferred to initiate extradition proceedings for the return of the person;
    (d) The person transferred shall receive credit for service of the sentence being served in the State from which he or she was transferred for time spent in the custody of the State Party to which he or she was transferred.
12. Unless the State Party from which a person is to be transferred in accordance with paragraphs 10 and 11 of this article so agrees, that person, whatever his or her nationality, shall not be prosecuted, detained, punished or subjected to any other restriction of his or her personal liberty in the territory of the State to which that person is transferred in respect of acts, omissions or convictions prior to his or her departure from the territory of the State from which he or she was transferred.
13. Each State Party shall designate a central authority that shall have the responsibility and power to receive requests for mutual legal assistance and either to execute them or to transmit them to the competent authorities for execution. Where a State Party has a special region or territory with a separate system of mutual legal assistance, it may designate a distinct central authority that shall have the same function for that region or territory. Central authorities shall ensure the speedy and proper execution or transmission of the requests received. Where the central authority transmits the request to a competent authority for execution, it shall encourage the speedy and proper execution of the request by the competent authority. The Secretary-General of the United Nations shall be notified of the central authority designated for this purpose at the time each State Party deposits its instrument of ratification, acceptance or approval of or accession to this Convention. Requests for mutual legal assistance and any

communication related thereto shall be transmitted to the central authorities designated by the States Parties. This requirement shall be without prejudice to the right of a State Party to require that such requests and communications be addressed to it through diplomatic channels and, in urgent circumstances, where the States Parties agree, through the International Criminal Police Organization, if possible.

14. Requests shall be made in writing or, where possible, by any means capable of producing a written record, in a language acceptable to the requested State Party, under conditions allowing that State Party to establish authenticity. The Secretary-General of the United Nations shall be notified of the language or languages acceptable to each State Party at the time it deposits its instrument of ratification, acceptance or approval of or accession to this Convention. In urgent circumstances and where agreed by the States Parties, requests may be made orally but shall be confirmed in writing forthwith.
15. A request for mutual legal assistance shall contain:
    (a) The identity of the authority making the request;
    (b) The subject matter and nature of the investigation, prosecution or judicial proceeding to which the request relates and the name and functions of the authority conducting the investigation, prosecution or judicial proceeding;
    (c) A summary of the relevant facts, except in relation to requests for the purpose of service of judicial documents;
    (d) A description of the assistance sought and details of any particular procedure that the requesting State Party wishes to be followed;
    (e) Where possible, the identity, location and nationality of any person concerned; and
    (f) The purpose for which the evidence, information or action is sought.
16. The requested State Party may request additional information when it appears necessary for the execution of the request in accordance with its domestic law or when it can facilitate such execution.
17. A request shall be executed in accordance with the domestic law of the requested State Party and, to the extent not contrary to the domestic law of the requested State Party and where possible, in accordance with the procedures specified in the request.
18. Wherever possible and consistent with fundamental principles of domestic law, when an individual is in the territory of a State Party and has to be heard as a witness or expert by the judicial authorities of another State Party, the first State Party may, at the request of the other, permit the hearing to take place by video conference if it is not possible or desirable for the individual in question to appear in person in the territory of the requesting State Party. States Parties may agree that the hearing shall be conducted by a judicial authority of the requesting State Party and attended by a judicial authority of the requested State Party.
19. The requesting State Party shall not transmit or use information or evidence furnished by the requested State Party for investigations, prosecutions or judicial proceedings other than those stated in the request without the prior consent of the requested State Party. Nothing in this paragraph shall prevent the requesting State Party from disclosing in its proceedings information or evidence that is exculpatory to an accused person. In the latter case, the requesting State Party shall notify the requested State Party prior to the disclosure and, if so requested, consult with the requested State Party. If, in an exceptional case, advance notice is not possible, the requesting State Party shall inform the requested State Party of the disclosure without delay.
20. The requesting State Party may require that the requested State Party keep confidential the fact and substance of the request, except to the extent necessary to execute the request. If the requested State Party cannot comply with the requirement of confidentiality, it shall promptly inform the requesting State Party.
21. Mutual legal assistance may be refused:
    (a) If the request is not made in conformity with the provisions of this article;

(b) If the requested State Party considers that execution of the request is likely to prejudice its sovereignty, security, *ordre public* or other essential interests;
(c) If the authorities of the requested State Party would be prohibited by its domestic law from carrying out the action requested with regard to any similar offence, had it been subject to investigation, prosecution or judicial proceedings under their own jurisdiction;
(d) If it would be contrary to the legal system of the requested State Party relating to mutual legal assistance for the request to be granted.

22. States Parties may not refuse a request for mutual legal assistance on the sole ground that the offence is also considered to involve fiscal matters.
23. Reasons shall be given for any refusal of mutual legal assistance.
24. The requested State Party shall execute the request for mutual legal assistance as soon as possible and shall take as full account as possible of any deadlines suggested by the requesting State Party and for which reasons are given, preferably in the request. The requesting State Party may make reasonable requests for information on the status and progress of measures taken by the requested State Party to satisfy its request. The requested State Party shall respond to reasonable requests by the requesting State Party on the status, and progress in its handling, of the request. The requesting State Party shall promptly inform the requested State Party when the assistance sought is no longer required.
25. Mutual legal assistance may be postponed by the requested State Party on the ground that it interferes with an ongoing investigation, prosecution or judicial proceeding.
26. Before refusing a request pursuant to paragraph 21 of this article or postponing its execution pursuant to paragraph 25 of this article, the requested State Party shall consult with the requesting State Party to consider whether assistance may be granted subject to such terms and conditions as it deems necessary. If the requesting State Party accepts assistance subject to those conditions, it shall comply with the conditions.
27. Without prejudice to the application of paragraph 12 of this article, a witness, expert or other person who, at the request of the requesting State Party, consents to give evidence in a proceeding or to assist in an investigation, prosecution or judicial proceeding in the territory of the requesting State Party shall not be prosecuted, detained, punished or subjected to any other restriction of his or her personal liberty in that territory in respect of acts, omissions or convictions prior to his or her departure from the territory of the requested State Party. Such safe conduct shall cease when the witness, expert or other person having had, for a period of fifteen consecutive days or for any period agreed upon by the States Parties from the date on which he or she has been officially informed that his or her presence is no longer required by the judicial authorities, an opportunity of leaving, has nevertheless remained voluntarily in the territory of the requesting State Party or, having left it, has returned of his or her own free will.
28. The ordinary costs of executing a request shall be borne by the requested State Party, unless otherwise agreed by the States Parties concerned. If expenses of a substantial or extraordinary nature are or will be required to fulfil the request, the States Parties shall consult to determine the terms and conditions under which the request will be executed, as well as the manner in which the costs shall be borne.
29. The requested State Party:
(a) Shall provide to the requesting State Party copies of government records, documents or information in its possession that under its domestic law are available to the general public;
(b) May, at its discretion, provide to the requesting State Party in whole, in part or subject to such conditions as it deems appropriate, copies of any government records, documents or information in its possession that under its domestic law are not available to the general public.

30. States Parties shall consider, as may be necessary, the possibility of concluding bilateral or multilateral agreements or arrangements that would serve the purposes of, give practical effect to or enhance the provisions of this article.

Article 47

Transfer of criminal proceedings

States Parties shall consider the possibility of transferring to one another proceedings for the prosecution of an offence established in accordance with this Convention in cases where such transfer is considered to be in the interests of the proper administration of justice, in particular in cases where several jurisdictions are involved, with a view to concentrating the prosecution.

Article 48

Law enforcement cooperation

1. States Parties shall cooperate closely with one another, consistent with their respective domestic legal and administrative systems, to enhance the effectiveness of law enforcement action to combat the offences covered by this Convention. States Parties shall, in particular, take effective measures:
   (a) To enhance and, where necessary, to establish channels of communication between their competent authorities, agencies and services in order to facilitate the secure and rapid exchange of information concerning all aspects of the offences covered by this Convention, including, if the States Parties concerned deem it appropriate, links with other criminal activities;
   (b) To cooperate with other States Parties in conducting inquiries with respect to offences covered by this Convention concerning:
      (i) The identity, whereabouts and activities of persons suspected of involvement in such offences or the location of other persons concerned;
      (ii) The movement of proceeds of crime or property derived from the commission of such offences;
      (iii) The movement of property, equipment or other instrumentalities used or intended for use in the commission of such offences;
   (c) To provide, where appropriate, necessary items or quantities of substances for analytical or investigative purposes;
   (d) To exchange, where appropriate, information with other States Parties concerning specific means and methods used to commit offences covered by this Convention, including the use of false identities, forged, altered or false documents and other means of concealing activities;
   (e) To facilitate effective coordination between their competent authorities, agencies and services and to promote the exchange of personnel and other experts, including, subject to bilateral agreements or arrangements between the States Parties concerned, the posting of liaison officers;
   (f) To exchange information and coordinate administrative and other measures taken as appropriate for the purpose of early identification of the offences covered by this Convention.
2. With a view to giving effect to this Convention, States Parties shall consider entering into bilateral or multilateral agreements or arrangements on direct cooperation between their law enforcement agencies and, where such agreements or arrangements already exist, amending them. In the absence of such agreements or arrangements between the States Parties concerned, the States Parties may consider this Convention to be the basis for mutual law enforcement cooperation in respect of the offences covered by this Convention. Whenever appropriate, States Parties shall make full use of agreements or arrangements, including

international or regional organizations, to enhance the cooperation between their law enforcement agencies.

3. States Parties shall endeavour to cooperate within their means to respond to offences covered by this Convention committed through the use of modern technology.

Article 49

Joint investigations

States Parties shall consider concluding bilateral or multilateral agreements or arrangements whereby, in relation to matters that are the subject of investigations, prosecutions or judicial proceedings in one or more States, the competent authorities concerned may establish joint investigative bodies. In the absence of such agreements or arrangements, joint investigations may be undertaken by agreement on a case-by-case basis. The States Parties involved shall ensure that the sovereignty of the State Party in whose territory such investigation is to take place is fully respected.

Article 50

Special investigative techniques

1. In order to combat corruption effectively, each State Party shall, to the extent permitted by the basic principles of its domestic legal system and in accordance with the conditions prescribed by its domestic law, take such measures as may be necessary, within its means, to allow for the appropriate use by its competent authorities of controlled delivery and, where it deems appropriate, other special investigative techniques, such as electronic or other forms of surveillance and undercover operations, within its territory, and to allow for the admissibility in court of evidence derived therefrom.
2. For the purpose of investigating the offences covered by this Convention, States Parties are encouraged to conclude, when necessary, appropriate bilateral or multilateral agreements or arrangements for using such special investigative techniques in the context of cooperation at the international level. Such agreements or arrangements shall be concluded and implemented in full compliance with the principle of sovereign equality of States and shall be carried out strictly in accordance with the terms of those agreements or arrangements.
3. In the absence of an agreement or arrangement as set forth in paragraph 2 of this article, decisions to use such special investigative techniques at the international level shall be made on a case-by-case basis and may, when necessary, take into consideration financial arrangements and understandings with respect to the exercise of jurisdiction by the States Parties concerned.
4. Decisions to use controlled delivery at the international level may, with the consent of the States Parties concerned, include methods such as intercepting and allowing the goods or funds to continue intact or be removed or replaced in whole or in part.

Chapter V Asset Recovery

Article 51

General provision

The return of assets pursuant to this chapter is a fundamental principle of this Convention, and States Parties shall afford one another the widest measure of cooperation and assistance in this regard.

Article 52

Prevention and detection of transfers of proceeds of crime

1. Without prejudice to article 14 of this Convention, each State Party shall take such measures as may be necessary, in accordance with its domestic law, to require financial institutions within its jurisdiction to verify the identity of customers, to take reasonable steps to determine

the identity of beneficial owners of funds deposited into high-value accounts and to conduct enhanced scrutiny of accounts sought or maintained by or on behalf of individuals who are, or have been, entrusted with prominent public functions and their family members and close associates. Such enhanced scrutiny shall be reasonably designed to detect suspicious transactions for the purpose of reporting to competent authorities and should not be so construed as to discourage or prohibit financial institutions from doing business with any legitimate customer.

2. In order to facilitate implementation of the measures provided for in paragraph 1 of this article, each State Party, in accordance with its domestic law and inspired by relevant initiatives of regional, interregional and multilateral organizations against money-laundering, shall:
   (a) Issue advisories regarding the types of natural or legal person to whose accounts financial institutions within its jurisdiction will be expected to apply enhanced scrutiny, the types of accounts and transactions to which to pay particular attention and appropriate account-opening, maintenance and record-keeping measures to take concerning such accounts; and
   (b) Where appropriate, notify financial institutions within its jurisdiction, at the request of another State Party or on its own initiative, of the identity of particular natural or legal persons to whose accounts such institutions will be expected to apply enhanced scrutiny, in addition to those whom the financial institutions may otherwise identify.
3. In the context of paragraph 2(a) of this article, each State Party shall implement measures to ensure that its financial institutions maintain adequate records, over an appropriate period of time, of accounts and transactions involving the persons mentioned in paragraph 1 of this article, which should, as a minimum, contain information relating to the identity of the customer as well as, as far as possible, of the beneficial owner.
4. With the aim of preventing and detecting transfers of proceeds of offences established in accordance with this Convention, each State Party shall implement appropriate and effective measures to prevent, with the help of its regulatory and oversight bodies, the establishment of banks that have no physical presence and that are not affiliated with a regulated financial group. Moreover, States Parties may consider requiring their financial institutions to refuse to enter into or continue a correspondent banking relationship with such institutions and to guard against establishing relations with foreign financial institutions that permit their accounts to be used by banks that have no physical presence and that are not affiliated with a regulated financial group.
5. Each State Party shall consider establishing, in accordance with its domestic law, effective financial disclosure systems for appropriate public officials and shall provide for appropriate sanctions for non-compliance. Each State Party shall also consider taking such measures as may be necessary to permit its competent authorities to share that information with the competent authorities in other States Parties when necessary to investigate, claim and recover proceeds of offences established in accordance with this Convention.
6. Each State Party shall consider taking such measures as may be necessary, in accordance with its domestic law, to require appropriate public officials having an interest in or signature or other authority over a financial account in a foreign country to report that relationship to appropriate authorities and to maintain appropriate records related to such accounts. Such measures shall also provide for appropriate sanctions for non-compliance.

Article 53

Measures for direct recovery of property

Each State Party shall, in accordance with its domestic law:

(a) Take such measures as may be necessary to permit another State Party to initiate civil action in its courts to establish title to or ownership of property acquired through the commission of an offence established in accordance with this Convention;

(b) Take such measures as may be necessary to permit its courts to order those who have committed offences established in accordance with this Convention to pay compensation or damages to another State Party that has been harmed by such offences; and
(c) Take such measures as may be necessary to permit its courts or competent authorities, when having to decide on confiscation, to recognize another State Party's claim as a legitimate owner of property acquired through the commission of an offence established in accordance with this Convention.

Article 54

Mechanisms for recovery of property through international cooperation in confiscation

1. Each State Party, in order to provide mutual legal assistance pursuant to article 55 of this Convention with respect to property acquired through or involved in the commission of an offence established in accordance with this Convention, shall, in accordance with its domestic law:
   (a) Take such measures as may be necessary to permit its competent authorities to give effect to an order of confiscation issued by a court of another State Party;
   (b) Take such measures as may be necessary to permit its competent authorities, where they have jurisdiction, to order the confiscation of such property of foreign origin by adjudication of an offence of money-laundering or such other offence as may be within its jurisdiction or by other procedures authorized under its domestic law; and
   (c) Consider taking such measures as may be necessary to allow confiscation of such property without a criminal conviction in cases in which the offender cannot be prosecuted by reason of death, flight or absence or in other appropriate cases.
2. Each State Party, in order to provide mutual legal assistance upon a request made pursuant to paragraph 2 of article 55 of this Convention, shall, in accordance with its domestic law:
   (a) Take such measures as may be necessary to permit its competent authorities to freeze or seize property upon a freezing or seizure order issued by a court or competent authority of a requesting State Party that provides a reasonable basis for the requested State Party to believe that there are sufficient grounds for taking such actions and that the property would eventually be subject to an order of confiscation for purposes of paragraph 1(a) of this article;
   (b) Take such measures as may be necessary to permit its competent authorities to freeze or seize property upon a request that provides a reasonable basis for the requested State Party to believe that there are sufficient grounds for taking such actions and that the property would eventually be subject to an order of confiscation for purposes of paragraph 1(a) of this article; and
   (c) Consider taking additional measures to permit its competent authorities to preserve property for confiscation, such as on the basis of a foreign arrest or criminal charge related to the acquisition of such property.

Article 55

International cooperation for purposes of confiscation

1. A State Party that has received a request from another State Party having jurisdiction over an offence established in accordance with this Convention for confiscation of proceeds of crime, property, equipment or other instrumentalities referred to in article 31, paragraph 1, of this Convention situated in its territory shall, to the greatest extent possible within its domestic legal system:
   (a) Submit the request to its competent authorities for the purpose of obtaining an order of confiscation and, if such an order is granted, give effect to it; or

(b) Submit to its competent authorities, with a view to giving effect to it to the extent requested, an order of confiscation issued by a court in the territory of the requesting State Party in accordance with articles 31, paragraph 1, and 54, paragraph 1(a), of this Convention insofar as it relates to proceeds of crime, property, equipment or other instrumentalities referred to in article 31, paragraph 1, situated in the territory of the requested State Party.

2. Following a request made by another State Party having jurisdiction over an offence established in accordance with this Convention, the requested State Party shall take measures to identify, trace and freeze or seize proceeds of crime, property, equipment or other instrumentalities referred to in article 31, paragraph 1, of this Convention for the purpose of eventual confiscation to be ordered either by the requesting State Party or, pursuant to a request under paragraph 1 of this article, by the requested State Party.

3. The provisions of article 46 of this Convention are applicable, mutatis mutandis, to this article. In addition to the information specified in article 46, paragraph 15, requests made pursuant to this article shall contain:

   (a) In the case of a request pertaining to paragraph 1(a) of this article, a description of the property to be confiscated, including, to the extent possible, the location and, where relevant, the estimated value of the property and a statement of the facts relied upon by the requesting State Party sufficient to enable the requested State Party to seek the order under its domestic law;

   (b) In the case of a request pertaining to paragraph 1(b) of this article, a legally admissible copy of an order of confiscation upon which the request is based issued by the requesting State Party, a statement of the facts and information as to the extent to which execution of the order is requested, a statement specifying the measures taken by the requesting State Party to provide adequate notification to bona fide third parties and to ensure due process and a statement that the confiscation order is final;

   (c) In the case of a request pertaining to paragraph 2 of this article, a statement of the facts relied upon by the requesting State Party and a description of the actions requested and, where available, a legally admissible copy of an order on which the request is based.

4. The decisions or actions provided for in paragraphs 1 and 2 of this article shall be taken by the requested State Party in accordance with and subject to the provisions of its domestic law and its procedural rules or any bilateral or multilateral agreement or arrangement to which it may be bound in relation to the requesting State Party.

5. Each State Party shall furnish copies of its laws and regulations that give effect to this article and of any subsequent changes to such laws and regulations or a description thereof to the Secretary-General of the United Nations.

6. If a State Party elects to make the taking of the measures referred to in paragraphs 1 and 2 of this article conditional on the existence of a relevant treaty, that State Party shall consider this Convention the necessary and sufficient treaty basis.

7. Cooperation under this article may also be refused or provisional measures lifted if the requested State Party does not receive sufficient and timely evidence or if the property is of a *de minimis* value.

8. Before lifting any provisional measure taken pursuant to this article, the requested State Party shall, wherever possible, give the requesting State Party an opportunity to present its reasons in favour of continuing the measure.

9. The provisions of this article shall not be construed as prejudicing the rights of bona fide third parties.

Article 56

Special cooperation

Without prejudice to its domestic law, each State Party shall endeavour to take measures to permit it to forward, without prejudice to its own investigations, prosecutions or judicial proceedings, information on proceeds of offences established in accordance with this Convention to another State Party without prior request, when it considers that the disclosure of such information might assist the receiving State Party in initiating or carrying out investigations, prosecutions or judicial proceedings or might lead to a request by that State Party under this chapter of the Convention.

Article 57

Return and disposal of assets

1. Property confiscated by a State Party pursuant to article 31 or 55 of this Convention shall be disposed of, including by return to its prior legitimate owners, pursuant to paragraph 3 of this article, by that State Party in accordance with the provisions of this Convention and its domestic law.
2. Each State Party shall adopt such legislative and other measures, in accordance with the fundamental principles of its domestic law, as may be necessary to enable its competent authorities to return confiscated property, when acting on the request made by another State Party, in accordance with this Convention, taking into account the rights of bona fide third parties.
3. In accordance with articles 46 and 55 of this Convention and paragraphs 1 and 2 of this article, the requested State Party shall:
   (a) In the case of embezzlement of public funds or of laundering of embezzled public funds as referred to in articles 17 and 23 of this Convention, when confiscation was executed in accordance with article 55 and on the basis of a final judgement in the requesting State Party, a requirement that can be waived by the requested State Party, return the confiscated property to the requesting State Party;
   (b) In the case of proceeds of any other offence covered by this Convention, when the confiscation was executed in accordance with article 55 of this Convention and on the basis of a final judgement in the requesting State Party, a requirement that can be waived by the requested State Party, return the confiscated property to the requesting State Party, when the requesting State Party reasonably establishes its prior ownership of such confiscated property to the requested State Party or when the requested State Party recognizes damage to the requesting State Party as a basis for returning the confiscated property;
   (c) In all other cases, give priority consideration to returning confiscated property to the requesting State Party, returning such property to its prior legitimate owners or compensating the victims of the crime.
4. Where appropriate, unless States Parties decide otherwise, the requested State Party may deduct reasonable expenses incurred in investigations, prosecutions or judicial proceedings leading to the return or disposition of confiscated property pursuant to this article.
5. Where appropriate, States Parties may also give special consideration to concluding agreements or mutually acceptable arrangements, on a case-by-case basis, for the final disposal of confiscated property.

Article 58

Financial intelligence unit

States Parties shall cooperate with one another for the purpose of preventing and combating the transfer of proceeds of offences established in accordance with this Convention and of promoting ways and means of recovering such proceeds and, to that end, shall consider establishing a financial intelligence unit to be responsible for receiving, analysing and disseminating to the competent authorities reports of suspicious financial transactions.

Article 59

Bilateral and multilateral agreements and arrangements

States Parties shall consider concluding bilateral or multilateral agreements or arrangements to enhance the effectiveness of international cooperation undertaken pursuant to this chapter of the Convention.

Chapter VI Technical Assistance and Information Exchange

Article 60

Training and technical assistance

1. Each State Party shall, to the extent necessary, initiate, develop or improve specific training programmes for its personnel responsible for preventing and combating corruption. Such training programmes could deal, inter alia, with the following areas:
   (a) Effective measures to prevent, detect, investigate, punish and control corruption, including the use of evidence-gathering and investigative methods;
   (b) Building capacity in the development and planning of strategic anticorruption policy;
   (c) Training competent authorities in the preparation of requests for mutual legal assistance that meet the requirements of this Convention;
   (d) Evaluation and strengthening of institutions, public service management and the management of public finances, including public procurement, and the private sector;
   (e) Preventing and combating the transfer of proceeds of offences established in accordance with this Convention and recovering such proceeds;
   (f) Detecting and freezing of the transfer of proceeds of offences established in accordance with this Convention;
   (g) Surveillance of the movement of proceeds of offences established in accordance with this Convention and of the methods used to transfer, conceal or disguise such proceeds;
   (h) Appropriate and efficient legal and administrative mechanisms and methods for facilitating the return of proceeds of offences established in accordance with this Convention;
   (i) Methods used in protecting victims and witnesses who cooperate with judicial authorities; and
   (j) Training in national and international regulations and in languages.
2. States Parties shall, according to their capacity, consider affording one another the widest measure of technical assistance, especially for the benefit of developing countries, in their respective plans and programmes to combat corruption, including material support and training in the areas referred to in paragraph 1 of this article, and training and assistance and the mutual exchange of relevant experience and specialized knowledge, which will facilitate international cooperation between States Parties in the areas of extradition and mutual legal assistance.
3. States Parties shall strengthen, to the extent necessary, efforts to maximize operational and training activities in international and regional organizations and in the framework of relevant bilateral and multilateral agreements or arrangements.
4. States Parties shall consider assisting one another, upon request, in conducting evaluations, studies and research relating to the types, causes, effects and costs of corruption in their respective countries, with a view to developing, with the participation of competent authorities and society, strategies and action plans to combat corruption.
5. In order to facilitate the recovery of proceeds of offences established in accordance with this Convention, States Parties may cooperate in providing each other with the names of experts who could assist in achieving that objective.
6. States Parties shall consider using subregional, regional and international conferences and seminars to promote cooperation and technical assistance and to stimulate discussion on

problems of mutual concern, including the special problems and needs of developing countries and countries with economies in transition.

7. States Parties shall consider establishing voluntary mechanisms with a view to contributing financially to the efforts of developing countries and countries with economies in transition to apply this Convention through technical assistance programmes and projects.
8. Each State Party shall consider making voluntary contributions to the United Nations Office on Drugs and Crime for the purpose of fostering, through the Office, programmes and projects in developing countries with a view to implementing this Convention.

Article 61

Collection, exchange and analysis of information on corruption

1. Each State Party shall consider analysing, in consultation with experts, trends in corruption in its territory, as well as the circumstances in which corruption offences are committed.
2. States Parties shall consider developing and sharing with each other and through international and regional organizations statistics, analytical expertise concerning corruption and information with a view to developing, insofar as possible, common definitions, standards and methodologies, as well as information on best practices to prevent and combat corruption.
3. Each State Party shall consider monitoring its policies and actual measures to combat corruption and making assessments of their effectiveness and efficiency.

Article 62

Other measures: implementation of the Convention through economic development and technical assistance

1. States Parties shall take measures conducive to the optimal implementation of this Convention to the extent possible, through international cooperation, taking into account the negative effects of corruption on society in general, in particular on sustainable development.
2. States Parties shall make concrete efforts to the extent possible and in coordination with each other, as well as with international and regional organizations:
   (a) To enhance their cooperation at various levels with developing countries, with a view to strengthening the capacity of the latter to prevent and combat corruption;
   (b) To enhance financial and material assistance to support the efforts of developing countries to prevent and fight corruption effectively and to help them implement this Convention successfully;
   (c) To provide technical assistance to developing countries and countries with economies in transition to assist them in meeting their needs for the implementation of this Convention. To that end, States Parties shall endeavour to make adequate and regular voluntary contributions to an account specifically designated for that purpose in a United Nations funding mechanism. States Parties may also give special consideration, in accordance with their domestic law and the provisions of this Convention, to contributing to that account a percentage of the money or of the corresponding value of proceeds of crime or property confiscated in accordance with the provisions of this Convention;
   (d) To encourage and persuade other States and financial institutions as appropriate to join them in efforts in accordance with this article, in particular by providing more training programmes and modern equipment to developing countries in order to assist them in achieving the objectives of this Convention.
3. To the extent possible, these measures shall be without prejudice to existing foreign assistance commitments or to other financial cooperation arrangements at the bilateral, regional or international level.
4. States Parties may conclude bilateral or multilateral agreements or arrangements on material and logistical assistance, taking into consideration the financial arrangements necessary for the

means of international cooperation provided for by this Convention to be effective and for the prevention, detection and control of corruption.

Chapter VII Mechanisms for Implementation

Article 63

Conference of the States Parties to the Convention

1. A Conference of the States Parties to the Convention is hereby established to improve the capacity of and cooperation between States Parties to achieve the objectives set forth in this Convention and to promote and review its implementation.
2. The Secretary-General of the United Nations shall convene the Conference of the States Parties not later than one year following the entry into force of this Convention. Thereafter, regular meetings of the Conference of the States Parties shall be held in accordance with the rules of procedure adopted by the Conference.
3. The Conference of the States Parties shall adopt rules of procedure and rules governing the functioning of the activities set forth in this article, including rules concerning the admission and participation of observers, and the payment of expenses incurred in carrying out those activities.
4. The Conference of the States Parties shall agree upon activities, procedures and methods of work to achieve the objectives set forth in paragraph 1 of this article, including:
   (a) Facilitating activities by States Parties under articles 60 and 62 and chapters II to V of this Convention, including by encouraging the mobilization of voluntary contributions;
   (b) Facilitating the exchange of information among States Parties on patterns and trends in corruption and on successful practices for preventing and combating it and for the return of proceeds of crime, through, inter alia, the publication of relevant information as mentioned in this article;
   (c) Cooperating with relevant international and regional organizations and mechanisms and non-governmental organizations;
   (d) Making appropriate use of relevant information produced by other international and regional mechanisms for combating and preventing corruption in order to avoid unnecessary duplication of work;
   (e) Reviewing periodically the implementation of this Convention by its States Parties;
   (f) Making recommendations to improve this Convention and its implementation;
   (g) Taking note of the technical assistance requirements of States Parties with regard to the implementation of this Convention and recommending any action it may deem necessary in that respect.
5. For the purpose of paragraph 4 of this article, the Conference of the States Parties shall acquire the necessary knowledge of the measures taken by States Parties in implementing this Convention and the difficulties encountered by them in doing so through information provided by them and through such supplemental review mechanisms as may be established by the Conference of the States Parties.
6. Each State Party shall provide the Conference of the States Parties with information on its programmes, plans and practices, as well as on legislative and administrative measures to implement this Convention, as required by the Conference of the States Parties. The Conference of the States Parties shall examine the most effective way of receiving and acting upon information, including, inter alia, information received from States Parties and from competent international organizations. Inputs received from relevant non-governmental organizations duly accredited in accordance with procedures to be decided upon by the Conference of the States Parties may also be considered.

7. Pursuant to paragraphs 4 to 6 of this article, the Conference of the States Parties shall establish, if it deems it necessary, any appropriate mechanism or body to assist in the effective implementation of the Convention.

Article 64
Secretariat

1. The Secretary-General of the United Nations shall provide the necessary secretariat services to the Conference of the States Parties to the Convention.
2. The secretariat shall:
   (a) Assist the Conference of the States Parties in carrying out the activities set forth in article 63 of this Convention and make arrangements and provide the necessary services for the sessions of the Conference of the States Parties;
   (b) Upon request, assist States Parties in providing information to the Conference of the States Parties as envisaged in article 63, paragraphs 5 and 6, of this Convention; and
   (c) Ensure the necessary coordination with the secretariats of relevant international and regional organizations.

Chapter VIII Final Provisions

Article 65
Implementation of the Convention

1. Each State Party shall take the necessary measures, including legislative and administrative measures, in accordance with fundamental principles of its domestic law, to ensure the implementation of its obligations under this Convention.
2. Each State Party may adopt more strict or severe measures than those provided for by this Convention for preventing and combating corruption.

Article 66
Settlement of disputes

1. States Parties shall endeavour to settle disputes concerning the interpretation or application of this Convention through negotiation.
2. Any dispute between two or more States Parties concerning the interpretation or application of this Convention that cannot be settled through negotiation within a reasonable time shall, at the request of one of those States Parties, be submitted to arbitration. If, six months after the date of the request for arbitration, those States Parties are unable to agree on the organization of the arbitration, any one of those States Parties may refer the dispute to the International Court of Justice by request in accordance with the Statute of the Court.
3. Each State Party may, at the time of signature, ratification, acceptance or approval of or accession to this Convention, declare that it does not consider itself bound by paragraph 2 of this article. The other States Parties shall not be bound by paragraph 2 of this article with respect to any State Party that has made such a reservation.
4. Any State Party that has made a reservation in accordance with paragraph 3 of this article may at any time withdraw that reservation by notification to the Secretary-General of the United Nations.

Article 67
Signature, ratification, acceptance, approval and accession

1. This Convention shall be open to all States for signature from 9 to 11 December 2003 in Merida, Mexico, and thereafter at United Nations Headquarters in New York until 9 December 2005.

2. This Convention shall also be open for signature by regional economic integration organizations provided that at least one member State of such organization has signed this Convention in accordance with paragraph 1 of this article.
3. This Convention is subject to ratification, acceptance or approval. Instruments of ratification, acceptance or approval shall be deposited with the Secretary-General of the United Nations. A regional economic integration organization may deposit its instrument of ratification, acceptance or approval if at least one of its member States has done likewise. In that instrument of ratification, acceptance or approval, such organization shall declare the extent of its competence with respect to the matters governed by this Convention. Such organization shall also inform the depositary of any relevant modification in the extent of its competence.
4. This Convention is open for accession by any State or any regional economic integration organization of which at least one member State is a Party to this Convention. Instruments of accession shall be deposited with the Secretary-General of the United Nations. At the time of its accession, a regional economic integration organization shall declare the extent of its competence with respect to matters governed by this Convention. Such organization shall also inform the depositary of any relevant modification in the extent of its competence.

Article 68
Entry into force

1. This Convention shall enter into force on the ninetieth day after the date of deposit of the thirtieth instrument of ratification, acceptance, approval or accession. For the purpose of this paragraph, any instrument deposited by a regional economic integration organization shall not be counted as additional to those deposited by member States of such organization.
2. For each State or regional economic integration organization ratifying, accepting, approving or acceding to this Convention after the deposit of the thirtieth instrument of such action, this Convention shall enter into force on the thirtieth day after the date of deposit by such State or organization of the relevant instrument or on the date this Convention enters into force pursuant to paragraph 1 of this article, whichever is later.

Article 69
Amendment

1. After the expiry of five years from the entry into force of this Convention, a State Party may propose an amendment and transmit it to the Secretary-General of the United Nations, who shall thereupon communicate the proposed amendment to the States Parties and to the Conference of the States Parties to the Convention for the purpose of considering and deciding on the proposal. The Conference of the States Parties shall make every effort to achieve consensus on each amendment. If all efforts at consensus have been exhausted and no agreement has been reached, the amendment shall, as a last resort, require for its adoption a two-thirds majority vote of the States Parties present and voting at the meeting of the Conference of the States Parties.
2. Regional economic integration organizations, in matters within their competence, shall exercise their right to vote under this article with a number of votes equal to the number of their member States that are Parties to this Convention. Such organizations shall not exercise their right to vote if their member States exercise theirs and vice versa.
3. An amendment adopted in accordance with paragraph 1 of this article is subject to ratification, acceptance or approval by States Parties.
4. An amendment adopted in accordance with paragraph 1 of this article shall enter into force in respect of a State Party ninety days after the date of the deposit with the Secretary-General of the United Nations of an instrument of ratification, acceptance or approval of such amendment.

5. When an amendment enters into force, it shall be binding on those States Parties which have expressed their consent to be bound by it. Other States Parties shall still be bound by the provisions of this Convention and any earlier amendments that they have ratified, accepted or approved.

Article 70

Denunciation

1. A State Party may denounce this Convention by written notification to the Secretary-General of the United Nations. Such denunciation shall become effective one year after the date of receipt of the notification by the Secretary- General.
2. A regional economic integration organization shall cease to be a Party to this Convention when all of its member States have denounced it.

Article 71

Depositary and languages

1. The Secretary-General of the United Nations is designated depositary of this Convention.
2. The original of this Convention, of which the Arabic, Chinese, English, French, Russian and Spanish texts are equally authentic, shall be deposited with the Secretary-General of the United Nations.

In Witness Whereof, the undersigned plenipotentiaries, being duly authorized thereto by their respective Governments, have signed this Convention.

APPENDIX 30

UN Resolution Adopted by the General Assembly

[on the report of the Third Committee (A/51/610)]
Fifty-first session, Agenda item 101
51/59. Action against corruption

The General Assembly,

Concerned at the seriousness of problems posed by corruption, which may endanger the stability and security of societies, undermine the values of democracy and morality and jeopardize social, economic and political development,

Also concerned about the links between corruption and other forms of crime, in particular organized crime and economic crime, including money-laundering,

Convinced that, since corruption is a phenomenon that currently crosses national borders and affects all societies and economies, international cooperation to prevent and control it is essential,

Convinced also of the need to provide, upon request, technical assistance designed to improve public management systems and to enhance accountability and transparency,

Recalling the Inter-American Convention against Corruption,[1] adopted by the Organization of American States at the Specialized Conference for Consideration of the Draft Inter-American Convention against Corruption, held at Caracas from 27 to 29 March 1996,

Recalling also its resolutions 45/121 of 14 December 1990 and 46/152 of 18 December 1991, and Economic and Social Council resolutions 1992/22 of 30 July 1992, 1993/32 of 27 July 1993 and 1994/19 of 25 July 1994,

Recalling in particular its resolution 50/225 of 19 April 1996, adopted at its resumed session, on public administration and development,

Recalling Economic and Social Council resolution 1995/14 of 24 July 1995 on action against corruption,

Recalling also the work carried out by other international and regional organizations in this field, including the activities of the Council of Europe, the European Union, the Organisation for Economic Cooperation and Development and the Organization of American States,

1. Takes note of the report of the Secretary-General on action against corruption[2] submitted to the Commission on Crime Prevention and Criminal Justice at its fifth session;

2. Adopts the International Code of Conduct for Public Officials annexed to the present resolution, and recommends it to Member States as a tool to guide their efforts against corruption;

3. Requests the Secretary-General to distribute the International Code of Conduct to all States and to include it in the manual on practical measures against corruption,[3] to be revised and expanded pursuant to Economic and Social Council resolution 1995/14, with a view to offering both those tools to States in the context of advisory services, training and other technical assistance activities;

---

[1] See E/1996/99. [2] E/CN.15/1996/5.

[3] International Review of Criminal Policy, Nos, 41 and 42 (United Nations publication, Sales No. E.93.IV.4).

4. *Also requests* the Secretary-General to continue to collect information and legislative and regulatory texts from States and relevant intergovernmental organizations, in the context of his continuing study of the problem of corruption;

5. *Further requests* the Secretary-General, in consultation with States, relevant intergovernmental and non-governmental organizations, as well as in cooperation with the institutes comprising the United Nations Crime Prevention and Criminal Justice Programme network, to elaborate an implementation plan and submit it to the Commission on Crime Prevention and Criminal Justice at its sixth session, in conjunction with his report to be submitted pursuant to Economic and Social Council resolution 1995/14;

6. *Urges* States, relevant intergovernmental and non-governmental organizations, as well as the institutes comprising the United Nations Crime Prevention and Criminal Justice Programme network, to extend to the Secretary- General their full support in elaborating the implementation plan and in implementing paragraph 4 above;

7. *Urges* Member States carefully to consider the problems posed by the international aspects of corrupt practices, especially as regards international economic activities carried out by corporate entities, and to study appropriate legislative and regulatory measures to ensure the transparency and integrity of financial systems and transactions carried out by such corporate entities;

8. *Requests* the Secretary-General to intensify his efforts to closely cooperate with other entities of the United Nations system and other relevant international organizations and to more effectively coordinate activities undertaken in this area;

9. *Also requests* the Secretary-General, subject to the availability of extrabudgetary resources, to provide increased advisory services and technical assistance to Member States, at their request, in particular in the elaboration of national strategies, the elaboration or improvement of legislative and regulatory measures, the establishment or strengthening of national capacities to prevent and control corruption, as well as in training and upgrading skills of relevant personnel;

10. *Calls upon* States, relevant international organizations and financing institutions to extend to the Secretary-General their full support and assistance in the implementation of the present resolution;

11. *Requests* the Commission on Crime Prevention and Criminal Justice to keep the issue of action against corruption under regular review.

82nd plenary meeting
12 December 1996

Annex
International Code of Conduct for Public Officials

I. General Principles

1. A public office, as defined by national law, is a position of trust, implying a duty to act in the public interest. Therefore, the ultimate loyalty of public officials shall be to the public interests of their country as expressed through the democratic institutions of government.

2. Public officials shall ensure that they perform their duties and functions efficiently, effectively and with integrity, in accordance with laws or administrative policies. They shall at all times seek to ensure that public resources for which they are responsible are administered in the most effective and efficient manner.

3. Public officials shall be attentive, fair and impartial in the performance of their functions and, in particular, in their relations with the public. They shall at no time afford any undue preferential

treatment to any group or individual or improperly discriminate against any group or individual, or otherwise abuse the power and authority vested in them.

II. Conflict of Interest and Disqualification

4. Public officials shall not use their official authority for the improper advancement of their own or their family's personal or financial interest. They shall not engage in any transaction, acquire any position or function or have any financial, commercial or other comparable interest that is incompatible with their office, functions and duties or the discharge thereof.

5. Public officials, to the extent required by their position, shall, in accordance with laws or administrative policies, declare business, commercial and financial interests or activities undertaken for financial gain that may raise a possible conflict of interest. In situations of possible or perceived conflict of interest between the duties and private interests of public officials, they shall comply with the measures established to reduce or eliminate such conflict of interest.

6. Public officials shall at no time improperly use public moneys, property, services or information that is acquired in the performance of, or as a result of, their official duties for activities not related to their official work.

7. Public officials shall comply with measures established by law or by administrative policies in order that after leaving their official positions they will not take improper advantage of their previous office.

III. Disclosure of Assets

8. Public officials shall, in accord with their position and as permitted or required by law and administrative policies, comply with requirements to declare or to disclose personal assets and liabilities, as well as, if possible, those of their spouses and/or dependants.

IV. Acceptance of Gifts or Other Favours

9. Public officials shall not solicit or receive directly or indirectly any gift or other favour that may influence the exercise of their functions, the performance of their duties or their judgement.

V. Confidential Information

10. Matters of a confidential nature in the possession of public officials shall be kept confidential unless national legislation, the performance of duty or the needs of justice strictly require otherwise. Such restrictions shall also apply after separation from service.

VI. Political Activity

11. The political or other activity of public officials outside the scope of their office shall, in accordance with laws and administrative policies, not be such as to impair public confidence in the impartial performance of their functions and duties.

APPENDIX 31

Economic Community of West African States Protocol on the Fight Against Corruption[1]

Preamble

We, the Heads of State and Government of the Member States of the Economic Community of West African States (ECOWAS).

Considering that the aims and objectives of the Community are to achieve the integration of its members;

Mindful of the provisions of Article 5 of the revised Treaty calling on Member States to take all necessary measures to harmonise their strategies and policies and to refrain from any action that may hinder the attainment of the said objectives;

Recalling the provisions of Articles 48 and 49 of the Protocol relating to the Mechanism for Conflict Prevention, Management, Resolution, Peace keeping and Security that call on ECOWAS Member States to eradicate corruption and adopt measures for combating money laundering and to promote transparency, accountability and good governance within their territories;

Conscious of the grave consequences of corruption on investment, economic growth and democracy;

Convinced that transparency and good governance strengthen democratic institutions;

Recognising the role of States in the prevention and suppression of corruption;

Convinced that the success of the fight against corruption requires sustained cooperation in criminal matters;

Mindful of the ECOWAS Convention on Mutual Assistance in Criminal Matters and the Convention on Extradition;

Expressing satisfaction at the efforts of the United Nations Organisation, as well as the global efforts of international, regional and non-governmental organisations in the fight against corruption;

Convinced of the need to adopt preventive and suppressive measures to combat corruption and more particularly to take appropriate measures against persons who engage in acts of corruption in the exercise of their public and private functions;

Resolved to join the efforts of our States in the fight against corruption;

Have agreed as follows:

Article 1
Definitions

'Public official(s)' means any person who has been selected, appointed or elected and who performs public functions on a permanent or temporary basis.

'Public function' means any temporary or permanent, paid or honorary activity, performed by a natural or legal person in the name of the State or under its direction, control, and authority.

[1] The Protocol was signed on 21 December 2001. It has not yet entered into force.

The term 'State' comprises the national, provincial, regional, local, and municipal levels and other public agencies.

'Assets' means property of any kind, whether moveable or immovable, tangible or intangible, and any document or legal instrument demonstrating, purporting to demonstrate, or relating to ownership or other rights pertaining to such assets.

'Legal person(s)' means any entity having such status under the applicable national law and includes other public bodies and public international organisations.

'Treaty' means the revised ECOWAS Treaty dated 24 July 1993 and includes any amendments thereto;

'Member State(s)' means a Member State of the Community as defined in paragraph 2 of Article 2 of the Treaty;

'Authority' means the Authority of Heads of State and Government of ECOWAS established by Article 7 of the Treaty;

'Council' means the Council of Ministers established by Article 10 of the Treaty;

'Executive Secretary' means the Executive Secretary of ECOWAS appointed in accordance with the provisions of Article 18 of the Treaty;

'State Party or State Parties' means States which have acceded to this Protocol and includes ECOWAS Member States;

'Foreign Public Official' means any person exercising a public function in enterprises or a public establishment in another Member State;

'Community Court' means the Community Court of Justice established pursuant to Articles 6 and 15 of the Treaty;

'Predicate offence,' means any offence as a result of which proceeds have been generated that may become the subject of an offence as defined in Article 6 of this Protocol.

Article 2

Aims and Objectives

The aims and objectives of this Protocol are:

i) to promote and strengthen the development in each of the State Parties effective mechanisms to prevent, suppress and eradicate corruption;

ii) to intensify and revitalise cooperation between State Parties, with a view to making anti-corruption measures more effective;

iii) to promote the harmonisation and coordination of national anticorruption laws and policies.

Article 3

Scope

1. This Protocol shall be applicable whenever an act of corruption is committed or produces some effects in a State Party.
2. This Protocol shall also be applicable whenever a national institutional system fails to provide the most basic preventive measures enumerated in Article 5 below.

Article 4

Jurisdiction

1. Each State Party shall adopt the necessary measures to exercise its jurisdiction in respect of criminal offences established in accordance with Articles 6, 7 and 12 of this protocol as long as:
   a) the criminal offence was committed in its territory;
   b) the criminal offence was committed by one of its nationals or by a permanent resident.
2. A State Party in whose territory an alleged offender is found, and which does not extradite such person in respect of an offence to which the ECOWAS Convention on Extradition applies solely on the ground that he or she is one of its nationals, shall, at the request of the State Party seeking extradition, be obliged to submit the case without undue delay to its competent authorities for the purposes of prosecution.

3. Each State Party shall review its legislation with a view to ascertaining whether its current basis for jurisdiction is effective in the fight against the bribery of foreign public officials, and where it is not, it shall take appropriate remedial measures.
4. State Parties shall consult when more than one State Party asserts jurisdiction with a view to determining the most appropriate jurisdiction for prosecution.

Article 5
Preventive Measures

In order to realise the objectives set out in Article 2 above, each State Party shall take measures to establish and consolidate:

a) National laws, ethical guidelines, regulations and codes of conduct that would eliminate conflicts of interest, emphasise methods of recruitment based on merit and provide thorough measures aimed at guaranteeing reasonable standards of living;
b) transparency and efficiency in the procurement and disposal of goods, works and services and in the recruitment of personnel into the public service;
c) Laws and other measures deemed necessary to ensure effective and adequate protection of persons who, acting in good faith, provide information on acts of corruption;
d) Laws and regulations aimed at discouraging corruption of national and foreign officials;
e) participation of civil society and Non-Governmental Organisations (NGOs) in efforts to prevent and detect acts of corruption;
f) revenue collection systems that eliminate opportunities for corruption and tax evasion and provide for regulations which require companies and organisations to maintain adequate financial books and records and adhere to internationally accepted standards of accounting;
g) policies that oblige public officials to disclose assets, liabilities and copies of their income tax returns. The disclosure rules should be extended to at least the spouses and dependent children of the public officials. Provisions should be made to ensure that the information provided shall not be misused;
h) specialised anti-corruption agencies with the requisite independence and capacity that will ensure that their staff receive adequate training and financial resources for the accomplishment of their tasks;
i) freedom of the press and the right to information; and
j) policies to ensure that public officials do not take official decisions related to private business in which they have an interest.

Article 6
Acts of Corruption

1. This Protocol shall be applicable to the following acts of corruption:
   a) a public official demanding or accepting, either directly or indirectly through a third party, any object of pecuniary value such as a gift, offer, a promise or an advantage of any nature, whether for himself or for another person, in exchange for an act or an omission in the discharge of his duties;
   b) offering or giving a public official, either directly or indirectly, any object of pecuniary value such as a gift, a favor or an advantage, whether for himself or another person, in exchange for an act or an omission in the discharge of his duties;
   c) Any person who promises to offer or to grant directly or indirectly any undue advantage to any person who declares or confirms that he can exercise some influence on decisions or actions of persons occupying positions in the public or private sector, whether or not this influence had been exercised or not, or whether the supposed influence had the desired result or not;
   d) any person who declares or confirms that he can exercise some influence on decisions or actions of persons occupying positions in the public or private sector, whether the influence

is used or not, and whether or not the supposed influence had the desired result; and asking for or accepting directly or indirectly any undue advantage from whatever quarters;

e) a public official diverting from its initial purpose, either for his own benefit or for the benefit of another person, any assets, whether moveable or immoveable, or deeds and securities belonging to the State, an independent agency or an individual, given to the public official by virtue of his position and for the needs of the State for safe-keeping and for other reasons.

2. Each State Party shall adopt necessary legislative and other measures to make the acts of corruption enumerated in this Protocol criminal offences.
3. (a) A significant increase in the assets of a public official that he cannot reasonably explain in relation to his lawful earnings shall be considered an illicit enrichment and an act of corruption for the purposes of this Protocol among those State Parties for which it is a criminal offence.
   (b) Any State Party, for which illicit enrichment is not an offence, shall, provide such assistance to and cooperation with the other State Parties.
4. Each State Party shall adopt necessary legislative and other measures to establish as offences liable to criminal or other sanctions the following acts or omissions, in order to commit, or conceal the offences referred to in this Protocol:
   a) Creating or using an invoice or any other accounting document or record containing false or incomplete information.
   b) Unlawfully omitting to make a record of payment.
5. Each State Party shall adopt such legislative and other measures as may be necessary to establish as criminal offences the following acts:
   a) Promising to offer or giving public officials or employees of companies of the private sector, either directly or indirectly to themselves or to third parties, in order to carry out or abstain from carrying out an action in violation of their functions;
   b) Public officials or employees of companies of the private sector, asking for or receiving, directly or indirectly, bribes for themselves or third parties, bribes in order to carry out or refrain from carrying out an action in contravention of their duties.
6. Each State Party shall adopt necessary legislative and other measures to establish as criminal offences the act of aiding and abetting in any of the criminal offences established in accordance with this Protocol.
7. This Protocol shall also be applicable by mutual agreement between two or several State Parties, to any other act of corruption which is not included in these provisions.

Article 7

Laundering of proceeds of corruption and similar criminal offences

1. Each State Party shall adopt, in accordance with the fundamental principles of its national law, such legislative and other measures as may be necessary to establish as criminal offences:
   (a) (i) The conversion or transfer of assets, knowing that such assets are the proceeds of crime, for the purpose of concealing the illicit origin of the assets or of helping any person who is involved in the commission of the predicate offence to evade the legal consequences of his or her action;
   (ii) The concealment of the true nature, source, location, disposition, movement or ownership of or rights with respect to assets, knowing that such assets are the proceeds of crime;
   (b) Subject to the basic concepts of its legal system:
   (i) The acquisition, possession or use of assets, knowing at the time of receipt, that such assets are the proceeds of crime;

(ii) Participation in, association with or conspiracy to commit, attempts to commit, aiding and abetting in facilitating and concealing the commission of any of the offences established in accordance with this article.

2. (a) Each State Party shall seek to apply paragraph 1 of this Article and consider as predicate offences, those acts stipulated in articles 6, 7 and 12 of this Protocol;
   (b) For purposes of sub-paragraph (a), predicate offences shall include offences committed both within and outside the jurisdiction of the concerned State Party. However, offences committed outside the jurisdiction of a State Party shall constitute predicate offences only where the relevant conduct is a criminal offence under the domestic law of the State Party implementing or applying this Article had it been committed there.
   (c) If required by fundamental principles of the national law of a State Party, it may be provided that the offences set forth in paragraph 1 of this article do not apply to the persons who committed the predicate offences;
   (d) Knowledge, intent or purpose required as an element of an offence set forth in paragraph 1 of this article may be inferred from objective factual circumstances.

Article 8

Protection of witnesses

1. Each State Party shall take appropriate measures within its means to provide effective protection to witnesses in criminal proceedings who give testimony concerning offences covered by this Protocol from potential retaliation or intimidation and, as appropriate, for their relatives and other persons close to them.
2. The measures envisaged in paragraph 1 of this Article may include, inter alia, without prejudice to the rights of the defendant, including the right to due process:
   a) Establishing procedures for the physical protection of such persons, such as to the extent necessary and feasible, relocating them and permitting, where appropriate, non-disclosure or limitations on the disclosure of information concerning the identity and whereabouts of such persons;
   b) Providing evidentiary rules to permit witness testimony to be given in a manner that ensures the safety of the witness, such as permitting testimony to be given through the use of communications technology such as video links or other adequate means.
3. State Parties shall consider entering into agreements or arrangements with other States for the relocation of persons referred to in paragraph 1 of this article.
4. The provisions of this article shall also apply to victims insofar as they are witnesses.

Article 9

Assistance and protection of victims

1. Each State Party shall take appropriate measures within its means to provide assistance and protection to victims of offences covered by this Protocol, in particular in cases of threat, retaliation or intimidation.
2. Each State Party shall establish appropriate procedures to provide access to compensation and restitution for victims of offences covered by this Protocol.
3. Each State Party shall permit the views and concerns of victims to be presented and considered at appropriate stages of criminal proceedings in a manner not prejudicial to the rights of the defense.

Article 10

Sanctions and measures

1. Each State Party shall provide, in respect of those criminal offences established in accordance with this Protocol, effective, proportionate and dissuasive sanctions and measures, including,

when committed by natural persons, penalties involving deprivation of liberty which can give rise to extradition.

2. Each State Party shall ensure that legal persons held liable in accordance with Article 11, shall be subject to effective, proportionate and dissuasive criminal or non-criminal sanctions, including monetary sanctions.
3. Each State Party shall adopt such legislative and other measures as may be necessary to enable it to confiscate or otherwise deprive the instrumentalities and proceeds of criminal offences established in accordance with this Protocol, or assets the value of which correspond to such proceeds.

Article 11

Liability of legal persons

1. Each State Party shall adopt such measures as may be necessary, and consistent with its legal principles, to establish the liability of legal persons for participation in offences established in accordance with articles 6, 7 and 12 of this Protocol.
2. Subject to the legal principles of the State Party, the liability of legal persons may be criminal, civil or administrative.
3. Such liability shall be without prejudice to the criminal liability of the natural persons who have committed the offences.
4. Each State Party shall, in particular, ensure that legal persons held liable in accordance with this article are subject to effective, proportionate and dissuasive criminal or non-criminal sanctions, including monetary sanctions, disqualification from commercial activities, judicial winding-up orders, and placements under judicial supervision.

Article 12

Acts of corruption concerning foreign public officials

1. Each State Party shall prohibit and punish the act of offering or giving to a foreign public official, either directly or indirectly, any object of pecuniary value such as gifts, promises or favors, to compensate the public official for an act or an omission in the exercise of his official functions.
2. State Parties that have enacted laws making transnational corruption a criminal offence shall, for the purposes of this Protocol, consider such an act as an act of corruption while State Parties which have not passed such laws shall provide the necessary assistance and cooperation set out in this Protocol.

Article 13

Seizure and forfeiture

1. Each State Party shall adopt measures, where necessary, that would permit:
   a) the competent authorities to identify, locate and seize assets or items for eventual forfeiture;
   b) the forfeiture of proceeds from crimes established in accordance with the provisions of this Protocol or other assets whose value is equal to the value of the crime.
2. In order to implement the measures referred to in this Article, each State Party shall empower its courts to order the surrender or seizure of bank, commercial or financial documents and shall not invoke banking secrecy in order to refuse the assistance requested by another State Party.
3. The requesting State Party shall undertake to use the information provided only for the purposes for which it was required.
4. In accordance with their national laws, treaties and other relevant agreements, State Parties shall assist each other in the identification and seizure of the assets or items acquired or used in committing the crimes.

5. Subject to its national laws, a State Party may transfer all or a part of the assets specified in the first paragraph of this Article to another State Party which has assisted it in carrying out investigations or prosecuting the crime.

Article 14

Extradition

1. The criminal offences which come under the scope of application of this Protocol shall be considered as crimes leading to extradition and as forming part of the ECOWAS Convention on Extradition and any other extradition Treaties existing between the parties. The parties undertake to include such crimes in all extradition Treaties as crimes that may lead to extradition.
2. A State Party which receives an extradition request from another State Party with which it has not entered into any extradition treaty may consider this Protocol as the legal basis of its request in relation to offences which fall within the context of this Protocol.
3. State Parties, which do not require the existence of a Treaty before they execute an extradition order, shall recognise the crimes established in accordance with the provisions of this Protocol as crimes leading to extradition.
4. The extradition shall be carried out in accordance with the provisions of the laws of the requested State Party or of the extradition Treaties in force, including reasons for which the requested State Party is rejecting the extradition request.
5. Where the extradition request submitted in accordance with the provisions of this Protocol is rejected on the basis of the nationality of the person whose extradition is sought or because the requested State feels it is competent to handle the matter, the requested State shall hand over the case to its competent authorities as soon as possible, except where other arrangements have been concluded with the requesting State Party, and shall inform the requesting State Party promptly of the outcome.

Article 15

Mutual legal assistance and law enforcement cooperation

1. In accordance with the provisions of their national legislation and the Treaties in force, State Parties undertake to assist each other by expediting action on requests submitted by competent authorities and to take necessary measures to facilitate the procedures and formalities relating to investigation and prosecution of acts of corruption.
2. State Parties undertake to assist each other as much as possible in the area of law enforcement cooperation so as to strengthen measures to prevent, detect and suppress acts of corruption.
3. The provisions of this Protocol shall not in any way affect the bilateral and multilateral Treaties which govern mutual assistance in criminal matters. No provision of this Protocol shall be considered as denying a State Party the right to favor the forms of mutual assistance set out in its national laws in its dealings with another State Party.
4. State Parties shall consider concluding bilateral or multilateral agreements whereby, in relation to matters that are the subject of investigations, prosecutions or judicial proceedings in one or more State Parties, the competent authorities concerned may establish joint investigative bodies. In the absence of such agreements, joint investigations may be undertaken by agreement on a case-by-case basis. The State Parties involved shall ensure that the sovereignty of the State Party in whose territory such investigation is to take place is fully respected.
5. If permitted by the basic principles of its domestic legal system, each State Party shall take the necessary measures to allow for the appropriate use of other special investigative techniques, in accordance with its domestic laws.

6. For the purpose of investigating the offences covered by this Protocol, State Parties shall conclude, when necessary, appropriate bilateral or multilateral agreements for using such special investigative techniques.
7. In the absence of an agreement or arrangement as set forth in paragraph 6 of this Article, decisions to use such special investigative techniques at the international level shall be made on a case-by-case basis and may, when necessary, take into consideration financial arrangements and agreements with respect to the exercise of jurisdiction by the State Parties concerned.
8. State Parties shall not decline mutual legal assistance on the basis of Bank secrecy.

Article 16

Central authority

1. Within the framework of the cooperation and mutual assistance established in this Protocol, each State Party shall designate a Central Authority.
2. The Central Authorities shall be responsible both for formulating and receiving the requests for cooperation and assistance set out in this Protocol. They may establish direct lines of communication between themselves.

Article 17

Application in time

1. Acts of corruption committed before the entry into force of this Protocol may, at the request of State Parties, form the basis of judicial cooperation, on condition that national and international standards in the area of extradition are respected.
2. This provision shall in no way affect the non-retroactive nature of criminal law.

Article 18

Harmonisation of national legislation

1. State Parties undertake to develop and harmonise their national legislation with a view to realising the aims and objectives of this Protocol.

Article 19

Establishment of a technical commission

1. State Parties undertake to establish a Technical Commission, in accordance with the provisions of Article 22 of the revised ECOWAS Treaty, which shall be called the Anti-corruption Commission. The Commission shall:
   a) Monitor the implementation of this Protocol both at the national and sub-regional levels;
   b) Gather and disseminate information among State Parties;
   c) Regularly organise relevant training programmes;
   d) Provide State Parties appropriate additional assistance.
2. The Technical Commission shall comprise experts from the Ministries in charge of Finance, Justice, Internal Affairs and Security of States Parties.
3. The Technical Commission shall meet at least twice every year.
4. The Technical Commission shall establish an appropriate balance between the confidentiality and transparency of its activities, and its deliberations shall be conducted on the basis of consensus and cooperation amongst its members.
5. Reports of meetings of the Technical Commission shall be submitted to the Council of Ministers.

Article 20

Relations with other treaties

This Protocol repeals all preceding provisions relating to acts of corruption in all bilateral Treaties existing between two States Parties.

Article 21

Notification

In the course of application of the provisions of Articles 7, 13 and 18, the State Parties shall notify in advance, the Executive Secretariat of their domestic laws on these issues; which shall in turn inform the other State Parties.

Article 22

Ratification and entry into force

This Protocol shall enter into force upon ratification by at least nine (9) signatory States, in accordance with their respective constitutional procedures.

Article 23

Depository authority and registration

This Protocol and all instruments of ratification and accession shall be deposited with the ECOWAS Executive Secretariat which shall transmit certified true copies of this Protocol to all State Parties and notify them of the dates of deposit of the instruments of ratification and accession. The Executive Secretariat shall register this Protocol with the Organisation of African Unity, the United Nations Organisation and such other organizations as the Council may determine.

Article 24

Accession

Any non-ECOWAS Member State may accede to this Protocol.

Article 25

Amendments and revision

1. Any State Party may submit proposals for the amendment or revision of this Protocol.
2. All such proposals shall be submitted to the ECOWAS Executive Secretariat which shall notify State Parties not later than thirty (30) days after the receipt of such proposals. Amendments or revisions shall not be considered by the Authority unless State Parties shall have been given at least three (3) months notice thereof.
3. The amendments or revisions adopted by the Authority shall be submitted for ratification by all State Parties in accordance with their respective constitutional procedures. They shall enter into force in accordance with Article 89 of the Treaty.

Article 26

Denunciation

1. This Protocol shall be concluded for an indefinite period of time. It may, however, be denounced by any State Party. The instrument of denunciation shall be deposited with the Executive Secretariat. The Protocol shall cease to have any effect on State Parties that have denounced it one year after the instrument of denunciation has been deposited.
2. During the period of one year, the denouncing State shall continue to comply with the provisions of this Protocol and shall be bound by its obligations under this Protocol.

Article 27

Settlement of disputes

1. Any dispute which may arise between the State Parties regarding the interpretation or application of this Protocol shall be amicably settled through direct agreement.
2. In the event of failure to settle the dispute, the matter may be referred to the Community Court of Justice by a party to the dispute, a State Party or the Authority, and the decision of the Community Court of Justice shall be final.

APPENDIX 32

Global Anti-Money-Laundering Guidelines for Private Banking

Wolfsberg[1] AML Principles

(1st revision, May 2002)

The following major International Private Banks

ABN AMRO Bank N.V.
Bank of Tokyo-Mitsubishi Ltd.
Barclays Bank
Citigroup
Credit Suisse Group
Deutsche Bank AG
Goldman Sachs
HSBC
J.P. Morgan Private Bank
Santander Central Hispano
Société Générale
UBS AG

have agreed to the following principles as important global guidance for sound business conduct in international private banking.

Acknowledgement

The banks collaborated with a team from Transparency International[2] who invited two international experts to participate, Stanley Morris[3] and Prof. Mark Pieth.[4] Transparency International and the experts regard the principles as an important step in the fight against money laundering, corruption and other related serious crimes.

30.10.2000 www.wolfsberg-principles.com

[1] Wolfsberg is the location in Switzerland where an important working session to formulate the guidelines was held.

[2] Transparency International (TI) is a Berlin based non-governmental organization, dedicated to increasing government accountability and curbing both international and national corruption. TI is active in more than 70 countries. TI was represented by its founder and Chairman of the Board, Peter Eigen and the Chairman of their US chapter, Fritz Heimann.

[3] Stanley E. Morris is an international Consultant on Anti Money Laundering issues. He was head of FinCEN and a member of the Financial Action Task Force on Money Laundering (FATF).

[4] Prof. Mark Pieth is a law professor in Basel, Switzerland. He is Chairman of the OECD Working Group on Bribery and Corruption and a former member of the Financial Action Task Force on Money Laundering (FATF).

Preamble

The following guidelines are understood to be appropriate for private banking relationships. Guidelines for other market segments may differ. It is recognized that the establishment of policies and procedures to adhere to these guidelines is the responsibility of management.

1 Client acceptance: general guidelines

1.1 General

Bank policy will be to prevent the use of its worldwide operations for criminal purposes. The bank will endeavor to accept only those clients whose source of wealth and funds can be reasonably established to be legitimate. The primary responsibility for this lies with the private banker who sponsors the client for acceptance. Mere fulfilment of internal review procedures does not relieve the private banker of this basic responsibility.

1.2 Identification

The bank will take reasonable measures to establish the identity of its clients and beneficial owners and will only accept clients when this process has been completed.

1.2.1 Client

- Natural persons: identity will be established to the bank's satisfaction by reference to official identity papers or such other evidence as may be appropriate under the circumstances.
- Corporations, partnerships, foundations: the bank will receive documentary evidence of the due organization and existence.
- Trusts: the bank will receive appropriate evidence of formation and existence along with identity of the trustees.
- Identification documents must be current at the time of opening.

1.2.2 Beneficial owner

Beneficial ownership must be established for all accounts. Due diligence must be done on all principal beneficial owners identified in accordance with the following principles:

- Natural persons: when the account is in the name of an individual, the private banker must establish whether the client is acting on his/her own behalf. If doubt exists, the bank will establish the capacity in which and on whose behalf the accountholder is acting.
- Legal entities: where the client is a company, such as a private investment company, the private banker will understand the structure of the company sufficiently to determine the provider of funds, principal owner(s) of the shares and those who have control over the funds, e.g. the directors and those with the power to give direction to the directors of the company. With regard to other shareholders the private banker will make a reasonable judgement as to the need for further due diligence. This principle applies regardless of whether the share capital is in registered or bearer form.
- Trusts: where the client is a trustee, the private banker will understand the structure of the trust sufficiently to determine the provider of funds (e.g. settlor) those who have control over the funds (e.g. trustees) and any persons or entities who have the power to remove the trustees. The private banker will make a reasonable judgement as to the need for further due diligence.
- Unincorporated associations: the above principles apply to unincorporated associations.
- The bank will not permit the use of its internal non-client accounts (sometimes referred to as 'concentration' accounts) to prevent association of the identity of a client with the movement of funds on the client's behalf, i.e., the bank will not permit the use of such internal accounts in a manner that would prevent the bank from appropriately monitoring the client's account activity.

1.2.3 Accounts held in the name of money managers and similar intermediaries

The private banker will perform due diligence on the intermediary and establish that the intermediary has a due diligence process for its clients, or a regulatory obligation to conduct such due diligence, that is satisfactory to the bank.

1.2.4 Powers of attorney/Authorized signers

Where the holder of a power of attorney or another authorized signer is appointed by a client, it is generally sufficient to do due diligence on the client.

1.2.5 Practices for walk-in clients and electronic banking relationships

A bank will determine whether walk-in clients or relationships initiated through electronic channels require a higher degree of due diligence prior to account opening. The bank will specifically address measures to satisfactorily establish the identity of non-face-to-face customers.

1.3 Due diligence

It is essential to collect and record information covering the following categories:

- Purpose and reasons for opening the account
- Anticipated account activity
- Source of wealth (description of the economic activity which has generated the net worth)
- Estimated net worth
- Source of funds (description of the origin and the means of transfer for monies that are accepted for the account opening)
- References or other sources to corroborate reputation information where available.

Unless other measures reasonably suffice to do the due diligence on a client (e.g. favorable and reliable references), a client will be met prior to account opening.

1.4 Numbered or alternate name accounts

Numbered or alternate name accounts will only be accepted if the bank has established the identity of the client and the beneficial owner. These accounts must be open to a level of scrutiny by the bank's appropriate control layers equal to the level of scrutiny applicable to other client accounts.

1.5 Offshore jurisdictions

Risks associated with entities organized in offshore jurisdictions are covered by due diligence procedures laid out in these guidelines.

1.6 Oversight responsibility

There will be a requirement that all new clients and new accounts be approved by at least one person other than the private banker.

2 Client acceptance: situations requiring additional diligence/attention

2.1 General

In its internal policies, the bank must define categories of persons whose circumstances warrant additional diligence. This will typically be the case where the circumstances are likely to pose a higher than average risk to a bank.

2.2 Indicators

The circumstances of the following categories of persons are indicators for defining them as requiring additional_diligence:

- Persons residing in and/or having funds sourced from countries identified by credible sources as having inadequate anti-mony laundering standards or representing high risk for crime and corruption.

- Persons engaged in types of business activities or sectors known to be susceptible to money laundering.
- 'Politically Exposed Persons'. (frequently abbreviated as 'PEPs'.), referring to individuals holding or having held positions of public trust, such as government officials, senior executives of government corporations, politicians, important political party officials, etc., as well as their families and close associates.

2.3 Senior management approval

The banks' internal policies should indicate whether, for any one or more among these categories, senior management must approve entering into new relationships.

Relationships with Politically Exposed Persons may only be entered into with the approval from senior management.

3 Updating client files

3.1 The private banker is responsible for updating the client file on a defined basis and/or when there are major changes. The private banker's supervisor or an independent control person will review relevant portions of client files on a regular basis to ensure consistency and completeness. The frequency of the reviews depends on the size, complexity and risk posed of the relationship.

3.2 With respect to clients classified under any category of persons mentioned in 2, the banks internal policies will indicate whether senior management must be involved in these reviews.

3.3 Similarly, with respect to clients classified as set forth in 3.2, the bank.s internal policies will indicate what management information must be provided to management and/or other control layers. The policies should also address the frequency of these information flows.

3.4 The reviews of PEPs must require senior management's involvement.

4 Practices when identifying unusual or suspicious activities

4.1 Definition of unusual or suspicious activities

The bank will have a written policy on the identification of and follow-up on unusual or suspicious activities. This policy will include a definition of what is considered to be suspicious or unusual and give examples thereof.

Unusual or suspicious activities may include:

- Account transactions or other activities which are not consistent with the due diligence file
- Cash transactions over a certain amount
- Pass-through/in-and-out-transactions.

4.2 Identification of unusual or suspicious activities

Unusual or suspicious activities can be identified through:

- Monitoring of transactions
- Client contacts (meetings, discussions, in-country visits etc.)
- Third party information (e.g. newspapers, Reuters, internet)
- Private banker's/internal knowledge of the client's environment (e.g. political situation in his/her country).

4.3 Follow-up on unusual or suspicious activities

The private banker, management and/or the control function will carry out an analysis of the background of any unusual or suspicious activity. If there is no plausible explanation a decision will be made involving the control function:

- To continue the business relationship with increased monitoring
- To cancel the business relationship
- To report the business relationship to the authorities.

The report to the authorities is made by the control function and senior management may need to be notified (e.g. Senior Compliance Officer, CEO, Chief Auditor, General Counsel). As required by local laws and regulations the assets may be blocked and transactions may be subject to approval by the control function.

5 Monitoring

5.1 Monitoring Program

A sufficient monitoring program must be in place. The primary responsibility for monitoring account activities lies with the private banker. The private banker will be familiar with significant transactions and increased activity in the account and will be especially aware of unusual or suspicious activities (see 4.1). The bank will decide to what extent fulfillment of these responsibilities will need to be supported through the use of automated systems or other means.

5.2 Ongoing Monitoring

With respect to clients classified under any category of persons mentioned in 2, the bank.s internal policies will indicate how the account activities will be subject to monitoring.

6 Control responsibilities

A written control policy will be in place establishing standard control procedures to be undertaken by the various 'control layers' (private banker, independent operations unit, Compliance, Internal Audit). The control policy will cover issues of timing, degree of control, areas to be controlled, responsibilities and follow-up, etc.

An independent audit function (which may be internal to the bank) will test the programs contemplated by the control policy.

7 Reporting

There will be regular management reporting established on money laundering issues (e.g. number of reports to authorities, monitoring tools, changes in applicable laws and regulations, the number and scope of training sessions provided to employees).

8 Education, training and information

The bank will establish a training program on the identification and prevention of money laundering for employees who have client contact and for Compliance personnel. Regular training (e.g. annually) will also include how to identify and follow-up on unusual or suspicious activities. In addition, employees will be informed about any major changes in anti-money-laundering laws and regulations.

All new employees will be provided with guidelines on the anti-money-laundering procedures.

9 Record retention requirements

The bank will establish record retention requirements for all anti-money-laundering related documents. The documents must be kept for a minimum of five years.

10 Exceptions and deviations

The bank will establish an exception and deviation procedure that requires risk assessment and approval by an independent unit.

11 Anti-money-laundering organization

The bank will establish an adequately staffed and independent department responsible for the prevention of money laundering (e.g. Compliance, independent control unit, Legal).

APPENDIX 33

Law Commission Draft Corruption Bill

ARRANGEMENT OF CLAUSES

Draft of a Bill Entitled

An Act to make provision about corruption.

Be it Enacted by the Queen's most Excellent Majesty, by and with the advice and consent of the Lords Spiritual and Temporal, and Commons, in this present Parliament assembled, and by the authority of the same, as follows:—

Main Offences

1. Corruptly conferring an advantage

A person commits an offence if—

(a) he corruptly confers an advantage, or

(b) he corruptly offers or agrees to confer an advantage.

2. Corruptly obtaining an advantage

A person commits an offence if—

(a) he corruptly obtains an advantage, or

(b) he corruptly solicits or agrees to obtain an advantage.

3. Performing functions corruptly

A person commits an offence if he performs his functions as an agent corruptly.

Conferring and Obtaining

4. Meaning of conferring an advantage

(1) A person confers an advantage if—

(a) he does something or he omits to do something which he has a right to do, and

(b) the act or omission is done or made in consequence of another's request (express or implied) or with the result (direct or indirect) 20 that another benefits.

(2) An act or omission may be done or made in consequence of a person's request even if the nature of the act or omission, and the time it is intended to be done or made, are not known at the time of the request.

5. Meaning of obtaining an advantage

(1) A person obtains an advantage if—

(a) another does something or he omits to do something which he has a right to do, and

(b) the act or omission is done or made in consequence of the first person's request (express or implied) or with the result (direct or indirect) that the first person benefits.

(2) An act or omission may be done or made in consequence of a person's request even if the nature of the act or omission, and the time it is intended to be done or made, are not known at the time of the request.

Acting Corruptly

6. Conferring an advantage: meaning of corruptly

(1) A person who confers an advantage, or offers or agrees to confer advantage: an advantage, does so corruptly if—

(a) he intends a person in performing his functions as an agent to do an corruptly. act or make an omission, and

(b) he believes that if the person did so it would probably be primarily in return for the conferring of the advantage (or the advantage when conferred), whoever obtains it.

(2) A person who confers an advantage, or offers or agrees to confer an advantage, does so corruptly if—

(a) he knows or believes that in performing his functions as an agent a person has done an act or made an omission,

(b) he knows or believes that the person has done the act or made the omission primarily in order to secure that a person confers an advantage (whoever obtains it), and
(c) he intends the person known or believed to have done the act or made the omission to regard the advantage (or the advantage when conferred) as conferred primarily in return for the act or omission.

(3) For the purposes of subsection (1) the nature of the intended act or omission, and the time it is intended to be done or made, need not be known when the advantage is conferred or the offer or agreement is made.

(4) This section has effect subject to sections 10 and 11.

7. Obtaining an advantage: meaning of corruptly

(1) A person who obtains an advantage obtains it corruptly if—
(a) he knows or believes that the person conferring it confers it and corruptly.
(b) he gives his express or implied consent to obtaining it (in a case where he does not request it).

(2) A person who agrees to obtain an advantage agrees to obtain it corruptly if he knows or believes that the person agreeing to confer it agrees corruptly.

(3) A person who solicits an advantage solicits it corruptly if—
(a) he intends a person to confer it or agree to confer it, and
(b) he believes that if the person did so he would probably do so corruptly.

8. Performing functions: meaning of corruptly

(1) A person who performs his functions as an agent performs them corruptly if—
(a) he does an act or makes an omission primarily in order to secure that a person confers an advantage (whoever obtains it), and
(b) he believes that if the person did so he would probably do so corruptly.

(2) A person who performs his functions as an agent performs them corruptly if—
(a) he does an act or makes an omission when he knows or believes that a person has corruptly conferred an advantage (whoever obtained it), and
(b) he regards the act or omission as done or made primarily in return for the conferring of the advantage.

Agents and Principals

9. Meaning of agent and principal

(1) A person is an agent, and another is his principal for whom he performs functions, if—
(a) the first is a trustee and the second is a beneficiary under the same trust;
(b) the first is a director of a company and the second is the company;
(c) each is a partner in the same partnership;
(d) the first is a professional person (such as a lawyer or accountant) and the second is his client;
(e) the first is an agent and the second is his principal (taking agent and principal in the sense normally understood by lawyers);
(f) the first is the employee of the second.

(2) If subsection (1) does not apply a person is an agent, and another is his principal for whom he performs functions, if there is an agreement or understanding between them (express or implied) that the first is to perform the functions for the second.

(3) A person is an agent performing functions for the public if the functions he performs are of a public nature.

(4) Subsection (3) has effect even if the person has no connection with the United Kingdom, and 'public' is not confined to the public of the United Kingdom or of any part of it.

(5) A person may be an agent performing some functions for a principal and others for the public.
(6) As regards a given function, a person may be an agent performing it for a principal and the public.

Exceptions from Offences

10. Remuneration or reimbursement: no corruption

(1) If—
  (a) an advantage is conferred or an offer or agreement to confer an advantage is made, and
  (b) any of the following three conditions is satisfied, the advantage is not conferred corruptly or (as the case may be) the offer or agreement is not made corruptly.
(2) The first condition is that—
  (a) the functions concerned are performed only for a principal (and not the public), and
  (b) the advantage is conferred (or to be conferred) by or on behalf of the principal as remuneration or reimbursement in respect of the performance of the functions.
(3) The second condition is that—
  (a) the functions concerned are performed only for the public (and not a principal), and
  (b) the advantage is conferred (or to be conferred) on behalf of the public as remuneration or reimbursement in respect of the performance of the functions.
(4) The third condition is that—
  (a) some of the functions concerned are performed for a principal and others are performed for the public, or a given function is performed for a principal and the public, and
  (b) each element of the advantage is conferred (or to be conferred) by or on behalf of the principal, or on behalf of the public, as remuneration or reimbursement in respect of the performance of the functions.
(5) The functions concerned are the functions relating to the act or omission which is intended to be done or made, or is known or believed to have been done or made.
(6) References to the public are not confined to the public of the United Kingdom or of any part of it.

11. Principal's consent: no corruption

(1) If—
  (a) an advantage is conferred or an offer or agreement to confer an advantage is made, and
  (b) the following condition is satisfied,
  the advantage is not conferred corruptly or (as the case may be) the offer or agreement is not made corruptly.
(2) The condition is that—
  (a) the functions concerned are performed only for a principal (and not the public), and
  (b) the principal, or each of them if more than one, is aware of all the material circumstances and consents to the conferring of the advantage or the making of the offer or agreement.
(3) A person is to be treated as if he were aware of all the material circumstances, and consented to the conferring of the advantage or the making of the offer or agreement, if the defendant believes that—
  (a) he is aware of those circumstances and so consents, or
  (b) he would so consent if aware of those circumstances.
(4) For the purposes of subsections (2) and (3) consent may be given on a principal's behalf by any agent of the principal, but it does not count if in giving it the agent performs his functions as an agent corruptly.
(5) The functions concerned are the functions relating to the act or omission which is intended to be done or made, or is known or believed to have been done or made.

MISCELLANEOUS

12. Receiving benefit from corruption

(1) If—
  (a) an advantage is obtained corruptly by a person other than the agent concerned,
  (b) the agent receives a benefit which consists of or is derived from all or part of the advantage,
  (c) the agent knows or believes that the advantage was obtained corruptly and that the benefit consists of or is derived from all or part of the advantage, and
  (d) the agent gives his express or implied consent to receiving the benefit,
  (e) the agent commits an offence.

(2) The benefit may take any form and may be directly or indirectly derived.

13. Penalties

A person guilty of an offence under this Act is liable—

(1) on conviction on indictment, to imprisonment for a term not exceeding [ ] years;

(2) on summary conviction, to imprisonment for a term not exceeding 6 months or a fine not exceeding the statutory maximum or both.

14. Jurisdiction

In section 1(2) of the Criminal Justice Act 1993 (group A offences for purposes of provisions about jurisdiction) the following paragraph is inserted after paragraph (c)—

'(cc) an offence under the Corruption Act 1998;'.

15. Abolition of existing offences

(1) The common law offence of bribery is abolished. Abolition of existing offences.

(2) The Public Bodies Corrupt Practices Act 1889 shall cease to have effect. 1889 c. 69.

(3) In section 1(1) of the Prevention of Corruption Act 1906 (offences relating to corrupt transactions with agents) the words from 'If' to 'business; or' (in the second place where the latter words occur) are omitted.

(4) Section 2 of the Prevention of Corruption Act 1916 (presumption of corruption for certain offences) is omitted.

GENERAL

16. Repeals

The enactments mentioned in the Schedule are repealed to the extent specified.

17. Commencement

(1) Sections 1 to 16 and the Schedule apply in relation to acts or omissions done or made on or after the appointed day.

(2) If an act or omission is alleged to have been done or made over a period of two or more days, or at some time in a period of two or more days, it must be taken for the purposes of this section to have been done or made on the last of those days.

(3) The appointed day is such day as the Secretary of State appoints by 5 order made by statutory instrument.

18. Extent

This Act extends to England and Wales only.

19. Citation

This Act may be cited as the Corruption Act 1998.

SCHEDULE

Section 16 Repeals

Chapter	Short title	Extent of repeal
1889 c. 69.	Public Bodies Corrupt Practices Act 1889	The whole Act.
1906 c. 34.	Prevention of Corruption Act 1906	In section 1(1) the words from 'If' to 'business; or' (in the second place where the latter words occur). In section 1(2) the words 'expression "consideration" includes valuable consideration of any kind; the'.
1916 c. 64.	Prevention of Corruption Act 1916	Section 2. In section 4(3) the words from 'and the' to the end.
1948 c. 65.	Representation of the People Act 1948	Section 52(7).
1988 c. 33.	Criminal Justice Act 1988	Section 47(1).
1995 c. x.	London Local Authorities Act 1995	In Part I of the Schedule, the entry relating to the Public Bodies Corrupt Practices Act 1889.

APPENDIX 34

Government Reply to the Report from the Joint Committee On the Draft Corruption Bill Session 2002–03 HL Paper 157, HC 705

Introduction

The Draft Corruption Bill was published for pre-legislative scrutiny on 24 March 2003, and the Joint Committee's report on it was published on 31 July. The Joint Committee concurred with the Government that existing legislation is in an unsatisfactory state and reform is needed. However they did put forward a number of recommendations.

The Government is indebted to the Committee for the thoroughness of its work, the high level of commitment it has shown in preparing the report and for examining evidence from such a wide variety of stakeholders within such a demanding time-scale. It appreciates the depth and quality of the debate that arose from pre-legislative scrutiny and is grateful for the recommendations put forward and the opportunities for clarification.

We have considered at length all of the Committee's conclusions, in which there are four specific recommendations for change. In two cases we are able to take the recommendations on board exactly as the Committee has wished. We would like to consider a third further in discussion with the two Houses as it particularly concerns Parliament itself. However, as regards the central issue of the definition of corruption, we do have reservations on the proposal of the Joint Committee. Although we have made modifications to the definition to meet some of the issues of clarity and precision brought forward by the Committee itself or in evidence, we have not abandoned the agent/principal approach proposed by the Law Commission for reasons which we detail below.

We take the opportunity to express our thanks to Lord Slynn, the members of the Joint Committee and all those who submitted evidence to them. We are confident that the process of pre-legislative scrutiny has enabled significant improvements to the Bill to be made.

The next step is to continue the revision of the draft Bill with a view to introducing it in Parliament in due course.

The Conclusions and Recommendations of the Joint Committee and the Government Response to them

1 We are not persuaded that UK companies should be made explicitly liable for the actions of non-resident foreign subsidiaries and agents because the individuals—in many cases nationals of the countries concerned—will be subject to national law in that jurisdiction.

2 The case for a separate offence of trading in influence is not, in our view, convincing.

3 The draft Bill does not seem to us the appropriate vehicle for giving a statutory definition of misconduct in public office.

(1) We are grateful for the Committee's conclusions on the above three points. We fully agree with them.

4 Our overall conclusion, however, is that by adopting only the agent/principal approach the Bill does not proceed on the right basis and that corrupt acts outside that relationship ought to be included in the Bill.

5 The Committee has therefore concluded that the only way to address the problems which are inherent in the Bill (which arise from agent/principal model) is to move away from the definition of 'corruptly' in clause 5.

6 Having examined all these different models, we consider that (leaving aside related offences) the essence of corruption could be better expressed in the following terms:

> A person acts corruptly if he gives, offers or agrees to give an improper advantage with the intention of influencing the recipient in the performance of his duties or functions;
>
> A person acts corruptly if he receives, asks for or agrees to receive an improper advantage with the intention that it will influence him in the performance of his duties or functions.

7 As we have already indicated, it could be possible to substitute for 'improper advantage' the words 'advantage to which a person is not legally entitled'.

8 In the light of criticisms which have been made of it, we do not consider that the draft Bill should be left as it stands on the essential issue . . . We conclude that the Bill would still be obscure and satisfactory if the offences remain based on the concept of agency.

9 We believe that a Bill centred on a simple definition such as ours would be clearer and would work better. We also believe it would be more likely to receive general approval.

(2) We have carefully considered the views of the Joint Committee as concerns the central issue of the definition of corruption. Their criticisms on the definition of corruption are broadly two-fold. They relate to the clarity of the offence and the possibility that by adhering to the agent/principal construct, some corrupt acts will fall outside of the ambit of the offence. Although we share the Committee's concerns that the offence should be as far as possible clear and simple, we believe that clarity can only be achieved by setting out within the Bill the elements which make a transaction corrupt. We do not agree with the assessment that abandoning the agent/principal approach would make the offence clearer or easier to use, nor do we accept that the reliance on agent/principal makes the offence too narrow. Lastly, we submit that in some aspects the adoption of the Joint Committee's proposal would lead to an unacceptable narrowing of the law.

The Definition of Corruption in the Draft Bill

(3) The definition of corruption is based upon the agent/principal construct which has existed in corruption law since 1906 and is expressed in two instances of case law as: in the case of *Lindley* (1957) a dishonest intention to 'weaken the loyalty of the servants to their master and to transfer that loyalty from the master to the giver', and in *Calland* (1967) 'dishonestly trying to wheedle anagent away from his loyalty to his employer'.

(4) The agent/principal relationship is not a concept unique to the UK. Ireland, Canada and Australia have a similar structure to some of their offences of corruption and several countries, including Germany and Austria, have a concept of private sector corruption based around breach of duty, which is conceptually close to the agent/principal approach although not quite as broad. The breach of duty approach is present within all international instruments which address private sector corruption i.e. the Council of Europe Criminal Law Convention, the EU Joint Action and Framework Decision on Private Sector Corruption and the UN Convention on Corruption.

(5) The enormous difficulty in defining corruption is how to differentiate an offence of corruption from all kinds of legitimate giving and receiving of advantages that make up ordinary transactions of business and social life. It seems to us that there are broadly two ways of doing this. One is by qualifying the payment as 'improper' or 'undue' or, as under current law, qualifying the act by the adverb 'corruptly' and leaving it to the jury to determine what that means. If we were to take this approach it would have to be on the basis that we are satisfied that a uniform

understanding exists as to what constitutes a corrupt act. The other approach, which we are proposing, is to list the constituent parts of what makes an act corrupt by a series of tests.

(6) Whilst the approach which we have adopted does lead to a statute which is visually fairly complex and which may well not be immediately understood by a layman, it will lead to more uniform conclusions as to whether a given action is corrupt. The underlying principles are logical, straightforward and easily understood. We think that we have got the balance right in proposing a wide coverage of behaviour, but excluding acceptable levels of corporate hospitality, legitimate advertising, and receiving gifts in the private sector where the principal gives consent. We also believe that it will be possible for courts to give jurors clear instructions to steer them through the corruption tests within the Bill leading to consistency of conviction. Examples of such instructions were included in the Memorandum by Lord Falconer submitted to the Joint Committee.

(7) We would argue strongly that there is no consistent understanding throughout society of what constitutes a corrupt act. In common parlance the word 'bribe' is used to describe almost any kind of advantage with an aim to influence a person. A person might say to another: 'if I bribe you by taking you to dinner, would you help me make these deliveries?', or 'a bicycle for your birthday is a bribe to make you work for your exams.' In the world of business it is difficult to know what constitutes a bribe: is it corrupt for an employee to accept a fishing trip from a supplier who wants to build up a relationship between the two firms, to go to a product launch in an expensive hotel or to accept a gift of thanks after a contract has been awarded? Without guidance as to what makes a transaction corrupt, we cannot expect uniformity of conviction or even prosecution. An ambiguous offence could lead to unfairness, only the very obvious cases being prosecuted and continuing uncertainty particularly in the business community as to what is or is not bribery.

(8) Within the Bill there are two main elements of the offence which help to clarify what constitutes corrupt behaviour. These are the requirement that the advantage is intended as the *primary* motivator, and the provision that, in the private sector, principal's consent exempts the conferring of an advantage from the criminal law of corruption.

(9) The concept of 'primarily' is straightforward and should be easily understood by juries. For example (taking the example given by the Joint Committee at paragraph 94), a person C gives an advantage to A hoping that in doing so he might influence A to buy supplies from his (C's) company. Let us say that the advantage is a 'free gift' of minimal value, such as an item of promotional stationery. The only reason for C to give A promotional stationery is to influence him in the performance of his functions—the stationery has advertising slogans on it and C hopes the slogans will stick in A's mind when he is making the decision as to which company to buy from. A, of course, understands this when he accepts the stationery. However, C does not believe that it will be *primarily* the stationery that will influence A to buy a product from him. It is the concept *primarily* that stops this everyday transaction from being corrupt. However, if the advantage is a large sum of money conferred secretly into A's bank account, then the *primarily* test would render the action corrupt. In Lord Falconer's Memorandum to the Joint Committee, he noted that a similar concept is used in NHS guidelines: hospitality should be *secondary* to the purposes of a meeting.

(10) Likewise the concept of the defence of principal's consent (which exists in the private sector only) is an important restriction on the definition of what is considered corrupt behaviour. Giving a waiter an extra large tip in the hope that he would be influenced to give more attentive service next time the tipper patronised the restaurant would be saved from being corrupt in the draft Bill by concept of principal's consent.

(11) To take another example to illustrate the above two concepts, we could consider a person who works in the financial services industry. Such a person is frequently given advantages in the form of commission by third parties in order to influence him to advise clients to buy certain

financial products. So how would it be possible to differentiate a corrupt payment from a non-corrupt one? If the duty that the financial advisor has towards his principal (his client) is not subverted, then he will advise his client to buy a product because it suits the client's needs, not primarily because of the commission that he receives. Secondly, the commission would not be corrupt if the client is aware of all that it is reasonable for him to be aware and the client consents, since the bond of loyalty has not been broken.

Widening the Approach beyond Agent/Principal

(12) The Joint Committee suggests that by abandoning the agent/principal concept, it would be possible to encompass a much greater field of activities within the private sector, including corruption by heads of business and receiving of bribes sanctioned by the agent's principal, and that it would make the definition of corruption less complex. All references to the agent/principal concept would be removed from the Bill and the Bill would apply equally to the private and public sectors.

(13) Attractive though the simplicity of their proposal might be, we do not think that it would be wise to abandon the agent/principal construct and the basic premise that corruption is subversion of loyalty to a principal. The vast majority of those who submitted evidence to the Committee, to the Home Office in response to the White Paper or to the Law Commission in response to its consultation document did not propose such a radical rethink. As Lord Falconer put it (Q460) 'it is difficult to think of occasions when the essence of corruption is not cheating on the person who you should be looking after'.

(14) We have seen no evidence of activities of bribery outside of the agent/principal relationship which are morally reprehensible enough to be criminalised but which do not fall in the ambit of other statutes. We believe that the case mentioned by the Joint Committee at paragraph 87 of their report, in which the owner of one firm gives money to the owner of another firm in order to induce him not to tender for a particular contract, would be covered where done dishonestly by the criminal offence of bid rigging under the Enterprise Act 2002. As for the Joint Committee's suggestion that 'bribery' which is sanctioned by a principal should be a criminal offence, we do not agree. If an employer in the private sector agrees that his employee can receive a payment or other advantage, then there is no reason for making the conferring of that payment a criminal offence. The purpose of the law on corruption in such situations is to protect the employer, but where he agrees to the 'corruption', he does not need protection. As the Law Commission notes, it is difficult to argue how a commercial agent who accepts a gift with the knowledge and consent of his principal should be liable to sanction by the criminal law. The principal is not being cheated on. As concerns public functions, as explained above, principal's consent is not a defence.

(15) By going beyond agent/principal, the Joint Committee definition would cover a variety of innocent situations such as small scale corporate hospitality designed to influence the recipient, advantages given or received in social life, even activities such as tipping a waiter, subject to the caveat 'improper'. As the Law Commission said of 'corruptly': 'for a term that is not statutorily defined to be included in the definition of an offence, we must be confident that its generally understood meaning is unequivocal and that that unequivocal meaning is the meaning we would like imported into the offence'. No workable definition of 'improper', which has meanings ranging from 'incorrect' to 'unsuitable' or 'unbecoming' has, however, been mooted. It is not entirely clear what the definition proposed by the Joint Committee: 'advantage to which a person is not legally entitled' means. But if it means that as long as there is some legal basis for the advantage, including any form of agreement between the parties, there is no corruption, then it is a charter for corruption. As we argued above, we believe that there would not be consistency amongst jurors as to whether anything but the most blatant cases of corruption are 'improper'. In effect in the draft Bill we define 'corruptly' or 'improper' through tests of whether the advantage is

the primary motivator and whether there is principal's consent. Consider once more the examples in paragraphs 9 and 10 above. In the absence of any definition of 'improper' could we really be sure that juries would come to the same conclusion?

The Narrowing of the Law that would Follow Adoption of the Joint Committee Definition

(16) Much of the complexity of the Bill derives from the need to cover a variety of complex situations. In some areas, adopting the offence proposed by the Joint Committee would entail a narrowing of the law—as follows:

—The proposed offence does not cover the situation where a bribe is offered not to the person whose behaviour it is intended to influence but a third party. For example if a person gives a bribe through an intermediary in order to influence someone to do something (for example giving a bribe to the wife of a public official in order to influence the latter to give a contract), it would neither be possible to prosecute the wife who is the recipient of the bribe, nor the official who has kept his side of the bargain and given a contract.

—The Joint Committee's definition does not address the behaviour in the Bill's clause 3 offence: performing functions corruptly. If a person, for example, gives a contract to a company primarily because he has heard that the company gives corrupt rewards in return for the awarding of contracts, such behaviour is covered by the draft Corruption Bill but not the Joint Committee definition.

—If the Joint Committee's proposal were adopted, it would be necessary to prove that the recipient receives (asks for or agrees to receive) the advantage *with the intention* that it would influence him in the performance of his duties or functions. Thus a recipient of a bribe could claim that he received the bribe but that he did not intend it to influence him in any way and thus is not guilty of an offence, for example he took the bribe but did not intend to carry out his side of the bargain. It would clearly be undesirable if the law did not condemn, for example, an official who accepts a bribe having promised to give a passport in return, even if he never intends to carry out his side of the bargain.

Whilst some redrafting of the Joint Committee definition could iron out these lacunae, doing so would inevitably make the definition lengthier and more complex.

10 We consider it would be better if the Joint Committee recommendations were followed and a Parliamentary Privilege Bill dealing with all these matters were brought forward.

(17) We have noted the views of the Joint Committee. Discussions are taking place between officials in the Cabinet Office and the House authorities about the case for a Parliamentary Privilege Bill and what it might contain.

11 We therefore recommend that Clause 12 be narrowed. This would apply only to the words or actions of an MP or peer in the case were he is the defendant . . . We also recommend that, to the extent that the words or actions of an MP or peer are admissible for or against him, they should also be admissible for or against all co-defendants in respect of corruption offences based on the same facts.

12 We recommend that Clause 12 be redrafted on the lines set out in paragraph 135.

(18) We have carefully considered the views of the Joint Committee as concerns the scope of clause 12. This is a delicate and complex constitutional issue. A balance must be found between the desirability of lessening any evidential bar to prosecution which might lead to a guilty person going unpunished, and the need to ensure that there is no impediment to the freedom of speech in Parliament. In looking at this, we submit that the two do not always run at odds with each other. In the particular case of corruption, the ability to use parliamentary proceedings in evidence might be a factor which enhances the freedom of speech, by making sure that a person

does not speak in Parliament as a result of a corrupt bargain. As concerns the specific question of removing witnesses from the scope of the derogation from privilege, whilst we take the Joint Committee's point that witnesses may lack parliamentary experience, it is also true that whereas a disciplinary system exists for MPs who receive corrupt advantages for speaking before Parliament, in practice there is no way of dealing with a witness who speaks to a Committee as a result of a corrupt bargain if, as may well be the case, his words are essential to the prosecution.

(20) However we appreciate the force of the Joint Committee's concerns on this. As this is a matter which directly affects the working practices of Parliament, we would like to take the opportunity to listen further to the two Houses on this point before coming to a firm conclusion. We would particularly welcome the chance to look at the concerns raised by the Joint Committee in more detail.

13 We recommend that Clause 17 be replaced by a requirement for the consent to be given by Director of Public Prosecutions or one nominated deputy.

(21) We are pleased to concur with the Joint Committee and are exploring the options as to how to make necessary provision in the Bill.

14 We recommend that the Government gives further consideration to the question of whether the Clause 15 exemption for intelligence agencies is so wide that Clause 15 risks non-compliance with the UK's international obligations.

(22) We thank the Joint Committee for this recommendation. Having acted upon recommendation 15, we consider that we have met the Committee's concerns in this regard.

15 We also recommend that the Government considers whether Clause 15 should be amended so that the exemption for activities of the intelligence agencies applies only to acts or omissions done or made in the interests of national security or preventing or detecting serious crime.

(23) We are grateful for this recommendation and have made the necessary change in the Bill.

Corruption

Draft Legislation

Cm 5777

CORRUPTION

Draft Legislation

Presented to Parliament by the
Secretary of State for the Home Department
by Command of Her Majesty
March 2003

CM 5777 **£7.25**

CORRUPTION
Publication of Draft Clauses

Contents **Page**

FOREWORD BY LORD FALCONER

Corruption is potentially devastating. If it is not kept in check, it has the potential to cause serious damage to government and business – indeed to every aspect of economic and social life. We need to be constantly on our guard against corruption – it is a complex crime, by its very nature insidious and its effects stretch across international borders. Corruption world-wide weakens democracy, harms economies, impedes sustainable development and can undermine respect for human rights by supporting corrupt governments, with widespread destabilising consequences. We are duty-bound to promote high standards of fairness and propriety and to ensure that UK citizens do not contribute to corruption either at home or abroad.

The Corruption Bill should be seen in the context of a multi-faceted strategy to tackle corruption both at home and internationally. In the last few years, a number of important changes to the law have been made. These include:

- The Anti-terrorism, Crime and Security Act 2001, which extends UK jurisdiction to corruption offences committed abroad by UK nationals and incorporated bodies.
- The Proceeds of Crime Act 2002, which strengthens the law on money laundering and sets up an Assets Recovery Agency to investigate and recover assets and wealth obtained as a result of unlawful activity.

In the international sphere, the UK is at the forefront of efforts to tackle corruption. We are active members of the Organisation for Economic Co-operation and Development (OECD)'s Working Group on Bribery and of GRECO – the Council of Europe anti-corruption body. We support the development of EU wide minimum standards on corruption, and are currently negotiating along with our UN partners a UN Convention against Corruption. We intend to ratify the Council of Europe Criminal Law Convention on Corruption in the near future. Finally, the UK leads a number of initiatives internationally, including the development of the Extractive Industries Transparency Initiative, which seeks to encourage transparency over payments and revenues arising from the exploitation of natural resources and, through the UK development assistance programme and EU Phare programme, is helping a wide range of developing and transition countries tackle corruption.

So what does the Bill do and how will it contribute to combating corruption? Existing corruption law, drawn from a range of sources from as far back as 1889, is outdated. In its 1998 report, the Law Commission describes it as "obscure, complex, inconsistent and insufficiently comprehensive". It can be difficult for our law enforcement authorities to use and the inconsistency, lack of definition and various lacunae might lead to corrupt individuals' being acquitted. It shies away from the most important question – it does not have a definition of what acting corruptly actually means.

The Bill is drafted on the basis of a Law Commission report. It modernises the law by bringing together all offences of corruption in a single statute and addressing existing lacunae. It defines what is meant by "acting corruptly" and ensures that the law on corruption applies equally to all. Following the recommendation of the Joint Committee on Parliamentary Privilege of June 1999, in the event of a corruption prosecution, MPs and Peers will no longer be subject to the protection of parliamentary privilege – under which evidence of proceedings in Parliament is not admissible in court. In addition, the Bill amends civil law to enable ratification of the Council of Europe Civil Law Convention on Corruption, which aims to ensure that those who have suffered damage as a result of acts of corruption are able to defend their rights and interests.

Corruption law is a complex, intricate and sensitive field and the reform proposed is far reaching. I would therefore invite all those with expertise or interest in this area to offer their views on our legislative proposal. We will consider your comments before introducing the Bill to Parliament.

Charles Falconer

CORRUPTION BILL

EXPLANATORY NOTES

INTRODUCTION

1. These explanatory notes relate to the Corruption Bill as published in draft on 24 March 2003. They have been prepared by the Home Office and the Lord Chancellor's Department in order to assist the reader of the Bill and to help inform debate on it. They do not form part of the Bill and have not been endorsed by Parliament.

2. These notes need to be read in conjunction with the Bill. They are not, and are not meant to be, a comprehensive description of the Bill. So where a clause does not seem to require any explanation, none is given.

3. Parts 1 and 2 of the Bill extend only to England, Wales and Northern Ireland. *Clauses 29 and 30* extend only to Scotland.

TERRITORIAL APPLICATION: WALES

4. The Bill applies to Wales as it does to the rest of the jurisdiction. It does not change the position as regards the National Assembly of Wales.

BACKGROUND

Reform of Criminal Law

5. The Government's policy on the reform of the criminal law of corruption was set out in the White Paper, *Raising Standards and Upholding Integrity: the Prevention of Corruption (Cm 4759, June 2000)*. It takes fully into account the Law Commission report *Legislating the Criminal Code: Corruption (Law Com No 248, 1998)*. The Corruption Bill modernises and simplifies the law, replacing the overlapping and at times inconsistent provisions on corruption with a single, clear statute. It removes a possible incompatibility with ECHR (the presumption of corruption as concerns employees of the Crown, public bodies etc). It also acts on a recommendation from the Joint Committee on Parliamentary Privilege as regards evidence in corruption cases *(HL Paper 43 and HC 214, March 1999, paragraph 167)*.

Amendments to Civil Law

6. The Bill amends civil law to enable ratification of the Council of Europe Civil Law Convention on Corruption *(ETS No 174)*. The aim of the Convention is to require parties to the Convention to provide in their internal law for effective remedies for persons who have suffered damage as a result of corruption, in order to enable them to defend their rights and interests, including the possibility of obtaining compensation for damage.

SUMMARY

7. The Bill is in three parts.

- *Part 1:* establishes the offences of corruption, including what is meant by the term "corruptly". It explains what is meant by the terms 'agent' and 'principal'. The scheme is based on the Law Commission report referred to above. Part 1 also includes provision *(clause 12)* setting aside Parliamentary

Privilege in cases involving offences under the Bill and provision conferring extra-territorial jurisdiction as regards corrupt acts committed abroad by UK nationals and incorporated bodies. The new offences apply in England and Wales and Northern Ireland.

- *Part 2:* makes changes to the law in England, Wales and Northern Ireland governing the limitation periods for civil actions relating to corrupt conduct. It clarifies that the provisions of section 32 of the Limitation Act 1980 and Article 71 of the Limitation (Northern Ireland) Order 1989 regarding actions based on the fraud of the defendant also extend to corrupt conduct. It provides for a limitation period for actions based on the corrupt conduct of the defendant, including actions relating to trust property, of ten years from the date the corrupt conduct occurred. It defines a corrupt conduct for these purposes as conduct which constitutes an offence under Part 1 of the Bill.
- *Part 3:* makes provision for Scotland on proceedings in the UK Parliament equivalent to *clause 12* and also contains general provisions.

COMMENTARY ON CLAUSES

Part 1: Offences

Clause 1: Corruptly conferring an advantage

8. *Clause 1* makes it an offence to confer an advantage corruptly – this is equivalent to the offence of "active bribery" in international law. The meaning of 'conferring an advantage' is explained in *clause 4*. The term 'corruptly' is explained in *clauses 5, 6 and 7*.

9. An offence is committed under this clause even if the advantage is not in fact conferred but is only offered or if there is only an agreement to confer an advantage.

Clause 2: Corruptly obtaining an advantage

10. *Clause 2* makes it an offence to obtain an advantage corruptly – this is equivalent to the offence of "passive bribery" in international law. The meaning of 'obtaining an advantage' is explained in *clause 8*, and the meaning of 'corruptly' in *clause 9*. The offence is committed even if the advantage is not in fact obtained, but is only solicited or there is only an agreement to obtain it.

Clause 3: Performing functions corruptly

11. *Clause 3* makes it an offence to perform functions as an agent corruptly. In many instances, an agent who performs functions corruptly, for example, by awarding a contract to a person in return for a bribe, will commit an offence under *clause 2*. However, this will not always be the case and this clause ensures that he commits an offence even if, for example, he awards the contract only in the hope of a later reward (which he does not, in the event, receive). The term 'agent' is defined in *clause 11*, and includes persons in both the public and private sectors. The meaning of 'corruptly' in this context is set out in *clause 10*.

Clause 4: Meaning of conferring an advantage

12. *Clause 4* establishes the meaning of conferring an advantage. The first limb of the test is set out in *subsection (1)(a)*. It covers any act – for example, a person providing another with a free holiday. It also covers omissions to act, but only where the person omitting to act has a right to do so (for example, he omits to enforce a debt owing to

him) or a duty to do so (for example, he omits to enforce a debt owing to his employer that he has a duty to enforce by virtue of his employment). The second limb of the test is set out in *subsection (1)(b)*. The act or omission must be done or made in consequence of another's request whether the request is express or implied (for example, an employee requests that a supplier give him tickets to a football match or hints that he would like such tickets) or the effect of the act or omission must be that another benefits directly or indirectly (for example, where the omission is a failure to enforce a debt, the person who owed that debt will benefit from it).

13. *Subsection (2)* ensures that the definition of conferring an advantage is wide enough to cover the situation where the nature or timing of the act or omission is not known at the time of the request, for example, where an employee requests a supplier to look favourably on the job application that his son may make in the next few months (in return for which he will grant the supplier a contract). If the supplier acted as requested, he would be conferring an advantage on the employee since he would be acting in consequence of the employee's request. This would be the case even though, at the time he made the request, the employee was not altogether specific about what was wanted.

Clause 5: Conferring an advantage: meaning of corruptly

14. *Clause 5* is a key provision since it establishes what it means to confer an advantage corruptly.

15. *Subsection (1)* concerns the conferring of an advantage (or agreement or offer to confer an advantage) in return for influencing the future functions of an agent. For example, company C, which supplies components, may pay money to a purchasing agent to show favour to it in awarding a contract. The payment is corrupt if:

- company C intends the purchasing agent to perform his purchasing functions for his employer company, B, by awarding company C the contract *(paragraph (a))*;
- company C believes that if the purchasing agent awards it the contract it will be primarily in return for the money. It makes no difference who actually obtains the money – for example, it might be paid to the agent's partner *(paragraph (b))*;
- the exception provided in *clause 6* does not apply as company C is not acting on behalf of the purchasing agent's principal – i.e. his company, B *(paragraph (c))*;
- the exception provided in *clause 7* does not apply as company B does not consent *(paragraph (d))*.

16. *Subsection (2)* concerns the conferring of an advantage (or offer or agreement to confer an advantage) as a reward for functions carried out by the agent in the past. For example, a person (C) pays money to a planning officer (A) who has helped ensure that he obtained planning permission for a bungalow. The money is conferred corruptly if:

- C knows or believes that A has helped ensure that C receives planning permission while acting in the course of his duties as a public agent *(paragraph (a))*;
- C knows or believes that A has done this primarily in order that money (or another advantage) is paid to someone (not necessarily to A) *(paragraph (b))*;
- C intends A to regard the money as having been given in return for the award of planning permission *(paragraph (c))*;

- The exception provided in *clause 6* does not apply as C is not acting on behalf of the public *(paragraph (d))*;
- The exception provided in *clause 7* does not apply *(sub-paragraph (e))* since *clause 7* can never apply to functions which are performed for the public *(clause 7(1)(a))*.

17. As noted above, it results from *subsections (1)(b) and (2)(b)* that the person obtaining the advantage need not necessarily be the agent whose conduct it is sought to influence or reward. This approach ensures that behaviour where an agent has an interest in a third party (such as the agent's spouse) receiving a benefit will be covered. It is not necessary for the advantage to be of direct benefit to the person upon whom it is conferred.

18. *Subsection (3)* ensures that the exact nature of the act or omission which is to be carried out in return for the advantage does not need to be known at the time the advantage is conferred. It is sufficient if the briber's intention is to influence the agent's conduct at some indeterminate future time, even if he cannot yet foresee the exact circumstances in which the agent's conduct may be influenced. For example an NGO might bestow a gift on a member of the board of a charitable trust that distributes grants to NGOs, intending that, if in the future there is a relevant grant, the member of the board would look more favourably upon the application from the NGO primarily because of the gift.

19. There is no specific provision made for intermediaries. Under the general principles of our law, an intermediary may be charged with aiding and abetting or, depending on the circumstances, as a principal offender.

Clause 6: Acting on behalf of principal or public: no corruption

20. *Clause 6* is the first of the exemption clauses. It is needed because if a corrupt intention could consist *solely* of an intention to induce an agent to perform his or her functions as an agent in return for the conferring of an advantage, a person who paid a salary to an employee on behalf of his employer would be committing a corruption offence.

21. *Clause 6* is divided according to whether the functions concerned are performed for a principal, for the public or for both. The functions concerned may be performed both for a principal and the public *(subsection (4))*, for example, where an employee works for a privatised utilities company. The functions concerned are the functions referred to in *clause 5(1)(a) and (2)(a)* – i.e. they are the functions which the person conferring the advantage intends to influence or reward.

Clause 7: Principal's consent: no corruption

22. *Clause 7* is the second of the exemption clauses. Its effect is to exclude from the offences any case where the agent's principal knows of all the material circumstances surrounding the conferring of the advantage and gives his consent. For example, if the owners of a business charge unusually large "commissions" or "special payments" to guarantee prompt or otherwise superior service, this would not be corruption but, in effect, an open and extra charge on customers who are free to pay it or take their business elsewhere.

23. *Subsection (1)(a)* makes clear that this exception can never apply if the functions are performed for the public, even if the agent also acts for a principal in performing those functions. For example, a barrister has a professional duty as an officer of the court and is therefore performing a public function as well as acting for his client. The

client's consent for him to receive an advantage to act in breach of his duty to the court would be immaterial. *Subsection (1)(b)* stipulates that *each* of the principals (if there are more than one) should be aware of the material circumstances and consent to the conferring of the advantage. This excludes the possibility of an agent being bribed by one principal to act against the interests of another.

24. *Subsection (2)* extends the exemption in *subsection (1)* to take account of the fact that the defendant may have a mistaken but genuine belief about the principal's consent. *Subsection (2)(a)* covers the case where the defendant believes that the relevant principal knows all the material circumstances and consents to what is done. *Subsection (2)(b)* covers the case where the defendant believes that the principal would consent if he were aware of the circumstances.

25. It may not always be convenient for the principal himself to give consent, so *subsection (3)* provides that this may be done by an agent of the principal. For example, a company (the principal) may give an employee (an agent) power to decide whether gifts offered to other employees should be accepted or not. But this does not apply where the person with authority to give consent performs his functions as an agent corruptly, thereby committing an offence under *clause 10* – i.e. he gives the consent primarily in return for or in anticipation of a corrupt advantage.

Clause 8: Meaning of obtaining an advantage

26. *Clause 8* explains the meaning of obtaining an advantage. It is almost the exact reverse of *clause 4* which sets out the definition of conferring an advantage and everything said in the note on that clause applies here too. It is to be noted that, by virtue of *subsection (1)(b)*, a person may obtain an advantage without even indirectly benefiting from it. For example, if a person requests another to make a payment to charity, he obtains an advantage because the other person has done something (made a payment) in consequence of his request. Further, there is nothing in *clause 8* which requires the person who obtains the advantage to be the agent whose functions are being influenced or rewarded.

Clause 9: Obtaining an advantage: meaning of corruptly

27. *Clause 9(1)* establishes what it means to obtain an advantage corruptly. The definition depends on the definition of conferring an advantage corruptly which is set out in *clauses 5, 6 and 7*. There are two limbs of the test in clause 9(1). Firstly, the person obtaining the advantage must know or believe that the person conferring the advantage is doing so corruptly – i.e. is committing an offence under *clause 5*. So if an agent who obtains an advantage does not believe that the person conferring the advantage is doing so for the purpose of influencing him, he does not obtain the advantage corruptly. Secondly, the person obtaining the advantage must give his express or implied consent to obtaining it. So if another person transfers a large sum to an agent's bank account when the agent expressly requested him not to, the agent does not commit an offence even though he knows that the person transferring the money is doing so for the purpose of influencing his functions as an agent.

28. *Subsections (2) and (3)* make similar provision in respect of what it means to agree to obtain an advantage corruptly and what it means to solicit an advantage corruptly.

Clause 10: Performing functions: meaning of corruptly

29. *Clause 10* establishes what it means to perform functions as an agent corruptly. *Subsection (1)* broadly covers the situation where an agent acts in the hope of future

corrupt advantage. *Subsection (2)* broadly covers the situation where an agent acts to reward an advantage that has already been corruptly conferred. As with *clause 9*, this clause depends on the definition of conferring an advantage corruptly which is set out in *clauses 5, 6 and 7*. An example of the situation covered by subsection (1) would be where an agent grants a contract primarily in order to secure that the supplier to whom he grants it will fly him to Rome for the weekend and he believes that if the supplier did so, he would meet the criteria of *clause 5(2)* (essentially, that the supplier would intend the agent to regard the trip to Rome as conferred primarily in return for the contract). The same example can be used to illustrate subsection (2). If an agent grants a contract to a supplier when he knows or believes the trip to Rome last month paid for by the supplier was intended to lead to the granting of the contract and he regards the contract as granted primarily in return for the trip to Rome, then he is performing his functions corruptly.

Clause 11: Meaning of agent and principal

30. *Clause 11* establishes the meaning of the terms 'agent' and 'principal'. The definition at *subsection (1)(a)* is broad and covers many different situations, for example, a director's agreement to perform functions for a company, an employee's agreement to perform functions for his employer, an accountant's agreement to perform functions for his client etc. It does not, however, include a person who unilaterally performs functions for another without the other's agreement, as corruption is understood in terms of the potential breach of a relationship of trust, which is unlikely to exist in a relationship which is not based on any kind of mutual understanding. *Subsections (1)(b) and (1)(c)* add relationships which do not fall within subsection (1)(a), but nonetheless should be covered since there is a relationship of trust.

31. *Subsection (2)(a) and (b)*, and *subsection (4)* make it clear that it is immaterial if the agent (including an agent performing functions for the public) or principal have no connection with the United Kingdom. So a UK national (see *clause 13*) who bribes a Saudi Arabian employee of a Saudi Arabian company in Saudi Arabia will commit an offence under this Bill.

32. *Subsection (3)* provides a definition of an agent performing functions for the public. It reflects the approach also used in section 6(3) of the Human Rights Act 1998 in which "public authority" is not exhaustively defined and is said to include "..any person certain of whose functions are functions of a public nature". The definition is based on the nature of the functions as opposed to the body concerned, thus ensuring a wide coverage reflecting better the current situation in which the boundaries between the public and private sector are increasingly fluid.

Clause 12: Proceedings in Parliament

33. This clause implements a recommendation made by the Joint Committee on Parliamentary Privilege *(HL Paper 43 and HC 214, March 1999, paragraph 167)*. Its effect is to make evidence admissible in proceedings for a corruption offence (as defined in *subsection (2)*) notwithstanding Article 9 of the Bill of Rights 1689 which prevents proceedings in Parliament being impeached or questioned in a court.

Clause 13: Corruption committed outside the UK

34. This clause creates extra-territorial offences in respect of acts and omissions done abroad by UK nationals (as defined in *subsection (4)*) and bodies incorporated in any part of the UK which would be corruption offences (as defined in *subsection (3)*) if

done in England and Wales or Northern Ireland. It also enables such offences to be prosecuted in England and Wales or Northern Ireland, even though they take place outside the UK.

35. As regards legal persons, the clause applies to any body incorporated under the law of any part of the UK *(subsection (1)(a))*. It thus applies not only to companies but also, for example, to limited liability partnerships.

Clause 14: Jurisdiction

36. *Subsection (1)* provides that the new corruption offences will be Group A offences for the purposes of Part I of the Criminal Justice Act 1993. Part I of the 1993 Act provides that a person may be guilty of a Group A offence where any "relevant event" occurred in England and Wales. A "relevant event" is defined as "any act or omission or any other event (including any result of one or more acts or omissions) proof of which is required for prosecution of the offence". In the case of corruption a 'relevant event' might be for example the offer, the agreement to accept, or the acceptance of a bribe, or even simply the supply of information corruptly. So the effect of *clause 14* is that where, for example, A who is abroad telephones B in England and offers him a bribe, A would be committing an offence under *clause 1(b)*.

37. *Subsection (2)* makes parallel provision for Northern Ireland by amending the Criminal Justice (Northern Ireland) Order 1996.

Clause 15: Authorisations for intelligence agencies; Clause 16: Authorisations: supplementary

38. The effect of these two clauses is that acts carried out by persons on behalf of the security and intelligence agencies (the Security Service, the Secret Intelligence Service and GCHQ) will not constitute offences of corruption if they are authorised by the Secretary of State. This new authorisation system is closely based on section 7 of the Intelligence Services Act 1994.

39. *Subsections (4) to (6) of clause 15* set out the conditions for the issue of authorisations: most importantly, the Secretary of State must be satisfied that any act he authorises will be necessary for the discharge of the relevant agency's functions and that the nature and likely consequences of the act will be reasonable, having regard to the purposes for which it is done. *Subsection (7) of clause* 15 gives the Secretary of State power to grant different types of authorisations, including class authorisations.

40. *Clause 16* makes supplementary provision regarding the authorisations. *Subsection (11)* amends the Regulation of Investigatory Powers Act 2000 to ensure that the exercise of this new system will be kept under review by the Intelligence Services Commissioner

Clause 17: Consent to prosecution

41. *Subsection (1)* provides that no proceedings for a corruption offence (as defined in *subsection (4)*) may be started in England and Wales without the consent of the Attorney General. (Under the Law Officers Act 1997, any function of the Attorney General may be exercised by the Solicitor-General).

42. *Subsections (2), (3) and (5)* address the position in Northern Ireland, which is complicated by the fact that the Justice (Northern Ireland) Act 2002 is soon to come into force. Once section 22 of that Act is commenced the intention is that consent to the prosecution of offences which do not fall in the excepted field should rest with the Director of Public Prosecutions for Northern Ireland.

Clause 18: Penalties

43. This clause provides that the maximum penalty for an offence under the Bill on conviction on indictment will be 7 years' imprisonment and/or an unlimited fine. The maximum penalty on summary conviction will be 6 months' imprisonment and/or a fine not exceeding the statutory maximum (currently £5000). (The effect of the current Criminal Justice and Sentencing Bill will be to raise the 6 month threshold for indictable offences to 51 weeks.)

Clause 19: Abolition of existing offences etc

44. This clause contains repeals:

- *Subsection (1)* abolishes the common law of bribery, which is superseded by the offences in the Bill.
- *Subsection (2)* repeals the Public Bodies Corrupt Practices Act 1889 for the same reason.
- *Subsection (3)* repeals most of the Prevention of Corruption Act 1906 for the same reason. However it leaves in place the third offence in section 1 of the 1906 Act, as this is an offence of fraud, rather than corruption.
- *Subsection (4)* repeals the Prevention of Corruption Act 1916 except for those provisions which are related to the third offence in section 1 of the 1906 Act.
- *Subsection (5)* repeals section 178(c) of the Licensing Act 1964. This provision outlaws the bribery of constables by holders of a justice's licence. It equates to the offence in this Bill of corruptly conferring an advantage. Section 178(c) also covers attempts to bribe. The Bill covers offers and agreements *(clause 1(a))*; if an attempt is anything other than an offer or agreement, then it would be covered by section 1 of the Criminal Attempts Act 1981.
- *Subsection (6)* repeals paragraph 3 of Schedule 11 to the Local Government and Housing Act 1989. This provision amends the 1916 Act but has never been brought into force. As the amendment is directed at ensuring certain housing companies run by local authorities are public bodies for the purposes of the 1889 and 1916 Acts it will be redundant when these Acts are repealed.

Clause 21: Commencement: Part 1

45. *Subsection (1)* provides that this Part shall have effect only in relation to acts or omissions after the implementation date.

46. *Subsection (2)* makes transitional provision, for dealing with cases which straddle the implementation date. It provides that the date which determines which law shall apply shall be the last date on which an act or omission is alleged to have been done.

47. *Subsection (3)* gives the Secretary of State power to make an order setting the implementation date for this Part.

Part 2: Limitation

Clause 22: Postponement of limitation periods

48. *Subsections (1) to (6)* amend section 32 of the Limitation Act 1980. Section 32 provides that, where an action is based on the fraud of the defendant, or any fact relevant to the right of action has been concealed by the defendant, the limitation period begins on the date when the claimant discovered, or could reasonably have

discovered, the fraud or concealment. Subsections (1) to (6) clarify that these provisions also extend to corrupt conduct on the part of the defendant.

49. *Subsection (7)* amends section 32 of the 1980 Act to provide that an action based on the corrupt conduct of the defendant shall not be brought after the expiration of ten years from the date the corrupt conduct occurred. The Council of Europe Convention requires that civil proceedings relating to corruption must not be commenced after the end of a limitation period of not less than 10 years from the date of corruption. The 1980 Act does not currently specify a longstop period after which an action cannot be taken. The period of ten years reflects the longstop period proposed generally for civil actions by the Law Commission in its report *Limitation of Actions (Law Com No 270)*.

Clause 23: Actions in respect of trust property

50. *Clause 23* applies the ten year longstop period introduced by *subsection (7)* of *Clause 22* to actions in respect of trust property which are based on corrupt conduct. This is because a case involving corruption may also involve a fraudulent breach of trust. The provisions on actions in respect of trust property in section 21 of the 1980 Act currently contain no longstop period.

Clause 24: Meaning of corrupt conduct

51. *Clause 24* defines corrupt conduct for the purposes of the 1980 Act as conduct which constitutes an offence under Part 1 of the Bill. This comprises corruptly conferring an advantage, corruptly obtaining an advantage, and performing functions corruptly.

Clause 25: Postponement of time limits; Clause 26: Actions in respect of trust property; Clause 27: Meaning of corrupt conduct

52. *Clauses 25 to 27* insert equivalent provisions to those contained in *Clauses 22 to 24* in the Limitation (Northern Ireland) Order 1989.

Clause 28: Commencement: Part 2

53. *Clause 28(1)* provides for *Clauses 22 to 27* to apply to actions in relation to which the cause of action or right of action accrues on or after the commencement day. *Clause 28(2)* provides that the commencement day is the last day of the period of two months starting with the day on which the Act is passed.

Part 3: Miscellaneous and General

Clause 29: Proceedings in Parliament: Scottish Offences

54. This clause makes equivalent provision in respect of the Scottish offences of bribery and corruption as *clause 12* makes in respect of offences of corruption under the Bill. This particular change in the law relates to the Parliament of the United Kingdom and therefore to aspects of the constitution, reserved by paragraph 1(c) of Part I of Schedule 5 to the Scotland Act 1998. It is therefore not within the legislative competence of the Scottish Parliament to make, for Scotland, provision comparable to that for England and Wales in *clause 12* and hence there is no need to invoke the Sewel convention.

55. *Subsection (1)* is similar to *clause 12 (1)* but makes reference to proceedings for a crime or offence specified in *subsection (2)*.

56. *Subsection (2)* specifies the offences of bribery and corruption under Scots law. It is not necessary to make reference to attempts as under Scots law a reference to the

crime includes a reference to an attempt to commit the crime. Furthermore, section 293 of the Criminal Procedure (Scotland) Act 1995 provides that aiding, abetting, counselling, procuring and inciting the commission of a statutory offence is itself an offence. In relation to the common law element of the crime of bribery and corruption all parties involved in the commission of a crime are, at common law, equally guilty whatever part they may have played in the commission of the crime.

57. *Subsection (3)* ensures that the clause applies to the Scots offences whether or not they are constituted by section 69 (2) (a) of the Criminal Justice (Scotland) Act 2003. This section relates to bribery and corruption and is analogous to *clause 13*.

58. *Subsections (4) – (6)* repeat the effect of *clause 21* in respect of this clause.

Clause 30: Authorisation for intelligence agencies: Scotland

59. This clause extends the new authorisation system under *clauses 15 and 16* to cover corruption offences under Scots law. The intelligence agencies are concerned with national security, which is a reserved matter under the Scotland Act (Schedule 5, Part 2, Section B8).

Clause 32: The Crown

60. This clause ensures that the offences in Part 1 apply to persons in the public service of the Crown, for example, civil servants.

SCHEDULE

61. The schedule provides for repeals and revocations. The most important of these have been explained under *clause 19*. The reasons for the other repeals are:

Representation of the People Act 1948

Section 52 (7) of this Act amended the 1889 Act and will be redundant following the repeal of the 1889 Act.

Electoral Law Act (Northern Ireland) 1962

Section 112 (3) of this Act amended paragraphs (c) and (d) of section 2 of the 1889 Act and will be redundant following the repeal of the 1889 Act.

Local Government Act (Northern Ireland) 1972

Schedule 8 paragraph 1 of this Act amended section 7 of the 1889 Act and will be redundant following the repeal of the 1889 Act.

Criminal Justice Act 1988

Section 47 (1) of this Act amended the 1889 Act and will be redundant following the repeal of the 1889 Act.

Criminal Justice (Evidence etc) (Northern Ireland) Order 1988

Article 14(1) of this Order amended paragraph (a) of section 2 of the 1889 Act and will be redundant following the repeal of the 1889 Act.

Anti-terrorism, Crime and Security Act 2001

Part 12 of this Act has been replaced by provisions in Part 1 of this Bill – in particular *clause 11 (2) and (4) and clause 13*. The repeal of section 128(1)(b) is consequential on the repeal of Part 12.

FINANCIAL EFFECTS OF THE BILL

62. The Bill's provisions have negligible expenditure provisions for Government Departments.

PUBLIC SERVICE MANPOWER EFFECTS OF THE BILL

63. The Bill has a negligible impact on public sector manpower.

SUMMARY OF THE REGULATORY APPRAISAL

64. No RIA is necessary, as the regulatory impact is likely to be negligible.

EUROPEAN CONVENTION ON HUMAN RIGHTS

65. Section 19 of the Human Rights Act 1998 requires the Minister in charge of a Bill in either House of Parliament to make a statement about the compatibility of the provision of the Bill with the Convention (as defined by section 1 of that Act). The statement has to be made before second reading.

66. We do not think that there is anything in the draft Bill that conflicts with the Convention. Indeed, it repeals a provision of existing legislation (section 2 of the Prevention of Corruption Act 1916), which risks being deemed as incompatible.

COMMENCEMENT

67. Part 1 of the Bill and *clause 29* will be brought into force by commencement order. Part 2 of the Bill will commence two months after Royal Assent, in accordance with *clause 28*.

COMMENTS

68. The Bill will now be subject to pre-legislative scrutiny by a Joint Committee of both Houses of Parliament. Any enquiries or comments relating to the scrutiny procedure should be addressed to:

Richard Dawson
Committee Office Scrutiny Unit
House of Commons
London SW1P 3JA

Or by e-mail to: scrutiny@parliament.uk
Tel: 020 7 219 8363
Fax: 020 7 219 8361

You may also care to address comments and any other enquiries to:

Corruption Bill Team
Room 321
Home Office
50 Queen Anne's Gate
London SW1H 9AT

Or by e-mail to: Anna.Hodgson@homeoffice.gsi.gov.uk
Tel: 020 7273 4424
Fax: 020 7273 4345

Corruption Bill

CONTENTS

PART 1

OFFENCES

Corruption offences

Conferring an advantage

Obtaining an advantage

Performing functions

Agents and principals

Miscellaneous

A

BILL

TO

Make provision about corruption.

BE IT ENACTED by the Queen's most Excellent Majesty, by and with the advice and consent of the Lords Spiritual and Temporal, and Commons, in this present Parliament assembled, and by the authority of the same, as follows:—

PART 1

OFFENCES

Corruption offences

1 Corruptly conferring an advantage

A person commits an offence if—

(a) he corruptly confers an advantage, or

(b) he corruptly offers or agrees to confer an advantage.

2 Corruptly obtaining an advantage

A person commits an offence if—

(a) he corruptly obtains an advantage, or

(b) he corruptly solicits or agrees to obtain an advantage.

3 Performing functions corruptly

A person commits an offence if he performs his functions as an agent corruptly.

Conferring an advantage

4 Meaning of conferring an advantage

(1) A person confers an advantage if—

(a) he does something (for example, makes a payment) or he omits to do something which he has a right or duty to do;

(b) the act or omission is done or made in consequence of another's request (express or implied) or with the result (direct or indirect) that another benefits.

(2) An act or omission may be done or made in consequence of a person's request even if the nature of the act or omission, and the time it is intended to be done or made, are not known at the time of the request.

5 Conferring an advantage: meaning of corruptly

(1) A person (C) who confers an advantage, or offers or agrees to confer an advantage, does so corruptly if—

(a) he intends a person (A) to do an act or make an omission in performing functions as an agent of another person (B) or as an agent for the public;

(b) he believes that if A did the act or made the omission it would be primarily in return for the conferring of the advantage (or the advantage when conferred), whoever obtains it;

(c) the exception provided by section 6 does not apply;

(d) the exception provided by section 7 does not apply.

(2) A person (C) who confers an advantage, or offers or agrees to confer an advantage, does so corruptly if—

(a) he knows or believes that a person (A) has done an act or made an omission in performing functions as an agent of another person (B) or as an agent for the public;

(b) he knows or believes that A has done the act or made the omission primarily in order to secure that a person confers an advantage (whoever obtains it);

(c) he intends A to regard the advantage (or the advantage when conferred) as conferred primarily in return for the act or omission;

(d) the exception provided by section 6 does not apply;

(e) the exception provided by section 7 does not apply.

(3) For the purposes of subsection (1) the nature of the intended act or omission, and the time it is intended to be done or made, need not be known when the advantage is conferred or the offer or agreement is made.

6 Acting on behalf of principal or public: no corruption

(1) The exception provided by this section applies if any of the following three conditions is satisfied.

(2) The first condition is that—

(a) the functions concerned are performed only for a principal (B) and not for the public;

(b) C is acting on behalf of B.

(3) The second condition is that—

(a) the functions concerned are performed only for the public and not for a principal;

(b) C is acting on behalf of the public.

(4) The third condition is that—
 (a) some of the functions concerned are performed for a principal (B) and others are performed for the public, or a given function is performed for a principal (B) and the public;
 (b) each element of the advantage is conferred (or to be conferred) by C acting on behalf of B or of the public (or of both).

(5) The functions concerned are the functions referred to in section 5(1)(a) or (2)(a).

(6) References to the public are not confined to the public of the United Kingdom or of any part of it.

7 Principal's consent: no corruption

(1) The exception provided by this section applies if—
 (a) the functions concerned are performed only for a principal and not for the public;
 (b) the principal, or each of them if more than one, is aware of all the material circumstances and consents to the conferring of the advantage or the making of the offer or agreement.

(2) A person is to be treated as if he were aware of all the material circumstances, and consented to the conferring of the advantage or the making of the offer or agreement, if the defendant believes that—
 (a) he is aware of those circumstances and so consents, or
 (b) he would so consent if aware of those circumstances.

(3) For the purposes of subsections (1) and (2) consent may be given on a principal's behalf by any agent of the principal, but it does not count if in giving it the agent performs his functions as an agent corruptly.

(4) The functions concerned are the functions referred to in section 5(1)(a) or (2)(a).

Obtaining an advantage

8 Meaning of obtaining an advantage

(1) A person obtains an advantage if—
 (a) another does something (for example, makes a payment) or he omits to do something which he has a right or duty to do;
 (b) the act or omission is done or made in consequence of the first person's request (express or implied) or with the result (direct or indirect) that the first person benefits.

(2) An act or omission may be done or made in consequence of a person's request even if the nature of the act or omission, and the time it is intended to be done or made, are not known at the time of the request.

9 Obtaining an advantage: meaning of corruptly

(1) A person who obtains an advantage obtains it corruptly if—
 (a) he knows or believes that the person conferring it confers it corruptly, and

(b) he gives his express or implied consent to obtaining it (in a case where he does not request it).

(2) A person who agrees to obtain an advantage agrees to obtain it corruptly if he knows or believes that the person agreeing to confer it agrees corruptly.

(3) A person who solicits an advantage solicits it corruptly if—

(a) he intends a person to confer it or agree to confer it, and

(b) he believes that if the person did so he would do so corruptly.

Performing functions

10 Performing functions: meaning of corruptly

(1) A person who performs his functions as an agent performs them corruptly if—

(a) he does an act or makes an omission primarily in order to secure that a person confers an advantage (whoever obtains it);

(b) he believes that if the person did so he would do so corruptly.

(2) A person who performs his functions as an agent performs them corruptly if—

(a) he does an act or makes an omission when he knows or believes that a person has corruptly conferred an advantage (whoever obtained it);

(b) he regards the act or omission as done or made primarily in return for the conferring of the advantage.

Agents and principals

11 Meaning of agent and principal

(1) A person is an agent, and another is his principal for whom he performs functions, if—

(a) there is an agreement or understanding between them (express or implied) that the first is to perform the functions for the second;

(b) the first is a trustee and the second is a beneficiary under the same trust;

(c) the first and the second are partners in the same partnership.

(2) It is immaterial if-

(a) the functions of the first person have no connection with the United Kingdom;

(b) the affairs or business of the second person (or the functions of the second partner) have no connection with the United Kingdom.

(3) A person is an agent performing functions for the public if the functions he performs are of a public nature.

(4) Subsection (3) has effect even if the person has no connection with the United Kingdom, and "public" is not confined to the public of the United Kingdom or of any part of it.

(5) A person may be an agent performing some functions for a principal and others for the public.

(6) As regards a given function, a person may be an agent performing it for a principal and the public.

Miscellaneous

12 Proceedings in Parliament

(1) No enactment or rule of law preventing proceedings in Parliament being impeached or questioned in any court or place out of Parliament is to prevent any evidence being admissible in proceedings for a corruption offence.

(2) These offences are corruption offences—
  (a) an offence under this Part;
  (b) an attempt, conspiracy or incitement to commit an offence under this Part;
  (c) aiding, abetting, counselling or procuring the commission of an offence under this Part.

13 Corruption committed outside the UK

(1) This section applies if—
  (a) a national of the United Kingdom or a body incorporated under the law of any part of the United Kingdom does or omits to do anything in a country or territory outside the United Kingdom;
  (b) the act or omission would, if done or made in England and Wales or Northern Ireland, constitute a corruption offence.

(2) In such a case—
  (a) the act or omission constitutes the offence concerned;
  (b) proceedings for the offence may be taken in England and Wales or Northern Ireland;
  (c) the offence may be treated for incidental purposes as having been committed at a place in England and Wales or Northern Ireland.

(3) These offences are corruption offences—
  (a) an offence under this Part;
  (b) an attempt, conspiracy or incitement to commit an offence under this Part;
  (c) aiding, abetting, counselling or procuring the commission of an offence under this Part.

(4) A national of the United Kingdom is an individual who is any of these—
  (a) a British citizen, a British overseas territories citizen, a British National (Overseas) or a British Overseas citizen;
  (b) a person who under the British Nationality Act 1981 (c. 61) is a British subject;
  (c) a British protected person within the meaning of that Act.

14 Jurisdiction

(1) In section 1(2) of the Criminal Justice Act 1993 (c. 36) (group A offences for purposes of provisions about jurisdiction) the following paragraph is inserted after paragraph (c)—

"(cc) an offence under Part 1 of the Corruption Act 2003;".

(2) In Article 38(2) of the Criminal Justice (Northern Ireland) Order 1996 (S.I. 1996/3160 (N.I. 24)) (group A offences for purposes of provisions about

jurisdiction) the following sub-paragraph is inserted after sub-paragraph (c)—
"(cc) an offence under Part 1 of the Corruption Act 2003;".

15 Authorisations for intelligence agencies

(1) Subsection (2) applies if, apart from that subsection, a person would commit a corruption offence in doing an act or making an omission.

(2) The person does not commit a corruption offence if the act or omission done or made is authorised to be done or made by virtue of an authorisation given by the Secretary of State.

(3) The Secretary of State may give an authorisation under subsection (2) only if he is satisfied that the conditions in subsections (4) to (6) are met.

(4) The first condition is that—
  (a) any acts or omissions which may be done or made in reliance on the authorisation will be necessary for the proper discharge of a function of the Security Service, the Secret Intelligence Service or GCHQ, or
  (b) the operation in the course of which any such acts or omissions may be done or made will be necessary for the proper discharge of such a function.

(5) The second condition is that there are satisfactory arrangements in force to secure—
  (a) that no act or omission will be done or made in reliance on the authorisation beyond what is necessary for the proper discharge of a function of the Security Service, the Secret Intelligence Service or GCHQ, and
  (b) that, in so far as any acts or omissions may be done or made in reliance on the authorisation, their nature and likely consequences will be reasonable, having regard to the purposes for which they are done or made.

(6) The third condition is that—
  (a) there are satisfactory arrangements in force under section 2(2)(a) of the Security Service Act 1989 (c. 5) and sections 2(2)(a) and 4(2)(a) of the Intelligence Services Act 1994 (c. 13) with respect to the disclosure of information obtained by virtue of this section, and
  (b) any information obtained by virtue of an act or omission done or made in reliance on the authorisation will be subject to those arrangements.

(7) An authorisation under subsection (2) may in particular—
  (a) relate to one or more specified acts or omissions, to acts or omissions of a specified description or to acts or omissions done or made in the course of a specified operation;
  (b) be limited to one or more specified persons or to persons of a specified description;
  (c) be subject to specified conditions.

(8) "Specified" means specified in the authorisation.

(9) These offences are corruption offences—
  (a) an offence under this Part;
  (b) an attempt, conspiracy or incitement to commit an offence under this Part;

(c) aiding, abetting, counselling or procuring the commission of an offence under this Part.

(10) "GCHQ" has the meaning given by section 3(3) of the Intelligence Services Act 1994 (c. 13).

16 Authorisations: supplementary

(1) This section applies to an authorisation under section 15(2).

(2) An authorisation may be given only under the hand of—
(a) the Secretary of State, or
(b) a senior official.

(3) But an authorisation may be given under the hand of a senior official only if—
(a) the case is urgent;
(b) the Secretary of State has expressly authorised the giving of the authorisation;
(c) a statement of that fact is endorsed on the authorisation.

(4) An authorisation ceases to have effect—
(a) at the end of the period of 6 months starting with the day on which it was given, if it was given under the hand of the Secretary of State;
(b) at the end of the second working day after the day on which it was given, if it was given under the hand of a senior official.

(5) Subsection (4) does not apply if the authorisation is renewed under subsection (6) before the day on which it would otherwise cease to have effect.

(6) The Secretary of State may renew an authorisation for a period of 6 months starting on the day on which it would otherwise cease to have effect, if at any time before that day he considers it necessary for the authorisation to continue to have effect for the purpose for which it was given.

(7) Subsection (6) may apply more than once.

(8) A renewal under subsection (6) must be made under the hand of the Secretary of State.

(9) The Secretary of State must cancel an authorisation if he is satisfied that an act or omission authorised by virtue of it is no longer necessary.

(10) In this section—
"senior official" has the meaning given by section 81 of the Regulation of Investigatory Powers Act 2000 (c. 23);
"working day" means any day other than a Saturday, a Sunday, Christmas Day, Good Friday or a day which is a bank holiday under the Banking and Financial Dealings Act 1971 (c. 80) in any part of the United Kingdom.

(11) In section 59(2) of the Regulation of Investigatory Powers Act 2000 (matters to be kept under review by Intelligence Services Commissioner) after paragraph (a) insert—
"(aa) the exercise by the Secretary of State of his powers under sections 15 and 16 of the Corruption Act 2003;".

17 Consent to prosecution

(1) No proceedings for a corruption offence may be started in England and Wales except with the consent of the Attorney General.

(2) No proceedings for a corruption offence may be started in Northern Ireland before the relevant date except with the consent of the Attorney General.

(3) No proceedings for a corruption offence may be started in Northern Ireland on or after the relevant date except with the consent of the Director of Public Prosecutions for Northern Ireland.

(4) These offences are corruption offences—
- (a) an offence under this Part;
- (b) an attempt, conspiracy or incitement to commit an offence under this Part;
- (c) aiding, abetting, counselling or procuring the commission of an offence under this Part.

(5) The relevant date is the date on which section 22(1) of the Justice (Northern Ireland) Act 2002 (c. 26) comes into force (Attorney General for England and Wales no longer Attorney General for Northern Ireland).

18 Penalties

A person guilty of an offence under this Part is liable—
- (a) on conviction on indictment, to imprisonment for a term not exceeding 7 years or a fine or both;
- (b) on summary conviction, to imprisonment for a term not exceeding 6 months or a fine not exceeding the statutory maximum or both.

19 Abolition of existing offences etc.

(1) The common law offence of bribery is abolished.

(2) The Public Bodies Corrupt Practices Act 1889 (c. 69) shall cease to have effect.

(3) In section 1 of the Prevention of Corruption Act 1906 (c. 34) (offences relating to corrupt transactions with agents)—
- (a) in subsection (1) the words from "If any agent" to "business; or" (in the second place where the latter words occur) are omitted;
- (b) subsection (4) is omitted.

(4) In the Prevention of Corruption Act 1916 (c. 64)—
- (a) section 2 (presumption of corruption for certain offences) is omitted;
- (b) in section 4(2) (meaning of "public body") the words "(including authorities existing in a country or territory outside the United Kingdom)" are omitted.

(5) In section 178 of the Licensing Act 1964 (c. 26) paragraph (c) and the word "or" immediately preceding it (bribery) are omitted.

(6) Paragraph 3 of Schedule 11 to the Local Government and Housing Act 1989 (c. 42) (amendment of 1916 Act) is omitted.

General

20 Repeals and revocations

The Schedule contains repeals and revocations.

21 Commencement: Part 1

(1) Sections 1 to 20 and the Schedule apply in relation to acts or omissions done or made on or after the appointed day.

(2) If an act or omission is alleged to have been done or made over a period of two or more days, or at some time in a period of two or more days, it must be taken for the purposes of this section to have been done or made on the last of those days.

(3) The appointed day is such day as the Secretary of State appoints by order made by statutory instrument.

PART 2

LIMITATION

England and Wales

22 Postponement of limitation periods

(1) Section 32 of the Limitation Act 1980 (c. 58) (postponement of limitation period in case of fraud etc.) is amended as follows.

(2) In the sidenote after "fraud," insert "corrupt conduct,".

(3) In subsection (1) after paragraph (a) insert—

"(aa) the action is based on the corrupt conduct of the defendant; or".

(4) In subsection (1) after "discovered the fraud," insert "corrupt conduct,".

(5) In subsection (3) after "fraud" insert ", corrupt conduct".

(6) In subsection (4)(a)—

(a) after "case of fraud" insert ", corrupt conduct";
(b) after "party to the fraud" insert "or corrupt conduct";
(c) after "believe that the fraud" insert ", corrupt conduct".

(7) After subsection (5) insert—

"(6) An action based on the corrupt conduct of the defendant shall not be brought by virtue of subsection (1) above after the expiration of ten years from the date on which the corrupt conduct occurred."

23 Actions in respect of trust property

In section 21 of the Limitation Act 1980 (time limit for actions in respect of trust property) after subsection (1) insert—

"(1A) Subsection (1) above does not apply if the action is based on the corrupt conduct of the trustee."

24 Meaning of corrupt conduct

In section 38(1) of the Limitation Act 1980 (c. 58) (interpretation) after the definition of "action" insert—

""corrupt conduct" means conduct which constitutes an offence under Part 1 of the Corruption Act 2003;".

Northern Ireland

25 Postponement of time limits

(1) Article 71 of the Limitation (Northern Ireland) Order 1989 (S.I. 1989/1339 (N.I. 11)) (postponement of time limit in case of fraud etc.) is amended as follows.

(2) In the heading after "fraud," insert "corrupt conduct,".

(3) In paragraph (1) after sub-paragraph (a) insert—

"(aa) the action is based on the corrupt conduct of the defendant; or".

(4) In paragraph (1) after "discovered the fraud," insert "corrupt conduct,".

(5) In paragraph (3) after "fraud" insert ", corrupt conduct".

(6) In paragraph (4)(a)—

(a) after "case of fraud" insert ", corrupt conduct";

(b) after "party to the fraud" insert "or corrupt conduct";

(c) after "believe that the fraud" insert ", corrupt conduct".

(7) After paragraph (5) insert—

"(5A) An action based on the corrupt conduct of the defendant may not be brought by virtue of paragraph (1) after the expiration of ten years from the date on which the corrupt conduct occurred."

26 Actions in respect of trust property

In Article 43 of the Limitation (Northern Ireland) Order 1989 (S.I. 1989/1339 (N.I. 11)) (time limit for actions in respect of trust property) after paragraph (1) insert—

"(1A) Paragraph (1) does not apply if the action is based on the corrupt conduct of the trustee."

27 Meaning of corrupt conduct

In Article 2(2) of the Limitation (Northern Ireland) Order 1989 (S.I. 1989/1339 (N.I. 11)) (interpretation) after the definition of "conventional rent" insert—

""corrupt conduct" means conduct which constitutes an offence under Part 1 of the Corruption Act 2003;".

Commencement

28 Commencement: Part 2

(1) Sections 22 to 27 apply to actions in relation to which the cause of action or right of action accrues on or after the commencement day.

(2) The commencement day is the last day of the period of two months starting with the day on which this Act is passed.

PART 3

MISCELLANEOUS AND GENERAL

Miscellaneous

29 Proceedings in Parliament: Scottish offences

(1) No enactment or rule of law preventing proceedings in Parliament being impeached or questioned in any court or place out of Parliament is to prevent any evidence being admissible in proceedings for a crime or offence mentioned in subsection (2).

(2) The crimes and offences are—

(a) as a crime at common law, bribery or accepting a bribe;

(b) the offences under section 1 of the Public Bodies Corrupt Practices Act 1889 (c. 69) (corruption in office);

(c) the first two offences under section 1 of the Prevention of Corruption Act 1906 (c. 34) (bribes obtained by or given to agents).

(3) Subsection (1) applies whether or not the crime or offence is constituted by virtue of section 69(2)(a) of the Criminal Justice (Scotland) Act 2003 (asp 00) (bribery and corruption committed outwith United Kingdom).

(4) This section applies in relation to acts or omissions done or made on or after the appointed day.

(5) If an act or omission is alleged to have been done or made over a period of two or more days, or at some time in a period of two or more days, it must be taken for the purposes of subsection (4) to have been done or made on the last of those days.

(6) The appointed day is such day as the Secretary of State appoints by order made by statutory instrument.

30 Authorisations for intelligence agencies: Scotland

Sections 15 and 16 apply in relation to a crime or offence mentioned in section 29(2) as they apply in relation to a corruption offence (as defined by subsection (9) of section 15).

General

31 Extent

(1) Parts 1 and 2 do not extend to Scotland, except as applied by section 30.

(2) Sections 29 and 30 extend to Scotland only.

32 The Crown

(1) Part 1 binds the Crown, subject to subsections (2) to (6).

(2) No contravention by the Crown of a provision of Part 1 makes the Crown criminally liable.

(3) But the High Court may, on the application of a person appearing to the court to have an interest, declare unlawful an act or omission of the Crown which constitutes a contravention of a provision of Part 1.

(4) Despite subsection (2), the provisions of Part 1 apply to persons in the public service of the Crown as they apply to other persons.

(5) Subsections (1) to (4) do not affect Her Majesty in her private capacity.

(6) The reference in subsection (5) to Her Majesty in her private capacity includes a reference to Her Majesty in right of her Duchy of Lancaster and to the Duke of Cornwall.

33 Citation

This Act may be cited as the Corruption Act 2003.

SCHEDULE

Section 20.

Repeals and Revocations

Short title and chapter	*Extent of repeal or revocation*
Public Bodies Corrupt Practices Act 1889 (c. 69)	The whole Act.
Prevention of Corruption Act 1906 (c. 34)	In section 1(1) the words from "If any agent" to "business; or" (in the second place where the latter words occur). In section 1(2) the words "expression "consideration" includes valuable consideration of any kind; the". Section 1(4).
Prevention of Corruption Act 1916 (c. 64)	Section 2. In section 4(2) the words "(including authorities existing in a country or territory outside the United Kingdom)". In section 4(3) the words from "and the" to the end.
Representation of the People Act 1948 (c. 65)	Section 52(7).
Electoral Law Act (Northern Ireland) 1962 (c. 14)	Section 112(3).
Licensing Act 1964 (c. 26)	In section 178, paragraph (c) and the word "or" immediately preceding it.
Local Government Act (Northern Ireland) 1972 (c. 9).	In Schedule 8, paragraph 1.
Criminal Justice Act 1988 (c. 33)	Section 47(1).
Criminal Justice (Evidence, Etc.) (Northern Ireland) Order 1988 (S.I. 1988/1847 (N.I. 17))	Article 14(1).
Local Government and Housing Act 1989 (c. 42)	In Schedule 11, paragraph 3.
Anti-terrorism, Crime and Security Act 2001 (c. 24)	Part 12. Section 128(1)(b).

Printed in the UK by The Stationery Office Limited
on behalf of the Controller of Her Majesty's Stationery Office
Id 133884 03/03 001069 832371

Corruption – Draft Legislation

TSO

Published by TSO (The Stationery Office) and available from:

Online
www.tso.co.uk/bookshop

Mail, Telephone, Fax & E-mail
TSO
PO Box 29, Norwich NR3 1GN
Telephone orders/General enquiries 0870 600 5522
Order through the Parliamentary Hotline *Lo-Call* 0845 7 023474
Fax orders 0870 600 5533
Email book.orders@tso.co.uk
Textphone 0870 240 3701

TSO Shops
123 Kingsway, London WC2B 6PQ
020 7242 6393 Fax 020 7242 6394
68-69 Bull Street, Birmingham B4 6AD
0121 236 9696 Fax 0121 236 9699
9-21 Princess Street, Manchester M60 8AS
0161 834 7201 Fax 0161 833 0634
16 Arthur Street, Belfast BT1 4GD
028 9023 8451 Fax 028 9023 5401
18-19 High Street, Cardiff CF10 1PT
029 2039 5548 Fax 029 2038 4347
71 Lothian Road, Edinburgh EH3 9AZ
0870 606 5566 Fax 0870 606 5588

TSO Accredited Agents
(See Yellow Pages)

and through good booksellers

TSO

INDEX